A Guide to the
Historical and Archaeological Publications
of Societies in England and Wales,
1901–1933

A Guide to the
Historical and Archaeological
Publications of Societies
in England and Wales,
1901-1933

compiled for the

Institute of Historical Research

by

E. L. C. MULLINS

UNIVERSITY OF LONDON
THE ATHLONE PRESS
1968

Published by
THE ATHLONE PRESS
UNIVERSITY OF LONDON
at 2 Gower Street, London WC1

Distributed by Constable & Co Ltd
12 Orange Street, London WC2

Canada
Oxford University Press
Toronto

U.S.A.
Oxford University Press Inc
New York

485 11094 6

Printed in Great Britain by
WESTERN PRINTING SERVICES LTD
BRISTOL

Foreword

This volume lists and indexes the titles and authors of books and articles bearing upon the history and archaeology of England and Wales, the Isle of Man and the Channel Islands, issued to their members between the years 1901 and 1933 inclusive by more than four hundred local and national societies located within these areas. Earlier in origin, as well as more limited in scope and different in plan, it is complementary to *Writings on British History, 1901–1933* (5 vols. in 7, Jonathan Cape, for the Royal Historical Society), and is continued by *Writings on British History, 1934*, the first of a series of volumes compiled for the same Society and publisher by Mr A. T. Milne, comprising society as well as non-society publications.

The provision of some kind of bibliographical aid whereby the publications of societies with historical and archaeological interests might become more generally known was among the earliest services to scholarly inquiry to be undertaken by the Institute of Historical Research. Following upon a discussion opened by Miss E. Jeffries Davis during the third interim Anglo-American Conference of Historians in 1924, the Institute, jointly with the Congress of Archaeological Societies, appointed a committee to devise and prepare a *Guide* which would meet the needs of historians and archaeologists alike. The committee immediately began to assemble and make available to readers at the Institute typewritten lists of relevant publications arranged by societies. Requiring no special skill, as Miss Jeffries Davis put it, the listing was soon seen to be more laborious and more extensive than had been anticipated. By 1928 the number of societies known to merit inclusion in the *Guide* exceeded 300 and was still growing; several societies were of considerable antiquity and the lists of their publications extremely long. But what caused the committee most distress was its inability to draw up for the proposed *Guide* 'a scheme which would satisfy permanently the interests of all concerned'. Abandoning perfection, it resolved to publish, as an interim measure, the existing lists, amplified along lines suggested by Miss Jeffries Davis and brought down to the end of 1928, with an index. The committee also resolved, the Institute and the Congress agreeing, to keep the *Guide* up-to-date by means of annual supplements, with cumulative indexes, to be issued with the Institute's *Bulletin*. The first of these supplements, listing societies' publications during 1929, appeared with no. 23 of the *Bulletin* in November 1930, being followed, while the preparation of lists for the main volume slowly progressed, by five more on the same plan; the seventh, for the publications of 1935, had to be 'radically different from its predecessors' because of the decision by the Royal Historical Society to begin its series of *Writings* with a volume for the year 1934. This decision, besides progressively eroding the usefulness of the supplements, implied that 1933 rather than 1928 should become the terminal date for the lists in the *Guide* itself. Accordingly, to the special committee set up by the Institute in 1948 to consider the resumption of work after the austerity of war and immediate post-war years, there seemed to be only one course: to appoint an editor to complete the *Guide*, with 1933 as its *terminus ad quem* and, since some limitation in the other direction could not be avoided, 1901 as its *terminus a quo*, and to discontinue the supplements: the thirteenth and last, for the years 1942–6, was issued with no. 64 of the *Bulletin* in November 1948.

The decision to begin the *Guide* with the publications of 1901 had the effect of consigning to the archives of the Institute a considerable part of the work already done on what had long been known as 'the Parsloe Guide'. Mr C. G. Parsloe began his association with the Institute in the session of 1922–3 when, while Franks Student in Archaeology, he became one of the two research librarians on its staff. From 1925 until his retirement from the post of Secretary and Librarian of the Institute in 1943 he was actively involved with the proposed *Guide*, compiling, with others, among whom was Miss Zirphie Faiers, later Mrs Parsloe, the lists of publications described above, and himself editing twelve of the thirteen annual supplements, the first five with Mrs Parsloe's assistance. The Committee of the Institute gratefully recognizes its obligation to Mr and Mrs Parsloe for laying the foundation upon which the present *Guide* has been built.

Above all, the Committee expresses its gratitude to Mr E. L. C. Mullins for undertaking in 1949 the completion of the *Guide* in its revised form and carrying the task through at the sacrifice of so many of his leisure hours. Mr Mullins was assisted for over three years by Miss Sonia F. Hodge (Mrs R. J. Knecht) and for two years by Miss Mary E. Mardo (Mrs Stansfield). To them, as well as to the members of the Guide Sub-Committee meeting under the chairmanship of successive Directors of the Institute, and to the present Secretary and Librarian, Mr A. T. Milne, grateful acknowledgments are made. The Board of the Athlone Press has shown much forbearance and understanding during the delays that have befallen the work, while from the Board's Secretaries, the late Mr W. D. Hogarth and his successor, Mr A. M. Wood, and their staffs, has come much patient encouragement. To all who have been associated with the *Guide* since it was first suggested more than forty years ago, the Committee offers its thanks.

A. G. Dickens
Director, Institute of Historical Research

Acknowledgements

The compiler gladly acknowledges his obligation to those who preceded him in this work and to all who assisted him to complete it. He is specially grateful to Mrs Knecht and Mrs Stansfield who, as Miss Hodge and Miss Mardo, drafted most of the lists of publications and nearly all the index slips, and to his friends in the Institute of Historical Research and the University of London Library for allowing him to draw upon their professional ability in bibliography and indexing. He also recalls the help he received from Mr E. H. Milligan, librarian of the Society of Friends, and that Mr A. R. Hewitt, librarian and curator of the United Grand Lodge of England, brought many masonic societies to his notice and made their publications available to him. The staff of the Reading Room of the British Museum cheerfully produced, by the barrow-load, far more volumes for inspection than the following pages enumerate. For the typographical merit of the *Guide* the compiler is indebted to Mr James Price and his successor at the Athlone Press, Mr Wolfgang Klär, and to the staff of Western Printing Services Ltd.

Explanatory Notes

THE LISTS. The *Guide* is selective only in the sense that the books and articles listed in it lie within the limits described in the first sentence of the Foreword, broadly interpreted. Titles have commonly been shortened by the abbreviation or omission of words. Additions by the compiler are enclosed in square brackets. Authors' personal names, indicated by initials in the lists, are given in full in the Index of Authors if they have been ascertained. All works may be assumed to be written in the language of their titles.

THE INDEXES. To facilitate reference to the lists from the General Index and Index of Authors, a number has been allotted to each volume in the lists and a letter of the alphabet to each article within a volume. For the twenty-seventh and subsequent articles as far as the fifty-second, the letter is doubled, and trebled where there are fifty-three articles or more. Numbers and letters appear in the lists in heavy type. An asterisk against a number or letter in the indexes means that the indicated volume-title or article-title contains more than one mention of the person, place, or subject indexed. Both indexes are constructed on the 'letter by letter' principle, so 'Artillery' comes before '*Art of Love*', 'Boers' before 'Boer War', 'Higham Ferrers' before 'High Beach', and 'Roman camps' before 'Roman Catholics'.

ABBREVIATIONS. Most of the abbreviations employed are in common use or of readily apparent significance. They include the following: abp = archbishop; adm. = admiral; Ann. = Annual; Ant. = Anthony; Antiq. = Antiquarian; Archaeol. = Archaeological; archd. = archdeacon; Archit. = Architectural; Assn = Association; bn = battalion; bp = bishop; bpric = bishopric; card. = cardinal; cath. = cathedral; cent. = century; chwdns = churchwardens; chyd = churchyard; commr = commissioner; Ctss = Countess; D. = Duke; dist. = district; doc. = document; Dchss = Duchess; E. = Earl; Econ. = Economic; edn = edition; Fd = Field; Ft = Foot; Harl. = Harleian; Hist. = Historical; Inst. = Institute; Jos. = Joseph; Jnl = Journal; Lt = Light; Lt. = Lieutenant; Lit. = Literary; Marg. = Margaret; Mq. = Marquess; Mic. = Michael; Nat. = Natural; Nath. = Nathaniel; nr = near; prec. = precentor; Procs = Proceedings; Publs = Publications; Philosoph. = Philosophical; Rec. = Record; reg. = register; Rpts = Reports; Regt = Regiment; Sci. = Scientific; sec. = secretary; ser. = series; Trans. = Transactions; Univ. = University; Vct = Viscount; Vctss = Viscountess; Yr. = Year.

Contents

Contents

Contents

Contents

Contents

Publications

ABERAFAN AND MARGAM DISTRICT HISTORICAL SOCIETY

Founded 1924, to foster interest in local history.

Transactions, 1928–33 (5 vols. 1928–33):

1 Vol. for 1928.

a Y plygain [Christmas morning candle-mass], by J O'Brien. [In English]

b The effect of the Romans on the Welsh language, by L. Ll. Brookes.

c Aberafan and district, 1637–87, by T. Richards.

d 'Capel y papistiaid': the last of the old Catholic chapels of Glamorgan, by J. O'Brien.

e The arms of Aberafan as depicted on the 15th cent. borough mace, by R. G. Williams.

f Coity castle in the days of Owen Glyndwr, by R. G. Williams.

g The Stradling family and St. Donat's church, by J. O'Brien.

h Notes on Cowbridge, by W. T. Gwyn.

i The Punpcius Carantorius stone, by A. J. Richard.

j The charters of Afan, by J. T. Jones.

k Romantic career of great Welsh bard and scholar [Dr. Sion Dafydd Rhys], by R. G. Williams.

l Notes on [the history of] Afan.

m Carreg Cennen castle [Carmarthenshire].

n Stone monuments in Afan, by J. O'Brien.

o The antiquities of Llangynwyd and Margam mountain.

p Ewenny priory and church.

q St. Bride's Major.

r Notes on old china, by R. T. C. Bevan.

s Merthyr Mawr church.

t The ancient monasteries of Neath, by J. O'Brien.

u The Cistercian order: 800th anniversary in Britain, by J. O'Brien.

2 Vol. for 1929.

a The feudal system, by O. S. Thomas.

b The river names of the district, by A. J. Richard.

c Margam and district in the 18th and 19th cent., by A. J. Richard.

d Coity castle connections: links with Tudor times, by R. G. Williams.

e An interesting 18th cent. document [a register of enclosed lands belonging to the borough of Aberafan, 1788], by J. T. Jones.

f The Mansells of Briton Ferry, by G. B. Hammond.

g Leland and the rivers Ogmore, Alun and Ewenny, by R. G. Williams.

h Cwmavon and St. Michael's church, by J. O'Brien.

i Llanstephan [castle, Carmarthenshire], by A. J. Richard.

j Courts of justice at Aberavon in the middle ages, by J. O'Brien.

k Folk-tales of the district, by A. J. Richard.

l Great floods of the past [at Aberafan], by J. O'Brien.

m The folk-lore of Avan: death omens and funeral and burial customs, by J. O'Brien.

3 Vol. for 1930.

a Sea pilotage: its local and general history, by F. G. Knott.

b A list of early published views of the Port Talbot district, by M. Phillips.

c Tudor Wales, by E. E. Hughes.

d Antiquarian remains in the Afan district, by J. O'Brien.

e Some south Glamorgan lexicographers [Dr. Sion Dafydd Rhys; Rev. Thomas Richards; Rev. John Walters; Rev. William Jones; Edward Williams], by A. H. Price. [Contd. in vol. for 1932–3]

f The story of local inns: names and signs of Aberavon inns, by J. O'Brien.

g Discovery of a 'mass-dial' at Ewenny [priory], by R. G. Williams.

h Vale of Glamorgan sketches, by R. G. Williams: (1) Old Beaupre, (2) St. Hilary, (3) The Basset-Mansel tomb at Llantrithyd, (4) Flemingston, (5) St. Athan, its manor and church, (6) Eglwys Brewis. [Contd. in vols. for 1931–2 and 1932–3]

4 Vol. for 1931–2.

a Notes on the fisheries of the Avan district, by J. O'Brien.

b A list of books, pamphlets, and contributions to periodicals relating to or having reference to the Port Talbot district, comp. M. Phillips.

c Prominent Aberavon citizens of a century ago, by J. O'Brien.

d Early Christian monuments of the British Isles, by A. J. Richard.

e Aberavon and district about 1700 [extracts from Edward Lhwyd's 'Parochialia'].

f Church bells and their uses, by J. O'Brien.

g Early mining records of the district, by M. Phillips. [Contd. in vol. for 1932–3]

h Local elementary education in 1847 [in the parishes of Margam, Baglan, Michaelston-super-Avon, and Llangonoyd].

5 Vol. for 1932–3.

a The itinerary of Nicholas Carlisle [being extracts relating to the Aberafan and Margam district from his *Topographical Dictionary of the Dominion of Wales*, 1811], by J. O'Brien.

b St. Roque's chapel, Merthyrmawr, by R. G. Williams.

c Early development of the iron and tinplate industries in the Port Talbot district [1253–1850], by M. Phillips.

d Caerphilly castle: the most remarkable military fortress in Great Britain, by E. R. Lewis.

e Water mills of Avan and Margam, by J. O'Brien.

f The medieval borough and its freedom, by J. T. Jones.

g Folklore of the district, by M. Phillips.

AFRICAN SOCIETY

Founded 1901, to investigate the usages, institutions, customs, religions, antiquities, history and languages of the native races of Africa; to facilitate the commercial and industrial development of the continent; and to form a central institution for the study of African subjects, and the diffusion of knowledge relating to such subjects. The Journal includes numerous articles additional to those listed below bearing upon the economic and political development of British African territories.

Journal, vols. 1–32 (1901–33):

6 Vol. 1.

a The African Association of 1788, by W. Sinclair.
b A century of exploration in South Africa, by G. Lacy.

7 Vol. 4.

a The Gold Coast when Edward IV was king [1461–83], by J. M. Sarbah.
b Dutch and English on the Gold Coast in the 18th cent., by M. Nathan.

8 Vol. 14.

a Some effects of the war [1914] upon British and German trade in South Africa, by H. Birchenough.
b Rhodesia and the war [1914], by H. W. Fox.
c The conquest of Togoland [1914], by W. A. Crabtree.

9 Vol. 15.

a German South-West African campaign [1914–15], by M. H. Park.
b Campaign on German East Africa–Rhodesia border [1914–16], by J. J. O'Sullevan.

10 Vol. 16.

a Some account of the various editions of the Gold Coast ordinances [1860–1916], by Sir W. B. Griffith.

11 Vol. 17.

a The revision of the Berlin Act [1885], by A. B. Keith.

12 Vol. 18.

a The East-African campaign [1914–18].

13 Vol. 19.

a General Botha, by R. C. Hawkin.
b Great Britain in West Africa, by W. A. Crabtree.

14 Vol. 20.

a The Cape to Cairo railway, by R. Williams.

15 Vol. 22.

a Africa and historical research, by A. P. Newton.

16 Vol. 23.

a Early educational experiments on the Gold Coast, by Evelyn C. Martin.

17 Vol. 24.

a The parliamentary tour in South Africa [1924], by J. H. Thomas.
b The work of the East Africa commission [1924], by W. G. A. Ormsby-Gore.

18 Vol. 25.

a Empire settlement in Africa in its relation to trade and the native races, by G. H. Nicholls.
b Henry Barth [explorer], by E. W. Bovill.

19 Vol. 26.

a The Blue Nile, and irrigation, by H. Weld.
b The parliamentary visit to Nigeria [1927–8], by W. Elliot.

20 Vol. 28.

a The parliamentary visit to Tanganyika, 1928, by A. A. Somerville, E. Ramsden, W. Paling, and R. H. Morris.
b Eastern and central Africa: House of Lords debate on the report of commission on closer union [13 Mar. 1929].
c Conference on forced and contract labour [held by the British League of Nations Union, Mar. 1929, and addressed by L. S. Amery, Earl Buxton, W. Ormsby-Gore, and others].

21 Vol. 29.

a The South African protectorates [Transvaal, Orange Free State, and Natal], by J. A. I. Agar-Hamilton.
b The silent trade of Wangara [the trans-Saharan gold trade], by E. W. Bovill.
c Nigeria in the 'nineties, by Sir H. L. Galway.
d English contributions to the study of African languages, by Alice Werner.

22 Vol. 30.

a The parliamentary visit to Northern Rhodesia, 1930, by J. A. Parkinson, H. L. Boyce, and P. J. Pybus.
b The Jameson raid [a review of the book of this title by H. M. Hole], by Earl Buxton.
c Land policy and economic development in Kenya [a memorandum submitted to the joint parliamentary committee upon closer union in the East African territories], by C. Speller.

23 Vol. 31.

a Land policy and economic development in Kenya, by Sir E. Grigg.
b The report of the joint select committee on closer union in East Africa.
c Mary Kingsley.
d The life of Mary Kingsley [a review of the biography by Stephen Gwynn], by R. S. Rattray.
e The river Niger: Macgregor Laird and those who inspired him, by H. S. Goldsmith.

24 Vol. 32.

a Education and race relations, by Lord Lugard.
b Lord Cromer [a review of the biography by the Marquis of Zetland], by Lord E. Gleichen.
c Egypt since Cromer [a review of the book of this title by Lord Lloyd of Dolobran], by Lord E. Gleichen.

ALCHEMICAL SOCIETY

Founded 1912, for the study of works and theories of the alchemists in all their aspects, philosophical, historical, and scientific, and all matters relating thereto.

Journal, vols. 1–3 (1913–15):

25 Vol. 2.

a Some English alchemical books, by J. Ferguson.
b Roger Bacon, by B. R. Rowbottom.

ALCUIN CLUB

Founded 1897, to promote the study of the history and use of the Book of Common Prayer.

Collections, vols. 3–29 (1901–32):

26 Vols. 3, 4, 8, 12. Pontifical services. 4 vols. 1901–8. [Vols. i–ii illustrated from miniatures of the 15th and 16th cent., with notes and liturgical introd. by W. H. Frere; vol. iii illustrated with woodcuts of the 16th cent., with notes by F. C. Eeles; vol. iv illustrated with woodcuts of the 16th cent., with notes by A. Riley]

27 Vol. 6. Edwardian inventories [of church goods] for Bedfordshire, ed. F. C. Eeles from transcripts by J. E. Brown. 1905.

28 Vol. 7. Edwardian inventories for Huntingdonshire, ed. Mrs. S. C. Lomas from transcripts by T. Craib. 1906.

29 Vol. 9. Edwardian inventories for Buckinghamshire, ed. F. C. Eeles from transcripts by J. E. Brown. 1908.

30 Vol. 10. Fifty pictures of Gothic altars, selected and described by P. Dearmer. 1910.

31 Vol. 11. The Sarum missal in English, newly translated by F. E. Warren. 2 vols. 1913.

32 Vol. 13. A history of the use of incense in divine worship, by E. G. C. F. Atchley. 1909.

33 Vols. 14-16. Visitation articles and injunctions of the period of the Reformation. 3 vols. 1910. [Vol. i: Historical introd. and index, ed. W. H. Frere; vol. ii: 1536-58, ed. W. H. Frere with assistance of W. M. Kennedy; vol. iii: 1559-75, ed. W. H. Frere]

34 Vol. 17. Traditional ceremonial and customs connected with the Scottish liturgy, by F. C. Eeles. 1910.

35 Vol. 18. The rationale of ceremonial, 1540-43, with notes and appendices and an essay on the regulation of ceremonial in the reign of Henry VIII, with four facsimiles of handwritings, by C. S. Cobb. 1910.

36 Vol. 19. Illustrations of the liturgy: thirteen drawings of the celebration of holy communion in a parish church, by C. O. Skilbeck, with notes and introd. by P. Dearmer. 1912.

37 Vol. 20. Edwardian inventories for the city and county of Exeter, transcribed by Beatrix F. Cresswell. 1916.

38 Vol. 21. The sacrament reserved: a survey of the practice of reserving the eucharist, with special reference to the communion of the sick, during the first twelve centuries, by W. H. Freestone. 1917.

39 Vol. 22. The ornaments of the ministers, as shown on English monumental brasses, by H. J. Clayton. 1919.

40 Vol. 23. Chantry certificates for Oxfordshire, ed. and transcribed by Rose Graham; and Edwardian inventories of church goods for Oxfordshire, ed. Rose Graham from transcripts by T. Craib. 1920.

41 Vol. 24. Illustrations of the occasional offices of the church in the middle ages from contemporary sources, collected and described by H. S. Kingsford. 1921.

42 Vols. 25-27. Elizabethan episcopal administration: an essay in sociology and politics, by W. P. M. Kennedy. 3 vols. 1924. [Vols. ii and iii contain visitation articles and injunctions]

43 Vol. 28. Studies in early Roman liturgy, by W. H. Frere. I: The kalendar. 1930.

44 Vol. 29. Historical survey of holy week: its services and ceremonial, by J. W. Tyrer. 1932.

Tracts, nos. 1-20 (1901-32):

45 No. 4. The parish clerk, and his right to read the liturgical epistle, by C. Atchley. *P.* 1903.

46 No. 6. The people's prayers: some considerations on the use of the litany in public worship, by E. G. C. F. Atchley. *P.* 1906.

47 No. 7. The sign of the cross in the western liturgies, by E. Beresford-Cooke. *P.* 1907.

48 No. 8. The 'Interpretations' of the bishops and their influence on Elizabethan episcopal policy, with an appendix of the original documents, by W. M. Kennedy. *P.* 1908.

49 No. 10. The bread of the eucharist, by R. M. Woolley. 1913.

50 No. 18. Cassock and gown [a survey of clerical dress], by H. J. Clayton. 1929.

ALDERSHOT MILITARY SOCIETY

Founded 1887, to enable officers to meet, hear the views and opinions of others, and express their own on the current military topics of the day.

Publications, *of which only the following have been seen:*

51 Vol. 83. The British in the Iberian peninsula, 1808-14, as illustrating sea power and strategy, by T. M. Maguire. *P.* [1905?].

52 Vol. 105. A sketch of the British occupation of Buenos Aires [1806] and the revolt of the Spanish colonies in South America, in the early part of the 19th cent., by A. J. Godley. *P.* [1910?].

ANCIENT MONUMENTS SOCIETY

Founded 1924, to encourage the study and conservation of ancient monuments, historic buildings and ancient craftsmanship in Lancashire and the north of England.

Publications:

53 Year Book, 1926 (1926).

a List of buildings in England and Wales in the charge of H.M. Office of Works, transferred under the Ancient Monuments Act, 1913, comp. Sir F. Baines.

b List of the more important historic crown buildings administered and maintained by H.M. Office of Works, comp. Sir F. Baines.

c List of monuments in the northern and north-western counties of England and in Wales scheduled for protection by the commissioners of works in pursuance of section 12 of the Ancient Monuments Consolidation and Amendments Act, 1913.

d Suggestions for amendment of the Ancient Monuments Act, 1913, forwarded to the first commissioner of H.M. Works, etc.

e List of county Ancient Monuments committees and hon. correspondents in the north and north-western counties of England and in Wales appointed by the Ancient Monuments Boards of England or Wales, to assist the staff of the Department of Ancient Monuments and Historic Buildings.

f List of archaeological and kindred societies in the northern counties of England and in Wales.

ANGLESEY ANTIQUARIAN SOCIETY AND FIELD CLUB

Founded 1911, for the practical study of archaeology, natural science, art, literature, history, and kindred subjects, so far as they pertain to Anglesey; also the preservation of historical documents, ancient monuments, rare birds and plants, and objects of geological or other scientific interest in the Island.

Transactions, 1913-14, 1920-33 (16 vols. [1913-33])

54 Vol. for 1913.

a Prehistoric remains of the Penmaenmawr [Caernarvonshire] uplands, by W. B. Lowe.

ANGLO-BELGIAN UNION

Founded 1918, to educate both peoples in the knowledge of each other and to promote the friendly relations existing between the two countries.

Anglo-Belgian Notes, vols. 1–8 (1921–31), contd. as Annual Reports, vols. 9–10 (1932–3):

73 Vol. 1.

a The Anglo-Belgian defensive treaty [1922].
b The Historical Congress at Brussels [1923], by J. Holland Rose.
c Flanders and England in history, by H. de Sagher.

74 Vol. 3.

a L'attaque de Zeebrugge, le 23 avril 1918, par A. E. M. G. Stinglhamber.

75 Vol. 7.

a The Walloon church in Southampton, by Euphemia Torry.
b The old capital of England [Winchester], by Florence Freer.

ANGLO-DANISH SOCIETY

Founded 1924, to promote intercourse between British people interested in Denmark and Danes resident in Great Britain; to assist in the encouragement of artistic, commercial, literary, scientific and social relations between the two countries; to promote any Anglo-Danish schemes which, in the opinion of the council, may further the work of the Society.

Anglo-Danish Journal, vols. 1–8 or nos. 1–33[1] (1926–34):

76 Vol. 3.

a Bones of Rothwell [Northants.], by W. Melville.
b *Berlingske Tidende*, by S. Poulsen. [Includes the newspaper's account of the battle of Copenhagen, 1801, the account in *The Times* of 17 Apr. 1801, and despatches and letters by Lord Nelson]

77 Vol. 8.

a London's livery companies, by R. J. Blackham.
b Oxford and St. Frideswide, by Ethel C. Williams.
c Greenstead church: a memory of Viking days, by Ethel C. Williams.

ANGLO-HELLENIC LEAGUE

Founded 1913, for the prevention of misunderstanding between the British and Hellenic peoples and the improvement of social, commercial and political relations of the two countries.

Pamphlets, nos. 1–57 (1914–30):

78 No. 24. England in the Balkans: Hellenic note on British policy [1914–15], by J. Mavrogordato. *P.* 1916.

79 No. 36. The Anglo-Hellenic alliance: speeches by Mr. Winston Churchill, the Greek minister, and Viscount Bryce at the Mansion House, June 27, 1918. *P.* 1918.

80 No. 57. Correspondence of Commodore Hamilton during the Greek war of independence, with introd. by J. Gennadius. *P.* 1930.

Extra publication:

81 The English in Athens before 1821, by W. Miller. *P.* 1930.

[1] Nos. 3, 4, 5, and 7 (parts of vols. 1 and 2) have not been seen.

ANGLO-NORMAN LITERARY CIRCLE

Founded 1929, as the Jersey branch of the British Association of Literary Amateurs, to give practical encouragement to literary talent throughout the Channel Islands.

Anglo-Norman Review, nos. 1–18 (1929–31):

82 No. 1.

a A visit to Jersey 300 years ago, by G. H. Le Neveu [from Peter Heylyn's account of his visit, 1628].

83 No. 3.

a Some 17th cent. letters [between Elie Dumaresq, Thomas Carey, and Cardin Fautrat], by Julia Marett. [Contd. in no. 4]
b The king's dinners at the Chief Pleas in Guernsey, by Edith F. Carey.

84 No. 14.

a Admiral Philip d'Auvergne, duc de Bouillon [d. 1816], by C.J.P.

ANGLO-RUSSIAN LITERARY SOCIETY

Founded 1893, to promote the study of the Russian language and literature.

Proceedings, nos. 29–89 (1901–21):

85 No. 29.

a Our Russian guests in 1799–1800, by W. C. Bridge.

86 No. 33.

a Two Anglo-Russian philanthropists [John and Walter Venning], by Miss R. Venning.

87 No. 35.

a Mr. Heard's Lancastrian school in Russia.

88 No. 62.

a John Howard, the prison reformer, by E. A. Cazalet.

89 No. 63.

a Russia and England in the great war, 1795–1815, by E. G. Rason.

90 No. 67.

a The Eldorado of Canute the Great, by E. G. Rason [Russian trade as the source of Canute's wealth]

ANGLO-SWEDISH LITERARY FOUNDATION

Founded 1927, for the encouragement of cultural intercourse between Sweden and the British Isles through the promotion and diffusion of knowledge and appreciation of the literature and art of Sweden in the British Isles.

Publications:

91 Erik Gustaf Geijer: impressions of England, 1809–10. Comp. from his letters and diaries with introd. by A. Blanck, translated by Elizabeth Sprigge and C. Napier. 1932.

ANTIQUARIAN ASSOCIATION OF THE BRITISH ISLES

Founded 1930, to popularise antiquities of every description; to illustrate them; to show ancient influence on modern life and conditions; and to create a greater desire to preserve things of the past.

Journal, vols. 1–3 (1930–32):

92 Vol. 1.

a Early colonial currency in America.

b Verulam, by H. Johnston.

c Hog-back stones, by J. C. Wall.

d Weapons of the British, by H. Swift.

e Keltic torcs, by L. Scott.

f Graffiti: mediaeval signs, drawings and writings, by E. V. Paterson.

g The Carthusians in pre-Reformation England, by E. R. Power.

h The pyx veil or sindon at Hessett, Suff., by Sybil Andrews.

i A funeral achievement, by M. A. Morton.

j Local markstones, roads and trackways [particularly in Beccles and district, Suff.], by R. C. Dunt.

93 Vol. 2.

a The Suffolk cloth trade in the 15th and 16th centuries, by Barbara McClenaghan.

b The tithe barn at Harmondsworth, Mdx., by P. Arnold.

c Norman castles of Suffolk, by R. Graham.

d Timber framed towers, by J. C. Wall.

e Proof of ancient track alignment, by A. Watkins.

f Castles [barbican, drawbridge, fosse or moat], by W. Wahul. [Contd. in vol. 3, the portcullis]

g A chronology of some of the principal events which affected the coinage of ancient Britain, by A. E. Robinson.

h False and imitation Roman coins: notes on moulds found and coins manufactured elsewhere than in the imperial mints, by A. E. Robinson. [Contd. in vol. 3]

i Weapons of the British bronze age, by H. Swift.

j The Lollards' tower [Lambeth Palace and St. Paul's cathedral], by C. Jackson.

k The sanctity of squeezing [through perforated stones, shrines, etc.], by J. C. Wall.

94 Vol. 3.

a Were Britons cannibals?, by C. H. Everitt.

b Badges [chiefly royal, 12th–18th cent.], by M. A. Morton.

Extra publication:

95 The four shrines of St. Thomas at Canterbury, by J. C. Wall. *P.* 1932.

ARCHAEOLOGICAL AND ARCHITECTURAL SOCIETY OF DURHAM AND NORTHUMBERLAND

Founded 1861, as the Architectural and Archaeological Society of Durham and Northumberland, to visit and describe places of archaeological interest. Title changed to the above form in 1908, though not altered on Transactions.

Transactions, vols. 5–6 (1907–12):

96 Vol. 5.

a [Calder abbey and St. Mary's church, Gosforth, Cumb.]

b [Blyth priory, Notts.]

c [Durham castle.]

d Heighington church, by J. F. Hodgson.

e The Galilee well at Durham, by J. T. Fowler.

f Drawings of parts of the cathedral, Durham, made at the end of the 18th cent., by W. Greenwell.

g Church of St. John the Baptist, Edlingham, Northumb., by W. H. Knowles.

i Some four- and five-lighted north-country 'Decorated windows', including all those in co. Durham, by J. F. Hodgson.

j Barford chapel [nr. Gainford], by R. H. Edleston.

k Sockburn church, by W. H. Knowles.

l Belsay castle, by A. E. Middleton.

97 Vol. 6.

a Aycliffe church revisited: some further notes with illustrations, by J. F. Hodgson.

b Account of a visit to Durham in 1825, by Sir S. Glynne.

c Alnwick Castle, by C. J. Bates.

d Fonts and font covers [in co. Durham], by J. F. Hodgson.

e Distinctive marks of the coins of the bishopric of Durham, by J. T. Fowler.

f Churches of Escomb, Jarrow, and Monkwearmouth, by J. F. Hodgson.

g Monumental effigy near the north door of Durham cathedral, by J. T. Fowler.

h Dedication of the parish church of Staindrop, by T. Romans.

ARCHITECTURAL AND ARCHAEOLOGICAL SOCIETY FOR THE COUNTY OF BUCKINGHAM

Founded 1847, to promote the study of the architecture, archaeology, the general history and natural history and arts of Buckinghamshire.

Records of Buckinghamshire, or papers and notes on the history, antiquities, and architecture of the county; together with the proceedings of the Architectural and Archaeological Society for the county of Buckingham, vols. 8–10 (1897–1910), contd. as Records of Buckinghamshire, vols. 11–12 (1911–33):

98 Vol. 8.

a Church plate of Buckinghamshire, by J. L. Myres.

b Church bells of Buckinghamshire, by E. J. Payne.

c Stained glass from Westlington House, Dinton, by G. F. Lee.

d The parish church of High Wycombe, 3rd notice [previous notices in vol. 7, and] extracts from the churchwardens' and overseers' accounts, by R. S. Downs.

e Inventories of the parish church of All Saints, and of the chapel of the Blessed Virgin Mary, Wycombe [1475–1552], by W. H. St. J. Hope.

f Population returns for Buckinghamshire, 1676, by W. H. Summers.

g Church of St. Mary, Stoke Mandeville, by J. Parker.

h Intra-mural monuments and other inscriptions of Gt. Marlow church, transcribed by A. H. Cocks.

i Proceedings. [Includes an account of the buried Roman city at Silchester, by J. Parker]

j Norman doorways in co. Buckingham, by C. E. Keyser.

k Bletchley [parish] register, by W. Bradbrook.

l A paper from a family deed-chest [relating to Jesuit missionaries, 1592], by J. W. Garrett-Pegge.

m Discovery of a stone coffin in Turville church, by A. H. Cocks.

n The Giffards, pt. 2, by J. Parker. [Pt. 1 in vol. 7]

o Proceedings. [Includes accounts of Hitcham manor and church and Burnham church]

p Notes on place-name endings in Buckinghamshire, by C. F. J. Bourke.

q An account of the church of St. Mary at Turville, and of its recent restoration and enlargement, by W. A. Forsyth.

r Intra-mural monuments of Turville church, by A. H. Cocks.

s Armorial ceiling at Fenny Stratford church, by W. Bradbrook.

t The Benedictine nunnery of Little Marlow, by C. R. Peers.

u 'Tring, Wing and Ivinghoe' [being an attempt to establish the date and authorship of a stanza of which these names form the first line], by E. J. Payne.

v Monumental brasses formerly in Great Marlow church, by M. Stephenson.

w Church of St. Bartholomew, Fingest, by W. A. Forsyth.

x Delafield's manuscript notes on Fingest [comp. in the early 18th cent.], by J. Parker.

y Notes on the history of the manor and church of Hedsor, by Lord Boston.

z Burnham abbey, by H. Brakspear.

aa Church of St. Nicholas, Ibstone, by W. A. Forsyth.

bb A curious piece of church furniture [an oak chest probably connected with the Sandys family of the Vyne, in Hambleden church], by J. C. Fox.

99 Vol. 9.

a Notes on the architectural history of the parish church of All Saints, Wycombe, by W. H. St. J. Hope.

b Wavendon parish register, by W. Bradbrook.

c The church of St. Lawrence, Old Bradwell, by E. S. Harris.

d Letters [to Browne Willis from Dr. Tanner, bishop of St. Asaph, and Dr. Benson, bishop of Gloucester] and notes from the Cole manuscripts, ed. W. Bradbrook.

e Proceedings. [Includes accounts of Twyford and Hillesden]

f The political aspect of Buckinghamshire, by the Earl of Rosebery.

g The ancient hundreds of Buckinghamshire, by A. M. Davies.

h Church of St. Michael, Stewkley, by W. A. Forsyth.

i Proceedings. [Includes accounts of North Marston church and Master John Schorne, fl. *c.* 1290–1314]

j Upton-cum-Chalvey parish register, by E. L. Reynolds.

k Bletchley monuments and epitaphs, by W. Bradbrook.

l Old coins: recent finds in or near High Wycombe, by R. S. Downs.

m The Wooburn version of the Mummers' play, by A. H. Cocks.

n Eton College, by J. Parker.

o Exploration of a 'natural barrow' at Stone, by A. H. Cocks [with a note on the human remains, by W. Wright].

p A semi-underground hut in Walton Road, Aylesbury, by A. H. Cocks.

q Hitcham church, by W. Niven.

r Bucks. churches. [Brief notes on repairs, etc.]

s Note on a palimpsest brass at Twyford, by M. Stephenson.

t Richard Bowle's book [relating to the restoration of the interior of Chesham parish church, 1606], ed. J. W. Garrett-Pegge. [Contd. in vol. 10. Richard Bowle, d. 1626, sometime auditor of the estates of the dukes of Bedford]

u Prehistoric pit-dwellings at Ellesborough, by A. H. Cocks.

v Pew formerly on the old rood-loft, High Wycombe, by F. Skull.

w Notes on some recently-discovered mural paintings at Little Hampden church, by C. E. Keyser.

x Anglo-Saxon burials at Ellesborough, by A. H. Cocks.

y A hoard of bronze implements from New Bradwell, by A. H. Cocks.

z The Royal Latin School, Buckingham (chapel of St. John Baptist), by J. T. Harrison.

100 Vol. 10.

a The Danes' ditches at Danesfield (Medmenham), by A. H. Cocks.

b Aston Abbotts parish register, by W. Bradbrook.

c Stowe and its 'gardens', by W. Niven.

d Parish church of All Saints, High Wycombe, by E. D. Shaw.

e Bronze or latten foot of a portable cross, Stoke Poges, by W. Niven.

f Little Marlow church [drawings and historical notes by F. T. H. White], by W. Niven.

g Disused church of St. Mary the Virgin, Stoke Mandeville, by W. Niven.

h Notes on the court rolls of the rectorial manor at Waddesdon, by A. Ballard.

i A former vicar of Marlow, 1753–1801: John Mortimer Cleobury, by W. Niven.

j Excavations at Norbury camp, Whaddon Chase, by J. Berry and W. Bradbrook.

k Bucks. 17th cent. trade tokens, by W. Crouch.

l The church loft, West Wycombe, by W. Niven.

m Note on two palimpsest brasses at Marsworth, by M. Stephenson.

n A 14th cent. subsidy list for Stone [1335–37], by F. G. Gurney.

o Schedule of payments [of Peter's pence] from the archdeaconry of Buckingham, 1460, by F. W. Ragg.

p Sir William Borlase's benefactions to Marlow [1628], by W. Niven.

q Two 15th cent. neighbours in Edlesborough [of the Rufford family], and some coats of arms, by F. G. Gurney.

r Notes on correspondence relating to High Wycombe [1756–62], by E. L. Reynolds.

s A record of the archdeaconry courts of Buckingham during part of 1521, by F. W. Ragg.

t Masworth church, and deductions from discoveries made therein, 1881–1906, by F. W. Ragg.

u Wing: extracts from churchwardens' accounts [inventories, 1527 and 1552].

v Mr. Weller's collection of Bucks. prints and drawings, by A. H. Cocks.

w Eustace Mascoll: brass in Farnham Royal church [1564/5], by F. C. Carr-Gomm.

x Schedule of tenths and fifteenths of the archdeaconry of Buckingham [1529?], by F. W. Ragg.

y An Eton bill of the 17th cent., by A. H. Cocks.

101 Vol. 11.

a Newton Longville parish books [extracts from accounts of churchwardens and overseers of the poor, 17th–19th cent.], by W. Bradbrook.

b A meeting-place of the early Quakers in Buckinghamshire, by Mrs. G. Eland.

c Fragment of folio ms. of archdeaconry courts of Buckinghamshire, 1491–95, by F. W. Ragg.

d A shorthand 'inventor' of 300 years ago [Thomas Arkisden, fl. 1633], by W. J. Carlton.

e The manor of Great Horwood [procedure of the court baron].

f Clifton Reynes parish account book [extracts, 1665–1723], by W. Bradbrook.

g Association oath rolls for Buckinghamshire, *c.* 1696, by W. Gandy.

h Newton Longville parish register [extracts, 1560–1840], by W. Bradbrook.

i The original charter of Aylesbury: notes on a contemporary copy, by E. Hollis.

j Hillesden account-book, 1661–7 [extracts by G. Eland].

k Tickford priory, by F. W. Bull.

l A Hughenden vicar and his perambulations [John Batchler, 1713–65], by C. Disraeli.

m Easter offerings and small tithes, 1616 [at Hanslope].

n Some early instruments of Tickford priory [12th cent.], by G. H. Fowler.

o A political ballad of the 17th cent., by G. Eland.

p The inclosure of Drayton Parslow [1797], by G. Eland.

q Excavations in Bulstrode camp, by C. Fox and L. C. G. Clarke.

r Manor court rolls of Fenny Stratford [1373–95] and Etone (Bletchley) [1371–84], by W. Bradbrooke.

s Three land-charters of Monks Risborough [13th–15th cent.], by G. H. Fowler.

t Excavations at Danesborough camp, by J. Berry.

u The royal arms in churches, by W. Bradbrook.

v Extents of the royal manors of Aylesbury and Brill, *c.* 1155, by G. H. Fowler.

w The building of Winslow Hall [*c.* 1700], by G. Eland.

102 Vol. 12.

a Concerning an 18th cent. village fire [Marsh Gibbon] and a Bucks. spa, by Margaret M. Verney.

b Fenny Stratford in the 17th cent. [from accounts of overseers of the poor], by W. Bradbrooke.

c Notes on four Bucks. parishes in the archdeaconry of St. Albans [concerning wills and clergy, 1420–88, of Aston Abbots, Little Horwood, Granborough, and Winslow], by A. J. Clear.

d Churchwardens' accounts of Quinton [extracts, 1668–1735], by G. Eland.

e The building of the county hall, Aylesbury [and county gaol, 1720–40], by G. R. Crouch.

f Remains of former church at Chalfont St. Peter, by E. C. Rouse.

g The rector of Bletchley, 1715–27 [Edward Wells], by W. Bradbrooke.

h Haddenham during the civil war [local tax collections and expenses, with notes by Sir C. Firth].

i The parish of Granborough, by C. E. Martin.

j The antiquity of Buckinghamshire, by C. R. Peers.

k Mural paintings in Chalfont St. Giles church, by E. C. Rouse.

l A 16th cent. will [of John Purefoy, 1579], ed. F. G. Gurney.

m Note-books of William Lowndes [1679–1709], ed. G. Eland.

n Notes on Bledlow parish church, by C. O. Skilbeck.

o Recent discoveries at King John's lodge, Wraysbury, by G. H. Fowler.

p Farm accounts, late 14th cent., by E. Hollis.

q An Eton boy's letters [1793].

r An early boundary dispute [North Crawley, 12th cent.], by G. H. Fowler.

s Decorative paintings of the 16th and early 17th cent. in Bosworth House, Wendover, by F. W. Reader.

t The reparation of Bletchley church, 1710, by W. Bradbrooke.

u A funeral in 1765, by G. Eland.

v The iconography of Bucks., by M. R. James.

w A Norman manor house [Boothby Pagnell, Lincs.], by F. W. Bull.

x Lord Chesterfield at Eythrope [three letters, 1778–88, ed. G. Eland].

y Little Missenden wall paintings [pre-Reformation], by E. W. Tristram.

z Some additional trade tokens of Bucks., by E. Hollis.

aa Lewis Atterbury, a Buckinghamshire rector in the 17th cent., by A. L. Browne.

bb A 15th cent. library list [of John Morden, rector of Emberton, 1390–1410].

cc Tudor mural paintings in the lesser houses in Bucks., by F. W. Reader.

dd Mural paintings at Dorney and Aston Clinton, Little Missenden addenda, by E. C. Rouse.

103 Index to Records of Bucks., vols. 1–10. 1928.

ARCHITECTURAL AND TOPOGRAPHICAL SOCIETY

Founded 1908, to make and publish a survey of objects of architectural and archaeological interest in the British Islands. Dissolved 1908.

Publications:

104 The Architectural and Topographical Record, Mar.–Dec. 1908 (4 nos. 1908).

a Dorset, parish of Worth Matravers, by W. I. Travers.

b Dorset, parish of Corfe, by W. I. Travers.

c Bucks., parish of Dorney, by C. O'Brien and W. I. Travers.

d Dorset, parish of Studland, by W. I. Travers.

e Dorset, parish of Church Knowle, by W. I. Travers.

f Bucks., parish of Boveney, by G. S. Mileham and W. I. Travers.

g Dorset, parish of Tyneham, by W. I. Travers.

h Dorset, parish of Steeple.

i Dorset, parish of Kimmeridge, by W. I. Travers.

j Kent, parish of Longfield, by C. E. Lovell.

ARCHITECTURAL ASSOCIATION

Founded 1847, to promote and afford facilities for the study of architecture, and to serve as a medium of communication between the members and others interested in the progress of architecture.

Architectural Association Notes, vols. 16–19 [1901?–1904?], contd. as Journal, vols. 20–49 [1905?–34]:

105 Vol. 16.

a The 19th century [its architectural revivals in England], by J. M. Brydon.

b Life, work and influence of Sir William Chambers, by J. M. Ross.

c John Loughborough Pearson, R.A., by W. D. Caröe.

d Cathedral church of St. Mary-the-Virgin, Lincoln, by S. L. Crosbie.

e Notes on the life and work of Sir Arthur W. Blomfield, A.R.A., (1) by R. T. Blomfield, (2) by S. J. Nicholl.

106 Vol. 17.

a Life, work, and influence of Sir John Vanbrugh, by G. H. Lovegrove.

b Sir George Gilbert Scott, R.A., by A. W. N. Burder.

c Sir Charles Barry, R.A., by H. H. Statham.

d George Edmund Street, R.A., by G. H. F. Prynne.

107 Vol. 18.

a John Francis Bentley: a sketch from memory, by E. I. Bell.

b English monumental brasses of the 13th, 14th, and 15th cent., by A. Oliver.

c William Burges, A.R.A., by P. L. Marks.

d The Royal Architectural Museum: an outline history, by J. P. Seddon.

e Life, work, and influence of Robert Adam and his brothers, by J. Swarbrick. [Appendices in vol. 19]

108 Vol. 20.

a Westminster [a brief historical account], by A. H. Ryan-Tenison.

b Village churches, by A. N. Wilson.
c Life, work, and influence of Sir J. Soane, by A. E. Bullock.
d Old manor houses, by J. A. Gotch.

109 Vol. 21.

a Towers and spires [of English churches], by W. H. Bidlake.
b A comparison between the mediaeval architecture of England and France, by G. H. West.
c The London club house of last century, by A. W. Soames.
d History and development of chimneys, by G. Sanderson.
e The Mansion House: an historical outline, by C. Pinsent.

110 Vol. 22.

a Regent Street [its development], by M. E. Macartney.

111 Vol. 23.

a Sir C. Wren's city of London churches, by A. Keen.
b Oxford [an architectural survey], by E. Warren.
c Some notes on English domestic work of the Renaissance, by H. Tanner.
d The development of house planning, 1300–1900, by L. M. Gotch.

112 Vol. 24.

a Inigo Jones and Wren, by H. W. Brittan.
b George Devey and his work, by J. Williams.
c The development of English brickwork, by H. F. Murrell.

113 Vol. 25.

a A comparison between English and continental ironwork, by J. S. Gardner.
b Life and work of William Butterfield, by E. S. Harris.
c The mediaeval house, by J. A. Gotch.
d Georgian architecture, by M. Bunney.
e The architecture of Bath, by M. A. Green.

114 Vol. 26.

a Sir John Soane, by A. E. Bullock.

115 Vol. 27.

a Some thoughts on Jacobean architecture, by A. T. Bolton.
b Alfred Stevens, by E. F. Strange.

116 Vol. 29.

a The serious art of Thomas Rowlandson, by S. Image.

117 Vol. 30.

a Some notes on Chelsea, by W. H. Godfrey.

118 Vol. 31.

a Some letters from the front [1915–17. Contd. in vol. 32].

119 Vol. 32.

a Some famous coaching inns.

120 Vol. 35.

a Sir John Vanbrugh, by G. M. Aylwin.

121 Vol. 37.

a Ham House and its history, by D. Dovetail.
b The study of English architecture of the 17th and 18th cent., by H. S. Goodhart-Rendel.

122 Vol. 38.

a Sun dials or mass markers on old English churches, by G. E. Bunce.

123 Vol. 39.

a The evolution of the architectural competition, by H. V. Lanchester.

b A brief discourse concerning the three chief principles of magnificent buildings: viz. solidity, conveniency, and ornament, by Sir Balthazar Gerbier D'Ouvelly. Printed in London 1662. [An extract]
c The preservation of old buildings, by B. Oliver.

124 Vol. 40.

a Old Norwich, by E. H. Buckingham.

125 Vol. 41.

a London development, by W. R. Davidge.

126 Vol. 42.

a Discourses on art, by Sir Joshua Reynolds. [Extracts from addresses, 1769–74]

127 Vol. 43.

a Lectures on architecture, by Sir John Soane. [Delivered 1809–37. Contd. in vol. 44]
b Roman excavations at Ashtead [Surrey], by A. W. G. Lowther.

128 Vol. 44.

a A Cistercian monastery in Somerset [St. Mary's, Old Cleeve], by E. L. Bird.

129 Vol. 45.

a Excavation of a Roman settlement on Ashtead common, by A. W. G. Lowther.

130 Vol. 46.

a The architectural work of the order of St. John of Jerusalem in Malta, by Anne J. Cook.

131 Vol. 47.

a Aerial surveying and archaeology, by O. G. S. Crawford.
b The Architectural Association, 1847–1931, by F. R. Yerbury.
c Evolution of the sailing ship, by R. M. Taylor.
d The planning of London, by W. R. Davidge.
e Money, the cause and the remedy of the economic crisis [1931–2], by R. Eisler.
f Norwich from a stranger's viewpoint, by R. Atkinson.

132 Vol. 48.

a Should the monuments be removed from Westminster abbey?, by W. F. Norris.
b The Abbey monuments and the press.
c Dr. Eisler and the gold crisis, by F. Wigglesworth.
d Town and country planning under the Act of 1932, by S. D. Adshead.

133 Vol. 49.

a Window glass: its influence on English architectural design: a theory, by M. L. Anderson.

ARTHURIAN SOCIETY

Founded 1927, to foster the study of Arthurian legend and romance by research. Incorporated with the Society for the Study of Mediaeval Languages and Literature, 1932.

Arthuriana, vols. 1–2 (1929–30):

134 Vol. 1.

a Sir Thomas Malory and the *Piteous History of the Morte of King Arthur*, by Marjorie B. Fox.
b *Chievrefueil* and Thomas' *Tristan*, by E. S. Murrell.

135 Vol. 2.

a Merlin in the Arthurian prose cycle, by Marjorie B. Fox.
b Recent methods of textual criticism, by M. Dominica Legge.
c On textual criticism, with special reference to Anglo-Norman, by A. Ewert.

ARUNDEL CLUB

Founded 1904, for the publication of reproductions of works of art in private collections and elsewhere. Dissolved 1917.

Portfolios, 1904–16 (13 portfolios [1904–16]):

136 For 1904.

a Legend of St. Etheldreda, English school, 15th cent., 2 plates.

137 For 1906.

a Penelope Arabella Bettesworth, by Sir J. Reynolds.

138 For 1907.

a Thomas Howard, Earl of Arundel, by P. van Somer.
b Alathea Talbot, Countess of Arundel, by P. van Somer.
c Henry Howard, Earl of Surrey, by G. Streetes.
d A scullion of Christchurch, Oxford, by J. Riley [1646–1691].
e Miss Montagu, by T. Gainsborough.
f Portrait of Mrs. Besaguliers, by W. Hogarth.

139 For 1908.

a Portrait of Miss Elizabeth Bunn (Mrs. Meymott).
b Charles Towneley, the collector, in his library, with his marbles (now in the British Museum), by Zoffany.
c Portrait groups of members of the Popple and Ashley families, by W. Hogarth.
d Portrait said to be that of William West, 1st Lord Delawarr, attributed to G. Streetes.
e South Gate, Yarmouth, by J. S. Cotman.
f The apotheosis of the Duke of Buckingham, by Rubens

140 For 1909.

a Portraits of Richard Kempenfelt, Sir Samuel Cornish, and Thomas Parry, esq., by J. Zoffany.

141 For 1910.

a Portrait of the Hon. Augusta Phipps, by Gainsborough

142 For 1911.

a Portrait of the Duke of Richmond and Lennox, by Van Somer.
b Portrait of the Countess of Bedford (?), by Van Dyck.
c Portrait of Mrs. Charles Cocks, by Sir J. Reynolds.
d Portrait of Lady Decies and child, by Sir J. Reynolds.
e Portrait of Master Philip Cocks, by Romney.
f Portrait of Countess Castiglione, by G. F. Watts.

143 For 1912.

a King Charles I, by Sir A. Van Dyck.
b Portrait of John Somers Cocks, by G. Romney.
c Anne, Lady Cocks, daughter of Reginald Pole, esq., by G. Romney.
d Philip Yorke, first Earl of Hardwicke, by Sir H. Raeburn.

144 For 1913.

a Portrait of Henry Howard, Earl of Surrey, Flemish school.
b Morton Hall, Cheshire, by J. S. Cotman.

145 For 1915.

a The Earl and Countess of Arundel, by Van Dyck (?).
b Portrait of Peregrine Bertie, 11th Baron Willoughby d'Eresby, Portuguese school.
c Mary Panton, Duchess of Ancaster, by T. Hudson.
d Portrait of Prince Rupert, by Gainsborough.
e Portrait of Clementina Sarah, Lady Willoughby d'Eresby, by Sir T. Lawrence.

146 For 1915.

a The Earl of Arundel with his grandson, by Van Dyck.
b Mrs. Barton Booth, by J. Ellys.
c Lady Hamilton, by Romney.

ASSOCIATED ARCHITECTURAL SOCIETIES

Reports and Papers read at the meetings of the Architectural Societies,[1] vols. 25–40 [1900–33]:

147 Vol. 25.

a Early Lincolnshire inquisitions *post mortem*, by W. O. Massingberd.
b The Heneage family [a history by the Rev. William Oates, rector of Benniworth, 1733], with preface by A. R. Maddison.
c Notes on the ecclesiastical history of the deanery of Graffoe during the 15th and 16th cent., by R. E. G. Cole. [Pt. 2: 17th–18th cent. Contd. for 18th–19th cent. in vol. 26]
d Churches visited in the excursion from Gainsborough, July, 1899, by A. F. Sutton. [Includes: Blyton, St. Martin; Laughton, All Saints; Scotton, St. Genevieve; Scotter, St. Peter; Northorpe, St. John-the-Baptist; Kirton-in-Lindsey, St. Andrew; Blyborough, St. Alkmond; Corringham, St. Lawrence; Saundby, St. Martin; Sturton, St. Peter; East Retford, St. Swithin; West Retford, St. Michael; Clayworth, St. Peter]
e Derby china, by W. O'Neill.
f Early monastic writers of Worcester, by J. K. Floyer.
g Parish clerks and some duties of parish clerks and sextons in pre-Reformation times, by H. Kingsford.
h Severn End, Worcester [and Sir Nicholas Lechmere], by L. Sheppard.
i History of Rous Lench [Worcs.], by W. K. W. Chafy.
j Pre-historic man in Holderness, by T. Sheppard.
k A description of the churches visited in the excursion from Peterborough, July, 1900, by A. F. Sutton. [Irthlingborough, St. Peter; Higham Ferrers, St. Mary the Virgin; Rushden, St. Mary the Virgin; Stanwick, St. Lawrence; Raunds, St. Peter; Lowick, St. Peter; Castor, St. Kyneburga; Fotheringhay, St. Mary the Virgin and All Saints; Oundle, St. Peter; Warmington, St. Mary the Virgin]
l Martin Lister, M.D., F.R.S., by R. W. Goulding.
m Royalist papers [1643–51] relating to the sequestration of the estates of Sir Lewis Watson, knight and baronet, afterwards first Baron Rockingham of Rockingham Castle, during the civil wars in England, by S. T. Winckley.
n Parish registers of Ratby, co. Leicester, 1695–1710, transcribed by H. Hartopp.
o Parish registers of Houghton-on-the-Hill, co. Leicester, 1582–1639, transcribed by H. Hartopp, ed. S. T. Winckley.
p Some unpublished documents [c. 1220–1636] relating to Noseley, co. Leicester, ed. H. Hartopp. [Contd. in vol. 26]
q Institutions to benefices in the diocese of Lincoln, 1547–70: calendar no. 11, nos. 832–1327, by C. W. Foster.
r The *vellum quadragesimale*, or Lenten veil, by F. R. Fairbank.

[1] Bedfordshire Archit. and Archaeol. Soc. (to vol. 30, pt. 1), Lincolnshire Archit. and Archaeol. Soc., Northampton and Oakham Archit. and Archaeol. Soc., Leicestershire Archit. and Archaeol. Soc., Worcestershire Archaeol. Soc., and Yorkshire Archit. Soc.

s Church bells of Worcestershire, pt. 1: mediaeval period, by H. B. Walters.

t Historical notes relating to the parish of Kempsey [Worcs.], by R. C. Purton.

u Remarks on some characteristics of north Northamptonshire churches, by R. P. Brereton.

148 Vol. 26.

a A description of the churches visited in the excursion from Boston, by A. F. Sutton. [Swineshead, St. Mary; Donington, St. Mary and the Holy Rood; Bicker, St. Swithin; Quadring, St. Margaret; Wigtoft, SS. Peter and Paul; Wyberton, St. Leodegarius; Frampton, St. Mary; Kirton, SS. Peter and Paul; Algarkirk, SS. Peter and Paul; Sutterton, St. Mary; Gosberton, SS. Peter and Paul; Surfleet, St. Laurence; Pinchbeck, St. Mary]

b Lincoln cathedral charters, translated with notes by W. O. Massingberd. [Contd. in vol. 27]

c Alien priories of Worcestershire, by J. W. Willis Bund.

d The order of coronation, by Earl Beauchamp.

e History of the parish of Hartlebury [Worcs.], by D. Robertson.

f Bishop [Thomas] Cobham, 1317–27: his monumental work in Worcester cathedral, by Mrs. O'Grady.

g Renaissance architecture in Northamptonshire, by J. A. Gotch.

h Anglo-Saxon remains found at North Luffenham, co. Rutland, by V. B. Crowther-Beynon.

i The lords lieutenant of Leicestershire, by W. G. D. Fletcher.

j Clerks of the peace and lieutenancy for co. Leicester, by W. J. Freer.

k Some notes for a history of Potter Hanworth [Lincs.], by Kate Norgate and M. H. Footman.

l Note on family of Peacock of south Lincolnshire.

m [History of Boston grammar school, in the 14th cent.], by A. F. Leach.

n Ancient fonts on the wolds of East Riding, by E. M. Cole.

o The lords lieutenant and county officials of Northamptonshire, by C. A. Markham.

p Some notes on the parochial history of Brixworth [Northants.], by A. K. Pavey. [Contd. in vol. 28]

q Extracts from and notes on the parish registers of Misterton, co. Leicester, by W. Bradbrook.

r An account of recent discoveries of Roman remains at Rothley Temple, Leics., and in Leicester, by W. J. Freer.

s History of the parish of Inkberrow [Worcs.], by W. Bradbrook.

t Fonts in the archdeaconry of Worcester, by W. Walters.

u Gleanings from parish records [17th–18th cent., chiefly from Stoulton, Worcs.], by H. Kingsford.

v 'Jacob's Well' [an inn], Trinity Lane, York, by J. Solloway.

149 Vol. 27.

a Churches visited in the excursion from Sleaford, June, 1903, by A. F. Sutton. [Heckington, St. Andrew; Hale Magna, St. John the Baptist; Helpringham, St. Andrew; Swaton, St. Michael; Horbling, St. Andrew; Billingborough, St. Andrew; Folkingham, St. Andrew; Silk Willoughby, St. Denis; Sleaford, St. Denys; Ewerby, St. Andrew; Billinghay, St. Michael; Ruskington, All Saints]

b The tower of Irthlingborough church, by W. T. Brown.

c Fotheringhay church: its building and its present (1903) condition, by R. P. Brereton.

d Books that amused and taught the children of olden days [from 1475], by Mrs. Berkeley.

e Life of the Rev. James Wilmot, D.D., vicar of Barton-on-the-Heath and Alcester, Warwicks., fellow of Trinity College, Oxford, 1726–1807, by J. W. Willis Bund.

f Transcript and translation of signet bill conferring a baronetcy upon Richard Halford, esq., of Wistow, Leics., 16 Dec. 1641.

g Anglo-Saxon remains found at North Luffenham, Rutland, previously to 1900, by V. B. Crowther-Beynon.

h The King's pool; the royal fishpond of Fosse, York, by T. P. Cooper.

i Churches visited from Wisbech, by A. F. Sutton. [Elm, All Saints; Emneth, St. Edmund; Tilney All Saints; Terrington, St. Clement; Walpole St. Peter; West Walton, St. Mary; Walsoken, All Saints; Wisbech, St. Peter; Long Sutton, St. Mary; Tydd, St. Giles; Leverington, St. Leonard]

j The priory of St. Catherine without Lincoln, of the order of St. Gilbert of Sempringham, by R. E. G. Cole.

k The making and un-making of a Lincolnshire estate, by A. R. Maddison. [A history of the Maddison family]

l Short notes as to Rothwell priory, by F. W. Bull.

m Recent discoveries of Roman and Anglo-Saxon remains at Kettering, by F. W. Bull.

n Some of the great houses of Northamptonshire, by J. A. Gotch.

o Notes on some unrecorded Saxon work in and near Northamptonshire, by R. P. Brereton.

p The manor house, Yardley Hastings [Northants.], by C. A. Markham.

q The monastery and guesten hall of Worcester, by C. J. Houghton.

r Subsidies of the clergy in the archdeaconry of Leicester in the 17th cent., by A. P. Moore. [With transcripts]

s The Renaissance in Leicestershire (with illustrations), by J. A. Gotch.

t Notes on the will of a mediaeval archdeacon [William Donne, archdeacon of Leicester, fl. 1354–85], by A. P. Moore.

u Leicester marriage licences: an abstract of marriage bonds and allegation books preserved in the registry of the archdeaconry of Leicester, 1570–1729, transcribed and indexed by H. Hartopp. [Contd. in vols. 28 and 29]

v York bell founders, by G. Benson.

150 Vol. 28.

a Copledike [family] of Harrington [13th–17th cent.], by W. O. Massingberd. [With transcripts of documents]

b Brunaburh, 937: identification of this battle site in north Lincolnshire, by A. Hunt.

c The Roman pavement at Horkstow [Lincs.], by A. Hamilton Thompson.

d The priory or house of nuns, of St. Mary of Brodholme [Lincs.], of the order of Prémontré, by R. E. G. Cole. [With transcripts of documents]

e Where was Sidnacester?, by E. M. Sympson. [An attempt to identify the site of the see of the bishops of Lindsey]

f Architectural drawings of Lincoln cathedral in Norman times, by J. J. Smith.

g History and architecture of St. Martin's church, Leicester, by S. J. W. Sanders.

h The Sawyers of Kettering, by F. W. Bull.

i The reredos, the church of the Blessed Virgin, Dallington [Northants.], by T. C. Beasley.

Proceedings of the ecclesiastical courts in the archdeaconry of Leicester, 1516–35, by A. P. Moore. [With transcripts]

k Dovecotes of Worcestershire, by Mrs. Berkeley.

l The de Montfords of Beaudesert [12th–13th cent.], by F. W. Evans.

m The city of Worcester during the great civil war, 1642–1646, by J. W. Willis Bund.

n York churches, with special reference to an anonymous visit made to them in the year 1843, by J. Solloway.

o Notes on the history of the church of St. John the Evangelist, York, by T. A. Brode.

p The royal borough of Torksey [Lincs.], its churches, monasteries, and castle, by R. E. G. Cole.

q Some special features of Somersetshire churches, by H. Cayley.

r Shakespeare in the country and in the town, by A. Ewen. [On Shakespeare's material environment at Stratford, in his journeying to London, and in London itself]

s The royal palace at Colly Weston [Northants.], by Amy Tasker.

t The sequestration papers of Edward Farnham, of Quorndon [1645–6], by W. G. D. Fletcher.

u Kyre Wyard, Worcs. [the house and the Pytts family], by Mrs. Baldwyn-Childe.

v Old timbered houses [in Worcester], by W. K. Shirley.

w Constantine the Great: 'the greatest of all Yorkshire-men', by J. Solloway. [An attempt to establish York as the birthplace of Constantine]

x Some early civic wills of York [1385–1406, transcripts with translations], by R. B. Cook.

151 Vol. 29.

a The Tournays of Caenby [Lincs.], by A. R. Maddison. [With pedigree and abstracts of charters and deeds]

b Pre-Conquest church-towers in north Lincolnshire, by A. Hamilton Thompson.

c A description of the churches visited in the excursion from Grimsby, June, 1907, by A. Sutton. [Grimsby, St. James; Great Coates, St. Nicholas; Immingham, St. Andrew; Killingholme, St. Denis; Ulceby, St. Nicholas; Old Clee, Holy Trinity]

d An 18th cent. squire [Sir Justinian Isham, bt., 1687–1737], his journals and letters, by H. I. Longden.

e Judicial combat, by W. B. Shoosmith.

f A mediaeval legend of St. Peter's, Northampton [relating to St. Ragener], by R. M. Serjeantson.

g Some notes on the wall paintings of Slapton church [Northants.], by E. F. Leach.

h Leicestershire livings in the reign of James I, by A. P. Moore.

i Ancient sculptures at Barton-le-Street [church], Yorks., by H. E. Ketchley.

j Old parish account books [1580–1800] of St. John the Evangelist, York, by T. A. Brode.

k Some Worcestershire churches, by J. Amphlett.

l Roman cardinals [with benefices] at Lincoln, by C. Moor.

m Low side windows of Northamptonshire churches, by C. A. Markham.

n Some Wiltshire houses, by Alice Dryden. [Includes Wardour Castle, South Wraxall manor house, Longford, Longleat, and Wilton]

o The metropolitan visitation of Archbishop Laud [1634, with particular reference to Leicestershire], with an appendix containing transcripts of documents in ecclesiastical suits of the period, and other papers, by A. P. Moore.

p Early history of the family of Farnham, of Quorndon, by W. G. D. Fletcher.

q Some Devonshire church screens, by H. Congreve.

r Wylde [family] of Worcestershire, by L. Bullock.

s Staindrop [Yorks.] with its historical associations, by W. J. Milburn.

t Parish of Holy Trinity, Goodramgate, York: the constables' book, 1636–1736, by G. Benson.

u The Romano-British bishops of York: which was their church?, by J. Solloway.

152 Vol. 30.

a Parish church of All Saints, Winteringham [Lincs.], by J. T. Fowler.

b Church plate of the diocese of Lincoln, by E. M. Sympson.

c Some Lincolnshire faculties, 1663–93, by R. E. G. Cole.

d Admissions to benefices in the diocese of Lincoln, 1587–1660, as recorded in the bishops' certificates returned to the barons of the exchequer, by C. W. Foster.

e The church of Oundle, by R. M. Serjeantson.

f Builders of Peterborough cathedral, by W. Fickling.

g The White friars of Northampton, by R. M. Serjeantson.

h Ancient sundial at Churchill-in-Oswaldslow, near Worcester, by L. Sheppard.

i Two fragments of geometrical treatises found in Worcester cathedral library, by J. M. Wilson.

j The Commandery, Worcester, by L. Sheppard.

k The restored churches of Worcestershire, by J. W. Willis Bund.

l Inkberrow [Worcs.]: parochial records of local government in 1657, by W. Bradbrook. [Extracts from records, 17th–19th cent.]

m St. Mary's abbey, York, by J. Solloway.

n Old clockmakers and watchmakers of York, by T. P. Cooper.

o Marriage contracts or espousals in the reign of Elizabeth, by A. P. Moore.

p Pipewell abbey, Northants., by H. Brakspear.

q Description of the churches visited from Alford, June, 1910. [Addlethorpe, St. Nicholas; Hogsthorpe, St. Mary; Mumby, St. Peter; Huttoft, St. Margaret; the Bolle monuments in Haugh church; Alford church; Saleby church; Strubby church; Maltby church; and others]

r Notes on the history of Well [Lincs.], by E. H. R. Tatham.

s Military effigies at Maltby and Belleau in Lincolnshire, by F. P. Barnard.

t The rectors of Gilmorton [Leics.], including some notes on the parish, by M. Bloxsom.

u Chantry certificates for Leicestershire returned under the Act of 37 Henry VIII, cap. iv, with introd. and supplementary documents, by A. Hamilton Thompson.

v Note on some of the bosses in the cloisters of Worcester cathedral, and in particular on the Jesse tree in the south cloister, by J. M. Wilson.

w Notes on 'the sculptured Worcester rood' occupying one of the spandrils at the east end of the south aisle in the Ladye chapel of Worcester cathedral, by Mrs. O'Grady. [Note by J. M. Wilson]

x The Saxon wall and the monastic ruins near the south-west corner of Worcester cathedral, by L. Sheppard.

y Some Anglo-Saxon antiquities from Bricklehampton, co. Worcester, by F. T. Spackman.

z A monograph on St. John's chapel, Worcester cathedral, by Earl Beauchamp.

aa Notes on the dials or circles on the south door jambs of Stoulton church, near Worcester, from materials supplied by the Rev. Hamilton Kingsford, M.A., by J. M. Wilson.

bb A 17th cent. rogue [John Seamour, fl. 1661, impostor], by J. W. Willis Bund.

cc Holy Trinity church, Goodramgate, York: extracts from the churchwardens' accounts, 1557–1819, by G. Benson.

dd The primate of England [an account of the struggle for precedence between the archbishops of York and Canterbury], by J. Solloway.

ee William de Rothwell [d. *c.* 1361] and his brass [in Rothwell church, Northants.], by R. M. Serjeantson.
ff Hatchments, by C. A. Markham.

153 Vol. 31. (*See also no.* **6442** *below*)

a Dr. Robert Sanderson, rector of Boothby Pagnell, 1619–60, died bishop of Lincoln, 1663, by G. G. Walker.
b Township self-government in Denton, Lincs., by A. Welby.
c The manor and rectory of Kettlethorpe in the parts of Lindsey, by R. E. G. Cole. [List of rectors, 1220–1910]
d Chantry certificates for Northamptonshire [1546–48], ed. with introd. by A. Hamilton Thompson.
e Ashby-de-la-Zouch castle [its history and architecture], by T. H. Fosbrooke.
f Place-names of Leicestershire, by W. Watts.
g The Franciscans or Grey friars of Worcester, by L. Sheppard.
h Notes on building stones used in Worcester cathedral, by J. M. Wilson, with the assistance of L. Sheppard and W. Forsyth.
i Worcestershire bridges, by J. W. Willis Bund.
j Churchwardens' accounts of St. Martin-cum-Gregory, York, 1560–1670 [and the churchwardens' book, 1670–1754], described by G. Benson.
k Some early civic wills of York, by R. B. Cook. [Previous article in vol. 28. Contd. in vols. 32–35]
l The battle of Hatfield [Campodonum, 633] and royal hunting lodge, by W. A. Mathews.
m Observations on Gervase Holles' Lincolnshire notes, 1634–42, by R. E. G. Cole.
n The chantry house in the Newarke [Leicester]: its origin and associations, by S. H. Skillington.
o Edwardian inventories for Leicestershire, by E. H. Day.
p The Bretts of Rotherby, by W. D. Bushell.
q The three Ancient Monuments Bills of 1912, by W. J. Freer.
r The origin and history of the de Senlis family, grand butlers of France and earls of Northampton and Huntingdon, by R. M. Serjeantson.
s The restoration of the long-lost brass of Sir Wm. Catesby [d. 1472?], by R. M. Serjeantson.
t Barnwell castle, Northants. [its history and architecture], by C. A. Markham.
u Some remarks on Prince Arthur's chantry in Worcester cathedral, by Mrs. E. McClure.
v Little Malvern priory, by F. T. Marsh.
w Introductory notes on some of the ancient mss. now shown in Worcester cathedral, by J. M. Wilson.
x The legendary history of Worcestershire, by J. W. Willis Bund.

154 Vol. 32. (*See also no.* **6443** *below*)

a Excavations on the site of Bardney abbey, by C. E. Laing.
b Notes on the history of the abbey of St. Peter, St. Paul, and St. Oswald, Bardney, by A. Hamilton Thompson.
c Two Worcestershire murders [1660, 1707], by J. W. Willis Bund.
d St. Swithin's church, Worcester, by G. Cogswell.
e Some 12th cent. paintings on the vaulted roof of the chapter house of Worcester cathedral, by J. M. Wilson.
f Notes on a Worcester service book now in Exeter cathedral library, by J. K. Floyer.
g Descriptive account of some fragments of mediaeval embroidery found in Worcester cathedral, by H. B. Southwell.
h [Drayton House, Northants.], by S. G. S. Sackville.
i Sanctuaries [sanctuary seekers in Northants.], by R. M. Serjeantson.

j Notes on the Saviles, lords of the manor of Blaby, Leics., by W. H. Bailey.
k The history of the hospital and the new college of the Annunciation of our Lady in the Newarke, Leicester, by A. Hamilton Thompson. [Contd. in vol. 33]
l Notes on Barholme church, Lincs., by G. M. Livett.
m Tombstone inscriptions from Bardney abbey, comp. C. E. Laing, revised by J. T. Fowler.
n Repairs and excavations at Tattershall castle, 1912–14, by A. Hamilton Thompson.
o S. Gilbert of Sempringham: a short sketch of his life and work, by E. C. Griffith.
p Was the effigy of King John in Worcester cathedral originally coloured, or gilt?, by J. M. Wilson.
q Some old wills [including that of Thomas Warmstry, dean of Worcester, 1665], by G. F. Adams.

155 Vol. 33.

a Proceedings relative to the canonization of Robert Grosseteste, bishop of Lincoln, by R. E. G. Cole.
b Pluralism in the mediaeval church; with notes on pluralists in the diocese of Lincoln, 1366, by A. Hamilton Thompson. [Contd. in vols. 34–36]
c Extracts from the accounts and correspondence of Henry Gladwell [steward to Lord George Germain], kept at Drayton during the 18th cent., by S. G. S. Sackville.
d Court rolls of Higham Ferrers, by R. M. Serjeantson. [With notes on town and duchy of Lancaster officials. Contd. in vol. 34]
e The Austin canons of Bridlington, by J. Solloway.
f Architectural and historical notes on the church and parish of Sedgeberrow, Worcs., by F. T. Marsh.
g An antiquarian inventory [or suggested plan for the preservation of local antiquities], by J. W. Willis Bund.
h Proceedings relative to the canonization of John de Dalderby, bishop of Lincoln, by R. E. G. Cole.
i Sermons in Lincoln cathedral [the history and arrangement of preaching turns], by J. O. Johnston.
j Castle Ashby [its architectural history], by J. A. Gotch.
k Worcestershire roads, by J. W. Willis Bund.
l The Bigges of Lenchwick [16th–17th cent.] and their tombs in Norton church, Evesham, by E. A. B. Barnard.

156 Vol. 34.

a Inventories of [Lincolnshire] church goods, 1548, by C. W. Foster.
b A 14th cent. pilgrimage, by J. W. Willis Bund.
c Notes on the misericords in Worcester cathedral, by H. B. Southwell.
d John de Wyke, prior of Worcester, 1301–17: some early glimpses of the early years of his priorate from the *liber albus*, by J. M. Wilson. [Includes the priorate of Wulstan de Bransford, 1317–39]
e Leicestershire documents [feet of fines and extracts from curia regis rolls] *temp.* King John, by A. Hamilton Thompson. [Contd. to 1272 in vol. 35]
f Some papal provisions in the cathedral church of Lincoln, 1306–20, by R. E. G. Cole.
g A Benedictine abbey [Peterborough] in the middle ages, by A. Hamilton Thompson.
h Mediaeval hospitals and alms of Peterborough, by W. T. Mellows.
i Worcestershire and Westminster [relations between the county and abbey to the 13th cent.], by J. W. Willis Bund.
j Notes on church floors, by Mrs. E. Gutch.

157 Vol. 35.

a Masons' marks on Worcester cathedral, by C. B. Shuttleworth.

vacancies of the episcopal see and during the visitations of the diocese by the archbishops of Canterbury as metropolitans, with collations to benefices made by the archbishops *jure devoluto*, from the archiepiscopal registers in the library of Lambeth Palace, 1279–1532, by A. Hamilton Thompson.

c St. Leonard's hospital, York, by G. Benson.

d 17th and 18th cent. domestic architecture of Stamford, by H. F. Traylen.

e Social and economic conditions in the Holland division of Lincolnshire, 1640–60, by Gladys M. Hipkin.

f The family of Gervase Holles, by A. C. Wood.

g The Mansion House, or official residence of the lord mayor of York, by T. P. Cooper.

h Roman site at Sharaoh, near Nobottle, Brington, Northants., by H. O. Cavalier.

i Pottery and coins [from the Nobottle excavation], by B. H. St. J. O'Neil.

j Tithe barn of Croyland abbey, Wellingborough, by J. W. Fisher.

163 Index to vols. 20–25 (1889–1900) of Reports and Papers of the Associated Architectural Societies, by G. T. Harvey. 1905.

164 Index to vols. 26–36 (1901–22) with which is incorporated an index of the articles in vols. 1–25 of Reports and Papers of the Associated Architectural Societies, by C. W. Foster and R. C. Dudding. *P.* 1929.

BACON SOCIETY

Founded 1886, (1) to encourage the study of the works of Francis Bacon; also his character, genius, and life; his influence, and the tendencies and results of his writing; (2) to encourage the general study of the evidence in favour of his authorship of the plays commonly ascribed to Shakespeare, and to investigate his connection with other works of the period.

Baconiana, new ser., vols. 9–10 or nos. 33–40 (1901–2):

165 Vol. 10.

a The parentage of Francis Bacon, by P. Woodward.

b 'The parentage of Francis Bacon', by G. Stronach.

Baconiana, 3rd ser., vols. 1–21 or nos. 1–81 (1903–34):

166 Vol. 1.

a Francis Bacon and his knowledge of field sports.

b Francis Bacon, the statesman: illustrations of his methods of working, by G. James.

c Bacon and Essex, by G. Stronach.

d Sixteenth century copyright, by C. Y. C. Dawbarn.

e The raison-d'être of mediaeval papermarks, by W. Krisch.

167 Vol. 2.

a Sixteenth century grammar schools, by P. Woodward.

b Notes on the state of religion in Shakespeare's day, by H. Bayley.

c The migration of woodblocks.

168 Vol. 3.

a Education in the universities [in the 16th cent.].

b The charges against Lord St. Alban, by P. Woodward.

169 Vol. 5.

a Masque music in Bacon's time, by Alice C. Bunten.

170 Vol. 6.

a An interesting letter to young Francis Bacon [from Sir Thomas Bodley, *c.* 1577].

b [Transcript of an agreement concerning the division of the rent of an inn at Chelmsford, formerly the property of Benedict Barnham, father of Bacon's wife, *c.* 1621]

c Letter by Sir Thomas Bodley [to Sir Francis Bacon, 1607].

171 Vol. 8.

a Bacon as an East Anglian M.P.

b *Newes from Spayne.* [Extracts from a tract published in 1620]

172 Vol. 9.

a The mystery of Francis Bacon, by W. T. Smedley.

b Bacon in France, by Alicia A. Leith.

c Francis Bacon's appointment as K.C., by H. Hardy.

d John Barclay's *Argenis* and Bacon's secret life, by G. C. Cuningham.

e Bacon in Italy, by Alicia A. Leith.

173 Vol. 10.

a Burghley and Bacon, by W. T. Smedley.

b Bacon's Warwickshire relations, by H. Hardy.

c Francis Bacon as treasurer of Gray's Inn, by H. Hardy. [Contd. in vol. 11]

174 Vol. 11.

a Francis Bacon and the rectory at Cheltenham, by H. Hardy.

b The dates of Spenser's birth and death, by G. C. Cuningham.

c Jottings on Lord Bacon: references to Bacon's death, and the desecration of his tomb, by Alice C. Bunten. [Contd., with particular reference to Sir Thomas Meautys, in vol. 12, and to mss. at Lambeth Palace, in vol. 13]

175 Vol. 12.

a Did Bacon die in 1626?, by P. Woodward.

b Bacon and Portugal, by Alicia A. Leith.

c Something about Arundel House, Highgate, by Alicia A. Leith.

d Chief events in the life of Sir Thomas Meautys, brother of Lady Jane Cornwallis and 2nd cousin to Sir Thomas Meautys, secretary to Lord Bacon, by Alice C. Bunten.

176 Vol. 13.

a Francis Bacon, born 22 Jan. 1560/1, by W. T. Smedley.

b The problem of Shakespeare's marriage explained by the canon law, by H. Hardy.

c Thomas Heywood, by W. T. Smedley.

d The story of Robert Devereux, Earl of Essex.

e Churchwardens' accounts [St. Martin-in-the-Fields], by G. C. Cuningham.

f Bacon's expenses, by P. Woodward.

g Notes on 'Bacon's expenses', by W. T. Smedley.

h Copy of the will of Sir Nicholas Bacon, lord keeper of the great seal.

177 Vol. 14.

a Robert, Earl of Essex, by G. C. Cuningham.

b Did Bacon die in 1626?, by G. C. Cuningham.

178 Vol. 15.

a Thomas Lodge, by P. Woodward.

b Bacon's death and burial, by G. C. Cuningham.

179 Vol. 16.

a Bishop Thirlby and Shakespeare's house in Blackfriars, by H. Hardy.

b Bacon's death in 1647, by H. A. W. Speckman.

c The Bacon family.

180 Vol. 17.

a Did Bacon die in 1626?, by Alicia A. Leith.

181 Vol. 18.

a An historical sketch of Canonbury tower, by H. Seymour.

b Biographers of Bacon, by Sir J. A. Cockburn.

c Notes on Anthony Bacon's passports of 1586, by Alice C. Bunten.

d Francis Bacon and Gray's Inn, by Sir D. P. Barton, bt.

182 Vol. 19.

a Notes on Bacon and Edward Alleyn of Dulwich College, by Alice C. Bunten.

b Kimbolton Castle chronicles, by Sir J. A. Cockburn.

183 Vol. 20.

a Robert, second Earl of Essex, by P. Woodward.

b John Barclay's *Argenis*: a reprint of the key published by 'Sir Robert Le Grys', 1629.

c The interrogatories of Francis Bacon, by M. F. Bayley. [Contd. in vol. 21]

184 Vol. 21.

a The origin of freemasonry, by L. Biddulph.

b Dugald Stewart [Scottish mathematician and philosopher] on the sublime genius of Francis Bacon, by Alicia A. Leith.

c The Bacon pedigree, by Mrs. Foggitt *née* Gertrude Bacon.

d Francis Bacon and the money-lenders [*c.* 1590–1607], by C. L'E. Ewen.

BANGOR WELSH MSS. SOCIETY

Founded 1907, for transcribing and publishing original documents relating to Wales.

Publications, vols. 1–8 (5 vols. 1908–14):

185 Vol. 1. Gwaith barddonol Howel Swrdwal a'i fab Ieuan, gan J. C. Morrice. 1908. [The poetical works of Howel Swrdwal and his son Ieuan, by J. C. Morrice]

186 Vol. 2. Vita sancti Tathei and Buched seint y Katrin, by H. I. Bell. 1909. [The life of St. Tatham from a 13th cent. ms., and the Welsh life of St. Catherine from a 15th cent. ms., both in the British Museum]

187 Vols. 3, 4. Casgliad o waith Ieuan Deulwyn, gan I. Williams. 1909. [The works of Ieuan Deulwyn collected from various sources, by I. Williams]

188 Vol. 5. Detholiad o waith Gruffydd ab Ieuan ab Llewelyn Vychan, gan J. C. Morrice. 1910. [Selections from the work of Gruffydd ab Ieuan ab Llewelyn Vychan by J. C. Morrice from mss. in the British Museum]

189 Vols. 6–8. Gwaith Dafydd ab Edmwnd. 1914. [The poems of Dafydd ab Edmwnd, collected from various sources by Thomas Roberts]

BAPTIST HISTORICAL SOCIETY

Founded 1908, to promote historical research as to Baptists, especially in the British Isles.

Transactions, vols. 1–7 (1908–21):

190 Vol. 1.

a Early Welsh Baptist doctrines, set forth in a ms. ascribed to Vavasor Powell [d. 1670], ed. C. Burrage.

b Letter to William Carey, jun., [from] William Carey, D.D. [1812].

c Baptists and Bartholomew's day [1662], by W. T. Whitley.

d William Vidler, Baptist and universalist [1758–1816], by F. W. Butt-Thompson.

e Porton Baptist church [Wilts.], 1655–85, by A. Tucker.

f Instructions to a missionary [Jabez Carey, from William Carey, 1814].

g First impressions of Bristol [1826], by W. Robinson.

h The Serampore mission [1836], by J. Foster.

i An unrecorded first edition of Bunyan, by J. C. Foster.

j A 17th cent. Baptist church: Bromsgrove, by J. Ford.

k Leonard Busher, Dutchman [fl. 1611–14], by W. T. Whitley.

l Baptist literature till 1688. [Contd. in vol. 2]

m Original sin, feet-washing, and the New Connexion. [Letter from Daniel Dobel, 1771]

n Dr. Carey and the *Baptist Magazine* [1815].

o Printing Ryland's funeral sermon [letter from Robert Hale to Joseph Gutteridge, 1825], ed. J. Stuart.

p Militant Baptists, 1660–72.

q The Baptist licenses of 1672.

r Old Wisbech records.

s Sutton-in-the-Elms and Arnesby.

t Benjamin Stinton [d. 1719] and his Baptist friends.

u Stinton's historical researches.

v Records of the Jacob–Lathrop–Jessey church, 1616–41.

w Rise of the Particular Baptists in London, 1633–44.

x Debate on infant baptism, 1643.

y The Jacob–Jessey church, 1616–78.

191 Vol. 2.

a A sabbatarian pioneer: Dr. Peter Chamberlen [1601–83], by J. W. Thirtle.

b The Hubbard–How–More church, from Gould's copy of Stinton's *Repository*.

c Circular letter of the Berkshire Association, 1707.

d [James] Mursell's preparation for college. [Letter from John Ryland, 1820]

e The contents of Stinton's *Repository*.

f The Baptist interest under George I, by J. Evans.

g Thomas Newcomen: inventor and Baptist minister, 1663–1729, by J. Ford.

h 'A trve and short declaration, both of the gathering and joining together of certain persons (with John More, Dr. Theodore Naudin, and Dr. Peter Chamberlen) and also of the lamentable breach and division which fell amongst them', ed. C. Burrage. [Records of Anabaptists in London, *c.* 1652–4]

i Seeking a change. [Letters from Richard Adams to John Howe and to the Baptists at Whitchurch, 1709]

j The Fifth Monarchy movement, by A. J. D. Farrer.

k Thomas Tryon, 1634–1703, by J. C. Foster.

l The origins of modern Baptist denomination, by G. P. Gould. [Issued as supplement to vol. 2, no. 3]

m Memorials of the Treacher family, by W. J. Collins.

n Baptist churches till 1660. [County lists, England and Wales]

o The Bunyan christening, 1672, by W. T. Whitley.

192 Vol. 3.

a Salisbury and Tiverton about 1630 [records respecting Baptists], ed. A. Tucker and H. B. Case.

b Bampfield's plan for an educated ministry [*c.* 1680].

c The Helwys family, by W. H. Burgess.

d The revival of immersion in Holland and England, by W. T. Whitley.

e Haddenham [Bucks.] and two Peter Tylers, by G. Loosley.

f Early days at Eythorne [the Baptist community there], by W. T. Whitley.

g A Hertfordshire worthy: Jonas Thurrowgood, of Hitchin [d. 1753], by W. B. Gerish.

h The 'Johnsonian Baptists', by R. Dawbarn.

i William Mitchill's *Jachin and Boaz*, 1707, ed. W. E. Blomfield.

i Daniel Noble [d. 1783].
j The Stinton *Repository* of 1712.
k The Wallis house [Kettering], 1792, by W. T. Whitley. [The early history of Baptists in Northamptonshire]
l The late Midland College, by W. J. Avery.
m Early Baptists in Hampshire, by W. T. Whitley.
n Welsh Baptists till 1653.
o London preaching about 1674.
p Origin of the General Baptist Missionary Society, by J. G. Pike and A. Dakin.
q New light on Dr. Carey [missionary, d. 1834], by S. P. Carey.
r The Baptist Board, by A. J. Payne.
s English in Amsterdam about the time of John Smyth [*c.* 1600–10], by W. T. Whitley.
t The English career of John Clarke, Rhode Island [*c.* 1660].
u Prosecutions of Worcestershire dissenters under the Stuarts.

198 Vol. 2.

a Continental Anabaptists and early English Baptists, by W. T. Whitley.
b The relation between English Baptists and the Anabaptists of the Continent, by A. J. D. Farrer.
c The Lincolnshire conference of the New Connexion, 1791–1803, by T. R. Hooper.
d Andrew Fuller, 1754–1815, by G. Laws.
e Abraham Greenwood, 1749–1827, by A. S. Langley.
f Baptists in east Kent, by W. T. Whitley.
g The value of denominational history, by H. W. Robinson. [Based on an unpublished discipline book, 1689–1723, of a London Baptist church formed by Hanserd Knollys]
h George Fox and Roger Williams: a battle of giants [Rhode Island, 1671–3], by H. J. Cowell.
i Former secretaries of the Baptist Union [1811–98], by C. M. Hardy.
j *The Gospel Minister's Maintenance vindicated.* [Summary of the book by Benjamin Keach]
k A student's programme in 1744, ed. J. C. Ryland.
l The Morgans of Birmingham [19th cent.], by F. W. Butt-Thompson.
m Midland [Baptist] churches of 1651.
n [The Baptists in] hamlets in Surrey and Sussex.
o An early recruit from the clergy [Samuel Oates, d. 1683].
p Catholic holy days and Puritan sabbaths, by W. T. Whitley.
q Baptists in the Weald [of Kent].

199 Vol. 3.

a A Baptist student: John Collett Ryland, by H. W. Robinson.
b Stony Stratford [Baptist church], by W. T. Whitley.
c The church covenant of the Particular Baptist church, meeting in the Horse Fair, Stony Stratford, Bucks. [John Goodrich, pastor, 1790].
d The Indulgence of 1687 in Wales, by J. M. Jones.
e Richard Baxter, the director of souls, by A. S. Langley.
f The centenary of the Baptist Building Fund, by S. J. Price.
g Wales under the penal code, 1662–87. [Review of book by Thomas Richards]
h Dr. Thomas Thomas, of Pontypool [d. 1881], by E. W. P. Evans. [Review of biography by T. Morgan]
i Three hundred years of Baptist life in Coventry. [Review of book by Irene Morris].
j Baptist beginnings in the West Riding, by D. Glass.
k Capel-y-ffin, by D. Attwater. [Extracts from a Breconshire Baptist register]
l Baptist gleanings in Stafford.

m Baxter's work, by W. H. Haden.
n A pilgrimage to Bessell's Green [Kent], by T. R. Hooper.
o A Baptist soldier, William Allen [fl. 1647–60], by H. W. Robinson.
p Some notable names in midland Baptist history, by A. S. Langley.
q John Gibbs, 1627–99, by M. F. Hewett.
r Broadmead's call to Robert Hall. [Letters, 1825]
s Burnham's group of churches.
t Gower Street chapel [London].
u Bunyan relics, by C. B. Cockett.

200 Vol. 4.

a John Bunyan, by G. O. Griffith. [Review of biography by R. H. Coats]
b Cromwell and America, by H. J. Cowell.
c The experience of John Ryland [1770], ed. H. W. Robinson.
d Colonel Thomas Blood [d. 1680], by W. T. Whitley.
e Early years of the Baptist Union, by S. J. Price.
f General Baptists in Surrey and Sussex. 1: Lewes–Ditchling, by W. T. Whitley; 2: Outwood, by T. R. Hooper.
g Bunyan the Baptist, by J. H. Thomas.
h Early Baptist movements in Suffolk, by A. J. Klaiber.
i Serampore and its college, by W. T. Whitley.
j Mrs. Judson on her husband's imprisonment in Burma: a letter to Mrs. J. Deakin of Glasgow [1826].
k *The Baptists of London*, by W. T. Whitley. [A review by John W. Ewing]
l John Smyth [fl. 1590] and the freedom of faith, by H. W. Robinson.
m Baptists of Liverpool in the 17th cent., by O. Knott. [Pt. 1 only]
n William Law, controversialist and mystic [b. 1686], by J. B. Middlebrook.
o Reminiscences of the abolition of religious tests in the universities of Oxford and Cambridge, by J. A. Aldis.
p Col. Sir Jerome Sankey, M.P., Ph.D. [fl. 1655].
q Coxe Feary, founder of Bluntisham [Baptist church, Hunts.], by A. E. Willings.
r Sutcliff's academy at Olney.
s Wales under the Indulgence, 1672–5. [Summary of a book by Dr. T. Richards].
t Bristol Baptist College: the 250th anniversary.
u Henry Miller of Warbleton, 1729.
v Newport, Isle of Wight [Baptist churches].
w A Sussex lay preacher seeing camp meetings in America. [From the diary and letters of John Burgess, 1785–1819]
x Giles, father and sons. [William, b. 1771; William, b. 1798; John Eustace, b. 1805]
y Dr. John Gill's confession of 1729, by S. J. Price.
z Sutton in Ashfield [Baptist churches].

201 Vol. 5.

a Reminiscences of the Rev. John Aldis [fl. 1850] of Maze Pond [Bermondsey], by J. A. Aldis.
b Prisoners [including Baptists] in Devon and Cornwall in 1672.
c The Bloody assizes of 1685.
d Repairing a meeting-house in 1720 [at Horsleydown], by S. J. Price.
e The influence of Whitefield on Baptists, by W. T. Whitley.
f 'Brother [John] Giles' becomes a recognised minister [1789], by S. J. Price.
g Sidelights from an old minute book [of Spurgeon's tabernacle, 1719–1806], by S. J. Price.
h Baptist trust deeds, by S. J. Price.

i Baptists in a Huguenot temple, La Patente church, Spitalfields [Brown's Lane chapel].
j Early relations of Horton academy and Rawdon college [Yorks.] with Lancashire, by A. C. Underwood.
k Newport Pagnell Baptists, by F. W. Bull.
l J. C. Ryland as schoolmaster, by W. T. Whitley.
m Bunhill Fields [London]: the place and the records, by W. T. Whitley.
n *Distressed Sion relieved*, 1689 [by Benjamin Keach].
o Little Wild Street [chapel, London].
p The Blight family, by S. J. Price.
q A treasurer and his college [James Smith, of Melbourne and the Academy of the New Connexion, Nottingham, 1764–1847], by W. T. Whitley.
r James Foster, D.D., 1697–1753, by F. Beckwith.
s Sandhurst [Baptist chapel, Kent] bicentenary.
t John Miles in Wales, 1649–63.
u Early Baptists at Nottingham.
v Thurlaston [Baptist chapel, Leics.], 1784, by H. W. Fursdon.
w Ann Hasseltine Judson's letters, 1818–22.

202 Vol. 6.

a Bow [London] men and their [Baptist] church, by F. W. Butt-Thompson.
b Calendar of letters, 1742–1831, collected by Isaac Mann.
c The first Leeds Baptist church, by F. W. Beckwith.
d Richard Thomas of Harley Wood [d. 1772], by F. G. Hastings.
e Dissenting academies, 1662–1820, by S. J. Price.
f The story of Methodist union, by A. W. Harrison.
g Toc H (Talbot House), by J. R. Lewis.
h The Deputies of the dissenters [1730–1930].
i Henry Hills, official printer [fl. 1640–1700].
j John Stutterd of Colne [Lancs., d. 1818].
k The Spurgeon centenary.
l Locke and the spirit of toleration, by E. W. P. Evans.
m John Clifford [d. 1923, of Westbourne Park chapel, London].

Extra publications:

203 The church books of Ford or Cuddington and Amersham, Bucks., ed. W. T. Whitley. 1912.

204 The Baptists of Yorkshire, being the centenary memorial volume of the Yorkshire Baptist Association. 1912. [The single-volume edition of this and the following, no. 205, stated to have been published by the Society under the title 'Baptists in Yorkshire, Lancashire, Cheshire and Cumberland: augmented edition of two Association volumes [1913]' has not been seen]

a Baptist principles before the rise of Baptist churches, by H. W. Robinson.
b Baptist churches of Yorkshire in the 17th and 18th cent., by W. E. Blomfield.
c The present Baptist churches of Yorkshire, by J. B. Morgan and C. E. Shipley.
d The Yorkshire Baptist Association, by J. Haslam.

205 Baptists of north-west England, 1649–1913. Prepared for the Lancashire and Cheshire Association by W. T. Whitley. 1913.

206 The works of John Smyth, fellow of Christ's College, 1594–8. Tercentenary edn. with notes and biography by W. T. Whitley. 2 vols. 1915.

207 The Baptists of London, 1612–1928, by W. T. Whitley. [Published with the help of the London Baptist Association, 1928]

208 Calvinism and evangelism in England, especially in Baptist circles, by W. T. Whitley. *P.* [1933].

BARROW NATURALISTS' FIELD CLUB AND LITERARY AND SCIENTIFIC ASSOCIATION

Founded 1876, for the study of the natural history, history, and antiquities of the district around Barrow and Low Furness.

Annual Reports and Proceedings, vols. 15–20 (1901–13):

209 Vol. 15.

a Notes on a socketed bronze celt, by H. Gaythorpe.

210 Vol. 16.

a The old forest laws and their influence on English scenery and the character of the English people, by H. G. Pearson.

211 Vol. 17.

a Conishead priory, and Harlesyde Isle or Chapel Island, by H. Gaythorpe.
b Dalton castle and church, and Ireleth chapel, by H. Gaythorpe.
c Gleaston castle.
d Rampside, by H. Gaythorpe.
e The Walney fords, by H. Gaythorpe.
f Millom church and castle: Arnaby school, by H. Gaythorpe.
g Urswick: the stone walls, by H. Gaythorpe.
h William Close: surgeon, apothecary, historian, musician [d. 1813], by H. Gaythorpe.
i The village of Barrow in the parish of Dalton-in-Furness: owners and occupiers in 1843, by W. B. Kendall.
j The village of Barrow: supplementary notes, by H. Gaythorpe.
k Recent archaeological discoveries in Furness, by H. Gaythorpe.
l The pele of Fotheray [Foulney Island], by T. K. Fell.
m Dendron: the history of a Furness village, by A. J. Humphris.

212 Vol. 18.

a Waste of coastline, Furness and Walney, in 1,000 years, by W. B. Kendall.
b Furness abbey in the days of the monastery, by H. G. Pearson.
c Swarthmoor Friends' meeting house: its history and associations, by H. Gaythorpe.

213 Vol. 19.

a Muchland and its owners, by W. B. Kendall.

Annual Reports and Proceedings, new ser., vols. 1–2 (1929–33):

214 Vol. 1.

a Furness before the coming of the monks, by P. V. Kelly.

BASKERVILLE CLUB

Founded 1903, for the encouragement of bibliographical studies by publications and otherwise. Dissolved 1931.

Publications, nos. 1–2 (1904–14):

215 No. 2. Bibliography of the work of John Donne, dean of St. Paul's, by G. Keynes. 1914.

BATH NATURAL HISTORY AND ANTIQUARIAN FIELD CLUB

Founded 1855, to make excursions round Bath with the view of investigating the natural history, geology, and antiquities of the neighbourhood. Dissolved c. 1910.

Proceedings, vol. 9–vol. 11, no. 3 (1901–9):

216 Vol. 9.

a The purpose, the age and the builders of Stonehenge, by E. S. Maskelyne.

b Notes on ancient British remains found in a lias quarry at Tyning, Radstock, by J. McMurtrie.

c A Roman villa discovered at Northstoke, by C. W. Shickle.

d Some heraldic tiles in the Bath Literary Institute, by C. W. Shickle.

e Notes on Roman pavement found at the Royal United Hospital [Bath], by T. Browne.

f The Denys family and their connection with the manors of Alveston, Siston and Dyrham [Glos.], by T. S. Bush.

g Summary of proceedings [including accounts of visits to Blenheim Palace, Broughton Castle, and Compton Wynyates, and Stonehenge and Old Sarum].

h Keynsham briefs [1750–1822], by C. W. Shickle.

i Notes on the borough of Bath and the hundred of Bath Forinsecum, by T. W. Whale.

j The manor house, Colerne [Wilts.], by W. E. Blathwayt.

k Summary of proceedings and excursions [including accounts of visits to Silbury and Avebury, Colerne and Lucknam, Worcester, Evesham and Broadway, and Sherborne, Dorset].

l Notes on an old map of the parish of Walcot [1740], by C. W. Shickle.

m Subsidy roll of Somerset, 13 Henry IV [1411–12], by C. W. Shickle.

n Romano-British remains found at Kilmersdon Lane quarry, Radstock, by J. McMurtrie.

o Summary of proceedings and excursions [including accounts of visits to Chepstow and Tintern, Oxford and Great Haseley, and Bristol].

p The guild of Merchant Taylors in Bath, by C. W. Shickle.

q Notes on the tumbrel, cucking and ducking stools, by T. S. Bush.

r Notes on a box at St. Peter's church, Bristol, by T. S. Bush.

s Notes on a socketed bronze celt, by H. Gaythorpe.

t Summary of proceedings and excursions [including accounts of visits to Malmesbury and Charlton Park, Cirencester, and Devizes and Bromham].

217 Vol. 10.

a William Smith, LL.D., the father of British geology, by H. Woodward.

b Notes on an old building at Witham, by W. Gill.

c Ancient Roman coins discovered at Bathwick, by C. W. Shickle.

d The principles of the Somerset Domesday, by T. W. Whale.

e Summary of proceedings and excursions [including accounts of visits to Chew Magna and Stanton Drew].

f Thomas Linley [d. 1795]: his connection with Bath, by E. Green.

g Richard Brinsley Sheridan: his connection with Bath, by E. Green.

h Thomas Mathews [d. 1820]: his connection with Bath, by E. Green.

i Notes on ancient stone crosses of Somerset, by E. J. Appleby.

j C. S. Calverley and a tomb at Southstoke, by M. H. Scott.

k Bath token issues of the 18th cent., by S. Sydenham.

l Summary of proceedings and excursions [including accounts of visits to Berkeley Castle, Iron Acton, Yate and Horton, Montacute and Stoke-sub-Hambdon, and Bristol].

m Richard Brinsley Sheridan and Thomas Linley: their residences at Bath, by E. Green.

n Accounts of the city [of Bath] train bands, by C. W. Shickle.

o Ancient interments at Newton St. Loe, near Bath, by J. P. E. Falconer.

p Bath tokens of the 19th cent. and their issuers, by S. Sydenham.

q Summary of proceedings and excursions [including accounts of visits to the Forest of Dean, Wardour Castle and Caerwent].

r John Wilkes and his visits to Bath, by E. Green.

s Bath city and traders' tokens issued during the 17th cent., by S. Sydenham.

t Summary of proceedings and excursions [including an account of a visit to Bridgwater].

218 Vol. 11.

a Excavations on the so-called Via Julia, and on Lansdown, by A. T. Martin.

b Summary of proceedings and excursions [including an account of a visit to Langport].

c Cardinal Adrian, bishop of Bath and Wells, by C. W. Shickle.

d An archdeacon of Bath in the 12th cent. [Petrus Blesensis or Peter of Blois], by F. Shum.

e Bath pleasure gardens of the 18th cent. issuing metal admission tickets, by S. Sydenham.

f Rev. George Webbe [1641], rector of Bath and bishop of Limerick, by C. W. Shickle.

g Bits about Combe down, by A. Richardson.

h Summary of proceedings and excursions [including an historical account of Malmesbury and accounts of visits to Westbury and Edington, Longleat and Wedmore].

BATH RECORDS SOCIETY

Founded c. 1921.

Publications:

219 Ancient deeds belonging to the corporation of Bath, 13–16 cent., translated and epitomised by C. W. Shickle. 1921.

BEDFORD ARTS CLUB

Founded 1903, to promote social intercourse amongst men interested in science, art, and literature.

Arts Club series, nos. 1–4:

220 No. 1. Chicksands priory: its monastic and later possessors, by W. C. Massey. *P.* 1905.

221 No. 2. The great siege of Bedford castle [1224]: a chapter of local history, comp. from original and contemporary records, by A. R. Goddard. *P.* 1906.

222 No. 3. Chantry certificates for Bedfordshire: a transcript of the return made by the commissioners in the reign of Edward VI, with introd. by J. E. Brown; institutions of chantry priests in Bedfordshire, by F. A. Page-Turner. [1903]

223 No. 4. 'Ouse's silent tide'—Cowper [being an account of the history of the Great Ouse], by C. F. Farrar. *P.* [1910]

BEDFORDSHIRE HISTORICAL RECORD SOCIETY

Founded 1912, to collect and to make accessible materials for the history of the county.

Octavo publications, vols. 1-15 (1913-33):

224 Vol. 1.

a The Beauchamps, barons of Bedford, by C. G. Chambers and G. H. Fowler.
b Clerical subsidies in the archdeaconry of Bedford, 1390-2 and 1400-1, by J. E. Brown.
c Domesday notes, by G. H. Fowler. [Contd. in vol. 5]
d A lease of Caddington manor in 1299, by C. G. Chambers.
e Sir William Harper [d. 1574], by F. A. Page-Turner.
f Early charters of the priory of Chicksand, by G. H. Fowler.
g Notes on two trades [strawplaiting, brickmaking], by W. Austin.
h Roll of the justices in eyre at Bedford, 1202, by G. H. Fowler.
i Some records of Northill college, by C. G. Chambers. [Contd. in vol. 2]

225 Vol. 2.

a Bedfordshire wills and administrations [1379-1627] proved at Lambeth Palace and in the archdeaconry of Huntingdon, by F. A. Page-Turner.
b The Beauchamps, barons of Eaton, by G. H. Fowler.
c Ancient Bedfordshire deeds, by F. A. Page-Turner. [Contd. in vols. 4 and 8]
d Bedfordshire charters in the Missenden cartulary, by G. H. Fowler.
e The Brown e family of Arlesey, by F. A. Page-Turner.
f Markets and fairs of Luton, by W. Austin.
g The assessment of knight service in Bedfordshire, by J. E. Morris. [Contd. in vol. 5]
h *Materies genealogica* [notes relating to Beds. families from monuments and registers in other counties], by F. A. Page-Turner.
i An early Bedfordshire taxation [1237], by Mrs. Hilary Jenkinson.
j A commutation of villan services [*c.* 1216-40], by W. Austin.
k Records of knight service in Bedfordshire, by G. H. Fowler.

226 Vol. 3.

a Roll of the justices in eyre at Bedford, 1227, by G. H. Fowler.
b Domesday water mills of Bedfordshire, by W. Austin.
c The king's larderer of Meppershall, by Mrs. Hilary Jenkinson.
d Recruiting of militia, 1798.

227 Vol. 4.

a Will of Roger Benetheton [of Colmworth], 1438-9, by R. M. Serjeantson.
b Ancient indictments, 1341-2, by G. H. Fowler.
c Selections from jury lists [1780-1830], by J. E. Brown.

228 Vol. 5.

a St. John [family] of Southill, by F. A. Page-Turner.
b Some Saxon charters, by G. H. Fowler.
c A late example of a deodand [1758], by W. Austin.
d The Hillersdens of Elstow, by F. A. Page-Turner.
e Grant of free warren to Newnham priory [1385], by J. Hamson.
f Cutenho, Farley hospital, and Kurigge [in the parish of Luton], by W. Austin.

g Munitions in 1224 [at the siege of Bedford castle], by G. H. Fowler.
h The Becher family of Howbury, by F. A. Page-Turner.
i Yttingaford and the 10th cent. bounds of Chalgrave and Linslade, by F. G. Gurney.
j The paper register of St. Mary's, Bedford, 1539-58, ed. A. G. Kealey.
k Calendar of inquisitions *post mortem* [1250-71], by G. H. Fowler.

229 Vol. 6. Calendar of feet of fines for Bedfordshire, preserved in the Public Record Office, of the reigns of Richard I, John and Henry III, ed. G. H. Fowler. 1919. [Contd. for the reign of Edward I, with some earlier fines, in vol. 12]

230 Vol. 7. Calendar of pipe rolls in the reign of Richard I, for Buckinghamshire and Bedfordshire, 1189-99, by G. H. Fowler and M. W. Hughes. 1923. [Published in conjunction with the Archit. and Archaeol. Soc. for the County of Buckingham]

231 Vol. 8.

a Stagsden and its manors, by J. S. Elliott.
b Three records of the alien priory of Grove and the manor of Leighton Buzzard, by R. Richmond.
c Harlington churchwardens' accounts [with transcript 1677-89], by J. H. Blundell.
d Some Bedfordshire assessments for the taxation of a ninth, 1297, by Mrs. Hilary Jenkinson.
e Institutions to ecclesiastical benefices in the county of Bedford, 1535-1660, by C. W. Foster.
f Declaration of common rights: Eaton Bray and Totternhoe, 1475, by F. Puttnam.
g 'Catsbrook' at Biscot near Luton, by W. Austin.
h Wingate of Streatley and Harlington, by J. H. Blundell.

232 Vol. 9.

a The Shefford beaker: *c.* 1800 B.C., by C. Fox.
b The Morteyn family in Bedfordshire, by G. A. Moriarty.
c The shire of Bedford and the earldom of Huntington, by G. H. Fowler.
d The later descent of Wingate of Harlington, by J. H. Blundell.
e The disseisins of Falk de Breauté at Luton, by G. H. Fowler and M. W. Hughes.
f An Elizabethan inquisition concerning bondmen, by S. Peyton.
g Roll of the justices in eyre, 1240, by G. H. Fowler.
h List of Bedfordshire apprentices, 1711-20, by Mrs. Hilary Jenkinson.
i The commune of Bedford [charter, late 12th cent.], by F. M. Stenton.
j Hand list of Bedfordshire county muniments.

233 Vol. 10. A digest of the charters preserved in the cartulary of the priory of Dunstable, by G. H. Fowler. 1926.

234 Vol. 11.

a The honour of Old Wardon, by W. Farrer, introd. J. Tait.
b Early records of Turvey and its neighbourhood: Drayton and Halstead charters, by G. H. Fowler.
c Ecclesiastical troubles in Dunstable, *c.* 1616 [concerning Edward Alport, minister], by S. Peyton.
d Inventory of Toddington manor house, 1644, by J. H. Blundell.

235 Vol. 12.

a Belverge of Sharpenhoe, by J. H. Blundell.
b Meeting places of Stodden and Redbournstoke hundreds, by F. G. Emmison. [A note on the meeting place of Manstead hundred appears in vol. 8]

c The writer of the warrant for the arrest of John Bunyan, by F. G. Emmison.

d Bedfordshire bells, *c.* 1710, comp. L. H. Chambers.

236 Vol. 13. Cartulary of the abbey of Old Wardon, by G. H. Fowler. 1930.

237 Vol. 14.

a Windmills of Bedfordshire, past and present, by J. S. Elliott.

b Nowers of Wymington, by E. St. J. Brooks.

c Some Bedfordshire wills at Lambeth [1387–1570] and Lincoln [1319–1533], by Mrs. Hilary Jenkinson and G. H. Fowler.

d Account roll of the manor of Clapham Bayeux, 1333–4, by F. G. Emmison.

238 Vol. 15.

a Relief of the poor at Eaton Socon, 1706–1834, by F. G. Emmison.

b Tithe at Pavenham, 1759–60, by C. D. Linnell.

Quarto memoirs, vols. 1–3:

239 Vol. 1. Bedfordshire in 1086: an analysis and synthesis of Domesday book, by G. H. Fowler. 1922.

240 Vol. 2. Four pre-enclosure village maps, by G. H. Fowler. 1928–36. [Strip map of Oakley Reynes, 1795, with introd. to the study of field maps. Pre-enclosure map of Renhold, 1781. Strip map of Aspley Guise, *c.* 1745, with analysis of the enclosure award, 1761. Strip map of Eversholt, 1764, with notes on strip map of Houghton Regis, 1762]

241 Vol. 3. Rolls from the office of the sheriff of Beds. and Bucks., 1332–34, by G. H. Fowler. 1929.

BERKSHIRE ARCHAEOLOGICAL SOCIETY

Founded 1840, as the Berkshire Ashmolean Society, for the publication of original documents, the examination of historic sites and ancient buildings, the encouragement of historical and architectural study, and restoration of historical monuments. Reconstituted in 1871 as the Berkshire Archaeological and Architectural Society.

Berks., Bucks., and Oxon. Archaeological Journal, new ser., vol. 6–vol. 34, no. 1 (1900–30),[1] *contd.* as Berkshire Archaeological Journal, being the journal of the Berkshire Archaeol. Soc., vol. 34, no. 2–vol. 37 (1930–3):

242 Vol. 6.

a Norman doorways in Berkshire, by C. E. Keyser.

b Thomas Southam [d. 1403–4], archdeacon of Berks. and Oxon., by H. R. H. Southam.

c Early Berkshire wills, from the P.C.C., ante 1558, by G. F. T. Sherwood. [Previous pts. in vols. 2–3 (1892–5), and in new series, vols. 1, 3–5. Contd. in vols. 7 and 20]

d A tour through Buckinghamshire, by A. J. Foster. [Contd. in vols. 7–10]

e History of Wantage, by P. H. Ditchfield.

f Norman doorways in Buckinghamshire, by C. E. Keyser.

g Oxfordshire church goods [from inventories, *temp.* Edward VI], by N. Hone. [Contd. in vols. 8–10]

---

[1] Published in connection with the Berks. Archaeol. Soc., Maidenhead and Thames Valley Antiq. Soc. (to vol. 17), Newbury District Field Club, Oxford Archit. and Hist. Soc. (to vol. 24), Oxford Ladies Archaeol. and Brass-rubbing Soc. (to vol. 31), Oxford Univ. Antiq. Soc. (to vol. 24), Oxfordshire Archaeol. Soc. (to vol. 24), and Windsor and Eton Scientific and Archaeol. Soc. (from vol. 25).

h History of Compton Wynyates, by W. Money.

i Index to Berkshire marriage registers, by Mrs. J. H. Cope. [Contd. in vols. 7–9]

j Cookham church, by Sir G. Young. [Contd. in vol. 7]

243 Vol. 7.

a Notes on Broughton Castle, by Lord Say and Sele.

b A tentative list of objects of prehistoric and early historic interest in the counties of Berks., Bucks., and Oxford, comp. B. C. Windle.

c History of the sarsens, by T. R. Jones.

d The Denchworth missal [containing genealogical data of the Hyde family], by H. B. Hyde.

e Mortimer in olden time [with particular reference to a Saxon tombstone in St. Mary's church], by C. L. Cameron.

f The Devil's Highway [Roman road] between Bagshot and Silchester, by G. A. Kempthorne.

g History of Faringdon, by P. H. Ditchfield. [Contd. in vol. 8]

h County collections for Berkshire, by G. F. T. Sherwood. [Contd. in vol. 8]

i The Kendrick family, by G. Kendrick. [See also 'Notes and queries' in vol. 8, no. 2]

j Churchwardens' accounts of the parish of St. Mary, Thame, commencing in 1442, by W. P. Ellis. [Contd. in vols. 8–14, 16, 19–20]

244 Vol. 8.

a History of Littlecote [hall], by W. Money.

b Index to Bradfield parish marriage register, 1559–1813, from original transcriptions by Emma E. Cope. [Contd. in vol. 9]

c Notes and queries. [Includes: St. Mary's church, Reading]

d History of Hungerford, by P. H. Ditchfield.

e Church plate of Berkshire. [Contd. in vols. 9 and 10]

245 Vol. 9.

a Fifield in Benson, Oxon., by J. E. Field.

b Somerton church, Oxon.

c Alard, *rector scholarum* of Oxford, 1211, by H. Salter.

d Esegarstona (Esgarston) versus East Garston, by F. T. Wethered.

e Rural parochial records, by G. C. Peachey.

246 Vol. 10.

a Old Southcote manor, by E. W. Dormer.

b Index to Ruscombe parish marriage register, 1559–1812 (men's names only), transcribed by Ll. Treacher.

c History of Maidenhead, by P. H. Ditchfield.

d The Roman city of Silchester, by W. H. St. J. Hope.

e Notes on Berkshire parishes, extracted from the chartulary of Oseney abbey, by H. Salter.

f Beating the bounds of Brightwalton, by G. C. Peachey.

g Some notes on the Domesday survey of Berkshire, by J. E. Field.

h Some notes on the Abingdon chronicle, by J. E. Field.

i An old corner of Bucks. [West Wycombe], by E. W. Dormer. [Contd. in vol. 11]

247 Vol. 11.

a Cookham church. Relic of a long lost monument [to Edmund Stockton, vicar], by S. Darby.

b Bulstrode and the Templars, by W. H. W. Powell.

c A palimpsest brass recently replaced in Binfield church, with notes on other palimpsest brasses in Berkshire, by M. Stephenson.

d Prehistoric remains in the Thames valley, by E. Margrett.

e Some notes on the parish of Ruscombe, Berks., by Ll. Treacher. [Contd. in vol. 12] f Will of Richard Turnor of Binfield, Berks. [1558], by M. Stephenson.

g Architectural account of the churches of Sparsholt and Childrey, Berks., by C. E. Keyser.

h Bisham abbey, by E. W. Dormer. [Contd. in vols. 12 and 13]

i Saxon charters of Brightwell, Sotwell and Mackney, Berks., by J. E. Field. [Contd. in vol. 12]

j Sutton Courtenay [manor farm], by C. Lynam.

248 Vol. 12.

a The advowson of St. Peter's, Wallingford, 1638–70, by G. F. T. Sherwood.

b St. Ann's well and chapel, Caversham, by E. Margrett.

c Notes on the churches of Letcombe Regis and Letcombe Bassett, by C. E. Keyser.

d God's hostels: two ancient English almshouses [at Quainton, near Aylesbury, and St. Mary's hospital, Chichester, by I. G. Sieveking].

e The real Sir Henry Lee, of Ditchley [d. 1611], by Viscount Dillon.

f Baulking church, Berks., by W. H. Hallam.

g Architectural account of the churches of Buckland, Hinton Waldrist and Longworth, by C. E. Keyser. [Contd. in vol. 13]

h The Wilcotes family, by W. F. Carter. [Contd. in vol. 13]

249 Vol. 13.

a The discovery of human remains in the Forbury, Reading, by W. Ravenscroft.

b Earmundeslea at Appleton, Berks. [in Saxon charters], by J. E. Field.

c Early history of Maidenhead bridge: an historical parallel, by E. H. Young. [*Quo warranto* proceedings against the corporation of Maidenhead with reference to market dues, *temp.* James I]

d Some Buckinghamshire parishes formerly included in the archdeaconry of St. Albans, by H. R. W. Hall. [Extracts from 16th cent. churchwardens' returns, etc. Contd. in vols. 14–16]

e Stanton Harcourt and its manor, by W. Money.

f The priory of Poghley, by H. Salter.

g A military study of the conquest of Britain by the English. Abbreviated report of a lecture by P. T. Godsal.

250 Vol. 14.

a Wanderings in Buckinghamshire, by A. J. Foster. [Contd. in vols. 15 and 16]

b Feet of fines for Berkshire, extracted by L. J. A. Pile. [Contd. in vols. 15–17, and 19–20]

c Architectural account of the churches of Cholsey and South Moreton, by C. E. Keyser.

d The old conduit at Whitley, Reading, by E. Margrett.

e The Dunch family of Little Wittenham, by W. Money.

f White Waltham and Shottesbrook in the middle ages, by F. T. Wethered.

g The Stapleton brass at Ipsden, Oxon., by J. E. Field.

h Notes on Steventon, Berks., by W. Money.

i Notes on the manor houses of Sutton Courtenay, by P. H. Ditchfield.

251 Vol. 15.

a Architectural account of the churches of North Moreton, Brightwell, Little Wittenham, and Long Wittenham, by C. E. Keyser.

b Berkshire court rolls, by N. J. Hone. [Contd. in vols. 16 and 17]

c The yew and the bow, by E. W. Dormer.

d The last days of Hurley priory, by F. T. Wethered.

e The seven churches of Oxford, by T. Barns.

252 Vol. 16.

a Notes on the churches of Boxford, Avington, Ashbury, Uffington, and Longcot, by C. E. Keyser.

b A churchwardens' account book [for Spelsbury, Oxfordshire, 1525–1703], by J. Oldfield.

c St. Katherine's hospital and chapel in Regent's Park, London. Abridgment of a paper by H. M. Poynter.

d Extracts from the parish registers of Oxfordshire, transcribed by J. Oldfield. [Contd. in vol. 17]

e Cookham church. [By Sir G. Young, with criticisms by G. P. G. Hills]

f History of Bisham abbey, by Sir H. V. Neale. [Contd. in vol. 17]

253 Vol. 17.

a Notes [mainly architectural] on the churches of Aldermaston, Padworth, Englefield, and Tidmarsh, by C. E. Keyser.

b Registers of St. Margaret's, Westminster [and] churchwardens' accounts, by F. T. Wethered. [Extracts]

c The manor of Earley Regis, otherwise Earley Whiteknights, Berks. [1840].

d 'Blacking' in Berkshire [poaching in Windsor Forest 1722–3], by G. A. Kempthorne.

254 Vol. 18.

a Notes [mainly architectural] on the churches of Steventon, Harwell, Didcot, and Hagbourne, by C. E. Keyser.

b Phipps families of Berkshire, by H. R. Phipps.

c An old Hurley priory deed, 1306, by F. T. Wethered.

d Church briefs [from Little Wittenham parish registers], by J. Oldfield.

e The manorial descent of Frilsham, by J. H. Round.

f The church of Blewbury, by J. W. Dodgson. [Contd. in vol. 19]

g St. Edward the Confessor: an offering of baudekins by the prior of Hurley [Sanson de Eswelle] at his shrine, Oct. 13, 1238, by F. T. Wethered.

h 18th cent. remedies, by Emily J. Climenson.

i Notes on the topography of North Moreton, Berks., chiefly from the rolls of the manorial courts, by J. E. Field. [Contd. in vol. 19]

255 Vol. 19.

a Notes [mainly architectural] on the churches of Hanney, Lyford, Denchworth, and Charney Bassett, by C. E. Keyser.

b List of briefs in the parish register [and churchwardens' accounts] of Ruscomb [1661–80].

c Warfield and Hurley, Berks., by F. T. Wethered.

d Warfield church.

e Sandhurst, Berks., by G. A. Kempthorne. [Contd. in vols. 20–24]

f Manor courts [rules of procedure from the manor of Stanton Harcourt, Oxon.], by J. Oldfield.

g History of the parish of Beenham, by Mary Sharp. [Contd. in vols. 20–23]

256 Vol. 20.

a Notes [mainly architectural] on the churches of Stanford-in-the-Vale, Hatford, and Shellingford, and the chapels of Goosey and Baulking, by C. E. Keyser.

b Bishops' transcripts [of parish registers, Oxford diocese], by J. Oldfield.

c The Shiplake virtuoso [Henry Constantine Jennings, d. 1819], by Emily J. Climenson.

257 Vol. 21.

a Notes [mainly architectural] on the churches of Frilsham, Yattendon, Ashampstead, Hampstead Norreys, and Aldworth, by C. E. Keyser.

b The Washington arms and pedigree, by Mrs. Suckling.

i Notes on the manor and manor house of Bulmershe, Berks., by E. W. Dormer.

268 Vol. 32.

a Some early Checkendon documents [1314–1552], by A. H. Cooke.

b The Beaver monument in Wokingham churchyard, by B. Long.

c Wokingham: the origin and spelling of the name, by A. T. Heelas.

d Wayland's smithy, Berks., by C. R. Peers and R. A. Smith. [Ancient monument. Contd. in vol. 33]

269 Vol. 33.

a Shroud brasses of Berkshire, by H. T. Morley.

b Architectural and historical notes on the church of St. Mary the Virgin, Silchester, by P. H. Ditchfield.

270 Vol. 34.

a Salisbury cathedral, by P. H. Ditchfield.

b Two early Englefield deeds [1329, 1421], by F. Turner.

271 Vol. 35.

a Long Wittenham church [with list of clergy], by J. W. Walker.

b Will of Anthony Blagrave the younger, of Bulmershe Court, Sonning, 1653.

c Coats of arms in Berkshire churches, by P. S. Spokes. [Contd. in vols. 36 and 37]

d Maidenhead thicket [or frithe].

e Brasses and mural monuments in Shinfield church and links with Tavistock, Ely, and Exeter, by Meta E. Williams. [Contd. in vol. 37]

f A rent roll of the suppressed priory of Goring, 1546, by A. H. Cooke.

g The raid on Beaumes manor, Shinfield, Berks., Good Friday, 1347, by Nora Alexander.

272 Vol. 36.

a Architectural history of St. Matthew's church, Harwell, by J. W. Walker.

b A Berks. enclosure by mutual consent, 1794 [in the manor of Bulmershe].

c A Romano-British building at Knowl Hill, Berks., by W. A. Seaby.

d C. R. Sherbourne's Berkshire views [early 19th cent.], by E. Axon.

e Swan-marks of Berkshire, by N. F. Ticehurst.

f An Elizabethan swainmote court roll of Finchampsted bailiwick, by G. A. Kempthorne.

g Notes on the Braybrooke family of Brightwalton, by W. Bradbrooke.

273 Vol. 37.

a The Windsor Forest turnpike, by A. T. Heelas.

b The name 'Berkshire', by G. W. B. Huntingford.

c Records of the judicial proceedings against William Penn and William Mead in London, June 1670–May 1671, by H. Bowler.

d A vanished Berkshire family [Cowslade], by Lucy A. B. Harrison.

e Discovery of mediaeval walling in Broad Street, Reading, by W. A. Seaby.

BIBLIOGRAPHICAL SOCIETY

Founded 1892, to print books and papers dealing with different aspects of bibliography, and generally to promote bibliographical research.

Transactions, vols. 5–15 (1901–20):

274 Vol. 5.

a The Rawlinsons [Thomas, d. 1725, and Richard, d. 1755] and their collections, by W. Y. Fletcher.

b Printers, stationers, and book-binders of York to 1600, by E. G. Duff.

c History of English handwriting, 700–1400, by E. M. Thompson.

275 Vol. 6.

a Notices of English stationers in the archives of the city of London, by H. R. Plomer.

b Notes on English illustrated books, by A. W. Pollard.

c Elizabethan cypher-books, by A. J. Butler.

d Curriculum and text-books of English schools in the first half of the 17th cent., by F. Watson.

e Bibliography of the writings of Christopher Smart [d. 1771], with biographical references, by G. J. Gray.

276 Vol. 7.

a Initial letters in early English printed books, by C. Sayle.

b Books mentioned in wills, by H. R. Plomer.

c Bagford's notes on bookbindings, by C. Davenport. [John Bagford, d. 1716]

d The bibliography of some devotional books printed by the earliest English printers, by F. A. Gasquet.

e Some early guide-books, by G. F. Barwick.

277 Vol. 8.

a Dr. Johnson as a bibliographer, by H. B. Wheatley.

b Some Durham book-lovers, by R. S. Faber.

c History of the chapter library of Canterbury cathedral, by M. Beazeley.

278 Vol. 9.

a Books and bookmaking in early chronicles and accounts, by F. A. Gasquet.

b Signs of booksellers in St. Paul's churchyard, by H. B. Wheatley.

c The library of Henry Savile, of Banke [Yorks., d. 1617], by J. P. Gibson.

d English 15th cent. broadsides, by E. G. Duff.

279 Vol. 10.

a Magazines of the 18th cent., by G. F. Barwick.

280 Vol. 11.

a Dryden's publishers, by H. B. Wheatley.

b Daniel and the emblem literature [16th and 17th cent.], by G. R. Redgrave.

c Richard Schilders [d. 1634] and the English Puritans, by J. D. Wilson.

d Descriptive catalogues of maps, by Sir H. G. Fordham.

e Notes on English books printed abroad, 1525–48, by R. Steele.

f Magazines of the 19th cent., by G. F. Barwick.

g English herbals, by J. F. Payne.

281 Vol. 12.

a A [proposed] bibliography of modern British history since 1485, by H. R. Tedder.

b Notes on the bibliography of Pope, by G. A. Aitken.

c Books of secrets [or craft 'mysteries'], by J. Ferguson.

d The inventory of incunabula in Great Britain and Ireland, by E. Crous.

e Notes on bibliographical evidence for literary students and editors of English works of the 16th and 17th cent., by R. B. McKerrow.

282 Vol. 13.

a Road books and itineraries bibliographically considered, by Sir H. G. Fordham. [With a catalogue for Gt. Britain and Ireland to 1850]

b Reynold Wolfe [printer, d. 1573], by C. Sayle.

c New lights on [the works of Thomas] Chatterton, by Sir E. Clarke.

d Claudius Hollyband and his *French Schoolmaster* and *French Littelton*, by A. W. Pollard.

e English current writing and early printing, by H. Jenkinson.

283 Vol. 14.

a Notes on the bibliography of Matthew Prior, by G. A. Aitken.

b Shakespeare's editors, 1623–20th cent., by H. B. Wheatley.

c The City Printers [Pynson, d. 1530–Arthur Taylor, d. 1870], by C. Welch.

d Robert Adam, F.R.S., F.S.A., architect to George III and to Queen Charlotte, as a bibliographer, publisher and designer of libraries, by A. T. Bolton. [With details of books sold from his library]

e Autograph mss. of Anthony Mundy [playwright, d. 1633], by Sir E. M. Thompson.

284 Vol. 15.

a The family letters of Oliver Goldsmith, by Sir E. Clarke.

b John Rastell [d. 1536], printer, lawyer, venturer, dramatist, and controversialist, by A. W. Reed.

c The writings of Sir James Ware [d. 1666] and the forgeries of Robert Ware [d. 1696], by P. Wilson.

d The small house and its amenities in the architectural hand-books of 1749–1827, by Katharine A. Esdaile.

e Regulation of the book trade [in London] before the proclamation of 1538, by A. W. Reed.

f Hand-list of scientific mss. in the British Isles dating from before the 16th cent., by Dorothea W. Singer.

g General index, vols. 11–15.

285 Transactions, general index, vols. 1–10. 1910. [The index to vols. 11–15 is included in vol. 15 above]

Transactions, 2nd ser., vols. 1–14 (1920–34), incorporating The Library, 4th ser.:

286 Vol. 1.

a Travesties of Shakespeare's plays, by R. F. Sharp.

b A portrait of Alexander Pope, by R. Crawfurd.

c Early printers and booksellers of Winchester, by A. C. Piper.

d The division of rare English books between England and the United States, by A. W. Pollard.

e The first edition of Ben Jonson's *Every Man out of his Humour*, by W. W. Greg.

f *An Apology of Private Mass*, 1562, by A. Esdaile.

g Some books by Sir Samuel Morland [d. 1695], by G. R. Redgrave.

h Anthony Munday and his books, by M. St. C. Byrne.

i The printing of Fielding's works, by J. P. de Castro.

287 Vol. 2.

a Samuel Pepys's Spanish books, by S. Gaselee.

b Notes on the bibliography of three 16th cent. English books connected with London hospitals, by Sir D'A. Power.

c Use of the galley in Elizabethan printing, by R. B. McKerrow.

d Early railway time tables, by E. H. Dring.

e Eliot's Court [London] printing house, 1584–1674, by H. R. Plomer.

f Author and publisher in 1727—*The English Hermit*, by A. Esdaile. [Discusses relations between the author and publisher of this play]

g The Royal mss. at the British Museum, by M. R. James. [Review of Warner and Gilson, *British Museum Catalogue of Western Manuscripts*, 1921]

h Cambridge printing [1521–1921], by A. W. Pollard. [Reviews of commemorative books]

i Notes upon the mss. library at Holkham, by C. W. James.

j Worcester cathedral library, from the report of Canon J. M. Wilson to the dean and chapter, 1921.

k Dr. Johnson as a bibliographer, by E. G. Millar.

288 Vol. 3.

a Elizabethan handwritings: a preliminary sketch, by H. Jenkinson.

b 'The Refusal of ye Hand. A Mock-heroical poem' [*c.* 1723], by G. C. M. Smith.

c Richard Pynson, glover and printer, by H. R. Plomer.

d The first English printers and their patrons, by H. B. Lathrop.

e Notes on the history of copyright in England, 1662–1774, by A. W. Pollard.

f The licensing of the *Mirror for Magistrates*, by Eveline I. Feasey.

g Eliots Court press, by H. R. Plomer.

h Thomas Heywood's *Art of Love* lost and found, by A. M. Clark.

i Notes on Shakespeare's printers and publishers, with special reference to the poems and *Hamlet*, by H. Farr.

j William Strahan [printer, d. 1785] and his ledgers, by R. A. Austen-Leigh.

k The two issues of Day's *Isle of Gulls*, 1606, by W. W. Greg.

289 Vol. 4.

a Elizabethan spelling as a literary and bibliographical clue, by A. W. Pollard.

b Anthony Munday's spelling as a literary clue, by M. St. C. Byrne.

c The editor of Sir Thomas More's English works, William Rastell, by A. W. Reed.

d William Caxton's stay at Cologne, by A. W. Reed.

e John of Basing's 'Greek' numerals, by W. W. Greg.

f The fifth edition of Burton's *Anatomy of Melancholy*, by E. G. Duff.

g An Elizabethan printer [Richard Field] and his copy, by W. W. Greg.

h Milton, Salmasius, and Dugard, by F. F. Madan.

i The importation of books into England in the 15th and 16th cent.: an examination of some customs rolls, by H. R. Plomer.

j The surreptitious edition of Michael Drayton's *Piers Gaueston*, by J. W. Hebel.

k Notes on 18th cent. bookbuilding, by R. W. Chapman.

l Massinger's autograph corrections in *The Duke of Milan*, 1623, by W. W. Greg.

m Letters and booklists of Thomas Chard (or Chare) of London, 1583–4, by R. Jahn.

n Early documents connected with the library of Merton College, by P. S. Allen.

o An early [English, 1577] translation of Seneca, by M. St. C. Byrne.

290 Vol. 5.

a Border-pieces used by English printers before 1641, by R. B. McKerrow.

b More Massinger corrections, by W. W. Greg.

c Italian books printed in England before 1640, by H. Sellers.

d Nicholas Ling [printer, fl. 1580–1607] and *Englands Helicon*, by J. W. Hebel.

e Massinger corrections, by A. H. Cruickshank.

f The building up of the British Museum collection of incunabula, by A. W. Pollard.

g Anthony Trollope and his publishers: a chapter in the history of 19th cent. authorship, by M. Sadleir.

h Thomas Churchyard's spelling [*c.* 1600], by M. St. C. Byrne.

i Lost literature of medieval England, by R. W. Chambers.

j The first illustration to 'Shakespeare', by E. K. Chambers. [Early 17th cent. drawings on a ms. of *Titus Andronicus*]

k 'Paterson's Roads.' Daniel Paterson, his maps and itineraries, 1738–1825, by Sir H. G. Fordham.

l Elizabethan printers and the composition of reprints, by R. B. McKerrow.

291 Vol. 6.

a English illuminated mss. [Abstract of paper dealing with the 10th–13th cent. by E. G. Millar]

b *The Spanish Tragedy*—a leading case?, by W. W. Greg.

c Anthony Munday's romances of chivalry, by G. R. Hayes.

d Writings of Charles Sayle: a list, by G. J. Gray.

e The Oxford Press, 1650–75, by F. Madan.

f Prompt copies, private transcripts, and the 'playhouse scrivener', by W. W. Greg.

g John Ogilby, 1600–76: his *Britannia* and the British itineraries of the 18th cent., by Sir G. H. Fordham.

h Matthew Parker, by E. C. Pearce.

i The Motte editions of *Gulliver's Travels*, by H. Williams. [See also notes by the same in vol. 9]

j Walkley's piracy of Wither's poems, 1620, by P. Simpson.

k John Clement [d. 1572] and his books, by A. W. Reed.

l The riddle of [Ben] Jonson's chronology, by W. W. Greg.

m The Stationers' company's records [a synopsis to the close of the 18th cent.].

n Sir John MacAlister [founder of *The Library*, d. 1925]: reminiscences by A. W. Pollard.

292 Vol. 7.

a English translations of Portuguese books before 1640, by H. Thomas.

b Anthony Munday's romances: a postscript, by G. R. Hayes.

c Derby his hand—and soul, by W. W. Greg. [The handwriting of William Stanley, sixth Earl of Derby, d. 1642]

d Some aspects of copyright, 1700–80, by A. S. Collins.

e The Birchley Hall [Wigan] secret [Roman Catholic] press, by A. J. Hawkes.

f Was Nicholas Udall the author of *Thersites*?, by A. R. Moon.

g Ralph Crane, scrivener to the King's players, by F. P. Wilson.

h The unity of John Norden: surveyor and religious writer, by A. W. Pollard.

i The 1574 edition of Dr. John Caius's *De antiquitate Cantabrigiensis academiae libri duo*, by H. R. Plomer.

j *A Hundreth Sundry Flowers*, by W. W. Greg. [See also letter in vol. 8]

k Birchley—or St. Omers?, by C. A. Newdigate. [On the Birchley Hall secret press]

l The King's printers. [Documents relating to the appointment of a printer for Ireland, 1617–18, ed. R. Steele]

m Greek mss. in England before the Renaissance, by M. R. James.

n Some notes on the Stationers' registers, by W. W. Greg.

o Caxton on the continent, by W. J. B. Crotch.

p An inventory of paper, 1674, by R. W. Chapman.

293 Vol. 8.

a *The Birth of Mankind or the Woman's Book* [editions and printers of, since 1540], by Sir D'A. Power.

b *Keep the Widow Waking*: a lost play by Dekker, by C. Sisson.

c Two hitherto unrecorded editions of *Robinson Crusoe*, by H. C. Hutchins.

d The library of Dover priory: its catalogue and extant volumes, by C. R. Haines.

e Relations between London and Edinburgh printers and stationers (–1640), by F. S. Ferguson.

f Richard Tottell [printer, d. 1593], his life and work, by H. J. Byrom.

g The Cambridge University press and John Siberch [*c.* 1520], by G. J. Gray.

h Books and readers, 1591–4, by G. B. Harrison.

i The [Edward] Whitchurch compartment in London and Mexico, by Lucy E. Osborne. [On a woodcut border used *c.* 1550]

j Library regulations of a medieval college [Merton], by H. W. Garrod.

294 Vol. 9.

a Marks as signatures, by C. Sisson.

b Caxton's son-in-law [Gerard Crop], by W. J. B. Crotch.

c A Chester bookseller's lawsuit, 1653, by R. Stewart-Brown. [Concerning Richard Thropp, stationer]

d The new Caxton indulgence [issued by John Sant, abbot of Abingdon, 1476], by A. W. Pollard.

e Percy's *Reliques*, by L. F. Powell.

f Notes on English printing in the Low Countries (early 16th cent.), by Miss M. E. Kronenberg.

g Importation of Low Country and French books into England, 1480 and 1502–3, by H. R. Plomer.

h *A pore Helpe* and its printers, by M. C. Lenthicum.

i Later editions of Quarles's *Enchiridion*, by W. L. Ustick.

j Some aspects of Sheridan bibliography, by R. C. Rhodes.

k An interruption in the printing of the First Folio, by E. E. Willoughby.

l *Troilus and Cressida*, 1609, by P. Alexander.

m *Eastward Ho*, 1605, by Chapman, Jonson, and Marston: bibliography and circumstances of production, by R. E. Brettle.

n Further notes on Shakespeare's sonnets, by J. A. Fort.

o Oxford oddments, by F. Madan. [University Press accounts, 1672–9; play-acting at or near Oxford after the civil war; etc.]

p The date of Shakespeare's 107th sonnet, by J. A. Fort.

q The Stationers' company and censorship, 1599–1601, by E. Kuhl.

295 Vol. 10.

a The early editions of Thomas Dekker's *The Converted Courtezan or The Honest Whore*, by M. Baird. Pt. 1. [See also correspondence in same vol.]

b The *Christian Hero* by Richard Steele: a bibliography, by R. Blanchard.

c Travel and topography in 18th cent. England: a bibliography of sources for economic history, by G. E. Fussell and Constance Goodman.

d Edward Allde [fl. 1600] as a typical trade printer, by R. B. McKerrow.

e The extent of literacy in England in the 15th and 16th cent.: notes and conjectures, by J. W. Adamson.

f Some poetical miscellanies of the early 18th cent., by I. A. Williams.

g Sources of early English paper-supply, by E. Heawood.

h Extant autograph material by Shakespeare's fellow-dramatists, by Henrietta C. Bartlett.

i The library of the Royal College of Physicians in the Great Fire, by Eleanore Boswell.

j The revels books of 1604–5, and 1611–12, by T. W. Baldwin.

k English 17th cent. almanacks, by E. F. Bosanquet.

l St. Germain's *Doctor and Student*, by S. E. Thorne.

m Rowe's edition of Shakespeare, by A. Jackson.

296 Vol. 11.

a Notes on some early [16th cent.] plays, by W. W. Greg.
b Some bibliographical notes on Massinger, by A. K. McIlwraith.
c Keep the widow waking, by G. B. Harrison. [On Judith, or Doll, Phillips, a London cozener, 1595]
d Grafton and [his residences in] the London Grey Friars, by C. J. Sisson.
e Richard Robinson's *Eupolemia* and the licensers, by R. B. McKerrow.
f Two John Taylor mss. at Leonard Lichfield's press, by Marjorie Rushforth.
g Towards a text of Browne's *Britannia's Pastorals*, by G. Tillotson.
h An early printed account book [1582], by E. F. Bosanquet.
i Sir John Hayward's troubles over his *Life of Henry IV*, by Margaret Dowling.
j Thomas Walkley and the Ben Jonson 'Works' of 1640, by F. Marcham.
k Papers used in England after 1600, by E. Heawood.
l The growth of the Peele canon, by T. Larson. [A bibliography of the works of George Peele, fl. 1590]
m John Wayland, printer, scrivener, and litigant [d. 1572], by H. J. Byrom.
n Some notes on the library of printed books at Holkham, by C. W. James.
o Thomas Walkley and the Ben Jonson 'Works' of 1640, by W. W. Greg.
p A playbill of 1687, by Eleanore Boswell.

297 Vol. 12.

a Richard Field, printer, 1589–1624, by A. E. M. Kirwood.
b Alexander Read, physician and surgeon, 1580–1641: his life, works and library, by W. Menzies.
c Elizabethan almanacks and prognostications, by C. Camden, jr.
d The abridgements of the statutes, 1481?–1551?, by J. D. Cowley.
e John Evelyn as bibliophil, by G. Keynes.
f The *Metamorphosis of Aiax* and its sequels, by A. E. M. Kirwood.
g More bibliographical notes on Marston, by R. E. Brettle.
h The Elizabethan printer and dramatic mss., by R. B. McKerrow.
i Note concerning 'Mistress Crane' and the Martin Marprelate controversy, by Julia N. McCorkle.
j Extant mss. printed from by W. de Worde with notes on the owner, Roger Thorney [mercer, of London, d. 1498], by G. Bone.
k Three ms. notes by Sir George Buc [master of the revels, d. 1623], by W. W. Greg.
l The authorship of *The Prayse of Nothing* [1585], by R. M. Sargent.
m An English bookbinder's ticket, *c.* 1610?, by A. W. Pollard.
n Egidius van der Erve [of Emden, fl. 1550] and his English printed books, by F. Isaac.
o The printing of John Dowland's *Second Booke of Songs or Ayres* [1600], by Margaret Dowling.
p Gabriel Naudé and John Evelyn, with some notes on the Mazarinades, by the Earl of Crawford and Balcarres.

298 Vol. 13.

a Bibliographical clues in collaborate plays [by Anthony Munday and Henry Chettle, *c.* 1598], by M. St. C. Byrne.
b The mss. of St. George's chapel, Windsor, by M. R. James.

c King Henry VI's claim to France in picture and poem, by B. J. H. Rowe.
d The library of a physician [Claver Morris, of Wells] *c.* 1700, by E. Hobhouse.
e King Richard II's books, by Edith Rickert.
f The personal prayer-book of John of Lancaster, Duke of Bedford [d. 1435], by E. F. Bosanquet.
g Wayland's edition of *The Mirror for Magistrates*, by W. A. Jackson.
h Subscription publishers prior to Jacob Tonson [d. 1736], by Sarah L. C. Clapp.
i A publishing agreement of the late 17th cent. [concerning Henry More's theological works], by R. B. McKerrow.
j Milton autographs established, by H. C. H. Candy.
k The booksellers and printers of Richmond, Surrey [1726–1926], by A. C. Piper.
l *If You Know Not Me, You Know Nobodie*, and *The Famous Historie of Sir Thomas Wyat*, by Mary F. Martin. [Concerning the authorship of these plays]
m Smollett's works as printed by William Strahan, with an unpublished letter of Smollett to Strahan [1759], by L. M. Knapp.
n Travel and topography in 17th cent. England: a bibliography of sources for social and economic history, by G. E. Fussell and V. G. B. Atwater.
o Translations for the Elizabethan middle class, by L. B. Wright.
p The Vesalian compendium [of anatomy] of Geminus [printer and surgeon *c.* 1545] and Nicholas Udall's translation: their relation to Vesalius, Caius, Vicary, and de Mondeville, by S. V. Larkey.
q A cancel in Southerne's *The Disappointment*, 1684, by C. Leech.
r Parliament and the press, 1643–7, by W. M. Clyde. [Contd. in vol. 14]

299 Vol. 14.

a Books and readers, 1599–1603, by G. B. Harrison.
b Pen-and-ink corrections in mid-17th cent. books, by G. and A. Tillotson.
c Samuel Pepys, his shorthand books, by W. J. Carlton.
d Elizabethan roman and italic types, by F. Isaac.
e Astrological prognostications of 1583, by R. Pruvost.
f Edmund Spenser's first printer, Hugh Singleton, by H. J. Byrom.
g English imprints, after 1640, by P. H. Muir.
h Three little Tudor books [Xenophon's *Treatise o Household* i.e. the *Œconomicus*, Philip More's *The Hope of Health*, and *The Viniard of Devotion*], by E. F. Bosanquet.
i The chronology of Milton's handwriting, by Helen Darbishire.
j John Wolfe, printer and publisher, 1579–1601, by H. R. Hoppe.
k Architectural design on English title-pages, by W. H. Smith.
l *Dives et Pauper* [*c.* 1405], by H. G. Pfander.
m Thomas Heywood's play on 'The Troubles of Queen Elizabeth' [or, *If You Know Not Me, . . .*], by G. N. Giordano-Orsini.
n Newcome's Academy and its plays, by E. A. Jones.
o The bibliographical approach to Shakespeare: notes on new contributions, by A. W. Pollard.
p John Martin, 1789–1854, illustrator and pamphleteer, by T. Balston.
q English circulating libraries, 1725–50, by A. D. McKillop.

300 General index, 2nd ser., vols. 1–10. 1932. [These and other vols. published by the Bibliographical Society and the Library Association up to 1932 are indexed in

George W. Cole, *An Index to Bibliographical Papers*, 1877–1932 (Bibliographical Society of America, 1933)]

Supplements to the Transactions, nos. 1–8:

301 No. 1. Lists of mss. formerly owned by Dr. John Dee, with preface and identifications, by M. R. James. *P.* 1921.

302 No. 2. Spanish books in the library of Samuel Pepys, by S. Gaselee. *P.* 1921.

303 No. 4. A bibliography of English character-books, 1608–1700, by Gwendolen Murphy. 1925.

304 No. 5. Lists of mss. formerly in Peterborough abbey library, with preface and identifications, by M. R. James. 1926.

305 No. 6. A bibliography of the works of John Bunyan, by F. M. Harrison. 1932.

306 No. 7. A handlist of mss. in the library of the Earl of Leicester at Holkham Hall, abstracted from the catalogues of William Roscoe and Frederic Madden and annotated by S. De Ricci. 1932.

307 No. 8. The printing of the First Folio of Shakespeare, by E. E. Willoughby. 1932.

Illustrated monographs, nos. 9–21:

308 No. 10. Early Oxford bindings [to *c.* 1640], by S. Gibson. 1903.

309 No. 11. The earliest English music printing: a description and bibliography of English printed music to the close of the 16th cent., by R. Steele. 1903.

310 No. 12. A chart of Oxford printing, '1468'–1900, with notes and illustrations, by F. Madan. 1904.

311 No. 13. The earlier Cambridge stationers and bookbinders and the first Cambridge printer, by G. J. Gray. 1904.

312 No. 15. A census of Caxtons, by S. De Ricci. 1909.

313 No. 16. Printers' and publishers' devices in England and Scotland, 1485–1640, by R. B. McKerrow. 1913.

314 No. 17. English printed almanacs and prognostications: bibliographical history to 1600, by E. F. Bosanquet. 1917.

315 No. 18. Fifteenth century English books: a bibliography of books and documents printed in England and of books for the English market printed abroad, by E. G. Duff. 1917.

316 No. 20. Early editions of Euclid's *Elements*, by C. Thomas-Stanford. 1926.

317 No. 21. Title-page borders used in England and Scotland, 1485–1640, by R. B. McKerrow and F. S. Ferguson. 1932.

Facsimiles and illustrations, nos. 1–3:

318 No. 2. English and Scottish printing types, 1501–35, 1508–41, collected and annotated by F. Isaac. 1930.

319 No. 3. English and Scottish printing types, 1535–58, 1552–58, collected and annotated by F. Isaac. 1932.

Other publications (octavo and quarto series):

320 A list of masques, pageants, etc. supplementary to a list of English plays, by W. W. Greg. 1902.

321 Abstracts from the wills of English printers and stationers, 1492–1630, by H. R. Plomer. 1903.

322 A century of the English book trade: short notices of all printers, stationers, book-binders, and others connected with it from 1457–1557, by E. G. Duff. 1905.

323 Short catalogues of English books printed before 1641. No. 1: Books in Archbishop Marsh's library, Dublin, by N. J. D. White. 1905.

324 Alien members of the book-trade during the Tudor period, being an index to those whose names occur in the returns of aliens, letters of denization, and other documents published by the Huguenot Society, with notes by E. J. Warman. 1906.

325 Abstracts from the wills and testamentary documents of binders, printers, and stationers of Oxford, 1493–1638, by S. Gibson. 1907.

326 A dictionary of the booksellers and printers who were at work in England, Scotland, and Ireland, 1641–67, by H. R. Plomer. 1907.

327 A dictionary of printers and booksellers in England, Scotland and Ireland and of foreign printers of English books, 1557–1640, ed. R. B. McKerrow. 1910.

328 Hand-lists of books printed by London printers, 1501–1556. Pt. iii by E. G. Duff, W. W. Greg, R. B. McKerrow, and A. W. Pollard; pt. iv by E. G. Duff, H. R. Plomer, and A. W. Pollard. Pts. iii–iv, 1905–13. [Pts. i and ii, published 1895–6, and also pt. iii, bear the temporary title 'Hand-lists of English printers']

329 List of English editions and translations of Greek and Latin classics printed before 1641, by Henrietta R. Palmer, with introd. by V. Scholderer. 1911.

330 A list of English tales and prose romances printed before 1740, by A. Esdaile. 1912.

331 A bibliography of the writings in prose and verse of Samuel Taylor Coleridge, by T. J. Wise. 1913.

332 A hand-list of English books in the library of Emmanuel College, Cambridge, printed before 1641, by G. H. Watts and P. W. Wood. 1915.

333 Abstracts from the wills and testamentary documents of printers, binders, and stationers of Cambridge, 1504–1699, by G. J. Gray and W. M. Palmer. 1915.

334 A register of middle-English religious and didactic verse, by C. Brown. 2 vols. 1916–20.

335 A bibliography of the writings in prose and verse of Walter Savage Landor, by T. J. Wise and S. Wheeler. 1919.

336 Coleridgeiana, being a supplement to the bibliography of Coleridge, by T. J. Wise. *P.* 1919.

337 A dictionary of printers and booksellers at work in England, Scotland and Ireland, 1668–1725, by H. R. Plomer with others, ed. A. Esdaile. 1922.

338 A bibliography of the writings in prose and verse of George Meredith, by M. B. Forman. 1922.

339 Meredithiana, being a supplement to the bibliography of Meredith, by M. B. Forman. 1924.

340 A short-title catalogue of books printed in England, Scotland and Ireland and of English books printed abroad, 1475–1640, comp. A. W. Pollard and G. R. Redgrave, with the help of G. F. Barwick and others. 1926.

341 Records of the court of the Stationers' company, 1576–1602, from register B, ed. W. W. Greg and Eleanore Boswell. 1930.

342 A dictionary of printers and booksellers at work in England, Scotland and Ireland, 1726–75, by H. R. Plomer, G. H. Bushnell, E. R. McC. Dix. 1932. [For additional notes see no. 1748a below]

BIBLIOGRAPHICAL SOCIETY OF LANCASHIRE

Founded 1900, to stimulate interest in bibliographical topics by meetings and by the publication of facsimiles of unique books, especially English printed books. Dissolved 1903.

Publications:

343 Commemoracio lamentacionis siue compassionis Beate Marie. Reproduced in facsimile from the unique copy printed at Westminster by William Caxton, with introd. by E. G. Duff. 1901.

344 English printing on vellum to the end of the year 1600, by E. G. Duff. *P.* 1902.

345 On the difficulty of correct description of books, by Augustus De Morgan [1853], with introd. by H. Guppy. *P.* Reprinted from the Library Association Record, 1902.

346 Suggestions for the description of books printed between 1501 and 1640, by J. P. Edmond. *P.* Reprinted from the Library Association Record, 1902.

BIRKENHEAD LITERARY AND SCIENTIFIC SOCIETY

Founded 1857, for the study of literature and philosophy, science, and the fine arts. Dissolved 1928.

Inaugural addresses:

347 Old century progress and new century problems, by W. T. Rogers. *P.* 1901.

348 The study of history, by G. R. Anderson. *P.* 1902.

349 Utopia, ancient and modern: a study in evolution, by H. E. Davies. *P.* 1906.

350 Fifty years: a retrospect, by D. MacIver. *P.* 1906. [Changes of thought and life in the last half-century]

351 The writing of history in relation to life and literature, by S. R. Dodds. *P.* 1914.

352 The interpretation and use of history, by W. H. Jefferson. *P.* 1916.

353 Interpretations of history, by W. G. Jones. *P.* 1922.

354 Folk song and folk story, by E. G. Browne. *P.* 1925.

Other publications:

355 History of the Society, 1857–1907, by R. S. Marsden. 1907.

BIRMINGHAM AND MIDLAND INSTITUTE: BIRMINGHAM ARCHAEOLOGICAL SOCIETY

Founded 1870, as the Archaeological Section of the Birmingham and Midland Institute, for the encouragement of archaeological research and record in the Midland area, and particularly in the counties adjacent to Birmingham. Title changed to present form in 1916.

Transactions, Excursions and Report, vols. 26–41 (1901–16), *contd. as* Transactions and Proceedings, vols. 42–55 (1917–33):

356 Vol. 26.
a Manduessedum Romanorum: Mancetter, by A. Chattaway.
b Mediaeval or 'tithe' barns, by F. B. Andrews.
c Some notes on Domesday book, especially that part of it which relates to the county of Warwick, by B. Walker.
d The study of topography, by H. S. Thompson.

357 Vol. 27.
a Excursions, 1900. [Includes accounts of the churches of Clifton-Campville and Little Malvern]
b Middleton Hall, Warwicks., by E. de Hamel.
c Chipping Campden, by J. Crouch.
d Birmingham springs and wells, by H. S. Pearson.

358 Vol. 28.
a Excursions, 1901. [Includes an account of Stoke Golding church]
b Mediaeval seals of Worcestershire, by F. B. Andrews.
c Mummers and minstrels, by W. Hale.
d The manor and castle of Weoley, by F. S. Pearson.

359 Vol. 29.
a Excursions, 1902. [Includes accounts of the churches of Tong and Knowle]
b The antiquity of iron in Britain, by C. J. Hart.
c The manufacture of wrought plate in Birmingham, with notes upon old Birmingham silversmiths, by A. Westwood.
d Alkerton church and its sculptures, by H. S. Pearson.
e Chaddesley Corbett and the Roman Catholic persecution in Worcestershire in connection with the Titus Oates plot, in the reign of Charles II, by J. Humphreys.

360 Vol. 30.
a Two Warwickshire muniment rooms [at Compton Verney and Warwick Castle], by J. H. Bloom.
b Birmingham trades and industries in the last century, by C. J. Woodward.
c The Wyntours of Huddington and the Gunpowder plot, by J. Humphreys.
d A note on Francis Eginton [d. 1805, painter on glass].

361 Vol. 31.
a Excursions, 1905. [Includes an account of Wootton Wawen church]
b The hundreds of Warwickshire, by B. Walker.
c The Habingtons of Hindlip and the Gunpowder plot, by J. Humphreys.
d The evolution of church chancels, by R. H. Murray.

362 Vol. 32.
a Two days' excursion to Silchester, Avebury and Silbury Hill, 1906, by J. A. S. Hanbury.
b Beaudesert [castle site] and the De Mountfords, by F. W. Evans.
c Early earthworks, dykes, and hollow roads of the upland of Barr and Sutton Coldfield, by G. B. Benton.
d Low side windows of Warwickshire churches, by F. T. S. Houghton.
e Meon Hill [prehistoric camp] and its treasures, by T. R. Hodges.

363 Vol. 33.
a The development and design of the [church] tower and spire, by W. H. Bidlake.
b Some records mostly of the Fairfax family during the 17th cent., by C. F. Crowder.
c Notes on Welford church, Glos., by C. J. Woodward.
d Excursions, 1907. [Includes accounts of St. Kenelm's chapel and St. John the Baptist church, Halesowen, and Bushwood Hall, Lapworth]

364 Vol. 34.

a The evolution of the English rood screen, by B. Camm.
b Romanesque and Gothic doorways, by W. H. Bidlake.
c Excursions, 1908. [Includes accounts of Tutbury castle and church]
d Churchwardens' accounts of the parish of Northfield [1606–1730], by F. S. Pearson.
e Early masonry [of unknown origin] at Broom: a report by E. Smith.

365 Vol. 35.

a Hales Owen abbey at the end of the 15th cent., by W. E. Davis-Winstone.
b A midland architect and his work in the 15th cent., by J. Amphlett.
c The Benedictine abbey of Evesham, by F. B. Andrews.
d Excursions, 1909. [Includes an account of Abbey Dore, Herefs.]
e Grafton Manor and its history, by J. Humphreys.
f Prehistoric flint factory at Great Packington, Warwicks., by T. C. Cantrill.

366 Vol. 36.

a Old views of Birmingham, by H. S. Pearson.
b The Oak house, West Bromwich, by W. H. Kendrick.
c The navigation of the Avon, together with some notes on its Worcestershire bridges and mills, by P. G. Feek.
d Excursions, 1910. [Includes accounts of Mere Hall, Lincoln cathedral, Deerhurst abbey and chapel, and Kinlet church]
e Half-timbered houses in Worcestershire, by F. B. Andrews.
f Some notes on Roman Lincoln, by A. Smith.

367 Vol. 37.

a The incorporation of Evesham: the story of the formation of a municipal borough in the 17th cent., by E. A. B. Barnard.
b Stoke Prior church, by C. Stockdale.
c Monumental effigies in the churches of Worcestershire, by J. Humphreys.
d Excursions, 1911. [Includes accounts of Salisbury cathedral and the churches of Higham Ferrers, Raunds, and Irthlingborough]
e Norman work in the churches of Worcestershire, by J. Humphreys.

368 Vol. 38.

a Bond's and Ford's hospitals, Coventry, by W. H. Bird.
b Birmingham markets and fairs, by W. Barrow.
c Town houses of timber structure in Worcestershire, by F. B. Andrews.
d Excursions, 1912. [Includes accounts of Merevale abbey and Dudley castle and priory]
e Burford parish church (Salop) and the Cornewall monuments, by E. C. L. McLaughlin.

369 Vol. 39.

a Stone lecterns at Abbots Morton, Crowle, and Wenlock, by F. T. S. Houghton.
b Edgbaston, by P. B. Chatwin. [Includes a survey of the lordship, 1701]
c Excursions, 1913. [Includes accounts of Claverley church and Maxstoke castle and priory]
d Kyre Wyard, by P. B. Chatwin.
e Early [17th and 18th cent.] periodical literature, by J. A. S. Hanbury.
f Notes on the history of midland waterways, by H. R. Hodgkinson.
g Some remains of the bronze age at Mathon, by J. E. H. Blake.

370 Vol. 40.

a Uriconium, by J. Humphreys. [Reports and notes on excavations at Wroxeter occur in several vols. of the Society's *Transactions*]
b The old houses of Tewkesbury, by F. B. Andrews.
c Excursions, 1914. [Includes accounts of Great Malvern priory church and the churches of Monk's Kirby, Newbold-on-Avon, and Wolston]
d Ceawlin, the second Bretwalda, and the conquest of the midlands, by P. T. Godsal.
e New Street [Birmingham], by H. S. Pearson.

371 Vol. 41.

a Notes on some Worcestershire flint instruments, by W. H. Edwards.
b The story of St. Chad's gospels, by H. E. Savage.
c Cleeve Prior, by J. Humphreys.
d Local enclosures, by B. Walker.
e Archaeological notes in the valley of the upper waters of the river Avon, by P. B. Chatwin.

372 Vol. 42.

a Ancient bridges, fords and ferries [in Warwicks.], by J. A. Cossins.
b Low side windows of Worcestershire churches, by F. T. S. Houghton.
c Some street names in Birmingham, by H. New.

373 Vol. 43.

a The Sheldon tapestry maps of Worcestershire, by J. Humphreys.
b Bretforton [church], by J. E. H. Blake.
c Warwickshire fonts, by F. T. S. Houghton.
d Westwood, Worcs., by F. B. Andrews.
e Woollas Hall, Worcs., by F. B. Andrews.
f Legends of the Severn, by J. W. Willis Bund.
g Finger rings, by T. G. Barnett.
h The Melvill book of roundels, by G. Bantock and H. O. Anderton.

374 Vol. 44.

a The Elizabethan estate book of Grafton Manor, near Bromsgrove, with particulars of the rebuilding of the mansion in 1568–9, ed. J. Humphreys.
b Church of S. Eadburgh in Broadway, by R. Price and C. E. Bateman.

375 Vol. 45.

a Warwick registers: notes on English history as told by account books and parish registers at Warwick, by T. Kemp.
b Parochial and other chapels of co. Worcester, together with some account of the development of the parochial system in the county, by F. T. S. Houghton.
c Forest of Feckenham, by J. Humphreys.
d Ancient Stafford, by T. J. Davies.
e Excursions, 1919. [Includes an account of Hagley Hall]

376 Vol. 46.

a Strategy of the battle of Evesham [1265], by A. Hayes.
b Selly manor house: an architectural description, by W. A. Harvey.
c The holders of the manor of Selly, by F. T. S. Houghton.
d Roman roads of south Birmingham, by G. Cadbury.
e Field names in the parish of Feckenham, by W. E. Davis-Winstone.
f William Hamper [d. 1831], by H. S. Pearson.

377 Vol. 47.

a The family of Muchgros, by F. T. S. Houghton.
b Monumental effigies in co. Warwick, by P. B. Chatwin. [Contd. in vols. 48 and 49.]

c Report of the excursions . . . 1921. [Includes accounts of Coughton Court and Bromsgrove church]

378 Vol. 48.

a The mediaeval builder and his methods, by F. B. Andrews.
b Origin and development of the English castle, by H. Baker.
c Old buildings round Bredon hill [Worcs.], by H. Humphreys.

379 Vol. 49.

a Saltways of Droitwich district, by W. T. Whitley.
b Excavation of an Anglo-Saxon cemetery at Bidford-on-Avon, Warwicks, 1922–3, by J. Humphreys. [Contd. in vol. 50]
c Report on the Sheldon chapel, Beoley church, by R. Price.
d Notes on triptychs at Besford, Worcs., and elsewhere, by F. T. S. Houghton.

380 Vol. 50.

a The Turton family, by C. S. James.
b Ancient maps and atlases, by W. A. Cadbury.
c The painted panels at Strensham, by F. T. S. Houghton.
d Sheldon tapestries, by J. Humphreys.
e Report of the summer meetings, 1924. [Includes accounts of Guy's Cliffe, Warwick, and Breedon church, Leics.]

381 Vol. 51.

a Scratch dials, by E. Horne.
b Gravestones in midland churchyards, by J. E. H. Blake.
c Astley church and its stall paintings, by F. T. S. Houghton.
d Note on Roman buildings at Droitwich, by H. R. Hodgkinson.
e The crypt of Berkswell church, Warwicks., by P. B. Chatwin.

382 Vol. 52.

a Saxon charters of Worcestershire, by G. B. Grundy. [Contd. in vol. 53]
b Kenilworth abbey [excavations, 1890, 1922–3], by E. Carey-Hill.
c Notes on the Rea valley, by B. Walker.
d Imitations of early (1st–2nd cent.) sigillata shapes by late (3rd–5th cent.) Romano-British potters, by T. May.
e The misericords of Coventry, by Mary D. Harris.
f The heath mill, Birmingham [*temp.* Hen. VIII], by W. Barrow.
g Excavations on Corley camp, near Coventry, by P. B. Chatwin.
h Prehistoric cooking site and camping ground in Sutton Park, Warwicks., excavated 1926, by W. L. Burrows.
i Roman villa, Bays meadow, Droitwich, by H. R. Hodgkinson.
j Report of the summer meetings, 1927. [Includes an account of Dorchester abbey church]

383 Vol. 53.

a The Saxon settlement in Worcestershire, by G. B. Grundy.
b Early Coventry, by P. B. Chatwin.
c Recent discoveries in the Beauchamp chapel, Warwick, by P. B. Chatwin.
d Notes on painted windows of the Beauchamp chapel, Warwick, by P. B. Chatwin.
e Notes on musical instruments figured in windows of the Beauchamp chapel, Warwick, by W. Bentley.
f Excavation at Mancetter, 1927, by B. H. St. J. O'Neil.
g Pershore abbey, Worcs.: excavations, 1929–30.
h Hartshill castle and neighbourhood, by P. B. Chatwin.

384 Vol. 54.

a Salt-ways, by F. T. S. Houghton.
b The Hawkesworth papers, 1601–60, with notes on Col. Joseph Hawkesworth at Warwick and Kenilworth castles, by E. Carey-Hill.
c Wanderings of Charles II in Staffordshire and Shropshire, by H. P. Kingston.
d Roman finds at Baginton, near Coventry, by P. B. Chatwin.

385 Vol. 55.

a Further notes on the mediaeval builder, by F. B. Andrews.
b Mss. relating to Birmingham in the city reference library, by L. Chubb.
c The Herlands and other carpenters [14th–17th cent.], by F. B. Andrews.
d The Ravenhurst [estate], Camp Hill, Aston-juxta-Birmingham, by B. Walker.
e Wixford church, Warwicks.: its brass and painted glass, by P. B. Chatwin.
f Registers of the churches of the Holy Cross and of St. Andrew of Pershore [described], by F. B. Andrews.
g A ms. plan of Birmingham [*c.* 1821] in the Library of Congress, Washington, D.C., by B. Walker.

386 Index to Transactions, vols. 1–41, 1870–1915. *P.* 1918. [Supersedes Index to Transactions, vols. 1–31, 1870–1905, issued in 1907]

BLACKWELL AND DISTRICT SCIENTIFIC AND LITERARY SOCIETY

The Derbyshire Naturalists' Quarterly, vols. 1–2 (1900–2):[1]

387 Vol. 1.

a The antiquity of man, by W. J. P. Burton.

388 Vol. 2.

a The lake village at Glastonbury, and the Scottish lake dwellings, by Mrs. Meade-Waldo.
b Antiquities of Derbyshire, by W. M. Wilson.
c Pre-historic remains at Harlyn Bay, near Padstow, Cornwall, by W. J. P. Burton.

BOURNEMOUTH NATURAL SCIENCE SOCIETY

Founded 1904, as Bournemouth and District Society of Natural Science in succession to an earlier Society, to promote science in all its branches by means of lectures, field meetings, the reading and discussion of papers, and the formation of sections of its members devoted to any particular branch of the Society's work.

Proceedings, vols. 1–25 (1909–33):

389 Vol. 1.

a John Prophete [fl. 1387–1409], D.D., rector of Ringwood, Hants, by G. Brownen.
b The Roman villa at Hemsworth, Dorset, by H. Le Jeune.
c Place names in Dorset: their association with the geography of the county, by W. J. Stanton.

390 Vol. 2.

a The growth of the English language, by S. Wood.
b Sopley church, by A. Scott.

[1] Issued in association with the Bakewell and District Naturalists' Field Club and the Matlock Field Club.

c The association of some Dorset place-names with the history of the county, by W. J. Stanton.

391 Vol. 3.

a Mediaeval costume, as illustrated by the monuments in Wimborne minster, by Ida M. Roper.

392 Vol. 4.

a The Berkeleys of Bisterne, etc., Hants: their homes and their chauntries, by G. Brownen.

393 Vol. 5.

a Flowers in stone as applied to church architecture, by Ida M. Roper.

b Godlingston manor: its history and archaeology, by L. V. C. Homer.

394 Vol. 8.

a Church of St. Nicholas, Studland, by H. S. Solly.

395 Vol. 11.

a Old maps of Hampshire, Dorset, and Wiltshire, by H. Sumner.

b Surnames, by J. E. Kelsall.

c Hampshire and Kent contrasted and compared, by R. Y. Banks.

d Old Wardour castle, by H. S. Solly.

396 Vol. 12.

a Ancient earthworks in the Bournemouth district, by H. Sumner.

b Earthworks in the Bournemouth district south of the river Stour, by W. G. Wallace.

397 Vol. 13.

a Excavations on St. Catherine's hill, Christchurch, by W. G. Wallace.

398 Vol. 14.

a Barrows on Ibsley common, by H. Sumner.

399 Vol. 18.

a Roman housing in south Britain (near Bournemouth), 253–378, by H. Sumner.

400 Vol. 20.

a The bronze and early iron ages, by E. H. Goddard.

401 Vol. 21.

a Recent additions to the historical records of West Parley and neighbourhood, by C. D. Drew.

402 Vol. 22.

a Coombs ditch and Bokerley dyke reviewed, by H. Sumner.

403 General index to the Proceedings, 1903–23, comp. J. R. White. *P.* 1927.

Other publications:

404 A natural history of Bournemouth and district, including archaeology, topography, municipal government, climate, education, fauna, flora and geology, by members of the Society, ed. Sir D. Morris. 1914.

BRADFORD HISTORICAL AND ANTIQUARIAN SOCIETY

Founded 1878, to encourage and assist in the preservation of all matters of historical, archaeological and general antiquarian interest relating to the city of Bradford and its neighbourhood.

Bradford Antiquary, new ser., vols. 2–6, *or* pts. 6–31 (1901–40):

405 Vol. 2.

a Non-sepulchral earthworks of Yorkshire, by Mrs. E. Armitage.

b West Riding cartulary: a collection of ancient documents chiefly from the Hemingway mss., transcribed and abstracted by A. Federer. [Previous article in vol. 1. Contd. in vol. 3]

c The original home of the Pilgrim Fathers [Bawtry and Austerfield, Yorks., and Scrooby, Notts.], by B. Dale.

d Burial register of Bradford parish church, transcribed by T. T. Empsall. [Previous part in vol. 1. Contd. in vol. 3]

e Kirkgate chapel, Bradford, and its associations with Methodism, by J. N. Dickons.

f Bradford militia assessments, June and Sept. 1716 (from the Hemingway mss.).

g Pre-historic antiquities of the Bradford district, by B. Wood.

h Ministers of the parish church of Bradford and its three chapels during the Puritan revolution, by B. Dale.

i An assessment for raising £199 5s. 2d., charged upon Bradford, for his Majesty's use, 1727.

j The Layton family, of Rawdon [Yorks.], by W. Cudworth.

k James Nayler [d. 1660], the mad Quaker, by B. Dale.

l Plans of Bradford, by S. O. Bailey.

m The first Bradford bank, by W. Cudworth.

n Hawksworth Hall and its associations, by H. Speight.

o Bradford churchwardens, comp. from the parish church records, by W. Cudworth.

p The story of the Turvin coiners, by C. A. Federer.

q Vestiges of the Celts in the West Riding, by J. H. Rowe.

r The first Bradford waterworks, by W. Cudworth.

s Ministers of parish churches and chapels round about Bradford during the Puritan revolution, by B. Dale.

t Turrets and milecastles of the Roman wall in Northumberland, by P. Ross.

u The Cholmleys of Whitby, by R. T. Gaskin.

v Annals of an old Yorkshire village [Thornton], by J. Gregory.

w John Hall, 'doctor', of Kipping [d. 1709], by B. Dale.

x Vicar of Bradford v. Bradford parish church lecturer: a chapter of local ecclesiastical history, 1728–33.

y Hubberholme and its ancient church.

z Coniston-with-Kilnsey: its history and antiquities.

406 Vol. 3.

a The duchy of Lancaster and the manor of Bradford, by H. F. Killick.

b Baildon: some of its ancient and modern features, by W. Scruton.

c The Bradford newspaper press, by B. Wood.

d Robin Hood: myth or mystery?, by C. A. Federer.

e The forgotten manor of Exley, by W. A. Brigg.

f The Laycocks of the parish of Kildwick, by J. A. and J. B. Laycock.

g Memoirs of Capt. John Hodgson of Coalleyn Hall, near Halifax; touching his conduct in the civil wars, and his troubles after the restoration.

h Bradford manor court rolls, by H. Speight.

i The earlier daughter churches of Bradford parish church, by L. Dawson.

j Some Claphams of note, by J. A. Clapham.

k Bradford in 1832. [Plan]

l Shipley in 1800. [Plan]

m The place-names Menston and Manningham, by J. H. Rowe.

n The Friends of Lothersdale, and the story of their sufferings, by W. Scruton.

s The Craven way; or the Roman road from York to Carlisle via Settle, by F. Villy.

t The manor of Harden [chiefly in the 17th cent.], by C. Whone.

u The lost hamlet of Cockan, by W. Robertshaw.

v Wycoller causeway, by F. Villy.

w Notes on local clergy in Reformation times, by H. I. Judson.

x The Roman road beyond Long Preston and the position of a hoard of coins, by F. Villy.

y Bradford tradesmen's tokens of the 17th cent., by W. E. Preston.

z Quaker sketches [relating to Nidderdale, 17th–18th cent.], by H. R. Hodgson.

aa The manor of Clayton, by W. Robertshaw. [Appendix 1: Miscellaneous notes relating to the Clayton family. Appendix 2: Boundaries of the manor of Clayton, *c.* 1775]

bb Antiquarian notes, by F. Villy. [Wycoller causeway; Castlestead, Pately Bridge; Roads over Blackstone Edge from Lancashire to Yorkshire]

cc Notes on a 16th cent. Keighley muster roll, by H. I. Judson.

dd A local conversation piece, by W. Robertshaw. [Portrait of Edward Rookes Leeds, of Royds Hall, d. 1785, and his four daughters, by Arthur Devis, d. 1787]

ee Pedigree of the family of Bolling, of Chellow and Ilkley, in the parishes of Bradford and Ilkley.

ff The manor of Chellow, by W. Robertshaw.

gg An Addingham millstone quarry, by W. E. Preston.

hh Two local sundials, by L. R. A. Grove. [At Tong Hall and Wyke manor house]

ii The Roman road south-west from Bainbridge, by F. Villy.

Local Record series, vols. 1–2:

410 Vol. 1. Wills proved in the court of the manor of Crosley, Bingley, Cottingley, and Pudsey, in co. York, with inventories and abstracts of bonds, ed. W. E. Preston. 1929 [1914–29].

411 Vol. 2. West Yorkshire deeds, ed. and indexed by W. Robertshaw. 1936 [1931–6].

BRADFORD SCIENTIFIC ASSOCIATION

Founded 1875, to encourage the spread of scientific knowledge generally, and of its local application in particular by means of lectures, etc., and for the investigation and study of local geology, archaeology, flora, fauna, etc. The Society suspended operations from 1882 to 1884.

Bradford Scientific Journal, vols. 1–3 (1904–12):

412 Vol. 1.

a The Romans at Ilkley, by W. Cudworth.

b Unique Yorkshire cave implement, by W. Cudworth.

c The discovery of a cinerary urn on Baildon moor, by W. E. Preston.

d The ethnographical significance of some Yorkshire place names, by B. Wood.

413 Vol. 2.

a Prehistoric remains on the moors near Kildwick, by J. J. Brigg.

b The Manchester-Ilkley Roman road between Cockhill and Ilkley, by F. Villy.

414 Vol. 3.

a An unrecorded Roman road and camp at Swinden, near Hellifield, by E. E. Gregory.

b Bolton priory, by H. E. Wroot.

c Excavations at Castlestead ring, near Cullingworth, by F. Villy.

d Prehistoric remains in the Shipley glen district, by B. Wood.

e Prehistoric remains at Thorpe, by J. Crowther.

f An old Bradford botanist [Dr. Richard Richardson, 1741], by H. E. Wroot.

BRIGHTON AND HOVE ARCHAEOLOGICAL CLUB

Founded 1906, to promote the study of local antiquities with a view to the proper recording and preservation of the same.

Brighton and Hove Archaeologist, nos. 1–3 (1914–26):

415 No. 1.

a Notes on a survey of Hollingbury camp, by H. S. Toms.

b Notes on the church of St. Michael, Up Marden, Sussex, by O. H. Leeney.

c A rental of the manor of Preston in the reign of Edward VI, by C. Thomas-Stanford.

d Ancient trackways near Saddlescombe, with notes on pottery found on Newtimber hill, by E. Curwen and E. C. Curwen.

e The forest of Anderida: some of the scenes and history of 'the Weald', by T. G. Leggatt.

f Ancient parish churches near the river Ouse, by J. S. North.

g A 17th cent. document ['copy of court-roll' of Brighthelmston, 1645], by Mabel Russell-Davies.

h Records of local and other Roman coins, by H. S. Toms.

416 No. 2.

a The Hove tumulus, by E. Curwen and E. C. Curwen.

b The *circus* on Buckland bank [Falmer], by A. H. Allcroft. [Contd. in no. 3]

c Brighton steine and the Danes in Sussex, by W. C. Wallis.

d Notes on Celtic road and lynchets on Truleigh hill, by R. P. R. Williamson.

e Valley entrenchments west of the Ditchling road, by H. S. Toms.

f Tomb of Edward Elrington [d. 1515] at Preston, by C. Thomas-Stanford.

g Surveys of Thundersbarrow camp and Thunder's steps [near Kingston-by-Sea], by R. Gurd and W. J. Jacobs, with notes by H. S. Toms.

h Our windmills [chiefly in Sussex], by W. Law.

417 No. 3.

a Roman villa at Preston, by H. S. Toms and G. Herbert.

b Port's road, the ancient road of Portslade, by E. Curwen and E. C. Curwen.

c Valley entrenchments east of the Ditchling road, by H. S. Toms.

d Constables and headboroughs, by F. Harrison.

e The Bartholomew's property, Brighthelmston, 1547–92, by J. S. North. [Deeds relating to land of St. Bartholomew's chapel]

f Brighthelmston church and the chapel of St. Bartholomew, by W. C. Wallis.

g Our ancient dovecotes [chiefly in Sussex], by W. Law.

BRIGHTON AND HOVE NATURAL HISTORY AND PHILOSOPHICAL SOCIETY

Founded 1854, as the Brighton and Sussex Natural History Society, to promote the study of natural history, geology, the physical and applied sciences, and philosophy. Title changed to the above form in 1898.

Abstracts of Papers read before the Society together with the Annual Report, 1901–33 (30 vols. 1901–33):

418 Vol. for 1901.

a The pottery of prehistoric and Roman Britain, by H. S. Toms.

b Roger Bacon: a chapter in the history of science in the 13th cent., by R. J. Ryle.

419 Vol. for 1902.

a Some prehistoric camping grounds near Brighton, by H. S. Toms.

420 Vol. for 1903.

a Hollingbury camp [Brighton], by H. S. Toms.

421 Vol. for 1905.

a History of the South Downs, by J. H. A. Jenner.

422 Vol. for 1907.

a Pigmy flint implements found near Brighton, by H. S. Toms.

423 Vol. for 1909.

a Twenty years' history of the Society, 1888–1908, by H. Davey.

b Shoreham.

424 Vol. for 1915.

a John Selden, 1584–1654, by A. O. Jennings.

425 Vol. for 1918.

a Round the Sussex border: 1. Sussex and Kent, by H. Davey. [Contd. for the Sussex–Surrey and Sussex–Hampshire borders in vol. for 1919–20]

b The Anglo-Saxons in Sussex, by A. F. Griffith.

426 Vol. for 1919–20.

a Edward Gibbon, 1737–94, by C. Thomas-Stanford.

427 Vol. for 1921–2.

a Joseph Priestley, the hero of the 18th cent., by A. W. Oke.

428 Vol. for 1925.

a Dr. Gideon Mantell [d. 1852], by S. Spokes.

b Snail-eaters of late cave days, by H. S. Toms.

429 Vol. for 1927.

a The Piltdown skull, by Sir A. S. Woodward.

BRISTOL AND GLOUCESTERSHIRE ARCHAEOLOGICAL SOCIETY

Founded 1876, to collect and classify original and existing information on the antiquities of the district, and thus to accumulate materials for county history; to establish a library to assist the study of antiquities; to promote such an interest throughout the district in the monuments of its past history as shall tend to their preservation.

Transactions, vols. 24–54 (1902–33):

430 Vol. 24.

a Proceedings at Winterbourne, Almondsbury, Over Court, and Westbury-on-Trim, 1901. [Brief historical accounts]

b Proceedings at Chipping Campden, 1901. [Includes accounts of the churches of All Saints and St. Lawrence, Evesham, and of Chipping Campden, Quinton, Mickleton, and Buckland churches]

c The Halleway chauntry at the parish church of All Saints, Bristol, and the Halleway family, by E. G. C. F. Atchley.

d Architecture of Hayles abbey, by H. Brakspear.

e Bristol city coat of arms, by F. Were.

f The family of Catchmay, by W. T. Allen.

g A note on Hidcote House, by S. G. Hamilton.

h Aust, the place of meeting [of St. Augustine and the British bishops], by C. S. Taylor.

i Hospital of St. John, Bristol, by J. Latimer.

j Sir John Fortescue [d. *c.* 1476], buried at Ebrington, Glos., by Anne M. Welch.

k The grammar school, Campden, by F. B. Osborne.

l Heraldry in Red Lodge, Bristol, by F. Were.

m Aust and Wiclif, by J. Baker.

n Bristol archaeological notes for 1901, by J. E. Pritchard. [Further reports, relating to miscellaneous discoveries, in vols. 26, 27, 29–32]

o Remains of a Roman villa, discovered at Brislington, Bristol, Dec. 1899, by W. R. Baker.

p The high cross at Gloucester, by C. H. Dancey.

q Maces, swordbearer, and swords of the city of Gloucester, by C. H. Dancey.

r King Alfred and his family in Mercia, by C. S. Taylor.

431 Vol. 25.

a Proceedings at Yatton, Wrington, and Banwell, 1902. [Brief historical accounts]

b Proceedings at Tewkesbury, 1902. [Includes accounts of Tewkesbury abbey church, and of Great Malvern, Little Malvern, and Deerhurst churches]

c The monks of the monastery of St. Mary, at Tewkesbury, by E. R. Dowdeswell.

d On certain rare monumental effigies, by A. Hartshorne.

e Bristol cathedral heraldry, by F. Were.

f Monumental effigies in Bristol and Gloucestershire, by A. Hartshorne.

g List of monumental effigies in Bristol and Gloucestershire, ed. Mary E. Bagnall-Oakeley. [Further lists appear in vols. 26–34]

h Heraldry [in the churches of Winterbourne, Almondsbury, Ashchurch, All Saints' Evesham, Wickamford, Chipping Campden, Ebrington, Quinton, Mickleton, Long Marston, Buckland, and Broadway], by F. Were.

i The story of two Lantonys [in Monmouthshire and at Gloucester], by W. St. C. Baddeley.

j Deerhurst, Pershore, and Westminster, by C. S. Taylor.

k The arrangement of the chancel at Deerhurst, by R. H. Murray.

l The grave of Bishop Carpenter [of Worcester, d. 1476, being two short letters, 1902, relating to the disappearance of his remains].

432 Vol. 26.

a Proceedings at Malmesbury and Sherston, 1903.

b Proceedings at Gloucester, 1903. [Includes historical accounts of Gloucester and Caerwent]

c Incidents in the early history of Gloucester, by F. A. Hyett.

d The maire of Bristow is kalendar: its list of civic officers collated with contemporary legal mss., by J. Latimer.

e The stained glass art of the 14th cent., by St. C. Baddeley.

f Heraldry in Tewkesbury abbey, by F. Were.

g The battle of Tewkesbury, 1471, by W. Bazeley.

h The Mercers' and Linen Drapers' company of Bristol, by J. Latimer.

i The crypt church, Gloucester, sometimes called St. Mary of South Gate, by by C. H. Dancey.

j Osric of of Gloucester, by C. S. Taylor [Investigation of the tradition identifying Osric, king of the Hwiccii, with Osric, king of Northumbria, fl. 718–29]

k Notes on Roman roads, with an account of excavations on the Fosse road at Radstock and on a road near North Stoke, Bath, by J. McMurtrie.

l The so-called King's Board at Tibberton Court, near Gloucester, by M. H. Medland.

433 Vol. 27.

a Proceedings at Bredon, Strensham, and Pershore, 1904.

b Proceedings at Hereford, 1904. [Includes accounts of Hereford cathedral and of Ewias Harold, Abbey Dore, Madley, Ludlow, and Leominster churches]

c Early connection between the [cathedral] churches of Gloucester and Hereford, by J. W. Leigh.

d The church and monastery of Abbey Dore, Herefs., by R. W. Paul.

e Bristol cathedral: the choir screen, by R. H. Warren.

f The date of Wansdyke, by C. S. Taylor.

g The Painswick or Ifold villa, by W. St. C. Baddeley.

h Some Gloucestershire manuscripts now in Hereford cathedral library, by L. E. G. Brown.

i On the parish records of the church of All Saints, Bristol, by E. G. C. F. Atchley.

j Heraldry read at Bredon, Strensham, Pershore, Dumbleton, and Didbrook, by F. Were.

k Old church of St. Thomas the Martyr, Bristol, by C. S. Taylor.

l Bristol hotwells, by L. M. Griffiths.

434 Vol. 28.

a Proceedings at Berkeley and North Nibley, 1905. [Chiefly an account of Berkeley Castle]

b Proceedings at Cheltenham and Worcester, 1905. [Includes accounts of Worcester cathedral and Cheltenham and Bishop's Cleeve churches]

c Monastic and kindred institutions of Bristol and Gloucestershire, by J. Mitchinson.

d Some ancient deeds relating to the manor of Southam, near Cheltenham, by E. R. Dowdeswell.

e The misereres in Gloucester cathedral, by O. W. Clark.

f Heraldic notes of the spring excursion to Berkeley Castle, by F. Were.

g Notes on heraldry in churches, by F. Were. [Includes parish churches of Badgworth, Brockworth, Witcombe, Tredington, Bishop's Cleeve and Cheltenham, and Southam chapel]

h The ancient tolzey and pie poudre courts of Bristol, by S. D. Cole.

i Notes on the [heraldic] visitations of Gloucester, by E. Conder.

j Index to the heraldry in Bigland's *History of Gloucestershire*, with notes by F. Were.

435 Vol. 29.

a Proceedings at Chepstow, St. Briavels, and Tintern, 1906.

b Proceedings at Bristol, 1906. [Includes brief accounts of buildings of historical interest in Bristol, Clapton, Weston-in-Gordano, Clevedon, Chelvey, Dyrham camp, Cold Ashton and Marshfield]

c Exhibition of old Bristol plans, Bristol coinage, antiquities, etc., at the conversazione on July 17th, 1906.

d Religious houses of Bristol and their dissolution, by C. S. Taylor.

e Certain Roman remains at Watercombe, near Bisley, by St. C. Baddeley.

f On early and mediaeval libraries and the evolution of the bookroom and the bookcase, by T. W. Williams.

g Gilbert de Laci (?1108–1163) and Pain FitzJohn (–1137): the de Laci pedigree (Gloucestershire and Herefordshire branch).

h Notes on the purlieus of the forest of Dean, by E. Conder.

i On a Roman road from Old Sarum to Uphill and its structure at Chewton Mendip, where cut through in 1906, by J. McMurtrie.

j Notes on the iron ore mines of the forest of Dean, and on the history of their working, being the substance of an address by W. H. Fryer.

k Grant by Sir John Benet of Doyly, Mdx., Knight of the Bath, to the master, fellows and scholars of Pembroke College, Oxford, made the 10th November in the eight and twentieth year (1676) of the reign of our sovereign lord Charles II, by F. Were.

436 Vol. 30.

a Proceedings at Northleach and Chedworth, 1907. [Includes an account of the Chedworth villa]

b Proceedings at Cirencester, 1907. [Includes accounts of Cirencester, Ashton Keynes, and Cricklade churches]

c The modern status of archaeology and the hopes of archaeology in relation to certain dark periods in Britain, by W. St. C. Baddeley.

d The archaeology of tradition, by E. S. Hartland.

e Silver plate and insignia of the city of Gloucester, by C. H. Dancey.

f Priory of St. Guthlac, Hereford, by S. E. Bartleet.

g Mediaeval chapels of Bristol, by R. H. Warren.

h Notes on a leaden vessel [possibly a lavabo] in Gloucester museum, by A. C. Fryer.

i A skeleton and other relics lately found in a Romano-British settlement at Radstock, by J. McMurtrie, with notes on the skull by J. Beddoe.

j Witcombe villa [and Roman Gloucester], by W. St. C. Baddeley.

k The Lond or Loud brass in St. Peter's church, Bristol, by C. E. Boucher. [Robert Lond, priest and schoolmaster, fl. 1426–69]

l Note on the printed text of William Worcester [1415–1482?], by C. S. Taylor.

m The heraldry of some of the citizens of Bristol between 1662 and 1688, by E. Conder and F. Were.

437 Vol. 31.

a Proceedings at Newent, 1908. [Includes brief historical accounts of Dymock, Kempley, Newent, and Pauntley]

b Proceedings at Cardiff, 1908. [Includes brief accounts of Llandaff cathedral, Caerphilly and Cardiff castles, Llantwit church, and Ewenny priory]

c Early connection between Glamorgan and Gloucestershire, by W. Bazeley.

d Gloucestershire mediaeval libraries, by T. W. Williams.

e The Smyths of Ashton Court, by L. U. Way.

f Caerphilly castle, by J. S. Corbett.

g St. John's church, Cardiff, by J. Ballinger.

h Gloucestershire fonts, by A. C. Fryer. [Contd. in vols. 32–34, 36–42, 44, 46–49, with index in vol. 49 and additional note in vol. 50]

i Head of an early 14th cent. effigy in St. Philip's church, Bristol, by A. C. Fryer.

j Notes on the heraldry seen at [Dymock, Kempley, and Pauntley churches], by F. Were.

438 Vol. 32.

a Proceedings at Standish, Moreton Valence, Frampton and Leonard Stanley, 1909.

b Proceedings at Evesham, 1909. [Includes brief accounts of buildings of historical interest in Evesham, Fladbury, Wyre, Pershore, Elmley Castle, and Beckford]

h Parish church of S. Edward, Stow-on-the-Wold, by T. Overbury.
i Some early Selwyns, by C. Swynnerton.
j Glass-making in Bristol, by A. C. Powell.
k The ruined chapel at Brownshill, Chalford, and the chapel of Pagenhill, by Mary A. Rudd.
l Notes on the family of Bradeston, by R. Austin.
m Ancient stained glass in Gloucestershire churches, by S. Pitcher.

454 Vol. 48.

a Proceedings at Gloucester [etc.], 1926. [Includes an account of Tewkesbury abbey]
b Proceedings at Bristol, 1926. [Includes accounts of the churches of Winterbourne and Berkeley]
c Local history. Presidential address by A. Hamilton Thompson.
d The Roman pavement at Woodchester, by St. C. Baddeley.
e Sir John Hudleston, constable of Sudeley [d. 1512], by C. R. Hudleston.
f Berkeley Castle, by St. C. Baddeley.
g Letters and verse written to John Smyth of Nibley on the completion of his Berkeley history [c. 1636], by R. Austin.
h St. Peter's hospital, Bristol, by J. J. Simpson.
i Archives of the corporation of Bristol, by Miss N. D. Harding.
j The Pithay, Bristol: Norman pottery and wall, by J. E. Pritchard.
k Ashleworth: ecclesiastical records [abstracted from various sources, more particularly from the papers of F. S. Hockaday, 12th–19th cent.].
l The recently discovered church at Grafton near Beckford and the churches of Great Washbourne and Stoke Orchard, by W. H. Knowles.
m Rectors of Cotes or Coates, by J. D. Thorp.
n Old plans and views of Bristol, by J. E. Pritchard.
o Church of St. Nicholas of Myra, Ozleworth, Glos., by L. Wilkinson, T. Overbury, and W. St. C. Baddeley.
p Ashleworth church, by T. Overbury.

455 Vol. 49.

a Proceedings at Hereford, 1927. [Includes accounts of Abbey Dore, Grosmont, Skenfrith, Eaton Bishop, and Weobley]
b The dispossessed religious of Gloucestershire, by G. Baskerville. [Additional note in vol. 52]
c Berkeley Castle, by the Earl of Berkeley.
d The Campden mystery [the 'murder' of William Harrison, 1660, and his reappearance], by Sir F. Hyett.
e A 17th cent. house and chimney piece in Small Street, Bristol, by H. C. M. Hirst.
f Deerhurst priory church, including the excavations, 1926, by W. H. Knowles.
g Flaxley grange and St. White's, by May H. Ellis.
h Effigies of the Stratford family, at Farmcote, Glos., by Ida M. Roper.
i Gloucestershire cartulary. I: Concerning the priory of Stanley St. Leonards, by C. Swynnerton.
j Painted glass in the lord mayor's chapel [St. Mark's church], Bristol, by G. McN. Rushforth.

456 Vol. 50.

a Proceedings at Ashchurch[etc.], 1928. [Includes accounts of Woollas Hall and Elmley Castle]
b Proceedings at Stroud, 1928. [Includes accounts of Painswick, Beverstone, Uley camp, and Frampton-on-Severn]
c The development of architecture in Gloucestershire to the close of the 12th cent., by W. H. Knowles.

d Church of St. Nicholas, Ashchurch, by W. H. Knowles.
e The Severn-god and Lydney, by St. C. Baddeley.
f A post-Roman settlement near Frampton-on-Severn, by St. C. Baddeley.
g History of the manor of Coates, Glos., with some account of families connected with it, and descent of the owners, by J. D. Thorp.
h The builder of Southam [Sir John Hudleston, d. 1547] and some deeds connected with the estate, by C. R. Hudleston.
i Archaeology of Longtree hundred, by R. J. Burton.
j The story of Dauntsey [Wilts.], by G. McN. Rushforth.

457 Vol. 51.

a Proceedings at Charfield [etc.], 1929. [Includes accounts of St. James's (old) church, Charfield; St. Mary's, Yate; and Chipping Sodbury]
b Proceedings 1929. [Includes accounts of earthworks in Lydney Park and Caerleon]
c Lydney, Glos. Presidential address by Lord Bledisloe.
d Notes on some old Gloucestershire maps, by A. C. Painter. [Additional note in vol. 52]
e Battle of Dyrham, 577, by St. C. Baddeley.
f Grant of arms to Queen Elizabeth's hospital, Bristol, 1591, by W. Leighton.
g Tyndall's park, Bristol, Fort Royal and the Fort house therein, by G. Parker.
h Sir George Onesiphorus Paul [prison reformer, d. 1820], by Sir F. Hyett.
i The bridges of Gloucester and the hospital [of St. Bartholomew] between the bridges, by May H. Ellis. [With list of priors of St. Bartholomew's]
j Abstracts of deeds relating to Chalford and Colcombe, by Mary A. Rudd.
k Ebbworth manor [charters, 12th–13th cent.], by St. C. Baddeley.
l Archaeology of Bisley hundred, by R. J. Burton.
m Belas Knap long barrow, Glos., by W. J. Hemp.
n Belas Knap long barrow, Glos.: excavations, 1929, by Sir J. Berry. [Excavations, 1930, in vol. 52]
o Clock and watch makers of the 18th cent. in Gloucestershire and Bristol, comp. F. Buckley and G. B. Buckley.
p Members of parliament for Gloucestershire and Bristol, 1900–29, by Sir F. Hyett and C. Wells.

458 Vol. 52.

a Proceedings at Teddington [etc.], 1930. [Includes accounts of Hayles abbey, Winchcombe church, and Sudeley castle]
b Proceedings, 1930. [Includes accounts of Broughton castle and church, Bloxham church, Great Tew, and Chipping Norton]
c Teddington church, Worcs., in which are structural fragments from Hayles abbey, by W. H. Knowles.
d Robert de Todeni [d. 1088] and his heirs, by A. L. Browne.
e Lists of Bristol ships, 1571 and 1572, by J. W. Damer-Powell.
f Notes on portions of a late and secondary Roman road-system (c. 220–390) in Gloucestershire, by St. C. Baddeley.
g Elkstone church, Glos., by W. H. Knowles.
h Prehistoric and Roman site at Barnwood near Gloucester, by Elsie M. Clifford.
i The Roman-British temple, Chedworth, by St. C. Baddeley.
j Warkworth [Northants.], by G. McN. Rushforth.
k Some ecclesiastical wills [of the abbots and priors of suppressed Gloucestershire monasteries], by G. Baskerville.

459 Vol. 53.

   a Proceedings at Micheldean [etc.], 1931. [Includes accounts of Goodrich castle and English Bicknor]

   b Proceedings, 1931. [Includes accounts of Langford, Bampton, and Minster Lovel]

   c The wool trade and the woolmen of Gloucestershire. Presidential address by J. J. Simpson.

   d Roof bosses in Gloucester cathedral, by C. J. P. Cave.

   e Early road planning in the middle Cotswolds, by A. C. Painter.

   f Hill, Glos., by H. Jenner-Fust. [With list of vicars and description of manorial records]

   g Church of S. John Baptist, Inglesham, Wilts., by W. H. Knowles.

   h A 16th cent. monument in Westbury-on-Trym church [of Miles Wilson, d. 1567, and Elizabeth Revell, d. 1581], by Ida M. Roper and C. R. Hudleston.

   i Tudor relief-portrait in stone at Prinknash, Glos., by St. C. Baddeley.

   j Early lords of Little Rissington, by A. L. Browne.

   k The west wall of Glevum, by St. C. Baddeley.

   l Gloucester Roman research committee: report, 1931-32.

460 Vol. 54.

   a Proceedings, 1932. [Includes accounts of Slymbridge, Dursley, and Horton Court]

   b Proceedings, 1932. [Includes accounts of Bristol cathedral and the lord mayor's chapel (St. Mark's church), Bristol]

   c Hugh Westwood [of Chedworth, d. 1559], by A. C. Painter.

   d Medieval Cirencester, by E. A. Fuller.

   e The Grey Friars, Gloucester, by Vera M. Dallas.

   f Arms of St. Augustine's abbey, Bristol, by G. McN. Rushforth.

   g Arms of St. Mark's or the Gaunts' hospital, Bristol, by G. McN. Rushforth.

   h Arms and badges of Edward Stafford, 3rd Duke of Buckingham, by R. Jeffcoat.

   i Arms of the dean and chapter of Bristol, by H. de Candole.

   j Manor of Charlton Kings, later Ashley, by F. B. Welch.

   k The Black Friars at Gloucester, by W. H. Knowles.

   l Minchinhampton custumal [c. 1300] and its place in the story of the manor, by C. E. Watson.

461 General index to vols. 21-40 (1897-1917), with subject-index to the illustrations in vols. 1-40, comp. R. Austin. 1919.

462 General index to vols. 41-50 (1918-29), with subject-index to illustrations, comp. R. Austin. 1930.

463 General index to vols. 51-60 (1931-9), with separate index to illustrations, and places visited by the Society, 1876-1939. 1942.

Additional vols.:

464 Catalogue of books, pamphlets and mss. from the library of the Rev. David Royce, presented by Mrs. Royce to the Society, 1902; with a memoir of Mr. Royce by W. Bazeley. [1903]

465 Church plate of Gloucestershire; with extracts from the chantry certificates relating to the county by the commissioners of 2 Edward VI (1548), and from the returns of church goods in 6 and 7 Edward VI (1552-3), ed. J. T. Evans. 1906.

466 Descriptive catalogue of the printed maps of Gloucestershire, 1577-1911, with biographical notes, by T. Chubb. 1912.

BRISTOL RECORD SOCIETY

Founded 1929, to make available something of the wealth of historical material contained in the city archives, and in the collections of lay and ecclesiastical corporations.

Publications, vols. 1-4:

467 Vol. 1. Bristol charters, 1155-1373, ed. Miss N. D Harding. 1930.

468 Vols. 2, 4. The great red book of Bristol, ed. E. W. W. Veale. Vols. i-ii. 1931-3. [Vol. i: Introd. (pt. 1): Burgage tenure in mediaeval Bristol; vol. ii: Text (pt. 1). Vols. iii-iv, being pts. 2 and 3 of text, were published in 1937-50]

469 Vol. 3. Bristol corporation of the poor: selected records, 1696-1834, ed. Emily E. Butcher. 1932.

BRITISH ACADEMY FOR THE PROMOTION OF HISTORICAL, PHILOSOPHICAL AND PHILOLOGICAL STUDIES

Founded 1902, to promote the study of the moral and political sciences, including history, philosophy, law, politics and economics, archaeology and philology.

Proceedings, 1903-32 (18 vols.[1] 1905?-33?):

470 Vol. for 1903-4.

   a John Locke as a factor in modern thought, by A. C. Fraser.

   b Locke's theory of the state, by Sir F. Pollock.

   c Lord Acton, by J. Bryce. [Also W. A. J. Archbold on Acton as a Cambridge professor, and H. R. Tedder on Acton as a book-collector]

   d Dr. S. R. Gardiner, by C. H. Firth.

   e Mr. Lecky, by Sir S. Walpole.

   f Sir Leslie Stephen, by F. W. Maitland.

471 Vol. for 1905-6.

   a The Romanization of Roman Britain, by F. J. Haverfield.

   b Frederick William Maitland, by Sir F. Pollock.

472 Vol. for 1907-8.

   a Knight's fees, by P. Vinogradoff.

   b An unrecognized Westminster chronicler, 1381-94, by J. Armitage Robinson.

   c Milton as an historian, by C. H. Firth.

   d George Joachim, first Viscount Goschen, by Viscount Milner.

   e Sir Spencer Walpole, by Sir A. C. Lyall.

473 Vol. for 1909-10.

   a The nave of Westminster, by R. B. Rackham.

   b Column and line in the Peninsular war, by C. W. C. Oman.

474 Vol. for 1911-12.

   a Andrew Lang, by P. Hume Brown.

475 Vol. for 1913-14.

   a The study of modern history in Great Britain, by C. H. Firth.

   b The present state of mediaeval studies in Great Britain, by T. F. Tout.

   c Notes on the organisation of the mason's craft in England, by W. Cunningham.

   d Roger Bacon, by Sir J. E. Sandys.

[1] All articles in these vols. were also issued separately.

e Some results of research in the history of education in England, by A. F. Leach.

f Thomas Hodgkin, by T. F. Tout.

476 Vol. for 1915-16.

a Presidential addresses by Viscount Bryce. [Remarks occasioned by the 1914 war]

b The Academ Roial of King James I, by Ethel M. Portal.

c Primitive man, by G. Elliot Smith.

477 Vol. for 1917-18.

a Neglected British history, by W. M. Flinders Petrie.

b Sir Walter Raleigh's *History of the World*, by C. H. Firth.

c Relations of the House of Savoy with the court of England, by F. de Filippi.

d Evelyn, Earl of Cromer, by Lord Sanderson.

e P. Hume Brown, by G. Macdonald.

478 Vol. for 1919-20.

a Englishmen and Italians: some aspects of their relations past [mainly 19th cent.] and present, by G. M. Trevelyan.

b Shakespeare and the makers of Virginia [the Virginia Company], by Sir A. W. Ward.

c World history, by Viscount Bryce.

d The political significance of *Gulliver's Travels*, by C. H. Firth.

e Seals and documents, by R. L. Poole.

f Early English magic and medicine, by C. Singer.

g The tangled skein: art in England, 1800-1920, by Sir R. Blomfield.

h William Cunningham, by W. R. Scott.

i F. Haverfield, by G. Macdonald.

479 Vol. for 1921-3.

a English place-name study: its present condition and future possibilities, by A. Mawer.

b John Dryden and a British Academy, by O. F. Emerson.

c The beginning of the year in the middle ages, by R. L. Poole.

d The Elizabethans and the empire, by A. F. Pollard.

e The study of early municipal history in England, by J. Tait.

f National policy and naval strength, 16th to 20th cent., by H. W. Richmond.

g William Byrd, 1623-1923, by Sir W. H. Hadow.

h Adam Smith, by W. R. Scott.

i Introduction of the Observant friars into England, by A. G. Little.

j A romanesque relief in York minster, by E. Maclagan.

k Beginnings of a modern capital: London and Westminster in the 14th cent., by T. F. Tout.

l The philosophy of history, by A. S. Pringle-Pattison.

m Lord Reay, 1839-1921, by Viscount Bryce.

480 Vol. for 1924-5.

a Early correspondence of John of Salisbury, by R. L. Poole.

b English primitives [examples of medieval painting], by T. Borenius.

c The winning of the initiative by the House of Commons, by W. Notestein.

d Lord Shelburne and the founding of British-American goodwill, by C. W. Alvord.

e Sir Adolphus William Ward, 1837-1924, by T. F. Tout.

f Sir Paul Vinogradoff, 1854-1925, by W. S. Holdsworth.

g Sir James Henry Ramsay, 1832-1925, by T. F. Tout.

481 Vol. for 1926.

a English ornament in the 7th and 8th cent., by C. R. Peers.

b Chaucer and the rhetoricians, by J. M. Manly.

c The saga and the myth of Sir Thomas More, by R. W. Chambers.

d The great game in Asia [the activities of British political agents, soldiers, explorers, and others], 1800-44, by H. W. C. Davis.

e Linguistic evidence and archaeological and ethnological facts, by J. Fraser.

f Viscount Bryce of Dechmont, 1838-1922, by H. A. L. Fisher.

g Charles Lethbridge Kingsford, 1862-1926, by A. G. Little.

482 Vol. for 1927.

a Mediaeval paintings at Westminster, by W. R. Lethaby.

b The Danes in England, by F. M. Stenton.

c John Bagnell Bury, 1861-1927, by N. H. Baynes.

483 Vol. for 1928.

a Machiavelli and the Elizabethans, by M. Praz.

b Roger Bacon, by A. G. Little.

c The Whig historians, by H. A. L. Fisher.

d The Welsh chronicles, by J. E. Lloyd.

e Edward Armstrong, 1846-1928, by W. H. Hutton.

f Richard Burdon Haldane (Viscount Haldane of Cloan), 1856-1928, by A. S. Pringle-Pattison, with additional note by Viscount Dunedin.

484 Vol. for 1929.

a Wales and archaeology, by R. E. M. Wheeler.

b Sir Sidney Lee, 1859-1926, by C. H. Firth.

c Charles Plummer, 1851-1927, by P. S. Allen, with additions by F. M. Stenton and R. I. Best.

d Sir Edward Maunde Thompson, 1840-1929, by F. G. Kenyon.

e Thomas Frederick Tout, 1855-1929, by F. M. Powicke.

485 Vol. for 1930.

a Wandering Englishmen in Italy [late 16th cent. onwards], by Mrs. G. M. Trevelyan.

b Robert Grosseteste and the *Nicomachean Ethics*, by F. M. Powicke.

c The art of Geoffrey Chaucer, by J. L. Lowes.

d Bretons et Anglais aux Ve et VIe siècles, par F. Lot.

e Sir Henry Spelman and the *Concilia*, by F. M. Powicke.

f Sir George Otto Trevelyan, bt., 1838-1928, by B. Williams.

g Lord Rosebery, 1847-1930, by J. Buchan.

h Arthur James Balfour (Earl of Balfour), 1848-1930, by F. G. Kenyon.

i Sir Israel Gollancz, 1863-1930, by F. G. Kenyon.

486 Vol. for 1931.

a Cardinal Pole's manuscripts, by E. Lobel.

b Bulgarian and other atrocities, 1875-8, in the light of historical criticism, by H. Temperley.

c Sir Richard Temple, bt., 1850-1931, by R.E.E.

487 Vol. for 1932.

a Some problems in medieval historiography, by G. G. Coulton.

b The poems of Llywarch Hên, by I. Williams.

c Cynewulf and his poetry, by K. Sisam.

d Viscount Dillon, 1844-1932, by C. Ffoulkes. [Reprinted in vol. 12 of the *Journal* of the Soc. for Army Historical Research]

488 Index to vols. 1-20, 1901-34. [1937?]

Supplemental papers, nos. 1-6:

489 No. 2. Roman Britain in 1913, by F. Haverfield. 1914.

490 No. 3. Roman Britain in 1914, by F. Haverfield. 1915.

491 No. 4. The Saxon bishops of Wells: a historical study in the 10th cent., by J. Armitage Robinson. [1918?]

492 No. 5. St. Oswald and the church of Worcester, by J. Armitage Robinson. [1919?]

493 No. 6. Roman Britain, 1914–28, by Sir G. Macdonald. [1931?]

Records of social and economic history of England and Wales, vols. 1–8:

494 Vol. 1. Survey of the honour of Denbigh, 1334, ed. P. Vinogradoff and F. Morgan. 1914.

495 Vols. 2, 3. The register of St. Augustine's abbey, Canterbury, commonly called the black book, ed. G. J. Turner and H. E. Salter. 2 vols. 1915–24.

496 Vol. 4. (i) A terrier of Fleet, Lincs. [1316], from a ms. in the British Museum, ed. Nellie Neilson. (ii) An 11th cent. inquisition of St. Augustine's, Canterbury, by A. Ballard. 1920.

497 Vol. 5. Documents illustrative of the social and economic history of the Danelaw, ed. F. M. Stenton. 1920.

498 Vol. 6. Account book of a Kentish estate [Godinton], 1616–1704, ed. Eleanor C. Lodge. 1927.

499 Vol. 7. Cartulary and terrier of the priory of Bilsington, Kent, ed. Nellie Neilson. 1928.

500 Vol. 8. Feudal documents from the abbey of Bury St. Edmunds, ed. D. C. Douglas. 1932.

Other publications:

501 The Caedmon manuscript of Anglo-Saxon biblical poetry, Junius xi in the Bodleian Library, introd. Sir I. Gollancz. 1927.

502 Britain's tribute to Dante in literature and art: a chronological record of 540 years, by P. Toynbee. [1921]

503 Somerset historical essays, by J. Armitage Robinson. 1921.

  a William of Malmesbury on the antiquity of Glastonbury.
  b The Saxon abbots of Glastonbury.
  c The first deans of Wells.
  d Early Somerset archdeacons.
  e Peter of Blois [archdeacon of Bath].
  f Bishop Jocelin and the interdict.

BRITISH ARCHAEOLOGICAL ASSOCIATION

Founded 1843, for the encouragement and prosecution of researches into the arts and monuments of the early and middle ages.

Journal, new ser., vols. 7–39 (1901–34):

504 Vol. 7.
  a Early defensive earthworks, by I. C. Gould.
  b The site of London beyond the border [i.e. in Essex] a thousand years ago, by W. S. Lach-Szyrma.
  c Proceedings of the 57th congress, at Leicester, 1900. [Includes notes on Groby Hall and castle; and on Ulverscroft priory, by G. Patrick]
  d Notes on Hadrian's wall, by R. H. Forster.
  e The abbey of St. Mary de Pratis, Leicester, by C. H. Compton.
  f Two Norfolk villages [East and West Rudham], by H. J. Dukinfield Astley.
  g Kirby Muxloe castle, by J. A. Gotch.
  h Zoology on brasses, chiefly from Gloucestershire examples, by C. T. Davis.

  i Lutterworth, by G. Patrick.
  j A group of transitional Norman fonts (north-east Cornwall), by A. C. Fryer.
  k Wycliffe, by W. S. Lach-Szyrma.
  l Roman roads in Leicestershire, by Colonel Bellairs.
  m Chaucer as illustrating English mediaeval life, by W. S. Lach-Szyrma.
  n St. Nicholas church, Leicester, by C. Lynam.
  o The early lords of Belvoir, by W. A. Carrington. [Contd. in vol. 8]

505 Vol. 8.
  a The history of Northumberland. Inaugural address by T. Hodgkin.
  b Statutes of Durham cathedral, by G. W. Kitchin.
  c Proceedings of the 58th congress, at Newcastle-upon-Tyne, 1901. [Includes notes on Newcastle cathedral and castle, Warkworth castle, and Hexham priory]
  d The President and Council of the North, by C. H. Compton.
  e Some recently discovered earthworks, the supposed site of a Roman encampment at Cottenham, Cambs., by C. H. Evelyn-White.
  f The underground strong-room at Richborough, by A. R. Goddard.
  g Early history and associations of Lindisfarne, or Holy Island, by H. J. Dukinfield Astley.
  h Canterbury's ancient coinage, by S. W. Kershaw.
  i Lindisfarne priory, by H. J. Dukinfield Astley.
  j Notes on Flemish brasses in England, by A. Oliver.

506 Vol. 9.
  a Britain's burse, or the New Exchange [Strand, London], by T. N. Brushfield.
  b Hulne priory, Alnwick, Northumberland, by G. Patrick.
  c Proceedings of the 59th congress, Westminster and Home Counties, 1902. [Includes notes on St. Margaret's, Westminster; and Cobham church, Kent, by G. Payne]
  d The archaeology of woad: an account of its history from early times to the beginning of the 19th cent., with reference to the principal books on the subject, by C. B. Plowright.
  e The castle of Dunstanburgh [Northumb.], by C. H. Compton.
  f The 'Galilee' considered as a place of sanctuary; with a suggestion as to the term 'Galilee', and some remarks on the so-called 'sanctuary knocker', by C. H. Evelyn-White.
  g Chislehurst [Kent] caves and dene-holes, by W. J. Nichols. [Contd. in vol. 10]
  h Notes on the granges of Margam abbey [Glam.], by T. Gray. [Contd. in vol. 11]
  i Oatlands in Weybridge, by S. W. Kershaw.
  j Mining tribes of ancient Britain, by W. S. Lach-Szyrma.

507 Vol. 10.
  a Richard Masters, parson of Aldyngton [Kent], 1514–58, by A. D. Cheney.
  b Some early defensive earthworks of the Sheffield district, by I. C. Gould.
  c Notes on Sheffield manor house, by T. Winder.
  d Proceedings of the 60th congress, at Sheffield, 1903. [Includes notes on Sheffield parish church, Blyth priory church, Steetley chapel, Barlborough Hall, and Beauchief abbey]
  e St. Christopher and some representations of him in English churches, by Mrs. Collier.
  f Wingfield manor [Derbys.?], by J. B. Mitchell-Withers.
  g Notes on the forest of Galtres [Yorks.], by S. W. Kershaw.

h Laughton-en-le-Morthen church, Yorks., by T. Rigby.
i Roche abbey, Yorks.: its history and architectural features, by H. J. Dukinfield Astley.
j Rotherham church [Yorks.], by E. I. Hubbard.
k Sheffield cutlery and the poll-tax of 1379, by R. E. Leader.

508 Vol. 11.

a The boy bishop (*episcopus puerorum*) of medieval England, by C. H. Evelyn-White.
b Bath stone, by T. S. Cotterell.
c Proceedings at the 61st congress, at Bath, 1904. [Includes notes on Dyrham church]
d Notes on Durham and other north-country sanctuaries, by R. H. Forster.
e Bath old bridge and the chapel thereon, by E. Green.
f Lacock abbey [Wilts.]: notes on the architectural history of the building, by C. H. Talbot.
g The Saxon church at Bradford-on-Avon, by H. J. Dukinfield Astley.
h Lacock church [Wilts.], by C. H. Talbot.

509 Vol. 12.

a Notes on the brasses of Berkshire, by A. Oliver.
b Reading abbey, by J. B. Hurry.
c Villa Faustini (Antonine *Itinerary*, 5 and 9), by C. H. Compton.
d History of Wallingford [Berks.], by J. E. Field.
e A short account of Ufton Court [Berks.], by Miss Sharp.
f History of Abingdon, by P. H. Ditchfield.
g St. Clether: his chapel and holy wells [in the Inny valley, Cornwall], by Mrs. Collier.
h The walls of Wallingford, by I. C. Gould.
i The chapel of the hospital of St. James, Wigginton, Tamworth [Staffs.], by C. Lynam.
j The isle of Ictis and the early tin trade, by E. Green.
k The tenth *iter* [of the Antonine *Itinerary*] and the Roman stations in the north of England, by R. H. Forster.
l Relics of the old Cornish language, by W. S. Lach-Szyrma.
m Proceedings of the 63rd congress, at Nottingham, 1906. [Includes notes on the tombs in Bottesford church]
n The Roman city of Corstopitum, near Corbridge-on-Tyne.
o Roman remains at Glasfryn, Tremadoc, Carnarvonshire.
p Notes on Whitehall and the Strand [London], by A. Oliver.
q Earthworks of the moated mound type, by T. D. Pryce.

510 Vol. 13.

a Waltham abbey: its early history and architecture, by E. G. Tooker.
b Turgot, prior of Durham [d. 1115], by R. H. Forster.
c The walls of Nottingham, by J. G. N. Clift.
d Some Nottinghamshire strongholds, by I. C. Gould.
e John Alcock [d. 1500], a notable bishop of the 15th cent., by Mrs. Collier.
f Adel church [Leeds], by C. S. Buckingham.
g Norman architecture of Nottinghamshire, by C. E. Keyser.
h Maiden castle, Dorchester, by J. G. N. Clift.
i Notes on Maiden castle, by R. H. Forster.
j Neolithic implements from Dorset, by J. G. N. Clift.
k Wolfeton House [Dorset], by A. Bankes.
l Monumental brasses of Dorsetshire, by W. de C. Prideaux.
m Selby abbey [Yorks.], by C. H. Compton.

511 Vol. 14.

a Corbridge excavations, 1907, by R. H. Forster. [Contd. for 1908-9 in vols. 15-16]

b Wareham [Dorset], by J. G. N. Clift.
c Notes on the municipal seals exhibited at the Weymouth congress, by A. Oliver.
d Kilpeck [Herefs.], and its church, by C. S. Buckingham.
e Deneholes, etc., by T. V. Holmes.
f Notes on the Hangman's Wood deneholes [Grays, Essex], by R. H. Forster.
g A criticism of the Hangman's Wood denehole report, by J. G. N. Clift.
h Notes on deneholes, by J. W. Hayes.
i Camden's opinion on the use and purpose of deneholes, by J. G. N. Clift.
j Wilfrid's church at Hexham [Northumb.], by R. H. Forster.
k John Halle [d. 1479], merchant and mayor of Salisbury, by Mrs. Collier.
l Notes on some sculptured Norman tympana and lintels, by C. E. Keyser.
m Brass of Edward Cranford [d. 1431, in St. John's church, Puttenham, Surrey], by J. G. N. Clift.

512 Vol. 15.

a The forest of Cumberland, by F. H. M. Parker.
b Earthworks of the hill-spur type, by A. G. Chater.
c Somerset club brasses, by E. Green.
d Boadicea's battle [*v*. Suetonius Paulinus, A.D. 61], by R. H. Forster.
e Stoke d'Abernon brasses, by J. G. N. Clift.
f A study in 'eoliths', by J. G. N. Clift.
g Notes on Warkworth [Northumb.], by R. H. Forster.

513 Vol. 16.

a The topography of the Carmelite priory of London, by A. W. Clapham.
b Carausius and Allectus, by R. H. Forster.
c The library at St. Mary's, Warwick, by W. T. Carter.
d Coventry leet book, by [Mary] D. Harris.
e Proceedings of the 66th congress, at Warwick, 1910. [Includes notes on Warwick Castle, corporation insignia, the 'Black Book' of Warwick, and the 16th cent. 'Book of John Fisher']

514 Vol. 17.

a Notes on customs and constitutions of cathedrals of the old foundation, with special reference to Chichester, by G. P. G. Hills.
b Warwickshire in the civil wars of the 17th cent., by M. H. Bloxham.
c How to write parochial and college histories, by W. S. Lach-Szyrma.
d Tattershall castle. [By P. H. Ditchfield. See also under 'Archaeological notes' in vol. 20]
e Note on finds [of Roman gold coins] at Corstopitum, by R. H. Forster.
f The ancient church of St. Helen, Bishopsgate, by R. H. Barton.
g Notes on the history of Southwark cathedral, by R. R. Bristow.
h Church of St. Olave, Hart Street, by B. Corcoran.
i Proceedings of the congress in London, 1911 [held in conjunction with the London and Middlesex Archaeol. Soc.]
j History and description of Bow church, Cheapside, by A. W. Hutton.
k The Tower of London, by C. H. Hopwood.
l Priory church of St. John at Clerkenwell, by H. W. Fincham.

515 Vol. 18.

a Architectural account of Bredon church, Worcs., by C. E. Keyser.

b Historical account of Canonbury tower, by H. W. Fincham.

c Priory of Austin Friars, London, by W. A. Cater.

d Proceedings of the congress at Gloucester, 1912. [Includes notes on Gloucester cathedral; the history of Gloucester, by F. A. Hyett; and Winchcombe]

e Notes on a sanctuary knocker at St. Nicholas' church, Gloucester, by C. E. Keyser.

f Margidunum, a Roman fortified post on the Fosse Way: excavations of 1910–11, by T. D. Pryce.

g Berkeley Castle, by W. Bazeley.

516 Vol. 19.

a Palaeolithic figures of flint found in the old river alluvia of England and France and called figure stones, with some of the literature on the subject and an account of its progress, by W. M. Newton.

b Notes [mainly architectural] on the churches of Little Bytham and Egleton, by C. E. Keyser.

c Sudeley castle, by W. Bazeley.

d Deerhurst church and Saxon chapel, by W. Bazeley.

e Corbridge excavations, 1912, by R. H. Forster.

f The city of London and its dragons, by J. Dallas. [Armorial bearings of London]

g Cambridgeshire dykes, by T. McK. Hughes.

h Stourbridge fair, by P. H. Ditchfield.

i Horham Hall, Essex, by A. P. Humphry.

j Proceedings of the 70th congress, at Cambridge, 1913. [Includes notes on Trinity College, Audley End, Saffron Walden church, Maddingley Hall, and the churches of Swavesey and Willingham]

k History of Christ's Hospital, London, by W. Lempriere.

l The Bartlow hills [or barrows], by C. G. Brocklebank.

m St. Mary's church, Warwick, and its services, immediately after the dissolution of the collegiate chapter, 1545, by T. Kemp.

n Some letters from William Camden, by W. A. Cater.

517 Vol. 20.

a Notes [mainly architectural] on the churches of Ampney Crucis, Ampney St. Mary's, and Ampney St. Peter's, by C. E. Keyser.

b The romance of Grime's Graves, by H. J. Dukinfield Astley.

c Cardinal Wolsey's college, Ipswich, by C. Caine.

d The archbishop's manors in Sussex, by S. W. Kershaw.

e Proceedings of the 71st congress, at Canterbury, 1914. [Held in conjunction with the Kent Archaeol. Soc. Includes notes on St. Augustine's abbey and St. Martin's church, Canterbury; Barfreston church; St. Martin's priory and the castle, Dover; the church of SS. Mary and Ethelburga, Lyminge; Saltwood castle; and Hythe church]

f Richborough castle, by Lord Northbourne.

g Notes on the keep, Dover castle, by Lieutenant Peck. [Written 1870]

h Notes on the manor houses of Hertfordshire, by A. W. Anderson.

i Steyning church, Sussex, by P. M. Johnston.

j Sandwich and the Old House, by J. A. Macmeikan.

k Church of St. Nicholas, Ash, by R. H. Goodsall.

l Early London: facts and theories, by F. Lambert. [Review of *London*, by Sir Laurence Gomme, and *Prehistoric London; its Mounds and Circles*, by E. O. Gordon]

518 Vol. 21.

a Notes [mainly architectural] on the churches of Brize Norton and Black Bourton, in the county of Oxford, by C. E. Keyser.

b Some account of the Barbers' company, and the plate, pictures and charters at Barber-Surgeons' hall [London], by F. Weston.

c Additional notes on London sculptured and carved signs, coats-of-arms, and inscriptions, by P. Norman.

d Whitby abbey, by P. H. Ditchfield.

e Further notes on the Austin friary of London; with some account of the origin of the mendicant orders, by W. A. Cater.

f Proceedings of the 72nd congress, in the Isle of Wight, 1915. [Includes notes on Carisbrooke castle and church, the history and archives of Newport, and Brading church]

g Excavations in the crypt of the church of St. Mary-le-Bow, Cheapside, by F. Lambert.

h The mediaeval church and crypt of St. Mary of the Arches, otherwise known as St. Mary-le-Bow, by W. A. Cater.

i Architectural notes on the crypt of St. Mary-le-Bow, by E. S. Underwood.

j Notes on the church of St. Mary, Brading, by Dr. Whitehead.

k All Saints', Newchurch, by F. Bamford.

l History of Newport, Isle of Wight, by Miss Hearn.

m List of earthwork enclosures, by J. G. N. Clift. [For Northumberland, Cumberland, Westmorland, Durham and Huntingdonshire. Issued as appendix to pts. 1 and 2 of this vol.]

519 Vol. 22.

a Architectural description of Bampton church, Oxfordshire, by C. E. Keyser.

b Ancient recipes and old-world cures, by B. F. Collier.

c Aquae Sulis, by S. R. Forbes.

d The art of trephining among pre-historic and primitive peoples: their motives for its practice and their methods of procedure, by T. W. Parry. [With a note by G. Elliot Smith]

e Battle of La Hogue, 1692: extract from the parish registers of Northwood, Isle of Wight, by S. Andrews.

f History of the parish church of S. Botolph, Ruxley, Kent, by F. C. Elliston-Erwood.

g Notes on the parish registers of Newport, Isle of Wight, by S. Andrews.

h The flight of St. Frideswide, by G. E. C. Rodwell.

i Kingston, Isle of Wight, church and manor-house, by G. E. Jeans.

j Earthworks at Charlton, London, S.E., with a report on some excavations made therein, by F. C. Elliston-Erwood.

k A Kentish hundred: pleas of the Crown for the hundred of Ruxley [1227], with a running commentary, by W. H. Mandy.

l Church of St. Michael, Southampton, by W. G. Horseman.

m Shalfleet and its church, by P. G. Stone.

520 Vol. 23.

a Notes [mainly architectural] on the churches of Seaton, Rutlandshire, and Wakerley and Wittering, Northants., by C. E. Keyser.

b La Roche d'Andeli and Château-Gaillard, fortified 1196–8 and besieged 1203–4, by C. Roessler de Graville.

c Holland House and Earl's Court: their history and topography, by W. Derham.

d Excavations in the crypt of St. Mary-le-Bow, by W. A. Cater [with additions by E. S. Underwood].

e Early man in Norfolk, by H. J. Dukinfield Astley.

f Roger, bishop of Salisbury, chancellor and justiciar of England, 1102–39, comp. W. H. Butcher.

g Proceedings of the 74th congress, at Brighton, 1917. [Includes notes on St. Nicholas's church, Brighton, Clayton church, the history of Brighton, by P. H. Ditchfield, New Shoreham church, and Chichester cathedral]

521 Vol. 24.

a Notes [mainly architectural] on the churches of South Stoke, North Stoke, Ipsden, and Checkendon, Oxon., by C. E. Keyser.

b Studland church, and some remarks on Norman corbel-tables, by P. M. Johnston.

c The war [1914–18] and archaeologists, by P. H. Ditchfield.

d Old pewter, its history and interest, from a collector's standpoint, by F. Weston.

e The Merchant Taylors' company and its hall, by H. L. Hopkinson.

f The Fordwich stone and its legend, by W. Derham.

g 'Castram ad divisas': the castle at the boundaries [Devizes, Wilts.], by W. H. Butcher.

h The Tallow Chandlers' company: its origin and a sketch of its history, by A. C. Knight.

i Proceedings of the 75th congress, in London, 1918. [Includes notes on Westminster School, Chaldon church, Surrey, and the Temple church]

522 Vol. 25.

a Notes on the architecture of the churches of Great Rollright, Hook Norton, and Wigginton, Oxon., by C. E. Keyser.

b The cathedral and priory of St. Mary of Coventry and an approximate restoration of the plan of the church, by T. F. Tickner.

c Mediaeval bestiaries and their influence on ecclesiastical decorative art, by G. C. Druce. [Contd. in vol. 26]

d St. Mary of Westcheap, London, called Newchurch, including a topographical study of the Mansion House area, Cornhill to Cheapside, by W. A. Cater.

e Proceedings of the 76th congress, at Colchester, 1919. [Includes notes on Holy Trinity church, and the 'Marquis of Granby', Colchester; Dedham church; local Roman remains in Colchester museum; the churches of Halstead and Castle Hedingham; and Long Melford]

f Abbey of St. John the Baptist, Colchester, by G. Rickword.

g Notes on the origin and location of the church of St. Giles, Colchester, by W. A. Cater.

h The Roman occupation of Colchester, by T. Stevens.

i Legends of Coel and Helena, by W. G. Benham.

j The story of the siege of Colchester, 1648, by A. M. Jarmin.

523 Vol. 26.

a Notes on the architecture of the churches of Brigstock and Stanion, Northants., by C. E. Keyser.

b The Roman wall of Colchester, by P. Laver.

c Abbey of Lilleshall, by W. G. Clark-Maxwell.

d Proceedings of the 77th congress, at Shrewsbury, 1920. [Includes notes on Shrewsbury abbey church; the castle and St. Lawrence's church, Ludlow; Much Wenlock priory; the churches of Tong, High Ercall, Battlefield, and St. Mary's, Shrewsbury]

524 Vol. 27.

a Proceedings of the 78th congress, at Lincoln, 1921. [Includes notes on Bardney abbey; Thornton abbey; St. Botolph's church, Lincoln; and Heckington church]

b The Roman conquest and occupation of Lincolnshire, by A. Hunt.

c Gainsborough Old Hall, by P. H. Ditchfield.

d Temple Bruer, Lincs., by H. A. Peake.

e Heckington church, by C. A. Norris.

f A visit to the churches of Croughton, Northants., and Hanwell, Horley, and Hornton, Oxon., by C. E. Keyser.

g Manx pigmy flints, by C. H. Cowley.

h Insignia of the city of Lincoln, by J. G. Williams.

525 Vol. 28.

a Proceedings of the 79th congress, at Bath, 1922. [Includes notes on Bath abbey church, and Bradford-on-Avon]

b The Premonstratensian abbey of Langley, Norfolk, with report on excavations, by F. C. Elliston-Erwood.

c Heraldry as a science, by Emma E. Cope.

d Priory of St. Mary of Prittlewell, by W. A. Cater.

e The Cluniac order and its English province, by Rose Graham.

f The charters of Bath, by R. W. Falconer.

g The king of Bath [Richard Nash, d. 1761].

h Recent discoveries at Colchester castle, by A. M. Jarmin.

i Deneholes and chalk mines, by J. W. Hayes.

526 Vol. 29.

a Proceedings of the 80th congress, at York, 1923. [Includes notes on York minster, Fountains abbey, Pickering church, and Selby abbey]

b Parish church of St. John the Baptist, Knaresborough, by A. A. Gibson.

c Kirkham abbey, by C. V. Collier.

d Kirby Underdale church, by W. R. Shepherd.

e Windows of York minster, by F. Harrison.

f The York school of glass-painting, by J. A. Knowles.

g Parish church of Kirkburn, by A. J. Parkes.

h Beverley minster, by R. H. Whiteing.

i True deneholes, by A. J. Philip.

j Further report on the earthworks at Charlton, London, by F. C. Elliston-Erwood.

527 Vol. 30.

a The monastery of Battle, by Rose Graham.

b [Leaden] font in Brookland church, by G. C. Druce.

c Architectural history of Appledore church, Kent, by F. C. Elliston-Erwood.

d Romanesque ornament in England: its sources and evolution, by P. M. Johnston.

e Maserfield battle, 642: battlefields of Lincolnshire: identification of site in north-west Lincolnshire, by A. Hunt.

f The walls of Rye and Winchelsea, by P. H. Ditchfield.

g Luton parish church, by T. G. Hobbs.

528 Vol. 31.

a Proceedings of the 82nd congress, at Norwich, 1925. [Includes notes on the churches of St. Peter Mancroft, Norwich, and Ranworth; Spixworth Hall, and Norwich cathedral]

b Hospital of St. Giles, Norwich, by F. W. Bennett-Symons.

c St. Gregory's church, Norwich, by E. A. Kent, from notes by J. Jessopp.

d Carrow abbey, by Ethel M. Colman.

e South Burlingham, by E. A. Kent, from notes by B. Cozens-Hardy.

f Wymondham church, by R. V. Reyner.

g South Lopham church, by C. Upcher.

h Great Yarmouth town walls, by R. H. Teasdel.

i The tolhouse at Great Yarmouth, by R. F. E. Ferrier.

j Grey Friars' cloisters, Great Yarmouth, by F. R. B. Howards.

k St. Olave's priory [Herringfleet], by E. A. Kent.

l Great Dunham church, by J. F. Williams.

m Provincial museums: Reading, by P. H. Ditchfield; Grange Wood, Croydon, by E. A. Martin [with additional note in vol. 32].

n Castleacre, by H. J. Dukinfield Astley.

o The battle of 'Assandun': where was it fought?, by M. Christy. [Correspondence in vol. 32]

k SS. Peter and Paul, Keddington, a notable church, by W. H. Turnbull.

l Prehistoric settlement on Hinksey hill, near Oxford, by J. N. L. Myres [with reports by C. Hawkes and G. R. de Beer].

m Excavations in the city of London, 1930, by Q. Waddington.

534 Vol. 37.

a Proceedings of the 88th congress, at Peterborough, 1931. [Includes notes on Peterborough cathedral; the churches of Alwalton, Warmington, and Oundle; and Thorney abbey]

b Mural paintings in houses, with special reference to recent discoveries at Stratford-on-Avon and Oxford, by P. M. Johnston.

c Southchurch Hall, by J. F. Nichols.

d Some great houses of Northamptonshire, by J. A. Gotch.

e A holiday journal of 1774 [kept by Lord Orford, relating to the fen district and Whittlesey mere], by E. G. Swain.

f The date and orientation of Stonehenge, by R. H. Cunnington.

g Cattle droving between Scotland and England, by W. Thompson.

h The screen in St. Mary's church, Attleborough, Norf.

i Frisia and its relations with England and the Baltic littoral in the dark ages, by N. T. Belaiew.

j In the palmy days of Boston: the hospitallers of St. John, and the men of St. Botulph, at Skirbeck, by W. T. Whitley.

535 Vol. 38.

a Proceedings of the 89th congress, at Weymouth, 1932. [Includes notes on Bindon abbey, Barnston manor house, Corfe castle, Woodsford castle, Wolfeton House, and Beaminster church]

b 17th cent. architecture of Stamford and district, by H. F. Traylen.

c Tilbury fort, by J. W. Burrows.

d The honour of Belvoir, by A. L. Browne.

e Bicknoller church, west Somerset, by F. C. Eeles.

f Two inventories [of relics, plate, jewels, etc. belonging to the priory] in the library of Worcester cathedral, transcribed and ed. J. E. H. Blake.

g The humours of archaeology, or, the Canterbury congress, 1844, and the early days of the Association, by E. R. Taylor.

h Romano-British Baldock: past discoveries and future problems, by W. P. Westell and E. S. Applebaum.

i A mediaeval roof in St. John's College, Oxford, by A. J. Taylor.

j Sanctuary in medieval London, by Isobel D. Thornley.

k Sanctuary boundaries and environs of Westminster abbey and the college of St. Martin-le-Grand, by Marjorie B. Honeybourne.

l The crypt at Whitefriars, London, by S. Toy.

536 Vol. 39.

a Proceedings of the 90th congress, at Nottingham, 1933. [Includes notes on the church of St. Mary the Virgin, Nottingham, Wollaton Hall, Newstead abbey, Bolsover castle, Blyth church, Worksop priory church, Welbeck abbey, Woodborough church, Bottesford church, Belvoir Castle, Southwell minster, Newark castle and church of St. Mary Magdalene, and Nottingham castle]

b The pre-Fire towers of Sanctae Mariae de arcubus [St. Mary-le-Bow, London], by W. A. Cater.

c Roman villa at Magor farm, near Camborne, Cornwall, by B. H. St. J. O'Neil.

d Carved capitals of Southwell minster, by W. J. Conybeare.

e Cholesbury camp [Bucks.], by D. Kimball.

f Lead fonts in England, with some reference to French examples, by G. C. Druce.

g Excavations at Wilbury hill [Herts.] in 1933, by E. S. Applebaum. [With an account of some iron age finds]

h The forbears of Sir Henry Powle [1630–92] of Shottesbrooke, speaker of the Convention parliament and master of the rolls, by A. L. Browne.

i Vestiges of pre-Roman London, by Q. Waddington.

537 General index to vols. 43–52, 1887–96. 1915.

538 General index to new series, vols. 1–25, 1895–1919, with subject index to illustrations and list of places visited by the Association, comp. R. Austin. 1924.

BRITISH ASSOCIATION FOR THE ADVANCEMENT OF SCIENCE

Founded 1831, to give a stronger impulse and a more systematic direction to scientific inquiry; to promote the intercourse of those who cultivate science in different parts of the British Empire with one another and with foreign philosophers; to obtain more general attention for the objects of science and the removal of any disadvantages of a public kind which impede progress. The Reports of Meetings include proceedings, transactions of sections, addresses by presidents, section presidents, and others, reports on the state of science, reports of committees, and accounts of meetings of delegates from corresponding societies. Where no author is named in the following list the title relates to the report of a committee.

Reports of Meetings, 1901–33 (33 vols. 1901–33):

539 Vol. for 1901.

a Silchester excavation. [Further reports in vols. for 1902 and 1903]

b The age of stone circles. [Further reports in vols. for 1902, 1903, 1905–9, 1912–15, and 1922]

c Excavations at Arbor Low [Derbys.], Aug. 1901, by H. St. G. Gray.

d Stone implements at Arbor Low, by H. Balfour.

e Report on human skeleton found in the stone circle of Arbor Low in 1901, by J. G. Garson.

f Women's labour. [Further reports in vols. for 1902 and 1903]

g On research in geographical science, by H. R. Mill.

540 Vol. for 1902.

a The Roman fort at Gellygaer [Glam.].

541 Vol. for 1903.

a The lake village at Glastonbury. [Further reports in vols. for 1904–15, 1922 and 1923]

b Address by Sir W. de W. Abney [on the state and education in science in the second half of the 19th cent.].

542 Vol. for 1904.

a Excavations on Roman sites in Britain. [Further reports in vols. for 1906 and 1908–19]

b Address by H. Lamb [on the place of G. G. Stokes in the development of mathematical physics].

c Address by H. Balfour [on the contribution to anthropology made by Lane Fox].

543 Vol. for 1905.

a Address by A. R. Forsyth [on some scientific centenaries, including the publication in 1605 of *The Advancement of Learning* and Halley's prediction in 1705 of the return of the comet in 1758].

544 Vol. for 1906.

  a Excavations at the Stripple Stones [on Bodmin moors], Cornwall, by H. St. G. Gray.

  b Lead mining in Yorkshire, by J. Backhouse.

  c Labourers and the land: Yorkshire [1901], by R. E. Turnbull.

  d Address by Sir G. T. Goldie [on the progress of geography since 1881].

545 Vol. for 1907.

  a Notes on the survey of the Fernacre and Stannon stone circles [Bodmin moors], Cornwall, by H. St. G. Gray.

  b Exploration of the 'Red Hills' of the east coast salt marshes.

  c Address by W. J. Ashley [on the past history and present position of political economy in Great Britain].

  d Address by S. P. Thompson [on the development of engineering and its foundation on science].

546 Vol. for 1908.

  a Avebury excavations, 1908, by H. St. G. Gray. [Further report in vol. for 1909]

  b Trade unionism in the tin-plate industry [c. 1873–1903], by J. H. Jones.

  c Address by D. Clerk [on the development of the science of thermodynamics].

  d Halley's comet, by H. H. Turner.

547 Vol. for 1909.

  a Address by J. L. Myers [on the influence of anthropology on the course of political science].

548 Vol. for 1910.

  a The amount and distribution of income (other than wages) below the income-tax exemption limit in the United Kingdom.

  b The poverty figures, by D. H. Macgregor. [Criticism of the inquiries by Booth, Rowntree, and Chiozza Money]

  c Notes on the history of Sheffield wages [in 19th cent.], by G. H. Wood.

549 Vol. for 1911.

  a Prehistoric site at Bishop's Stortford. [Further reports in vols. for 1912 and 1913]

  b Avebury excavations. [Further reports in vols. for 1915 and 1922 by H. St. G. Gray]

  c The claim of Sir Charles Bell to the discovery of motor and sensory nerve channels, by D. Waller. [An examination of the original documents of 1811–30]

  d Economic aspects of the introduction and establishment of a British beet-sugar industry, by S. Stein.

  e Notes on the stature, etc., of our ancestors in east Yorkshire, by J. R. Mortimer.

  f A Roman fortified post on the Nottinghamshire Fosseway: note on the excavations of 1910–11, by T. D. Pryce.

  g Catalogue of destructive earthquakes, by J. Milne.

550 Vol. for 1912.

  a Curricula and educational organisation of industrial and Poor-law schools.

  b The road problem, by Sir J. H. A. Macdonald.

  c Discovery of a neolithic cemetery at La Motte, Jersey, by R. R. Marett.

  d Early associations for promoting agriculture and improving the improver, by T. H. Middleton.

551 Vol. for 1913.

  a Excavations on Roman sites in Britain. [With report on excavations in the ancient hill fort (Dinorben) in Parc-y-meirch Wood, Kinmel Park, Abergele, by W. Gardner. Other reports occur in vols. for 1912, 1915, and 1923]

  b Excavations on the site of Viroconium at Wroxeter, by J. P. Bushe-Fox. [Further report in vol. for 1915]

552 Vol. for 1914.

  a Exploration of the palaeolithic site known as La Cotte de St. Brelade, Jersey. [With summary of paper on this subject by R. R. Marett. Further reports in vols. for 1915–18]

  b The history of the endeavour to co-ordinate the work of local scientific societies in Great Britain, by Sir G. Fordham.

553 Vol. for 1915.

  a Interim report of the conference on outlets for labour after the war. [Dealing particularly with the employment of women. The greater part of the transactions of the conference were published as *Credit, Industry, and the War* (1915), no. 586 below]

554 Vol. for 1916.

  a Industrial unrest: abstract of report.

  b Replacement of men by women in industry: abstract of report.

  c Effects of the war on credit, currency, and finance: abstract of report.

555 Vol. for 1917.

  a Science in secondary schools.

  b Money-scales and weights, by T. Sheppard. [Reprinted in Yorkshire Numismatic Soc. *Transactions*, vol. ii]

556 Vol. for 1918.

  a The 'free-place' system [and its effects upon secondary education].

557 Vol. for 1919.

  a Address by Sir H. Bell, bt. [on increasing post-war expenditure and its problems].

  b Chemical warfare, by H. Hartley.

  c Roads ancient and modern, by Lord Montagu.

558 Vol. for 1920.

  a Address by C. T. Heycock [on the development of knowledge of metallic alloys].

  b Address by J. H. Clapham [on comparisons of the economic condition of Europe after the great wars of a century ago with its condition in 1920].

  c The evolution of topographical and geological maps, by T. Sheppard.

  d List of papers bearing upon the zoology, botany, and prehistoric archaeology of the British Isles, issued during June–Dec. 1919, by T. Sheppard. [Contd. in vols. for 1921–5]

559 Vol. for 1921.

  a Effects of the war on credit, currency, finance, and foreign exchanges. [Further report in vol. for 1922]

560 Vol. for 1922.

  a Fuel economy, the utilisation of coal, and smoke prevention.

561 Vol. for 1923.

  a Population and unemployment, by Sir W. Beveridge.

  b Transport and its indebtedness to science, by Sir H. Fowler.

  c The distribution of bronze age implements. [Further reports in vols. for 1928, 1930, 1931, and 1933]

562 Vol. for 1924.

  a Chemistry and the state, by Sir R. Robertson.

  b A retrospect of free-trade doctrine, by Sir W. Ashley.

c A hundred years of electrical engineering, by G. W. O. Howe.

d Health and physique through the centuries, by F. C. Shrubsall.

e Conservation of sites of scientific interest, by J. L. Myres.

563 Vol. for 1925.

a Fifty years' evolution in naval architecture and marine engineering, by Sir A. Denny, bt.

564 Vol. for 1926.

a Kent's cavern, Torquay. [Further reports in vols. for 1927–33]

565 Vol. for 1929.

a Utility of geological surveys to colonies and protectorates of the British Empire, by Sir A. E. Kitson.

b Public regulation of wages in Great Britain, by H. Clay.

566 Vol. for 1930.

a A state experiment in chemical research [the Chemical Research Laboratory, Bushey Park], by G. T. Morgan.

b National parks: a résumé of the position, by P. Abercrombie.

567 Vol. for 1931.

a Michael Faraday and the theory of electrolytic conduction, by Sir H. Hartley.

b Educational development, 1831–1931: a centenary survey and a forecast, by Sir C. G. Robertson.

c The changing outlook in agriculture, by Sir E. J. Russell.

d Derbyshire caves. [Further report in vol. for 1933]

e A retrospect of wireless communication, by Sir O. Lodge.

568 Vol. for 1932.

a The contacts of geology: the ice age and early man in Britain, by P. G. H. Boswell.

b Britain's access to overseas markets, by R. B. Forrester.

c Sheep-farming: a distinctive feature of British agriculture, by R. G. White.

d The British Association standards of resistance, 1865–1932, by Sir R. T. Glazebrook and L. Hartshorn.

e A scientific survey of York and district, by various authors. [Includes chapters on prehistoric archaeology, Roman excavations, historical geography, and industries]

569 Vol. for 1933.

a What is tradition?, by Lord Raglan.

b The development of the national system of education, by J. L. Holland.

c General science in school. [Includes an historical review and is followed by a report on science teaching in adult education]

d A scientific survey of Leicester and district, by various authors.

Handbooks, etc., to places selected for annual meetings:

570 Southport: handbook of the town and district. 1903.

571 Historical and scientific survey of York and district, ed. G. A. Auden. 1906.

572 Guide to Leicester and district. [1907].

573 Handbook and guide to Sheffield, ed. W. S. Porter and A. T. Watson. 1910.

574 Handbook and guide to Portsmouth, ed. J. C. Nicol. 1911.

575 Birmingham meeting: excursions guide book. 1913.

576 Handbook for Birmingham and neighbourhood, ed. G. A. Auden. 1913.

577 Manchester in 1915, ed. H. M. McKechnie. 1915.

578 Official handbook to Newcastle and district, ed. G. R. Richardson and W. W. Tomlinson. 1916.

579 Handbook to Cardiff and neighbourhood, by various authors, ed. H. M. Hallett. 1920.

580 Handbook to Hull and the East Riding of Yorkshire, ed. T. Sheppard. 1922.

581 Merseyside: handbook to Liverpool and district, ed. A. Holt. [1923].

582 Natural history of the Oxford district, ed. J. J. Walker. 1926. [Includes chapters on early and modern settlement]

583 Leeds meeting: general handbook, ed. C. B. Fawcett. 1927.

584 Leeds meeting: handbooks for excursions. 1927. [Pamphlets]

585 Scientific survey of Leicester and district, by various authors, ed. P. W. Bryan. 1933.

Other publications:

586 Credit, industry and the war; being reports and other matter presented to the section of economic science and statistics, 1915, ed. A. W. Kirkaldy, preface by W. R. Scott. [1915].

587 Labour, finance, and the war; being the results of inquiries arranged by the section of economic science and statistics, 1915–16, ed. with preface by A. W. Kirkaldy. [1916].

588 Industry and finance: war expedients and reconstruction; being the results of enquiries arranged by the section of economic science and statistics, 1916–17, ed. A. W. Kirkaldy. [1918].

589 Industry and finance, supplementary volume; being the results of inquiries arranged by the section of economic science and statistics, 1918–19, ed. A. W. Kirkaldy. 1920.

590 Monetary policy [1913–21]; being the report of a sub-committee on currency and the gold standard . . . reproduced with minor alterations by the members of the sub-committee: J. H. Clapham, C. W. Guillebaud, F. Lavington, D. H. Robertson. 1921.

591 British finance during and after the war, 1914–21. [Investigations of a committee of the section of economic science and statistics] co-ordinated by A. H. Gibson, ed. A. W. Kirkaldy. 1921.

592 British labour: replacement and conciliation, 1914–21; being the result of conferences and investigations by committees of [the section of economic science and statistics], pt. 1 co-ordinated and revised by Miss L. Grier and Miss A. Ashley, pt. 2 ed. A. W. Kirkaldy. 1921.

593 Down House: here Darwin thought and worked for 40 years and died, 1882. *P.* [1929].

594 London and the advancement of science, by various authors. 1931. [Introductory survey followed by chapters entitled 'The learned societies','Education in London', 'Government and scientific research', 'The Royal Observatory, Greenwich', 'Kew Gardens and the John Innes Institution', 'The development of medicine in London', 'The museums of London' and 'A brief history of the London makers of scientific instruments']

BRITISH INSTITUTE OF PHILOSOPHICAL STUDIES

Founded 1925, to bring leading exponents of the various branches of philosophy into direct contact with the general public.

Journal of Philosophical Studies, vols. 1–5 (1926–30), contd. as Philosophy, vols. 6–8 (1931–3):

595 Vol. 2.

a The social philosophy of Smith's *Wealth of Nations*, by J. Laird.
b Some aspects of the materialist conception of history, by O. de Selincourt.

596 Vol. 3.

a The limits of historical knowledge, by R. G. Collingwood.
b A century of philosophy at University College, London, by G. D. Hicks.

597 Vol. 5.

a Hobbes' philosophy and its historical background, by Z. Lubienski.
b Historical causes, by A. Coates.
c The Earl of Balfour [d. 1930], by A. Wolf.

598 Vol. 6.

a Science, history, and philosophy, by G. de Ruggiero.
b Reality in history, by Hilda D. Oakeley.

599 Vol. 7.

a History and sociology, by M. Ginsberg.

600 Vol. 8.

a Two philosophers of the Oxford Movement [J. H. Newman and W. G. Ward], by C. C. J. Webb.
b A pluralistic view of history, by A. Coates.

BRITISH NUMISMATIC SOCIETY

Founded 1903, to encourage and promote numismatic science, particularly in connection with Great and Greater Britain and the English-speaking races. Archaeology, history, heraldry, art, and genealogy, in so far as they affect numismatics, are within the objects.

British Numismatic Journal and Proceedings, vols. 1–10 (1905–14) and vols. 11–20 (forming 2nd ser., vols. 1–10, 1916–32):

601 Vol. 1. (*See also no. 6453 below*)

a Buried treasure: some traditions, records and facts, by W. J. Andrew.
b Notes on three British gold coins, recently found near Abingdon, by B. Roth.
c The regal sceatta and styca series of Northumbria, by A. B. Creeke.
d The first coinage of Henry II, by N. Heywood.
e The Colchester hoard [chiefly 13th cent.], by G. Rickword.
f Notes on the coinage of Edward IV suggested by a recent find of coins, by L. A. Lawrence.
g The Henry VIII medal or pattern crown, by J. E. T. Loveday.
h Finds of clippings of silver coins, by B. Roth.
i Brief musings on the exurgat money, by F. Stroud.
j The coinage of William Wood for the American colonies, 1722–33, by P. Nelson.

k The Spanish dollar as adapted for currency in our West Indian colonies, by J. B. Caldecott.
l Notes on private tokens, their issuers and die-sinkers, by S. H. Hamer. [Contd. in vols. 2 and 3]
m Treasure trove, the Treasury, and the trustees of the British Museum, by P. W. P. Carlyon-Britton.
n Find of Roman coins at Peterborough, by J. C. Hill.

602 Vol. 2. (*See also no. 6454 below*)

a The sceatta and styca coinage of the early archbishops of York, by A. B. Creeke.
b The Oxford mint in the reign of Alfred, by P. W. P. Carlyon-Britton.
c The Saxon, Norman and Plantagenet coinage of Wales, by P. W. P. Carlyon-Britton.
d Concerning the evolution of some reverse types of the Anglo-Norman coinage, by W. S. Ogden.
e A numismatic history of the reigns of William I and II, by P. W. P. Carlyon-Britton. [Contd. in vols. 3–10]
f Historical notes on the first coinage of Henry II, by P. W. P. Carlyon-Britton.
g Portraiture of the Stuarts on the royalist badges, by Helen Farquhar.
h The obsidional money of the great rebellion (1642–9), by P. Nelson.
i The mail coach and its halfpennies, by H. A. Parsons.
j The Anglo-Saxon moneyer Torhtulf and characteristics of die-sinking, by L. A. Lawrence.
k Table of English gold coins, 1649–1820, by P. Nelson.

603 Vol. 3 (*See also no. 6455 below*)

a Find of ancient British coins at South Ferriby, near Barton-on-Humber, Lincs., by B. Roth.
b Find of Roman bronze coins on the Little Orme's Head, North Wales, by W. S. Ogden. [Contd. in vols. 6 and 9]
c The kingdom and coins of Burgred [852–74], by N. Heywood.
d The inscription on the Oxford pennies of the *Ohsnaforda* type, by A. Anscombe.
e A remarkable penny of King Alfred, by L. A. Lawrence.
f Cornish numismatics, by P. W. P. Carlyon-Britton.
g The busts of James I on his silver coinage, by H. W. Morrieson.
h The royal farthing tokens: Pt. I, 1613–36, by A. E. Weightman.
i Some notes on the great recoinage of William III, 1695–9, by P. Nelson.
j Patterns and medals bearing the legend IACOBUS III, or IACOBUS VIII, by Helen Farquhar.
k Art and the coins of England, by H. A. Parsons.

604 Vol. 4. (*See also no. 6456 below*)

a The influence of war on the coinage of England, by H. W. Morrieson.
b The Berkeley [Glos.] mint, by P. W. P. Carlyon-Britton.
c The 'Gothabyrig' mint, by P. W. P. Carlyon-Britton.
d Portraiture of Tudor monarchs on their coins and medals, by Helen Farquhar.
e A remarkable gold coin of Henry VIII, by L. A. Lawrence.
f English silver coins of James I, by H. W. Morrieson. [Further notes in vol. 9]
g Early Australian coinage, by A. Chitty.
h Bronze coinage of Queen Victoria, by A. E. Weightman.
i Some Roman brass coins found at Lincoln, by N. Heywood.
j A leaden cross bearing a styca impression, and other antiquities found at York, by G. A. Auden.
k Anglo-Saxon computation of historic time in the 9th cent., by A. Anscombe. [Contd. in vol. 5]
l Leaden tokens, by J. B. Caldecott and G. C. Yates.

605 Vol. 5. (*See also no.* 6457 *below*)

a The Roman mint and early Britain, by W. S. Ogden.

b The gold mancus of Offa, king of Mercia, by P. W. P. Carlyon-Britton.

c A penny of St. Æthelberht, king of East Anglia, by P. W. P. Carlyon-Britton.

d On some coins of the 10th cent. found in the Isle of Man, with special reference to a penny of Anlaf struck at Derby, by P. W. P. Carlyon-Britton.

e Find of mediaeval cut halfpence and farthings at Dunwich, by E. R. H. Hancox.

f The cross as a mint-mark, by J. S. Shirley-Fox.

g Portraiture of Stuart monarchs on their coins and medals, by Helen Farquhar. [Contd. in vols. 6–11]

h Some copper coins issued by the English East India Company and other European powers in Southern India, by R. P. Jackson.

i The pattern halfpennies of 1788 and 1790 by J. P. Droz, by S. Bousfield.

j Evolution of portraiture on the silver penny, by W. J. Andrew.

606 Vol. 6.

a The coinage of Prasutagus, king of the Icenians, by H. Laver.

b 'Uncertain' Anglo-Saxon mints and some new attributions, by P. W. P. Carlyon-Britton.

c The Winchcombe mint [Glos.], by P. W. P. Carlyon-Britton.

d A numismatic history of the reign of Stephen, 1135–54, by W. J. Andrew. [Contd. in vols. 8 and 10]

e Die-making in the 12th cent., by J. S. Shirley-Fox.

f Numismatic history of the reigns of Edward I, II and III, by H. B. E. Fox and J. S. Shirley-Fox. [Contd. in vols. 7–10]

g Coin weights, by L. A. Lawrence.

h 17th cent. tokens of Northamptonshire, by W. C. Wells. [Contd. in vols. 7, 8, and 10]

607 Vol. 7.

a A remarkable hoard of silver pennies and halfpennies of the reign of Stephen, found at Sheldon, Derbys., 1867, by W. J. Andrew.

b Shakespeare's portraiture: printed, graven, and medallic, by W. S. Ogden.

c A parcel of stycas from the York find, 1842, by N. Heywood.

d Notes on some interesting British medals, by C. Winter.

608 Vol. 8. (*See also no.* 6458 *below*)

a Attribution of the ancient British coins inscribed Dias or Deas, by P. W. P. Carlyon-Britton.

b Names of old-English mint-towns: their original form and meaning and their epigraphical corruption, by A. Anscombe. [Contd. in vols. 9 and 10]

c St. Cuthbert's pennies, by Lord Grantley. [Contd. in vols. 9 and 10]

d A penny of Æthelred, sub-regulus of Mercia, son-in-law of Ælfred the Great, by P. W. P. Carlyon-Britton.

e A penny of Llywelyn, son of Cadwgan, of the type of the second issue of William Rufus, by P. W. P. Carlyon-Britton.

f Find of late Plantagenet groats, by L. A. Lawrence.

g Coinage of Mary Tudor, 1553–8; illustrated from the Public Records, by H. Symonds.

h A glance inside the mint of Aberystwyth in the reign of Charles I, by H. Symonds.

i Medals and campaigns of the 43rd Foot, now 1st battalion the Oxfordshire and Buckinghamshire Light Infantry, by W. J. Freer.

609 Vol. 9. (*See also no.* 6459 *below*)

a The Dunwich mint, by H. A. Parsons.

b The long-cross coinage of Henry III and Edward I, by L. A. Lawrence. [Contd. in vols. 10 and 11]

c Mint-marks and denominations of the coinage of James I as disclosed by the trials of the pyx, with historical comments on the procedure and notes on the mint accounts of the period, by H. Symonds.

d The Chester mint of Charles I, by H. Symonds.

610 Vol. 10. (*See also no.* 6460 *below*)

a Coins of Æthelred I of Northumbria, by H. A. Parsons.

b The earliest noble of Richard II, by P. W. P. Carlyon-Britton.

c Documentary evidence for the English royal coinages of Henry VII and Henry VIII, by H. Symonds.

d Notes on the mint at Aberystwyth in the reign of Charles I, by H. M. Morgan.

e The coinage of Aberystwyth, 1637–42, by H. W. Morrieson.

f The 45th: 1st Nottinghamshire regiment, 'The Sherwood Foresters', their honours and medals, by F. E. Burton.

g A unique naval relic of 1742: the Callis medal, by C. Winter.

h Find of English half-groats of Henry VII in co. Wicklow, by J. B. S. MacIlwaine.

i Find of English coins of the Tudor and Stuart periods in co. Wexford, by G. R. Francis.

j A Washington token, by W. C. Wells. [John Washington, carrier, *c.* 1650–60]

611 Vol. 11. (*See also no.* 6461 *below*)

a Find of Anglo-Saxon stycas at Lancaster, by N. Heywood.

b Some coins of Sigtuna inscribed with the names of Æthelred, Cnut and Harthacnut, by H. A. Parsons.

c The Anglo-Saxon coins of Harthacnut, by H. A. Parsons.

d The short-cross coinage, 1180–1247, by L. A. Lawrence.

e English coinages of Edward VI, by H. Symonds.

f Petition 'for the restoring of farthing tokens: 1644', by F. P. Barnard.

g Gold coins issued from the mint at Oxford, 1642–6, by P. Nelson.

h Contemporary evidence against the attribution of obsidional money to isolated fortresses in the time of Charles I, by W. J. Andrew.

i 'Seventeenth century tokens of Northamptonshire': a note on Lamport or Langport, by H. Symonds.

j The 38th regiment of Foot, now the 1st battalion the South Staffordshire regiment, by W. J. Freer.

612 Vol. 12. (*See also no.* 6462 *below*)

a The coins of Archbishop Eanbald II of York, by H. A. Parsons.

b A hoard of coins of William the Conqueror in a trench in the war area, by R. C. Carlyon-Britton.

c Royal charities. Pt. i: Angels as healing-pieces for the king's evil, by Helen Farquhar. [Contd. in vol. 13]

d Silver coins of Edward VI, by H. W. Morrieson.

e Silver coins of the Tower mint of Charles I, by G. R. Francis. [Contd. in vols. 13–15]

f Coins of the Shrewsbury mint, 1642, by H. W. Morrieson. [A revision appears in vol. 14]

g A Granby medal [1765, awarded by the Marquess of Granby to cadets at the Royal Military Academy, Woolwich], by H. W. Morrieson.

h Gold collars, medals and crosses granted to British officers by the crown of Portugal in the Peninsular war, by C. Winter.

i Lt.-Col. Richard Brunton's Portuguese decorations for the Peninsular war, by A. A. Payne. [Additional notes in vol. 14]

j Relics of Lt.-Col. Thomas Lloyd [d. 1813], of the 94th regiment (now the 2nd battalion the Connaught Rangers), by C. Winter.

k Waterloo medals, by C. Winter.

l The Royal Irish regiment, by C. Winter.

613 Vol. 13.

a Symbols and double names on late Saxon coins, by H. A. Parsons.

b Royal charities. Pt. ii: Touchpieces for the king's evil, by Helen Farquhar. [Contd. as pts. iii and iv in vols. 14 and 15]

c Masonic tokens of the 18th cent., by H. W. Morrieson.

d Medallic illustrations of naval history, by the Marquess of Milford Haven.

e Medals of the 77th regiment, now the 2nd battalion the Duke of Cambridge's own Middlesex regiment, by C. Winter.

614 Vol. 14. (*See also no.* 6463 *below*)

a Odilo, a Northumbrian moneyer of the 9th cent., and his issues, by A. Anscombe.

b The first coinage of Henry II, by L. A. Lawrence.

c Find of French deniers and English pennies of the 12th cent., by Lord Grantley and L. A. Lawrence.

d A portion of a set of silver counters exhibiting London criers and their cries, by L. A. Lawrence.

e The centenary of our modern coinage instituted in February, 1817, and the issues which preceded it in George III's reign, by H. W. Morrieson.

f Examples of engraved coins selected from a collection formed by Mrs. Ella Pierrepont Barnard. ['Love tokens']

g London as illustrated upon the great seals, upon medals, and in allied engravings, by W. Martin.

615 Vol. 15.

a Coins of Harold I, by H. A. Parsons.

b The prototype of the first coinage of William the Conqueror, by H. A. Parsons.

c A remarkable penny of Henry II, by P. W. P. Carlyon-Britton.

d Two tragedies, a mediaeval charm, and a note on the mint of Rhuddlan, by W. J. Andrew. [On 13th cent. coins found in graves at Winchester and Dyserth]

e Halfpennies and farthings of Henry VIII, by R. Carlyon-Britton.

f A review of the coinage of Charles II, by H. W. Morrieson.

g Coinage of Ireland during the rebellion, 1641–52, by F. W. Yeates. [Additional notes in vol. 16]

616 Vol. 16.

a Some notes on a coin of Anlaf from the Derby mint, by G. R. Francis.

b Chronological sequence of the types of Eadweard the Martyr and Æthelraed II, by P. W. P. Carlyon-Britton.

c Remarks on hoards of late Anglo-Saxon coins, by H. A. Parsons.

d A penny of the armed-figure type with the title COM in the reign of Stephen, by Lord Grantley.

e The Calais mint, 1347–1470, by A. S. Walker.

f English piedforts and their purposes, by L. A. Lawrence.

g An unpublished variety of groat of the first coinage of Henry VIII, by R. Carlyon-Britton.

h James I crowns: new discoveries, by G. R. Francis.

i The coinage of Oxford, 1642–6, by H. W. Morrieson. [Contd. in vol. 20]

j Royal charities, 2nd series: The maundy, by Helen Farquhar. [Treats of royal almsgiving and the coins used. Contd. in vols. 17–20]

k A series of portrait plaques in thin silver, struck in Stuart times, technically called shells or clichés, by Helen Farquhar.

l Jacobite drinking glasses and their relation to Jacobite medals, by G. R. Francis.

617 Vol. 17. (*See also no.* 6464 *below*)

a The Northampton and Southampton [Anglo-Saxon] mints, by W. C. Wells. [Contd. in vols. 19 and 20]

b Hoard of coins of Æthelraed II found in Ireland, by W. C. Wells.

c Assays and imitations, foreign and native, of the late Saxon period, 975–1066, by H. A. Parsons.

d The sequence of mint-marks preceding, during, and succeeding the restoration of Henry VI, by R. C. Carlyon-Britton.

e Some portrait-medals struck between 1745 and 1752 for Prince Charles Edward, by Helen Farquhar.

f The attribution of the 'BR' monogram on Charles I's coins, by H. W. Morrieson.

g Orders, decorations and medals given to the British navy, army and flying force in the great war [1914–18], by W. J. Freer.

h South Notts Yeomanry medals, by F. E. Burton.

i Gold and silver medals of the East India Company, by C. Winter.

618 Vol. 18.

a The last coinage of Henry VII, by R. Carlyon-Britton.

b Rose farthing tokens [*temp.* Charles I], by E. Rogers.

c The dress of Elizabeth as shown on her early silver coins, 1558–61, by H. W. Morrieson.

d The Shrewsbury medal [issued to Royalists, 1643]: a note upon military medals of the mid-17th cent., by Helen Farquhar.

e The coinage of Bristol, 1643–5, by H. W. Morrieson.

f Table of the silver coins of the Tower mint of Charles I, by H. W. Morrieson.

g The Army of India medal [1799, or 1803, to 1826], by C. Winter.

h Medals of the Royal Fusiliers, City of London regiment, by C. Winter.

i Notes on a collection of money-scales and other coin-weighing appliances, by V. B. Crowther-Beynon.

j An 18th cent. coin-clipper, by V. B. Crowther-Beynon.

k Buckinghamshire trade tokens issued in the 17th cent., by J. O. Manton. [Contd. in vols. 19 and 20. Overprints of these articles were issued as an extra vol. 'by J. O. Manton and E. Hollis' by the Bucks. Archit. and Archaeol. Soc., 1933]

619 Vol. 19.

a The Richborough coin inscribed 'Domino Censaurio Ces.', by A. Anscombe.

b The Anglian coins of Cnut the Great, by H. A. Parsons.

c Some coins of Henry I, by P. W. P. Carlyon-Britton.

d The coinage of Lundy, 1645–6, by H. W. Morrieson.

e 18th and 19th cent. tokens of Northamptonshire, by W. C. Wells.

f Pitt Clubs and their badges, by S. A. Garnett.

620 Vol. 20.

a Numismatic sidelights on the battle of Brunanburh, 937, by W. J. Andrew.

b Edward the Elder pennies with façade of a building, by G. D. Lumb.

c Coins commemorating the rebuilding of York, 921–5, by W. J. Andrew.

d 'Fastolfi moneta', 'Fastolfes mot', and the like, on coins of Eadgar *rex Anglorum*, by A. Anscombe.

e Stockbridge, an Anglo-Saxon mint, by W. J. Andrew.

f The first authorised issue of Edward the Confessor, by H. A. Parsons.

g *Quando moneta vertebatur*: the cand e of coin-types in the 11th cent.; its bearing on mules ovhangerstrikes, by G. C. Brooke.

h The mints of Rye and Castle Rising in the reign of Stephen, by W. J. Andrew.

i Some notes on 'Peny-yard pence', by V. B. Crowther-Beynon.

j The coinage of Combe Martin, 1647–8, by H. W. Morrieson.

k Addenda to the coinages of Thomas Bushell [of Aberystwyth], by H. W. Morrieson.

l A review of the pattern broads of Charles II, by E. C. Carter.

m The Bombay pice struck by the English East India Company during the reign of Charles II, by H. A. Parsons.

n War medals issued for services in India, 1852–1924, also the first and second issue of the Most Eminent Order of the Indian Empire, by C. Winter.

o Treasure trove, by G. C. Brooke.

Other publications:

621 Catalogue of lantern-slides and negatives belonging to the Royal Numismatic Soc. and the British Numismatic Soc. 1930.

BRITISH RECORD SOCIETY LIMITED

Founded 1888, as the British Record Society, taking over the work of the Index Library, to publish records and documents and calendars of records and documents in Great Britain and Ireland, and to take measures for the protection, preservation, and custody of such records and documents. 'Limited' added to the title in 1892.

Index Library, vols. 23–61 and 63:

622 Vols. 23, 37, 48. Abstracts of Wiltshire *inquisitiones post mortem* returned into the court of chancery. 3 vols. 1901–14. [In conjunction with the Wiltshire Archaeol. and Nat. Hist. Soc. Vol. i: 1625–42, ed. G. S. Fry and E. A. Fry; vol. ii: 1242–1326, ed. E. A. Fry; vol. iii: 1327–77, abstracted by Ethel Stokes]

623 Vol. 24. Calendar of wills and administrations in the archdeaconry court of Lewes in the bishopric of Chichester, together with those in the archbishop of Canterbury's peculiar jurisdiction of South Malling and the peculiar of the deanery of Battle, comprising together the whole of the eastern division of Sussex and the parish of Edburton in west Sussex, Henry VIII—Commonwealth, comp. W. H. Hall. 1901.

624 Vols. 25, 43, 44, 54, 61. Index of wills proved in the prerogative court of Canterbury, and preserved in the principal probate registry, Somerset House, London. Vols. iv–viii, 1901–36. [Vol. iv: 1584–1604, comp. S. A. Smith, ed. E. A. Fry; vol. v: 1605–19, comp. Ethel Stokes; vol. vi: 1620–9, ed. R. H. E. Hill; vol. vii: 1653–6, ed. T. M. Blagg and Josephine S. Moir; vol. viii: 1657–60, ed. T. M. Blagg. In progress, 1958. Vols. i–iii, for 1383–1583, were published in 1893–8.]

625 Vols. 26, 36. Abstracts of *inquisitiones post mortem* for the city of London returned into the court of chancery. Vols. ii–iii, 1901–8. [In conjunction with the London and Middlesex Archaeol. Soc. Vol. ii: 1561–77, ed.

S. J. Madge; vol. iii: 1577–1603, ed. E. A. Fry. Vol. i: 1485–1560, was published in 1896]

626 Vol. 27. Calendars of wills and administrations relating to co. Leicester, proved in the archdeaconry court of Leicester, 1495–1649, and in the peculiars of St. Margaret, Leicester, Rothley, Groby, Evington, and the unproved wills, etc., previous to 1801, all preserved in the probate registry at Leicester, transcribed and indexed by H. Hartopp. 1902. [In conjunction with the Leicestershire Archaeol. Soc. For continuation see no. 640 below]

627 Vols. 28, 41, 52, 57. Calendars of Lincoln wills, ed. C. W. Foster. 4 vols. 1902–30. [Vol. i: 1320–1600; vol. ii: 1601–52; vol. iii: administrations in Lincoln consistory court, 1540–1659; vol. iv: wills and administrations in the archdeaconry of Stow, peculiar courts, and miscellaneous courts. Title-pages vary]

628 Vols. 29, 32. Index of chancery proceedings (Reynardson's division) preserved in the Public Record Office, 1649–1714, ed. E. A. Fry. 2 vols. 1903–4. [Vol. i: A–K; vol. ii: L–Z]

629 Vols. 30, 40, 47. Abstracts of *inquisitiones post mortem* for Gloucestershire returned into the court of chancery during the Plantagenet period. 3 vols. 1903–14. [Numbered iv–vi in continuation of the series for the reign of Charles I, published 1893–9. Vol. iv: 1236–1300, ed. S. J. Madge; vol. v: 1302–58, ed. E. A. Fry; vol. vi: 1359–1413, abstracted by Ethel Stokes]

630 Vols. 31, 39. Calendar of wills and administrations in the consistory court of the bishop of Worcester; also marriage licences and sequestrations deposited in the probate registry at Worcester, ed. E. A. Fry. 2 vols. 1904–10. [In conjunction with the Worcestershire Historical Soc. Vol. i: 1451–1600; vol. ii: 1601–52]

631 Vol. 33. Calendar of marriage licences issued by the Faculty Office, 1632–1714, ed. C. E. Cokayne and E. A. Fry. 1905.

632 Vol. 34. Calendar of wills proved in the consistory court of the bishop of Gloucester. Vol. ii: 1660–1800, ed. E. A. Fry and W. P. W. Phillimore. 1907. [Vol. i: 1541–1650, was published in 1895]

633 Vols. 35, 46. Calendars of wills and administrations relating to the counties of Devon and Cornwall, preserved in the probate registry at Exeter, ed. E. A. Fry. 2 vols. 1908–14. [In conjunction with the Devonshire Association. Title-pages vary. Vol. i: in the court of the principal registry of the bishop of Exeter, 1559–1799, and of Devon only, in the court of the archdeacon of Exeter, 1540–1799; vol. ii: in the consistory court of the bishop of Exeter, 1532–1800]

634 Vol. 38. Leicestershire marriage licences; being abstracts of the bonds and allegations for marriage licences preserved in the Leicester archdeaconry registry, 1570–1729, ed. H. Hartopp. 1910. [Also published in the Associated Architectural Societies' *Reports and Papers*]

635 Vol. 42. Calendars of Huntingdonshire wills, 1479–1652, comp. W. M. Noble. 1911. [With Hunts. archdeaconry marriage licences 1610–14 and one for 1517]

636 Vol. 45. Calendar of wills and administrations in the court of the archdeacon of Taunton, pts. 1–2: wills 1537–1799, ed. E. A. Fry. 1912.

637 Vol. 45a. Calendar of wills and administrations in the court of the archdeacon of Taunton, pt. 3: administrations, 1596–1799; pt. 4: wills in the royal peculiar of

Ilminster, 1690–1857, ed. E. A. Fry. 1921. [Generally occurs bound as part of no. 641 below]

638 Vol. 49. Calendar of wills in the consistory court of the bishop of Chichester, 1482–1800, ed. E. A. Fry. 1915.

639 Vol. 50. Index of wills and administrations in the probate registry at Canterbury, 1396–1558, 1640–50, transcribed and arranged by H. R. Plomer. 1920. [In conjunction with the Kent Archaeol. Soc., Records Branch]

640 Vol. 51. Index to wills and administrations proved and granted in the archdeaconry court of Leicester, 1660–1750, and in the peculiars of St. Margaret, Leicester, and Rothley; and the Rutland peculiars of Caldecott, Ketton and Tixover, and Liddington prior to 1821, in the probate registry at Leicester, transcribed and indexed by H. Hartopp. 1920. [Continues no. 626 above]

641 Vol. 53. Calendars of wills and administrations relating to Dorset, ed. G. S. Fry. 1922. [Supplements vol. 22. For Taunton and Ilminster wills, etc., issued as part of this vol. see no. 637 above]

642 Vols. 55, 63. Index to the act books of the archbishops of Canterbury, 1663–1859, comp. E. H. W. Dunkin, extended and ed. C. Jenkins and E. A. Fry. 2 vols. 1929–38. [Vol. i: A–K; vol. ii: L–Z]

643 Vols. 56, 59. Calendar of wills, administrations and accounts relating to Cornwall and Devon in the connotorial archidiaconal court of Cornwall (with which are included the records of the royal peculiar of St. Burian) now in the district probate registry at Bodmin, ed. R. M. Glencross. 2 vols. 1929–32. [Vol. i: 1569–1699; vol. ii: 1700–99. Title-page of vol. ii reads 'consistorial archidiaconal court of Cornwall']

644 Vols. 58, 60. Abstracts of Nottinghamshire marriage licences, ed. T. M. Blagg and F. A. Wadsworth. 2 vols. 1930–5. [Vol. i: archdeaconry court, 1577–1700, peculiar of Southwell, 1588–1754; vol. ii: archdeaconry court, 1701–53, peculiar of Southwell, 1755–1853]

BRITISH SCHOOL AT ROME

(Faculty of Archaeology, History and Letters)

Founded 1901, to afford facilities for British students of Roman archaeology, history and letters by offering studentships and maintaining a hostel and library in Rome.

Papers, vols. 1–12 (1902–32):

645 Vol. 6.

a Thomas Jenkins [painter and dealer in antiquities, d. 1797] in Rome, by T. Ashby.

646 Vol. 7.

a The grand tour of an Elizabethan [the journal of Sir Edward Unton's tour kept by Richard Smith, 1563], by A. H. S. Yeames.

647 Vol. 12.

a Two groups of documents relating to John Baliol [king of Scotland, d. 1315] from the Vatican archives, by Annie I. Cameron.

BRITISH SOCIETY OF FRANCISCAN STUDIES

Founded 1906, to promote the study of Franciscan history and literature, and in particular to print original documents and treatises based on original research relating to Franciscan history and the religious life of the middle ages generally.

Publications, vols. 1–17:

648 Vol. 1. Liber exemplorum ad usum praedicantium, saeculo XIII compositus a quodam fratre minore Anglico de provincia Hiberniae, secundum codicem Dunelmensem editus per A. G. Little. 1908.

649 Vol. 2. Fratris Johannis Pecham quondam archiepiscopi Cantuariensis tractatus tres de paupertate, cum bibliographia ediderunt C. L. Kingsford, A. G. Little, F. Tocco. 1910.

650 Vol. 3. Fratris Rogeri Bacon compendium studii theologiae, edidit H. Rashdall; una cum appendice de operibus Rogeri Bacon edita per A. G. Little. 1911.

651 Vol. 4. Part of the *Opus Tertium* of Roger Bacon, including a fragment now printed for the first time, ed. A. G. Little. 1912.

652 Vol. 5. Collectanea Franciscana I, ediderunt A. G. Little, M. R. James, H. M. Bannister. 1914.

a Brother William of England, companion of St. Francis, and some Franciscan drawings in the Matthew Paris mss., by A. G. Little.

b Description of a Franciscan ms., formerly in the Phillipps library, by A. G. Little.

c Library of the Grey friars of Hereford, by M. R. James.

d Short notice of some mss. of the Cambridge friars, now in the Vatican library, by H. M. Bannister.

e Records of the Franciscan province of England, by A. G. Little.

653 Vol. 6. The Grey friars of London: their history, with the register of their convent and an appendix of documents, by C. L. Kingsford. 1915.

654 Vol. 10. Collectanea Franciscana II, ediderunt C. L. Kingsford et alii. 1922.

a Notes on documents in the cathedral library at Canterbury relating to the Grey friars, by C. Cotton.

b Friar Alexander and his historical interpretation of the apocalypse [1242], by G. P. Gilson.

c List of libraries prefixed to the catalogue of John Boston [of Bury, fl. 1410] and the kindred documents, by M. R. James.

d Additional material for the history of the Grey friars, London, by C. L. Kingsford.

e Friar Henry of Wodestone [fl. 1270] and the Jews, by A. G. Little.

655 Vol. 12. The order of Minoresses in England, by A. F. C. Bourdillon. 1926.

656 Vol. 14. Fratris Rogeri Bacon de retardatione accidentium senectutis, cum aliis opusculis de rebus medicinalibus, nunc primum ediderunt A. G. Little, E. Withington. 1928.

657 Vol. 15. S. Louis of Toulouse and the process of canonisation in the 14th cent., by Margaret R. Toynbee. 1929

658 Vol. 16. Franciscan philosophy at Oxford in the 13th cent., by Dorothea E. Sharp. 1930.

Extra series, vols. 1–3:

659 Vol. 1. Franciscan essays, by P. Sabatier and others. 1912.

a Franciscans at Oxford, by A. G. Little.

660 Vol. 2. The Grey friars of Canterbury, 1224–1538, by C. Cotton; with a chapter on the remains of the friary and its restoration, by R. H. Goodsall. 1924.

661 Vol. 3. Franciscan essays, II, by F. C. Burkitt, H. E. Goad, A. G. Little. 1932.

a Chronicles of the mendicant friars, by A. G. Little.

BRITISH SOCIETY OF MASTER GLASS-PAINTERS

Founded 1921, to promote, encourage, assist and carry out whatever may tend to elevate the art or craft of glass painting and staining; to take all necessary steps for the preservation of the ancient glass of this country; to collect and disseminate professional information.

Journal, vols. 1–5 (1924–34):

662 Vol. 1.

a Recently discovered window at Chelsea [old church], by C. Hosken.

b The association of flint chippings with fragments of old glass found in mediaeval glasshouses at Chiddingfold, Surr., by Mrs. Halahan.

c Materials of the mediaeval glass painter, by N. Heaton.

d Ancient painted glass in London, by F. S. Eden.

e 15th cent. Jesse window at St. Margaret's church, Margaretting, by P. C. Haydon-Bacon.

f The medieval glass painter as a copyist, by J. D. Le Couteur.

g Mediaeval methods of employing cartoons for stained glass, by J. A. Knowles.

h The glazing of St. Stephen's chapel, Westminster, 1351–2, by L. F. Salzman. [Contd. in vol. 2]

i Imitation stained glass, ancient and modern, by J. A. Knowles.

j History of the York school of glass-painting, by J. A. Knowles. [Contd. in vols. 2–5]

k A delineator of ancient painted glass: John Browne of York, 1793–1877, by G. Benson.

663 Vol. 2.

a Glass painters' advertisements, by J. A. Knowles.

b Glass painters of Birmingham: Francis Eginton, 1737–1805; William Raphael Eginton, 1778–1834; Joseph Hornblower [fl. 1770], and others.

c Long Melford church, Suff., and its portrait glass: a mediaeval portrait gallery, by J. D. Le Couteur.

d English importations of foreign stained glass in the early 19th cent., by B. Rackham.

e Medieval glazing accounts [1221–1537], by L. F. Salzman. [Contd. in vol. 3]

f Ancient glass in the churches of Eaton Bishop and Madley, Herefs., by G. Marshall.

g William Fowler, artist and antiquary [d. 1832], by B. G. Binnall.

h Heraldic painted glass at the Law Society's hall, London, by F. S. Eden.

i Sale of the 16th cent. glass from the chapel of Ashridge Park, Herts.

664 Vol. 3.

a Lewis Foreman Day, designer and writer on stained glass [d. 1910], by D. M. Ross.

b Early 17th cent. portraits in stained glass at Oxford, by Mrs. R. L. Poole.

c Bernard Dinninghof, 16th cent. glass-painter and architect, by S. D. Kitson.

d N. H. J. Westlake [painter and writer, d. 1921], by Margaret Westlake.

e Some fragments of stained glass in south Yorkshire and Derbyshire, by J. B. Himsworth.

f Frederick Drake, glass-painter of Exeter [d. 1920], by Daphne Drake.

g Mediaeval glass in Oriel College chapel, by G. McN. Rushforth.

h Ancient stained glass at Stanford-on-Avon, by F. S. Eden.

i Early glass-workers in north Staffordshire, by T. Pape. [Contd. in vol. 4]

665 Vol. 4.

a 15th cent. glass in Somerset, by C. Woodforde.

b Early painted glass in Messingham church, by P. B. G. Binnall.

c Old stained glass in south Yorkshire and Derbyshire, by J. B. Himsworth.

d Marks on the glass at Wells: a discussion by J. Armitage Robinson, E. Horne, and J. A. Knowles.

e The great west window at Wells, by J. Armitage Robinson.

f Old stained glass in Oxfordshire, by E. S. Bouchier.

g Medieval glass in Elsing church, Norf., by C. Woodforde.

h Some heraldic glass in Norwich, by E. A. Kent.

i Clayton and Bell. [John R. Clayton, d. 1913, and Alfred Bell, d. 1895, partners in the firm of glass and mural painters]

j Renaissance glass, by W. Butterworth sen.

k Mediaeval stained glass in Cornwall and Brittany, by G. H. Doble.

666 Vol. 5.

a Schools of glass-painting in King's Lynn and Norwich in the middle ages, by C. Woodforde.

b Further notes on ancient glass in Norfolk and Suffolk, by C. Woodforde.

c Essex glass-painters in the middle ages, by C. Woodforde.

d Stained glass in the middle ages, by L. B. Saint.

e Mediaeval stained glass designers, by J. A. Knowles.

f 15th-century [glass] in Bardwell church, Suff., by H. Wilkinson.

g Painted glass in Saxlingham Nethergate church, Norf., by C. Woodforde.

h W. E. Chance [d. 1923], and the revived manufacture of coloured glass, by T. Stokes.

i The penancer's window in the nave of York minster: a discussion between J. T. Hardman and J. A. Knowles.

Extra publication:

667 Some stained glass windows executed within the past 20 years. 1930. [A directory]

BUCKINGHAMSHIRE PARISH REGISTER SOCIETY

Founded 1902, by the Committee of the Architectural and Archaeological Society for the county of Buckingham, to print old parish registers of the county under the supervision of that Society. Dissolved 1917.

Publications, vols. 1–20:

668 Vol. 1. Register of Walton (near Bletchley), 1598–1812, [transcribed by W. Bradbrook, index by E. Cookson. 1902].

669 Vol. 2. Register of Thornton, 1562–1812. 1903.

670 Vol. 3. The earliest register of Great Marlow, 1592–1611. Transcribed by A. H. Cocks. 1904.

671 Vol. 4. A transcript of the first volume, 1538–1636, of the register of Chesham, with introductory notes, appendices, and index, by J. W. Garrett-Pegge. 1904.

672 Vols. 5, 8. Register of Woughton-on-the-Green, 1558–1718, 1718–1812, transcribed, indexed and ed. W. Bradbrook; pt. 2 indexed by E. Cookson. 2 vols. [1906–8].

673 Vols. 6, 7, 10, 12, 13. Register of Olney, 1665–1812, transcribed by O. Ratcliff, indexed by O. Ratcliff and E. Cookson, introd. by T. Wright. 5 vols. [1907–10].

674 Vols. 9, 16. Register of Stoke Poges, 1563–1653, transcribed by E. L. Reynolds. 2 vols. [1908]–12.

675 Vol. 11. Register of Mentmore, 1685–1829, transcribed and indexed by Mrs. C. H. Parez. 1909.

676 Vol. 14. Register of Raventone, 1568–1812, transcribed and indexed by O. Ratcliff. [1911?].

677 Vol. 15. Aston Abbots, 1559–1837, Edgcott, 1538–1837. [1912, being vol. i, new series, Buckinghamshire baptisms, marriages and burials, ed. W. Bradbrook]

678 Vol. 17. Drayton Parslow, 1559–1837, transcribed by C. F. Clark. [1913, being vol. ii, new series, as above]

679 Vols. 18, 19. Register of Wing, 1546–1812, transcribed by A. V. Woodman. 2 vols. 1914–15.

680 Vol. 20. Register of Addington: baptisms and burials, 1558–1837; marriages, 1558–1908, transcribed by R. Ussher, indexed and ed. W. Bradbrook. 1916.

BURNLEY LITERARY AND SCIENTIFIC CLUB

Founded 1873, for the instruction and mental recreation of its members by means of original papers, discussions, and conversation of a literary and scientific character.

Transactions, vols. 16–37 (1902–13):

681 Vol. 16.
a Alfred Tennyson: a man amongst men, by F. H. Hill.
b David Garrick, by J. O. S. Thursley.
c The development of Shakespeare's fame since his death, by J. T. Foard.
d Pendle Forest, with special reference to its old mansions, by J. Greenwood.

682 Vol. 17.
a Roman Ribchester, by J. Garstang.
b Jonathan Swift, by F. J. Grant.
c Urns found in east Lancashire, and the implements associated with the men who made them, by W. H. Sutcliffe.
d Excursion to Ribchester.

683 Vol. 18.
a Oliver Cromwell, the greatest Englishman of his time, by F. H. Hill.
b The romance of the Ver [Herts.], by J. Morphen.
c Lord Nelson, by W. Lancaster.

684 Vol. 19.
a Sir Jonas Moore, knight [d. 1679], of Pendle Forest, by J. A. Laycock.
b Philip Gilbert Hamerton—a man [d. 1894], by C. Hargreaves.

685 Vols. 20, 21.
a Westminster abbey, by T. R. Pickering.
b Edmund Spenser, the poet's poet, by A. W. Fox.
c Winchester—the old capital of England, by W. L. Grant.
d Shakespeare's London, by H. Fishwick.
e The evolution of English caricature, by H. D. Herald.

686 Vol. 22.
a Lady Mary Wortley Montagu, 1689–1762, by F. J. Grant.
b George Borrow, by T. Wilson.

687 Vol. 23.
a The battle of Brunanburgh [937], by T. Booth.
b The beginnings of English colonization, by W. S. Matthews.
c Milton, by A. Pearson.

688 Vol. 25.
a Dr. Johnson, by G. S. Ritchie.

689 Vol. 26.
a The Cinque ports, by J. Perkins.
b Historical associations of the river Calder, by J. Allen.

690 Vol. 27.
a St. Paul's cathedral, by J. Perkins.
b Oliver Goldsmith, by G. S. Ritchie.
c Dr. Johnson, by C. S. Sargisson.
d Mrs. Gaskell and Knutsford, by G. A. Payne.
e Henry de Laci, the great Earl of Lincoln: the last Norman baron who owned Burnley and district, by S. Compston.

691 Vol. 28.
a Charles Darwin: his life and work, by A. Wilmore.
b Chester in history, by A. E. Simpson.
c General Wolfe, by H. L. Joseland.
d Ruined abbeys of Yorkshire, by J. Beauland.
e The deans of Whalley, by J. Brownbill.

692 Vol. 29.
a Robert Louis Stevenson, by H. Marwick.
b The beginnings of the English bible, by H. Guppy.

693 Vol. 30.
a Local relics of palaeolithic man, by J. Whitham.
b The singing-pew of bygone days, by S. Compston.
c Coleridge the poet, by T. W. Meredith.
d Detached thoughts on ecclesiastical architecture [12th–15th cent.], by A. A. Bellingham.
e William Morris: artist and craftsman, by T. Foster.

694 Vol. 31.
a The Club, 1873–1913: a retrospect, by F. J. Grant.
b Palaeoliths found in the Burnley valley, by J. Whitham.
c The development of English pottery, by J. Burton.

695 Vol. 32.
a Of the 'humanity' of certain locally found east Lancashire palaeoliths, by J. Whitham.
b The Waterloo campaign, by J. T. Marquis.

696 Vol. 34.
a Charlotte Brontë, by F. Ratcliffe.
b The halmot court of Ightenhill, by W. Parker.
c Edwin Waugh [d. 1890], by R. J. Gordon.

697 Vol. 35.
a Edward Fitzgerald, of Omar Khayyám fame, by S. Smith.
b Old homesteads in Lancashire and Cheshire, by J. H. Crabtree.
c Thomas Edward Brown [d. 1897], national poet of the Isle of Man, by W. H. Kneen.
d Charles Lamb, by T. Bank.

698 Vol. 36.
a Yatefield and Woodtop [Burnley] in the 18th cent., by W. H. Hall.

699 Vol. 37.
a Glimpses into the story of the Fylde, by G. A. Wood.

BURTON-ON-TRENT NATURAL HISTORY AND ARCHAEOLOGICAL SOCIETY

Founded 1876, to promote and encourage the practical study of natural history, archaeology, general science and literature.

Transactions, vols. 5–7 (1903–14):

700 Vol. 5.

a The great bridge of Burton-on-Trent, by H. A. Rye.
b Notes on Burton abbey plan, by H. A. Rye.
c Tapestry at Haddon Hall, by H. A. Rye.
d The ancient industries of Cannock Chase, by G. M. Cockin.
e Notes on excavations of the foundations of the old Burton bridge.

701 Vol. 6.

a Annals of Burton abbey, by R. T. Robinson.
b Sinai Park [formerly part of Burton abbey], by H. A. Rye.
c Abbots of Burton-on-Trent, 1004–1540, comp. G. Appleby.

702 Vol. 7.

a Vernon monuments [in Tong church, Salop.], by H. A. Rye.
b The Blount family, Nether Hall [Burton], and Lady Paulet's almshouses, by G. Appleby. [Followed by additional notes on Lady Paulet, d. 1593, and her benefactions]
c A visit to the Roman wall in connection with the Monk's bridge, by H. A. Rye.
d Rugeley in early Georgian times, by G. M. Cockin.

CALVINISTIC METHODIST HISTORICAL SOCIETY

Founded 1914, to promote a scientific study of the history and literature of Calvinistic Methodism.

Journal, vols. 1–18 (1916–33):[1]

703 Vol. 1.

a A bibliography of Welsh Calvinistic Methodism. [See also 'Harrisiana' below and bibliography in vol. 10]
b Teithiau Howel Harris i Ogledd Cymru [the journeys of Howel Harris into North Wales], gan R. Bennett.
c A sidelight on the history of Daniel Rowland, by J. H. Davies.
d Dechreuad Methodistiaeth Caerfyrddin [the beginnings of Carmarthen Methodism], gan M. H. Jones.
e Daniel Rowland: contemporary descriptions, 1746 and 1835, by J. H. Davies.
f Richard Tibbott, 1719–98, by R. Bennett. [His diary, in Welsh. Contd. in vols. 2–4]
g Harrisiana: a bibliography. [Contd. in vols. 2 and 3, and in vol. 5 under the title 'Bibliography of Welsh Methodism'. See also vol. 13]
h Methodistiaeth fore tref Caerfyrddin [early Methodism of Carmarthen town], gan M. H. Jones.

704 Vol. 2.

a Sasiynau Caerfyrddin [Carmarthen preaching sessions 1819–67], gan M. H. Jones.
b Pregeth y Parch. Daniel Rowland yn Llangeitho, Rhog. 21, 1782. [Sermon preached by Daniel Rowland at Llangeitho, 21 Dec. 1782]

[1] Vol. 21 (1936) has an index to the first twenty vols.

c Cyfarfod misol sir Fflint [Flintshire monthly meeting, 1826–7], gan R. Bennett.
d Local histories of Welsh Methodism: a bibliography. [In Welsh. Contd. in vol. 3]
e Hunangofiant y Parch. Hopkin Bevan, Llangyfelach, 1765–1839 [autobiography of Rev. Hopkin Bevan], gan J. J. Morgan.
f *The Christian Amusement* and *The Weekly History* [early Calvinistic Methodist newspapers, *c.* 1741], by M. H. Jones. [Contd. in vols. 3 and 4]
g Hanes Methodistiaeth yn Lerpwl [history of Welsh Methodism in Liverpool], gan O. J. Owen. [Contd. in vol. 3]
h The baptismal [non-parochial] register of Water Street chapel, Carmarthen: a description by W. D. Rowlands.
i John Elias a charcharorion rhyfel yn 1811 [John Elias and Welsh prisoners of war in France in 1811], gan H. Lewis.
j The Trevecka mss. supplement. [Letters of Howell Harris, and extracts from his Latin diaries. Contd. in supplements to vols. 3, 5, 6, 9 and 11]

705 Vol. 3.

a Cychwyniad Methodistiaeth Fflint [the beginnings of Methodism in Flintshire], gan J. D. Jones. [Contd. in vol. 5]
b William Williams, Pantycelyn [preacher and hymn-writer, 1716–91], by M. H. Jones.
c The printed works of Williams, Pantycelyn, by J. H. Davies.
d Llawysgrifau Williams Pantycelyn yn Athrofa'r Bala. [Williams Pantycelyn mss. in Bala College], gan J. T. A. Jones.
e Chapel Ed, Goetre, by A. Morris.
f Howell Davies [preacher], by R. Bennett.

706 Vol. 4.

a The Moravians and the [Welsh] Methodists [in the 18th cent.], by M. H. Jones.
b Benjamin La Trobe's preface to the 'auto-biography' of Howell Harris. [La Trobe, Moravian preacher and editor, fl. 1765–86]
c Letters to Howell Harris: mss. in Bala College library, by J. T. A. Jones.
d Taith trwy Wynedd [a journey through part of North Wales, 1751], gan R. Bennett.
e A relic of the past: Morgan Howell's pulpit chair at Rock chapel, Blackwood, by A. Morris.
f Y Ty Round (where the Rock services were first held), by D. W. Williams. [The Round House, Rock, in 1839, with supplementary note by A. Morris]
g Llawysgrifau John Elias yn Athrofa'r Bala. [John Elias mss. in Bala College]
h John Lewis, printer of *The Weekly History*, by M. H. Jones. [Extracts from letters, 1740–7. Contd. in vol. 5 as 'John Lewis, "printer to the religious societies" ']
i Y Parch. Thomas Charles [1755–1814] a Methodistiaeth Lerpwl [Rev. T. Charles and Liverpool Methodism], gan O. J. Owen.
j Who was Williams Pantycelyn's tutor at Llwynllwyd?, by D. Edmondes-Owen.
k 'An account of the Progress of the Gospel', by M. H. Jones. [The continuation of *The Weekly History*, also issued by John Lewis, of Bartholomew Close, London, 1743–8. Contd. in vol. 6, vol. 10 under the title 'The First Calvinistic Methodist newspaper', and vol. 11 as 'The Christian History', which concludes the list of letters, 1740–5, relating to Wales and Welsh revivalists, contained in the London, Glasgow, and Boston editions, and mentioned in earlier articles]
l Yr erledigaeth gyntaf ar y Methodistiaid yng Ngwrecsam.

[The first persecution of the Methodists in Wrexham, *c.* 1747]
m Extracts from the diary of Howell Harris for 1749.

707 Vol. 5.

a George Whitefield yn ei berthynas a Methodistiaeth Cymru [Whitefield's relations with Welsh Methodism], gan M. H. Jones.
b Y pregaethwyr cyntaf a wasanaethodd Fethodistiaid Caerfyrddin [the earliest preachers serving Carmarthenshire Methodism], gan M. H. Jones.
c Moravian chapels in Wales.
d The hour glass at 'Y Burthyn' chapel, near Cowbridge [with references from Howell Harris's diary relating to Aberthyn chapel], by M. H. Jones.
e Llythyrau y Parch. Thomas Charles. [Letters of the Rev. T. Charles, 1779–88]
f Methodistiaeth Gwrecsam yn y llysdy [Wrexham Methodists charged with holding an illegal conventicle, 1648], gan R. Bennett.
g 18th cent. hymn books [chiefly Welsh, and their suggested English sources], by M. H. Jones.
h Llenyddiaeth wrth-Fethodistaidd a dadleuol. [Anti-Methodist and polemical literature, 18th–19th cent.]

708 Vol. 6.

a Ffurf wreiddiol emynau Ann Griffiths [original form of the hymns of Anne Griffiths, 1780–1805], gan D. M. Lewis.
b An account book, 1773: Aburthyn chapel, Glam.
c Taith Thos. William i'r gogledd yn 1751, a gwahoddiad i Howel Harris yn 1764. [Thomas William's journey to the north in 1751 and an invitation to Howell Harris to continue preaching in Wales]
d Griffith Jones, Llanddowror, a'r Methodistiaid [relations between the founder of Welsh charity or circulating schools, rector of Llanddower, d. 1761, and the Methodists, with a bibliography for his life and work], gan M. H. Jones. [Contd. in vol. 9]
e Peter Williams [Welsh preacher and writer, 1722–96], by J. H. Davies.
f Lewis Evan, Llanllugan [Welsh preacher, contemporary of Howell Harris], by R. Bennett.
g Prif ffeithiau bywyd a gwaith Ieuan Gwyllt [the life and work of the Rev. John Roberts, 1822–77, Welsh preacher, writer, musician], gan M. H. Jones.

709 Vol. 7.

a Portraits of Howell Harris, by J. Ballinger.
b Evan Roberts a 'theulu' Trefecca. [Evan Roberts and the Trevecka 'family'. Includes letters by Howell Harris, 1755]
c Diary of a journey by Rev. Griffith Jones, Llanddowror, and Sir John Philipps, bt., to Scotland [*c.* 1718].
d Morgan John Rhys yn ei gysylltiad a Threfecca. [Morgan John Rhys, Welsh preacher and writer, 1760–1804, and his connection with Trevecka]
e Ymgais at uno'r ffrydiau Methodistaidd cyntaf: Wesley, Whitefield, a Howell Harris, mewn cyd-ymgynghoriad yn 1749. [An attempt to unite the first Methodist movements: Wesley, Whitefield, and Howell Harris in conference, 1749]
f Llyfryddiaeth Peter Williams. [Bibliography of Peter Williams, with additions in 'Briwsion hanes']
g The Tabernacle church, Haverfordwest, by J. Phillips.
h Connexional archives. [Books and mss. bearing on the history of Calvinistic Methodists, deposited with or acquired by the Society. Contd. in vols. 8–14, 17–18]
i Derbyniad John Jones, Talysarn, i'r gymdeithasfa [the admission of John Jones into the preachers' convention, 1822], gan R. Bennett.

j Ysgrif-lyfr John Lewis Butler, ysgolfeistr, Woodstock. [Notes on preachers and sermons, 1829–42, kept by John Lewis Butler, schoolmaster, of Woodstock]

710 Vol. 8.

a Ein cyffes ffydd, 1823–1923 [the Calvinistic Methodist confession of faith, 1823–1923], gan E. O. Davies. [With bibliography by M. H. Jones]
b John Elias and John Davies of Fronheulog [near Llandderfel].
c John Davies, Fronheulog a'i ohebwyr [John Davies and his correspondents, with letters of John Elias], gan J. T. A. Jones. [Followed by a list of Fronheulog mss. at Bala College]
d Teulu'r Tyddyn [notes on the Bowen family, of Tyddyn Gwyddfyd in the parish of Llandinam], by R. Bennett.
e Dydd-lyfr y Parch. Robert Jones, Rhoslan [diary of Rev. R. Jones, of Rhoslan, 30 Apr. 1809–4 Oct. 1818], gan H. Hughes.
f Howell Harris a Chymdeithas Amaethyddol Brycheiniog. [Howell Harris and the Brecon Agricultural Society]
g The itinerary of Howell Harris, Trevecka, compiled from his diary and letters; and in which are traced his journeys through Wales and parts of England as a Methodist evangelist 1735–73. First instalment, 1735–45, ed. M. H. Jones. [Issued as supplement. Second instalment, 1746–52, and third instalment, 1753–73, were issued as supplements to vols. 10 and 12]

711 Vol. 9.

a Y Parch. Dafydd Jones, Llangan [Rev. David Jones, of Llangan, 1735–1810, Welsh preacher], by T. Beynon.
b Nodion o sir Benfro. [Notes from Pembrokeshire, on the old chapel at Caerfarchell, and a letter from the Rev. Ebenezer Richard, of Tregaron, to the Rev. William Morris, of St. Davids, 1832]
c Teulu Trevecca [the Trevecka community], gan M. H. Jones.
d Talgarth [Brecon] parish registers and the Trevecka family.

712 Vol. 10.

a Y flwyddyn 1751 fel trobwynt yn hanes Methodistiaeth [the year 1751 as a turning point in Methodist history], gan M. H. Jones.
b An account of tracts and pamphlets on the doctrines of grace published by Hervey, Sandeman, Wesley, and others, 1755–73, by J. C. Whitebrook.
c Sir Ddinbych a theulu Trefecca [Denbighshire and the Trevecka community], by W. Williams.
d Marriage agreement of Simon Lloyd, Bala, and Sarah Bowen, Trevecca [1755].
e Cysegrleocdd Methodistiaid Caerfyrddin a'r cylch [sanctuaries of the Methodists of Carmarthen and district], gan M. H. Jones.
f Hen deulu Trefecca: darganfod llawysgrif newydd. [The discovery of a new ms. relating to the Trevecka community]
g Llyfryddiaeth argraffu ac argraffwyr Cymru [bibliography of Welsh printing and printers], gan M. H. Jones.
h Hanes Methodistiaeth ym Mhontyberem, sir Gaerfyrddin [history of Methodism in Pontyberem, Carmarthenshire], gan H. Edwards.
i Descendants of Joseph, Thomas, and Howell Harris, of Trevecka.

713 Vol. 11.

a William Ellis, Maentwrog [19th cent.], by D. D. Williams.

b How the records of the Calvinistic Methodist pres-
  byteries are kept, by M. H. Jones.
c Cof-lyfr Capel Afan, gogledd Aberteifi. [Record book of
  Capel Afan, north Cardiganshire, 1859–79]
d Gyfylchi a Jerusalem, Pontrhydyfen: trydydd jubili,
  1776–1926 [Gyfylchi and Jerusalem chapels, Pontrhydyfen, third jubilee], gan T. Beynon.
e A journal of the Welsh associations, 1778–97 [being
  Nathaniel Rowland's minute-book].
f Cymdeithasfa Aberystwyth Ebrill, 1849 [Aberystwyth
  convention, April 1849], gan E. Evans.
g Methodistiaith fore yn y gogledd: darganfod llythyrau
  newydd. [Early Methodism in the north: discovery of
  new letters, 1738–72]

714 Vol. 12.

a John Foulkes Jones [b. 1826], gan R. Bennett.
b Extracts relating to Welsh Methodism [1806–38], by
  T. Sylvanus.
c Dechreuad a chynnydd Methodistiaeth yn nhref Llanrwst [beginning and development of Methodism in
  Llanrwst], gan W. Williams.
d William Davies, Castellnedd, 1727–87 [preacher], by
  T. Beynon.
e Trefollwyn-Trefecca. Methodistiaeth fore ym Mon
  [early Methodism in Anglesey], gan R. Mathews.
f Daniel Rowland of Llangeitho: sources and literature
  for the study of his life and work, by M. H. Jones.
  [With additions in 'Miscellanea' and in vol. 13]
g Lle'r Parch. Daniel Rowland ym mysg emynwyr cyfnod
  'Aleluia' Pantycelyn [the place of Rev. Daniel Rowland
  among the hymn-writers of Williams Pantycelyn's
  'Aleluia' period], gan D. M. Lewis.
h Llyfr cyhoeddiadau Aberddawen, o Ion. 4, 1807–
  Hyd. 10, 1813 [the preaching appointments book,
  Aberddawen, 4 Jan. 1807–10 Oct. 1813], gan J. O.
  Evans.
i Y Parch. James Hughes (Iago Trichrug), yr esboniwr:
  llythyrau o'i eiddo in llyfrgell Athrofa'r Bala. [Letters
  of the Rev. James Hughes, biblical commentator, in
  Bala College library, written 1831–43]
j Baptismal registers [extracts]: 1. Broadmead, Bristol;
  2. Llanpumsaint, by M. H. Jones.
k Richard Jones, Llanrwst 1753–1836 [Methodist elder],
  gan W. Williams.
l Hen lyfrau cofnodion eglwysi: (a) Caergeiliog, Mon;
  (b) Rhydlwyd, Lledrod, Ceredigion. [Old church note
  books of Caergeiliog, 1781–1801, and Rhydlwyd, 1863–
  1874, gan R. Lewis]

715 Vol. 13.

a John Ellis, y cerddor, 1760–1839 [John Ellis, musician],
  gan W. Williams.
b Sypyn o hen lythyrau diddorol. [A sheaf of interesting
  old letters, 1819–60, signed William Charles (1848),
  J. Evans (1860), John Rowlands (1819), Roger Edwards
  (1847), Hugh Hughes (1848), Richard Humphreys
  (1849), and others]
c Canmlwyddiant ail gapel Twynllanau, Llanddeusant
  [the second centenary of Twynllanau chapel, Llan-
  ddeusant], gan T. Beynon.
d Cymanfa gyffredinol Aberdar a'r Gymdeithas Hanes.
  [Aberdare General Convention and the Historical
  Society, 1928]
e Llyfryddiaeth hanes bywyd a gwaith Howell Harris
  [bibliography of the life and work of Howell Harris, the
  bibliography in English], gan M. H. Jones.
f Joseph Harris, Trefecca [mathematician, inventor,
  author; elder brother of Howell Harris. In Welsh].
g Richard Thomas, un o'r cynghorwyr bore a phregethwr
  cyntaf Mon [Richard Thomas, one of Anglesey's first

preachers, contemporary of Howell Harris], gan R.
  Lewis.
h Nodion cyfundebol, 1790–1849. [Denominational notes
  arranged from the papers of T. Sylvanus]

716 Vol. 14.

a Casgliadau argraffedig o emynau cyn 'Aleluia' Pantycelyn, 1744. [Collections of hymns published before
  Williams Pantycelyn's 'Aleluia', 1744]
b *The Christian Standard*: the first Forward Movement
  newspaper, by D. W. Williams. [List of chief contents,
  1891–3]
c Ein cyfansaddiad: trem yn ol ac ymlaen [our constitution: a glance backward and forward], gan E. O.
  Davies. [See synopsis in English below]
d A synopsis of the moderator's valedictory address, 1929.
  Our constitution: past and future. [Followed by bibliographical notes]
e John William Fletcher [vicar of Madeley and superintendent of Lady Huntingdon's college] 1729–85: bicentenary of his birth.

717 Vol. 15.

a Trevecca and its colleges [with list of students, 1842–62].
b Eglwys yr Alban: blynyddoed mawr [the Presbyterian
  Church of Scotland: historic years], gan E. O. Davies.
c An interesting legal document throwing light on early
  Welsh Methodism [1837].
d Y Parch. William Jones, Rhuddlan, 1779–1844, gan
  W. Williams.
e Emynyddiaeth Cymru: rhagflaenwyr Williams Pantycelyn. [The hymnology of Wales: precursors of Williams
  Pantycelyn]
f Caniadau y brodyr. [Songs of the brethren, being early
  Methodist hymns]
g Robert Jones, Rhoslan, 1745–1829 [schoolmaster, author,
  preacher], gan D. D. Williams.
h Llawysgrifau Wheldon, coleg y gogledd: disgrifiad a
  chatalog. [The Wheldon mss., referring to Robert Jones,
  19th cent. minister and editor, his family and friends]
i Briwsion. *The Monthly Herald*, the religious miscellany
  and intelligencer of the Calvinistic Methodist, 1857
  July–1858 June. 12 numbers. Chief items [a list].
j Castleton: the home of Edward Coslet [Methodist
  preacher, d. 1828], by A. Morris.
k Hen offeiriad Methodistaidd ac ordeiniad, 1811. [An
  old Methodist priest and ordination, by D. D. Williams.
  Refers to Thomas Jones, ordained 1774, author of
  *The Welsh Looking Glass . . . by a person who has travelled
  through that country at the close of the year* 1811].
l Methodism in the area included in the diocese of Bangor
  during the middle and latter half of the 18th cent., by
  D. D. Williams. [Contd. in vol. 16]
m Odfeuon dwyieithog Howel Harris [Howell Harris's
  bilingual religious meetings], gan R. Bennett.
n Peter Roberts, Llansannan, 1770–1829 [Methodist
  preacher].
o Y Parch. William Hughes, Racine, Llanrwst, 1813–83
  [Methodist preacher], gan W. Williams.
p George Whitefield's letter to Howell Harris [1741], by
  T. Beynon.
q Trem ar y modd y datblygodd addysg Cymru: cyfraniad
  Gruffydd Jones, Llanddowror, i addysg ei wlad [a
  glance at the development of Welsh education: the
  contribution of Griffith Jones, Llanddowror, to the
  education of his country, by D. D. Williams].
r Robert Raikes, 1735–1811 [founder of the English
  Sunday School movement], gan D. B. Jones.
s Methodism in Anglesey [1749 and 1776], by D. D.
  Williams.

t Nodiadau ar rai emynau [notes on some hymns], gan J. O. Evans.

u Oddeutu muriau Caer [around Chester's walls], gan M. Parry.

718 Vol. 16.

a Y modd y caed y testament Cymraeg cyntaf. [How we obtained the first Welsh Testament, by D. D. Williams]

b Coflyfr John Roberts, Llangwm, am 1810 a rhan o 1812 [the memoranda book of the Rev. John Roberts, Llangwm, for 1810 and part of 1812], gan R. Morris.

c Sidelights on early Calvinistic Methodist story, from *John Wesley—the Master Builder*, by A. Morris.

d Yr hen gymdeithasfaoedd [the old (18th cent.) Conventions], gan R. Bennett.

e 'Yr ymarfer o dduwioldeb' ['The practice of Godliness': some religious books of the 17th–18th centuries], gan Clwydydd.

f Dyddiaduron y Parch. Morgan Howell [diaries of the Rev. Morgan Howell, 1825–52], gan J. O. Evans.

g Yr interliwdiau fel ffynonellau hanes. [The 'interludes', or 18th cent. plays, as historical sources, by D. D. Williams]

h Angladd Dafydd Dackin [the funeral of Dafydd Dackyn, a Methodist worthy, 1842], gan R. Bennett.

i Dechreuad y diwygiad Methodistaidd yng Nghymru [the beginnings of the Methodist revival in Wales], gan J. P. Williams.

j Amddiffyniad i'r Methodistiaid [defence of the Methodists, against the charge of Jacobinism during the French revolution and Napoleonic wars, gan D. D. Williams.

k Morfa Bach, Cydweli [Morfa Bach, a farm near Kidwelly, visited by Howell Harris], by T. Beynon.

l Moravians and Methodists: a sidelight on their early relations, by Elnith Griffiths.

m Llythyr Evan Moses. [A letter by Evan Moses, 1755]

n Un o lyfrau Pantycelyn a'r cysylltiadau [one of Williams Pantycelyn's books and its associations], gan H. Edwards.

o Lleoedd o ddiddordeb hanesyddol yng Ngheredigion. [Places of historical interest in Ceredigion, or Cardiganshire, by D. D. Williams]

p Methodistiaeth a chaniadaeth [Methodism and singing], gan J. P. Williams.

q A Moravian's diary: William Holland's journey through South Wales, 1746, by Elnith R. Griffiths. [Contd. in vol. 17, where the date 1742 in the title should read 1747]

r Llythyrau. [Letters of Anne Williams, later the wife of Howell Harris, 1741–2, and of D. Elias, 1749]

719 Vol. 17.

a Y Piwritaniaid. [The Puritans, by D. D. Williams]

b Ewyllys Morgan Rhys, yr emynydd. [The will of Morgan Rhys, hymn-writer, 1779]

c Ein caniadaeth gynulleidfaol [our congregational singing], gan Clwydydd.

d Athroniaeth Methodistiaeth. [Methodist philosophy, by D. D. Williams]

e Y prifathro Thomas Charles Edwards ar 'Effeithiau ymneilltuaeth yng Nghymru' [Principal Thomas Charles Edwards on 'The effects of Nonconformity in Wales'], gan D. D. Williams.

f Y goror [Methodism in the Welsh border *c.* 1815], gan R. Bennett.

g The original copy of the Constitutional Deed [1826], by R. Roberts.

h Eglwyseg, by H. L. Jones. [The growth of the Methodist community in Eglwyseg, Merionethshire]

i Hen lythyrau. [Old letters, 1845–6]

j Canmlwyddiant geni Islwyn a Cheiriog [the centenary of the birth of Islwyn and Ceiriog, Welsh poets of the 19th cent.], gan D. D. Williams.

k Methodistiaeth ym mhapurau Thomas Morgan, Henllan [Methodism in the papers of Thomas Morgan, Henllan, 1720–99], gan R. T. Jenkins.

l Catalogue of Welsh books in the Trevecca library. [Contd. in vol. 18]

m Briwsion. Hen groniclau Mallwyd, gan W. R. Jones. [Old Mallwyd chronicles, i.e. church accounts, 1821–39. Contd. in vol. 18]

n Llythyrau Trefecca [Trevecca letters: an evaluation by D. D. Williams].

o Ebeniana, by K. Monica Davies. [On the poet, Eben Fardd. In English]

p Clynnog Fawr yn Arfon. [St. Beuno and his monastery at Clynnog Fawr, by D. D. Williams]

q Rhai emynwyr ail gyfnod y diwygiad [some hymn-writers of the second phase of the Methodist revival], gan J. P. Williams.

r Hanes dechreuad yr ysgol sabothol ym Melin-y-Coed, Llanrwst. [History of the beginning of Melin-y-Coed Sundayschool]

720 Vol. 18.

a Rhai o elfennau llwyddiant Methodistiaeth galfinaidd yn Liverpool [some factors making for the success of Calvinistic Methodism in Liverpool], gan D. D. Williams.

b Sasiwn y Bala, Mehefin 1839 [the Bala convention, June 1839], gan Clwydydd.

c Emynyddiaeth Cymru [Welsh hymnology], gan D. W. Williams.

d Canmlwyddiant marw Richard Jones o'r Wern, 1772–1833 [centenary of the death of Richard Jones of the Wern, preacher, hymn-writer, patriot], gan D. D. Williams.

e Achlysurol flwyddolion [anniversaries, or notable dates in Methodist history], gan J. Y. Evans.

f The Oxford Movement and Wales, 1833–45, by D. D. Williams.

g The Calvinistic Methodist or Presbyterian Church of Wales Bill: 'Proof of evidence', by E. O. Davies. [Brief history of the Welsh Calvinistic Methodist Connection, and discussion of desired amendments to the Constitutional Deed, prepared for parliament]

h Y dyddiadur Methodistaidd am 1854 [the Methodist diary for 1854], gan R. Morris.

i Trem ar hanes y cyfundeb [a glance at the history of the denomination], gan D. D. Williams.

j Trwyddedu a chofrestru pregethwyr ac addoldai Methodistiaid sir Drefaldwyn, 1795–1811 [the licensing and registering of Methodist preachers and chapels in Montgomeryshire, 1795–1811], gan R. Bennett.

k Y Parch. Lewis Jones, y Bala, 1807–54 [Rev. Lewis Jones, of Bala], gan Clwydydd.

CAMBRIAN ARCHAEOLOGICAL ASSOCIATION

Founded 1846, to examine, preserve, and illustrate the ancient monuments and remains of the history, language, manners, customs, and arts of Wales and the Marches.

Archaeologia Cambrensis, 6th ser., vols. 1–20 (1901–20):

721 Vol. 1.

a Llantrissant castle, by J. S. Corbett.

b Llancaiach House, by C. Wilkins.

c Two Kelto-Roman finds in Wales, by J. R. Allen.

d Ynys Seiriol [or Puffin Island, off the south-east extremity of Anglesey], by H. Hughes.

e Some parallels between Celtic and Indian institutions, by G. H. Jones.

f Welsh records, by J. P. Yeatman. [Contd. from 5th ser., vol. 17. Pedigrees by G. Hughes, fl. 1634]

g Notes on the older churches in the four Welsh dioceses, by Sir S. R. Glynne. [Contd. from 5th ser., vol. 17; contd. in vol. 2 below. Sir Stephen Glynne, d. 1874]

h Some carved wooden spoons made in Wales, by J. R. Allen.

i A destroyed Tudor building in Wrexham, by A. N. Palmer.

j Architectural history of the cathedral church of St. Deiniol, Bangor, by H. Hughes. [Contd. in vols. 2 and 4]

k The family of Jenkins [Sir Leoline Jenkins, *c.* 1623-85], by H. F. J. Vaughan.

l Wanten or Wanton dyke [Montgomeryshire], with some remarks on upper and lower 'short dykes', by J. M. E. Lloyd.

m Dolforwyn castle, and its lords, by R. Williams.

722 Vol. 2.

a Old farm-houses with round chimneys near St. David's, by J. R. Allen.

b Prehistoric interments near Cardiff, by J. Ward.

c Camps and earthworks of the Newtown district [Montgomeryshire], by D. R. Thomas.

d Llandenny parish church, Monmouthshire, by G. E. Halliday.

e The oldest parish registers in Pembrokeshire, by J. Phillips. [Contd. in vols. 3 and 5]

f Discoveries at Llangendierne church, Carmarthenshire, by T. P. Clark.

g Church of St. Michael, Llanfihangel Glyn Myfyr, Denbighshire, by H. Hughes.

h Crug yr Avon: Glamorgan's lone sentry-box, by J. Griffith.

i Flintshire subsidy roll, 1593, by D. R. Thomas.

j Cairn and sepulchral cave at Gop, near Prestatyn, by B. Dawkins.

k The chevron and its derivatives: a study in the art of the bronze age, by J. R. Allen.

l Notes on Llandaff parish, by G. E. Halliday.

m The Wogans of Boulston, by F. Green.

n Exploration of a pre-historic camp in Glamorganshire, by H. W. Williams.

o Adventures of a Denbighshire gentleman [Roger Myddelton] of the 17th cent. in the East Indies, by A. N. Palmer.

723 Vol. 3.

a Exploration of Clegyr Voya [Pembrokeshire], by S. Baring-Gould.

b Roman forts in S. Wales, by F. Haverfield.

c The early settlers of Brecon, by E. Anwyl.

d Survey of the lordship of Haverford, 1577, by H. Owen.

e The removal of the cross of Iltyd at Llantwit Major, Glam., by G. E. Halliday.

f Montgomeryshire screens and rood-lofts, by D. R. Thomas.

g The hermitage of Theodoric [Glam.], and the site of Pendar, by T. Gray.

h The *Golden Grove Book* of pedigrees, by E. Owen.

i Pre-Norman cross-base at Llangefelach, Glam., by J. R. Allen.

j History of the old parish of Gresford in the counties of Denbigh and Flint, by A. N. Palmer. [Contd. in vols. 4 and 5]

k Forgotten sanctuaries: being some thoughts on the vanished crosses and chapels in St. John's parish, Brecon, by Gwenllian E. F. Morgan.

l Note on a perforated stone axe-hammer found in Pembrokeshire, by J. R. Allen.

m Llangurig church, Montgomeryshire, by D. R. Thomas.

n Ancient British camps, etc., in Lleyn, co. Carnarvon, transcribed by E. Owen [from a ms. written in 1871 by J. G. Williams of Pwllheli].

o Incised cross-stone at Ystafell-Fach, Brecknockshire, and the tradition of an ancient town, by W. T. G. Lewis.

p The early life of St. Samson of Dol [*c.* 525-93], by W. D. Bushell.

q Gileston church, Glam., by G. E. Halliday.

r St. Brychan, king, confessor, by S. Baring-Gould and J. Fisher.

724 Vol. 4.

a An exploration of some of the cytiau [huts] in Tre'r Ceiri [Caerns.], by S. Baring-Gould and R. Burnard.

b Is 'Porth Kerdin' in Moylgrove [Pembrokeshire]?, by A. W. Wade-Evans.

c Partrishow church, Breconshire, by D. R. Thomas.

d Some traces and traditions round Llangybi [relating to St. Cybi and St. Cybi's well], by W. Williams.

e 'Penreth', by A. Hall. [An attempt to trace the location of a bishop's see of this name, mentioned in 1537]

f The origin of the Peverils, by J. P. Yeatman.

g Church of St. John the Baptist, Newton Nottage, Glam., by G. E. Halliday.

h The *Vaidre Book* [antiquarian notes written *c.* 1580-1610 by George Owen], ed. H. Owen. [Contd. in vol. 5]

i Brynllys castle and church [Brecon.].

j Early settlers of Carnarvonshire, by E. Anwyl.

k Church of Saints Mael and Sulien, Cwm, Flints., by H. Hughes.

l Caerwent, by M. L. Dawson.

m The cross of Irbic at Llandough, Glam., by J. R. Allen.

n Glimpses of Elizabethan Pembrokeshire, by J. Phillips.

o Discovery of cinerary urn at Staylittle, near Llanbrynmair, Montgomeryshire, by E. K. Jones and E. R. Vaughan.

p Aberystwyth castle: excavations in 1903, by H. Hughes.

725 Vol. 5.

a Early Cardiganshire, by J. W. Willis Bund.

b Find of British urns near Capel Cynon, Cardiganshire, by J. Davies.

c Discovery of an early Christian inscribed stone at Treflys, Carnarvonshire, by J. R. Allen.

d The Roman inscription at Carnarvon, by J. E. Lloyd.

e Find of late-Celtic bronze objects at Seven Sisters, near Neath, Glam., by J. R. Allen.

f Old stained glass in St. Beuno's church, Penmorva, by C. E. Breese.

g The church of Penbryn, and its connections and associations, by D. P. Williams.

h Criccieth castle, by H. Hughes.

i Pre-historic human skeletons found at Merthyr Mawr, by D. Hepburn.

j Llandecwyn [Merionethshire] inscribed stone, by C. E. Breese. [See also vol. 6 below.]

k Llantwit Major church, by G. E. Halliday.

l Some notes on medieval Eifionydd [Caerns.], by J. E. Lloyd.

726 Vol. 6.

a The Ordovices and ancient Powys, by D. R. Thomas.

b Discovery of prehistoric hearths in South Wales, by T. C. Cantrill and O. T. Jones.

c Allen's 'Pembrokeshire', by E. Laws. [Joseph Allen, fl. 1792]

d Welsh wooden spoons with ornamental carving and love-symbols, by J. R. Allen.

e Some sacramental vessels of earthenware and of wood, by D. R. Thomas.

f The house of Scotsborough, near Tenby, by E. Laws.

g Early settlers of Cardigan, by E. Anwyl.

h The Llandecwyn inscribed stone, by E. Anwyl. [See also vol. 5 above]

i Religious and social life of former days in the vale of Clwyd as illustrated by the parish records, by J. Fisher.

j Wenlock priory, by W. G. Clark-Maxwell.

k Roman remains, Penydarren Park, Merthyr Tydfil, by F. T. James.

l Notes on old Radnor church, by E. Hartland.

m The town of Holt, co. Denbigh: its castle, church, franchise, demesne, fields, etc., by A. N. Palmer. [Contd. in vols. 7-9]

n The exploration of Pen-y-Gaer, above Llanbedr-y-Cenin [Caerns.], by H. Hughes.

o Note on the defences of Pen-y-Gaer, by W. Gardner.

p Pen-y-Gorddyn, or Y Gorddyn Fawr [Denbighshire], by H. Hughes.

q Hen Dre'r Gelli: a buried pre-historic town in the Rhondda valley, by J. Griffith.

r Note of an ancient cope belonging to St. Martin's church, Laugharne, Carmarthenshire, by G. G. T. Treherne.

s Treflys church, Carnarvonshire, by H. Hughes.

t Painted panels at Penmachno church, Carnarvonshire, by H. Hughes.

u Cardiganshire: its plate, records, and registers, by G. E. Evans. [Contd. in vols. 17 and 18]

727 Vol. 7.

a Report on excavations at Tre'r Ceiri [Caerns.], in 1906, by H. Hughes.

b Llansaint [Carmarthenshire], by G. E. Evans.

c Epigraphic notes by Sir J. Rhys. [On inscribed stones at Llansaint and Llandawke, Carmarthenshire; Nevern, Pembrokeshire; and Treflys and Llystyn Gwyn, near Brynkir station, Caerns.]

d Report on the 60th annual meeting, at Carmarthen, 1906. [Includes notes on Llanstephan castle, Carmarthenshire, by J. Williams]

e Report on excavations at Coelbren [Brecon], by W. Ll. Morgan.

f Roman remains at Cwmbrwyn, Carmarthenshire, by J. Ward.

g Llanstephan castle.

h The pilgrims' church at Llanfihangel Abercowin [Carmarthenshire], by W. Davies.

i Notes on Eglwys Cymmyn, Parc-y-Ceryg Sanctaidd, and Llandawke, by G. G. T. Treherne.

j Carmarthen in early Norman times, by J. E. Lloyd.

k The Capel Mair stone [Llangeler, Carmarthenshire], by Sir J. Rhys.

l St. Peter's church, Carmarthen, by T. E. Brigstocke.

m Notes on the east window of the church of All Saints, Gresford, by E. A. Fishbourne.

n The early settlers of Carmarthen, by E. Anwyl.

728 Vol. 8.

a The early settlers of Anglesey, by E. Anwyl.

b Roman Cardiff, by J. Ward. [Contd. in vols. 13 and 14]

c Report of the 61st annual meeting, at Llangefni, 1907. [Includes notes on Llanbabo church.]

d A discovery of Roman coins on the Little Orme's Head, by W. Gardner.

e The Flemish bell of St. Nicholas at Nicholaston church, Gower, by G. E. Halliday.

f Excavations at Din Lligwy [Anglesey], by E. N. Baynes. [Contd. in vol. 85]

g Merddyn Gwyn barrow, Pentraeth [Anglesey], by H. Hughes.

h An island of the saints [Isle of Caldey, off Pembrokeshire], by W. D. Bushell.

i Antiquities on the sandhills at Merthyr Mawr, Glam., by M. Evanson.

j Glazed pebbles in an old building near Llanbedr, Merionethshire, by C. E. Breese.

k Tintern abbey, by J. G. Wood. [Contd. in vol. 9]

l The Bryngwyn tumuli [Flints.], by P. Stapleton. [Contd. in vol. 9]

m Monumental effigies, Pembrokeshire, by E. Laws and E. H. Edwards. [Contd. in vols. 9, 11, and 12]

n Berw [Anglesey].

o Ten days' tour through the Isle of Anglesea [*sic*], Dec. 1802, by Rev. John Skinner. [With notes by E. N. Baynes. Issued as supplement to vol. 8]

729 Vol. 9.

a Old Monmouth, by J. H. Matthews.

b The Skenfrith cope [preserved in the Roman Catholic church, Monmouth], by R. H. Morris.

c Inscription on the pillar of Eliseg, near Llangollen, by A. H. Sayce.

d Report of the 62nd annual meeting, at Monmouth, 1908. [Includes notes on Newland and Staunton churches, Glos.; Trelleck, Caerwent, White castle, and Skenfrith castle, Mon.; and Pembridge castle, Herefs.]

e A semi-subterranean columbarium, Llanthony, by I. Gardner.

f Notes on the alien Benedictine priory of St. Nicholas and St. John the Evangelist in Monkton, Pembroke, by E. Laws.

g The excavation of Lligwy cromlech, Anglesey, by E. N. Baynes.

h Exploration of Moel-y-Gaer, Bodfari [Flints.].

i Note on the discovery of pre-historic hearths at Swanlake [Pembrokeshire], by A. L. Leach.

j The Maen Pebyll, Mynydd Hiraethog, Denbighshire, by W. B. Halhed.

k The early settlers of Monmouth, by E. Anwyl.

l The Harfords of Bosbury [Herefs.], by Alice Harford.

m Excavation of two barrows at Ty'n-y-Pwll, Llanddyfnan, Anglesey, by E. N. Baynes.

n Wooden altars, with reference to the reputed wooden altar in the church at Llaneilian, Anglesey, by C. R. B. King.

o Find of Roman coins on the Little Orme, N. Wales, by W. S. Ogden. [Contd. in vol. 15]

p Chepstow castle and the barony of Striguil, by A. Morris.

q The shell-mounds on Laugharne Burrows, Carmarthenshire, by T. C. Cantrill.

r Roman building at Glasfryn, Tremadoc, Caerns., by C. E. Breese and E. Anwyl.

730 Vol. 10.

a Pen-y-Corddyn, near Abergele, by W. Gardner

b Report of the 63rd annual meeting, at Chester, 1909. [Includes notes on the cathedral and churches of St. John and St. Mary-on-the-hill, Chester, and Bunbury church]

c Isycoed, co. Denbigh, by A. N. Palmer.

d The hut-circles on Gateholm, Pembrokeshire, by T. C. Cantrill.

e The Sandbach crosses [Cheshire], by G. F. Browne.

f Y Garn Llwyd, erroneously called the Gaer Llwyd [a cromlech in Monmouthshire], by J. G. Wood.

g The family of De Braose, by W. H. Davey.

h Discovery of pre-historic burial-ground in Cardiganshire [Llanwenog], by E. L. Thomas. [Contd. in vol. 12]

i Llantilio Crossenny church [Mon.], by Sir H. M. Jackson.

j The charters of the city of Chester, by R. H. Morris.

k Roman roads in Cheshire, by Miss M. V. Taylor.

l The Scotti and Picti in the *Excidium Britanniae*, by A. W. Wade-Evans.

m Dolmens of the Channel Islands, by W. F. Bushell.

n Origin of the *Annales Cambriae*: the true date of St. David's death, by E. W. B. Nicholson.

731 Vol. 11.

a The Cistercian abbey of Cwm Hir [Radnorshire], by E. H. Day.

b The burial of Llewelyn ap Gruffydd [d. 1282], by R. H. Morris.

c Cil Ivor camp [Glam.], by W. Ll. Morgan.

d Recent excavations at Siamber Wen, near Dyserth, Flints., by K. D. Beste.

e An implement of crystalline quartz, from Freshwater West, Pembrokeshire, by A. L. Leach.

f Report of the 64th annual meeting, at Llandrindod Wells, 1910. [Includes notes on Llanbadarn Fawr church and Llanavan Fawr]

g Notes on some Radnorshire place-names, by E. Anwyl.

h The Saxones in the *Excidium Britanniae*, by A. W. Wade-Evans.

i The investiture of the Prince of Wales, by R. H. Morris.

j Pre-historic cooking-places in South Wales, by T. C. Cantrill and O. T. Jones.

k Amongst the Prescelly [stone] circles, by W. D. Bushell.

l Excavations, Roman station, Llandrindod Wells, by R. W. Thomas.

m *Anglia Wallia* (Queen's Remembrancer's Roll, Memoranda, 4 Eliz. Hilary, membrane 133). [An account of all Welsh harbours etc.]

n Pre-historic cooking-places in the Pembrokeshire and Carmarthenshire coasts, by A. L. Leach.

732 Vol. 12.

a Medieval house, Dyserth, Flints., by R. Cochrane.

b Pre-historic remains on the uplands of north Carnarvonshire, by W. B. Lowe.

c Certain fixed points in the pre-history of Wales, by B. Dawkins.

d Report on the 65th annual meeting, at Abergele, 1911. [Includes notes on Rhuddlan abbey and castle, and Bettws y Coed]

e Prehistoric remains on Penmaenmawr (known as Braich y Ddinas): report on the survey and excavations, by H. Hughes. [Contd. in 6th ser., vols. 13 and 15; 7th ser., vols. 2 and 3]

f Excavations at the Praetorium at Castell Collen [Llandrindod Wells] 1911, by H. Lewis.

g Pre-historic flint factory discovered at Aberystwyth, by R. Thomas.

h Roman roads in North Wales, by W. B. Halhed.

i Pre-historic remains, Llanbedr, Merionethshire, by L. D. Buxton.

j Notes on the spiral ornament in Wales, by R. H. Morris.

k Dyserth castle, by T. Edwards.

l Charles Heath of Monmouth, author, printer, and publisher [d. 1831], by W. Haines.

m The Price families of Plas Iolyn and Gilar [near Pentrevoelas, Denbighshire], by W. B. Lowe. [See also letter in vol. 14, Miscellanea, by T. Ll. Jones]

n The castle of Senghenydd [Glam.], by W. Ll. Morgan.

733 Vol. 13.

a Ewenny priory, or St. Michael of Ogmore, by St. C. Baddeley.

b Llewelyn ap Gruffydd [d. 1282], and the lordship of Glamorgan, by J. E. Lloyd.

c Report of the 66th annual meeting, at Cardiff, 1912. [Includes notes on Caerleon, Llantwit Major, and the castles of Caerphilly and Cardiff]

d Welsh archaeology and anthropology, by H. J. Fleure.

e Folk-speech of Monmouth and neighbourhood, by J. H. Matthews. [See also letter by I. Gardner in Miscellanea]

f Bacon Hole, Gower, by W. Ll. Morgan.

g Distribution of neolithic implements in northern Flintshire, by T. A. Glenn.

h Excavations in the ancient hill fort, Parc y Meirch Wood, Kinmel Park [Denbighshire], by W. Gardner.

i Pre-historic cooking places in Anglesey, by E. N. Baynes.

j Ancient Welsh measures of capacity, by A. N. Palmer.

k Military aspects of the Roman occupation of Caerleon, by A. Mackworth.

l Haverfordwest castle, by J. W. Phillips.

m Harlech castle, by H. Hughes.

n Excavation of tumuli in Eglwys Bach, Denbighshire, by W. Gardner.

o Carnarvon castle: reconstruction of the interior.

p Ancient glass in Dolwyddelan church, by H. Hughes.

q Three ancient inscriptions [on stones at Nevern, Pembrokeshire, and Rhydowen, Carmarthenshire], by Sir J. Rhys.

r Stone implements from soil-drifts and chipping-floors, etc. in south Pembroke, by A. L. Leach.

s Excavations at Kerry, Montgomeryshire, by F. S. Wright.

734 Vol. 14.

a Excavations at Castell Collen, Llandrindod Wells, by H. G. Evelyn-White.

b Antiquities of Wilts., by E. H. Goddard.

c The retreat of the Welsh from Wiltshire, by W. B. Dawkins.

d Report on the 67th annual meeting, at Devizes, 1913. [Includes notes on the Wansdyke, Avebury, Silbury hill, Edington church, Battlesbury camp, Winterbourne Stoke barrows, Stonehenge, Old Sarum, Devizes, and Bradford-on-Avon Saxon church]

e Excavations at Cae Gaer, Llangurig, by F. N. Price.

f Some place-names in the locality of St. Asaph, by J. Fisher.

g Exploration of neolithic station near Gwaenysgor, Flints., by T. A. Glenn.

h Recent discoveries at Clynnogfawr [Caerns.], by B. Stallybrass.

i Welsh materials for English history, by J. H. Matthews.

j The friars in Wales, by Ruth C. Easterling.

k 'Our Lady of Penrhys' [Ystradyfodwg, Glam.], by J. Ward.

l The lordship of Ruthin [Denbighshire]: its survey, with some extracts from the records, by J. Fisher.

m The family of De la Roche, by H. Owen.

735 Vol. 15.

a Haverfordwest in the civil war, by J. Phillips.

b Raglan castle, by I. Gardner.

c Prehistoric and historic remains at Dyserth castle, by T. A. Glenn.

d Robert Parry's diary [1559-1613].

e Llantwit Major, Glam., excavations, by J. W. Rodger.

f Flint chipping-floors in south-west Pembrokeshire, by T. C. Cantrill. [See also letter in Miscellanea]

g A budget of war letters two centuries old [1708-9, 1714, 1746, 1749, 1799].

h Wales in the time of Queen Elizabeth: *De presenti statu totius Walliae* [a tract written in the latter part of Elizabeth's reign], ed. J. Fisher.

i The St. Nicholas chambered tumulus, Glam., by J. Ward. [Contd. in vol. 16]

churches of Llangennith, Llanddewi, Port Eynon, and Llangyfelach]

**Archaeologia Cambrensis, 7th ser., vols. 1–8
(1921–8):**

741 Vol. 1.

a Problems of pre-historic chronology in Wales, by R. E. M. Wheeler.

b Excavations at Segontium [by A. G. K. Hayter for 1920, and R. E. M. Wheeler for 1921. Contd. in vols. 2 and 3 for 1922].

c The Scandinavian settlement of Cardiff, by D. R. Paterson.

d Pen y Gaer, near Llangollen.

e Druidism, by A. G. Edwards.

f Three monastic houses of South Wales [Whitland abbey, Carmarthenshire; the abbey of St. Dogmael and the priory of Haverfordwest, Pembrokeshire], by A. W. Clapham.

g St. Asaph cathedral, by E. W. Lovegrove.

h The ancient hill fort on Moel Fenlli, Denbighshire, by W. Gardner.

i 'Clede Mutha' [the mouth of the Clyde and not of the Cleddy at Milford Haven], by C. A. Seyler.

j Excavation of bronze-age tumulus, near Gorsedd, Holywell, Flints., by H. Williams.

k Funeral helmet and spurs of Archbishop John Williams [d. 1650] at Llandegai [Caerns.], by W. J. Hemp and V. Farquharson.

l Excavation of a megalithic tomb in Breconshire [at Ffostill near Talgarth], by C. E. Vulliamy. [Contd. in vol. 3]

m Report of the 75th annual meeting, at Ruthin, 1921. [Includes notes on Denbigh priory and castle; Dinorben hill fort, Parc y Meirch, Kimnel Park; Mold church; Hawarden church and castle; St. Peter's church, Ruthin; St. Winefride's well, Holywell; and Basingwerk abbey]

n St. Peter's church, Ruthin, by E. W. Lovegrove.

o The houseling pew in Rug chapel [Flints.], by I. Gardner.

p Ruthin corporation records: extracts transcribed by J. Fisher.

742 Vol. 2.

a Neolithic stone axes of Graig Lwyd, Penmaenmawr, by S. H. Warren.

b The pre-Norman settlement of Glamorgan, by D. R. Paterson.

c The register of Benedict, bishop of Bangor, 1408–17, transcribed by A. I. Pryce.

d The ancient hill fort known as Caer Drewyn, Merionethshire, by W. Gardner.

e An earthwork at Bryn Glas near Carnarvon, by R. E. M. Wheeler.

f Ithel Vychan [fl. 1301–23] of Halkyn [Flints.], and some of his descendants, by T. A. Glenn.

g The locality of the battle of Mynydd Carn, 1081, by Sir E. D. Jones.

h Notes on some early Welsh inscriptions, by R. A. S. Macalister.

i The Welsh woollen industry in the 16th and 17th cent., by Caroline A. J. Skeel. [Contd. for the 18th and 19th cent. in vol. 4. See also correspondence in vol. 4, Miscellanea]

j Haverfordwest priory: report on the excavations, 1922, by A. W. Clapham.

k Romano-British site at Rhostryfan, Caerns., by H. Williams. [Contd. in vol. 3]

l St. David's cathedral, by E. W. Lovegrove.

m The town seal of Haverfordwest, by W. J. Hemp.

n Heraldic tablets in Holywell church, by T. A. Glenn.

o Report of the 76th annual meeting, at Haverfordwest, 1922. [Includes notes on Haverfordwest castle and St. Mary's church; St. David's; and Nevern church]

743 Vol. 3.

a Painscastle [Radnorshire], and its story, by M. L. Dawson.

b Wales and the Avignon papacy, by J. R. Gabriel.

c The Benedictine priory of St. Mary, Cardiff, by R. H. D'Elboux.

d An ancient shell-heap near Maes-y-Garnedd, Merionethshire, by S. Smith and Annie S. Williams.

e Maen Pebyll long cairn [Mynydd Hiraethog, Denbighshire], by W. J. Hemp.

f Sarum manual in Hereford cathedral library, by J. Fisher.

g Oswestry as a link between England and Wales, by J. E. Lloyd.

h A Roman site in Pembrokeshire, by R. E. M. Wheeler.

i Problems of Welsh archaeology, by H. J. Fleure.

j A short study in Welsh genealogy: the lineage of the Rev. Griffith Jones [d. 1761], vicar of Llanddowror [Carmarthenshire], by G. T. Thomas.

k A tumulus at Garthbeibio, Mont., by R. E. M. Wheeler.

l Lleyn antiquities [Caerns.], by E. Davies.

m Pigmy flints found at Newport, Pembrokeshire, by R. Thomas.

n The tithe map of Dwygyfylchi [Caerns.], by I. E. Davies.

o Report of the 77th annual meeting, at Oswestry, 1923. [Includes notes on Montgomery castle and church, Powis castle, Welshpool church, Llanrhaiadr ym Mochnant church, the records of Chirk, co. Denbigh (14th–16th cent.), and Meifod church]

p Oswestry charters and corporation plate, by R. Ll. Kenyon.

744 Vol. 4.

a Early charters of Swansea and Gower, by C. A. Seyler. [Contd. in vol. 5]

b Pre-historic remains in N. Carnarvonshire, by W. B. Love.

c A cave at Craig-y-Nos, Abercrave, Brecon, by R. H. D'Elboux.

d Llanfaes friary [Anglesey], and its mystery monuments, by C. R. Hand.

e Exchequer tallies in the National Museum of Wales, by J. R. Gabriel.

f Berain in co. Denbigh, by H. H. Hughes.

g The Cistercian abbey of Cwm Hir [Radnorshire], immediately before the dissolution, by E. H. Day.

h Llanfilo (St. Beilio), Brecon, by W. D. Carỏe.

i Rare celts from Wales, by W. J. Hemp.

j Excavations at Haverfordwest priory, by E. A. R. Rahbula.

k Arrow stones and other incised stones in north Carnarvonshire and north Denbighshire, by W. B. Lowe.

l The chancel of Beaumaris church, by C. R. Hand.

m A polished stone celt from the neighbourhood of the Llandegla sepulchral caves [Denbighshire], by H. P. Lewis.

745 Vol. 5.

a Two beakers of the early bronze age recently discovered in South Wales; with a record of the distribution of beaker-pottery in England and Wales, by C. Fox.

b Two studies in the history of the diocese of Bangor: (i) the rectory of Llandyrnog [Denbighshire], 17th cent., (ii) the appropriation of the Llandinam [Mont.] comportions, 1683–5, by T. Richards.

c Two effigies in Montgomery church, by W. J. Hemp.

d The chapel traditionally attributed to St. Patrick, Whitesand Bay, Pembrokeshire, by A. B. Badger and F. Green.

e The roads of North Wales, 1750–1850, by A. H. Dodd.

f Pre-Norman cross and cross-base in Diserth church, by H. H. Hughes.

g Notes on four sepulchral vessels of the bronze age from North Wales, by C. Fox.

h A 'late Celtic' bronze mirror from Wales, by C. Fox.

i The vanished tombs of Brecon cathedral, by Gwenllian E. F. Morgan.

j A burial place of dwellers in the Upper Taf valley, near Whitland, Carmarthenshire, in the bronze age, by C. Fox.

k Rhos and Rhufoniog [Denbighshire] pedigrees, by G. P. Jones.

l The Roman fort at Caerhun, Caerns., by W. Gardner.

m Dinas, Llanfairfechan: excavations, by H. H. Hughes and W. B. Lowe.

n St. David and Glastonbury, by A. W. Wade-Evans.

o Excavations at Castell Taliorum, St. Illtyd, Llanhilleth, Mon., by T. Lewis.

p Medieval place-names, by A. Jones.

q Llandaff cathedral: a bibliography *raisonné*, by H. M. Thompson.

r Canoe discovered in Llangorse lake [Brecon], by C. Fox.

s Report of the 79th annual meeting, at Llandeilo Fawr, **1925**. [Includes notes on Dynevor castle, Brecon cathedral, and the Gaer, Brecon; Llandilo church, and Talley abbey]

746 Vol. 6.

a A bronze age barrow on Kilpaison Burrows, Rhoscrowther, Pembrokeshire, by C. Fox.

b The carving on Maen Achwyfan [cross, Flints.], by H. H. Hughes.

c The Ysceifiog circle and barrow, Flintshire, by C. Fox.

d The Nab Head chipping floor [St. Brides, Pembrokeshire], by J. P. Gordon-Williams.

e The old poor-law in North Wales, by A. H. Dodd.

f Offa's dyke: a field survey, by C. Fox. [Contd. in vols. 7–8, and 84–86]

g Peculiar east windows in some Anglesey churches, by G. G. Holme.

h Native hill-forts in North Wales and their defences, by W. Gardner.

i Excavations on the site of the Roman fort at Caerhun, by P. K. B. Reynolds. [Contd. in vols. 7, 84–86]

j Welsh Celtic bells, by J. Fisher.

k Early bronze hanging-bowl found at Cerrig-y-Druidion [Denbighshire], by E. Davies.

l Bardsey island and its saints, by J. Fisher.

m Early bronze age finds in the Dyfi basin [Darowen, Mont.], by I. C. Peate.

n Brychan, by G. P. Jones.

o Lead coffin found at Rhuddgaer, Anglesey, by H. H. Hughes.

p Report on the excavation of the chapel of St. Justinian, St. David's, by E. J. Boake.

q Report of the 80th annual meeting, at Pwllheli, 1926. [Includes notes on Clynnog church, Caerns.]

747 Vol. 7.

a The Capel Garmon chambered long cairn, by W. J. Hemp.

b A settlement of the early iron age (La Tène I sub period) on Merthyr Mawr Warren, Glam., by C. Fox.

c A La Tène I brooch from Wales [Merthyr Mawr], with notes on the typology and distribution of these brooches in Britain, by C. Fox.

d Llanrhychwyn church [Caerns.], and its painted windows, by H. H. Hughes.

e Four Roman bronze vessels found at Glyn Dyfrdwy, co. Denbigh, by W. Gardner.

f Further excavations at the Graig Lwyd neolithic stone axe factory [Penmaenmawr], by H. G. O. Kendall.

g Excavations on the Kerry hills, Mont., by J. E. Daniel, E. E. Evans, and T. Lewis.

h Kenfig castle, by A. J. Richard.

i Casting of bells at Whitford, for Caerwys church, Flints. [1662–8], by D. H. Williams.

j Abbey Dore church, Herefs., by R. Paul.

k Road-books of Wales; with a catalogue, 1775–1850, by Sir G. Fordham.

l Excavations of the Powysland Club at the Forden Gaer [Mont.], by F. N. Pryce and T. D. Pryce. [Contd. in vols. 84 and 85]

m Castle of Deudraeth [Merionethshire], by T. E. Morris.

n Church of Kilpeck, Herefs., by I. Gardner.

o Caerleon excavations, by V. E. Nash-Williams. [Contd. in vol. 84]

p Pembrokeshire church presentments [1684], by G. E. Evans.

q Report of the 81st meeting, at Hereford, 1927. [Includes notes on Hereford cathedral, vicars' college, and Wye bridge; Leominster priory church; Pembridge church; and Kilpeck church and castle]

748 Vol. 8.

a The Caerleon amphitheatre: a summary, by Tessa V. Wheeler.

b Giraldus Cambrensis: *Speculum Duorum*, by W. S. Davies.

c Corston beacon: an early bronze age cairn in south Pembrokeshire, by C. Fox.

d Distribution maps and early movements into Britain, and their relation to legendary history, by S. Harris.

e 14th cent. stoup belonging to St. Mary's church, Brecon, by Gwenllian E. F. Morgan.

f Rice and Thomas, sons of John ap Rice Wynn [d. 1577?], of Ceirchiog, Anglesey, by C. Gwyn. [Contd. in vol. 85, Miscellanea]

g A La Tène shield from Moel Hiraddug, Flintshire, by W. J. Hemp.

h Ancient inscriptions of Wales, by R. A. S. Macalister.

i Landscape and history in mid-Glamorgan, by H. J. Randall.

j Early bronze age burial from Stormy down, Pyle, Glam., by W. F. Grimes.

k A beaker-burial from Ludchurch, Pembrokeshire, by W. F. Grimes.

l Report of the 82nd annual meeting, at Port Talbot, 1928. [Includes notes on Margam abbey]

Archaeologia Cambrensis (*continuing the above*), vols. 84–88 (1929–33):

749 Vol. 84.

a Ancient monuments of the Isle of Man, by P. M. C. Kermode.

b Ancient inscriptions of the south of England, by R. A. S. Macalister.

c North Wales coal industry during the industrial revolution, by A. H. Dodd.

d Cinerary urns found at Plâs Penrhyn, Anglesey, by E. N. Baynes.

e Two Welsh-Manx Christmas customs, by J. Fisher.

f Margam abbey, by H. E. David.

g Burial mounds in the parish of Llanboidy, Carmarthenshire, by W. F. Grimes.

h Report of the 83rd annual meeting, at Douglas, I.o.M., 1929. [Includes notes on Kirk Maughold]

750 Vol. 85.

a The romance of place-names, by J. J. Kreen.

b Notes on the political history of early Powys, by G. P. Jones.

c The Roman legionary fortress at Caerleon: report on the excavations, by C. Hawkes. [Contd. in vols. 86–88 by V. E. Nash-Williams]

d Ancient churches of Anglesey, by H. H. Hughes.

e Crank yn How, an early Christian and Viking site at Lezayre, Isle of Man, by J. R. Bruce and W. Cubbon.

f A beaker burial from Llannon, Carmarthenshire, by I. C. Peate.

g Beuno sant [a translation of *Buchedd Beuno*, the life of St. Beuno], by A. W. Wade-Evans.

h The fort of Dinas Emrys, by C. E. Breese.

i Church of S. Cybi, Holyhead, by H. H. Hughes.

j Excavations of a house-site on Gateholm, Pembrokeshire, by T. C. Lethbridge and H. E. David.

k Four early Christian stones from South Wales, by V. E. Nash-Williams.

l The fortified hill-settlement at Llanmelin, Mon., by V. E. Nash-Williams.

m Report on the 84th annual meeting, at Menai Bridge, Anglesey, 1930. [Includes notes on Beaumaris church and castle, Caer Leb, Plas Berw (an early 17th cent. house), and Llangadwaladr church]

751 Vol. 86.

a Find of gold nobles at Borth, Cardigans., by G. C. Brooke.

b The Levelinus inscription at Pentrefoelas, by R. A. S. Macalister.

c Geological report on Uriconium, by T. C. Cantrill.

d Bonedd y Saint, E. [*The descent of the Saints*, copy written 1485], by A. W. Wade-Evans.

e Aberystwyth, by J. E. Lloyd.

f Excavations at Caerwent, by W. F. Grimes.

g The chambered cairn of Bryn Celli Ddu [Anglesey], by W. J. Hemp.

h The smaller cairn at Bryn Celli Ddu, by R. S. Newall.

i Report of the 85th annual meeting, at Lampeter, 1931. [Includes notes on Strata Florida abbey and Llanbadarn Fawr church]

752 Vol. 87.

a The background of history in north-eastern Wales, by F. J. North.

b A new inscribed stone found at Barmouth, by B. H. St. J. O'Neil.

c The Nantgarw pottery and its products: an examination of the site, by I. J. Williams.

d Craig Gurtheyrn hill fort, Llanfihangel ar Arth, Carmarthenshire, by W. Gardner.

e The Llancarfan charters, by A. W. Wade-Evans.

f Church of S. Mary Magdalene, Gwaenysgar, Flints., by H. H. Hughes.

g Surface flint industries around Solva, Pembrokeshire, by W. F. Grimes.

h The erroneous position of Llandovery on 16th cent. maps of the British Isles, by R. A. Pelham.

i The chancel arch, Llangristiolus church, Anglesey, by G. G. Holme.

j The Ogmore castle inscription, by I. Williams.

k Pedigree roll of Sir William Meredith of Stansty, 1604, by W. J. Hemp.

l Excavation of a hut site at Parc Dinmor, Penmon, Anglesey, by C. W. Phillips.

m Llanerfyl [Mont.], reliquary and reredos, by H. H. Hughes.

n Kitchen-middens on Giltar Point, near Tenby, by A. L. Leach.

o Ffridd Faldwyn hill-fort, near Montgomery, by W. Gardner.

p 'Castell Odo' [near Aberdaron, Caerns.], by C. E. Breese.

q Aberdovey and the Spanish invasion in 1597, by A. S. Davies.

r Report of the 86th annual meeting, at Newtown, 1932. [Includes notes on Llanwnog church and Montgomery castle]

753 Vol. 88.

a Early Welsh line and mezzotint engravers, by I. J. Williams.

b An investigation into the problem of the sand dune areas on the South Wales coast, by L. S. Higgins.

c Pottery from the Lligwy burial chamber, Anglesey, by S. Piggott.

d Ancient measures of capacity, by A. Jones.

e Plas Ucha, Llangar, Merioneth, by L. Monroe.

f Priory Farm cave, Monkton, Pembrokeshire, by W. F. Grimes, with a report on the human and animal remains by L. F. Cowley.

g The Roman west wall at Caerwent, by V. E. Nash-Williams.

h The chambered tomb of Pant-y-Saer, Anglesey, by W. L. Scott.

i Stone implements from the Nab Head, St. Bride's, Pembrokeshire, by A. L. Leach.

j Early iron age hill-fort at Llanmelin, near Caerwent, with a note on the distribution of hill-forts and other earthworks in Wales and the Marches, by V. E. Nash-Williams.

k Report of the 87th annual meeting, at Cardiff, 1933. [Includes notes on Cardiff castle, Llandaff cathedral, Caerphilly castle, Llandough cross, Llancarfan church, and the church of St. Woollos, Mon.]

Supplements to Transactions:

754 Parochialia: being a summary of answers to 'Parochial Queries, in order to a geographical dictionary, etc., of Wales' issued by Edward Lhwyd [1660–1709], ed. R. H. Morris. 1909–11.

755 Original documents: 1: Add. Roll 26596, Brit. Mus., the account of Sir Edward Stradelynge, chamberlain of South Wales for 1431–3. 2: Add. Charters 7198, the condition of the royal castles in North and South Wales, 14 Ed. III [1341]. 3: Add. Roll 26595, the account of William de Ffrodesham, chamberlain of North Wales, Mich. 17 Rich. II to Mich. 18 Rich. II [1393–4]. 1913–15.

756 Tours in Wales (1804–13) by Richard Fenton, ed. J. Fisher. 1917.

757 *Menevia Sacra* [a description and history of St. David's cathedral], by Edward Yardley, S.T.B., archdeacon of Cardigan, 1739–70, ed. F. Green. 1927.

CAMBRIDGE ANTIQUARIAN SOCIETY

Founded 1839, to collect and print information relative to the history and antiquities of the university, county, and town of Cambridge.

Proceedings, with communications made to the Society, vols. 10–33 (1901–33):

758 Vol. 10.

a Astbury the potter [d. 1743] and Voyez the modeller [fl. *c.* 1769], by J. W. L. Glaisher.

b The Icknield way, by W. H. Bullock-Hall.

c Two series of paintings formerly at Worcester priory, by M. R. James.

d A tinder-box attributed to Shakespeare, by C. E. Sayle.

e Seals of the commonalty and of the mayor of Cambridge, by T. D. Atkinson.

f Sculptures on the south portal of the abbey church at Malmesbury, by M. R. James.

g Sculptures at Lincoln cathedral, by M. R. James.

h Note on a supposed Romano-British settlement at Odsey, by H. G. Fordham.

i The potter's field at Horningsea, with a comparative notice of the kilns and furnaces found in the neighbourhood, by T. McK. Hughes.

j Some indications of a Roman potter's field near Jesus College, by T. McK. Hughes.

k Exhibition of dated pieces of Nottingham stoneware and sgraffiato ware, by J. W. L. Glaisher.

l The sepulchral brass of St. Henry of Finland [d. *c.* 1158], by M. R. James.

m St. Urith of Chittlehampton, by M. R. James.

n Excavations in the War Ditches near Cherry Hinton, by T. McK. Hughes. [Another article on these ditches by the same occurs later in this vol.]

o Some earthworks at Boxworth and Knapwell, by T. McK. Hughes.

p Ancient horse-shoes, by T. McK. Hughes.

q St. Mary's church, Swaffham Prior, by C. P. Allix.

r Arbury [earthwork], by T. McK. Hughes. [Another article by the same occurs in vol. 11]

s Work done to the library of Exeter cathedral in 1412 and 1413, by J. W. Clark.

t Two pieces of furniture in Exeter cathedral, formerly used for the protection of books, by J. W. Clark.

u University wills at Peterborough, by C. J. B. Gaskoin.

v Place-names of Huntingdonshire, by W. W. Skeat.

w A charter relating to Anglesey abbey, by J. E. Foster.

x The chapel of the hospital of St. John, Duxford (Whittlesford Bridge), by C. E. Sayle.

y Mortuary roll of the abbess of Lillechurch, Kent, by C. E. Sayle.

z Two wheel-desks: the one in the church of S. Nicholas, Great Yarmouth; the other in the Bibliothèque de l'Arsenal, Paris, by J. W. Clark.

aa A description of the cast room of the university library, Cambridge, as built by Bishop Rotheram, written by William Cole, M.A., in 1759, by J. W. Clark.

bb Apostle spoons, by H. D. Catling.

cc Exhibition of objects found in or near Barrington [dating from prehistoric to medieval times], by J. W. E. Conybeare.

dd Documents relating to the dissolution of the monastery of Thornton Curtis in co. Lincoln left by the Rev. Charles Parkyn to Pembroke College, Cambridge, written out and abstracted by E. H. Minns.

759 Vol. 11.

a Iter V and Iter IX of Antonine as seen from Fowlmere, by A. C. Yorke.

b Some English verses written in a 15th cent. service-book, with a paraphrase and notes, by J. W. Clark.

c On charitable foundations in the university called chests; with a transcript and translation of the deed of foundation and statutes of the earliest of these, the Neel Chest, 1344, by J. W. Clark.

d Cambridgeshire maps: annotated list of the pre-survey maps of the county, 1579–1800, by H. G. Fordham.

e Ickleton church and priory, by A. R. Goddard.

f An Elizabethan bushel measure, by W. B. Redfern.

g Survey of the King's Ditch at Cambridge in 1629, by T. D. Atkinson.

h Some consecration crosses in East Anglian churches, by T. D. Atkinson.

i Hobson's connection with the so-called Hobson's watercourse, by J. E. Foster.

j A village tragedy of fifty years ago [in which Abraham Green was killed by Nehemiah Perry, of Strethall, Essex, in 1849], by G. Wherry.

k Loggan's *Habitus Academici*, by H. D. Catling.

l A badge of the Cambridge Volunteers of 1798 belonging to Mr. J. G. Mortlock, by J. E. Foster.

m A late Roman settlement near Somersham, Hunts., by J. C. F. Fryer and G. L. Keynes.

n The shambles at Shepton Mallet, by F. J. Allen.

o Cambridgeshire maps, by H. G. Fordham. [Contd. in vol. 12]

p The Norman origin of Cambridge castle, by W. H. St. J. Hope.

q A biography of John Bowtell, 1753–1813; and of John Bowtell his nephew, 1777–1855, by A. B. Gray.

r Some ancient trenches and interments near Shepreth, by T. McK. Hughes.

s The superficial deposits under Cambridge, and their influence upon the distribution of the colleges, by T. McK. Hughes.

t On the section seen and the objects found during excavations on the site of the old Bird Bolt hotel, by T. McK. Hughes.

u Notes on the proctor's halberd and other insignia, by W. L. H. Duckworth.

v Some old playing-cards [probably 16th cent. French] found in Trinity College, by W. M. Fletcher. [Another article by the same, on more playing-cards found in Cambridge, occurs in vol. 18]

w Account of a palaeolithic site in Ipswich, by Nina F. Layard.

760 Vol. 12.

a Notes on the gold armilla found in Grunty Fen, together with Mr. Isaac Deck's original account of its discovery, by A. von Hügel.

b The Round Moat [British earthwork] at Fowlmere, by A. C. Yorke.

c Excavations in King's Lane [Cambridge], by T. McK. Hughes.

d 14th cent. wall-painting in Lolworth church, representing the incredulity of St. Thomas, by G. M. Benton.

e Rings under the eaves of old houses [used in connection with fire-hooks], by G. E. Wherry.

f Two book covers, with chains, found in the tower of St. Benedict's church, Cambridge, by J. W. Clark.

g Stone coffins and skeletons discovered at Thetford, Norfolk, by G. M. Benton.

h A wall-painting in Babraham church, by T. D. Gray.

i Excavations at Earith Bulwarks, by G. L. Keynes and H. G. Evelyn-White.

j Skeletons recently found at the 'war ditches', Cherry-Hinton, by F. G. Walker.

k Contents of a tumulus excavated at Lord's Bridge, near Cambridge, by F. G. Walker.

l Rood screens in Cambridgeshire, by F. B. Bond. [Contd. in vol. 13]

m Report on the excavations at Barton [earthwork], by F. G. Walker.

n A tumulus recently explored on Newmarket heath, by C. P. Allix and T. McK. Hughes.

761 Vol. 13.

a The corrupt spelling of Old English names, by W. W. Skeat.

b Old houses in Cambridge [with particular reference to

Barnwell priory and the School of Pythagoras], by T. D. Atkinson.

c History of a site in Senate House Yard with some notes on the occupiers, by J. W. Clark and J. E. Foster.

d Hoard of [late Celtic and Romano-British] metal found at Santon Downham, Suffolk, by R. A. Smith.

e Early university property, by H. P. Stokes.

f The connection of the church of Chesterton with the abbey of Vercelli, by J. E. Foster.

g Some notable church towers of Cambridgeshire and their relation to the principal towers of England, by F. J. Allen.

h An ancestor's escape from France after the revocation of the Edict of Nantes, by C. P. Allix. [An account of the establishment in England of Pierre Allix, 1641–1717, of Alençon, canon and treasurer of Salisbury cathedral]

i The shops at the west end of Great St. Mary's church, Cambridge, by G. J. Gray.

j Four ms. books of accounts kept by Joseph Mead, B.D., fellow of Christ's College, with his pupils between 1614 and 1633, by J. Peile.

k Ancient footgear, by W. B. Redfern.

l Greek coins and Syrian arrowhead dug up in a Roman cemetery at Godmanchester, by F. G. Walker.

m The Zodiac club [founded by members of the university in 1725], by R. Bowes.

762 Vol. 14.

a Hair and wig powdering from early days, by W. B. Redfern.

b Human bones found on the site of the Augustine friary, Bene't Street, Cambridge, by W. I. Pocock and W. L. H. Duckworth.

c The problem as to changes in the course of the Cam since Roman times, by W. Cunningham.

d The ship in the windows of King's College chapel, Cambridge, by H. H. Brindley and A. H. Moore.

e Grantchester and Cambridge [a study in etymology], by W. W. Skeat.

f The ford and bridge of Cambridge, by A. Gray.

g Roman roads into Cambridge, by F. G. Walker.

h The old mills of Cambridge, by H. P. Stokes.

i Notes on an ancient seal [found near Anglesey priory, Bottisham, and probably owned by Master Lawrence de St. Nicholas, fl. 1190–1244] presented in 1910 to the Society by Edward Hailstone.

j Notes on two bronze pins recently found in and near Cambridge, by F. G. Walker.

763 Vol. 15.

a The ship in the St. Christopher window in Thaxted church, with remarks on early methods of reefing sails, by H. H. Brindley.

b The late survival of a Celtic population in East Anglia, by A. Gray.

c The Wandlebury legend [first told by Gervase of Tilbury in the 13th cent., later associated with Gogmagog], by A. Gray.

d Recently discovered neolithic site at Gamlingay, Cambs., by F. G. Walker.

e Cambridge parish workhouses, by H. P. Stokes.

f Some consecration crosses [in Exeter cathedral and Glastonbury abbey], by T. D. Atkinson.

g The sign of the Cromwell Arms, Ely, by T. D. Atkinson.

h Inn signs painted by Richard Hopkins Leach [d. 1851], by T. D. Atkinson.

i Excavations in the tumuli at Bourn, Cambs., 1909, by F. G. Walker.

j Excavations at Magdalene College, Cambridge, 1910, by F. G. Walker.

k Excavations near Latham Road, Trumpington, by F. G. Walker.

l Cambridgeshire doctors in the olden time, by W. M. Palmer.

m A village [Fowlmere] in the making, by A. C. Yorke.

764 Vol. 16.

a The origin of St. Mary's gild in connection with Corpus Christi College, Cambridge, by J. P. Rushe.

b Church spires of Cambridgeshire, by F. J. Allen.

c The earliest inventory of Corpus Christi College, by M. R. James.

d Roman and Saxon remains from Grange Road, Cambridge, by F. G. Walker.

e Report on human remains from Hyning, Westmld., by W. L. Duckworth.

f College dons, country clergy, and university coachmen, by W. M. Palmer. [From Cambridgeshire probate records at Peterborough, with an account of these records, and extracts from 16th cent. inventories, especially those relating to private libraries]

765 Vol. 17.

a Roman pottery kilns at Horningsea, Cambs., by F. G. Walker.

b The reformation of the corporation of Cambridge, July 1662, by W. M. Palmer.

c Mediaeval and 16th cent. ships in English churches, by H. H. Brindley.

766 Vol. 18.

a Flints [their formation and types], by T. McK. Hughes.

b Ships in the Cambridge 'Life of the Confessor' [i.e. the 13th cent. ms. known as *La Estoire de Seint Aedward le Rei*], by H. H. Brindley.

767 Vol. 19.

a Objects found in the King's Ditch under the Masonic Hall, by T. McK. Hughes.

b The maker of the iron gates at Clare College [1713–14], by J. R. Wardale.

c Notes on Cambridgeshire witchcraft, by Catherine E. Parsons.

d Medieval graffiti, especially in the eastern counties, by G. G. Coulton.

768 Vol. 20.

a Wayside crosses in Cambridge, by H. P. Stokes.

b The Cambridge bellmen, by H. P. Stokes.

c Cambridgeshire materials for the history of agriculture, by W. Cunningham.

d Arretine fragments in Cambridgeshire (Barrington and Foxton), by F. J. Haverfield.

e Roman and Saxon antiquities found near Kettering, by F. R. G. Hief.

f English Gothic foliage sculpture, by S. Gardner.

g Animals in mediaeval sculpture, by G. C. Druce.

h Notes on the hearth taxes for Cambridge, 1664 and 1674, by E. Powell.

i Dr. Dale's visits to Cambridge, 1722–38, by T. McK. Hughes.

j Early clay tobacco-pipes found near Barton Road, Cambridge, by H. Scott.

769 Vol. 21.

a The 12th cent. *pulpitum* or roodloft formerly in the cathedral church of Ely; with some notes on similar screens in English cathedral and monastic churches, by Sir W. St. J. Hope.

b Ancient church bells in Cambridge, by A. H. F. Boughey.

c The muniments of King's College, by J. Saltmarsh.

d The Barnwell canons and the papal court at Avignon, by J. M. Gray. [On the attempt of Simon de Sagio to secure the priorate, 1349]

e Fenland waterways, past and present: South Level district, by G. Fowler.

f Excavations in the bed of the Old Cam at Quaveney (Rollers Lode), by T. C. Lethbridge and G. Fowler.

g Huts of the Anglo-Saxon period, by T. C. Lethbridge and C. F. Tebbutt. [On huts at St. Neots and at Waterbeach and Mildenhall]

h Anglo-Saxon burials at Soham, Cambs., by T. C. Lethbridge.

i The Stokes and Hailstone mss. [in the Society's library], by W. M. Palmer.

Octavo series, nos. 34–52:

782 No. 34. Christ Church, Canterbury. 1: Chronicle of John Stone, monk of Christ Church, 1415–71. 2: Lists of the deans, priors and monks of Christ Church monastery. Ed. and comp. W. G. Searle. 1902.

783 No. 35. Churchwardens' accounts of St. Mary the Great, Cambridge, 1504–1635, ed. J. E. Foster. 1905.

784 No. 36. Place-names of Cambridgeshire, by W. W. Skeat. P. 1901. [2nd edn. 1911]

785 No. 37. Calendar of the feet of fines relating to the county of Huntingdon levied in the king's court, 1194–1603, ed. G. J. Turner. 1913.

786 No. 38. Verses formerly inscribed on twelve windows in the choir of Canterbury cathedral, reprinted from the ms., with introd. and notes by M. R. James. 1901.

787 No. 39. Cambridge gild records, ed. Mary Bateson, with preface by W. Cunningham. 1903.

788 No. 40. Annals of Gonville and Caius College, by J. Caius, ed. J. Venn. 1904.

789 No. 41. The chaplains and chapel of the university of Cambridge, 1256–1568, by H. P. Stokes. 1906.

790 No. 42. Place-names of Bedfordshire, by W. W. Skeat. 1906.

791 No. 43. The riot at the great gate of Trinity College, Feb. 1610/11, by J. W. Clark. 1906.

792 No. 44. Outside the Trumpington gates before Peterhouse was founded: a chapter in the intimate history of mediaeval Cambridge, by H. P. Stokes. 1908.

793 No. 45. Esquire bedells of the university of Cambridge, from the 13th to the 20th cent., by H. P. Stokes. 1911.

794 No. 46. Place-names of Suffolk, by W. W. Skeat. 1913.

795 No. 47. Outside the Barnwell gate, by H. P. Stokes. 1915.

796 No. 48. Vetus liber archidiaconi Eliensis [relating to the archdeacon's office and duties], ed. C. L. Feltoe and E. H. Minns. 1917.

797 No. 49. Mediaeval hostels of the university of Cambridge (with a special history of Borden Hostel), together with chapters on Le Glomery Hall and the master of Glomery, by H. P. Stokes. 1924.

798 No. 50. A history of the Wilbraham parishes (Great and Little) in the county of Cambridge, by H. P. Stokes. 1926.

799 No. 51. Index to Proceedings, vols. 9–24, including subjects and authors of quarto and octavo publications, 1895–1922. P. 1927.

800 No. 52. Notes on Bodleian mss. relating to Cambridge, Pt. i: Town and university, by F. Madan. Pt. ii: County, by W. M. Palmer. 1931.

Quarto new series, nos. 1–4:

801 No. 1. The dual origin of the town of Cambridge, by A. Gray. P. 1908.

802 No. 2. King's Hostel, Trinity College, Cambridge, by W. D. Caröe. P. 1909.

803 No. 3. Recent excavations in Anglo-Saxon cemeteries in Cambridgeshire and Suffolk: a report comp. and illustrated by T. C. Lethbridge. 1931.

804 No. 4. The School of Pythagoras (Merton Hall), Cambridge, by J. M. Gray. 1932.

Other publications:

805 Charters of the borough of Cambridge, ed. for the council of the borough of Cambridge and the Society by F. W. Maitland and Mary Bateson. 1901.

806 Luard memorial series: records of the university. Vols. ii–iii, ed. Mary Bateson. 1903. [Vol. ii: Grace book B, pt. 1, containing proctors' accounts etc., 1488–1511. Vol. iii: Grace book B, pt. 2, 1511–44. Vol. i: Grace book A, 1454–88, was published in 1897; subsequent vols., published by the Cambridge University Press, are not associated with the name of Dr. Luard]

807 Catalogue of the first exhibition of portraits in the Society's collection and of Cambridge caricatures to 1840, held in the Fitzwilliam Museum. P. 1908.

808 [Map of] Roman roads in Cambridgeshire, by F. G. Walker. 1 sheet. [1910?]

809 Exhibition of Stuart and Cromwellian relics, and articles of interest connected with the Stuart period, at the Guildhall, Cambridge, 1911. [1911].

810 Cambridge under Queen Anne; illustrated by memoir of Ambrose Bonwicke [d. 1714] and diaries of Francis Burman [1702] and Zacharias Conrad von Uffenbach [1710], ed. with notes by J. E. B. Mayor, preface by M. R. James. 1911.

811 Monumental inscriptions and coats of arms from Cambridgeshire, chiefly as recorded by John Layer, about 1632, and William Cole, between 1742 and 1782, ed. W. M. Palmer. 1932.

CAMBRIDGE HISTORY SOCIETY

Founded 1922, to promote historical study and research and intercourse among historical students in Cambridge.

Cambridge Historical Journal, vols. 1–4 (1923–34):

812 Vol. 1.

a A lost Caesarea, by J. B. Bury. [On the provincial divisions of Roman Britain]

b Peacemaking, old and new, by Sir E. Satow. [With additional note]

c The miller and the baker: a note on commercial transition, 1770–1837, by C. R. Fay.

d The growth of an agrarian proletariat, 1688–1832: a statistical note, by J. H. Clapham.

e Russia and *The Times* in 1863 and 1873, by W. F. F. Grace.

f Plea rolls of the medieval county courts, by H. Jenkinson.

g The resignation of Lord Palmerston in 1853: extracts from unpublished letters of Queen Victoria and Lord Aberdeen, by B. K. Martin.

h Note on modern diplomatic, colonial, and other records at present available for study at Cambridge, by H. W. V. Temperley.

i The marshalsy of the eyre, by Helen M. Cam. [With additional note]

j British policy in the publication of diplomatic documents under Castlereagh and Canning, by C. K. Webster and H. W. V. Temperley.

k The Eastern crisis of 1840: extracts from the unpublished papers of Lord John Russell, by G. P. Gooch.

l Lord Elgin in India, 1862–3, by J. L. Morison.

m Tithe surveys as a source of agrarian history, by J. H. Clapham.

n Some additions to the ms. records of Cambridge, by H. W. V. Temperley. [With additional note. Contd. in vol. 2]

o The editorial methods of Sir Adolphus Ward. 1: The Cambridge Modern History, by Sir S. Leathes. 2: The Cambridge History of British Foreign Policy, 1922–3, by G. P. Gooch.

p Adam Smith's project of an empire, by E. A. Benians.

813 Vol. 2.

a The English wool trade in the reign of Edward IV, by Eileen Power.

b Edmund Burke and the origins of the theory of nationality, by A. B. C. Cobban.

c The diary of a country gentleman [Sir John Knatchbull] in 1688, by P. C. Vellacott.

d John de Warenne and the *quo warranto* proceedings in 1279, by G. Lapsley.

e Edward I's exercise of the right of presentation to benefices as shown by the patent rolls, by R. A. R. Hartridge.

f The distribution of assignment in the treasurer's receipt roll, Michaelmas, 1346–65, by A. Steel.

g The late Professor J. B. Bury. 1: An impression, by J. P. Whitney. 2: His views on the science of history, with a recent letter on personal bias in the writing of history.

h The legal status of markets, by L. F. Salzman.

i The effect of Becket's murder on papal authority in England, by Z. N. Brooke.

j Note on the origin of Lord John Russell's despatch of Oct. 16, 1839, on the tenure of Crown offices in the colonies, by J. R. M. Butler.

k Canada and the repeal of the corn laws, by D. L. Burn.

l Settlement and removal in Cambridgeshire, 1622–1834, by Ethel M. Hampson.

m The law of nations and the common law of England: a study of 7 Anne, cap. 12, by E. R. Adair.

n Lord Granville's unpublished memorandum on foreign policy, 1852, by H. Temperley.

814 Vol. 3.

a *Acta episcoporum* [12th cent.], by F. M. Stenton.

b Appropriation of parish churches during the reign of Edward III, by Kathleen Wood-Legh.

c Capitalism and the decline of the English gilds, by T. H. Marshall.

d British West India commerce as a factor in the Napoleonic war, by J. Holland Rose.

e Anglo-Russian relations, 1815–40, by C. W. Crawley.

f The first complete exploration of Hudson's Bay: Pierre Esprit Radisson and Médard Chouard Groseilliers, by Irene M. Harper.

g The duel between Castlereagh and Canning in 1809, by C. K. Webster and H. Temperley. [With an additional note]

h Unpublished letters of Wellington, July–Aug. 1812, by I. J. Rousseau.

i Col. Campbell's report on Egypt in 1840, with Lord Palmerston's comments, by F. S. Rodkey.

j China, England and Russia in 1860, by T. S. Tsiang.

k The customary poor-law of three Cambridgeshire manors, by Frances M. Page.

l The office of receiver-general on the estates of King's College, by J. Saltmarsh.

m A Hungarian magnate [Count Stephen Széchenyi the elder] at Cambridge in 1787, by H. Marczali.

n Peterborough and Barcelona, 1705: narrative and diary of Col. John Richards, by G. M. Trevelyan.

o Macartney in Russia, 1765–7, by W. F. Reddaway.

p Palmerston and the Clayton-Bulwer treaty [1850], by G. F. Hickson.

q Sir Henry Bulwer and the United States archives, by J. D. Ward.

815 Vol. 4.

a Some aspects of the history of chantries during the reign of Edward III, by Kathleen L. Wood-Legh.

b Bankruptcy before the era of Victorian reform, by E. Welbourne.

c The relationship between the treasury and the excise and customs commissioners, 1660–1714, by Doris M. Gill.

d Mayors of the staples [after 1353], by E. E. Rich.

e Locke *versus* Lowndes, by C. R. Fay.

f British policy towards parliamentary rule and constitutionalism in Turkey, 1830–1914, by H. Temperley.

g List of officials of the staple of Westminster [1353–1532], by E. E. Rich.

h A 13th cent. market town: Linton, Cambs., by J. H. Clapham.

i Monastic foundation charters of the 11th and 12th cent., by V. H. Galbraith.

j Great Britain and Poland, 1762–72, by W. F. Reddaway.

k Lord Augustus Loftus and the Eastern crisis of 1875–8, by B. H. Sumner.

l Documents illustrating Anglo-Spanish trade between the commercial treaty of 1667 and the commercial treaty and the Asiento contract of 1713, by Jean McLachlan.

CAMBRIDGE UNIVERSITY LAW SOCIETY

Founded 1920, to promote interest in legal subjects among law students in the University.

Cambridge Law Journal, vols. 1–5 (1921–35):

816 Vol. 1.

a *Execrabilis* in the common pleas: further studies, by T. F. T. Plucknett.

b Evolution of the law of blasphemy, by C. Kenny.

c History of conspiracy and abuse of legal procedure, by R. Pound. [Review of two vols. by P. H. Winfield]

d The new rules of pleading of Hilary term, 1834, by W. S. Holdsworth.

e F. W. Maitland, by W. W. Buckland.

817 Vol. 2.

a Gossip about legal history: unpublished letters of Maitland and Ames, with introd. by H. D. Hazeltine.

b English private law, 1870–1920, by Sir F. Pollock.

c Reprisals as a measure of redress short of war, by S. Maccoby.

d The Dominions and their mother country, by C. Kenny.

e The Book of Assizes, by W. C. Bolland.

818 Vol. 3.

a Appeal in English law, by the Rt. Hon. Lord Justice Atkin.

b Bacon, by W. S. Holdsworth.
c The Imperial Conference [1926] and the constitution, by E. Jenks.
d The happy state of the modern law student, by Mr. Justice Mackinnon. [On aspects of the study of law in earlier times]
e Trusts for sale, by J. M. Lightwood.
f Dr. Johnson and the Old Bailey, by T. Mathew.
g Parliament and the Dominions: a retrospect, by R. L. Schuyler.

819 Vol. 4.

a The Dominions and the United Kingdom, by G. G. Phillips.
b Some aspects of Blackstone and his *Commentaries*, by W. S. Holdsworth.
c Blackstone's *Commentaries*, by A. V. Dicey.

820 Vol. 5.

a Notes on the office of Master of the Rolls, by Lord Hanworth.
b Sir Edward Coke, by Sir W. Holdsworth.

CAMBRIDGESHIRE AND HUNTINGDONSHIRE ARCHAEOLOGICAL SOCIETY

Founded 1900, to promote antiquarian study and research in connection with Cambridgeshire (including the Isle of Ely) and Huntingdonshire.

Transactions, vols. 1–5 (1904–37):

821 Vol. 1.

a The Aldreth causeway, its bridge and surroundings, by C. H. Evelyn-White.
b Swavesey priory, by W. M. Palmer and Catherine E. Parsons.
c The Cardyke, by A. Bull.
d Earthworks at Cottenham, Cambs., the supposed site of a Roman camp or settlement, by C. H. Evelyn-White.
e The bridge and bridge-chapel of St. Ives, Hunts., by C. H. Evelyn-White.
f Swavesey (St. Andrew) church, by C. H. Evelyn-White.
g Over (St. Mary) church and manor, by C. H. Evelyn-White.
h The term 'Galilee' as applied to the western portion of church buildings and its possible connection with sanctuary use, by C. H. Evelyn-White.
i A Norman church in the Isle of Ely [Stuntney], by C. H. Evelyn-White.
j Stuntney church, by F. T. Mullett.
k St. John's hospital, Huntingdon, by F. G. Vesey.
l Notes on the early history of Shingay, Cambs., by W. M. Palmer.
m A book of church accounts relating to certain 'balks' in the common fields of Rampton, Cambs. [18th–19th cent.], ed. C. H. Evelyn-White.
n Parish registers of Rampton, Cambs. 1599–1812, ed. C. H. Evelyn-White.
o Some account of the parish and church of Warboys, Hunts., by S. I. Ladds.
p Ramsey abbey and the parish church, by R. Black.
q Some notes on the church of St. John the Baptist, Wistow, Hunts., by W. M. Noble.
r Village gilds of Cambridgeshire, by W. M. Palmer.
s Church of the Holy Cross, Bury, Hunts., with some account of the image of St. Mary the Virgin, by C. H. Evelyn-White.

822 Vol. 2.

a Brampton, Hunts., by S. I. Ladds.
b The priory and church of St. Neots, Hunts., by W. Emery.
c Stow Longa (St. Botolph), Hunts., by G. E. Sharland.
d Eynesbury and its church, by W. Emery.
e Great Paxton, Hunts., by A. G. Cane.
f Carved bench-ends in Eynesbury church, Hunts., by C. H. Evelyn-White.
g The story of Cottenham, Cambs., by C. H. Evelyn-White.
h Some Norman doorways in Cambridgeshire and Huntingdonshire displaying sculptured *tympana*, by C. H. Evelyn-White.
i Ickleton church, by J. W. E. Conybeare.
j Notes from the parish books of Great Paxton, Hunts., by A. G. Cane.
k Notes from the church-wardens' books of Great Gransden, Hunts., by A. J. Edmonds.
l Notes from the registers and church-wardens' accounts of St. Mary, Over, Cambs., by T. Normandale.
m Chesterford [Essex, British and Roman remains], by T. McK. Hughes.
n St. Andrew's church, Sutton, Isle of Ely, by M. Sheard.
o Some of the principal documents in Cottenham church, by A. Bull.
p Incumbents of county of Huntingdon, by W. M. Noble. [Contd. in vol. 3]
q Leighton Bromswold, the church and lordship, by H. B. Maling.
r Bourn church, by F. R. Williams.
s Ely St. Mary's: the chantry, Cromwell House, St. John's hospital, by K. H. Smith.

823 Vol. 3.

a A poaching affray at Castle Camps in 1556, by C. E. Parsons.
b Great Staughton, Hunts., by H. G. Watson.
c Wisbech parish church, by F. B. Ward.
d Notes on Huntingdon, by F. G. Vesey.
e William Dowsing's destructions in Cambridgeshire [churches, 1643], by J. G. Cheshire.
f Notes on Graveley church, by O. P. Fisher.
g Discovery of an ancient boat in Warboys Fen, by W. M. Noble.
h All Saints' church, Long Stanton, Cambs., by H. B. Woolley.
i Notes on a pamphlet concerning the ownership of 'The Delf's' at Haddenham, Isle of Ely, 1653, by A. Bull.
j Great Stukeley church, Hunts., by S. I. Ladds.
k Briefs in Farcet parish [1664–1722], by E. G. Swain.
l The Devil's ditch, by R. Stephenson.
m Burwell, its castle, etc., by W. O'F. Hughes.
n Sawtry abbey, Hunts., by S. I. Ladds.

824 Vol. 4.

a Haddon church, Hunts., by A. Chaplin.
b Guilden Morden parish church, by A. L. Williams.
c Steeple Morden church, Cambs., by E. Y. Orlebar.
d Excavations at Emmanuel Knoll, Godmanchester Hunts., by S. I. Ladds.
e Bourn bridge [Cambs.], by Catherine E. Parsons.
f Great Catworth, Hunts., by A. W. M. Weatherly.
g Hildersham church, Cambs., by P. R. Phillips.
h Cardinal Pole's visitation, 1556: an abstract of that part relating to the archdeaconry of Huntingdon, translated (from Strype's *Ecclesiastical Memorials*), by H. P. Pollard.
i Cartulary of the priory of St. Mary, Huntingdon, ed. W. M. Noble.
j Abbot's Ripton briefs [1709–47], ed. E. H. Vigers.

k Records of the archdeaconry of Huntingdon [a catalogue], by W. M. Noble and S. I. Ladds.

l The prior's house, Ely, by R. H. Kennett.

m Croxton church, Cambs., by W. Simons.

n Iron age pottery and associated objects in the museum of the Huntingdon Institution, by J. R. Garrood.

o Romano-British village sites in Colne and Somersham, Hunts., by C. F. Tebbutt.

p Episcopal visitation returns, Cambridgeshire (diocese of Ely), 1638–62, by W. M. Palmer. [Contd. to 1665 in vol. 5]

825 Vol. 5.

a The monastery of Ely, by S. I. Ladds.

b A Romano-British village in Huntingdonshire [Sawtry Judith parish], by J. R. Garrood.

c The borough of Huntingdon and Domesday book by S. I. Ladds.

d Rogues, vagabonds and sturdy beggars, by E. H. Vigers. [Extract from Little Stukeley register, *temp.* Chas. II]

e Swan-marks of Cambs. and Hunts., by N. F. Ticehurst.

f The Tournai slab [depicting St. Michael] at Ely, by S. I. Ladds.

g Burgesses of Huntingdon [1765–1826], by G. Proby.

h Preliminary report on excavation at Houghton, Hunts., by C. M. J. Coote.

i Churchwardens' bills or returns for the deanery of Barton, Cambs., for Michaelmas, 1554, by W. M. Palmer.

j Excavations at Eynesbury Conygear, by C. F. Tebbutt.

k Domesday woodland in Huntingdonshire, by H. C. Darby.

l Stone and bronze implements from Castle Hill farm, Wood Walton, by J. R. Garrood.

m An ancient bell at Old Weston, Hunts., by S. I. Ladds.

n Protestation returns for Huntingdonshire [1641], by G. Proby.

o Enclosures at Ely, Downham, and Littleport, 1548, by W. M. Palmer.

p A medieval chapel at Salome Lodge, Leighton, Hunts., by J. R. Garrood.

q Huntingdonshire windmills, by C. F. Tebbutt.

r Roman Godmanchester, by J. R. Garrood.

Other publications:

826 Autumn excursion, 1922. Melbourn, Fowlmere, and Shepreth. *P.* 1922. [Historical and antiquarian notes]

CANTERBURY AND YORK SOCIETY

Founded 1904, to print copies, abstracts, and indexes of the bishops' registers and other ecclesiastical records in the provinces of Canterbury and York.

Publications (*completed vols. only*), vols. 1–37:

827 Vols. 1, 3, 4. Rotuli Hugonis de Welles, episcopi Lincolniensis, 1209–35. 3 vols. 1907–9. [Vol. i ed. with introd. by W. P. W. Phillimore; vols. ii–iii ed. F. N. Davis. In conjunction with the Lincoln Record Soc., 1912–14]

828 Vol. 2. Registrum Thome de Cantilupo, episcopi Herefordensis, 1275–82, transcribed by R. G. Griffiths, with introd. by W. W. Capes. 1907. [In conjunction with the Cantilupe Soc., 1906]

829 Vol. 5. Registrum Ade de Orleton, episcopi Herefordensis, 1317–27, transcribed and ed. with introd. A. T. Bannister. 1908. [In conjunction with the Cantilupe Soc., 1907]

830 Vol. 6. Registrum Ricardi de Swinfield, episcopi Herefordensis, 1283–1317, transcribed and ed. W. W. Capes. 1909. [In conjunction with the Cantilupe Soc., 1909]

831 Vol. 7. Registrum Radulphi Baldock, Gilberti Segrave, Ricardi Newport, et Stephani Gravesend, episcoporum Londoniensium, 1304–38, transcribed and ed. R. C. Fowler. 1911.

832 Vol. 8. Registrum Johannis de Trillek, episcopi Herefordensis, 1344–61, transcribed and ed. with introd. by J. H. Parry. 1912. [In conjunction with the Cantilupe Soc., 1911]

833 Vol. 9. Registrum Thome de Charlton, episcopi Herefordensis, 1327–44, ed. W. W. Capes. 1913. [In conjunction with the Cantilupe Soc., 1912]

834 Vol. 10. Rotuli Roberti Grosseteste, episcopi Lincolniensis, 1235–53, transcribed and ed. F. N. Davis. 1913. [In conjunction with the Lincoln Record Soc., 1914. Includes institutions by Henry de Lexington, 1254–8, in the archdeaconry of Huntingdon]

835 Vol. 11. Lincoln episcopal records in the time of Thomas Cooper, bishop of Lincoln, 1571–84, ed. C. W. Foster. 1913. [In conjunction with the Lincoln Record Soc., 1912]

836 Vols. 12, 13. Register of John de Halton, bishop of Carlisle, 1292–1324, transcribed by W. N. Thompson, with introd. by T. F. Tout. 2 vols. 1913. [In conjunction with the Cumberland and Westmorland Antiq. and Archaeol. Soc., 1913]

837 Vol. 14. Registrum Ludowici de Charltone, episcopi Herefordensis, 1361–70, ed. J. H. Parry. 1914. [In conjunction with the Cantilupe Soc., 1913]

838 Vol. 15. Registrum Willelmi de Courtenay, episcopi Herefordensis, 1370–75, ed. W. W. Capes. 1914. [In conjunction with the Cantilupe Soc., 1913]

839 Vol. 16. Registrum Johannis Whyte, episcopi Wintoniensis, 1556–9, with a prefatory note by W. H. Frere. 1914.

840 Vols. 17, 24, 33. Visitations of religious houses in the diocese of Lincoln, ed. A. Hamilton Thompson. 2 vols. in 3. 1915–27. [Vol. i: injunctions and other documents from the registers of Richard Flemyng and William Gray, bishops of Lincoln, 1420–36; vol. ii (2 pts.): records of visitations held by William Alnwick, bishop of Lincoln, 1436–49. In conjunction with the Lincoln Record Soc., 1914–23]

841 Vol. 18. Registrum Johannis Gilbert, episcopi Herefordensis, 1375–89, transcribed and ed. J. H. Parry. 1915. [In conjunction with the Cantilupe Soc., 1913]

842 Vols. 19, 30. Registrum Johannis de Pontissara, episcopi Wyntoniensis, 1282–1304, transcribed and ed. C. Deedes. 1 vol. in 2. 1915–24. [In conjunction with the Surrey Record Soc., 1913–24]

843 Vol. 20. Registrum Johannis Trefnant, episcopi Herefordensis, 1389–1404, ed. W. W. Capes. 1916. [In conjunction with the Cantilupe Soc., 1914]

844 Vol. 21. Registrum Roberti Mascall, episcopi Herefordensis, 1404–16, transcribed by J. H. Parry, with introductory note by C. Johnson. 1917. [In conjunction with the Cantilupe Soc., 1916]

845 Vol. 22. Registrum Edmundi Lacy, episcopi Herefordensis, 1417–20, transcribed J. H. Parry, and ed. A. T. Bannister. Registrum Thome Poltone, episcopi Herefordensis, 1420–22, transcribed W. W. Capes. 1918.

[In conjunction with the Cantilupe Soc., 2 vols. 1916–17. The Cantilupe Soc. edition of the Poltone register has a memoir of Canon Capes]

846 Vol. 23. Registrum Thome Spofford, episcopi Herefordensis, 1422–48, ed. A. T. Bannister. 1919. [In conjunction with the Cantilupe Soc., 1917]

847 Vol. 25. Registrum Ricardi Beauchamp, episcopi Herefordensis, 1449–50; registrum Reginaldi Boulers, episcopi Herefordensis 1441[1450]–53; registrum Johannis Stanbury, episcopi Herefordensis, 1453–74, ed. A. T. Bannister. 1919. [In conjunction with the Cantilupe Soc., 3 vols. 1917–18]

848 Vol. 26. Registrum Thome Myllyng, episcopi Herefordensis, 1474–92, ed. A. T. Bannister. 1920. [In conjunction with the Cantilupe Soc., 1919]

849 Vol. 27. Registrum Ricardi Mayew, episcopi Herefordensis, 1504–16, ed. A. T. Bannister. 1921. [In conjunction with the Cantilupe Soc., 1919]

850 Vol. 28. Registrum Caroli Bothe, episcopi Herefordensis, 1516–35, ed. A. T. Bannister. 1921. [Includes abstracts of the registers of Edward Foxe, 1535–9, and Edmund Bonner, 1539. In conjunction with the Cantilupe Soc., 1921]

851 Vol. 29. Chapters of the Augustinian canons [1231–1578], ed. H. E. Salter. 1922.

852 Vol. 31. Rotuli Ricardi Gravesend diocesis Lincolniensis [1258–79], transcribed, ed. and indexed by F. N. Davis, with additions by C. W. Foster and A. Hamilton Thompson, and introd. by A. Hamilton Thompson. 1925. [In conjunction with the Lincoln Record Soc., 1925]

853 Vol. 32. Registrum Thome Wolsey cardinalis ecclesie Wintoniensis administratoris [1529–30], transcribed F. T. Madge and H. Chitty, and ed. with introd. by H. Chitty. 1926.

854 Vol. 34. Registrum Simonis de Sudbiria diocesis Londoniensis, 1362–75. Vol. i, transcribed and ed. R. C. Fowler. 1927. [Vol. ii was published in 1938]

855 Vols. 35, 36, 39. Registrum Matthei Parker, diocesis Cantuariensis, 1559–75, transcribed E. Margaret Thompson and ed. W. H. Frere. 1 vol. in 3. 1928[1907]–33.

856 Vol. 37. Registra Stephani Gardiner [1531–47] et Johannis Poynet [1551–2] episcoporum Wintoniensium, transcribed and ed. H. Chitty with introd. by H. E. Malden and H. Chitty. 1930.

CANTILUPE SOCIETY

Founded 1905, to print the episcopal registers and other records of the diocese of Hereford to 1539. Dissolved 1921. The Hereford registers distributed by the Society were issued in conjunction with the Canterbury and York Soc. (q.v.) though with title-pages in English and generally with different publication dates. In the following list nos. 858 and 859 were privately printed but are commonly catalogued among the Society's publications.

Publications:

857 Charters and records of Hereford cathedral [to 1421], transcribed and ed. with introd. by W. W. Capes. 1908.

858 Diocese of Hereford: institutions, etc., 1539–1900, comp. A. T. Bannister. 1923.

859 Index to the registers of the diocese of Hereford, 1275–1535, comp. E. N. Dew. 1925.

CARADOC AND SEVERN VALLEY FIELD CLUB

Founded 1893, by the amalgamation of the Caradoc Field Club and the Severn Valley Naturalists' Field Club, to encourage the study of natural history and archaeology, particularly in the county of Shropshire.

Transactions, vols. 3–9 (1901–35):

860 Vol. 3.

  a Roman baths at Bath, by E. S. Cobbold.

861 Vol. 4.

  a Prehistoric man in Shropshire, by T. Auden.

  b Shrewsbury hermits and anchorites, by Miss H. M. Auden.

  c Life in Stratford[-upon-Avon], 10th–16th cent., by J. H. Bloom.

862 Vol. 5.

  a Shrewsbury castle and walls, by J. W. Heath.

  b Lake dwellings at home and abroad, by F. A. Allen.

  c Two Shropshire naturalists [J. F. M. Dovaston, d. 1854, and R. A. Slaney, d. 1862], by H. E. Forrest.

  d Town walls of Shrewsbury, by R. E. Davies. [A summary of a second paper by R. E. Davies is also in this vol.]

  e The town walls of Shrewsbury, by J. A. Morris.

  f Gleanings from Shropshire registers, by Miss H. M. Auden.

  g Stapleton church, by H. E. Forrest.

  h The Quarry, Shrewsbury, by J. W. Heath.

863 Vol. 6.[1]

  a John Talbot, first Earl of Shrewsbury, by Barbara Clay-Finch.

  b The study of old roads, by Miss Auden.

  c Cicely Neville, the rose of Raby [b. 1415, later Duchess of York], by Barbara Clay-Finch.

  d Phillips' *History of Shrewsbury*, by J. Barker. [Extracts from the ms. original]

  e Notes on timber houses, by H. E. Forrest.

  f Raglan and Monmouth. [Notes by H. E. Forrest on the first and second Marquess of Worcester]

  g Some historic oaks of Shropshire, by J. Barker.

  h The Rowley family, by H. E. Forrest.

  i History of Shrewsbury abbey, by H. E. Forrest.

  j Old St. Chad's church [Shrewsbury], by H. E. Forrest.

  k Visit to St. Julian's and St. Alkmund's churches [Ludlow], by H. E. Forrest.

864 Vol. 7.

  a Carreghofa. [Notes of papers by H. E. Forrest and C. I. Littlehales on the Welsh portion of Llanymynech parish]

  b Berwick. [Notes by H. E. Forrest on the descent of the manor of Aldemere, otherwise Berwick]

  c Corvedale. [Notes by H. E. Forrest on the family of Baldwin of Elsich, Diddlebury, and Aston, and on the Lutley family of Broncroft]

  d Hawkstone. [Notes by H. E. Forrest on Soulton Hall and on the castle and fortifications at Wem, and by W. J. Creak on the grammar school]

  e Marrington. [Notes by H. E. Forrest]

  f Sheep and early man in Britain, by H. E. Forrest.

  g Place-names of the Wealdmoors, by E. W. Bowcock.

  h Early brickwork in England, by H. E. Forrest.

  i Roman roads in Shropshire, by H. E. Forrest.

865 Vol. 8.

  a The Lees of Shropshire and Virginia, by H. E. Forrest.

---

[1] No. 5 of this vol. not seen.

b Shropshire surnames, by Miss H. M. Auden.
c Life of St. Wistan, by M. Gepp.
d Four prospects of Shrewsbury [*c.* 1710], by J. Bowen.
e Roman roads in Wales, by H. E. Forrest.
f Field names, by Miss H. M. Auden.
g The river Severn, by J. Franklin.
h Tintern abbey. [Notes of a visit]
i Tong, Boscobel, and Moseley. [Notes of a visit, with particular reference to Tong church and its vestry library]
j Longnor. [Notes on Longnor by Miss H. M. Auden and H. E. Forrest, and by Miss Auden on Leebotwood]
k Linley Hall and Bishop's Castle. [Includes notes by H. E. Forrest on Blunden Hall and the Blunden family of Bishop's Castle]

866 Vol. 9.

a Early enclosures in Shropshire, by Miss H. M. Auden.
b Old Oswestry.
c The Manor House, All Stretton. [Notes by T. E. Price-Stretche]
d Old roads, by Miss H. M. Auden.
e Shrewsbury in the time of Queen Elizabeth, by J. A. Morris.
f Clun in the middle ages, by H. C. Jones.
g The cattle trade between Wales and England in the middle ages, by H. C. Jones.
h Mediaeval cultivation, by Miss H. M. Auden.
i The Haughmond doe, a traditional song in the parish of Upton Magna, written *c.* 1590–1600.
j Condover, by Miss H. M. Auden.
k Uriconium, by J. A. Morris.
l Shropshire worthies, by Miss H. M. Auden.
m Field meeting, Claverley. [Includes an account of Ludstone]
n Excursion to Aston Botterel.
o Field meeting, Bitterley. [Includes an account of Whitton Court]
p Early iron industries in Shropshire, by G. Potts.
q Early history of the Clun valley, by H. C. Jones.
r Navigation of the upper Severn [from the 12th cent.], by A. S. Davies.
s The port of Bridgnorth, by W. Watkins-Pitchford.
t England in the time of Caractacus [1st cent.], by H. E. Forrest.
u Field meeting, Moreton Old Hall.
v Social life in the Abbey Foregate [Shrewsbury, 1843], by Miss H. M. Auden.
w Flints of the Clun valley, by H. C. Jones.

CARDIFF NATURALISTS' SOCIETY

Founded 1867, to promote the study of natural history, archaeology, other sciences, and the arts, with special reference to Wales and Monmouthshire.

Report and Transactions, vols. 32–64[1] (1901–33):

867 Vol. 33.

a Presidential address to the archaeological section [on the early history of Cardiff], by J. S. Corbett.
b Place names of the Cardiff district, by J. H. Matthews.
c Notes upon the psalter of Ricemarch, by T. H. Thomas.
d Notes on the great flood of January 20th, 1607 [in Monmouthshire], by C. H. James.

868 Vol. 35.

a The Roman fort of Gellygaer in Glamorgan excavated by the Society 1899–1901, by J. Ward. [Reprinted in

[1] A general index to vols. 1–70, by H. M. Mallett, was issued with vol. 70, for 1938, in 1941.

Man, vol. iii, published by the Royal Anthropological Institute]

869 Vol. 36.

a Folk-lore of South Wales, by T. H. Thomas.
b Member lordships of Glamorgan, by J. S. Corbett.

870 Vol. 37.

a Pre-historic human skeletons found at Merthyr Mawr, Glam., by D. Hepburn.
b 'Calvary' crosses [gravestones], Glamorgan, by T. H. Thomas.

871 Vol. 38.

a Castell Morgraig: the situation, exploration and remains, by J. Ward.
b Masonry and architecture [of Castell Morgraig], by J. W. Rodger.
c Historical data [concerning Castell Morgraig], by J. S. Corbett.
d Pontypool Japan ware [history of], by T. H. Thomas.

872 Vol. 39.

a Ecclesiastical buildings of Llantwit Major, by J. W. Rodger.
b Notes as to Llantwit Major, by J. S. Corbett.
c Churches and castles in Glamorgan, by E. Seward.

873 Vol. 40.

a The Castell field at Craig Llwyn, Lisvane, Glam., by E. Seward.

874 Vol. 41.

a Stones in the parish of Merthyr Mawr, Glam., by M. Evanson.
b Notes on Roman remains in the Society's district, by J. Ward.

875 Vol. 42.

a The Roman fort of Gellygaer: the baths, by J. Ward.
b Dinaspowys, by J. S. Corbett.

876 Vol. 43.

a Sydenham Edwards of Usk, painter and draughtsman of natural history [d. 1819], by B. H. Thomas.
b Welsh records in foreign libraries, by T. Matthews.

877 Vol. 44.

a Stone cross slabs of South Wales and Monmouthshire, by J. W. Rodger.
b The Roman fort at Gellygaer: the annexe, by J. Ward. [Vol. 46 contains an account of discoveries made in 1913]

878 Vol. 45.

a 15th cent. coroner's account for Glamorgan [1425–6, in translation], by J. S. Corbett.

879 Vol. 46.

a The great wind-storm of Oct. 27, 1913, by Max A. Wright.
b Recent discoveries of Roman work at Cardiff castle, by J. Ward.

880 Vol. 47.

a Llantwit Major excavations, by J. W. Rodger. [With geological notes by T. C. Cantrill. See also short article in vol. 45]

881 Vol. 50.

a Castell Coch, by J. S. Corbett.
b Roman remains: Cardiff racecourse, by J. Ward.

882 Vol. 51.

a The geographical background to Welsh Arthurian stories, by F. T. Howard.

883 Vol. 52.

a The leek: national emblem of Wales, by Eleanor Vachell.

884 Vol. 54.

a Early Cardiff: with a short account of its street-names and surrounding place-names, by D. R. Paterson.

885 Vol. 55.

a Roman buildings and earthworks on the Cardiff race-course, by R. E. M. Wheeler.

886 Vol. 56.

a Glamorgan: papers and notes on the lordship and its members, by J. S. Corbett, ed. D. R. Paterson, 1925. [On the history of the lordship, Llantwit Major, Dinas-powys, and numerous Glamorgan manors, and on early Cardiff, its medieval churches and population, etc.]

887 Vol. 57.

a Radyr, by C. Morgan.
b Early photography, by Sir T. M. Franklen.

888 Vol. 59.

a The Beaupré porch [at the manor house, Beaupré], by C. Fox.
b Welsh vineyards, by A. A. Pettigrew.

889 Vol. 60.

a Diamond jubilee of the Society.
b History of the Cardiff Naturalists' Society, by A. W. Sheen. [See also '1895–1926: a retrospect', by R. W. Atkinson in this vol.]

890 Vol. 61.

a Some notes on the brown and the black rat in the city and port of Cardiff, by C. Matheson.
b Mithraism in Wales [in Roman times], by V. E. Nash-Williams.

891 Vol. 63.

a The lordship of Cardiff, by W. Rees.
b Old St. Mary's church, Cardiff, by D. R. Paterson.

892 Vol. 64.

a From Giraldus Cambrensis to the geological map, by F. J. North. [On the evolution of geological science]

CARDIGANSHIRE ANTIQUARIAN SOCIETY

Founded 1909, to explore every avenue connected with old Cardiganshire and to publish the results.

Transactions and Archaeological Record, vols. 1–2 ([1911]–15), *contd. as* Transactions, vols. 3–9 (1924–33):

893 Vol. 1.

a First [and second] county gathering at Strata Florida. [Summaries of addresses on the history and architecture of the abbey by E. Tyrrell-Green and others]
b Visit to Talley abbey. [Summaries of addresses on its history and architecture by J. W. Willis Bund and others]
c Meeting at Gogerddan. [Summaries of addresses by E. Lewes and others]
d Visit to Lampeter. [Includes an address on the grammar school by D. Samuel, and another on Cardiganshire dialects by H. M. Williams]
e Visit to Loventium and Llanddewi-Brefi. [Summaries of addresses]
f Hafod Ychtryd [manor-house, and its owners].

g Rhai o olion hynafiaethol plwyf Llanddewi Brefi. [Antiquities of the parish of Llanddewi Brefi]
h The Quakers in Cardiganshire. Crynwyr Llanddewi Brefi. [The Quakers in Llanddewi Brefi. In Welsh]
i Pedigree of the Werndriw family.
j St. Gwenog: her church and her well [at Llanwenog], by J. Morris.
k History and traditions of the neighbourhood of High-mead [Llanwenog], by J. C. Davies.
l Cardiganshire fonts, by E. Tyrrell-Green. [Contd. in vol. 2]
m A tribute to the early church, by T. A. Levi.
n Carved work in Cardiganshire churches, by E. Tyrrell-Green. [Contd. in vol. 2]
o Dedications of Cardiganshire churches, by J. Morris. [Contd. in vol. 2]
p Brittany and Cardiganshire, by J. C. Davies.
q Cwm Cynfelin [Aberystwyth] and Llangorwen church, by D. Samuel.
r Teifi-side antiquities, by E. Tyrrell-Green. [Contd. in vol. 2]
s Old Cardiganshire houses, by D. E. Davies. [Contd. in vol. 2]
t Unveiling of a monument [to the Rev. Thomas Phillips, D.D., 1772–1842, and his academy] at Neuaddllwyd.

894 Vol. 2.

a The royal mint, Aberystwyth, by G. E. Evans.
b Tir y werin, Ceredigion. [Common, or public, land in Cardiganshire]
c The story of Llangranog, by Miss E. E. Hope.
d Monuments to Cardiganshire worthies. I: Lewis Edwards [d. 1887]. II: Henry Richard [d. 1888].
e Vanished and vanishing Cardiganshire.

895 Vol. 3.

a An old system of numeration found in south Cardiganshire, by D. Thomas.
b Bibliography of printed literature relating to the local history of the parishes of Cardiganshire [Aberystwyth and Tregaron districts only].

896 Vol. 4.

a The birth and growth of Aberayron, by J. M. Howell.
b The people of Cardiganshire, by H. J. Fleure. [Summary of contributions in *Transactions*, 1915–16, of the Hon. Soc. of Cymmrodorion and in the Royal Anthropological Institute *Journal*, 1916, with additions]
c A regional survey of north Cardiganshire prehistoric earthworks, by I. T. Hughes.
d Ty Dawns ['The dance house', or place for Sunday games, near Swyddffynnon], by R. O. Jones.
e Notes on Llanarth and neighbourhood, by R. E. Bevan. [Followed by extracts from the diaries of the Rev. John Pugh, d. 1763, and his son John Pugh, d. 1796]

897 Vol. 5.

a Sculptured stones of Cardiganshire, by R. A. S. Macalister.
b Cantref y Gwaelod [the legendary district engulfed by the sea in Cardigan Bay], by D. J. Davies. [In English]
c The Penllwyn [bronze-age] urn: notes of a lecture by C. Fox.
d Some historical associations of Penllwyn, by M. H. Jones.
e The introduction of metal into Wales, by H. Peake.
f Old Aberystwyth, by E. Evans.
g Some remains of the 'lost' Goidelic language of Cardiganshire, by D. Thomas.
h Archaeological investigations in the vicinity of Llanddewi-Brefi and Llanfair-Clydogau, by T. Lewis.

i Twm Shôn Cati [the bard and genealogist, properly called Thomas Jones, alias Moetheu, 1530–1620?], gan R. I. Davies.

898 Vol. 7.

a Archaeology and ethnology, by A. C. Haddon.
b Port books of the port of Cardigan in Elizabethan and Stuart times [with an abstract of extant port books, 1603–1709. Contd. in vol. 9].
c Rhai o grefftau Ceredigion [some crafts of Cardiganshire], gan I. C. Peate.
d Rhydlan Deifi with Maenor Crug y Whyl and the surrounding district, by D. C. Evans.
e Bronze objects of the bronze age found in Cardiganshire, by A. R. Sansbury.
f Parish church of Llanllwchaiarn, by H. Evans.
g Llandysiliogogo: the parish church and district, by D. E. Thomas.
h Fairs in Cardiganshire, by J. E. J. Jones.
i Some south Cardiganshire earthworks, by I. T. Hughes.
j Excavations at Pen-y-Glogau, south Cardiganshire, by S. J. Jones and D. E. Davies.

899 Vol. 8.

a Pilgrim routes to Strata Florida, by S. M. Powell.
b Strata Florida abbey, by R. O. Jones.
c Taliesin, by Mary Williams.

900 Vol. 9.

a Some observations on hill-top camps, by I. T. Hughes.
b Cribyn Clottas: some hill-top camps, by D. C. Evans.
c Nevern, by T. Y. Lewis.

901 Index to the Transactions, ed. D. G. Griffiths. 1953. [Prepared at the instance of the Cardiganshire Joint Library Committee. Does not cover vols. 6, 10, 14, each of which was issued as a complete vol. with its own index]

CARMARTHENSHIRE ANTIQUARIAN SOCIETY AND FIELD CLUB

Founded 1905, for the practical study of archaeology, etc., pertaining to Carmarthenshire in particular and West Wales in general.

Transactions, vols. 1–24 ([1905]–33):

902 Vol. 1.

a A contribution towards the history and development of Castell Carreg Cennen, by A. Stepney-Gulston.
b Carmarthen: the Grey friars, 1536, by G. E. Evans.
c Priory of St. John the Evangelist, Carmarthen, by G. E. Evans.
d Books printed at Carmarthen.
e John Ross, printer [of Carmarthen, fl. 1764–1811].
f Abergwili [church], by G. E. Evans.
g Kidwelly. Borough of Kidwelly. [A true copy of the chief rent of the said borough, together with the owners and occupier's names (*sic*), 1780]
h Garnfawr [Newchurch, and its cairn], by A. Ll. Davies.
i Continental records of the 13th and 14th cent. [Entries relating to Carmarthenshire in the] Papal registers, rolls series, by M. L. Dawson.
j Abergwili: notes on its canons, 1296–1336 [being entries from the Papal registers], by G. E. Evans.
k Carmarthen, 1764–97 [a manuscript chronicle by John Vaughan], by G. E. Evans.
l Carmarthen: the Cambrian Society, 1818, by G. E. Evans.

903 Vol. 2.

a Meyrick's library and school [at Carmarthen], by G. E. Evans. [Edmund Meyrick, sometime vicar of St. Peter's church and treasurer of St. David's cathedral, d. 1713]
b The brethren of Bishop Rudd's hospital and almshouse. [Anthony Rudd, bishop of St. David's, 1549?–1615]
c Story of Welsh literature for King Louis Philippe: unpublished report of Count Villemarqué [1839].
d N.W. Carmarthenshire antiquities, by M. H. Jones.
e Carmarthen tithes, by T. W. Barker.
f Sir Thomas Powell's grammar school, by G. E. Evans. [Sir Thomas Powell, bt., 1664–1720, of Broadway, co. Carmarthen, and Coldbrook, co. Monmouth]
g [The lordship of] 'St. Clare' [or St. Clears], by G. E. Evans.
h Llanfihangel-Aber-Cywyn old parish church, commonly known as the 'Pilgrim's church', by D. C. Evans.
i Principal John Rhys' lecture on inscribed stones [with special reference to Carmarthenshire], by M. H. Jones.
j Eglwys Cymmin [church], by G. G. T. Treherne.
k Notes relating to the town and county of Carmarthen [in the 19th cent., from the diaries of Griffith Harris, of Carmarthen], by M. H. Jones.
l Copy of answers given by Thos. Bishop, esq., to the queries of Mr. Austin, one of the municipal commissioners, relating to the borough of Llandovery, Jan. 1834.
m John Griffiths, clericus [d. 1825]: his curious register and diary [relating to Llandysilio parish, 1759–95], by G. E. Evans.
n The free grammar school of Queen Elizabeth, Carmarthen, 1576–1856, by G. E. Evans.
o Rise and growth of Methodism in Carmarthen, by M. H. Jones. [Contd. in vol. 3]
p Letters of Nicholas Claggett, bishop of St. David's (1731–42) to Dr. Browne Willis.
q List of Carmarthenshire clergy [*c.* 1580–*c.* 1750].
r Burgesses of the county borough of Carmarthen, by G. E. Evans. [Contd. in vol. 3]

904 Vol. 3.

a Carmarthenshire manor houses: a description of Abermarlais and Dinevor in 1532, by F. Green. [Survey taken after the attainder of Sir Rhys ap Griffith, 1531]
b Carmarthen castle, by Ella Armitage.
c St. Peter's church, Carmarthen, by T. E. Brigstocke.
d Carmarthen castle, by H. S. Holmes.
e Genealogical notes on sheriffs of Carmarthenshire, by E. Allen. [Contd. in vol. 4]
f Newcastle Emlyn castle in 1532, by F. Green. [Continuation of survey taken after Sir Rhys ap Griffith's attainder]
g Letters of Adam Ottley, bishop of St. David's (1713–23), to Browne Willis, transcribed by J. T. Evans.
h The benefice of St. Peter's, Carmarthen, with a list of vicars, by Jessie Spurrell.
i Llanllwni: notes towards its parish history, by G. E. Evans. [Contd. in vol. 4]
The Mansels of Margam, Motlyscwm and Iscoed, by E. J. Waters.
k History of Lammas-street chapel, Carmarthen, by J. Thomas.

905 Vol. 4.

a Dolaucothi: its Roman remains, and Ogofau gold mine, by H. M. Lloyd.
b Carmarthenshire 'people called Quakers', by G. E. Evans.
c Talley abbey, by W. Spurrell
d Pembrey parish church, by D. Jones.

e Carmarthenshire place-names. [Contd. in vol. 5]

f Carmarthen parliamentary surveys, 1650–53.

g [Edward] Higgins [1725–67, house-breaker]: his false reprieve and execution at Pensarn.

h Llandovery and Llanfair-y-Bryn, 1710 [extracts from Archdeacon Edward Tenison's ms. *Visitatio Archidiaconatus Maridunensis*], by G. E. Evans.

i Carmarthenshire and early telescopes, by A. Mee. [Some account of Sir William Lower, d. 1615, and John Protheroe, fl. 1608–24]

j Roman 'finds' in Carmarthenshire.

k Rhoscrowther church [Pembrokeshire], by W. D. Caröe.

l Parish registers: county of Carmarthen. [Extracts from a copy of 'Abstract of the answers and returns . . . parish register abstract', 1831]

m Owen Glyndwr and his times, by J. L. Phillips.

n Traces of the Romans in the Taf valley and its vicinities, by J. Ll. James.

o Address on church registers at St. Clears, by C. F. Owen.

p Centenary of T. Brigstocke [1809–81], the Welsh painter, by T. H. Thomas.

906 Vol. 5.

a Eglwys Cymmin, church of St. Margaret Marlos [transcripts from the parish registers, etc. Concluded in vol. 8].

b Roman Dolaucothy, by F. Haverfield.

c The statute of the Carmarthen Eisteddfod, 1451, by M. H. Jones.

d Llangadock—mediaeval and otherwise, by H. M. Lloyd.

e Carmarthenshire directory of 1794, by A. W. Matthews.

f Penpiccillion [estate, Llanstephan, Carmarthenshire, and its owners], by G. E. Evans.

g Will of Anthony Rudd, bishop of St. David's (and Rudd charity, 1614).

h Griffith Jones's schools in Conwil-Elvet and Abernant [1737–61], by H. E. Lewis.

i Carmarthen: St. John's priory, by G. E. Evans.

j Talley abbey, by J. W. Willis Bund.

k Caermartren [Carmarthen]: subsidy rolls, 1628, by A. W. Matthews. [Addenda in vol. 6]

l Y Garn Goch [stone 'camp', Carmarthenshire], by D. C. Evans.

m Mysteries of the Carmarthenshire hill tops: great 'British camp' at Cwmrheiddol, by H. C. Tierney.

n Field names [in Pembrey parish], by E. E. Morgan. [Contd. in vol. 7]

o Highways of Carmarthenshire, 1765, by A. W. Matthews. [Contd. in vol. 6]

p Lay subsidy rolls [relating to Carmarthenshire], from Elizabeth to William and Mary, by A. W. Matthews.

907 Vol. 6.

a A few place-names in the Aman valley considered, by E. A. Jones. [Contd. in vol. 7]

b Notes on digging in a tumulus on Bigning mountain, Castle Lloyd, by J. Ward.

c Carmarthenshire: accounts of a poll tax for 1689–90, by A. W. Matthews.

d Rowland and William Gwynn, Taliaris, and Sir John Stenpey, bt., 1647–54, by G. E. Evans.

e Carmarthenshire sequestration commissioners, 1650–54: plague at Carmarthen [1651], by G. E. Evans.

f Notes on some mayors of the county borough of Carmarthen, by G. E. Evans.

g 'Cath' place names, by T. Matthews.

h Roman Carmarthen.

i Rivers in Carmarthenshire described in 1586 [in Holinshed's *Chronicles*, vol. 1].

908 Vol. 7.

a Kidwelly shell-mounds on the Burrows, by G. E. Evans.

b Early Carmarthenshire non-conformity, by M. H. Jones.

c County portraits [belonging to the Vaughans, earls of Carbery, at Golden Grove], by G. E. Evans.

d Borough of St. Clears: commissioners' report, 1833.

e Carmarthenshire wills, 1480–1604, by A. W. Matthews.

f Carmarthenshire nonparochial registers.

g Episcopal returns of Welsh nonconformist ministers and of their whereabouts in 1665, by G. L. Turner.

h The King's school: Gray friars, Carmarthen, 1545, by A. W. Matthews. [Contd. in vol. 8]

i Carmarthenshire place-names, copied from tithe apportionments in the diocesan registry at Carmarthen.

j Carmarthenshire taxation, 1560–61: eastern district, by A. W. Matthews.

k Lloyds of Tregeyb, 1610: copy of [17th cent. Breton] manuscript and translation into English by A. B. Thomas.

l Carmarthen bibliography [of printed books. Contd. in vols. 8 and 9]

m A short topographical sketch [of Carmarthen], by W. Waters.

n Election squibs [1831], by G. E. Evans.

o Carmarthen Eisteddfod, 1819: its secretary, Rev. David Rowland. [Transcripts of letters. Contd. in vol. 8]

909 Vol. 8.

a Calendar of chancery proceedings [relating to Carmarthenshire], series II, 1558–1621. [Contd. to 1660 in vol. 9]

b 'Free and voluntary present', Elvet hundred, 1662. [Transcripts from lay subsidy rolls]

c Index to the seats of Carmarthenshire, with names of owners as engraved upon the map drawn by Thomas Kitchin, *c.* 1730–40, by G. R. Brigstocke.

d Pembrey parish registers, by G. E. Evans.

e Pembrey church, by W. D. Caröe.

f The Carmarthenshire militia, 1793–9: unpublished letters.

g References to Carmarthen in early Welsh literature, extracted and comp. by M. H. Jones. 1: The Black Book of Carmarthen. [Contd. in vol. 9]

h Llanfair-ar-y-bryn parish, 1670: assessment of hearth tax.

i Llanfihangel-Abercowin church.

j Landing of the French [at Fishguard, Pembrokeshire], 1797: an unpublished contemporary ms.

k List of pedigrees of South Wales, etc., printed by Sir T. Phillips, bt., and preserved in the Bodleian Library.

l Carmarthen hearth tax, 1670: Lansadwrin, Llangadock, and the part of Llandilo Fawr parish in Perfedd. [Other parishes covered in vols. 9 and 10]

910 Vol. 9

a Carmarthen rent roll, 1575.

b Carmarthen court leet, 1657.

c Talley parish register, 1685–1808.

d A Carmarthenshire farm and its ecclesiastical associations: Bettws old church and graveyard.

e Carmarthenshire and other Welsh families commemorated in Bath abbey, by C. H. Glascodine.

f Llanarthney parish vestry book, 1799–1807.

g Carmarthenshire obituary [from the *Gentleman's Magazine*], 1731–95, by A. W. Matthews.

h Llanarthney church warden's book, 1802–29, by G. E. Evans.

i A survey of lands of Charles I in Cathinog, 1650 [transcript from parliamentary surveys relating to Carmarthenshire], by A. W. Matthews.

j Prebend of Mydrim and Llanvihangel, 1572: a relief against a bond.

k Carmarthenshire births, deaths, and marriages, July–Dec. 1817, by A. W. Matthews. [Contd. to June 1819, in vols. 10, 12 and 13]

l Carmarthen events, Jan.–June, 1818, by A. W. Matthews. [Contd. to June 1819, in vols. 10 and 11]

m The Edwardian inventories [1549–52], by E. H. Day.

n Carmarthenshire obituaries, 1622–1789, by A. W. Matthews.

o Roads to Carmarthenshire, 1698 [extracts from Ogilby's *Britannia or the Kingdom of England and Dominion of Wales actually survey'd*], by A. W. Matthews.

911 Vol. 10.

a A survey of the principality of Denevour, 1651 [transcript from parliamentary surveys], by A. W. Matthews.

b Carmarthen priory, 1115–1900.

c Welsh Wesleyan Methodism in Carmarthenshire in the early 19th cent., by E. E. Morgan.

d Llanllawddog register of births, marriages, and deaths, by R. E. Williams.

e Rhyd-y-gors [the estate, and its owners], by Jessie Spurrell.

f Pedigree of the Edwardes of Rhyd-y-gors.

g Llanllawddog parish vestry book, by R. E. Williams.

h Carmarthen castle mount. [Report by W. Ll. Morgan and W. Spurrell]

i Carmarthen: plea of a messuage in St. Mary Street, 1653, by A. W. Matthews.

j Llanfynydd parish [churchwardens' accounts] 1684, by G. E. Evans.

k Llanllawddog church, by R. E. Williams.

l Carmarthen: a shipping dispute, 1652, by A. W. Matthews.

m Place-names in the parishes of Newchurch, Llangunnor, and Llandefeilog.

n A survey of lands of Charles I in Maenor Deilo, 1650, by A. W. Matthews.

o Churchwardens' presentments [in Carmarthenshire], 1684, by G. E. Evans. [Contd. in vol. 11]

912 Vol. 11.

a Kidwelly: St. Nicholas chantry lands, 1641, by A. W. Matthews.

b Carmarthenshire: survey of wood belonging to duchy of Lancaster, 1608, by A. W. Matthews.

c Carmarthenshire: silver roll, March, 1655, by A. W. Matthews. [Contd. in vol. 13]

d The priory of St. John the Evangelist, and Griffith Leyson, D.C.L., of Carmarthen, by G. T. Thomas. [Extracts from the wills of Griffith Leyson, proved 1555, and of Joyce Gamage, his widow, proved 1586]

e Churchwardens' presentments [in Carmarthenshire], 1705. [Contd. in vol. 12]

f Llanllawddog: a marriage settlement, 1702, now at Derllwyn, by R. E. Williams.

g Carmarthen tin works and its founder [Robert Morgan, d. 1778], by G. E. Evans.

h Genealogical pamphlets of Wales, by A. W. Matthews.

i Killy Carw lands, in Llangendeirne, 1693: bill of complaint [from chancery proceedings], by A. W. Matthews.

j Humphrey Toy, mayor of Carmarthen, 1557 [and his will], by G. T. Thomas.

k The lordship of St. Clears, and the Traney manors [i.e. Traney March, Traney Morgan, and Traney Clinton], by G. T. Thomas.

913 Vol. 12.

a Llanllawddog parish: fields etc.

b The chantry of St. Catharine, Carmarthen, by E. Owen.

[Reports of two commissions issued to inquire into a lawsuit relating to this property between Griffith Tucker and Thomas Reynolds, 1539]

c Llanybyther: ancient monuments, by H. Davies-Evans.

d Williams Pantycelyn, by G. E. Evans.

e Pencarreg: Jenken v. William, 1642 [from chancery proceedings], by A. W. Matthews.

f Carmarthen printers, 1840–61: declarations as to printing presses, by G. E. Evans.

g Fenton's tours in Wales, 1804–10.

h Papal registers: entries relating to the diocese of St. David's, by H. C. Tierney.

i Carmarthenshire ship money, 1635–40 [extracts from state papers], by A. W. Matthews.

j Llandilo: land of Kily Werne, 1689 [extracts from chancery proceedings], by A. W. Matthews.

914 Vol. 13.

a History of nonconformity in Laugharne: the Congregationalists, by D. M. Thomas.

b Catalogue of chancery proceedings [relating to Carmarthenshire], 1613–1714 (Bridges series), extracted by A. W. Matthews.

c A fine old Welsh gentleman [Thomas Johnes, of Hafod] who died April 23rd, 1816, by W. C. Gaze.

d Carmarthenshire rates in King's books, 1690, by A. W. Matthews.

e Carmarthenshire cases of debt, 1732 [from Carmarthenshire plea rolls], by A. W. Matthews.

f Kidwelly [churchwardens' presentments], 1787, by G. E. Evans.

g Carmarthenshire bishop's transcripts, 1671.

h Carmarthen silver roll, 1655, by A. W. Matthews.

i References to Carmarthenshire in old Welsh literature: poems of Lewis Glyn Cothi, by M. H. Jones.

j A dispute over lands in Newchurch, 1694 [from chancery proceedings], by A. W. Matthews.

k The Coygan bone cave, by F. C. Wardle and G. E. Evans.

l The grammar schools of Carmarthen to 1576, by L. S. Knight.

m Bronze vessel found near Tenby, 1834, by G. E. Evans.

n Sir 'Harry' Vaughan, the elder, 1587?–1659? [royalist], by G. E. Evans.

915 Vol. 14.

a Llanegwad [presentment], 1717.

b Churchwardens' presentments [Carmarthenshire], 1720, by G. E. Evans.

c Manor of Mallaine [parliamentary survey] 1650, by A. W. Matthews.

d Carmarthenshire and the Reformation movement, by T. H. Lewis.

e Llanfynydd [churchwardens' presentments], 1789, by G. E. Evans.

f Survey [parliamentary] of the crown manor of Mab Utryt, 1650, by A. W. Matthews.

g Llanfihangel Uch Gwili chapel, 1792 [churchwardens' presentments], by G. E. Evans.

h Carmarthenshire presentments, 1671–2 and 1678–9, by G. E. Evans.

i Letters of the Rev. Griffith Jones [d. 1761] to Madame Bevan. [Contd. in vol. 15]

916 Vol. 15.

a Churchwardens' presentments [Carmarthenshire] 1790. [Contd. in vol. 16]

b Napps circle in Pendine, by A. H. Allcroft.

c Journal of tour in Carmarthenshire, 1767 [by Sir Joseph Banks].

d The circle on Pwll mountain in Marros, by A. H. Allcroft.

e Notes of an epigraphic pilgrimage in south west Wales, by R. A. S. Macalister. [A survey of inscribed stones]

f John Butt, M.P., native of Carmarthen, 1400–52, by A. W. Matthews.

g Carmarthen borough accounts, 1824–5.

h Llangevelech, Tirdunkin chapel: annals and registers.

i Carmarthen: Lammas Street chapel foundation stone laying, 1826, by G. E. Evans. [With notes on Stephen Hughes, nonconformist minister, fl. *c.* 1662–72, and others]

j Carmarthen inns and their land lords, 1802, by G. E. Evans.

k Prehistoric Carmarthenshire: the light thrown by place-names, by M. H. Jones. [Contd. in vol. 16]

917 Vol. 16.

a Bibliography of the works of the Rev. Griffith Jones, Llanddowror, by M. H. Jones.

b Carmarthenshire schools, 1705–59, by G. E. Evans.

c Carmarthenshire in the bronze and iron age, by M. H. Jones.

d Manor of Elvet [Carmarthenshire: miscellaneous mss., 1736–67].

e Roman Carmarthenshire.

f Norman Carmarthenshire.

g Romano-British Carmarthenshire.

h Royal Carmarthenshire Militia, 1803–31. [Extracts from regimental orders, etc. Contd. in vol. 17]

i Dug-out canoes in Wales: when and how found, by G. E. Evans.

j Llanedy [church], by J. R. Gabriel.

k David Davies, 1796–1801 [a Carmarthen student, and Unitarian minister at Neath].

918 Vol. 17.

a Eglwys Cymmyn church, by G. G. T. Treherne.

b Carmarthen priory ruins as a workhouse, 1758, by G. E. Evans.

c Carmarthenshire collations, 1753–61, by G. E. Evans.

d Will of Sir Thomas Powell, bt. [of Broadway, Carmarthenshire, d. 1720], by G. E. Evans.

e Beynon-Heslop duel, Newcastle Emlyn, 1814. [Notes taken by one of the judges during the trial]

f An 18th cent. pocket book [1752] of the roads and post towns in England and Wales, by M. H. Jones.

g St. Hernin [and some legends associated with him], by M. L. Dawson.

h The state sword of Carmarthen, by G. E. Evans.

i [The history of Carmarthen bridge, by G. E. Evans]

j Carmarthen: documents relating to the town from earliest times to the close of the reign of Henry VIII. [Comp. E. A. Lewis. Contd. in vol. 18]

k Rev. Griffith Jones, Llanddowror, 1683–1761, by M. H. Jones. [A bibliography]

l Rev. Griffith Jones, Llanddowror: his lineage, by M. H. Jones.

m Ieuan Brydydd Hir [or Evan Evans, d. 1789, Welsh poet and antiquary] at Carmarthen: an unpublished letter, 1781, by G. E. Evans. [Further letters in vol. 18]

919 Vol. 18.

a Roman pottery from Carmarthen, by R. E. M. Wheeler.

b Ruined chapels in Carmarthenshire: Llanegwad parish, by J. R. Gabriel.

c The Soppit psalter, by P. E. Hook.

d West Wales manuscripts: schedule of deeds presented by G. E. Evans to the National Library of Wales.

e Laugharne parish church, by J. P. G. Williams.

f Laugharne: bells cast locally, by J. P. G. Williams.

g Carmarthen archdeaconry court: caveats re administration of effects of deceased persons. [Contd. in vols. 19 and 20]

920 Vol. 19.

a West Wales Quakers, 1793. [Extracts from the diary of John Grubb, of Clonmel, Ireland]

b Agriculture and Industry Society, Carmarthen, 1800, by G. E. Evans.

c 'Laugharneshire', by G. T. T. Treherne. [Miscellaneous notes]

d Kidwelly. [List of mayors and bailiffs]

e Roman coins: two forgotten hoards, by G. E. Evans. [Referring to the finds at Bwlch-bach farm, Nanteos, 1841, and Rhiwarthenisaf farm, 1881]

f Roman road from Carmarthenshire to Pennal: notes by D. Paith Jones, 1884–6, of Llanbadarn Fawr, ed. G. E. Evans.

g Kilpaison (Kilpatrick's ton) bronze age cemetery, by J. P. G. Williams.

h Whitland abbey excavations.

i Briefs, 1682–1731 [issued upon the occasions of a fire in Presteigne, Radnorshire, 1682, the fall of the tower of Quatford church, Shropshire, 1713, and the repairing of Llandaff cathedral, 1731].

j The Cistercian order, by G. A. Taylor.

k Eugenia and Mary Morgan, Carmarthen, 1795–6. [Selections from letters by Anne Blome, of Castle Piggin, Abergwili, to Eugenia, d. 1841, and Mary, d. 1840, daughters of Charles Morgan]

l Newcastle Emlyn: the church of Holy Trinity, by G Evans.

m Llandovery: confirmation of the borough charter [1587].

921 Vol. 20.

a Carmarthen portsearcher, 1630. [The appointment of David Rees]

b An 'encrusted' urn of the bronze age from Penllwyn, near Aberystwyth, by C. Fox.

c Giraldus Cambrensis, by A. L. Congreve.

d The Picton relics [relating to General Sir Thomas Picton].

e Sir Henry Vaughan, the elder, 1587?–1660? [Abstracts of the wills of Sir Henry Vaughan, the elder, and his son, Sir Henry Vaughan, the younger, d. 1676, with an inventory of the goods of the latter]

f Pembrey parish: early industrial efforts, by R. G. Thomas.

g The Morgan (Furnace) papers, 1764–1839, by G. E. Evans. [Extracts from letters of the Morgan family, of Furnace House, Carmarthen]

h Extracts from *The Cambrian and General Advertiser for the Principality of Wales,* 1806–37.

i The Society of Sea Serjeants, 1726–60 [composed of natives of the counties of Cardigan, Carmarthen, Glamorgan and Pembroke. Contd. in vol. 21].

922 Vol. 21.

a Llandyssul parish: part of a late Celtic bronze collar, by G. E. Evans.

b Erasmus Williams' letter book, Carmarthen, 1775–80.

c John Nash [d. 1835], a Carmarthen resident.

d Carmarthen borough constabulary, 1658–1835: watchmen, constables, crime, by G. E. Evans.

e Carmarthen notes, 1765–1827 [being extracts from the minutes or order books of the corporation], by G. E. Evans.

f Carmarthen council's fishing experiments, 1804–8, by G. E. Evans.

g Carmarthen address to H.R.H. the Prince Regent, 1819, by G. E. Evans.

923 Vol. 22.

a Carmarthenshire pedigrees [from 'Edwards Collection of Welsh pedigrees' in the Bodleian Library].

b Primary visit of [Charles] Moss, bishop of St. David's, 28 July 1768. [A list of clergy in the deaneries of Gower, Llandilo and Llangadock, Kidwelly and Carmarthen]

c A Carmarthen diary [1852–64, of the Rev. Titus Evans], by G. E. Evans.

d [Thomas] Burgess, bishop of St. David's: presentation of the 'Cambrian vase' 1825, by G. E. Evans.

e Laugharne: extension of churchyard: early graves, by J. P. G. Williams.

f Carmarthen wine, beer and mineral water trade. [Extracts from a thesis by H. J. Evans, with notes by G. E. Evans]

g Baines, the forger, 1818, by G. E. Evans.

924 Vol. 23.

a Old mines of north Carmarthenshire, by J. F. Jones.

b Llanarthney and Llanddarog: final concord, 1644, by G. E. Evans.

c Llandybie district lime industry. [Substance of a thesis by J. G. Jones]

d Llangeler parish: notes on some of its ancient monuments, by F. Jones.

e Laugharne Independent congregation, 1752–74, by G. E. Evans.

f Carmarthenshire in the register of Edward the Black Prince, 1346–48.

g A Carmarthen broadside, 1832 [entitled *Descriptive Catalogue of the Conservative Club*], by G. E. Evans.

h Carmarthen schools, 1825–6, by G. E. Evans.

i 'Rebecca Riots': unpublished letters, 1843–4, ed. G. E. Evans.

j Penboyr parish book [1749–67].

k The episcopal chapel, Abergwili Palace, by G. E. Evans. [Contd. in vol. 24]

l The Cwmgwili manuscripts. [Extracts selected by G. E. Evans. Contd. in vol. 24]

925 Vol. 24.

a Llandovery charter, by J. F. Jones. [Miscellaneous notes]

b A Llandefeilog worthy [David Daniel Davies, d. 1841, physician], by C. Spurrell.

c Common law records, Carmarthenshire, by J. F, Jones.

d George Phetiplace, justice of South Wales, 1574–7, M.P. for Buckingham, 1552–3, by A. L. Browne.

e Roman roads of Carmarthenshire, by S. O'Dwyer.

f Harcourt of Carmarthen, and of Danyparc, Brecon.

g The records of St. David's diocese [their destruction], by G. E. Evans.

h Carmarthen doctors, by C. Spurrell.

i Field day in 'the Griffith Jones country'. [Includes notes on Merthyr Derllys, Mydrim and Llanddowror churches and parish histories, and the *apologia* of Griffith Jones to the bishop of St. David's, 1715]

926 Index to the Transactions, vols. 1–12, of the Carmarthenshire Antiquarian Field Club. 1928.

Other publications:

927 Yr Encilion or The Journal of the Carmarthenshire Antiquarian Society and Field Club, vol. 1, pts. 1–2. 1912. [No more published]

a Carmarthen castle, by Sir J. Hills-Johnes.

b Carmarthen local events, 1547–1836 [comp. from the corporation order books and a ms calendar of the name; of mayors, bailiffs, and sheriffs from 1400, by G. E. Evans].

c A study of Carmarthen place-names in their historical setting, by M. H. Jones.

d Lewis Glyn Cothi [fl. 1450–86, Welsh poet], by E. Lewes.

e Poems by Lewis Glyn Cothi, by H. E. Lewis.

f A bibliography or compilation of data for the history of Carmarthen.

CATHOLIC RECORD SOCIETY

Founded 1904, to transcribe, print, and index the Catholic registers of baptisms, marriages and deaths, and other old records of the faith, chiefly personal and genealogical, since the Reformation, in England and Wales.

Publications, vols. 1–33:

928 Vol. 1. Miscellanea I. 1905.

a Dr. Nicholas Sander's report to Cardinal Moroni [relating to the change of religion in England, ?1561; Latin text and translation, ed. J. H. Pollen]

b Official lists of prisoners for religion during the reign of Queen Elizabeth, ed. J. H. Pollen. [Contd. in vol. 2]

c Conclusion of the autobiography of Father William Weston, S.J. [for 1589–1603], ed. J. H. Pollen.

d Martyrdom of the Ven. John Boste. [Letter from the Ven. Christopher Robinson, 1594, to the Ven. Richard Dudley]

e Three state letters concerning Catholics during the reign of Charles I, 1626. [Relation of a brawl at the arrest of Catholics resorting to mass at Durham House; letter from Sir John Coke to Lord Conway about the arrest of a priest at Newington; letter of protection for John Colleton, priest]

f Note-book of John Southcote, D.D., 1623–37, ed. J. H. Pollen.

g Genealogical note-book of the Venerable Arthur Bell, O.S.F., martyr, 1638. [Latin]

h The Huddleston obituaries [being anniversaries noted by Dom John Dionysius Huddleston, O.S.B., *temp.* civil war], ed. J. Gillow.

i The Napper family register [being extracts from the common-place book of Edmund Napper, of Holywell, Oxford, b. 1679], ed. J. Gillow.

j Family notes of Thomas Owst's descendants, the Smiths of Drax [18th–19th cent., with a licence to travel, 1745].

k Family notes of Wilks, Sherlock, Lewys, etc. [18th–19th cent.].

l Registers of the Catholic mission of Winchester, 1721–1826. [Latin transcript by R. Palmer, ed. E. Burton]

m Catholic registers: Cowdray, Easebourne and Midhurst [1745–62, 1779–1822. Latin transcript by R. Palmer, ed. J. S. Hansom].

n Catholic registers of Perthir in the county of Monmouth, 1758–1818, ed. J. H. Matthews.

929 Vol. 2. Miscellanea II. 1906.

a Four papers relative to the visit of Thomas Sackville, afterwards Earl of Dorset, to Rome in 1563–4. [Latin, with translation. The testimonial by Bishop Goldwell and others ed. H. D. Grissell; the Vatican papers ed. J. H. Pollen]

b The memoirs of Father Robert Persons, ed. J. H. Pollen. [Partly Latin and Italian, with translation. Contd. in vol. 4]

c Records relating to Catholicism in the South Wales marches, 17th and 18th cent., ed. J. H. Matthews.

d Catholic registers of Towneley Hall, Lancs. (baptisms and marriages); by the Rev. Thomas Anderton, 1705–27; with the chaplain's stipendiary accounts, 1705–20; also some account of the terrier of Martholme, 1667, and the chaplain's commemorations at mass, 1706–22; ed. J. Gillow.

e Petition of Denis Molony [d. 1726] to parliament to be allowed to practise at the bar, ed. A. Molony.

f Catholic registers of Cheam, Surrey [1755–88], ed. J. S. Hansom.

g Catholic registers of Wootton Wawen, Warwicks. [1765–1843], ed. J. S. Hansom.

h Registers of the Catholic mission of S. Oswald, Bellingham, Northumb. (formerly Hesleyside), 1794–1837, contrib. J. S. Hansom.

930 Vol. 3. Miscellanea III. 1906.

a Queen Elizabeth's license [1576] to Richard Hoghton to visit his brother Thomas Hoghton, an exile for his 'blessed conscience', ed. J. Gillow.

b Tower bills, ed. J. H. Pollen. [Accounts by the lieutenant of the Tower for the maintenance of prisoners, 1575–89. Contd. for 1595–1681, with Gatehouse certificates, 1592–1603, in vol. 4]

c The life and martyrdom of Mr. Maxfield, priest, 1616, ed. J. H. Pollen. [With six letters of the martyr and an account of his relics]

d Memoir of Edmund Mathew [*alias* Pointz, d. 1667, while a pupil in the English seminary of St. Omers], ed. J. H. Pollen.

e Recusants of Masham, Yorks. [being extracts from the act books of the peculiar court of Masham], ed. J. S. Hansom.

f Three letters relating to the treatment of Catholic prisoners in Wisbech castle, 1615.

g Letters of the Archpriest Harrison relative to the appointment of an agent at the Roman curia, etc., transcribed and translated by J. G. Dolan.

h A Chapter necrology, Oct. 1670–Feb. 1678 [the obituary kept by the Rev. Alexander Holt *alias* Rigby], annotated J. Gillow.

i Catholic registers of Holywell, Flintshire [1698–1829], contrib. P. Hook.

j Catholic registers of Nidd Hall, N.R. of York, 1780–1823, contrib. R. Trappes-Lomax.

k The old registers of the Catholic mission of Llanarth in co. Monmouth, 1781–1838, transcribed by J. H. Matthews.

l Register of St. Joseph's chapel, Trenchard Lane (now Street), Bristol, 1778–1808, ed. J. S. Hansom.

931 Vol. 4. Miscellanea IV. 1907.

a Lord Burghley's map of Lancashire, 1590, annotated J. Gillow.

b Catholic chaplaincies and families in the north during the 18th cent.: notes and memoirs by Father John Laurenson, S.J., chaplain at Brough Hall, Yorks., 1808, contrib. J. Gerard.

c Family notes of Knights of Lincolnshire, ed. J. S. Hansom.

d Documents at Everingham [chiefly relating to recusants in Yorkshire, 1663–6], contrib. C. J. S. Spedding.

e Catholic registers of Holme-on-Spalding-moor, E.R. York [1744–1840], ed. J. S. Hansom.

f Catholic registers of Robert Hall and Hornby, co. Lancaster, 1757–1851, contrib. W. Wrennall.

g The nuns of the Institute of Mary at York, 1677–1825, contrib. J. S. Hansom.

h Papist returns for the city of York and part of the Ainsty, 1735, contrib. J. S. Hansom.

i Catholic registers of York Bar convent chapel, being the conventual chapel of the Institute of Mary, outside Micklegate Bar, 1771–1826, contrib. J. S. Hansom.

j Catholic registers of Courtfield in the parish of Welsh Bicknor, Mon., 1773–1832, contrib. J. H. Matthews.

k Fr. John Birkett [d. 1680], confessor in Lancaster castle, and the recent discovery of documents, by J. Gillow.

932 Vol. 5. Unpublished documents relating to the English martyrs. Vol. i: 1584–1603, collected and ed. J. H. Pollen. 1908.

933 Vol. 6. Miscellanea V. 1909.

a English Benedictine nuns in Flanders, 1598–1687: annals of their five communities, by Lady Abbess Anne Neville [d. 1689], ed. Mary J. Rumsey.

b Will of Christopher Stonehouse of Dunsley in the parish of Whitby, a noted recusant [*c.* 1564–1631], contrib. J. S. Hansom.

c List of convicted recusants in the reign of Charles II [comp. 1671], ed. J. S. Hansom.

d Catholic registers of the domestic chapel formerly at Crondon Park, Essex [*c.* 1759–1831], with some notes relating to Hopcar, Lancs., contrib. F. A. R. Langton and J. S. Hansom; introd. W. H. Cologan.

e Registers of the Catholic chapel, Lulworth Castle, Dorset [1755–1840]: historical notes by J. Gillow.

934 Vol. 7. Miscellanea VI. 1909.

a Bedingfeld papers, contrib. J. H. Pollen. [Relating to members of the Bedingfeld family in the 17th and 18th cent., with the Catholic baptismal register of Oxburgh, 1791–1811, a census of Oxburgh Catholics, 1790–1804, and notes on the Bedingfelds of Oxburgh]

b Monmouthshire recusants, 1719, contrib. J. H. Matthews.

c Obituary notes of Abbess Newsham [d. 1889], of St. Clare's abbey, Darlington, ed. J. S. Hansom.

d Everingham papists, 1767, ed. J. S. Hansom.

e Catholic registers of St. Mary's domestic chapel, Everingham Park, Yorks. [1771–1884], with historical notes by J. Gillow.

f Catholic registers of St. Elizabeth's church, Richmond, Surrey [1794–1839].

g Catholic registers of the domestic chapel at Callaly Castle, Northumb., 1796–1839.

h Catholic registers of the domestic chapel at Slindon House and St. Richard's church, Slindon, Sussex [1698–1840].

i Catholic registers of the domestic chapel at Waterperry manor house, Oxon., and St. Clement's church, Oxford, 1701 ?–1834, with historical notes by Mrs. Bryan Stapleton.

j Genealogical supplement to the Bedingfeld papers, contrib. R. T. Bedingfeld.

935 Vol. 8. The diary of the 'Blue Nuns' or order of the Immaculate Conception of Our Lady, at Paris, 1658–1810, ed. J. Gillow and R. Trappes-Lomax. 1910.

936 Vol. 9. Miscellanea VII. 1911.

a Thomas Wiseman of Wimbish, Essex: his *inquisitio post mortem*, 1586, with some notes of his family, contrib. F. J. A. Skeet.

b Correspondence of Cardinal Allen [1579–85], contrib. P. Ryan.

c Particulars of priests in England and Wales, 1692, contrib. R. Stanfield.

d Official papers relating to Catholic recusants, ed. J. S. Hansom. [George Turner, physician, 1596; Francis Richardson, 1603; Thomas Marrow, 1603; John Kitchyn, sailor ?, 1603; John Clark, 1608 or 9; John Wentworth *alias* Hydalgo, priest, 1637]

e Proceedings against Catholics for attending mass at the Spanish Embassy on Palm Sunday, 1614, annotated by J. S. Hansom.

f Thomas, first Lord Arundell of Wardour, and his proposal to settle the manor of Christchurch-Twineham on the church, 1638, ed. J. S. Hansom.

g Some records of the Monmouth mission [from 1716], contrib. J. H. Matthews.

h Confession of John Hambly, priest, 1586, contrib. J. L. Whitfield.

i Notes of the Eccles family of Meanfields [Winwick], Lancs., contrib. J. P. Smith.

j Catholic registers of Liverpool, now St. Mary's, Highfield Street, 1741–73, ed. J. S. Hansom, notes by J. Gillow.

k The English Benedictine nuns of the convent of Our Blessed Lady of Good Hope in Paris, now at St. Benedict's priory, Colwich, Staffs.: notes and obituaries, 1652–1861, ed. J. S. Hansom.

937 Vols. 10, 11. The Douay college diaries, third, fourth and fifth, 1598–1654, with the Rheims report, 1579–80, ed. E. H. Burton and T. L. Williams. 1 vol. in 2. 1911.

938 Vol. 12. Obituaries. 1913.

a Obituaries of secular priests, 1722–83, contrib. R. Stanfield.

b *Laity's Directory* obituaries, 1773–1839, contrib. J. S. Hansom.

c Catholic memorial inscriptions, contrib. J. H. Matthews.

939 Vol. 13. Miscellanea VIII. 1913.

a Records of the [English Benedictine] abbey of Our Lady of Consolation at Cambrai [now Stanbrook], 1620–1793, ed. J. Gillow.

b Two lists of influential persons apparently prepared in the interests of Mary, Queen of Scots, 1574 and 1582, ed. J. B. Wainewright.

c Narrative of the martyrdom of the Ven. Thomas Holland, S.J., 1642, contrib. E. R. James.

d Papers from the Courtfield muniments [1641 etc. mainly concerned with an indictment for harbouring a priest], contrib. J. H. Matthews.

e Addresses of the stations in England served by the Jesuit fathers, 1727–34, contrib. R. Trappes-Lomax.

f Account book of Mr. Ralph Clavering, 1763–4, contrib. R. Trappes-Lomax.

g Boys at Liège academy, 1773–91: their parents or guardians, and the pensions paid, contrib. R. Trappes-Lomax.

h Minute-book of the Roman Catholic Club London], 1793–8, contrib. J. S. Hansom.

i Registers of Fr. Thomas Worthington, O.P., kept in Lancashire, 1713–17, contrib. J. S. Hansom.

j Catholic registers of Danby, West Witton, and Leyburn, Yorks., 1742–1840, with notes of the Scrope family, 1663–1754, contrib. J. S. Hansom, notes by J. Gillow.

k Rev. Pierce Parry's private baptismal registers at Claxby and Oscott, 1755–66, contrib. J. Gillow.

l Catholic registers of Britwell-Prior or Brightwell, Oxon., 1765–88, contrib. J. Edge.

m Catholic registers of Isleworth, Mdx., 1746–1835, contrib. J. S. Hansom, notes by J. Gillow.

n Catholic registers of Newport, Salop, 1785–1846, contrib. C. Giles, notes by J. Gillow.

o Catholic registers of Culcheth, Lancs., 1791–1825, contrib. J. Donohoe, notes by J. Gillow.

p Catholic registers of Southworth Hall, Lancs., 1795–1827, contrib. J. Donohoe, notes by J. Gillow.

940 Vol. 14. Miscellanea IX. 1914.

a Annals of the English college, Seville, with an account

of other foundations [at Valladolid, St. Lucar, Lisbon and St. Omers, 1589–95, an unfinished memoir by Fr. Persons, S.J., in 1610], contrib. J. H. Pollen.

b Registers of the English Poor Clares at Gravelines, including those who founded filiations at Aire, Dunkirk, and Rouen, 1608–1837, contrib. W. M. Hunnybun, ed. J. Gillow.

c Register book of professions etc., of the English Benedictine nuns at Brussels and Winchester, now at East Bergholt, 1598–1856, ed. J. S. Hansom.

d Rosary Confraternity lists [relating to Bornhem, 1706–1778, and the north of England, 1738–1813], contrib. B. Jarrett.

e Catholic registers of Capheaton, Kirkwhelpington, Northumb., 1769–85, contrib. C. J. S. Spedding, notes by J. R. Baterden.

f Catholic registers of Biddleston Hall, Alwinton, Northumb., the seat of the Selby family, 1767–1840, contrib. J. S. Hansom, notes by J. R. Baterden.

g Catholic registers of Pylewell House, Lymington, Hants, 1805–40, and Rook Cliff, Milford-on-Sea, Hants, 1813–15, contrib. J. S. Hansom, notes by J. Gillow.

h Catholic registers of the Rev. Monox Hervey, *alias* John Rivett, *alias* John Moxon [in Oxon., London, Yorks., and co. Montgomery, 1729–56], contrib. J. S. Hansom.

i Official documents [1745–6], supplementing the Rev. Monox Hervey's registers, contrib. J. S. Hansom.

941 Vols. 15, 16. Lancashire registers, I–II: The Fylde [1763–1851], ed. J. P. Smith. 1 vol. in 2. 1913–14

942 Vol. 17. Miscellanea X. 1915.

a Records of the English canonesses of the Holy Sepulchre of Liège, now at New Hall [Essex], 1652–1793, ed. R. Trappes-Lomax.

b Registers of the English Benedictine nuns of Pontoise, now at Teignmouth, 1680–1713.

c Official documents relating to an enquiry as to the estate of Robert Charnock of Leyland, priest, left for 'superstitious uses', 1687, contrib. G. E. Hine.

d Catholic registers of Harvington Hall, Chaddesley-Corbett, Worcs., a chaplaincy of the Throckmortons, 1752–1823, contrib. E. H. Burton, notes by J. Gillow.

e Catholic registers of Linton-upon-Ouse, Newton-upon-Ouse, near York [1771–1840], contrib. J. S. Hansom, notes by J. Gillow.

f Catholic registers of the domestic chapel of the Browne-Mostyn family at Kiddington, Oxon., 1788–1840, contrib. H. H. Ball, notes by the Hon. Mrs. B. Stapleton.

g Catholic registers of St. Peter's, Woolston, Warrington, 1771–1834, ed. J. S. Hansom, notes by J. Gillow.

943 Vol. 18. Recusant roll, no. 1, 1592–3 (Exchequer, lord treasurer's remembrancer, Pipe office series), contrib. Muriel M. C. Calthrop. 1916.

944 Vol. 19. Miscellanea XI. 1917.

a Obituary notices of the nuns of the English Benedictine abbey of Ghent in Flanders [and at Preston, Lancs.], 1627–1811.

b Register book of St. Gregory's college, Paris, 1667–1786, contrib. E. H. Burton.

c Catholic registers kept by the Rev. Bruno Cantrill, O.S.F , in London (?), 1726–55, contrib. C. R. Lindsay.

d Six Catholic marriage registers kept by the Rev. Joseph Alexius Smallwood, O.S.F., in London (?), 1730–50, contrib. C. R. Lindsay.

e Catholic registers kept by the Rev. Arthur Pacificus Baker, O.S.F., Lincoln's Inn Fields, London, 1747–73, contrib. C. R. Lindsay.

f Catholic registers of the church at Lincoln's Inn Fields, London: an instalment of baptisms and marriages from 1759, with collections of previous entries, contrib. C. R. Lindsay, notes by Johanna H. Harting [and J. S. Hansom].

945 Vol. 20. Lancashire registers, III: Northern part [1762–1855], ed. J. P. Smith. 1916.

946 Vol. 21. English martyrs, vol. ii: The Ven. Philip Howard, Earl of Arundel, 1557–95, ed. J. H. Pollen and W. MacMahon. 1919.

947 Vol. 22. Miscellanea XII. 1921.

a Diocesan returns of recusants for England and Wales, 1577, contrib. P. Ryan.
b Two letters of Bishop Barnes [on recusancy, 1570 and 1585], contrib. J. H. Pollen.
c Recusants and priests, Mar. 1588, contrib. J. H. Pollen.
d Prisoners in the Fleet, 1577–80, contrib. J. H. Pollen.
e The archpriest controversy, contrib. R. Stanfield.
f John Mawson, layman, martyr, 1612, and some Catholic Mawsons, contrib. J. Mawson.
g Register book of the Catholic chapel, Market Rasen, Lincs., 1797–1840, contrib. G. F. Engelbach.
h Catholic registers of Knaresborough, 1765–1840, contrib. T. G. Cummins, G. F. Engelbach, and J. S. Hansom.
i Catholic registers of Costessey or Cossey Hall, Norf., the seat of the Jerningham family, 1785–1821, contrib. J. P. Smith, notes by E. H. Burton and J. S. Hansom.
j Catholic registers of the domestic chapel of the Goring, Biddulph, and Wright family at Burton House, Suss., 1720–1855, contrib. Bernardine Fish, ed. J. S. Hansom.
k Addenda to Market Rasen registers, etc., contrib. J. S. Hansom.
l Michael Tirrye, B.A., schoolmaster, recusant [*c.* 1590], contrib. J. S. Hansom.

948 Vol. 23. Lancashire registers, IV: Brindle and Samlesbury [1722–1840], presented by J. P. Smith. 1922.

949 Vol. 24. The English Franciscan nuns, 1619–1821, and the Friars Minor of the same province, 1618–1761, ed. R. Trappes-Lomax. 1922.

950 Vol. 25. Dominicana. 1925.

a Letters of Philip, Cardinal Howard, 1645–94, contrib. B. Jarrett, with addenda contrib. R. C. Wilton.
b English Dominican papers [1619–1829] and obituary roll [1661–1827], contrib. R. Bracey.
c English Dominican books and papers, contrib. B. Jarrett.
d Records of nuns of the second order [1661–1797].
e The Rev. William Lister, O.P.: letter concerning his identity from the Rev. Robert Fisher to the Rev. Christopher Bagshawe, 1597 or 1598, contrib. B. Jarrett.
f Catholic registers of the Rev. James Dominic Darbyshire, O.P., at Standish and Borwick Hall, Warton, Lancs., 1728; Gifford Hall, Suff., 1728; and Ugbrooke Park, Devon, 1736–55. Contrib. B. Jarrett. [In Flemish]
g Catholic registers of Aston-Flamville, Leics., 1759–67, contrib. E. Henson, notes by W. Gumbley.
h Catholic baptisms at Carshalton, Surr., by Fr. John Ambrose Woods, O.P., 1798–9, contrib. J. S. Hansom.

951 Vol. 26. Miscellanea XIII. 1926.

a Some letters and papers of Nicholas Sander, 1562–80, contrib. J. B. Wainewright.
b Catholic registers of Hammersmith, Mdx., 1710–1838, contrib. Johanna H. Harting. [Corrections in vol. 27]

c Catholic registers kept by Fr. Peter Antoninus Thompson, O.P., at Stonecroft, as chaplain to the Gibson family, from 1715; at Hexham and Stonecroft, Northumb., conjointly, from 1721; at Hexham alone, from 1734; and by other Dominicans, 1754–1826, transcribed by J. Stark, ed. J. R. Baterden.
d Catholic registers of Stonecroft, Northumb., kept by the Dominicans after its separation from Hexham, 1737–1821, transcribed by J. Stark, ed. J. R. Baterden.
e Catholic registers of the secular mission of Hexham at Cockshaw, Northumb., 1753–1832, transcribed by J. Stark, ed. J. R. Baterden.

952 Vol. 27. Miscellanea [XIV]. 1927.

a Catholic registers of Brambridge (afterwards Highbridge) mission, Hants, 1766–1869, transcribed and ed. R. C. Baigent. [Postscript at end of vol.]
b Catholic registers of the domestic chapel at Arundel Castle, afterwards at the public chapel at Arundel, 1749–1835, followed by a list of burials in the FitzAlan chapel at Arundel (other than those mentioned in Tierney's *History of Arundel*), and a private register of burials there since 1866, transcribed and ed. F. J. A. Skeet.
c Catholic registers of Abergavenny, Mon., 1740–1838, ed. J. H. Canning, introd. by E. H. Willson.
d Account of the life and death of Brother Alexis, called in the world Robert Graeme, a Scotch gentleman, d. 1701; a contemporary translation of the 1703 French edition, contrib. G. F. Engelbach.
e A list of guests at Everingham Park, Yorks., Christmas, 1662, contrib. R. C. Wilton.

953 Vol. 28. The Douay college diaries: The seventh diary, 1715–78, preceded by a summary of events, 1691–1715, ed. E. H. Burton and E. Nolan. 1928 [1929].

954 Vol. 29. The English college at Madrid, 1611–1767, ed. E. Henson. 1929.

955 Vol. 30. Registers of the English college at Valladolid, 1589–1862, ed. E. Henson. 1930 [1931].

956 Vol. 31. Lancashire registers, V: Fernyhalgh, Goosnargh, and Alston Lane [1771–1856], ed. R. L. Smith. 1932.

957 Vol. 32. Miscellanea [XV]. 1932 [1933].

a Life of Francis Tregian, written in the 17th cent. by Francis Plunkett, Cistercian monk, contrib. Mrs. P. A. Boyan.
b Catholic registers of Kendal, Westmld., 1762–1840, with notes on the mission of Dodding Green from 1706, ed. J. R. Baterden.
c Catholic registers of Reading, 1780–1840, and Woodley Lodge, 1802–69, transcribed and ed. R. E. Scantlebury.
d Catholic registers of Robert Hall and Hornby, Lancs., 1762–1818: supplementary article contrib. J. P. Smith.
e Archbishop Blackburn's visitation returns of the diocese of York, 1735, contrib. R. Trappes-Lomax.
f Some hostile 'true reports' of the martyrs [six tracts relating to martyrdoms between 1581 and 1643], contrib. C. A. Newdigate.

958 Vol. 33. Memorials of Father Augustine Baker and other documents relating to the English Benedictines, ed. J. McCann and H. Connolly. 1933.

Other publications:

959 Ten years' work of the Society, by J. H. Pollen. *P.* 1914.
960 The Catholic Record Society. *P.* n.d. [Mss. printed by the Soc., being a résumé of the contents of vols. 1–46]

CHAUCER SOCIETY

Founded 1867, to do honour to Chaucer, and to let the lovers and students of him see how far the best unprinted mss. of his works differed from the printed texts. Subscriptions ceased in 1910, though parts of works then unfinished were issued from time to time until at least as late as 1924.

Publications, 1st ser., *including:*

961 No. 82. The romaunt of the rose: a reprint of the first printed [English] edition by William Thynne, 1532, ed. F. J. Furnivall. 1911.

962 No. 89. Specimen extracts from the nine known unprinted mss. of Chaucer's 'Troilus' and from Caxton's and Thynne's first editions, ed. Sir W. S. McCormick and R. K. Root. 1914.

963 Nos. 95, 96. The Cambridge ms. Dd. 4.24 of Chaucer's Canterbury tales, completed by the Egerton ms. 2726 (the Haistwell ms.), ed. F. J. Furnivall. 1 vol. in 2. 1902 [1901–2].

964 No. 97. Specimens of all the unprinted mss. of the Canterbury tales, pt. 9: The clerk's tale and headlink, put forth by F. J. Furnivall, with introd. by J. Koch. 1902. [Pts. 1–5: The pardoner's tale, and pts. 6–8: The clerk's tale, were published 1890–1900]

965 No. 98. The mss. of Chaucer's 'Troilus', with collotype facsimiles of the various handwritings, by R. K. Root. 1914.

966 No. 99. The textual tradition of Chaucer's 'Troilus', by R. K. Root. 1916.

Publications, 2nd ser., *including:*

967 No. 33. Richard Brathwait's comments, in 1665, upon Chaucer's tales of the miller and the wife of Bath, ed. with introd. by Caroline F. E. Spurgeon. 1901.

968 No. 34. A new ploughman's tale: Thomas Hoccleves, legend of the Virgin and her sleeveless garment, with a spurious link, ed. from ms. CLII, Christ Church, Oxford (Chaucer's Canterbury tales), by A. Beatty; paralleled with another copy of Mr. Israel Gollancz's edition of Hoccleve's minor poems, pt. 2 (E.E.T. Soc.), from the Ashburnham quarto ms. 133. *P.* 1902.

969 No. 35. The pardoner's prologue and tale, by Geoffrey Chaucer: a critical edition by J. Koch. 1902.

970 No. 36. Analogues of Chaucer's Canterbury pilgrimage (April 1386) and his putting-up joust-scaffolds, etc., in West-Smithfield (May, 1390), being the expenses of the Aragonese ambassadors in England, 1415, and the cos. of erecting scaffolds, etc., in West-Smithfield, 1442, ed F. J. Furnivall and R. E. G. Kirk. *P.* 1903.

971 No. 37. The development and chronology of Chaucer's works, by J. S. P. Tatlock. 1907.

972 No. 38. The evolution of the Canterbury tales, by W. W. Skeat. *P.* 1907.

973 No. 39. Studies in Chaucer's 'Hous of fame', by W. O· Sypherd. 1907.

974 No. 40. The origin and development of the story of Troilus and Criseyde, by K. Young. 1908.

975 No. 41. The Harleian ms. 7334 and revision of the Canterbury tales, by J. S. P. Tatlock. *P.* 1909.

976 No. 42. The date of Chaucer's 'Troilus', and other Chaucer matters, by G. L. Kittredge. 1909.

977 No. 43. The eight-text edition of the Canterbury tales, with remarks upon the classification of the mss. and upon Harleian ms. 7334, by W. W. Skeat. 1909.

978 No. 45. A study of the miracle of Our Lady, told by Chaucer's prioress, by C. Brown. 1910.

979 No. 46. Lydgate's Siege of Thebes, ed. from all the known mss. and the two oldest editions, by A. Erdmann. Pt. i: Text. 1911. [Also published by the Early English Text Soc., extra series, no. 108. No. 125 in the same series contains introd. and notes]

980 No. 47. A detailed comparison of the eight mss. of Chaucer's Canterbury tales, as completely printed in the publications of the Society, by J. Koch. 1913.

981 Nos. 48–50, 52–56. Five hundred years of Chaucer criticism and allusion, 1357–1900, by Caroline F. E. Spurgeon, with supplement containing additional entries, 1868–1900. 7 vols. (nos. 49 and 50 being one vol.), 1914–24.

982 No. 51. The scene of the franklin's tale visited, by J. S. P. Tatlock. 1914.

CHELTENHAM SCIENCE SOCIETY

Founded 1877, as the Cheltenham Natural Science Society, to further the study of science. Title changed to the above form in 1921.

Proceedings, new ser.,[1] vol. 1–vol. 5, pt. 1 (1907–30):

983 Vol. 1.
a Handicrafts of pre-historic man, by Miss M. A. Reid.
b A supposed Roman circus on Cleeve hill, by E. T. Wilson.
c Notes on a supposed Roman circus, by C. Callaway.
d The Romans on the Cotteswolds: why the camps were occupied, by L. Richardson.
e Brickearths, pottery and brickmaking in Gloucestershire, by L. Richardson and R. J. Webb.

984 Vol. 2.
a Flints of the Cotteswolds and their users, by E. T. Wilson.
b Notes on the north and mid-Cotteswold flints, by J. W. Gray.
c The evolution of Gothic architecture, by C. I. Gardiner.
d Long-barrow men of the Cotswolds, by E. T. Wilson.

985 Vol. 3.
a Notes on the long barrow race beyond the Cotteswolds, by E. T. Wilson.
b Church glass, by A. J. de H. Bushnell.
c Excursion to Uley, by A. J. de H. Bushnell.
d Summary of a lecture [on British prehistoric monuments], by A. M. McAldowie.

986 Vol. 4.
a The history of scientific discovery [as illustrated by the discovery of the circulation of the blood], by F. J. Cole.

[1] None of the 1st ser., mostly reprinted from *The Cheltenham Examiner*, has been seen; the vol. for 1904–5 is reported to include 'Gloucestershire and ancient British history', by J. Evans.

CHESTER AND NORTH WALES ARCHITECTURAL, ARCHAEOLOGICAL AND HISTORIC SOCIETY

Founded 1849, as the Architectural, Archaeological and Historic Society of the county, city and neighbourhood of Chester, for the collection and publication of archaeological and historical information relating to the city and county of Chester and the neighbourhood. The following variations of the title occur at different periods: Chester Archaeological and Historical Society; Chester Architectural, Archaeological and Historic Society; Chester and North Wales Archaeological and Historic Society.

Journal, new ser., vols. 8–30 (1902–33):

987 Vol. 8.

a Cotes monument, once set up in St. John's church, Chester, by S. C. Scott.
b A defence of the liberties of Chester, 1450, by H. D. Harrod.
c The Chester Rows, by H. D. Harrod.
d The nave roof of the church of St. Mary-on-the-Hill [Chester], by E. Barber.
e A descriptive account of Roman and other objects from various sites in Chester and district, 1898–1901, by R. Newstead.
f An extended list of potters' stamps on the red-glazed Roman ware (popularly known as Samian) found at Chester; with the chief forms of stamping briefly classified, by F. H. Williams.
g Early lead miners brought from the High Peak to work in Flintshire, by H. Taylor.

988 Vol. 9.

a The cloisters of Chester cathedral, by E. Barber.
b Ludlow and the masque of Comus [performed at Ludlow castle, 1634], by J. C. Bridge.
c Chester cathedral: the stalls, misereres and woodwork of the choir, by E. Barber.
d Chester miracle plays, some facts concerning them, and the supposed authorship of Ralph Higden, by J. C. Bridge.
e The south transept of Chester cathedral, by E. Barber.
f Discovery of Ralph Higden's tomb, by E. Barber.
g Notes on four leaden weights of supposed Roman origin in the Grosvenor museum, Chester, by T. May.

989 Vol. 10.

a Gleanings from the muniment room of the town hall, Chester (Stuart period), by R. H. Morris.
b Chester in the 12th and 13th cent.; being notes on recently discovered documents relating to the city, dating from 1178, by W. F. Irvine.
c Ancient glass in the church of St. Mary-on-the-Hill [Chester], by E. Barber.
d St. Werburgh and her shrine, by E. Barber.
e George Lloyd, D.D., bishop of Chester, 1605–16, by F. Sanders.
f Ten early Chester deeds, 1270–1490, by H. Taylor.

990 Vol. 11.

a Churchwardens' accounts of the parish of St. Bridget, Chester, 1811–47, by E. Barber.
b 'The Cheshire regiment', or 22nd regiment of Foot, by F. Simpson.
c On 'peculiars', with special reference to the 'peculiar' of Hawarden, by W. E. B. Whittaker.
d Horns, by J. C. Bridge.
e Notes on the architecture of Basingwerk abbey, Flintshire, by E. Hodkinson.

991 Vol. 12.

a Chester cathedral: the Jacobean work, by E. Barber.
b Churchwardens' accounts of St. Martin's, Chester, 1683–1816, by E. Barber.
c The Glynnes of Hawarden, by W. E. B. Whittaker.

992 Vol. 13.

a Bishop Chadderton's visitation articles [1581], ed. F. Sanders.
b Notes on Chester street-names past and present (northern section), by G. W. Haswell.
c Notes on Chester street-names, past and present, by W. E. Brown.
d Notes on the history of St. Mary's nunnery, Chester, by W. F. Irvine.
e John Bird, D.D., bishop of Chester, 1541–54, by F. Sanders.
f Chester cathedral: some details of its architecture often unnoticed, by E. Barber.

993 Vol. 14.

a Notes on the coins of the Potter-Meols collection, by F. W. Longbottom.
b Chester mystery plays, by H. Gollancz.
c Quakers in Chester under the Protectorate, by F. Sanders.
d The river Dee, by F. Simpson.
e Two Cheshire soldiers of fortune of the 14th cent.: Sir Hugh Calveley, and Sir Robert Knolles, by J. C. Bridge.
f Three Chester Whitsun plays, with introd. and notes by J. C. Bridge. [1: The salutation and Nativity. 2: The play of the Shepherds. 3: The adoration of the Magi]

994 Vol. 15.

a The Cheshire gentry in 1715: drawn from the Ashley Hall portraits at Tatton, by Earl Egerton of Tatton.
b Diary of Nehemiah Griffith, esq., of Rhual, Mold, for 1715, ed. J. C. Bridge.
c The 1715 rebellion: letters from John Rutherford, a Scottish prisoner of war at Liverpool, and William Elliott, esq., relative to his release.
d Church of All Saints, Gresford: a guess at its architectural history, by E. A. Fishbourne.
e Acton church and Dorfold Hall [Cheshire]: a description in 1907, by J. Hall.
f Parish registers of Burton, by P. F. A. Morrell.
g The St. Oswald's reredos, and the frescoes in Chester cathedral, by E. Barber.

995 Vol. 16.

a A recently discovered section of the Roman wall a Chester, by R. Newstead.
b The pentice and other ancient law courts in Chester, by Sir H. Lloyd.
c Discovery of three documents relating to the family of the Randle Holmes of Chester, by H. Taylor.
d Some early 18th cent. brasses in Ince church, by F. G. Slater.
e St. Plegmund and his connection with Cheshire, by E. Barber.
f The conquest of Britain by the Angles in the light of military science, by P. T. Godsal.
g Chester cathedral: the mosaics, by E. Barber.
h A preliminary note of the Roman remains discovered in Chester during 1909.

996 Vol. 17.

a Trade and customs of Chester in the 17th and 18th cent. as shown in some old parish registers, by E. Barber.
b The feodary's returns for Cheshire, 1576, by J. Hall.

c Story of Ince in the 18th cent. extracted from the parish records and other sources, by F. G. Slater.

d The baptistry of the cathedral [Chester], by E. Barber.

e Report on the Earwaker ms. collection in the Grosvenor museum library, Chester, by J. Hall.

f Inventory of [Chester] corporation plate, insignia, and regalia.

g Painting in the church of St. Mary-on-the-Hill, Chester, by E. Barber.

997 Vol. 18.

a Parkgate: an old Cheshire port, by E. Barber.

b Royal charters and grants to the city of Chester, by J. Hall. [With list of expenses relating to the 1685 charter]

c A Roman urn from Wroxeter in the Grosvenor museum, and other pottery of the 1st cent. A.D., by R. C. Bosanquet.

d George Cotes, bishop of Chester, 1554–55, by F. Sanders.

e City guilds or companies of Chester, with special reference to that of the barber-surgeons, by F. Simpson.

f Ancient boat in Baddiley mere, by E. Barber.

998 Vol. 19.

a Cilcain and its parish church, by F. Simpson.

b Organists of Chester cathedral, 1541–1644 and 1663–1877, by J. C. Bridge.

c The Berringtons of Cheshire, by J. H. E. Bennett.

d The 16th cent. abbots of St. Werburgh's, Chester; some notes on documents relating to the abbey and other religious houses of Cheshire; and a mediaeval guide book to Chester, by Miss M. V. Taylor.

e The ancient abbey of Vale Royal, by J. H. Cooke.

999 Vol. 20.

a City guilds of Chester: the Smiths, Cutlers and Plumbers' company, by F. Simpson.

b Notes on the Chester hand or glove, by R. Stewart-Brown.

c Two letters by the Beverley family of Huntington near Chester [1598 and 1644], by J. Hall.

d Items of expenditure from 16th cent. accounts of the Painters, Glaziers, Embroiderers and Stationers' company, with special reference to the 'Shepherds' Play', by J. C. Bridge.

e Two Elizabethan chamberlains of the palatinate of Chester [Robert Dudley, Earl of Leicester, and Henry, Earl of Derby], by J. H. E. Bennett.

f A Roman centurion of the 20th legion, by H. Taylor.

1000 Vol. 21.

a Leche House, Chester, by F. Simpson. [Includes an inventory, 1639]

b Chester's oldest newspaper [*The Chester Weekly Journal*], by H. Taylor.

c Cheshire and 'the Fifteen', by J. H. E. Bennett.

d Chester newspapers about 100 years ago, by J. Hall.

e Chester Welsh printing, by M. Parry. [With list of ballads, 1752–1800]

f City gilds of Chester: the Skinners and Felt-makers' company, by F. Simpson.

g Holy Trinity church, Chester: records of three centuries [1532–1837], by L. M. Farrall.

h Chester cathedral: recent work in the cloisters and refectory, by E. Barber.

1001 Vol. 22.

a A deed of transfer of family property [in Chester] by Randle Holme III and Randle Holme IV in 1690, by H. Taylor.

b Five letters of Henry Maynwaring of Chester, merchant,

to Thomas Trafford, esq., of Bridge Trafford, co. Chester, 1588–9, by P. H. Lawson.

c Kenrick Edisbury, surveyor of the navy, 1632–8, and his descendants; being a brief account of the family of Edisbury of Marchwiel, co. Denbigh, by J. C. Bridge.

d City gilds of Chester: the Bricklayers' company, by F. Simpson.

e The execution of criminals in Cheshire, by R. S. Brown. [On the liability of the sheriffs of the city and co. of Chester, mainly in 19th cent., with an addendum by H. Taylor]

f Some early deeds relating to land on the north side of Eastgate Street, Chester [14th–16th cent.], by R. M. Montgomery.

g The abbey church of St. Werburgh, Chester, in pre-Norman times, by G. W. Haswell.

h Matthew Henry's chapel, by W. W. Tasker.

i Hatton Hall [near Waverton], by J. H. E. Bennett.

1002 Vol. 23.

a Chester Blue Coat hospital, by F. G. Wright.

b Arms and inscriptions sometime in the church of St. Bridget, Chester, by J. H. E. Bennett.

c The mediaeval stall-end in Hawarden parish church and contemporary panels in Eastham church, by W. F. J. Timbrell.

d A short account of the life of George Clarke, lieutenant-governor of New York, 1736–45, by R. H. Linaker.

1003 Vol. 24.

a The Grey friars of Chester, by J. H. E. Bennett [with additions by A. Hamilton Thompson].

b Family memoranda of the Stanleys of Alderley, 1590–1601 and 1621–7, by P. H. Lawson.

c The cult of Mithra in Deva, by W. J. Williams.

d Catalogue of Roman coins in the Chester museum, comp. J. T. Davies and F. W. Longbottom.

1004 Vol. 25.

a Siege of Chester, 1643–6, by R. H. Morris; ed. and completed by P. H. Lawson. 1923.

1005 Vol. 26.

a Report on Roman potters' marks found in Chester, by A. G. K. Hayter.

b The trade of Chester in the reigns of the three Edwards, by H. J. Hewitt.

c Mediaeval oak coffins at Nantwich. [Part of a report by F. Simpson]

d Chester castle, 907–1925, by F. Simpson.

e Commonplace-book of John Crewe of Utkinton, Ches., c. 1640–50, by P. H. Lawson.

f Jupiter Tanarus, by R. G. Collingwood. [On a Roman altar found in Chester, 1653]

1006 Vol. 27.

a 13th cent. crypt, Bridge Street, Chester, by F. Simpson.

b Royal Oak inn, Chester, by F. Simpson.

c Communications and transport in mediaeval Cheshire, by H. J. Hewitt.

d Records of archaeological finds at Chester, by R. Newstead.

e Schedule of Roman remains of Chester, with maps and plans, by P. H. Lawson. [Contd. in vol. 29]

1007 Vol. 28.

a Diary of George Booth of Chester [d. 1719] and Katherine Howard, his daughter, of Boughton, near Chester, 1707–64, by G. P. Crawfurd.

b The family of Proby in Chester and Ireland, by G. P. Crawfurd.

c A few Cheshire worthies [Richard Taylor, d. 1827; Joseph Hemingway, d. 1837; George Cuitt the younger, d. 1854; John Musgrove, b. 1785; William Cole, junior, d. 1892; William Tasker, d. 1852; Frances Wilbraham, d. 1905; James Harrison, d. 1866], by F. Simpson.

d Druidism, by A. G. Edwards.

e The Troutbeck family [of Cheshire], by J. Brownbill.

f The Stuart kings and Chester corporation, by H. T. Dutton.

g A letter of confraternity of the Grey friars, Chester [to Nicholas Kerke, 1479], by J. H. E. Bennett.

1008 Vol. 29.

a Roman amphitheatre at Chester, by R. Newstead and J. P. Droop.

b The S.E. corner of the Roman fortress, Chester, by R. Newstead and J. P. Droop.

c Early man in the Cheshire plain, by W. J. Varley.

1009 Vol. 30.

a Excavations at Heronbridge, 1930–31, by J. A. Petch. [With a report on human remains by E. Davies]

b The Watling street at Heronbridge, by W. J. Williams.

c The old Dee bridge at Chester, by R. Stewart-Brown. [With note by P. H. Lawson]

d The Newgate and Wolf's tower (now Thimbleby's tower), by F. Simpson.

e Constructional design of church timber roofs in Cheshire, Denbighshire and Flintshire, by F. H. Crossley.

f Roman ditch at Heronbridge, by W. J. Williams.

1010 Subject-indexes to the old series, vols. 1–3, 1849–85, and new series, vols. 1–18, 1887–1911. *P.* 1912.

1011 Subject-index and index of authors to vols. 18–28, 1911–29, of new series, comp. W. J. Varley and Joan Varley. *P.* 1929.

CHESTER SOCIETY OF NATURAL SCIENCE, LITERATURE AND ART

Founded 1871, to promote the study of natural science, literature and art.

Thirtieth–Fifty-ninth Annual Report and Proceedings (1901–30):

1012 51st Report.

a Charles Kingsley and the Chester naturalists, by Sir W. A. Herdman.

Other publications:

1013 The formation [by Charles Kingsley] of the Chester Society of Natural Science, Literature, and Art, and an epitome of its subsequent history, by J. D. Siddall. *P.* 1911.

CHETHAM SOCIETY

Founded 1843, for the publication of historical and literary remains connected with the palatine counties of Lancaster and Chester.

Remains Historical and Literary connected with the palatine counties of Lancaster and Chester, new ser., vols. 44–90:

1014 Vol. 44. Act book of the ecclesiastical court of Whalley, 1510–38, ed. Alice M. Cooke. 1901.

1015 Vols. 45, 51. History of the ancient chapel of Stretford in Manchester parish, including sketches of the township of Stretford, together with notices of local families and persons, by H. T. Crofton. Vols. ii and iii, 1901–3. [Vol. i was published in 1899]

1016 Vols. 46, 48. Portmote or court leet records of the borough or town and royal manor of Salford, 1597–1669, transcribed and ed. J. G. de T. Mandley. 2 vols. 1902. [Additions in vol. 80]

1017 Vol. 47. Chetham miscellanies, new ser., vol. i. 1902.

a Inventories of goods in the churches and chapels of Lancashire, 1552, ed. H. Fishwick and J. E. Bailey. Pt. 3: Amounderness and Lonsdale hundreds. 1902. [Continues 1st ser., vols. 107–113, published in 1879–88]

b An exhortation for contributions to maintain preachers in Lancashire, by George Walker, B.D., rector of St. John Evangelist's, Watling Street, London (c. 1641), with introd. by C. W. Sutton. 1901.

c The wonderful child: tracts issued in 1679 relating to Charles Bennett of Manchester, alleged to speak Latin, Greek, and Hebrew, when three years old without having been taught, ed. W. E. A. Axon. 1901.

d Mosley family: memoranda [mainly 17th cent.] of Oswald and Nicholas Mosley of Ancoats, from the Manchester sessions ms. in the free reference library Manchester, ed. with genealogical introd. by E. Axon. 1902.

1018 Vols. 49, 50. Life of Humphrey Chetham [d. 1653], founder of the Chetham hospital and library, by F. R. Raines and C. W. Sutton. 1 vol. in 2. 1903.

1019 Vols. 52–55. History of Newton chapelry in the ancient parish of Manchester, including sketches of the townships of Newton with Kirkmanshulme, Failsworth, and Bradford, but exclusive of the townships of Droylsden and Moston, together with notices of local families and persons, by H. T. Crofton. 3 vols. in 4. 1904–5.

1020 Vols. 56, 57, 64. Chartulary of Cockersand abbey of the Premonstratensian order printed from the original in the possession of Sir Thomas Brooke, transcribed and ed. W. Farrer. Vol. iii, pts. 1–3, 1905–9. [Vols. i and ii, each in 2 pts., were published as vols. 38, 39, 40, and 43, in 1898–1900]

1021 Vols. 58, 59. Materials for the history of the church of Lancaster, ed. W. O. Roper. Vols. iii and iv, 1906. [Vols. i and ii were published as vols. 26 and 31, in 1892–4]

1022 Vol. 60. History of the parish of Lytham in the county of Lancaster, by H. Fishwick. 1907.

1023 Vols. 61, 62. Materials for the history of Lancaster, by W. O. Roper. 1 vol. in 2. 1907.

1024 Vol. 63. Chetham miscellanies, new ser., vol. ii. 1909.

a Broughton near Manchester: its topography and manor court, by H. T. Crofton. 1909.

b The apostolical life of Ambrose Barlow, O.S.B. [1585–1641], ed. from the original ms. in the Manchester University library by W. E. Rhodes. 1908.

c A Manchester assessment of 1648, with introd. by E. Broxap. 1909.

1025 Vol. 65. Tracts relating to the civil war in Cheshire, 1641–59, including Sir George Booth's rising in that county, ed. J. A. Atkinson. 1909.

1026 Vols. 66–68. Records of Blackburn grammar school, ed. G. A. Stocks. 1 vol. in 3. 1909.

1027 Vol. 69. The township booke of Halliwell [accounts, 1640–1762], transcribed and ed. A. Sparke. 1910.

1028 Vol. 70. Poems of John Byrom, ed. A. W. Ward. Vol. iii, with appendix of unpublished letters by and to Byrom.

1912. [Continues vols. 29, 30, 34 and 35, published in 1894-5]

1029 Vol. 71. Survey of the manor of Rochdale in the county of Lancaster, parcel of the possessions of the rt. worshipful Sir Robert Heath, knt., His Majesty's attorney general, made in 1626, ed. H. Fishwick. 1913.

1030 Vol. 72. History of Leagram: the park and the manor, by J. Weld. 1913.

1031 Vol. 73. Chetham miscellanies, new ser., vol. iii. 1915.
  a Documents relating to the plague in Manchester in 1605, with other memoranda, 1593-1606, ed. W. E. A. Axon. 1909.
  b Survey of the manor of Penwortham in 1570, transcribed and ed. C. W. Sutton. 1914.
  c List of clergymen, etc., in the diocese of Chester, 1691, recorded at the first visitation of Nicholas Stratford, bishop of Chester, ed. with introd. by John Brownbill. 1915.

1032 Vols. 74, 76, 78. Coucher book of Furness abbey. Vol. ii, pts. 1-3, ed. J. Brownbill. 1915-19. [Continues vols. 9, 11 and 14, published in 1886-7, ed. J. C. Atkinson]

1033 Vol. 75. Domesday survey of Cheshire, ed. with introd., translation and notes by J. Tait. 1916.

1034 Vol. 77. Lancashire quarter sessions records, ed. with introd. and notes by J. Tait. Vol. i: 1590-1606. 1917.

1035 Vols. 79, 82. Chartulary or register of the abbey of St. Werburgh, Chester, ed. with introd. and notes by J. Tait. 1 vol. in 2. 1920-3.

1036 Vol. 80. Chetham miscellanies, new ser., vol. iv. 1921.
  a Dunkenhalgh deeds, c. 1200-1600, ed. G. A. Stocks and J. Tait. 1921.
  b Extracts from Manchester churchwardens' accounts, 1664-1710, by E. Broxap. 1921.
  c The new court book of the manor of Bramhall, 1632-57, by H. W. Clemesha. 1921.
  d Latin verses and speeches by scholars of the Manchester grammar school, 1640 and 1750-1800, ed. A. A. Mumford. 1921.
  e Records of some Salford portmoots in the 16th cent., ed. J. Tait. 1921.

1037 Vol. 81. Place-names of Lancashire, by E. Ekwall. 1922.

1038 Vol. 83. Taxation in Salford hundred, 1524-1802, ed. with introd. and notes by J. Tait. 1924.

1039 Vol. 84. Calendar of county court, city court and eyre rolls of Chester, 1259-97, with an inquest of military service, 1288, ed. with introd. by R. Stewart-Brown. 1925.

1040 Vol. 85. History of the township and manor of Clayton-le-Moors, co. Lancaster, by R. Trappes-Lomax. 1926.

1041 Vol. 86. Economic history of Rossendale, by G. H. Tupling. 1927.

1042 Vol. 87. Plea rolls of the county palatine of Lancaster: roll I [1401 etc.], ed. J. Parker. 1928.

1043 Vol. 88. Mediaeval Cheshire: an economic and social history of Cheshire in the reigns of the three Edwards, by H. J. Hewitt. 1929.

1044 Vol. 89. Diary and letter book of the Rev. Thomas Brockbank, 1671-1709, ed. R. Trappes-Lomax. 1930.

1045 Vol. 90. Chetham miscellanies, new ser., vol. v. 1931.
  a History of the township of Arkholme in co. Lancaster, comp. W. H. Chippindall. 1931.

  b Some Ewood deeds [1541-1823], by T. Woodcock. 1931.
  c The hundred of Leyland in Lancashire, by T. C. Porteus. 1931.
  d Narrative of the indictment of the traitors of Whalley and Cartmell, 1536-7, by J. E. W. Wallis. 1931.

CHURCH HISTORICAL SOCIETY

Founded 1896, to deal with the crisis in Anglicanism caused by the papal condemnation of Anglican orders. Dissolved 1916.

Publications, *including:*

1046 No. 65. Typical English churchmen, from Parker to Maurice. A series of lectures ed. W. E. Collins. 1902.
  a Matthew Parker, by H. Gee.
  b Richard Hooker, by A. J. Mason.
  c William Chillingworth, by H. Rashdall.
  d James Ussher, by E. W. Watson.
  e John Bramhall, by W. E. Collins.
  f Jeremy Taylor, by H. H. Henson.
  g Gilbert Burnet, by H. W. C. Davis.
  h Joseph Butler, by H. Wace.
  i William Warburton, by J. N. Figgis.
  j Charles Simeon, by C. H. Simpkinson.
  k Henry Phillpotts, by E. C. S. Gibson.
  l Frederick Denison Maurice, by W. E. Collins.

1047 No. 78. Typical English churchmen, ser. 2: From Wyclif to Gardiner. 1909.
  a John Wyclif, by J. N. Figgis.
  b William of Wykeham, by W. A. Spooner.
  c William Courtenay, by T. S. Holmes.
  d Cardinal Beaufort, by L. B. Radford.
  e Cuthbert Tunstall, by G. H. Ross-Lewin.
  f Stephen Gardiner, by J. Gairdner.

1048 No. 71. Thomas Becket: a lecture by W. E. Collins. *P.* 1902.

1049 No. 72. Puritan manifestoes: a study of the origin of the Puritan revolt, with a reprint of the *Admonition to the Parliament*, and kindred documents, 1572, ed. W. H. Frere and C. E. Douglas. 1907.

1050 No. 73. Three chapters in recent liturgical research, by J. Wickham Legg. 1903. [Two chapters, on the *Missa Catachumenorum* or 'Table prayers', and on relics in the consecration of altars, contain slight references to England]

1051 No. 79. Church and state in England before the Conquest, by W. E. Collins. *P.* 1903.

1052 No. 94. The peculium: an endeavour to throw light on some of the causes of the decline of the Society of Friends, especially in regard to its original claim of being the peculiar people of God, by T. Hancock. 2nd edn. revised, with introd. by W. E. Collins. 1907.

CHURCH HISTORICAL SOCIETY

Founded 1929. The earlier Society (q.v.) did not publish after 1909 and was dissolved in 1916.

Publications, new ser., *including:*

1053 The Carthusian order in England, by E. Margaret Thompson. 1930.

1054 Studies in English Puritanism from the Restoration to the Revolution, 1660-1688, by C. E. Whiting. 1931.

1055 Sitting for the psalms: an historical study, by C. F. Rogers. *P.* 1931.

1056 A history of the church in Blackburnshire, by J. E. W. Wallis. 1932. [Chiefly concerned with the parishes of Blackburn and Whalley]

1057 The renewed church of the United Brethren, 1722–1930, by W. G. Addison. 1932. [With special reference to the Moravian church in England]

1058 The King's book, or a necessary doctrine and erudition for any Christian man, 1543, with introd. by T. A. Lacey. 1932.

1059 The Reformation and the Irish episcopate, by H. J. Lawlor. 2nd edn., *P.* 1932. [First published 1906]

1060 Anglican orders (English): the bull of His Holiness Leo XIII, Sept. 13, 1896, and the answer of the archbishops of England, Mar. 29, 1897. *P.* 1932.

1061 Anglican orders (Latin). *P.* 1932. [Latin edition of the above]

1062 Canterbury administration: the administrative machinery of the archbishopric of Canterbury illustrated from original records, by Irene J. Churchill. 2 vols. 1933.

1063 Saint Wulstan, prelate and patriot: a study of his life and times, by J. W. Lamb. 1933.

CLAPHAM ANTIQUARIAN SOCIETY

Founded 1923, to collect and preserve records, literary and pictorial, of Clapham.

Publications:

1064 Catalogue of an exhibition illustrating Clapham past and present, held Jan. 31st, 1925. *P.* [1925].

1065 Clapham and the Clapham sect. 1927. [Reprinted from the *Clapham Observer*]
  a History of Clapham from Manning and Bray's *History of Surrey*; also a list of the rectors with notes and additions, by T. C. Dale.
  b Clapham before 1700, by R. de M. Rudolf.
  c The Clapham sect, by R. de M. Rudolf.
  d Clapham Park, Surrey: the story of its homes, roads and past residents, by J. H. M. Burgess.
  e Old Clapham today, by G. S. Maxwell.
  f The Atkins family, by T. C. Dale.
  g Clapham Common in the reign of Charles II, by T. C. Dale.
  h Some matters concerning the Clapham estate of William Hewer [d. 1715], by T. C. Dale.

CLAPTON ARCHITECTURAL CLUB

Founded 1890, for the study of architecture. Dissolved 1905.

Proceedings, 1901–3 (3 vols. 1901–3):

1066 Vol. for 1901.
  a The basis of Gothic art [a discussion as to the origin of medieval Gothic architecture], by E. S. Prior.
  b Ely cathedral, by C. C. Makins.
  c St. Peter's church, Northampton.
  d Church of the Holy Sepulchre, Northampton.
  e Queen Eleanor's cross [on the London road, south of Northampton].
  f Church of All Saints, Earls Barton, by L. Barrett.
  g Architectural notes on Lynn Regis [i.e. King's Lynn], by Gertrude Mitchell.
  h The marshland churches [of Norfolk].

1067 Vol. for 1902.
  a Architectural notes on Canterbury, by S. Gardner.
  b Church of St. John the Baptist, Shottesbrooke, by G. I. Mitchell.
  c Church of St. Michael, Bray, by G. I. Mitchell.
  d Newark, by H. S. Kingsford.
  e Southwell, by H. S. Kingsford.

1068 Vol. for 1903.
  a Architectural notes [on New Shoreham, Old Shoreham, Broadwater, and Sompting churches], by S. Gardner.
  b Church of St. Peter, Iver [Bucks.], by S. Hebert.
  c Churches of St. Martin, West Drayton; St. Mary, Harmondsworth; SS. Peter and Paul, Harlington, by M. E. Pitcairn.
  d Church of St. Mary the Virgin, Hayes [Mdx.], by C. Pagan.

CLASSICAL ASSOCIATION

Founded 1903, to promote the development and maintain the well-being of classical studies.

Proceedings, vols. 1–30 (1904–33):

1069 Vol. 9.
  a Roman London, by F. J. Haverfield. [Summary]

1070 Vol. 20.
  a Prehistoric remains of the Bristol district, by Mrs. Dobson. [Summary]
  b Caerwent, by A. T. Martin. [Summary]
  c Corinium Dubunorum, by St. C. Baddeley. [Summary]

1071 Vol. 21.
  a Some mediaeval travellers to Rome, by Caroline Skeel.

1072 Vol. 25.
  a Roman London, by R. E. M. Wheeler. [Summary]

1073 Vol. 26.
  a Excavations at Caerleon, by V. E. Nash-Williams. [Summary]

1074 Vol. 29.
  a Agricola in Britain, by Sir G. Macdonald.
  b John Barclay's *Argenis*, by W. H. Semple. [Summary]

1075 Year's Work in Classical Studies, 1906–33 (26 vols. 1907–33).
  The following vols. include sections on Roman Britain: vols. 1–2 (1906–7) by F. Haverfield; 3–4 (1908–9) by H. B. Walters; 5–11 (1910–16), 13 (1918–19), 15 (1921–1922), 17 (1923–4), 19 (1925–6), and 21 (1927–8) by F. A. Bruton; 23 (1930) by R. G. Collingwood.

Classical Review,[1] vols. 24–47 (1910–33):

1076 Vol. 24.
  a Excavations at Gellygaer, by D. A. Salter.

1077 Vol. 26.
  a 17th cent. archaeological explorer [William Petty] and his methods, by Rachel Poole.

1078 Vol. 27.
  a Castell Collen fort, by H. G. Evelyn-White.

[1] Purchased by the Association in 1909. The *Classical Review*, vols. 1–23, 1887–1910, and the *Classical Quarterly*, vols. 1–3, 1907–9, were independent publications

1079 Vol. 30.

a The 18th cent. in Latin verse [as reflected in the epilogues to Westminster School Latin plays], by D. M. Low.

1080 Vol. 34.

a When did Agricola become governor of Britain?, by J. G. C. Anderson.

1081 Vol. 42.

a A new Roman governor of Provincia Britannia, by D. Atkinson.

1082 Vol. 46.

a Latin poets in the British parliament [a study of quotation and allusion in debates], by C. A. Vince.

b Bede and Vegetius, by C. W. Jones. [See also note by J. L. Myres in vol. 47]

Classical Quarterly,[1] vols. 4-27 (1910-33):

1083 Vol. 4.

a John of Salisbury and the classics, by W. C. Summers.

1084 Vol. 12.

a A 7th cent. English edition of Virgil, by N. F. G. Dall·

1085 Vol. 16.

a Juvenal in Ireland?, by R. K. McElderry.

1086 Vol. 21.

a An English commentary on Ovid [compiled by Thomas of Walsingham from earlier writers], by F. W. Hall.

CLASSICAL ASSOCIATION, MANCHESTER AND DISTRICT BRANCH

Founded 1904, to promote the development and maintain the well-being of classical studies in Manchester and the district.

Publications:

1087 Melandra castle: being the report for 1905, ed. R. S Conway, with introd. by E. L. Hicks. 1906.

1088 Second annual report. The Roman fort at Manchester, ed. F. A. Bruton. 1909.

1089 Second annual report, supplementary vol. Excavations at Toothill and Melandra, with proceedings of the branch, ed. F. A. Bruton. 1909.

1090 Roman coins of Manchester, by R. S. Conway, J. Mac-Innes, and G. C. Brooke. [1909].

1091 Roman fort at Ribchester, ed. J. H. Hopkinson. *P.* 1911. 2nd edn., *P.* 1916; 3rd edn., revised and enlarged by D. Atkinson, *P.* 1928.

CLEVELAND NATURALISTS' FIELD CLUB

Founded 1881, for the practical study of natural history, science, archaeology and antiquities.

Proceedings, vols. 1-4 (1896-1932):

1092 Vol. 1.

a Some account of the remains of Norman architecture in Cleveland churches, by R. Lofthouse.

b Prehistoric Middlesbrough, by W. Y. Veitch.

c [Portion of an] effigy found at Normanby, by T. M. Fallow.

[1] Purchased by the Association in 1909. The *Classical Review*, vols. 1-23, 1887-1910, and the *Classical Quarterly*, vols. 1-3, 1907-9, were independent publications.

d On the former occurrence of the seal in the Tees estuary, and on the adjoining coast, by R. Lofthouse.

e Whorlton-in-Cleveland, by J. C. Fowler.

f Discoveries at Liverton church, by T. M. Fallow.

g 'Flint Jack', his life-history, by W. G. Clarke. [Edward Simpson, b. 1815, fabricator of ancient implements]

1093 Vol. 2.

a History of Easby, by J. Hawell.

b Monumental brasses of Cleveland, by T. M. Fallow.

c Notes [relating to Ingleby Greenhow, etc.], by J. Hawell.

1094 Vol. 3.

a Ancient church or chapel of Coatham, by T. M. Fallow. [Extracted from *Christ's Church, Coatham, Parish Magazine*, 1896, by J. M. Meek]

b Notes made during the restoration of Ingleby church, by P. Huntington.

c Coast erosion, by J. J. Burton.

d Cleveland in English history, by J. S. Calvert.

e Roseberry Topping in fact and fiction, by J. J. Burton.

f Origin of the Cleveland Naturalists' Field Club, by J. S. Calvert.

1095 Vol. 4.

a Archaeological excavations for 1927 [at Whorlton and Eston Nab].

b History of natural history societies in Middlesbrough, by J. W. R. Punch.

c A few Cleveland place names, by R. B. Turton.

d Floods in the Esk valley in July 1930, by J. W. R. Punch.

CLIFTON ANTIQUARIAN CLUB

Founded 1884, for the investigation of antiquities, especially of those in the surrounding country. Dissolved 1912.

Proceedings, vols. 5-7 (1901-12):

1096 Vol. 5.

a Ecclesiastical seals of Bristol, pt. 3, by R. H. Warren. [Previous pts. in vol. 3]

b Notes on the Clifton, Burwalls and Stokeleigh camps, by C. Ll. Morgan.

c Clifton in 1746 [a survey of the manor], by J. Latimer.

d Ancient bronze figure from Aust cliff, Glos., by F. Ellis.

e The transference of Bath [to Mercia], by G. F. Browne.

f Archaeological notes for 1900, by J. E. Pritchard. [Also notes for 1901-2 in same vol.]

g Notes on a collection of old silver spoons, by A. Trapnell.

h Braun's map of Bristol [1572], commonly called Hoefnagle's, by R. H. Warren.

i The Roman road on Durdham down, by A. T. Martin.

j Remains of a Roman villa discovered at Brislington, Bristol, 1899, by W. R. Barker.

k President's address [on the vale of Gloucester as described by William of Malmesbury], by G. F. Browne.

l Remains of a Roman well at Brislington, Bristol, by W. R. Barker.

m Four bronze implements from Coombe Dingle, Glos., by A. E. Hudd.

n Tiles of Bristol cathedral, by R. H. Warren.

o The *Supplementum Chirurgiae* [or *Supplement to the Marrow of Chirurgiae*, etc., 1655, by James Cooke, of Warwick, d. 1688, physician and surgeon], by G. Parker.

p Mural decorations in a dormitory of the Old Deanery, College Green, Bristol, by W. W. Hughes.

q The exploration of Romano-British cities, with especial reference to the excavations now in progress in Caerwent, by A. T. Martin.

r St. Augustine's abbey, Bristol: the work of Abbot Knowle, 1298–1332, by R. H. Warren.
s Some Roman coins from Caerwent, by A. E. Hudd.
t President's address [on Irish influences on early Malmesbury], by G. F. Browne.
u Ancient Bristol documents, nos. 16 to 20: notes on five deeds dated 1370 to 1408, by J. Latimer.
v Architecture of the later Renaissance in Bristol, by A. Harvey.
w Two medals to commemorate the surrender of Bristol, 1643, by C. B. Fry.
x Roman colours, with special reference to those used in wall-paintings at Caerwent, by A. C. Fryer.
y The alleged arms of John Whitson [d. 1629, alderman of Bristol], by J. Latimer.

1097 Vol. 6.

a Open-air pulpit at Magdalen College, Oxford, by J. G. Tetley.
b The choir screen of Bristol cathedral, by R. H. Warren.
c St. Edmund in stained glass, by G. H. Leonard.
d Some sculptured stone-work and encaustic tiles at Westbury-on-Trym, by A. Harvey.
e Some Roman remains from Monmouthshire, by A. E. Hudd.
f Costume of an effigy [14th cent.] at Winterbourne, Glos., by Ida M. Roper.
g Some Norman remains of St. Augustine's abbey, Bristol, by C. Lynam.
h Some old glass from Temple church, Bristol, representing St. Katherine of Alexandria and other saints, by A. E. Hudd.
i The lost font of St. Werburgh's church, Bristol, by A. C. Fryer.
j King Charles II at Abbots-Leigh, Sept. 12–16, 1651, by J. Rowley.
k The Beardmore collection of ancient arms and armour, by H. C. Batten.
l Aldhelm crosses in Somerset and Wilts., by G. F. Browne.
m The treasury of the abbey of St. Augustine, Bristol, by R. H. Warren.
n Polygonal naves at the churches of Ozleworth and Swindon, Glos., by A. Harvey.
o St. Augustine's abbey, Bristol: the east end of Abbot Knowle's Lady chapel, by R. H. Warren.
p Notes on 32 pages of a temporale of the 14th cent., in the possession of the bishop of Bristol, by G. F. Browne.
q A Brecon cresset-stone, by A. C. Fryer.
r An [Irish] ecclesiastical table [possibly 13th cent.], by A. C. Fryer.
s Ancient Bristol documents, 21: a deed of 1364, by R. H. Warren.
t Armorial bearings of the city of Bristol, by W. R. Barker.
u Sculptures from Newgate and Lawford's Gate, Bristol, by R. H. Warren.
v Recent discoveries at Westbury-on-Trym parish church, by A. Harvey.
w The arms of Lyons, of Long Ashton, Somerset, by R. W. Paul.
x Ancient Bristol documents, 22: a dispute over a party-wall in Bristol, 1482, by A. E. Hudd.
y Licenses granted by bishops of Bristol to practitioners in medicine and surgery, by G. F. Browne.
z The Bristol portrait of Sebastian Cabot, by W. R. Barker.

1098 Vol. 7.

a Richard Ameryk and the name America, by A. E. Hudd.
b Some rare books and mss. in the Bristol reference library, by E. R. N. Matthews.

c Old iron chest discovered in the basement of the Dutch House, Bristol, by W. R. Barker.
d The Skinner chair in the Bristol museum, by W. R. Barker.
e The Bristol pageant, 1820, by W. R. Barker.
f Ancient Bristol documents, 23: a deed of William Borton, or Burton, abbot of St. Augustine's, Bristol, 1528, ed. A. E. Hudd and R. H. Warren.
g The vaulting of the church of St. Mary, Redcliff, by A. Harvey.
h 'Bristol-red', by Ida M. Roper.
i Sword-belts on Bristol effigies, by A. C. Fryer.
j Cresset-stones in the Isle of Man, by A. C. Fryer.
k Ancient Bristol documents, 24: the original foundation charter of St. Ewen's church, Bristol, 12th cent., ed. R. T. Cole.
l Bristol merchant marks, by A. E. Hudd.
m Roman coins from Caerwent, by A. E. Hudd.
n Index [to all vols.].

COMMONS, OPEN SPACES AND FOOTPATHS PRESERVATION SOCIETY

(Commons Preservation Society)

Founded 1865, to give advice and assistance in the compilation of permanent records of all local commons, open spaces, and public rights of way. The Reports and Journal are concerned with the Society's activities in parliament, the courts of law, etc., and contain brief historical matter relating to the lands and jurisdictions involved.

1099 Report of proceedings, 1899–1912 (7 vols. 1902–[1912?]).
1100 Journal, vols. 1–3 (1927–34).

Other publications:

1101 Commons, forests and footpaths, by Lord Eversley. 1910. [A revised and enlarged edn. of *English Commons and Forests*, 1894, by the same author, then the Rt. Hon. G. Shaw Lefevre]

CONGREGATIONAL HISTORICAL SOCIETY

Founded 1899, to promote the study of and interest in the history of Congregationalism.

Transactions, vols. 1–12 (1901–36):

1102 Vol. 1.

a Non-parochial registers in Yorkshire, by B. Dale.
b Dr. [Isaac] Watts' church-book [being the register and minute-book of the Bury Street chapel, London], by T. G. Crippen.
c From a diary of the Gurney family: a fellow prisoner with John Bunyan, by C. S. Horne. [Brief extracts relating to the Gurneys and to Thomas Marsom, nonconformist minister, imprisoned with Bunyan, from a ms. volume by William Brodie Gurney, 1845]
d Early nonconformist bibliography, by T. G. Crippen. [Contd. in vol. 2]
e Congregationalism in Manchester: its beginnings and development, by H. Shaw.
f John Bunyan and Thomas Marsom, by J. Brown. [See also the reply to this article by W. H. G. Salter in this vol.]
g Devonshire and the Indulgence of 1672, by E. Windeatt.

h The Puritans in Devon [with particular reference to *The Joint-testimonie of the Ministers of Devon*, 1648], by E. Windeatt.

i An unpublished letter of Dr. Isaac Watts [to the congregation of the Bury Street chapel, 1713], by T. G. Crippen.

j Robert Browne and his *Treatise of Reformation* [printed at Middleburgh, 1582. Transcript, with introd. by T. G. Crippen. Also published separately, *P.* 1903]

k Lists of the early separatists [16th cent.], by F. J. Powicke.

l Notes and queries. [A forgotten chapter of early nonconformist history, with reference to women preachers]

m The Trendall papers; with some new facts relating to Archbishop Laud. [John Trendall, 'free mason' of London, fl. 1639]

n Historical points of contact between English and Scottish Congregationalism, by J. Stark.

o James Nayler [d. 1660], the mad Quaker, by B. Dale.

p William III and the nonconformists. [A private letter, 1692, relating to fines levied upon dissenters]

q Incipient Congregationalism in Halifax. [A letter relating to the origin of the Square church, 1763]

r The Bourton[-on-the-water] church-covenant [1655, being a Baptist confession of faith].

s Isaac Watts' family bible.

t Hampshire Congregationalism, by G. Brownen.

u Recovery of a lost treatise [now known as *A New Year's Guift*], by Robert Browne.

v Dr. Thomas Gibbons' diary [1749–85], by W. H. Summers. [Contd. in vol. 2]

w Congregationalism in Birmingham, from material supplied by J. Rutherford.

x Prison correspondence of an ejected minister [Robert Franklin, 1630–84].

y Gainsborough old hall and the pilgrim church, by E. McKnight.

z Memorials of old Devonshire nonconformity. [Transcripts of two 17th cent. letters]

aa Evangelization in Wales, 1690. [Letters from Hugh Owen, d. 1699, itinerant preacher, to Richard Stretton, minister at Haberdashers' Hall, 1677–1712]

bb The Indulgence, 1672. [A draft]

1103 Vol. 2.

a Welsh nonconformity in 1672, by G. L. Turner.

b John Ball [nonconformist minister, d. 1745] of Honiton, by G. E. Evans.

c London ministers in 1695. [Transcript of a ms. list]

d London Congregational Board [organized in 1727. Transcripts from the minutes, 1727–71].

e The Marprelate tracts. Summary of a paper by W. Pierce.

f The date of Penry's *Aequity*, by A. Gordon.

g Bibliography of Congregational church history, by T. G. Crippen.

h A remarkable letter of Joseph Hussey [d. 1726, nonconformist minister].

i The last days of a renegade [being a letter to Robert Nelson from Robert Ferguson, 1714].

j A remarkable Puritan manuscript [written by Giles Wiggenton, fl. 1569–92, vicar of Sedbergh, and others, *c.* 1550–90].

k Robert Browne's ancestors and descendants, by F. I. Cater.

l The Brownists in Amsterdam. [A list of marriages of English residents, 1598–1617]

m The church of the Pilgrim Fathers: an examination of the claims of the church in Old Kent Road (formerly in Union Street), Southwark, to that designation, by E. E. Cleal.

n Nonconformity in Trowbridge: Silver Street chapel, by W. Scamell.

o New facts relating to Robert Browne, by F. I. Cater.

p History of early Congregationalism in Leeds, by B. Dale.

q Nonconformity in Carnarvonshire in 1672, by G. L. Turner.

r A letter of Henry Barrow to Mr. Fisher from the Fleet prison, Dec. 1590, by F. J. Powicke.

s The chapel in Ropemakers' Alley (Little Moorfields), by S. B. Atkinson.

t Conventicles in East Anglia, 1669.

u The church of the Pilgrim Fathers [being a further attempt to discover its true modern representative], by T. G. Crippen.

v Four causes of separation, by Henry Barrowe. [Transcript of an unpublished treatise from the Wiggenton ms. in the Congregational library]

w Memoir of Robert Mackenzie Beverley [d. 1868, by Mary S. Rowntree, with a list of his publications].

x The Bury St. Edmunds church covenants [1646, with a list of the works of Samuel Chidley, Commonwealth lawyer and nonconformist]

y A pastoral letter from prison, by John Greenwood [*c.* 1586].

z History of the church in Southwark, founded 1616. [From the ms. collection of Benjamin Stinton]

aa List of persons burned for heresy in England [1210–1611], by W. H. Summers.

bb The examination of Giles Wiggenton [at Lambeth, 1584]; now first printed from his own autograph memoranda in the Congregational library.

cc The experiences of Mary Franklin [wife of a nonconformist minister, d. 1713].

dd Early non-conformity in Yarmouth, by G. E. Evans.

ee History of a church in Southwark [1621–1705], from the Gould ms.

ff A new portrait of Richard Baxter [in the possession of the Standerwick family], by J. W. Standerwick.

gg Richard Frankland [d. 1698] and his academy [at Rathmell, Yorks.], by T. G. Crippen.

1104 Vol. 3.

a Nonconformity in Leek, by J. Lovatt.

b Richard Frankland, by B. Dale.

c Wiggenton's [satirical] *Visitation*.

d The story of Congregationalism in Longdon and Lichfield, by A. J. Stephens.

e The apostolic labours of Capt. Jonathan Scott [d. 1807], by D. Macfadyen.

f Academical discipline in the 18th cent. [being a report relating to the academy of the Congregational Fund Board in Tenter Alley, Moorfields, 1712–44].

g Chapel building under the Stuarts [being a contract for the building of a meeting-house in Nightingale Lane, London, 1682].

h Burton-on-Trent [nonconformist church], by J. S. Iliff.

i Early Baptists in London [1633–44], being a further extract from the Gould ms.

j The ancient meeting-house at Ravenstonedale, by B. Dale and T. G. Crippen.

k Ebenezer church, West Bromwich. Revised and abridged from a paper by W. Kelly.

l Puritans and Presbyterians in the Channel Islands, by E. Le Brun.

m Bury Street chapel [transcript of a ms. relating to its building, 1709–10].

n Robert Browne and the Achurch parish register, by F. I. Cater.

o Memorials of Dr. [Philip] Doddridge [d. 1751].

p Historic [nonconformist] communion plate.

q Hanover chapel, Peckham.

during the primacy of Archbishop Sancroft, 1678–90. [Transcribed by C. E. Woodruff from the Tanner mss. in the Bodleian Library]

m Letters of Thomas Jollie, 1629–1703, ejected minister of Altham, Lancs., to Oliver Heywood.

n Origin of the Congregational Fund Board. [Transcripts by T. G. Crippen from the Board's first minute book, containing its proceedings, 1695–9]

o Samuel Cradock, cleric and pietist, 1620–1706, and Matthew Cradock, first governor of Massachusetts, by J. C. Whitebrook.

p The excommunication of Robert Browne and his will, by F. I. Cater.

q A view of English nonconformity in 1773 [a general list of dissenting churches in each county and of petitioning ministers, taken from 'Thompson's list' in Dr. Williams's Library].

r Early nonconformity in Nottinghamshire [17th and early 18th cent.], by H. F. Sanders.

s Williamson's spy book [containing informers' reports, 1663–5], by G. L. Turner.

t The old meeting-house at Staplehurst [Kent, 1647–1824].

u The rise of lay preaching in Holland [and its influence on English religious refugees, 1592–1677], by W. T. Whitley.

v [English] preachers in the Netherlands in 1634, by J. C. Whitebrook.

w The number of the ejected ministers [with particular reference to Walker's *Sufferings of the Clergy*].

x Richard Baxter, Roger Morrice, and Matthew Sylvester, by A. Peel. [Information concerning Richard Baxter's library transcribed from a ms. in Dr. Williams's Library]

y Reminiscences of the old dissent at Witham [Essex, 1585–1822], by R. W. Dixon.

z *Mar-Martine* [1589, a reply to *Martin Marprelate*, reputed to be the joint production of John Lily and Thomas Nash, printed in full; also a rejoinder *Marre Mar-Martin*].

1107 Vol. 6.

a William White: an Elizabethan Puritan [and his writings], by A. Peel.

b Early nonconformist academies. [Bethnal Green, Highgate and Clerkenwell, Newbury, Whitehaven and Bolton, Pinner, Hoxton, Tiverton, Kibworth, Warrington (by T. G. Crippen), Heckmondwike, Northowram, Dudley, Newbury, and Sheriff Hales]

c Congregationalists and the *Great Ejectment* [a correction], by G. L. Turner.

d Particulars of Congregationalist ministers ejected in 1660 and 1662 [from various contemporary sources].

e A note on Penry's last years, by T. Gasquoine.

f Statistics of the Church of England, 1603. [Transcripts from mss. in the British Museum]

g White's *Century* [a précis of *The First Century of scandalous malignant Priests*, by John White, 1643].

h Old Gravel Lane meeting [house, east London, and its pastors, 1718–1883].

i 'Of the name of Puritans' [transcribed from a ms. commonplace book, of unknown authorship, *c.* 1620–40].

j Dr. John Stoughton the elder [*c.* 1589–1639, Puritan divine and settler in Massachusetts], by J. C. Whitebrook.

k The oldest English missionary society [the 'Corporation for the promoting and propagating the Gospel of Jesus Christ in New England' or 'The New England company'; its history from 1649], by J. Massie.

l Works by three Nottingham worthies: John Barret, John Whitlock, and William Reynolds [published 1658–1714], contrib. by S. Jones.

m London nonconformity in 1810 [from *The Protestant Dissenters' Almanack and Annual Register for the year of our Lord 1811*; also a list of dissenting chapels in and near Manchester, 1810, from the same].

n Early Independency in Essex, by A. Goodall.

o Remains of Thomas Jollie [d. 1703, ejected minister of Altham, Lancs. Literary fragments transcribed from Collectanea Hunteriana in the British Museum].

p List of clergy in Wales ejected by the 'Propagators', fl. 1649 (gathered from Walker's *Sufferings of the Clergy*, etc.).

q Nonconformist places of worship licensed under the Toleration Act 1689, by J. Nichol.

r Congregational Fund Board. [Transcript of the rules and orders of meetings for encouraging the preaching of the Gospel in England and Wales, revised 5 Feb. 1738]

s Samuel Smith of Stannington [pastor d. 1761, and his miscellaneous religious writings], by T. G. Crippen.

t Calamy as a biographer, by A. Gordon.

u Kinsfolk of Robert Browne in Cambridgeshire.

v A rare separatist pamphlet [the *Advertisement* of Jean de L'Ecluse, separatist printer of French origin, 1612, printed in full].

w The 'New Conformists' [subscribers to the Act of Uniformity, 1662].

x The Surrey mission [1797–1874].

y *An Antidote against the Contagious Air of Independency*, 1644. [Pamphlet, printed in full]

z Henry Roote and the Congregational church of Sowerby, near Halifax, 1645, communicated by T. W. Hanson.

aa From the Bury Street church records. [Transcript of the customs of a London church in worship and discipline, 1723].

bb Puritanism in the Peak [William Bagshaw, 'the apostle of the Peak', d. 1702, pastor of Ashford, and his successors].

cc The origin of nonconformity in Sheffield, by R. E. Leader. [Also printed in Hunter Archaeol. Soc. *Transactions*, vol. 3]

dd 'Protestant society for the protection of religious liberty' [founded 1811].

ee Bushell [family] of Frodsham [Bishopsgate and Barbados, in the 17th cent.], by J. C. Whitebrook.

ff The Antinomian controversy, by J. H. Colligan.

gg Puritanism in little England beyond Wales [i.e. south Pembrokeshire, from the 16th cent.], by A. J. Grieve.

hh Congregationalism in the Fen country. [Transcripts, 1692–1722, from a ms. journal of George Doughty, pastor. Contd. in vol. 7]

1108 Vol. 7.

a The clerical subsidy, 1661. [Transcripts from the subsidy rolls for the dioceses of Worcester, Oxford, Bristol, St. David's and Llandaff, arranged in a classified summary, showing ejected ministers]

b Arianism and the Exeter assembly [1717–19], by F. J. Powicke.

c St. Mary's chapel, Broadstairs [a Congregational church and its pastors].

d Puritanism in Wharfedale [in the 17th cent.], by G. S. Briggs.

e Thomas Hall [d. 1665, Presbyterian] of King's Norton [with a list of his writings].

f The Congregational church at Barking [in the 17th and 18th cent.], communicated by S. Wilding.

g Early nonconformity at Godalming [including extracts from the journal of Lawrance Lee, butcher, of Godalming, b. 1668], communicated by J. H. Norris.

h Will of the Rev. William Berman [1703, lecturer at St. Thomas's, Southwark, until ejected], by G. L. Turner.

i The story of the Western college, Bristol [founded as a Congregationalist academy in 1752], by C. C. Johnstone.

j The Salters' Hall controversy [1719, relating to Arianism], by F. J Powicke.

k Nonconformity in Staffordshire, 1660–70, by A. G. Matthews.

l Rise and progress of Congregationalism in Worcestershire, by W. Wimbury.

m Independency in little England beyond Wales [from 1660], by A. Grieve.

n The Gainsborough bible [once belonging to Thomas Gainsborough, the artist], by C. H. Vine.

o Henry Jacob's church in New England: a tercentenary memorial. [An account of the off-shoots of the Jacob fellowship, 1616, both in London, and in Scituate and Barnstaple West, Mass.]

p The Canterbury church-book. [Transcripts from Canterbury Congregational church records, 1642–1691, with brief account of the pastors]

q John Magee [d. 1743] a venturesome divine [and his relations with Presbyterianism in Northern Ireland], by A. Gordon.

r The Salters' Hall assembly and the advices for peace, March 1719 [relating to the Arian controversy], by F. J. Powicke.

s Congregational hymnody.

t John Alden, of the *Mayflower* [an attempt to identify his place of origin], by Charlotte Skinner.

u State prayers [1637–1714]: the Niblock collection. [Contd. in vols. 8 and 9]

v Brief historical sketch of the church of Christ meeting in Helen's Lane, Colchester, by Rev. Joseph Herrick, pastor there 1814–65.

w Taunton school [founded 1845 for nonconformists], by G. E. Colthurst.

x The Book of Sports. [Transcript of the first issue, with the title-page of the second edition and the two added paragraphs]

y John Warner, M.A.: a forgotten nonconformist leader in southwest Hampshire, 1646–68.

z The Ancient Merchants' lecture [founded originally at Pinners' Hall, London, 1672].

aa The London Itinerant Society [founded in 1796 to propagate the Gospel in the locality within twenty miles of London].

bb An unpublished letter of Oliver Heywood [c. 1697, concerning one Richard Dugdil, reputed to be 'possessed'].

cc Ordination, primitive and Congregational, by T. G. Crippen.

dd The defeat of Lord Sidmouth's Bill, 1811, by V. Bartlett. [An eyewitness account by Rev. John Nelson Goulty, Congregational minister]

ee William Cudworth [leader of 'The hearers and the followers of the Apostles'] and his connexion, 1717–63 [with a list of his publications], by J. C. Whitebrook.

ff The diary of an ejected minister. [Extracts from the diary of Rev. Francis Chandler in the Collectanea Hunteriana, 1661–6]

gg Old nonconformist academies [Hungerford and Exeter].

1109 Vol. 8.

a Voyagers in the *Mayflower* [their places of origin, dates of death, and other personal details; also a similar list of voyagers in the *Fortune*, 1621, and the *Anne*, 1623].

b A select bibliography of the Pilgrim Fathers of New England, by W. Pierce.

c *The Presbyterian Paternoster, Creed and Ten Commandments* [an anonymous broadsheet, 1681, and the prosecution subsequent to its publication], by G. L. Turner.

d 'The heads of agreement, 1691' [assented to by the united ministers in and about London formerly called Presbyterian and Congregational. Printed in full].

e The Fakenham theological seminary [1837–53, with list of students].

f Religious liberty 110 years ago. [Cases of prosecution of nonconformists, 1811–21]

g The mate of the *Mayflower* [John Clark], by W. T. Whitley.

h The psalmody of the Pilgrims, by T. G. Crippen.

i *The Females Advocate* [a plea that women be granted rights equal to men in Congregational or Baptist church government. Summary of a pamphlet of unknown date].

j A Puritan publisher, John Bellamy [d. 1654, and some of his publications].

k *Asinus Onustus: the Asse overladen.* [Summary of a pamphlet printed in 1642, attacking ecclesiastical abuses]

ml Myles Standish [d. 1655?], by B. Nightingale.
The Abolishing of the Book of Common Prayer. [Summary of a pamphlet, printed in 1641, itself the substance of a book from the ministers of Lincoln diocese to James I, 1605]

n Edward Winslow, 1595–1655, by W. T. Whitley.

o Religious life in the 17th cent. as illustrated by the Southampton documents, by W. Camfield.

p Ministerial co-operation in Yorkshire, 1787. [Rules to be observed by ministers engaged in preaching the monthly lectures, with notes on the subscribers]

q *Concerning Periwigs: Signs of Apostacy Lamented.* [A pamphlet by Benjamin Bosworth, a New England Puritan, 1693]

r Whitefield and Congregationalism, by C. E. Watson.

s The old Scottish Independents [or 'Daleites': their origin c. 1768, and their relations with Benjamin Ingham, d. 1772, and the Inghamites].

t *A Whip for an Ape* [or *Martin displaied*: an anti-Martinist publication in the Marprelate controversy, accredited to John Lyly. Date unknown].

u Congregational benefactors to the deaf, contributed by S. Oxley. [The Rev. John Townsend, d. 1826; the Rev. T. H. Gallaudet, U.S.A., d. 1851; the Rev. T. Arnold, d. 1897]

v *The Lineage of Locusts* [or *the Pope's pedigree*: an undated broadside from a Puritan tract attributed to Anthony Gilby, d. 1585].

w The Morisonian controversy [between the Presbyterian church of Scotland and James Morison, d. 1893, founder of the Evangelical Union].

x Early Independents and the visible church, by M. Dorothea Jordan.

y Correspondence of Sir Edward Harley, K.B., 1624–1700 and Rev. Francis Tallents, 1619–1708. [Letters, 1689–1700, annotated by A. S. Langley]

z *The Lofty Bishop, the Lazy Brownist and the Loyal Author.* [Printed 1640. From a volume of broadsides in the British Museum]

aa An Elizabethan episcopal register [of John Whitgift, archbishop of Canterbury], by C. Jenkins.

bb The Associate Congregations, London, 1805 [their rules and regulations], by T. G. Crippen.

cc Letters of Dr. Philip and Mrs. Doddridge [1745–7], transcribed by T. G. Crippen.

1110 Vol. 9.

a Gleanings from the Castle Hill church book, Northampton [1694–1770], by H. N. Dixon.

b The Independents of 1652, by F. J. Powicke.

c Nonconformity in Hull [17th–19th cent.], by A. E. Trout.

d The history and teaching of Carrs Lane, Birmingham, by H. F. Keep. [Carrs Lane Calvinistical Independent church, founded 1748] e Nicholas Lockyer [d. 1685]: a half-forgotten champion of Independency, by T. G. Crippen.

f Thomas Raffles of Liverpool [d. 1863, Independent minister], by G. S. Veitch.

g Some hymns and hymnbooks [with particular reference to Dr. Barrett's *Hymnal*, 1887], by B. L. Manning.

h Contributions of the nonconformists to the building of the Mansion House [London, 1739–*c.* 1755], by W. Pierce

i John Moore of Tiverton [d. 1730, dissenting minister; with extracts from his diary and cash-book], by T. G. Crippen.

j The Congregational Historical Society: a survey, 1900–1925, by A. J. Grieve.

k A Puritan moderate: Dr. Thomas Thorowgood, S.T.B. 1595–1669, rector of Grimston, Little Massingham, and Great Cressingham, Norf. [transcript of his 'diary', 1642–54], by B. Cozens-Hardy.

l Dr. Lewis Du Moulin's 'Vindication of the Congregational way'. [Transcript of ms. by Lewis Du Moulin, d. 1680, physician, one-time Camden Professor of History at Oxford, and Calvinistic author, with notes by F. J. Powicke]

m The beginning of Congregationalism in Newfoundland [1760–1800], by D. L. Nichol.

n The covenant and confession of faith [of Blanket Row church, Hull, 1770. Printed in full].

o John Howard [prison reformer], by R. G. Martin.

p A censored letter: William Hooke in England to John Davenport in New England, 1663 [concerning the religious situation in England and Scotland. Introd. and notes by A. G. Matthews].

111 Vol. 10.

a John Wyclif: an address by A. Peel.

b Robert Browne's will. [Brief introduction by A. G. Matthews]

c *Manductio ad Ministerium; or the Angels preparing to sound the Trumpets*, by Dr. Cotton Mather, F.R.S., 1726, abridged and annotated by H. H. Oakley.

d Letters of Rowland Hill [d. 1833], William Jay [d. 1853], and Robert Morrison [d. 1834, relating to church and family matters, with introd. by A. Peel].

e The Wharton correspondence, by A. G. Matthews. [An account of the relations between Philip Wharton, 4th Baron Wharton, d. 1696, and (i) Thomas Gilbert, Independent minister, (ii) the tutors of Wharton's sons; based on letters in the Rawlinson and Carte mss.]

f Why Sir Andrew Aguecheek 'had as lief be a Brownist as a Politician': a note on Shakespeare's *Twelfth Night*, Act III, Sc. 2, by H. H. Oakley.

g Some forgotten London benefactors [i: Arthur Shallet, founder of Gravel Lane charity school, Southwark, 1687. ii: Thomas Cranfield, d. 1837, pioneer of charity schools], by W. J. P. Wright.

h John Gibbs [d. 1698, vicar of Newport Pagnell], by F. W. Bull.

i Letters [1: John Newton, d. 1807, of Olney and St. Mary Woolnoth, London, to 'Mr Aaron Cass'; 2: Rev. Matthew Wilks, Moorfields tabernacle, to James Sherman, Castle St., Reading, afterwards of Surrey chapel; 3: Charles James Blomfield, d. 1857, bishop of London, to E. H. Barker; 4: Louis Kossuth, the Hungarian patriot, to J. J. Colman. Norwich].

j The Forbes library, Southgate chapel, Gloucester [originally in the possession of James Forbes, d. 1712, first nonconformist minister in Gloucester], by A. T. S. James.

k Ambrose Barnes [d. 1710], a Newcastle Puritan, by R. S. Robson.

l Whitefield and the newspapers, 1737–41. [Extracts from London newspapers relating to Whitefield]

m The Rev. Richard Baxter's relation to Oliver Cromwell as exhibited in his own words, copied from Part 1 of his autobiography, with introductory essay and notes by F. J. Powicke.

n Boston and 'the great migration' [from England, 1628–1640], by D. Chamberlin.

o A Congregational church's first year, 1804–5 [the early history of Clapton Park chapel, London], by A. Peel.

p The earliest Sunday school [founded in Dursley tabernacle, Glos., by William King], by H. I. Frith.

q Yorkshire [nonconformist] academies and the United college [Bradford, founded 1888], by E. J. Price.

r The Dursley Sunday schools established in 1784, by R. Austin. [Supplement to the article by H. I. Frith, above]

s A Congregational church's first pastorate: Clapton Park, London, 1804–49, by A. Peel.

t Dale of Birmingham [Robert William Dale, d. 1895, Congregational minister], by H. F. Keep.

u A Congregational church as seen in its minutes: Clapton Park, 1849–1929, by A. Peel.

v Rodborough tabernacle. [A letter giving an account of the origin of the church at Rodborough, Glos., in the later 18th cent., written by John Knight, d. 1860, 'the good old man, or patriarch of Whiteshill']

1112 Vol. 11.

a Hymns of the Rev. T. G. Crippen [d. 1929], with introd. by A. Peel.

b The 'free churches' of Norwich in Elizabethan and early Stuart times, by H. N. Dixon.

c Dissenting academies: a neglected chapter in the history of English education, by E. J. Price. [An account of nonconformist educational pioneers in the 17th and 18th cent.]

d Mary Rowles Jarvis [d. 1930?, Congregational poet], by R. Dunkerley.

e The romance of a colonial [nonconformist] church [founded at Cape Town, *c.* 1806, by the 93rd regiment, the Argyll and Sutherland Highlanders], by G. Walker.

f Mr. Pepys and nonconformity, by A. G. Matthews.

g The centenary of Congregationalism in Australia [1830–1930], by C. B. Cockett.

h An early nonconformist father of freedom: John Jackson of Brentford [d. 1693], by A. A. Walmsley.

i The works of Richard Baxter [a bibliography], by A. G. Matthews.

j Nonconformity in the middle ages, by W. T. Whitley. [Hermits, monks, and friars represented as departures from conventional medieval Christianity]

k Two letters of Edmund Calamy [to the Rev. George Benson, Abingdon, Berks., 1723–6].

l Monumental brasses, communion plate, church bells, [in English churches, dated 1640–60], by W. J. P. Wright.

m The Savoy confession. [Reprint of the concluding portion of *A Declaration of the Faith and Order in the Congregational churches in England*; agreed upon at the Savoy, Oct. 12, 1658]

n The *Christian Witness*. [The preface by Dr. John Campbell, nonconformist minister, to the first number of the *Christian Witness*, 1844, the first official periodical of the Congregational Union of England and Wales]

o The Puritan spirit through the ages, by G. F. Nuttall.

p An old Yorkshire congregation, South Cave Congregational church [an historical account, 17th–20th cent.], by A. E. Trout.

q Her brother's keeper: some passages in the life of Margaret Oliphant [d. 1897, authoress, and her relations with her brother, William Wilson], by R. S. Robson.

r Two John Sheffields: the Rev. John Sheffield of St. Swithin's, London Stone [d. 1680, ejected minister] and the Rev. John Sheffield of Southwark [d. 1726], with the publications of both, by J. C. Whitebrook.

s The autobiography of David Everard Ford [d. 1875, Congregational minister. Extracts from the original ms. ed. A. Peel]

t A hundred years of ministerial training, by A. J. Grieve. [Congregational training institutions at work in and since 1831]

u Cromwell's toleration, by G. F. Nuttall.

v Collections for the Piedmontese, 1655. [A list of collections in Leicestershire parishes, comp. W. J. P. Wright from Nichols's *History of Leicestershire*]

1113 Vol. 12.

a Some notes on Staffordshire nonconformity [in the 17th and early 18th cent.], by A. G. Matthews.

b Extract from Robert Browne's *Booke which sheweth.* [127 of the original 185 questions and answers, selected and modernised by W. Walker, with introd. by A. J. Grieve]

c Letters written to J. M. Hodgson [minister, principal of Edinburgh Theological Hall, d. 1916, chiefly from his father John Hodgson, selected by G. F. Nuttall].

d The Dutch church in Norwich [being transcripts of articles taken from the Book of Orders for strangers in Norwich, 1569–80], ed. S. S. Slaughter.

e Was [Oliver] Cromwell an iconoclast?, by G. F. Nuttall.

f Some early Scottish Independents [in the 17th cent.], by G. D. Henderson.

g Early Puritanism and separatism in Nottingham, by H. F. Sanders.

h Willingham church [Cambs.]: Congregational, 1662–1798; Baptist, 1798–1934, by W. T. Whitley.

i The Sub Rosa [a private society of Congregational ministers, founded 1781], by A. Peel.

j Co-operation of Presbyterians and Congregationalists: some previous attempts, by A. Peel.

k Chronicles of a book society connected with the Congregational church, Clavering, 1787–1933, by Daisy Sanders.

l Private schools, 1660–89, by W. T. Whitley.

m Congregationalism in Ashburton [Devon, 1672–1934], by T. G. Crippen.

n Calvin's *Institute of Christian religion* in the imprints of Thomas Vautrollier [1567–87], by J. C. Whitebrook.

o Schools within the diocese of York in 1743, by W. T. Whitley.

p Rowland Hill and the theatre [being a copy of a broadsheet written by Hill, 1774], by A. Peel.

q George Cokayn [d. 1672, Congregational minister], by C. B. Cockett.

r Benson [Oxon.] free church, by G. F. Nuttall.

s The Lollard movement after 1384: its characteristics and continuity, by G. F. Nuttall.

t Anabaptism in England during the 16th and 17th cent., by D. B. Heriot.

u Henry Richard [d. 1888] and [international] arbitration, by G. V. Jones.

v Miscellaneous mss. [on 19th cent. Congregationalism] from New College, London, by A. Peel.

w The Presbytery of Wandsworth [1570], by S. W. Carruthers.

x Dr. Johnson and the nonconformists, by A. G. Matthews and G. F. Nuttall.

Extra publications:

1114 A 'New years guift', an hitherto lost treatise by Robert Browne, the father of Congregationalism, in the form of a letter to his uncle, Mr. Flower, written Dec. 31st, 1588 (old style), and now first published. Ed. with introd. by C. Burrage. *P.* 1904.

1115 Relics of the Puritan martyrs. 1593: Four principall and waighty causes for separation, by Henry Barrowe; a pastoral letter, written from prison, and part of a controversial epistle by John Greenwood. Ed. from a contemporary ms. by T. G. Crippen. *P.* 1906.

CONGRESS OF ARCHAEOLOGICAL SOCIETIES IN UNION WITH THE SOCIETY OF ANTIQUARIES OF LONDON

Founded 1888, to consider means of promoting the better organization of antiquarian research; and the preservation of ancient monuments and records.

Publications:

1116 Reports of the committee on ancient earthworks and fortified enclosures, 1904–20. 15 *Ps.* [1904–20]. *Contd. as*

1117 The year's work in archaeology, no. 1: 1921. *P.* 1922. *Contd. as*

1118 Reports of the earthworks committee. Accounts, reports of the council and of the congresses for the years 1922–3. 2 *Ps.* 1923–4. *Contd. as*

1119 Reports of the 32nd–37th congress and of the earthworks committee for 1924–9. 6 *Ps.* 1925–30. *Contd. as*

1120 Report of the 38th congress and of the earthworks and research committees for 1930. *P.* 1931. *Contd. as*

1121 Report of the 39th congress and of the research committee for 1931. *P.* 1932.

1122 Index of archaeological papers published in 1900, comp. G. L. Gomme. 1901. [Also for papers published 1901–3, by the same; for 1904–7 by B. Gomme; for 1908 by A. Gomme; and for 1909–10 under the direction of W. Martin. 9 vols. 1902–14. Eight similar vols. or pamphlets for the period 1891–9 were issued 1892–1900]

1123 Provisional scheme for recording ancient defensive earthworks and fortified enclosures. [1903].

1124 Scheme for recording ancient defensive earthworks and fortified enclosures. *P.* 1903. [Appendix II issued 1905; revised edn. 1910]

1125 Directions for recording churchyard inscriptions. 2 *Ps.* [1907].

1126 On a scheme for rendering the charters and mss. in the various repositories available for county purposes, by W. A. Copinger. *P.* [1907].

1127 Index of archaeological papers, 1665–1890, ed. G. L. Gomme. 1907.

1128 Index of reports of the earthworks committee for 1905–1926. 1927.

COTTESWOLD NATURALISTS' FIELD CLUB

Founded 1846, as the Cotteswold Naturalists' Club, to promote the systematic investigation of the natural history and antiquities of the district. Title changed to the above form in 1859.

Proceedings, vols. 13–24 (1899–1933):

1129 Vol. 13.

a Evolution in the monastic orders, by J. Bellows.

b Roman work at Chepstow, by J. Bellows.

c The camps at Minchinhampton, by E. N. Witchell.
d Survivals of Roman architecture in Britain, by J. Bellows.
e Common fields at Upton St. Leonard's and the recent inclosure (1897), by E. C. Scobell.

1130 Vol. 14.
a The England of the time of the War of Independence [1775–83], by J. Bellows.

1131 Vol. 15.
a Some further evidence of the Roman occupation of Gloucester, by M. H. Medland.
b Evidences of ancient occupation on Cleeve hill [Glos.], by J. W. Gray and G. W. S. Brewer.

1132 Vol. 16.
a [The battle of Burford, Oxon., *c.* 752, by J. Sawyer]

1133 Vol. 17.
a Note on a long barrow near Bisley, by A. E. W. Paine·
b The water supply of Gloucester: historical note and appendix: acts of parliament, reports and other papers, by R. Austin.

1134 Vol. 18.
a Notgrove long barrow, by G. B. Witts. [Reprinted from the *Cheltenham Ladies' College Magazine*, 1882]
b The Gloucester and Berkeley canal, by A. J. Cullis.
c The court of attachments, forest of Dean, and the office of verderer, by M. W. Colchester-Wemyss.

1135 Vol. 19.
a Leonard Stanley, Stanley Monachorum or Stanley St. Leonard, by W. St. C. Baddeley.
b Salt: its origin, uses and folk-lore, by W. St. C. Baddeley.

1136 Vol. 20.
a The Crickley hill (Birdlip) late Celtic finds of 1879, by W. St. C. Baddeley.
b Miserden and its owners, by W. St. C. Baddeley.
c Notes on a Romano-British burial-ground (*sepulcretum*) at Barnwood, near Gloucester, by R. Austin, with a note on pottery found there, by W. St. C. Baddeley.
d Ancient Cirencester, by W. St. C. Baddeley.

1137 Vol. 21.
a Churchdown and Mattesdune before the Norman conquest, by W. Bazeley.
b On an ampulla, or flask, borne by pilgrims to the shrine of St. Menas, Abu Menas, Lower Egypt [with notes on English shrines], by W. Bazeley.
c An alchemist's laboratory in Gloucester [and the medieval manufacture of glass], by G. Embrey.
d Durham and Gloucester: connexions and contrasts, personal, archaeological and naturalist, by H. Gee.
e Find of Roman coins on Haresfield beacon, 1837, by W. Bazeley.

1138 Vol. 22.
a Excavations on Leckhampton hill [earthwork], Cheltenham, 1925. Reports by E. J. Burrow, W. H. Knowles, A. E. W. Paine and J. W. Gray.
b 'Walton spa', near Tewkesbury, by L. Richardson.
c 'Stow spa', near Stow-on-the-Wold, by L. Richardson.
d The Hyde spa, Prestbury, near Cheltenham, by L. Richardson.
e 'Malvern waters', by L. Richardson, with historical note by F. C. Morgan.
f Discovery of a Romano-British interment at Stratton near Cirencester, by E. C. Sewell.

1139 Vol. 23.
a Caerleon and Caerwent and the Roman occupation of South Wales, by V. E. Nash-Williams.
b Origin and history of the English horse-shoe, by R. W. Murray.
c Notes on flint weapons and tools from Northumbria, by A. Watts.
d A horse-shoe and luck, by R. W. Murray.

1140 Vol. 24.
a Roman mosaic pavements at Corinium, by E. C. Sewell.
b Discovery of a beaker near Woodchester, by C. I. Gardiner.
c Recent discoveries [pre-Roman] in the Stroud valley: an address to the Cotteswold Club on Mar. 25, 1930, by C. I. Gardiner.
d The Thames and Severn canal, by F. C. Warren.

1141 Contents of the Proceedings, vols. 1–14, 1847–1903. *P.* 1904. [Issued as Supplement to vol. 14]

1142 Index to the Proceedings, vols. 1–17, 1846–1912, comp. R. Austin. *P.* 1913.

COUNCIL FOR THE PRESERVATION OF RURAL ENGLAND

Founded 1926, to organise concerted action to secure the protection of rural scenery, etc.; to act as a centre for advice and information upon such matters; to arouse, form and educate public opinion in order to ensure the promotion of these objects.

Publications:

1143 The scenery of England: a study of harmonious grouping in town and country, by V. Cornish. 1932. [Contains some historical references]

COUNCIL FOR THE PRESERVATION OF RURAL ENGLAND, CORNWALL BRANCH

Publications:

1144 Cornwall: a survey of its coast, moors, and valleys with suggestions for the preservation of amenities, by W. H. Thompson, with notes on the antiquities of Cornwall by C. Henderson. 1930.

COUNCIL FOR THE PRESERVATION OF RURAL ENGLAND, DEVON BRANCH

Publications:

1145 Devon: a survey of its coast, moors and rivers with some suggestions for their preservation, by W. H. Thompson, with a preface by the Hon. Sir J. Fortescue. 1932. [Includes notes on the antiquities of Devon]

COUNCIL FOR THE PRESERVATION OF RURAL ENGLAND, 'PENN COUNTRY' BRANCH

Founded 1931

Publications:

1146 The Penn country of Buckinghamshire [1933?].
a An outline of our heritage [an historical sketch of the 'Penn country'], by G. Eland.
b The romance of the Penn country, by R. M. Robinson. [Historical incidents]

c Roads, footpaths, and old ways, by the Hon. Sir F. Mackinnon.

d Churches in the Penn country, by C. H. Biddulph-Pinchard.

e Hughenden [manor] and Disraeli, by C. Disraeli.

f The Quakers, by S. Graveson.

g Poets of the Penn country, by A. F. Fremantle.

COUNCIL FOR THE
PRESERVATION OF RURAL ENGLAND
THAMES VALLEY BRANCH

Publications:

1147 The Thames valley from Cricklade to Staines: a survey of its existing state with some suggestions for its future preservation, by the Earl of Mayo, S. D. Adshead, and P. Abercrombie, with the assistance of W. H. Thompson. 1929.

COUNCIL FOR THE
STUDY OF INTERNATIONAL RELATIONS

Founded 1915, to promote the impartial study of the various problems arising out of the relations between different countries. Dissolved 1917?.

Publications:

1148 Fifty years of Europe: a study of international relations leading up to the great war, by J. H. Harley. *P.* [1915].

Aids to study, nos. 1–7:

1149 No. 1. Notes on the countries at war, by H. Clay. *P.* [1916].

1150 No. 2. Outline syllabuses for the use of members of study circles and preparatory classes on some problems of the war, by A. Greenwood and H. Clay. *P.* [1916].

1151 No. 3. British foreign policy: a scheme of study, by H. Clay. *P.* [1916].

1152 No. 4. The causes of the war: what to read. *P.* [1916].

1153 No. 5. 'War and democracy': a scheme of study, by H. Clay. *P.* [1916].

1154 No. 6. The British Empire: a scheme of study, by E. M. Wrong. *P.* [1916].

1155 No. 7. International relations: a scheme of study, by H. Clay. *P.* [1916].

Aids to study, new ser., nos. 1–2:

1156 No. 1. Parliament and foreign policy, by J. F. S. Mac-Neill. *P.* 1917.

1157 No. 2. The Foreign Office and the foreign services abroad. *P.* 1917.

CROYDON NATURAL HISTORY AND
SCIENTIFIC SOCIETY

Founded 1870, as the Croydon Microscopical Club, to bring together those interested in science and in particular in the natural history and archaeology of the district. Title changed to Croydon Microscopical and Natural History Club in 1877, and to the above form in 1902.

Proceedings and Transactions, vols. 5–9 (1900–27), *contd. as* Proceedings, vol. 10 ([1928]–35):

1158 Vol. 5.

a Stone and bronze celts recently discovered in Croydon and neighbourhood, by N. F. Robarts.

b The life of Thomas Edwards [naturalist, d. 1886], by J. Epps.

c Recent discoveries [chambered tombs] at Waddon, Surr., by G. Clinch.

1159 Vol. 6.

a Flints found at Waddon marsh, by H. D. Gower.

b Croydon Bourne flows, by B. Latham.

c Notes on Bermondsey abbey, by N. F. Robarts.

d The British town of Wallington in the 1st cent. B.C., by N. F. Robarts.

e A chapter in the history of Croydon [mortality rates in the 19th cent.], by B. Latham.

f Eolithic implements in Surrey, by N. F. Robarts.

1160 Vol. 7.

a Roman remains in Southwark, by N. F. Robarts.

b Report on earthworks at Henley Wood, Chelsham [1911].

1161 Vol. 8.

a Token money in Croydon, by E. A. Martin.

b Vanishing rural handicrafts in the neighbourhood of Croydon, by W. H. Mills.

c Ancient monuments in Surrey, with special reference to those in the district round Croydon, by F. Campbell-Bayard.

d The hamlet of Coombe, by W. H. Mills.

e Records of underground water and Croydon Bourne flows, by B. Latham.

f The Wickham bourne, by W. Whitaker.

g Addington: its antiquities and traditions, by W. H. Mills.

1162 Vol. 9.

a Surrey, London, and the Saxon conquest [with an appendix on the course of the Roman road through Croydon], by A. F. Major. [Also published as a pamphlet, 1920]

b The Saxon settlement of north-east Surrey, by A. F. Major.

c Circular churchyards, by A. H. Allcroft.

d Geology and lines of transport in the Croydon district, by G. M. Davies.

1163 Vol. 10.

a Notes on field-names of Addington parish, by W. H. Mills.

b Worth, Suss., by G. J. B. Fox. [An account of the church and parish]

c The Grand Surrey Iron Railway [first section opened 1803].

d English copper coins and counterfeits, by L. F. Hammond.

e A Roman road through Kent, Surrey, and Sussex [Addington to Ashdown Forest], by J. Graham.

f Report on Saxon cemetery at the junction of Mitchley Avenue and Riddlesdown Road, near Riddlesdown, Purley, by L. B. Escritt.

g Report on human remains from near the corner of Mitchley Avenue and Riddlesdown Road, Purley, by Miss M. L. Tildesley.

h Croydon village community [until the 11th cent.], by H. W. Knocker.

CUMBERLAND AND WESTMORLAND ANTIQUARIAN AND ARCHAEOLOGICAL SOCIETY

Founded 1866, for the investigation, description and preservation of the antiquities, archaeology and historical records of Cumberland, Westmorland and Lancashire north-of-the-sands.

Transactions, new ser., vols. 1–33 (1901–33):

1164 Vol. 1.

a Bishop Nicolson's diaries, by H. Ware. [Contd. in vols. 2–5. Additional notes and corrections in vol. 6 'Addenda antiquaria'. William Nicolson, d. 1726, bishop of Carlisle and Derry, archbishop of Cashel]

b Report of the Cumberland excavation committee for 1900, by F. Haverfield. [Contd. for 1901–3 in vols. 2–4]

c Gerard Lowther's house, Penrith (Two Lions Inn): its purchase by him, descent, and social life associated with its subsequent owners, by G. Watson. [Gerard Lowther, d. 1597]

d The Nelsons of Penrith, by G. Watson.

e On a brass found in Arthuret church, by R. Bower.

f Cawmire or Comerhall, by H. S. Cowper.

g A contrast in architecture, by H. S. Cowper. Pt. 1: Primitive quadrangular structures. Pt. 2: The sod hut, an archaic survival.

h The forgotten dedication of Great Orton church, Cumb., by F. H. M. Parker.

i Pedigree of Wastell of Wastell Head; with a memoir of General [Philip] Honywood [d. 1785] of Howgill Castle, by F. H. M. Parker.

j A letter of 1745 [from Henry Holme to John Honywood, relating to Jacobites in the neighbourhood of Kendal], by J. Whiteside.

k Ormshed [Ormside] and its church, by J. Brunskill.

l Little Strickland chapel, by J. Whiteside.

m An ancient British village in Kentmere, by J. A. Martindale.

n Witherslack church and manor, by F. R. C. Hutton.

o The Chambers family of Raby Cote, by F. Grainger. [With a note on armorial stones at Raby Cote, by T. H. Hodgson]

p Matterdale church and school, by J. Whiteside.

q Swindale chapel, by J. Whiteside.

r Kentmere Hall, by J. Cropper.

s Some notes respecting Kentmere Hall, by J. F. Curwen.

t Pre-Norman cross-fragment from Glassonby, by W. G. Collingwood.

u Fragments of an early cross at the abbey, Carlisle, by W. G. Collingwood.

v Tumulus at Grayson-lands, Glassonby, Cumb., by W. G. Collingwood.

w Bones from Grayson-lands tumulus, Glassonby, by H. Barnes, with remarks by Sir W. Turner.

x Roman fort on Hardknott: supplementary notes [to the article in *Transactions*, vol. 12, original series], by C. W. Dymond.

1165 Vol. 2.

a Some notes on Lowthers who held judicial offices in Ireland in the 17th cent., by Sir E. T. Bewley. [Sir Gerard Lowther, d. 1624; Sir Lancelot Lowther, d. 1637; Sir Gerard Lowther, d. 1660]

b Recent Roman finds at Waterhead, Windermere, by H. S. Cowper.

c An ancient village near Threlkeld, by C. W. Dymond and T. H. Hodgson.

d Exploration of 'sunken kirk', Swinside, Cumb., with incidental researches in its neighbourhood, by C. W. Dymond.

e Report on excavations at the Holy Well, Gosforth, by W. G. Collingwood.

f Early sculptured stones at Gosforth, Ponsonby, [Beckermet] St. Bridget's, Haile, and Egremont, by C. A. Parker.

g Bells at Gosforth, Irton, and Waberthwaite, by C. A. Parker.

h A pre-Norman shaft, recently found at Great Clifton church, by R. M. Lidbetter.

i A gold ring found at Maryport, by J. Little.

j Sculptured basin found at Drumburgh, by A. Sparke.

k Shap church, by J. Whiteside.

l Mardale chapel and the Holmes of Mardale, by J. Whiteside.

m The marriage of Sir Hugh de Louthre [b. *c.* 1287] and Margaret de Whale, by F. M. H. Parker.

n The battle of Stainmoor [*c.* 954] in legend and history, by W. G. Collingwood.

o St. Cuthbert's church, Bewcastle, by J. F. Curwen.

p Wharton Hall, Westmld., by J. F. Curwen and J. Wharton.

q The military road in Cumberland [begun in 1753], by T. H. Hodgson.

r Church bells in the archdeaconry of Furness: Colton, Kirkby Ireleth, Broughton, Woodland, and Seathwaite, by H. Gaythorpe.

s Gosforth in the chartulary of St. Bees, by W. N. Thompson.

t Notes during the restoration of Whicham church, by W. S. Sykes.

u Notes on a charter of Richard de Lucy (*c.* 2 John), by W. Farrer.

v Holme Cultram chapels, by F. Grainger.

w Calendar of charitable trusts in the diocese of Carlisle, 1736–1865, by J. Wilson.

x Ring-marked stones at Glassonby and Maughonby, by J. J. Thornley.

y Proceedings. [Includes accounts of Sherburn hospital, Durham, and Ravenstonedale church]

z Addenda antiquaria. [Includes an account of excavations at Foldsteads, near Kirkbampton]

1166 Vol. 3.

a On the bishop's license [to practise medicine, surgery, and midwifery], by H. Barnes.

b Romano-British fibulae and other objects from Brough, by H. S. Cowper.

c Some notes on the hermitage at Conishead priory, Lancs., by J. F. Curwen.

d South and (part of) south-west Cumberland in the chartulary of St. Bees, by W. N. Thompson.

e Stone implements found at Braystones, Cumb., with remarks on probable neolithic settlements in the neighbourhood, by W. H. Watson.

f Early Brampton Presbyterianism, 1662–1780, by H. Penfold.

g Extracts from acts of the privy council relating to Cumberland and Westmorland, 1558–68, by T. H. Hodgson.

h Paines [manorial court penalties] made at Shap [16th–18th cent.], by J. Whiteside.

i Chancellor [Richard] Burn [d. 1785] and the Quakers, by J. Whiteside.

j The Sixteen Men of Holme Cultram, by F. Grainger.

k Caernarvon castle [Cumb.], a forgotten stronghold, by C. A. Parker.

l [Bullet] mould from Gill, St. Bees, by C. A. Parker.

m Gosforth Hall, by C. A. Parker and J. F. Curwen.

n Bewley Castle, by J. Wilson and Sir E. T. Bewley.

o The Burdetts of Bramcote and the Huttons of Penrith, by G. Watson.

1173 Vol. 10.

a Manor of Hutton John in 1668, by J. H. Colligan.

b Church of St. Oswald the king, Warton, Lancs., by J. K. Floyer.

c A pair of gaufering irons, by Mrs. T. H. Hodgson.

d Three relics of the 17th and 18th cent., by Mrs. and Miss Hodgson. [1: A bible of 1602 with prayer-book and psalter of 1605; 2: Silver cup, late 16th or early 17th cent.; 3: A French couteau-de-chasse *c.* 1745]

e Liddel mote, by J. F. Curwen.

f Extinct Cumberland castles, pt. 2, by T. H. B. Graham. [Crew, Kirklinton, Rockcliffe, Downhall, Collinson, and Monk castles]

g Townfields of Cumberland, by T. H. B. Graham. [Contd. in vol. 13]

h Rectors of Workington, by T. Iredale.

i Old statesman families of Irton, Cumb., by C. Moor.

j The family of Dalston, by F. Haswell.

k Piel castle, Lancs., by J. F. Curwen.

l Rampside Hall, by C. P. Chambers and H. Gaythorpe.

m The Rampside [Viking] sword; with notes on the church and churchyard of Rampside in Furness, by H. Gaythorpe.

n A pre-Norman cross-shaft from Urswick church, by W. H. Collingwood.

o Dalton castle, by H. Gaythorpe.

p The Askews of Marsh grange, by J. Brownbill and H. Gaythorpe.

q An exploration of the [interment] circle on Banniside moor, Coniston, by W. G. Collingwood.

r Coniston Hall, by W. G. Collingwood.

s Germans at Coniston in the 16th cent., by W. G. Collingwood.

t De Lancaster [family], by F. W. Ragg.

u Proceedings. [Includes accounts of the runes on the lost head of Bewcastle cross and a cup-and-ring-marked stone from Honey Pots farm, near Edenhall]

1174 Vol. 11.

a The border manors [comprised in the baronies of Liddel, Burgh-upon-Sands, Levington, and Gilsland, and the manor of Scaleby], by T. H. B. Graham.

b The barony of Liddel and its occupants [to early 17th cent.], by T. H. B. Graham.

c A Virginian colonist [William Nelson, d. 1772, son of Thomas Nelson of Penrith, d. 1745], by J. H. Colligan.

d Officers of the diocese of Carlisle: the archdeacons, officials principal, vicars general and chancellors, by J. E. Prescott.

e Castle How, Peel Wyke [earthwork], by J. F. Curwen.

f Isel Hall, by J. F. Curwen.

g Cockermouth castle [its owners to 1649, and its present state], by J. F. Curwen.

h The old Hall, Cockermouth, by J. H. Martindale.

i Hewthwaite Hall, Cockermouth, by J. H. Martindale.

j The Askews and Penningtons of Seaton, by C. Moor.

k The town's book of Biggar, Isle of Walney, 1830–95, by H. G. Pearson.

l Luking-tongs: their meaning and use [in weeding], by Mary L. Armitt.

m Shap registers [described, with extracts], by Elizabeth Noble.

n Find of Roman coins near Brougham castle, by A. J. Heelis.

o The Kaber Rigg plot [or Atkinson's rebellion], 1663, by F. Nicholson.

p Extinct Cumberland castles, pt. 3, by T. H. B. Graham. [Includes Dunmallok, Wolsty, Drumburgh, Burgh, Bewcastle, Triermain, and Askerton castles]

q Mauld's Meaburn, the Alston mines, and a branch of the Veteriponts [being an enquiry into the 12th–15th

cent. estates of part of the Veteripont family], by F. W Ragg.

r Mauld's Meaburn and le Fraunceys and de Hastings, by F. W. Ragg.

s Cotton Julius F. vi. Notes on Reginald Bainbrigg of Appleby [antiquary, d. 1606], on William Camden [antiquary, d. 1623] and on some Roman inscriptions, by F. Haverfield.

t High Head castle, Cumb., by J. H. Martindale.

u Recent finds in Whittington parish, Kirkby Lonsdale, by A. Moorhouse.

v The milecastle on the wall of Hadrian at Poltcross burn, by J. P. Gibson and G. Simpson, with contributions by R. C. Bosanquet and H. H. E. Craster.

w A rune-inscribed Anglian cross-shaft at Urswick church, by W. G. Collingwood.

x Roman inscriptions from Cumberland, by F. Haverfield.

1175 Vol. 12.

a The development of Inglewood, and an account of the Skeltons of Armathwaite and the Restwolds of High Head, by F. H. M. Parker.

b A cross-shaft of the Viking age at Kirkby Stephen, by W. G. Collingwood.

c The debatable land [the Scottish border to the 18th cent.], by T. H. B. Graham. [Contd. in vol. 14]

d The de Levingtons of Kirklinton, by T. H. B. Graham.

e The Rumney cup [a 15th cent. silver gilt mazer], by A. W. Rumney.

f A 17th cent. charm, by C. A. Parker.

g Trostermount-on-Ullswater, by J. F. Curwen.

h Capulside or Cappleside Hall, Beetham, by J. F. Curwen.

i Middleton Hall, Westmld., by J. F. Curwen.

j Little Strickland Hall and its owners, by D. Scott.

k Newby Hall, by R. M. Rigg.

l Cliburn Hall, by F. Haswell.

m Cliburn church, by C. Wright.

n Clifton Hall and its owners, by E. Jackson.

o Caerthannoc or Maidencastle, Soulby fell, by H. Maclean.

p Maybrough and King Arthur's round table, by A. J. Heelis.

q Anglian cross-shafts at Dacre and Kirkby Stephen, by W. G. Collingwood.

r Extinct Cumberland castles, pt. 4, by T. H. B. Graham. [Includes Kirkoswald, Irthington, Sowerby, Linstock, and Drawdykes in Stanwix castles]

s North Lonsdale after the Restoration [being letters, etc., received by Sir Roger Bradshaigh, J.P., D.L., 1660–76], by W. Farrer.

t Manor of Bardsea [and its owners the Anderton family], by H. I. Anderton.

u Report on excavations at the 'Druids' circle', Birkrigg in the parish of Urswick, Sept. 1911, by C. Gelderd and J. Dobson. [For 1921 report see vol. 22]

v Report on an ancient settlement at Stone Close, near Stainton-in-Furness, by J. Dobson.

w St. Anthony's chapel, Cartmell fell, by J. F. Curwen.

x Painted glass at St. Anthony's chapel, Cartmell fell, by J. T. Fowler.

y Mauld's Meaburn and Newby: de Veteriponts, le Franceys and de Vernon, by F. W. Ragg. [Mainly charters supplementing and continuing the articles in vol. 11 above]

z An ancient enclosure and interment on Heaves fell, by T. M'K. Hughes.

aa Interments near Hyning, Westmld., by T. M'K. Hughes.

bb Proceedings. [Includes notes on Morland church; the Castlestede, near Hornby, Lancs.; and the churches of Lancaster and Heysham]

1176 Vol. 13.

a Annals of Liddel [12th–13th cent.], by T. H. B. Graham.
b Report on recent explorations at Dog Holes, Warton Drag, by J. W. Jackson.
c Notes on Westmorland assize roll, 1256, by A. P. Brydson.
d Ings registers [described], by G. E. P. Reade.
e The parish of Warwick, by T. H. B. Graham.
f The fortified church of St. John the Baptist, Newton Arlosh, by J. F. Curwen.
g 17th cent. silver spoon [stamped with four Tudor roses on the stem], by L. E. Hope.
h Report of the excavations at Papcastle [Roman camp], 1912, by R. G. Collingwood.
i Earthwork on Allen Knott, Applethwaite, Windermere, by R. G. Collingwood.
j *The Fatal Nuptiall*, a tract (by Richard Braithwaite?) on the Windermere ferry accident, 1635, by W. G. Collingwood.
k The [original Elizabethan] seal of the grammar school, Penrith, by F. Haswell.
l S. Michael's, Addingham, by T. W. Stephenson.
m Old Eden bridges at Great Salkeld, by C. J. Gordon.
n Voreda, the Roman fort at Plumpton Wall [near Penrith], by F. Haverfield.
o The earlier owners of Edenhall [12th–15th cent.], by F. W. Ragg.
p Edenhall church and its glass, by B. G. R. Hale and F. Haswell.
q Hayton castle, Aspatria, by J. H. Martindale.
r The abbey of St. Mary, Holme Cultram: recent investigations and notes on the ancient roof, by J. H. Martindale.
s Kirkbampton church, by J. H. Martindale.
t Crosscanonby church, by W. J. Marsh.
u Crosscanonby Hall, by J. B. Bailey.
v Aikton church, by H. Barnes.
w Notes on the vicars of Kirkoswald since the Commonwealth, by T. C. Hughes.
x Excavations on the line of the Roman wall in Cumberland, 1909–12, by F. G. Simpson, F. Haverfield, H. H. E. Craster, and P. Newbold.
y Proceedings. [Includes notes on the Bewcastle cross]

1177 Vol. 14.

a Shap and Rosgill and some early owners [12th–15th cent.], by F. W. Ragg.
b Calendar of original deeds at Tullie House [Carlisle], by J. Wilson. [Confined to deeds in Latin relating to Cumberland and Westmorland, 1461–1716]
c Pedigree of the family of Porter of Bolton, Cumb., by C. A. Parker.
d Note-book of William Thomson of Thornflatt, J.P. for Cumberland during the Commonwealth, by P. H. Fox. [Contains records of marriages, 1656–7, and of other business]
e The college of Kirkoswald and the family of Fetherstonhaugh, by Mrs. Fetherstonhaugh and F. Haswell.
f Manor of Corby [12th–18th cent.], by T. H. B. Graham.
g Discovery of a bloomery at Lindale church, near Grange-over-Sands, by J. W. Jackson.
h The granges of Holm Cultram [1150–1538], by W. Baxter.
i The Cumberland yeoman in past times, by F. Grainger.
j Postern door of Carlisle castle, by J. H. Martindale.
k Chrism crosses, St. Kentigern's church, Crosthwaite, Keswick, by H. D. Rawnsley. [Contd. in vol. 16]
l An award of 1535 relating to Adelaide hill, Windermere, the boundaries of the manor of Windermere in 1614, and a rental of 1675, by G. Browne.
m Church of St. Michael, Hawkshead, by J. F. Curwen.

n Church of St. Oswald, Grasmere, by J. F. Curwen.
o Calder abbey gold coins [Edward III nobles], by C. A. Parker.
p A submerged church in the river Eden, by C. J. Gordon.
q The caves known as Isis Parlis [near Brougham], by A. J. Heelis.
r De Culwen [being documents and pedigrees relating the Curwen family, 12th–15th cent.], by F. W. Ragg.
s Report on the exploration of the Roman fort at Ambleside, 1913, by F. Haverfield and R. G. Collingwood, with a preliminary report of exploration in Mar.–Apr., 1914, by R. G. Collingwood and L. B. Freeston. [Reports for 1914–15, by R. G. Collingwood are in vols. 15 and 16]
t Some Birkrigg barrows [near Ulverston], by C. Gelderd, J. Randall, and J. Dobson.
u Proceedings. [Includes notes on St. Bees grammar school, and Muncaster church]

1178 Vol. 15.

a The Kirkbrides of Kirkbride [12th–16th cent.], by T. H. B. Graham.
b The manor court of Egremont [being an account of the ruins of the court house, with extracts from court records, 17th–18th cent.], by C. Caine.
c Poor relief in Cumberland in the 17th and 18th cent., by F. Grainger.
d Recent observations [chiefly solar] at the Keswick stone circle, by W. D. Anderson.
e Folk-lore of Isis Parlis and the Luck of Edenhall, by C. E. Golland.
f Old building in King's Arms Lane, Carlisle, by J. H. Martindale.
g Early crosses at Carlisle, Bewcastle, and Beckermet, by W. G. Collingwood.
h Roman milestone found near Appleby in 1694 and lately refound, by F. Haverfield.
i Catalogue of Roman inscribed and sculptured stones, earthenware, etc., discovered in or near the Roman fort at Maryport, and preserved at Netherhall, by J. B. Bailey, with introd. and additions by F. Haverfield. [See also vol. 26]
j Proceedings. [Includes notes on the owners of Randalholme manor house, Alston; Whitley Castle Roman camp; and Over Denton church]

1179 Vol. 16.

a The grammar school of Carlisle, by J. E. Prescott.
b Original name of Hayes castle, by J. Wilson.
c The family of Denton, by T. H. B. Graham.
d The citadel, Carlisle, by G. D. Oliver.
e The family of de Richmond, constables of Richmond castle, and their connection with Corby, by W. H. Chippindall.
f Castle dairy, Kendal, by J. F. Curwen.
g Early Lowther and de Louther [12th–15th cent.], by F. W. Ragg.
h The Osmotherleys of Cumberland, by J. Skelton.
i Two 14th cent. documents illustrating Robert Bruce's raid in Furness and Lonsdale, 1322, by H. G. Pearson.
j Patterdale [church] pewter flagon, by J. F. Curwen.
k The Castle Rock of St. John's vale, by W. G. Collingwood.
l Tombstone of Ranulf, Lord de Dacre of Gillesland [d. 1461] in Saxton churchyard, by J. L. Bouch.
m More Kirkby notes: Kirkby v. Benbow, by H. S. Cowper. [On the court-martial of Col. Richard Kirkby ordered by Admiral Benbow, 1703]
n Fresh light on the family of Robert de Eglesfeld, founder of the Queen's College, Oxford, by J. R. Magrath.

o An Anglian cross at Tullie House, by W. G. Colling-wood.

p Roman notes, by F. Haverfield.

q Addenda antiquaria. [On Roman coins; 16th and 17th cent. deeds and conveyances; 17th cent. nonconformists, etc. Similar brief notes occur in other vols.]

1180 Vol. 17.

a Nunnery, by T. H. B. Graham. [On the convent at Armathwaite, and the owners of the property after the dissolution]

b The manor of Melmerby, by T. H. B. Graham. [Contd. in vol. 20]

c The Lancaster canal, by J. F. Curwen.

d The borough court of Egremont [its officers, jurisdiction, and records], by C. Caine.

e Dr. [Hugh] Todd's account of the city and diocese of Carlisle, by J. H. Martindale.

f Ancient oak recently restored to St. Mary's, Carlisle, by J. H. Martindale.

g The McMechan chap-books in the Jackson library, Carlisle, by H. Barnes.

h Knitting-sticks, by C. A. Parker.

i A reconsideration of Gosforth cross, by C. A. Parker and W. G. Collingwood.

j Catalogue of Roman pottery in the museum, Tullie House, Carlisle, by T. May and L. E. Hope.

k Five Strathclyde and Galloway charters: four concerning Cardew, and one the Westmorland Newbigging, by F. W. Ragg.

l The first days of Carlisle, by F. Haverfield and D. Atkinson.

1181 Vol. 18.

a The chorography, or a descriptive catalogue of the printed maps, of Cumberland and Westmorland, by J. F. Curwen.

b Mountain names, by W. G. Collingwood. [Also see note in vol. 20, 'Addenda antiquaria']

c A cross-socket, aumbry-niche and piscina at Holy Trinity, Millom, Cumb., by R. D. Ellwood.

d The family of de Mulcaster, by T. H. B. Graham.

e Manor of Blakhale, by T. H. B. Graham.

f Five [medieval] documents concerning Sizergh, Strick-land, and Barton, by F. W. Ragg.

g Pedigree of the family of Docker of Keld (Shap), Bampton, Newby, and Gosforth, by G. Lissant.

h Penrith castle: suggestions and notes from the patent rolls, by J. F. Curwen.

i Recent discoveries [among papers of the Clifford family] in the muniment rooms of Appleby Castle and Skipton Castle, by D. Scott.

j Six documents [16th–17th cent.] relating to Westmor-land and south Cumberland, by N. N. Thompson.

k The Roman mile calculated from the milestones south-east of Carlisle, by P. Ross.

l The Roman name of Birdoswald fort, by F. Haverfield. [With additional note in 'Addenda antiquaria']

m Proceedings. [Includes notes on Carlisle castle]

1182 Vol. 19.

a The Tullie House fibulae, by F. Haverfield.

b The Roman road in Eskdale, by C. R. B. McGilchrist. [With note by F. Haverfield]

c Sir Robert Parvyng, knight of the shire for Cumberland, and chancellor of England [d. 1343], by J. R. Magrath.

d Farlam and Cumwhitton [manors, and their early his-tory], by T. H. B. Graham.

e The eastern fells [being the early history of Castle-carrock, Cumrew, and Renwick], by T. H B. Graham. [Contd. for Kirk Croglin and Little Croglin in vol. 20, and for other villages in vols. 21 and 22]

f A charter of Peter de Brus III, 1246–60 [relating to Kirkeby in Kendale], by J. F. Curwen.

g Mediaeval Knipe; Gnype Cundal and Gnype Patrick, by F. W. Ragg.

h Hearth tax return, 22 Charles II, Kendal barony, by E. Conder.

i The family of the Right Rev. Edmund Law, D.D., by Sir A. Law.

j Elizabethan weights in the Carlisle museum, by L. E. Hope.

k Proceedings. [Includes notes on Carlisle castle]

1183 Vol. 20.

a The Roman road north of Low Borrow bridge, to Brougham castle, Westmld., by P. Ross.

b Beggar's Breeches, Grange fell, Cartmel, by R. O'N. Pearson. [On the origin of four fields, the rent of which was used for poor relief]

c Carlatton [its early history], by T. H. B. Graham.

d Manor of Ainstable, by T. H. B. Graham.

e The Giant's Thumb [a stone cross at Penrith], by W. G. Collingwood.

f Lengleys: Asby Parva, Asby Cotesford and Highhead, by F. W. Ragg.

g Walney chapel, by H. Gaythorpe.

h Cartmel priory church, by J. F. Curwen.

i Some pre-Reformation clergy of Windermere, by A. P. Brydson.

j The provisioning of Roman forts, by F. Haverfield, with an appendix by R. G. Collingwood.

k Old Carlisle, by F. Haverfield.

l Some papers from Bardsea Hall muniment chest, by T. N. Postlethwaite.

m Calendar of papers and documents [17th–18th cent.] in the possession of Mr. James Burrow, Hill Top, Cros-thwaite, near Kendal, by Sir S. H. Scott, bt.

n The Glaisters of Scotland and Cumberland, by J. Glaister.

o Proceedings. [Includes notes on Bellbridge Old House, and Ambleside fort]

1184 Vol. 21.

a Explorations in the Roman fort at Ambleside, 1920, and at other sites on the tenth *iter*, by R. G. Collingwood.

b Travels of Sir Guilbert de Launoy in the north of England and elsewhere, 1430, by O. H. North.

c Old Salkeld, by T. H. B. Graham.

d Cumberland ports and shipping in the reign of Elizabeth, by P. H. Fox.

e The Cowpers of Aldingham in the 16th and early 17th cent., by H. S. Cowper.

f James Jackson's diary, 1650–83, by F. Grainger.

g Lanercost foundation charter, by T. H. B. Graham. [Contd. in vol. 22]

h Scaleby [manor and its early owners], by T. H. B. Graham.

i Fountains abbey and Cumberland, by W. P. Haskett-Smith.

j 13th cent. Keswick, by W. G. Collingwood.

k Helton Flechan, Askham and Sandford of Askham, by F. W. Ragg.

l Greenrigg, Caldbeck [a farmhouse connected with the family of John Dalton, chemist], by J. S. Parkin.

m The fair at Ravenglass; with a note on the village cross, by C. Caine.

n Notes on a Roman wall discovered in the courtyard of the Blue Bell inn, Scotch Street, Carlisle, by H. Redfern.

o Addenda antiquaria. [Includes a list of the inhabitants of Caldbeck, 1642]

p Proceedings. [Includes notes on the Roman wall near Birdoswald, by H. Hodgson]

1202 Vol. 14. Place-names of Cumberland and Westmorland, by W. J. Sedgefield. 1915. [University of Manchester, English series, no. 7. Issued to the Society by arrangement]

1203 Vol. 15. The Gosforth district: its antiquities and places of interest, by C. A. Parker. New edition, revised by W. G. Collingwood. 1926. [First edition published independently, 1904]

Tract series, nos. 7-12:

1204 No. 7. The Beetham repository, 1770, by William Hutton, vicar of Beetham, 1762-1811, ed. J. R. Ford [with a sketch of the life of the Rev. W. Hutton by J. O. Crosse]. 1906.

1205 No. 8. Elizabethan Keswick: extracts from the original account books, 1564-77, of the German miners, in the archives of Augsburg, transcribed and translated by W. G. Collingwood. 1912.

1206 No. 9. Bibliography of the dialect literature of Cumberland and Westmorland, and Lancashire north-of-the-Sands, by A. Sparke. 1907.

1207 No. 10. Records of Queen Elizabeth grammar school, Penrith, by P. H. Reaney. 1915.

1208 No. 11. Memoirs of Sir Daniel Fleming [d. 1701], transcribed by R. E. Porter and ed. W. G. Collingwood. 1928.

1209 No. 12. Edward Wilson of Nether Levens, 1557-1653, and his kin, by R. P. Brown. 1930.

Chartulary or Record series, vols. 2-8:

Vol. 2. The register of John de Halton, 1292-1324. [See Canterbury and York Soc., no. 836 above]

Vol. 3. Register of the priory of St. Bees. [See Surtees Soc., no. 5680 below]

1210 Vols. 4, 5. Records relating to the barony of Kendale, by W. Farrer, ed. J. F. Curwen. 2 vols. 1923-4.

1211 Vol. 6. Records relating to the barony of Kendale, vol. iii, by J. F. Curwen. 1926. [In conjunction with the Westmorland County Council]

1212 Vol. 7. Register and records of Holm Cultram, by F. Grainger and W. G. Collingwood. 1929. [Calendar of the abbey cartulary, with papers on the history of the parish to the 19th cent.]

1213 Vol. 8. Later records relating to north Westmorland or the barony of Appleby, by J. F. Curwen. 1932.

Parish Registers series:

1214 Registers of the parish church of Dacre, Cumb., 1559-1716, transcribed by H. Brierley. 1912.

1215 Registers of Milburn, Westmld., 1679-1812, transcribed by H. Brierley. 1914.

1216 Registers of Warcop, Westmld., 1597-1744, transcribed by J. Abercrombie. 1914.

1217 Registers of the parish church of St. Giles, Great Orton, Cumb., 1568-1812, transcribed by W. F. Gilbanks. 1915.

1218 Registers of the parish church of Barton, Westmld.: baptisms and marriages, 1666-1812; burials, 1666-1830. Transcribed by H. Brierley. 1917.

1219 Registers of the parish church of Skelton, Cumb., 1580-1812, transcribed by H. Brierley and R. M. Richardson. 1918.

1220 Registers of Kendal, Westmld., transcribed by H. Brierley. 1921-2. [Pt. 1: Baptisms, 1558-87; pt. 2: Marriages and burials, 1558-87; baptisms, 1591-5. Vol. ii,

containing pt. 3: Baptisms, 1596-9, 1607-31; marriages and burials, 1591-9, was published in 1952]

1221 Registers of Brough under Stainmore, 1556-1812, transcribed by H. Brierley. 1923-4.

1222 Registers of Millom, Cumb., 1591-1812, transcribed by J. F. Haswell. 1925.

1223 Registers of Middleton-in-Lonsdale, Westmld. 1670-1812, transcribed by J. F. Haswell. 1925.

1224 Registers of Whicham, 1569-1812, transcribed by J. F. Haswell. 1926.

1225 Registers of Bridekirk, 1584-1812, transcribed by J. F. Haswell. 1927.

1226 Registers of Newbiggin, Westmld., 1571-1812, transcribed by J. F. Haswell. 1927.

1227 Registers of Crosthwaite. 4 vols. 1928-31. [Vol. i: 1562-1600; vol. ii: 1600-1670, transcribed by H. Brierley; vol. iii: baptisms and marriages, 1670-1812; vol. iv: deaths, 1670-1812, transcribed by H. Brierley and F. Haswell]

1228 Registers of Cliburn, 1565-1812, transcribed by J. F. Haswell. 1932.

1229 Registers of Lowther, 1540-1812, transcribed by J. F. Haswell. 1933.

Other publications:

1230 Supplement to Old Church Plate in the Diocese of Carlisle, by Mrs. H. Ware. 1908.

1231 The book of the pilgrimage of Hadrian's Wall, July 1st to 4th, 1930, comp. R. G. Collingwood. n.d. [Also issued by the Soc. of Antiquaries of Newcastle-upon-Tyne]

CYMDEITHAS HANES ANNIBYNWYR CYMRU

(Welsh Independents Historical Society)

Founded 1923.

Y Cofiadur, sef cylchgrawn Cymdeithas Hanes Annibynwyr Cymru, rhifyn 1-9 (7 vols. 1923-32):

1232 Rhifyn 1.

  a Ysgrifau Thomas Morgan, Henllan. [Calendar, largely in English, of the writings of Thomas Morgan, d. 1799]

  b Llyfr eglwys y Cilgwyn. [Kilywyn church book: lists of ministers and other miscellaneous 18th cent. entries, in English]

  c Anghydffurfwyr ac Ymneilltuwyr cyntaf Cymru, gan T. Shankland. [On the earliest nonconformists and separatists in Wales, mainly pre-1650]

1233 Rhifyn 2.

  a Cyfamodau eglwys Llanbrynmair. [Covenants, or declarations of religious association, of Llanbrynmair church, 1733 and 1798]

1234 Rhifyn 3.

  a Morgan Llwyd a Llyfr y Tri Aderyn, gan W. J. Gruffydd. [Morgan Llwyd and the Book of the Three Birds, 17th cent.]

  b Eglwysi Henllan a Rhydyceisiaid, gan D. M. Lewis. [The churches of Henllan and Rhydyceisiaid, with a contemporary tract on the separation of the two churches during 1707-9]

1235 Rhifyn 4.

a Stephen Hughes a'i gyfnod, gan G. J. Williams. [On Stephen Hughes, 17th cent., and his time]

1236 Rhifyn 5 a 6.

a Beddfaen John Williams, Ty'n y Coed, gan W. G. Williams. [Gravestone of John Williams, 17th cent. Caernarvonshire nonconformist]

b Henry Maurice: piwritan ac annibynnwr, gan T. Richards. [Henry Maurice, 17th cent. Puritan and Independent]

1237 Rhifyn 7.

a Lle'r Ffiniau yn natblygiad annibyniaeth yng Nghymru, gan I. C. Peate. [The place of the Marches in the development of Independency in Wales]

b Trysorfa cyfarfodydd chwarterol a misol yr independiaid, gan J. M. Prytherch. [Summary, partly English, of the minutes of the quarterly and monthly meetings of the Independents, 1796–1839]

1238 Rhifyn 8 a 9.

a Emynwyr cynnar yr annibynwyr yng Nghymru, gan H. E. Lewis. [Early Welsh Independent hymnologists]

b Y parch. Edward Williams, 1750–1813, gan D. E. Williams. [On the Rev. Edward Williams, with transcripts of letters in English referring to the removal of the training college from Abergavenny to Oswestry, and notes on some of the college's early students]

CYMDEITHAS HANES BEDYDDWYR CYMRU
(Welsh Baptists Historical Society)

Founded 1901, to promote the study of the history of the Baptists in Wales and in other countries, and to encourage the publication of books dealing with the history of the Baptist church in Wales.

Trafodion (22 vols. 1906–33):

1239 Cyfrol am 1906–7.

a Rhestr o ddefnyddiau hanes diwygiad 1904–5 a ddaeth i law mewn atebiad i gylch-lythyr y Gymdeithas. [A list of material dealing with the history of the 1904–5 revival]

b Diwinyddiaeth Bedyddwyr Cymru yn y C18 yng ngoleu eu hemynyddiaeth, gan H. C. Williams. [The theology of Welsh Baptists in the 18th cent. in the light of their hymnology]

c Cyfraniad Bedyddwyr Cymru i gerddoriaeth hyd y flwyddyn 1850, gan W. Evans. [The contribution made by Welsh Baptists to music up to 1850: a list of hymnologists and their work]

1240 Cyfrol am 1907–8.

a Thomas Llewelyn, gan S. Morris. [Thomas Llewelyn, d. 1793: his scholarship and religious activities, and a copy of his will]

b Cerddorion Bedyddiedig Cymru, ac eraill fuont o wasanaeth i gerddoriaeth yn ystod y Ganrif ddiweddaf, gan W. C. Evans. [Welsh Baptist musicians and others who were of service to music in the last century]

1241 Cyfrol am 1908–9.

a Rhai o'r prif egwyddorion a ddelir ac a gynhelir gan Eglwys Crist yng Nghymru a gam enwir Ailfedyddwyr, gan T. Shankland. [Some main principles held and maintained by the Church of Christ in Wales, falsely called Anabaptists. A ms. of the mid-17th cent.]

b Pennod o hanes Titus Lewis: ei lafur geinidogaethol, gan E. T. Jones. [A chapter from the life of Titus Lewis, d. 1811: his work as a minister]

1242 Cyfrol am 1909–10.

a Timothy Thomas: ei lafur llenyddol, gan B. Humphreys. [Timothy Thomas: his literary work, 1720–68, dealing with the various theological controversies of the age]

1243 Cyfrol am 1910–11.

a John Myles: ymchwil i hanes ei fywyd yng Nghymru, gan T. Shankland. [John Myles: research into the history of his life in Wales, 1620–84. Throws light on Puritanism in South Wales during the civil war and the Protectorate]

1244 Cyfrol am 1911–12.

a Y Beibl Cymraeg, gan P. Williams. [The Welsh bible: the history of its translation, its translators, and its influence, literary and spiritual, on Wales]

b Pregeth y Parch. Enoch Francis yng nghymmanfa Llangloffan, 1729. [Sermon delivered at the assembly at Llangloffan in 1729 by Rev. Enoch Francis]

c Ewyllys David Davies, Castellnedd. [The will of David Davies, Neath]

1245 Cyfrol am 1912–13.

a Robert Morgan o Llandeilo-Talybont, gan J. Edwards. [Robert Morgan of Llandilo-Talybont; one of the leaders of the Baptists in the 17th cent.]

b Joseph Harris a chychwyniad llenyddiaeth gyfnodol yng Nghymru, gan T. Shankland. [Joseph Harris, d. 1825, and the beginning of periodical literature in Wales; a history of the growth of periodical literature, and his contribution to it]

1246 Cyfrol am 1913–14.

a Nefydd o'r Blaenau, gan T. Morgan. [Nefydd of Blaenau, d. 1872: the man and his work as a minister]

b Rhai o weinidogion cyntaf Cilfowyr a'i canghennau, gan E. T. Jones. [Some of the first ministers of Cilfowyr and its sister churches, in the 18th cent.]

1247 Cyfrol am 1916–19.

a Bedyddwyr Cymru yng Nghyfnod Lewis Thomas, gan T. Richards. [Baptists in Wales, at the time of Lewis Thomas: a history of nonconformist groups, Baptists in particular, in S. Wales, 1660–1700]

b Bedyddwyr Llangyfelach, gan W. R. Watkin. [The Baptists of Llangyfelach]

1248 Cyfrol am 1920–21.

a Athrawiaeth y Drindod a pherson Crist yng Nghymru yn ystod y ddeunawfed ganrif, gan J. Jenkins. [The doctrine of the Trinity and the person of Christ in Wales during the 18th cent.]

b Dialogous a'i awduriaeth. [*Dialogous*, 18th cent. religious work, and its authorship]

1249 Cyfrol am 1922.

a Llythyr y Gymanfa, gan E. K. Jones. [The assembly's letter to the various chapels; origins and use since 1650]

b Awduriaeth emynau, gan T. Shankland. [The authorship of hymns]

1250 Cyfrol am 1923.

a Bywyd a llafur y Parch. Evan Evans, Cefn Mawr a Llundain, 1773–1827, gan T. Frimston. [The life and work of the Rev. Evan Evans, Cefn Mawr and London, 1773–1827]

1251 Cyfrol am 1924.

  a Declarasiwn 1687: tipyn o'i hanes a barn Cymru am dano, gan T. Richards. [The Declaration of Indulgence, 1687: its history and effect on Welsh nonconformists]

1252 Cyfrol am 1925.

  a Bedyddwyr parthau uchaf Sir Aberteifi, gan T. R. Morgan. [The Baptists of the upper parts of Cardiganshire: a history of the rise of Baptism and a survey of various chapels in the area]

1253 Cyfrol am 1926.

  a Miles Harri, gan R. Jones. [Miles Harri, d. 1775, his life and work as a Baptist minister in South Wales in the first half of the 18th cent.]

1254 Cyfrol am 1927.

  a J. P. Davies, Tredegar, a'i gyfraniad i ddiwinyddiaeth ei gyfnod. [J. P. Davies, Tredegar, d. 1832, and his contribution to the theology of his age]

1255 Cyfrol am 1928.

  a Cefndir hanes eglwys Ilston, 1649–60, gan D. R. Phillips. [Background history of the Ilston chapel, 1649–1660]

  b Barddoniaeth Elizabeth Crebar, gan Gwili. [The poetry of Elizabeth Crebar]

  c Y Diwygiad Methodistaidd a'r Hen Ymneilltuwyr, gan T. Richards. [The Methodist revival and the old nonconformists]

1256 Cyfrol am 1929.

  a Bedyddwyr bore Sir Fflint, gan E. Williams. [The early Baptists of Flintshire: the rise of Baptist chapels in Flintshire in the 17th, 18th and early 19th cent.]

  b Ffyrdd a therfynau, gan T. Richards. [Roads and boundaries: their significance in the rise of nonconformity in northern Cardiganshire]

1257 Cyfrol am 1930.

  a Y Parch. J. Williams, y Rhos, a'i Gyfraniad i Addysg a Chrefydd Cymru, gan W. Thomas. [The Rev. J. Williams, of Rhos, d. 1856, and his contribution to education and religion in Wales]

  b William Richards o Lynn, gan R. T. Jenkins. [William Richards, of Llynn, d. 1818: his theology and politics]

  c J. R. Jones o Ramoth a'r Ysgol Sul, gan B. Owen. [J. R. Jones of Ramoth, fl. 1796–1818, and the Sunday school]

1258 Cyfrol am 1931.

  a Dafydd Hughes, y Cenhadwr i'r Gogledd, gan T. Bassett. [Dafydd Hughes, missionary of the north, d. 1806: a survey of his work in North Wales]

  b Briwsion o hanes y Bedyddwyr Cyffredinol Cymreig, gan R. T. Jenkins. [Fragments of the history of the Common Welsh Baptists in the late 18th and early 19th cent.]

  c Jones o Ramoth a'r Ysgol Sul, gan J. D. Davies. [Jones of Ramoth and the Sunday school]

  d Hen lyfr cyfrifon aelodau eglwys Cefnbychan, gan E. K. Jones. [The old account book of the members of Cefnbychan chapel, in the first quarter of the 19th cent.]

1259 Cyfrol am 1932.

  a Y Parch. Dafydd Jones, Caerfyrddin, gan E. T. Jones. [The Rev. Dafydd Jones, Caerfyrddin, d. 1841, his work in the ministry, and as historian of the Baptist church in South Wales]

  b Hanes Bedyddwyr Llandyfan, gan J. T. Jones. [A history of the Baptists of Llandyfan, 1785–1825]

  c The Baptists and Welsh Wesleyan Methodism, 1830–1860, by A. H. Williams. [In English]

1260 Cyfrol am 1933.

  a Bedyddwyr Penfro, gan W. Rees. [Pembrokeshire Baptists in the 18th and 19th cent.]

  b Benjamin Price y Cyrmo Bach. [Benjamin Price, d. 1856]

  c Antinomiaeth Vavasor Powell, gan R. G. Williams. [The Antinomianism of Vavasor Powell, d. 1670]

Other publications:

1261 Llythyrau oddiwrth y gymanfa at yr egwysi. [Letters from the Conference to the chapels, 1760–90, pt. 1, ed. T. Shankland. 1910]

DARTFORD DISTRICT ANTIQUARIAN SOCIETY

Founded 1910, to encourage the study of local antiquities, and to examine and record, as far as possible, all evidence of historic and prehistoric remains of antiquarian interest within the district.

Publications:

1262 Excavations on a Roman site at Northfleet, by W. H. Steadman. *P.* 1913. [Reprinted from the *Dartford Antiquary*, vol. 1]

1263 The village of Stone and its Druidical circle in prehistoric times, by F. de P. Castells. *P.* [1915]. [Reprinted from the *West Kent Advertiser*]

1264 The architectural history of Dartford church, with a note on the memorial brasses, by F. V. Baker. *P.* 1918.

1265 Excavation at a Romano-British occupation site in Stone wood, Greenhithe, described and illustrated by W. B. Peake, with foreword by E. C. Youens. *P.* 1919.

1266 The old Roman road in west Kent (from Greenwich to Springhead), by F. de P. Castells. *P.* [1920]. [Reprinted from the *Dartford Chronicle*]

1267 Luddesdown: the story of a Kentish manor. Archaeological, architectural and historical, by W. B. Peake; appendix on geology and botany of the district, by S. Priest; and a note on the early architectural features of Luddesdown Court, by A. Cumberland. 1920.

Transactions, nos. 1–3 (1931–3):

1268 No. 1.

  a Church of St. John the Baptist, Sutton-at-Hone, Kent, by R. Marchant.

  b Ancient almshouses of Dartford, by F. V. Baker.

  c Early history of paper-making in Dartford, by A. C. Tagg.

  d Some results of the 1925 excavations at Roman site at Farningham, by S. Priest in collaboration with A. Cumberland.

  e The manorial system in early Norman times, by Miss E. Newnham. [With particular reference to Stone with Littlebrook]

  f Reminiscences of Dartford, by R. W. Jackson.

  g The life of Richard Trevithick [d. 1833], by E. Hesketh.

  h Heath Lane ancient brick kiln, by S. Priest.

  i Ancient and modern surveying, by C. H. Webb.

1269 No. 2.

  a Horton Kirby. [From the notebook of Edward Cresy, 1857]

  b Franks [a Tudor house on the river Darenth, built by the Bathurst family], by D. Wolfe.

1270 No. 3.

a Hut circles at Stone: report by F. C. Elliston-Erwood.
b Foots Cray church (All Saints), by W. H. G. Smith.
c Shire Hall, Wilmington, by A. C. Tagg.
d Meopham church: 14th and 15th cent. stained glass, by C. H. Golding-Bird.
e Georgian social life [in Dartford and district], by H. Aldous.

DERBYSHIRE ARCHAEOLOGICAL AND NATURAL HISTORY SOCIETY

Founded 1878, to examine, preserve and illustrate the archaeology and natural history of the county of Derby.

Journal, vols. 23–45 (1901–23):

1271 Vol. 23.

a Court rolls of Baslow, commencing 13 Ed. II (1319–20), by C. Kerry. [Contd. from vol. 22]
b Notes on a pre-historic burial-place at Megdale, near Matlock bridge, by J. Ward.
c Royal aids for co. Derby, *temp.* Elizabeth, ed. W. A. Carrington.
d Records of co. Derby, by W. A. Carrington.
e The lost manor of Mestesforde [Matlock], by B. Bryan.
f Proceedings in Winster church regarding the consanguinity of the parties to the marriage of two of the Staffords of Eyam, 1308, by C. E. B. Bowles.
g Depositions in action for trespass brought by Henry Furniss against Robert Eyre [1611], ed. C. E. B. Bowles.
h Melandra castle [Roman station], by J. Garstang.
i Report of the excavations [at Melandra castle], 1889–1900, by R. Hamnett.
j Note on the most recent discoveries in Repton church crypt, by F. C. Hipkins.
k Early defensive earthwork on Comb Moss, by I. C. Gould.

1272 Vol. 24.

a Tissington well-dressing, by Mrs. Meade-Waldo.
b Subsidy for the hundred of Scarsdale, 1599, ed. W. A. Carrington.
c Mam Tor [earthwork] near Castleton, by I. C. Gould.
d [Petitions, depositions, etc.] concerning the commons and waste lands in various townships in the High Peak [17th cent.], ed. C. E. B. Bowles.
e A lease of Bradshaw Hall and lands, in lieu of a will, from William Bradshawe to Henry, his son and heir, 1478, ed. C. E. B. Bowles.
f Proceedings prior to the divorce of Godfrey Bradshawe and Margaret Howe, 1554, ed. C. E. B. Bowles.
g Recent discovery of gravestones at St. Peter's church, Derby, by G. Bailey. [Contd. in vol. 25]
h Deeds, etc., enrolled, co. Derby [1 Edw. VI–14 Eliz.], by W. A. Carrington.
i The state of Repton manor from the reign of Henry I to that of Henry V, by F. C. Hipkins.
j A Derbyshire brawl in the 15th cent., by H. Kirke.
k The chartulary of the abbey of Dale, by J. C. Cox. [Extracts]
l The ancient font of Smalley church, by P. H. Currey.

1273 Vol. 25.

a Bradshaw Hall and the Bradshawes. 1: The hall, by E. Gunson. 2: The Bradshawes of Bradshaw, by C. E. B. Bowles.
b The church of Norbury, by J. C. Cox.
c Notes on two pre-Norman cross shafts found at Norbury, in 1902, by J. R. Allen.

d Catalogue of pictures at Hardwick Hall; and an account of the heraldry in the various rooms and on the tapestry at Hardwick, by Lord Hawkesbury.
e Notes on old Buxton and district, by W. Turner.
f Roman weights found at Melandra, by T. May. [Contd. in vol. 28]
g Carl's wark [a prehistoric fortress on Hathersage moor], by I. C. Gould.
h Duffield forest in the 16th cent., by F. Strutt and J. C. Cox.
i Derbyshire fonts, by G. le B. Smith. [Contd. in vols. 26–29]
j The Saxon window in Muggington church, by P. H. Currey.

1274 Vol. 26.

a Denby Old Hall and its owners. 1: The hall, by P. H. Currey. 2: The owners of Denby Old Hall, by R. J. Burton.
b Expenses of the shrievalty during the summer assize of 1631, by C. E. B. Bowles.
c Arbor Low stone circle: excavations, 1901 and 1902, by H. St. G. Gray.
d History and chartulary of the abbey of Darley, and of the oratory of St. Helen, Derby, by J. C. Cox.
e Old English village life as illustrated at Barrow and Twyford, by W. Baxter.
f 13th cent. seal of Roger de Carsington, by Mrs. Meade-Waldo.
g Derby municipal muniments, by C. E. B. Bowles.
h Roman Brough-Anavio, by J. Garstang, with notes on the inscribed tablet, and on the Romano-British name of Brough, by F. Haverfield.
i The Peak in the days of Anne, by H. Kirke.
j Discovery of an early interment at Stanley Grange, by C. Kerry.

1275 Vol. 27.

a Extracts from book of accounts of lady's waiting woman for moneys disbursed in clothes, etc., for Elizabeth, Countess of Devonshire and family, 1656–62, ed. F. Brodhurst.
b Church of St. Helen's, Darley Dale, by J. C. Cox.
c Tideswell and Tideslow [Derbyshire place-names], by T. N. Brushfield.
d Cavalier's sword found at Egginton, by R. L. Farmer.
e Two Derbyshire wills of the 16th cent. [of Johanne Holme, 1506, and Wyllam Howlme, 1520], ed. H. E. Currey.
f Manors of Derbyshire, by C. E. B. Bowles.
g Breadsall priory. 1: The priory, by P. H. Currey. 2: The history of Breadsall priory, by J. C. Cox.
h Origin of the Shirleys [of Eatington] and the Gresleys [of Drakelowe], by J. H. Round.
i Shallcross and Yeardsley Halls. 1: Shallcross, Whaley bridge, by E. Gunson. 2: Yeardsley Hall, Furness vale, by E. Gunson.
j The Shall-cross: a pre-Norman cross, now at Fernilee Hall, by W. J. Andrew.
k Accounts of John Bagshaw of Abney Grange, in the reign of George I, by A. Hughes.

1276 Vol. 28.

a South Sitch, Idridgehay, by P. H. Currey.
b The religious pension roll of Derbyshire, *temp.* Edward VI, ed. J. C. Cox.
c Little Hucklow: its customs and old houses, by S. O. Addy.
d The owners of Shallcross, by W. H. Shawcross.
e Peverel's castle in the Peak, by H. Kirke.
f Winster market house, by H. C. Heathcote.

g Some early Chapel-en-le-Frith charters [1323–1434], by W. B. Bunting.

1277 Vol. 29.

a Church and village of Monyash, by J. C. Cox.

b Henovere and the church of Heanor: notes on the chartulary of Burton abbey and the chronicle of Dale abbey, by R. J. Burton.

c Guising and mumming in Derbyshire, by S. O. Addy.

d A note on Brough and Bathumgate [the Roman road from Brough to Buxton], by S. O. Addy.

e Grant by Sir John Benet, to Pembroke College, Oxford, of certain rents in Derbyshire [1676], by C. E. B. Bowles.

f Sir William Cavendish, d. 1557, by F. Brodhurst.

g Some notes on Arbor Low and other Lows in the High Peak, by T. A. Matthews. [Further notes in vol. 33]

h Manor of Abney: its boundaries and court rolls, by C. E. B. Bowles.

i Brazen alms-dish, Tideswell, by G. le B. Smith.

1278 Vol. 30.

a Sir Sampson Meverill of Tideswell, 1388–1462, by J. M. J. Fletcher.

b Derbyshire in 1327–8: being a lay subsidy roll, ed. J. C. Cox.

c Dorothy Vernon, heiress of Haddon [b. 1545], by G. le B. Smith.

d Names of Derbyshire and Staffordshire barrows, by S. O. Addy.

e Snitterton bull ring, by G. le B. Smith.

f Notes on some Derbyshire antiquities from Samuel Mitchell's memoranda [1824–5], by J. Ward.

g Court rolls of the manor of Holmesfield [with a breviate of the customs of the manor], by H. C. Fanshawe.

h Weston-on-Trent church, by R. L. Farmer.

i Trial of George Busby, priest, at Derby, 1681, by H. Kirke.

j Elizabeth Hardwycke, Countess of Shrewsbury, 1520–1608, by F. Brodhurst.

k The Staffords of Eyam, by C. E. B. Bowles.

l Derbyshire and other horn-books, by W. Bemrose.

m Bakewell font, by C. T. Abraham.

n Excavations at the Roman camp of Melandra, 1906–7, by R. Hamnett.

1279 Vol. 31.

a Haselbarow Hall and its owners, by S. O. Addy.

b A Derbyshire cavalier [Lewis Kirke, d. 1663], by H. Kirke. [Contd. in vol. 32]

c Zouch of Codnor, by R. J. Burton.

d Derbyshire heraldic notes, by F. Were.

e Swarkestone bridge, by G. Bailey.

f Stafford of Eyam: Foljambe charter [1467], by C. E. B. Bowles.

g Will of George Talbot, 4th Earl of Shrewsbury, 1468–1538, by F. Brodhurst.

h Harborough cave, near Brassington. 1: Description of the excavations, by W. S. Fox. 2: Description of the finds, by R. A. Smith.

i Selections from assize roll, Derbyshire, 4 Edward III, by J. C. Cox.

j A note on sanctuaries, by J. C. Cox.

k Ford Hall, Chapel-en-le-Frith, and Banner Cross, near Sheffield, by W. J. Andrew and E. Gunson.

l The owners of Ford Hall from the 13th to the 20th cent., by W. H. Greaves-Bagshawe.

m Heraldic stained glass, Hassop Hall, by A. P. Shaw. [Contd. in vol. 32]

n Coal raising in the 17th cent., by C. E. B. Bowles.

1280 Vol. 32.

a Bishop Pursglove of Tideswell [d. 1579], by J. M. J. Fletcher.

b A Derbyshire visitation manuscript, 1687, by H. Lawrance.

c Willelmus Barbae Aprilis [fl. *c.* 1111–72], by B. Tacchella.

d Early deeds of Repton school [*c.* 1220–1446], by J. C. Cox.

e Ancient court of minstrels at Tutbury, by H. Kirke.

f Dr. Johnson in Derbyshire, by H. Kirke.

g Roman road between Little Chester and Minning Low, by W. Smithard.

h Ravencliffe cave, by W. S. Fox and C. H. Read.

i 'The Sixteen' of Heanor, by R. J. Burton.

j History and customs of lead-mining in the wapentake of Wirksworth, by Mrs. Meade-Waldo.

1281 Vol. 33.

a Promontory forts of Derbyshire, by E. Tristram.

b An aristocratic squabble [between the Earl and Countess of Shrewsbury, *temp.* Elizabeth], by H. Kirke.

c The 'harbour' and barrows at Arbour-Lows, by S. O. Addy.

d Will of Sir John Cavendish, 1381, with the causes which led to his death, by F. Brodhurst.

e Bradwell lead mining customs: some original documents, by S. Evans.

f Stydd preceptory and the military religious orders, by R. L. Farmer.

g Notes on the Roman roads called Batham gate and Doctor gate, by W. Smithard.

h Bishop Durdent [d. 1159] and the foundation of Derby school, by B. Tacchella.

i Roman camp near Coneygrey House, Pentrich, by W. Smithard.

j Derbyshire cave-men of the Roman period, by W. S. Fox.

k Churchwardens' accounts [1729–1805], Chapel-en-le-Frith, by H. Kirke.

l The Wolley mss.: an analysis by J. C. Cox. [Contd. in vols. 34 and 35]

m Mackworth castle, by G. Bailey.

n Some records of an 18th cent. benefit society [Tideswell Humane Friendly Indefatigable Union Society], by J. M. J. Fletcher.

1282 Vol. 34.

a Notes on an ancient pack-horse bridge at Coxbench, by P. H. Currey.

b Tunsted of Tunsted, by H. Kirke.

c Survey of the soake and manor of Wirksworth [1649], by W. H. Arkwright.

d A Lancastrian raid in the wars of the roses [treason indictments, 1453–4], with introd. by W. J. Andrew and E. M. Poynton. [Contd. in vol. 35]

e [Bronze age] cinerary urn found near Eyam, by R. S. M. O'Ferrall.

f Extracts from Dalby's feodary, 1451, by S. O. Addy.

g Some old charters and deeds [early Henry III–1684], by C. E. B. Bowles.

h Note on discoveries at Repton priory and church, by J. C. Cox.

i Fin Cop prehistoric fort, by E. Tristram.

j Place-names at or near Derby, by W. Smithard.

k The Gells of Hopton, by Mrs. Meade-Waldo. [Additions and corrections by P. L. Gell in vol. 35]

l Melandra castle excavations, 1908–11, by H. Lawrance.

m William Newton 'the minstrel of the Peak' [d. 1830], by J. M. J. Fletcher.

1283 Vol. 35.

a Dr. Clegg, minister and physician [of Chapel-en-le-Frith] in the 17th and 18th cent., by H. Kirke.

b Notes on the antiquities of Stanton-by-Dale, by R. J. Burton.

c Records and traces of old roads near Derby, by W. Smithard.

d The ossiferous cave at Langwith, by E. H. Mullins, with report on a cranium found at Langwith cave, by A. Keith.

e Some galleries in Tideswell church, by J. M. J. Fletcher.

f Excavation at Repton, by J. C. Cox. [Reprinted from the *Athenaeum*]

g Vignettes of St. Guthlac, as reproduced in the windows of Repton school library, by H. Vassall.

h Arms of the gentlemen of Derbyshire, 1569, by H. Lawrance. [Contd. in vol. 36]

1284 Vol. 36.

a The [1688] Revolution house at Whittington, by H. Kirke.

b Bakewell Easter roll [of tithe payments], 1348, ed. S. O. Addy.

c Exsuperius [a Christian name], by W. Maples.

d Derby borough rental [1611], by H. E. Currey.

e Ancient guide posts, by J. Simpson.

f A budget [or collection of deeds and parish records] from Repton, by J. C. Cox.

g Place-names of Derbyshire, by B. Walker. [Contd. in vol. 37]

1285 Vol. 37.

a Notes on two churches visited by the Society, 1914 [Castle Donington and Lockington, Leics.], by R. L. Farmer.

b 'Rectory manors' in Derbyshire, by S. O. Addy.

c The Spatemans of Roadnook, by A. H. Prior.

d Some [Derbyshire] menhirs, by T. A. Matthews.

e Megalithic remains [of a stone circle] on Bilberry Knoll, Matlock, by J. Simpson.

f Stone circle known as the 'Bull ring' at Dove Holes [near Buxton], and the mound adjoining, by E. Tristram.

g Mam Tor earthwork [near Castleton], by E. Tristram.

h Destruction [by suffragettes, 1914] of All Saints, Breadsall, by J. C. Cox.

1286 Vol. 38.

a Bolsover castle, by P. H. Currey.

b The midland circuit [late 18th cent. assize records], by H. Kirke.

c Churches of Roman Britain, by P. L. Gell.

d Roman Buxton, by E. Tristram.

e The church wall at Norton as a measure of taxation, by S. O. Addy.

f Wirksworth china, by T. L. Tudor.

g Village cross at King's Newton, by T. L. Tudor.

h Old court-house at Alfreton, by W. Stevenson.

i Chellaston alabaster, by R. L. Farmer.

j Wirksworth grammar school and almshouse, by C. E. B. Bowles.

k Registers of Glossop parish church, 1620–1812, by H. Lawrance. [Contd. in vol. 39]

l Derbyshire Elizabethan depositions, and a proof of coming of age of 1300, by J. C. Cox.

1287 Vol. 39.

a Registers and churchwardens' accounts of the parish of Duffield, by J. C. Cox.

b Stafford of Botham, by C. E. B. Bowles.

c Charles Cotton [d. 1687], by H. Kirke.

d Blackwell, and its sculptured cross, by W. Stevenson.

e The rebuilding of the nave of Glossop church, 1914–15, by H. Lawrance.

f Notes on the vicars of Tideswell during the 16th and 17th cent., by J. M. J. Fletcher.

g Ashover and the Wheatcrofts, by S. O. Addy.

h The river Trent, by T. B. F. Eminson.

i The chapel in the forest [Chapel-en-le-Frith], by H. Kirke.

j Notes on an old churchwardens' account book (1598–1718) of St. Werburgh in Derby, by T. L. Tudor. [Contd. in vols. 40 and 41]

1288 Vol. 40.

a The abbey of Dale, by J. C. Cox.

b House-burial, with examples in Derbyshire, by S. O. Addy. [Contd. in vols. 41 and 42]

c Pinxton castle [earthwork], by W. Stevenson.

d Heraldry of the visitation of Derbyshire, 1611, by H. Lawrance.

e Registers of the parish of Kedleston, 1600–1812, by Ll. Ll. Simpson.

f Royal visitors to Derbyshire, by J. C. Cox.

g Some notes on North Wingfield church, by W. Stevenson.

h The home of the Deincourts, by G. Griffin.

1289 Vol. 41.

a Notes on the history of Tideswell and its manor, by J. M. J. Fletcher.

b The earliest registers of the parish of Weston-upon-Trent, 1565–1605, by Ll. Ll. Simpson.

c Some notes on the family of Woodrofe, by H. Kirke.

d Derbyshire grammar schools, with a description of the seals used by those which have been incorporated, by H. Lawrance.

e Pleasley church, by W. Stevenson.

1290 Vol. 42.

a Sir Henry Vernon of Haddon [d. 1515], by H. Kirke.

b Heraldry of Dugdale's visitation of Derbyshire, 1662–3, by H. Lawrance.

c The river Dove, by T. B. F. Eminson.

d The south court of Codnor castle, by W. Stevenson.

e Kirk Langley church: two 'restorations', by R. L. Farmer.

1291 Vol. 43.

a Barton Blount and the civil war, by A. M. Auden.

b C. R. Sherborne's Derbyshire views [a list of late 18th and early 19th cent. drawings].

c Antiquities on Beeley moor, by H. Chadwick.

d Some account of the family of Powtrell of West Hallam, by H. Lawrance.

e Ancient font at Wilne, by G. Bailey.

f Chesterfield. 1: The parish church, by H. Ryde. 2: Gilds and corporation insignia, by W. Jacques.

1292 Vol. 44.

a Some notes on the minor poets of Derbyshire, by H. Kirke.

b An outline of the coinage of Britain, with special reference to Derby mintages, to 1066, by J. O. Manton.

c Repton, Northworthy (Derby), and Wirksworth, by T. L. Tudor.

d Taxation by the oxgang in the subsidy roll for Scarsdale and the High Peak, 1603, by S. O. Addy.

1293 Vol. 45.

a The Brailsford cross, by W. G. Collingwood.

b Recent excavations at Repton priory, by A. Hamilton Thompson.

c Manor of Beeley, by H. Chadwick.

d Wills at Somerset House relating to Derbyshire [15th–16th cent.], ed. S. O. Addy.

e An enquiry into the origin of the family of Stathum, by S. P. H. Statham.

f Pedigrees of Brownell of Hallamshire and north Derbyshire, by S. O. Addy.

Journal, new ser., vols. 1–6 (1924–33):

1294 Vol. 1.

a Glossary of words used by Derbyshire lead-miners during the past 250 years, by F. Williamson.

b Recent restoration of Wilne church, by P. H. Currey.

c Heraldry of Ferrers, by H. Lawrance.

d Mediaeval military effigies in Derbyshire, by H. Lawrance and T. E. Routh. [Contd. in vol. 2]

e Derbyshire lead weights, by S. O. Addy.

f Notes on Domesday tenants and under-tenants in Derbyshire, by S. P. H. Statham.

g The family of Duckmanton, by S. P. H. Statham.

h 'Little John's grave' [at Hathersage] and the lawful village perch, by S. O. Addy.

i Monastic settlements in the Peak forest, by H. Kirke.

1295 Vol. 2.

a A famous pew in Ashburne church [associated with Dr. John Taylor and Dr. Johnson], by E. A. Sadler.

b Chelmorton and other deeds [15th and 16th cent.].

c Heraldry of Willoughby, by H. Lawrance.

d Later descendants of Domesday holders of land in Derbyshire, by S. P. H. Statham. [Contd. in vols. 3 and 5]

e Notes on Walker's *Place-names of Derbyshire*, by F. Williamson. [Contd. in vol. 3]

f Bronze age pottery from Stanton moor, by W. S. Fox.

g French prisoners in Ashbourne [1812–14], by E. A. Sadler. [Contd. in vol. 3, with a note on French prisoners in England]

h Roman coins from Little Chester, by A. C. Knight.

1296 Vol. 3.

a Ravencliffe cave, by W. S. Fox.

b Arbor Low and the holed stone, by B. Barham.

c Hoard of 14th cent. pennies and foreign sterlings found at Derby, 1927, by J. O. Manton.

d Note on lynchets in Derbyshire, by W. H. Young.

e An Aethelstan penny (925–941) [minted at Derby], by J. O. Manton.

1297 Vol. 4.

a Excavations at barrows on Stanton moor, by J. P. Heathcote.

b Derby pot manufactory known as Cockpit Hill pottery [chiefly in 18th cent., with a chronological table of pottery and porcelain manufacture in Derby], by F. Williamson.

c Inventory of the contents of Markeaton Hall, made by Vincent Mundy, 1545; annotated by W. G. Clark-Maxwell.

1298 Vol. 5.

a Will of Lionel Tylney, lead-miner and merchant, d. 1653, by H. Lawrance.

b Bridge and chapel of St. Mary at Derby, by P. H. Currey. [Additional notes by F. Williamson]

c The earliest records of Ashbourne grammar school [1585–1610], by E. A. Sadler.

1299 Vol. 6.

a Letters of a Derbyshire squire [F. N. C. Mundy, of Markeaton, d. 1815] and poet [Rev. P. Williams, d. 1830] in the early 19th cent., ed. W. G. Clark-Maxwell.

b Derbyshire clergy: additions to the Rev. J. C. Cox's lists, comp. W. E. Godfrey.

c The mansion, Ashbourne, by E. A. Sadler.

d John, Lord Frescheville of Staveley [d. 1682], by A. C. Wood.

e Repton [priory] charters [12th–16th cent.].

1300 Index [1st ser.], vols. 1–25, prepared by the Hon. F. Strutt. [1912].

DEVON AND CORNWALL RECORD SOCIETY

Founded 1904, for the transcription and printing of records concerning the counties of Devon and Cornwall.

Publications:

1301 Calendar of *inquisitiones post mortem* for Cornwall and Devon, 1216–1649, comp. and ed. E. A. Fry. 1906.

1302 Registers of Parkham [1537–1812], transcribed by J. I. Dredge, with introd. by E. Hensley. 1906.

1303 Register of baptisms, marriages and burials of Ottery St. Mary, Devon, 1601–1837, transcribed and ed. H. Tapley-Soper. 1 vol. in 2. 1908–29.

1304 Subsidy rolls, muster and hearth tax rolls, and probate calendars of the parish of St. Constantine (Kerrier), Cornwall. 1910.

1305 Registers of baptisms, marriages and burials of the city of Exeter. 2 vols. 1910–33. [Vol. i: The cathedral, 1593–1813, transcribed and ed. W. U. Reynell-Upham and H. Tapley-Soper. Vol. ii: All Hallows, Goldsmith Street, 1561–1837; St. Pancras, 1664–1837; St. Paul, 1562–1837, transcribed and ed. H. Tapley-Soper]

1306 Devon feet of fines. 2 vols. 1912–39. [Vol. i: 1196–1272, ed. O. J. Reichel. Vol. ii: 1272–1369, ed. O. J. Reichel, F. B. Prideaux, and H. Tapley-Soper]

1307 Register of baptisms, marriages and burials of Branscombe, Devon, 1539–1812, transcribed and ed. H. Tapley-Soper and E. Chick. 1913.

1308 Cornwall feet of fines. 2 vols. 1914–50. [Vol. i: 1195–1377, ed. J. H. Rowe. Vol. ii: 1377–1461. The preface announced as part of vol. ii was not published]

1309 Register of baptisms, marriages and burials of Falmouth, Cornwall, 1663–1812, transcribed and ed. Susan E. Gay and Mrs. H. Fox. 1 vol. in 2. 1914–15.

1310 Register of Edmund Lacy, bishop of Exeter, 1420–55, pt. ii: the *registrum commune*, transcribed and summarised by C. G. Browne, annotated and ed. O. J. Reichel. 1915. [Published in conjunction with William Pollard & Co. Ltd., Exeter. Pt. 1, ed. F. C. Hingeston-Randolph, was published in 1909 by Messrs. Pollard who, in association with George Bell & Son, London, were responsible for several other medieval registers of Exeter diocese]

1311 Register of baptisms, marriages and burials of Parracombe, Devon, 1597–1836, transcribed by A. J. P. Skinner, with preface by J. F. Chanter. 1917.

1312 The description of the citie of Excester, by Iohn Vowell *alias* Hoker, transcribed and ed. W. J. Harte, J. W. Schopp, H. Tapley-Soper. 1 vol. in 3. 1919–47. [Pt. 1, introd. and index, was published in 1947]

1313 Register of baptisms, marriages and burials of Hemyock, Devon, 1635–1837, with the bishop's transcripts for the years 1602, 1606, 1609, 1611, 1617, 1625, 1626, 1633,

1636, and a list of the rectors and chaplain priests, transcribed by A. J. P. Skinner. 1923.

1314 Register of baptisms, marriages and burials of Lustleigh, Devon, 1631–1837, and extracts from the bishop's transcripts, 1608–1811, transcribed and ed. H. Johnson and H. Tapley-Soper. 1927–30.

1315 Register of baptisms, marriages and burials of Colyton, Devon, 1538–1837, transcribed and ed. A. J. P. Skinner. 1 vol. in 2. 1928.

1316 Register of baptisms, marriages and burials of Halberton, Devon, 1605–1837, transcribed and ed. C. A. T. Fursdon. 1930–31.

1317 Register of baptisms, marriages and burials of Hartland, Devon, 1558–1837, transcribed and ed. J. I. Dredge and R. P. Chope. 1930–34.

1318 Register of marriages, baptisms, and burials of Widecombe-in-the-Moor, Devon [1560–1837], transcribed and ed. E. C. Wood and H. Tapley-Soper. 1938. [In progress 1933]

1319 Parish of Topsham, Devon. Marriages, baptisms and burials, 1600–1837, from the parochial register [etc.], transcribed and ed. H. Tapley-Soper. 1 vol. in 2. 1938. [In progress 1933]

1320 Register of marriages, baptisms and burials of the parish of St. Mary, Truro, Cornwall, 1597–1837, transcribed and ed. Susan E. Gay, Mrs. H. Fox, Stella Fox, H. Tapley-Soper. 1 vol. in 2. 1940. [In progress 1933]

DEVON ARCHAEOLOGICAL EXPLORATION SOCIETY

Founded 1928, to promote the science of comparative archaeology, prospection and excavation.

Proceedings, vols. 1-2 (1929-36):

1321 Vol. 1.

a Our prehistoric camps, by C. A. R. Radford.
b The problem of Roman Exeter, by V. E. Nash-Williams.
c Stone-age site [Beer] in south-east Devon, by Gertrude MacA. Woods.
d Reports on excavations at Hembury fort, Devon, by Dorothy M. Liddell. [For 1930–32]
e Hembury fort and the primitive road system of east Devon, by G. Sheldon.
f The Rolling Stone on Gittisham hill, by F. C. Tyler.
g Exeter excavations, 1931, by E. Montgomerie-Neilson and L. A. D. Montague.
h Report on the underground passages in Exeter.
i The Yelland stone row, by E. H. Rogers.

1322 Vol. 2.

a Frithelstock priory and the parish church, by C. A. R. Radford.
b Excavations in a dry valley in Beer, S.E. Devon, by Gertrude and R. MacA. Woods.
c Report of the Exeter excavation committee. [1: Introduction and conclusions, by E. Montgomerie-Neilson. 2: Report on the excavations, 1932–3. 3: Description of the finds, 1932–3, by E. Montgomerie-Neilson and L. A. D. Montague]
d St. Katherine's priory, Exeter, by A. W. Everett.
e Three Levalloisian flakes from Broom, Chard [Som.], by Mary D. Nicol.

f Report on the excavations at Hembury fort, 1934–35, by Dorothy M. Liddell.
g Report of the Exeter excavation committee [for 1934–5. Includes surveys of the foundation of Roman Exeter and of its defences, and an account of excavations in St. John's school, by L. A. D. Montague].
h Bronze age urns from Honiton, by C. T. Shaw.
i Tiles and other objects found at Frithelstock priory, by C. A. R. Radford.
j Roman-British antiquities found at Topsham, by L. A. D. Montague.
k Palaeolithic implement from Exeter and a note on the Exeter gravels, by R. Pickard.
l The 'fort' of Oldaport, by F. Cottrill.
m Report of the Exeter excavation committee [for 1936. Includes an account of Roman remains in the cathedral close].
n Neolithic site on Haldon, by E. H. Willock.
o Ancient man in Devon, by J. R. Moir.
p Unreported mounds on Woodbury common, by G. E. L Carter.

DEVONSHIRE ASSOCIATION FOR THE ADVANCEMENT OF SCIENCE, LITERATURE AND ART

Founded 1862.

Transactions, vols. 33-65 (1901-33):

1323 Vol. 33.

a 'Hands across the sea', by Sir R. Lethbridge. [The history and distribution of Devonshire families in the empire and America]
b Twentieth report of the barrow committee. [Contd. in vols. 34–65]
c Eighteenth report of the committee on Devonshire folk lore. [Further reports in vols. 34–39, 43, 49, 57, 59–61, 63–65]
d Seventh report of the Dartmoor exploration committee. [Previous reports in vols. 26–31. Contd. in vols. 34–38]
e Tenth report of the committee on Devonshire records. [Previous reports in vols. 21–26, 28–29, and 31. Contd. in vols. 34, 58 and 59]
f Financial diary of a citizen of Exeter [John Hayne the younger], 1631–43, by T. N. Brushfield.
g Index to printed literature relating to the antiquities, history, and topography of Exeter, by M. Adams.
h Fragmentary notes on French prisoners in the west of England and other places in the early part of the 19th cent., by J. D. Prickman.
i Edmund and Richard Tremayne, by Mrs. G. H. Radford. [Edmund, d. 1582, clerk of the privy council Richard, d. 1584, treasurer of Exeter cathedral]
j Adventures of the *Ann* of the port of Exeter, 1803–6, by W. F. C. Jordan.
k Early register of the parish of Fen Ottery, 1596–1680, by F. B. Dickinson.
l Extracts from the Red Book and notes on the pipe rolls of Henry II [relating to Devon], by T. W. Whale.
m Neighbours of North Wyke [an account of old houses in the district], by Ethel Lega-Weekes. [Contd. in vols. 34–37]
n Some earthworks in the South Hams probably concerned in the Irishmen's raid [1069], and others in the immediate neighbourhood belonging to Judhel de Totnais, by E. A. S. Elliot.
o Apprenticeship indentures from Stockleigh English parish chest, by J. Erskine-Risk.

p Antiquities of Ockery and Roundhill, Dartmoor, by A. B. Prowse.

q Notes on the district probate registry at Exeter, by Frances B. Troup. [With descriptive list of calendars at the registry]

r Modus [decimandi or tithe modus] for the parish of Kenton, confirmed at the castle of Exeter, 1606, by W. P. S. Bingham.

s Totnes: its mayors and mayoralties, pt. 2, by E. Windeatt. [Pt. 1 in vol. 32. Contd. in vols. 34 and 36–38]

t A hitherto undescribed granite cross on the 'Abbots' Way', Dartmoor, by A. B. Prowse.

u The Devonshire Domesday, by O. J. Reichel. 5: The hundreds of Devon. 6: Domesday identifications, pt. 1. [Pts. 1–4 in vols. 26–28, and 30. Further notes in vol. 34]

v A chapter in the history of the chapel of St. James, Okehampton, by J. D. Prickman.

w Notes on Kingsbridge documents, etc., by W. Davies.

x Ford [near Newton Abbot] and its associations, by R. W. Cotton.

y Churches of Colyton and Shute, and the Pole monuments there, by A. J. Jewers.

1324 Vol. 34.

a The disappearing stone monuments of Dartmoor, by R. Burnard.

b The Bideford and Okehampton railway of 1831, by Sir R. Lethbridge.

c History of the church at Bideford and some of its rectors, by R. Granville.

d The long bridge of Bideford, by A. G. Duncan.

e Extracts from a Devonshire lady's notes of travel in France in the 18th cent., by O. J. Reichel. [Transcripts from a ms. by Jane Parminter, d. 1810]

f John Sixtinus [d. 1519], archpriest of Haccombe, by T. N. Brushfield.

g Index to Domesday analysis (vol. 28), and Testa de Nevill tax roll (vol. 30), with corrections, by T. W. Whale.

h Index to printed literature relating to North Devon, by M. Adams.

i A forgotten episode in Devon county history [relating to the descent of the Dowrish family estates], by J. Erskine-Risk.

j Early nonconformity in Bideford, by Miss Wickham.

k Early history of the manor of Hartland, by R. P. Chope.

l Raleghana, by T. N. Brushfield, pt. 4: Sir Henry de Ralegh, *ob.* 1301. [Previous pts. in vols. 28, 30 and 32. For continuation see vols. 35–39]

m Devonshire screens and rood lofts, by F. B. Bond, assisted by A. L. Radford. [Contd. in vol. 35]

n Inventories of the collegiate churches of the Holy Cross, Crediton [1524 and 1545], and Our Blessed Lady of Ottery [1545], by H. M. Whitley.

o 'Giffard's jump' [being chiefly an account of the Giffard family], by H. F. Giffard.

p Muniments of the corporation of Totnes, pt. 2, by E. Windeatt. [Pt. 1 in vol. 32]

1325 Vol. 35.

a Our four parishes: Sidbury, Sidmouth, Salcombe Regis, and Branscombe, by J. Y. A. Morshead.

b Date of the Domesday survey: and use of some of its terms, by T. W. Whale.

c Biography of John Bodley [d. 1591], father of Sir Thomas Bodley, by Frances B. Troup.

d Molland [parish] accounts, with an introductory note on the evolution of parishes, by Sir J. B. Phear.

e R. D. Blackmore and *Lorna Doone*, by J. F. Chanter.

f Nicholas Radford, 1385(?)–1455 [and his murder by Sir Thomas Courtenay], by Mrs. G. H. Radford.

g The hundred of Budleigh in the time of Testa de Nevil, 1244, illustrated by the hundred roll of 3 Edward I, 1274, the geld roll of 1084, and a list of its Domesday representatives, by O. J. Reichel.

h A local antiquary: being some reminiscences of the late Peter Orlando Hutchinson, esq., of Sidmouth [d. 1897], by H. G. J. Clements.

i Sidbury church, by W. Cave.

j The ancient family of Wyke of North Wyke, by W. Wykes-Finch.

k The stone rows of Dartmoor, by R. H. Worth, pt. 6. [Previous pts. by R. N. Worth in vols. 24–28. Contd. in vols. 38, 40, 43, 50]

l An original article on the pilchard fishery at Borrough Island by Colonel Montagu a hundred years ago [*c.* 1810], with supplementary notes to the present time, by E. A. S. Elliot.

m Raleghana, pt. 5: The history of Durham House, London.

n Allhallows church, Goldsmith Street, Exeter: notes by H. Reed.

o Some bits of an old borough [Great Torrington], by G. M. Doe.

p Manors in Devon, 1755, by J. B. Pearson.

q An analysis of the Exon. Domesday in hundreds, by T. W. Whale. [Supplement in vol. 36]

r Pedigree of Sir Thomas Bodley, with notes, by Frances B. Troup.

s Church dedications in Devonshire, by D'O. W. Oldham.

1326 Vol. 36.

a Ancient Teignmouth, by W. C. Lake.

b Sir John Davie, fifth baronet of Creedy, 1707–27, by Sir R. T. White-Thomson.

c Jocelin de Brakelond and the *servicium debitum*, by O. J. Reichel.

d Rock inscriptions at Beardown [being the work of Edward Atkyns Bray, d. 1857, vicar of Tavistock], by A. B. Prowse.

e [English] hand-made lace and net: ebb and flow, by Constance Lee.

f St. Mary's church, Totnes: some notes respecting alterations made in the structure and fittings during the latter part of the 19th cent., by C. R. B. King.

g Raleghana, pt. 6: *The History of the World*, by Sir Walter Ralegh: a bibliographical study.

h Autobiography of Martin Dunsford [d. 1807], historian of Tiverton, by G. L. Dunsford.

i Sketch of the history of the church and manor of South Molton, by Helen Saunders.

j West Teignmouth church, dedicated to St. James the Less, by Mrs. M. I. Jordan. Pt. 2: The church lands, the act of parliament, 1815, and the new church, by W. F. C. Jordan.

k Some Hatherleigh worthies of the 17th cent., by Sir R. Lethbridge.

l Hallsands and Start Bay, by R. H. Worth. [An account of the damage sustained by the fishing village of Hallsands following dredging operations begun in 1897. Supplement in vol. 41]

m Some doubtful and disputed Domesday identifications, by O. J. Reichel.

n The hide examined, by Sir J. B. Phear.

o Parish clerks of Barnstaple, 1500–1900; with a survey of the origin and development of the order of parish clerks and their status at different periods, by J. F. Chanter.

p Some notes on the church and parish of Churston Ferrers, by M. Adams.

q Registry required by act of parliament for burial in woollens in Stockleigh English, by J. Erskine-Risk.

r Index to the names of persons found in monumental inscriptions in Devonshire churches, copied in the years 1769–93, by T. Wainwright.

1327 Vol. 37.

a First report of the church plate committee. [Further reports in vols. 38, 39, 42, 44, 45, 47–56, 59]
b The pack-horse on Dartmoor, by R. Burnard.
c Lydford town, by Mrs. G. H. Radford.
d Sidelights on the work and times of a great west-country prelate [Bartholomew, bishop of Exeter, 1159–1183] in the 12th cent., by O. J. Reichel.
e The lady of the isle: Isabella de Fortibus [d. 1293], Countess of Albermarle and Devon, by Frances Rose-Troup.
f History of the Exon Domesday, by T. W. Whale.
g Raleghana, pt. 7: Three state documents relating to the arrest and execution of Sir W. Ralegh in 1618. [Contd. in vol. 38]
h The rude stone monuments of Exmoor and its borders, by J. F. Chanter and R. H. Worth. [Contd. in vol. 38]
i The earlier sections of Testa de Nevil relating to Devon done into English with an index, by O. J. Reichel.
j Dartmoor: a note on graves, by T. A. Falcon.
k The manors of Bicton and Kingsteignton, by J. B. Pearson.
l Sir Thomas Tyrwhitt [d. 1833] and Princetown, by J. Brooking-Rowe.
m Index of references to Dartmoor and its borders contained in the Transactions, vols. 1–30, by A. B. Prowse.

1328 Vol. 38.

a The parishes of Lynton and Countisbury, by J. F. Chanter. 1: Introductory, antiquities, historical sketch, and manors. 2: Family and ecclesiastical history, and local legends.
b On certain documents relating to the history of Lynton and Countisbury, by J. F. Chanter.
c Notes on North Devon pottery of the 17th, 18th and 19th cent., by T. Charbonnier.
d Pigmy flint implements in North Devon, by T. Young.
e Pages from a [19th cent.] manuscript history of Hatherleigh, by J. C. Martin. [Contd. in vols. 41, 43, and 45]
f Fees of Earl Hugh de Courtenay [d. c. 1422], by T. W. Whale.
g Early descent of Devonshire estates belonging to the honours of Mortain and Okehampton, by O. J. Reichel.
h Supposed currency bars, found near Holne Chase camp, by P. F. S. Amery.
i Ancient oak altar in St. Peter's church, Tawstock, by C. R. B. King.
j Old Tiverton or Twyford, by Emily Skinner.
k Private chapels of Devon: ancient and modern, by D'O. W. Oldham.
l The [Dartmoor] forest bounds near Princetown, by A. B. Prowse.
m Raleghana, pt. 7: Three state documents relating to the arrest of Sir W. Ralegh in 1618.
n Church wardens' accounts of South Tawton, by Ethel Lega-Weekes. [Contd. in vols. 39–41]

1329 Vol. 39.

a Membury church, by F. E. W. Langdon.
b The Courtenay monument [to Margaret Beaufort, wife of Thomas Courtenay, 5th Earl of Devon], in Colyton church, by Mrs. G. H. Radford.
c Concerning some old habits and decaying industries formerly prevalent in the west of England, and more particularly in the county of Devon, by W. H. Thornton.
d The ancient population of the forest of Dartmoor, by R. Burnard.

e Church of Chulmleigh, North Devon, by J. B. Pearson.
f Burg de Tiverton and the town leat, by Emily Skinner.
g Misereres of Exeter cathedral, by Kate M. Clarke. [Contd. in vol 40]
h Raleghana, pt. 8: The execution of Sir Walter Ralegh and some of the events that followed it.
i Pedigree of family of Walrond of Bovey, Seaton, and Beer, by A. J. P. Skinner.
j Swainmote courts of Exmoor, and the Devonshire portion and purlieus of the forest, by J. F. Chanter.
k Notes on some traditions concerning the brief visit of Cromwell and Fairfax to Bovey Tracey and its neighbourhood, 1646, by W. H. Thornton.
l Coins and tokens of Devon, by A. J. V. Radford.
m Churches and church endowments in the 11th and 12th cent., by O. J. Reichel.

1330 Vol. 40.

a King's Teignton fair, by P. Jackson.
b The hundred of Haytor in the time of Testa de Nevil, 1244, with notes and an index, by O. J. Reichel. [Supplement, taken from hundred rolls, 3 Edw. I, in vol. 50]
c Leaves from the notebook of John Risdon [d. 1716], of Netherton manor and West Teignmouth, by Mary H. Jordan.
d The constitution of the Merchants' company in Totnes 1579–93, by E. Windeatt.
e 'The Rundlestone' [being part of a menhir formerly standing in a hamlet of that name], by A. B. Prowse.
f 'Devon on guard', 1759–1815, by J. W. Lee.
g On the occurrence of human remains of neolithic age near Croyde, by T. Young.

1331 Vol. 41.

a The Wyses and Tremaynes of Sydenham [Marystow], by Mrs. G. H. Radford.
b Bere Alston as a parliamentary borough, by J. J. Alexander.
c Ralegh miscellanea, by T. N. Brushfield. [Contd. in vol. 42]
d Inventory of the goods and chattels of Richard Bevys, late mayor of Exeter, 1603, transcribed by E. A. Donaldson.
e A batch of old deeds relating to Buckland Filleigh [13th–16th cent.], by O. J. Reichel.
f Ornamental lime-plaster ceilings and the plasterer's craft in Devonshire, by J. T. Fouracre.
g Wembury: its bay, church, and parish, by H. M. Evans. [Contd. in vol. 42]
h The [St. Mary] Magdalen lands of West Teignmouth, by Mary H. Jordan.
i County armaments in Devon in the 16th cent., by Ethel Lega-Weekes.

1332 Vol. 42.

a A short history of Cullompton, by M. T. Foster.
b Church of St. Andrew, Cullompton, by E. S. Chalk.
c The hundred of Sulfretona or Hairidge in early times, by O. J. Reichel.
d Tavistock as a parliamentary borough, by J. J. Alexander. Pt. 1: 1295–1688. [Contd. in vol. 43]
e The town, village, manors, and church of Kentisbeare, by E. S. Chalk.
f The manors, parish, and churches of Blackborough, *alias* All Hallows, by E. S. Chalk.
g Counsellor John Were of Silverton, and the siege of Exeter, 1645–6, by J. H. Ward.
h Cillitona: the land of the wife of Hervius [or Hervei de Helion], by Emily Skinner. [An attempt to identify Southwood with Cillitona in the Domesday hundred of Tiverton]

i Visitations of Devonshire churches [1301-30], by H. M. Whitley.

j Christianity in Devon before 909, by J. F. Chanter.

k A further sketch of Bishop's Teignton, by W. F. C. Jordan.

l Notes on Venn [house] in the parish of Bishop's Teignton, by Mary H. Jordan.

1333 Vol. 43.

a Presidential address [on Devonshire in the palaeolithic and neolithic ages and the bronze age], by R. Burnard.

b Borough of Clifton-Dartmouth-Hardness and its mayors and mayoralties, by E. Windeatt. [Contd. in vols. 44-46]

c Foundation and early history of Dartmouth and Kingswear churches, by H. R. Watkin.

d Dr. George Oliver [antiquary, d. 1861] on Dartmouth and its churches, by E. Windeatt.

e John Flavell [d. 1691]: a notable Dartmouth Puritan and his bibliography, by E. Windeatt.

f Early history of the hundred of Cadelintona or Colridge, by O. J. Reichel.

g Church goods commission in Devon, 1549-52, by Beatrix F. Cresswell. [Extracts from original inventories]

h An ancient British trackway, by T. J. Joce.

i 'The lord Dynham's lands' [a survey taken in 1566 for Henry Compton], by R. P. Chope.

j Inventory of church goods of Saint Kieran's church, Exeter, 1417 [with translation], by H. M. Whitley.

k Dartmouth as a parliamentary borough, by J. J. Alexander. [Supplementary note in vol. 61]

1334 Vol. 44.

a William Pengelly [d. 1894], F.R.S., F.G.S., father of the Devonshire Association, by Hester F. Julian (née Pengelly). [Contd. in vols. 45-47]

b Records of St. Nicholas' priory, Exeter, by Kate M. Clarke.

c Illustrations of municipal history from the act book of the chamber of the city of Exeter, 1559-1588, by W. J. Harte. [Contd. in vols. 45 and 46]

d 14th cent. stained glass of Exeter cathedral, by F. M. Drake.

e Fight at Clyst in 1455 [between Thomas Courtenay, Earl of Devon, and William Bonville], by Mrs. G. H. Radford.

f Exeter bond of association [1584], with some notes on the signatures, by Beatrix F. Cresswell.

g Domesday hundred of Wenford or Wonford, by O. J. Reichel.

h Hundred of South Tawton in early times, by O. J. Reichel.

i Devon county members of parliament, by J. J. Alexander. [Contd. in vols. 45-50, and 57]

j Plymouth china [and its manufacture by William Cookworthy, d. 1780], by Mrs. G. H. Radford. [Reprinted in *Devonian Year Book* for 1920]

k Tithe commutation in Exbourne in the 17th cent., by Sir R. Lethbridge.

l Kalenders and the Exeter trade-gilds before the Reformation [from the 11th cent.], by Frances Rose-Troup.

m Corporation of Exeter estate in Ireland, 1654-6, by J. B. Pearson.

n Exeter goldsmiths' guild, by J. F. Chanter.

o Account of the Hospitium de le Egle [Exeter], by Ethel Lega-Weekes.

p Drake's treasure, by E. T. Clifford. [Reprinted in *Devonian Year Book* for 1913]

q Maritime trade of Exeter in mediaeval times, by H. M. Whitley.

r Rectors of St. Leonard's, Exeter, since the Commonwealth, by T. C. Hughes.

s William Wykes, 'first recorder of Exeter' (14th cent.) and Wykes, sheriff of Devon, by Ethel Lega-Weekes.

t Aulnager in Devon, by R. P. Chope.

u Exeter and Dartmouth road [an ancient trackway], by T. J. Joce.

v Survey of Old Burrow camp [earthwork], by H. St. G. Gray.

w Life of Joanna Southcott [prophetic authoress, d. 1814], by C. Lane.

x Bibliography of Joanna Southcott, by C. Lane.

1335 Vol. 45.

a Buckfast abbey and its relation to Kingsbridge, by W. Davies.

b Extracts from the leger book and other ancient documents of the abbey of Buckfast, by J. F. Chanter.

c Hundred of Stanborough or Dippeforda in the time of Testa de Nevil, 1243, by O. J. Reichel. [With a supplement]

d Totnes and the civil war, by E. Windeatt.

e Romano-British inscribed stone between Parracombe and Lynton, by J. F. Chanter.

f Sanctuary in Devon, by H. M. Whitley.

g Baptismal fonts of Devon, by Kate M. Clarke. [Contd. in vols. 46-48, 50-54.]

h Savery, Newcomen, and the early history of the steam-engine, by R. Jenkins. [Contd. in vol. 46]

i Dawlish parish church [in 12th-15th cent.], by Flora Jordan.

j Freemans [family] of Ashburton, Buckfastleigh, Bovey-Tracey, etc., by Ethel Lega-Weekes.

k Some Devonshire field-names, with suggestions as to their signification, by E. Stanbury.

1336 Vol. 46.

a Tavistock abbey, by Mrs. G. H. Radford.

b Some notes on Tavistock history, by J. J. Alexander. [Contd. in vol. 47]

c Charter of Tavistock [1682], by Mrs. G. H. Radford.

d Hundred of Lifton in the time of Testa de Nevil, 1243 by O. J. Reichel.

e Hundred of Tavistock in early times, by O. J. Reichel.

f Mines and mining in the Tavistock district [1810-1901], by M. Bawden.

g History of Whitchurch, by W. N. P. Beebe.

h Crowndale [and the Drake family], by J. J. Alexander.

i Stray notes on Dartmoor tin-working [chiefly 17th cent.], by R. H. Worth.

j St. Urith of Chittlehampton: a study in an obscure Devon saint [her origin and the church of that name], by J. F. Chanter.

k Activities of 'The National Society of Colonial Dames of America', more particularly with reference to certain Devonians, by Sir R. T. White-Thomson. [Old silver in American churches and its donors]

l Use of a Norse standard of measurement by the Normans in 11th and 12th cent. buildings, as exemplified in the structure of Torre abbey and the churches of Kingskerswell and Cockington, by H. R. Watkin.

m 'A mother of men': the Countess Gytha [wife of Godwin, Earl of Wessex], by Barbara Clay-Finch.

n Vicarages in Devon [owners of the churches in 1535, patrons and impropriators in 1831], by J. B. Pearson.

o Anglian invasion of Devon, with some notes on the place-name '-worthy', by J. M. Martin.

1337 Vol. 47.

a Churchyard and wayside crosses in the neighbourhood of Exeter, by Beatrix F. Cresswell.

b Hundred of Exminster in early times, by O. J. Reichel.

c Early history of the principal manors in Exminster hundred, by O. J. Reichel.

d Prudum, Produm, etc. [family of], of Exeter; and the first city seal [13th cent.], by Ethel Lega-Weekes.

e Berry Pomeroy castle, by H. M. Whitley.

f Walrond screen in Seaton church [its armorial bearings], by A. L. Radford.

g Secret of the Fosse Way [its terminal in Devon], by T. J. Joce.

h Bideford under the restored monarchy; with extracts from a 'sessions of the peace book' for the borough of Bideford, 1659–88, by A. G. Duncan.

i Hooker's *Synopsis Chorographical of Devonshire*, by W. J. Blake.

1338 Vol. 48.

a First report of the committee on bibliography. [An earlier report was issued separately in 1916—see below. Subsequent reports in vols. 49–65. The bibliography, kept by the Society, relates to the county and, in 1932, numbered more than 600,000 slips]

b Athelstan myth [his activities in the west], by J. J. Alexander.

c History of Puslinch [near Yealm estuary], by J. Y. A. Morshead.

d Totnes castle and walled town, by H. M. Whitley.

e Robert Wenyngton [mid-15th cent.]: an old 'sea-dog' of Devon, by E. T. Clifford. [Reprinted in the *Devonian Year Book* for 1917]

f Canon in residence [and organization of the chapter], by J. B. Pearson.

g Southcott of Dulcishayes, Kilmington: an extension of the pedigree as given by Vivian, page 698, comp. A. J. P. Skinner.

h Kairpen-Huelgoit, which is called Exeter, by J. M. Martin. [Accounts and discussion of a so-called siege by Vespasian]

1339 Vol. 49.

a Barnstaple goldsmiths' guild, with some notes on the early history of the town, by J. F. Chanter.

b Early 17th cent. plaster ceilings of Barnstaple, by B. W. Oliver.

c Ancient church needlework in Devon, by Beatrix F. Cresswell.

d New light on Sir Richard Grenville, by R. P. Chope. [1: The projected South Seas voyage. 2: The North Devon fleet against the Armada. Reprinted in the *Devonian Year Book* for 1918]

e Notes on the musical history of Barnstaple [ecclesiastical and secular], by H. J. Edwards.

f Barnstaple and its three sub-manors: part of the inland hundred of Braunton, by O. J. Reichel.

g Charles, Prince of Wales, at Barnstaple [1645], and his hostess [Grace Beaple], by J. F. Chanter.

h History of the drama in Barnstaple [15th–19th cent.], by S. Harper.

1340 Vol. 50.

a Proceedings at the fifty-seventh annual meeting. [Includes accounts of Greenway house and the Gilberts; Dittisham parish and church]

b A great Devonian: William Briwer [d. 1226, founder of Torre abbey; his origin, ancestry and birth-place, etc.], by H. R. Watkin.

c Palaeontological and archaeological 'finds' in Kent's cavern, by Hester F. Julian.

d Haccombe [manor and family], by A. W. Searley. [Contd. in vols. 51–57]

e Portraits of the Sainthill family formerly in Bradninch manor house [16th–18th cent.], by A. L. Radford.

f Original [Celtic] main road west of Exeter, by T. J. Joce.

g Chapter in the history of the Peter or Petre family of Devon [16th–17th cent.], by H. Tapley-Soper.

h Last of the Dynhams [brief account of the family and of Sir John Dynham, d. 1501], by R. P. Chope. [Reprinted in the *Devonian Year Book* for 1923]

i Otterton notebook [originally the property of Richard Duke, of Otterton, d. 1733], by J. J. Alexander.

j Devonshire place-names [parishes], by J. F. Chanter.

k Bideford poor and poorhouses, 1830–40, by A. G. Duncan.

l Two Devonshire papists [Anthony Floyer and Henry Carew] in the time of Queen Elizabeth, by J. K. Floyer.

1341 Vol. 51.

a Charles Kingsley, by H. R. Gamble.

b When the Saxons came to Devon, by J. J. Alexander. [Contd. in vols. 52–54, and 56]

c Memorandum of flint implements found on Dartmoor, by T. V. Hodgson.

d Study of place- and field-names, by Frances Rose-Troup.

1342 Vol. 52.

a Sir John Bowring, first president of the Devonshire Association, by Hester F. Julian.

b Sir Henry Wentworth Acland, president of the first Totnes meeting, by Hester F. Julian.

c Joseph Pitts of Exeter, ?1663–?1739 [first English traveller to Mecca], by Cecily Radford.

d Origin and upgrowth of the English parish, illustrated by material taken from the Exeter episcopal registers [15th cent.], by O. J. Reichel.

e Investigation of place-names, by A. B. Prowse.

f Saint Loye's [chapel], East Wonford, by Ethel Lega-Weekes.

1343 Vol. 53.

a Devon wills of the 16th and 17th cent., by Sir O. A. R. Murray.

b James Anthony Froude, president of the Devonport meeting, and his brother, William Froude, F.R.S., by Hester F. Julian.

c Heraldry in relation to the Courtenay tomb in Colyton church, by Lady Radford.

1344 Vol. 54.

a The place of Damnonia [south-west peninsula of Britain] in British England, by Sir H. E. Duke.

b First report of the ancient monuments committee [Contd. in vols. 55–65]

c Beginnings of Crediton, 550–780, by J. F. Chanter.

d Manor and hundred of Crediton, by O. J. Reichel.

e Notes on the vicars of Crediton since the Commonwealth, by T. C. Hughes.

f Hugh Deane, clerk to the governors of the corporation [of Crediton], 1551–83, by Beatrix F. Cresswell.

g Henry de Bracton: a plea for remembrance, by Lady Radford.

1345 Vol. 55.

a First report of the mediaeval bell committee.

b Irish invasion of Devon [1067–8], by J. J. Alexander.

c Some more bits of an old borough [regalia and armorial bearings of Great Torrington], by G. M. Doe.

1346 Vol. 56.

a Presidential address [containing an account of Ashburton from prehistoric times to 19th cent.], by J. S. Amery.

b Vicars of Ashburton since the Commonwealth, by T. C. Hughes.

c Some artistic remains of Buckfast abbey [abbatial throne and miscellaneous 15th cent. wood-carvings], by J. Stephan.

d Baste walls of Totnes, by C. F. Rea.

e Recorders of Totnes, and the courts civil and criminal, of the unreformed borough, by W. B. Faraday.

1347 Vol. 57.

a Celtic Devon, by J. F. Chanter.

b Short account of the Okehampton market, by E. H. Young.

c History of Okehampton grammar school [1610-1806], by W. Hunter.

d Notes on vicars of Okehampton [16th-20th cent.], by T. C. Hughes.

e Note on Jasper Mayne [d. 1672, cleric, poet and royalist], by E. T. Abell.

f Gidleigh castle, by J. S. Amery and R. H. Worth.

g Building of Totnes parish church [15th-19th cent.], by C. F. Rea.

h Southcomb [family] of Rose Ash [rectors, 1675-1854], by W. H. Wilkin. [Contd. in vol. 62]

1348 Vol. 58.

a Hartland abbey [its history to the dissolution], by R. P. Chope.

b Orleigh: an ancient house [and its owners, particularly the Dennis and Davie families], by W. H. Rogers.

c Borough or Burrough [house], in Northam and its inhabitants [Borough, Leigh, Berry, Downe and Barton families], by J. F. Chanter.

d Some literary associations of Celtic and Saxon Devon, by F. A. Perry. [Reprinted in the *Devonian Year Book* for 1929]

e North Devon in Elizabethan times, by G. M. Doe.

f Early history of Bradley manor, near Newton Abbot [12th-13th cent.], by H. R. Watkin.

g Notes on Membury [the parish, church, registers and churchwardens' book], by W. H. Wilkin. [Contd. in vols. 59-61]

h Early boroughs of Devon [historical account from 893], by J. J. Alexander.

i Early archpriests at Haccombe [13th-14th cent.], by A. W. Searley.

j Some South Devon surnames, by C. F. Rea.

k Note on Dartmoor place-names, by R. H. Worth.

1349 Vol. 59.

a History of Ford abbey [12th-20th cent.], by C. Sherwin.

b Old Traine in Modbury: the house and its early owners [Scoos and Swete families, 15th-18th cent.], by J. L. E. Hooppell.

c The earliest southern way from Exeter [pre-Roman track], by T. J. Joce.

d Miss Burney in Devonshire [1773, 1788, 1791], by Ursula Radford.

e Exeter members of parliament, by J. J. Alexander. [Contd. in vols. 60-62]

f Vicars of Winkleigh since the Commonwealth, by T. C. Hughes.

g Barnstaple, Bideford and Torrington during the civil war, by I. Rogers.

1350 Vol. 60.

a Proceedings at the 67th annual meeting. [Includes accounts of Cleeve abbey and of Dunster castle and church]

b Early printing in Devon, by Lady Radford.

c Castle of Barnstaple, by B. W. Oliver.

d Hugh Squier's school, South Molton, by W. W. Joyce.

e Bishop Grandisson: student and art-lover [his gifts of books and vestments to Exeter cathedral, and accounts of decorative work done for him in the cathedral], by Frances Rose-Troup.

f Okehampton during the civil war, 1642-6, by E. H. Young.

g Notes on the history of the parishes of Nymet Tracey, *alias* Bow, with Broad Nymet, by Barbara M. H. Carbonell. [Includes accounts of Nymet Tracey and Broad Nymet churches and lists of rectors]

h History of the hundred in Devon, by G. E. L. Carter.

1351 Vol. 61.

a First report of the archaeological section. [Contd. in vols. 62-63]

b Second report on early history of Devon, by J. J. Alexander. [Includes a chronological summary of events in Devon, 800-940. Previous report in vol. 53]

c Frithelstock priory [c. 1220-1545], by R. P. Chope. [Reprinted in Devon Archaeol. Exploration Soc. *Proceedings*, vol. 2]

d Lost chapel of St. Clare at Hardness, Dartmouth, by H. R. Watkin. [On the probable site of chapel and cemetery, with a history of the foundation and purpose of the chapel and a schedule of mediaeval references thereto]

e Gallants Bowers [derivation of the place-name], by Ethel Lega-Weekes.

f New Edgar charter [A.D. 962] and the South Hams, by Frances Rose-Troup.

g Story of the chapel of St. James the Apostle at Okehampton, by E. H. Young.

h Suggested route from Exeter to the great central trackway (Dartmoor), by R. Pickard.

i Devonshire village (Feniton) in the olden days [an account from Saxon times], by H. W. Watson.

1352 Vol. 62.

a First report on the parliamentary representation o Devon, by J. J. Alexander. [Contd. in vol. 65]

b First report of the parochial history section. [Contd. in vols. 63-65]

c First report of the place-name section. [Contd. in vols. 63-65]

d Notes on the tinners of Devon and their laws, by Lady Radford.

e Stone remains in Drewsteignton, by F. C. Tyler.

f Holcombe by Dawlish [manor, 998-1069], by Frances Rose-Troup.

g Barnstaple borough [and its links with King Athelstan], by B. W. Oliver.

h Great Torrington church troubles in Tudor times, by G. M. Doe.

i Some Devonshire farm names, by Earl Fortescue.

j Trackways near Cotley castle (British earthwork), by R. Pickard.

k 'The Yarty' [a brief account of the river with historical allusions], by W. H. Wilkin.

l Hartland parish records [described], by Isobel D. Thornley.

1353 Vol. 63.

a The monasteries of Devonshire, by J. H. B. Masterman.

b Ancient monastery of St. Mary and St. Peter at Exeter [680-1050], by Frances Rose-Troup.

c Copleston of Offwell [rectors of Offwell from 1773], by W. H. Wilkin.

d An unrecorded royal visit to Exeter [Henry IV and Joan of Navarre in 1403], by Cecily Radford.

e Admission to citizenship in 14th cent. Exeter, by Muriel E. Curtis.

f Demolition of ancient buildings of Exeter during the last half century [from 1877], by H. Reed.

g The Nymet area [derivation of the place-names 'Nymet' and 'Nympton' in central North Devon], by Barbara M. H. Carbonell.

h Goatpath [ancient trackway from Great Haldon to Staverton], by T. J. Joce.

i William Davy, priest and printer [d. 1826], by Ursula Radford.

j A municipal charity [account of the Town and Alms Lands Charity of Great Torrington], by G. M. Doe.

k Beginnings of Lifton [during the Anglo-Saxon period], by J. J. Alexander.

l Flint implement of palaeolithic type from Dartmoor, by R. H. Worth.

m Blowing houses in the valley of the Walkham (moorland), by R. H. Worth.

n Thomas Benet, M.A., Reformation martyr of Exeter [1531] *alias* Master Dusgate, fellow of Corpus Christi College, Cambridge, by Mrs. R. G. Tapley-Soper (*née* Connor).

1354 Vol. 64.

a The Saxon conquest and settlement [of south Britain], by J. J. Alexander.

b Memories and antiquities of Paignton, by W. G. Couldrey.

c Paignton in the Pembroke survey [1567], by J. E. B. Churchward.

d Sir Thomas Louis, bt., Knight of Maria Theresa and Knight of Ferdinand in Sicily, rear-admiral of the white squadron [d. 1807], by G. D. Woollcombe.

e Pomeroys of Berry Pomeroy, by J. Scanes.

f Blowing-houses in the valleys of the Sheepstor brook and the Glaze-brook, by R. H. Worth.

g Prehistoric monuments of Scorhill, Buttern hill and Shuggledown (Shoveldown), by R. H. Worth.

h Date of the Dartmoor antiquities, by C. W. Pilkington-Rogers.

i Devon barns, by Lilian Sheldon.

j Hereditary sheriffs of Devon [descendants of Baldwin the Sheriff and of Richard de Redvers], by Frances Rose-Troup.

k The bishop's chapel of St. Faith at Exeter, by Ethel Lega-Weekes.

l Exeter swords and hat of maintenance, by H. Lloyd-Parry.

m Early printed plans of Exeter, 1587–1724, by K. M. Constable.

n Some evidence of trade between Exeter and Newfoundland to 1600, by W. J. Harte.

o Holbeton church reviewed, by J. J. Beckerlegge.

p Great Torrington quarter sessions, 1686–1836, by G. M. Doe.

q Radford of Lapford [rectors of Lapford and Nymet Rowland], by W. H. Wilkin.

r Vicars of Knowstone-cum-Molland, 1767–1915, by W. H. Wilkin.

s Anglo-Saxon Devon, by G. E. L. Carter.

1355 Vol. 65.

a William Froude [d. 1879, engineer and naval architect], his life and work, by Sir W. S. Abell.

b Beginnings of Ilfracombe [and the Saxon settlement of Devon], by J. J. Alexander.

c The loyal saddler of Exeter [John Cooke, d. 1840], by Ursula Radford.

d Devon toll-houses, by Lilian Sheldon.

e Blowing-houses in the valleys of the Sheepstor brook, the Meavy, the Erme, and the Avon, by R. H. Worth.

f Weathering of Exeter's wall and buildings, by R. Pickard.

g Building stones of ancient Exeter, by F. T. Howard.

h Modern water supply of Exeter [since 1693], by A. Kneel and R. Pickard.

i East and north Devon place-names, by J. J. Alexander.

j Custos and college of the vicars choral of the choir of the cathedral church of St. Peter, Exeter, and their close, by J. F. Chanter.

k Borough English and burgage tenure, by G. E. L. Carter.

l Devon charters and the threefold obligation, by Frances Rose-Troup.

m Some Axminster worthies [17th and 18th cent.], by W. H. Wilkin.

Extra volumes:

Calendars of wills and administrations relating to Devon and Cornwall. 2 vols. 1908–14. [See no. **633** above]

1356 Guide to the Reports and Transactions, first series, vols. 1–30, by H. G. H. Shaddick. 1909.

1357 Committee on bibliography. Report of the hon. secretary for the period ended 13 Dec. 1915. *P.* [1916].

1358 Key to the Transactions, vols. 1–60, by R. P. Chope. 1928.

1359 The hundreds of Devon (supplementary). The hundreds of Tiverton, Hemyock, Halberton, South Molton, Roborough, Axminster, Axmouth, Black Torrington, Plympton, and Ermington in early times, by O. J. Reichel, ed. F. B. Prideaux. 1928–33.

1360 Index to folk-lore in the Transactions, vols. 1–60, by R. P. Chope. 1929.

1361 Parochial histories of Devonshire, no. 1: Okehampton, comp. E. H. Young. [?1932].

1362 Reports and Transactions of the Devonshire Association, vols. 61–70. General index, comp. A. A. Fursdon. 1951.

DICKENS FELLOWSHIP

Founded 1902, to knit together in a common bond of friendship lovers of Charles Dickens.

Publications:

1363 Publication no. 1. Charles Dickens: the story of his life and writings, by B. W. Matz. *P.* [Reprinted from *Household Words*, 1902]

1364 The Dickens house, 48 Doughty Street, London, W.C.1. *P.* [1926].

1365 Dickens: the story of the life of the world's favourite author, by W. Dexter. 1928.

1366 The Dickensian, a quarterly magazine for Dickens lovers, vols. 1–29. (1905–33). [Contains articles bearing on the life and times of Charles Dickens]

1367 Index to the first thirty vols. [of the *Dickensian*], 1905–34. 1935.

DORSET NATURAL HISTORY AND ARCHAEOLOGICAL SOCIETY

Founded 1875, as the Dorset Natural History and Antiquarian Field Club, to promote and encourage an interest in the study of the physical sciences generally and archaeology, especially the natural history of Dorset and its antiquities, prehistoric records, and ethnology. Above title taken in 1928 on amalgamating with the Dorset County Museum.

Proceedings, vols. 22–54 (1901–33):

1368 Vol. 22.

a Cerne and Minterne meeting. [Includes accounts of Minterne church, Minterne House and its tapestry, and Cerne church and abbey]

b Exeter and Torquay meeting. [Includes accounts of Exeter guildhall, cathedral, and cathedral library, and Kent's cavern, Torquay]

c West Purbeck meeting. [Includes accounts of Creech barrow, Barnestone manor house, and Great Tyneham house]

d Meeting in the neighbourhood of Salisbury. [Includes accounts of Britford church, Longford castle, and Downton moot]

e A critical and material examination of the hill-fortress called Eggardun, by H. C. March and H. S. Solly.

f Cerne abbey barn, by H. J. Moule.

g Water supply of ancient Dorchester, dating probably from Roman times, by Major Coates.

h Some notes on Major Coates' discovery of the ancient water supply of Dorchester, by W. M. Barnes.

i The giant and the maypole of Cerne, by H. C. March.

j Eponymous families of Dorset, by G. R. Elwes.

1369 Vol. 23.

a Portland meeting. [Includes an account of Wyke Regis church]

b The form and probable history of Saxon church architecture, by W. M. Barnes.

c Ancient memorial brasses of Dorset, by W. de C. Prideaux. [Contd. in vols. 25, 27–29, 32, 34–37, and 40]

1370 Vol. 24.

a Shaftesbury meeting. [Includes an account of Shaftesbury abbey]

b Milton Abbey meeting. [Includes an account of Milton abbey church]

c Topography of old Dorset, by A. Pope.

d King John's house at Tollard Royal [Wilts.], by W. M. Barnes.

e William Cuming, M.D., 1714–87, by W. B. Stone.

f The problem [of the origin] of lynchets, by H. C. Marsh.

g Church bells of Dorset, by J. Raven. [Contd. in vols. 25–27]

h The Roman villa at Fifehead Neville, by G. H. Engleheart.

1371 Vol. 25.

a The old town of Milton Abbey, by H. Pentin.

b Dorset gaol and the Monmouth rebellion, by S. E. V. Filleul.

c Commentary on some parts of the account of Sherborne abbey and school given in Hutchins' *Dorset*, vol. iv, 3rd ed., by W. B. Wildman.

d Charles II in the Channel Islands, by J. S. Udal.

e Club notes and discussions. [Includes: 1: The declaration of an indulgence at St. Catherine's chapel, Milton abbey. 2: Incised slab in Milton abbey church].

f Church goods, Dorset, 1552, ed. W. M. Barnes. [Contd. in vol. 26]

1372 Vol. 26.

a Liscombe: its chapel, monastic house, and barn, by H. Pentin.

b Barrow-digging at Martinstown, near Dorchester, 1903, by H. St. G. Gray and C. S. Prideaux.

c Notes on old church bands and village choirs of the past century, by F. W. Galpin.

d Brownsea island, by C. van Raalte.

e Some Milton antiquities, by H. Pentin.

1373 Vol. 27.

a First summer meeting. [Includes accounts of Bindon abbey and Lulworth castle]

b Second summer meeting. [Includes accounts of Wimborne minster and Kingston Lacy]

c Cross-legged effigies in Dorset, by S. Heath.

d Rolls of the court baron of the manor of Winterborne Waste *alias* Monkton, by W. M. Barnes.

e Dorset chantries, by E. A. Fry. [Contd. in vols. 28–31]

1374 Vol. 28.

a Fourth summer meeting. [Includes an account of Ford abbey]

b Roman pavements, by H. C. March.

c Notes on the parish and church of Piddletrenthide, by C. W. H. Dicker.

d The Pepys of south Dorset: a diarist in the reign of William III [John Richards, of Warmwell, d. 1721], by W. B. Barrett.

e Whitchurch Canonicorum, by D. H. Stubbs.

f Cartulary of Cerne abbey, commonly known as the Red Book of Cerne (Camb. Univ. Lib.), ed. with English translation by B. F. Lock. [Contd. in vol. 29]

g 14th cent. life in Bridport, as shewn by wills in the borough archives, by R. G. Bartelot.

h Coins struck in Dorset during the Saxon, Norman and Stuart periods, by H. Symonds.

i The liberty and manor of Frampton: rolls of the court leet and court baron, ed. W. M. Barnes.

j Queen Eleanor crosses, by A. Pope.

k William Knapp [d. 1768, parish clerk of Poole and composer of hymn tunes], by S. E. V. Filleul.

l The Lady Margaret [d. 1509], Countess of Richmond and Derby, and her connection with Wimborne minster, by W. J. Fletcher.

m Some Dorset church towers, by R. G. Brocklehurst.

1375 Vol. 29.

a Architectural history of the parish church of St. Mary at Cerne, by C. W. H. Dicker.

b Town cellars at Poole, by W. K. Gill.

c Dorset tokens of the 18th and 19th cent., and medals of various periods, by H. Symonds.

d Additions to and amendments of the Dorset section of Dr. Williamson's edition (1889) of W. Boyne's *Trade Tokens issued in the 17th century*, by H. Symonds.

e Hilton church, by E. H. H. Lee.

f Catalogue of sepulchral pottery [found in barrows] in the Dorset county museum, by J. E. Acland.

g The ritual of barrows and circles, by H. C. March.

h Some Dorset bridges, by R. G. Brocklehurst.

i Reports on the excavations at Maumbury Rings, by H. St. G. Gray. [Contd. in vols. 30 and 31]

1376 Vol. 30.

a First summer meeting. [Includes an account of Ford abbey]

b Last summer meeting. [Includes an account of Scoles manor]

c The Roman villa at Hemsworth, by G. H. Engleheart.

d Some British and Romano-British coins found in Dorset, by H. Symonds.

e The status of peasantry in Portland, by Mrs. K. Warry.

f Some ancient customs of the manors of Stratton and Grimston, by A. Pope.

g Mediaeval floor-tiles of St. George's church, Fordington, by R. G. Bartelot.

h Tarrant Gunville [manorial descent, 11th–16th cent.], by E. A. Fry.

i Sequence and evolution of architectural styles in the

church of Fordington St. George, Dorchester, by J. Feacey.

j Registrum abbathiae de Middeltone [Milton], in scaccario (Bodl. ms. James, 23), with English translation by B. F. Lock.

1377 Vol. 31.

a Some Dorset privateers, by H. Symonds.
b The birthplace of Matthew Prior, scholar, poet and dramatist, by J. M. J. Fletcher.
c The Normans in Dorset, by C. W. H. Dicker.
d The Pitt family of Blandford St. Mary, by A. C. Almack.
e Story of the Bettiscombe skull [and the Pinney family], by J. S. Udal.
f Weymouth and Melcombe Regis in the time of the great civil war, by W. B. Barrett.

1378 Vol. 32.

a First summer meeting: West Dorset. [Includes notes on Melplash Court]
b Second summer meeting: Gillingham, Mere, and Stourhead.
c Third summer meeting: the mid-Piddle valley [including Walterson or Waterston manor].
d Two-days' meeting at Winchester. [Includes notes on Headborne Worthy and St. Cross]
e Sir George Somers [fl. c. 1580] and his family, by F. J. Pope.
f The manor, hundred and priory courts of Cranborne, 1725–35, by H. Symonds.
g History of the Dorchester gallows, by S. E. V. Filleul.
h Notes on the history of the Dorset Volunteer Force, by Sir W. Watts.
i Calendar of Dorset deeds presented to the Club in 1909 by E. A. Fry.
j Note on an old house at Piddletown lately taken down, by C. W. H. Dicker.
k Some Saxon saints of Wimborne, by J. M. J. Fletcher.
l Notes on mediaeval enamelled armorial horse trappings, with special reference to a Weymouth find, by W. de C. Prideaux.

1379 Vol. 33.

a Notes on some surveys of valley entrenchments in the Piddletrenthide district, by H. S. Toms.
b A comparison of Dr. Stukeley's account of the Roman amphitheatre at Dorchester with the results of the excavations, 1908–10, by J. E. Acland.
c The mystery of Corfe, by J. G. N. Clift. [On the death of Edward the Martyr, 978]
d Bridport harbour through seven centuries, by H. Symonds.

1380 Vol. 34.

a Second summer meeting: Marlborough. [Includes notes on Avebury]
b Fourth summer meeting: the Cerne valley. [Includes notes on Charminster church]
c Scando-Gothic art in Wessex, by H. C. March.
d Dorset assizes in the 17th cent., by F. J. Pope.
e Ancient earthworks of Cranborne Chase, by H. Sumner.
f Interim report on excavations at Maumbury Rings, Dorchester, 1912. [Further report in vol. 35]
g Dorset weather lore, by J. S. Udal.
h Sherborne brewers in 1383, by E. A. Fry.
i The marriage of St. Cuthburga, afterwards foundress of the monastery at Wimborne, by J. M. J. Fletcher.
j Roman villas discovered in Dorset: their sites and the relics found therein which throw light upon the civil life of their occupants, by T. E. Usherwood.

1381 Vol. 35.

a Second summer meeting: the New Forest. [Includes sites of Romano-British potteries at Sloden and Island's Thorn]
b Third summer meeting: Malmesbury and Lacock.
c On the relics left by Philip and Joan of Castile in 1506 at Wolfeton House, and preserved in the writer's family, by O. Pickard-Cambridge.
d Chained books in Dorset and elsewhere, by J. M. J. Fletcher.
e Sandsfoot and Portland castles, by H. Symonds.
f A Dorset inventory of 1627 [being the goods of William Edmonds *alias* Younge, yeoman], by N. M. Richardson.
g Thomas Gerard of Trent [d. 1634/5], his family and his writings, by E. H. Bates Harbin.
h Dorset 'buttony', by J. E. Acland.
i Folk-lore and superstitions still obtaining in Dorset, by E. A. Rawlence.

1382 Vol. 36.

a Second summer meeting: Christchurch, Hants.
b Notes on excavations at Dorchester on the site of the Roman defences, by J. E. Acland.
c Some old village jokes and games which obtained in the Blackmore Vale in the last century, by E. A. Rawlence.
d A Dorset worthy: William Stone, royalist and divine, 1615–85, by J. M. J. Fletcher.
e Early man in Dorset, by H. S. Solly.
f The augmentation books, 1650–60, in Lambeth Palace library, by E. A. Fry.
g Reports on excavations at Dewlish, 1914.

1383 Vol. 37.

a 'The man in the wall' at Wimborne minster, by J. M. J. Fletcher.
b List of Dorset barrows opened by Mr. E. Cunnington or described by him, comp. J. E. Acland.
c Sundry folk-lore reminiscences relating to man and beast in Dorset and the neighbouring counties, by E. A. Rawlence.
d The silk industry in Wessex, by H. Symonds. 1: The throwing-mills at Sherborne and their owners. 2: Domestic economics in the 18th cent.
e Edge tools in early Britain, by the Rev. W. Barnes, rector of Came, d. 1886, ed. J. E. Acland.
f Pre-Saxon civilization in Dorset, by Ellen E. Woodhouse.
g Old Portland, by H. Pentin.

1384 Vol. 38.

a Second summer meeting. [Includes summary of an address by J. M. J. Fletcher on a 1403 churchwardens' roll of Wimborne minster]
b Walks and avenues of Dorchester, when and by whom planted, by A. Pope.
c Dorset soldiers of the Tudor and early Stuart periods, by F. J. Pope.
d The Portland reeve staff and court leet, by J. E. Acland.
e Wessex minsters, by A. C. Almack.
f Leaden coffin found at Cann, near Shaftesbury, by H. St. G. Gray.
g Opening of the round barrow at Melcombe Bingham, by C. Ashburnham.
h A Dorset royal peculiar [Wimborne minster], by J. M. J. Fletcher.
i Dorset children's doggerel rhymes, by H. Pentin.

1385 Vol. 39.

a Commercial day book of John Richards of Warmwell [merchant, fl. 1687–1721, sometime of London], by W. N. Sturt.

b Some unrecorded deans of Wimborne minster, by J. M. J. Fletcher.

c Notes on coins believed to have been struck at Sandsfoot castle and Weymouth in 1643–4, by H. Symonds.

d Pipe leases for Dorset [16th–early 19th cent.], by E. A. Fry.

e Notes on Dorset 'restored' churches, by A. C. Almack. [Contd. in vol. 40]

1386 Vol. 40.

a First winter meeting. [Includes note by J. M. J. Fletcher on a 14th cent. ms. *Regimen animarum* at Wimborne minster]

b Tomb of King Ethelred in Wimborne minster, by J. M. J. Fletcher.

c Notes on the history of Chardstock [Devon], by E. S. Rodd.

1387 Vol. 41.

a First summer meeting: Abbotsbury.

b Second summer meeting: Wimborne Minster.

c Dorset Volunteers during the French wars, 1793–1814, by H. Symonds.

d Sandsfoot castle, Weymouth, by W. C. Norman.

e Some old inns of Wimborne, by E. K. Le Fleming.

f A glimpse of Weymouth and the war, 1802–3, by W. O. Cockcraft.

g Tudor houses in Dorset and the contemporary life within them, by V. L. Oliver.

h General index to the Dorset Field Club Proceedings, vols. 1–41, by H. Pouncy.

1388 Vol. 42.

a Second summer meeting. [Includes summary of an address by R. G. Bartelot on King John's castle at Eggardon]

b First winter meeting. [Includes summary of an address by J. M. J. Fletcher on 'The archdeacon of Dorset's book', 18th cent.]

c Eggardun hill, by H. S. Solly.

d The Helstone, by V. L. Oliver.

e Travels of Peter Mundy in Dorset, 1635, by N. M. Richardson.

f Church screens of Dorset, by E. T. Long.

g The founding of Dorchester, Massachusetts, and the Rev. John White [d. 1648], by J. E. Acland.

1389 Vol. 43.

a First summer meeting: Corfe castle.

b Second summer meeting: Sherborne. [Includes notes on the old and new castles and the abbey church]

c Third summer meeting: Shaftesbury.

d The Black Death in Dorset, 1348–9, by J. M. J. Fletcher.

e Dorset church woodwork, by E. T. Long.

f Notes on Whitcombe church, by M. P. Maturin.

g Evidence for an Anglo-Saxon mint at Bridport, by H. Symonds.

h Priest's chamber on Lyme Regis bridge, by W. Wingrave.

i Ancient stained glass in Dorset churches, by E. T. Long.

j Calendar of mss. relating to manors in Sturminster Marshall, comp. H. Symonds.

1390 Vol. 44.

a First summer meeting: Edington.

b Third summer meeting: Worth Matravers and St. Aldhelm's Head. [Includes notes on Scoles and the Scoville family]

c Sir Thomas Dackomb, priest, rector of Tarrant Gunville, 1549–67, a Dorset bibliophile, by J. M. J. Fletcher.

d Dorset church towers, by E. T. Long.

e The pre-Roman and Roman occupation of the Weymouth district, by V. L. Oliver.

f Additional notes on two 16th cent. Dorset clergymen [Thomas Dackomb and William Kethe], by J. M. J. Fletcher.

g Dorset church fonts, by E. T. Long.

h Notes on some Dorset churches, by Sir S. Glynne. [Contd. in vol. 45]

1391 Vol. 45.

a First summer meeting: Cranborne Chase. [Includes notes on Bokerly dyke and Cranborne church]

b Second summer meeting: Bridport. [Includes notes on Whitchurch Canonicorum]

c Fourth summer meeting: Beaminster district. [Includes notes on Netherbury church]

d Notes on exhibits in the Dorset county museum relating to the Napoleonic era, 1793–1815, by J. E. Acland.

e The SS collar in Dorset and elsewhere, by J. M. J. Fletcher. [Also published separately, *P*. 1924]

f Armorial bearings in old houses of Dorset, by J. S. Udal.

1392 Vol. 46.

a The Roman aqueduct at Dorchester, by P. Foster.

b Pre-Reformation Dorset church monuments, by E. T. Long.

c The [early 14th cent.] Holewale brass at Askerswell, by V. L. Oliver.

d The Mautravers brass [to John, Baron Mautravers, d. 1365] at Lytchett Matravers, by V. L. Oliver.

e Rev. Henry John Richman, headmaster of Dorchester grammar school and rector of Holy Trinity church and of St. Peter's [d. 1824], by J. M. J. Fletcher.

f Bronze age, or earlier, lynchets, by H. S. Toms.

g Rev. William Barnes [d. 1886] as an engraver, by V. L. Oliver.

1393 Vol. 47.

a Second summer meeting: Wells and Glastonbury.

b Third summer meeting: Poole and Poole harbour. [Includes notes on Scaplen's Court, Poole]

c 13th cent. steelyard weights, by G. D. Drury.

d A century of Dorset documents [mainly from the consistory court, Wimborne minster, 1557–1670], by J. M. J. Fletcher.

e A trio of Dorset worthies [Stanley Gower, rector of Holy Trinity, Dorchester, 1647–60; Samuel Cromleholme, d. 1672, headmaster of the grammar school, also of St. Paul's school, London; Humphrey Gower, d. 1711, vice-chancellor of Cambridge university], by J. M. J. Fletcher.

f Some Dorset deeds in the John Rylands Library, comp. R. Fawtier.

g The almshouses of St. George in Poole, by H. P. Smith.

h William Knapp, the Dorset composer [*c*. 1729–68], by H. P. Smith.

1394 Vol. 48.

a Second summer meeting: Hod hill and Hambledon hill. [Includes an address by A. Pope on Dorset 'clubmen' in Aug. 1645]

b Third summer meeting: Bride valley. [Includes notes on Puncknowle and Stratton]

c St. Peter's, Church Knowle, by G. D. Drury.

d West country bankers, 1750–1825, by H. Symonds.

e Mediaeval iron fire-backs, by J. E. Acland.

f Heart burials and some Purbeck marble heart-shrines, by G. D. Drury.

g Records of the turnpike trustees of the Poole, Wimborne and Cranborne trust, by E. K. Le Fleming.

h Some Abbotsbury records, by E. H. T. Atkinson.

i Dorset clocks and clock-makers, by R. G. Bartelot.

1395 Vol. 49.

a First summer meeting: Minterne, Folke, and Perse Caundle.

b Fourth summer meeting: Stour vale and Blandford. [Includes notes on Sturminster Marshall]

c Tarrant Crawford, and the founder of Salisbury cathedral [Bp. Richard Poore], by J. M. J. Fletcher. [Also published separately. *P.* 1928]

d An additional calendar of Dorset deeds, by V. L. Oliver. [Contd. in vols. 50, 52, and 53]

e Notes on the church of St. John the Baptist, Bere Regis, by H. W. Crickmay.

f West Woodyates manor, by F. B. Eastwood.

g Description of Romano-British pavement originally found in 1903 and re-discovered on Oct. 5th, 1927, in the foundry yard on the south side of the High Street, Fordington, by O. C. Vidler.

h English alabaster tables in Dorset, by E. T. Long.

i Friendly societies and their emblems, by R. Hine.

j Poole's ancient admiralty court, by H. P. Smith.

k Roofs of Dorset churches, by E. T. Long.

1396 Vol. 50.

a First summer meeting: Forde abbey, Hawkchurch, and Wootton Fitzpaine.

b Second summer meeting: upper Yeo valley. [Includes notes on Clifton Maybank, Wyke Grange, and Trent]

c Third summer meeting: Wimborne district. [Includes notes on Gussage St. Michael, Gussage All Saints, and Knowlton]

d Fourth summer meeting: neighbourhood of Dorchester. [Includes notes on Puddletown church]

e Roman villa at Fifehead Neville, by V. L. Oliver.

f Ancient mural paintings in Dorset churches, by E. T. Long.

g The division of the commons of West Parley and West Moors [1633], by C. D. Drew.

h Disc barrows of Dorset, by V. L. Oliver.

i Ancient monuments in Dorset scheduled under the Act of 1913, up to May 1928, comp. V. L. Oliver.

1397 Vol. 51.

a First summer meeting: Salisbury and Old Sarum. [Includes notes on the cathedral, churches, and old houses, and an address on the history of the church in Wessex]

b Second summer meeting: Lyme Regis district. [Includes notes on Whitchurch Canonicorum]

c Third summer meeting: Marnhull, Shaftesbury, and Iwerne Minster.

d Fourth summer meeting: Milton Abbey, Hilton, and Bingham's Melcombe.

e Hoard of Roman coins from Jordan hill, Weymouth, by F. S. Salisbury.

f 14th cent. effigies in Horton church: with observations on sword-grasping figures, by G. D. Drury.

g Chettle Down earthwork: an ancient pond, by H. S. Toms.

h Early iron age site at West Parley, by C. D. Drew. [Correction in vol. 52]

i Romano-British pottery from Dudsbury, by C. D. Drew.

j All Saints', Hilton, by G. D. Drury.

k St. Andrew's, Bingham's Melcombe, by G. D. Drury.

1398 Vol. 52.

a First summer meeting: Christchurch and the lower Stour valley. [Includes notes on West Parley church]

b Third summer meeting: Purbeck. [Includes notes on Worth Matravers and Kingston church]

c Fourth summer meeting: Crewkerne, Ham hill, Barrington Court, and South Petherton.

d Fifth summer meeting: Corton, Portesham, Waddon, and the Helstone.

e Iron age and Romano-British settlement at Milborne St. Andrew, by Mrs. Pleydell-Railston, with notes on the site and pottery by C. D. Drew.

f The Havelland brass [John Havelland, d. 1607, and family] at Langton Matravers church, by G. D. Drury. [With pedigree and notes on the Havelland family]

g Dorset church dedications, by E. T. Long.

h Combs ditch and Bokerly dyke reviewed, by H. Sumner.

i Agricultural riots in Dorset in 1830, by W. H. P. Okeden.

j The occupation of the Hamworthy peninsula in the late Keltic and Romano-British periods, by H. P. Smith.

1399 Vol. 53.

a First summer meeting: Dorchester. [Includes an address by Lord Hanworth on manorial records]

b Third summer meeting: West Chelborough and Chantmarle. [Includes notes on Benville manor]

c Fourth summer meeting: Shaftesbury and Farnham.

d Fifth summer meeting: Eggardon and Loders. [Includes notes on Toller Fratrum and Toller Porcorum churches]

e Religious houses of Dorset, by E. T. Long.

f A few [Roman] coins found at Dorchester, by O. C. Vidler.

g Notes on the outer bounds of Cranborne Chase, by T. Dayrell-Reed.

h On writing a parish history, and sources of information within the county of Dorset, by C. D. Drew.

i An Anglo-Saxon burial on Hardown hill [near Morecombelake], by W. Wingrave.

j Early ecclesiastical effigies in Dorset, by G. D. Drury.

k Excavations at Jordan hill, 1931, by C. D. Drew.

1400 Vol. 54.

a Fourth summer meeting: Hod hill, Hammoon, and Sturminster Newton. [Includes notes on Sturminster castle]

b Sir John Strangwayes's account of his estate in verse [1650. Included in the presidential address by Lord Ilchester at the annual general meeting]

c The 6th cent. helmet unearthed at Hamworthy in 1932, by H. P. Smith.

d The Hamworthy section of the branch Roman road from Badbury Rings to Poole harbour, by H. P. Smith.

e Excavations at Jordan hill and Preston [Roman villa], 1932, by C. D. Drew.

f Bindon abbey charter, 1313, by G. D. Drury.

g Lady St. Mary church, Wareham, by P. M. Johnston.

h Late bronze age urnfield at Kinson, by J. B. Calkin.

i Romano-British occupation site at Badbury Rings, by W. G. Wallace.

1401 List of the officers, members, and rules, and a general index of the papers, etc., published in vols. 1–26 of the Proceedings, comp. H. Pouncy. 1906.

1402 Index to authors of papers, etc., published in vols. 1–55 of the Proceedings, comp. E. R. Sykes. *P.* 1941.

DUGDALE SOCIETY

Founded 1920, to promote and foster the study of Warwickshire history, topography and archaeology.

Publications, vols. 1–12:

1403 Vols. 1, 3, 5, 10. Minutes and accounts of the corporation of Stratford-upon-Avon and other records, 1553–1620, transcribed by R. Savage, with introd. and notes by

E. I. Fripp. Vols. i–iv, 1921–9. [Vol. i: 1553–66; vol. ii: 1566–77; vol. iii: 1577–86; vol. iv: 1586–92]

1404 Vol. 2. Abstract of the bailiffs' accounts of monastic and other estates in the county of Warwick under the supervision of the court of augmentation for the year ending Michaelmas 1547, translated by W. B. Bickley, with introd. by W. F. Carter. 1923.

1405 Vols. 4, 7, 12. Records of King Edward's School, Birmingham. Vols. i–iii, 1924–33. [Vols. i and ii with introds. by W. F. Carter; vol. iii ed. W. F. Carter and E. A. B. Barnard. Vol. iv, ed. P. B. Chatwin, was published in 1948]

1406 Vol. 6. Lay subsidy roll for Warwickshire of 6 Edward III (1332), translated and ed. with introd. by W. F. Carter; with three early subsidy rolls for Stratford-upon-Avon, and an extract from an assize roll of 1323, ed. F. C. Wellstood. 1926.

1407 Vol. 8. Registers of Edgbaston parish church, 1636–1812, vol. i, transcribed and ed. with introd. by C. S. James, 1928. [Vol. ii was published in 1936]

1408 Vol. 9. Register of Walter Reynolds, bishop of Worcester, 1308–13, ed. R. A. Wilson. 1928. [In conjunction with the Worcestershire Hist. Soc.]

1409 Vol. 11. Warwickshire feet of fines, vol. i: 1195–1284, abstracted by Ethel Stokes, ed. F. C. Wellstood, with introd. and indexes by F. T. S. Houghton. 1932. [Vols. ii–iii were published in 1939–43]

Occasional papers, 1–3:

1410 No. 1. The ancient records of Coventry, by Mary D. Harris. *P.* 1924.

1411 No. 2. The preservation and interpretation of ancient records, by the Rt. Hon. Lord Hanworth. *P.* 1929.

1412 No. 3. Dr. Thomas's edition of Sir William Dugdale's *Antiquities of Warwickshire*, by H. M. Jenkins. *P.* 1931.

DURHAM AND NORTHUMBERLAND PARISH REGISTER SOCIETY

Founded 1897, to print and index the ancient parish registers of Durham and Northumberland down to the year 1812. Dissolved 1926.

Publications, 5a–36:

1413 Nos. 5a, 5b. Registers of Bothal with Hebburn, Northumb., 1678–1812, transcribed by W. Ellis, indexed and ed. H. M. Wood. 2 vols. 1901.

1414 No. 6. Registers of Ryton, co. Durham: marriages, 1581–1812, transcribed, indexed and ed. J. Baily. 1902.

1415 No. 7. Registers of Ingram, Northumb.: baptisms, 1696–1812; marriages, 1684–1812; burials, 1682–1812, transcribed by A. C. C. Vaughan, indexed and ed. H. M. Wood. 1903.

1416 No. 8. Registers of Edlingham, Northumb., 1658–1812, transcribed by Miss K. A. Martin, indexed and ed. H. M. Wood. 1903.

1417 No. 9. Registers of St. Margaret's, Durham: marriages, 1558–1812, transcribed, indexed and ed. H. Roberson. 1904.

1418 No. 10. Registers of Whitburn, co. Durham: baptisms, 1611–1812; marriages and burials, 1579–1812, transcribed, indexed and ed. H. M. Wood. 1904.

1419 Nos. 11, 16. Registers of Berwick-upon-Tweed, Northumb., transcribed by E. Dodds, indexed and ed. H. M. Wood. 2 vols. 1905–7. [Vol. i: baptisms, 1574–1700. Vol. ii: marriages, 1572–1700]

1420 No. 12. Registers of Middleton St. George, co. Durham: baptisms, 1652–1812; marriages and burials, 1616–1812, transcribed, indexed and ed. H. M. Wood. 1906.

1421 No. 13. Registers of Bishop Middleham, co. Durham, 1559–1812, transcribed, indexed and ed. R. Peacock. 1906.

1422 No. 14. Registers of Alnham, Northumb.: baptisms, 1688–1812; marriages, 1705–1812; burials, 1727–1812, transcribed by W. Nall, indexed by Mrs. H. M. Wood. 1907.

1423 No. 15. Registers of Lesbury, Northumb.: baptisms and burials, 1690–1812; marriages, 1689–1812, transcribed by J. Bolam, ed. R. Peacock, indexed by H. M. Wood. 1907.

1424 No. 17. Registers of St. Mary in the South Bailey, Durham: baptisms, 1560–1812; marriages and burials, 1559–1812, transcribed and indexed by H. M. Wood, ed. W. Greenwell. 1908.

1425 No. 18. Registers of Coniscliffe, co. Durham: baptisms and marriages, 1590–1812; burials, 1591–1812, transcribed by Miss Edleston, indexed and ed. H. M. Wood. 1908.

1426 No. 19. Registers of Whorlton, co. Durham: baptisms, 1626–1812; marriages, 1713–1812; burials, 1669–1812, transcribed by Miss Edleston, indexed and ed. H. M. Wood. 1908.

1427 No. 20. Registers of Beadnell, Northumb.: baptisms and burials, 1766–1812; marriages, 1767–1812, transcribed by Miss K. A. Martin, indexed and ed. H. M. Wood. 1909.

1428 No. 21. Registers of Whalton, Northumb., 1661–1812, transcribed by J. Walker, indexed and ed. H. M. Wood. 1909.

1429 No. 22. Registers of Seaham, co. Durham: baptisms, 1646–1812; marriages, 1652–1812; burials, 1653–1812, transcribed and indexed by H. M. Wood, ed. R. Peacock. 1910.

1430 No. 23. Registers of Dalton-le-Dale, co. Durham, 1653–1812, transcribed and ed. G. W. A. Firth, indexed by W. Leighton. 1910.

1431 No. 24. Registers of Corbridge, Northumb.: baptisms, 1654–1812; marriages, burials, 1657–1812, transcribed by H. M. Wood, ed. R. Peacock. 1911.

1432 No. 25. Registers of Halton, Northumb.: baptisms, burials, 1654–1812; marriages, 1654–1769, transcribed by H. M. Wood, ed. R. Peacock, indexed by W. Leighton. 1911.

1433 No. 26. List of parochial and non-parochial registers relating to Durham and Northumberland, by H. M. Wood. *P.* 1912.

1434 No. 27. Registers of St. Mary-le-Bow, Durham: baptisms, burials, 1571–1812; marriages, 1573–1812, transcribed and ed. H. M. Wood. 1912.

1435 No. 28. Registers of the cathedral church of St. Nicholas, Newcastle-upon-Tyne: marriages, 1574–1812, transcribed and ed. H. M. Wood. 1914.

1436 Registers of Castle Eden, Durham: baptisms, 1661–1812; marriages, 1698–1794; burials, 1696–1812, transcribed and ed. F. G. J. Robinson, indexed by A. E. and G. M. F. Wood. *P.* 1914.

1437 No. 30. Registers of Sherburn Hospital: baptisms, 1692–1812; marriages, 1695–1763; burials, 1678–1812, transcribed by H. M. Wood, indexed by A. E. Wood, ed. D. S. Boutflower. *P.* 1914.

1438 No. 31. Registers of Chatton, Northumb., 1712–1812, transcribed by H. M. Wood, indexed by A. R. Green. 1915.

1439 No. 32. Registers of St. Nicholas' church, Durham, vol. i: marriages, 1540–1812, transcribed by H. M. Wood, ed. W. Bothamley. 1918.

1440 No. 33. Registers of Meldon, Northumb.: baptisms, 1706–1812; marriages, 1727–1812; burials, 1716–1812, transcribed, indexed and ed. H. M. Wood. *P.* 1918.

1441 No. 34. Registers of Ilderton, Northumb.: baptisms, 1724–1812; marriages, 1727–1812; banns, 1754–1812; burials, 1727–1812, transcribed, indexed and ed. J. C. Hodgson. *P.* 1918.

1442 No. 35. Registers of Winston, Durham: baptisms, 1572–1812; marriages, 1574–1812; banns, 1754–1809; burials, 1573–1812, transcribed by Miss A. Edleston, indexed by T. Porteus. 1918.

1443 No. 36. Registers of Long Houghton, Northumb.: baptisms, marriages, burials, 1646–1812; banns, 1754–1805, transcribed, indexed and ed. H. M. Wood. 1926.

DURHAM HISTORICAL SOCIETY

Founded 1901, to promote the study of local antiquities and history.

Publications:[1]

1444 Brooke Foss, Dunelm: a memorial [being the life of Brooke Foss Westcott, bishop of Durham, d. 1901], by J. W. Fawcett. 1901.

1445 Parish registers of Muggleswick containing baptisms, marriages and burials, 1784–1812, transcribed, annotated and indexed by J. W. Fawcett. 1906.

1446 Parish registers of All Saints' church, Lanchester; vol. i: baptisms, marriages and burials, 1560–1603, transcribed, annotated, and indexed by J. W. Fawcett. 1909.

1447 Parish registers of St. Cuthbert's church, Satley, containing baptisms, marriages and burials, 1560–1812, gravestone inscriptions, local pedigrees, etc., transcribed, annotated, and indexed by J. W. Fawcett. 1914.

DYSERTH AND DISTRICT FIELD CLUB

Founded 1911, for the study of natural science and archaeology.

Proceedings, 1913–32 (20 vols. 1914–33):

1448 Vol. for 1913.
  a Ancient British hill fort at Kinmel Park.
  b Mia Hall [an historical account of the locality], by T. Edwards.
  c The hill fortress of Caer Lleon.
  d Pre-historic remains on Penmaenmawr uplands, by W. B. Lowe.

[1] The Society also published a periodical, *The Durham Antiquary*, but this has not been seen.

1449 Vol. for 1914.
  a Days in merrie Sherwood, with glimpses of Ivanhoe land, by J. W. Ellis.
  b Tremeirchion and district. [Tremeirchion church and caves and prehistoric remains]

1450 Vol. for 1915.
  a The Welsh cult of the holy well, by J. Fisher.
  b Whitford and Downing. [Includes an account of Whitford church, Downing Hall, and Thomas Pennant, d. 1798]
  c Ruins of Basingwerk abbey, by W. L. Hobbs.

1451 Vol. for 1916.
  a Church of St. Mary Magdalene, Gwaenysgor, by A. F. Smith.
  b Dyserth castle, by W. L. Hobbs.

1452 Vol. for 1917.
  a Welsh place-names, by E. Davies.

1453 Vol. for 1918.
  a The orientation of ancient monuments, by W. L. Hobbs.

1454 Vol. for 1920.
  a Local building traditions and materials of Snowdonia, by H. H. Hughes.

1455 Vol. for 1922.
  a Flintshire pre-Norman history, by J. F. Sharp.

1456 Vol. for 1924.
  a Roman coins, by E. Davies.
  b Some evidences of 'early man' within and near to the northern portion of the vale of Clwyd, by F. G. Smith.
  c Report on a human skeleton found in peat at Prestatyn, Flints., by Sir A. Keith.
  d Siamber Wen [a ruined medieval dwelling] with plan, by H. V. Goold.

1457 Vol. for 1925.
  a Welsh church bells in history and legend, by J. Fisher.
  b Offa's and Watt's dykes in north-east Wales, by C. Dodd.

1458 Vol. for 1926.
  a St. Beuno and his church at Clynnog [Caerns.], by W. B. Jones.
  b Early man: recent researches, by F. G. Smith.
  c Beaumaris castle and Penmon priory, by H. H. Hughes.
  d Tremeirchion [church], by D. L. Jones.
  e Some notes on recent prehistoric discoveries at Prestatyn, by F. G. Smith.

1459 Vol. for 1927.
  a The congregation of Savigny and Basingwerk abbey, by E. W. Lovegrove.
  b Marie Stuart: a psychological study by C. A. Sainte-Beuve, by E. Montag.
  c Charter of Rhuddlan, 1284.

1460 Vol. for 1928.
  a How Wales became a principality, with special reference to Flintshire, by M. J. Hughes.
  b Points of archaeological interest in Flintshire, by E. Davies.

1461 Vol. for 1929.
  a Wales in the middle ages, by J. E. Lloyd.
  b 'Heu Ddinbych', Hiraethog moors [ruins of unknown origin].
  c Some caves [in Derbyshire] and the Club's cave at Gwaenysgor [with an account of their prehistoric remains], by J. W. Jackson.

1462 Vol. for 1930.
a Hill forts of North Wales, by H. Higgins.
b Norman influence in the foundation of Welsh dioceses, by J. F. Sharp.
c Uriconium or Viroconium [a brief account of the remains].
d The story of Kilhweh and Olwen, from the *Mabinogion* [and its relation to Arthur], by H. Higgins.

1463 Vol. for 1932.
a Visit to Cefn and other local caves [with accounts of their prehistoric remains], by J. W. Jackson.
b Mines and miners in Flintshire, by C. Williams.

EALING SCIENTIFIC AND MICROSCOPICAL SOCIETY

Founded 1877, as the Ealing Microscopical and Natural History Club, to promote the study of science. Title changed to Ealing Microscopical and Natural History Society in 1883, to Ealing Natural Science and Microscopical Society in 1894, and to the above form in 1904.

24th–56th Annual Report, with Transactions (1901–33):[1]

1464 25th Report.
a Recent discoveries in relation to prehistoric man in Ealing, by J. A. Brown.

1465 31st Report.
a The life of prehistoric man on the Downs, by A. J. and G. Hubbard.

1466 32nd Report.
a Prehistoric man: 1, The dwellings of neolithic man, by A. J. Hubbard; 2, Crockern Tor, Dartmoor, a prehistoric seat of parliament, by G. Hubbard.

1467 36th Report.
a Middlesex in Roman times, by M. Sharpe.

1468 37th Report.
a Fossil man, by A. S. Woodward. [An account of the Piltdown skull]
b Gilbert White and Selborne, by W. M. Webb.
c Ancient Hanwell, by A. Beasley.

1469 38th Report.
a The Domesday survey of Middlesex, by M. Sharpe.
b Gothic architecture in England and France, by H. W. Bennett.
c A brief survey of the English coinage, by L. A. Lawrence.

1470 40th Report.
a The Glastonbury lake-village, by H. St. G. Gray.

EARLY ENGLISH TEXT SOCIETY

Founded 1864, to print old and middle English texts.

Original series:

1471 No. 14. King Horn, Floris and Blauncheflur, The assumption of Our Lady. First ed. in 1866 by J. R. Lumby; re-ed. with introd., notes, and glossary, by G. H. McKnight. 1901.

[1] The 41st–48th and 52nd Reports have not been seen.

1472 No. 15. Political, religious and love poems (some by Lydgate, Sir Richard Ros, Henry Baradoun, Wm. Huchen, etc.) from the archbishop of Canterbury's Lambeth ms. no. 306, and other sources, with a fragment of the romance of *Peare of Provence and the fair Maguelone*, and a sketch, with the prolog and epilog, of the romance of *The knight Amoryus and the lady Cleopes*, by John Metham, scholar of Cambridge, 1448–9, ed. F. J. Furnivall. 1903. [Re-ed. from edition of 1866]

1473 No. 117. Minor poems of the Vernon ms. Pt. 2 (with a few from the Digby mss. 2 and 86), ed. F. J. Furnivall. 1901. [Pt. 1, ed. C. Horstmann, was published as no. 98, 1892]

1474 No. 118. The lay folks' catechism, or the English and Latin versions of Archbishop Thoresby's instructions for the people; together with a Wycliffite adaptation of the same, and the corresponding canons of the council of Lambeth [1281], with introd., notes, glossary and index, by T. F. Simmons and H. E. Nolloth. 1901.

1475 Nos. 119, 123. Robert of Brunne's 'Handlyng Synne', 1303, with those parts of the Anglo-French treatise on which it was founded, William of Wadington's 'Manuel des Pechies', re-edited from mss. in the British Museum and Bodleian libraries by F. J. Furnivall. 1 vol. in 2. 1901–3.

1476 No. 120. Three middle-English versions of the rule of St. Benet and two contemporary rituals for the ordination of nuns, ed., with introd., notes and glossaries, by E. A. Kock. 1902.

1477 Nos. 121, 122. The Laud Troy book, a romance of about 1400, now first edited from the unique ms. (Laud misc. 595) in the Bodleian Library, Oxford, with introd., notes and glossary, by J. E. Wülfing. 1 vol. in 2. 1902–3.

1478 No. 124. Twenty-six political and other [15th cent.] poems (including 'Petty Job') from the Oxford mss. Digby 102 and Douce 322, ed., with introd. and glossarial index, by J. Kail. 1904.

1479 Nos. 125, 128. Medieval records of a London city church (St. Mary at Hill) 1420–1559, transcribed and ed. with facsimiles and introd. by H. Littlehales. 1 vol. in 2. 1904–5.

1480 Nos. 126, 127. An alphabet of tales: an English 15th cent. translation of the *Alphabetum narrationum* of Etienne de Besançon, from Additional ms. 25719 of the British Museum, ed. Mary M. Banks. 1 vol. in 2. 1904–5.

1481 Nos. 129, 130, 142. The English register of Godstow nunnery, written about 1450, ed. with introd. by A. Clark. 1 vol. in 3. 1905–11.

1482 Nos. 131, 136. The Brut, or the chronicles of England, ed. from ms. Rawl. B.171, Bodleian Library, etc., by F. W. D. Brie, with introd., notes, and glossary. 1 vol. in 2. 1906–8.

1483 No. 132. The works of John Metham, including the Romance of Amoryus and Cleopes, ed. H. Craig. 1916.

1484 Nos. 133, 144. The English register of Oseney abbey, written about 1460, ed. with introd. and indexes by A. Clark. 1 vol. in 2. 1907–13.

1485 Nos. 134, 135, 138, 146. The Coventry leet book, or mayor's register, containing the records of the city court leet or view of frankpledge, 1420–1555, with divers other matters, transcribed and ed. Mary D. Harris. 1 vol. in 4. 1907–13.

1486 No. 135b. Piers the plowman and its sequence. Contributed to *The Cambridge History of English Literature* by J. M. Manly. 1908.

1487 No. 137. Twelfth century homilies in ms. Bodley 343, ed. A. C. Balfour. Pt. 1: Text and translation. 1909.

1488 No. 139. Treatises of fistula in ano, haemorrhoids, and clysters, by John Ardene, from an early 15th cent. ms. translation, ed. with introd., notes, etc., by D'A. Power. 1910.

1489 Nos. 139b–e. The Piers plowman controversy. 1910. [Four works, separately paged]

  a Piers plowman the work of one or of five: J. J. Jusserand's first reply to J. M. Manly. From *Modern Philology*, Jan. 1909.

  b J. M. Manly's reply to J. J. Jusserand. From *Modern Philology*, June 1909.

  c J. J. Jusserand's second reply to J. M. Manly. From *Modern Philology*, Jan. 1910.

  d The authorship of Piers plowman, by R. W. Chambers. From *The Modern Language Review*, Jan. 1910.

1490 No. 140. John Capgrave's lives of St. Augustine [of Hippo] and St. Gilbert of Sempringham, and a sermon, ed. J. J. Munro. 1910.

1491 No. 141. The middle-English poem, Erthe upon erthe, ed. with introd., notes, and glossary, by Hilda M. R. Murray. 1911.

1492 No. 143. The prose life of Alexander, from the Thornton ms., ed. J. S. Westlake. 1913.

1493 Nos. 145, 147, 183. The northern passion [a poem written in the north of England at the end of the 13th and beginning of the 14th cent., to instruct the laity in religion], ed. Frances A. Foster; supplement ed. W. Heuser and Frances A. Foster. 3 vols. 1913–30.

1494 No. 148. A 15th cent. courtesy book ['to teche every man . . . to serve a lorde or mayster'], ed. R. W. Chambers, and two 15th cent. Franciscan rules [for the third order, of penitents, and the second order, of St. Clare], ed. W. W. Seton. 1914.

1495 No. 149. Lincoln diocese documents, 1450–1544 [extracts from episcopal registers, including wills and probate records, leases of prebendal estates, church and chantry agreements, disciplinary acts of the bishop, widows' vows, estates of the see, etc.], ed., with notes and indexes, by A. Clark. 1914.

1496 No. 150. The Old English version of the enlarged rule of Chrodegang together with the Latin original; an Old English verse and Prose, B. M. Add. ms. 39574, ed., with with the Latin original; an interlinear Old English rendering of the epitome of Benedict of Aniane, ed. A. S. Napier. 1916.

1497 No. 151. The lanterne of light [early 15th cent. Lollard tract], ed. Lilian M. Swinburn. 1917.

1498 No. 152. Early English homilies from the 12th cent. ms. Vesp. D. xiv, ed. Rubie D.-N. Warner. 1917.

1499 Nos. 153, 154. Mandeville's Travels, translated from the French of Jean d'Outremeuse, ed. P. Hamelius. 2 vols. 1919–23. [Vol. i: Text. Vol. ii: Introd. and notes]

1500 No. 155. The Wheatley ms.: a collection of middle-English verse and prose, B.M. Add. ms. 39574, ed., with introd. and notes, by Mabel Day. 1921.

1501 No. 156. The Donet [a didactic dialogue on the Christian religion] by Reginald Pecock, D.D., bishop of St. Asaph and Chichester, now first ed. from ms. Bodl. 916 and collated with *The poore mennis myrrour*, by Elsie V. Hitchcock. 1921.

1502 No. 157. The Pepysian gospel harmony [*c.* 1400], ed. Margery Goates. 1922.

1503 No. 158. Meditations on the life and passion of Christ from B.M. Add. Ms. 11307 [a compendium of lyric themes of middle-English religious poetry, *c.* 1350–*c.* 1450], ed. Charlotte D'Evelyn. 1921.

1504 No. 159. Vices and virtues, being a soul's confession of its sins, with reason's description of the virtues: a middle-English dialogue of about 1200 A.D., ed. with introd., translation, notes and glossary, from Stowe ms. 240 in the B.M., by F. Holthausen. Pt. 2: Notes and glossary. 1921. [Pt. 1, text and translation, was issued as no. 89 in 1888]

1505 No. 160. The Old English version of the Heptateuch, Aelfric's treatise on the Old and New Testament, and his preface to Genesis, ed. from all existing mss. and fragments, with introd. and three appendices, together with a reprint of *A Saxon treatise concerning the Old and New Testament, now first published in print with English of our times by William L'Isle of Wilburgham* (1623), and the Vulgate text of the Heptateuch, by S. J. Crawford. 1922.

1506 No. 161. Three Old English prose texts in ms. Cotton Vitellius A.xv, ed. with introd. and glossarial index by S. Rypins. 1924. [A spurious letter of Alexander the Great to Aristotle, Wonders of the east, and Life of St. Christopher, with their Latin texts]

1507 No. 162. Pearl, Cleanness, Patience, and Sir Gawain [four 14th cent. English poems], reproduced in facsimile from ms. Cotton Nero A.x in the B.M. With introd. by Sir I. Gollancz. 1923. [Reprinted 1931]

1508 No. 163. The book of the foundation of St. Bartholomew's church in London, the church belonging to the priory in West Smithfield, ed. from the original ms. in the B.M., Cotton Vespasian B.ix, by Sir N. Moore, bt. 1923. [A translation, *c.* 1400, of the Latin original, *c.* 1180]

1509 No. 164. The folewer to the Donet, by Reginald Pecock, D.D., bishop of St. Asaph and Chichester, now first ed. from B.M. Roy. ms. 17 D. ix, with introd. on Pecock's language and style, by Elsie V. Hitchcock. 1924. [A sequel to the Donet, no. 1501 above]

1510 No. 165. The famous historie of Chinon of England, by Christopher Middleton [1597], to which is added *The assertion of King Arthure*, translated by Richard Robinson [1582] from Leland's *Assertio inclytissimi Arturii*, together with the Latin original, ed. with introd., notes, and glossary, by W. E. Mead. 1925.

1511 No. 166. A stanzaic life of Christ compiled [at Chester in the 14th cent.] from Higden's *Polychronicon* and the *Legenda aurea*, ed. from ms. Harley 3909 by Frances A. Foster. 1926.

1512 No. 167. 'Dialogus inter militem et clericum' [by William of Occam], Richard FitzRalph's sermon 'Defensio curatorum', and Methodius, 'The bygynnyng of the world and the end of worldes', by John Trevisa, vicar of Berkeley, ed., with introd. on the mss., Trevisa's life and works, and a study of the language, by A. J. Perry. 1925. [The first two are given in Trevisa's English translation; the third is a translation formerly ascribed to him]

1513 No. 168. The book of the ordre of chyvalry, translated and printed by William Caxton from a French version of Ramón Lull's *Le libre del orde de cauayleria*, together with Adam Loutfut's Scottish transcript [1494], Harleian ms. 6149, ed. A. T. B. Byles. 1926. [With appendix, 'Making of knyghte of the Bathe']

1514 No. 169. The southern passion, ed. from Pepysian ms. 2344, Magdalene Coll., Cambridge, with introd., notes and glossary, by Beatrice D. Brown. 1929. [Narrative poem, *c.* 1275–85, on the Passion, Resurrection, and Ascension]

1515 No. 170. Boethius, *De consolatione philosophiae*, translated by John Walton, canon of Oseney [*c.* 1410], ed., with introd., notes and glossary, by M. Science. 1927.

1516 No. 171. The reule of Crysten religioun [1443], by Reginald Pecock, D.D., bishop of St. Asaph and Chichester, now first ed. from Pierpont Morgan ms. 519, by W. C. Greet. 1927.

1517 No. 172. The seege or batayle of Troye: a middle English metrical romance, ed. from mss. Lincoln's Inn 150, Egerton 2862, Arundel xxii, with Harley 525 included in the appendix, by Mary E. Barnicle. 1927.

1518 No. 173. The pastime of pleasure, by Stephen Hawes: a literal reprint of the earliest complete copy, 1517, with variant readings from the editions of 1509, 1554, and 1555, with introd., notes, glossary and indexes by W. E. Mead. 1928.

1519 No. 174. The middle-English stanzaic versions of the life of Saint Anne, ed. R. E. Parker. 1928. [From texts in Minnesota University, Trinity College, Cambridge, and the Bodleian Library]

1520 No. 175. The eclogues of Alexander Barclay, from the original edition by John Cawood, ed., with introd. and notes, by Beatrice White. 1928.

1521 No. 176. The prologues and epilogues of William Caxton, by W. J. B. Crotch. 1928. [With considerable biographical introd.]

1522 No. 177. Byrhtferth's manual (A.D. 1011), now ed. for the first time from ms. Ashmole 328 in the Bodleian Library, with introd., translation, sources, [etc.] and plates, by S. J. Crawford. Vol. 1: Text, translation, sources and appendices. 1929. [Concerned with astrology, chronology, numerology. No more published]

1523 No. 178. The revelations of Saint Birgitta, ed. from the 15th cent. ms. in Princeton University, by W. P. Cumming. 1929.

1524 No. 179. The castell of pleasure, by William Nevill: the text of the first issue of the poem with variant readings from the reprint of 1518, with introd., notes and glossary, by Roberta D. Cornelius. 1930.

1525 No. 180. The apologue of Syr Thomas More, knyght, ed., with introd. and notes, by A. I. Taft. 1930. [More's defence of his controversial religious works, 1533]

1526 No. 181. The dance of death, ed. from mss. Ellesmere 26/A.13 and B.M. Lansdowne 699, collated with the other extant mss. by Florence Warren; introd., notes, etc., by Beatrice White. 1931.

1527 No. 182. Speculum Christiani: a middle-English religious treatise of the 14th cent., ed. from all the known mss. and one old edition, with introd., notes [etc.] and appendices, by G. Holmstedt. 1933.

1528 No. 184. The poems of John Audelay, ed. with introd., notes and glossary, by Ella K. Whiting. 1931. [Early 15th cent.]

No. 185. See Extra series, 93, no. **1544** below.

1529 No. 186. The life and death of Sr Thomas Moore, knight, sometymes lord high chancellor of England, written in the tyme of Queene Marie by Nicholas Harpsfield, L.D., ed. from eight mss, with collations, notes, etc., by Elsie V. Hitchcock; introd. on the continuity of English prose, a life of Harpsfield, and notes, by R. W. Chambers; with appendices, including the Rastell fragments, chiefly concerning Fisher; the news letter to Paris, describing the trial and death of More; More's indictment; and More's epitaph. 1932.

1530 No. 187. The vulgaria [Latin text-book] of John Stanbridge [d. *c.* 1510] and the vulgaria of Robert Whittington [b. *c.* 1480], ed. with introd. and notes by Beatrice White. 1932.

1531 No. 188. The siege of Jerusalem, ed. from ms. Laud. Misc. 656 with variants from all other extant mss. by E. Kölbing and Mabel Day. 1932. [15th cent. Based on the legendary siege of Jerusalem by Titus]

1532 No. 189. The book of fayttes of armes and of chyvalrye, translated and printed by William Caxton from the French original by Christine de Pisan, ed. A. T. P. Byles. 1932. [Re-issued with corrections, 1937]

1533 No. 190. English mediaeval lapidaries, by Joan Evans and Mary S. Serjeantson. 1933. [Treatises dealing with the symbolism and virtues of precious stones]

1534 No. 191. The seven sages of Rome (southern version), ed. K. Brunner. 1933. [Middle English]

Extra series:

1535 Nos. 77, 83, 92. The pilgrimage of the life of man, Englisht by John Lydgate, 1426, from the French of Guillaume de Deguileville, 1330, 1355, ed. F. J. Furnivall, with introd., notes, glossary, and indexes, by Katharine B. Locock. 1 vol. in 3. 1899–1901.

1536 Nos. 81, 82. The English works of John Gower, ed. from mss. with introd., notes, and glossary, by G. C. Macaulay. 2 vols. 1900-1.

1537 Nos. 84, 89. Lydgate's Reson and sensuallyte, ed. from the Fairfax ms. 16 (Bodleian) and the Additional ms. 29,729 (Brit. Mus.) by E. Sieper. 2 vols. 1901-3. [Vol. i: The mss., text (with side-notes by Dr. Furnivall), glossary. Vol. ii: Studies and notes]

1538 No. 85. The poems of Alexander Scott, ed. from the Bannatyne ms. in the Advocates' library, Edinburgh, and the Maitland ms. in the library of Magdalene College, Cambridge, by A. K. Donald. 1902.

1539 No. 86. The poems of William of Shoreham, ab. 1320, vicar of Chart-Sutton, re-ed. from the unique ms. in the British Museum, by M. Konrath. 1902.

1540 No. 87. Two Coventry Corpus Christi plays. 1: The shearmen and taylors' pageant, re-ed. from the edition of Thomas Sharp, 1825; and 2: The weavers' pageant, re-ed. from the ms. of Robert Croo, 1534; with a plan of Coventry and appendixes containing the chief records of the Coventry plays, by H. Craig. 1902.

1541 No. 88. Le morte Arthur, a romance in stanzas of eight lines, re-ed. from ms. Harley 2252, in the British Museum, with introd., notes, glossary and index of names, by J. D. Bruce. 1903.

1542 No. 90. English fragments from Latin mediaeval service-books with two coloured facsimiles from medieval prymers, ed. H. Littlehales. *P.* 1903.

1543 No. 91. The Macro [morality] plays. 1: Mankind (ab. 1475); 2: Wisdom (ab. 1460); 3: The castle of Perseverance (ab. 1425), ed. F. J. Furnivall and A. W. Pollard. 1904.

1544 Nos. 93, 112. Merlin, a middle-English metrical version of a French romance, by Henry Lovelich, skinner and citizen of London, ab. 1450, ed. from the unique ms. 80 in Corpus Christi College, Cambridge, with introd., notes, and glossaries, by E. A. Kock. 1 vol. in 3. 1904–32. [Pt. 3 was issued as original series, vol. 185, in 1932]

1545 No. 94. Respublica, 1553, a play on the social condition of England at the accession of Mary, ed. L. A. Magnus. 1905.

1546 No. 95. The legend of the holy grail, its sources, character and development, by Dorothy Kempe: the introd. to and Pt. 5 of Henry Lovelick's verse 'History of the holy grail'. 1905. [Pts. 1–4, were published as nos. 20, 24, 28 and 30, 1874–78]

1547 No. 96. Mirk's festival: a collection of homilies, by Johannes Mirkus (John Mirk), ed. from Bodl. ms. Gough eccl. top. 4, with variant readings from other mss., by T. Erbe. Pt. 1. 1905.

1548 Nos. 97, 103, 106, 126. Lydgate's Troy book (1412–20), ed. from the best mss. with introd., notes, and glossary, by H. Bergen [with side notes by F. J. Furnivall]. 2 vols. in 4. 1906–35.

1549 No. 98. Magnyficence: a moral play by John Skelton, ed. R. L. Ramsay, from the edition in Univ. library, Cambridge, with introd., notes, and glossary. 1908.

1550 No. 99. The romance of Emaré, re-ed. from the ms., with introd., notes, and glossary, by Edith Rickert. 1908.

1551 No. 100. The middle-English Harrowing of Hell and Gospel of Nichodemus, now first ed. from all the known mss., with introd. and glossary, by W. H. Hulme. 1907.

1552 No. 101. Songs, carols, and other miscellaneous poems, from the Balliol ms. 354, Richard Hill's commonplace-book [early 16th cent.], ed. R. Dyboski. 1908.

1553 No. 102. The *Promptorium parvulorum*: the first English-Latin dictionary, ed. from the ms. in the chapter library at Winchester, with introd., notes, and glossaries, by A. L. Mayhew. 1908.

1554 No. 104. The non-cycle mystery plays, together with the Croxton play of the Sacrament and the Pride of Life, re-ed. from the manuscripts by O. Waterhouse. 1909.

1555 No. 105. The tale of Beryn, with a prologue of the merry adventure of the pardoner with a tapster at Canterbury, re-ed. from the Duke of Northumberland's unique ms. by F. J. Furnivall and W. G. Stone, with an English abstract of the French original and Asiatic versions of the tale, by W. A. Clouston; plans of Canterbury in 1588, and the road thither from London in 1675, etc. 1909.

1556 No. 107. The minor poems of John Lydgate, ed. from all available mss., with an attempt to establish the Lydgate canon, by H. N. MacCracken. Pt. 1: The Lydgate canon; religious poems. 1911.

1557 Nos. 108, 125. Lydgate's Siege of Thebes, ed. from all the known mss. and the two oldest editions, pt. 1 by A. Erdmann, pt. 2 by A. Erdmann and E. Ekwall. 2 vols. 1911–30.

1558 No. 109. The middle-English versions of Partonope of Blois, ed. A. T. Bödtker. 1912.

1559 No. 110. Caxton's Mirrour of the world [a translation from the 13th cent. *Image du monde*], ed. O. H. Prior. 1913.

1560 No. 111. The history of Jason, translated from the French of Raoul le Fevre by William Caxton, *c.* 1477, ed. J. Munro. 1913.

1561 No. 113. Poems by Sir John Salusbury [d. 1612] and Robert Chester [b. 1566], with introd. by C. Brown. 1914. [Also published as Bryn Mawr College monographs, no. 14]

1562 No. 114. The gild of St. Mary, Lichfield, being ordinances of the gild and other documents, ed. F. J. Furnivall. 1920. [Contents include: Ordinances, 1387, translated from Latin 1583; Sir Humfrey Stanley's ordinances, 1486; Dean Heywood's reform of 'Our Lady's alms-chest', 1486; charters of the Lichfield tailors, 1576 and 1697; ordinances of the Lichfield smiths, 1601 and 1630; ordinances of the Lynn tailors, 1449; Southampton tailors' petitions, 1406–7 and 1468]

1563 No. 115. The Chester plays, pt. 2, re-edited by Dr. Matthews. 1916. [Pt. 1, ed. Hermann Deimling, 1893]

1564 No. 116. The Pauline epistles, contained in [late 14th cent.] ms. Parker 32, Corpus Christi College, Cambridge, ed. Margaret J. Powell. 1916.

1565 No. 117. The life of Fisher [bishop of Rochester, d. 1535], transcribed from ms. Harleian 6382 by R. Bayne. 1921. [Supplementary to Extra series, no. 27, 1876]

1566 No. 118. The earliest arithmetics in English, ed. with introd. by R. Steele. 1922. [15th cent. tracts on arithmetic]

1567 No. 120. Ludus Coventriae, or the plaie called Corpus Christi (Cotton ms. Vespasian D. viii), ed. Katherine S. Block. 1922.

1568 Nos. 121–124. Lydgate's Fall of Princes, ed. H. Bergen. 2 vols. in 4. 1924–7.

1569 List of publications. 1: Classified survey. 2: Order of publications. 1931.

EAST DERBYSHIRE FIELD CLUB

Founded 1902, for the study of botany, entomology, and pond life, geology, archaeology and general subjects.

Transactions [Year Book], 1903–23, 1931 (22 vols.[1] 1904?–24?, 1932?):

1570 Vol. for 1903.
a All Saints' church, Wingerworth, by E. W. Brown.
b Early man in Derbyshire, by W. T. G. Burr.
c Winfield manor house, by W. Jacques.

1571 Vol. for 1904.
a The Athens of the Peak [Eyam], by F. D. Udall.
b The Roman fort at Brough, by W. Jacques.

1572 Vol. for 1905.
a George Eliot's associations with Wirksworth, by F. D. Udall
b The Bateman collection [of finds from Derbyshire barrows], by S. Steele.
c Stavely in past days, by W. L. Coleman.

1573 Vol. for 1906.
a Stone circle and tumuli on Eyam moor, by W. T. Burr.

[1] No others found.

b The village of Pentrich and its revolution, by G. Griffin. [Armed rising organized by Jeremiah Brandreth and Thomas Bacon, 1817]
c Markland Grips [camp], by W. Jacques.

1574 Vol. for 1907.

a Flowers of history, by W. L. Coleman. [Floral emblems, national and otherwise]
b Lead mining in Derbyshire, by G. Griffin.
c Langwith cave [and its prehistoric remains], by E. H. Mullins.

1575 Vol. for 1908.

a Some notes on Youlgreave, by W. L. Coleman.

1576 Vol. for 1909.

a Ogston Hall, by G. M. R. Turbutt.
b Newbold chapel, by J. Sharkey.

1577 Vol. for 1910.

a Creswell crags [and their prehistoric remains], by W. T. G. Burr.
b Roman Derbyshire, by W. Jacques.
c Some by-paths of Derbyshire history [from Saxon times to the 15th cent.], by W. Jacques.
d A visit to Romeley Hall, by A. Court.
e Some decayed and lost industries of Clay Cross and neighbourhood, by G. Griffin.

1578 Vol. for 1911.

a Dethick, by W. Jacques.
b Hardwick Hall, by F. Brodhurst.
c Spital [Chesterfield] and Sutton Scarsdale, by W. Jacques.

1579 Vol. for 1912.

a Eyam, by W. Jacques.

1580 Vol. for 1913.

a Lead mining in Derbyshire, by W. Jacques.
b Arbor Low [stone circle], by W. T. G. B[urr].
c Dale abbey, Morley and Stanton, by W. L. Coleman.
d Bolsover castle, by W. Jacques.

1581 Vol. for 1914.

a Beauchief abbey, by W. Jacques.
b The pitsteads in Lindway Spring wood [Ashover], by E. Watkins.
c Place names.
d Royal forests of Derbyshire, by W. Jacques.

1582 Vol. for 1915.

a Chesterfield parish church, by H. Ryde.
b Development of the safety lamp, by G. Forster.
c Whitwell, by W. L. Coleman.
d Steetley chapel, by W. L. Coleman.
e The fortress of Carlwark, Hathersage, by N. Roden.
f Bradwell: the 'Broadwall' of the Peak, by S. Evans.

1583 Vol. for 1916.

a Wingerworth church, by H. Ryde.
b An Ashover worthy [Leonard Wheatcroft, 1706], by H. Peck.
c Dronfield church, by W. T. Groocock.
d Hault Hacknall church, by H. Peck.
e The growth of the lace industry, by Mrs. Longden.

1584 Vol. for 1917.

a Notes on North Wingfield church, by W. Stevenson.
b Old Brampton church, by E. C. Mackenzie.
c Development of the English parish church, by J. C. Bedwell.
d The Fanshawes and Fanshawe gate, by W. Jacques.

1585 Vol. for 1922.

a Some gleanings toward a history of Ashover, by H. Peck
b Some Derbyshire bridges, by W. L. Coleman.

1586 Vol. for 1923.

a Brimington, by W. T. G. Burr.

1587 Vol. for 1931.

a Evening outing to Dronfield church, by W. T. Groocock.
b Outing to Newstead abbey [Notts.], by V. Brelsford.
c Creswell caves [and their prehistoric remains], by V Brelsford.
d Lecture by W. L. Coleman [on Elizabeth Hardwick, Countess of Shrewsbury, d. 1608].

EAST HERTS ARCHAEOLOGICAL SOCIETY

Founded 1898, to collect and publish information on the history and antiquities of the district.

Transactions, vols. 1–8 (1901–34):

1588 Vol. 1.

a Chadwell spring, by W. F. Andrews.
b Scott's grotto, Amwell, by R. T. Andrews.
c Amwell Magna, by W. B. Gerish.
d Ware priory, by R. Walters.
e Stortford castle, by J. L. Glasscock.
f St. Michael's church, Bishop's Stortford, by H. T. Lane.
g Thorley church, by J. E. I. Proctor.
h Sawbridgeworth church, by H. A. Lipscomb.
i St. Leonard's church, Bengeo, by W. B. Gerish.
j Sacombe church, by R. T. Andrews.
k Watton church, by W. F. Andrews.
l Grant of the manor of Aston to Reading abbey [1136], by W. Brigg.
m Opening of a barrow in Easneye wood, by J. Evans.
n Furneaux Pelham, by R. T. Andrews.
o Some church chests in east Hertfordshire, by J. A. Tregelles.
p The Roman station at Braughing.
q Church of St. Mary, Hitchin, by G. Lucas and W. Millard.
r A note on the Ermine street in Hertfordshire, by R. B. Croft.
s Ancient buildings at Ware, by R. T. Andrews.
t Standon, by W. d'A. Crofton.
u Hospice of the Knights Hospitallers at Standon, by J. A. Brown.
v The parish of Broxbourne, by J. Salwey.
w The leper hospital, Hoddesdon, by R. T. Andrews and W. B. Gerish.
x John Loudon McAdam, the great road-maker, by T. Salkield.
y St. Lawrence's church, Wormley, by S. Austin.
z Great Munden church, by A. J. Tuck.
aa Little Munden, by Clara E. Sworder.
bb The Eleanor cross at Waltham and its sister crosses, by J. Tydeman.
cc St. Peter's church, Bennington, by W. Mills.
dd Insignia and plate of Hertford corporation, by J. B. Caldecott.

1589 Vol. 2.

a Grant of a market to Buntingford, 1541, by T. T. Greg.
b Opening of a barrow at Broxbournebury, 1901, by Sir J. Evans.
c Rawdon House, Hoddesdon, by J. A. Hunt.

1595 Vol. 8.

 a A Hertfordshire miscellany, by E. E. Squires.
 b Romano-British objects from 'Foxholes', near Hitchin, by W. P. Westell.
 c Abstract of the act book of the archdeacon of Huntingdon's court [Herts. cases, 1590–96], by F. G. Emmison.
 d The Knighton family of Bayford, Herts., and Little Bradley, Suff., by H. C. Andrews.
 e Notes on Aspenden, Wakeley and Berksdon churches, and Aspenden Hall, by A. Jackson.
 f Excursions, 1928. [Includes notes on Furneaux Pelham Hall]
 g Excursions, 1929. [Includes notes on Broxbourne, its churches and their builders; Balls Park, Hertford; the Mount, Sandon; and Kelshall]
 h Sidelights on brasses in Hertfordshire churches, by H. C. Andrews.
 i The holy springs of Waltham abbey at Wormley, by G. H. Bushby.
 j Recent discoveries at St. Mary's church, Baldock, by H. J. Gray.
 k Notes on the church of St. Mary the Virgin, and the school, Standon, by J. Chapman.
 l The Ashwell museum, by J. M. Bray.
 m Excursions, 1930. [Includes notes on Gilston and its manors, Overhall and Netherhall, and their owners; and on Upp Hall, Braughing]
 n Excursions, 1931. [Includes notes on Harmer Green and some of its families]
 o Brief studies in the manorial and economic history of Much Hadham, by Lydia L. Rickman.
 p The old Blue-Coat school, Ware, by W. H. Lee.
 q A Hertfordshire receiver-general [in 1690], by B. S. Harvey.
 r Ashwell: a 16th cent. fresco, by H. C. Andrews.
 s Excursions, 1932. [Includes notes on Bayford, Brickendon, Little Hormead, Albury, Sandridge church, and Nomansland, a common between Sandridge and Wheathampstead]
 t Excursions, 1933. [Includes notes on Wyddial manor and its hall]

Extra publication:

1596 Place-names of Hertfordshire, by W. W. Skeat. 1904.

EAST KENT SCIENTIFIC AND NATURAL HISTORY SOCIETY

Founded 1857, as the East Kent Natural History Society, for the collection and diffusion of practical and theoretical knowledge respecting natural history, in all its branches, both in relation to the particular district, and the general science. Title changed to above form in 1898.

Reports and Transactions, ser. 2, vols. 1–13 (1901–13):

1597 Vol. 2.

 a Coins and Christianity, by S. Webb. [Contd. in vol. 3]

1598 Vol. 3.

 a Battlefields of Kent, by H. Housman.

1599 Vol. 4.

 a Early history of Canterbury monastery, by A. J. Galpin.
 b Canterbury pilgrim signs, by F. Bennett-Goldney.

1600 Vol. 7.

 a Caesar's invasion of Kent, by F. Bennett-Goldney.
 b Charles Dickens and Canterbury, by A. C. Turley.

1601 Vol. 8.

 a Presidential address [on the Society's jubilee], by S. Harvey.

1602 Vol. 9.

 a Mediaeval craftsmen, by W. J. Jennings.
 b Miniature portraits, by F. Bennett-Goldney.

1603 Vol. 10.

 a Norman architecture in East Kent churches, by T. Underhill.

1604 Vol. 11.

 a Coastal changes in Kent and Sussex, by L. H. Evans.

EAST RIDING ANTIQUARIAN SOCIETY

Founded 1893, for the study of the history and archaeology of East Yorkshire and the preservation of the antiquities therein.

Transactions, vols. 9–27 (1902–34):

1605 Vol. 9.

 a The ms. account and memorandum book of a Yorkshire lady [Mary Worsley, d. 1737], by Lord Hawkesbury.
 b Duggleby Howe, by E. M. Cole.
 c Notes on the ancient model of a boat, and warrior crew, found at Roos, in Holderness, by T. Sheppard.
 d Some further gleanings from old Burlington [notes on Bridlington, 1620–70], by C. V. Collier.
 e The East Riding portion of an heraldic ms. relating to Yorkshire preserved in the library of Sir Tatton Sykes, transcribed by C. V. Collier and annotated by A. S. Scott-Gatty.

1606 Vol. 10.

 a Holderness wills extracted from the probate registry at York, by W. Brown. [Contd. in vol. 11]
 b Notes on some ancient East Riding families and their arms, by A. E. Ellis. [Previous pt. in vol. 6. Contd. in vols. 11 and 12]
 c Incised alabaster slab in Harpham church, by M. Stephenson.
 d East Riding portraits: catalogues of some collections of portraits in houses in the East Riding, by Lord Hawkesbury.
 e Account of the discovery of Roman remains at Langton, by J. R. Mortimer.
 f Additional note on the Roos Carr images, by T. Sheppard.
 g William Stapleton and the Pilgrimage of Grace [1536], by J. C. Cox.
 h Ancient fonts on the wolds of East Riding, by E. M. Cole.

1607 Vol. 11.

 a *Optimus est qui optime facit*: a chapter in the family [history] of Best, of Elmswell [Emswell], by H. Lawrance.
 b Catalogue of portraits, miniatures, etc., at Castle Howard, by Lord Hawkesbury.
 c Portraits, etc., at Naworth Castle, Cumb., in the possession of the Earl of Carlisle, 1903.
 d Hayton notes, by Lord Hawkesbury.

1608 Vol. 12.

 a Report of proceedings. [Includes notes on Saltmarshe]
 b Portraits at Langton Hall in the possession of Francis Best Norcliffe, by H. Lawrance.

c Stovin's manuscript, by C. V. Collier. [An account of Hatfield Chase by George Stovin, d. 1780. Contd. in vol. 13]

d Elmswell [Emswell]: a note on the spelling of the name, by H. Lawrance.

1609 Vol. 13.

a Report of proceedings. [Includes notes on Halsham church]

b Catalogue of portraits, miniatures, etc. at Kirkham Abbey, in the possession of Lord Hawkesbury, 1905.

c Catalogue of [East Riding] portraits at 2, Carlton House Terrace [London].

d Roman remains at Harpham, by C. V. Collier.

e Some Howdenshire villages, by P. Saltmarshe. [Contd. in vols. 15 and 16]

1610 Vol. 14.

a Roman coins found on the wolds, by E. M. Cole.

b Note on the place-name 'Filey', by W. H. Stevenson.

c Notes on Scarborough castle, by W. Stevenson.

d The Cliffords and Boyles of Londesborough, with special reference to the Burlington vault in Londesborough church, by R. C. Wilton.

e Notes on the more important archaeological discoveries in east Yorkshire, by T. Sheppard.

f East Yorkshire subsidy rolls, 2 Charles I, by Eleanor Lloyd.

1611 Vol. 15.

a Poll-tax roll of the East Riding, with some account of the Peasant revolt of 1381, by J. C. Cox.

b How Rowley in Yorkshire lost its population in the 17th cent., and how Rowley in Massachusetts was founded, by A. N. Cooper.

1612 Vol. 16.

a Some Anglo-Saxon vases in the Hull museum, by T. Sheppard.

1613 Vol. 17.

a The Aske family, by P. Saltmarshe.

b Stature of early man in east Yorkshire, by J. R. Mortimer.

c Pre-historic boat from Brigg, by T. Sheppard.

d Hull and east Yorkshire tradesmen's tokens, by W. Sykes.

1614 Vol. 18.

a Origin and formation of English surnames, by P. Saltmarshe.

b The priory of Haltemprice, by J. C. Cox.

c Recent find of coins, etc., in the river Hull, by T. Sheppard. [Reprinted in Yorkshire Numismatic Soc. *Transactions*, vol. i]

d Danes' Graves, by J. R. Mortimer.

e Documents at Burton Agnes [hall, 13th–16th cent.], by C. V. Collier. [Contd. in vol. 19]

1615 Vol. 19.

a East Yorkshire history in plan and chart, by T. Sheppard.

b Notes on some East Riding disputes [*temp.* Edw. IV and Charles I], by C. V. Collier.

c East Riding levies for the Scotch wars in the reigns of Edward II and III, with remarks on the feudal system, by P. Saltmarshe.

d Trade gilds of Beverley, by J. M. Lambert.

1616 Vol. 20.

a The arms of Hull, by T. Sheppard.

b York boy bishops, by A. A. R. Gill.

c Notes on Thorganby, E. Yorks., by P. Saltmarshe.

d Excavations at Peaseholm, Scarborough, by T. Sheppard.

1617 Vol. 21.

a East Riding muster roll, 1625, by T. Sheppard.

b Archdeacons of the East Riding, by A. A. R. Gill.

c Documents at Scampston [14th–16th cent.], by C. V. Collier.

d Old wills from Harpham, preserved at Scampston [13th–16th cent.], by W. Brown.

e Whitby arms, by G. Buchanan.

f Interior of St. Mary's parish church, Scarborough, prior to its restoration, by W. H. Fowler.

g St. Mary's church, Scarborough, by C. Cooper.

1618 Vol. 22.

a Documents at Everingham [14th–16th cent.], by C. V. Collier.

b Danes' dyke, by T. Sheppard.

c Whaling relics, by T. Sheppard.

d The old Hull grammar school. [Protests against the proposed demolition, 1916]

1619 Vol. 23.

a River banks of Howdenshire, their construction and maintenance in ancient days, by P. Saltmarshe.

b Ancient drainage in Howdenshire, by P. Saltmarshe.

c Aldbrough church, Holderness, by G. F. Twycross-Raines.

d Origin of the materials used in the manufacture of pre-historic stone weapons in east Yorkshire, by T. Sheppard.

e A new light on old Hull, by W. Stevenson.

1620 Vol. 24.

a Origin of heraldry, by P. Saltmarshe.

b Andrew Marvell tercentenary celebrations [at Hull, 1921, with an address by Sir A. K. Rollit].

c Lowthorpe and its collegiate church of St. Martin, by C. V. Collier.

d Saxon gold ring found at Driffield, east Yorks., by T. Sheppard.

e An ancient calendar [staff almanac, or primstaff].

f Old Hull and East Riding deeds [14th–17th cent.], ed. C. V. Collier.

g Recent prehistoric finds in east Yorkshire.

h Ancient mazes at Harpham and Pompeii compared, by T. Sheppard.

i Roman remains at Middleton-on-the-Wolds.

1621 Vol. 25.

a Place-names of the East Riding, by J. Nicholson.

b Land tenure in the past, with special mention of some East Riding properties, by P. Saltmarshe.

c Press gang times in the East Riding, by A. A. R. Gill.

d Local archaeological notes.

1622 Vol. 26.

a Early means of transport in the East Riding, by T. Sheppard.

b Wyke-upon-Hull in 1293, by J. Bilson.

c Meaux abbey, by T. Sheppard [with appendix by G. K. Beaulah on paving tiles].

d Ancient land tenures in Howdenshire, by P. Saltmarshe.

1623 Vol. 27.

a Roman kilns and pottery near Holme-on-Spalding moor, by T. Sheppard.

b The Roman pottery at Throlam, Holme-on-Spalding moor, east Yorks., by P. Corder.

c Architectural gems of east Yorkshire, by T. Sheppard.
d Rare Yorkshire 17th cent. tokens, by T. Sheppard.
e Local history from the Howdenshire poll tax roll [1379, with population figures for 1921], by P. Saltmarshe.
f A Hull historic celebration [of the 600th anniversary of the city's charter, 1931, with an address by J. Drink-water].
g Hull shipping pictures [catalogued, with illustrations].
h An Anglo-Saxon necklace from Yorkshire, by C. Green.
i Early pottery on the Yorkshire wolds.
j An Anglian cinerary urn from Hibaldstow, Kirton-in-Lindsey, by C. Green.
k Excavations at Brough-on-Humber, by P. Corder.

1624 Index to the first twenty vols., by J. C. Cox.[1] *P.* 1919.

EASTBOURNE NATURAL HISTORY, PHOTOGRAPHIC AND LITERARY SOCIETY

Founded 1867, as the Eastbourne Natural History Society, to unite lovers of natural history, science, photography, and literature, and especially to investigate and record the fauna and flora of the district. The words 'and Literary' were added in 1908, the word 'Photographic' in 1912.

Transactions, and Journal, new ser., vols. 3–10 (1895?–1933):

1625 Vol. 3.
a Archaeological discoveries in Sussex during the past year [1893–4], by H. M. Whitley.
b The enduring charm of Isaac Walton, by T. Bradfield.
c Sussex legends and folk-lore, by H. M. Whitley.
d The growth of an English city, being an account of the early topographical development of Norwich, by W. Hudson.
e Mural paintings in Sussex churches, by P. M. Johnston.
f Settlement of the East Sussex downs in Saxon times, by W. Hudson.

1626 Vol. 4.
a Some notes on the Cinque ports, especially Hastings and its members, by W. Hudson.
b Differences between English and French Gothic art, by G. H. West.
c The older prehistoric races of Sussex, by W. J. L. Abbott.
d Charles Darwin, by J. C. Miller.
e Old Sussex iron-work, by W. R. Butterfield.
f Pevensey and its Lincolnshire echo [the Roman stations of Pevensey, Ancaster and Saltersford], by H. Preston.

1627 Vol. 5.
a The associations of Gilbert White with Ringmer, by E. J. Bedford.
b A brief history of the Society, by E. J. Bedford. [Further article by Miss Jay in vol. 8]
c A record of the valley-side entrenchment in Bramble Bottom, Eastdean, by H. S. Toms.
d Exceit and Cuckmere: the recently discovered church; probable derivations of the two names.
e Parson Darby's hole [a cavern excavated in a cliff near Beachy Head by the Rev. Jonathan Darby, d. 1726], by Winifred Jay. [Further article by R. Morris in vol. 7]

1628 Vol. 7.
a Historical archaeology [of Sussex], by L. F. Salzmann.
b Some historic bye-paths near Eastbourne, by A. A. Evans.

[1] Not seen.

c Some Eastbourne place-names, by W. Budgen.
d A record of the Mill Fields valley entrenchment and covered way, Willingdon hill, by H. S. Toms.
e Some notes on Roman Eastbourne, by W. Budgen.

1629 Vol. 8.
a The mote at Eastbourne: what it was and where it was, by W. Budgen.
b Roman road from Eastbourne to Jevington, by W. Budgen.
c The Roman circus in Britain, by A. H. Allcroft.
d Bridges and water mills of the Cuckmere, by W. Budgen.
e Andrew Borde of Pevensey, by A. A. Evans.

1630 Vol. 9.
a A suggestion as to the border-land between palaeoliths and pre-palaeoliths, by H. Morris.
b The story of Compton Place, by W. Budgen.

ECONOMIC HISTORY SOCIETY

Founded 1926, to promote the study and teaching of economic history; and the issue of an Economic History Review.

Economic History Review, vols. 1–4 (1927–34):

1631 Vol. 1.
a Rise and development of economic history, by N. S. B. Gras.
b The Merchant Adventurers' company in the reign of Elizabeth, by G. Unwin.
c Financial organization of the manor, by A. Elizabeth Levett.
d The small landowner, 1780–1832, in the light of the land tax assessments, by E. Davies.
e A neglected aspect of the relations between economic and legal history, by W. S. Holdsworth. [Interrelation of the rules of English law and economic conditions illustrated by reference to Elizabethan labour legislation, the agitation against monopolies *temp.* Eliz. I and James I, and developments in land law]
f Northamptonshire wage assessments of 1560 and 1667, by Bertha H. Putnam.
g List of books and articles on the economic history of Great Britain and Ireland, published 1925–7. [Contd. for following years in vols. 2–4]
h Russian work on English economic history, by E. A. Kosminsky.
i Credit in medieval trade, by M. Postan.
j War trade and trade war, 1701–13, by G. N. Clark.
k Development of the cotton industry in France and the Anglo-French treaty of commerce, 1860, by A. L. Dunham.
l Significance of the corn laws in English history, by C. R. Fay.

1632 Vol. 2.
a Jethro Tull and the 'new husbandry' of the 18th cent., by T. H. Marshall.
b Place of Bronterre O'Brien in the working-class movement, by A. Plummer.
c Winchester [diocese rent] rolls and their dating [1208–1453], by W. H. Beveridge.
d Aulnage accounts [i.e. taxes paid on cloth produced for sale in 15th cent.]: a criticism, by Eleanora M. Carus-Wilson.
e Records of a Derbyshire colliery, 1763–79, by G. W. Daniels and T. S. Ashton.
f The industrial revolution and discontent, by J. L. Hammond.

g Alien merchants and the English crown in the later 14th cent., by Alice Beardwood.

h Dutch and English merchant shipping in the 17th cent., by Violet Barbour.

i Early 14th cent. petition from the tenants of Bocking to their manorial lord [the prior and convent of Christ Church, Canterbury], by J. F. Nichols.

j The Normandy chamber of commerce and the [Anglo-French] commercial treaty, 1786, by H. Sée.

k Select bibliography of the economic history of Wales, by J. F. Rees and W. Rees.

1633 Vol. 3.

a The hundred rolls of 1279–80 as a source for English agrarian history, by E. Kosminsky.

b Benjamin Gott [d. 1840] and the industrial revolution in Yorkshire, by H. Heaton.

c The repeal of the apprenticeship clauses of the statute of apprentices [1814], by T. K. Derry.

d Letter of Adam Smith to Henry Dundas, 1789, by W. R. Scott.

e The Hanse, Cologne, and the crisis of 1468, by F. R. Salter.

f Poor relief accounts of two rural parishes [Northill and Eaton Socon] in Bedfordshire, 1563–98, by F. G. Emmison.

g Bibliography of Scottish economic history, by W. H. Marwick.

h British policy and colonial money supply [late 17th–early 18th cent.], by C. Nettels.

i English traders at Aleppo, 1658–1756, by G. Ambrose.

j A dealer in wardrobe bills [Walter of Yarmouth, 1346], by G. Sayles.

k Select bibliography of Irish economic history, by P. L. Prendeville. [Contd. in vol. 4]

l Masons and apprenticeship in mediaeval England, by D. Knoop and G. P. Jones.

m Accounts of an 18th cent. merchant: the Portuguese ventures of William Braund [mainly in the bullion trade and marine insurance, 1756–63], by Lucy S. Sutherland.

n Labour at Thornborough: an 18th cent. estate, by Elizabeth W. Gilboy. [A study of agricultural wages from the estate accounts, 1749–73]

o Early farming journals, by G. E. Fussell.

1634 Vol. 4.

a English agriculture under Charles II: the evidence of the Royal Society's 'enquiries', by R. Lennard.

b Some aspects of joint stock companies, 1844–1900, by G. Todd.

c Note on the statute of labourers, by A. Elizabeth Levett.

d Origins and early development of the Merchant Adventurers' organization in London as shown in their mediaeval records, by Eleanora M. Carus-Wilson.

e Some experiments in company organization in the early 17th cent., by F. J. Fisher.

f The cotton famine on the continent, 1861–5, by W. O. Henderson.

g Tithe commutation as a factor in the gradual decrease of landownership by the English peasantry [1793–1815], by V. Lavrovsky.

h The limited companies of 1866–83, by H. A. Shannon.

i Some English settlers in Genoa in the late 12th cent., by R. L. Reynolds.

j London silkwomen of the 15th cent., by Marian K. Dale.

k Studies in bibliography. 1: Mediaeval capitalism, by M. Postan. 2: Modern capitalism, by R. H. Tawney.

l Labour conditions in Essex in the reign of Richard II, by Nora Kenyon.

m Oxfordshire poor law papers [prior to 1834], by C. R. Oldham.

Bibliographies and pamphlets:

1635 No. 1. The industrial revolution, 1750–1850: a select bibliography, by Eileen Power. *P.* [1928].

1636 No. 2. Air photography and economic history: the evolution of the corn-field, by E. C. Curwen. *P.* [1928].

Reprints of economic history classics:

1637 No. 1. England's treasure by forraign trade, by Thomas Mun. Reprinted from the first edition of 1664. *P.* 1928.

ENGLISH ASSOCIATION

Founded 1906, to promote the due recognition of English as an essential element in the national education; to discuss methods of teaching English and the correlation of school and university work; to encourage and facilitate advanced study in English literature and language; and to unite all those who are interested in English studies.

Essays and Studies by members of the English Association, vols. 1–17 (1910–33):

1638 Vol. 1.

a English place-names, by H. Bradley.

1639 Vol. 2.

a The particle *ing* in place-names, by H. Alexander.

1640 Vol. 4.

a Some unconsidered elements in English place-names, by A. Mawer.

b Defoe's *True born Englishman* [text of the first edition, 1700], by A. C. Guthkelch.

1641 Vol. 5.

a English place-names and Teutonic sagas, by F. W. Moorman.

1642 Vol. 6.

a The 'Caedmonian' Genesis, by H. Bradley.

b South-eastern and south-east midland dialects, by H. C. Wyld.

1643 Vol. 7.

a Thomas Parnell; or, What was wrong with the 18th cent., by A. H. Cruickshank.

b A contemporary light upon John Donne, by J. Sampson.

1644 Vol. 8.

a On the meanings of certain terms in Anglo-Saxon charters, by G. B. Grundy.

b *The Felon Sew* [a mock heroic poem of the 15th cent. with some account of its transcriber, Ralph Rokeby], by G. H. Cowling.

1645 Vol. 9.

a The Trojans in Britain [Geoffrey of Monmouth's 'History', and English historians], by G. Gordon.

b The original language of the 'Ancren Riwle', by Dorothy M. E. Dymes.

1646 Vol. 10.

a Marlowe's map [the geography of Marlowe's plays in relation to 16th cent. cartography], by Ethel Seaton.

b A life of Bishop Corbett, 1582–1635, by J. E. V. Crofts.

c Reason and enthusiasm in the 18th cent., by O. Elton.

1647 Vol. 13.

a John of Salisbury, by Helen Waddell.

b Sir Thopas: a satire [by Geoffrey Chaucer, and its possible object, the Flemings], by J. M. Manly.

1648 Vol. 15.

a Thomas Purney [b. 1695]: a forgotten poet and critic of the 18th cent., by H. O. White.

1649 Vol. 16.

a John Donne and contemporary preachers: their preparation of sermons for delivery and for publication, by J. Sparrow.

b A 17th cent. ms. of poems by Donne and others, by H. H. Wood.

1650 Vol. 17.

a Keats and politics, by H. G. Wright.

b The L'Estrange-Peacock correspondence [letters between Thomas Love Peacock and Thomas L'Estrange, Belfast solicitor, 1860–63, and between L'Estrange and Edith Nicholls, granddaughter of Peacock, 1873–5], by H. F. B. Brett-Smith.

1651 The Year's Work in English Studies, vols. 1–12 (1921–33).

All vols. contain reports on publications relating to English language and literature issued in the period under review.

Pamphlets:

1652 No. 19. John Bunyan, by C. H. Firth. *P.* 1911.

1653 No. 30. Wordsworth's patriotic poems and their significance to-day, by F. S. Boas. *P.* 1914.

1654 No. 35. The 18th cent. [its literature and thought], by W. P. Ker. *P.* 1916.

1655 No. 60. Fanny Burney, by Edith J. Morley. 1925.

1656 No. 67. Lord Macaulay, the pre-eminent Victorian, by S. C. Roberts. *P.* 1927.

1657 No. 73. Colloquial language of the Commonwealth and Restoration, by Margaret Williamson. *P.* 1929.

1658 No. 84. William Shenstone and his friends, by Marjorie Williams. *P.* 1933.

1659 No. 86. The old English newspaper, by Mrs. H. Richardson. *P.* 1933.

ENGLISH CERAMIC CIRCLE

Founded 1927, as English Porcelain Circle, to increase the knowledge of early English porcelain by communications and discussions. Title changed to above form in 1931.

English Porcelain Circle Tr ansactions, nos. 1–4 (1928–32):

1660 No. 1.

a The earliest references to Chelsea porcelain, by H. B. Gardner.

b Caughley porcelain before 1772, by A. Hurst.

c Sources of underglaze-blue decoration [of early porcelain], by F. C. Dykes.

1661 No. 2.

a Soft paste Bristol porcelain, and the intimate relationship of the factory at Lowdin's Glass House [Bristol] with Limehouse and Worcester [18th cent.], by W. Elliot.

b Early allusion to English porcelain: Gouyn's will and some Chelsea models, by H. B. Gardner. [Charles Gouyn, London jeweller, 18th cent.]

c Liverpool porcelain, by B. Rackham.

d The early work of Planché and Duesbury, by Mrs. MacAlister.

1662 No. 3.

a Inscribed and dated Lowestoft porcelain [with classified list of pieces], by A. J. B. Kiddell.

b The Chelsea birds [and *The Natural History of Uncommon Birds*, 1743, by George Edwards], by H. B. Gardner.

c Recent discoveries. [Includes: A note on the Limehouse china factory, by A. J. Toppin; Old porcelain wall-brackets, by O. Glendenning; Inscribed and dated 'scratch-cross' pieces, by H. E. Rhodes]

d A few facts about Derby pattern books: Billingsley figure and landscape subjects, by W. H. Tapp. [William Billingsley, 18th cent.]

1663 No. 4.

a Cross-currents in English porcelain, glass and enamels [and the connection between the paintings on them], by H. Read.

b A Chelsea figure of Æsop [and its possible model].

c Sir Hans Sloane's plants on Chelsea porcelain, by H. B. Gardner.

d The trustworthiness of J. T. Smith [author of *Nollekens and his Times*, 1828], by Mrs. A. Esdaile.

e Porcelain as a side-light on Battersea enamels [the identification of Battersea and Bilston enamels], by B. Rackham.

f Notes on Janssen, and the artists at the Battersea factory, by A. J. Toppin. [Sir Stephen Theodore Janssen, merchant, lord mayor and chamberlain of London, d. 1777]

g Supplementary notes on the Battersea factory [the site of Janssen's enamel factory], by B. Rackham.

h John and Robert Brewer, the Derby painters [John Brewer, d. 1816, Robert Brewer, d. 1857, and their paintings on china], by W. H. Tapp.

English Porcelain Circle monograph:

1664 William Duesbury's London account book, 1751–3, with foreword by R. L. Hobson, and introd. by Mrs. D. MacAlister. 1931.

English Ceramic Circle Transactions, no. 1 (1933):

1665 No. 1.

a English saltglazed stoneware [from 1671], by W. B. Honey.

b Bristol biscuit plaques [from the factory of Richard Champion, late 18th cent.], by W. Elliot.

c Contributions to the history of porcelain-making in London, by A. J. Toppin. [Includes: The Kentish Town china factory, 18th cent.; James Giles, enameller, d. 1780; Nicholas Crisp, jeweller and potter, b. *c.* 1704]

d Early Staffordshire china [and its manufacturers], by Mrs. D. MacAlister.

e Invisible writing on English porcelain, by F. Hurlbutt.

ENGLISH FOLK DANCE AND SONG SOCIETY

Founded 1911, as the English Folk Dance Society, to disseminate knowledge of English folk dances, folk music, and singing games, and to encourage the practice of them in their traditional forms. Above title taken in 1932 on amalgamation with the Folk Song Society, which published music.

Journal, vol. 1 (1914–15):

1666 Vol. 1, nos. 1–2.

a Bibliography of the morris dance, by P. Lucas.

b The folk dance in English literature, by R. J. E. Tiddy.

Journal, 2nd ser., nos. 1–4 (1927–31):

1667 No. 1.

  a Fifteen years' progress [of the Society], by W. D. Croft.
  b The Lancashire rush-cart and morris-dance, by Anne G. Gilchrist.
  c English country-dances: a summary of views as to their nature and origin.

1668 No. 2.

  a Th' owd lass of Coverdill, and other sword-dance fragments, by M.K.

1669 No. 3.

  a Observations on the sword-dance and mummer's play, by D. Kennedy.

1670 No. 4.

  a Herefordshire for a morris dance, by Joan Sharp. [Account of the pamphlet *Old Meg of Herefordshire for a Mayd-Marian and Hereforde-Towne for a Morris Daunce*, 1609]

Journal [new ser.], vol. 1 (1932–3):

1671 Vol. 1, nos. 1–2.

  a Lambkin: a study in evolution [of a Scottish and Northumbrian ballad].
  b Molly [or morris] dancing in East Anglia, by J. Needham and A. L. Peck.
  c Carved morris-dance panel from Lancaster castle, by Anne G. Gilchrist.

E.F.D.S. News, nos. 1–34 (1921–33):

1672 No. 8.

  a Circumspice [an account of the work of Cecil James Sharp].

1673 No. 10.

  a Pepys on dancing [being principally accounts of and references to dancing in the Diary. Contd. in no. 11]
  b Morris dancing in Nottinghamshire in the 17th cent.: extracts from the act book of the archdeacon's court [1618].
  c The Northumbrian small-pipes, by E. P. Booker.

1674 No. 11.

  a May Day, by Muriel L. M. Maltby-Stevenson.

1675 No. 30.

  a Northumberland bagpipes, by G. V. B. Charlton.

ENGLISH MONUMENTAL INSCRIPTIONS SOCIETY

Founded 1911, to collect and publish inscriptions upon sepulchral monuments, etc.

Register of English Monumental Inscriptions, vols. 1–2 (1911–14):

1676 Vol. 1.

  a Monumental inscriptions in the church of St. Bartholomew at Orford, Suff., 1911, by H. W. B. Wayman. [Includes transcripts of wills. Also issued separately. *P. 1911*]
  b Churchyard inscriptions from Aldham, Suff., 1901, by C. Partridge.
  c Churchyard inscriptions from Layham, Suff., 1901, by C. Partridge.
  d Monumental inscriptions, in the church [and churchyard] of Swefling, Suff., 1907, by H. W. B. Wayman.

  e Monumental inscriptions in the church at Wantisden, Suff., 1907, by H. W. B. Wayman.
  f Churchyard inscriptions from Wantisden, by H. W. B. Wayman.
  g Inscriptions from the churchyard of St. Mary, Denham, Bucks., 1912, by T. W. Oswald-Hicks.
  h Monumental inscriptions within the church at Woughton-on-the-Green, Bucks., 1909, by W. Bradbrook.
  i Inscriptions from the churchyard at Woughton-on-the-Green, by W. Bradbrook.
  j Churchyard inscriptions from parishes in the hundred of Samford and county of Suffolk.

1677 Vol. 2.

  a Monumental inscriptions within the churchyard [and church] of St. Botolph, Bradenham, Bucks., 1913, by T. W. Oswald-Hicks.
  b Monumental inscriptions within the church [and churchyard] of St. Bartholomew, Fingest, Bucks., 1913, by T. W. Oswald-Hicks.
  c Monumental inscriptions within the church [and churchyard] of Holy Trinity, Great Woolstone, Bucks., 1911, by W. Bradbrook.
  d Monumental inscriptions within the church [and churchyard] of Holy Trinity, Little Woolstone, Bucks., 1911, by W. Bradbrook.
  e Monumental inscriptions within the church [and churchyard] of St. Mary, Belstead, Suff.
  f Monumental inscriptions in the church of St. Peter, Freston, Suff., 1908.
  g Churchyard inscriptions from Freston, by C. R. Durrant.
  h Monumental inscriptions from the graveyard of the Congregational chapel, Southwold, Suff., 1908, by D. Roper.
  i List of forty original licenses for marriages solemnized at the Rev. Alexander Keith's 'New' chapel in Mayfair [1746–53], and at St. George's church, Hanover Square, London [from 1830], by T. W. Oswald-Hicks.
  j Monumental inscriptions within the church [and churchyard] of St. John Baptist, Little Missenden, Bucks., 1912, by L. H. Chambers.
  k Monumental inscriptions within the church [and churchyard] of St. Michael, Walton, Bucks., 1909, by W. Bradbrook.
  l Yorkshire monumental inscriptions: a list of 84 transcripts printed and in ms., compiled from a revised report of the Yorkshire Archaeological Society, 1913.
  m Monumental inscriptions in the churchyard of the parish church of St. Edmund, Southwold, Suff., 1908.
  n Monumental inscriptions within the church [and churchyard] of St. Luke, Stoke Hamond, Bucks., 1913, by W. Bradbrook.
  o Suffolk monumental inscriptions: table of printed transcripts.
  p Abstracts of Suffolk wills proved in the prerogative court of Canterbury, 1383–1604, by H. W. B. Wayman. [A Calendar of Suffolk wills proved in P.C.C., 1384–1604, comp. C. W. S. Randall Cloke, ed. T. W. Oswald-Hicks, was issued separately in 1913]

ENGLISH PLACE-NAME SOCIETY

Founded 1923, to carry out the survey of English place-names inaugurated under the auspices of the British Academy in 1922.

Publications:

1678 No. 1, pt. 1. Introduction to the survey of English place-names, ed. A. Mawer and F. M. Stenton. 1924. [Contains chapters by O. G. S. Crawford E. Ekwall,

W. J. Sedgefield, F. M. Stenton, J. Tait, H. C. Wyld assisted by Mary S. Serjeanston, and R. E. Zachrisson]

1679 No. 1, pt. 2. The chief elements used in English place-names: being the second part of the introduction to the survey of English place-names, ed. A. Mawer. 1924.

1680 No. 2. Place-names of Buckinghamshire, by A. Mawer and F. M. Stenton. 1925.

1681 No. 3. Place-names of Bedfordshire and Huntingdonshire, by A. Mawer and F. M. Stenton. 1926.

1682 No. 4. Place-names of Worcestershire, by A. Mawer and F. M. Stenton, in collaboration with F. T. S. Houghton. 1927.

1683 No. 5. Place-names of the North Riding of Yorkshire, by A. H. Smith. 1928.

1684 Nos. 6, 7. Place-names of Sussex, by A. Mawer and F. M. Stenton with the assistance of J. E. B. Gover. 1 vol. in 2, 1929–30. [Pt. i: Rapes of Chichester, Arundel, and Bramber. Pt. ii: Rapes of Lewes, Pevensey, and Hastings]

1685 Nos. 8, 9. Place-names of Devon, by J. E. B. Gover, A. Mawer, and F. M. Stenton. 1 vol. in 2, with separate case of maps, 1931–2. [For notes on Devon place-names by Sir A. Mawer, see Philosophical Soc. *Transactions* for 1931–33 (published 1933)]

1686 No. 10. Place-names of Northamptonshire, by J. E. B· Gover, A. Mawer, and F. M. Stenton. 1933.

EPIDEMIOLOGICAL SOCIETY OF LONDON

Founded 1850, to promote the investigation of epidemic diseases. In 1907 the Society became the Epidemiological Section of the Royal Society of Medicine.

Transactions, new ser., vols. 20–26 (1901–7):

1687 Vol. 20.

a Plague in Britain in the 19th cent. [with special reference to Glasgow, 1900], by A. K. Chalmers.

1688 Vol. 23.

a Industrial anthrax, 1899–1903, by T. M. Legge.

1689 Vol. 24.

a Phthisis rates [in Great Britain, 19th cent.]: their significance and their teaching, by A. Ransome.

1690 Vol. 26.

a On tuberculosis [with particular reference to the period 1880–1900], by J. Tatham.

Extra publication:

1691 The commemoration volume, containing an account of the foundation of the Society, and of the commemoration dinner, together with an index of the papers read at its meetings, 1855–1900. 1902.

ESSEX ARCHAEOLOGICAL SOCIETY

Founded 1852, to promote the study and preservation of the history and antiquities of Essex.

Transactions, new ser., vols. 8–21 (1903–34):

1692 Vol. 8.

a Two Essex incised slabs [at Middleton, to James Samson, priest, 1349, and at Bradwell-juxta-Coggeshall, to a priest, 1349], by M. Christy and E. B. Smith.

b Ship-money in Essex, 1634–40, by W. C. Waller.

c Some interesting Essex brasses, by M. Christy and W. W. Porteous. [Contd. from vol. 7. Further articles in vols. 9 and 10]

d The Milbournes of Great Dunmow, by T. Milbourn.

e Essex field-names, collected and arranged by W. C. Waller. [Contd. from vol. 7. Further articles in vol. 9]

f Archaeological notes. [Includes: Fyfield church, and the chapel at Havering-atte-Bower]

g General meeting, April, 1900. [Includes an account of the ancient rampart through Lexden park]

h Mediaeval Colchester: town, castle and abbey, from mss. in the British Museum, by H. J. Dukinfield Astley.

i Wallbury camp, Great Hallingbury, by I. C. Gould.

j The castle of Stansted Montfitchet, by H. Laver.

k An extinct county family: Wroth of Loughton Hall, by W. C. Waller. [Contd. in vol. 9]

l The Order of the Hospital in Essex, by J. H. Round.

m Helion of Helion's Bumpstead, by J. H. Round.

n The manor of Colne Engaine, by J. H. Round.

o Colchester bays, says and perpetuanas [all fabrics], by E. Howard.

p Quarterly meeting, June, 1900. [Includes accounts of Nevenden church; the site of the Danish camp at Benfleet; and South Benfleet church]

q Quarterly meeting, Aug. 1900. [Includes an account of Latton hill mound, Harlow]

r Lawford church, by E. K. Green.

s Churches of Great and Little Bromley, by H. H. Minchin.

t Stukeley's 'temple' [earthwork] at Navestock, by I. C. Gould.

u Archaeological notes. [Includes notes on a 12th cent. charter of Alice of Essex; the Tregoz family of Tolleshunt Tregoze; and the manors of Wethersfield and Pleshey and 'Plesingho']

v Quarterly meeting, Oct., 1901. [Includes an account of the chapel formerly at Brentwood]

w Records of Tiltey abbey: an account of some preserved at Easton Lodge, by W. C. Waller. [Contd. in vol. 9]

x Some Essex brasses recently refixed, by M. Christy and W. W. Porteous.

y Oliver's Thicks rampart: an earthwork near Colchester, by H. Laver.

z Archaeological notes. [Includes notes on the descent of Thorrington, and the church and glebe of Willingale Doe]

1693 Vol. 9.

a Parish church of St. Mary the Virgin, Kelvedon (Easterford), by E. F. Hay.

b Bures mount [possibly of Norman origin], by I. C. Gould.

c Quarterly meeting, Aug. 1902. [Includes an account of Great Tey church and its early 19th cent. restoration]

d The 15th cent. vestry and priest's chamber in Hatfield Broad Oak church, by F. W. Galpin.

e Roman remains discovered in making the public park at Colchester castle, by H. Laver.

f Taxations of Colchester, 1296 and 1301 [with transcripts of the original documents], by G. Rickword.

g Notes on the discovery of ancient vessels on a Roman site at Braintree, by J. W. Kenworthy.

h Family and arms of [Dr. William] Gilbert of Colchester [d. 1603], by S. P. Thompson.

i A note on the hundred of Ongar, by W. C. Waller.

j Great Chesterford church, by F. Chancellor.

k The Repell ditches, Saffron Walden, by I. C. Gould.

l Chancel arch of White Notley church, by C. Lynam.

m The Capells at Rayne, 1486–1622, by W. Minet. [Appendices including abstracts of deeds relating to the manor of Rayne]

w John Wilbye, madrigalist [d. 1638], by F. Skeet.

x Wyncoll family, by L. C. Sier. [Contd. in vol. 12]

y Kingdom of the East Saxons and the tribal hidage, by G. Rickword. [See also article by the same in vol. 12]

z Quarterly meeting, July, 1909. [Includes account of Laindon church]

aa Quarterly meeting, Sept. 1909. [Includes accounts of Witham, Little Braxted, Great Braxted, Little Totham, Great Totham, and Wickham Bishops churches]

bb Copford church, by H. Laver.

cc Armorial glass and badges in Harlow church, by J. G. Bradford.

dd Early lords of Shelley [manor, 12th cent.], by J. H. Round.

1696 Vol. 12.

a Some walls at Waltham abbey, by J. French.

b Early domestic decorative wall-paintings recently found in Essex [chiefly 16th cent.], by M. Christy and G. Maynard.

c Quarterly meeting, Sept. 1910. [Includes accounts of Colne Engaine, Wakes Colne, Colne Priory, and Earls Colne churches]

d Benedictine abbey of Barking: a sketch of its architectural history and an account of recent excavations on its site, by A. W. Clapham. [Reprinted by the Morant Club, 1911]

e Great Birch [manor], Easthorpe, and the Gernons [12th–13th cent.], by J. H. Round.

f 'Ings' and 'gings' of the Domesday survey, especially Fryerning, by Mrs. A. Christy.

g Manor of Great Myles's, Kelvedon Hatch [and its owners], by H. Clifford.

h Papers read at the quarterly meeting, June, 1910. [Includes accounts of Moyns manor and its owners, and of Steeple Bumpsted and Hempstead churches]

i Papers read at the quarterly meeting, July, 1910. [Includes accounts of Lambourne Hall and church; Rolls Park, Chigwell and Chigwell church]

j Rayleigh castle: new facts in its history and recent explorations on its site, by E. B. Francis.

k Excavation of Lexden mount [Roman tumulus], by H. Laver and F. W. Reader. [Reprinted by the Morant Club, 1912]

l Stray notes on Essex fines [chiefly Christian names in 13th cent.], by W. C. Waller.

m Manor of Theydon Mount [in 13th cent.], by J. H. Round.

n Household expenses of Sir Thomas Barrington [stewards' accounts, 1622–67], by F. W. Galpin.

o Quarterly meeting, July, 1912. [Includes accounts of Rainham, Wennington, Aveley, South Ockendon, and North Ockendon churches]

p Roman colonization [of Britain], by T. Stevens.

q Religious gilds of Essex [with transcripts of some certificates], by R. C. Fowler.

r A 14th-cent. pluralist: Richard de Drax, rector of Harlow, by W. C. Waller.

s Court House, or 'Old Town Hall', at Barking, by A. W. Clapham.

t Family of Strangman, by J. H. Round.

u Gosfield church and hall, by H. L. Elliot.

v Descent of West Horndon [manor, *temp.* Edward II], by J. H. Round.

w Three more Essex incised slabs, by M. Christy.

x All Saints, Colchester, by A. Weddell.

y Earliest Essex medical man [*temp.* Henry II], by J. H. Round.

z Essex churches, by F. Chancellor. [Contd. in vols. 13 and 14]

1697 Vol. 13.

a Books bearing on Essex history, by J. H. Round.

b Tilbury fort [1539–1672], by G. Biddell.

c Monumental brasses of Colchester, by M. Christy, W. W. Porteous and E. B. Smith.

d Church of St. Clement, West Thurrock: a sketch of its architectural history and an account of recent excavation on its site, by A. W. Clapham. [Reprinted by the Morant Club, 1913]

e John Doreward's chantry, Bocking [founded 1397], by J. H. Round.

f Manorial customs in West Mersea and Fingringhoe [with a transcript of customary, 1497], by W. G. Benham.

g Lionel de Bradenham [*temp.* Edward III] and Colchester, by J. H. Round.

h Rent-roll of Sir Henry Marney of Layer Marney [1499], with introd. and notes by G. Rickword.

i Colchester town ditch, by A. M. Jarmin.

j Friday Hill [Chingford] and the Boothbys, by W. C. Waller.

k The opening of the Romano-British barrow on Mersea island, by S. H. Warren. [Reprinted by the Morant Club, 1913]

l Embezzled church goods of Essex [transcripts from inventories of goods sold by 1548], by E. P. Dickin.

m Briefs at Tollesbury, 1707–31, by A. Clark.

n Token coinage of Essex in the 17th cent., by W. Gilbert. [Contd. in vol. 14]

o Augustinian priory of Little Leez and the mansion of Leez Priory, by A. W. Clapham.

p On the opening of a mound [medieval?] at Chadwell St. Mary, by M. Christy and F. W. Reader. [Reprinted by the Morant Club, 1914]

q Opening of Plumberow mount [Romano-British], in Hockley, by E. B. Francis. [Reprinted by the Morant Club, 1914]

r White Notley Hall and church, by W. Chancellor.

s Bequests relating to Essex extracted from *Calendar of wills proved and enrolled in the court of Husting, London,* with additional notes by A. B. Bamford. [Contd. in vol. 14]

t White Notley Hall [its descent and the Smith family], by J. H. Round.

u Augustinian priory church of Little Dunmow: a sketch of its architectural history and an account of recent excavations on its site, by A. W. Clapham. [Reprinted by the Morant Club, 1914]

v On certain carvings in Saffron Walden church, by G. M. Benton.

w Layer Marney tower [1500–25], by W. Chancellor.

x Archaeological notes. [Includes: Manorial customs in West Mersea, etc.: the tenants' destruction of the ancient records of the manor, *c.* 1381, by W. G. Benham]

1698 Vol. 14.

a Early Georgian inventory [of Isaac Lemyng Rebow, 1735], with introd. and notes by G. Rickword.

b Excavation of the site of a mediaeval pottery at Mill Green, Ingatestone, by M. Christy and F. W. Reader. [Reprinted by the Morant Club, 1915]

c Layer Marney church, by F. Chancellor.

d Court rolls of Colchester [1405–6], by I. H. Jeayes.

e Eastwood parish church: St. Lawrence and All Saints, by F. B. Johnston.

f Eastwood: extracts from *Ecclesiae Essexienses,* by W. H. King.

g New Hall Park, Boreham [descent of the estate, 1738–1802], by L. C. Sier.

h Stangate priory, by W. Howard-Flanders.

i North Weald Basset [manor] and the Essex family [13th cent.], by J. H. Round.

c Some omissions in Newcourt's *Repertorium* [1621–37], by H. Smith. [Contd. in Archaeological notes]

d Wall-paintings in Essex churches, by G. M. Benton. [Contd. in vols. 18 and 20, and completed in vol. 21 by E. W. Tristram and G. M. Benton]

e Archaeological notes. [Includes: The 'Brightlingsea' family, by J. H. Round; Pant or Blackwater river, by R. C. Fowler]

f The making of Brentwood [the origins of the town as deduced from 12th cent. charters], by J. H. Round.

g The Pamphilons: an Essex family of violin makers [17th and 18th cent.], by W. Minet.

h Land-owners and place-names [in Essex], by P. H. Reaney.

i The Goshalms [family and the origin of the name, 13th cent.], by J. H. Round.

j Archaeological notes. [Includes: Berryfield, Colchester, the origin of the name and the extent of the area, by P. Laver; Broomfield church and its original deeds, by R. C. Fowler; Late bronze and early iron age pottery discovered at Shalford, by G. M. Benton; Roman burial group discovered at West Mersea, by G. M. Benton]

k The Essex and Suffolk border, by J. H. Round. [Some problems relating to parishes in that locality]

l Notes on the coast, shipping, and sea-borne trade of Essex, 1565–77, by E. P. Dickin.

m Some Essex monastic seals, by R. C. Fowler.

n Gernon, Garland, and Garnish [the interrelation of the place-names], by P. H. Reaney.

o Navestock [manor, and its medieval connection with St. Paul's cathedral], by J. H. Round.

p The Roman fort in the parish of Bradwell-juxta-Mare, by Miss M. V. Taylor.

q Domestic wall-paintings at Bocking [16th cent.], by E. T. Bond.

r Medieval graffiti in Steeple Bumpstead and other Essex churches, by G. M. Benton.

1702 Vol. 18.

a 'Gryme's Dyke', or the outward trench of Wyldenhey, by J. H. Round. [The article in vol. 11 submitted to record evidence]

b Wall-paintings [domestic, 16th and early 17th cent.] at East and West Hanningfield, by A. B. Bamford.

c Fulk Basset's register and the Norwich taxation [1254], by R. C. Fowler.

d Two large groups of marsh-mounds on the Essex coast [and their possible origin], by M. Christy and W. H. Dalton. [Reprinted, with additions, by the Morant Club, 1925]

e Archaeological notes. [Includes: 'Bygades', the origin of its name and other names on the Essex coast, by J. H. Round; 'Alfledenesse', the identification of the place and its owners, by J. H. Round; Miles Graye of Colchester and Saffron Walden, the 17th cent. bell-founder, by G. M. Benton; Roman pavement uncovered at Colchester, by G. M. Benton]

f The abbey church and claustral buildings of Tilty, by F. W. Galpin.

g Early English wall inscriptions at Colchester [Durlston House, late 15th or early 16th cent.], by W. G. Benham.

h Appointments to Essex benefices by commissioners of the great seal, 1649–54, by H. Smith.

i Ballingdon Hall and the Eden family [17th cent.], by C. F. D. Sperling.

j The Essex hundred-moots: an attempt to identify their meeting-places, by M. Christy.

k Pewter communion vessels of Essex churches, by W. J. Pressey. [With list of those possessed by Essex churches, 1926]

l Edwins Hall and the Sandys family [16th cent.], by R. C. Fowler.

m Find of Roman pottery at Harlow, by A. G. Wright.

n Dedham tombstones [of Edmund Chapman, d. 1602, and John Rogers, d. 1636, lecturers in the church], by G. H. Rendall.

o The manor of Borley, 1308, by G. F. Beaumont.

p An early Roman burial group, by M. R. Hull. [Pottery found at Lexden]

q Early history of the Society and of the Colchester and Essex museum, by G. M. Benton.

r Wall-paintings at Quendon Hall, by G. M. Benton. [Religious subjects, late 16th or early 17th cent.]

s Archaeological notes. [Includes: The font at Rainham, by M. Christy]

1703 Vol. 19.

a Records of the archdeaconries of Essex and Colchester [1540–1707], by W. J. Pressey.

b Widdington church, by G. M. Benton.

c An early Essex subsidy [1237–8], by R. C. Fowler.

d Deeds from a parish chest [Writtle, 1330–1706], by I. H. Jeayes.

e Archaeological notes. [Includes: Heraldic glass formerly at Bicknacre priory, by G. M. Benton; Bocking and Stisted manors, origins of their names and early accounts of them, by J. H. Round; Notes on Roman jewellery found at Lexden, by E. J. Rudsdale; The manor of Borley and its early descent, by J. F. Nichols]

f The earliest map showing Essex [by Christopher Saxton, 1576], by M. Christy.

g Essex place-names study, by P. H. Reaney.

h The destroyed church of St. Lawrence, East Donyland, by G. M. Benton.

i Customs and services on an Essex manor (Netteswell), in 13th cent., by J. L. Fisher.

j Roman tombstone found in Colchester, by M. R. Hull.

k Archaeological notes. [Includes: Great Tey churchyard fence, with a list of persons liable for its repair, 1668, by C. F. D. Sperling; Henry III in Essex, 1235, by J. H. Round; The Colchester Sphinx, by M. R. Hull; Discovery of Roman remains at Colchester, 1927, by E. J. Rudsdale]

l Winter meetings at Colchester. [Includes abstract of a lecture on windmills, with notes on those in Essex]

m The Witham desk-hanging and the Latton altar frontal [16th and 17th cent.], by G. M. Benton.

n 'Cesterwald' [identification of the locality], by J. H. Round.

o The barony of Little Easton and the family of Hastings [chiefly 13th cent.], by L. Landon.

p Sunecastre, or the camp [Saxon or Danish] at Asheldham, by P. G. Laver.

q A balance sheet of St. Osyth's abbey [1491], by R. C. Fowler.

r Parkes farm, Gestingthorpe, by D. W. Clark and G. M. Benton.

s Archaeological notes. [Includes: A Roman coffin from Rainham, by G. W. Farmer; Discoveries at Fingringhoe church, being blocked medieval windows, by G. M. Benton]

t Quarterly meeting and excursion, July, 1928. [Includes accounts of Tollesbury church and parish prison]

u A recently discovered wall-paper at Colchester [c. 1730], by H. Jenkinson.

v Prehistoric sites at Finchingfield, by J. G. Coverton.

w An early rector of Stock [Master Gregory, of Ginge Joyberd church, 13th cent.], by J. H. Round.

x Antiquities from Essex in the Ashmolean Museum, Oxford, by E. Thurlow Leeds. [Palaeolithic to Anglo-Saxon objects]

ESSEX FIELD CLUB

Founded 1880, as Epping Forest and County of Essex Naturalists' Field Club, for the study and investigation of the natural history, geology, and archaeology of the county of Essex. Title changed to above form in 1882.

Essex Naturalist, vols. 11–24 (1900–35):

e Queen Elizabeth's lodge, Epping forest: notes on the original construction and use of the building, by W. W. Love.

f Christopher Saxton, draughtsman of the oldest known map of Essex, by J. Avery.

1709 Vol. 12.

a Palaeolithic implements from the low-level drift of the Thames valley, chiefly from Ilford and Grays, by J. P. Johnson.

b The coming of age of the Essex Field Club: a record of local scientific work, 1880–1901, by R. Meldola.

c Neolithic implements from the North Downs near Sutton, Surrey, by J. P. Johnson.

d Anent a forest lodge in 1444, by W. C. Waller.

e Notes on 'dug-out' boats in the ancient marshes of the Lea and the Thames.

f Eolithic implements from the plateau gravel around Walderslade, Kent, by J. P. Johnson.

1710 Vol. 13.

a Tree trunk water pipes, by T. V. Holmes.

b The palaeolithic period in the Thames basin, by J. P. Johnson.

c Charcoal burning in Essex, by T. S. Dymond.

d Wooden water-pipes at Clerkenwell, London, by F. W. Reader.

e Origin of the term 'sarsen stones', by T. V. Holmes.

f Remains of a supposed pile-dwelling at Woodham Walter, by M. Christy.

g Evidences of prehistoric man in west Kent, by J. R. Larkby.

h Essex worthies, 4: George Edwards, the Stratford naturalist [d. 1773], by J. Avery.

1711 Vol. 14.

a Notes on the pile-dwelling site at Skitts hill, Braintree, by F. W. Reader.

b A whale at Mersey [Mersea] in 1299, by J. E. Harting.

c Exploration of some 'red-hills' in Essex, with remarks upon the objects found, by W. Cole.

d Straw-plaiting: a lost Essex industry, by I. C. Gould.

e History of salt-making in Essex, by M. Christy.

1712 Vol. 15.

a Miscellaneous denehole notes, by T. V. Holmes.

b Denehole at Gravesend, by T. V. Holmes.

c The woodlands of Essex [history of], by J. C. Shenstone.

d Wells on Fowlness island, ancient and modern, by W. H. Dalton.

e The eastern boundary stones of the forest of Waltham: supplementary note, by R. Meldola.

f Some unexplored fields of Essex archaeology, by J. French.

g Notes on a human skeleton, found at Foxearth, by J. M. Wood.

h History of the mineral waters and medicinal springs of Essex, by M. Christy and May Thresh. [Reprinted with additions as Special Memoir, no. 4, 1910]

1713 Vol. 16.

a The re-afforestation of Hainault (part of the old forest of Waltham), by F. Dent and T. S. Dymond. [Includes the history of Hainault forest]

b Notes on the palaeolithic and neolithic implements of east Essex, by S. H. Warren.

c Charcoal burners in Epping forest; their primitive huts and the formation of hut-circles, by S. H. Warren.

d Notes on a bone object found at Braintree, and on some similar objects found elsewhere, by F. W. Reader.

e Notes on a prehistoric deposit at Loughton, by S. H. Warren.

f Dr. Benj. Allen (1663–1738) of Braintree: a forgotten Essex naturalist, by M. Christy. [Further article in vol. 17]

g A pre-historic interment near Walton-on-Naze, by S. H. Warren.

h A neolithic floor in the bed of the Crouch river, and other discoveries near Rayleigh, by F. W. Reader. [Reprinted by the Morant Club, 1911]

i On the correlation of the pre-historic 'floor' at Hull-bridge with similar beds elsewhere, by S. H. Warren. [Reprinted by the Morant Club, 1911]

1714 Vol. 17.

a Past and present history of Colchester corporation water works with relation to underground water, by J. M. Wood.

b John Ray [d. 1705], Samuel Dale [d. 1739], and Benjamin Allen [d. 1738, naturalists]: a eulogy, by G. S. Boulger.

c Nineteen letters [1704–11, relating to scientific matters] from the Rev. Wm. Derham to Dacre Barrett, of Belhus, by T. Barrett-Lennard.

d Notes on human skull found at Wendon, by G. Maynard, with a report on the cranium, by A. Keith.

1715 Vol. 18.

a The dating of early human remains, by S. H. Warren.

b Chigwell Row medicinal springs: a late 18th cent. account of them, by (?) William Martin Trinder, ed. M. Christy.

c Notes on the low-level gravels of the river Lea and their palaeolithic implements, by A. Wrigley.

d Notes upon the palaeolithic implements from Wanstead Park, by C. Butcher.

e John Gibbs [d. 1892]: an Essex botanist, by M. Christy.

f E. G. Varenne [d. 1887], of Kelvedon, botanist: some local anecdotes and reminiscences, by A. Hills.

1716 Vol. 19.

a Samuel Dale, of Braintree, botanist, and the Dale family: some genealogy and some portraits, by M. Christy.

b Annotated copy of Richard Warner's *Plantae Wood-fordienses* [with notes on Benjamin Meggot Forster, d. 1829, the annotator, and his brothers], by P. Thompson.

c Recent discovery of a dene-hole at Grays, by P. Thompson.

d Another annotated copy of Warner's *Plantae Wood-fordienses* [with notes on the annotator, Edward Forster, d. 1849], by P. Thompson.

e Æneas Macintyre [fl. 1825–36]: a forgotten Essex botanist, by M. Christy.

f Samuel Harsnett, archbishop of York, by G. Rickword.

1717 Vol. 20.

a The sparrow-hawk (*accipiter nisus*) and the goshawk (*astur gentilis*) in litigation in the 12th and 13th cent., by W. E. Glegg.

b Jabez Legg [d. 1867]: a forgotten local worthy, by J. Avery.

c Some neolithic sites in the upper valley of the Essex Cam, by G. Morris.

d Richard Warner [Woodford botanist, d. 1775], by G. S. Boulger.

e Richard Warner as viewed by Kalm [Swedish botanist, d. 1779], by B. D. Jackson.

f A third annotated copy of Richard Warner's *Plantae Woodfordienses* [with notes on the annotator, Thomas Furly Forster, d. 1825], by P. Thompson.

1718 Vol. 21.

a Palaeolithic and neolithic implements from the Thames valley and elsewhere, by S. H. Warren.

b The Willingales [family] of Loughton: to whom do we owe Epping forest?, by P. Thompson. [An account of resistance to enclosure of the forest in the late 19th cent.]
c Excavations in pillow mounds [iron age] at High Beach, by S. H. Warren.
d Essex rivers and their names, by M. Christy.

1719 Vol. 22.

a Report on excavations in Loughton camp, Epping forest, by S. H. Warren.
b Short history of the Essex Field Club, as recorded for the most part in the minutes of its council, by P. Thompson. [Also issued separately as Special Memoir, no. 7, *P.* 1930]

1720 Vol. 23.

a Subsidence of the Thames estuary since the Roman period, at Southchurch, by A. G. Francis.
b Faraday and his influence on our everyday life, by W. Bridger.

1721 Vol. 24.

a Palaeolithic industries of Clacton and Dovercourt districts, by S. H. Warren.
b Some Essex doctors [William Harvey, d. 1657; John Fothergill, d. 1780; Joseph Lister, d. 1912; Sir Morell Mackenzie, d. 1892], by S. J. Barns.
c Reminiscences of Lord Lister, by Gulielma Lister.
d The past history of the forest of Essex, by R. Coles.
e An afternoon tour of West Ham. [Includes accounts of West Ham church and Stratford Langthorne abbey]
f Visit to Layer Marney. [Includes accounts of Layer Marney Towers and Layer Marney church, by S. J. Barns]
g Visit to Horham Hall and the Thaxted district. [Account of Horham Hall by S. J. Barns]
h History of mycology in Essex, by J. Ramsbottom.
i History of Essex heronries, by W. E. Glegg.
j An afternoon tour of Woodford. [Includes an account of what used to be Higham Benstead manor house, by S. J. Barns]

1722 The Essex Naturalist: general index to vols. 1–22, 1887–1930, comp. and ed. S. J. Barns.

Essex Museum handbooks:

1723 Handbook to the collection of prehistoric objects in the Essex Museum of Natural History, Passmore Edwards Museum, by F. W. Reader. *P.* 1901.

1724 An account of Queen Elizabeth's lodge, Chingford, and of the Epping Forest museum. *P.* 1925.

Special memoirs:

1725 No. 5. Pre-history in Essex as recorded in the journal of the Essex Field Club, by S. H. Warren. 1918.

EXETER DIOCESAN ARCHITECTURAL AND ARCHAEOLOGICAL SOCIETY

Founded 1841, *as the Exeter Diocesan Architectural Society, for the diffusion of information on architectural and archaeological subjects. Title changed to above form in* 1893 *or* 1894.

Transactions, 3rd ser., vol. 2–vol. 5, pt. 1 (1901–33):

1726 Vol. 2.

a Our parish registers, by F. B. Dickinson.
b Salcombe Regis church, by J. Newnham.

c Report of district meeting at Newton Abbot and neighbourhood, by R. M. Fulford. [Includes an account of Haccombe church]
d Vestries, by J. Newnham.
e Report of the annual excursion. [Includes accounts of Poughill church and Stratton church]
f All Saints, Kenton: supplementary notes, by W. P. S. Bingham. [Contd. from vol. 1]
g Ecclesiastical and antiquarian notes on church of St. Mary, Exbourne, Devon, by D'O. W. Oldham.
h District meeting, Sherborne, by J. Newnham. [Includes an account of the abbey]
i Notes on the manor and church of Broadhempston, by M. Adams.
j Parishes and parishioners [of the diocese of Exeter] of six hundred years ago, by E. V. Freeman.
k Rise of the parochial system in England, by O. J. Reichel.
l Peter's pence, by E. V. Freeman.
m Hennock church and parish, by R. M. Fulford.
n The resuscitation of Gothic, by S. M. Nourse.
o Symbolic art as illustrated by the romanesque font at St. Marychurch, by Miss M. Gray.
p Heraldic stained glass in Ashton church, by F. M. Drake.
q Report of the visit to Dunster and Cleeve abbey, by J. Jerman.

1727 Vol. 3.

a The [parish] registers of England, by C. Square.
b Notes on ancient ecclesiastical needlework with reference to some local vestments, by J. Jerman.
c Report on the visit to St. Germans and Plymouth, 1906, by J. Jerman. [Includes an account of St. Germans church]
d The Carew monuments in Exeter cathedral, by R. Granville.
e Some 14th cent. customs of the cathedral church of Exeter, by C. G. Browne.
f Chained books and libraries in Devonshire parish churches, by Beatrix Cresswell.
g The Renaissance, by S. Nourse.
h Church of St. James the Less, Honeychurch, by Edith K. Prideaux.
i Church of St. Mary the Virgin, Rewe, by G. O. Apthorp.
j Survey of Devonshire churches, by Beatrix F. Cresswell.
k Illustrated notes on 15th cent. alabasters from South Huish church, Devon, by P. Nelson and Edith K. Prideaux.
l Carved bench-ends in Devon, by Kate M. Clarke.
m The chalice and paten, as illustrated by the church plate of the archdeaconry of Barnstaple, by J. F. Chanter.

1728 Vol. 4.

a The Kirkham monument in Paignton church, by G. McN. Rushforth.
b Grandisson's *Legenda Sanctorum* [14th cent. ms.], by J. F. Chanter.
c Hemyock castle, by C. Sherwin.
d Tavistock abbey, by Lady Radford.
e Bishop's Court [manor house, Clyst], by J. F. Chanter.
f Footprints of medieval life in a mid-Devon district [i.e. the parishes of Spreyton and Hittisleigh], by E. V. Freeman.
g Wall paintings in Exeter cathedral, by H.S.
h Chapel of St. John the Baptist, formerly at Thorverton, by H.S.
i Church houses, by J. B. Hyde.
j The story of the cloisters of Exeter cathedral, 1250–1930, by J. F. Chanter.
k Windows of the church of St. Neot, Cornwall, by

G. McN. Rushforth, with appendix by M. H. N. C. Atchley.

l Pages from a missal annotated by Bishop Grandisson, by H. E. Bishop.

1729 Vol. 5, pt. 1.

a The custos and college of the vicars choral of the choir of the cathedral church of St. Peter, Exeter, and their close, by J. F. Chanter.

EX-LIBRIS SOCIETY

Founded 1891, for the systematic collection and arrangement of book-plates, etc.

Journal, vols. 11–18 (1901–8):

1730 Vol. 11.

a The Medmenham friars [a brief account of some members of the Hell Fire Club founded by Sir Francis Dashwood], by W. Bolton.

b Hewer, by A. J. Jewers. [Notes on Hewer Edgley Hewer of Clapham, Surrey, d. 1728. Contd. in vol. 12]

c 'Ex Libris of Queen Victoria of England.' [Brief summary of an article in *Ex-Libris Zeitschrift*, vol. 11, 1901]

1731 Vol. 12.

a Book-plates of Sir Philip Sydenham [d. 1739], by C· Johnson.

b Ireland book-plates, by W. Bolton. [With some account of Samuel Ireland, d. 1800, author and engraver, and of William Ireland, d. 1835, forger of Shakespeare documents]

c Exeter cathedral library, and its book-plates, by W. H. K. Wright.

d Book-plates of New College, Oxford, by J. H. Smith.

e Sir Horace Mann and the Walpoles, by W. Bolton.

f Rev. Dr. Thomas Bray [d. 1730] and the parochial libraries [founded by him in England and Maryland], by F.J.T.

g Borlase [family] book-plates, by A. J. Jewers.

h Sir John Hill [d. 1775, author], by G. C. Peachey.

i A Lord Proprietor of Carolina, by A. A. Bethune-Baker. [Brief account of William, Earl of Craven, d. 1697]

j Book-plates of Fleming of Rydal [with notes on the family], by G. C. Peachey.

1732 Vol. 13.

a The Hopton family and their book-plates, by W. M. Birch.

1733 Vol. 14.

a Marryat bookplates, by C. T. Davis. [With notes on Captain Marryat and his family]

b Bookplates of Swire of Cononley, by G. C. Peachey.

c Francis Garden, engraver [fl. *c.* 1745, and some of his American book-plates and their owners], by F. E. Marshall. [Further note in vol. 17 by C. Johnson]

1734 Vol. 15.

a An 18th cent. Leicestershire church library [founded at Ashby-de-la-Zouch, by Thomas Bate, d. 1727, rector of Swarkeston, Derbys.], by J. P. Rylands.

b Price-Cleveland book-plate [notes on the families of Cleveland of Birkenhead and Price of Bryn-y-Pys, Flints.], by A. H. Arkle.

c James Pierot [of Bermuda, silversmith, fl. *c.* 1780]: an interesting plate, by E. S. Potter.

d Shakespeare's coat of arms, by J. Vinycomb.

e Book-plates of Jesus College, Oxford, by J. H. Smith.

1735 Vol. 16.

a Book-plates of Grylls [family], by A. C. G. Grylls.

b Book-plates of Wadham College, Oxford, by J. H. Smith.

c English royal heraldry. [Summary of a paper by C. Davenport]

d Joseph Holland, 1585 [an attempt to identify the owner of the book so named], by G. H. Viner.

e Wright [family] book-plates, by A. J. Jewers. [Contd. in vol. 17]

1736 Vol. 17.

a A London silversmith of the 18th cent. [extracts from the account book of George Coyte, fl. 1771–77], by E. F. Strange. [Reprinted from the *Connoisseur*]

1737 Vol. 18.

a A brief sketch of the Ettrick family, by E. Maughan-Ettrick.

b Book-plates of J. Skinner, of Bath [18th cent.], by C. Johnson. [Further article by J. H. Smith]

c Matthew Skinner [18th cent.] of Exeter [and his book-plates], by C. Johnson.

d Sir Jeffry Wyattville [d. 1840, architect, and his book-plate], by A. B. Grimaldi.

1738 General index to the Journal, vols. 1–12, 1890–1902, comp. W. H. K. Wright. 1904.

FEDERATION OF OLD CORNWALL SOCIETIES

The first Old Cornwall Society was founded in 1920, to keep Cornwall Cornish, by interesting Cornish people in everything, past and present, that gives character to Cornwall.

Old Cornwall, vols. 1–2 (1925–36):

1739 Vol. 1.

a The preservation of ancient monuments in Cornwall, by H. Jenner.[1]

b Cornish mines and miners, by A. K. H. Jenkin.[1]

c Cornish family mottoes, by R. M. Nance.[1]

d Cornwall and the smuggling trade, by A. A. Clinnick.

e Cornish wrestling, by H. Pascoe.

f Some notes on the wool trade in Cornwall, by J. N. Rosewarne.

g Parson Drake's Cornish [marriage] certificate [17th cent.], by R. M. Nance.

h The Redruth and Chacewater railway, by two old Cornwallites.

i Mock mayors in Cornwall, by W. T. Martin.

j A Cornish letter, 1711, from the Gwavas mss. [Oliver Pender to William Gwavas, about the Cornish of Edward Lhuyd], ed. R. M. Nance.

k Scraps from old maps [of Cornwall], by A. P. Jenkin.

l Cornish crosses in the Redruth district, by W. T. Martin.

m A true story of Tintagel [the imprisonment of John of Northampton, ex-mayor of London, 1384], by M. G. Pearse.

n Notes on old-time Camborne, by F. J. Stephens.

o Flint hunting in Camborne, by J. Thomas.

p John Keigwin's Cornish translation of Charles I's letter of thanks to the county of Cornwall [1643], by R. M. Nance.

[1] Not seen.

q Rowlandson in Cornwall, by J. A. D. Bridger.
r A market-day adventure in 1704 [John Sandys and a French privateer], by G. A. Kempthorne.
s The criss-cross-row, by R. M. Nance. [On rhymed alphabets]
t An old Cornish carol book [1797], by T. Miners.
u Some old names on Black-more, by C. Henderson.
v Quaint houses in Cornwall, by J. C. Hoare.
w Pendennis castle down to 1700, by W. T. Hooper.
x Street-names of Penzance, by S. C. Julyan.
y The gorsedd of Boscawen-un, by H. Jenner.
z The bounds of Zennor [1613], by C. Henderson.
aa A Cornish letter from John Boson to William Gwavas, 1710, ed. R. M. Nance.
bb Games at Manaccan, by F. J. Roskruge.
cc Lynchets in west Cornwall, by W. T. Martin.
dd The mummers' play in west Cornwall, by T. Miners.
ee A little Looe smuggling and a few Looe ghosts, by E. S. Shapcott.
ff Scilly under the Godolphins [16th–19th cent.], by J. E. Hooper.
gg Goon-Norman downs [and the stone circle there], by C. Henderson.
hh William Bottrell [writer, d. 1881] and some of his characters, by J. H. Rowe.
ii Billy Foss [of Land's End, early 19th cent.] and his fellow-rhymesters, by R. M. Nance.
jj Twelve Men's moor, by C. Henderson.
kk A St. Ives mackerel-boat, 1814, by R. M. Nance.
ll 'Garland day' at Looe, by Miss E. Hicks.
mm Wreckers at Mullion in the 18th cent., by Katharine N. Welman.
nn Two Cornish surnames [Tippet and Tripconey], by C. Henderson.
oo Some Looe customs and incidents of last century, by E. S. Shapcott.
pp Missing Cornish crosses, by C. Henderson.
qq Parlooe cross, by C. K. C. Andrew.
rr Recent discoveries in the Redruth district, by S. A. Opie.

1740 Vol. 2.
a Ralph Allen [d. 1764], by J. C. Hoare.
b 'Parson Hawker' of Morwenstow [Robert Stephen Hawker, vicar, 1834–75], by W. G. Harris.
c Remembrances of life on a farm, by W. J. Charke. [The routine and implements of a Cornish farm]
d Nicholas Boson and Richard Angwyn [17th cent.], by C. Henderson.
e Trewoof [the house and its owners, 13th–17th cent.], by Anne Pool.
f Daniel Gumb, the Cornish cave-man mathematician [d. 1777], by W. H. Paynter.
g Old fishing ways at Looe, by R. Pearce.
h The Langford charity [at St. Cleer], by E. Chirgwin.
i Notes taken in Zennor and Morvah [relating to wayside crosses and stones], by F. C. Hirst.
j Henry Quick, the Zennor poet [d. 1857], by W. H. Eva.
k An historic Cornish wreck: the loss of H.M.S. *Anson*, 1807, by C. K. C. Andrew.
l Elements of Cornish archaeology, by F. C. Hirst.
m Ancient stone circle at Duloe, by C. K. C. Andrew.
n Report on the underground passages at Weeth, Camborne, by C. A. R. Radford.
o St. Erth rood screen in Somerset, by C. K. C. Andrew.
p Notes on the Cornish priories, by G. A. Kempthorne.
q Bodanan [manor, in St. Teath], by Anne Pool.
r The probable parentage of Dorothy Pentreath [d. 1777], by W. T. Hoblyn.
s Domesday book and east Cornwall, by W. M. M. Picken.
t Rialton, by C. G. Henderson.
u Bishop Rock [lighthouse], by J. E. Hooper.

FIRST EDITION CLUB

Founded 1922, to serve the interests and convenience of bibliophiles.

Book Collector's Quarterly, nos. 1–12 (1900–33):

1741 No. 1.
a Robert Burton his book, by H. Jackson.
b Lord Birkenhead as book-collector, by J. V. Thompson.
c The Brotherton library [Leeds] and its founder, by J.W.

1742 No. 2.
a Verses on the death of Dr. Swift, by H. Davis.

1743 No. 3.
a Note on the first editions of *Manfred*, by J. C. Butterwick.

1744 No. 4.
a On collecting Jacobite books and prints, by T. Borenius.
b The old trumpeter of Liberty Hall [Dr. William King, principal of St. Mary Hall, Oxford, d. 1763, with a bibliography of his writings], by H. Williams.
c Music printing, 1473–1701, by D. Flower.

1745 No. 6.
a Notes on the early years of cloth binding, by J. Carter
b Publishers' binding: cloth, by W. Bowyer.
c Gothic script types in England, by A. F. Johnson.
d Ichabod Dawks [fl. 1680–1716] and his script type, by H. Carter.

1746 No. 7.
a Authors and copyright in the 19th cent., with unpublished letters from Wilkie Collins, by D. Flower.

1747 No. 8.
a The publications of the Sette of Odd Volumes, by V. Holland.

1748 No. 9.
a 18th cent. booksellers, by R. W. Chapman. [Notes additional to the English section in *A Dictionary of the Printers and Booksellers who were at work in England, Scotland and Ireland, 1726–75*, Bibliographical Soc. 1932]
b William Somerset Maugham: some bibliographical observations, by P. H. Muir. [Contd. in no. 10]

1749 No. 10.
a The first issue of *The Birmingham Gazette* [1741], by W. Bennett.
b Bibliography of the privately printed opuscula issued to members of the Sette of Odd Volumes, by V. Holland.

1750 No. 11.
a A man with a nose: George Augustus Sala [writer, d. 1896], by R. Straus.
b Jane Austen's library, by R. W. Chapman.
c Illustrated series of the 'nineties: the Cranford series, by T. Balston.

1751 No. 12.
a John Locke's library, by Helen C. Hughes.
b George Saintsbury: a check list, by W. Leuba.
c On collecting the *Vicar of Wakefield*, by H. T. Kirby.

Other publications:

1752 Bibliographical catalogue of the first loan exhibition of books and mss. held by the Club, 1922. 1922. [Includes a complete list of books illustrated by Hugh Thomson]
1753 A reply to Z [i.e. to a letter contributed anonymously (possibly by John Wilson) to *Blackwood's Magazine*,

Aug. 1818], by William Hazlitt, with introd. by C. Whibley. 1923.

1754 Bibliography of first editions of books by William Butler Yeats, comp. A. J. A. Symons. *P.* 1924.

1755 Bibliography of first editions of published and privately printed books and pamphlets by Austin Dobson, comp. A. Dobson, with preface by Sir E. Gosse. 1925.

1756 Bibliographical catalogue of Byron first editions, proof copies and mss. of books by Lord Byron exhibited at the fourth exhibition held by the Club, Jan. 1925. 1925.

1757 Twenty letters to Joseph Conrad, with introd. by G. Jean-Aubry. 12 *Ps.* 1926. [From Arnold Bennett, James Gibbons Huneker, Stephen Crane, Edw. Garnett, Geo. Gissing, Rudyard Kipling, Hen. James, H. G. Wells, Constance Garnett, E. V. Lucas, John Galsworthy]

1758 The Ravenna journal, by George Gordon Byron, 6th Lord Byron, mainly compiled in 1821 and now for the first time issued in book form, with introd. by Lord Ernle. 1928.

1759 Select bibliography of the principal modern presses, public and private, in Great Britain and Ireland, by G. S. Tomkinson, with introd. by B. H. Newdigate. 1928.

1760 Catalogue of the fifty books of the year 1928, selected and shown by the Club. *P.* 1929.

1761 Book clubs and printing societies of Great Britain and Ireland, by H. Williams. 1929. [Chiefly concerned with societies, etc., publishing in the fields of history and historical sources, literature, literary and religious texts, bibliography, and fine editions]

1762 Exhibition of the fifty best books, 1930. *P.* 1930.

1763 Catalogue of an exhibition of fifty books published during 1930 and selected by a committee of members of the Club. *P.* 1931.

1764 Catalogue of books, newspapers, etc., printed by John Bell, b. 1745, d. 1831, of *The British Library*, *The Morning Post, Bell's Weekly Messenger*, etc., and by John Browne Bell, b. 1779, d. 1855, son of the above, founder of *Bell's New Weekly Messenger, The News of the World*, etc., exhibited at the Club. 1931.

FLINTSHIRE HISTORICAL SOCIETY

Founded 1911, for the collection and publication of archaeological and historical information and materials relating to the county, and the excavation and preservation of the remains of antiquity and other objects of interest found in the county.

Publications, vols. 1-11 :

1765 Vol. 1. Flintshire: its history and records, by T. F. Tout. *P.* [1911].

1766 Vol. 2. Cilcain and its parish church, by F. Simpson. 1912.

1767 Vol. 3. Flintshire ministers' accounts, 1301-28, extracted from the accounts of the chamberlains of Chester and ed. A. Jones. 1913.

1768 Vol. 4.
 a The Glynnes of Hawarden, by W. E. B. Whittaker. [Originally published by the Chester and North Wales Archaeol. Soc., 1906]

b An index to wills proved at the peculiar court of Hawarden, and to miscellaneous papers relating to the same court (now at the St. Asaph court of probate), 1554-1800, comp. and ed. J. H. E. Bennett and P. H. Lawson. [1914. Also issued separately]

1769 Vol. 5. Journal, 1914-15.
 a Anian of Nanneu, O.F.P., prior of Rhuddlan, bishop of St. Asaph, 1268-93, by Ruth C. Easterling.
 b Dominican bishops of St. Asaph, by W. Gumbley.
 c The Dominican priory of Rhuddlan, by W. Gumbley.
 d William Fresney, O.P., archbishop of Rages (Edessa), 1263-90, by W. Gumbley.
 e The Dominican friary of Rhuddlan.
 f A 15th cent. document of Rhuddlan [an extent or list of burgesses and tenements, 1428], by A. Jones.
 g A Flintshire royal princess [Elizabeth, daughter of Edward I], by H. Taylor.

1770 Vol. 6. Journal, 1916-17.
 a Edward I and the co. of Flint, by J. E. Lloyd.
 b Altar plate in the church of St. Mary, Hawarden, by J. Timbrell.
 c The lords of Mold, by H. Taylor.
 d Hawarden grammar school, by W. B. Jones.
 e Articles for the surrender of Flint castle to the parliamentary forces, 1646, by H. Taylor.
 f Early 17th cent. sepulchral slab in Rhuddlan churchyard, by P. H. Lawson.

1771 Vol. 7. Journal, 1919-20.
 a The church of St. Mary Magdalene, Gwaenysgor, by A. W. Beer.
 b Altar plate in the church of St. John-the-Baptist, Hawarden, by W. F. J. Timbrell.
 c Hawarden deeds [15th cent.], by W. B. Jones.
 d The monastery of Basingwerk at the period of its dissolution, by E. Owen.
 e Note on 'Tegeingl', by M. J. Hughes from a lecture by H. Taylor.

1772 Vol. 8. Flint pleas, 1283-5, ed. J. G. Edwards. 1921.

1773 Vol. 9.
 a Sir George Wynne, bt., M.P. (Flint district boroughs, 1727-41), by H. Taylor, Miss V. H. Wynne-Eyton and W. B. Jones. [Contd. in vol. 11 by H. Taylor]
 b The palatinate of Chester and Flint. [The preface to Public Record Office *Lists and Indexes*, no. 40]
 c Petitions to Edward I by the burgesses of Flint, 1295-1300, by A. Jones.
 d Excursion to the castles of Flint, Ewloe and Hawarden. [Notes of address by H. Taylor]
 e Roman Flintshire, by M. V. Taylor, with a note on a road from St. Asaph to Holywell by W. J. Hemp.

1774 Vol. 10.
 a Flint excavation report, being an account of some trial trenches dug at Pentre, 1923, by D. Atkinson and M. V. Taylor. *P.* 1924.
 b Report on the excavations at Pentre, Flint, during 1924 by J. A. Petch and M. V. Taylor. *P.* 1925.

1775 Vol. 11.
 a Flintshire in Domesday book, by J. Tait.
 b An indenture of 1549 [grant to John, Earl of Warwick, of land in Axton and Picton], ed. M. J. Hughes.
 c Piers Mostyn the first, of Talacre [b. *c.* 1495], by Lord Mostyn.
 d Dyserth freeholders, 1291/2-1570, and other notes, by T. A. Glenn.
 e The arms of Flintshire, by H. Taylor.

f An early Flint deed [charter of Madoc Felauth, of Coleshill, to William, son of William of Doncaster, 1304].

g Ancient stained and painted glass in Flintshire, by W. B. Jones.

h An autobiography of John Boydell, engraver [d. 1804], ed. W. B. Jones.

i Flint borough election, 1697, by H. Taylor.

Record series, nos. 1–2:

1776 No. 1. Calendar of the Coleman deeds relating to Flint-shire [1384–1884], ed. J. G. Edwards. [1924? Reprinted from the National Library of Wales *Calendar of Deeds and Documents*, vol. i, 1921]

1777 No. 2. Flintshire ministers' accounts, 1328–53, ed. D. L. Evans. 1929.

FOLK-LORE SOCIETY

Founded 1878, for the systematic and comparative study of the oral culture and traditions of the folk, both as regards their origin and their present social functions.

Folk-Lore (incorporating the Archaeological Review and the Folk-Lore Journal), vols. 12–44 (1901–33):

1778 Vol. 12.

a Folklore notes from south-west Wilts. [chiefly Hill Deverill and Longbridge Deverill], by J. H. Powell.

b Folklore of Lincolnshire, by Mabel Peacock.

c Garland day at Castleton [Derbys.], by S. O. Addy.

1779 Vol. 13.

a Folklore notes from St. Briavels [Glos.], by L. M. Eyre.

b Stray notes on Oxfordshire folklore, comp. P. Manning. [Contd. in vol. 14]

c Folklore in the Kennet valley [Wilts.], by L. Salmon.

1780 Vol. 15.

a Notes on the Stamford [Lincs.] bull-running, by Mabel Peacock.

1781 Vol. 16.

a Folklore of the Wye valley, by Margaret Eyre.

b The legend of Merlin, by M. Gaster.

1782 Vol. 19.

a Local traditions of the Quantocks, by C. W. Whistler.

1783 Vol. 21.

a English charms of the 17th cent., by M. Gaster.

1784 Vol. 22.

a Hampshire folklore, by D. H. M. Read.

1785 Vol. 23.

a The game of 'thread the needle' and custom of church clipping, by Miss J. B. Partridge.

b 17th cent. cures and charms, by A. R. Wright.

c Cotswold place-lore and customs, by Miss J. B. Part-ridge.

d Guy Fawkes' day, by Charlotte S. Burne.

1786 Vol. 24.

a Oxfordshire village folklore, 1840–1900, by Angelina Parker. [Contd. in vol. 34]

b Ceremonial customs of the British gipsies, by T. W. Thompson.

c Breconshire village folklore, by M. E. Hartland.

1787 Vol. 25.

a 'Bringing in the fly', by P. Manning. [Additional note in vol. 26]

b Souling, clementing, and catterning: three November customs of the western midlands, by Charlotte S. Burne.

1788 Vol. 26.

a Catalogue of Brand material. [Notes on calendar customs for an intended new edition of Brand's *Popular Anti-quities*. Contd. in vols. 27–29]

1789 Vol. 27.

a Mabinogion, by J. Baudis. [On the arrangement of Welsh folk-tales]

b Examples of folk-memory from Staffordshire, by S. A. H. Burne.

c The folklore of Shakespeare, by H. B. Wheatley.

d Bibliography of the writings of Sir Laurence Gomme on anthropology and folklore, by Alice B. Gomme.

1790 Vol. 28.

a Organisations of witches in Great Britain, by Margaret A. Murray.

1791 Vol. 31.

a Witches and the number 13, by Margaret A. Murray.

b Folklore of Somerset, [by various contributors].

c Glastonbury and the Grail legend, by Mary A. Berkeley. [Additional note in vol. 33]

d The Derbyshire mumming play of 'St. George and the dragon'; or, as it is sometimes called, 'The Pace Egg', collected by Gwen John (1921).

1792 Vol. 37.

a St. Walstan, a Norfolk popular saint, by H. W. Howes.

1793 Vol. 39.

a Some folklore incidents in Shakespeare, by H. C. Lake.

b Besom wedding in the Ceiriog valley [and elsewhere], by W. R. Jones.

c Berkshire mummers' plays and other folklore, by S. Piggott.

1794 Vol. 40.

a Norfolk folklore, by M. R. Taylor.

b Mummers' plays from Berkshire, Derbyshire, Cumberland, and Isle of Man, by S. Piggott.

1795 Vol. 41.

a Mummers' plays from Middlesex, by L. F. Newman.

1796 Vol. 42.

a Precious stones in middle-English verse of the 14th cent., by I. P. J. Heather.

1797 Vol. 43.

a Frodsham soul-caking play, by M. W. Myres.

b English folk dances: their survival and revival, by Maud Karpeles, with note by Joan Evans.

c The murderers of St. Thomas Becket in popular tradition, by T. Borenius.

d Some notes on the folklore of upper Calderdale, by F. H. Marsden.

e An account of the Haxey hood game [1932], by Ethel H. Rudkin.

1798 Vol. 44.

a Iconographical peculiarities in English medieval ala-baster carvings, by W. L. Hildburgh.

b Lincolnshire folklore, by Ethel H. Rudkin.

County Folklore, vols. 2–7:

1799 Vol. 2. Examples of printed folklore concerning the North Riding of Yorkshire, York and the Ainsty, collected and ed. Eliza Gutch. 1901.

1800 Vol. 4. Examples of printed folklore concerning Northumberland, collected by Marie C. Balfour and ed. N. W. Thomas. 1904.

1801 Vol. 5. Examples of printed folklore concerning Lincolnshire, collected by Eliza Gutch and Mabel Peacock. 1908.

1802 Vol. 6. Examples of printed folk-lore concerning the East Riding of Yorkshire, collected and ed. Eliza Gutch. 1912.

Other publications:

1803 Bibliography of (anthropology and) folklore, 1905–7. Containing works published within the British Empire. Comp. N. W. Thomas. 3 vols. 1906–8. [Vols. ii–iii were published in conjunction with the Royal Anthropological Institute of Great Britain and Ireland]

1804 The handbook of folklore. New edn., revised and enlarged by Charlotte S. Burne. 1914. [Based on the edn. by Sir Laurence Gomme, 1890]

1805 Proverb literature: a bibliography of works relating to proverbs, ed. W. Bonser from materials left by T. A. Stephens. 1930.

1806 Jubilee congress of the Folk-Lore Society, 1928: papers and transactions. 1930.

  a English gypsy marriage and divorce rites, by T. W. Thompson.

  b Survivals of folk-belief in modern Wales, by T. G. Jones.

  c The fragments [of folklore] that are left in north-east Cornwall, by Barbara C. Spooner.

  d The Arthurian legend, by J. A. MacCulloch.

  e Animals in Manx folklore and song, by Mona Douglas

FRIENDS HISTORICAL SOCIETY

Founded 1903, for the publication of original document and articles on the history of Quakerism.

Journal, vols. 1–30 (1903–33):

1807 Vol. 1.

  a The handwriting of George Fox, by I. Sharp.

  b Our recording clerks. 1: Ellis Hookes, *c.* 1657–81, by N. Penney.

  c The case of William Gibson [d. 1734], by I. Sharp and N. Penney.

  d The Quaker family of Owen, by J. J. Green.

  e William Dewsbury and John Whitehead to George Fox 1654, by I. Sharp and N. Penney.

  f Contemporary account of the last illness and death of George Fox never before published, by J. J. Green.

  g Our recording clerks. 2: Richard Richardson, 1681–9, by N. Penney.

  h Abstract of the journal of Edmund Peckover's travels in North America and Barbados [1742–3].

1808 Vol. 2.

  a Letter of Margaret Fox to her daughters Sarah and Susanna, 1677, by I. Sharp.

  b Meetings in Yorkshire, 1668.

  c Remarks on letter in cypher from Francis Howgill to George Fox [1654], by J. G. Birch.

  d The settlement of London yearly meeting [1654–1904].

  e Joseph Rule, the Quaker in white [d. 1770], by J. J. Green.

  f Edmund Peckover, ex-soldier of the Commonwealth and Quaker, by E. Josephine Penrose.

  g Extracts from the bishop of Chester's visitation for 1665, relating to Friends, by W. F. Irvine. [Contd. in vol. 3]

  h Will of Margaret Fox [d. 1702].

1809 Vol. 3.

  a Disused [Friends'] burial grounds in south Yorkshire, by C. Brady.

  b David Lloyd [d. 1731], by J. S. Walton.

  c King's briefs, the forerunners of mutual insurance societies, by J. Cadbury.

  d Memoirs of Barbara Hoyland [d. 1829], addressed to her children.

  e 'Esquire Marsh' [Richard Marsh, d. 1672], by J. J. Green.

1810 Vol. 4.

  a Our bibliographers. 1: John Whiting, 1656–1722, by I. Sharp.

  b American letters of Edmund Peckover [1742–3].

  c Friends at Newbury, Berks., by W. H. Summers.

  d Presentations of Quakers in episcopal visitations, 1662–1679, by G. L. Turner. [Contd. in vols. 5–7, 10–16, 18, and 25]

  e Quaker allusions in the diary of Samuel Pepys. [Contd. in vols. 5–6]

  f William Hitchcock to John and Amy Harding, 1687, by G. Cope. [Letter]

  g An unpublished letter of Hannah Penn, née Callowhill, second wife of William Penn, addressed to Thomas Story [1715], by J. J. Green.

  h Early meetings in Nottinghamshire, by Emily Manners.

1811 Vol. 5.

  a Westmorland and Swaledale seekers in 1651, by W. C. Braithwaite.

  b Extracts from the minute book of the sufferings of Friends in Mansfield and the surrounding district, by Emily Manners.

  c Reminiscences of the Friends' meeting, Manchester [early 19th cent.].

  d A glimpse of ancient Friends in Dorset, by Elizabeth B. Rutter.

  e Some Quaker teachers in 1736, by W. E. A. Axon.

  f Records respecting John and Margaret Lynam in England and Maryland [fl. 1670].

  g Richard Cubham of Bickerstaffe, yeoman [d. 1709].

  h The defection of John Scanfield [fl. 1686].

1812 Vol. 6.

  a Quakerism in the Isle of Man [1664–71].

  b Meetings in Ely, Cambridge and Huntingdon, 1668.

  c The Somerby estate, the chief endowed property of the quarterly meeting of Leicester and Rutland, by Mary Radley and Henrietta Ellis.

  d Captain Thomas Taylor, of Brighouse, co. York, yeoman [d. 1684], by J. J. Green.

  e A short account of John Reckless [d. 1679] and his family, by Emily Manners.

  f George Fox's knowledge of Hebrew, by Mary G. Swift.

  g The Quakers in Greystoke parish, Cumb. by J. H. Colligan.

1813 Vol. 7.

  a Correspondence of Anne, Viscountess Conway, 'Quaker Lady', 1675, by J. J. Green.

  b Letters to William Penn, from Worcester prison, 1674.

  c Early Friends at Poulner, Hants, by H. W. Sanders.

  d Notes on American descendants of John Reckless [d. 1679], of Nottingham, by J. Emlen.

1814 Vol. 8.

  a Our bibliographers. 2: Morris Birkbeck, 1736–1816, by I. Sharp.

  b A school [conducted by Quakers] in Ilchester jail, 1662.

  c William Dewsbury, to Margaret Fell, 1655. [Letter]

d Alexander Parker [d. 1688/9], by D. Abbatt.
e Joseph Green (1690–1740), the friend of Thomas Story, by J. J. Green.
f Vision seen by Thomas Richardson in Wisbech jail, 1663.
g Ancient simplicity [concerning the families of Hiron and Tydmarsh in the 17th cent.].
h Friends in Danby dale, Yorkshire.
i Sydney Parkinson [c. 1745–71] and his drawings, by W. F. Miller.
j Notes on the life of Edmond Waller [fl. 1698], by Evelyn Roberts.
k Minutes concerning William Penn's declaration of intention of marriage, and the marriage of George Fox [1669], by A. N. Brayshaw.
l Extracts relating to Friends [1654–8] from the *State Papers* of John Thurloe, by Elsie M. Smith.

1815 Vol. 9.

a The American journey of George Fox, 1671–3, from a ms. in the Bodleian Library.
b Thirnbeck mss. [Letters of Fell family, 1654–1720]
c The Cambridge edition of *The Journal of George Fox*. [Addenda and corrigenda. Contd. in vols. 10–17, 19–24, 26, 28, and 30]
d Divine guidance. [Incidents in the life of Thomas Wagstaffe, d. 1802]
e Some expenses of a northern counties yearly meeting held in Lancashire in 1786, by D. Abbatt.
f *The dying words of Ockanickon.* [A tract of 1682]
g Calendar of contents of a volume known as 'Bristol mss. v.' [Letters and papers of George Fox and other early Friends]
h Extracts from State Papers Domestic, 1664–9, by A. Gordon.

1816 Vol. 10.

a Margaret Meakins [d. 1692], and the plague of London, by J. J. Green.
b Documents relating to James Nayler [d. 1660].
c Early Friends on the eastern shore of Virginia.
d A literary circle in Sheffield in 1816: extract from a letter by Sarah Smith of Sheffield to her sister, Rebecca Shorthouse of Birmingham.
e [Letters to Sarah Smith, 1813–29].
f Notes relating to Elizabeth Heath, of Mansfield [d. 1693], foundress of Heath's charity, by Emily Manners.
g Letters to Daniel Wheeler [Quaker missionary] from his family in Russia, 1832–3.
h Dr. Lettsom's rural fete at Grove Hill, Camberwell [1801], by J. J. Green.
i Extracts from the diary of Abiah Darby [1716–94. Contd. in vol. 26]
j Women writers among Friends of the 17th cent. and later.
k Account of an early business journey of John Hill Lovell, 1822.
l An account of ministering Friends from Europe who visited America, 1656–1793.
m The conversion of Joseph Phipps [of York, d. 1787].
n George Fox to William Penn, 1674–8. [Letters. Contd. in vol. 11]
o John Matern [c. 1640–80], schoolmaster.
p Richard Shackleton to Abiah Darby, 1784. [Letter]
q Record of Friends travelling in Ireland, 1655–1765. [Contd. for 1756–1861 in vols. 15 and 16]
r Thomas Bennet [d. 1764], schoolmaster, of Pickwick, Wilts.
s A Stuart [Jane Stuart, d. 1742] among the Quakers, by Mabel R. Brailsford.
t Friends in Nova Scotia, 1785. [Correspondence between Friends of London and Philadelphia]

1817 Vol. 11.

a Our bibliographers. 3: Joseph Smith, 1819–96, by I. Sharp.
b Sad news from Virginia, 1674. [Letter referring to Friends from Bristol]
c Women's meetings in Cornwall in the early days of the Society, by R. H. Fox.
d Joseph Rule, the Quaker in white, by R. H. Fox.
e Nathaniel Wilmer (c. 1650–1711), Quaker merchant and shipowner of London, and friend of William Penn; with some account of his bible, by J. J. Green.
f Benjamin Furly [d. 1716], Quaker merchant, and his statesmen friends, by C. R. Simpson.
g Benjamin Furly and his library, by C. R. Simpson.
h Visions of John Adam, 1712.
i George Fox to Margaret Fox, from Worcester and London, 1673–4. [Letters]
j Friends in Montgomeryshire. [Meeting houses and burial grounds]
k A journey of Margaret Fox into Yorkshire, 1672.
l Abraham manuscripts [relating to Fell family, 1653–1712].
m Friends in Radnorshire. [Meeting houses and burial grounds]
n George IV and Thomas Shillitoe, by F. C. Clayton. [See also vol. 13 under title 'Standing before kings']
o Stockton meeting house, 1814–1914, by J. W. Steel.

1818 Vol. 12.

a Mercy Ransom, née Bell, 1728–1811, of London, Croydon, and Hitchin, by J. J. Green.
b Friends in Denbighshire. [Meeting houses and burial grounds]
c Isabel Yeamans [fl. 1664–1704], by Charlotte F. Smith.
d Certificate granted to Daniel Wheeler, jun., by Emperor Nicholas I, 1840.
e Reminiscences of William Forster and Stephen Grellet [1845–54], by J. L. Baily.
f William Hobson, of Markfield, Tottenham, 1752–1840, the Quaker builder of the Martello towers, etc., by J. J. Green.
g Elizabeth Hooton [d. 1672], by W. C. Braithwaite.
h John Whiting and Sarah Hurd [1683–1722], by M. Ethel Crawshaw.
i Description of a dinner party at Woburn Abbey attended by Queen Victoria [1841].
j John Bellers [d. 1725]—lost and found, by I. Sharp.
k John Bellers in official minutes, by C. R. Simpson.
l Deputation to Queen Victoria on her accession.
m The Barnes family of Cumberland, by I. Sharp.
n Burton [or Monk Bretton] burial ground, south Yorkshire.

1819 Vol. 13.

a Some incidents in the life of John Salkeld, 1672–1739.
b Notices relating to Friends in the *Gentleman's Magazine*, 1731–89, by J. J. Green. [Contd. in vols. 15, 16, and 27]
c Richard Smith and his journal, 1817–24, by J. D. Crosfield. [Contd. in vol. 14]
d Elizabeth Fry to Alderman Wood, M.P. [Letters, 1825]
e Dr. Fothergill to Henry Zouch, 1778. [Letter]
f Two 18th cent. pocket-books. [Diaries of Sarah Fox and John Storer]

1820 Vol. 14.

a Note on some early records of Quakers near Harrogate [17th–18th cent.], by W. J. Kaye.
b Two letters from David Livingstone [1858–60].
c Notes on the travels of Aaron Atkinson in America, 1698–99.
d Elizabeth Robson [d. 1843], by J. J. Green.

e Richard Lindley [d. 1785] and his writings.

f A private view of London yearly meetings in sessions of 1818 and 1825.

g Life and writings of Charles Leslie, M.A., non-juring divine. [Review of a life of this opponent of Quakerism, d. 1722]

h Michael Yoakley's charity [London and Margate], by R. H. Marsh.

i Friends in Carmarthenshire, by G. E. Evans. [Meeting houses and burial grounds]

j William Jenkyn [d. 1685, of Christchurch and St. Anne's, Blackfriars, London], ejected minister.

k The family of Flounders.

1821 Vol. 15.

a An Irishman at London yearly meeting in 1794. [Extracts from the diary of John Lecky, of Cork, d. 1839]

b Diary of James Backhouse, 1747–52.

c Travels of William Baldwin in America, 1709.

d [Letters to and from William Cowper]

e St. Albans meeting: notes on the past, by E. Marsh.

f Notes on the family of Roger Haydock [d. 1696].

g Bracy Clark, F.L.S., 1771–1860.

h Nathaniel Morgan and the Duke of Gloucester, 1822, by Margaret Sefton-Jones.

i 'Concerned in ye late warre.' [Censure on a Friend, from the Somersetshire quarterly meeting books, 1685. Two similar cases are described in vol. 12]

j A tract attributed to George Fox, by Margaret E. Hirst.

1822 Vol. 16.

a Letters of Hilary Prach and John G. Matern [1676].

b The journey [to London and Yorkshire] of John and Anna Perry [of Ipswich] in 1789.

c John Harrison [of Liverpool] at London yearly meeting in 1789.

d John Howard on Ackworth [Quaker] school [1789].

e Records [1761–1821] of James Jenkins.

f Wedding dresses in 1765.

g 'London yearly meeting during 250 years.' [Additions to the volume of addresses]

h London yearly meeting in 1833.

i Bail-dock (or bale-dock), by A. N. Brayshaw.

j Isaac Blackbeard and his 'Book of Three Leaves', 1783, by J. T. Sewell.

k Glimpses of family life in 1832 [from the journal compiled (? by Ralph Neild) while travelling with John Wilbur].

l 'The Beacon', ed. J. E. Clark. [Letters of James Clark of Street, Somerset, 1835]

m The Rev. Colonel John Wigan [fl. 1649–65], by W. T. Whitley.

n Wilkinson-Storyism in Wiltshire, c. 1680, by R. Barrow.

1823 Vol. 17.

a Schooldays [at Rochester] in the twenties: a reminiscence for my grandchildren, by C. Tylor, 1895, with additional notes. [Contd. in vol. 18]

b John Thomas of Bristol [d. 1827] and the Kennet and Avon canal.

c Foreshadowings of Quakerism.

d John Bellers and his work, by C. R. Simpson.

e A vision [by Joseph Fry, of Bristol, d. 1787].

f The remarkable religious experience of Edmund Gurney, of Norwich, 1723–96.

g London yearly meeting, 1836. [Extracts from letters by John Southall, d. 1862]

h Notes on the life of Emma Marshall [d. 1899].

i Benjamin Huntsman, 1704–76, and the casting of steel.

1824 Vol. 18.

a Devonshire House reference library, with notes on early printers and printing in the Society of Friends, by Anna L. Littleboy. [Also issued separately, 1921]

b The theatre and Barclay's 'Apology'. [From the ms. journal of Joseph Woods, 1805]

c 'First publishers of truth' in Norwich: A booke of ye sufferings of the people of God cald Quakers in the citty of Norwich [1654].

d Public Friends in business: letter [1738] from David Hall [of Skipton] to James Wilson of Kendal.

e The third marriage of William Allen, F.R.S., 1827. [Contd. in vol. 19]

f The father [John Taylor, d. 1817] of the founder of the *Manchester Guardian*, by J. W. Graham.

g London yearly meeting, 1838.

h Warner Mifflin [of Virginia, d. 1798] refused certificates for London yearly meeting.

i Burial in woollen.

j Nicholas Naftel, 1762–1842.

1825 Vol. 19.

a A Pennsylvania loyalist's interview with George III. [1784. From ms. diary of Samuel Shoemaker]

b The case of William Batkin [court-martialled as a 'conscientious objector', 1841]

c The convincement of John Coughen, 1663.

d Treffry, of Devon and Cornwall.

e Leading the way, being a series of brief sketches of Quaker inventions and of Friends who led the way in various directions. [Contd. in vols. 20, 22–24]

f Edward Haistwell's diary of the travels of George Fox, 1677–8.

g The first publishers of truth—a study, by E. E. Taylor.

h On behalf of the king, 1745. [Letter from Thomas Savage, of Clifton, Westmld., describing the retreat of Prince Charles Edward]

i Journal of William Robson. [Extracts, 1817–18]

1826 Vol. 20.

a Visit of Priscilla Green [d. 1877] to Lord Mount Edgcumbe, by J. J. Green.

b Joseph Sams, schoolmaster, bookseller and virtuoso [d. 1860], by N. Penney.

c A few remarks on the Society of Friends at St. Austell, Cornwall, by Elizabeth Fardon.

d Letters [1772–6] from Joseph Gurney to Joseph Gurney Bevan.

e Reflections on London women's y[early] m[eeting], 1826. [Letter from Margaret Crosfield]

1827 Vol. 21.

a George Fox and 16th cent. bibles, by H. J. Cadbury.

b 'The Forty Five.' [Extracts from letters, 1745–6]

c Early 19th cent. evangelism.

d 'Every man at Nature's table has a right to elbow-room.' George Harrison [of Wandsworth] to David Holt [of Manchester], 1819.

e Gleanings from minute books of the quarterly meeting of Sussex [1668–1803], by Maude Robinson.

f A Quaker newswriter. [Richard Cockin, d. 1845. Contd. in vols. 22, 23 and 26]

g Establishment of the meeting for sufferings, 1676 [in London].

h Diary of a London Quaker apprentice [Edward Binyon], 1765–8.

i B. Kaye's journal to and at ye yearly meeting, London, 1787.

j Northern yearly meeting, 1777. [Letter from Joseph King]

1828 Vol. 22.

a Friends and the French prophets [in England, early 18th cent.].

b The Quaker family of Bevan.
c The Gurneys of Lakenham grove [Norwich].
d On turning plain. [Extracts from late 18th cent. journals, etc., about Quaker dress]
e Quakerism in Staffordshire.
f Dorothy Ripley [d. 1831], unaccredited missionary. [Contd. in vol. 23]
g Anecdotes of Benjamin Lay [d. 1759].
h Joseph Woods to William Matthews. [Letters, 1786–99]

1829 Vol. 23.

a The story of a great literary venture [1727–55, concerning abstracts of the sufferings of Friends].
b Bridewell hospital and James Nayler [1657–9].
c Yearly meeting at Longtown, 1780.
d Friends' meeting house in Bristol about 1850.
e The Reed family, with special reference to Rachel Reed [d. 1845], her visitors, and her friendship with Stephen Grellet.

1830 Vol. 24.

a A Darlington schoolboy's diary [kept by Thomas Whitwell, 1827–8].
b Another literary venture: Anthony Purver's translation of the bible, 1764.
c London yearly meeting, 1779.
d Two Lincoln worthies [Robert Craven, fl. 1656–70; Abraham Morrice, fl. 1672–1705]
e Excerpts from journal of William Savery, relating to Swarthmoor meeting and Swarthmoor Hall [1797], ed. F. R. Taylor.

1831 Vol. 25.

a William Sewel to William Penn, 1696. [Letter]
b An old time Quaker stenographer [Laurence Steel, d. *c.* 1684], by W. J. Carlton.
c The Brewin brothers of Cirencester [Robert, b. 1805; Thomas, b. 1809; William, b. 1813], by W. S. Harmer. [Reprinted from the *Wilts and Gloucestershire Standard*]
d The life of Joseph Metford, 1776–1863. [Extracts from his autobiography]
e Aldam manuscripts. [Extracts from 17th cent. Quaker mss. Contd. in vol. 26]
f Friends and the Emperor Alexander. [Letters from Thomas Clarkson to his wife, 1814, describing the Czar's visit to a London Quaker meeting]
g Thomas Curtis to Mary Fisher, 1655. [Letters]

1832 Vol. 26.

a An account of the birth, education, and sufferings for the truth's sake of that faithful Friend, Elizabeth Andrews [d. 1718].
b Letter from Richard Hubberthorne concerning George Fox and James Nayler [addressed to Margaret Fell, 1656].
c Death of the Emperor Alexander. [Letter from Daniel Wheeler to Thomas Shillitoe, 1826]
d Elizabeth Fry and the convict ships. [Letter to James Backhouse, 1832]
e Letters of William Forster of Tottenham [1775–8. Contd. in vol. 27].
f Durham county Friends' school. [Extracts from minutes, 1809–31]
g Elizabeth Fry—'Public property'. [A letter, 1841, on the unauthorized publication of a book]
h John Audland to George Fox, 1654. [Letter]
i Loss by fire: a brotherly appeal [to assist victims of a fire near Newbury, Berks., 1699].

1833 Vol. 27.

a Our recording clerks: Benjamin Bealing, 1689–1737;

Benjamin Bourne, 1737–46, 1748–57; Joseph Besse, 1746–8.
b Extracts from the A. R. Barclay mss. [17th cent. letters, including several to George Fox. Contd. in vols. 28 and 31]
c An original letter of Thomas Carlyle [discussing the relative interest for biographical study of the lives of George Fox and John (or Robert) Lilburne].
d Stephenson, of Westmorland and Cumberland.
e George Fox and James Nayler.
f Historians criticized. [Letters from David Hume and Thomas Leland to Elizabeth and Richard Shackleton of Ballitore, 1770–3]
g 'Finch versus Batger.' Do religious acts constitute worship? [An account of the suit of Henry Finch of Reading, d. 1805, upon his expulsion from a quarterly meeting]
h Sir Walter Scott to Mary Leadbeater, 1811. [Letter referring to his poetry]
i Discipline beyond sea, 1668. [Instructions, presumably by George Fox]
j History of 'The Quiet Hour' [the painting by B. R. Haydon], by J. L. Nichalls.

1834 Vol. 28.

a George Fox's library, by J. L. Nichalls.
b Our recording clerks: Jacob Post, 1757; Robert Bell, 1757–9; William Weston, 1759–73; Thomas Gould 1773–83; John Ady, 1783–1811.
c London yearly meeting, 1753.
d Extracts from the journal of Joseph Fry, 1833–57.
e Thomas Shillitoe's interview with William IV and his queen [1832].
f Elizabeth Fry in Newgate.

1835 Vol. 29.

a Quakerism on moor and wold. [Address by Arthur Rowntree, based on Quaker records of Scarborough and Whitby, 1669–1786]
b The Gurney mss. [Selections from a collection of letters, 1750–1850, dealing with literature, politics, and social reform. Contd., with reference to the Gurneys of Keswick, 1771–5, in vol. 30]
c Our recording clerks: William Manley, 1811–44.
d George Fell and the story of Swarthmoor Hall, by N. Penney. [Contd. in vol. 30]
e George Fox's library: further identifications, by H. J. Cadbury. [Contd. in vol. 30]
f New light on Fanny Henshaw's convincement, by S. Hobhouse.

1836 Vol. 30.

a Our recording clerks: James Bowden, 1844–57, and the era of the registers.
b Luke Howard on early travel by rail [1833-42].
c Scrivener Alsop and the Friends' school and workhouse [Clerkenwell, 1778–83].
d 'Pen pictures of London yearly meeting, 1789–1833': corrections and additions. [See no. 1845 below]

Supplements, nos. 1–17:

1837 Nos. 1–5. 'The first publishers of truth', being early records (now first printed) of the introduction of Quakerism into the counties of England and Wales, ed. N. Penney with introd. by T. Hodgkin. 1907 [1904–7].

1838 No. 6. John ap John [d. 1697] and early records of Friends in Wales, comp. W. G. Norris, ed. N. Penney 1907.

1839 No. 7. Thomas Pole, M.D. [d. 1829], by E. T. Wedmore, with notes by N. Penney. 1908.

1840 Nos. 8–11. Extracts from state papers relating to Friends, ed. N. Penney, with introd. by R. A. Roberts. 1910–13. [1st series: 1654–8. 2nd, 3rd, and 4th series: 1659–72. See article by G. L. Turner in *Journal*, vol. 10]

1841 No. 12. Elizabeth Hooton, first Quaker woman preacher, 1600–72, by Emily Manners, with notes by N. Penney. 1914.

1842 No. 13. Tortola: a Quaker experiment in the tropics, by C. F. Jenkins. 1923.

1843 No. 14. Record of the sufferings of Quakers in Cornwall, 1655–86, transcribed and ed. N. Penney, with introd. by L. Violet Hodgkin (Mrs. J. Holdsworth). 1928.

1844 No. 15. Quaker language, by T. E. Harvey. *P.* 1928.

1845 Nos. 16–17. Pen pictures of London yearly meeting, 1789–1833, being extracts from the notes of Richard Cockin, James Jenkins and others, ed. N. Penney, with introd. by T. E. Harvey. 1929–30. [For corrections and additions see no. 1836d above]

1846 No. 18. Psychical experiences of Quaker ministers, collected by J. W. Graham, introd. by F. E. Pollard. *P.* 1933.

FRIENDS OF CANTERBURY CATHEDRAL

Founded 1927, to bind together all who love Canterbury cathedral and desire to take some part in preserving it for posterity.

First–Sixth Annual Report (1928–33):

1847 1st Report.
a The water tower, by C. Cotton.

1848 2nd Report.
a The badge in heraldry and in the cathedral.
b The water tower, by W. D. Caroë. [Reprinted as Canterbury Papers, no. 1. *P.* 1929]

1849 3rd Report.
a Canterbury cathedral: the chapel of All Saints, by W. D. Caroë.
b Edward the Black Prince.

1850 4th Report.
a King Henry IV.

1851 5th Report.
a Christ Church gateway, with some account of the royal, noble and knightly families whose arms are carved thereon.
b Priory of Christ Church, Canterbury: monks and their books.

1852 6th Report.
a Canterbury cathedral north transept window, by B. Rackham.
b Notes on royal and primatial autographs [of Edward V, Princess Elizabeth of York, Henry VII, and Archbishop Bourchier].
c The Canterbury psalter and its parent, the Utrecht psalter, by M. R. James.
d Canterbury cathedral tapestries at Aix-en-Provence.

1853 Index to Annual Reports, 1928–32. *P.* [Issued with Sixth Annual Report, 1933]

1854 Index to Annual Reports, 1933–7. *P.* [Issued with Tenth Annual Report, 1937]

Canterbury Cathedral Chronicle, nos. 1–16 (1928–33):

1855 No. 1.
a The 700th anniversary of Archbishop Stephen Langton.

1856 No. 5.
a St. Thomas of Canterbury: the man and the martyr.

1857 No. 7.
a Hubert Walter, 1141–1205: priest, lawyer, soldier, statesman, archbishop.

1858 No. 8.
a The times of Prior Henry of Eastry, 1284–1331.

1859 No. 9.
a Archbishop Simon Sudbury: a tragedy of Tower Hill.

1860 No. 11.
a Some famous pilgrims to Canterbury [13th–14th cent.].

1861 No. 12.
a The care of old buildings, by Sir C. Peers.

1862 No. 13.
a Archbishop Warham and his tomb.
b William Warham, archbishop of Canterbury, 1503–32. [Extracts from an address by C. Jenkins]

1863 No. 14.
a The death of King Edward IV, April 9th, 1483.
b The Reculver columns [in Canterbury cathedral].

1864 No. 16.
a Simon Mepham, archbishop of Canterbury, 1328–33.
b William Laud, translated to the archbishopric of Canterbury, Sept. 19th, 1633, beheaded at Westminster, Jan. 10th, 1645. [With an address by T. G. Gardiner]

1865 Index to Canterbury Cathedral Chronicle, nos. 1–12. *P.* [Issued with Sixth Annual Report, 1933].

Canterbury Papers, nos. 1–3:

1866 No. 2. The Warriors' chapel and the Buffs, by F. W. Tomlinson. *P.* 1929.

1867 No. 3. On the burning and repair of the church of Canterbury, 1174, from the Latin of Gervase, a monk of the priory of Christ Church, Canterbury, ed. C. Cotton. *P.* 1929. [2nd edn. 1932].

GEOGRAPHICAL ASSOCIATION

Founded 1893, to help teachers and citizens to appreciate the life of peoples in all regions of the world and to study the physical setting of that life in past and present.

Geographical Teacher, vols. 1–13, *contd. as* Geography, vols. 14–18 (1901–33):

1868 Vol. 1.
a Physical conditions and exploration as illustrated by Australia, by A. W. Andrews.

1869 Vol. 3.
a Orography and history, by E. W. Dann.

1870 Vol. 4.
a The economic historical geography of a county, illustrated by Essex and Cumberland, by Nora E. Mac-Munn.

b Hints towards teaching the historical geography of Britain, by H. J. Snape.

c Historical geography of East Anglia. 1: The western borders, by P. M. Roxby. [Contd. in vol. 5]

1871 Vol. 5.

a Exchanges of products between the New and the Old Worlds [and the rôle of Englishmen in developing chinchona and rubber plantations], by Sir C. R. Markham.

b Roads to the north [from London], by J. Fairgrieve.

c Geography of early London, by G. L. Gomme.

1872 Vol. 6.

a Highways of England [a survey from prehistoric times], by G. Montagu.

b The fenland [an historical survey of its drainage], by W. J. Willcock.

1873 Vol. 7.

a Suggestions for investigations in human geography in Britain, by H. J. Fleure and W. E. Whitehouse.

b The docks of London, by J. W. Page.

c Agricultural geography of England on a regional basis. Pt. 1, by P. M. Roxby [with particular reference to the works of William Marshall, agriculturist, d. 1818]. Pt. 2: Yorkshire, by E. Marjorie Ward. [Contd. in vol. 8]

d Prehistoric primitive man in Western Europe, by J. Fairgrieve.

1874 Vol. 8.

a Agricultural geography of England on a regional basis. 3: Staffordshire, by A. Angelbeck. [Contd. in vol. 9]

b Historical geography of the Weald as exemplified round Tonbridge, by Mabel S. Elliott.

c Historical geography of the west country woollen industry, by R. H. Kinvig.

d The Cinque ports and their coastline, by E. Marjorie Ward.

1875 Vol. 9.

a Sites of old cathedral cities of England and Wales, by Rachel M. Fleming.

1876 Vol. 10.

a 13th cent. town planning in Salisbury, by L. M. Hardy.

b Geographical position of Chester [and its development since the Roman period], by F. T. Howard.

c Place names of the Empire, by Sir C. Lucas.

d A regional study of north east England, by C. B. Fawcett.

e Monmouthshire as a border county, by E. Chivers.

1877 Vol. 11.

a Forms of mediaeval settlements in England, by W. Page.

b Iron industry of South Wales, by A. E. Trueman.

c Evolution of the south west [of England], by W. S. Lewis.

d London and Westminster contrasted, by Hilda Ormsby. [A study of geographical influences upon the determination of the sites]

1878 Vol. 12.

a Influence of geographical factors on agricultural activities of a population [in Britain], by Sir J. Russell.

b Types and materials of houses in England, by H. Batsford.

c Gloucester, by F. T. Howard. [The development of the city from the Roman period]

d The island [of Britain] and the Empire, by Sir C. P. Lucas.

e British climate in historic times, by Sir R. Gregory.

f Ancient maritime trade of Exeter, by W. S. Lewis.

1879 Vol. 13.

a Voyage de Guernsey à Rome pour le jubilé, 1500, by S. Harris. [The route of a pilgrimage made by some Guernsey men. In English]

b Pontefract, by E. W. Gilbert.

c Some sources for the history of exploration, by J. N. L. Baker.

d A study of rural settlements in south-west Wales, by E. G. Bowen.

e Regional surveys [of Britain: a list of institutions having materials].

f Short bibliography of the county of Hertford, by Mary S. Aslin.

g Critical analysis of the census returns of Merthyr Tydfil area, by A. Davies. [Fluctuations in population, 1801–1921]

h The Highland openfield system [and its evolution], by Isabel F. Grant.

i Bibliography of Hampshire basin with special reference to Southampton, ed. O. H. T. Rishbeth.

1880 Vol. 14.

a Aspects of the development of Merseyside [from the 13th cent.], by P. M. Roxby.

b Geography of settlements in south-west Lancashire, by H. King.

c Bibliography of Staffordshire with a list of maps, by C. E. Redmill.

d Geographic background to the Roman occupation of Britain, by J. Holmes.

e Early settlements in the upper Thames basin, by E. Thurlow Leeds.

1881 Vol. 15.

a Tinplate migration in the Vale of Neath [chiefly in the 19th cent.]: a study in economic geography, by H. C. Darby.

b Norwich and its region [a brief historical account].

c Skipton—a study in site value [from the Roman period], by A. and S. E. Raistrick.

d Geographical aspects of administrative areas, by H. J. E. Peake. [An inquiry into the relations between administrative areas and geographical features in England]

e The paper-making industry in Somerset [from the 18th cent.], by W. W. Jervis and S. J. Jones.

f Some aspects of the development of Tees-side [from the 19th cent.], by K. H. Edwards.

1882 Vol. 16.

a Newhaven and Seaford: a study in the diversion of a river mouth [from the 16th cent.], by F. G. Morris.

b Some intimate Bristol connections with the overseas Empire, by E. W. Lennard.

c Growth of population in the east Warwickshire coalfield [1801–1921], by C. E. Redmill.

d Historical geography of Bristol, by S. J. Jones.

1883 Vol. 17.

a Some medieval sources for the study of historical geography [with particular reference to Sussex], by R. A. Pelham.

b Early Christianity in the British Isles: a study in historical geography, by E. G. Bowen.

1884 Vol. 18.

a The Fylde [Lancashire: an historical account of the agricultural development of the region], by R. E. Thompson.

b Wareham [a brief historical account].

GILBERT WHITE FELLOWSHIP

Founded 1918, to continue the work of Gilbert White in the study of natural history and antiquities.

Pamphlets, nos. 1–7:

1885 No. 1. Inaugural meeting. [Includes: Blackfriars, a note by the way, by W. Martin] *P.* 1918.

1886 No. 2. The Rev. Gilbert White as a botanist, by Sir D· Prain. *P.* 1923.

1887 No. 3. The Rev. Gilbert White and moral history, by Sir D. Prain. *P.* 1924.

1888 No. 5. In Gilbert White's time, by Sir A. D. Hall. *P.* 1927. [On life at Oxford and the English countryside in the 18th cent.]

1889 No. 7. Since Gilbert White—two centuries of change, by Sir E. J. Russell. *P.* 1932. [On changes in scientific method]

Extra publication:

1890 Catalogue of exhibition commemorating the bicentenary of Gilbert White, 1720–1920, held at 6, Queen Square, W.C., Sept., 1920. *P.* 1920.

GLAMORGAN SOCIETY, LONDON

Founded 1902?, to foster interest in the history and the traditions of the county and principality.

Historical Sketches of Glamorgan: papers read before the Society, 2 vols. (1907–12):

1891 Vol. 1.
  a Morgannurg [Glamorganshire] in Tudor times, by Sir D. Brynmor-Jones.
  b A hero of Glamorgan [Phillip Jones, d. 1674], by W. Ll. Williams.
  c Another hero of Glamorgan [Sir Thomas Morgan, d. *c.* 1679], by W. Ll. Williams.
  d Early history of the see of Llandaff, by D. Bryant.

1892 Vol. 2.
  a The marcher lordship of Glamorgan, by D. Bryant.
  b Glamorgan in the times of the civil wars, by J. L. Phillips.
  c A Glamorgan worthy of the 18th cent. [the Rev. Richard Price, d. 1791], by H. Prosser.
  d Sir Henry Morgan, buccaneer [d. 1688], by J. L. Phillips.

GLASTONBURY ANTIQUARIAN SOCIETY

Founded 1886, for the establishment and support of a museum at Glastonbury.

Publications:

1893 Proceedings for 1904 (1906).
  a The village of Street, by W. S. Clark.
  b Streets, highways, and byeways of Glastonbury, by J. G. L. Bulleid.
  c St. Gildas, by J. Clark.
  d Municipal history of Glastonbury, by C. Grant.
  e Municipal life of Glastonbury: the bi-centenary of the borough. (From the *Central Somerset Gazette*.)
  f Lord Chancellor King, first recorder of Glastonbury, by C. Grant. [Peter King, Baron King of Ockham, d. 1734]
  g The recorders of Glastonbury, by C. Grant.

  h The church of St. Benignus, Glastonbury, by C. Grant.
  i A light in the dark ages [St. Dunstan], by T. G. Crippen.

1894 The Glastonbury lake village: a full description of the excavations and the relics discovered, 1892–1907, by A. Bulleid and H. St. G. Gray. 2 vols. 1911–17. [Vol. i with introductory chapter by R. Munro. Vol. ii with chapters on the human and animal remains, by W. B. Dawkins and J. W. Jackson; the bird-bones, by C. W. Andrews; and plants, by C. Reid]

GLOUCESTER CATHEDRAL SOCIETY

Founded 1882, to promote an intelligent interest in Gloucester cathedral among all classes. The Society's activities ended in 1897 but funds permitted the publication of part 2 of their last volume in 1928.

Publications:

1895 Records of Gloucester cathedral, vol. 3, ed. W. Bazeley and R. Austin. 1897–1928.
  a Gloucester Cathedral Society, 1895–6. [Includes: Cameos from the history of Gloucester cathedral, by W. Bazeley; and a description of the great east window]
  b Notes on the early English Lady chapel, built by Ralph and Olympias de Wylington, 1224, by W. Bazeley.
  c The beginnings of English Christianity, by W. Bright.
  d A register book for [the parish of] St. Mary de Lode [Gloucester], 1656–59.
  e St. Nicholas' church, Gloucester, by M. H. Medland.
  f The organ of Gloucester cathedral, by W. Bazeley.
  g Notes on the Benedictine abbey of St. Peter at Gloucester, by W. H. St. J. Hope.
  h Notes on the Chaworth (de Cadurcis) tombs in the chapter house of Gloucester cathedral, by St. C. Baddeley.
  i Headmasters and ushers of the King's (College) school, Gloucester, 1541–1841, by J. N. Langston, with editorial note by R. Austin.

GREENWICH AND LEWISHAM ANTIQUARIAN SOCIETY

Founded 1920, by the amalgamation of the Greenwich Antiquarian Society and the Lewisham Antiquarian Society, to study and record such evidences of historic and prehistoric interest as may be found in Greenwich and Lewisham or within a convenient distance thereof.

Transactions, vols. 2–31 (1920–30):[1]

1896 Vol. 2.
  a The Greenwich parish register, 1615–36/7, by J. E. G. de Montmorency. 1920.

1897 Vol. 3.
  a Building of the Royal Hospital at Greenwich, by A. D. Sharp.
  b The old church of St. Mary, Lewisham, by A. R. Martin.
  c Greenwich in the 13th cent., by J. E. G. de Montmorency.
  d Roman remains from Greenwich park, with special reference to pottery now at the Greenwich central library, by F. C. Elliston-Erwood. [Also issued separately]
  e Discoveries on the line of the Watling street at Shooters Hill, by F. C. Elliston-Erwood.

[1] Continuing the *Transactions* of the Greenwich Antiquarian Society.

f Notes on mediaeval Greenwich and Lewisham, by W. H. Mandy.
g Weremansacre and the nucleus of Greenwich, by J. E. G. de Montmorency.
h The alien priory of Lewisham, by A. R. Martin.
i History of the Greenwich Antiquarian Society, by H. W. Ord. [Reprinted as *The Study of Local History*]
j The story of the Greenwich armoury, by A. D. Sharp.
k Saxon barrows in Greenwich park, by A. R. Martin.
l Greenwich and north America, with special reference to the part played by Maj.-General James Wolfe, by M. C. Matthews.
m Alfonso Ferrabosco, 1575?–1627, court musician, by J. W. Kirby.
n Early Greenwich schools and schoolmasters.
o Heraldic shields in the founder's window in the chapel of Trinity hospital, Greenwich, by Lucy B. Ellis.
p Charitable institutions of Greenwich parish, one hundred years ago [early 19th cent.], by M. C. Matthews.
q Trinity hospital, Greenwich, by P. K. Kipps.

GREENWICH ANTIQUARIAN SOCIETY

Founded 1905, to study and record such evidences of historic and prehistoric interest as may be found in Greenwich, or within a convenient distance thereof. Amalgamated with the Lewisham Antiquarian Society in 1920 to form the Greenwich and Lewisham Antiquarian Society.

Publications:

1898 Transactions, vol. 1[1] (1907–15).
a Presidential address [on the archaeological and historical interest of the district], by H. Jones.
b Early and mediaeval records of Greenwich, by J. E. G. de Montmorency.
c Church of St. Alfege, Greenwich, from early times to 1710, by L. L. Duncan.
d Greenwich mss. and maps in the British Museum, by J. E. G. de Montmorency.
e Greenwich records in the [Public] Record Office, by J. E. G. de Montmorency.
f List of books, pamphlets, views, plans, etc., relating to Greenwich, with press marks, as found in the reading room of the British Museum, comp. F. W. Nunn.
g Pre-historic and Roman Greenwich, by J. E. G. de Montmorency.
h Notes from Kent assize rolls relating to Greenwich and neighbourhood [13th–19th cent.], by W. H. Mandy. [Includes extracts from subsidy rolls, and from the court rolls of Greenwich and Lewisham manors, relating to the hundred of Blackheath. Pt. 4 has a translation of the pleas of the crown for Blackheath hundred at Canterbury assizes, 1279]
i Greenwich: its origin and early history, by J. M. Stone.
j Blackheath and Greenwich place-names, by J. E. G. de Montmorency.
k Greenwich history as told by Venetian records, by J. M. Stone.
l Greenwich: its underground passages, caverns, etc., by J. M. Stone.
m Romano-British defences south-east of London, by J. E. G. de Montmorency.
n Greenwich and Blackheath in times of war, by H. W. Ord.
o Greenwich as an ancient fishing port, by Mrs. T. Norledge.
p Prehistoric Greenwich, by J. E. G. de Montmorency.

[1] For subsequent vols. see Greenwich and Lewisham Antiquarian Society.

Special publication:

1899 No. 1. A brief history of the church of St. Alphege, Greenwich, with some account of its ancient organ, by J. E. G. de Montmorency. *P.* 1910. [2nd edn., 1923, by Greenwich and Lewisham Antiquarian Soc.]

GROTIUS SOCIETY

Founded 1915, to afford facilities for discussion of the laws of war and peace, and for interchange of opinions regarding their operation, and to make suggestions for their reform, and generally to advance the study of international law.

Problems of the War, vols. 1–4; *contd. as* Problems of Peace and War, vols. 5–18 (1916–33):

1900 Vol. 1.
a Position of enemy merchantmen [with particular reference to the British merchant navy 1914–16], by C. Stubbs.

1901 Vol. 3.
a Treaties of peace [in the war of the Spanish Succession, the Napoleonic wars, the Anglo-American war and the Crimean war], by Sir G. Bower.
b Black list [the position of war-time commerce in relation to the Trading with the Enemy Act, 1915], by J. E. G. de Montmorency.

1902 Vol. 4.
a Note on the construction of the definition of 'British subject' in sect. 1 of the Nationality Act, 1914, by Sir F. Piggott.
b A maxim and a wrong deduction [an account of Britain's attitude to the doctrine of 'free ships, free goods'], by Sir G. Bower.
c Divergencies between British and other views on international law, by G. Kaeckenbeeck.

1903 Vol. 5.
a Grotius in England [1613]: his opposition there to the principles of the *Mare liberum*, by W. S. M. Knight.

1904 Vol. 8.
a Dominion status, by M. Nathan.

1905 Vol. 9.
a The Anglo-French Tunis dispute [1922–3], by W. Latey.

1906 Vol. 10.
a Foundations of modern prize law [Lord Stowell and the prize court], by H. Potter.

1907 Vol. 11.
a The Locarno pact, Oct. 15–Dec. 1, 1925, by W. R. Bisschop.

1908 Vol. 12.
a Mandates: how they are working [a survey of British mandated territories, 1927], by D. C. Lee.
b National minorities in the British Empire, by F. Ll. Jones.

1909 Vol. 13.
a The Paris pact, otherwise called the Kellogg pact, by C. J. Colombos.

1910 Vol. 13.
a Relations of the executive and the judiciary [in Britain], by F. T. Grey.

1911 Vol. 16.
a Aliens in Great Britain [1793–1919], by E. S. Roscoe.

b Expatriation as practised in Great Britain, by R. S. Fraser.

1912 Vol. 17.

a The international status of India, by L. Sundaram.
b The Iraq treaty, 1930, by S. G. Vesey-Fitzgerald.

1913 Vol. 18.

a The Anglo-American conception of due process of law, by W. J. Heyting.

Texts for Students of International Relations:

1914 No. 4. Quakers and peace, with introd. and notes by G. W. Knowles. 1927. [Contains extracts from Quaker writings, 1654–1920]

1915 No. 6. Jeremy Bentham's 'Plan for an universal and perpetual peace', with introd. by C. J. Colombos. 1927.

GYPSY AND FOLK-LORE CLUB

Founded 1912, to promote fellowship among those interested in gypsies and gypsies themselves; to encourage study of, and conversation in the Romani language; to promote a greater interest in the study of folk-lore generally. Dissolved 1916?.

Romanitshels', Didakais and Folk-lore Gazette, vols. 1–3 (1912–16):

1916 Vol. 1.

a The Graal legend and its exponents, by D. F. de l'H. Ranking.
b The gypsies: an outline sketch, by R. A. S. Macfie.
c Notes on the Boss pedigree, by G. Hall.

Extra publication:

1917 Catalogue of books, pamphlets, prints, old broadsides, etc., comprised in the gypsy-lore section of the library of the Club. *P.* 1912.

GYPSY LORE SOCIETY

Founded 1888, to promote and co-ordinate research into the history, language, ethnology, and folk lore of the gypsy race wherever it is found. Revived in 1907 and in 1921, after lapses.

Journal, new ser., vols. 1–9 (1907–16):

1918 Vol. 1.

a Supplementary annals of the gypsies in England before 1700, by H. T. Crofton. [See also 3rd ser., vol. 6]
b A gypsy tract from the 17th cent. [*Strange and certain news from Warwick, or the king of the gypsies dreadful tragedy*, 1673], ed. W. E. A. Axon.
c The tinkers, by C. G. Leland.
d Borde's *Egipt speche* [being a Romani vocabulary from *The fyrst boke of the introduction of knowledge, c.* 1550], by H. T. Crofton.
e The state *versus* the gypsy [chiefly in Europe, but with reference to the Movable Dwellings Bill, 1908], by W. M. Gallichan.
f Affairs of Egypt, 1892–1906 [being notes on the gypsies in England, etc.], by H. T. Crofton. [Contd. for following years in vols. 2, 3, and 5]

1919 Vol. 2.

a A [Spanish] gypsy's letter to George Borrow, 1838, by W. I. Knapp.

b Whiter's *Lingua Cingariana*, by Lady A. Grosvenor. [Walter Whiter, d. 1832, philologist and rector of Hardingham, Norf.]
c Drab [poison used by gypsies for killing pigs], by J. Myers. [See also note in vol. 3]
d The former costume of the gypsies, by H. T. Crofton.
e Notes and queries. [Includes: 17: Gypsy parliaments, by E. O. Winstedt; 30: Gypsies or 'potters', of Natland, near Kendal, *c.* 1821, by H. T. Crofton]
f English gypsies in 1596, by J. Sampson.
g Pedigree of Matthew Wood [gypsy narrator of folk-tales].

1920 Vol. 3.

a Borrow's gypsies, by T. W. Thompson.
b A pilgrim's progress, by Lady A. Grosvenor. [On the Rev. T. W. Norwood, fl. 1854–63, and his Romani studies]

1921 Vol. 4.

a Maj.-gen. John Staples Harriott [d. 1839, and his Romani vocabulary], by W. F. Prideaux.
b Jacob Bryant [antiquary, d. 1804]: an analysis of his Anglo-Romani vocabulary, with a discussion of the place and date of collection and an attempt to show that Bryant, not Rüdiger, was the earliest discoverer of the Indian origin of the gypsies, by J. Sampson.
c Notes and queries. [Includes: 35: The Wood family outside Wales, by E. O. Winstedt; 37: Gypsies at Helmdon, Northants., by E. O. Winstedt]

1922 Vol. 5.

a Sir Thomas Browne on the gypsies, by A. Symons. [Extract from *Pseudodoxia Epidemica*]
b Samuel Roberts of Park Grange, Sheffield, 1763–1848 [philanthropist, and his relations with gypsies], by S. Roberts.
c Clara Heron [d. 1889], by G. Hall.
d Roberts' vocabulary [of gypsy words].

1923 Vol. 6.

a Gypsy dances [in England in the 19th cent.], by E. O. Winstedt and T. W. Thompson.
b Notes and queries. [Includes: 20: Gypsies at Aylesbury. by E. O. Winstedt; 48: Gypsy depredations in 1819, in Northamptonshire, by W. E. A. Axon; 55: Inverto Boswell again, by E. O. Winstedt]
c The gypsy coppersmiths' invasion [of England] of 1911–13, by E. O. Winstedt.

1924 Vol. 7.

a Early British gypsies [in the 16th and 17th cent.], by E. O. Winstedt.
b Preface to the Heron pedigree, by G. Hall.
c Notes on the Heron pedigree collected by George Hall, by W. H. R. Rivers.

1925 Vol. 8.

a Tom Taylor's Anglo-Romani vocabulary, by A. Russell.
b Lucas's [Anglo-Romani] vocabulary, by A. Russell.

1926 Vol. 9.

a The Norwood gypsies [17th–19th cent.] and their vocabulary, by E. O. Winstedt.
b Bright's Anglo-Romani vocabulary, by A. Russell.

Journal, 3rd ser., vols. 1–12 (1922–33):

1927 Vol. 1.

a The uncleanness of women among English gypsies, by T. W. Thompson.
b Notes on English gypsy christian names, by E. O. Winstedt. [Contd. in vol. 2]

c Notes and queries. [Includes: 4: Some gypsy records from the 16th and 17th cent., by T. W. Thompson]

d The gypsy Grays as tale-tellers: being an introduction to the second series of some English gypsy folk-tales, by T. W. Thompson.

1928 Vol. 2.

a Notes and queries. [Includes: 3: Foreign travellers and English gypsies, in the 18th cent.]

b Consorting with and counterfeiting Egyptians [English official documents of the 16th cent.], ed. T. W. Thompson.

c Anglo-Romani gleanings, 1: From families frequenting Wales. [Chiefly genealogies and grammatical survivals. Contd. in vol. 3: From London-side gypsies; vol. 4: From Hampshire gypsies; and vol. 8: From East Anglian gypsies]

1929 Vol. 3.

a English gypsy death and burial customs, by T. W. Thompson. [Additional notes in vol. 9]

b Charles Godfrey Leland [d. 1903, president of the Gypsy Lore Soc.], by D. MacRitchie.

c Witherite [a form of barium carbonate used by gypsies for killing pigs], by T. W. Thompson.

d Samuel Fox [d. 1870, vicar of Morley and Smalley, Derbys.], and the Derbyshire Boswells, by T. W. Thompson.

1930 Vol. 4.

a Collecting folk-melodies from gypsies in Herefordshire, by Ella M. Leather, with note by T. W. Thompson.

b English gypsy folk-medicine: some unedited notes, by T. W. Thompson.

c Irvine's vocabulary [of Anglo-Romani, 1819].

d Notes and queries. [Includes: 15: Joshua Scamp and Edward Buckland, gypsies, executed in 1801 and 1821 respectively]

1931 Vol. 5.

a Gypsy marriage in England, by T. W. Thompson. [Contd. in vol. 6]

b Notes on the gypsies [chiefly superstitions], by E. Wittich.

c The dialect of the Derbyshire gypsies, compiled in the parish of Smalley by the Rev. Samuel Fox, 1832–3, and ed. J. Sampson.

1932 Vol. 6.

a Tales in a cottage, by T. W. Thompson. [An account of Reuben Brinkley, gypsy, and of gypsy life in the 19th cent.]

b Notes on Dr. J. Sampson's *The Dialect of the Gypsies of Wales*, by B. Gilliat-Smith.

c Notes and queries. [Includes: 2: Rutland and Leicestershire gypsy tombs; 7: Addenda to Crofton's *Early Annals of the Gypsies in England*]

d Gypsies as highwaymen and footpads.

1933 Vol. 7.

a Gleanings [concerning gypsies] from constables' accounts and other sources [in the 16th and 17th cent.], by T. W. Thompson.

b Groome's letters to [Bath] Smart and Crofton [mainly in the 1870's].

c Some gypsy notes [including parallels between Welsh and Welsh gypsy], by W. E. Collinson.

d Gypsies who hunted with the Badsworth hounds [c. 1830–40], by T. W. Thompson.

e Some potential sources for the early history of the gypsies in England, by H. Hall, with select classified list of the same sources by Marjorie F. Hall.

1934 Vol. 8.

a Additional notes on English gypsy uncleanness taboos, by T. W. Thompson.

1935 Vol. 9.

a Lamentations for the dead: a Welsh gypsy belief and its parallels, by Dora E. Yates.

b Notes and queries. [Includes: 1: Gypsies in political disturbances with particular reference to the Gordon riots, 1780]

c Welsh sources for gypsy history, by J. G. Davies.

d Gypsies in Wales, by R. W. Jones.

e An East Anglian Romani vocabulary of 1798, ed. J. Sampson.

f Illustrations of English gypsy law, by T. W. Thompson.

1936 Vol. 10.

a David Townsend's *Gypsies of Northamptonshire* [1877], by H. W. Saw.

b Notes and queries. [Includes: 8: *Caraboo: a narrative of a singular imposition, practised . . . by Mary Willcocks, . . . alias Caraboo, princess of Javasu*, 1817]

c The Wood family. 1: Early records, by E. O. Winstedt. [Contd. in vols. 11–13 by J. Sampson]

d English gypsies as bell-hangers, by T. W. Thompson.

1937 Vol. 11.

a John Sampson, 1862–1931 [librarian of Liverpool university library and Romani scholar], by Andreas.

b Gypsy [Frederick] Draper, 1797–1902, by R. L. Hine.

1938 Vol. 12.

a 'Pestiferous carbuncles' [gypsies] in Somerset, by W. G. W. Watson.

b A mixed marriage [1830, between Nehemiah Perry, of Strethall, near Saffron Walden, and Sarah Shaw, gypsy], by T. W. Thompson.

Monographs, nos. 1–5:

1939 No. 1. A gypsy bibliography, by G. F. Black. 1914. [A provisional issue of this work appeared in 1909]

1940 No. 2. Index of old series, journal of the Gypsy Lore Society, by A. Russell. *P.* 1914.

HAKLUYT SOCIETY

Founded 1846, to print rare and valuable voyages, travels, naval expeditions, and other geographical records.

Publications, 2nd ser., nos. 6–72:

1941 No. 6. The strange adventures of Andrew Battell of Leigh, in Angola and the adjoining regions. Reprinted from *Purchas his pilgrimes*. Ed., with notes and history of Kongo and Angola, by E. G. Ravenstein. 1901.

1942 No. 11. Early Dutch and English voyages to Spitsbergen in the 17th cent., ed. with introd. and notes, by Sir W. M. Conway. 1904.

1943 No. 12. A geographical account of countries round the bay of Bengal, 1669–79, by Thomas Bowrey, ed. Sir R. C. Temple, bt. 1905.

1944 No. 16. Journal of John Jourdain, 1608–17, describing his experiences in Arabia, India, and the Malay archipelago, ed. W. Foster. 1905.

1945 Nos. 17, 35, 45, 46, 55. Travels of Peter Mundy, in Europe and Asia, 1608–67, ed. Sir R. C. Temple, bt. Vols. i–iv, 1907–25. [Vol. i: Travels in Europe, 1608–28. Vol. ii: Travels in Asia, 1628–34. Vol. iii, pt. 1: Travels in England, western India, etc., 1634–7; pt. 2: Travels in Achin, etc., 1638. Vol. iv: Travels in Europe, 1639–47.

A further vol. (vol. v) containing travels in S.W. England, with a diary of events in London, 1658–63, and in Penryn, 1664–7, was published as no. 78 in 1936]

1946 Nos. 19, 20, 39. A new account of East India and Persia, being nine years' travels, 1672–81, by John Fryer, ed. W. Crooke. 3 vols. 1909–15.

1947 Nos. 26, 27. Storm van 's Gravesande: the rise of British Guiana, comp. from his despatches by C. A. Harris and J. A. J. De Villiers. 2 vols. 1911.

1948 No. 34. New light on Drake: a collection of documents relating to his voyages of circumnavigation, 1577–80, translated and ed. Zelia Nuttall. 1914.

1949 No. 52. Journal of William Lockerby, sandalwood trader in the Fijian islands, 1808–9, with introd. and other papers connected with the earliest European visitors to the islands, ed. Sir E. Im Thurn and L. C. Wharton. 1925.

1950 Nos. 53, 68. The life of the Icelander, Jón Ólafsson, traveller to India, written by himself and completed about 1661, with a continuation by another hand up to his death in 1679, translated from the Icelandic edition by Bertha S. Phillpotts. 2 vols. 1923–32. [Vol. i: 1593–1622, ed. the translator. Vol. ii: 1618–79, ed. Sir R. Temple, bt., and Lavinia M. Anstey. Includes accounts of visits to England]

1951 No. 56. Colonising expeditions to the West Indies and Guiana, 1623–67, ed V. T. Harlow. 1925.

1952 No. 57. Francis Mortoft his book, being his travels. through France and Italy, 1658–9, ed. M. Letts. 1925.

1953 No. 58. The papers of Thomas Bowrey, 1669–1713 Pt. 1: Diary of a tour in Holland and Flanders, 1698; pt. 2: The story of the *Mary Galley*, 1704–10. 1927.

1954 No. 60. A relation of a voyage to Guiana, by Robert Harcourt, 1613, with Purchas' transcript of a report made at Harcourt's instance on the Marrawini district, ed. with introd. and notes by Sir C. A. Harris. 1928.

1955 No. 62. Spanish documents concerning English voyages to the Caribbean, 1527–68, selected from the archives of the Indies at Seville by Irene A. Wright. 1929.

1956 No. 63. The desert route to India, being the journals of four travellers [William Beawes, Gaylard Roberts, Bartholomew Plaisted, and John Carmichael] by the great desert caravan route between Aleppo and Basra, 1745–51, ed. D. Carruthers. 1929.

1957 No. 64. New light on the discovery of Australia, as revealed by the journal of Captain Don Diego de Prado y Tovar, ed. H. N. Stevens, with annotated translations from the Spanish by G. F. Barwick. 1930.

1958 Nos. 65, 70. Select documents illustrating the four voyages of Columbus, including those contained in R. H. Major's *Select Letters of Christopher Columbus*, translated and ed., with additional material, introd. and notes, by C. Jane. 2 vols. 1930–33. [Vol. i: First and second voyages. Vol. ii: Third and fourth, with supplementary introd. by Eva G. R. Taylor]

1959 No. 66. Relations of Golconda in the early 17th cent., ed. W. H. Moreland. 1931. [Includes William Methwold's 'relation' from *Purchas his Pilgrims*]

1960 No. 67. Travels of John Sanderson in the Levant, 1584–1602, with his autobiography and selections from his correspondence, ed. Sir W. Foster. 1931.

1961 No. 69. A brief summe of geographie, by Roger Barlow [dedicated to Henry VIII], ed. with introd. and notes, by Eva G. R. Taylor. 1932.

1962 No. 71. Documents concerning English voyages to the Spanish main, 1569–80, by Irene A. Wright. 1932. [Contains Spanish documents selected from the archives of the Indies at Seville, and English accounts reprinted]

1963 No. 72. Bombay in the days of Queen Anne, being an account of the settlement written by John Burnell, with introd. and notes by S. T. Sheppard, to which is added Burnell's narrative of his adventures in Bengal, with introd. by Sir W. Foster and notes by Sir E. Cotton and Lavinia M. Anstey. 1933.

Extra series:

1964 The texts and versions of John de Plano Carpini and William de Rubruquis [13th cent. friar travellers] as printed for the first time by Hakluyt in 1598, together with some shorter pieces, ed. C. R. Beazley. 1903.

1965 Prospectus and list of members, with list [and index] of publications and maps [issued 1847–1934]. *P.* 1934, [Similar indexes were published in 1905, 1907, 1912, 1918, 1927, and 1930]

HALIFAX ANTIQUARIAN SOCIETY

Founded 1900, *to encourage and assist in the preservation of all matters of historical, archaeological and general antiquarian interest primarily relating to the old parish of Halifax and the adjoining places.*

Papers, Reports, etc. 1902–33 (31 vols.):

1966 Vol. for 1902.

a Life of Dr. Haldesworth [fl. 1507–56], vicar of Halifax, by J. Lister. [Contd. in vols. for 1903–8]
b Heralds' visits to Halifax: heraldic bearings of Halifax gentry, by J. W. Clay.
c Antiquarians at Midgley: Kershaw House, Brearley Hall, and Luddenden church.
d Historical sketch [of Sowerby], by H. P. Kendall.
e Greetland's ancient halls [Sunny Bank, High Trees, Crowstone Hall, and Barkisland Hall], by J. Lister.
f Prehistoric man in Halifax parish: discovery of an ancient stone circle at Walshaw Dean.
g Visit to Kirklees priory and Hartshead church.
h The antiquities of Elland.
i Halifax surnames: their source and significance as found in the poll-tax returns for Halifax, 1379], by C. Crossland.
j Sowerby in olden times [being constables' accounts] 1629–42, by H. P. Kendall. [Contd. to 1708 in vols. for 1903–6]

1967 Vol. for 1903.

a Local prehistoric man, by T. Wilkinson.
b The [Halifax] court leet and court baron, by J. Seed. [With an account of the origin and early history of the court leet, by J. H. Ogden]
c Heptonstall in the middle ages, by J. H. Ogden.
d Saltonstall, Warley, by T. Sutcliffe.
e Northowram old halls [Westercroft, Cinderhills and the Whitley family, and Coley Hall], by M. Pearson.
f Three old homesteads: Broadbottom [near Hawksclough], Fallingroyd, and Mayroyd [in Wadsworth], by J. H. Ogden.

1968 Vol. for 1904–5.

a Private tokens: the issuers and die-sinkers, by S. H. Hamer.

b A moorland township: Wadsworth in ancient times, by J. H. Ogden.

c Over-Shibden [or Shibden valley: the Hazelhurst homesteads, Hangingroyd and its owners, and Upper Shibden Hall], by M. Pearson.

d Burlees and Old Town [Wadsworth], by J. H. Ogden.

e Ancient halls of Norland, by H. P. Kendall. [Includes Binroyde, Upper Wat Ing, Norland Hall, and Butterworth End]

f Two Halifax vicars: wills and inventories of Richard Hooke [1688] and Edmund Hough [1690], by E. W. Crossley.

g Halifax parish church: an early chapter of its history [12th–13th cent.], by J. Lister.

h Some lessons from old buildings as seen from local examples, by J. F. Walsh. [Brief historical survey]

i Building the Piece hall [Halifax, 1775]. The estimated cost: builders' prices in Halifax 130 years ago.

j Antiquarians at Ovenden. [Includes accounts of Nathaniel Priestley's house, Park House, Ovenden Hall, Mixenden Hall and Holdsworth House]

k Excursion to Shelf. [Shelf Hall, High Bentley, Lower High Bentley, and Dean House, and their owners]

l Woodhall and Copley Hall, Skircoat. [The estates and their owners]

m Excursion to Rishworth. [Goat House and the grammar-school, Rishworth Hall, Upper Cockroft, and Lower Cockroft]

n The Royds of Rishworth, by R.

o Rastrick chapel and school: their early history, by J. Lister.

1969 Vol. for 1906.

a Tokens issued by the overseers of the poor and the workhouse authorities, by S. H. Hamer.

b Early owners of Godley [or Shibden grange], by J. Lister.

c Famous Sowerby mansion: White Windows [and its owners], by M. P. Kendall.

d Bentley Royd [Sowerby: the estate and its owners].

e Wood Lane Hall [Sowerby, and its owners].

f Ancient Shibden mansions, by M. Pearson. [Staups House, Field House, Salterlea, Damhead, and their owners]

g Halifax parish church: features of its architecture, by H. E. Savage.

1970 Vol. for 1907.

a The English coinage [and former methods of its production], by S. H. Hamer.

b Rare book in Halifax [a 15th cent. printed copy of *Sermones tredecim universales*, by Michael of Hungary], by H. E. Savage.

c Extracts from some Elland records [churchwardens' accounts], 1729–1804, by S. H. Hamer.

d Extracts from old Warley township accounts [18th–19th cent.], by T. Sutcliffe.

e Horley Green [estate, Northowram, and the Drake family], by J. Lister.

f High Sunderland [estate, Northowram, and the Sunderland family], by J. Lister.

g Lower Deerplay [estate, Sowerby?, and its owners, with notes on the Priestley family of Soyland], by E. W. Crossley.

h Shibden Hall, Southowram [and the Otes family], by J. Lister.

i Todmorden antiquities: the 'old church' of St. Mary's and Todmorden Hall, by J. Holder.

j The Crossleys and Scaitcliffe [estate], by W. Ormerod.

k Crossleys of Scaitcliffe, by E. W. Crossley.

l John Brearcliffe, the antiquary [d. 1682]: the Brearcliffe family, by T. W. Hanson. [Further articles on John Brearcliffe in connection with the Halifax gibbet, and with Halifax parish church under the Commonwealth, appear in vols. for 1908 and 1909 respectively]

1971 Vol. for 1908.

a Township records in Todmorden district, by J. Holden

b A Halifax gibbeting [of Richard Hopkinson, 1505, with earlier instances of executions], by E. W. Crossley.

c The two Willow halls [Skircoat]: Upper and Lower, by H. P. Kendall.

d Heptonstall [church], by H. P. Kendall.

e Norcliffe in Southowram: antiquarian rambles, by J. Lister. [Notes on the Norcliffe, Rookes, Brighouse, and Rossendale families]

f Antiquarian rambles: Southolme in Southowram [and its occupiers], by J. Lister.

g Walterclough, in Southowram [the estate and its owners], by J. Lister.

h Smith House, in Lightcliffe [and its owners], by J. H. Turner.

i Cliffe Hill, in Lightcliffe [the estate and its owners], by J. H. Turner. [With notes on members of the Cliffe family, 1272–1539]

j Lightcliffe church, by J. H. Turner.

k Halifax parish church: the 17th cent. woodwork, by H. E. Savage.

1972 Vol. for 1909.

a Local incidents in the civil war, by H. P. Kendall. [Contd. in vol. for 1910]

b Old free chapels in the parish of Halifax, by J. Lister.

c Notes on some chantry endowments in the parish of Halifax, by E. W. Crossley.

d Cragg coiners [fl. 1767–82]: excursion to Turvin, by T. W. Hanson.

e Blackstone Edge roads: excursion to Blackstone Edge, by H. P. Kendall.

f Stoney-royd [Southowram: the estate and its owners], by J. Lister.

g Siddal Hall (Upper and Lower), by J. Lister. [The estates and their owners]

h Far or Old Siddall Hall [and its owners], by J. Lister.

i Backhall [Southowram: the estate and its owners], by J. Lister.

j Shibden homesteads: excursion to Shibden, by S. H. Hamer.

k Halifax bibliography and authors, pt. 1, by C. Crossland. [Contd. in vols. for 1910–15]

1973 Vol. for 1910.

a Halifax gibbet law, by J. Lister.

b Life and letters of Sir William Fawcett, K.C.B. [d. 1804], by J. Lister. [Contd. in vols. for 1911, 1913, and 1914]

c Ovenden Wood [estate and its owners], by T. W. Hanson.

d Shibden Hall: the Waterhouse family, by J. Lister.

e Old Haugh End [Sowerby: the estate and its owners], by H. P. Kendall.

f Sowerby Hall [and its owners], by H. P. Kendall.

g Ball Green [Sowerby?: the estate and its owners], by H. P. Kendall.

h Rookes Hall and Upper and Lower Rookes, Hipperholme [the estates and their owners], by W. B. Trigg and L. Tolson.

i Dr. Favour [d. 1624, vicar of Halifax] as Protestant disputant, by T. W. Hanson.

1974 Vol. for 1911.

a Norland Hall [a descriptive account of the house], by H. P. Kendall.

b Old Halifax circulating library, 1768–1866, by E. P. Rouse.

c The civil war as affecting Halifax and the surrounding towns, by H. P. Kendall.

d Birks and Brackenbed [the estate, Birks Hall and its owners, 1540–1888], by T. W. Hanson.

e Little Brackenbed [house and its owners], by T. W. Hanson.

f Brackenbed Grange [and its owners], by T. W. Hanson.

g The Roman ford at Longbottom, by H. P. Kendall.

h Long Causeway crosses, from Yorkshire to Lancashire, by A. Newell.

i Wadsworth homesteads [the Akroyd estate in the township of Wadsworth], by H. P. Kendall.

j Ibbotroyd [estate and an inventory of James Ashworth of Ibbotroyd, 1699].

k History of Shibden mill, by J. Lister.

l *Antiquitie triumphing over Noveltie*, by Dr. Favour [d. 1624] sometime vicar of Halifax, by T. W. Hanson.

1975 Vol. for 1912.

a The oldest Halifax inn, 'one of the fairest inns in England': 'The Union Cross', formerly 'The Cross', by J. Lister.

b Halifax old and new [before 1800], by S. Nicholl.

c Roman evidences in the parish of Halifax, by H. P. Kendall.

d Excursion to Pontefract, by H. P. Kendall. [An account of the castle, with an account of siege-pieces of the castle and provincial tokens of the town issued in 17th cent., by S. H. Hamer]

e Grindlestone Bank, Ovenden Wood [the estate and its owners], by T. W. Hanson.

f The Jumples, Illingworth [the estate and its owners].

g Edwards of Halifax: a family of book-sellers, collectors and book-binders, by T. W. Hanson. [William Edwards, d. 1808, and his descendants]

h Some local gleanings from the bookstalls, by H. E. Savage. [Accounts of William Heaton, weaver and poet, b. ?1805; early topography of Halifax; a 1796 edition of Oliver Heywood's sermons; and other miscellaneous items concerning Halifax]

i Tokens of Lichfield, by S. H. Hamer.

j Tokens and medals of Halifax and district, by S. H. Hamer.

1976 Vol. for 1913.

a Two old Sowerby Bridge houses [Lower Hollins in Warley and Broadgates, alias Underbank, and the Waterhouse family], by H. P. Kendall.

b Mereclough Bottom [an account of the mill in Sowerby Bridge and its owners], by H. P. Kendall.

c Fields in Norland [the house and its owners], by H. P. Kendall.

d Sowerby Croft [the house and its owners], by H. P. Kendall.

e The Harper Royds [the houses and their owners], by H. P. Kendall.

f Visit to Shibden Hall: the Waterhouse family [in 16th cent.], by J. Lister.

g Binroyd in Norland [the house and the Brigg family], by H. P. Kendall.

h Visit to Warley, by T. Sutcliffe. [Slode House and the Farrar family; Shaw Booth House and the Appleyard family; Peacock House; Bank House and the Brooksbank family]

i The Ovenden Heights [houses and their owners at Cockhill and Soilhill], by T. W. Hanson.

j Ancient plaster work [from Binroyd farmstead, Norland, 1670].

k Hearth and window taxes, by C. Clegg. [Includes a list

of returns in Halifax and Southowram, 1664–5, and in Halifax, 1666]

l Halifax exercises [theological conferences *temp.* James I–Charles II, with notes on the ministers concerned], by T. W. Hanson.

1977 Vol. for 1914.

a The Waterhouse lecture [established in 1642 by Nathaniel Waterhouse, to provide monthly sermons in Halifax church and its 12 chapels], by T. W. Hanson.

b William Booth, the Perry Barr forger [and his trial and execution, 1812], by S. H. Hamer.

c Bankhouse in Skircoat [the house and its owners], by H. P. Kendall.

d Exley Hall, Southowram [and its owners], by J. Lister.

e Hathershelf, Sowerby [the estate and its owners], by H. P. Kendall.

f Higgin Chamber, Sowerby [the estate and its owners], by H. P. Kendall.

g Quickstavers in Sowerby [the estate and its owners], by H. P. Kendall.

h Warley mill, by T. Sutcliffe.

i Old Warley houses [the Roebucks, the Grange and Newland, and their owners], by T. Sutcliffe.

j Halifax directories [from 1781], by J. L. Cox.

k The naming of the Hebble [brook], by T. W. Hanson.

1978 Vol. for 1915.

a Halifax church, 1640–60, by T. W. Hanson. [Contd. in vol. for 1916]

b Sowerby bridge and Stirk bridge, by H. P. Kendall.

c Sowerby Bridge old church, by H. P. Kendall.

d Gleanings from local [Halifax and district] Elizabethan wills, by H. P. Kendall.

e History of Shibden Hall [and its owners], by J. Lister. [Contd. in vols. for 1916, 1917, and 1921–6]

f Upper Swift Place in Soyland [and the Dyson and Hoyle families], by H. P. Kendall.

g Beeston Hirst and Thrum Hall in Soyland [and the Royde family], by H. P. Kendall.

h Baitings in Soyland [and the Priestley family], by H. P. Kendall.

i Bradford parish church and Bolling Hall.

j Sowerby Ramble [the township and its origin] and Erringden Park, by A. Newell.

k Mankinholes [village and its history], by A. Newell.

l Stock Lane House, Warley, and the Oldfield family, by T. Sutcliffe.

m The Hollins [house] in Warley, and its families, by T. Sutcliffe.

n Turnpikes and tollbars, by C. Clegg.

o Tokens of the 18th cent. issued by artists, booksellers, engravers and printers, by S. H. Hamer.

1979 Vol. for 1916.

a Making Place in Soyland and the Hill family, by H. P. Kendall.

b Warley worthies, by T. Sutcliffe.

c The Royd in Soyland [the house and its owners], by H. P. Kendall.

d Blackshaw Clough in Soyland [the house and its owners], by H. P. Kendall.

e Eastwood [estate] and the Eastwood family, by A. Newell.

f Higher and Lower Ashes [houses and their owners], by A. Newell.

g The Manchester–Ilkley Roman road [particularly the portion within the old parish of Halifax and the adjacent part of Lancashire], by J. H. Hoyle.

h Diary of a grandfather [Cornelius Ashworth, of Waltroyd Wheatley, d. 1821], by T. W. Hanson.

d Notes and comments on Halifax churchwardens' accounts 1620–1714, by J. W. Houseman. [Contd. for 1714–1800 in vol. for 1926, for 1714–1832 in vol. for 1927]

e Some remarkable clocks, with some reference to the makers, by S. H. Hamer.

1989 Vol. for 1926.

a The Mixenden treasure [attempts to discover it, 1510], by T. W. Hanson.

b Tour through Lower Warley [with accounts of Cooper House, Magson House, Greystokes and Shepherd House, and their owners], by T. Sutcliffe.

c Everill Shaw in Heptonstall [the house and estate, and its owners], by H. P. Kendall.

d The forest of Sowerbyshire, by H. P. Kendall.

1990 Vol. for 1927.

a The Bache in Warley [the house (now Beech House), and estate, and its owners], by H. P. Kendall.

b Brownhirst [house and estate] and the Bairstows, by W. B. Trigg.

c Sod House Green [near Ovenden, and its owners], by W. B. Trigg.

d Abel cross and the hamlet of Shackleton [also the manor of Shackleton, its descent, and Mansfield House, Shackleton, and its owners], by H. P. Kendall.

e Elland churchwardens' accounts [17th and early 18th cent.], by E. W. Crossley. [Contd. for 1700–50, in vol. for 1929]

f Some local [Halifax] star chamber cases, by J. Lister.

1991 Vol. for 1928.

a Halifax hunts and huntsmen, by H. P. Kendall.

b History of the Halifax parish church organs, by J. W. Houseman.

c A tour in Midgley [miscellaneous notes on its houses and families], by T. Sutcliffe.

d Cross Stone [an account of Cross Stone road, and church], by A. Newell.

e Halifax builders in Oxford [John Akroyd, d. 1613; John Bentley, d. 1615, their brothers and others], by T. W. Hanson.

f Some Ovenden houses [Threapcroft, Newhouse, and Watkinson Hall, and their owners], by W. B. Trigg.

1992 Vol. for 1929.

a Kebroyd in Soyland [estate and the Foxcroft family], by H. P. Kendall.

b Local heraldry [armorial bearings of families in and about Halifax], by R. Bretton.

c Development of local government in the parish of Halifax 1760–1848, by J. W. Houseman.

d Ryecroft, Illingworth [the estate and its owners], by W. B. Trigg.

e Excursion to Clitheroe, Waddington Old Hall, Stony-hurst College and Whalley, by T. Sutcliffe.

f Stannary End, formerly Tymeley Bent [the house and its owners], by T. Sutcliffe.

g Rastrick grave rental, 1710–1836.

h Early British trackways, by H. Whitaker.

i Jeremy Bentley, first M.P. for Halifax [1654], by T. W. Hanson.

1993 Vol. for 1930.

a Rental of the freeholders and copyholders of Halifax, 1587–8, transcribed and ed. H. P. Kendall.

b The high street of Halifax 200 years ago, by T. W. Hanson.

c Redacre, Redicarre, in Wadsworth [the estate and its owners], by G. Dent.

d Local township records: Hipperholme-cum-Brighouse [in the parish of Halifax], 1813–29, by J. W. Houseman.

e Hamer collection of Halifax tokens (17th cent.)

f The Halifax coalfield, by W. B. Trigg. [Contd. in vol. for 1932]

1994 Vol. for 1931.

a The plague in Halifax parish [1551, 1631 and 1645], by H. P. Kendall.

b Heraldry of Halifax parish church, by R. Bretton.

c The Rayners of Norland, by H. P. Kendall and W. B. Trigg.

d Birchenlee Carr or Birckenlee Carr [in Wadsworth, the house and estate and their owners], by G. Dent.

e Dialect on the map: some Calder Valley place names, by W. B. Crump.

1995 Vol. for 1932.

a Some little local histories [including notes on Halifax inns and extracts from 18th cent. autobiographies], by T. W. Hanson.

b Greave list of Sowerby for 1624 [the rental of the steward of the manor], by H. P. Kendall.

c The Stepps in Warley [the house and estate and the owners], by H. P. Kendall.

d Some of our local people named 'Holroyde', by H. Wright.

e Northowram Hall [and estate, and its owners], by W. B. Trigg.

f Prehistoric remains in Barkisland, by A. T. Long-botham.

g Old Ripponden: the Height and the Chappel [the estate and its owners], by J. H. Priestley.

h Our local [Halifax and district] railways, by C. Clegg.

i Local township records: Shelf [in the parish of Halifax] 1714–1841, by J. W. Houseman.

1996 Vol. for 1933.

a The Lumb in Soyland [the house, estate, and its owners], by H. P. Kendall.

b Wadsworth Royd in Wadsworth [the estate and its owners], by G. Dent.

c Lambert House, Elland [the house, estate and owners], by A. T. Longbotham.

d Pyke House, Littleborough [the house, estate and owners], by W. B. Trigg.

e Mills of the Ryburn valley [employed for corn, wool, cotton and paper from the 13th cent.], by J. H. Priestley.

f Industrial water supply of Ovenden [from the end of the 18th cent.], by W. B. Trigg.

g Slead Hall [the house and its owners], by H. T. Clay.

1997 Index of papers and excursions to Dec. 1926, comp. C. Clegg. *P.* [1927 ?]

1998 Index of Transactions (titles and subjects), 1901–41, comp. R. Bretton. [1942].

Record series, vols. 1–3:

1999 Vol. 1. Poll tax (lay subsidy) 2 Richard II, 1379, parish of Halifax, in the wapentake of Morley, reprinted from *Yorkshire Archaeological Journal*, vol. 6, with notes on local returns; also rental of Halifax and Heptonstall, 1439, by J. Lister and J. H. Ogden. [1906].

2000 Vol. 2. Extent (or survey) of the graveships of Rastrick, Hipperholme and Sowerby, 1309, copied and translated by J. Lister, with notes of identification by H. P. Kendall. 1914.

2001 Vol. 3. Architecture of the church of St. John the Baptist, Halifax, by F. Barber, ed. H. P. Kendall. *P.* 1917.

HALIFAX SCIENTIFIC SOCIETY

Founded 1874, for the cultivation of science.

Halifax Naturalist and Record of the Society, vols. 5–8 (1901–4):

2002 Vol. 5.

  a Origin of some Halifax surnames, by C. Crossland.
  b 'Noyful fowles and vermyn' [being entries in various churchwardens' accounts, etc., of payments for the destruction of vermin and birds of prey], by J. Longbottom.
  c Early Halifax bibliography, by J. H. Turner. [Contd. in vol. 6]

2003 Vol. 6.

  a The Haley Hill Literary and Scientific Society, by J. J. Aves.

2004 Vol. 7.

  a Upper Saltonstall: an old-world mountain hamlet, by J. Longbottom.
  b Place names in the parish of Halifax in relation to surrounding natural features, by C. Crossland.
  c Halifax water supply in 1761, by C. J. Fox.
  d A flint workshop on Boulsworth hill, by P. Whalley.
  e An old-time winnower [machine], by J. Longbottom.

2005 Vol. 8.

  a Examples of 17th cent. plaster work, by H. P. Kendall.
  b Ancient local porches and doorways, by H. P. Kendall.
  c Masons' marks, with local examples, by J. Longbottom.

HAMPSHIRE FIELD CLUB AND ARCHAEOLOGICAL SOCIETY

Founded 1885, as the Hampshire Field Club, for the study of the natural history and antiquities of the county. Title changed to above form in 1898.

Papers and Proceedings, vols. 4–12 (1899–1934):

2006 Vol. 4.

  a Bentworth and its historical associations, by T. W. Shore, with architectural notes by R. M. Lucas.
  b Short list of some tumuli in north Hampshire, by S. Andrews.
  c The west gate of Winchester, by W. H. Jacob, with architectural notes by N. C. H. Nisbett.
  d The old church, St. Lawrence, Ventnor, by W. R. Odell.
  e West gate house, Southampton, with a notice of the town walls and gates, by G. W. Minns.
  f Heraldry and exterior decoration of the Bargate, Southampton, by B. W. Greenfield, with architectural notes by R. M. Lucas.
  g Physical geology and early archaeological associations of the neighbourhood of Cheriton, by T. W. Shore.
  h Earlstone manor house, Burghclere, by W. Money.
  i Old water courses and mills of Romsey, by E. Buckell.
  j Saxon sepulchral monument at Whitchurch, by G. W. Minns.
  k Font at Barton Stacey, by G. W. Minns.
  l An ancient deed between the abbot of Titchfield and the monks of Quarr [1266], by E. S. Prideaux-Brune.
  m Neolithic implements from the neighbourhood of Southampton, by W. Dale.
  n King Arthur and the round table at Winchester, by T. W. Shore.
  o Gilbert White of Selborne, by Linda Gardiner.
  p Itinerary of the ministry of Gilbert White compiled from some of his sermons, by G. W. Minns.

  q Ashmansworth church, by W. Money, with a description of the mural paintings by C. Keyser.
  r An account of some recent discoveries in Romsey abbey, by J. C. Yarborough.
  s Funeral garlands at Abbotts Ann, by G. W. Minns.
  t The manor of Woodgarston and some documents relating thereto [12th cent.–1416], by R. F. Bigg-Wither.
  u The Roman station of Clausentum at Bitterne.

2007 Vol. 5.

  a Origin of Southampton Water with some account of its earliest navigators, by T. W. Shore.
  b Site of the battle of Aclea, 851, by C. Cooksey.
  c Some notes on Warnford church, by N. C. H. Nisbett.
  d Dummer [with Kempshot], by S. Andrews.
  e Bonchurch parish, by J. Whitehead.
  f Notes on Woolmer forest, by T. W. Shore.
  g Notes on Warblington, by T. W. Shore.
  h Bevis Mount, by F. J. C. Hearnshaw.
  i Second supplement to Hampshire bibliography, by R. G. Davis. [Contd. from vol. 3]
  j Maritime trade of Southampton in the 17th cent., by F. W. Camfield.
  k Carisbrooke church and priory, by J. Groves.
  l The discovery of an Anglo-Saxon cemetery at Droxford, by W. Dale.
  m Notes on some armorial bearings on the presbytery screens, Winchester cathedral, by N. C. H. Nisbett.
  n The priory and manor of Appuldurcombe, Isle of Wight, by J. L. Whitehead.
  o Some relics discovered near the site of the ancient castle of Southampton, by C. F. Cooksey.
  p Remarks on an old map of a portion of the ancient parish of Titchfield, by G. W. Minns.
  q Notes on some Roman urns found at Winchester, by W. H. Jacob.
  r The court leet of Southampton, by F. J. C. Hearnshaw.
  s Notes on recent publications concerning Hampshire, by O. Gilbert. [Contd. in vol. 6]
  t Chapel of St. Nicholas in Castro, Carisbrooke, by P. Stone.
  u Prisoners of war at Winchester [1778–94], by G. N. Godwin.
  v Norman doorways of Hampshire and the Isle of Wight, by J. F. Guyer.
  w A Roman villa at Little Lippen wood, near West Meon (excavated 1905–6), by A. M. Williams.
  x Inventory of the goods and chattels of Sir Richard Worsley, of Appuldurcombe, 1566, by J. L. Whitehead, with an appendix of notes by Elinor R. Aubrey.
  y Notes on a ruined building in Warnford park, by N. C. H. Nisbett.
  z Some extracts from the papal archives relating to the diocese of Winchester, by Mrs. H. Dawson.
  aa Southwick priory, by G. H. Green.
  bb Some notes on Broadlands in the parish of Romsey Infra, by Mrs. Suckling.

2008 Vol. 6.

  a An old Southampton newspaper [*Hampshire Chronicle or Winchester, Southampton and Portsmouth Mercury*, 1772–1774], by T. L. O. Davies.
  b Some notes on the manor of Stanbridge Earls in the parish of Romsey Extra, by Mrs. Suckling.
  c The Meon valley, by H. W. Trinder.
  d Recent treet changes in Southampton, by R. M. Lucas.
  e Genealogical and other notes relating to the De Insula, otherwise de l'Isle, de Lisle, or Lisle family, by J. L. Whitehead.
  f Romsey abbey and town: a transition document, 1539–41, by H. G. D. Liveing.

g The manors and churches of Laverstoke and Freefolk by Sir W. W. Portal.

h Eling, by T. Thistle.

i Farley Chamberlayne and its associations, by Mrs. Suckling.

j Letter concerning Wonston in the 10th cent., by the Hon. F. H. Baring.

k Industrial organisation in Southampton during the 17th cent., by F. W. Camfield.

l Genealogical and other notes relating to the de Estur family of the Isle of Wight, by J. L. Whitehead.

m The Hamble river, by H. W. Trinder.

n Note on Richard Mountaine and William Haskoll, of Winchester, [18th cent.] engravers of book-plates, by C. D. Sherborn.

o Danebury, by J. P. Williams-Freeman.

p The making of the New Forest, by the Hon. F. H. Baring.

q West Saxon occupation of Hampshire, by F. Clarke.

r Some humorous aspects of life in Southampton during the 17th cent., by F. W. Camfield.

s List of Hampshire earthworks, classified according to the schedule of the earthworks committee, by J. P. Williams-Freeman.

2009 Vol. 7.

a Rental of Wymering: early 14th cent. deed, with translation of a part, by R. F. Bigg-Wither.

b Hampshire flints: demarcation of the stone ages, by W. Dale.

c The Hampshire portion of the Devil's highway [part of Roman road on northern boundary of Hampshire], by G. A. Kempthorne.

d Notes on Roman roads in the south of Hants, by J. P. Williams-Freeman.

e Some fine Hampshire fonts, by Emma Swann.

f Beauworth [and a find of William I 'Pax' pennies, 1833].

g Tudor Winchester from civic mss., by W. H. Jacob.

h Notes on the monument in Winchester cathedral, originally marking the burial place of the heart of Ethelmar [d. 1261], by N. C. H. Nisbett.

i Three interesting Hampshire brasses [of Sir John Lysle, d. 1407; John Prophete, d. *c.* 1416; William and Anne Complyn, d. 1498], by E. Beaumont.

j The old Lymington salterns, by W. Ravenscroft.

k Lords of the manor of Farley Chamberlayne, by Mrs. Suckling.

l Arms of lords of Farley from 1346.

m History of the Benedictine priory of Monk Sherborne, by Florence Davidson.

n An ancient interment at Kingsclere, by W. Money. [See below]

o Norman doorways in churches in the northern part of Hampshire, by C. E. Keyser.

p William the Conqueror's march through Hampshire in 1066, by the Hon. F. H. Baring.

q Quaker burial grounds at Baughurst, by Florence A. G. Davidson.

r Historical notes on the parish of Yateley, by J. H. Stilwell.

s The Kingsclere skeleton, by O. G. S. Crawford.

t Roche Court and its former owners, by Miss Skinner.

u Lavant near Alton, by H. Bury.

v Boldre church, Hants, by W. Ravenscroft.

w The [library] catalogue of Titchfield abbey, ed. J. H. Cope.

x Church goods in Hampshire, 1552, ed. J. H. Cope. [Contd. in vol. 8]

2010 Vol. 8.

a Notes on some blacksmiths' legends and the observance of St. Clement's day, by G. P. G. Hills.

b Cowes castle, by Sir W. Portal.

c The Royal Yacht Squadron, by Sir W. Portal.

d The Aclea(h). 1: Of the battle in 851; 2: Of the synods in 782, etc., by F. H. Baring. [On the possible identification of Acleah with Oakley, Hants]

e Old track from Walbury camp to Tidbury Ring, by C. Burne.

f Roman building at Grateley, by J. P. Williams-Freeman.

g Some Hampshire rectors, by Mrs. Cope.

h Notes on the ancient painted glass in Winchester cathedral, by J. D. Le Couteur.

i The misereres of Hampshire, by Emma Swann.

j Architectural account of West Sherborne (Pamber) priory church, by C. E. Keyser.

k Church goods in Hampshire (Winchester College), 1553, transcribed by H. Chitty.

l The ancient yew tree in South Hayling churchyard, by J. G. Sandeman.

m Notes from Newport leet records, *re* curfew, watch and ward, etc., by J. L. Whitehead.

n An unrecognised charter of Alverstoke [948], by J. C. Hughes.

o Some notes on the Solemn League and Covenant in England, with special reference to the parish of Long Sutton, by C. R. S. Elvin.

p Stansted Park and its owners, by A. C. Piper.

q Notes on the remains of ancient painted glass in Stoke Charity church, by J. D. Le Couteur.

r An unrecorded type of circular earthwork in the New Forest, by H. Kidner.

s Hampshire church bells, by J. L. Whitehead.

t Medieval relics from a mysterious interment at Winchester, by W. J. Andrew.

u Church goods in Hampshire in 1549, transcribed by T. Craib, with additional notes by J. H. Cope. [Contd. in vol. 9]

2011 Vol. 9.

a Some notes on the manor of East Tytherley, by Mrs. Suckling.

b Winchester College bells and belfries, by H. Chitty.

c Reminiscences of the city of Winchester 70 years ago [*c.* 1850], by T. Stopher.

d New Forest round barrows which do not conform to either of the three standard types, by H. Kidner.

e History of the drainage of the Hampshire basin and the relation of prehistoric man to that history, by R. W. Hooley.

f The antiquity of man in Hampshire, by O. G. S. Crawford, J. R. Ellaway, and G. W. Willis.

g Excavations at Roundwood during 1920, by O. G. S. Crawford.

h Excavations at Rancombe, near Shorwell, Isle of Wight, Aug. 1920, by O. G. S. Crawford.

i Roman buildings and other antiquities in a district of N.W. Hants, by G. H. Engleheart.

j A cross-base at Winchester, by W. G. Collingwood.

k On place-names in general, and the Hampshire place-names in particular, by G. B. Grundy.

l Hampshire perambulations [or bounds, 13th–16th cent.], by H. Chitty and O. G. S. Crawford.

m An unrecorded brass in Winchester cathedral [14th cent.], by A. Snell.

n Oh! the mistletoe bough [the connexion of the story with Marwell Hall, Hants], by C. Forman.

o Field notes [of archaeological discoveries] Basingstoke district, by J. R. Ellaway, G. W. Willis, and H. Rainbow.

p Palaeoliths from Great Pan farm [near Shide], Isle of Wight, by H. F. Poole.

q Excavation of a mound at Christchurch, by H. St. G. Gray.

r Old roads in central Hants, by C. F. C. Hawkes.

s An account of Alresford, written by Sir George Brydges Rodney, *c.* 1768–82, ed. H. Sumner.

t Notes on the shrine of St. Swithun, by J. D. Le Couteur and D. H. M. Carter.

2012 Vol. 10.

a Excavation of a barrow on St. Catherine's hill, Niton, Isle of Wight, by G. C. Dunning.

b An undisturbed early neolithic site near Sandown, Isle of Wight, by H. F. Poole.

c Ancient road from Purlieu to Lepe, by I. Sanders.

d Staircases (including some Hampshire examples), by W. E. Troke.

e Wills preserved in the probate registry at Winchester: Hants will abstracts, commencing 1502[–1505], by J. C. Smith.

f Excavations at Armsley, by H. S. W. Edwardes.

g Hallstatt pottery from Winchester, by R. W. Hooley.

h Norden's survey of medieval coppices in the New Forest, 1609, by H. Sumner.

i The field archaeology of Doles, by H. S. L. Dewar.

j Low side windows of Hampshire churches, by A. R. Green. [With list and descriptions]

k Excavation of an early bronze age village on Worthy down, Winchester, by R. W. Hooley. 1: Description of the site, prepared for publication by M. L. Tildesley. 2: Description of the finds, prepared for publication by G. C. Dunning.

l Report on human remains found by R. W. Hooley at Worthy down, 1921, by Sir A. Keith.

m Ancient maps of Great Britain, with special reference to Hampshire, by Sir C. Close.

n Painted lid of a reliquary chest or altar chest [1320–35] in Winchester cathedral, by A. R. Green.

o Notes on two excavations in Hampshire [Chilworth Ring earthwork, 1928, and Roman house at Lodge farm, North Warnborough, 1929–30], by Dorothy M. Liddell.

p Weights and measures of the city of Winchester, by Edith E. Wilde.

q Two bronze age discoveries in Hants [at Brown Candover and Hinton Ampner], by H. T. White.

r Notes on a Roman villa at Havant, by F. Warren.

2013 Vol. 11.

a St. Catharine's hill, Winchester, by C. F. C. Hawkes, J. N. L. Myres, C. G. Stevens. [Excavations and history]

2014 Vol. 12.

a Report on the first excavations at Oliver's Battery [near Winchester] 1930, by W. J. Andrew. [Followed by report on the second excavations, 1931]

b The Winchester Anglo-Saxon bowl, and bowl-burial, by W. J. Andrew.

c Gravel and flint implements of Bleak down, Isle of Wight, by H. F. Poole.

d Roof bosses in the nave aisles, Winchester cathedral, by C. J. P. Cave.

e A Hampshire plot [planned 1586 in protest against scarcity of corn and sowing of woad], by H. T. White.

f Two examples of sculptured alabaster panels now remaining in Hampshire churches, by A. R. Green.

g The ecclesiastical court house of the hundred of East Meon, by P. M. Horder.

h Tumuli on Netley hill, Bursledon, by C. F. Fox.

i The Belgae through Hampshire?, by J. P. Williams-Freeman. [On the suggested Belgic invasion of Britain, *c.* 50 B.C.]

j Excavations at Meon hill [Houghton parish], by Dorothy M. Liddell.

k Note on a Romano-British refuse pit at Swanwick, by C. Fox.

l The coast of Hampshire, by J. P. Williams-Freeman.

m Hampshire in early maps and early road-books, by E. G. Box.

n Note on a hoard of iron currency-bars found on Worthy down, Winchester, by R. W. Hooley.

o A vanished castle: an attempt to reconstruct the castle of Southampton from observation, analogy and documentary evidence, by P. G. Stone.

2015 Supplement to vol. 6 (1911).

a Relics of old Southampton, by G. W. Minns.

b Notes on the manor of Knighton, I. of W. and the early manor lords, 1066–1343, by J. L. Whitehead. [Contd. in vols. 7 and 8]

c Arms [of high stewards, recorders, and others] in the town hall at Romsey, by Mrs. Suckling.

d Prehistoric, Roman, and Saxon Nursling, by O. G. S. Crawford.

e Leland in Hampshire in or about 1535–43, by G. W. Minns.

f Henri, second Marquis de Ruvigny, Earl of Galway [d. 1720]: an unknown grave, by G. W. Minns.

Extra publication:

2016 Shore memorial volume. Hampshire papers on the natural history and antiquities of the county and other miscellanea [published and unpublished] by the late T. W. Shore, ed. G. W. Minns. 1908–11.

a Anglo-Saxon Hampshire charters.

b Gemots: early councils and parliaments held in Hampshire [–1393].

c Old ironworks in Hampshire.

d Geology and Hampshire industries.

e Celtic earthworks in Hampshire.

f Traces of old agricultural communities in Hampshire.

g Old roads and fords of Hampshire.

h The basis of Hampshire history.

i Saxon and Norman churches in Hampshire and the Isle of Wight.

j Prehistoric weapons and implements.

k Roman roads and remains in Hampshire.

l Surviving traces of the West Saxon conquest of Hampshire.

m Orientation of churches in Hampshire.

n 'Wishing wells.'

o Decayed Hampshire manufactures.

p Observations on some prehistoric earthworks and tumuli of Hampshire.

q An ancient burial ground in Southampton and its probable identification (St. Andrews?).

r Ancient site of Southampton.

s Ancient Venetian trade with Southampton.

t Ancient watergate of Southampton castle.

u The Southampton common.

v Southampton street and place names.

w The geology of Bramdean valley and the antiquarian associations of Woodcote manor.

x Ellingham, Moyles Court and ancient Hampshire courts.

y Odiham.

z The Meon country.

aa Micheldever.

bb Boarhunt, and some of its early land tenures.

cc Hambledon and the forest of Bere.

dd The Hampshire Field Club at Farley Chamberlayne.

ee Farley Mount.

ff Sherborne priory.

gg Some aspects of Hampshire life in the middle ages.

hh Bramshaw and its neighbourhood.

ii Hayling island.

jj Overton and its neighbourhood.
kk Barton Stacey.
ll Notes on Eling.
mm Notes on Chalton and Catherington
nn Somborne and Stockbridge.
oo Ancient parish of Hound.
pp Rockbourn and its early associations.
qq Broughton.
rr Notes on Wellow.

HAMPSTEAD ANTIQUARIAN AND HISTORICAL SOCIETY

Founded 1897, for the study and recording of antiquarian and historical matters, especially in regard to the borough of Hampstead.

Transactions, 1900–5 (4 vols., 1901–7):

2017 Vol. for 1900.

a Notes on Jack Straw; and the Commonwealth ministers at Hampstead, by W. Urwick.
b Abbé Morel [d. 1852] and the Holly Place chapel, by C. E. Maurice and B. W. Smith.
c A short history of St. Mary's, Holly Place, by C. J. Munich.
d Two eminent occupants of Golder's Hill [Mark Akenside, d. 1770, poet and physician, and Jeremiah Dyson, d. 1776, civil servant and politician], by J. Werge.
e The office of coroner past and present; with the account of a remarkable inquest [1833, after a Chartist riot], by G. D. Thomas.

2018 Vol. for 1901.

a Hampstead at the beginning of last century, by E. Bond.
b Historical sketches connected with an old city church [Holy Trinity, Minories], by S. Kinns.
c The fame of King Alfred, by J. W. Hales.
d England's 'Gounour [Governor] by yonde the see', *c.* 1463–70 [William Caxton], (1) in the City; (2) in the house of the English nation at Bruges; (3) at the Burgundian court, by A. N. Butt.

2019 Vol. for 1902–3.

a The Hampstead Long Room, by E. E. Newton.
b Swakeleys, Mdx.—its history and associations, by H. B. Wheatley.
c A Hampstead invalid and a Hampstead doctor (Gay and Arbuthnot), by C. E. Maurice.
d Stonehenge: old theories and new discoveries, by Mabelle Holmes.
e Wyldes [house] and its story, by Mrs. A. Wilson.

2020 Vol. for 1904–5.

a St. Katharine's royal hospital, past and present, 1148–1904, by A. L. Peile.
b Three celebrities of North End [Lord Chatham, Miss Mulock (Mrs. Craik), and Miss Eliza Meteyard], by C. E. Maurice.
c Kilburn priory, by C. J. Munich.
d Crosby Hall, by A. N. Butt.

HARLEIAN SOCIETY

Founded 1869, for the publication of the heraldic visitations of counties, and manuscripts relating to genealogy, family history, and heraldry.

Visitation section, publications, vols. 48–85:

2021 Vols. 48, 49. Obituary prior to 1800 (as far as relates to England, Scotland, and Ireland), compiled by Sir William Musgrave and entitled by him 'A general nomenclator and obituary, with reference to the books where the persons are mentioned, and where some account of their character is to be found', ed. Sir G. J. Armytage. Vols. v–vi, 1901. [Vols. i–iv, numbered 44–47, were published in 1899–1900]

2022 Vols. 50–52, 55. Lincolnshire pedigrees, ed. A. R. Maddison. 1 vol. in 4. 1902–6.

2023 Vol. 53. Visitations of Sussex, 1530 and 1633–4, ed. W. B. Bannerman. 1905.

2024 Vol. 54. Visitation of Kent, begun 1663, finished 1668, ed. Sir G. J. Armytage. 1906.

2025 Vols. 56, 57. Four visitations of Berkshire, 1532, 1566, 1623, and 1665–6, ed. W. H. Rylands. 2 vols. 1907–8.

2026 Vol. 58. Visitation of the county of Buckingham, 1634, ed. W. H. Rylands. 1909.

2027 Vol. 59. Pedigrees made at the visitation of Cheshire, 1613, and some other contemporary pedigrees, ed. Sir G. J. Armytage and J. P. Rylands. 1909. [In conjunction with the Record Soc., Lancashire and Cheshire]

2028 Vol. 60. Visitation of Surrey, begun 1662, finished 1668, ed. Sir G. J. Armytage. 1910.

2029 Vol. 61. Visitation of Suffolk, begun 1664 and finished 1668, ed. W. H. Rylands. 1910.

2030 Vol. 62. Visitation of the county of Warwick, 1682–3, ed. W. H. Rylands. 1911.

2031 Vol. 63. Staffordshire pedigrees based on the visitation made 1663–4, ed. Sir G. J. Armytage and W. H. Rylands. 1912.

2032 Vol. 64. Pedigrees from the visitation[s] of Hampshire, 1530, 1575, 1622, 1634, ed. W. H. Rylands. 1913.

2033 Vol. 65. Middlesex pedigrees as collected by Richard Mundy, ed. Sir G. J. Armytage. 1914. [For 1593 and 1634]

2034 Vol. 66. Grantees of arms named in docquets and patents to the end of the 17th cent., in mss. in the British Museum and elsewhere, alphabetically arranged by Joseph Foster, ed. W. H. Rylands. 1915.

2035 Vols. 67, 68. Grantees of arms named in docquets and patents between the years 1687 and 1898, preserved in various mss., collected and alphabetically arranged by Joseph Foster, ed. W. H. Rylands. 1 vol. in 2. 1916–17.

2036 Vols. 69–72. Allegations for marriage licences in the archdeaconry of Sudbury, Suffolk, ed. W. B. Bannerman and G. G. B. Bannerman. 2 vols. in 4. 1918–21. [Pt. i: 1684–1754. Pt. ii: 1755–81. Pt. iii: 1782–1814. Pt. iv: 1815–39]

2037 Vol. 73. Visitation of Rutland, 1681–2, partly ed. W. H. Rylands and completed by W. B. Bannerman. 1922.

2038 Vols. 74, 75. Visitations of Kent taken in 1530–1, 1574 and 1592, ed. W. B. Bannerman. 2 vols. 1923–4.

2039 Vols. 76, 77. A collection of miscellaneous grants, crests, confirmations, augmentations and exemplifications of arms in the mss. in the British Museum and elsewhere, ed. W. A. Littledale. 1 vol. in 2. 1925–6.

2040 Vols. 78, 79. An index of persons named in early chancery proceedings, Rich. II (1385) to Edw. IV (1467) preserved in the Public Record Office, London, ed. C. A. Walmisley. 2 vols. 1927–8.

2041 Vols. 80–84. Knights of Edward I. Notices collected by C. Moor. 5 vols. 1929–32.

2042 Vol. 85. Visitation of Norfolk, 1664, ed. and annotated by A. W. H. Clarke and A. Campling. Vol. i, 1933. [Vol. ii, numbered 86, was published in 1934]

Register section, publications, vols. 28–63:

2043 Vol. 28. Registers of the abbey church of SS. Peter and Paul, Bath, ed. A. J. Jewers. Vol. ii, 1901. [Vol. i, numbered 27, was published in 1900]

2044 Vols. 29, 30. Registers of St. Vedast, Foster Lane [1558–1837], and of St. Michael le Quern [1685–1837], London, ed. W. A. Littledale. 2 vols. 1902–3.

2045 Vol. 31. Registers of St. Helen's, Bishopsgate, London [1575–1837], ed. W. B. Bannerman. 1904.

2046 Vol. 32. Registers of St. Martin Outwich, London [1670–1873], ed. W. B. Bannerman. 1905.

2047 Vols. 33–37. Registers of St. Paul's church, Coven Garden, London [1653–1853], ed. W. H. Hunt. 5 vols. 1906–9.

2048 Vols. 38–41. Registers of St. Bene't and St. Peter, Paul's Wharf, London [1607–1837], ed. W. A. Littledale. 4 vols. 1909–12.

2049 Vol. 42. Registers of St. Mildred, Bread Street [1658–1853], and of St. Margaret Moses, Friday Street [1558–1850], London, ed. W. B. Bannerman. 1912.

2050 Vol. 43. Registers of All Hallows, Bread Street [1538–1892], and of St. John the Evangelist, Friday Street [1653–1822], London, ed. W. B. Bannerman. 1913.

2051 Vols. 44, 45. Registers of St. Mary le Bowe, Cheapside, All Hallows, Honey Lane, and of St. Pancras, Soper Lane, London [1538–1852], ed. W. B. Bannerman. 1 vol. in 2. 1914–15.

2052 Vol. 46. Registers of St. Olave, Hart Street, London, 1563–1700, ed. W. B. Bannerman. 1916.

2053 Vols. 47, 48, 51–57. Registers of marriages of St. Mary le Bone, Mdx., 1668–1812, and of Oxford Chapel, Vere Street, St. Mary le Bone, 1736–54, ed. W. B. Bannerman and R. R. B. Bannerman. 9 vols. 1917–27.

2054 Vols. 49, 50. Registers of St. Stephen's Walbrook, and of St. Benet Sherehog, London [1557–1860], ed. W. B. Bannerman. 1 vol. in 2. 1919–20.

2055 Vol. 58. Register of St. Mary Mounthaw, London, 1568–1849, ed. W. B. Bannerman. 1928.

2056 Vols. 59, 60. Register of St. Mary Somerset, London [1557–1853], ed. W. B. Bannerman. 2 vols. 1929–30.

2057 Vols. 61, 62. Registers of St. Mary the Virgin, Aldermanbury, London [1538–1722], ed. W. B. Bannerman. 1 vol. in 2. 1931–2.

2058 Vol. 63. Register of St. Matthew, Friday Street, London, 1538–1812, and the united parishes of St. Matthew and St. Peter Cheap, marriages 1754–1812, ed. A. M. B. Bannerman. 1923.

HARROW ARCHITECTURAL CLUB

Founded 1899, *for the study of architecture.*

Proceedings, 1904–33 (1904–33):

2059 Vol. for 1904.
  a Chichester cathedral: a table of the styles of masoncraft used from 1090 to *c*. 1450, with extracts from documents and other notes, by E. S. Prior.

2060 Vol. for 1905.
  a Figure sculpture of Lincoln cathedral, by A. Gardner.

2061 Vol. for 1906.
  a Elias de Dereham [d. 1245], by W. D. Bushell.
  b Origins of English Gothic, by S. Gardner.

2062 Vol. for 1907.
  a The fiction of Anglo-Saxon architecture, by W. P. Nevill.

2063 Vol. for 1908.
  a Fonts, by S. Gardner.

2064 Vol. for 1909.
  a Architectural notes on some churches near Maldon, by Gertrude Mitchell.

2065 Vol. for 1911.
  a Birds and beasts in church architecture, by G. C. Druce.

2066 Vol. for 1912.
  a English architecture from the 11th to the 17th cent., by Ethel Charles.

2067 Vol. for 1915.
  a Old bridges, by A. Vallance.
  b Great church towers of England, by F. J. Allen.

2068 Vol. for 1922.
  a English school of alabaster sculpture, by A. Gardner.

2069 Vol. for 1925.
  a Cobham collegiate church, Kent, by A. Vallance.

2070 Vol. for 1926–7.
  a Castles, by H. S. Braun.

2071 Vol. for 1933.
  a Mediaeval fashions [in dress, etc.] from monuments, by A. Gardner.

HASTINGS AND ST. LEONARDS NATURAL HISTORY SOCIETY

Founded 1893, *for the promotion of the study of natural history.*

Hastings and East Sussex Naturalist, vols. 1–4 (1906–33):

2072 Vol. 1.[1]
  a Gilbert White and Sussex, by W. H. Mullens.
  b Neolithic man in the forest of Anderida, by H. W. Feilden.

2073 Vol. 2.
  a The Piltdown skull, by C. Dawson.

2074 Vol. 3.
  a Prehistoric Hastings, by A. Belt.
  b Some local heron history, by N. F. Ticehurst.
  c Some more local heron history, by N. F. Ticehurst.
  d William Markwick [d. 1813]: a biographical sketch and notes on his natural history manuscripts now in the Hastings museum, by W. H. Mullens.
  e The ancestry of William Markwick, by J. E. Ray.

2075 Vol. 4.
  a Thomas Parkin, 3 Feb. 1845–10 Oct. 1932, by A. Belt.

[1] Vol. 1 not seen.

HENRY BRADSHAW SOCIETY

Founded 1890, to print liturgical mss. and rare editions of service books, and illustrative documents, on an historical and scientific basis; preference being given to those which bear upon the history of the Book of Common Prayer, or of the Church of England.

Publications, vols. 20–71:

2076 Vols. 20, 22. *Ordinale Sarum sive directorium sacerdotum, auctore Clemente Maydeston* [fl. 1410], transcribed by W. Cooke, and ed. C. Wordsworth. 1 vol. in 2. 1901–2.

2077 Vol. 21. Facsimiles of *Horae de Beata Maria Virgine*, from English mss. of the 11th cent., ed. E. S. Dewick. 1902.

2078 Vols. 23, 28. Customary of the Benedictine monasteries of St. Augustine, Canterbury, and St. Peter, Westminster, ed. Sir E. M. Thompson. 2 vols. 1902–4.

2079 Vol. 24. The benedictional [written late 10th cent. at Winchester] of Archbishop Robert, ed. H. A. Wilson. 1903.

2080 Vol. 25. The clerk's book of 1549 [relating to the office and duties of parish clerks], ed. J. Wickham Legg. 1903.

2081 Vols. 26, 40, 46. The Hereford breviary, ed. W. H. Frere and L. E. G. Brown. 3 vols. 1904–15.

2082 Vol. 27. Tracts on the mass [13th–16th cent.], ed. J. Wickham Legg. 1904.

2083 Vol. 34. The order of the communion, 1548: a facsimile of the British Museum copy, ed. H. A. Wilson. 1908.

2084 Vols. 37, 38, 63. *Ordinale Exon.*, ed. J. N. Dalton. Vols. i–iii, 1909–26. [Vol. iv was published as no. 79 in 1940]

2085 Vol. 39. The pontifical of Magdalen College, ed. H. A. Wilson. 1910.

2086 Vol. 41. English orders for consecrating churches [etc] in the 17th cent., ed. with introd. and notes by J. Wickham Legg. 1911.

2087 Vols. 45, 56. The Leofric collectar. 1 vol. in 2. 1914–21. [Vol. i, with appendix containing a litany and prayers, ed. E. S. Dewick. Vol. ii, the collectar compared with that of St. Wulfstan, together with kindred documents of Exeter and Worcester, ed. from the papers of E. S. Dewick by W. H. Frere]

2088 Vols. 47, 48. The psalter and martyrology of Ricemarch [11th cent.], ed. H. Jackson Lawlor. 2 vols. 1914.

2089 Vol. 50. Cranmer's liturgical projects, ed. J. Wickham Legg. 1915.

2090 Vol. 51. The Canterbury benedictional, ed. R. M. Woolley. 1917.

2091 Vol. 55. The calendar of St. Willibrord: a facsimile, with transcription, introd., and notes, ed. H. A. Wilson. 1918.

2092 Vols. 59, 60. The Gilbertine rite, ed. R. M. Woolley. 2 vols. 1921–2.

2093 Vol. 64. The benedictional of John Longlonde, bishop of Lincoln [d. 1547], ed. R. M. Woolley. 1927.

2094 Vols. 65, 66. The *ordinale* and customary of the Benedictine nuns of Barking abbey, ed. J. B. L. Tolhurst. 1 vol. in 2. 1927–8. [Vol. ii with notes by Laurentia McLachlan]

2095 Vols. 69, 70. The monastic breviary of Hyde abbey, Winchester, ed. with liturgical introd., notes and indices, by J. B. L. Tolhurst. Vols. i–ii, 1932–3. [Vols. iii–vi were issued as nos. 71, 75, 76, and 90, 1934–42]

HERTFORDSHIRE NATURAL HISTORY SOCIETY AND FIELD CLUB

Founded 1875, as the Watford Natural History Society and Hertfordshire Field Club, for the investigation of the meteorology, geology, botany, zoology, ethnology, pre-Norman archaeology and topography, of the county of Hertford. Title changed to above form in 1879.

Transactions, vols. 10–19 (1898–1934):

2096 Vol. 10.
  a Notes on place-names and field-names of the parish of Watford, by P. Manning.
  b Classified subject-index to principal contents of the first twelve volumes [i.e. vols. i–x, and two vols. issued by the Watford Natural History Soc., 1875–80], 1875–1901.

2097 Vol. 11.
  a Hertfordshire maps: a descriptive catalogue of the maps of the county, by Sir H. G. Fordham. [1579–1789. Contd. in vol. 12 (1790–1841), vol. 13 (1842–1900, with additions and corrections), and vol. 15 (further additions)]

2098 Vol. 12.
  a Sun-dials and their mottoes, by L. Evans.
  b Some Hertfordshire naturalists and their work, by B. D. Jackson.
  c The history of botanic illustration, by B. D. Jackson.
  d A neolithic belt found near Berkhamsted common, by Sir J. Evans.

2099 Vol. 13.
  a A recent palaeolithic discovery [flints] near Rickmansworth, by Sir J. Evans.
  b Hertfordshire earthquakes, by J. Hopkinson.
  c Notes on Berkhamsted castle, by D. Montgomerie.

2100 Vol. 14.
  a Recent discoveries of palaeolithic implements in Hertfordshire and Bedfordshire, by Sir J. Evans.
  b 'Burnt Oak' and other notable trees in the neighbourhood of Watford, by D. Hill.
  c St. Albans and its neighbourhood: an account of the topography, geology, hydrology, climate, flora, fauna and archaeology of the district, with a guide to the Hertfordshire county museum, by members of the Society, ed. J. Hopkinson.

2101 Vol. 15.
  a Recent discoveries of prehistoric horse remains in the valley of the Stort, by A. Irving.
  b Classified subject-index to the principal contents of the Transactions, 1875–1914.

2102 Vol. 16.
  a Roads and travel before railways in Hertfordshire and elsewhere, by Sir H. G. Fordham.
  b Two ancient East Anglian industries: cultivation and manufacture of woad and manufacture of gun-flints, by C. Oldham.
  c Skulls of the wild boar from the Roman level at St. Albans, by G. E. Bullen.

2103 Vol. 17.
  a Oyster shells from the site of Verulam, by G. E. Bullen.

2104 Vol. 18.

a Payments for 'vermin' by the Berkhamsted church-wardens [17th–18th cent.], by C. Oldham.

b Changes in Hertfordshire flora: a consideration of the influence of man, by E. J. Salisbury.

c Survey of the Society's work, 1875–1925, by T. E. Jones.

2105 Vol. 19.

a Payments for 'vermin' by some Hertfordshire church-wardens [17th–19th cent.], by C. Oldham.

b History of the Hertfordshire Natural History Society, 1875–1933, by W. J. Cox.

HISTORIC SOCIETY OF LANCASHIRE AND CHESHIRE

Founded 1848, for the furtherance of historical research generally and with reference to the two counties in particular; and to keep a written record of historical facts and modern changes for the benefit of posterity.

Transactions, vols. 51–84[1] (1901–33):

2106 Vol. 51.

a Cheshire in Domesday book, by J. Brownbill.

b Brief historical notes on the churches of St. George and St. John, Liverpool, by H. Peet.

c Records of the Jews in Liverpool, by B. L. Benas.

d Freemasonry in Lancashire and Cheshire (17th cent.), pt. 2: Chester, by W. H. Rylands. [Contd. from vol. 50]

e Warrington church plate, by T. S. Ball.

f Notes on some of the places, traditions, and folklore of the Douglas valley, by W. F. Price.

g George Preston [of Holker Hall, fl. 1618] and Cartmel priory church, by T. J. Cooper.

h Origin of the name Pilkington, by J. Pilkington.

2107 Vol. 52.

a Excavations on the site of the Romano-British *civitas* at Wilderspool, 1899–1900, by T. May.

b The Domesday survey of south Lancashire, by J. H. Lumby.

c Henry Brown: a Liverpool attorney of the 18th cent., by G. T. Shaw.

d Church plate in Manchester cathedral and the parish churches of Preston and Lymm, by T. S. Ball.

e Some features of Roman military defensive works, by J. Garstang.

f Lancashire hearth taxes [1662], by W. F. Irvine.

g Origin of the Irelands of Hale, by W. F. Irvine.

h Sir Thomas Johnson [d. 1729, M.P., of Liverpool], by Edith M. Platt.

i The Poole family of Poole Hall in Wirral, by Margaret E. Poole.

j On the Rigodunum of Ptolemy, by J. Garstang. [An attempt to identify the Roman station with Lancaster]

k Calendar of printed grants of arms, grants of crests, grants of augmentations, and exemplifications of arms, by J. P. Rylands.

2108 Vol. 53.

a Ancient ironworks of Coniston lake, by W. G. Colling-wood.

b The barony of Grelley [11th–14th cent.], by W. Farrer.

c Mediaeval fonts of the hundreds of West Derby and Wirral, by J. W. Ellis.

d Origin of the mayoral allowance at Liverpool and Chester, by J. Elton.

e Notes on the old halls of Wirral [including Leasowe

[1] Vols. 51–78 are also described as 'new series', vols. 15–42.

Castle, Bidston, Storeton, Bromborough, Puddington, Gayton, and Thurstaston], by W. F. Irvine.

f Distribution of surnames in Lancashire in the 16th and 17th cent., by H. Fishwick.

g Notes on the parish of Woodchurch, by W. F. Irvine and F. C. Beazley.

h Liverpool lists of emigrants to America, 1697–1706, by J. Elton.

i List of Roman remains from Ribchester, by J. Garstang.

j The Ribchester temple, by J. Garstang.

2109 Vol. 54.

a Rise and growth of Blackpool, 1592–1792, by C. Roeder.

b Ancient church dedications in Cheshire and south Lancashire, by J. Brownbill.

c Chester, Birkenhead, and Liverpool in the patent and close rolls of the 3 Edwards, by J. H. Lumby.

d Chapel of St. Mary del Key, Liverpool, by J. Elton. [Historical account, *c.* 1257–1745]

e Early recorded mayors of Liverpool [1351–1481]: an original list with documentary authorities, by J. Elton.

f Notes on the Merchant Taylors' schools at Great Crosby, Lancs., by T. Goffey.

g Early charters of the Knights Hospitallers [*c.* 1180–*c.* 1230] relating to Much Woolton, near Liverpool, by R. Gladstone.

h The Ribchester 'temple', by F. Haverfield.

i The Hemans' memorial tablet. [Correspondence relating to the birthplace of Mrs. Hemans, poetess, d. 1835]

j Lancashire Catholicism. [From an 'Account of Papists within the diocese of Chester', 1767]

k Index to vols. 1–51, 1849–1900, prepared by F. C. Beazley.

2110 Vols. 55 and 56.

a Notes on the history of Hall i' th' wood [Tonge] and its owners, by W. F. Irvine.

b Abbey of St. Werburgh, Chester, in the 13th cent., by Miss E. K. McConnell.

c Abbeystead in Wyresdale, and its endowed school, by W. O. Roper.

d Extracts from the Liverpool corporation records, 1541–1701, by Edith M. Platt.

e Birkenhead priory reparation [1896], by A. M. Robinson.

f William the son of Adam, first recorded mayor of Liverpool [fl. 1351–83], by J. Elton.

g Old flour mills of Wirral, by E. M. Abraham.

h Some notes on Heysham church and parish, by E. M. Grafton.

i Chester and Liverpool in the patent rolls of Richard II and the Lancastrian and Yorkist kings [Henry IV, Henry VI, and Edward IV], by J. H. Lumby.

j Excavations on the Romano-British site at Wilderspool and Stockton Heath, 1901–4, by T. May.

k Notes on the parish church of St. Wilfred, Standish, by W. F. Price.

l Warrington in 1580: the Easter roll of moneys due to the rector of Warrington, 22 Elizabeth, by J. P. Rylands.

m Stone axe found at Weston Point [near Runcorn], by W. Handley.

n Temporary licence to bury in St. Nicholas's cemetery, Liverpool, and commission of dedication, 1361–2.

2111 Vol. 57.

a Early fee-farm leases of Liverpool, by R. Muir.

b The old rectory house and rectory of Warton, by J. K. Floyer.

c Notes on some unchronicled Liverpool banks, by J. Hughes.

d The 'going-out' of Prince Charlie in 1745: some local lights on a well-known episode, by F. S. Banner.

e Lancashire and Cheshire in English literature up to about 1700, by R. H. Case.

f Monumental and other inscriptions in the churches of Stoak, Backford, and Thornton-le-Moors, in co. Chester, by J. P. Rylands and F. C. Beazley.

2112 Vol. 58.

a An account of £2000 levied upon the county of Lancaster for the use of the parliamentary army in 1643-4, by H. Fishwick.

b Excavations on the Romano-British site at Wilderspool, 1905, by T. May.

c Further notes on Standish church and its chantries, by Mrs. A. C. Tempest.

d Heraldry of Ormskirk church, by J. Bromley.

e An old Liverpool captain and his ship [Daniel Wilcox d. 1789, of the *Hero*], by A. H. Arkle.

f Some armorial house-tablets in Lancashire, by W. F. Price and J. P. Rylands. [Contd. in vol. 60]

g Exemplification and confirmation of the Booth arms and quarterings by Robert Cooke, esquire, Clarenceux king of arms, to William Booth, esquire, of London, 1 April 1580, communicated by W. H. Rylands.

h History of Liverpool directories, 1766-1907, by G. T. Shaw.

i Registers of St. Mary's, Birkenhead, 1721-1812, ed. F. C. Beazley.

2113 Vol. 59.

a Notes on the parish of Burton in Wirral, by F. C. Beazley.

b The manor of Rufford and the ancient family of Heskeths, by W. G. Proctor.

c Notes on the Benedictine abbey of Séez: its English lands and charters, by Miss E. M. Grafton.

d Pugin and the rebuilding of Winwick chancel, by W. A. Wickham.

e A report on Liverpool castle, 2 Oct. 1559, by R. Gladstone.

f The disafforestation of Wirral [1376], by R. Stewart-Brown.

g Liverpool in the reign of Anne, 1705 and 1708, from a rate assessment book of the town and parish, giving one of the earliest known lists of inhabitants, with their respective holdings according to streets, by H. Peet. [With map]

2114 Vol. 60.

a The ancient parish of Croston: a historical retrospect, by W. G. Proctor. [Contd. in vol. 62]

b An account of the oil-painting 'Liverpool in 1680', with notes on the Peters family of Platbridge and Liverpool, by R. Stewart-Brown.

c Some notes on Aughton, by W. A. Wickham.

d Heraldry of the font at Holt [Denbighshire], by E. E. Dorling.

e Some old books on Southport, by F. H. Cheetham.

f Three touches of a Lancashire parish [Up-Holland] with national history [the rebellion of Thomas of Lancaster, the dissolution of the monasteries, and the civil war], by G. F. Wills.

g Some Cheshire heraldic documents, by W. H. Rylands. [Grant of crest to Sir Hugh Cholmondeley, 1547; exemplification of arms, etc., to Sir Thomas Venables, 1560; grant of augmentation to Sir Piers Legh, 1575; grant of supporters to Robert Cholmondeley, 1661]

h Lancashire recusants, about 1630, by J. Brownbill.

i God's Providence house, Liverpool, by W. F. Irvine.

2115 Vol. 61.

a Some notes on Billinge [church], by W. A. Wickham.

b The tower of Liverpool with some notes on the Clayton family of Crooke, Fulwood, Adlington, and Liverpool, by R. Stewart-Brown.

c Elizabeth Farren [d. 1829], Countess of Derby, by R. J. Broadbent.

d The Poor law in Liverpool, 1681-1834, by W. L. Blease.

e Liverpool during the civil war, by Edith M. Platt.

f Selections from the Moore papers [17th cent., relating to Liverpool], transcribed by R. Stewart-Brown.

g Index to papers and communications, vols. 52-61.

2116 Vol. 62.

a Merchants' marks and other mediaeval personal marks, by J. P. Rylands.

b Notes on the Hesketh pedigree, by W. G. Procter.

c Some notes on Hindley chappell, by W. A. Wickham.

d Some Cheshire heraldic documents from the Ashmole manuscripts, by W. H. Rylands.

e Maps and plans of Liverpool and district by the Eyes family of surveyors, with particulars of some 37 local surveys, etc. [1725-1856], by R. Stewart-Brown.

f Richard Brooke of Handford *vel* Handforth and Liverpool, F.S.A. [d. 1861]: some notes concerning his lineage and connections, by R. C. Lockett.

2117 Vol. 63.

a Liverpool almshouses, by H. Peet.

b The Herdman drawings of old Liverpool, by R. Stewart-Brown.

c Eccleston church in Leyland, by F. H. Cheetham.

d The Brownlow family of Hall i' th' wood, by H. I. Anderton.

e Misericords in Lancashire and Cheshire churches, by A. Wolfgang.

f Moore of Bankhall, by R. Stewart-Brown.

g Sir Roger Bradshaigh's letter-book [1660-76].

h Early mayors of Lancaster [1338-1508; bailiffs from 1246].

i Some Lancashire and Cheshire heraldic documents, by W. H. Rylands.

j Wirral census, 1811, by A. H. Arkle.

2118 Vol. 64.

a Early coffee houses of Liverpool, by A. H. Arkle.

b A contest for the wardenship of Manchester [1466], by J. Brownbill.

c Ancient screens in Cheshire and Lancashire churches, by A. Wolfgang.

d Church discipline after the Restoration, by W. F. Irvine.

e Canting arms in Cheshire, by E. E. Dorling.

f The Overchurch chalice [early 17th cent.], by F. C. Beazley.

g The royal manor and park of Shotwick, by R. Stewart-Brown.

h Some notes on chapter-houses, by W. A. Wickham.

i A narrative of the '15 [from a ms. in the possession of W. Pedder, 1912], by Dorothy Fitzherbert-Brockholes (Mrs. Longueville).

j Old Swan charity school [Liverpool], by J. Hoult.

k Obits of the Radcliffes of Ordsall [1548-78].

l The last ancress of Whalley [Isolda Heton, 1437].

m A Blackburnshire puture roll [c. 1440-62], ed. H. I. Anderton.

n Acton church [near Nantwich] seating arrangements [1635].

o Tarporley in 1755.

p Lancashire recusants and Quakers [temp. Charles II].

q Note on a palimpsest brass in Hawarden church, by M. Stephenson.

2119 Vol. 65.

   a A Liverpool castle token, by C. R. Hand.
   b St. Nicholas's church, Liverpool: its architectural history, by H. Peet. [With appendix on the chapel of St. Mary del Key]
   c Notes on Childwall, by R. Stewart-Brown.
   d An armorial bench-end in Hawarden church, by J. P. Rylands.
   e North Meols church, by F. H. Cheetham.
   f Edge Lane Hall [Liverpool], by C. R. Hand.
   g Lancashire jottings. [Contd. in vols. 66, 67, 69 and 73]
   h Malpas grammar school [its foundation, 1528].

2120 Vol. 66.

   a Notes on Shotwick, by F. C. Beazley.
   b The brothers Beattie and their drawings of old Liverpool [1845–1913], by C. R. Hand.
   c The Southport of 60 years ago, by E. R. Beattie.
   d 15th cent. angels bearing shields of arms, from Aughton church, by P. Nelson.
   e Anglian cross-head at Aughton and other recent discoveries there, by W. A. Wickham.
   f Church of St. Michael-on-Wyre in Amounderness, by F. H. Cheetham.
   g Mediaeval bedposts in Broughton church, Chester, by W. F. J. Timbrell.
   h Old St. Nicholas's, Liverpool, by J. Brownbill.
   i Holford Hall, by A. Wolfgang.
   j Will of Thomas Holden of Holden, 1441, by J. C. Smith.
   k Will of Nicholas Blundell, 1736 [of Little Crosby].

2121 Vol. 67.

   a Captain William Latham [fl. 1808–25] and the Calderstones, by C. R. Hand.
   b Will of Mrs. Ann Molyneux, with three codicils [1728], by H. Peet.
   c The [clipper ship] *Red Jacket* and its 'Sapling' [a periodical issued 1855], by A. H. Arkle.
   d Ancient alabasters at Lydiate, by P. Nelson.
   e Roll of the mock corporation of Farnworth in Widnes [18th cent.], by C. Madeley.
   f Equestrian aquamaniles, by P. Nelson.
   g Cockersand chapter-house, by W. A. Wickham.
   h Bells of St. Peter's church, Liverpool, by R. T. Bailey.
   i Martin Hall, Burscough, by J. Bromley.
   j Monumental inscriptions in Melling church, Liverpool, by F. H. Cheetham.
   k Patents of arms to the Butlers of Bewsey and Kirkland, by J. P. Rylands.
   l Memorial inscriptions in Hawarden parish church, by W. B. Jones.

2122 Vol. 68.

   a Joseph Williamson: 'the king of Edge hill' [fl. 1804–41], by C. R. Hand. [Contd. in vol. 79]
   b The townfield of Liverpool, 1207–1807, by R. Stewart-Brown.
   c Early Liverpool printers, by A. H. Arkle.
   d Stallwork in Cheshire, 1915, by F. H. Crossley.
   e Heraldic memorials of the Hulton family, in Deane church, Lancs., by J. P. Rylands.
   f Some heraldic wood-carvings, by P. Nelson.
   g Chantry of St. John Baptist at Bailey, by C. A. Newdigate.
   h Architectural description [of the chapel at Bailey], by F. H. Cheetham.
   i The mediaeval Blackburn pax, by R. T. Bailey. [With list of surviving English paxes]
   j Mediaeval music, by A. W. Pollitt. [Contd. in vol. 69]
   k Elizabeth Stuart, Queen of Bohemia, 1596–1662, by W. H. Williams.

   l Arms and crest of John Westby, 1560, by J. P. Rylands.
   m Plea roll pedigrees.

2123 Vol. 69.

   a Church screens of Cheshire, by F. H. Crossley.
   b The Norris chapel at Childwall, by C. R. Hand.
   c Who was 'William Stainford, abbot'?, by C. A. Newdigate. [Reputedly of Cockersand, 1393]
   d Some unusual English alabaster panels, by P. Nelson.
   e Monuments at Bunbury church, Ches., by J. P. Rylands and F. C. Beazley. [Contd. in vol. 70]

2124 Vol. 70.

   a Remains of mediaeval stallwork in Lancashire, by F. H. Crossley.
   b The Liverpool court of passage [or borough court], by W. Peel.
   c Manchester cathedral screens, by H. A. Hudson.
   d Allotment of a seat in Blackburn church [1687–1723], by J. Livesey.

2125 Vol. 71.

   a Speke Hall, by H. Winstanley.
   b Stanlawe Grange at Aigburth, by C. R. Hand.
   c A Stanley coffer, 1678, by R. T. Bailey.
   d Recently recovered plans of old St. Nicholas's church, Liverpool, by H. Peet. [With an appendix relating to the sale of a pew, 1773]
   e Dame Mary Moore [fl. 1675], by W. F. Irvine.
   f Impressions of armorial seals of Cheshire gentry made by Elias Ashmole in 1663, by J. P. Rylands.
   g Two mediaeval alabasters, by P. Nelson.

2126 Vol. 72.

   a Mediaeval roofs of Manchester cathedral, by H. A. Hudson.
   b Travelling post [*i.e.* with hired horses], by J. Hoult.
   c Journal of John Hough [d. 1797], lord of the manor of Liscard, by E. C. Woods.
   d Woodwork of English alabaster retables, by P. Nelson.
   e Some Lancashire wills [William Crookall of Bispham, 1603; Nicholas Bray of Liverpool, 1559; John Molyneux of Liverpool, 1698], ed. J. P. Rylands.
   f Norris deeds concerning Liverpool [14th–17th cent.].
   g Lancashire chancery depositions.

2127 Vol. 73.

   a Early Liverpool coaching, by A. H. Arkle.
   b Three local [i.e. near Liverpool] windmills, by C. R. Hand.
   c The Kirkby font, by F. C. Larkin.
   d Carvings of mediaeval musical instruments in Manchester cathedral, by H. A. Hudson.
   e Leasowe Castle: its owners and history, by E. C. Woods.
   f 14th cent. English alabaster of the Blessed Virgin, by P. Nelson.
   g Crosse family of Wigan, Chorley, and Liverpool, by R. Stewart-Brown and F. C. Beazley.
   h Abstracts of deeds relating to the sale of pews in St. Nicholas's church, Liverpool, by H. Peet.
   i The lost [Domesday] manor of Thirnby, by W. H. Chippindall.

2128 Vol. 74.

   a Maghull chapel, by F. H. Cheetham.
   b Rector [Henry] Wolstenholme [d. 1771] and his memorial tablet, by H. Peet.
   c Reliquae of St. Peter's church, Liverpool, by H. Peet.
   d Manchester cathedral: the screens of the nave chantries, by H. A. Hudson.
   e Wirral watersheds and river-systems and their influence on local history, by E. H. Rideout.

f Saint Catherine panels in English alabaster at Vienna, by P. Nelson.
g Early railways in south-west Lancashire, by W. H. Williams.
h Lord Harington [d. 1458], and Conishead.
i Fitton obits, by R. Stewart-Brown.
j Notes on the Brooke and Brock families of Cheshire, by F. C. Beazley.
k Index to vols. 62–71. [Vol. 86, published 1935, contains the index to vols. 72–85]

2129 Vol. 75.

a The parish of Thurstaston [its history], by F. C. Beazley.
b Sculptured Clayton arms at Otterspool, formerly in Water Street, Liverpool, by R. T. Bailey.
c Blowick: the name and the place, by F. H. Cheetham.
d Crannogs, by F. O. Blundell.
e An English 15th cent. alabaster reredos of St. Edmund, by P. Nelson.
f Cheshire pedigrees, by T. Price.
g The ancient manors of Whittington, by W. H. Chippindall.

2130 Vol. 76.

a Mediaeval monumental effigies remaining in Cheshire, by F. H. Crossley.
b Four Liverpool clippers, by F. C. Beazley.
c The 'French chapel' in Scotland Road [Liverpool], 1804–32, by A. de Curzon.
d Notes on North Meols, by F. H. Cheetham.
e Ormskirk grammar school: the first minute-book, 1613–1890, by J. R. Bate.
f Old-time Lancashire chalices, by F. O. Blundell.
g Wirral field-names, by E. H. Rideout.
h The Chester mystery plays, by G. W. Mathews.
i John Fletcher [printer, fl. 1784–1831] and *The Stranger in Chester* [by J. H. Hanshall, 1816], by C. R. Hand.

2131 Vol. 77.

a A masque at Knowsley [1640/1, written by Sir Thomas Salusbury], by R. J. Broadbent.
b The [Liverpool] Athenaeum book-plate, by F. G. Blair.
c John de Winwick [d. 1359] and his chantry in Huyton church, by F. Crooks.
d Prescot watch-making in the 18th cent., by J. Hoult.
e Sites of ancient villages in Wirral, by E. H. Rideout.
f Euxton market [and its charter, 1301], by E. C. Woods.
g Wirral records of the 17th cent., by F. C. Beazley. [Additional note in vol. 78]

2132 Vol. 78.

a Fire insurance in Liverpool, by P. C. Brown.
b Euxton chapel, by F. H. Cheetham.
c Notes on the early Crooks of Crook, Whittle-le-Woods, by F. Crooks.
d Hospital of St. John at Chester, by R. Stewart-Brown.
e Further notes on the Penkett family, by E. C. Woods.
f Bell ringing orders at Preston church, 1587–8, by F. H. Cheetham.
g Excavations at Hilbre, 1926, by R. Newstead.
h Liverpool's second directory, 1767, by G. T. Shaw.

2133 Vol. 79.

a The old custom house, Liverpool, by E. H. Rideout.
b Some notes on the Liverpool election of 1806, by G. W. Mathews.
c Prescot in Tudor times, by J. Hoult.
d Smuggling in Wirral, by E. C. Woods.
e The ancient chest of St. Nicholas's church, Liverpool, by H. Peet.

f The Chester companies and the old quay, by Edna Rideout.
g Excavations on the site of Liverpool castle, 1927, by F. C. Larkin.

2134 Vol. 80.

a Huskisson and Liverpool, by G. S. Veitch.
b Henry Park, surgeon [d. 1831], and his register, by F. C. Beazley.
c The granges of Furness abbey, with special reference to Winterburn-in-Craven, by Annie Cottam.
d Account book of the new haven, Chester, 1567–8, by Edna Rideout.
e Heraldry of Huyton church, by F. Crooks.
f Bye-laws of Ashton-under-Lyne, by E. H. Rideout.
g Some notes on Robert Williamson, printer and stationer of Liverpool [fl. 1752–63], by A. H. Arkle.
h Later records of the Jews in Liverpool, by B. B. Benas.
i Pedigree of Statham [Liverpool and New Zealand branch] from 1716, by R. Stewart-Brown.

2135 Vol. 81.

a Crosby Hall, Lancs., by F. H. Cheetham.
b Notes on the parish and church of Harthill, by G. W. Mathews.
c 'A pretended voyage to America', by Edna Rideout. [On Christopher Carleill's trading proposition to the merchants of Chester, 1583]
d Poor law administration in North Meols in the 18th cent., by E. H. Rideout.
e Emigration to British North America under the early passenger acts, 1803–42, by Kathleen A. Walpole.
f Mrs. Charles Tinsley, novelist and poet [d. 1885], a little-known Lancashire authoress, by H. Peet.

2136 Vol. 82.

a Development of the Liverpool warehousing system [chiefly in the 18th cent.], by E. H. Rideout.
b Mr. Serjeant Spankie [d. 1842], by G. S. Veitch.
c The *Kitty's Amelia*, the last Liverpool slaver [lost, 1809], by C. R. Hand.
d A legacy to S. Mary del Key, 1509 [including a collar of SS, by Thomas Barrowe, the King's cook], by F. C. Beazley.
e The pool of Liverpool [the harbour and its history], by R. Stewart-Brown.
f An Altcar tithes dispute in the 14th cent., by Annie Cottam.
g Thomas Steers [architect, d. 1750], the engineer of Liverpool's first dock: a memoir, by H. Peet.

2137 Vol. 83.

a North Meols church, by F. H. Cheetham.
b The Wavertree enclosure act, 1768, by Ina Leach.
c Rodney Street, Liverpool, by Edna Rideout. [On its inhabitants and associations, with particular reference to A. H. Clough, poet, and notes on house numbering in early Liverpool directories]
d Armorial seal of William de Faryngton [14th cent., with descent of the Faryngton family], by F. Crooks.
e Stationers, booksellers and printers of Chester to about 1800, by R. Stewart-Brown.
f Lancashire witches, 1612 and 1634, by Mildred Tonge.
g Monument to Sir Thomas Hesketh, bt. [d. 1778], at Rufford, by F. H. Cheetham.

2138 Vol. 84.

a The episode of the Irish beef [imported from Ireland, 1723, and seized in accordance with the navigation acts], by E. H. Rideout.

b Records of the court baron of North Meols, 1640 and 1643, with observations on the North Meols court leet, 1884–1926, by F. H. Cheetham.

c The cotton famine in Lancashire [1861–5], by W. O. Henderson.

d The court leet of Prescot, by F. A. Bailey.

e Lancashire and Cheshire briefs in a Rutland parish [Hambleton, 1707–48], by F. H. Cheetham.

f Township papers of Great Sankey, Lancs., by G. A. Dunlop and E. H. Rideout.

HISTORICAL ASSOCIATION

Founded 1906, *for the advancement of the study and teaching of history.*

Leaflets, 1–92:

2139 No. 1. Source-books. [Bibliography. 1907]

2140 No. 2. Some books on the teaching of history in schools. [Bibliography. 1907].

2141 No. 3. Summary of historical examinations affecting schools, including matriculation examinations and entrance scholarships. [1906. Revised edns. issued, apparently annually, until 1920].

2142 No. 4. Address by the Right Hon. James Bryce on the teaching of history in schools. [1907].

2143 No. 5. Brief bibliography of British history for the use of teachers. [1907].

2144 No. 6. Books upon general history, ancient history, and European history. [Bibliography. 1907].

2145 No. 7. Supplementary reading. [Bibliography, for British history. 1907]

2146 No. 8. Books on colonial history: the history of the British Empire. [Bibliography. 1907].

2147 No. 9. Bibliography of Exeter. 1908.

2148 No. 10. Address by Thomas Hodgkin on the teaching of history in schools. 1908.

2149 No. 11. The teaching of local history, by W. M. Childs, etc. 1908.

2150 No. 12. Illustrations, portraits, and lantern slides, chiefly for British and modern history. 1908. [Bibliography]

2151 No. 13. Historical maps and atlases. 1908. [Bibliography]

2152 No. 14. Bibliography of London. 1908.

2153 No. 15. The teaching of civics in public schools, by G. T. Hankin. 1909.

2154 No. 16. The revolutionary and Napoleonic era. 1909. [Bibliography]

2155 No. 17. An experiment in the teaching of history, by Winifred Mercier. 1909.

2156 No. 18. Recent British history, being the history of the United Kingdom, 1815–1909. 1910. [Bibliography]

2157 No. 19. Methods of teaching history in schools. 1910.

2158 No. 20. School historical libraries, by F. J. Weaver. 1910. [List of suggested items]

2159 No. 21. Brief bibliography of Scottish history for the use of teachers, by H. W. Meikle. 1910. [Revised 1921]

2160 No. 22. Development of the castle in England and Wales, by F. M. Stenton. 1910. [With bibliographical note and classified list of castles]

2161 No. 23. Brief bibliography of Irish history, by Constantia Maxwell. 1911. [Revised 1921 as 'A short bibliography of Irish history']

2162 No. 25. Short bibliography of the history of Sheffield, by E. Curtis. 1911.

2163 No. 26. On the educational value of history, by A. F. Pollard. 1911.

2164 No. 28. Some influences of the geography of Northumberland upon its history, by G. H. Thomson. 1912.

2165 No. 29. History of Europe from 1815 and of the United States from 1783. 1912. [Bibliography]

2166 No. 32. An essay on English monasteries, by Rose Graham. 1913. [With brief bibliography and notes on monastic plans by W. H. St. J. Hope]

2167 No. 33. Bibliography of English economic history, by J. H. Clapham. 1913. [Revised 1920]

2168 No. 35. Brief bibliography of British constitutional history, by W. S. McKechnie. 1914.

2169 No. 36. History and the present war, a short bibliography for the use of teachers of history. 1914.

2170 No. 37. The value of history as a factor in moral education, by A. Mary Baylay. 1915.

2171 No. 38. Norman London, by F. M. Stenton; medieval London, by C. L. Kingsford. 1915.

2172 No. 39. Supplementary bibliography of the war, by F. J. C. Hearnshaw. 1915.

2173 No. 42. Bibliography of political theory, by A. J. Carlyle and G. P. Gooch. 1916.

2174 No. 44. Bibliography of mediaeval history, 400–1500, by Beatrice A. Lees. 1917. [Cf. no. **2195** below]

2175 No. 45. The teaching of history and the use of local illustrations [with examples from Hitchin and neighbourhood], by F. Seebohm. 1918.

2176 No. 46. List of selected books relating to the history of the British Empire overseas suitable for the use of schools and students, by A. P. Newton. 1918. [Revised 1923, 1929]

2177 No. 47. Bibliography of social history, by Ethel H. Spalding. 1919.

2178 No. 49. Brief bibliography of Welsh history for the use of teachers, by J. E. Lloyd. 1921.

2179 No. 50. Time charts, by Helen M. Madeley. [1921].

2180 No. 51. Historical novels, by C. H. Firth. 1922.

2181 No. 52. Bibliography of modern history, 1500–1789, by Lillian M. Penson. 1922.

2182 No. 53. Roman Britain, especially as illustrated by the excavations at Caerwent, by A. T. Martin.

2183 No. 54. Short bibliography of architecture, for the use of teachers of history and others, by A. Stratton. 1923.

2184 No. 55. Bibliography of church history, by J. P. Whitney. 1923.

2185 No. 56. The congress of Vienna, 1814–15, and the conference of Paris, 1919. [1923].

a A comparison of their organisation and results, by C. K. Webster.

b Attempts at international government in Europe; the period of the congress of Vienna (1814–25); and the period since the treaty of Versailles (1919–22), by H. W. V. Temperley.

c A note on the Corfu incident (1923).

d A select bibliography.

2186 No. 57. The English parish church, by S. Gardner. [1924].

2187 Nos. 58, 61. Bibliography of naval history, by G. Callender. 2 pts. 1924–5. [Pt. 1: 1485–1714; pt. 2: 1739–1919]

2188 No. 59. Short list of books on world history, by J. A. White, etc. 1924.

2189 No. 62. Foreign policy and the Dominions [1883–1925], by W. J. Harte. 1925.

2190 No. 65. Brief summary of diplomatic events from the German armistice to Locarno [1925], with references to diplomatic documents, by H. Temperley. 1926.

2191 No. 66. Parish history and records, by A. Hamilton Thompson. Revised edition, 1926. [First published by the S.P.C.K., 1919]

2192 No. 67. The evidence of the Casket letters, by C. A. Mitchell. 1927.

2193 No. 68. Short bibliography of modern European history, 1709 [1789]–1926, by H. Temperley and Lillian M. Penson. 1927.

2194 No. 69. The study of history in schools as a training in the art of thought, by F. C. Happold. 1927.

2195 No. 70. Short bibliography of medieval history, 400–1500, by Beatrice A. Lees. 1927. [Revised 1934]

2196 No. 72. Short bibliography of local history, by A. Hamilton Thompson. 1928.

2197 No. 73. The Norman conquest, by D. C. Douglas. 1928.

2198 No. 74. The teaching of pre-history in schools, by Dina P. Dobson. 1928.

2199 No. 75. Short bibliography of English constitutional history, by Helen M. Cam and A. S. Turberville. 1929.

2200 No. 77. The English captivity of James I, King of Scots (1406–24), by E. W. M. Balfour-Melville. 1929.

2201 No. 78. Church and state in England in the 18th cent., by N. Sykes. 1930.

2202 No. 79. The philosophy of history [a survey of its development from the 16th cent.], by R. G. Collingwood. 1930.

2203 No. 80. Selected epigraphs: the inaugural lectures of the Regius Professors of Modern History at Oxford and Cambridge since 1841, by L. S. Wood. 1930.

2204 No. 81. A village history exhibition as an educational factor [an example from Cowden, Kent, in 1922], by G. Ewing. 1930.

2205 No. 82. List of illustrations for use in history teaching in schools. 1930.

2206 No. 83. The manor [in medieval England], by Miss L. C. Latham. 1931.

2207 No. 85. Site of the battle of Bannockburn, by T. Miller. 1931.

2208 No. 87. Owain Glynn Dŵr (Owen Glendower), by J. E. Lloyd. 1932.

2209 No. 88. European arms and armour, by C. J. Ffoulkes. 1932.

2210 No. 89. Control of foreign policy in the British Commonwealth of Nations [1883–1932], by W. J. Harte. 1932.

2211 No. 90. Medieval education in England, by R. B. Hepple. 1932.

2212 No. 92. Methods of chronology, by A. E. Stamp. 1933.

English History in Contemporary Poetry, nos. 1–5:

2213 No. 1. The 14th century, by H. Bruce. 1914.

2214 No. 2. Lancaster and York, 1399–1485, by C. L. Kingsford. *P.* 1913.

2215 No. 3. The Tudor monarchy, 1485–1588, by N. L. Frazer. 1914.

2216 No. 4. Court and parliament, 1588–1688, by F. J. C. Hearnshaw. *P.* 1913.

2217 No. 5. The 18th century, by C. L. Thomson. 1914.

Constitutional Documents, nos. 1–6:

2218 No. 1. The coronation charter of Henry I, 1100, ed. F. J. C. Hearnshaw. *P.* [1914].

2219 No. 2. Magna Carta, 1215, ed. F. J. C. Hearnshaw. *P.* [1914].

2220 No. 3. The Petition of Right, 1628, ed. F. J. Weaver. *P.* [1914].

2221 No. 4. Habeas corpus Act, 1679, ed. F. J. C. Hearnshaw. *P.* [1914].

2222 No. 5. The Bill of Rights, 1689, ed. F. J. Weaver. *P.* [1914].

2223 No. 6. The Act of Settlement, 1701, ed. F. J. Weaver. *P.* [1914].

History, new ser., vols. 1–18 (1916–34):

2224 Vol. 1.

a The colonization of Ulster [*temp.* James I], by Constantia Maxwell.

b Fifty years of British foreign policy [1866–1916], by W. J. Harte.

c The growth of an imperial parliament, by A. F. Pollard. [A survey of British parliamentary development from the reign of Henry II, with particular reference to the problem of union with the Dominions]

d Ludlow: a study in local history, by J. E. Morris.

e The making of an imperial parliament, by R. Muir and D. O. Malcolm. [A criticism of the article by A. F. Pollard]

f A moss trooper [being a brief account of John Heron, of Crawley, fl. 1500–24], by Ruth Dodds.

2225 Vol. 2.

a The growth of an imperial parliament: a rejoinder, by A. F. Pollard.

b The Zulu problem of 1878–9 [and the Natal government], by A. F. Hattersley.

c Irish national tradition [and its expression in literature], by Alice S. Green.

d The history of education [and the lack of works upon it in Great Britain], by H. M. Beatty.

e The expulsion of the Long Parliament [1653, from contemporary accounts], by C. H. Firth.

f Historical revisions. 1: Magna Carta, by A. F. Pollard. 2: The real significance of the Armada's overthrow, by G. Callender. 4: The meaning of Protectorate in the British Empire, by C. P. Lucas.

g An Elizabethan prophecy [and its medieval origins], by C. W. Previté-Orton.

2226 Vol. 3.

a Historical revisions. 5: The two houses of parliament and their separation, by A. F. Pollard. 6: Warren Hastings and Macaulay's mis-representation of his character and government in Bengal, by J. W. Neill. 7: The effects of the Black Death on rural organization in England, by Eileen E. Power. 8: 'No taxation without representation': the origins of separatist tendencies in the American colonies in the 18th cent., by A. F. Pollard. 9: Geoffrey of Monmouth and the Brut as sources of early British history, by R. W. Chambers. [Contd. in vol. 4, with a rejoinder, by W. M. Flinders Petrie. Also a note on the text of Geoffrey of Monmouth, by R. W. Chambers]

b The naval campaign of 1587 [in Cadiz bay, with particular reference to English gunnery tactics], by G. Callender.

2227 Vol. 4.

a Historical revisions. 10: The battle of Flores, 1591, by G. Callender. 12: English craft gilds in the middle ages, by Eileen E. Power.

2228 Vol. 5.

a Historical revisions. 13: The battle of Bannockburn [1314], by T. F. Tout. 14: The Petition of Right, 1628, by E. R. Adair. 15: The balance of power: the origin and use of the phrase, by A. F. Pollard. 16: The Danes in England, by F. M. Stenton.

b Evolution of sea-power under the first two Tudors, by G. Callender.

2229 Vol. 6.

a The beginnings of colleges [at Cambridge], by A. Gray.
b Europe before the war [1871–1914], by G. P. Gooch.
c An essay in historical method: the Barbellion diaries [being a criticism of *Journal of a Disappointed Man* and *A Last Diary* by W. N. P. Barbellion], by A. F. Pollard.
d Social problems in the 19th cent. [in Britain], by C. R. Fay.
e The Dominions and foreign affairs, by A. F. Pollard.
f Historical revisions. 18: The Act of Treasons, 1352, by Isobel D. Thornley. 19: The study of English place-names, by F. M. Stenton.
g Illustrations of medieval commercial morality [in the 14th and 15th cent., with particular reference to the Company of Staplers of Calais], by A. S. Walker.
h London and its records, by Eliza Jeffries Davis.
i Barbellion's diaries, by H. R. Cummings. [A reply to the article by A. F. Pollard, with a note by A. F. Pollard]
j The Dutch and Walloons at Norwich [1564–1643, with reference to 'The Dutch and Walloon Strangers' Book'], by Kate Hotblack.
k Local war records [1914–18: report of the secretary to the Local War Records committee on the year's work, 1920–21].

2230 Vol. 7.

a Anglo-French trade relations under Charles II, by D. G. E. Hall.
b The monastery school at Jarrow [681–1083], by R. B. Hepple.
c Historical revisions. 22: The Pilgrim Fathers, by J. A. Williamson. 23: The number of casualties at Peterloo, 1819, by G. M. Trevelyan.
d Lord Bryce and modern democracies [an appreciation of his life and work], by A. F. Pollard.
e Historical revisions. 24: The Navigation Act of 1651, by G. N. Clark.

2231 Vol. 8.

a Historical revisions. 25: The Great Fire of London, 1666, by Eliza Jeffries Davis. 28: The great statute of *praemunire*, 1529, and its predecessors, what they ordained, by W. T. Waugh.
b On autographs [and their validity], by H. Jenkinson.
c The jewels lost in the Wash [1216], by A. V. Jenkinson.
d The recruiting of the Long Parliament, 1645–7, by R. N. Kershaw.
e Emancipation of slaves at the Cape [1828–34], by A. F. Hattersley.
f The centenary of Francis Parkman, 1823–93, by B. Williams.

2232 Vol. 9.

a Parliamentary analogies from the Channel Islands, by A. J. Eaglestone. [Development of the legislature in Jersey and Guernsey]
b Historical revisions. 30: The Vikings, by A. Mawer. 31: The general elections of 1784, by C. E. Fryer.
c What were the 'Provisions of Oxford' [1258]?, by E. F. Jacob.
d Italian influences on English history during the Renaissance, by Cecilia M. Ady.
e The overland route to India in the 18th cent., by H. L. Hoskins.

2233 Vol. 10.

a The allegory of *Robinson Crusoe*, by G. Parker. [*Robinson Crusoe* as Defoe's autobiography]
b Historical revisions. 33: Holland and England during the war of the Austrian succession, by P. Geyl. 34: Cathedral builders of the middle ages with particular reference to England, by A. Hamilton Thompson. 36: Roman Britain, by C. G. Parsloe.
c The West Saxon invasion and the Icknield way, by E. Thurlow Leeds.
d *Punch* [as a reflector of English views on foreign affairs, 1841–73], by C. S. S. Higham.
e Correspondence. [English sorcery trials, the inquisition and Saint Joan, by H. G. Richardson, with reply by Nellie Buckland]
f Hadrian's wall, by R. G. Collingwood.
g Sayings of Queen Elizabeth, by J. E. Neale.
h Medieval wills [chiefly from the 14th and 15th cent.], by Caroline A. J. Skeel.

2234 Vol. 11.

a History, English, and statistics, by A. F. Pollard. [Election to parliament *temp.* Edward I and Edward II]
b London during the civil war, by C. H. Firth.
c Geographical history of the Cinque ports, by J. A. Williamson.
d The teaching and practice of handwriting in England [from the Norman conquest], by H. Jenkinson.
e Historical revisions. 38: *Quo warranto* proceedings under Edward I, by Helen M. Cam. 39: The derivation of London, by Eliza Jeffries Davis. 40: Queen Caroline and the church, by N. Sykes.
f 'Re-election' and the medieval parliament [an answer to the article by A. F. Pollard], by J. G. Edwards.
g The evolution of the sentimental idea of empire [in the 19th cent. and afterwards]: a Canadian view, by A. R. M. Lower.

2235 Vol. 12.

a Everyday life in some medieval records [of the 13th cent.], by Hilda Johnstone.
b Historical revisions. 41: The household ordinance of 1279, by B. Wilkinson. 42: Movement of population during the industrial revolution, by J. L. Hammond.

43: Lord Salisbury and Turkey, by W. N. Medlicott.
44: The Spanish succession, 1697–1700, by R. Lodge.
c The birth of the London rate-payer [in the 17th cent.], by W. G. Bell.
d History in pantomime, by A. H. Dodd. [Material from pantomime books, 1831–79]

2236 Vol. 13.

a Historical revisions. 45: *Trimoda necessitas*, the possible meaning of the term, by Eliza Jeffries Davis. 47: The execution of the Great Charter, 1215, by C. G. Crump. 48: Roman London, by G. Macdonald.
b Beginning of English maritime enterprise [13th–15th cent.], by C. L. Kingsford.
c The diplomatic envoy [in the 16th cent., with particular reference to foreign accounts of Elizabeth and her court], by J. E. Neale.
d Gilbert Debenham [d. 1481]: a medieval rascal in real life, by Winifred I. Haward.

2237 Vol. 14.

a Historical revisions. 49: The medieval university of Oxford, by H. E. Salter. 50: The industrial revolution, by H. L. Beales. 51: Scutage, by Helena M. Chew. 52: The stop of the exchequer, 1672, by A. Browning.
b The city of Oxford in the middle ages, by H. E. Salter.

2238 Vol. 15.

a The freedom of the seas [and Britain's attitude to it, with particular reference to the League of Nations], by R. Webb.
b Wolsey, by L. T. Dibdin.
c A patronage feud in a pocket borough: Helston, Cornwall [1813, between the Duke of Leeds and Sir Christopher Hawkins], by H. S. Toy.
d Historical revisions. 54: The so-called Star Chamber Act, 1487, by C. H. Williams. 55: The maritime powers in the 18th cent.: an account of relations between Britain and Holland, by R. Lodge. 56: The Agreements of the People, 1647–9, by J. W. Gough.
e The church and religion in the age of Shakespeare, by C. Jenkins.
f The place of the king's household in English constitutional history, to 1272, by A. Steel.
g The New Poor Law [1834], by H. L. Beales.

2239 Vol. 16.

a The bestiary, by M. R. James.
b The strange story of Lady Grange [Rachel Chisly, d. 1745, her abduction and imprisonment by her husband, James Erskine, Lord Grange], by R. W. Seton-Watson.
c Historical revisions. 57: The Great Trek, 1835–7, by A. F. Hattersley. 58: The origin of English banking, by A. V. Judges. 59: The dates of foundation of the early British West Indian colonies, by J. A. Williamson. 60: The personal rule of Henry III and the aims of the baronial reformers of 1258, by R. F. Treharne.
d Changing views of the Renaissance [concerning its nature as a movement and the time of its inception]. Pt. 1 by E. F. Jacob. Pt. 2 by A. S. Turberville.
e The continental policy of Great Britain, 1740–60, by R. Lodge.

2240 Vol. 17.

a Correspondence. [The battle of Bannockburn, 1314, by J. E. Morris]
b Historical revisions. 61: The goldsmiths in *La Strada*, or Cheapside, London, 1497, by Eliza Jeffries Davis. 63: The use of carts in the 14th cent., in England, by J. F. Willard. 64: The British mainland colonies of America in the 18th cent., by H. H. Bellot.

c Music of the English church [a brief historical survey from the 10th cent.], by H. G. Ley.
d Macaulay's third chapter, by C. H. Firth. [Some revisions of Macaulay's view of English social life in the reigns of Charles II and James II]
e 'War guilt' in the peace treaty, by H. Temperley. [An examination of article 231 of the Versailles treaty, 1919–20, and of the German and Renouvin-Bloch interpretations]

2241 Vol. 18.

a Historical revisions. 65: The Methuen treaties of 1703, by R. Lodge. 66: Trade cycles in the 19th cent. in Britain, by W. O. Henderson. 67: The Seymour conversations, 1853 [with the Russian government], by G. B. Henderson. 68: Wellington and Louis-Philippe, 1830, by A. C. F. Beales.
b Peoples and cultures in pre-historic Europe, by V. G. Childe.
c The character of the Anglo-Saxon conquests: a disputed point [concerning the period of time in which they were accomplished], by R. Lennard.

Other publications:

2242 Outlines versus periods, by T. F. Tout. Reprinted from the *University Review*. [1907].

2243 Annual bulletin of historical literature, nos. 1–22, 1911–32. [1912]–1933. [Select lists of publications for each year, with comments]

2244 General index to bulletins, nos. 1–12, 1911–22, ed. H. Temperley. 1923.

2245 Pictures of parliament, by A. F. Pollard. Reprinted from *The Evolution of Parliament*. P. [1921].

2246 Oxford: a short illustrated historical guide, by E. A. G. Lamborn. P. 1929.

2247 Illustrations of Exeter civic seals. [Facs.] 6 sheets [1923].

HISTORICAL SOCIETY OF WEST WALES

Founded 1910, for the publication of historical records and articles relating to the counties of Pembroke, Carmarthen, and Cardigan. Dissolved 1931?.

West Wales Historical Records, vols. 1–14 (1912–29):

2248 Vol. 1.

a Genealogies of Cardiganshire, Carmarthenshire and Pembrokeshire families [Peniarth ms. 156. Contd. in vol. 2].
b Captain Jenkin Jones's diary [1819].
c Dynevor: materials illustrating the history of Dynevor and Newton to the close of the reign of Henry VIII, by E. A. Lewis. [Contd. in vol. 2]
d Pembrokeshire parsons, by F. Green and T. W. Barker. [Contd. in vols. 2–6]

2249 Vol. 2.

a Haverford records, by H. Owen.
b The Abermeurig family and its connections [the estate of Abermeurig and its owners], by J. H. Davies.
c Saunders [family] of Pentre, Tymawr, and Glanrhydw, by F. Green.

2250 Vol. 3.

a Carmarthen castle: a collection of historical documents from the earliest times to the close of the reign of Henry VIII, by E. A. Lewis. [Contd. in vol. 4]
b Cardiganshire freeholders in 1760, by J. H. Davies.

c The Barlows of Slebech, by F. Green.
d Marriage bonds and fiats of West Wales and Gower [from the diocesan registry at Carmarthen. Contd. in vols. 4–12]

2251 Vol. 4.

a Pembrokeshire lay subsidies [i.e., church briefs, 1543] by H. Owen.
b Old book-plates of West Wales, by H. M. Vaughan.
c The Musgraves of Llanina, by F. Green.

2252 Vol. 5.

a The Millingchamps of Cardigan, by H. M. Vaughan.
b Mayors of Pembroke [1381–1915].
c Carmarthen tinworks and its founder [Robert Morgan, fl. 1747–77], by F. Green.
d Walter [family] of Roch Castle, by F. Green.
e Household accounts of a Welsh peeress in the 18th cent. [Dorothy, Viscountess Lisburne], by H. M. Vaughan.

2253 Vol. 6.

a Early banks in West Wales, by F. Green.
b The Wogans of Pembrokeshire, by F. Green. [Contd. in vol. 7 with an appendix on the English branches of the Wogan family]

2254 Vol. 7.

a Rebecca in West Wales [the Rebecca riots of 1843 and 1844], by F. Green.
b The Dyers of Aberglasney, by F. Green.
c The Stepneys of Prendergast, by F. Green.
d Early wills in West Wales [1344–1551], by F. Green.
e Parish registers of West Wales, by F. Green.
f Registers of St. Peter, Carmarthen. [Contd. in vols. 8–14]
g Dr. Alban Thomas [d. 1771, physician, sometime assistant secretary and clerk to the Royal Society], by A. Evans.

2255 Vol. 8.

a Carmarthenshire under the Tudors, by T. H. Lewis.
b St. Mary's college at St. Davids [chantry certificate, 1548].
c Edward Richard [d. 1777] and Ystrad Meurig [school], by A. T. Fryer.
d Street names of St. Davids city, by F. Green.
e Stedman [family] of Strata Florida, by F. Green.
f Harries [family] of co. Pembroke, by F. Green.
g Manorial customs in co. Carmarthen [1554].
h Dewisland coasters in 1751 [with extracts from the log-book of Abel Hicks, shipowner, 1751–64], by F. Green.
i The Tuckers of Sealyham, by Mrs. C. O. Higgon and F. Green.
j The Edwardes of Sealyham, by Mrs. C. O. Higgon and F. Green.
k Lloyd [family] of Danyrallt, by F. Green.

2256 Vol. 9.

a Quakers of Pembrokeshire, by D. Salmon.
b Pembrokeshire in by-gone days [11th–17th cent.], by F. Green.
c Scurlock [family] of Carmarthen, by F. Green.
d Scourfield [family] of New Moat, by F. Green.
e Local history from a printer's file [the *Tivyside Advertiser*, Cardigan, 1825–65], by J. Ballinger. [Contd. in vols. 10 and 11]
f Pembrokeshire hearths in 1670 [hearth tax returns. Contd. in vols. 10 and 11]

2257 Vol. 10.

a Notes on the church and parish of Rudbaxton [with an appendix of monumental inscriptions], by J. R. P. Penn.

b The Pictons of Poyston, by F. Green.
c Captain T. Edwardes Tucker's diary [1813–14, in the Peninsula and France].
d Chapels of St. Patrick [Whitesand bay, Pembrokeshire] and St. Justinian [Porth Stinan], by F. Green and A. B. Badger.

2258 Vol. 11.

a Notes on the church and parish of Camrose, by J. R. P. Penn.
b Bowen [family] of Roblinston and Camrose [with a note on Bowen of Lochmeiler], by J. R. P. Penn and F. Green.
c The Fortunes of Leweston, by F. Green.

2259 Vol. 12.

a Pembrokeshire Quakers' monthly meeting, by D. Salmon.
b The castle and lordship of Llanstephan: historical documents relating to the castle, town, and lordship from the earliest times to the close of the reign of Henry VIII, comp. E. A. Lewis. [Mainly from National Library of Wales Add. ms. 459. Contd. in vol. 13]
c Some unpublished letters of Sir Thomas Picton [d. 1815], ed. E. Edwards. [Contd. in vol. 13]
d Heraldry in St. Peter's church, Carmarthen, by H. M. Vaughan.
e Cuny [family] of Welston and Golden, by F. Green.
f Holi'r Pwnc, gan J. Ballinger. [Sunday-school catechising in Wales. In English]

2260 Vol. 14.

a The French invasion of Pembrokeshire in 1797. [Official documents and private letters ed. D. Salmon]
b Symins [family] of Martell and Llanstinan, by F. Green.
c The sequestration of Dewisland [an estate of the bishop of St. Davids] by the Commonwealth.

HISTORY OF EXETER RESEARCH GROUP

Founded 1920, to prepare material necessary for a history of Exeter based on original authorities. Taken over by University College, Exeter, in 1929.

Monographs, nos. 1–5:

2261 No. 1. Lost chapels of Exeter, by Frances Rose-Troup. 1923.

2262 No. 2. The Anglo-Norman custumal of Exeter, ed. J. W. Schopp, with introd. by J. W. Schopp and Ruth C. Easterling. 1925.

2263 No. 3. The Franciscans and Dominicans of Exeter, by A. G. Little and Ruth C. Easterling. 1927.

2264 No. 4. The mediaeval council of Exeter, by B. Wilkinson, with introd. by Ruth C. Easterling. 1931.

2265 No. 5. Some disputes between the city and the cathedral authorities of Exeter, by Muriel E. Curtis. 1932.

HONOURABLE SOCIETY OF CYMMRODORION

Founded 1873 (being the third society to bear this name), for the improvement of education and the promotion of intellectual culture, by the encouragement of literature, science, and art, as connected with Wales.

Y Cymmrodor, vols. 14–43 (1901–33):

2266 Vol. 14.

a English law in Wales and the Marches, by H. Owen.
b The Broughtons of Marchwiel: contribution to the history of the parish of Marchwiel, by A. N. Palmer.

c Vita Sancti Kebie [St. Cybi], by S. B. Gould.
d Sidelights on Welsh Jacobitism, by J. A. Price.

2267 Vol. 15.

a Lewis Morris in Cardiganshire [1746–65], by D. Ll. Thomas.
b Saint Carannog [fl. 438], by S. B. Gould.
c Old county families of Dyfed: 1, The Wogans of Boulston [Pembrokeshire], by F. Green.

2268 Vol. 16.

a A Welsh insurrection [1529], by W. Ll. Williams.
b Old county families of Dyfed: 2, The Wogans of Merrion [Pembrokeshire], and Somersetshire, by F. Green.
c The holy grail: a discrimination of the native and foreign elements of the legend, by G. Y. Wardle. [Contd. in vol. 17]
d The two Hugh Owens, by H. R. Hughes and W. P. Williams. [See also *Transactions*, 1901–2, p. 128]

2269 Vol. 17.

a The silver plate of Jesus College, Oxford, by E. A. Jones·
b Peniarth ms. 37, ff. 61a–76b [ancient Welsh laws], ed. A. W. Wade-Evans.
c Correspondence of Dr. John Davies of Mallwyd with Sir Simonds d'Ewes [1640–41], ed. G. Hartwell-Jones.

2270 Vol. 18.

a Origin of the Welsh englyn and kindred metres, by J. Rhys.

2271 Vol. 19.

a The Vandals in Wessex, and the battle of Deorham [577], by E. W. B. Nicholson. [A postscript, entitled 'Gormund and Isembard', occurs in vol. 22]
b The Brychan documents, by A. W. Wade-Evans.
c Two charters of Henry VII [one to the inhabitants of Bromfield and Yale; the other to the inhabitants of Chirkland], ed. A. N. Palmer.
d An episode in the history of Clynnog church, by E. Owen.
e The Selby romance: an account of the Welsh claims to a Buckinghamshire estate [Whaddon Chase], by F. Green.

2272 Vol. 21.

a All around the Wrekin [the derivation of the names Viroconium and the Wrekin, and some notes on the pillar of Eliseg, Llangollen, and a sepulchral stone at Trallong, co. Brecon], by J. Rhys.
b The dynasty of Cunedag and the 'Harleian genealogies', by E. W. B. Nicholson.
c Iolo Goch's 'I Owain Glyndwr ar ddifancoll', by W. J. Gruffydd.
d Welsh folk-lore of the 17th cent. (apparitions, knockers, corpse candles), as illustrated by letters of John Lewis (Glaskeirig), the Rev. John Davies (Glenerglyn), Colonel W. Rogers (Hereford), the Rev. Samuel Jones (Coedreken), the Rev. Maurice Bedwell (Swansea), Daniel Higgs, Captain Samuel Foley, and the Rev. Richard Baxter, by W. E. A. Axon.
e Notes on certain Powysian poets [Madoc Benfras; David ap Edmund; Huw Morus; William Lleyn; Rhŷs Cain; Ieuan Llafar; Tudor Aled; Howel ap Sir Mathew; Howel Bangor], by A. N. Palmer.

2273 Vol. 22.

a The foreign aspect of Welsh records, by H. Hall.
b Parochiale Wallicanum, by A. W. Wade-Evans.
c The chronology of Arthur, by A. W. Wade-Evans.
d George Borrow's second tour of Wales [1857], by T. C. Cantrill and J. Pringle.

e On the 17th cent. ballad entitled 'A warning for all murderers', by W. E. A. Axon.

2274 Vol. 23. Celtic Britain and the pilgrim movement, by G. H. Jones. 1912.

2275 Vol. 24.

a Rhygyvarch's life of Saint David, by A. W. Wade-Evans. [Transcript, Latin, of the 11th cent. life, with English translation]
b Some old Welsh pedigrees, by A. Anscombe. [Peipiau Ercicg, Guoruodu Ercicg, and Iudon Guent; Mouric map Teudiric and some contemporaries; the descendants of Mouric map Teudiric, King of Glinissicg]
c A contribution to the commercial history of mediaeval Wales, with tabulated accounts, 1301–1547, by E. A. Lewis.
d The story of a Welsh education commission, 1846–7, by D. Salmon.
e Tribanan Morganwg. [Glamorganshire rhymes, in Welsh, from a collection sent by Jenkin Howell, Aberdare, to the National Eisteddfod of 1893]
f A Welsh version of the birth of Arthur [National Library of Wales, Llanstephan ms. 201 (15th cent.), with an English translation], by J. H. Davies.

2276 Vol. 25.

a Edward I's commission of enquiry of 1280–81: an examination of its origin and purpose, by J. E. Lloyd. [Postscript in vol. 26]
b The mediaeval market and fair in England and Wales, by Mrs. O. S. Watkins.
c Some unpublished prose miscellanies of George Borrow, by E. Rhys.
d Carmarthenshire gleanings (Kidwelly), comp. G. Evans. [Sanctuary lands and medieval customs in Kidwelly; Llansaint, Ecclesia omnium sanctorum, and Hawkin church; and notes on the borough of Kidwelly]
e Thomas Phillips [d. *c*. 1851]: founder of the collegiate institution of Llandovery, by W. B. Hamer.

2277 Vol. 26.

a The king's court of great sessions in Wales [1542–1830, its jurisdiction, officials, statutory changes, relations with other courts, etc.], by W. Ll. Williams.
b The Welsh inscriptions of Llanfair Waterdine [church], by Sir J. Rhys.
c Awdl i Rys ap Gruffudd jan Einion Offeiriad. Dosbach Einion ar Ramadeg a'i Ddyled i Ddonatus, gan I. Williams. [A poem dedicated to Rhys ap Gruffudd by Einion Offeiriad (priest), fl. 1300–50]
d The Welsh national emblem: leek or daffodil?, by A. E. Hughes. [Note in vol. 27]
e The ecclesiastical constitution of Wales on the eve of the Edwardine conquest, by J. A. Price.
f Welsh adventurers to the West Indies in the 16th cent. [with transcript of a ballad *Hanes Bagad o Gymry*, ed. Lieutenant William Peilyn, 1570]. Introd. by E. V. Evans.
g The ballad of the Welsh buccaneers (Llanddyfan text, 1654), ed. J. G. Davies, with some genealogical suggestions by the Hon. Mrs. Bulkeley-Owen.

2278 Vol. 27.

a The Benedictine abbey of St. Mary at St. Dogmaels, by H. M. Vaughan.
b The year of the reception of the Saxones, by A. W. Wade-Evans.
c Some insular sources of the *Excidium Britanniae* [written in the 8th cent.], by A. W. Wade-Evans.
d The fate of the structures of Conway abbey, and Bangor and Beaumaris friaries, by E. Owen. [With transcripts

from Exchequer K.R. Accounts concerning works
executed in north Wales 30–31 Henry VIII, 1539–40]

e Peniarth ms. 118, ff. 829–37. [An extract, written by
John David Rhys, *c.* 1600, referring to a mythical period
of Welsh history]. Introd., transcript, and translation by
H. Owen.

f Owen Glyndwr and the Welsh church [with an extract
from the 'Roll of the Welsh', *Calendar of Papal Registers,*
1406], by J. A. Price.

g Beau Nash: the Welsh dandy, by W. Ll. Williams.

h The application of electricity to practical uses: a Welsh-
man's contribution (the late Sir William H. Preece,
K.C.B., F.R.S. [d. 1913]), by Ll. Preece.

i Welshmen in the American war of independence, by
E. A. Jones.

2279 Vol. 28. Taliesin, by Sir J. Morris-Jones. 1918. [A
criticism of *Taliesin,* by J. G. Evans, in the series Early
Welsh Texts]

2280 Vol. 29.

a Strata Marcella abbey [Montgomeryshire] immediately
before and after its dissolution [1536], by E. Owen.

b Henry of Richmond's itinerary to Bosworth [1485], by
W. T. Williams.

c Andrew Boorde [fl. 1517–49] and the Welsh people, by
E. V. Evans. [Extracts from *The Fyrst Boke of the Introduction of Knowledge*]

d Welsh cathedral schools to 1600, by L. S. Knight.

e Two Welsh correspondents of John Wilkes [the Rev.
Evan Lloyd, d. 1776, and Robert Morris, d. 1797], by
E. A. Jones.

f The name of Cerdic [and its origin], by A. Anscombe.

2281 Vol. 30. Giraldus Cambrensis: *De invectionibus,* ed.
W. S. Davies. 1920. [Full Latin text with introd. and
index]

2282 Vol. 31.

a The Celt in ancient history, by G. H. Jones.

b Gildas and modern professors, by A. W. Wade-Evans.

c Origin of the Welsh grammar school, by L. S. Knight.

d Adam Usk's epitaph, by Sir J. Morris-Jones. [Notes on
an inscribed brass in Usk church, to Adam Usk, chronicler, d. *c.* 1430]

e Adam of Usk, by W. Ll. Williams.

f Cultural bases: a study of the Tudor period in Wales
[with an appendix of Welsh 16th cent. poems and
English translations], by T. G. Jones.

g Darnau o'v Efengylan, gan H. Lewis. [Fragments of
the Gospels, from ms. Havod 22, late 16th cent.], by H.
Lewis.

h The chapter of Llandaff cathedral, 1561–1668, by
C. A. H. Green.

i The speech [1575] of William Blethin, bishop of Llandaff
and the customs and ordinances of the church of
Llandaff, by J. A. Bradney.

2283 Vol. 32.

a Catraeth [Gododin] and Hirlas Owain: a study [of war
poems of the 6th? and 12th cent. attributed to Aneurin
and to Prince Owain Cybeiliog], with critical texts,
translations, and notes, by T. G. Jones.

b The story of Newcastle-Emlyn and Atpar to 1531, with
concluding survey, by G. Evans.

2284 Vol. 33. Segontium [Carnarvon] and the Roman occupation of Wales, by R. E. M. Wheeler. 1923.

2285 Vol. 34. Taliesin: or the critic criticized, by J. G. Evans.
1924. [A reply to Sir J. Morris-Jones's argument in
vol. 28 above]

2286 Vol. 35.

a A neglected Welsh triad [the *Tri unben llys Arthur* or
Three Sovereign Princes of the Court of Arthur, and its
relation to the early history of Mercia], by A. Anscombe.

b The 'Book of Basingwerk' and ms. Cotton Cleopatra
B.v, by A. Griscom. [Possible British or Armorican
sources for Geoffrey of Monmouth's *Historia Regum
Britanniae.* Contd. in vol. 36]

c The Scandinavian settlement in Ystrad Tywi [genea-
logical evidence], by G. P. Jones.

d Notes on the parish register of Merthyr Tydfil, 1703–63,
by F. T. James.

e The English element in the Perfeddwlad [Denbighshire,
after the Edwardian conquest], by T. P. Ellis.

f Some letters of Thomas Johnes of Hafod (1794–1807),
selected from the Cumberland papers, B.M., Add. mss.
36491–36516, by H. M. Vaughan.

2287 Vol. 36.

a The indiscretion of Anthony Wood [concerning an
anecdote relating to David Jenkins of Hensol in his
Athenae Oxonienses], by T. Richards.

b Denbigh castle, by W. J. Hemp.

c Some Jacobite relics at Peniarth in Merionethshire, by
H. M. Vaughan.

2288 Vol. 37. The Roman fort near Brecon, by R. E. M.
Wheeler. 1926.

2289 Vol. 38.

a Merioneth notes, by T. P. Ellis. [Includes notes on 1794
surveys of the Hengwrt and Nannau estates; the name
Dolgelly; a Hengwrt inventory of 1696 and Hengwrt
accounts, 1720–2; lands of Cymmer abbey; servile
tenures in Dolgelly; various wills; a projected sale of the
Hengwrt demesne in 1766; Ystumcolwyn rentals, Montgomery, 1756–88; and Merioneth roads]

b A synopsis of two tours in Wales in 1775, and in 1811,
by Sir Thomas Gery Cullum, bt.; and his son, the Rev.
Sir Thomas Gery Cullum, bt., transcribed by H. M.
Vaughan.

c The Wynn papers (1515–1690), a résumé and an appreciation [of the *Calendar of Wynn (of Gwydir) papers,
1515–1690, in the National Library of Wales and elsewhere,* 1926], by Marjorie F. Hall.

d The troubles of Dr. William Lucy [d. 1677, bishop of
St. David's], by T. Richards.

e Edmund Prys, archdeacon of Merioneth [d. 1623], by
A. O. Evans.

2290 Vol. 39.

a Ewloe [manor, Flintshire, and its owners], by J. E.
Lloyd.

b The castle of Ewloe and the Welsh castle plan, by
W. J. Hemp.

c Early Celtic missionaries, by G. H. Jones.

d A north Cardiganshire woollen yarn factory: its history,
machinery, trade and rural associations, with a note
on a family of Montgomeryshire millwrights [Davies],
by I. C. Peate.

e Legal references, terms and conceptions in the 'Mabinogion', by T. P. Ellis.

f Nicholas Robinson (1530?–85, bishop of Bangor), by
A. O. Evans. [Also issued separately, 1928]

g Letters to and from William Owen (Pughe) [antiquary],
1804–6, ed. E. V. Evans.

2291 Vol. 40.

a Katheryn of Berain [Katheryn Tudor, d. 1591]: a study
in North Wales family history, by J. Ballinger. [Also
issued separately, 1929]

b The ecclesiology of Anglesey, by E. Tyrrell-Green.

c Iron-work in the Teifi valley, by E. Tyrrell-Green.

d The importance and value of local records: the Dolgelly parish registers [1795–1898, including poor law administration, church affairs, municipal activities, and the school], by T. P. Ellis. Preliminary note by E. V. Evans.

e A Scottish surgeon in Wales in the 17th cent. [Alexander Reid, d. 1641], by Marjorie F. Hall.

f Two Welsh heraldic pedigrees [cast in the 16th cent. in 'target' form, for the Chaloner and Broughton families], with notes on Thomas Chaloner of Denbigh and Chester, Ulster king of arms [d. 1598], by W. J. Hemp.

g Notes on the arms of Bishop Nicholas Robinson [of Bangor, d. 1585], by W. J. Hemp.

h 'Mamwys' [a right acquired by a man through his mother, in Welsh tribal law]: textual references, by T. P. Ellis.

2292 Vol. 41. Holt, Denbighshire: the works-depot of the twentieth legion at Castle Lyons, by W. F. Grimes. 1930.

2293 Vol. 42.

a The Catholic church in the Welsh laws, by T. P. Ellis. [With two appendices on words and phrases of ecclesiastical import used in the Welsh laws, and on the close adherence of the Welsh laws to the *jus ecclesiasticum*]

b Three old foundations [the churches of St. Beuno, Clynrog, and St. Rhychwyn, Trefriw, Carnarvonshire, and St. Ceinwen, Dwyran, Anglesey], by A. O. Evans. [Also issued separately, 1930]

c A Caernarvonshire inventor: a note on the work of John Williams [or Ioan Madog, d. 1878], by I. C. Peate.

d Phylipiaid Ardudwy—a survey and a summary, by W. Ll. Davies. [The lives and works of a group of Welsh poets, John Phylip, d. 1620; Richard Phylip, d. 1641; Gruffydd Phylip, d. 1666; Phylip John Phylip, d. 1678 and William Phylip, d. 1670, of Ardudwy, Merionethshire]

2294 Vol. 43.

a The Croes Nawdd [a mediaeval Welsh relic of the Cross, and its erroneous connection with St. Neot], by E. Owen.

b Goronwy Owen and the College of William and Mary, by B. B. Thomas. [Goronwy Owen, master of the grammar school, College of William and Mary, Virginia, 1758–60]

c Some records of the free grammar school of Deythur, in co. Montgomery, 1690–1900, by C. Campbell.

d Noë, King of Powys [8th cent., and the pedigree of the princes of Brecknock], by P. C. Bartrum.

e A sequel to the French invasion of Pembrokeshire, by D. Salmon.

f Welsh surnames in the border counties of Wales [Ches., Salop, Herefs., Worcs., Glos., Monms., Somerset, Devon], by T. E. Morris.

Transactions, 1899–1933 (33 vols. 1901–33):

2295 Vol. for 1899–1900.

a Welsh cave legends and the story of Owen Lawgoch, by J. Rhys.

b Owen Lawgoch—Yeuain de Galles: some facts and suggestions, by E. Owen. [See also vol. for 1900–1]

c Canu Penillion, gan W. H. Williams. [Penillion singing—origins and development]

d Wales and the coming of the Normans (1039–93), by J. E. Lloyd.

2296 Vol. for 1900–1.

a The diplomatics of Welsh records, by H. Hall.

b Archbishop Peckham [d. 1292], by J. W. Willis Bund.

c Owain Lawgoch, by W. Ll. Williams, with a rejoinder by E. Owen. [See also vol. for 1899–1900]

2297 Vol. for 1901–2.

a The romance of Welsh education, by T. M. Williams.

b Welsh Catholics on the continent, by W. Ll. Williams.

2298 Vol. for 1902–3.

a The decay of tribalism in North Wales, by E. A. Lewis.

b Celtic art in pagan and Christian times, by J. R. Allen.

2299 Vol. for 1903–4.

a Sir Henry Morgan, the buccaneer [d. 1688], by W. Ll. Williams.

b Thomas Edwards o'r Nant, a'r Interliwdiau, gan I. Foulkes. [Thomas Edwards, d. 1810, and the Interludes]

c Prolegomena to the study of old Welsh poetry, by E. Anwyl.

2300 Vol. for 1904–5.

a The Brehon laws and their relation to the ancient Welsh institutes, by D. Brynmor-Jones.

b Yr Arwrgerdd Gymreig, gan R. A. Griffith. [The Welsh epic]

c Melodies of Wales [their history], by R. Bryan.

d Sir John Philipps [of Picton, d. 1736]; the Society for Promoting Christian Knowledge; and the charity school movement in Wales, 1699–1737, by T. Shankland.

2301 Vol. for 1905–6.

a Saxon, Norman and Plantagenet coinage of Wales, by P. W. P. Carlyon-Britton.

b Dafydd ap Gwilym a'i gyfnod, gan J. M. Rees. [Dafydd ap Gwilym, fl. 1340–90, and his age]

c Date and place of burial of Dafydd ap Gwilym, by Ll. Williams.

d Dafydd ap Gwilym—a further note, by J. H. Davies.

e Italian influence on Celtic culture, by G. H. Jones.

f Walter Map [fl. 1200], by W. L. Jones.

2302 Vol. for 1906–7.

a Some incidents in the life of Edward Lhuyd [d. 1709], by R. Ellis.

b The national emblem of Wales, by I. B. John.

c Welsh church dedications, by J. Fisher.

d Welsh bibliography and its aims, by J. H. Davies.

2303 Vol. for 1907–8.

a Welsh national melodies and folk-song, by J. Lloyd-Williams.

b The union of England and Wales, by W. Ll. Williams.

c Literary relationships of Dafydd ap Gwilym, by W. L. Jones.

2304 Vol. for 1908–9.

a The use and age of ancient stone monuments, by J. N. Lockyer.

b Tudur Aled [fl. 1480–1525, poet and Franciscan], by J. Morris-Jones.

c Military aspects of Roman Wales, by F. Haverfield.

d Howell Harris, citizen and patriot, by M. H. Jones.

2305 Vol. for 1909–10.

a The Roman fort at Caersws, Montgomeryshire, by R. C. Bosanquet.

b John Jones of Glan-y-Gors [d. 1821, writer of satirical songs in Welsh], by M. P. Jones.

c The book of Aneirin [and relations between Wales and north Britain in the post-Roman period, with a translation of the *Gododin*], by E. Anwyl.

d William Herbert, Earl of Pembroke [d. 1469], by H. T. Evans.

2306 Vol. for 1910–11.

a Megalithic remains of Anglesey, by E. N. Baynes.
b Pre-Reformation survivals in Radnorshire [with particular reference to local tradition], by D. E. Owen.
c The organization of Welsh historical and archaeological research, (1) by J. E. Lloyd; (2) by R. C. Bosanquet.
d Founders of the Cymmrodorion Society: a memorial to the Morusiaid [i.e. the Morris brothers: Lewis, d. 1765; Richard, d. 1779; William, d. 1763; John, d. 1740], by S. J. Evans.

2307 Vol. for 1911–12.

a The Hafod press, and Colonel Thomas Johnes [d. 1816], author and publisher, by H. M. Vaughan. [See additional notes in vol. for 1919–20]
b Welsh Catholic poetry of the 15th cent., by H. E. Lewis.
c The story of the ancient churches of Llandovery [the churches of Llandingat, Llangynfab, and Llanfair], by G. Evans.

2308 Vol. for 1912–13.

a The tradition of London in its Welsh aspect, by Sir L. Gomme.
b The Mabinogion [and the Arthurian tradition], by W. J. Gruffydd.
c The Welsh bard and the poetry of external nature, from Llywarch Hen to Dafydd ab Gwilym [9th?–15th cent.], by J. G. Davies.

2309 Vol. for 1913–14.

a The Celtic church—a tragedy in history, by H. D. M. Spence-Jones. [A history of the Celtic church, its doctrines, organization, building and liturgy]
b Dafydd ap Gwilym a'r Glêr, gan I. Williams. [Dafydd ap Gwilym, fl. 1340–90, and the itinerant bards]
c Bardism and romance: a study of the Welsh literary tradition, by T. Gwynn Jones. [The legal and social status of bards from the early Christian period, and their struggle with the romancers in the 13th cent. and later]

2310 Vol. for 1914–15.

a Suggestions for the study of Welsh history, by C. H. Firth.
b The use of local records, by Sir F. Pollock.
c Welsh local records: details and classified topographical list, by H. Hall.
d The theology of the early British church, with special reference to Fastidius ['a bishop of the Britons', 5th cent.?], by R. Morris.
e Life in Wales in mediaeval times, by Mary Williams.

2311 Vol. for 1915–16.

a Carnarvon castle, by C. R. Peers.
b Ancient Wales—anthropological evidences, by H. J. Fleure. [With appendices, being comments by L. Winstanley and T. G. Jones on a map of archaeological and anthropological distributions in western Europe by H. J. Fleure]
c The mediaeval lordship of Brecon, by W. Rees.

2312 Vol. for 1916–17.

a Foreign elements in Welsh mediaeval law, by Sir D. Brynmor-Jones.
b Church architecture of Wales, by E. Tyrrell-Green.
c Social and economic conditions in Wales and the Marches in the early 17th cent. as illustrated by Harl. ms. 4220, by Caroline A. J. Skeel.
d Felony in Edwardian Wales, by J. C. Davies.

2313 Vol. for 1917–18.

a Welsh nationalism and Henry Tudor [Henry VII], by W. G. Jones.
b Morgan Llwyd o Wyntdd, gan D. T. Evans. [Morgan Llwyd of Gwynedd, d. 1659]
c Nodiadau ieithyddol ar waith barddonol Pantycelyn, gan H. E. Lewis. [Notes on the grammar of the poetry of William Williams of Pantycelyn, d. 1791]

2314 Vol. for 1918–19.

a The Celtic circle-moot: some new facts and the inferences, by A. H. Allcroft.
b Types of baptismal fonts as illustrated by Welsh examples, by E. Tyrrell-Green.
c Owain Glyn Dwr: his family and early history, by J. E. Lloyd.
d The French linguistic influence in mediaeval Wales, by M. Watkin. [Contd. in vol. for 1919–20]

2315 Vol. for 1919–20.

a Welsh wit: mediaeval and modern, by E. Rhys.
b Mediaeval Welsh scriptures, religious legends, and Midrash, by J. Jenkins. [With an appendix giving various readings that occur in certain texts—Peniarth mss. 5 and 14, and Havod ms. 22—of 'Euangel Nicodemus']

2316 Vol. for 1920–1.

a Welsh Jacobitism, by H. M. Vaughan. [With a note on Welsh Jacobitism and Sir Watkin Williams Wynn, d. 1749, by J. A. Price]
b Roman and native in Wales: an imperial frontier problem, by R. E. M. Wheeler. [An inquiry into the nature and reasons for construction of hill camps by the native population in Roman Wales]
c 'Hill top camps' with special reference to those of north Cardiganshire, by R. W. Sayce.
d The connection of Celtic with classical studies, by W. R. Roberts.

2317 Vol. for 1921–2.

a Ecclesiology of Pembrokeshire, by E. Tyrrell-Green.
b Harlech castle, by C. R. Peers.
c Beirniadaeth lenyddol yng Nghymru, gan R. J. Rowlands. [Literary criticism in Wales, 19th and early 20th cent.]
d Beirniadaeth lenyddol yng Nghymru, gan D. T. Evans. [Literary criticism in Wales, its history]

2318 Vol. for 1922–3.

a The Puritan visitation of Jesus College, Oxford, and the principalship of Dr. Michael Roberts (1648–57), by T. Richards.
b Edmund Prys: archdeacon of Merioneth, priest, preacher, poet (1544–1623), by A. O. Evans. [Also issued separately, 1924]
c Goronwy Owen and his bicentenary, 1723–1923, by E. V. Evans.

2319 Vol. for 1923–4.

a Gerald of Wales on the survival of Welsh, by W. R. Roberts.

2320 Vol. for 1924–5.

a The Whitford leases: a battle of wits, by T. Richards. [Sir Roger Mostyn's application for a lease of the rectorial profits of Whitford, and the opposition by the dean and chapter of St. Asaph, 1668–74]

2321 Vol. for 1925–6.

a Welsh music in the Tudor period, by R. E. Roberts.

b Notes on the history of the principality of Wales in the time of the Black Prince, by D. L. Evans.

c Some 19th cent. letters [mainly by the Rev. Richard Humphreys, Calvinistic Methodist minister, d. 1863; Anne Humphreys, d. 1852, his wife; Jeanette Morgan, d. 1888, their daughter; and the Rev. Edward Morgan, minister, d. 1871], ed. E. M. Humphreys.

d Diogelu enwau lleoedd Cymni, gan D. A. Evans. [Safeguarding the place-names of Wales]

e Llyfryddicieth enwau lleoedd. [A bibliography of place-names, in English]

2322 Vol. for 1926–7.

a Hywel Dda: codifier [fl. 909–46], by T. P. Ellis.

b David Samwell (1751–98), surgeon of the *Discovery*, London-Welshman and poet, by W. Ll. Davies.

2323 Vol. for 1927–8.

a John Williams of Gloddaeth [d. 1650], lord keeper of the great seal of England, bishop of Lincoln, archbishop of York, and bencher of the ancient and honourable society of Grays Inn, by I. Bowen. [Appendices: Transcript of the original notebook of Lord Keeper Williams, July, 1622; *The Welsh-mans proposition to the arch-bishop of Yorke, commander in chiefe before Conoway castle in Wales*, etc., 1646; and transcript of documents relating to Westminster abbey, 1635]

b King Arthur's round table at Caerleon, by Tessa V. Wheeler. [A Roman amphitheatre constructed *c.* 80 A.D.

2324 Vol. for 1928–9.

a Nonconformist academies in Wales, 1662–1862, by H. P. Roberts.

b Lewis Bayly, bishop of Bangor (d. 1631), and Thomas Bayly (d. 1657) his son, by E. A. B. Barnard.

c The Honourable Society of Cymmrodorion [a brief history from 1751], by E. V. Evans.

2325 Vol. for 1929–30.

a The non-ferrous metallurgical industries of South Wales, and Welshmen's share in their development, by D. O. Evans. [With particular reference to the lead, copper, zinc and nickel industries and their history from the 16th cent.]

b The contribution of Welshmen to music [and drama], by J. L. Davies. [Historical survey, with brief accounts of some Welsh composers, singers, actors and actresses]

c Llangwyrfon and certain place names in Cardiganshire [and their association with Celtic religious ceremonies], by G. A. Stephens.

2326 Vol. for 1930–1.

a The second civil war in Wales [1648, with particular reference to John Poyer, Rowland Laugharne and Rice Powell, parliamentarians who later became royalists, and to Sir John Owen of Clenneney], by J. F. Rees.

b 'Perlau benthyg', gan H. Lewis. ['Borrowed pearls': a glance at 17th cent. prose]

2327 Vol. for 1931–2.

a The Royal Commission on Ancient Monuments in Wales and Monmouthshire and the antiquities of Glamorgan and Monmouthshire, by G. H. Jones.

b The voluntary system at work: a chapter in Welsh education, based on unpublished material, by I. Jones. [The work of the British and Foreign School Society in Wales, 1814–70; with appendices containing a list of British schools in North Wales, in 1852; correspondence between Robert Forster and John Phillips, 1856–60, and between John Phillips and John Bowstead, 1860–61; and a list of British schools in South Wales, 1860, etc.]

2328 Vol. for 1932–3.

a Development of modern Welsh secondary education, by T. I. Ellis. [The report of the Aberdare committee, 1881; the Intermediate and Technical (Wales) Act, 1889, and the Central Welsh Board; and the Bruce committee, 1919]

b Contributions of Welshmen to science, by T. I. Jones. [Biographical notes on Welsh scientists, 16th–20th cent., with lists of their publications]

Supplements to Transactions:

2329 Bibliography of Welsh ballads printed in the 18th cent., comp. J. H. Davies. 1911 [1908–11]. [Issued in conjunction with the Welsh Bibliographical Society]

2330 Index to the publications of the Society, by G. O. Williams. 1913.

2331 Goronwy Owen and his bicentenary. 1924.

2332 Darn o'r ffestifal (Liber festialis), gan H. Lewis. 1925. [Part of Liber festialis, a ms. from the third quarter of the 16th cent., by John Mirk]

2333 The religious census of 1676: an inquiry into its historical value, mainly in reference to Wales, by T. Richards. 1927.

Cymmrodorion Record series:

2334 No. 1. The description of Pembrokeshire [1603], by George Owen, of Henllys, lord of Kemes, ed. with notes and appendix by H. Owen. Pt. 3, 1906. [Pts. 1–2 were published in 1892–6; pt. 4 in 1936]

2335 No. 3. Gildae de excidio Britanniae, Fragmenta, Liber de paenitentia, accedit et Lorica Gildae. Gildas: the ruin of Britain, fragments from lost letters, the penitential, together with the Lorica of Gildas, ed. H. Williams. Pt. 2, 1901. [Pt. 1 was published in 1899]

2336 No. 4. Catalogue of mss. relating to Wales in the British Museum, comp. and ed. E. Owen. Pts. 2–4, 1903–22. [Pt. 1 was published in 1900]

2337 No. 5. Extent of all the lands and rents of the lord bishop of St. David's, 1326, usually called the Black Book of St. David's, ed. J. W. Willis Bund. 1902.

2338 No. 6. Episcopal registers of the diocese of St. David's 1397–1518. Vols. 1–2: Latin text, with translation and index, by R. F. Isaacson; vol. 3: a study of the published registers by R. A. Roberts. 2 vols. in 3. 1917–20.

2339 No. 7. Calendar of the public records relating to Pembrokeshire, ed. H. Owen. 3 vols. 1911–18.

2340 No. 8. Calendar of the register of the Queen's Majesty's council in the dominion and principality of Wales and the Marches of the same [1535] 1569–91, by R. Flenley. 1916.

2341 No. 9. Walter Map's *De Nugis Curialium*, translated by M. R. James, with historical notes by J. E. Lloyd, ed. E. S. Hartland. 1923.

2342 No. 11. The first extent of [the lordship of] Bromfield and Yale, 1315, by T. P. Ellis. 1924.

2343 No. 12. Welsh port books, 1550–1603, with an analysis of the customs revenue accounts of Wales for the same period, comp. and ed. with some introductory notes by E. A. Lewis. 1927.

Other publications:

2344 The lives of the British saints: the saints of Wales and Cornwall, and such Irish saints as have dedications in Britain, by S. B. Gould and J. Fisher. 4 vols. 1907–13.

2345 Evicting a community: the case for the preservation of the historical and beautiful valley of the Ceiriog in North Wales, by Sir A. T. Davies. *P.* 1923.

HUGUENOT SOCIETY OF LONDON

Founded 1885, for the interchange and publication of knowledge relating to the history of the Huguenots in France and adjoining countries, the Huguenot emigrations from France, the refugee settlements throughout the world, Huguenot genealogy and heraldry, and Huguenot church and other registers.

Proceedings, vols. 6–14 (1902–33):

2346 Vol. 6.

a Notes on the *Eikon Basilike*, with a reference to some French translations, by J. B. Medley.
b On the origin and early history [1718–37] of the French Protestant Hospital (La Providence) [London], by A. G. Browning. [Contd. for 1737–60, in vol. 8]
c Notes and queries. [Includes a transcript of the will of James Baudouin, d. 1738]
d Early Huguenot friendly societies, by W. C. Waller. [Contd. in vol. 8]
e Un chapitre de l'histoire des églises du refuge de l'édit de Nantes: les deux Patentes [la Patente de Soho and la Patente de Spitalfields], par F. de Schickler.

2347 Vol. 7.

a Foreign artists of the reformed religion working in London from about 1560 to 1660, by L. Cust.
b Notes on the city of London records dealing with the French Protestant refugees, especially with reference to the collections made under various briefs, by G. B. Beeman.
c Manuscripts in the University library, Cambridge, relating to Huguenots and other refugees, by E. Worman.
d Annals of a quiet family [Lafargue], by J. H. Philpot.
e Huguenot settlements and churches in the west of England, by C. E. Lart.
f The influence exerted by Huguenot refugees of the 17th and early 18th cent. upon the social and professional life of England, by A. G. Browning.

2348 Vol. 8.

a Notes on the sites and history of the French churches in London, by G. B. Beeman.
b William Séguier [d. 1843], first keeper of the National Gallery, by L. Cust.
c Notes upon the early history of the manufacture of paper in England, by G. H. Overend.
d A lost history of the Huguenots [by Charles Philpot, d. 1823, being chiefly an account of his life], by J. H. Philpot.
e Sir Samuel Romilly, by Sir W. J. Collins.
f Some Romilly notes, by H. Wagner.
g The worthies associated in the original administration of the Boislin trust [created by Isaac de Bérenger, sieur de Boislin, 1708], by H. Wagner.

2349 Vol. 9.

a Alicante: March 3, 1709, by E. B. Vignoles.
b The Régis family, by C. P. Stewart.
c Deeds relating to the Aufrère family, ed. C. P. Stewart.
d Pedigree of Duval, by H. Wagner.
e Luther [family], of Myles, Essex, by C. E. Lart.
f Miscellanea. [Notes on the Rev. John Roget, of Geneva, d. 1783, and on the D'Aulnis family]
g History of the Aufrères, by C. P. Stewart. [Contd. in vol. 11]

h Notes on the pedigree of Layard [with pedigree by H. Wagner].
i Notes and materials on religious refugees in their relation to education in England before the revocation of the edict of Nantes, 1685, by F. Watson.
j The Huguenot regiments [in British and other service after 1685], by C. E. Lart. [See also supplemental notes, by W. H. Manchée, in vols. 13 and 14]
k The ms. memoirs of Peter de Cosne, 1658–1748 [of Southampton], by E. B. Vignoles.
l Notes on the life and work of John Lewis Roget [d. 1908], by S. R. Roget.
m List of pensions to Huguenot officers in 1692, by H. Wagner.
n Pedigree of Majendie, by H. Wagner.

2350 Vol. 10.

a Wheler's chapel, St. Mary's, Spital Square [London], by W. H. Manchée.
b The de la Balle family of Guînes, by W. Minet.
c Epitaphs in the French nonconformist cemeteries of Peter St. and Stephen's Green, Dublin, transcribed by V. E. Smyth, 1912.
d Directors of the French hospital of La Providence [London], by H. Wagner.
e The 'mémoires pour mes enfans' of Marie Molinier, Baroness Montolieu de St. Hippolyte [d. 1777], by H. Wagner.
f The Labouchère pedigree, by H. Wagner.
g The family of Riou, by P. H. Ditchfield.
h The French church of Thorpe-le-Soken, by W. C. Waller.
i Memories of Spitalfields, by W. H. Manchée.
j Pedigree of de Viçose (or Viçouse), by H. Wagner.
k Notes on the pedigree of the English branch of Duroure [with pedigree by H. Wagner].
l The Huguenots in Ulster, by R. A. McCall.
m Notes on the pedigree of André [with pedigree by H. Wagner].
n Subject index to papers, notes, etc., in vols. 1–10.

2351 Vol. 11.

a Marylebone, and its Huguenot associations, by W. H. Manchée.
b Some Huguenot wills [1773–94], ed. E. H. Lefroy.
c Some account of the French refugee family of Courtauld, by R. W. Dixon.
d Notes on the pedigree of Garnault [with pedigree by H. Wagner].
e Notes on the pedigree of Agace [with pedigree by H. Wagner].
f The work of Theodore de Bry [c. 1528–98] and his sons, engravers, by M. S. Giuseppi.
g Huguenot clergy list, 1548–1916, by W. H. Manchée.
h Notes and jottings in connexion with the Montrésor pedigree [with pedigree by H. Wagner].
i The family of Blutte, by W. Minet.
j Dutch, Walloon, and Flemish clergy list, 1550–1874, by W. H. Manchée.
k George Dorée, citizen and weaver of London, 1844–1916, maker of Edward VII's coronation velvet, by W. H. Manchée.
l Notes on the pedigree of Boulier de Beauregard and Gilbert [with pedigree by H. Wagner].

2352 Vol. 12.

a Presidential address [on French Protestant refugees in the American colonies], by G. B. Beeman.
b École de charité française de Westminster [founded 1747], by Susan Minet. [Contd. in vol. 13]
c Hogarth and his friendship with the Huguenots, by W. H. Manchée.

2364 Vol. 25. Registers of the church of Le Carré and Berwick Street, 1690-1788, ed. W. and Susan Minet. 1921.

2365 Vol. 26. Registres des églises de la Savoye, de Spring Gardens, et des Grecs, 1684-1900, ed. W. and Susan Minet. 1922.

2366 Vol. 28. Registres des églises de la chapelle royale de Saint James, 1700-56, et de Swallow Street, 1690-1709, ed. W. and Susan Minet. 1924.

2367 Vol. 29. Registers of the churches of the Tabernacle, Glasshouse Street, and Leicester Fields, 1688-1783, ed. W. and Susan Minet. 1926.

2368 Vol. 30. Register of the church of Rider Court, 1700-[1747], ed. W. and Susan Minet. 1927.

2369 Vol. 31. Register of the church of Hungerford Market, later Castle Street [1688-1754], ed. W. and Susan Minet, with a sketch of its history, as of that of the Carré, founded on the *actes* of the two churches. 1928.

2370 Vol. 32. Registres des quatre églises du Petit Charenton [1701-5], de West Street [1693-1743], de Pearl Street [1698-1701], et de Crispin Street [1694-1716], ed. W. and Susan Minet. 1929.

2371 Vol. 33. Extracts from the court books of the Weavers' company of London, 1610-1730 [relating to foreign immigrants], made and ed. W. C. Waller. 1931.

2372 Vol. 35. A supplement to Dr. W. A. Shaw's *Letters of Denization* which formed vols. 18 and 27. 1932. [Contains an index to part of vol. 18 omitted from that vol. and additional naturalizations, 1709-11]

HULL SCIENTIFIC AND FIELD NATURALISTS' CLUB

Founded 1895 (by the amalgamation of the Hull Field Naturalists' Club and the Hull Scientific Club), for the investigation of the biology, ecology, and distribution of the fauna and flora of the East Riding of Yorkshire, and the prehistory of the district.

Transactions, vols. 1-4 (1898-1919):

2373 Vol. 1.
a Note on a bronze celt recently found in Holderness, by T. Sheppard.
b Pre-historic man in Holderness, by T. Sheppard.
c Bye-gone Hull naturalists. 1: George Norman, 1823-82, by T. Sheppard. 2: Adrian Hardy Haworth, F.L.S., 1767-1833.
d Bronze mould and hoard of bronze axes found at Hotham Carrs, east Yorks., by T. Sheppard.
e Notes on the history of the Driffield museum of antiquities and geological specimens, by J. R. Mortimer.

2374 Vol. 3.
a Evidences relating to [the history of] east Hull, by T. Blashill.
b Roman villa at Harpham, east Yorks., by T. Sheppard.
c Notes on a collection of Roman antiquities from South Ferriby, in north Lincs., by T. Sheppard. [Contd. in vol. 4]
d Bye-gone Hull naturalists. 3: William Spence, 1783-1860, by T. Sheppard.

2375 Vol. 4.
a The Roman, Angle, and Dane in east Yorkshire, by T. Sheppard.

b A list of 17th cent. tokens of Lincolnshire in the Hull museum, with descriptions of hitherto unpublished tokens and varieties, by T. Sheppard.
c Roman bronze coins found at South Ferriby, Lincs., by T. Pickersgill.
d Some glimpses of old Hull in the light of recent excavations, by T. Sheppard.
e An Anglo-Saxon cemetery at Hornsea, by T. Sheppard.
f Our German ancestors: an account of the Anglo-Saxon remains found in east Yorkshire, by T. Sheppard.

HUNTER ARCHAEOLOGICAL SOCIETY

Founded 1912, to promote the study of local history and antiquities and the publication of records, etc.

Transactions, vols. 1-4 (1914-37):

2376 Vol. 1.
a Joseph Hunter [d. 1861, assistant keeper of the Public Records, and his principal works], by C. Drury.
b Customs of Hallamshire, by S. O. Addy.
c Sheffield in the 14th cent.: two Furnival inquisitions [*post mortem:* Thomas de Furnival, 1332; William de Furnival, 1383], by E. Curtis.
d Lady's bridge, Sheffield, by J. R. Wigfull.
e Ye Racker way [bridle-road leading out of Sheffield], by T. W. Hall.
f The house at the church gates [Sheffield, and the owners of the church gates property], by R. E. Leader.
g The Rev. Alfred Gatty, D.D., vicar of Ecclesfield [d. 1900]: a bibliography, by W. T. Freemantle.
h An old 'Hallam Nether' rate book, 1780-97, by T. Winder.
i Archaeological finds in and around Hallamshire, by T. Winder.
j 'Treasure trove' in Sheffield: discovery of ancient coins [Henry VIII-James I], by S. G. Harrison.
k A book of feudal aids made for the Earl of Shrewsbury [John Talbot] in 1451, ed. S. O. Addy.
l The castle hill [near Sheffield, and its probable Celtic origin], by G. A. Garfitt.
m The court leet of the manor of Sheffield [with which is reprinted *A Charge to the Court Leet for the Manor of Sheffield in the County of York*, 1795].
n Joseph Jolly, a forgotten attorney [fl. 1696-1731], by R. E. Leader.
o Wentworth Woodhouse [a description of the house], by W. Dickie.
p Literature and archaeology in Sheffield a hundred years ago [illustrated from the *Northern Star and Yorkshire Magazine*, monthly periodical, 1817-19], by R. E. Leader.
q Records of the court baron of the manor of Sheffield [*liber finium customariorum*, 5 Edw. 1—18 Eliz.], translated by Sir A. S. Scott-Gatty.
r Notes on some remains of ancient heraldic glass and other heraldry in Ecclesfield church, by C. Drury.
s The forest of the Peak [an historical account], by J. H. Brooksbank.
t Some defensive earthworks in the neighbourhood of Sheffield, by S. O. Addy.
u Talks of the town [Sheffield]: place, parsons, publicans and people, by R. E. Leader.
v Conisborough and its castle, by C. F. Innocent.
w An early 19th cent. day-book [for a farm at Whiston, near Rotherham], by T. Winder.

2377 Vol. 2.
a Our old roads, by R. E. Leader.

b Extracts from grants of Rotherham manor [1207–1536].

c Some notes upon episcopal registers, by A. Hamilton Thompson.

d The old house [at Attercliffe] near Washford bridge [and the Roades family], by A. B. Shaw.

e Some Hallamshire [account and court] rolls of the 15th cent., by A. H. Thomas.

f Sale of presentations to a rectory and a vicarage [Handsworth and Ecclesfield, 1816].

g Early books of the parish register of Sheffield [1560–1703], by J. R. Wigfull.

h A cinerary urn of the bronze age from Dronfield Woodhouse [Derbys.], by A. L. Armstrong.

i The Ecclesfield nailers agreement [1733], by R. Butterworth.

j Stannington Hall, by S. O. Addy.

k Fox Lane [Holmesfield parish] and Whibbersley crosses, by G. H. B. Ward.

l Surveyors of the highways in the lower division of Ecclesfield [1812–23], by T. Winder.

m Ancient Attercliffe wills, 1550–1700, by A. B. Shaw.

n Ecclesfield notes, by D. T. Smith.

o Extracts from an 18th cent. book of accounts [connected with the property of the Bright family of Bannercross], ed. W. S. Porter.

p Rock sculptures in Derbyshire, by G. A. Garfitt.

q Bronze and stone celts found in Sheffield, by E. Howarth.

r Extracts from the note-book of William Dickenson [1574–77, bailiff for the Earl of Shrewsbury's manor of Sheffield], by J. R. Wigfull.

s High Bradfield [and the chapelry] in the Ronksley mss., by C. F. Innocent.

t A bronze palstave, four stone celts, and other prehistoric implements from Sheffield and district, by A. L. Armstrong.

u Hawksyard [Staffs., and two deeds, 1399 and 1568, relating to it], by T. W. Hall.

v Three Sheffield wills at Somerset House [of Sampson Lord, priest, 1537; Humphrey Pirrans, proved 1582; John Scolefeld, 1626], transcribed by S. O. Addy.

w Gray and Mason at Aston, by G. C. M. Smith. [Thomas Gray, d. 1771, poet, and William Mason, d. 1797, his biographer]

x The field-system of Wightwizle, by C. F. Innocent.

y A medallion of St. Francis of Paula [found in Milk Street, Sheffield], by J. R. Wigfull.

z Thomas Swyft [vicar of Ecclesfield, d. 1478], author of the *Catholicon Anglicum* [an English-Latin dictionary], by S. O. Addy.

aa A description of the town of Sheffield in my remembrance wrote in the year 1832 at the time the cholera was raging in Sheffield, by Joseph Woolhouse, ed. R. E. Leader.

bb Sheffield's ancient public trusts, 1304–1566, by J. B. Wheat.

cc An 18th cent. housekeeper's book [kept by Richard Hodgson, Unitarian minister and schoolmaster, d. 1816, and his daughter, Sarah], by T. Winder.

dd The history of Bishopsholme, Sheffield, by J. B. Wheat.

ee Customs of the manor of Sheffield [from an inquisition, 1650].

ff The underground passage in Manor Lane [Sheffield], by J. R. Wigfull.

2378 Vol. 3.

a Mediaeval English cutlery, by S. O. Addy.

b Will of Christopher Capper, 1636 [Sheffield tanner], ed. C. Drury.

c Castleton: its traditions, sayings, place-names, etc., by J. H. Brooksbank.

d Wilson [family] of Broomhead, by J. B. Wheat.

e House building in Elizabeth's days [accounts for building a house in Sheffield, 1575–6], by J. R. Wigfull.

f Notes on Arbor Low [neolithic stone-circle], by A. L. Armstrong.

g Old Attercliffe and Carbrook [as they were in mid-19th cent.], by G. R. Vine.

h William Addy [fl. 1618–85] and Nathaniel Stringer [c. 1645–86], stenographers, by S. O. Addy.

i The Sembly quest [Sheffield, an annual military muster by the tenants of the manor, with a document relating to it, 1601], by C. Drury.

j A visit to Sheffield in the 18th cent. [by Hester Newdigate], by J. E. Tyler.

k Excavations at Creswell crags, Derbyshire, 1924–6: the Pin Hole cave, by A. L. Armstrong. [Also for 1926–8. Report on excavations, 1928–32, in vol. 4]

l Letters and other papers relating to church affairs in Sheffield in the 18th cent., by C. V. Collier.

m The court leet of the manor of Sheffield [record of the court of April 1578].

n The bay as a unit of measurement, by J. R. Wigfull.

o Beauchief abbey, by W. H. Elgar.

p Walkley Hall [Sheffield, and its owners], by W. H. Elgar, C. Drury, E. G. Bagshaw, and J. A. Venn.

q Extracts from a late 18th cent. diary, 1795–1800 [of Arthur Elliott], by J. B. Wheat.

r Funeral biscuits, by C. V. Collier.

s The Hoole family of Sheffield and the Sandersons, by S. O. Addy.

t Thorpe Salvin [village], by C. F. Innocent.

u Steetley chapel, by J. R. Wigfull.

v Stage plays in Sheffield in 1581, by S. O. Addy.

w Facts about the making of Mortimer's Road [c. 1770, and notes on Ewden bridge], by G. H. B. Ward.

x Notes and queries [Darnall Hall, Sheffield; the forfeit feast established 1814, by the Cutlers' company; and the Barrack tavern, Sheffield].

y The Carrs of Southey and Dublin, by S. O. Addy.

z The Kirk Edge murder [1782]: the King on the prosecution of George Steade against Francis Fearne for murder and highway robbery, by J. B. Wheat.

aa The Crookes urn burial [bronze age discoveries made at Crookes, Sheffield], by J. W. Baggaley.

bb An early Sheffield school [from 16th cent. accountbooks of the church burgesses], by J. R. Wigfull.

cc A relic of Sheffield castle [bed of George, Earl of Shrewsbury, d. 1590], by C. Drury.

2379 Vol. 4.

a Sheffield castle: an account of discoveries made during excavations on the site, 1927–9, by A. L. Armstrong.

b 'Her Majesties manor of Ecclesall' [and depositions concerning it taken at Sheffield, 1587], by J. R. Wigfull.

c Garret gleanings [miscellaneous documents relating to Sheffield and district], by J. B. Wheat.

d The political reform movement in Sheffield [1779–95], by G. P. Jones.

e The clergy in the neighbourhood of Sheffield at the time of the civil war, by H. Lawrance.

f A bibliography of Sheffield history, by W. Odom.

g Influence of Sheffield upon the silversmith's craft, by S. W. Turner.

h Bronze and stone implements found in Sheffield and district, by J. W. Baggaley.

i Sheffield grammar school, 1604–1905: the masters, ushers, and alumni, by G. C. M. Smith.

j Broom Hall, Sheffield [and its owners], by J. R. Wigfull.

k Roche abbey charters: transcripts with introd. and notes, by S. O. Addy, ed. T. W. Hall.

l Discoveries at Beauchief [abbey], by S. O. Addy.

m The stock of the town of Sheffield [a gift of money entrusted to certain persons for the benefit of the poorer inhabitants of Sheffield by George Talbot, Earl of Shrewsbury, d. 1590], by Mary Walton.

n Cockshutt, by W. H. Elgar.

o Notes on the architectural history of Padley Hall, Derbys., by C. M. Hadfield.

p The Shrewsbury chapel [in Sheffield cathedral], by J. R. Wigfull.

q Sheffield grammar school, by J. R. Wigfull.

r Notes on Castleton [Derbys.], and its neighbourhood, by J. H. Brooksbank.

s English medieval painting, by J. Rothenstein.

t Local plumbers and glaziers [16th–18th cent.], by J. R. Wigfull.

u Masters of Staveley Netherthorpe grammar school [1587–1933], by W. E. Godfrey.

v Fanshawe Gate, Holmesfield, Derbys., by B. Fanshawe.

w The Longshaw earthworks [Derbys.], by W. M. Cole.

INCORPORATED SOCIETY FOR PROMOTING THE ENLARGEMENT, BUILDING, AND REPAIRING OF CHURCHES AND CHAPELS IN ENGLAND AND WALES
(Incorporated Church Building Society)

Founded 1818, to collect funds wherewith to make grants to aid in the provision of additional free church accommodation, and to aid in the reseating and repair of churches.

Church Builder, new issue, vols. 22–36 (1901–16):

2380 Vol. 22.

a Church of S. Botolph, Stow Longa, Hunts.

b S. Margaret's, Cley-next-the-sea [Norf.].

2381 Vol. 23.

a Swaffham Prior, Cambs., otherwise called Swaffham Two-churches: restoration of S. Mary's church.

b Ashton church, Devon.

2382 Vol. 24.

a Cudworth [Som.] and its church. [Contd. in vol. 26]

b Church of S. Michael, Lower Guiting, Glos.

c S. Peter's, Astley, Worcs.

d The ancient parish church of S. Peter and S. Paul, Swanscombe, Kent.

2383 Vol. 25.

a S. Mary's, Stoke by Nayland, Suff.

b Great and Little Hampton, near Evesham, Worcs.

c Northampton and its proposed new church.

d Fobbing church, Stanford-le-Hope, Essex.

e New Winchelsea church.

2384 Vol. 26.

a Clevedon parish church, Som.

b S. Mary's, Chepstow.

c Church of S. Andrew, Cleeve Prior, Worcs.

2385 Vol. 27.

a S. Peter's, S. Mary Bourne [Hants].

b Llandefalle church, Breconshire.

c S. Mary's, Wymondham, Norf.

2386 Vol. 28.

a Church of S. Andrew, Clifton Campville, near Tamworth, Staffs.

b Parish church of Leake [Yorks.].

2387 Vol. 29.

a Church of S. Peter and S. Paul, Lavenham.

2388 Vol. 30.

a S. Mary-the-Virgin, Ile Abbots [Som.].

b S. Peter's, Martley, Worcs.

c Church of S. Matthew, Shuttington, Warws.

d Church of S. Mary, Whaplode [Lincs.].

2389 Vol. 31.

a Church of S. Peter, Walpole [Norf.].

b Lavenham—the church and its builders, by W. D. Caröe.

2390 Vol. 32.

a S. Nicholas, Plumstead [Woolwich].

b Llanddewi Brefi parish church [Cardiganshire], by E. Lewes, with a note by W. D. Caröe.

c Chillington [Som.] and its church.

d Parish and church of Mold [Flints.].

2391 Vol. 33.

a S. Nicholas, Deptford: the Westminster abbey of the navy, by A. Hart.

2392 Vol. 34.

a Church of Little Steeping, Lincs., by W.E.B.

b S. Mary the Virgin, Speldhurst [Kent], and S. John the Evangelist, Groombridge [Suss.].

c Two Welsh mountain churches [St. Ishow, Partrishow, and St. Milberg, Llanfilo, Breconshire], by W. D. Caröe.

d S. Mary's, Leake, in the Lincoln marshes.

2393 Vol. 35.

a Church extension at Mortlake, by H. Monroe.

b Church of Clynnogfawr in Arfon [Carnarvonshire], by B. Stallybrass.

c The island and royal manor of Portland and its churches, by D. B. Griggs.

d All Hallows, Bardsey-cum-Rigton, Yorks.

e Church of S. Mary the Virgin, Tunstead, Norf., by P. M. Johnston.

f S. Giles', Northampton, by T. A. Gurney.

2394 Vol. 36.

a Croughton church, Northants.

b Stanley S. Leonard, Glos., by C. Swynnerton.

c Church of S. Mary, Hendon.

INFORMATION SERVICE ON INTERNATIONAL AFFAIRS

Founded 1924, as the Association for International Understanding, for the collection of information on international affairs and the objective and scientific study of the facts. Title changed to above form in July 1928. The Service was merged in the Information Department of the Royal Institute of International Affairs, 1930.

Information series, nos. 1–8:

2395 No. 1. Information on the permanent court of international justice, by J. W. Wheeler-Bennett. 1924.

2396 No. 1a. The world court in 1925: first annual supplement, by J. W. Wheeler-Bennett. *P.* 1926.

2397 No. 1b. The world court in 1926: second annual supplement, by M. Fanshaw. *P.* 1927.

2398 No. 1c. The world court in 1927: third annual supplement, by M. Fanshaw. *P*. 1928.

2399 No. 2. Information on the reduction of armaments, by J. W. Wheeler-Bennett, with introd. by Sir N. Malcolm. 1925.

2400 No. 3. Information on the problem of security, 1917–26, by J. W. Wheeler-Bennett and F. E. Langermann, with introd. by H. A. L. Fisher. 1927.

2401 No. 4. Information on the renunciation of war, 1927–28, by J. W. Wheeler-Bennett, with introd. by P. H. Kerr. 1928.

2402 No. 5. Information on the world court, 1918–28, by J. W. Wheeler-Bennett and M. Fanshaw, with introd. by Sir C. Hurst. 1929. [Nos. 1, 1a, 1b, and 1c combined and revised]

2403 No. 6. Information on the reparation settlement, being the background and history of the Young plan and the Hague agreements, 1929–30, by J. W. Wheeler-Bennett and H. Latimer, with foreword by Sir C. Addis. 1930.

2404 No. 7. Disarmament and security since Locarno, 1925–1931, being the political and technical background of the general disarmament conference, 1932, by J. W. Wheeler-Bennett, with introd. by Sir N. Malcolm. 1932.

2405 No. 8. The wreck of reparations, being the political background of the Lausanne agreement, 1932, by J. W. Wheeler-Bennett, with introd. by Sir W. Layton. 1933.

Bulletin of International News, vols. 1–10[1]
(1925–34):

2406 Vol. 4.

a Anglo-Egyptian relations exclusive of the Sudan, 1922–7. [Other articles on Anglo-Egyptian affairs after Feb. 1922 appeared in vols. 2 and 3]
b The limitation of navies.
c Outline of Anglo-Irak treaty relations, 1920–27.
d The Anglo-Egyptian treaty negotiations.

2407 Vol. 5.

a The Anglo-French naval compromise.
b Great Britain and the Washington Hours Convention [limiting the industrial working week to 48 hours].
c The Nile waters agreement [1929].
d Anglo-American relations and naval disarmament: a new phase.

2408 Vol. 6.

a The Anglo-Egyptian question [1927–30, with proposals for an Anglo-Egyptian settlement].
b The Hague conference, 1929.
c The Palestine mandate [with the Balfour declaration, 1917; selected articles of the mandate, confirmed in 1922; and the Churchill memorandum, 1922].
d Anglo-Soviet relations, 1918–29 [with the protocol of agreement, 1929, and the statement of M. Litvinoff, 1929].
e Anglo-American relations and the five power naval conference [1929, with the British government's invitation to the naval conference addressed to the United

[1] Vols. 1–3 appeared in typewritten duplicated parts (with the exception of vol. 3, no. 12, which was printed) and are now difficult to trace. A new (printed) series began with vol. 4, July 1927. From vol. 6 onwards the Bulletin was issued by the Information Dept. of the Royal Institute of International Affairs.

States, France, Italy and Japan, and the joint statement issued by Great Britain and the United States].
f Great Britain and the optional clause [attached to the statute of the permanent court of international justice arising out of the covenant of the League of Nations].
g The Hilton-Young and Wilson reports on East Africa.
h General Smuts and native policy in East Africa. [Brief summary of points made in the Rhodes memorial lectures, 1929, by General Smuts]
i British relations with Iraq [1927–9, with a memorandum by the secretary of state for the colonies on policy in Iraq].
j The five-power naval conference [1929–30].
k The second Hague conference [1930].
l The covenant and pact of the League of Nations. [With the existing text of the covenant, articles 12, 13, and 15; British proposed amendments; and amendments adopted by the committee of eleven. Contd. in vol. 7]
m Great Britain's international obligations.
n Temporary commercial agreement between his Majesty's government in the United Kingdom and the government of the Union of Soviet Socialist Republics [1930].

2409 Vol. 7.

a The League of Nations in 1929–30.
b Chronology of events in Malta, 1921–30.
c Great Britain and Palestine [1929–30].
d The draft convention for disarmament [1930].
e The imperial conferences of 1926–30 and the conduct of foreign policy.

2410 Vol. 8.

a Comparative tables to illustrate the position of the armaments of the great powers [1931].
b The report of the joint select committee on closer union in East Africa [1931], by R.C.M.A.
c The Statute of Westminster, by H. Latimer.
d Statements of policy in India and Burma, by R.C.M.A. [Summaries of statements made by the prime minister to (i) the Indian round-table conference at the close of its second session, Dec. 1931, and (ii) the Burma round-table conference at the final session, Jan. 1932]
e The disarmament conference [1932–3], by H. Latimer. [Contd. in vols. 9 and 10]
f The United States, Britain and the Shanghai question, by H. Latimer.

2411 Vol. 9.

a The Lausanne conference [1932], by J. Wheeler-Bennett and [pt. 2] S. A. Heald.
b The Indian communal decision [concerning the representation of the British Indian communities in the provisional legislature of India under the new constitution], by H. Latimer.
c The Persian government and the oil concession [to the Anglo-Persian oil company, and events following its cancellation, 1932], by H. Latimer.
d The four-power pact [between Great Britain, France, Germany and Italy, 1933; with the Mussolini draft, the Daladier draft, and the final draft], by J. W. Wheeler-Bennett.

2412 Vol. 10.

a The language problem in Malta.
b Great Britain and German re-armament, by J. W. Wheeler-Bennett.

Extra publication:

2413 The origins of the League covenant: documentary history of its drafting, by Florence Wilson, with introd. by P. J. N. Baker. 1928.

INSTITUTE OF BANKERS

Founded 1879, to facilitate the consideration and discussion of matters of interest to the profession; and to afford opportunities for the acquisition of a knowledge of the theory of banking.

Journal, vols. 22–54 (1901–33):

2414 Vol. 22.
 a Early Victorian coinage.
 b Effect of war on the prices of commodities, 1850–1900: essays by W. A. Cole and E. E. Gellender.
 c Emergency issues of notes and tokens consequent upon the passing of the Bank Restriction Act of 1797, by M. Phillips.

2415 Vol. 23.
 a Growth of London as the financial centre of the world, and the best means of maintaining that position, by E. W. Sykes.
 b Signs of old Lombard Street [at the coronation of King Edward VII].

2416 Vol. 24.
 a Relations of commercial geography and commercial history, by G. G. Chisholm.
 b The history of a banking house (Smith, Payne and Smiths), by H. T. Easton.

2417 Vol. 25.
 a An enquiry into the economic condition of the country [1904], by R. H. I. Palgrave.
 b An investigation into the relative influence of this country's free gold market and her free trade fiscal policy in bringing about her financial predominance; and the effects to be anticipated should preferential trading with her colonies and dependencies be adopted, by J. W. Hartley.

2418 Vol. 27.
 a The 'Maberly Phillips' collection of old bank-notes [Additions are listed in subsequent vols.]
 b History of banks and banking in Essex, by M. Christy.

2419 Vol. 28.
 a The difference between the conditions under which the Bank Act of 1844 operates now, and those prevailing in 1844, showing how far and in what directions the act is considered capable of amendment, by H. Tipper.

2420 Vol. 29.
 a A decade of bank amalgamations, 1897–1906, by D. Fraser.
 b Sidelights on banking history, by M. Phillips. [Contd. in vol. 31. Also issued separately, *P.* 1908]
 c Banking in ancient and mediaeval societies, by H. Tipper. [3 pts., the third dealing with England to 1688]
 d The history of companies' legislation in England in its practical aspect, and its effect upon our industrial and banking development, by S. E. Perry.
 e Early legislation on bankers' cheques, by W. McKewan.

2421 Vol. 31.
 a A critical survey of the literature of banking in the United Kingdom, by J. Darge.
 b The finance of war, by E. Crammond.

2422 Vol. 32.
 a Banking in Canada, by Sir E. Walker.

2423 Vol. 33.
 a The South Sea bubble, by M. Phillips.

2424 Vol. 34.
 a Some modern phases of British banking, 1896–1911, by D. D. Fraser.

2425 Vol. 36.
 a 'Jemmy' Wood of Gloucester [d. 1836], a famous country banker.
 b Historical survey of the position occupied by the Bank of England as regards the other banks of this country, the state, and the financial and commercial community generally, with especial reference to the present position of the Bank, by H. V. Burrell.

2426 Vol. 38.
 a Early Sheffield banks, by R. E. Leader. [Contd. in vol. 39]

2427 Vol. 40.
 a An examination of the Bank Charter Act of 1844 with a view to its amendment, by H. F. R. Miller.

2428 Vol. 41.
 a Before the coming of the manager: the life of a banker's clerk a century ago, by L. Le M. Minty.

2429 Vol. 45.
 a Glimpses of England a century ago [with particular reference to economic conditions, 1815–25], by H. J. Smith.

2430 Vol. 47.
 a Our mother tongue, by B. L. K. Henderson. [On the growth and value of the English dictionary]

2431 Vol. 54.
 a The work of the Stock Exchange, by Sir S. Killick. [Includes a brief historical account]

2432 General index to vols. 16–31, 1895–1910. 1911.

Other publications:

2433 Catalogue of the 'Maberly Phillips' collection of old bank-notes, drafts, etc., collected and mounted by Maberly Phillips. 1906.

INSTITUTE OF MARINE ENGINEERS

Founded 1899, to advance the science and practice of marine engineering.

Twelfth–Forty-fourth Annual Report, 1900–32, (or Transactions), being vols. 12–44 (1901–33):

2434 Vol. 12.
 a Twenty years of progress in cargo-boat machinery, by J. F. Walliker.
 b Sea-borne traffic [including its history], by J. Adamson.

2435 Vol. 17.
 a Development of the torpedo-boat destroyer, by W. J. Harding.

2436 Vol. 18.
 a The introduction of steam navigation, by J. H. Hulls.

2437 Vol. 19.
 a Early days of marine insurance, by T. F. Auckland.

2438 Vol. 20.
 a Artificial illumination, historical and practical, by A. E. Battle.
 b History of Lloyds, by T. F. Auckland.

2439 Vol. 22.

a History and practice of lubrication in marine engines, by J. V. Wilson.

2440 Vol. 25.

a Twenty years' progress in marine construction, by A. Gracie.

2441 Vol. 28.

a The Institute of Marine Engineers [a brief account of its foundation, 1889, and its activities], by J. Anderson.

2442 Vol. 31.

a The evolution in propulsion of the modern super-submersible torpedo boat, by N. H. Wood.
b History of the steamship, by J. Houston.
c Development of the internal combustion engine, by C. Baxter.

2443 Vol. 32.

a Marine engine curiosities of practice and experience, by A. E. Seaton. [An account of some 19th cent. steamships]

2444 Vol. 36.

a Development of steam and internal combustion machinery for propulsion, by E. G. Warne.

2445 Vol. 40.

a The practical value of the report of the heat engine and boiler trials committee, by G. J. Wells. [Includes an account of the development of steam engines in the 18th and 19th cent.]
b Notes. [An account of John Wilkinson, d. 1808, Staffordshire iron-master, from an article in the *Foundry Trade Journal*, March, 1928?, by T. B. Fowler]

2446 Vol. 41.

a Origin and development of heavy oil engines, by A. F. Evans.

2447 Vol. 43.

a William Symington, 1763–1831, the father of marine engineering. [Reprint of a pamphlet by Edgar C. Smith, published by the Institute with the collaboration of the Newcomen Society, 1931]
b A short history of marine refrigeration, by A. R. T. Woods.
c Safety valves [in 19th cent. steam locomotives and their development in marine engineering], by D. MacNicholl.

2448 Vol. 44.

a Hammers through the ages. [Reprint of the abstract of an address by E. K. Clark, in *Engineering*, 30 Oct. 1931]

2449 Catalogue of papers read and discussed, 1889–1927. P 1928. [A list of published papers and lectures, 1889–1919 appears in the 30th Annual Report]

INSTITUTE OF TRANSPORT

Founded 1919, to promote and encourage knowledge of traffic science and of the art of transport in all its branches.

Journal, vols. 1–15 (1920–34):

2450 Vol. 1.

a Roads: a review and a forecast, by Sir H. P. Maybury.

2451 Vol. 2.

a The Manchester ship canal as a factor in transport, by M. Stevens.
b History of roads, constructional requirements from the user point of view, systems of control, and taxation of road user, by C. H. Bressey.

c Historical survey of mechanical road transport, by C. le M. Gosselin.
d The problem of the canals, by Sir J. Eaglesome.
e Waterborne transport: an early form of traffic development with special reference to canals and inland waterways, by D. Ross-Johnson.

2452 Vol. 3.

a Evolution of the motor vehicle for goods and passenger service, by P. F. Smith.
b Development of commercial airways, by Sir H. White-Smith.

2453 Vol. 4.

a The work of the Aire and Calder Navigation, by W. H. Breach.

2454 Vol. 5.

a The Manchester ship canal, by E. Latimer.
b Roads and their maintenance: the incidence of taxation in relation thereto, by E. G. Garstang.
c The rating of railways and docks, by A. J. Brickwell.
d The port of Bristol in the past and in the present, by D. Ross-Johnson.

2455 Vol. 6.

a The problem of London traffic [an historical survey], by Sir L. Macassey.

2456 Vol. 7.

a The problem of the canals, by Sir J. Eaglesome.
b A hundred years of railway development, by R. Bell.
c Some financial and political aspects of highway development, by A. Hacking.
d State ownership of waterways, by H. D. Dickinson.

2457 Vol. 8.

a Growth and form in modern cities [with particular reference to London], by F. Pick.
b Transport in England: a brief historical survey, by C. G. Robertson.

2458 Vol. 9.

a Notes on highway administration, by W. J. Merrett.
b The development of transport facilities in the midlands during the first part of the 19th cent., by J. F. Rees.

2459 Vol. 10.

a Motor transport in the British postal service, by F. Lane.
b The Port of London Authority: a survey of twenty years' work and trade, by D. J. Owen.

2460 Vol. 11.

a Transport developments in 1929, by R. Bell. [Reports for 1930–32 occur in vols. 12–14]
b Achievements and possibilities of air transport, by F. H. Page.
c The port of London, by J. H. Estill.

2461 Vol. 12.

a Canals and inland waterways, by T. Abbott.

2462 Vol. 13.

a The progress and development of commercial aviation, by C. A. Barnard.
b Rationalisation on the London Midland and Scottish railway, by E. J. H. Lemon.

2463 Vol. 15.

a British coasting trade and its national importance, [including a short history of the subject], by J. R. Cowper.

b The state and shipping: the influence of the past on recent developments, by Sir A. Hurd.
c The Road Traffic Act, 1930 (pt. 4), by A. F. Nicholson.

INSTITUTION OF ROYAL ENGINEERS

Founded 1875, as the Royal Engineers Institute, for the general advancement of military science, and more particularly the promotion of the acquisition of historical and scientific knowledge in relation to engineering as applied to military purposes. Title changed to the above form in 1921.

Royal Engineers Journal, vols. 31–34 (1901–4):

2464 Vol. 31.
a The [Boer] war: retrospect of the war, by S. L. Norris.
b The [Boer] war: the defence of Christiana [the Transvaal, 1900–1], by W. H. Turton.
c Col. Sir George Charles Hoste, R.E. [d. 1845], by R. H. Vetch.
d Maj.-gen. Sir Charles Holloway, R.E. [d. 1827], by R. H. Vetch.

2465 Vol. 33.
a Another forgotten drill-book: extracts from *A Treatise of Military Discipline*, by Humphrey Bland, 9th ed. 1762, ed. R. L. McClintock.
b An 18th cent. letter book [from the C.R.E.'s office, Halifax, Nova Scotia, containing letters written 1789–1801].
c Another old letter book [from Fredericton, Nova Scotia, for the years 1802–9].
d Records of the South African war, 1899–1902: records of units. [Contd. in vol. 34]
e Old records of Chatham garrison [18th cent.], by G. H. Griffith.
f Corps archaeologia: Lt.-col. John Rutherfurd, commandant, Royal Staff Corps [d. 1813], by R. H. Vetch.
g Records of the China expedition, 1900–1.
h Records of Chatham and neighbourhood [18th cent.], by G. H. Griffith.
i Corps archaeologia: Sir Richard Lee [d. 1575], by R. H. Vetch.

2466 Vol. 34.
a Raids and invasions of British Isles from the time of the Romans to the present date, by O. E. Ruck.

Royal Engineers Journal, new ser., vols. 1–47 (1905–33):

2467 Vol. 1.
a Gordon and Gladstone, by D. C. Walker.
b The scientific study of military history, by F. N. Maude.

2468 Vol. 3.
a Historic influence of foreign policy on coast defences, by O. E. Ruck.
b The siege of Sebastopol: some conversations with Gen. Todleben and Sir John Burgoyne, by the Hon. G. Wrottesley.
c The frontiers of the British Empire, by T. M. Maguire.
d Notes on the Cobham oppidum [British oppidum, Cobham Park, Kent], by O. E. Ruck.
e A report on Halifax, Nova Scotia, by one of Wolfe's engineers [Capt. Hugh Debbieg, 1761], by B. R. Ward.

2469 Vol. 4.
a Archaeologia militaria: notes on Joyden's redoubt, Bexley, Kent, by O. E. Ruck.

b Oppida Cantiana: notes on Bigberry camp [Harbledown, Kent] and the Pilgrim's Way, by O. E. Ruck.
c Martello towers. [Extract from *The Times*, Oct. 1806]

2470 Vol. 5.
a The battle of Hastings, 14 Oct. 1066, by E. R. James.

2471 Vol. 7.
a Reminiscences of the siege of Delhi, 1857, by W. E. Warrand.
b Foundation of the Royal Engineer establishment at Chatham, by B. R. Ward.

2472 Vol. 8.
a The first mounted units of the corps organized at Chatham, by B. R. Ward.
b The R.E. headquarters mess [at Brompton barracks, Chatham, with biographical accounts of the subjects of the various portraits in the mess], by B. R. Ward. [Contd. in vol. 9]
c Volunteers in the 18th cent., by G. A. Brown.

2473 Vol. 9.
a The main underground telegraph system of Great Britain, by W. A. J. O'Meara.

2474 Vol. 10.
a The Fyers family, by R. H. Vetch. [Contd. in vols. 11, 12 (under the title 'Maj.-gen. Sir William Reid'), and 13]

2475 Vol. 11.
a Mobilization in the 16th cent.

2476 Vol. 12.
a Gibraltar under Moor, Spaniard, and Briton, by E. R. Kenyon. [Contd. in vol. 13]

2477 Vol. 13.
a The work of the R.E. in the China or 'Boxer' war of 1900–1, by F. T. N. S. Bowring.
b A report on Torres Vedras [made by Maj.-gen. Sir J. T. Jones in 1810].

2478 Vol. 14.
a The British military mission in Egypt, 1798–1802.
b Historical documents of Maj.-Gen. Sir J. T. Jones [dealing with the Peninsular war. Contd. in vols. 15 and 16].

2479 Vol. 15.
a A lady's experiences in the great siege of Gibraltar, being the diary from June 1, 1779 to June 13, 1781, of Mrs. Green, wife of Lt.-col. Green, chief engineer of Gibraltar (afterwards Lt.-gen. Sir William Green, chief engineer of Great Britain, 1786–1802). [Contd. in vol. 16]
b Lt.-col. Sir Richard Fletcher, bt. K.C.B., R.E. [d. 1813], by E. A. Macartney-Filgate.
c Centenary reminiscences of Sir Charles Pasley [d. 1861], by B. R. Ward.
d The R.E. Museum [an account of its history and contents], by W. A. Harrison.

2480 Vol. 16.
a An engineer officer under Wellington in the Peninsula: the diary and correspondence of Lieut. Rice Jones, R.E., 1808–12; with letters from distinguished officers at the seat of war in Portugal, Spain, France, Belgium, and America and afterwards, ed. the Hon. H. N. Shore. [Contd. in vol. 17]
b Pasley's 'Essay on the military policy of the British Empire': contemporary criticisms, 1810–13, by B. R. Ward.

c Some Royal Engineer orders at the siege of Gibraltar [1779–83].

d Military archaeology of Kent, by A. M. Henniker. [Includes accounts of prehistoric earthworks, Roman camps, warning beacons arranged in 1588, and the French project for the invasion of England, 1778]

2481 Vol. 17.

a Papers of Field Marshal Sir John Burgoyne, G.C.B. [d. 1871].

b The siege of Gibraltar. [Letter from Sir William Green, 1782]

2482 Vol. 18.

a Early Indian campaigns and the decorations awarded for them [1799–1849], by H. Biddulph. [Contd. in vol. 19]

2483 Vol. 19.

a Sieges and the defence of fortified places by British and Indian armies of the 19th cent., by Sir E. T. Thackeray. [Contd. in vols. 20–23]

b Baird Smith papers during the Indian mutiny.

c A note of the several transactions of the French in their attack of Fort St. George, and of the garrison in the defence of that place, 1758–9. [Contd. in vol. 20]

2484 Vol. 20.

a Some [19th cent.] war medals of the Bengal Sappers and Miners, by P. C. S. Hobart.

2485 Vol. 23.

a Passing thoughts on military architecture in the Thames defences [an historical account], by A. A. Crookshank.

2486 Vol. 24.

a The chapel of Milton Chantry, Gravesend, by A. A. Crookshank.

2487 Vol. 25.

a Famous engineers of the Allied armies: Kitchener, by B. R. Ward.

b Deeds of the Royal Engineers. [Contd. in vol. 26]

2488 Vol. 28.

a Climax of two great wars [a comparison of the situation in England in 1810–11 and 1918], by J. H. Rose.

2489 Vol. 29.

a Work by R.E. units in the war: extracts from reports of units to the Engineer-in-Chief, B.E.F.

b From the Curragh to the Aisne, 1914: a story of the 59th Field Company, R.E., by G. Walker. [Contd. in vol. 32, 'From the Aisne to Ypres, 1914']

c Field Marshal Sir Douglas Haig on the 'Features of the war' [being a reprint from the 4th supplement to the *London Gazette* of April 8, 1919, of Part II of Sir Douglas Haig's final despatch reviewing the whole war].

2490 Vol. 30.

a History of the Railways and Roads Training Centre, R.E., Longmoor [Hants], by H. M. Sinclair.

b The work of the Royal Engineers in the European war, 1914–19. [Contd. in vols. 31, 33, 38, 39. Also published separately. For details see no. **2514** below]

c The battle of the Somme. [Extracts from various reports on the work of the Royal Engineers in the battle, 1916. Contd. in vols. 31 and 33]

2491 Vol. 31.

a The battle of Arras. [Extracts from various reports on the work of the Royal Engineers in the battle, 1917]

2492 Vol. 33.

a The introduction of mechanical warfare on land and its possibilities in the near future, by J. F. C. Fuller.

2493 Vol. 34.

a The Ordnance Survey of the United Kingdom, by Sir C. Close.

2494 Vol. 35.

a Some famous engineer officers of the 19th cent., by Sir G. Scott-Moncrieff.

2495 Vol. 36.

a An outline of the Egyptian and Palestine campaigns, 1914–18, by Sir M. G. E. Bowman-Manifold. [Also published separately, in several editions]

2496 Vol. 37.

a Notes on railway work in East Africa, 1914–18, by H. L. Woodhouse.

b Organization of engineering works in the Great war, by Sir G. K. Scott-Moncrieff.

c Leaves from an old letter-book [Hongkong, 1847–63], by C. W. Davy.

d Lieut.-col. William Cuninghame of Enterkine [d. 1759], by F. E. G. Skey.

2497 Vol. 38.

a Notes on the early years of the Ordnance Survey with some account of its founders [1746–1846], by Sir C. F. Close. [Contd. in vols. 39 and 40. Also published separately, 1926]

b Operations of the 1st Division on the Belgian coast in 1917, by W. G. S. Dobbie.

c History of the 12th Company, Royal Engineers, by M. R. Caldwell. [Contd. in vol. 39. Also published separately, 1925]

d The decision to defend Kut-el-Amarah, by E. W. C. Sandes.

e The defence of Kut-el-Amarah [Dec. 1915–April 1916], by E. W. C. Sandes.

2498 Vol. 39.

a The Institution of Royal Engineers (1875–1925), by F. E. G. Skey.

b Battle honours of Royal Engineer units [1914–18. Contd. in vols. 40–43]

c Some unexpected problems worked out by the Royal Engineers during the 1914–18 war, by W. H. Grey.

d Notes by a chief engineer during the Great war of 1914–18, by W. B. Brown. [Contd. in vol. 40]

e Engineers in the retreat to Corunna [1808–9], by R. H. Dewing.

f Life and work of Col. [Alexander Ross] Clarke [d. 1914], by Sir C. Close.

2499 Vol. 40.

a Brief history of the Royal Engineers with cavalry in France during the war 1914–18, by W. H. Evans.

b The early days of M[echanical] T[ransport] and some ideas on its future, by A. Mason.

c History of the 20th (Field) Company, Royal Bombay Sappers and Miners, Great war, 1914–18, by H. W. R. Hamilton. [Contd. in vol. 41. Also published separately, 1926]

d An unofficial history of the Signal Service with the British Salonika force, 1915–18, by C. C. S. White. [Contd. in vol. 41]

e Lieut.-gen. William Spry [d. 1802].

2500 Vol. 41.

a Some Royal Engineers and their work in Africa, by H. L. Pritchard.

b Maj.-gen. A. Emmett [d. 1872] and Napoleon, by F. E. G. Skey.
c Experiences at Fourth Army headquarters: organization and work of the R.E. [1916–18], by Sir R. V. H. Buckland.
d The crossing of the Piave in 1918, by W. A. F. Kerrick.
e A contemporary account of the battle of Gujerat [1849], by Sir A. Cunningham.

2501 Vol. 42.

a The origin of tunnelling companies, R.E., by Sir J. Norton-Griffiths.
b The life-work of the Rt. Hon. Sir George Taubman-Goldie [d. 1925], by P. H. Kealey.
c The 23rd (Field) Company R.E. in the Great war, 1914–18, by R. L. Bond. [Contd. in vol. 43]
d The Bombay engineer officer of 1800, by A. Vincent.
e Reuters [an historical account], by Sir R. Jones.
f R.E. football in the early '70s, by Sir R. M. Ruck.
g Shakespeare and Elizabethan war propaganda, by B. R. Ward.

2502 Vol. 43.

a How British colonies are governed, by Sir S. H. Wilson. [Includes an historical account]
b Ancient land measures of Britain and Malta, by J. W. S. Sewell.
c Military mining in the Great war, by R. N. Harvey.
d Afghan wars [1839–42, 1878–81, 1919], by F. C. Molesworth.

2503 Vol. 44.

a The Elizabethan chronicle play as war propaganda, by B. R. Ward.
b A subaltern in the Indian mutiny: containing some letters of Lieut. Edward Talbot Thackeray, Bengal Engineers, afterwards Col. Sir E. T. Thackeray, 1836–1927, ed. C. B. Thackeray. [Contd. in vol. 45]
c Sir Charles Pasley, 1780–1861, his life: a sketch, by P. H. Kealey. [Contd. in vol. 45]

2504 Vol. 45.

a Sir Charles Pasley [and his experiments in] the manufacture of Portland cements, by A. D. Campbell.
b Sir Charles Pasley: the development of the pontoon, by I. S. O. Playfair.
c Marlborough's campaigns [1702–11], by A. C. Mitchell.
d Sir Charles Pasley: submarine work [the removal of wrecks by submarine explosions], by P. H. Kealey.

2505 Vol. 46.

a History of the 7th Field Company, R.E., during the war, 1914–18; with a short record of the movements and campaigns since the formation of the company [c. 1793], by H. A. Baker.
b Fifty years ago: the S.M.E. [School of Military Engineering], 1881–83, by Sir J. E. Edmonds.
c History of the Royal Engineer Yacht Club [1846–1932], by W. G. Fryer.

2506 Vol. 47.

a Maj.-gen. Charles George Gordon [d. 1885], by B. M. Allen.
b A soldier family [the Durnfords], by J. W. Lydekker.
c Diary of an R.E. subaltern with the B.E.F. in 1914, by B. K. Young.

Professional (occasional) papers, vols. 27–30 (1901–4):

2507 Vol. 27.

a The work of the Royal Engineers in Natal [1899–1900], by C. K. Wood.

b Recent developments in locomotive practice [including an account of 19th cent. developments], by C. J. B. Cooke.

2508 Vol. 28.

a Military ballooning in the British army [including an historical account], by C. M. Watson.
b The survey of India, by C. Strahan.

2509 Vol. 30.

a Pieter's Hill [battle, 1900]: a tactical study, by F. A. Molony.
b The blockhouse system in the South African war, by E. H. Bethel.

Professional papers, new ser., vols. 1–3 (1906–18):

2510 Vol. 3.

a The growth of the offensive in fortification, by J. C. Matheson.

Other publications:

2511 Detailed history of railways in the South African war, 1899–1902. 2 vols. 1904.

2512 History of submarine mining in the British army, by W. B. Brown. 1910.

2513 History of the Corps of Royal Engineers, by Sir C. M. Watson. Vol. iii [1886–1912], 1915. [Vols. i–ii by W. Porter were published 1889]

2514 The work of the Royal Engineers in the European war, 1914–19. 11 vols. 1921–7. [Vol. i: Bridging. Vol. ii: Chemical warfare. Vol. iii: Work in the field under the Engineer-in-Chief, B.E.F.; geological work on the western front. Vol. iv: Military mining. Vol. v: The Signal Service, 1914–18 (France), by R. E. Priestley. Vol. vi: Supply of engineer stores and equipment. Vol. vii: Work in the field in other theatres of war; Egypt and Palestine; water supply. Vol. viii: Water supply (France). Vol. ix: Work under the Director of Works (France). Vol. x: Work of the experimental section. Vol. xi: Miscellaneous, comp. G. H. Addison, including sections on organization and expansion of corps 1914–18, organization of engineer intelligence and information, camouflage service, concrete defence work and factories, forward communications, machinery, workshops and electricity, anti-aircraft searchlights, inundations, and training schools]

2515 A history of Royal Engineers cricket, by R. S. R. Kerr. 1925.

2516 Catalogue of the Royal Engineers corps library at the Horse Guards, Whitehall, London. 1929.

INTERNATIONAL INFORMATION COMMITTEE

Founded 1916?, for the preparation and publication of literature dealing with and explaining the British Empire.— its origins, constitution, resources, and general conditions. Dissolved 1919?.

International Information series, British empire section, vols. 1–5:

2517 Vol. 2. The defences of the Empire, by A. Hurd. 1917.

2518 Vol. 3. The commonwealth of Australia: its development and resources, by E. Lewin. 1917.

2519 Vol. 4. New Zealand, by G. H. Scholefield. 1917.

2520 Vol. 5. Canada: past, present, and future, by P. Hurd. 1918.

INTERNATIONAL SOCIETY OF PHILOLOGY, SCIENCE AND ARTS

Founded in Paris 1873, formally constituted 1875, for the advancement and encouragement of all branches of science, literature, music, and the fine arts generally, and particularly the science of philology.

The Philomath, nos. 201–280,[1] being old ser., vols. 17–26, or new ser., vols. 1–9 (1913–33):

2521 No. 201.

a Philology, by H. M. Léon. [Contd. as 'Philology and philologers' in nos. 202–5, 207–10, 212–13]

2522 No. 216.

a The famous 'Childe of Hale' [John Middleton, d. 1623], by H. M. Léon.

2523 No. 218.

a The authorship of the letters of Junius, by N. Sibley.

2524 No. 219.

a A Manx place name [Cronk-ny-iree-lhaa], by W. R. H. Caine and H. M. Léon.

2525 No. 229.

a Some Sussex folk tales, by A. Beckett.

2526 No. 246.

a Edwin Waugh [d. 1890], Lancashire's dialect laureate, by A. Clarke.

2527 No. 251.

a Notes on Crawley and Ifield, Suss., by H. M. Léon. [Contd. in no. 252]

2528 No. 268.

a The primitive Aryans and the Celts, by C. H. Betts.

2529 No. 269.

a History of the wool-combing industry in Yorkshire, by W. Haigh.
b Buckden palace: its romantic and fascinating history, by R. H. Edleston and H. M. Léon.

IPSWICH AND DISTRICT FIELD CLUB

Founded 1903. Amalgamated in 1924 with the Ipswich Scientific Society to form the Ipswich and District Natural History Society, q.v.

Journal, vols. 1–6 (1908–21):

2530 Vol. 2.

a Neolithic remains at Stuston, by A. Mayfield.

2531 Vol. 4.

a Workshop floor of lower-middle Aurignacian age discovered in Messrs. Bolton and Laughlin's brickyard at Ipswich, by J. R. Moir.

2532 Vol. 6.

a Excavation of two tumuli on Brightwell heath, by J. R. Moir.

[1] The first 200 numbers, in French, were published in Paris.

IPSWICH AND DISTRICT NATURAL HISTORY SOCIETY

Founded 1924, by the amalgamation of the Ipswich and District Field Club (q.v.) and the Ipswich Scientific Society (which did not publish), to encourage the study of natural history and all branches of science.

Journal, vol. 1 (1925–35):

2533 Vol. 1.

a The antiquity of man in Ipswich, by J. R. Moir.
b The Suffolk coast, by E. R. Cooper.
c Stone implements from a new angle, by J. R. Moir.
d World-wide prehistoric cultures, by J. R. Moir.
e Farmhouse life 50 years ago [in 1880 on a Suffolk farm], by E. R. Cooper.

IRON AND STEEL INSTITUTE

Founded 1869, to afford a means of communication between members of the iron and steel trades upon matters bearing upon their respective manufactures, excluding all questions connected with wages and trade regulations. The Journal contains, in addition to the articles listed, presidential addresses on various aspects of the history of the iron and steel industry.

Journal, vols. 59–127 (1901–33):

2534 Vol. 69.

a The early use of iron, by B. H. Brough.

2535 Vol. 77.

a Iron scrap, or the issue of an old shoe heel: being the origin of the discovery of pig boiling, by J. Hall. [Reprint of a pamphlet published in 1864]

2536 Vol. 78.

a Iron and steel industries of the Cleveland district during the last quarter of a century, by W. Hawdon.
b A description of Messrs. Bell Brothers' blast-furnaces, 1844–1908, by G. Jones.

2537 Vol. 85.

a Notes on a bloom of Roman iron found at Corstopitum (Corbridge), by Sir H. Bell.
b Notes on some remains of early iron manufacture in Staffordshire, by T. Turner.

2538 Vol. 94.

a The use of meteoric iron by primitive man, by G. F. Zimmer.

2539 Vol. 95.

a Origin and development of the railway rail in England and America, by G. P. Raidabaugh.

2540 Vol. 104.

a Manufacture of shells in Canada during the war, 1914–18, by H. W. B. Swabey and R. Genders.

2541 Vol. 109.

a Continuous rolling-mills: their growth and development, by J. P. Bedson.

2542 Vol. 112.

a Ancient [Roman] iron from Richborough and Folkestone, by J. N. Friend and W. E. Thorneycroft.

2543 Vol. 121.

a History of the cementation process of steel manufacture, pt. 1, by D. Brownlie. [On the work of William Ellyott and Mathias Meysey in England, c. 1600]

Other publications:

2544 Sketches and illustrations of the iron, steel and allied trades, with introduction, portraits, views and sketches of Buxton and the railway routes, ed. C. H. Bird-Davis. 1910.[1]

2545 Journal of the Iron and Steel Institute: subject and name index, ed. G. C. Lloyd. 3 vols. 1911–33. [Vol. i: For Journal, vols. 59–82, and Carnegie scholarship memoirs, vols. 1–2, with a note on the development of the Institute. Vol. ii: For Journal, vols. 83–104, and Carnegie scholarship memoirs, vols. 3–10. Vol. iii: For Journal, vols. 105–124, and Carnegie scholarship memoirs, vols. 11–20]

2546 Visit of the Institute to Cardiff, 1920. [1920. Includes sections on Cardiff and South Wales, and on the iron, steel, coal, and anthracite concerns of the district]

2547 Carnegie scholarship memoirs, vol. 12: Iron in antiquity, by J. N. Friend. 1926.

ISLE OF MAN NATURAL HISTORY AND ANTIQUARIAN SOCIETY

Founded 1879, as the Isle of Mann (later Man) Natural History and Antiquarian Society, for the practical study of natural history and antiquities, especially in the Isle of Man.

Yn Lioar Manninagh. Journal of the Society:

2548 Vol. 4 (1901–10).

a The Ronaldsway estate, by A. W. Moore.
b A sculptured stone recently discovered in Ramsey, and the story of Sigurd the Volsung, as illustrated on monuments in the Isle of Man, by P. M. C. Kermode.
c The Northern Manks and the Southern Manx Volunteers [early 19th cent.], by A. W. Moore.
d [Proceedings and transactions to 1905]

Proceedings and Transactions, new ser., vols. 1–3 (1906–34):

2549 Vol. 1.

a Castle Rushen [date of origin], by A. Rigby.
b Evidence on a clan system having existed in the Isle of Man, with the names and localities of the principal clans in the 16th cent., by J. Quine.
c Neolithic refuse at Poolvaish, by F. Swynnerton.
d Reports of the Archaeological Survey [appointed to investigate all the historic and prehistoric remains in the Isle of Man. Reports include accounts of ancient keeills or chapels, and rhullics or Christian burial grounds in the parishes of Marown, Patrick, German, Kirk Michael, Ballaugh, Jurby, Kirk Andreas, Kirk Bride, Lezayre, Maughold, and Kirk Lonan. Contd. in vol. 2].
e St. Trinian's [Marown], by P. M. C. Kermode.
f Historical note on St. Trinian's, by J. Quine.
g Tynwald, by P. M. C. Kermode.
h Historical note on Tynwald hill, by J. Quine.
i Castle Rushen [general description], by A. Rigby.
j St. German's, by J. Quine.
k The [Manx] sword of state: its origin, by B. E. Sargeaunt.
l The earliest inhabitants of the Isle of Man, by F. Swynnerton.
m Discovery of bi-lingual inscription at Knock-y-Doonee, Andreas, by P. M. C. Kermode.

[1] Not seen.

n Ruined chapel on St. Michael's island, by A. Rigby.
o Introduction to the study of church buildings in the Isle of Man earlier than the 11th cent., by P. M. C. Kermode.
p The Woodbourne treasure trove, 1894 [including various Manx coins and gold and silver ornaments of the 10th cent.], by P. M. C. Kermode.
q Heraldry, its rise and decadence, by F. R. Somerset.
r Excavation of a round barrow on Ballaterson Cronk, Maughold, by S. N. Harrison.
s Inquiry as to the conditions of the Isle of Man and its inhabitants in the 5th cent., by P. M. C. Kermode.
t The Celtic tribal system in the Isle of Man, by P. M. C. Kermode.
u Notes on the Manx abbey lands, by P. G. Ralfe.
v Peel Island and the shrine of St. Mochonna, by P. M. C. Kermode.
w Inscribed cross-slab from Keeill at Ballavarkish, Bride, by P. M. C. Kermode.
x Cronk Howe Mooar, or Cronk-y-Mur, by P. M. C. Kermode.

2550 Vol. 2.

a Prof. Edward Forbes [d. 1854], by P. M. C. Kermode, W. A. Herdman, and Sir A. Geikie.
b The historical ballad of Mannanan Beg Mac y Leirr, by W. Cubbon.
c A rune inscribed slab from Kirk Maughold; and the first figure of a Viking ship on a Manx monument, by P. M. C. Kermode.
d Anglian crosses in Maughold, by J. Quine.
e Notes on the Manx church and the founding of Rushen abbey, by J. Quine.
f Tynwald in ancient days [1691], by G. F. Clucas.
g Report on a skull and skeleton of a man found in a lintel grave near Port St. Mary, 1918, by A. Keith.
h Notes on charter of Godred II to St. Bees [c. 1175], by J. Quine.
i Notes on Kirk Maughold cross, by F. Swynnerton.
j Some further notes on the Maughold cross shields, etc., by F. Swynnerton.
k Remarks on the above [two] papers, by P. M. C. Kermode.
l Manx notes from Tudor Liverpool, by J. A. Twemlow. [1: Early spellings of the word 'Manx'. 2: A 16th cent. Manx apprentice at Liverpool. 3: 16th cent. governors and deputy-governors of the island. 4: The Isle of Man as a port of call between England and Ireland in the 16th cent.]
m Saynt Maholde and Saynt Michell [suit in court of augmentations c. 1540], ed. — Owen. [See also below]
n Manx place names: their philological and grammatical development, by J. J. Kneen.
o Note re discovery of cist with urn at Baroose, Lonan, 1919, by J. Quine.
p President's address [on a discussion between Governor Horne and the House of Keys on the defence of the island, 1715], by D. F. Quayle.
q Myles Standish [d. 1656], the Puritan captain: was he a Manxman?, by W. Cubbon.
r Notes on Manx smuggling, from a Scottish source [the *Gallovidian*], by P. G. Ralfe.
s President's address [on 'The address of the 24 Keys to Lord Derby, 1703/4'], by D. F. Quayle.
t Life and work of the Rev. J. G. Cumming, vice-principal of King William's College, Isle of Man [d. 1868], by E. H. Stenning.
u A Manx lead mine in the 13th cent., by P. G. Ralfe.
v St. Ninian [d. ?432], by J. Davidson.
w St. Peter's church, Peel, by J. J. Joughin.
x An early reference to Manx ecclesiastical antiquities [letter written in 1826], by J. J. Kneen.

ISLE OF WIGHT NATURAL HISTORY AND ARCHAEOLOGICAL SOCIETY

Founded 1919, as the Isle of Wight Natural History Society for the study of the geology, zoology, botany, meteorology and archaeology of the Island. Title changed to the above form in 1927.

Proceedings, vols. 1–2 (1921–38):

u General meeting, 17 Feb. 1934 [being a lecture on old Yarmouth by A. G. Cole].

v Excursion to Bonchurch. [Includes an account of the old church and parish]

w Excursion to Wootton. [Includes an account of the church]

x Excursion to Newchurch and Alverstone. [Chiefly an account of Newchurch church]

y Excursion to Quarr abbeys. [History and description of the old abbey]

z A Brading deed of the 13th cent.

aa Excursion to St. Catherine's hill. [Includes an account of the 14th cent. oratory on the summit]

bb Excursion to Carisbrooke. [Includes an account of the church]

cc Medieval documents of the Isle of Wight, by G. A. Sherwin.

dd Annual general meeting, 1936. [Includes an address on Roman Bath by G. A. Sherwin]

ee Excursion to the Roman villa and St. Thomas's church, Newport.

ff An outline of the mesolithic flint cultures of the Isle of Wight, by H. F. Poole.

gg Annual general meeting, 1937. [Includes an address on recent advances in archaeological research, by G. A. Sherwin]

hh Excursion to St. Lawrence and Niton. [Includes an account of the old church at St. Lawrence]

ii 12th cent. middens in the Isle of Wight, by H. F. Poole and G. C. Dunning.

JAPAN SOCIETY

Founded 1892, to promote mutual understanding and good feeling between the British and Japanese peoples, and the encouragement of the study of the Japanese language, literature, history, and folklore, and of Japanese matters generally.

Transactions and Proceedings, vols. 5–30 (1902–33):

2554 Vol. 6.

a The dawn of western influence in Japan, by W. Crewdson.

b In memory of Will Adams, the first Englishman in Japan, by A. Diosy.

2555 Vol. 7.

a England's record in Japan [in the 19th cent.], by J. H. Longfold.

b England's appreciation of Japanese art [in the 19th cent.], by M. B. Huish.

c The story of a forgotten decoration conferred by the British government [upon Japanese who helped to defend the British legation in 1861].

2556 Vol. 9.

a The Japan-British exhibition [1910. Catalogue of exhibits of the Society including brief transcripts and facsimiles of some documents relating to early trading by the E. India Company in Japan]

2557 Vol. 13.

a Log-book of William Adams, 1614–19, by C. J. Purnell.

2558 Vol. 16.

a The monument to Will Adams.

2559 Vol. 22.

a The British aviation mission in Japan [1921–3], by the Master of Sempill.

2560 Analytical index to vols. 1–10 of the Transactions. *P.* [1914?].

JERSEY SOCIETY IN LONDON

Founded 1896?, to foster interest in the history of the Channel Islands.

Occasional publications:

2561 No. 2. Halley's comet from the Norman point of view [an account of its appearance in 1066], by W. B. Brodrick. [1910?]

2562 No. 3. The settlement of Normandy with special reference to the Channel Islands, by G. F. B. De Gruchy. [1911].

2563 No. 5. Jersey [half a century ago]: my reminiscences, by W. L. De Gruchy. [1915?]

2564 No. 6. Jersey, by J. B. Payen-Payne, 1860, ed. de V. Payen-Payne. [1927?]

2565 No. 7. Victor Hugo in Jersey, by de V. Payen-Payne. [1930?]

JEWISH HISTORICAL SOCIETY OF ENGLAND

Founded 1893, for the promotion and organisation of research into, and study of, the history of the Jews of the British Empire.

Transactions, sessions 1899–1931, vols. 4–12 (1903–31):

2566 [Vol. 4.] 1899–1901.

a History of the 'Domus Conversorum', 1290–1891, by M. Adler.

b John Dury [fl. 1656] and the English Jewry, by S. Levy.

c Joachim Gaunse: a mining incident in the reign of Elizabeth, by I. Abrahams.

d The earliest Jewish prayers for the sovereign, by S. Singer.

e Sir I. L. Goldsmid [d. 1859] and the admission of the Jews of England to parliament, by L. Abrahams.

f Status of the Jews in England after the re-settlement, by L. Wolf.

g Some historical notes, 1648–80 [concerning the readmission of Jews to England], by C. H. Firth.

h Extracts from the close rolls [concerning Jews, 1279–88], ed. Ada Corcos.

i The Jewish monarch and Queen Elizabeth [marriage proposal from Teitan, King of Jerusalem], ed. I. Abrahams.

j Clifford's tower, York, by F. Haes.

2567 [Vol. 5.] 1902–5.

a The Jewry of the Restoration, 1660–64, by L. Wolf.

b Notes on Leicester Jewry, by S. Levy.

c Jews and coronations, by S. Singer. [Deals with Jews as personally affected by the coronation of English sovereigns and with Jewish influence upon the coronation service]

d The lost tribes and the return of the Jews to England, by A. M. Hyamson.

e The Baal Shem of London [Dr. Falk, d. 1782], by H. Adler.

f A note on the Bodleian bowl [a 13th cent. Jewish metal vessel], by I. Abrahams.

g The Disraeli family, by L. Wolf.

h Jewish calendars of the coaching days, by M. Myers.
i The Norwich day-book [transactions of the Norwich Jewish exchequer, 9–11 Henry III], ed. S. Levy.

2568 [Vol. 6.] 1908–10.

a Anglo-Jewish historiography, by S. Levy.
b King Alfred and Mosaic law, by F. Liebermann.
c The so-called conspiracy of Dr. Ruy Lopez [1594], by M. Hume.
d Anglo-Judaica: description of a collection of pamphlets and books illustrative of the interest in Jewish studies and of the progress of the Jewish cause in Christian England, by H. Gollancz.
e The Jewish congregation of Portsmouth, 1766–1842, by I. S. Meisels.
f An English voice on the emancipation of the Jews [anonymous pamphlet of 1767], by H. Hirschfeld.
g The Jew bill of 1753, by A. M. Hyamson.
h A contribution to the history of the readmission of the Jews, by H. Gollancz.
i Satirical and political prints on the Jews' naturalization bill, 1753, by I. Solomons.
j A supposed Jewish conspiracy in 1753, by S. Levy.
k Some ms. sidelights on Anglo-Jewish emancipation, by M. Myers.
l A note on some Anglo-Jewish law cases, by A. M. Friedenberg.
m Text of Mr. Robert Grant's bill, 1830 [for Jewish emancipation], by I. Abrahams.
n 'The deacon and the Jewess': prefatory note by I. Abrahams.
o The deacon and the Jewess: or, apostacy at common law, by F. W. Maitland.
p 'Josippon' in England, by L. Wolf. [A list of English editions, 1558–1706]

2569 [Vol. 7.] 1911–14.

a Presidential address [mediaeval Jewish and English scholarship], by S. A. Hirsch.
b The [medieval] Jews of Canterbury, by M. Adler.
c Crypto-Jews in the Canaries [16th–17th cent.], by L. Wolf.
d A Dutch burial-ground [Middelburg] and its English [17th cent. Jewish] connections, by I. Harris.
e Richard Cumberland [d. 1811] centenary memorial papers, by L. Zangwill.
f Jewish pioneers of South Africa, by S. Mendelssohn.
g Origin of the Jewish Historical Society of England, by L. Wolf.
h Lord George Gordon's conversion to Judaism, by I. Solomons.
i Jacob Kimchi and Shalom Buzaglo [18th cent.], by C. Duschinsky.
j Presidential address [Haham David Nieto, d. c. 1729], by M. Gaster.

2570 [Vol. 8.] 1915–17.

a The Hebrew treasures of England, by E. N. Adler.
b The [medieval] records of exchequer receipts from the English Jewry, by H. Jenkinson.
c The question whether a Jew can be lord chancellor of England, by H. S. Q. Henriques.
d The purchase of Hebrew books by the English parliament in 1647, by I. Abrahams and C. E. Sayle.
e Records of mss. and documents possessed by the Jews in England before the expulsion, by H. P. Stokes.
f Isaac Abendana's Cambridge mishnah [in Latin] and Oxford calendars [of Jewish festivals], by I. Abrahams.
g Notes on some contemporary references to Dr. Falk [d. 1782], the Baal Shem of London, in the Rainsford mss. at the British Museum, by G. P. G. Hills.

h Dr. Joseph Jacobs [d. 1913?]: memorial meeting. [Addresses and bibliography]
i Relationship between the Jews and the royal family of England in the 13th cent., by H. P. Stokes.
j Economic and financial position of the Jews in mediaeval England, by Sir L. Abrahams.

2571 [Vol. 9.] 1918–20.

a Proposals for special taxation of the Jews after the Revolution [1689], by H. S. Q. Henriques.
b The legal position of the Jews in pre-expulsion England, as shown by the plea rolls of the Jewish exchequer, by C. M. Picciotto.
c Ephraim Luzzatto, 1729–92 [poet], by Mrs. R. N. Salaman.
d Hebrew loyalty under the first four Georges, by I. Abrahams.
e Reflections on the history of the Anglo-Jewish community, by H. S. Q. Henriques.
f Perkin Warbeck and his Jewish master, by C. Roth.
g Some medieval notes, by H. Jenkinson.
h Tallies and receipt rolls, by H. Jenkinson.

2572 [Vol. 10.] 1921–23.

a The first London synagogue of the resettlement, established 1657, enlarged 1674, by W. S. Samuel.
b A Jewish family in Oxford in the 13th cent., by H. P. Stokes.
c The Jewish question in Anglo-Swiss diplomacy, by M. Lipton.
d Note on Isaac Abendana, by I. Abrahams.
e Historical associations of the ancient burial-ground of the Sephardi Jews [Mile End Road, London], by D. Bueno de Mesquita.
f Menasseh Ben Israel's marriage banns [1623], by S. Levy.
g The first record of the Hebra Guemilut Hasadim, London, 1678, by L. D. Barnett.

2573 Vol. 11. 1924–27.

a Jews in Elizabethan England, by L. Wolf.
b A Jewish aid to marry, 1221, by Helena M. Chew.
c New light on the resettlement, by C. Roth.
d The Jewish cemetery at Ballybough in Dublin, by B. Shillman.
e Amy Levy [poet, d. 1889], by B. Z. Lask.
f Francis Francia, the Jacobite Jew [b. 1675], by M. Lipton.
g Leone de Modena [17th cent.] and England, by C. Roth.

2574 Vol. 12. 1928–31.

a David Nieto [d. 1728] and some of his contemporaries, by I. Solomons.
b New material for the literary history of the English Jews before the expulsion, by A. Marmorstein.
c Jews of Bristol in pre-expulsion days, by M. Adler.
d The Jews of Malta, by C. Roth.
e Looking backward; looking forward. The Mocatta library and museum [in University College, London], by G. Tuck.

Other publications:

2575 Menasseh ben Israel's mission to Oliver Cromwell, being a reprint of the pamphlets published by Menasseh ben Israel to promote the re-admission of the Jews to England, 1649–56, ed. with introd. and notes by L. Wolf. 1901.

Select pleas, starrs, and other records from the rolls of the exchequer of the Jews, 1220–84, ed. J. M. Rigg. 1902. [In conjunction with the Selden Soc., no. 4860 below]

2576 A book of essays, by S. A. Hirsch. 1905.

  a Early English Hebraists: Roger Bacon and his predecessors.

2577 Calendar of the plea rolls of the exchequer of the Jews preserved in the Public Record Office. Vols. i–ii: 1218–1275, ed. J. M. Rigg. 1905–10.

2578 A history of the Jews of England, by A. M. Hyamson. 1908.

2579 Essay and speech on Jewish disabilities by Lord Macaulay, ed. with introd. and notes by I. Abrahams and S. Levy. 1909. [2nd edn. 1910]

2580 Studies in Anglo-Jewish history, by H. P. Stokes. 1913. [Relating, *inter alia*, to the Jews of Cambridge]

2581 Notes on the diplomatic history of the Jewish question, with texts of protocols, treaty stipulations and other public acts and official documents [1744–1917], by L. Wolf. 1919.

2582 Miscellanies, pt. 1. 1925.

  a The Bodleian bowl, by I. Abrahams.

  b A petition from Haslemere in 1753, by A. M. Hyamson.

  c Charles Dickens and Eliza Davis, by I. Solomons.

  d Extracts from the close rolls, 1289–1368, by H. P. Stokes.

  e Maria Fernandez de Carvajal, by L. Wolf.

  f Mrs. Brydges Willyams and Benjamin Disraeli, by L. Wolf.

  g Colonial commerce, by A. M. Friedenberg.

  h Passes issued to Jews, 1689–96, by I. Abrahams.

  i The Netherbury tombstone [and its Old-Hebrew inscription], by F. C. Burkitt.

  j Jews and the coral trade [18th cent.], by L. Wolf.

  k *Theodore Cyphon* [a novel, by George Walker, 1796], by I. Abrahams.

  l The Lehman-Goldsmid litigation [1784–5], by H. S. Q. Henriques.

  m The Northampton 'Donum' of 1194, by I. Abrahams. [With description of the membranes by H. Jenkinson]

  n Anglo-Judaica in the catalogue of the British Museum Hebrew mss., by I. Abrahams.

2583 Miscellanies, pt. 2. 1935.

  a Index to the Transactions, vols. 1–12, and Miscellanies, pt. 1.

2584 Jews in the Canary Islands: being a calendar of Jewish cases [1499–1808] extracted from the records of the Canariote Inquisition in the collection of the Marquess of Bute, translated from the Spanish and ed. with introd. and notes by L. Wolf. 1926.

2585 Starrs and Jewish charters preserved in the British Museum, with illustrative documents, translations, and notes, by I. Abrahams and H. P. Stokes, with additions by H. Loewe. 3 vols. 1930–32. [Vol. ii: supplementary notes and essays by H. Loewe, and other essays by F. A. Lincoln, W. Page, and A. Jackson. Vol. iii: index]

JOHNSON CLUB

Founded 1884, to meet four times a year to hear papers on Johnsonian subjects.

Publications:

2586 Johnson Club Papers, by various hands. 1920.

  a Dr. Johnson and Dr. [William] Dodd, by Sir C. Biron.

  b Dr. Johnson and Lord Monboddo, by E. Clodd.

  c Dr. Johnson on liberty, by E. S. P. Haynes.

  d Dr. Johnson's expletives, by S. L. Hughes.

  e Dr. Johnson and Ireland, by J. O'Connor.

  f Johnson's dictionary, by Sir G. Radford.

  g Dr. Johnson and the law, by E. S. Roscoe.

  h Dr. Johnson and the Catholic church, by the Hon. Sir C. Russell, bt.

  i Johnson's character as shown in his writings, by H. S. Scott.

  j Sir Joshua Reynolds, by L. C. Thomas.

  k Johnson and the theatre, by A. B. Walkley.

  l Johnson's monument and Parr's epitaph on Johnson, by H. B. Wheatley.

KENT ARCHAEOLOGICAL SOCIETY

Founded 1857, for the study of archaeology in all its branches, both secular and ecclesiastical, especially with relation to Kent, and the recording of new discoveries.

Archaeologia Cantiana, vols. 25–45 (1901–33):

2587 Vol. 25.

  a Maidstone church, by W. A. S. Robertson.

  b Leeds Castle, by F. V. James.

  c East Sutton church, by T. C. Oyler.

  d Researches and discoveries [chiefly Roman] in Kent, 1900–1, by G. Payne.

  e Romano-British interments at Lower Walmer, by C. H. Woodruff.

  f Visitations of the archdeacon of Canterbury [c. 1560–1712], by A. Hussey. [Contd. in vols. 26–28]

  g Dent-de-lion gatehouse, Margate, with a pedigree of the family of Pettit, by C. E. Woodruff.

  h Church of St. John the Baptist, Margate, by C. Cotton.

  i Dover chamberlains' accounts, 1365–7, by S. P. H. Statham.

  j 13th cent. wall-painting at Upchurch, by C. H. Woodruff.

  k St. Mary's church, Minster, Isle of Thanet: list of vicars, by T. S. Frampton.

  l Church plate in Kent, by C. E. Woodruff. [See also vols. 16 and 17. Contd. in vols. 26–28]

  m Sutton Valence castle, by H. Sands.

  n The chantry of John Denys [of Apulton, sheriff of London, 1360] in Ickham church, by T. S. Frampton.

  o Excavations at St. Austin's abbey, Canterbury. (i) The chapel of St. Pancras, by W. H. St. J. Hope. (ii) The church of SS. Peter and Paul, by C. F. Routledge. [See also vol. 26]

  p 19th cent. restorations at Stockbury church, by D. Twopenny.

  q An old map of Canterbury [c. 1570–71], attributed to G. Hoefnagel, by H. Sands.

  r Descriptive catalogue of documents belonging to the Society. [Mss. relating to (1) the Oxinden family, (2) the ferry-warden and ferry court of the Isle of Sheppey]

2588 Vol. 26.

  a Excavations at St. Augustine's abbey, Canterbury. (ii) The church of SS. Peter and Paul, and some adjacent monastic buildings, by S. Evans.

  b Further discoveries of late Celtic and Romano-Celtic interments at Walmer, by C. H. Woodruff.

  c Crayford church, by G. M. Livett.

  d Little Mote, Eynsford, with a pedigree of the Sybill family, by R. H. E. Hill.

  e Notes on the ancient stained glass, memorial brasses, and an altar-slab in the church of St. Mary, Great Chart, by H. W. Russell.

  f Architectural history of Great Chart church, with a

note on Ashford church and some local mouldings, by G. M. Livett.

g Ford manor house and lands in 1647 [parliamentary survey], by A. Hussey.

h Anecdotes of the Hasted family [1800], by Edward Hasted, transcribed by R. Cooke.

i Architectural history of High Halden church, by G. M. Livett.

j Notes on 19th cent. alterations to High Halden church; with extracts from the parish books and registers, by W. H. Rammell.

k The Palatines [and an attempt to settle some of them in villages in W. Kent, 1709], by R. Cooke.

l Note on [the Burlton brass in] Dartford parish church, by W. D. Haskett-Smith.

m Discovery of a supposed reliquary at St. James' in the Isle of Grain, by A. A. Arnold.

2589 Vol. 27.

a Bilsington priory, by C. H. Woodruff.

b Researches and discoveries [chiefly Roman] in Kent, 1902-4, by G. Payne.

c Ightham Mote, by H. Taylor.

d Pedigree of Selby of Ightham Mote, by T. C. Colyer-Fergusson.

e Notes on an early Cinque ports charter [1260], by F. F. Giraud.

f The barons of New Romney in parliament, by J. Stokes.

g Cobham college, by A. A. Arnold.

h Cobham and its manors, by A. A. Arnold.

i Letters of Edward Hasted to Thomas Astle [1735-1802], transcribed by R. Cooke, annotated by C. E. Woodruff.

j Calendar of ancient deeds [14th-17th cent., chiefly relating to Boughton Monchelsea] presented by Charles Marchant.

k The reparation of Rochester castle, by G. Payne.

l Ancient timber-framed house at Shorne next Gravesend, by G. M. Arnold.

m Notes on Bethersden, by A. J. Pearman.

n Note on the so-called tomb of the Countess of Athol in the cathedral church of Canterbury [and its identification as the tomb of Elizabeth Tryvet, d. 1433], by W. H. St. J. Hope.

o Faversham household inventory [of Elizabeth Aiscoughe], 1609, by A. Hussey.

p List of the rectors of Ripple, comp. H. L. Beardmore. [See also vol. 32]

q The leaden font at Brookland, by G. M. Livett.

2590 Vol. 28.

a Ashford church, by A. J. Pearman.

b Researches and discoveries in Kent, 1905-7, by G. Payne.

c Horsmonden church, by F. Grayling and A. Vallance.

d Folkestone parish church, with reference to its earliest portion, by W. L. Rutton.

e Mss. relating to Goudhurst and neighbourhood, transcribed by R. H. E. Hill. [Includes documents relating to the rebuilding of Goudhurst church tower, 1638, and lay subsidy returns for Goudhurst, 1642]

f Pedigree of the family of de Fynes, by W. L. King.

g Cinque ports: notes from minute books of the corporation of Faversham [1570-1740, so far as they relate to the town as a corporate member of the Cinque port of Dover], by F. F. Giraud.

h Herne. (i) Herne wills: abstracts [1396-1552/3], ed. A. Hussey. [Contd. in vol. 30]

i Stained-glass windows of Nettlestead church, by W. E. Ball.

j Nettlestead church. 1: Architectural notes, by G. M. Livett. 2: Extracts from notes by W. F. Cobb.

k Staplehurst register [1538-96], by J. S. F. Chamberlain.

l Bredhurst paten [possibly 13th cent.], by W. Gardner-Waterman.

m Architectural notes on Patrixbourne church, by G. M. Livett.

n The vicars, masters or provosts, and perpetual curates of the church of SS. Gregory and Martin, Wye, comp., with notes, by T. S. Frampton.

o Church of St. Peter at Pembury, by W. T. Storrs.

p Allington Castle, by Sir W. M. Conway.

q The Sybill arms at Little Mote, Eynsford [and the origin of the heraldic device of 'tiger and mirror'], by G. C. Druce.

r Sybill of Eynsford and Farningham, by R. H. E. Hill.

s Old chimney-piece from Back's House, Milton-by-Sittingbourne, by A. Vallance.

2591 Vol. 29.

a Proceedings, 1910. [Includes summaries of papers on Richborough castle, by W. H. St. John Hope and G. M. Livett; on the parish church of St. Mary the Virgin, Eastry, by C. D. Lampen; and on Woodnesborough church, by F. Savage]

b Researches and discoveries in Kent, 1908-10, by G. Payne.

c The owners of Allington Castle, Maidstone, 1086-1279, by Agnes E. Conway.

d A series of Kentish heraldic fire-backs, and the identification of the arms, by H. S. Cowper.

e Monastic chronicle lately discovered at Christ Church, Canterbury; with introd. and notes by C. E. Woodruff.

f 14th cent. court roll of the manor of Ambree, Rochester [with 'A rental of the mannours of Ambree, Frendesbury, Wouldham, Sharsted, and Darenth belonging to the dean and chapter of Rochester, anno 1683'], ed. A. A. Arnold.

g The Cobhams and Moresbys of Rundale and Allington, by G. O. Bellewes.

h The last Savages of Bobbing [with abstracts of wills], by G. O. Bellewes.

i Some timber-framed houses in the Kentish weald, by H. S. Cowper.

j Kentish annals in Lambeth library, by S. W. Kershaw.

k Chapels in Kent, by A. Hussey.

l Hospitals in Kent, by A. Hussey.

m An unpublished record of Archbishop Parker's visitation in 1573, ed. C. Jenkins.

n Notes from the parish registers of Maidstone, by H. Monckton.

o Notes on the great north window of Canterbury cathedral, by J. D. Le Couteur.

2592 Vol. 30.

a Proceedings, 1912. [Includes summaries of papers on old bridges, by A. Vallance; on Lympne castle, by A. Vallance; and on Lyminge church, by C. E. Woodruff]

b The poll tax in Rochester, Sept. 1660, ed. A. A. Arnold.

c Hospital of St. Mary of Ospringe, commonly called Maison Dieu, by C. H. Drake. [See also vol. 38]

d 17th cent. Kentish proverb, by E. P. B. Richardson.

e An account of a map of Kent dated 1596, by the Hon. H. Hannen. [See also vol. 31]

f Note on some 15th and 16th cent. Kentish wills, by H. S. Cowper.

g Chapel of St. John the Baptist, Smallhythe, by A. H. Taylor.

h Postling church, by A. Vallance.

i Postling church: supplemental notes, by G. M. Livett.

j An explanation of the Hythe bones, by F. G. Parsons.

k Note on an old house, West Street, Faversham, by A. Vallance.

l The oldest map of Romney marsh [1617], by F. W. Cock.

m The *Textus Roffensis* in chancery, 1633, by A. A. Arnold.

n Vicars of St. Mary, Westhythe, by T. S. Frampton.

o West Hythe church and the sites of churches formerly existing at Hythe, by G. M. Livett.

p Notes on Hythe church, by H. D. Dale.

q Architectural history of the church of St. Leonard, Hythe, by G. M. Livett.

r Late-Celtic discoveries at Broadstairs, by H. Hurd.

s Record of inquisition [into the value and disposal of hatters' goods], at Faversham, 29 Eliz., ed. F. F. Giraud.

2593 Vol. 31.

a Proceedings 1913–14. [Includes summaries of papers on the fittings of mediaeval churches, by A. Vallance; Westerham church, by F. W. Maude, G. M. Livett, and C. E. Woodruff; Sundridge church, by G. M. Livett; and on St. Nicholas church, Ash next Sandwich, by R. H. Goodsall]

b The manor house and great park of the archbishop of Canterbury at Otford, by C. Hesketh.

c Further notes from Kentish wills, by A. Hussey.

d The Stodmarsh plaster panels, by T. A. Lehfeldt.

e Daniel Defoe and Kent: a chapter in Capel-le-Ferne history, by W. Minet.

f Notes of the remains of Westenhanger House, Kent, by G. Clinch.

g St. Mary's, Westenhanger (church destroyed): rectors and patrons, by T. S. Frampton.

h Extracts from original documents illustrating the progress of the Reformation in Kent, by C. E. Woodruff.

i Two Headcorn cloth halls, by H. S. Cowper.

j Monumental brasses in Kent, by R. Griffin. [Contd. in vol. 32]

k 'The valley of Holmesdale': its evolution and development, by H. W. Knocker. [Contd. in vol. 40 (the village communities) and vol. 44 (the manor of Sundrish)]

l Extracts from some lost Kentish registers, from ms. clxxx, Society of Antiquaries, London, by L. L. Duncan.

m Some Kentish charities, 1594, by F. Lambarde.

n A Wealden charter of 814 (B.M. Harleian charter 83 A.I.), by H. S. Cowper.

o Rectors and vicars of St. Mildred's, Tenterden, by A. H. Taylor. [With documents relating to the parish]

p Further notes on Phil. Symonson, maker of the map of Kent dated 1576–96, by the Hon. H. Hannen.

q Researches and discoveries in Kent, 1912–15, by G. Payne.

r Roman remains at Hoo St. Werburgh, by J. J. Robson.

s Ancient walling of St. Augustine's, Canterbury, by C. Cotton.

t Recent discoveries at St. Austin's abbey, Canterbury, by Sir W. St. J. Hope. [Contd. in vol. 32]

2594 Vol. 32.

a Reculver and Hoath wills, by A. Hussey.

b Some early [*sede vacante*] visitation rolls preserved at Canterbury [1292–1328], by C. E. Woodruff. [Contd. in vol. 33]

c Churchwardens' accounts of St. Andrew, Canterbury, 1485–1625, by C. Cotton. [Contd. in vols. 33–36]

d Extracts from the letter-book of a Dover merchant [Isaac Minet], 1737–41, by W. Minet.

e The municipal records of Tenterden, by A. H. Taylor. [Contd. in vol. 33]

f Cinque ports, Faversham: copy of orders of Faversham wardmote for a cesse for shipping, 38 Eliz., and names of persons charged, ed. F. F. Giraud.

g The Nevill heaume at Birling, by F. H. Cripps-Day.

h Rectors of Ripple: additional notes and corrections [to list in vol. 27], by C. L. Feltoe.

2595 Vol. 33.

a Round-naved churches in England and their connexion with the orders of the Temple and of the hospital of St. John of Jerusalem, by Sir W. St. J. Hope.

b Bromley common, by P. Norman.

c Arms and armour seized at Knole during the civil war, by C. J. Phillips.

d Residences of the bishops of Rochester, by A. J. Pearman, G. A. Tait, and H. P. Thompson.

e Note on two grants of arms [to W. Weldisshe of Lynton, 1543, and to Robert Knight of Bromley, 1548], by R. Griffin.

f Lower Halstow church, by E. R. Olive.

g Researches and discoveries. 1: A mediaeval counter, by C. E. Woodruff. 2: Seal of the vicar of Reculver [*c.* 1310], by G. Clinch.

2596 Vol. 34.

a Ash wills, by A. Hussey. [Contd. in vols. 35–37]

b The lepers' hospital at Swainestrey, by R. Griffin.

c The Grey friars of Canterbury, by A. G. Little.

d Dover documents [15th–18th cent.], ed. J. B. Jones.

e Arden of Faversham, by L. Cust. [With additions relating to the abbey lands]

f St. Austin's abbey, Canterbury: Abbot Roger II, 1252–72, by R. U. Potts.

g Researches and discoveries in Kent, 1915–19.

2597 Vol. 35.

a Roman cemetery discovered at Ospringe in 1920, by W. Whiting. [Contd. in vols. 36–38]

b Queen Court, Rainham, and Queendown, Hartlip, by H. G. Faussett-Osborne.

c Architectural notes on Kingsdown church near Sevenoaks (St. Edmund), by F. C. Elliston-Erwood.

d The latest excavations at St. Augustine's abbey, by R. U. Potts.

e The earliest Rochester bridge: was it built by the Romans?, by A. A. Arnold.

f Rochester bridge: the Roman bridge in masonry, by J. J. Robson.

g Teynham church: architectural notes, by F. C. Elliston-Erwood.

2598 Vol. 36.

a The picture of Queen Ediva in Canterbury cathedral, by C. E. Woodruff.

b The family of William Longchamp, bishop of Ely, chancellor and justiciar of England, 1190–91, by Agnes E. Conway.

c Minster in Sheppey: notes on two brasses in the church, by R. Griffin.

d Abbot Foche's grace cup, by R. U. Potts.

e Note on the early history of Cranbrook school, by L. L. Duncan.

f Inscription in Little Chart church [relating to the arms of the Darell family of Yorks., Kent, and Wilts.], by R. Griffin.

g Notes on helmets in Little Chart church, by V. Farquharson.

h 14th cent. altarpiece from Sutton Valence, by R. P. Bedford.

i Index to vols. 20–35.

2599 Vol. 37.

a The 'Pilgrim's Way', its antiquity and its alleged mediaeval use, with special reference to that part of it in Kent, by F. C. Elliston-Erwood.

b Notes on the topography of Cranbrook church, by L. L. Duncan.

c Some early professions of canonical obedience to the see of Canterbury by heads of religious houses, by C. E. Woodruff.

d Harty church, Sheppey, by A. Vallance.

e The Maidstone sector of Buckingham's rebellion, Oct. 18, 1483, by Agnes E. Conway.

f The chronicles of William Glastynbury, monk of Christ Church, Canterbury, 1419–48, with introd. and notes by C. E. Woodruff. [Includes a description of choir windows]

g A contemporary list of the benefactions of Thomas Ikham, sacrist, to St. Austin's abbey, Canterbury, *c.* 1415, transcribed and translated by C. Cotton.

h The Giron seal found at Hackington, by A. Van de Put.

i An old timber house at Sundridge, by A. Vallance.

j Notes on the churches of Romney marsh, 1923, by F. C. Elliston-Erwood.

k Roman villa, Folkestone, by S. E. Winbolt. [Contd. in vol. 38]

l Saxon burial cross found in St. Austin's abbey, by R. U. Potts.

2600 Vol. 38.

a The siege of Maidstone rectory in 1297, by Rose Graham.

b Notes on the life of Sir John Baker of Sissinghurst, Kent [d. 1558], by F. V. Baker.

c 17th cent. survey of the estates of the dean and chapter of Canterbury in East Kent, by C. E. Woodruff.

d Sevenoaks: the manor, church, and market, by H. W. Knocker.

e House in Rochester High Street, numbered 69 and 71, by S. W. Wheatley.

f Old roads in East Kent and Thanet, by G. P. Walker.

g Lambarde's 'Carde of this shyre', by E. G. Box. [Contd. in vol. 39]

h Tombs of the kings and archbishops in St. Austin's abbey, by R. U. Potts.

i Hospital of St. Mary of Ospringe, commonly called Maison Dieu, by C. H. Drake. [See also vol. 30]

j Chapel of Our Lady in the crypt of Canterbury cathedral, by C. E. Woodruff.

k Eastry wills, by A. Hussey. [Contd. in vols. 39 and 40]

2601 Vol. 39.

a Letters to the prior of Christ Church, Canterbury [Henry of Eastry], from university students [13th cent.], by C. E. Woodruff.

b Some Jutish pottery found in Kent, by W. Whiting.

c Further Romano-British pottery found in Kent.

d Roman cemetery at St. Dunstan's, Canterbury.

e Odo, bishop of Bayeux and earl of Kent, by Sir R. Tower.

f The lost Wantsum channel: its importance to Richborough castle, by G. P. Walker.

g Rochester cathedral heraldry before 1800, by A. W. B. Messenger.

h William Lambarde's pedigree notes, by F. F. Lambarde.

i The Lambarde cup [property of the Drapers' company].

j Arms of the Drapers' company, by Miss M. A. Greenwood.

k Philipott's *Villare Cantianum*: a bibliographical note, by the Hon. H. Hannen.

l Roman site at Otford, by B. W. Pearce. [Contd. in vol. 42]

m Boley hill [earthwork], Rochester, by S. W. Wheatley. [See also vol. 41]

n Sir Thomas Wyatt's assault on Cooling castle, 30 Jan. 1554, by B. Cope.

o The engraved plate at Cooling castle, by A. Vallance.

2602 Vol. 40.

a Brasses in Barham church, by R. Griffin.

b A find of ancient gold coins at Westerham, by G. C. Brooke.

c The de Aldehams, by G. Ward.

d A crucifix from West Farleigh, by A. Vallance.

e Notes from a 14th cent. act-book of the consistory court of Canterbury, by C. E. Woodruff.

f Note on the plan of St. Augustine's abbey church, by R. U. Potts.

g Roman cemetery at St. Martin's hill, Canterbury, by W. Whiting and H. T. Mead.

h Roman site in the church field at Snodland, by N. C. Cook.

i Kentish men at the university of Padua [1618–1765], by F. W. Cock.

j List of the gentry of Kent in the time of Henry VII: some notes on the list communicated by J. Greenstreet in *Arch. Cant.*, vol. 11, by B. Cope.

k The family of Septvans, by Sir R. Tower.

l Wingham church, by A. Hussey and A. H. Taylor.

m Whitfield *alias* Beuesfeld [Saxon church, with notes on similar churches at East Ham, and Sutton near Dover— an additional note occurs in vol. 42], by G. M. Livett.

n Ringwould church, by F. C. Eeles, with supplementary notes by V. J. B. Torr.

2603 Vol. 41.

a The making of the great park at Otford, by G. Ward.

b Sweyn's camp [earthwork], Swanscombe, by A. H. A. Hogg.

c Notes on some early documents relating to the manor, church, and priory of Bilsington, Kent, by C. E. Woodruff.

d Sittingbourne wills [15th–16th cent.], by A. Hussey. [Contd. in vols. 42 and 43]

e Cranbrook church inventory, 1509, by A. Vallance. [Additional note in vol. 42]

f Church of Cliffe-at-Hoo, by A. R. Martin.

g Records of the courts of the archdeaconry and consistory of Canterbury, by C. E. Woodruff.

h The Easter sepulchre in Faversham church, by F. Lambarde.

i Jutish cemetery near Finglesham, Kent: report by W. P. D. Stebbing with introductory note by W. Whiting.

j Boley hill [earthwork], Rochester, after the Roman period, by S. W. Wheatley. [See also vol. 39]

k Notes on the architecture of Aldington church, Kent, and the chapel at Court-at-Street, called 'Bellirica', by F. C. Elliston-Erwood.

l Annals of the town and port of New Romney, with some extracts from the records of the town, by M. Teichman-Derville.

m Kentish bibliographical notes, by F. W. Cock.

n Bourne Park, near Canterbury, by W. H. Godfrey.

o Heraldic ledger stones, by N. E. Toke.

p Castle hill camp, Tonbridge. [Report on excavation, 1929, by S. E. Winbolt]

q Durolevum: the evidence of the coins [found near Ospringe, Kent, 1923–6], by G. C. F. Hayter and W. Whiting.

r East Wickham church, by T. F. Ford.

s The cross and platform at Richborough, by W. H. Elgar.

2604 Vol. 42.

a The New Romney and Cinque port records, by M. Teichman-Derville.

2608 General index to vols. 20–45. 1949. [Published as Archaeologia Cantiana, vol. 52]

Extra publication:

2609 Testamenta Cantiana: a series of extracts from 15th and 16th cent. wills relating to church building and topography. West Kent by L. L. Duncan; East Kent by A. Hussey. 2 vols. in 1. 1906–7.

KENT ARCHAEOLOGICAL SOCIETY, RECORDS BRANCH

Founded 1913, to supplement the work of the parent Society by printing documents or other materials relating to church, parochial, manorial and family history in the county; and to promote research work.

Kent records:

2610 Vol. 1. Parish registers and records in the diocese of Rochester: summary of information collected by the ecclesiastical records committee of the Rochester Diocesan Conference, with introd. by W. E. Buckland. 1912.

2611 Vol. 2. Handbook to Kent records; containing a summary account of the principal classes of historical documents relating to the county, and a guide to their chief places of deposit, comp. and ed. Irene J. Churchill. 1914.

2612 Vol. 3. *Sede vacante* wills: a calendar of wills proved before the commissary of the prior and chapter of Christ Church, Canterbury, during vacancies in the primacy, with transcripts of archiepiscopal and other wills of importance, comp. and ed. C. E. Woodruff. 1914.

2613 Vol. 4. Diocesis Roffensis: registrum Hamonis Hethe [1319–52], ed. C. Johnson. 1915–48. [In conjunction with the Canterbury and York Soc.]

2614 Vol. 5. Churchwardens' accounts of St. Nicholas, Strood, transcribed with introd. by H. R. Plomer, pt. 1: 1555–1600; pt. 2: 1603–62. 1927 [1915–27]. Churchwardens' accounts at Betrysden [Bethersden], 1515–73, transcribed with introd. by F. R. Mercer. 1928.

Vol. 6. Index of wills and administrations in the probate registry at Canterbury, 1396–1558, 1640–50. [See British Record Soc., Index Library, vol. 50, no. **639** above]

2615 Vol. 7. East Kent records: a calendar of some unpublished deeds and court rolls in the library of Lambeth Palace, with appendices referring especially to the manors of Knowlton, Sandown, South Court, and North Court, ed. Irene J. Churchill. 1922.

2616 Vol. 8. Calendar of institutions by the chapter of Canterbury *sede vacante*, ed. C. E. Woodruff, with additions and notes by Irene J. Churchill. 1923.

2617 Vol. 9. Index of wills proved in Rochester consistory court, 1440–1561, comp. L. L. Duncan, with introductory note and bibliography by F. W. Cock. 1924 [1924–6].

2618 Vol. 10. The Twysden lieutenancy papers, 1583–1668, ed. with introd. by Gladys Scott Thomson. 1926. [Papers of Sir Roger Twysden, d. 1672]

2619 Vol. 11. A Kentish cartulary of the order of St. John of Jerusalem, by C. Cotton. 1930.

2620 Vol. 13. Kent keepers of the peace, 1316–17, ed. with introd. by Bertha H. Putnam. 1933.

Other publications:

2621 Kentish monumental inscriptions: inscriptions at Tenterden, ed. L. L. Duncan. [1919].

2622 Monumental inscriptions in the churchyard and church of All Saints', Lydd, Kent, by L. L. Duncan, ed. A. Finn. [1927].

LANCASHIRE AND CHESHIRE ANTIQUARIAN SOCIETY

Founded 1883, to examine, preserve and illustrate ancient monuments and records, and to promote the study of history, architecture, literature, arts, customs and traditions, particularly as regards antiquities of Lancashire and Cheshire.

Transactions, vols. 18–47 (1901–32):

2623 Vol. 18.
a Ancient crosses of Lancashire: the hundred of Blackburn, by H. Taylor.
b Archery in Manchester in the 16th and 17th cent., by W. E. A. Axon.
c The first church at Furness, by H. Brakspear.
d The Domesday survey of north Lancashire and the adjacent parts of Cumberland, Westmorland, and Yorkshire, by W. Farrer.
e Exploration of prehistoric sepulchral remains of the bronze age at Bleasdale, by B. Dawkins.
f Proceedings. [Coins of the Cinque ports issued during the 18th cent., by N. Heywood; Ashbourne church, Derbys., by F. A. Bromwich]
g Bibliography of Lancashire and Cheshire antiquities and biography, 1900, by N. Hollins. [Contd. for 1901–3 in vols. 19–21]

2624 Vol. 19.
a Ancient forests, chases, and deer parks in Lancashire, by W. Harrison.
b Mottrum of Mottrum in the parish of Prestbury, by F. Renaud.
c Old castles of Lancashire, by H. Fishwick.
d Pre-historic and subsequent mining at Alderley Edge, with a sketch of the archaeological features of the neighbourhood, by C. Roeder.
e Hanging Bridge [Manchester]: an etymological examination, by H. T. Crofton.
f Ancient crosses of Lancashire: the hundred of West Derby, by H. Taylor.
g Proceedings. [Includes accounts of Wigan parish churc Upholland; and Leek parish church]

2625 Vol. 20.
a Ancient forests, chases and deer parks in Cheshire, by W. Harrison.
b Ashworth chapel, by H. Fishwick.
c Notes on food and drink in Lancashire and other northern counties, by C. Roeder.
d Hornbooks and ABCs, by W. E. A. Axon.
e A narrative concerning two castellated manor houses formerly existing in Macclesfield, with a corresponding chapter of Cheshire history, by F. Renaud.
f Old [stained] glass windows of Ashton-under-Lyne parish church, by G. A. Pugh.
g How Chat Moss broke out in 1526, by H. T. Crofton.
h Ancient crosses of Lancashire: the hundred of Amounderness, by H. Taylor.
i Proceedings. [Includes an account of Hoghton Tower Lancs.]
j General index to vols. 11–20.

2626 Vol. 21.

a Ancient crosses of Lancashire: the hundred of Lonsdale, by H. Taylor.
b Flint implements, by W. H. Sutcliffe.
c Notes on a bronze age barrow [Winwick, Lancs.], by T. May.
d Walter and Margaret Nugent [d. 1614 and 1631], by E. Axon.
e Maps and views of Manchester, by C. Roeder.
f The Newchurch[-in-Culcheth, Lancs.] communion cup, by H. A. Hudson.
g Proceedings. [Includes a paper on 'Abraham Hurst and Elias Hall, exponents of the old Lancashire notation in music', by S. Andrew, and descriptions of the Arbor Low stone circle, and the Roman camp at Brough, Derbys.]
h Catalogue of the old Manchester and Salford exhibition held at Manchester, 1904. [Catalogue for exhibition, 1909–10, in vol. 27]

2627 Vol. 22.

a Beginnings of the Manchester post-office, by C. Roeder.
b Two votive rag-branches and a prayer-stick in the Manchester museum, by W. E. A. Axon.
c Edwin Butterworth [d. 1848]: his life and labours, by G. Shaw.
d Ancient crosses of Lancashire: the hundred of Salford, by H. Taylor.
e Charters, documents, and insignia relating to the ancient manor and borough of Macclesfield, by W. H. Clarke.
f Notes on antiquarian discoveries in Macclesfield, by W. Astor.
g Tithe corn book for Manchester, etc., 1584, by H. T. Crofton.
h Extracts relating to Deansgate, Manchester, from the Newton manor court rolls, 1530–1687, by H. T. Crofton.
i Bishop Nicolson's visit to Manchester, 1704, by C. W. Sutton.

2628 Vol. 23.

a Catalogue of the portraits, etc., at Holker Hall, Lancs., in the possession of Victor C. W. Cavendish, by the Earl of Liverpool.
b Recent archaeological discoveries at Alderley Edge, by C. Roeder and F. S. Graves.
c William Crabtree's plan of the Booth Hall estate [Blakeley, Lancs., 1637], by E. Axon.
d Antiquarian notes from the Derbyshire border of Cheshire, by T. Kay. i: The Roosdyche of Whaley. ii: The Windybottom bridge. iii: The Torkington moat. iv: A loom weight from Melandra.
e 13th cent. ms. in the Bodleian Library (Rawlinson, C.317) formerly belonging to Cockersand abbey, and containing *exempla*, by W. E. A. Axon.
f The Manchester altar to *Fortuna Conservatrix*, by W. E. A. Axon.
g The beginnings of Manchester, by C. Roeder. [Contd. in the Proceedings of Vol. 24]
h The ancient churches, the Parsonage, Acres field, and Acres fair in Manchester, by C. Roeder.
i Agrimensorial remains found in Manchester [being an account of Roman land organisation], by H. T. Crofton.
j An ancient sculptured stone in Manchester cathedral, by J. J. Phelps.
k Proceedings. [Includes a description of Winwick, Lancs.]

2629 Vol. 24.

a Hiding holes in old houses, by F. Moss.
b Collegiation of Manchester church [1426], by J. Moyes.

c Dumplington and the Holcrofts, by H. T. Crofton.
d Gallo-Roman potters' marks on *terra sigillata* (Samian) ware, found at Lancaster and Quernmore, by Alice Johnson. [Contd. in vol. 27]
e Ornamented *terra sigillata* (Samian) pottery found at Lancaster, by T. May.
f Scarisbrick Hall, Lancs., by F. H. Cheetham.
g Pre-historic glimpses of Eddisbury hundred, Ches., by C. Roeder.
h Plenary indulgence granted at Manchester in 1477 to Adam de Chetham, by W. E. A. Axon.

2630 Vol. 25.

a Early maps of Lancashire and their makers, by W. Harrison.
b Moston and White Moss [Lancs.], by H. T. Crofton.
c Some Moston folk-lore, by C. Roeder.
d Kersal moor and Kersal Cell: a sketch from neolithic days to present times, by C. Roeder.
e Recent finds at Castleshaw, by S. Andrew.
f Mab's Cross: the legend of Mabel Bradshaigh in literature and tradition, by W. E. A. Axon.
g Ancient [stained] glass of the cathedral church of Manchester, by H. A. Hudson.
h Defensive earthworks and fortified enclosures of Cheshire, by W. Harrison.
i Note on the Bradshaigh roll [1647, with later additions], by E. Axon.
j Proceedings. [Includes an account of Nether Peover, Ches., and of a plan of Salford of 1740]

2631 Vol. 26.

a Early maps of Cheshire, by W. Harrison.
b Chetham hospital silver plate, by T. S. Ball.
c Brunanburgh [the site], by J. T. Marquis.
d A Cheshire squire who served Queen Elizabeth [Sir Edward Fitton, d. 1579], by G. Pearson.
e Scots and Manchester after the '45, by H. T. Crofton.
f A relic of Henry Newcome [d. 1695], by W. E. A. Axon.
g Humphrey Oldfield [d. 1690], a Salford benefactor, and his family, by C. T. Tallent-Bateman.
h Hyde's cross [Manchester], by R. B. Wild.
i James Butterworth of Oldham [d. 1837], by G. Shaw.
j Burscough priory [Lancs.], by F. H. Cheetham.
k Proceedings. [Includes summary of a paper on 'Some early English music printers and publishers', by H. Watson; accounts of Woodford church and halls, Ches., and Harborough cave, Derbys.; and a paper on Chetham's hospital, Manchester, by F. Moss]

2632 Vol. 27.

a Preliminary report on the exploration of 'Dog Holes' cave, Warton Crag, near Carnforth, Lancs., by J. W. Jackson. [Further reports in vols. 28 and 30]
b Harrison Ainsworth's paternal ancestors, by E. Axon.
c Local and personal medals relating to Manchester, by N. Heywood.
d A note on Chadkirk [Ches.], by E. Axon.
e The earthwork in Crow Holt wood, near Bramhall Hall, Ches., by F. Moorhouse.
f Henry Dunster [of Lancashire, d. 1659], first president of Harvard College, by E. Axon.
g Witch stones and charms in Clitheroe and district, by W. S. Weeks.
h The family of Humphrey Booth, founder of Salford chapel [d. 1676], by C. T. Tallent-Bateman.
i Proceedings. [Includes accounts of 'The Peel', Etchells, Ches.; Winwick, Lancs.; and Mobberley church, Ches.]

2633 Vol. 28.

a Lancashire possessions of the Knights of St. John of Jerusalem, by H. Fishwick.

b Charter relating to Ralph Langley, warden of Manchester [1485], by W. E. A. Axon.

c Leland's *Itinerary*, by W. Harrison.

d The Hatfield family of Manchester, and the food riots of 1757 and 1812, by F. Nicholson and E. Axon.

e Darcy Lever old hall, by F. H. Cheetham.

f Note on John de Claydon, parson of Manchester in the reign of Edward III, by W. E. A. Axon.

g John Lister [d. 1759], master of Bury grammar school, and his correspondents, by J. Lister.

h An inquiry into the structural development of Manchester cathedral, by H. A. Hudson.

i Slade Hall, by W. Charlton. [Some account of the structure and of its owners, the Siddall family]

j Proceedings. [Includes an account of the monastic remains at Ince and of Winfield manor]

2634 Vol. 29.

a The Christmas lights at Manchester cathedral [and the lighting of medieval churches in general], by H. A. Hudson.

b The Bleasdale find: prehistoric rath or stockaded camp of the bronze age, by S. E. Collinson.

c Cartmel Fell chapel, by F. H. Cheetham.

d Martin Hall, Burscough, Ormskirk, by F. H. Cheetham.

e Crosses at Sandbach [presumed to be 7th cent. Mercian], by N. Heywood.

f Some Lancashire church plate, by T. S. Ball. [Contd. in vol. 30]

g New facts concerning Thomas Deacon [d. 1753, nonjuring bishop], by H. Broxap.

h The royal shrine at Westminster as it may have been at the end of the 14th cent., with some suggestions for the use of colour in churches of the present day, by J. H. Gibbons.

i Note on a find [of a prehistoric implement] by Mr. T. R. Morrow in the alluvium of the Mersey at Irlam, by W. B. Dawkins.

j Harrison Ainsworth's maternal ancestors, by E. Axon. [With appendices on Harrison of Bankfield, Harrison of Chinley and Manchester, Cooper of Dukinfield, and Swarbreck of Roseacre]

k Alexander Greene (father, d. 1661, and son, d. 1666) and other Manchester postmasters [in the 17th cent.], by E. Axon.

l Proceedings. [Includes an account of Lyme Hall]

2635 Vol. 30.

a Pigmy flint implements: their provenance and use, by W. H. Sutcliffe, W. A. Parker, R. A. Gatty, and W. B. Dawkins.

b Tarleton chapel, in Leyland, Lancs., by F. H. Cheetham. [With appendices containing transcripts of 16th cent. documents relating to the chapel]

c Note on the plan of Prestwich church, by F. H. Cheetham.

d Further notes on Lancashire and Cheshire tokens, by N. Heywood.

e A Manx leather penny of the 18th cent., by N. Heywood.

f Early Manchester horse-races, by E. Axon.

g North Lancashire antiquities, by W. Harrison.

h The statutes merchant and the statutes staple locally illustrated, by C. T. Tallent-Bateman. [A statute staple of 1668 and a statute merchant of 1675]

i The Pembertons of Aspull and Philadelphia, and some passages in the early history of Quakerism in Lancashire, by W. E. A. Axon.

j Notes on the 'Garstang Trust' and their records, by T. C. Hughes. [With extracts from documents of the former corporation of Garstang]

k Warden [John] Huntingdon's rebus in Manchester cathedral, by H. A. Hudson.

l Excavation of the tumulus on Sponds hill, Ches., by W. J. Andrew.

m The north wall of the Roman fort at Manchester, by J. J. Phelps.

n Proceedings. [Includes an account of Vale Royal abbey and its site]

o General index to vols. 21–30.

2636 Vol. 31.

a Notes on the discovery of an apse at St. Mary's church, Lancaster, in 1911, and of other discoveries [being the foundations of an early apse at Overton church], by H. J. Austin.

b New Park, Lathom: a vanished residence of the earls of Derby, by F. H. Cheetham.

c Touch pieces and touching for the king's evil, by W. Charlton.

d Historical notes on the Society of Friends or Quakers in Manchester in the 17th cent., by R. Muschamp.

e Manchester improvements, 1775–6, by C. W. Sutton.

f The Roman road between Ribchester and Overborough, by W. Harrison.

g Lancaster church plate, by T. S. Ball.

h Some Cheshire papers of the year 1648 [chiefly orders issued by courts of general sessions], by C. W. Sutton.

i Report on animal remains found at the Roman fort at Manchester, by J. W. Jackson.

j Communion plate of St. Ann's church, Manchester, by T. S. Ball.

k Hancock family of Pendle, by W. Parker and S. W. Partington.

l Notes on the Huntingdon and Stanley brasses in Manchester cathedral, by H. A. Hudson. [John Huntingdon warden 1422–58. James Stanley, warden 1485–1509, bishop of Ely 1506–15]

m Proceedings. [Includes accounts of Bolton abbey, Steetley chapel, Notts., and Sawley abbey, Yorks.]

2637 Vol. 32.

a Church bells of Lancashire, by F. H. Cheetham. [Contd. in vols. 33–35, 37–40, and 45]

b Coins of Brigantia, and their prototypes, by N. Heywood.

c Ancient Chester goldsmiths and their work, by T. S. Ball.

d Robert Yates [d. 1678], rector of Warrington, by F. Nicholson and E. Axon.

e Card money, by W. Charlton.

f The Easter sepulchre recess at St. Mary's church, Stockport, by A. A. Brickhill.

g Proceedings. [Includes an account of Middleton church]

2638 Vol. 33.

a Some Chester civic treasures, by T. S. Ball.

b Thomas Barritt [saddler and antiquary, d. 1820, and some papers from his collection], by C. W. Sutton.

c Notes on Wilmslow parish registers [1558–1652], by R. Peel.

d List of the wardens of the college of Manchester, with remarks upon an old ms. catalogue and an early printed list, by H. A. Hudson.

e Gold pendant of early Irish origin [found near Manchester, 1772], by J. J. Phelps.

f John Chetham [d. 1746], of Chetham's *Psalmody*, by E. Axon.

g Rev. Joshua Stopford [d. 1675] and the Stopfords of Audenshaw, by F. Nicholson and E. Axon.

h Proceedings. [Includes an account of Chetham's hospital, Manchester]

2639 Vol. 34.

a Some legendary stories and folk-lore of the Clithero district, by W. S. Weeks. [Contd. in vol. 38]

b Organs and organists of the cathedral and parish church of Manchester, by H. A. Hudson.
c The history of a turnpike trust (Manchester and Wilmslow), by W. Harrison.
d N. G. Philips' *Views of old Halls and Castles of Lancashire and Cheshire*, by G. H. Rowbotham.
e Lees chapel, otherwise Hey chapel, in Lees, by C. E. Higson.
f Maundy Thursday observances and the royal maundy money, by W. Charlton.
g Captain John Charnley [d. 1834] of the *Thetis*, freeman of Lancaster, by T. C. Hughes.

2640 Vol. 35.
a Stallwork of Manchester cathedral, by H. A. Hudson.
b The mesne field in Lees, by C. E. Higson.
c The Briercliffes of Briercliffe, by R. D. and T. H. Briercliffe and E. Axon.
d Nonconformity in Lancashire in the 17th cent., by E. Axon.
e Jesus chapel, Manchester cathedral: licence for service [1506].

2641 Vol. 36.
a Misericords at Manchester cathedral re-examined, by H. A. Hudson.
b John Jones and Edmund Jones, vicars of Eccles, 1611–1662, by E. Axon.
c The Wardley skull [supposed to be that of the Venerable Ambrose Barlow], by E. Axon.
d Manchester cathedral: the 18th cent. iron-work of the quire, by H. A. Hudson.

2642 Vol. 37.
a Some old Manchester fonts, by H. A. Hudson.
b Richard Wroe, 1641–1717/8, warden of Christ's college, Manchester, by J. Clayton.
c Gibraltar [a former courtyard in Manchester], by G. R. Axon.
d Pre-Norman cross at Cheadle, by J. J. Phelps.

2643 Vol. 38.
a Ellenbrook chapel and its 17th cent. ministers, by E. Axon.
b The battle of Brunanburh, by J. B. McGovern.
c Note on the bells at Downham, supposed to have come from Whalley abbey, by W. S. Weeks.
d Note on Hyde Hall, Denton, by F. H. Cheetham.

2644 Vol. 39.
a The culinary use of Roman *mortaria* [with particular reference to those discovered in Britain], by J. J. Phelps.
b The quire parcloses of Manchester cathedral, by H. A. Hudson.
c Quick moor [and its division, 1625], by C. E. Higson.
d Some early Monton ministers [Edward Sill, d. 1689; Roger Baldwin, d. 1695; Thomas Crompton, d. 1699; Jeremiah Aldred, d. 1729], by E. Axon.
e Hough End Hall, a residence of the lords of the manor of Manchester, by J. Swarbrick.
f John Webster [d. 1682], author of *The Displaying of supposed Witchcraft*, by W. S. Weeks.
g Roger and Orion Adams, printers [of Manchester; Roger Adams, d. 1741; Orion Adams, d. 1797], by G. R. Axon.

2645 Vol. 40.
a The minute books of Chetham's hospital and library, Manchester, by A. F. Maclure. [Extracts, 1653–1850]
b Parson Coppock [b. 1719, Jacobite], by Beatrice Stott.
c Sequence and purpose of the Roman forts at Castleshaw, by I. A. Richmond.

d The abbey of St. Mary-of-the-Marsh at Cockersand, by J. Swarbrick.
e Major Hugh Hornby Birley [d. 1845]: notes by J. R. M. Albrecht.
f General index to vols. 31–40. [Vol. 50, published 1936, contains the general index to vols. 41–50]

2646 Vol. 41.
a Charles Clement Deacon [d. 1749] and William Brettargh [officers in the Young Pretender's army, 1745], by Beatrice Stott.
b Ribchester church and Stydd chapel: notes relating chiefly to recent discoveries, by I. Taylor.
c Clitheroe in the 17th cent., by W. S. Weeks. [Contd. in vols. 42 and 43]
d Old English drinking glasses and their makers, by L. M. Butterworth.
e Robert Thyer, Chetham's librarian, 1732–63, by E. Ogden. [See also vol. 47]
f Note on the first Manchester newspaper [*The Manchester Weekly Journal*], by G. R. Axon.
g Index to illustrations, vols. 1–40, by G. R. Axon.

2647 Vol. 42.
a Some notes on the history of spectacles, by Ll. Andrew.
b The informations laid against certain townsmen of Manchester in 1746, by Beatrice Stott.
c Dunham Massey Hall, by J. Swarbrick.
d Note on Warburton [parish] in the 18th cent., by E. Ogden.
e Lancashire printed books: a bibliography of all books printed in Lancashire down to the year 1800, comp. and ed. A. J. Hawkes, preface by the Earl of Crawford and Balcarres.

2648 Vol. 43.
a New York depositions in 1707–8 concerning a son and grandson of Roger Kenyon of Peel.
b The Society of Friends in the Lancaster district in the 17th cent., by R. Muschamp.
c Characteristics of stained glass, by W. Butterworth.
d Notes on the rectors of Halton, Lancs., since the Commonwealth, by T. C. Hughes.
e Some notes on the *Pietà*, by H. A. Hudson. [On English representations of Our Lady of Pity]

2649 Vol. 44.
a Creswell caves [and their prehistoric remains], by J. W. Jackson.
b The Boydell effigy [c. 1277] at Grappenhall, by J. J. Phelps.
c Old forests of Cheshire, by Mabel Woodcock.
d A limewood carving [of the Crucifixion, attributed to Grinling Gibbons] at Dunham Massey Hall, by J. Swarbrick.
e Early days of coal gas as an illuminant [with particular reference to the scale of charges made for the supply of gas in Liverpool in 1816], by M. A. Gibson.
f The Comberbach (Cheshire) version of the soul-caking play, by A. W. Boyd.
g Hatherlow chapel baptismal register, 1732–81, by G. R. Axon.

2650 Vol. 45.
a Token coinage of Great Britain, by D. Halstead.
b A chaplain's journal, 1825, by Ll. Andrew. [Extracts from a ms. by the Rev. Henry Fielding, chaplain of the New Bailey prison, Salford]
c The Society of Friends in the Bolton district, by R. Muschamp.
d Town books of Sevenoaks and Newton-by-Daresby, Ches., by A. W. Boyd.

2651 Vol. 46.

   a James Dawson and Thomas Syddall [Jacobites], by Beatrice Stott.

   b Early Manchester and Salford Friendly societies, by H. J. M. Maltby.

   c The surrender of the charters of the borough of Clitheroe in 1684, by W. S. Weeks.

   d The Society of Friends [in the Rossendale and Liverpool districts] in the 17th cent., with a few later notes, by R. Muschamp.

   e Some recent discoveries relating to the wood-work of Manchester cathedral, by H. A. Hudson.

   f Some 17th cent. Cheshire wills [of Edmund Warrington, 1637, James Warrington, 1646, and Jane Warrington, 1647, all of Wayley], by Mrs. L. M. Hollingworth.

2652 Vol. 47.

   a The value of [historical] records, by J. Parker.

   b Three dug-out canoes found at Warrington, by G. A. Dunlop.

   c Markland family deeds and papers [at Wigan], by A. W. Boyd.

   d Robert Thyer: family letters and some speeches, by E. Ogden.

   e Wigan's part in the civil war, 1639-51, by A. J. Hawkes.

   f Grappenhall: further notes on the church and the Boydells, by A. Hodgkinson.

   g The Yannes family, of Lees, by C. E. Higson.

   h Mass dials on Cheshire churches, by M. A. Gibson.

   i Notes on the development of the British warship, by A. E. W. Marsh.

   j Abbot Paslew [of Whalley] and the Pilgrimage of Grace, by W. S. Weeks.

   k Early days of bleaching [and bleachworks in England], by H. Johnson.

LANCASHIRE PARISH REGISTER SOCIETY

Founded 1897, to transcribe and publish the registers of the ancient parishes of the county.

Publications:

2653 Vols. 1, 10, 24. Registers of Bury. 2 vols. in 3. 1898-1905. [Vol. i, transcribed and ed. W. J. Löwenberg and H. Brierley, pt. 1: 1590-1616, pt. 2: 1617-46. Vol. ii: 1647-98, transcribed and ed. A. Sparke, the index by Fanny Wrigley]

2654 Vols. 6, 20. Registers of Croston, transcribed and ed. H. Fishwick, the index by Amy Wilson. 1 vol. in 2. 1900-4. [Vol. i, pp. 1-357: Christenings, 1543-1685; marriages, 1538-1727; burials, 1538-1685. Vol. ii, pp. 358-577: Marriages and burials, 1690-1727, and index. Another version of vol. i, covering a shorter period, has only 323 pp., including its own index]

2655 Vols. 8, 9. Registers of the church of St. James, Didsbury, transcribed and ed. H. T. Crofton and E. A. Tindall. 1 vol. in 2. 1900-1. [Pt. 1: 1561-1653. Pt. 2: 1654-1757]

2656 Vol. 11. Registers of Brindle, 1558-1714, transcribed and ed. K. Jacques and H. Brierley, the indexes by Alice Brierley. 1901.

2657 Vols. 12, 18. Registers of Middleton, transcribed, ed. and indexed by G. Shaw. 2 vols. 1902-4. [Vol. i: 1541-1664. Vol. ii: 1653-1729]

2658 Vol. 13. Registers of Ormskirk, 1557-1626, transcribed and ed. J. Arrowsmith, the indexes by Mrs. C. M. Royds and Mrs. H. Brierley. 1902.

2659 Vol. 14. Registers of Chipping, 1559-1694, transcribed, ed. and indexed by Alice Brierley. 1903.

2660 Vol. 15. Registers of Eccleston, 1603-94, transcribed and ed. J. Arrowsmith, the indexes by Joan Peacock. 1903.

2661 Vol. 16. Registers of Padiham, 1573-1653, transcribed and ed. J. A. Laycock, the indexes by Amy Wilson. 1903.

2662 Vol. 17. Registers of Colne, 1599-1653, transcribed and ed. T. B. Ecroyd, the indexes by A. E. Hodder. 1904.

2663 Vol. 19. Registers of Poulton-le-Fylde, 1591-1677, transcribed, ed. and indexed by W. E. Robinson. 1904.

2664 Vol. 21. Registers of Cockerham, 1595-1657. 1904.

2665 Vol. 22. Registers of Newchurch in the township of Culcheth, 1599-1812, transcribed and ed. W. J. Kaye and E. W. W. Kaye, the indexes by Amy Wilson. 1905.

2666 Vol. 23. Registers of St. Thomas the Martyr, Upholland, 1600-1735, transcribed and ed. Alice Brierley, the index by A. E. Hodder. 1905.

2667 Vol. 25. Registers of Eccles, 1564-1632, transcribed and ed. A. E. Hodder. 1906.

2668 Vol. 26. Registers of Ribchester, 1598-1694, transcribed, ed. and indexed by J. Arrowsmith. 1906.

2669 Vol. 27. Registers of St. Michael's on Wyre, 1659-1707, transcribed by H. Brierley, the index by Alice Brierley. 1906.
Registers of Woodplumpton, 1604-59, transcribed by H. Brierley, the index by Fanny Wrigley. 1906.

2670 Vol. 28. Registers of Cartmel, 1559-1661, transcribed by H. Brierley, the index by Amy Wilson and C. H. Brierley. 1907.

2671 Vol. 29. Registers of St. Michael's, Pennington in Furness, 1612-1702, transcribed by H. Brierley, the index by J. Arrowsmith. 1907.
Registers of Urswick in Furness, 1608-95, transcribed by H. Brierley. 1907.

2672 Vol. 30. Registers of Aldingham in Furness, 1542-1695, transcribed and ed. H. S. Cowper. 1907.
Registers of Coniston, 1599-1700, transcribed by H. Maclean and H. Brierley, the index by C. H. Brierley. 1907.

2673 Vols. 31, 55, 56. Registers of the cathedral church of Manchester, with introd. by E. Axon. 2 vols. in 3. 1908-19. [Vol. i: 1573-1616. Vol. ii, pt. 1: Baptisms and marriages, 1616-55. Vol. ii, pt. 2: Burials 1616-53. Vol. ii transcribed by H. Brierley].

2674 Vols. 32, 57. Registers of Lancaster, transcribed by H. Brierley. 2 vols. 1908-20. [Vol. i: 1599-1690. Vol. ii: 1691-1748]

2675 Vol. 33. Registers of Lytham: baptisms and burials, 1679-1761; weddings, 1679-1754, transcribed by H. Brierley. 1908.
Registers of Bispham: baptisms, 1599-1754; burials and weddings, 1631-1754, transcribed and ed. W. E. Robinson. 1908.

2676 Vol. 34. Registers of Prestwich, 1603-88, transcribed by H. Brierley. 1909. [For continuation see no. **2691** below]

2677 Vol. 35. Earliest registers of Liverpool (St. Nicholas's church), 1660-1704; with some of the earlier episcopal transcripts, commencing in 1604, transcribed and ed. H. Peet. Also, report on the ecclesiastical records in the diocese of Liverpool. 1909.

2678 Vol. 36. Registers of Altham, 1596–1695, transcribed by H. Brierley. 1909.
Registers of Blackrod, 1606–1701, transcribed by T. H. Winder. 1909.

2679 Vol. 37. Registers of Walton-le-Dale, 1609–1812, transcribed by G. E. C. Clayton. 1910.

2680 Vol. 38. Registers of Chorley, 1548–1653, transcribed by E. McKnight and H. Brierley. 1910.

2681 Vol. 39. Registers of Blackley, near Manchester, 1655–1753, transcribed by H. Brierley. 1910.
Registers of Pilling: baptisms, 1630–1721; burials, 1685–1718; marriages, 1630–1719, transcribed by H. Brierley. 1910.

2682 Vol. 40. Registers of Tunstall: baptisms, 1626–1812; burials, 1627–1812; weddings, 1625–1812, transcribed by W. H. Kendall and H. Brierley. 1911.
Registers of Melling: baptisms, 1625–1721; burials, 1629–1721; weddings, 1636–1752, transcribed by H. Brierley. 1911.

2683 Vol. 41. Registers of Blackburn, 1600–1660, transcribed by H. Brierley. 1911.

2684 Vol. 42. Registers of Bolton-le-Sands, 1655–1736, transcribed by H. Brierley. 1911.
Registers of Over Kellet, 1648–1812, transcribed by W. Farrer. 1911.

2685 Vol. 43. Registers of Torver, near Coniston, 1599–1792, transcribed by H. Brierley. 1911.
Registers of Kirkby-in-Furness: baptisms, 1701–1812; burials, 1681–1812; marriages, 1728–1754, transcribed by H. Brierley. 1911.

2686 Vol. 44. Registers of Heysham: births and baptisms, deaths and burials, 1658–1813; marriages, 1659–1811, transcribed by H. Brierley. 1912.
Registers of Halton, 1592–1723, transcribed by H. Brierley. 1912.

2687 Vol. 45. Registers of Newchurch-in-Rossendale, 1653–1723, transcribed by A. Sparke. 1912.

2688 Vol. 46. Registers of Standish, 1560–1653, transcribed by H. Brierley. 1912.

2689 Vol. 47. Registers of Gorton, 1599–1741, transcribed by H. Brierley. 1913.
Registers of St. Lawrence, Denton, 1695–1757, transcribed by H. Brierley. 1913.

2690 Vol. 48. Registers of Preston, 1611–35, transcribed and ed. A. E. Hodder. 1913.
Registers of Broughton, near Preston: baptisms, 1653–1804; burials, 1653–1803; weddings, 1653–1759, transcribed and ed. A. E. Hodder. Indexes by R. Wilkinson. 1913.

2691 Vol. 49. Registers of Middleton, 1729–52, transcribed by H. Brierley. 1913.
Registers of Prestwich: baptisms and burials, 1689–1711; weddings to 1712, transcribed by H. Brierley. 1913.

2692 Vol. 50. Registers of Bolton: baptisms, 1573–4, 1590–1660; weddings, 1573, 1587–1660; burials, 1573–4, 1587–1660, ed. and indexed by A. Sparke. 1913.

2693 Vol. 51. Registers of Stalmine, 1583–1724, transcribed by Mrs. W. E. Robinson. 1914.

2694 Vol. 52. Registers of Penwortham, 1608–1753. 1915.

2695 Vols. 53, 54. Registers of Deane, ed. and indexed by A. Sparke. 1 vol. in 2. 1916–17. [Pt. 1: Baptisms and marriages, 1604, 1613–1750. Pt. 2: Burials, 1604, 1613–1750, and index]

2696 Vol. 58. Registers of Rochdale, 1642–1700, transcribed and indexed by H. Brierley. 1921.

2697 Vol. 59. Registers of Caton, 1585–1718, indexed by H. Brierley. 1922.
Registers of Claughton, 1701–1813, transcribed by H. Brierley. 1922.
Registers of Gressingham: baptisms, 1676–1812; marriages, 1691–1828; burials, 1678–1812, transcribed by H. Brierley. 1922.
Registers of Hornby, 1742–89, transcribed by H. Brierley. 1922.
Registers of Tatham, 1558–1812, indexed by H. Brierley. 1922.

2698 Vols. 60, 61. Registers of Radcliffe, transcribed by J. Clayton. 1 vol. in 2. 1922–3. [Pt. 1: Baptisms and burials, 1557–1783; marriages, 1560–1761. Pt. 2: Burials, 1558–1783, and indexes]

2699 Vol. 62. Marriage registers of Rochdale, 1701–1801. Transcribed by H. Brierley. 1924.

2700 Vol. 63. Parish registers of Garstang, 1567–1658. Transcribed by H. Brierley. 1925. [Contd. in no. **2705** below]

2701 Vol. 64. Parish registers of Goosnargh: baptisms and burials, 1639–1753; marriages, 1639–1812, transcribed by T. B. Boss and H. Brierley. 1926.

2702 Vol. 65. Parish registers of Ashton-under-Lyne: baptisms and marriages, 1594–1720; burials, 1596–1720, transcribed by H. Brierley. 1927–8.

2703 Vol. 66. Parish registers of North Meols, 1594–1731 transcribed by H. Brierley. 1929.

2704 Vol. 67. Parish registers of Thornton-in-Lonsdale, 1576–1812, transcribed by W. H. Chippindall. 1931.

2705 Vol. 68. Parish registers of Garstang, 1660–1734, transcribed by H. Brierley, indexed by A. Sparke. 1932.

2706 Vol. 69. Parish registers of Bentham, 1666–1812, transcribed by W. H. Chippindall. 1932.

2707 Vol. 70. Parish registers of Warrington, 1591–1653, transcribed by A. Sparke. 1933.

2708 Vol. 71. Parish registers of Ingleton and Chapel-le-Dale, 1607–1812, transcribed by W. H. Chippindall. 1933.

LEAGUE OF THE EMPIRE

Founded 1901, to inspire personal and active interest in the Empire as a whole, and to promote educational and friendly intercommunication between its different parts.

Monthly Record, nos. 1–28 (1904–6):

2709 No. 14.
a Men who have served the Empire in Africa. 1: Lord Napier of Magdala [d. 1890].

2710 No. 23.
a The chief stages in the growth of Greater Britain, by A. Phillips.

The Federal Magazine, nos. 29–115[1] (1907–18), *continuing the above:*

[1] Nos. 37–39 were issued as *Official Report of the Federal Conference on Education*, 1907; nos. 40–115 incorporate *The All-Red Mail.*

2711 No. 51.

a A transport cruise to the Cape in 1795, by E. M. O. Marshall. [Contd. in no. 52]

2712 No. 59.

a The Seychelles Islands: their discovery and history, by G. Mackay. [Contd. in no. 60]

2713 No. 61.

a The story of slavery in Saint Helena, by E. L. Jackson.

2714 No. 62.

a The story of the Falkland Islands, 1500–1842, by W. L. Allardyce. [Contd. in nos. 63–65]

2715 No. 70.

a A pioneer colonist's story [an emigrant to New Zealand, 1843–4], by C. A. Barnicoat. [Contd. in nos. 71–73]

2716 No. 72.

a The English coronation ceremony.

2717 No. 73.

a The Cinque ports country, by C. Hussey. [Contd. in nos. 74–76]

2718 No. 78.

a The story of Bermuda, by A. H. Watlington. [Contd· in nos. 79–81]

2719 No. 83.

a A brief memoir of Matthew Flinders [d. 1814].

2720 No. 91.

a Persons and places along the Pilgrims' Way from Southampton to Canterbury, by J. O. Bevan. [Contd. in no. 92]

2721 No. 105.

a Canada: an outline and bibliography of its history, by G. M. Wrong. [Contd. in no. 106]

League of Empire Review and Federal Magazine, new ser., nos. 1–14 (1922–6):

2722 No. 5.

a The British school and other centres of study in the Eternal City, by Mrs. A. Strong. [Contd. in nos. 6 and 7]

Textbooks:

2723 The British Empire: its past, its present, and its future, by A. F. Pollard. 1909.

2724 The British Empire and its history, by E. G. Hawke. 1911.

2725 The story of the Empire, by G. T. Hankin. 1911.

Other publications:

2726 The first British colonies, by F. A. Kirkpatrick. *P.* 1904.

2727 Lectures on British colonization and empire, first series (1600–1783), by F. A. Kirkpatrick, with introd. by H. E. Egerton. 1906.

2728 Empire-builders: a course of lectures by W. K. Stride, with introd. by H. E. Egerton. 1906.

LEEDS PHILOSOPHICAL AND LITERARY SOCIETY

Founded 1818, for the discussion of subjects associated with all branches of natural knowledge and of literature.

Proceedings, literary and historical section, vols. 1–3 (1925–35):

2729 Vol. 1.

a The date of *Hofuðlausn* [or Head-ransom, a poem by Egill Skallagrimsson, Icelandic skald], by E. V. Gordon.
b Two Roman milestones from north Yorkshire, by J. L. Kirk and H. A. Ormerod.
c The charters of Leeds, by A. Hamilton Thompson.
d A ms. from Cîteaux [including copies of two letters close of Edward I], by A. Hamilton Thompson.
e Excavations at Brough-by-Bainbridge [site of a Roman fort] in 1926, by R. G. Collingwood. [Contd. for 1928–9 in vol. 2, and for 1931 in vol. 3, by J. P. Droop and C. W. Jones]
f A collection of books in the library of the University of Leeds printed before the 19th cent., containing (a) translations from English into French, (b) books written in French on Great Britain and on British affairs, by R. Offor. [Contd. in vol. 2]

2730 Vol. 2.

a Estimates of the population and national resources of England in 1695, by A. S. Turberville.
b A ms. book of devotions in the collection of Professor H. A. Ormerod, with some notes on a fragment of a mortuary roll [of Robert Cutwolf, prior of Newstead in Sherwood forest, 1424–55] bound up with it, by A. Hamilton Thompson. [With transcripts of hymns from the book of devotions]
c Republicanism and the revolution of 1689, by A. S. Turberville.

2731 Vol. 3.

a Remarks on the Bainbridge [Roman] finds, 1928, –29, –31, by J. P. Droop.
b A Roman road south of Bainbridge, by B. H. St. J. O'Neil. [With a note by M. K. Clark]
c Latin additions to place- and parish-names of England and Wales, by B. Dickins.

Extra publication:

2732 The history of 100 years of life of the Leeds Philosophical and Literary Society, by E. K. Clark. 1924.

LEICESTER LITERARY AND PHILOSOPHICAL SOCIETY

Founded 1835, for the general cultivation of literature, science and art. The society had a section for archaeology and numismatics, later for archaeology, literature and economics, till 1894. An historical section was formed in 1922.

Transactions, new quarterly ser., vols. 5–34 (1898–1933):

2733 Vol. 5.

a The political ideas of Tennyson and Carlyle compared, by W. Whitaker.
b Garrick and his circle, by W. Archer.
c History of the geological section [of the Society], 1849–1900, by W. J. Hall.
d Wordsworth, by J. E. Stocks.

2734 Vol. 6.

a Discovery of a Roman villa near Rothley, Leics., in 1901, by W. T. Tucker.

2735 Vol. 8.

a Diary of Henry Crabb Robinson, by J. M. Gimson.

2736 Vol. 9.
a English art in the 18th cent., by B. J. Fletcher.
b Ancient and modern tools, by W. Taylor.

2737 Vol. 11.
a The old town hall library and its history, by J. E. Stocks.
b Leicestershire during the civil war, 1642-5, by E. W. Hensman.

2738 Vol. 12.
a 'Relief by the community', by G. W. Hope. [On the operation of the Poor Law, 1907]
b The Rev. Thomas Arthur Preston, rector of Thurcaston [naturalist, d. 1905], by W. Bell.

2739 Vol. 13.
a Sydney Smith, by A. W. W. Dale.

2740 Vol. 14.
a The Johnson bi-centenary, by W. A. Brockington.

2741 Vol. 16.
a Some thoughts on history, by F. B. Lott.

2742 Vol. 17.
a Presidential address [on the past, the present and the future of the Society], by A. V. Clarke.

2743 Vol. 25.
a Presidential address: some of Leicester's old charities, by Margaret Gimson.

2744 Vol. 27.
a Presidential address [the history of the Society], by J. H. Jaques.

2745 Vol. 30.
a Poor persons and the administration of justice, by C. Squire.

2746 Vol. 32.
a Presidential address [on monastic orders in England and Leicester abbey], by W. K. Bedingfield.

Extra publication:

2747 Presidential address: the state of the nation, by J. A. Hopps. *P.* 1918.

LEICESTERSHIRE ARCHAEOLOGICAL SOCIETY

Founded 1855, as the Leicestershire Architectural and Archaeological Society, to promote the scientific study of the history and antiquities of the city and county of Leicester, etc. Title changed to above form in 1917.

Transactions, vols. 9-17[1] (1900-33):

2748 Vol. 9.
a Calendars of Leicestershire administration bonds, transcribed by H. Hartopp. [1600-49, with records of peculiar courts previous to 1800. Contd. from vol. 8]
b St. Nicholas' church, Leicester, by C. Lynam.
c St. Andrew's church, Aylestone, by R. Goodacre.
d Supplementary remarks on Aylestone church and extracts from constable's accounts, 1671-1710, by H. S. Gedge.
e The abbey of St. Mary de Pratis, Leicester, by C. H. Compton.
f City of Gloucester: notes as to ancient charters, etc.

[1] A general index to vols. 1-20 (1855-1939) was issued as an extra publication in 1951.

2749 Vol. 10.
a Leicestershire men at the French wars of 1346-7, by W. G. D. Fletcher.
b An account of the battle of Willoughby Field [1648], co. Nottingham, by W. F. Beardsley.
c Notes, by A. Hamilton Thompson. [On the castle and St. Mary Magdalene's church, Newark, and All Saints' church, Coddington, Notts.; and on the Lincolnshire churches of All Saints, Beckingham, St. Helen, Brant Broughton, St. Peter, Navenby, and All Saints, Coleby]
d Notes, by A. Hamilton Thompson. [On the churches of St. Peter and St. Paul, Kettering; St. Edmund, Warkton; St. Mary, Weekley; St. Andrew, Geddington; SS. Peter and Paul, Stanion; St. Andrew, Brigstock; St. Peter, Oundle; St. Mary, Warmington; St. Mary, Tansor, St. Peter, Lowick, Drayton House and Lyveden, all in Northants.]
e Burrough camp, by E. H. Day.
f Note of two old leases of Leicester castle [1686 and 1705], by S. S. Partridge.
g Parish registers and records, by J. A. L. Beasley.
h Medals and campaigns of the 43rd Foot, now 1st battalion of the Oxfordshire and Buckinghamshire Light Infantry, by W. J. Freer.
i The manor of Hinckley in the late 18th cent., by H. J. Francis.

2750 Vol. 11.
a Short description of the original building accounts [1480-84] of Kirby Muxloe castle, Leics., recently discovered at the manor house, Ashby-de-la-Zouch, by T. H. Fosbrooke.
b Monasteries of Leicestershire in the 15th cent., by A. Hamilton Thompson.
c Kirby Muxloe castle.
d Token coinage of Leicestershire and Rutland in the 17th cent., by J. L. Young.
e Building accounts of Kirby Muxloe castle, 1480-84, ed., with introd. and notes, by A. Hamilton Thompson.
f The pipe roll for Leicestershire, 1199-1200, with selected pleas from the de banco rolls, 1338-63.
g The manors of Allexton, Appleby and Ashby Folville, by G. Farnham and A. Hamilton Thompson.

2751 Vol. 12.
a Rothley: the preceptory [of the Knights Templars], by T. H. Fosbrooke; the descent of the manor, by G. Farnham; the church, by J. W. Watts; the vicars of Rothley, by A. Hamilton Thompson.
b Star chamber proceedings: part of the evidence in a 16th cent. suit relating to Leicester and the forest of Leicester, with introd. and notes by S. H. Skillington.
c Potters Marston: the hall, by T. H. Fosbrooke; notes on the manor, by G. F. Farnham.
d Frolesworth: the church, by A. Herbert; notes on the descent of the manor, by G. F. Farnham.
e Claybrooke: the church, by A. Herbert; notes on the descent of the manor, by G. F. Farnham.
f The manor of Noseley, with some account of the free chapel of St. Mary, by G. F. Farnham and A. Hamilton Thompson.

2752 Vol. 13.
a The old town hall of Leicester, by T. H. Fosbrooke and S. H. Skillington, with a note on the stained glass in the mayor's parlour by A. B. McDonald. [Including sections on the medieval constitution and gilds of the borough]
b Rectors of the chapel and parish church of Noseley [-1661], by A. Hamilton Thompson.
c George Fox and Leicestershire, by Gertrude Ellis.

d The manor and advowson of Medbourne, 1086–1550, by G. F. Farnham and A. Hamilton Thompson.

e Hallaton: the church, by A. Herbert; notes on the descent of the manor, by G. F. Farnham.

f Hugh de Grentemesnil [d. *c.* 1098] and his family, by H. J. Francis.

g The manor, house, and chapel of Holt, by G. F. Farnham and A. Hamilton Thompson.

h Gaddesby: the church, by A. Herbert; notes on the manor, by G. F. Farnham.

2753 Vol. 14.

a The open fields of Leicester, by C. J. Billson.

b The castle and manor of Castle Donington, by G. F. Farnham and A. Hamilton Thompson, with an account of the church by A. Hamilton Thompson.

c Fenny Drayton and the Purefey monuments, by G. F. Farnham and A. Herbert. [With list of rectors]

d A corrody from Leicester abbey, 1393–4, with some notes on corrodies, by A. Hamilton Thompson.

e The extant certificates of Leicester gilds, with introd. and notes by S. H. Skillington.

f Notes upon a prehistoric contracted burial, discovered at Leire, co. Leics., 1926; also on an early sepulchral slab discovered at Ayleston church, by M. P. Dare.

g Notes on the manor of Ragdale, by G. F. Farnham.

h Ragdale Old Hall and church, by A. Hamilton Thompson.

i Stoke Golding: architectural notes on the church, by A. Hamilton Thompson; medieval manorial history, by G. F. Farnham.

2754 Vol. 15.

a Charnwood forest and its historians, by G. F. Farnham.

b Cemeteries of Roman Leicester in the light of recent discoveries, 1922–8, with particular reference to an eastern burial-ground uncovered in 1926–7, by M. P. Dare.

c Ashby-de-la-Zouch: architectural notes on the church, by A. Hamilton Thompson; extracts from the parish register, by H. Hartopp; the descent of the manor, by S. H. Skillington; manorial notes, by G. F. Farnham.

d Market Bosworth: architectural notes on the church, by A. Hamilton Thompson; the Harcourt family, by G. F. Farnham.

e The Leicester gild of tallow chandlers, by S. H. Skillington.

f Charnwood forest: the Charnwood manors, by G. F. Farnham. [Barrow-on-Soar, Mapplewell, Alderman Haw, Charley, Beaumanor, Groby, Ulverscroft, Whitwick, and Shepshed, with notes on Barrow church by A. Hamilton Thompson, and on Whitwick and Shepshed churches]

g Some notes on manors and manorial history, by A. Hamilton Thompson.

h The carved stones at Breedon on the Hill [church], Leics., and their position in the history of English art, by A. W. Clapham.

i Aldeby: a suggested identification in the Leicestershire Domesday, with a note on the site and church, by M. P. Dare.

2755 Vol. 16.

a Mr. Farnham's contribution to the history of Leicestershire, by A. Hamilton Thompson.

b Quenby: the manor and hall, by G. Farnham.

c Belgrave: architectural notes on the church, by A. Herbert; notes on the descent of the manor, by G. Farnham.

d The Skeffingtons of Skeffington: introductory narrative by S. H. Skillington; appendix [of documents] by G. F. Farnham.

e The chapel of St. Peter at Kirkby-upon-Wreak (Kirby Bellars): documents from the Lincoln episcopal registers, with introd. by A. Hamilton Thompson.

2756 Vol. 17.

a Prestwold and its hamlets in medieval times, by G. F. Farnham.

b An old Hazlerigg deed [1659], transcribed by Miss A. P. Deeley, with introd. by S. H. Skillington.

c The manor of Peckleton: introd. by S. H. Skillington; documentary abstracts by G. F. Farnham; architectural notes on the church by A. Herbert.

d The [G. F.] Farnham bequest [of notes and original documents] to the Leicester Museum muniment room, by G. K. Thomson; introd. by S. H. Skillington.

e Legends, folklore and dialect of Leicestershire, with an introduction on the general history of the county, by R. E. Martin.

f Ashby castle, by A. Herbert.

g Aylestone: the descent of the manor, by G. K. Thomson.

LEWISHAM ANTIQUARIAN SOCIETY

Founded 1885, to study, and as far as practicable to record, antiquities, with especial regard to the parish of Lewisham. Amalgamated with the Greenwich Antiquarian Society in 1920 to form the Greenwich and Lewisham Antiquarian Society, q.v.

Proceedings, 1899–1912 (3 vols. 1902–13):

2757 Vol. for 1899–1901.

a The maze of Maze Hill [Greenwich], Troy towns and Jerusalem roads, by W. E. Ball. [On the origin of these names for various types of mazes]

2758 Vol. for 1902–7.

a History of the borough of Lewisham, with an itinerary, by L. L. Duncan, with chapters on the geology of the district, by W. H. Griffin, and on the local authorities, by A. W. Hiscox. [Also issued separately, 1908]

2759 Vol. for 1908–12.

a Odds and ends of Lewisham history, by L. L. Duncan. [The tower of the parish church; the contents of a cottage in 1529; the goods of John Holard, Mrs. Colfe's father, 1576; the seizure of a mill in 1604 and what befell its captors; Romburgh: the story of a forgotten Lewisham name; Bellingham; the bounds of the manor of Lewisham and its subsidiary manors of Bankers and Shroffold, together with those of the manor of Lee]

Extra publication:

2760 A short history of Colfe's grammar school, Lewisham, by L. L. Duncan. P. [1902].

LIBRARY ASSOCIATION

Founded 1877, to promote and encourage bibliographical study and research.

Library Association Record, vols. 3–24 (1901–23):

2761 Vol. 3.

a The literary associations of Bath, by C. T. Macaulay.

b Paper-making in England, 1682–1714, by R. Jenkins.

c Some things of general interest in the Bristol medical library, by L. M. Griffiths. [Historical references to Bristol as a health resort]

d Literary and artistic associations of Plymouth and Devonport, by W. H. K. Wright.

2762 Vol. 4.

  a Edward Edwards [d. 1886, pioneer of the public library movement]: some notes on his life and work, by T. Greenwood.

  b Paper-making in England, 1714–88, by R. Jenkins.

  c Some institutions of Birmingham and neighbourhood, by R. K. Dent.

2763 Vol. 5.

  a John Baskerville [d. 1775, printer] and his work, by R. K. Dent.

  b Some public institutions of Leeds, by A. Tait.

  c Mediaeval libraries, with special reference to Bristol and its neighbourhood, by T. W. Williams.

2764 Vol. 6.

  a Leeds public free libraries, by T. W. Hand.

  b Library economy (chiefly continental) at the end of the 17th cent., by W. R. B. Prideaux.

  c Monastic libraries, by A. Morgan.

2765 Vol. 7.

  a The struggle for a public library in Newcastle-upon-Tyne [1854–80], by B. Anderton.

  b Old newspapers [chiefly English, 17th and 18th cent.], by G. Smith.

  c Some aspects of the work of Henry Bradshaw [d. 1886, librarian of the University of Cambridge], by C. F. Newcombe.

2766 Vol. 8.

  a Newspapers, by A. G. Burt.

  b The medical libraries of London, by W. R. B. Prideaux.

  c A survey of the public library movement in Bradford [1867–1906], by M. E. Hartley.

  d The Bradford Library and Literary Society [founded 1774], by W. Scruton.

  e The Bradford Mechanics' Institute library, by C. A. Federer.

2767 Vol. 9.

  a Bookbinding in England, by C. Davenport.

  b Booksellers' catalogues, by A. G. Burt.

2768 Vol. 10.

  a English and Scottish heraldry on books, by C. Davenport.

  b The Guildhall library: its history and present position, by E. M. Barrajo.

  c Brighton public libraries, museums and fine art galleries, by H. D. Roberts. [Brief historical account]

2769 Vol. 11.

  a Library economy in the 16th cent., by W. R. B. Prideaux.

  b Monastic book-making, by A. Morgan.

  c The library of University College, London, by R. W. Chambers.

2770 Vol. 12.

  a History of library associations, by W. W. Howe.

  b Dr. Thomas Bray [d. 1730, founder of the Society for Promoting Christian Knowledge and the Society for the Propagation of the Bible in Foreign Parts], by G. Smith.

2771 Vol. 13.

  a Exeter public library: an historical essay, by H. Tapley-Soper.

  b A critical account of the literature of the Indian mutiny, by K. N. Dhar.

  c Literature in the Manx language to the middle of the 19th cent., by G. W. Wood.

2772 Vol. 14.

  a Paper and publishing at the beginning of the 18th cent. [with particular reference to the printing of Ralph Thoresby's *Ducatus Leodiensis*, 1715], by R. Jenkins.

  b Monastic libraries of Wales, 5th to 16th cent., by D. R. Phillips.

  c Edward Edwards, by C. W. Sutton.

2773 Vol. 15.

  a John Collier [d. 1786, author and artist]: the man and his work, by R. J. Gordon.

  b Some 17th and 18th cent. [library] catalogues, by C. J. Purnell.

  c The story of the almanac, by H. G. Hayne.

  d Some literary associations of Bournemouth and neighbourhood, by C. H. Mate.

  e The debt of men of letters to libraries, by C. F. Newcombe.

2774 Vol. 16.

  a Some Lancashire diaries, by H. Fishwick.

  b Stoke Newington and English literature, by W. E. Baxter.

  c An account of the library of the Medical Society of London, by G. Bethell.

2775 Vol. 18.

  a Shakespeare in London, by W. Martin.

2776 Vol. 19.

  a The study of palaeography in England since 1873, by A. Hulshof.

2777 Vol. 20.

  a The national aspect of the Welsh records, by H. Hall.

2778 Vol. 22.

  a A monastic humanist of the 15th cent. [William Selling, prior of Christ Church, Canterbury]: a study in English Renascence book-collecting, by E. A. Savage.

  b The libraries of Norwich, by C. Nowell.

  c Norfolk bibliography, by G. A. Stephen. [A history of bibliography in Norfolk]

2779 Vol. 23.

  a Books in early wills, mainly 14th cent., by C. Jenkins.

  b The London Library, by C. J. Purnell.

2780 Vol. 24.

  a Collaboration in historical research, by Joan Wake. [On the ms. sources of local and national history]

Library Association Record, new ser., vols. 1–8 (1924–30):

2781 Vol. 1.

  a Sir Christopher Wren, builder of libraries.

  b Library architecture, by A. E. Richardson.

  c A working Shakespeare bibliography, by H. Sellers.

  d The science and romance of old mss., by Joan Wake.

2782 Vol. 2.

  a The rise and decline of the three-volume novel, by Mary Alexander.

2783 Vol. 3.

  a William Tyndale's place in English literature, by H. G. Wood.

2784 Vol. 4.

  a The Birmingham muniments: documents of earlier date than 1800 relating to Birmingham, preserved in the Birmingham reference library, with some notes on calendaring, by L. Chubb.

b Some account of Lincoln cathedral library, by W. H. Kynaston.

c Seventy-five years [of public libraries], 1850–1925, by H. Guppy.

d The preservation of a national literature [in England, from the 16th cent.], by A. Esdaile.

e Life in Elizabethan England [a bibliography], by Muriel St. C. Byrne.

2785 Vol. 5.

a Libraries and the study of local history, by A. Hamilton Thompson.

b The value of publications of archaeological societies to a public library, by E. W. Crossley.

2786 Vol. 7.

a A private library, by Lord Balniel. [An historical account of the Balcarres library, its growth and its contents]

Library Association Record, 3rd ser., vols. 1–3 (1931–3):

2787 Vol. 1.

a The mystery of the origins of typography, by M. Audin.

b A census of the known copies of Thomas Martyn's *Psyche*, 1797, by F. J. Griffin and C. D. Sherborn.

2788 Vol. 2.

a History of the copyright privilege in England, by R. Partridge.

2789 Vol. 3.

a Westminster abbey chapter library and muniment room.

b Private and public book collections [chiefly in the 19th cent.], by M. Sadleir.

Other publications:

2790 The Athenaeum subject index to periodicals, issued at the request of the Library Association, 1915, 1916. 2 vols. 1916–18. [The index for 1915 was first published in the form of class lists as supplements to *The Athenaeum*, 1915–16, and independently in 1916. A consolidated vol. comprising the material in the class lists rearranged in one alphabetical sequence and with numerous additional entries was published in 1916 as Vol. i: 1915. The index for 1916 appeared only as class lists, 1917–18. For the subjects covered by the lists, see below]

2791 Subject index to periodicals, issued at the request of the council of the Library Association, 1915–16. 1919. [Consolidated vol. in one alphabet]

2792 Subject index to periodicals, issued by the Library Association, 1917–19, 1920, 1921, 1922. 4 vols. 1920–26. [Class lists lettered:—A: Theology and philosophy (including folk-lore); B–E: Historical, political, and economic sciences; F: Education and child welfare; G: Fine arts and archaeology; H: Music; I: Language and literature, pt. 1, classical, oriental and primitive, pt. 2, modern European; K: Science and technology; L (in 1917–19 index only): List of periodicals indexed and author index. The class lists for 1915 (eleven) and 1916 (seven) deal with the same subjects but under slightly different titles]

2793 Subject index to periodicals, issued by the Library Association, 1926–32. 7 vols. 1928–33. [Indexes in single alphabet without classified divisions]

2794 [An index to bibliographical papers published by the Bibliographical Society and the Library Association, London, 1877–1932. See under Bibliographical Society, no. 300 above]

LINCOLN ENGINEERING SOCIETY

Founded 1923, to afford opportunities for professional discussion and to facilitate the interchange of ideas respecting improvements, or developments, in the various branches of engineering.

Annual Report and Proceedings, 1923–32 (6 vols. 1927–33):

2795 Vol. for 1923–6.

a Engineering progress during the last quarter of a century—and what of the next?, by L. W. Smith.

2796 Vol. for 1927.

a The history and the winning of coal, by E. C. Dunkerton.

2797 Vol. for 1931.

a Lincoln cathedral: a brief outline of its history and the special repairs, 1922–31, by R. S. Godfrey.

2798 Vol. for 1932.

a Over a century of public service: Lincoln corporation gas undertaking 1929–33, by G. Wright. [Short review of the history of Lincoln gas works 1830–1929, and a more detailed study of progress 1929–32]

LINCOLN RECORD SOCIETY

Founded 1910, to print records and documents relating to church, parochial, manorial, and family history.

Publications, vols. 1–28:

2799 Vol. 1. Lincolnshire church notes, made by Gervase Holles, 1634–42, ed. R. E. G. Cole. 1911.

Vol. 2. Lincoln episcopal records, 1571–8. [See Canterbury and York Soc., no. 835 above]

Vols. 3, 6, 9. Rotuli Hugonis de Welles, 1209–35. [See Canterbury and York Soc., no. 827 above]

2800 Vol. 4. Speculum dioeceseos Lincolniensis sub episcopis Gul. Wake et Edm. Gibson, 1705–23. Pt. 1: Archdeaconries of Lincoln and Stow, ed. R. E. G. Cole. 1913. [No more published]

2801 Vols. 5, 10, 24. Lincoln wills registered in the district probate registry at Lincoln, ed. C. W. Foster. 3 vols. 1914–30. [Vol. i: 1271–1526. Vol. ii: 1505–30. Vol. iii: 1530–2]

Vols. 7, 14, 21. Visitations of religious houses. [See Canterbury and York Soc., no. 840 above]

2802 Vol. 8. Visitation of co. Lincoln by Sir Edward Bysshe, 1666, ed. F. Green, with introd. by W. H. Rylands. 1917.

Vol. 11. Rotuli Roberti Grosseteste, 1235–53, necnon rotulus Henrici de Lexington, 1254–8. [See Canterbury and York Soc., no. 834 above]

2803 Vols. 12, 13, 15. Chapter acts of the cathedral church of St. Mary of Lincoln, ed. R. E. G. Cole. 3 vols. 1915–20. [Vol. i: 1520–36. Vol. ii: 1536–47. Vol. iii: 1547–59]

Vol. 16. Calendars of administrations, 1540–1659. [See British Record Soc., Index library vol. 52, no. 627 above]

2804 Vol. 17. Final concords of co. Lincoln from feet of fines in the Public Record Office, 1244–72, with additions, 1176–1250, ed. C. W. Foster. 1921.

2805 Vol. 18. Transcripts of charters relating to the Gilbertine houses of Sixle, Ormsby, Catley, Bullington, and Alvingham, ed., with a translation, from the King's Remembrancer's memoranda rolls, nos. 183, 185, and 187, by F. M. Stenton. 1922.

2806 Vol. 19. The Lincolnshire Domesday and the Lindsey survey, translated and ed. C. W. Foster and T. Longley, with introd. by F. M. Stenton, and appendixes of extinct villages by C. W. Foster. 1924.

Vol. 20. Rotuli Ricardi Gravesend, 1258–79. [See Canterbury and York Soc., no. 852 above]

2807 Vol. 22. The earliest Lincolnshire assize rolls, 1202–9, ed. Doris M. Stenton. 1926.

2808 Vol. 23. The state of the church in the reigns of Elizabeth and James I, as illustrated by documents relating to the diocese of Lincoln. Vol. i, ed. C. W. Foster. 1926. [No more published]

2809 Vols. 25, 26. Minutes of proceedings in quarter sessions held for the parts of Kesteven in co. Lincoln, ed. S. A. Peyton. 1 vol. in 2. 1931. [Vol. i: 1674–83. Vol. ii: 1683–95]

2810 Vols. 27, 28. The *registrum antiquissimum* of the cathedral church of Lincoln, ed. C. W. Foster. Vols. i–ii. 1931–3. [Vols. iii–vii were published in 1935–53]

Parish register section, vols. 1–9:

2811 Vols. 1, 3. Parish registers of Boston, copied by F. Besant and ed. C. W. Foster. 2 vols. 1914–15. [Vol. i: 1557–99. Vol. ii: 1599–1638]

2812 Vol. 2. Parish registers of St. Margaret in the Close, Lincoln, 1538–1837, ed. C. W. Foster, with introd. by R. E. G. Cole. 1915.

2813 Vol. 4. Parish registers of Grantham. Vol. i: 1562–1632, ed. C. W. Foster, with introd. by G. G. Walker. 1916. [No more published]

2814 Vol. 5. Parish registers of Alford and Rigsby, collated with and supplemented by the bishops' transcripts, 1538–1680, ed. R. C. Dudding. 1917.

2815 Vol. 6. Parish registers of Gainsborough. Vol. i: 1564–1640, ed. C. W. Foster. 1920. [No more published]

2816 Vol. 7. Parish registers of Bourne, 1562–1650, ed. C. W. Foster. 1921.

2817 Vol. 8. Parish registers of St. Peter at Gowts, Lincoln: baptisms, 1540–1837; burials, 1538–1837; marriages, 1826–1837, ed. R. C. Dudding. 1923.

2818 Vol. 9. Parish registers of the city of Lincoln: marriages, 1538–1754, ed. C. W. Foster. 1925. [St. Benedict, 1562–1753; St. Botolph, 1562–1753; St. John in Newport, 1743–53; St. Mark, 1561–1754; St. Martin, 1548–1754, St. Mary Magdalen, 1602–1753; St. Mary in Wigford, 1562–1754; St. Michael on the Mount, 1562–1754; St. Nicholas in Newport, 1602–1753; St. Paul in the Bail, 1565–1753; St. Peter at Arches, 1561–1753; St. Peter in Eastgate, 1562–1753; St. Peter at Gowts, 1538–1753; St. Swithin, 1562–1753]

LINCOLNSHIRE NATURALISTS' UNION

Founded 1893, to promote the study of every branch of natural history.

Transactions, vols. 1–8 (1905–35):

2819 Vol. 1.

a The pygmy flint age in Lincolnshire: a contribution to the ethnology of Lincolnshire, by A. Hunt.
b Pre-historic man in Lincolnshire, by A. Hunt.

2820 Vol. 2.

a History and present condition of the investigation of the land and fresh-water mollusca of Lincolnshire, by W. D. Roebuck. [A survey beginning with the work of Martin Lister, zoologist, d. 1712]
b Address [on the bibliography of Lincolnshire natural history], by W. D. Roebuck.

2821 Vol. 4.

a The lias [clay] brickyards of south-west Lincolnshire, by A. E. Trueman.
b The birds of Lincolnshire past, present and future, by F. L. Blathwayt.

2822 Vol. 6.

a Place-names on the map of Lincolnshire in relation to natural history, by S. C. Wood.

2823 Vol. 7.

a Martin Lister [d. 1712] and Lincolnshire natural history, by H. W. Kew.
b Ray's journey through Lincolnshire, 1661, by H. W. Kew. [John Ray, naturalist, d. 1705]

Extra publication:

2824 Romano-British remains at Saltersford, by H. Preston. P. [1915].

LINDSEY LOCAL HISTORY SOCIETY

Founded 1929, to bring together all those who are interested in local history and other cognate subjects.

Lincolnshire Magazine, vol. 1 (1932–4):

2825 Vol. 1.

a The beginnings of Lincolnshire, by J. W. F. Hill.
b Our villages. 1: Burton-upon-Stather, by H. E. Dudley.
c Studying local history at Old Bolingbroke, by C. Brears.
d Church of St. Mary, Winthorpe, by R. G. Finch.
e Moulton grammar school, by J. G. Westmoreland.
f The iron industry of north Lincolnshire, by G. R. Walshaw.
g Thornton abbey, by P. B. G. Binnall.
h Lincolnshire worthies. 1: Thomas Sutton [d. 1611, founder of Charterhouse], by F. W. Ives.
i Our villages. 2: Huttoft, by J. E. Gillott.
j 'Haxey Hood' game, by P. D. Taylor.
k A history of the Lincolnshire regiment (the 10th Foot), by R. D. Stokes.
l Fox-hunting in Lincolnshire [from the 18th cent.], by G. E. Collins.
m Wesley's travels in his native county [Lincolnshire], by L. G. H. Lee.
n Ancient glass in Lincolnshire. 1: Haydor, by C. Woodforde.
o Our villages. 3: Willoughton, by A. R. Bullivant.
p Lincolnshire folk-lore and legends, by C. Brears.
q Famous Lincolnshire organs. 1: The organs of Lincoln cathedral, by L. Elvin.
r The pleasures of flint-hunting [with an account of some flints discovered in Lincolnshire], by G. Taylor.
s Local history in a small school—Hatton, by C. A. S. Hobbins. [Notes relating to the village]
t Sanctuary knocker at Careby, by H. Walker.
u Brigg grammar school [founded 1674], by J. T. Daughton.
v Memories of old Winterton [in the second half of the 19th cent.], by Ellen L. Bennett.

w From fen to farm, from heath to husbandry, by G. E. Collins. [An account of the progress of land reclamation and stock-breeding in Lincolnshire]

x Lincolnshire worthies. 2: William Hilton, R.A. [d. 1839], by A. Garland.

y The later Renaissance architecture of Stamford and district, by H. F. Traylen.

z The city of Lincoln insignia, by J. W. F. Hill.

aa An early rotary pump [*c.* 1815, at Torksey], by G. L. Nutt.

bb Lincolnshire worthies. 3: St. Gilbert of Sempringham, by W. M. Wright.

cc Lincolnshire bells. 1: The art of change ringing, by R. Richardson.

dd Ancient glass in Lincolnshire. 2: Wrangle, by C. Woodforde.

ee Mablethorpe [an account of the village], by W. A. B. Jones.

ff Two colonial governors, Thomas Pownall [d. 1805, governor of Massachusetts Bay and of South Carolina], and Francis Bernard [d. 1779, governor of New Jersey and of Massachusetts Bay], by R. A. Humphreys.

gg Our villages. 4: Ancaster, by G. E. Orchard.

hh Famous Lincolnshire organs. 2: The organs of St. Botolph's, Boston, by L. Elvin.

ii Roman sites north of Lincoln: notes on several known and unknown, by Ethel H. Rudkin.

jj Caistor grammar school [founded 1630], by T. M. O. Cross.

kk Linen weaving at Appleby [a brief historical account], by H. E. Dudley.

ll Lincolnshire worthies. 4: Bennet Langton [d. 1801], Dr. Johnson's friend, by G. G. Walker.

mm Lincolnshire place names, by H. F. Allison.

nn The Lincolnshire census [1931], by F. W. Flower.

oo A lost battlefield: the site of the battle of Brunanburh, by H. E. Bryant.

pp Our villages. 5: Fulstow and Marshchapel, by W. Johnson.

qq Lincolnshire town and trade tokens issued in the 17th cent., by A. Smith.

rr City of Lincoln place names, by E. J. Abell.

ss The Jersey school at Lincoln, *c.* 1591–1830: an old-time scheme for relieving unemployment, by J. P. Alexandre.

tt Lincolnshire bells. 2: Church bells of Lincolnshire, by R. Richardson.

uu Lincoln City football club, 1884–1933, by G. H. Grosse.

vv St. Peter-at-Arches, Lincoln, by C. L. Exley.

ww Famous Lincolnshire organs. 3: The organs of St. Wulfram's church, Grantham, by L. Elvin.

xx Remembrance of things past: sixty years ago in a Lincolnshire village [Alvingham, 1872–9], by W. M. Childs.

yy A history of Lincoln school, by C. E. Young.

zz Newstead-on-Archolme priory, by C. L. Exley.

aaa Walesby church, by N. S. Harding.

bbb Ancient glass in Lincolnshire. 3: Tattershall, the history of the glass, by C. Woodforde.

LINGARD SOCIETY

Founded 1909, as the St. Thomas's Historical Research Society, for the encouragement of the study of historical matters of Catholic interest. Refounded in 1916 as the St. Thomas' Historical Society. Title changed to Lingard Society in 1923.

Lingard Papers, nos. 1–4:[1]

2826 No. 1. Regulars and the parochial system in mediaeval England, by E. Beck. Reprinted from the *Dublin Review*. P. 1923.

[1] Not seen.

2827 No. 2. Erasmus, by M. Wilkinson. Reprinted from the *Catholic Historical Review*. P. [1923].

2828 No. 3. Regulars and their appropriated churches in mediaeval England, by E. Beck. Reprinted from the *Catholic Historical Review*. P. [1923].

2829 No. 4. St. Edmund's College, Old Hall, by E. H. Burton. Reprinted from the *Catholic Historical Review*. P. [1923].

Lingard papers, new ser., nos. 1–16:[1]

2830 No. 1. John Lingard, 1771–1851, by J. Fletcher. Reprinted from the *Dublin Review*. P. [1925].

2831 No. 3. Witchcraft in England, by Letitia Fairfield. Reprinted from *The Tablet*. P. [1925].

2832 No. 6. England and the Council of Trent, by H. O. Evennett. Reprinted from the *Dublin Review*. P. [1927].

2833 No. 13. The policy of Henry III's later years [1585–9, particularly towards the Huguenots and Mary, Queen of Scots, with the despatches of Sir Edward Stafford to Walsingham, Burghley, and Queen Elizabeth], by M. Wilkinson. [1932].

2834 No. 14. Saint Dunstan, 909–988, by D. Pontifex. Reprinted from the *Downside Review*. P. [1933].

2835 No. 16. Canon law in mediaeval England, by R. O'Sullivan. Reprinted from the *Clergy Review*. P. [1933?].

LITERARY AND PHILOSOPHICAL SOCIETY OF LIVERPOOL

Founded 1812, for the study of literature, philosophy, the fine arts, natural history, and science.

Proceedings, vols. 55–68 (1901–26):

2836 Vol. 55.

a The birth of new nations during the Victorian reign, by J. M. Moore.

b Charles Lamb, by W. E. Sims.

c Aelfred the Great, king of England 1,000 years ago, by W. Wortley.

d Notes on observations of total solar eclipses, 1851–1900, by R. C. Johnson.

2837 Vol. 56.

a Utilitarianism in England during the 19th cent., by E. A. Wesley.

b Explanation of the origin and date of the heraldic term, coat of arms [including an account of the successive changes in the royal arms from the time of William the Conqueror], by J. B. Nevins.

c The foreign relations of Cromwell with France and Spain, by R. J. A. Shelley.

d Edward Gibbon [d. 1794], by W. E. Sims.

2838 Vol. 57.

a The Washington family [ancestors of George Washington], by A. E. Hawkes.

2839 Vol. 59.

a Cynewulf [9th cent. Saxon poet], by C. W. Stubbs.

b Cromwell in Lancashire, by R. J. A. Shelley.

2840 Vol. 60.

a William Roscoe [d. 1831] as the foster-father and founder of literature and the arts in Liverpool, by J. T. Foard.

[1] No. 12 not seen.

b Macaulay, the reforming Whig, by J. MacCunn.
c Thomas Carlyle, historian, philosopher, man of letters, by W. E. Sims.
d Sir Christopher Hatton [d. 1591], by A. E. Hawkes.
e The Black Death of 1348, by E. A. Wesley.

2841 Vol. 61.

a Walter Pater [d. 1894], by T. L. Dodds.
b Edward Fitzgerald [d. 1883]: a brief review of his life and character, by W. J. B. Ashley.
c The genesis and evolution of law, by B. B. Benas.

2842 Vol. 62.

a Hakluyt and voyages of discovery in Tudor times, by T. L. Dodds.
b The Schoolmen, by E. A. Wesley.

2843 Vol. 63.

a Prehistoric man in the light of recent discoveries, by W. H. Broad.
b The birthplace of Arthur Hugh Clough, by A. W. Newton.

2844 Vol. 65.

a A Liverpool physician and man of letters: James Currie, 1756–1805, by A. W. Newton.
b Human progress in the Christian era, by A. H. Bright.

2845 Vol. 67.

a Sir Anthony Panizzi [d. 1879, principal librarian, British Museum], by A. T. Brown.
b William Roscoe and problems of today, by the Earl of Crawford and Balcarres.
c The Platonic tradition in modern religious thought, by W. R. Inge.

2846 Vol. 68.

a William Blake [d. 1827], by G. W. Mathews.
b The politicians and the press, by Lord Beaverbrook. [The influence of newspapers on 20th cent. English politics, and the achievements of Lord Northcliffe in particular]

2847 An index to the proceedings of the Society, vols. 1–62, comp. A. W. Newton. 1912.

LITERARY AND PHILOSOPHICAL SOCIETY OF NEWCASTLE-UPON-TYNE

Founded 1793, to promote the study of language, literature, philosophy, science, history and the fine arts; and, in particular, to maintain a library, and to provide university extension and other educational lectures and classes for students in connection therewith.

Publications:

2848 Three lectures delivered to the Society on old Newcastle, its suburbs, and gilds, and an essay on Northumberland, by F. W. Dendy. 1921.

LIVERPOOL COMMITTEE FOR EXCAVATION AND RESEARCH IN WALES AND THE MARCHES

Founded 1907, for the full and systematic investigation of the early history of Wales by all the resources of modern historical archaeological science.

Publications:

2849 First annual report, 1908. (1909).

a A recently discovered section of the Roman wall at Chester, with appendices on a Roman concrete foundation in Bridge Street, and on a palaeolithic implement found at Chester, by R. Newstead.
b Preliminary report on some of the forts on the coast of North Wales, between Llandulas [Denbighshire] and the Rivals [Carnarvonshire], and in Anglesey, by H. S. Kingsford.
c Preliminary report on the antiquities of the Cader Idris district, by G. Clinch.
d Report on excavations on the Roman site at Caerleon, Monmouth, 1908, by H. G. Evelyn-White.

LIVERPOOL ECONOMIC AND STATISTICAL SOCIETY

Founded 1903, for the investigation, study, and discussion of economic questions, especially those relating to the trade and social conditions of the district, and generally the advance of economic and statistical science.

Transactions, 1903–14 (8 vols. 1903–14):

2850 Vol. for 1903–4.

a Report on the results of a special inquiry into the conditions of labour at the Liverpool docks [c. 1890–1900], by Eleanor Rathbone.

2851 Vol. for 1904–5.

a 'Dumping' [in the wheat milling industry in Britain, c. 1880–1900], by H. Rathbone.

2852 Vol. for 1905–6.

a Rise and growth of the movement for the protection of children [in the 19th cent. in Britain], by Frances Zanetti.

2853 Vol. for 1913–14.

a The first year's working of the Liverpool Docks Scheme [1912–13], by R. Williams. [Also published separately, 1914]

LIVERPOOL NATURALISTS' FIELD CLUB

Founded 1860, for the practical study of natural history in all its branches.

Proceedings, 1900–32 (33 vols. 1901–33):

2854 Vol. for 1918.

a Presidential address [on the history of plant collecting and herbaria], by W. S. Laverock.

2855 Vol. for 1919.

a Two giants [William Hooker, d. 1865, and Joseph Hooker, d. 1911, naturalists], by W. H. Holt.

2856 Vol. for 1920.

a English church woodwork, by J. J. Lewis.

2857 Vol. for 1921.

a The history and beauty of the Yorkshire dales, by Margaret Hughes.

2858 Vol. for 1923.

a The British Association for the Advancement of Science, by W. S. Laverock. [A brief historical account]

LIVERPOOL PHILOMATHIC SOCIETY

Founded 1825, for the attainment of knowledge by discussion.

Proceedings, vols. 46–77[1] (1901–32):

2859 Vol. 46.

a Annual dinner. [Address on Australian federation by the Earl Carrington]
b The life and works of Oliver Goldsmith, by W. F. Wilson.
c The constitution of the Australian commonwealth, by C. Wilson.
d Queen Elizabeth: her life and character, by F. Salisbury.

2860 Vol. 51.

a Life of a merchant prince [Sir Thomas Gresham] in Tudor times, by T. L. Dodds.

2861 Vol. 53.

a The making of Liverpool, by W. H. Saunders.

2862 Vol. 77.

a The Liverpool Philomathic Society, by C. H. Keet. [Brief selections from its records, 1861–84]

Other publications:

2863 The romance of the British road, by C. F. Elias. *P.* 1923.

2864 Dr. Samuel Johnson as traveller, by C. F. Elias. *P.* 1927.

LIVERPOOL WELSH NATIONAL SOCIETY

Founded 1885.

Transactions, 1900–12 (7 vols. [1901–12]):

2865 Vol. for 1900–1.

a Some Welsh literary curiosities [being a history of Welsh printing, publishing and literature from the 16th cent.], by J. Ballinger.
b Hen Farwriadau Cymru, gan J. Morris-Jones. [Old Welsh elegies sung in praise of Welsh leaders from 7th–19th cent., including Llywelyn the Great and Llywelyn the Last]
c The Welsh gypsies, by J. Sampson.

2866 Vol. for 1901–2.

a Some books of Welsh travel, by T. M. Williams.
b Edward I in Wales, by L. J. Roberts.
c Cymru Fu yn Liverpool yn y 19 ganrif, a chynt, gan R. W. Jones. [The Welsh in Liverpool in the 19th cent. and previously]

2867 Vol. for 1902–3.

a James Howell, the letter-writer, by H. E. Lewis.
b Cyfieithiad o Araith y Barwn Prys yn y Senedd yn erbyn i'r Brenin William III roddi yr Arglwyddiaethau yn Nghymru i'r Arglwydd Portland. [A translation of Robert Price's address given in Parliament against William III's intention to give the Welsh lordships to Lord Portland]

2868 Vol. for 1904–5 and 1908–9.

a Guron: being the result of a search for a lost son of Cenedog or Cunedda I, by O. Rhoscomyl.
b Vicar Prichard of Llandovery, by A. G. Edwards. [Rice Prichard, and the Welsh revivals of the 17th and 18th cent.]
c The roll of the Caerwys Eisteddfod of 1523, with introd. by J. H. Davies.

[1] Vols. 47–50, 54–76, and 78 have not been seen.

2869 Vol. for 1909–10.

a Cymru yn Llenyddiaeth Lloegr, gan T. G. Jones. [The Welsh in English literature, being an analysis of the different interpretations of the Welsh character in English literature, 13th–19th cent.]
b Land and people [being the influence of the geography etc. of Wales on its history], by J. E. Lloyd.
c Y Mabinogion, gan J. C. Morrice. [The Mabinogion]

2870 Vol. for 1910–11 and 1911–12.

a Bosworth Field: an episode of Welsh history [1485], by W. G. Jones.

LLANDUDNO, COLWYN BAY AND DISTRICT FIELD CLUB

Founded 1906, as the Llandudno and District Field Club, to encourage the study of natural history and archaeology, particularly in North Wales. Title changed to the above form in 1923.

Proceedings, vols. 1–17 (1906–33):

2871 Vol. 1.

a Presidential address. 1: The cromlech on the Great Orme. 2: The early Christian inscribed monument [Tyddyn Holland, Llandudno], by W. Gardner.

2872 Vol. 2.

a Puffin Island [an account of the ancient monastery].
b Ancient fortifications and ruins at Bryn Euryn, Llandrillo [yn Rhos] church and monks' chapel.
c Gyffin church and Llangelynin old church.
d Conway church.
e Eglwys Rhos otherwise Llanrhos [an account of the church].
f Deganwy castle.
g Pre-historic remains, Kendrick's cave, Great Ormes head, Llandudno, by G. A. Humphreys.
h Gloddaeth Hall.
i Llanrychwyn church.

2873 Vol. 3.

a Chester [St. John's church, the cathedral, the walls, the Rows].
b Cromlech at Capel Garmon.
c Roman road, Llanfairfechan to Caerhun.
d Penmon priory [Anglesey].
e Plas Mawr [Conway].
f Llanddulas church.
g Early man in Wales, by E. Anwyl.

2874 Vol. 4.

a Maenan Hall and Caer Oleu [prehistoric] camp.
b Visit to Segontium, the Roman city.
c Great Ormes head [being chiefly an account of prehistoric remains there].
d Rhuddlan priory, church, and castle.
e Mostyn Hall.
f Penrhos Lligwy [estate. Includes an account of the cromlech and of Diu Lligwy, Romano-British village].
g Y Corddyn [hill fortress].
h Caer Lleon: hill fortress, or hill-top camp, on Conway mountain.
i St. Tudno's church.
j Bryn Eisteddfod [objects of interest in the house and grounds].
k Llandrillo [yn Rhos] church, Capel Trillo, and the weir.
l Church screens, by G. A. Humphreys.

m Church plate, by G. A. Humphreys.
n Bangor cathedral, by J. R. Dawson.

2875 Vol. 5.

a Visit to Carnarvon castle, by E. Roberts.
b Conway castle, by G. A. Humphreys.
c Caerhun and Llanbedr[-y-Cenin] churches.
d Penrhyn quarries.
e Gwaenysgor church and cave, and the Gop [tumulus].
f Deganwy castle.
g Llanfairfechan churches.
h Sacred wells and fairy waters of Wales, by E. H. Guest.
i The beauty and romance of York, by C. E. Elcock.

2876 Vol. 6.

a Sarn Helen [Roman road from Caernarvon to Carmarthen].
b Gwydir castle, by W. B. Lowe.
c St. Marcellus, Whitchurch, near Denbigh.
d Ancient hill fort on Penygaer, near Llanbedr-y-Cenin.
e Caerhun Hall, and the Roman station of Conovium.
f Dyserth church, castle, and Siamber Wen [the probable ruins of a 13th cent. house].
g Penrhyn Old Hall.
h Llanrwst church and Gwydir chapel, by W. B. Lowe.
i Dolwyddelan church.
j The Mabinogion and its local associations, by Edith Guest.

2877 Vol. 7.

a Llansannan [church and parish].
b Llanelian church and Ffynnon Elian [the Llanelian cursing-well].
c Visit to excavations in the ancient hill fort in Parc-y-Meirch wood, Kinmel park, Abergele.
d Beaumaris castle.
e Tre'r Ceiri [prehistoric fortress].
f Cerrig Saethau (arrow stones), near Llanfairfechan.
g Conway town walls.

2878 Vol. 8.

a Llandegai church.
b Bodelwyddan church.
c St. Asaph cathedral.
d Gwern Engan [hut-circle village] near the Sychnant pass.
e The adventures of the northern party of Captain Scott's Antarctic expedition, 1910–13, by R. E. Priestley.
f Some dolmens of North Wales, by E. N. Baynes.
g Tomen-y-Mur [Roman fort near Caerhun], by H. Hughes.

2879 Vol. 9.

a Braich-y-Dinas [hill-fortress], Penmaenmawr, by H. H. Hughes.
b Llysfaen: notes by the Rev. T. Ll. Jones. [On the capture of Richard II, the parish church, and old homes and families]
c The church of St. Mary, Conway, by H. H. Hughes.

2880 Vol. 10.

a Neolithic stone axes of Graig Lwyd, Penmaenmawr, by H. Warren.
b Some recent discoveries of prehistoric remains in the uplands of north Carnarvonshire, by W. B. Lowe.
c Hut circles and various enclosures on the south-eastern slopes of Moel Faban, near Bethesda, by W. B. Lowe. [Reprinted in vol. 12]
d Notes on the position and distribution of hut circles, etc., in north Carnarvonshire, by W. B. Lowe.
e Notes on the site of Roman and other coins found on the north coast of Wales from Prestatyn to Carnarvon, by W. P. Lowe.

2881 Vol. 11.

a History of Llanddulas, by C. F. Roberts.
b History of Basingwerk abbey, by R. A. Thomas.
c Moel Fammau and Cilcain church, by W. B. Lowe.
d Church, etc., at Clynnog Fawr, by H. H. Hughes.
e Dinas, Llanfairfechan: excavations by the Club: report by H. H. Hughes and W. B. Lowe.
f Llandudno past and present, by F. Holland.
g Some prominent men in connection with the history of Llandudno, by J. Roberts.
h Llanfairfechan terriers [1749 and 1879].

2882 Vol. 12.

a Caer-y-Twr [hill-fortress] and the hut-circles at Ty Mawr on Holyhead mountain, by H. H. Hughes.
b Penmon priory, by G. G. Holme.
c Castell Aber Lleinawg, by G. G. Holme.
d Aberdaron and neighbourhood.
e Special note on Aberdaron church, by G. G. Holme.
f Llansannan, by W. B. Lowe.
g A herbal by William Salesbury, by E. S. Roberts.
h Penrhyn slate quarries, by W. B. Lowe.
i Cochwillan [house], near Llandegai, by H. H. Hughes.
j Welsh church bells, their history and legend, by J. Fisher.
k Life in a Cistercian abbey, by E. W. Lovegrove.
l Gloddaeth and Mostyn in olden times, by Lord Mostyn.
m Llanfairfechan [registers], by W. B. Lowe.

2883 Vol. 13.

a Penmynydd church and the table tomb, and Plas Penmynydd, the home of the Tudors, with a descriptive account of the development of sepulchral monuments from the time of the Norman conquest, and also of the knight's armour and the dress of the lady during this period [11th–15th cent.], with a pedigree of the Tudors of Plas Penmynydd, by G. G. Holme.
b Neolithic caves at Perthi Chwareu, near Llandegla.
c Excursion to Dwygyfylchi.
d Denbigh castle, by W. J. Hemp.
e Caer Lleion, or the fort on Conway mountain.
f Roman coins, by E. Davies.
g Prehistoric remains at Bryn Newydd, Prestatyn, by G. Smith.
h Prehistoric finds at Prestatyn, by G. Smith.

2884 Vol. 14.

a Puffin Island: the ancient remains, by H. H. Hughes.
b Llaniestyn and Llanfihangel churches, by G. G. Holmes.
c History of Flint castle, by W. J. Hemp.
d Ewloe castle, by W. J. Hemp.
e Hawarden (Penarlag) castle, by B. Jones.
f Excursion over the Penmaenmawr uplands.
g Pre-Norman work and its influence in North Wales, by H. H. Hughes. [An account of stone-carvings, particularly those on crosses]

2885 Vol. 15.

a Llanrhychwyn church, by H. H. Hughes.
b Llanbadrig church, by G. G. Holme.
c Capel Curig churches, by T. D. Jones.
d Valle Crucis abbey, by G. G. Holme.
e St. Asaph, by J. Fisher.
f Llaneilian church, by G. G. Holme.
g Llanfairfechan churches [St. Mary's parish church and Christ church], by H. L. North.
h Whitford [Whitford church, Maen Achwyfan, an inscribed stone, and inscribed stone at Downing Hall].
i Tre'r Ceiri [prehistoric fortress], Llanaelhaiarn.
j Caerhun. [A brief account of excavations on the site of the Roman fort of Kanovium]

k Ruthin, by J. Fisher.
l The ancient forts of Wales, by H. Higgins.
m The stone forts of Wales: who erected them?, by H. Higgins.

2886 Vol. 16.

a Llanrhychwyn church, by H. Higgins.
b Llangadwaladr church, Anglesey, by G. G. Holme.
c Aberffraw church, by G. G. Holme.
d Chirk castle, by C. E. Cope.
e Whitchurch, Denbigh [an account of the parish church], by C. A. R. Radford.
f Denbigh castle and town walls, by C. A. R. Radford.
g Denbigh friary, by C. A. R. Radford.
h The pre-Norman forts of eastern Wales (earthen), by H. Higgins.
i Sidelights on the pigmy [flint implements] workshop discovered at Prestatyn, by F. G. Smith.
j Kanovium [Roman fort near Conway], by P. K. B. Reynolds.
k The old turnpike, Penmaenmawr, by I. E. Davies.

2887 Vol. 17.

a Ffynnon Elian [St. Elian's well] and Llanelian church.
b Llanfair-yn-y-Cwmmwd church.
c Newborough church.
d Harlech castle and Tomen y Mur [Roman fort].
e Tomen y Rhodwydd [earthwork, c. 12th cent.] and Llanarmon church.
f Origin and ethnological composition of the Welsh people, by H. Higgins.
g Concerning currency, by F. G. Smith.
h Talacre and the Viking grave.
i Henllan church, Plas Heaton cave, tumulus and beaker.
j Beaumaris church and castle.
k Dinas Dinorwic [prehistoric fort].
l Church of St. Mary Magdalene, Gwaenysgor, Flintshire, by H. H. Hughes.
m The single ramparted defensive enclosures of Wales, by H. Higgins.
n The caves of North Wales [and their prehistoric remains], by J. W. Jackson.
o Old cottages at Dwygyfylchi and their associations, by I. E. Davies.

LODGE OF RESEARCH, No. 2429, LEICESTER

Founded 1892, for the publication of papers upon the history, antiquities, and symbols of the craft.

Transactions, 1902–33[1] (32 vols. 1903–33):

2888 Vol. for 1902–3.

a Catalogue of a collection of masonic curios belonging to the Freemasons' Hall, Leicester.
b Craft ritual [including its history], by W. B. Hextall.
c Masonic musicians and music, by W. H. Griffiths.

2889 Vol. for 1903–4.

a Masonic tracing-boards, by E. A. T. Breed.
b Freemasonry from 1600 to the Grand Lodge era [1717]: a sketch of the transition period, by W. J. Hughan.
c The Hiramic legend and the Ashmolean theory [an account of the history of the third degree in freemasonry], by W. B. Hextall.
d A review of the Transactions of the Lodge of Research from 1893 onwards, by G. D. Potts.

  [1] Vols. for 1900–1 and 1901–2 have not been seen.

2890 Vol. for 1904–5.

a Browning and freemasonry, by J. M. Dow.

2891 Vol. for 1905–6.

a The cathedral masons: a review of the Norwich records, by W. H. Jones.

2892 Vol. for 1906–7.

a Additional masonic degrees worked in England, by W. J. Hughan.
b Village freemasonry a century ago [in the 'Derbyshire' lodge constituted at Buxton, 1810, and the 'Lodge of Unity' constituted at Longnor in 1811], by S. Taylor.
c Freemasonry and Bacon's 'New Atlantis', by F. W. Billson.

2893 Vol. for 1907–8.

a The Royal Arch chapter of charity, Bristol, by C. Powell.
b History of freemasonry, by J. Johnstone.
c Some interesting masonic relics [including a report of a meeting of the Grand Lodge of England in 1732], by J. T. Thorp.
d Early literature of freemasonry, by G. W. Bain.

2894 Vol. for 1908–9.

a The guild merchant and other guilds and freemasonry, by S. P. Pick.
b Notes from the early proceedings of 'The Old King' Arms' lodge, no. 28 [London], by H. Hyde.
c Interesting items from the early records of 'St. Paul's' lodge, no. 43 [Birmingham], by G. D. Potts.
d William Hogarth and freemasonry, by W. B. Hextall.
e Freemasons' Hall, Leicester [erected 1859], by J. T. Thorp.

2895 Vol. for 1909–10.

a Some past and passing customs of the freemasons, by J. T. Thorp.

2896 Vol. for 1910–11.

a Freemasonry in the Leicestershire (17th) regiment, by W. Thomas. [Supplementary article in vol. for 1926–7.]
b Some incidents in the history of the Provincial Grand Lodge of Leicestershire and Rutland, by F. W. Billson.

2897 Vol. for 1911–12.

a Lodge no. 94 at the Ben Jonson's Head [Spitalfields, London], by J. T. Thorp.
b A masonic triad [William Preston, d. 1818; William Hutchinson, d. 1814; Dr. George Oliver, d. 1867], by W. B. Hextall.

2898 Vol. for 1912–13.

a Freemasonry as illustrated [by portraits] on the walls of the Freemasons' Hall, Leicester, by F. W. Billson.
b The office of grand steward, by A. Lole.
c Notes on the Leicestershire and Rutland masonic calendar, 1873–1913, by H. S. Biggs.

2899 Vol. for 1913–14.

a The masonic Union of 1813, by F. W. Billson.

2900 Vol. for 1914–15.

a The evolution of the masonic year-book, by J. T. Thorp,
b The masonic poem of c. 1390: a modernised transcript and some notes, by R. H. Baxter.

2901 Vol. for 1915–16.

a The consecration of lodge no. 336 [Plymouth], in 1808, by J. T. Thorp.
b Masonic music and musicians of the province of Leicestershire and Rutland, by W. J. Bunney.

2902 Vol. for 1916–17.

  a The Provincial Grand Mark lodge of Leicestershire and Rutland, by H. S. Biggs. [Contd. in vol. for 1917–18]

2903 Vol. for 1917–18.

  a Royal Arch masonry, by J. T. Thorp.

  b The Lodge of Research, no. 2429 (1892–1917): looking back and looking forwards, by J. T. Thorp.

  c The freemasons' 'pocket companions' of the 18th cent., by J. T. Thorp.

2904 Vol. for 1918–19.

  a Chapters from the history of the 'Howe and Charnwood' lodge, no. 1007 [Loughborough], 1864–89, by F. G. Fleeman.

2905 Vol. for 1919–20.

  a Augustus Frederick, Duke of Sussex, 1773–1843, by W. B. Hextall.

2906 Vol. for 1921–2.

  a Excerpts from the records of the Westminster and Keystone lodge, no. 10, by G. D. Potts.

  b Early Leicester freemasonry, by J. T. Thorp.

2907 Vol. for 1922–3.

  a Bibliography of Leicester freemasonry, by J. T. Thorp.

2908 Vol. for 1923–4.

  a On masons' marks in particular, and medieval craftsmen's marks in general, by W. N. Cheesman.

  b Livery companies of London, by J. H. Morton.

2909 Vol. for 1924–5.

  a The company of Masons of the city of London, by G. W. Daynes. [Contd. in vol. for 1925–6]

2910 Vol. for 1925–6.

  a The provincial grand masters of Leicestershire and Rutland, by F. G. Fleeman.

2911 Vol. for 1926–7.

  a Masonic emblems and symbols in Freemasons' Hall Leicester, by J. T. Thorp.

  b Was Robert Southey a freemason?, by W. J. Williams.

2912 Vol. for 1928–9.

  a The early years of the Grand Lodge of England, by G. W. Daynes.

  b Sir Christopher Wren—a wonderful freemason, by E. J. Liddiard.

  c Thoughts on the evolution of freemasonry, by G. B. Ellwood.

2913 Vol. for 1929–30.

  a Historical notes on Mark Grand Lodge and the Provincial Grand Mark Lodge of Leicestershire, by H. S. Biggs.

2914 Vol. for 1930–1.

  a The names of some Leicester lodges and their mottoes, by A. L. Macleod.

2915 Vol. for 1931–2.

  a Notes on the life of W. Bro. William Kelly, P.P.G.M. of Leicestershire and Rutland, by M. D. R. Richardson.

    Masonic Papers, nos. 1–5, by J. T. Thorp. (5 pts. 1901–15, being 'addenda' to the Transactions):

2916 No. 1.

  a George, 2nd Lord Rancliffe, provincial grand master of Leicestershire, 1812–50.

  b The Masonic Benefit Society of 1799.

  c Rev. Samuel Oliver [d. 1847].

2917 No. 2.

  a Exclusive private lodges.

  b The [fifth] Duke of Rutland's statue, Leicester.

  c The entered apprentice's song.

  d The engraved lists of lodges [issued annually 1723–78].

2918 No. 3.

  a Freemasonry in Leicestershire and Rutland.

2919 No. 4.

  a Warrant of lodge, no. 87 'Antients', held in the Leicestershire militia, 1761.

  b Freemasonry parodied in 1754 by Slade's *Free Mason examined*.

2920 No. 5.

  a The Triangular lodge at Rushton [Northants.].

  b Edward Oakley, architect, M.M. [fl. 1732].

  c The Royal Arch certificate of Admiral Sir Sidney Smith.

    Masonic Reprints: reproductions of masonic manuscripts, books, and pamphlets, with notes, vols. 1–14, ed. J. T. Thorp, 1907–31, being supplements to the Transactions:

2921 Vol. 1. *Masonry Dissected* [a pamphlet compiled and published by Samuel Prichard in 1730. See also vol. 12 below]; *A Defence of Masonry* [a pamphlet written by Martin Clare, 1730, in answer to the above]. 1907.

2922 Vol. 2. *Bruin in the Suds*, 1751 ['a poetical narrative' of an incident involving a vintner and a lodge of freemasons]. 1919.

2923 Vol. 3. *The Freemason's Accusation and Defence*, 1726 [an anonymous pamphlet attacking freemasonry]. 1920.

2924 Vol. 5. *Freemasonry the High-way to Hell*, 1768 [an anonymous pamphlet attacking freemasonry]; *Masonry the Turnpike-road to Happiness*, 1768 [an anonymous pamphlet written in answer to the above]. 1922.

2925 Vol. 6. *The Secrets of the Free-masons Revealed by a Disgusted Brother*, 1759 [an anonymous pamphlet attacking freemasonry]. 1923.

2926 Vol. 7. *The Complete Freemason, or Multa Paucis for Lovers of Secrets*, 1763–64 [mainly a history of freemasonry]. 1924.

2927 Vol. 8. *A Master-key to Freemasonry*, 1760 [an anonymous 'exposure' of freemasonry]. 1925.

2928 Vol. 9. *Rite ancien de Bouillon*: an old English ritual, 1740?. 1926.

2929 Vol. 10. *The Free Mason Examined*, 1754 [by Alexander Slade]. 1927.

2930 Vol. 11. *Solomon in All his Glory*, 1768 [an anonymous 'exposure' of freemasonry]. 1928.

2931 Vol. 12. *Masonry Dissected*, 1730 [a complete reproduction of the pamphlet a few pages of which were reprinted in vol. 1 above]. 1929.

    Other publications:

2932 History of freemasonry in Ashby-de-la-Zouch, 1809–1909, by J. T. Thorp. 1909. [Published as an 'addendum' to the *Transactions* for 1908–9]

2933 Bibliography of masonic catechisms and exposures [1717–1853], comp. J. T. Thorp. [Published as a supplement to the *Transactions* for 1928–9]

2934 Lodge no. 47, Macclesfield, 1764–1800, afterwards the Knights of Malta lodge, no. 50, Hinckley: historical notes and extracts from its book of minutes, comp. J. T.

Thorp. 1930. [Published as an 'addendum' to the *Transactions* for 1929–30]

2935 Origin of the English rite of freemasonry, especially in relation to the Royal Arch degree, by W. J. Hughan, ed. J. T. Thorp. New and revised edn. 1909, 3rd edn. 1925.

2936 Memorials of the masonic Union of 1813 consisting of an introduction on freemasonry in England, the articles of union, constitutions of the United Grand Lodge of England, 1815, and other official documents, etc., comp. W. J. Hughan, revised and augmented edition by J. T. Thorp. 1913.

LODGE QUATUOR CORONATI, No. 2076, LONDON

Founded 1884, to promote and diffuse the genuine principles of the art.

Ars Quatuor Coronatorum, being the Transactions of the Lodge, vols. 14–44 (1901–34):

2937 Vol. 14.
a The Alnwick lodge minutes [18th cent.], by W. H. Rylands.
b The miracle play, by E. Conder.
c Antony Sayer [d. 1741, first 'Grand Master of Masons'], by A. F. Calvert.

2938 Vol. 15.
a The building of Culham bridge [Berks., 15th cent.], by W. H. Rylands.
b Bro. Samuel Beltz, deputy assistant commissary general to the forces, 1783–1862, by E. A. Ebblewhite.
c Charter incorporating the trades of Gateshead, 1671, by W. H. Rylands.
d The old Swalwell lodge [co. Durham] and the harodim, by J. Yarker.
e Notes upon the craft guilds of Norwich with particular reference to the masons, by J. C. Tingey.
f Extracts from records of the corporation of Norwich [16th cent.], by W. Rye.

2939 Vol. 16.
a Notes on the legends of masonry, by W. H. Rylands.
b The degrees of pure and ancient freemasonry, by R. F. Gould.
c William of Wykeham, bishop of Winchester: architect and statesman, by E. Conder.
d Order of St. John of Jerusalem, England, by W. H. Rylands. [Various certificates etc. dating from 1826]
e Chichester [masonic] certificates, 18th cent., by J. T. Thorp.

2940 Vol. 17.
a Minutes of an extinct lodge [the Royal Sussex lodge, no. 720, 1820–32], by E. A. T. Breed.
b An account [of the expense] of rebuilding the cathedral church of St. Paul's, London, by J. W. Horsley.
c A glance at the records of two extinct Hull lodges [the Rodney lodge, no. 436, 1819–20, and the Phoenix lodge, no. 368, 1817–31], by G. L. Shackles.
d British Museum mss. relating to accounts of St. Paul's cathedral, by A. Oliver.

2941 Vol. 18.
a The Rev. Dr. [James] Anderson's non-masonic writings, 1712–39, by W. J. C. Crawley.
b Brother Moses Mendez, grand steward, 1738, by J. P. Simpson.

c Mock masonry in the 18th cent., by W. J. C. Crawley.
d A newly discovered version of the old charges [c. 1740], by F. W. Levander.
e Contemporary comments on the freemasonry of the 18th cent., by W. J. C. Crawley.

2942 Vol. 19.
a Old city taverns and masonry, by J. P. Simpson.
b A few historic notes relating to the Lodge of Prudent Brethren, no. 145 [18th–19th cent.], by H. Guy.
c J. Morgan and his *Phoenix Britannicus* [issued in periodical form, 1731], by H. Sirr. [See also vol. 26 below]
d Notes on the grand chaplains [of the grand masonic lodges] of England, by J. W. Horsley.
e Notes on some 18th cent. masonic documents, by F. E. Clarke.

2943 Vol. 20.
a John Cole [fl. 1788–1810, copper-plate printer], by W. J. Songhurst.
b Old London taverns and masonry, by J. P. Simpson.
c Proceedings against the Templars in France and England for heresy, etc., 1307–11, taken from the official documents of the period, by E. J. Castle.
d Notes on the metal work of St. Paul's cathedral, London, and Jean Tijou's designs and ironwork therein, by C. J. R. Tijou.
e The Great lodge, Swaffham, Norfolk, 1764–85, by H. Le Strange.

2944 Vol. 21.
a Some old [London] suburban taverns and masonry, by J. P. Simpson.
b Two editors of the *Book of Constitutions* [Rev. John Entick, d. 1773, and John Noorthouck, d. 1816], by E. L. Hawkins.
c Notes on the Society of Gregorians [18th cent.], by W. H. Rylands.
d The Henery Heade ms., 1675 [a copy of an old masonic charge], by E. L. Hawkins.
e The Taylor ms. [17th cent. masonic documents], by W. Watson.
f Early masons' contracts at Durham [1488], by E. H. Dring.
g Henry Yvele, the king's master mason, 1320–1400, by W. Wonnacott.

2945 Vol. 22.
a Notes concerning the masons' guild and the Marquis of Granby lodge of freemasons in the city of Durham, by H. Brown.
b The earliest years of English organized freemasonry, by A. F. Robbins.
c Notes on freemasonry in Cambridgeshire in the 18th cent., by A. R. Hill.
d Two old Oxford lodges [Lodge of Alfred in the university of Oxford, 1769–90, and the Constitution lodge, 1770–1789], by E. L. Hawkins.

2946 Vol. 23.
a Dr. [James] Anderson, [first compiler] of the *Constitutions*, by A. F. Robbins.
b The special Lodge of Promulgation, 1809–11, by W. B. Hextall.
c A chapter from the early history of the Royal Naval lodge, no. 59, by J. W. Horsley.
d The craft and its orphans in the 18th cent. [schools for orphans, etc., founded by freemasons], by W. J. C. Crawley.
e The Lodge of Reconciliation, 1813–16, by W. Wonnacott.

2947 Vol. 24.

a The old charges [of a freemason] and the Papal bulls [condemning them, 1738–1825], by W. J. C. Crawley.

b The Good Samaritans or Ark Masons in politics; with a note on some of their members, by J. C. Brookhouse. [An Ipswich society and the 1790 election]

c Summer outing, 1911, Wells and Glastonbury, by F. R. Taylor. [Includes descriptions of St. Cuthbert's church, Bishop Bubwith's almshouses, the cathedral and palace at Wells, and the abbey at Glastonbury]

2948 Vol. 25.

a The Jerusalem Sols and some other London societies of the 18th cent., by F. W. Levander.

b Notes on some masonic personalities at the end of the 18th cent., by G. P. G. Hills.

c Dr. Richard Rawlinson [d. 1755] and the masonic entries in Elias Ashmole's diary, by J. E. S. Tuckett.

d Summer outing, 1912. Headquarters: Newcastle-upon-Tyne, by F. R. Taylor. [Includes descriptions of various buildings etc. in Newcastle including the ancient bridge, the medieval walls, St. Andrew's church, the cathedral and the castle; also a description of Hexham abbey]

e Inaugural address [a survey of English printed masonic literature to 1750], by E. H. Dring.

2949 Vol. 26.

a The evolution of masonic ritual, by E. L. Hawkins.

b Further light on J. Morgan of the *Phoenix Britannicus*, by J. E. S. Tuckett. [See also vol. 19 above]

c Notes on the Rainsford papers in the British Museum, by G. P. G. Hills. [Correspondence and papers of General Charles Rainsford, d. 1809]

d Summer outing. East Sussex, by F. R. Taylor. [Includes descriptions of various places in Hastings, and of Battle abbey]

2950 Vol. 27.

a Some old time [18th cent.] clubs and societies, by W. B. Hextall.

b Orders and regulations for the company of Masons of the city of London in 1481 and the feast of the Quatuor Coronati, by E. Conder.

c The masonic certificates of Robert Partridge [d. 1817], by H. Le Strange.

d The story of the craft [i.e. freemasonry] as told in the *Gentleman's Magazine*, 1731–1820, by F. Armitage.

2951 Vol. 28.

a The *Collectanea* of the Rev. Daniel Lysons, F.R.S., F.S.A. [d. 1834], by F. W. Levander. [Contd. in vol. 29]

b Martin Clare and the *Defence of Masonry*, 1731, by W. Wonnacott.

c The Beswicke-Royds masonic ms. of the old charges [17th cent.]: an exact typographical reproduction with a short description, by R. H. Baxter.

2952 Vol. 29.

a The Friendly Society of Free and Accepted Masons [established 1737], by W. Wonnacott.

b The Worshipful Society of Apothecaries: a short sketch of the history of the society, by T. Carr.

c Sidelights on freemasonry from the autobiographies of John Britton, F.S.A. (1771–1857), and the Rev. Richard Warner (1763–1857), by G. P. G. Hills.

d 'Orator' [John] Henley, M.A., 1692–1756, by W. B. Hextall.

e John Wilkes, 1727–97, by A. F. Calvert.

2953 Vol. 30.

a The advent of Royal Arch masonry, by W. R. Kelly.

b A comparison of the regulations laid down in the *Book of Constitutions*, 1723–1819, by F. W. Levander.

c Admiral Sir William Sidney Smith, G.C.B. [d. 1840]: his naval career and other activities, by G. P. G. Hills.

d Charles, 2nd Duke of Richmond (grand master 1724–5) and some of his masonic associates, by W. Wonnacott.

2954 Vol. 31.

a The old charges and the ritual, by R. H. Baxter.

b An account of the minutes of the Royal lodge, 1777–1817, by G. P. G. Hills.

c An early will [dated 1725] of Philip, Duke of Wharton, by J. T. Thorp.

d List of articles contained in Ars Quatuor Coronatorum, vols. 1–30, with an enumeration and roll of authors, comp. R. H. Baxter.

2955 Vol. 32.

a Lodge no. 20, Antients [1753–6], by W. J. Songhurst.

b Notes on some trade guilds at Ludlow, by T. J. Salwey.

2956 Vol. 33.

a Fresh material for classifying the old charges, by H. G. Rosedale.

b Summer outing, 1920. Bristol and Malmesbury. [Includes a summary of a lecture on the history of Bristol and descriptions of the cathedral, Red Lodge, Temple church and St. Mary Redcliffe church, at Bristol, Sherston church, Malmesbury abbey, and Beverston castle and church]

2957 Vol. 34.

a The Sheffield Masonic Benefit Society [1804–34], by J. Stokes.

b The 'Colne' manuscripts of the old charges, by E. B. Beesley.

2958 Vol. 35.

a Summer outing, 1922. Sheffield. [Includes descriptions of Chesterfield parish church, Worksop priory, Roche abbey, Sheffield cathedral and Manor Lodge, and an account of the Corporation of Cutlers of Hallamshire, i.e. Sheffield]

b Notes on some Sheffield masonic worthies [James Woollen, d. 1814, John Richardson, d. 1840, and Godfrey Fox, d. 1833], by J. Stokes.

2959 Vol. 36.

a Notes on the trade companies of Kendal in the 16th and 17th centuries, by H. Poole.

b Anderson's *Constitutions* of 1723, by L. Vibert.

c Summer outing, 1923. Bath and neighbourhood. [Includes a description of St. Aldhelm's church, Bradford-on-Avon, by A. Y. Mayell]

d Notes upon the reports of the Historical Manuscripts Commission [containing material relevant to freemasonry], by G. W. Daynes.

60 Vol. 37.

a Masonic ritual and secrets before 1717, by H. Poole.

b The craft in the 18th cent.; old time manners and customs; reminiscences of a bi-centenary lodge: Old Dundee lodge [London], 1722–1924, by A. Heiron.

c Mr. Anthony Sayer, gentleman, first grand master of masons, 1717, by J. W. Hobbs.

2961 Vol. 38.

a The antiquity of the third degree [in freemasonry], by G. W. Bullamore.

b Alexander Pope [d. 1744] and freemasonry, by W. J. Williams.

c Some records of the lodge constituted at the Maid's Head, Norwich, in 1724, by G. W. Daynes.

2962 Vol. 39.

a St. John's lodge, no. 583, Henley-in-Arden, 1791–1811, by T. M. Carter.
b Masters' lodges, by A. Heiron.

2963 Vol. 40.

a Masonic song and verse of the 18th cent., by H. Poole.
b Masonic personalia, 1723–39: freemasons named in the Grand Lodge minute books, 1723–39, whose names also appear in the *Dictionary of National Biography*—a comparison showing probable identities, comp. W. J. Williams.
c The travelling masons and cathedral builders [10th–14th cent.], by J. W. Hobbs.
d Summer outing, 1927. Oxford. [Includes a history of freemasonry in Oxford and a list of Oxford wills and administrations of deceased freemasons, 1581–1730, comp. W. J. Williams]
e The [charter of] incorporation of the company of Freemasons, Carpenters, Joiners and Slaters of the city of Oxford, 12 Nov. 1604. [Transcript]
f Early freemasonry in the west of England as exemplified in Bath, Bristol and Exeter, by G. Norman.

2964 Vol. 41.

a Provincial warrants [i.e. warrants constituting a lodge issued by provincial grand masters], by T. M. Carter. [Contd. in vol. 42]
b Archbishop Becket and the Masons' company of London, by W. J. Williams.
c The Rev. Samuel Hemming [d. 1828], S.G.W. 1816, G.C. 1817, master of Lodge of Reconciliation, 1813–16, master of Lodge of Harmony: his life and work as citizen, schoolmaster and mason, comp. J. Johnstone.
d Summer outing, 1928. Exeter. [Includes a lecture on the history of Exeter by H. Lloyd-Parry and a paper on early freemasonry in Exeter by L. Vibert]
e The charter of incorporation of carpenters, masons, joiners, glaziers and painters of Exeter, 29 Mar. 1586. [Transcript]

2965 Vol. 42.

a Gild of masons at Lincoln, by W. J. Williams.
b Notes on the *Freemasons' Magazine or General and Complete Library*, a masonic periodical at the end of the 18th cent., by G. Elkington.
c Summer outing, 1929. Leeds. [Includes a sketch of the history of masonry in Leeds in the 18th cent., by H. Poole]
d Gild resemblances in the old ms. charges, by D. Knoop.

2966 Vol. 43.

a Freemasonry in Lewes [Suss.], prior to the union, by I. Grantham.
b The king's master masons [1243–1717], by W. J. Williams. [Includes a transcript of the charter of the Worshipful Company of Masons, 1677]

2967 Vol. 44.

a The first three years of the building of Vale Royal abbey [Cheshire], 1278–80: a study in operative masonry, by D. Knoop.
b Records of the 'Orthes' lodge in the Royal Warwickshire regiment of Foot, by S. J. Fenton.
c Freemasonry in Sheffield in the 18th cent., by D. Flather.
d Notes on three early documents relating to masons:
(i) A Vale Royal abbey building contract of 1359;
(ii) The sheriff of York's expenses taking masons [i.e. in

impressing masons], 1363; (iii) Wage list of the York minster masons, 1472, by D. Knoop and G. P. Jones.

Other publications:

2968 Quatuor coronatorum antigrapha. Masonic reprints of the Lodge, vol. 10. 1913.

a Minutes of the Grand Lodge of freemasons of England, 1723–39, with introd. and notes by W. J. Songhurst.

LONDON AND MIDDLESEX ARCHAEOLOGICAL SOCIETY

Founded 1855, to collect and publish archaeological information relating to the cities of London and Westminster, and the counties of London and Middlesex.

Transactions, new ser., vols. 1–7 (1892–1937):

2969 Vol. 1.

a Thirty-six years' work of the London and Middlesex Archaeological Society, by C. Welch.
b The palaces or town houses of the bishops of London, by W. S. Simpson.
c St. Paul's cathedral and its early literary associations, by C. Welch.
d Mercers' school, by J. Watney.
e History of the Innholders' company, by J. D. Mathews.
f Some account of the lord mayors and sheriffs of London during the 16th cent., by G. E. Cokayne.
g The ancient records and antiquities of the parishes of St. Swithin, London Stone, and St. Mary Bothaw, by J. G. White.
h St. James Garlickhithe, by H. D. Macnamara.
i Historical sketch of the Pewterers' company, by C. Welch.
j Discoveries made during the excavation for the foundation of the Safe Deposit Bank, Chancery Lane, by J. Sachs.
k St. Michael's church, Wood Street, by P. Norman.
l Notes on the records and history of the parish of St. Michael, Wood Street, by J. Christie.
m The Anglo-Saxon settlement round London and glimpses of Anglo-Saxon life in and near it, by T. W. Shore.
n Short account of Christ's Hospital, Newgate Street, by E. H. Pearce.
o Some account of the antique plate belonging to Christ's Hospital, by H. D. Ellis.
p The old parish church at Harmondsworth, by J. C. Taylor.
q A fragment of the Roman wall discovered in the Old Bailey, by J. Terry.
r A bastion of the wall of London in Cripplegate churchyard, by J. Terry.
s Enquiry as to the name of St. Mary Axe, by S. Darby.
t Anglo-Saxon London and its neighbourhood, by T. W. Shore.
u Certain neglected facts relating to English authors buried in St. Saviour's, Southwark, by F. G. Fleay.
v Notes on Pinner church and parish, by C. E. Grenside.
w History and antiquities of the Society of Apothecaries, by C. Welch.
x The crypts of the Guildhall, by W. R. Lethaby.
y The Ironmongers' company, its hall, records, plate, library, etc., by E. H. Nicholl.
z City archaeology: a retrospect and a glance forward, by C. Welch.

2970 Vol. 2.

a London's first conduit system: a topographical survey, by A. M. Davies.

j Roman London: Cheapside [excavations], by W. Martin.

k The Clerks' well: notes on the ancient well and the adjacent retaining wall of the Benedictine nunnery of St. Mary, Clerkenwell; the parish clerks and the plays they played at Clerks' well; Fagge's well and the Fackeswell brook, Cow cross, Smithfield, by A. Crow.

l Ralph Rowlet, goldsmith of London [d. 1571], by C. A. Bradford.

m The Sheldon tapestry map of London and vicinity [late 16th cent.], by W. Martin.

n A rediscovered Putney relic: an inscribed mounting-block, by W. Johnson.

o The roof of the hall of the Middle Temple and its repairs, by W. Martin.

p Stow commemoration, 1924: address by W. Martin.

q Pottery from Nicholas Lane, E.C., by E. Yates and A. G. K. Hayter.

r History of the Whitechapel bell-foundry, by A. D. Tyssen.

s The stone of destiny [in the coronation chair, Westminster abbey], by W. Martin.

t The making of Middlesex: its villages, fields and roads, by Sir M. Sharpe.

u The Mitre tavern in Fenchurch Street: a favourite house of Samuel Pepys, by K. Rogers.

v Clitterhouse manor, Cricklewood, Hendon, by F. Hitchin-Kemp.

w The Goose and Gridiron, St. Paul's Churchyard, by W. J. Williams. [Inn, demolished 1894]

x Exchequer documents relative to Shakespeare's residence in Southwark, by M. S. Giuseppi.

y Wyllyott's manor [Potters Bar], by A. H. Seabrook.

z Stow commemoration, 1925: address by C. L. Kingsford.

aa A link in the early history of London, by H. Sands. [Based on the pipe roll for 1130. Contd. in vol. 6]

bb Roman remains: Lombard Street—Gracechurch Street, by W. Martin.

cc Roman London: Brook's Yard [Upper Thames St.]: St. Mary's [*recte* St. Peter's, Paul's Wharf] churchyard; test-boring for St. Paul's.

dd A forgotten chapter in local history: St. Andrew's Holborn [and the extra-parochiality of the inns of court and chancery], by H. I. Whitaker.

ee The Old Hall of Lincoln's Inn, by W. Martin.

ff Stow commemoration, 1926: address by W. C. Edwards.

gg The Black friars in London: a chapter in national history, by W. Martin; architectural description by S. Toy.

hh A 17th cent. 'L.C.C.', by N. G. Brett-James. [Conflicts between the City corporation and the suburbs]

ii Huguenot Westminster, by W. H. Manchée.

jj Some ancient inns in Friday Street, by K. Rogers.

kk The mending of the Brynt bridge [at Hanwell, 1530], by Sir M. Sharpe and H. F. Westlake.

ll Mary, Queen of Scots and her execution. 1: Tradition and the Middle Temple, by W. Martin. 2: The execution, by J. Douglas. 3: Middle Temple ms. catalogued as 'Reports of cases by Bridgeman and Brock', by J. W. Gordon.

mm Latin in 'taphology', by Hilda Johnstone. [On the epitaph carved on the tomb of Bishop John Robinson, d. 1723, in Fulham parish churchyard]

nn Chancery Lane: Sir Nicholas Bacon's estate, by G. J. Turner.

oo 17th cent. house at Camberwell, by S. Toy.

pp Mr. Samuel Pepys, by Sir D'A. Power.

2974 Vol. 6.

a The parish and church of St. Martin Outwich, Threadneedle Street, by C. W. F. Goss.

b Notes on the history and topography of the Temple, London, by W. Martin.

c A speculative London builder of the 17th cent., Dr. Nicholas Barbon [d. 1698], by N. G. Brett-James. [See also 'Notes and queries' in this vol.]

d Benefactors' shields of arms in the nave of Westminster abbey, by J. B. Williamson.

e Judge Jeffreys' house in Aldermanbury: an historic City mansion, by M. M. Balfour.

f Two plans of the precinct and adjoining property of St. Mary Graces, by Marjorie B. Honeybourne.

g Blackfriars and *The Times*, by W. Martin. [On fragments of the Dominican priory discovered in Printing-house Square]

h John Stow commemoration. [Address by W. Bell]

i Sir Paul Pindar [d. 1650] and his Bishopsgate mansion, by C. W. F. Goss.

j The White Hart, Bishopsgate, by C. W. F. Goss.

k The London bills of mortality in the 17th cent., by N. G. Brett-James.

l Eton College property in Hampstead and adjacent parishes, by F. Marcham. [Transcript of 1755 survey]

m Court rolls of Hornsey [after 1603, described, with extracts], by W. McB. Marcham.

n London in 1689–90, from a ms. [by the Rev. Robert Kirk, d. 1692], transcribed by D. Maclean. [Contd. in vol. 7]

o List of Middlesex knights of the shire, 1295–1832. [See also 'Notes and queries' in this vol.]

p Sir Richard de Wyndesore [d. 1326], of Stanwell, by C. O. Banks.

q Notes on the Inner Temple gate house, by P. Norman.

r John Stow commemoration service. [Address by N. G. Brett-James]

s An account of the London and Middlesex Archaeological Society, 1855–1930, by C. W. F. Goss.

t Short history of the site of the Law Society's hall [Chancery Lane], by P. W. Chandler.

u Statue of King Charles I at Charing Cross, by H. G. Denoon.

v The Westminster guildhall and sanctuary.

w St. Andrew Undershaft, by P. M. Johnston.

x Sir Rowland Hayward [d. 1593], by Winifred Jay. [With transcripts of documents connected with his career]

y John Stow commemoration service. [Address by Sir M. Sharpe]

z Some extents and surveys of Hendon, by N. G. Brett-James. [With Latin transcript of a 1321 survey and the English version of the same made in 1606. Contd., with transcript of a 1574 survey, several maps, and 14th cent. farm accounts from Westminster abbey mss., in vol. 7]

aa Muswell Farm, or Clerkenwell Detached, by F. W. M. Draper.

bb St. Mary's church, Finchley, by E. H. Rann.

cc The White Bear, Cheapside.

2975 Vol. 7.

a Middlesex parishes and their antiquity, by Sir M. Sharpe.

b Earliest Ruislip, by H. Braun.

c William Dodington: a tragedy of St. Sepulchre's, Holborn, 1600, by C. A. Bradford.

d The extent of Edgeware, 1277, by D. G. Denoon and T. Roberts.

e Four eras in the Middlesex area [the prehistoric age, the Roman period, at the time of Domesday book, and at the end of the 19th century], by Sir M. Sharpe.

f Lord Ranelagh's house in Chelsea: an unrecorded work by Sir Christopher Wren, by C. G. T. Dean.

g The hundred of Gore and its moot-hedge, by H. Braun.

h Extents and surveys of Hendon, by N. G. Brett-James.

i Survey of the manor of Hendon by presentment of the homage, 8th May, 1635.

j The Pinner Grims Dyke, by H. J. W. Stone.

k Post-Roman London, by Sir M. Sharpe.

l Earthworks of north-west Middlesex, by H. Braun.

m The village of Crouch End, Hornsey, by W. McB. Marcham.

n The earliest mention of Bow church, by B. W. Kissan.

o London's first castle, by H. Braun.

p John Stow commemoration, 1936: address by C. W. F. Goss.

q The Norman castle [earthwork] of South Mymms, by C. L. Davis.

r Sanctuary at St. Sepulchre's, Holborn, *c.* 1499, by C. A. Bradford.

s Middlesex in Domesday book, by Sir M. Sharpe.

t Ancient customs of the manor of Hendon, 1685.

u Christopher Dodington [d. 1657], a patron of St. Sepulchre's church, Holborn, by C. A. Bradford.

v Chiltern castles: the Conqueror's flank march round London in 1066, by H. S. Braun.

w New facts concerning 'Clerkenwell Detached' at Muswell Hill, by W. McB. Marcham.

Other publications:

2976 Abstracts of *inquisitiones post mortem* for the city of London returned into the court of chancery. 3 vols. 1896–1908. [Pt. i: 1485–1561, ed. G. S. Fry. Pt. ii: 1561–77, ed. S. J. Madge. Pt. iii: 1577–1603, ed. E. A. Fry]

2977 Register of freemen of the city of London in the reigns of Henry VIII and Edward VI, translated and ed. with introd. and index by C. Welch. 1908.

2978 Churchwardens' accounts of the parish of Allhallows, London Wall, 1455–1536, transcribed and ed. C. Welch; to which is added a facsimile of 'The fruyte of redempcyon by Symon the Anker of London Wall emprynted by Wynkyn de Worde, 1514'. 1912.

LONDON DEVONIAN ASSOCIATION

Founded 1908, to foster a knowledge of the history, folklore, literature, music, art, and antiquities of the county.

London Devonian Year Book, 1910 (n.d.), *contd.* as Devonian Year Book, 1911–33 (33 vols. n.d.):

2979 Year Book for 1910.

a The family of Fortescue.

b The worthies of Devon. [Addenda in vol. for 1912]

c The origin of the Devonian race, by J. Gray.

2980 Year Book for 1911.

a The family of Northcote.

b The map of Devon, by G. E. L. Carter. [Includes an account of the historical geography of Devon]

c The Devonshire regiment and territorials, by R. P. Chope.

d Early history of Devon as told in the Anglo-Saxon chronicle, with notes from other sources selected by R. P. Chope.

2981 Year Book for 1912.

a The family of Giffard.

b The historical basis of Kingsley's *Westward Ho!*, by R. P. Chope.

c The mythical history of Devon. [Contd. in vols. for 1923, 1930]

2982 Year Book for 1913.

a A Devonian 'Common of saints', by Viscount St. Cyres. [An account of some Devonshire worthies]

b The civil war in the west [1642–6], by R. P. Chope.

c John Gay and the *Beggar's Opera*, by W. H. K. Wright.

d Thomas Newcomen, and the birth of the steam engine, by R. Jenkins.

2983 Year Book for 1914.

a Drake in history, song, and story, by W. H. K. Wright.

b The romance of Devon, by H. M. Whitley. [An historical account]

c Devonians in London, by R. P. Chope.

d Okehampton castle, by E. H. Young. [Contd. in vol. for 1915]

2984 Year Book for 1915.

a Devonshire dialect and humour, by R. P. Chope.

b Thomas Savery, F.R.S., engineer and inventor, by R. Jenkins.

c The saints of Devon, by J. F. Chanter. [Contd. in vol. for 1916]

d English folk-music, with special reference to the folksongs of the west country, by C. H. Laycock.

2985 Year Book for 1916.

a Farthest from railways: an unknown corner of Devon [Hartland point and parish], by R. P. Chope.

2986 Year Book for 1917.

a Drake's ship [*Pelican*, later *Golden Hind*].

b The opening of the Bristol and Exeter railway [1844].

c The Saxon conquest of Devon, by J. J. Alexander.

2987 Year Book for 1918.

a The first roll of worthies of Devon, by Nathaniel Carpenter [1589–1628?. An extract from his *Geography*, 1625]

b The North Devon railways and an early director [John Sharland, d. 1859].

2988 Year Book for 1919.

a The Devonshire regiment: *Semper fidelis*, by J. Fortescue.

b The last fight of the *Revenge*, by Sir Walter Ralegh.

c The shepherd of the ocean [Sir Walter Ralegh], by E. Gosse. [Reprinted from the *Fortnightly Review*]

d Raleghana.

e Some old farm implements and operations, by R. P. Chope.

2989 Year Book for 1920.

a Devon's greatest worthy, Sir Walter Ralegh, by R. P. Chope.

2990 Year Book for 1921.

a Mock processions [in Devonshire].

2991 Year Book for 1922.

a Devonshire wrastling and wrastlers.

b An old guide book [extracts relating to Devonshire from *A Guide to all the Watering and Sea-bathing Places*, 1803].

2992 Year Book for 1923.

a Some rural ways in bygone days, by R. P. Chope. [Social life in North Devon, *c.* 1870–80]

2993 Year Book for 1924.

a Six great Devonians: short character sketches [of Sir John Hawkins, Sir Francis Drake, Sir Humphrey Gilbert, John Churchill, Duke of Marlborough, Joseph Mallord William Turner, Captain Robert Falcon Scott], by 'London-Devonian'.

b Religious houses of Devon, by R. P. Chope.

c Memoirs of Haydon, the painter.

2994 Year Book for 1925.

a Hercules promontory: fact and fiction in the history of Hartland, by R. P. Chope.
b Parish church of Great Torrington, by G. M. Doe.

2995 Year Book for 1926.

a 'Devonians in London', by the Founder [J. Martin].
b Literary life in a Devonshire vicarage, 1822–57: Mr. and Mrs. T. Atkins Bray of Tavistock, by W. G. Harris.
c Tavistock goose fair, by J. J. Alexander.

2996 Year Book for 1927.

a The Devonshire club, 1765–1856.
b The birthplace of Sir Francis Drake, by J. J. Alexander.
c Clovelly dykes, by G. E. L. Carter. [Prehistoric earthworks]

2997 Year Book for 1928.

a Notes and gleanings. [Edgar Dewdney, d. 1916, by A. Sharpe; William Romaine Govett, d. 1848, by F. B. Boyce; Edmund Kean in Exeter, 1813, by W.H.W.]
b A calendar of Devon worthies, comp. H. Tapley-Soper.

2998 Year Book for 1929.

a Romance of journalism, by J. Martin. [Experiences of a journalist in Devon and Cornwall, 1863–70]
b The first empire builder: a great Devonian [Sir Walter Ralegh], by F. B. Boyce.
c The port of Bideford.

2999 Year Book for 1930.

a Devon settlers in London, by Annie G. Pike. [Reprinted from the *Western Morning News and Mercury*]
b Frithelstock priory: an appeal [including a brief historical account].
c 'Barnstaple bulldogs', by R. P. Chope. [A refutation of the claim that Barnstaple sent five ships against the Armada, 1588]
d Athelstan in the west of England, by J. J. Alexander.
e Place-names of Devon, by J. J. Alexander.
f A Tiverton worthy: John Cross (1819–61), painter, by A.F.C.

3000 Year Book for 1931.

a Ottery St. Mary, by Phillis M. Coleridge.

3001 Year Book for 1932.

a Municipal boroughs of Devon.
b 'Paignton' or ?, by W. G. Couldrey. [An account of the various spellings of the name]
c Exeter in 1761. [A letter written by Charles Lyttelton, dean of Exeter, to Sanderson Miller, of Radway, Warws.]
d [Robert] Southey's impressions of Devon [1799. Extracts from his *Common-place Book*, 4th ser.].

3002 Year Book for 1933.

a Folk-lore of the [Celtic] saints, by G. E. L. Carter.
b Bideford bridge, by W. H. Rogers.

LONDON NATURAL HISTORY SOCIETY

Founded 1914, by the amalgamation of the City of London Entomological and Natural History Society and the North London Natural History Society, for the study of natural history and kindred subjects, within a radius of about 20 miles around St. Paul's cathedral.

Transactions, 1914–20 (7 vols. 1915–21):

3003 Vol. for 1914.

a The City of London Entomological and Natural History Society [a brief sketch of its history], by A. W. Mera.
b The middle ages in the Wey valley, by E. Chapman.

London Naturalist, 1921–32 (12 vols. 1922–33):

3004 Vol. for 1924.

a In retrospect [recollections of the Haggerston Entomological Society, fl. 1858–9, from which the Society is descended], by E. Aris.
b Market crosses, by H. S. Stowell.

3005 Vol. for 1927.

a The wooden walls of Greensted nave: a note of interrogation, by E. Chapman.
b East window, Oxted church, by W. C. Forster.

3006 Vol. for 1928.

a Archaeological inspections, by G. J. B. Fox. [Accounts of churches at Laleham, Godalming, and West Horsley. Similar accounts for those of St. Sepulchre, Holborn, Kingsdown by Wrotham, and Darenth occur in the 1929 vol., Barking and Stoke D'Abernon in the 1930 vol., Shere and Chipping Ongar in the 1931 vol., and Laindon and Merton in the 1932 vol.]

3007 Vol. for 1930.

a Anglo-Saxon work in our churches, by J. E. S. Dallas.

3008 Vol. for 1931.

a Ongar castle, by W. C. Forster.

3009 Vol. for 1932.

a The Great North Wood, by W. C. Cocksedge. [On the Norwood Hills district, north of Croydon]
b A corner of Essex in the 18th cent. [from Romford to Waltham].

LONDON SHAKESPEARE COMMEMORATION LEAGUE

Founded 1902, as the London Shakespeare League, to promote and encourage the use of Shakespeare's own text and scene-sequence, the professional performances of Shakespeare's plays on an auditorium-stage, the establishment of an 'auditorium-stage' in London. Title changed to the above form in 1903.

Publications:

3010 The London Shakespeare League Journal, vol. 1, nos. 1–8 (1914–15), *contd. as* The Shakespeare League Journal, vol. 1, no. 9–vol. 8, no. 6 (1915–22), *contd. as* The Shakespeare Journal, vol. 8, no. 7– (1922–). None of these vols. has been seen.

3011 A note on James and Richard Burbage, by Mrs. C. C. Stopes. *P.* 1914.

3012 Shakespeare's profession, by W. Poel. A paper read before the Royal Society of Arts, ed. S. D. Headlam.[1] *P.* 1915.

3013 A chronology of Shakespeare's plays, shewing where they were acted in London, 1591–1642, by W. Poel. [Single-sheet chart. 1919.]

3014 Tercentenary of the publication of the first folio of Shakespeare's works, edited by John Heminge and Henry Condell, 1623: the prefatory pages of the first folio, with a comment by Sir S. Lee. *P.* 1923. [2 edns.]

3015 The London Shakespeare Commemoration League: its purpose and story, by S. R. Littlewood. *P.* 1928.

3016 A plea for the early texts, by W. Poel.[1] *P.* [n.d.].

[1] Not seen.

LONDON SOCIETY

Founded 1912, to stimulate a wider concern for the beauty of the capital city, the preservation of its charms, and the careful consideration of its development.

Journal, nos. 1–190 (1913–33):

3017 No. 13.
  a Queen Square, Bloomsbury, by P. Norman.

3018 No. 16.
  a Old Marylebone, by J. Slater.

3019 No. 31.
  a The story of Bethlehem hospital, by E. G. O'Donoghue.

3020 No. 35.
  a The Tower district of London, by C. H. Hopwood.

3021 No. 37.
  a The Barber Surgeons' hall.

3022 No 40.
  a Visit to the Drapers' company.

3023 No. 41.
  History of the Houses of Parliament, by T. Wilson.

3024 No. 44.
  The Worshipful Company of Stationers, by R. T. Rivington.

3025 No. 45.
  a London bridge, by W. D. Caröe. [Contd. in nos. 46 and 47]

3026 No. 49.
  a The Mercers' company and their hall [and plate], by D. Watney and F. D. Watney.

3027 No. 55.
  a The Brewers' hall, by E. Evans.

3028 No. 56.
  a The Roman wall of London, by P. Norman. [Contd. in no. 57]

3029 No. 59.
  a London before the great fire and now [1923], by H. A. Cox. [Contd. in no. 60]

3030 No. 65.
  a Visit to the Vintners' hall, by H. D. Truscott.

3031 No. 68.
  a An afternoon in old Highgate, by P. W. Lovell. [Contd. in no. 69. Also published separately, *P.* 1926]

3032 No. 70.
  a Shakespearean rambles, by T. Forrest. [An account of some places in London associated with Shakespeare and his plays. Contd. in no. 71]

3033 No. 71.
  a The city churches, their early date. The approximate date of the foundations of the city churches; a few examples of benefactions by medieval citizens; how the churches built by Wren after the great fire were paid for, by P. Norman.

3034 No. 81.
  a The Strand and the Adelphi: their early history and development, by J. Slater.

3035 No. 82.
  a Spas of old London and its vicinity, by S. Sunderland.

3036 No. 86.
  a Roman London, by P. Norman.

3037 No. 90.
  a The Merchant Taylors' hall, by H. L. Hopkinson.

3038 No. 93.
  a The great plague in London, by W. Bell.

3039 No. 96.
  a Westminster hall, by Sir F. Baines.

3040 No. 100.
  a The Tallow Chandlers' company, by M. F. Monier-Williams.

3041 No. 103.
  a Visit to Lincoln's Inn, by Sir T. R. Hughes.

3042 No. 105.
  a St. Helen's church, Bishopsgate: the Westminster abbey of the city, by S. T. H. Saunders.

3043 No. 108.
  a Visit to Canonbury tower.

3044 No. 113.
  a The Salters' company.

3045 No. 115.
  a Nicholas Hawksmoor [d. 1736], a London architect, by H. A. Tipping.

3046 No. 117.
  a The Worshipful Company of Haberdashers, by J. Eagleton.

3047 No. 120.
  a Visit to the Drapers' company. [An account of the London livery companies, by W. A. Thomson]

3048 No. 123.
  a The first city of London, by R. E. M. Wheeler. [Roman London]

3049 No. 125.
  a Hampton Court Palace: King Henry VIII's hall, by Sir F. Baines.

3050 No. 127.
  a Eltham Palace and Lodge.

3051 No. 128.
  a Church of St. Bartholomew the Great.
  b The Trinity hospital [Deptford], by H. Genochio.

3052 No. 132.
  a The order of the Hospital of St. John of Jerusalem, by H. W. Fincham. [The order in England; the building of the priory of St. John at Clerkenwell; St. John's gate; the priory church and its crypt]

3053 No. 137.
  a The Bank of England, by W. M. Acres.

3054 No. 139.
  a Visit to the church of St. Nicholas Cole-Abbey, by J. G. P. Meaden.

3055 No. 142.
  a Church of St. Mary Stratford atte Bow, by H. Greatbatch.

3056 No. 143.

a Apothecaries' hall.

3057 No. 144.

a *The Times* [a brief history], by J. Walter.
b Visit to Lansdowne House.

3058 No. 147.

a The Guards' chapel, Wellington barracks, by Sir N. Wilkinson.

3059 No. 148.

a Fickett's field [an account of the site now occupied by the Law Courts], by the Master Chandler.

3060 No. 151.

a The Armourers' and Brasiers' company, by H. P. Bodkin.

3061 No. 155.

a St. Stephen's church: historical notes by J. G. P. Meaden.

3062 No. 161.

a Visit to St. Margaret's church, Westminster, by W. H. Carnegie. [With additional notes from other sources]

3063 No. 163.

a Visit to Staple Inn.

3064 No. 164.

a Visit to the Chelsea physic garden, by W. Hales.

3065 No. 165.

a Church of St. Mary Aldermanbury.

3066 No. 166.

a Visit to Fulham Palace.

3067 No. 167.

a Visit to East Ham parish church [St. Mary Magdalen], by J. B. Carlos and P. M. Johnston.

3068 No. 170.

a St. Mary-le-Bow, by E. S. Underwood.

3069 No. 171.

a The Royal Exchange and the Royal Exchange Assurance, by E. de M. Rudolf.

3070 No. 176.

a Visit to Waltham abbey and Temple Bar, by A. Vallance.
b The story of St. Clement Danes.

3071 No. 178.

a London's debt to Wren, by B. Pite.

3072 No. 180.

a St. James' Palace and the Chapel Royal, by H. Genochio.

3073 No. 183.

a The story of the Mansion House, by S. Tatchell.

3074 No. 189.

a Barnard's Inn, Holborn, by B. C. Boulter.

Other publications:

3075 London city churches: their use, their preservation and their extended use. Containing historical notes by P. Norman. *P.* [1923].

3076 London's squares and how to save them. [1927].

LONDON SURVEY COMMITTEE

Founded 1894, as the Committee for the Survey of the Memorials of Greater London, to watch and register what still remains of beautiful or historic work in greater London. Title changed to the above form in 1915.

Monographs, nos. 3–13:

3077 No. 3. The old palace of Bromley-by-Bow, by E. Godman. [1902].

3078 No. 4. The Great House, Leyton, by E. Gunn. [1903].

3079 No. 5. Brooke House, Hackney, by E. A. Mann. [1904].

3080 No. 6. Church of St. Dunstan, Stepney, by W. C. Pepys and E. Godman. [1905].

3081 No. 7. East Acton manor house, by P. Norman. [1921].

3082 No. 8. Sandford manor, Fulham, by W. A. Webb. [1907].

3083 No. 9. Crosby Place, by P. Norman, with an architectural description by W. D. Caröe. [1908].

3084 No. 10. Morden College, Blackheath, by T. F. Green. [1916].

3085 No. 11. Eastbury manor house, Barking, by P. Norman. with drawings by H. V. C. Curtis. [1917].

3086 No. 12. Cromwell House, Highgate, by P. Norman. [1926].

3087 No. 13. Swakeleys, Ickenham, by W. H. Godfrey. [1933].

Survey of London [prepared by the Committee and published by the London County Council], vols. 2–14 (1909–31):

3088 Vols. 2, 4. Parish of Chelsea, by W. H. Godfrey. 2 vols. [1909–13].

3089 Vols. 3, 5. Parish of St. Giles-in-the-Fields; with drawings, illustrations and architectural descriptions, by W. E. Riley; ed. with introd. and historical notes by Sir L. Gomme. 2 vols. 1912–14.

3090 Vol. 6. Parish of Hammersmith, by members of the Committee. 1915.

3091 Vol. 7. The old church, Chelsea, by W. H. Godfrey. 1921.

3092 Vol. 8. Parish of St. Leonard, Shoreditch; with drawings, illustrations and architectural descriptions by G. T. Forrest; ed., with historical introd. and notes, by Sir J. Bird. 1922.

3093 Vol. 9. Church of St. Helen, Bishopsgate, by Minnie Reddan and A. W. Clapham. Pt. 1. 1924.

3094 Vols. 10, 13, 14. Parish of St. Margaret, Westminster; with drawings, illustrations and architectural descriptions by G. T. Forrest; ed., with historical notes, by M. H. Cox. 3 vols. 1926–31. [Pts. ii and iii: Neighbourhood of Whitehall]

3095 Vol. 11. The Royal Hospital, Chelsea, by W. H. Godfrey. 1927.

3096 Vol. 12. Church of All Hallows Barking, by Lilian J. Redstone and members of the Committee. 1929. [Vol. ii was published in 1934]

LONDON TOPOGRAPHICAL SOCIETY

Founded 1900 (taking over the effects of the Topographical Society of London, founded 1880), for the publication of material illustrating the history and topography of the city and county of London from the earliest times to the present day.

Publications, 11–66:

3097 No. 11. London Topographical Record, vol. 1 (1901).

a Mediaeval remains found at Blackfriars, 1900, by P. Norman .

b Some topographical notes of 1900, by T. F. Ordish. [Buildings demolished or threatened with demolition]

c The Strand improvement, by T. F. Ordish.

d An autograph plan by Wren [St. James's park near the Cock-pit 1677], by T. F. Ordish. [See also vol. 2]

e Note on Lincoln's Inn Fields [concerning houses designed by Inigo Jones], by H. B. Wheatley.

3098 No. 12. Plan of area now West Central part of London [*c.* 1648], by W. Hollar. 1 sheet. 1902.

3099 No. 13. London Topographical Record, vol. 2 (1903).

a 'An autograph plan by Wren', by W. L. Spiers. [See also vol. 1]

b Some demolitions in 1901, 1902, by J. P. Emslie.

c Church of the Friars Minor in London and the site of Christ's Hospital, by E. B. S. Shepherd.

d London buildings photographed, 1860–70, by P. Norman.

e Notes upon Norden and his map of London, 1593, by H. B. Wheatley.

f Pepys' London collection [in the Pepysian library, Cambridge], by W. R. Lethaby.

g Signs of old London, by F. G. H. Price. [Contd. in vols. 3–5]

h Hollar's map [of London, *c.* 1670–77], by W. R. Lethaby and R. Jenkyns.

3100 No. 14. View of London and Westminster by John Kip, *c.* 1710–20. 12 sheets. 1903.

3101 No. 15. Prospect of London and Westminster, taken at several stations to the southward thereof, by Robt. Morden and Phil. Lea [1682]. 12 sheets. 1904. [Also known as Ogilby and Morgan's plan]

3102 No. 16. London Topographical Record, vol. 3 (1906).

a Notes on Salway's plan of the road from Hyde Park Corner to Counter's Bridge [1811], by W. F. Prideaux. [Contd. in vol. 5]

b Address by F. G. H. Price [on archaeological discoveries made during demolitions in London].

c Changing London: notes on alterations in northern St. Marylebone during the last fifteen years [1905], by J. G. Head.

3103 No. 17. Plan of London, *c.* 1560–70, by Ralph Agas. 8 sheets. 1905.

3104 No. 18. An exact delineation of the cities of London and Westminster and the suburbs thereof, described by Richard Newcourt; Wm. Faithorne sculpsit [1658]. 8 sheets. 1905.

3105 No. 19. London, Westminster and Southwark, drawn and engraved by Wenceslaus Hollar, 1647. 7 sheets in 6. 1906.

3106 No. 20. London Topographical Record, vol. 4 (1907).

a Address [on the Roman wall], by P. Norman.

b Recent demolitions in Blackheath [1907], by G. H. Lovegrove. [Vanbrugh House and Vanbrugh Castle]

c Catalogue of the exhibition of maps, views, and plans of London exhibited at Drapers' hall, 1905, by B. Gomme.

3107 No. 21. Old St. Paul's: a section showing the choir with Wren's suggestion for a dome over the crossing and a new nave, dated 1666 [and a plan]. 2 sheets. 1908.

3108 Nos. 22, 26. An exact surveigh of the streets, lanes and churches contained within the ruines of the city of London, first described in six plats, by John Leake, etc. [1667]. 2 sheets. 1908–9.

3109 No. 23. London Topographical Record, vol. 5 (1908).

a London city churches that escaped the great fire, by P. Norman.

b Morden and Lea's plan of London 1682, by W. L. Spiers.

c Wren's drawings of old St. Paul's at All Souls' College, Oxford, by W. R. Lethaby.

3110 No. 24. The palace of Whitehall, 1683. 1 sheet. 1909.

3111 No. 25. London Topographical Record, vol. 6 (1909).

a Crosby Place, by P. Norman.

b Royal palace of Whitehall, by the Earl of Rosebery and W. L. Spiers.

c Notes on Visscher's view of London, 1616, by T. F. Ordish.

d Abstracts of documents relating to London from early chancery proceedings, and from the court of requests [15th–17th cent.], by P. Norman.

3112 Nos. 27, 29, 33. [Reproductions of unpublished drawings of London views, etc.] 21 sheets. 1910–13.

a Warders' lodging, Tower of London, by John Wykeham Archer, 1847.

b Church of St. Benet Fink as seen after the fire at the Royal Exchange, by John Wykeham Archer, 1843.

c *The Times* printing house, Printing House Square, Blackfriars, by John Wykeham Archer, 1851.

d The entrance court of Burlington House, looking towards Piccadilly, towards the house, by an assistant of Sir John Soane, about 1811.

e Colonnade in the entrance court of Burlington House, Piccadilly, looking east, by an assistant of Sir John Soane, about 1811.

f Cheyne Walk, Chelsea, by James Millar, 1776.

g The White Hart inn, Bishopsgate Street Without, by George Shepherd, *c.* 1810.

h The Grecian coffee house, Devereux Court, Strand, by George Shepherd, *c.* 1810.

i Beaufort Buildings, Strand, by George Shepherd, *c.* 1810.

j Carrington (formerly Gower) House, Whitehall, Sir William Chambers, architect, *c.* 1770: view of staircase, by George Basevi, 1813.

k Ashburnham House, Westminster, designed by Inigo Jones: view of staircase, by George Basevi, 1813.

l Views of the river from the gardens of Somerset House, looking east, and west, by Thomas Sandby.

m Church of St. Paul, Covent Garden, from the churchyard, by a pupil of Sir John Soane, *c.* 1820.

n Southwark iron bridge from Bankside, by E. W. Cooke.

o [Six drawings of London bridge], by E. W. Cooke.

3113 No. 28. London Topographical Record, vol. 7 (1912).

a Lanesborough House, by W. F. Prideaux.

b The monuments in Westminster abbey, by Lord Eversley.

c Earliest Westminster, by W. R. Lethaby.

d Account of the view of the palace of Whitehall from the river, 1683, by W. L. Spiers.

e Shakespeare at Whitehall, by E. Law.

f [Address by Lord Welby of Allington on the situation of the 'sporting apparatus' and cock-pit at Whitehall]

g Explanation of the plan of Whitehall, by W. L. Spiers.
h Notices of the palace of Whitehall in a letter from Sydney Smirke to Henry Ellis. [Reprinted from *Archaeologia*, xxv. 1832]

3114 No. 30. Roads out of London, being photographic reprints extracted from Ogilby's *Britannia*, 1675, with so much of his text as relates to them, ed. T. F. Ordish. 1911.

3115 No. 31. Prospect and map of London, showing the river Thames to Woolwich Reach, drawn by Jonas Moore in 1662. 1 sheet. 1912.

3116 No. 32. London Topographical Record, vol. 8 (1913).
a History of metropolitan roads, by T. F. Ordish.
b Notes on London views, by P. Norman.
c Disappearing London, by W. L. Spiers. [Contd. in vols. 9–11 and by P. Norman in vols. 12 and 13]
d The East India company at Crosby House, 1621–38, by W. Foster.

3117 Nos. 34, 36, 37, 41–44. Plan of the cities of London and Westminster, and borough of Southwark, with the contiguous buildings; from an actual survey taken by John Roque, and engraved by John Pine, 1737–46. 48 sheets + key. 1913–19.

3118 No. 35. London Topographical Record, vol. 9 (1914).
a Drawings of old and new London bridge and of Southwark bridge, by E. W. Cooke, with notes by P. Norman.
b Rocque's plan of London [1746], by H. B. Wheatley.
c Blake and London (with special reference to Lambeth), by T. F. Ordish.
d Index to the various printed publications of the Society and for the Record, vol. 1–8, by H. G. Head.

3119 No. 38. London Topographical Record, vol. 10 (1916).
a Queen Square, Bloomsbury, and its neighbourhood, by P. Norman.
b Extracts [of topographical interest] from *A brief historical relation of State affairs*, by Narcissus Luttrell (1678–1714), with notes by W. L. Spiers.
c Historical notes on mediaeval London houses, by C. L. Kingsford. [Contd. in vols. 11 and 12]
d Original plan of Durham House and grounds, 1626, by H. B. Wheatley.

3120 No. 39. Plan of the manor of Ebury, *c.* 1663–70. 1 sheet. 1915.

3121 No. 40. London Topographical Record, vol. 11 (1917).
a The site of 'The Theatre', Shoreditch: London's first playhouse, by W. W. Braines.

3122 No. 45. View of London bridge from east to west, by John Norden [engraved 1597]. 1 sheet. 1919.

3123 No. 46. London Topographical Record, vol. 12 (1920).
a Tallis's *Street views of London* [1838–40], by E. B. Chancellor.
b Stratford Place, by A. T. Bolton.

3124 No. 47. The west side of London bridge; the east side of London bridge, by Sutton Nicholls [*c.* 1710]. 1 sheet. 1921.

3125 No. 48. Tallis's London street views, exhibiting upwards of one hundred buildings in each number, the whole forming a complete stranger's guide through London: Bond Street, division I. [Facsimile reproduction, 1921]

3126 No. 49. View of London, engraved by Matthew Merian, 1638. 1 sheet. 1922.

3127 No. 50. [Unpublished drawings by Hollar.] 4 sheets. 1922.
a The river and City as seen from Milford Stairs.
b The Savoy.
c Somerset House.
d Durham House, Salisbury House, and Worcester House.
e York House.
f Suffolk House.
g Lambeth Palace in 1647.

3128 No. 51. London Topographical Record, vol. 13 (1923).
a Notes on the history of the Leadenhall, 1195–1488, by A. H. Thomas.
b Ancient Bradestrete identical with Threadneedle Street, by H. L. Hopkinson.
c Cheapside in its relation to the trades and crafts of London, by H. L. Hopkinson.
d London topographical gleanings, by C. L. Kingsford.
e The Pantheon in the Oxford road, James Wyatt, R.A., architect, 1770–72, by A. T. Bolton.

3129 Nos. 52, 53. Views of Westminster, sketched 1801–15 and drawn in water colours by William Capon [with Capon's descriptions annotated by P. Norman]. 1923–4.

3130 No. 54. A map drawn in 1585 to illustrate a law suit concerning Gelding's Close [Public Record Office, Exchequer special commissions, no. 1891]. 1 sheet. 1925.

3131 No. 55. Early history of Piccadilly, Leicester Square, Soho, and their neighbourhood, based on a plan [no. 3130 above], by C. L. Kingsford. 1925.

3132 No. 56. Drawings of buildings in area described [in no. 3131 above, together with a plan of west London *c.* 1710]. 1926.

3133 No. 57. London Topographical Record, vol. 14 (1928).
a The fortification of London in 1642/3, by N. G. Brett-James.
b The King's Head tavern, Leadenhall Street, by K. Rogers.
c Disappearing London: Regent Street, by A. T. Bolton.
d Rosamond ponds and the reservoir in the Green park, by P. Norman.
e The work of C. L. Kingsford (1862–1926) in London history and topography, by Eliza Jeffries Davis.

3134 No. 58. A plan of Nevill's Alley (Court), Fetter Lane, from a drawing in the British Museum [1670]. Copied from the plan by John Goslyng. 1 sheet. 1928.

3135 No. 59. Drawings of the inns of court and chancery made probably in the first half of the 18th cent., with notes by J. B. Williamson. 1928.

3136 No. 60. London Topographical Record, vol. 15 (1931).
a Two unknown names of early London wards, by J. Tait.
b Doctors Commons, by P. W. Chandler. [App. 1: Summary account of the Society of Doctors Commons, by Andrew Coltee Ducarel, 1753. App. 2: Church of St. Benet, Paul's Wharf, by W. H. Godfrey. App. 3: Doctors Commons, its title and topography, by Eliza Jeffries Davis]
c The rebuilding of Doctors Commons, 1666–72, by Edith A. Pickard and Eliza Jeffries Davis.
d Doctors Commons; the later history of the property to 1858, by Eliza Jeffries Davis.
e Nevill's Court, Fetter Lane: a commentary on Goslyng's plan (1670) issued by the London Topographical Society in 1928, by W. G. Bell.
f Particulars of properties in the city of London belonging to St. John's College, Oxford, by H. E. Salter.

3137 No. 61. Plan of the area lying east of St. Katherine's hospital (now St. Katherine's dock), *c.* 1590 (Public Record Office, M.P.B. 4). Reproduced from a tracing by Marjorie B. Honeybourne. 1 sheet. 1929.

3138 No. 62. London Topographical Record, vol. 16 (1932).

   a A plan of the site and buildings of St. Anthony's hospital, Threadneedle Street, *c.* 1530, by Rose Graham.

   b The precincts of the Grey Friars with some account of the adjoining property, including the church of St. Nicholas Shambles, its parsonage (the Butchers' hall) and the Earl of Northumberland's inn (the Bull and Mouth inn), by Marjorie B. Honeybourne.

   c Bread Street: its ancient signs and houses, by K. Rogers.

3139 No. 63. View of Greenwich, 1637, by Wenceslaus Hollar. 1 sheet. 1930.

3140 No. 64. Plan of crown property on the east side of Charing Cross between the former hospital of St. Mary Rounceval on the north and Scotland on the south. 1610. [Prepared for the suit Sir John Parker *v.* Richard Gardyner, etc. Public Record Office, Exchequer special commissions, no. 4186]. 1 sheet. 1930.

3141 No. 65. Plan of the manor of Walworth, and parish of Newington, Surrey, in the year 1681 [from the original in the possession of the dean and chapter, Canterbury]. 1932.

3142 No. 66. Plan of part of the map of London, comprising the estates of his grace the Duke of Bedford, in the parishes of St. Paul Covent Garden, St. Martin in the Fields, St. Giles in the Fields, St. George Bloomsbury, St. George the Martyr and St. Pancras, 1795. 1 sheet. 1933.

MALONE SOCIETY

Founded 1906, for the printing of dramatic texts and of documents relating to the English drama.

Reprints:

3143 *The Battle of Alcazar*, 1594 [by George Peele]. 1907.

3144 *The History of Orlando Furioso*, 1594 [by Robert Greene]. 1907.

3145 *The Interlude of Johan the Evangelist* [anon.]. *P.* 1907.

3146 *The Interlude of Wealth and Health* [anon]. *P.* 1907.

3147 *The History of King Leir*, 1605 [anon.]. 1907 [1908].

3148 The interlude of *Calisto and Melebea* [printed by John Rastell]. *P.* 1908.

3149 *The Tragedy of Locrine*, 1595 [anon.]. 1908.

3150 *The Life of Sir John Oldcastle*, 1600 [by Anthony Munday, Michael Drayton, Robert Wilson and Thomas Hathway]. 1908.

3151 *The Tragical Reign of Selimus*, 1594 [by Robert Greene ?]. 1908 [1909].

3152 *The Old Wives Tale*, 1595 [by George Peele]. *P.* 1908 [1909].

3153 The play of *Patient Grissell*, by John Phillip. 1909.

3154 *Iphigenia at Aulis*, translated by Lady Lumley. 1909.

3155 *The virtuous Octavia*, 1598 [by Samuel Brandon]. 1909 [1910].

3156 *Fidele and Fortunio, the two Italian gentlemen* [1584?]. 1909 [1910].

3157 *The Second Maiden's Tragedy*, 1611 [anon.]. 1909 [1910].

3158 *The Arraignment of Paris*, 1584 [by George Peele]. *P.* 1910.

3159 *Tom Tyler and his Wife* [anon.]. *P.* 1910.

3160 *The Wounds of Civil War*, by Thomas Lodge, 1594. *P.* 1910.

3161 *A Knack to Know an Honest Man*, 1596 [anon.]. 1910.

3162 *The Birth of Hercules* [anon.]. 1911.

3163 *Apius and Virginia*, 1575 [by R.B.]. *P.* 1911.

3164 *King Edward the First*, by George Peele, 1593. 1911.

3165 *The Comedy of George a Green*, 1599 [anon.]. 1911.

3166 *The Tragedy of Caesar's Revenge* [anon.]. 1911.

3167 *The Book of Sir Thomas More* [anon.]. 1911.

3168 *The Love of King David and fair Bethsabe*, by George Peele, 1599. 1912 [1913].

3169 *The Two Angry Women of Abington*, 1599 [by Henry Porter]. 1912 [1913].

3170 *The Weakest goeth to the Wall*, 1600 [anon.]. 1912 [1913].

3171 *Wily Beguiled*, 1606 [anon.]. 1912 [1913].

3172 *Englishmen for my Money*, 1616 [by William Haughton]. 1912 [1913].

3173 *The Resurrection of Our Lord* [anon.]. 1912 [1913].

3174 *Clyomon and Clamydes*, 1599 [anon.]. 1913.

3175 *Look about you*, 1600 [by Anthony Wadeson ?]. 1913.

3176 *A larum for London*, 1602 [anon.]. 1913.

3177 *The Contention between Liberality and Prodigality*, 1602 [anon.]. 1913.

3178 *The Wit of a Woman*, 1604 [anon.]. 1913.

3179 *The Tragedy of Mariam*, 1613 [by Lady Elizabeth Cary]. 1914.

3180 *The Cobler's Prophecy*, 1594 [by Robert Wilson]. 1914.

3181 *The Pedlar's Prophecy*, 1595 [anon.]. 1914.

3182 *Gesta Grayorum*, 1688 [anon.]. 1914 [1915].

3183 *The Tragedy of Tancred and Gismund*, 1591–2 [by Robert Wilmot]. 1914 [1915].

3184 *The Tragedy of Tiberius*, 1607 [anon.]. 1914 [1915].

3185 *The Welsh Embassador* [anon.]. 1920 [1921].

3186 *Every Man out of his Humour*, 1600 [by Ben Jonson]. 1920 [1921].

3187 *The Scottish history of James the Fourth*, 1598 [by Robert Greene]. 1921.

3188 *Antonio and Mellida*, and *Antonio's revenge*, by John Marston, 1602. 1921 [1922].

3189 *The Christmas Prince* [anon.]. 1922 [1923].

3190 *John a Kent and John a Cumber* [by Anthony Munday]. 1923.

3191 *The Spanish Tragedy*, with additions, 1602 [by Thomas Kyd]. 1925.

3192 *Edward the Second*, by Christopher Marlowe, 1594. 1925 [1926].

3193 *Alphonsus king of Aragon*, 1599 [by R. Greene ?]. 1926.

3194 *Friar Bacon and Friar Bungay*, by Robert Greene, 1594. 1926.

3195 *Edmond Ironside, or War hath made all Friends* [anon.]. 1927 [1928].

3196 *Believe as you list*, by Philip Massinger, 1631. 1927 [1928].

3197 *Fair Em* [anon.]. 1927 [1928].

3198 *The Blind Beggar of Alexandria*, by George Chapman, 1598. P. 1928 [1929].

3199 *The Massacre at Paris*, by Christopher Marlowe. 1928 [1929].

3200 *The Parliament of Love* [by Philip Massinger]. 1928 [1929].

3201 *The First Part of the Reign of King Richard the Second or Thomas of Woodstock* [anon.]. 1929.

3202 *The True Tragedy of Richard the Third*, 1594 [anon.]. 1929.

3203 *The Two Noble Ladies* [anon.]. 1930.

3204 *The Rare Triumphs of Love and Fortune* [anon.]. 1930 [1931].

3205 *King Johan*, by John Bale. 1931.

3206 *A Looking-glass for London and England*, by Thomas Lodge and Robert Greene, 1594. 1932.

3207 *The Launching of the 'Mary'*, by Walter Mountfort. 1933.

3208 *Jack Juggler* [anon.]. 1933.

Collections, vols. 1–2 (1907–31):

3209 Vol. 1.

a Notes on the Society's publications [with contributions by W. Bang and L. Brandin. Contd. in vol. 2].

b *Love Feigned and Unfeigned*, a fragmentary morality, prepared for press by A. Esdaile.

c *The Prodigal Son*, a fragment of an interlude printed *c.* 1530.

d The Elizabethan lords chamberlain, by E. K. Chambers.

e Dramatic records of the city of London: the Remembrancia, ed. E. K. Chambers and W. W. Greg.

f *Robin Hood and the Sheriff of Nottingham*, a dramatic fragment, *c.* 1475.

g A play of Robin Hood for May-games, printed by William Copland, *c.* 1560 [from his edition of *Gest of Robin Hood*].

h The play of Lucrece, a fragmentary interlude printed *c.* 1530.

i Dramatic records from the Lansdowne mss. [Burghley papers], ed. E. K. Chambers and W. W. Greg.

j *Albion knight*, an imperfect morality, printed by [Thomas] Colwell, *c.* 1566.

k *Temperance and Humility*, a fragment of a morality printed *c.* 1530.

l James I at Oxford in 1605: property lists from the University archives, ed. F. S. Boas and W. W. Greg.

m Dramatic records from the patent rolls: company licences [1574–1625], ed. E. K. Chambers and W. W. Greg.

n Bodenham's *Belvedere* [*or the Garden of the Muses*, 1600], quotations from *The virtuous Octavia* and *A Knack to Know an Honest Man*, by C. Crawford.

o *The Hunting of Cupid*, a lost play by George Peele.

p *The Cruel Debtor*, a fragment of a morality printed by Colwell, *c.* 1566. [Contd. in vol. 2]

q Notes on dramatic bibliographers, by W. W. Greg. [Contd. in vol. 2]

r A jotting by John Aubrey [possibly concerning Shakespeare], by E. K. Chambers.

s Two early player-lists [1: The Earl of Leicester's men, 1572; 2: Queen Elizabeth's men, 1588], by E. K. Chambers.

t Commissions for the Chapel [Royal, 1604, 1606], by E. K. Chambers.

u Plays of the King's men in 1641, by E. K. Chambers.

v Dramatic records from the privy council register, 1603–1642, ed. E. K. Chambers and W. W. Greg.

3210 Vol. 2.

a Blackfriars records [comprising (i) A general survey of the conventual buildings; (ii) Farrant's theatre; (iii) Burbage's theatre; (iv) Sale of the property adjoining Burbage's theatre], by A. Feuillerat.

b Four letters on theatrical affairs, ed. E. K. Chambers. [Thomas Cooper, dean of Christ Church and vice-chancellor of Oxford, to Robert, Earl of Leicester, 1569; Petruccio Ubaldini to Queen Elizabeth; Elizabeth, Countess of Derby, to Robert Cecil; Sir Thomas Lake, clerk of the signet, to Robert Cecil, 1608]

c The academic drama at Cambridge: extracts from college records [16th cent.], ed. G. C. M. Smith.

d The manuscript of *Sir Thomas More*.

e *Processus Satanae* [a fragment of a 16th cent. miracle play].

f *Somebody and others* [*or the spoiling of Lady Verity*. Fragments of a 16th cent. interlude].

g Players at Ipswich. [Extracts from the municipal records, 1553–1625]

h Dramatic records of the City of London: the repertories, journals and letter books, ed. Anna J. Mill and E. K. Chambers.

i Dramatic records: the Lord Chamberlain's office. [Extracts from the official records of the lord chamberlain of the household, in the Public Record Office, relating to plays and players, 1603–41, ed. Eleanore Boswell and E. K. Chambers]

Extra volumes:

3211 Two Elizabethan stage abridgements: *The Battle of Alcazar* and *Orlando Furioso*. [An essay in critical bibliography, by W. W. Greg.] 1922 [1923].

Designs by Inigo Jones for masques and plays at court. [See Walpole Soc. vol. 12, no. 5920 below]

MANCHESTER ASSOCIATION FOR MASONIC RESEARCH

Founded 1909, to attract and interest freemasons by means of papers and discussions upon the history, antiquities and symbols of freemasonry, and to print and circulate masonic papers and documents of general interest.

Transactions, vols. 1–22 ([1912?]–33):

3212 Vol. 1.

a The old charges of the British freemasons, by R. H. Baxter. [Collection of mss., 14th–19th cent.]

b Craft freemasonry in Bolton, 1732–1813, by F. W. Brockbank.

c The ancient lodge of Wigan, Antiquity, no. 178, by J. G. McConnell.

3213 Vol. 2.

a Ritual of the operative free masons, by T. Carr.

b The antiquity of freemasonry, by J. S. Derbyshire.

c The Chetwode Crawley ms. and its bearing on the question of masonic degrees, by R. H. Baxter.

3214 Vol. 3.

a Notes on the history of Manchester and Salford lodges, by C. W. Sutton.
b Royal Arch masonry, by C. P. Noar.
c The York lodge, 236, by W. R. Makins.
d De Quincey and the origin of freemasonry, by G. Atkinson.
e An exact typographical reproduction of the 'Langdale masonic ms.' of the old charges, with introd. by R. H. Baxter.

3215 Vol. 4.

a Some notes on the history of masonic ritual, by R. H. Baxter.
b Cestrian lodge, by T. S. Sheldon.
c English masonic pottery, by G. M. Garfitt.
d Index to vols. 1–4.

3216 Vol. 5.

a Records of the Royal Lancashire lodge, no. 116, held at Colne, Lancs., by J. S. Derbyshire.
b Notes on St. John's lodge, no. 191, Bury, by H. Woods and C. P. Noar.
c Loyal Masonic Volunteer Corps, 1803, by C. P. Noar.
d Masonic history, with suggestions for study and research, by J. T. Thorp.

3217 Vol. 6.

a Further notes on early freemasonry in Derbyshire including Royal Arch masonry, by J. O. Manton.

3218 Vol. 7.

a The Travelling Mark lodge of Ashton-under-Lyne, comp. from the minute-books, by C. P. Noar.
b Masonic research: its nature, object, uses, and limits, by H. Flint.

3219 Vol. 8.

a The reform of Grand Lodge [London], by F. W. Broadbent.
b Gravestone in Mellor churchyard, Derbys. [of Thomas Brierley, b. 1785], by J. O. Manton.
c A comparison of the old charges and the ritual [of freemasonry], by R. H. Baxter.
d The Quatuor Coronati lodge, its history and biographical notes on its deceased members, by R. H. Baxter.

3220 Vol. 9.

a Masonic china and glass, by J. G. Wallis.
b The French compagnonnage and the English operative masons, by F. Rees.
c Lodge no. 1, Philadelphia: further bye-laws and introductory remarks and comments, by C. Gough.

3221 Vol. 10.

a The evolution of our ritual before the union (1st degree) [of the Grand Lodge of England with the Ancients or Atholl masons, 1813], by H. G. Rosedale.
b Leaves from a mason's notebook, by J. P. Briscoe. [Miscellaneous notes on freemasonry]
c Early history of the ark mariners' degree, by W. W. Covey-Crump.
d Old masonic catechisms, by M. Rosenbaum.
e Wigan Grand Lodge, by C. Gough. [Contd. in vol. 12]

3222 Vol. 11.

a Robert Fludd [d. 1637] and freemasonry: a speculative excursion, by A. E. Waite.
b Lodge of Friendship, 44 [Manchester], by J. F. Sutton and C. W. Sutton.
c Wigan Grand Lodge and the Barnsley lodges, by C. Gough.

d Chapter of union, no. 507 (1824), Mellor, Derbys., by J. O. Manton.

3223 Vol. 12.

a Anderson's constitutions of 1723 [for the Grand Lodge, London], by L. Vibert.
b Old tracing or lodge boards, by E. H. Dring.
c Dr. Anderson's 'first charge' (1723) and its consequences: a tentative inquiry, by J. E. S. Tuckett.

3224 Vol. 13.

a A few sidelights on the collection of early masonic pottery and glass, by G. M. Garfitt.
b The basis of the third degree, by J. M. Dow.
c The Royal Arch degree, by J. Stokes.
d Fraternal communication between the Grand Lodges of England and Ireland in the 18th cent., by J. H. Lepper.
e Lodges and associations for masonic research in England, by R. H. Baxter.

3225 Vol. 14.

a Presidential address on Knight Templary, by A. G. W. Provart.
b The craft in the 18th cent. with special relation to Dermott's criticisms of the Moderns in the Dundee lodge [London], by A. Heiron.
c A list of Manchester lodges in 1794, by S. L. Coulthurst.

3226 Vol. 15.

a Engraved craft certificates of the Grand Lodges of the British empire, 1756–1925, by E. Pickstone.
b The Drinkwater mss. and some notes on the Tew group [of mss.], by H. Poole.
c Masonic tombs and burial places, by W. J. Williams.
d Lancashire lodges and masons mentioned in the first two Grand Lodge minute-books, 1723–39, by S. L. Coulthurst.
e Records of masonic activities in Manchester and Salford, as recorded in Manchester newspapers, 1759–1823, by S. L. Coulthurst.

3227 Vol. 16.

a The number of [masonic] degrees in 1723, by R. H. Baxter.
b Masonic instruction before 1813, by G. W. Daynes.

3228 Vol. 17.

a St. John's lodge, no. 583 (492 in 1792), Henley-in-Arden, 1791–1811, by T. M. Carter.
b Early practices of the Irish craft, by P. Crosslé.
c Freemasonry and social England in the 18th cent., by G. W. Daynes.

3229 Vol. 18.

a The fabric rolls of York minster [relating to the masons and their work, 14th–15th cent.], by T. O. Warburton.
b Romance and an old masonic songbook [*The Freemasons Melody*, 1818?], by E. Pickstone.
c Freemasonry 'east of Suez' [including British India, Ceylon, Penang and Singapore], by M. H. Houston.
d Hale's *Social Harmony* [1763: a collection of songs and catches, some concerned with freemasonry], by E. Pickstone.

3230 Vol. 19.

a The ritual of the Union and the ritual of to-day, by E. H. Cartwright.
b Archbishop Becket and the Masons' company of London, by W. J. Williams.
c Freemasonry in the two kingdoms [England and Scotland] before Grand Lodges: a comparison of the two systems, by L. Vibert.

3231 Vol. 20.

a Towards the sources of freemasonry, by J. M. Allan.
b Early freemasonry in Salford, by S. L. Coulthurst.
c Bro. John Crossley [d. 1830], first provincial grand master and first provincial grand superintendent of Holy Royal Arch masons of east Lancashire, by S. L. Coulthurst.

3232 Vol. 21.

a The mediaeval mason: a sketch of the times and the men, by T. Herdman.
b Early freemasonry in Chester: a recently discovered copy of ms. charges and other unpublished records, by S. L. Coulthurst.
c A Lodge of Friendship, 277, a link with the Grand Lodge of all England, at York, by F. L. Pick.

3233 Vol. 22.

a Presidential address, by P. Ridgway. [Extracts from the minute book of the Lodge of Friendship, no. 39, Manchester, 1755-79]
b Some notes on the appurtenances of the lodge room, by E. H. Cartwright.
c The Edinburgh Register House ms. [concerning freemasonry, 1696], by J. M. Allan.

Other publications:

3234 Early freemasonry in Derbyshire, with special reference to the Tyrian lodge, no. 253 [Derby], by J. O. Manton. 1913.

3235 The Quatuor Coronati lodge, no. 2076, of ancient, free, and accepted masons, London, by R. H. Baxter. 1918.

3236 A record of antiquities, and articles of masonic interest, belonging to the craft lodges and R.A. chapters of the province of east Lancashire, comp. and illustrated by E. B. Beesley, with an address delivered by the author in explanation of the illustrations. 1919.

3237 The history of the Wigan Grand Lodge, written and photographically illustrated by E. B. Beesley. 1920.

3238 Catalogue of books [in the library of the Association], comp. A. Sparke. 1924.

3239 Freemasonry in Lancashire, from the earliest time down to the partition of the province of Lancashire into two divisions, in 1825-6, written and photographically illustrated by E. B. Beesley. 1932.

3240 More masonry into men, the story of the Manchester lodge, and an index to the first 40 vols. of the Transactions (1909-50) by F. L. Pick, with foreword by Sir E. Rhodes. 1951.

MANCHESTER FIELD NATURALISTS' AND ARCHAEOLOGISTS' SOCIETY

Founded 1860, as the Manchester Field Naturalists' Society, to promote and popularise a taste for the study of natural history and archaeology. The words 'and Archaeologists'' were added in 1876.

Report and Proceedings, 1900-32 (33 vols. 1901-33):

3241 Vol. for 1900.

a A short review [of *England's Improvement by Sea and Land*, by Andrew Yarranton, 1677], by Sir W. H. Bailey.

3242 Vol. for 1910.

a Mellor pulpit and font [Ches.], by J. E. McDonald.

3243 Vol. for 1925.

a Dunham castle: its nature and its history, by J. E. McDonald.

3244 Vol. for 1927.

a Marple Hall.

3245 Vol. for 1930.

a Old Manchester.

MANCHESTER GEOGRAPHICAL SOCIETY

Founded 1884, to promote the study of all branches of geographical science, especially in its relations to commerce and civilisation.

Journal, vols. 17-44 (25 vols. 1901-29):

3246 Vol. 17.

a A short account of my adventures in Ashanti during the rebellion of 1900, by P. Grundy.

3247 Vol. 19.

a The Roman wall near Hexham, by J. J. Gleave.

3248 Vol. 20.

a St. John Baptist, Cirencester, and its 'Vice' [or church house], by C. H. Bellamy.

3249 Vol. 22.

a Orography and history, by E. W. Dann.
b An undiscovered country [Essex], and the English Holland, by M. W. Thompstone.

3250 Vol. 25.

a Kingston-upon-Hull Geographical Society, by J. H. Reed. [On the development of English geographical societies, particularly that of Manchester]

3251 Vol. 29.

a British East Africa protectorate: early history, development, the native tribes and their progress, by J. Ainsworth.
b The geography of east Yorkshire, illustrated by chart and plan, by T. Sheppard. [An historical account of coastal erosion in that area]
c The British Antarctic expedition, 1910-13, by E. R. G. Evans.

3252 Vol. 32.

a A half-century of geographical progress [c. 1860-c. 1910], by J. S. Keltie.

3253 Vol. 36.

a The geography of Britain at the time of the arrival of man, by Sir W. B. Dawkins.
b Some geographical factors in the evolution of navigation, by C. B. Fawcett.

3254 Vol. 37-38.

a The growth of the British empire, by A. Williams.

3255 Vol. 39-40.

a History of cartography, by W. H. Barker.
b Cheshire villages: some causes determining their location, by H. W. Ogden.
c Distribution of population in south-west Lancashire: its social significance, by H. King.
d The development of the alkali industry in the Mersey area, by H. Thomas.
e The exploration of Antarctica, by J. G. Hayes.

3256 Vol. 41–42.

a The city and port of Manchester, by W. H. Barker and W. Fitzgerald.

3257 Vol. 43.

a Foreword [on the history of Quarry Bank mill, near Wilmslow], by E. W. Greg.

b Geographical basis of the Lancashire cotton industry, by H. W. Ogden.

c Towns of south-east Lancashire, by W. H. Barker.

d The Ribble basin: the geography of industrial development, by W. Fitzgerald.

Other publications:

3258 University of Manchester and Manchester Geographical Society. Loan exhibition of old maps to be held in the Whitworth Hall of the Manchester University, January 1923. *P.* [1923?].

MANCHESTER LITERARY AND PHILOSOPHICAL SOCIETY

Founded 1781, as the Literary and Philosophical Society of Manchester, for the advancement of literature and science. Title changed to the above form between 1883 and 1887.

Memoirs and Proceedings, 4th ser., vols. 45–77 (1901–33):

3259 Vol. 45.

a Selections from the correspondence of Lieut.-col. John Leigh Philips [d. 1814], of Mayfield, Manchester, by W. B. Faraday. [Letters written by Capt. Samuel Cable, R.N., of Douglas, Isle of Man, d. 1804. Previous selections from the Philips correspondence appeared in vols. 3 and 44]

3260 Vol. 46.

a On the 'implements from the chalk plateau', in Kent, their character and importance, by R. D. Darbishire.

b Topographical distribution of mechanical inventions in co. Lancaster, and their influence on some British and foreign industries, by Sir W. H. Bailey.

3261 Vol. 48.

a The collection of apparatus used by Dalton, now in the possession of the Manchester Literary and Philosophical Society, by F. Jones.

3262 Vol. 50.

a Inaugural address [on the history of the Society], by Sir W. H. Bailey.

3263 Vol. 53.

a The dawn of human intention: an experimental and comparative study of eoliths, by A. Schwartz and Sir H. R. Beevor.

3264 Vol. 54.

a The development of the atomic theory, by A. N. Meldrum. [Contd. in vol. 55, with particular reference to the work of Dalton]

b Correspondence between Mrs. Hemans [d. 1835, poetess] and Matthew Nicholson [d. 1819], an early member of this Society, by F. Nicholson.

3265 Vol. 56.

a Observations upon the improvement of the physique of Manchester Grammar School boys during the last 30 years [1881–1910], by A. A. Mumford.

b Note on the earliest industrial use of platinum [in English pottery, *c.* 1790–1], by W. Burton.

3266 Vol. 57.

a A criticism of some modern tendencies in prehistoric anthropology, by W. H. Sutcliffe. [Comments by W. B. Dawkins occur later in the vol.]

b Bessemer, Göransson and Mushet: a contribution to technical history, by E. F. Lange. [Göran Fredrik Göransson, d. 1900, Swedish metallurgist; Robert Forester Mushet, d. 1891, metallurgist]

c Contributions to the history of science (period of Priestley-Lavoisier-Dalton), based on autograph documents, by K. Loewenfeld.

3267 Vol. 58.

a The old Manchester Natural History Society and its museum, by F. Nicholson.

b Controversies concerning the interpretation and meaning of the remains of the dawn-man found near Piltdown, by G. E. Smith.

3268 Vol. 59.

a The place of science in history, by J. MacLeod.

b John Dalton's lectures and lecture illustrations, by W. W. H. Gee, H. F. Coward, and A. Harden.

3269 Vol. 60.

a Relationship between the geographical distribution of megalithic monuments and ancient mines, by W. J. Perry, with remarks by G. E. Smith.

b The Society's house [in George Street, Manchester], by C. L. Barnes.

c A Lancashire worthy [James Wolfenden, b. 1754, mathematician], by C. L. Barnes.

d New phases of the controversy concerning the Piltdown skull, by G. E. Smith.

e The lake villagers of Glastonbury, by W. B. Dawkins.

3270 Vol. 62.

a Presidential address [on the history of the Society], by W. Thomson.

b Examples of pre-Roman bronze-plated iron from the Pilgrim's Way, by W. B. Dawkins.

3271 Vol. 63.

a Henry Wilde [d. 1919, electrical engineer], by W. W. H. Gee.

b The work and influence of Joule, by Sir E. Rutherford. [James Prescott Joule, d. 1889, physicist]

3272 Vol. 65.

a The work and discoveries of Joule, by Sir D. Clerk.

b Manx mines and megaliths, by W. H. Corkill.

c The problem of megalithic monuments and their distribution in England and Wales, by W. J. Perry.

d Samuel Oldknow [d. 1828], the first manufacturer of British muslins, by G. Unwin.

3273 Vol. 66.

a Some early autographs of John Dalton, by S. J. Hickson.

3274 Vol. 67.

a The rise of motive power and the work of Joule, by Sir C. A. Parsons.

b Four letters of John Dalton [to his brother Jonathan], by W. W. H. Gee.

3275 Vol. 68.

a Mediaeval metallurgy, by M. L. Becker.

b The Literary and Philosophical Society, 1781–1851, by F. Nicholson.

3276 Vol. 69.

a The life and work of Ludwig Mond [chemist, d. 1909], by H. B. Dixon.

3277 Vol. 73.

a John Benjamin Dancer [d. 1887], instrument maker and inventor, by H. Garnett.

3278 Vol. 74.

a Leaves from an old notebook: a record of some early experiments on the carbonisation of oil and coal, by Dr. W. Henry, F.R.S. (1808–24), by W. Buckley and A. McCulloch.

3279 Vol. 75.

a List of apparatus now in Manchester which belonged to Dr. J. P. Joule, F.R.S., with remarks on his mss., letters, and autobiography, by J. R. Ashworth.

b Caves of the Settle district, and their relation to the ice age, by J. W. Jackson.

3280 Vol. 76.

a Man's place in nature as shown by fossils, by Sir A. S. Woodward.

b Michael Faraday as a metallurgist, by F. C. Thompson.

MANCHESTER LITERARY CLUB

Founded 1862, to encourage the pursuit of literature and art; to promote research; to publish from time to time works illustrating or elucidating the art, literature and history of the county.

Papers, vols. 27–59 (1901–33):

3281 Vol. 27.

a Silas Told [d. 1779], by L. Clay.

b Caleb Talbot's [d. 1805] commonplace book, by J. Mortimer.

c Alfred the Great, by J. T. Foard.

d The matchless Orinda [Katherine Fowler, d. 1664], by A. W. Fox.

e John Ceiriog Hughes [b. 1832], by J. Davies.

f John Clieveland [poet, d. 1658], by A. W. Fox.

g Chaucer: the man and the time, by J. D. Andrew.

3282 Vol. 28.

a Lifting Tuesday [a Lancashire custom], by A. W. Fox

b Christopher Smart, 1722–71, by J. H. Swann.

c Lancashire novelists: Mrs. Gaskell, by J. Mortimer.

d Hydrington Prosecution Society, by J. E. Craven.

e Theodore Hook: author and humourist [d. 1841], by M. Bailey.

f The Mabinogion, by J. Davies.

g The work of the Spenser Society, by W. R. Credland.

3283 Vol. 29.

a Herbs from Gerard's garden [John Gerard, herbalist d. 1612], by A. W. Fox.

b The letters of Robert Louis Stevenson, by F. Smith.

c Pastor Moritz's visit to England in 1782, by J. J. Richardson.

d Mary, Queen of Scots: murderess or martyr, by J. T. Foard.

3284 Vol. 30.

a Ashbourne and Dr. Johnson, by J. Mortimer.

b James Heywood [d. 1776], by C. W. Sutton.

c Evolution of a city thoroughfare: Market Street, Manchester, by T. Swindells.

d Sir John Suckling [d. 1641], by A. W. Fox.

e The evolution of old songs, by N. Dumville.

f The second revival of wood engraving [1830s and '40s], by C. T. Tallent-Bateman.

3285 Vol. 31.

a The case of Thos. Doughty [executed by Drake for conspiracy, 1577], by E. E. Minton.

b The haven under the hill [Whitby], by T. Pratt.

c Old Deansgate [Manchester], by T. Swindells.

d The love story of Saint Bertram, by G. Milner.

e Some early Welsh romances, by J. Davies.

3286 Vol. 32.

a Herbert Spencer's autobiography, by E. Attkins.

b A quondam librarian [James Watson, d. 1820], by J. Mortimer.

c Nicholas Ferrar [d. 1637], by W. C. Hall.

d Manchester under the court leet, by T. Swindells.

e William Harvey: artist and book-illustrator [d. 1866], by C. T. Tallent-Bateman.

f The Thomas Greenwood library for librarians, by W. E. A. Axon.

g A chapter in the life of R. L. Stevenson, by T. Pratt.

3287 Vol. 33.

a A poet's wedding-journey [William Wordsworth's, 1802], by G. H. Bell.

b George Wither, 1588–1667, by W. C. Hall.

c Music in the time of the Tudors, by N. Dumville.

3288 Vol. 34.

a The love-letters of a regicide [Henry Marten, d. 1680] by A. W. Fox.

b Music in the time of the Stuarts, by N. Dumville.

c The early pencillings of Sir John Gilbert, R.A. [d. 1897], by C. T. Tallent-Bateman.

3289 Vol. 35.

a Thomas Platter: a 16th cent. scholar, by J. Mortimer.

b Samuel Laycock [d. 1893]: the man and his work, by G. Milner.

c George Ridding [d. 1904] and some Winchester days, by H. E. Campbell.

d Whistler: the man and his art, by W. Emsley.

e Francis Thompson [d. 1907], by W. C. Hall.

f In praise of Charles Darwin, by A. W. Fox.

3290 Vol. 36.

a Oliver Madox Brown, painter, poet, and novelist, by J. R. Williamson.

b Dr. Johnson as a book-lover, by W. E. A. Axon.

c Sir John Franklin [d. 1847]: an Arctic tragedy, by E. E. Minton.

d Dean Swift, by J. J. Richardson.

e Christopher Marlowe, by W. C. Hall.

f Dr. Johnson as a letter-writer, by J. J. Richardson.

g An election [in 1868] before the Ballot Act, by G. Elce.

h Samuel Williams, artist [d. 1853], by C. T. Tallent-Bateman.

3291 Vol. 37.

a Frederic, Lord Leighton, P.R.A., by E. E. Minton.

b William Shenstone, landscape gardener and man of letters [d. 1763], by A. W. Fox.

c John Trafford Clegg [b. 1857], by J. R. Williamson.

d Leaves from an old Manchester journal [the *Sphinx*, 1868–71], by J. Mortimer.

e William Henry Bartlett, artist and author [d. 1854], by C. T. Tallent-Bateman.

3292 Vol. 38.

a Dickens and Manchester, by J. Mortimer.

b Mr. Verdant Green, by H. E. Campbell. [On the author, Edward Bradley, d. 1889]

3293 Vol. 39.

a Some notes on Borrow: his books and personality, by B. A. Redfern.
b Folk songs of Lancashire, by T. Derby.
c Diary of an 18th cent. mariner [Aaron Thomas, 1798–9], by R. Peel.
d The poet of Manxland [Thomas Edward Brown, d. 1897], by B. A. Redfern.
e John Oliver Hobbes [Mrs. Craigie, d. 1906], by J. J. Richardson.
f Notes on the portraits of Thomas de Quincey, by J. A. Green.
g Helen Watson, a Lancashire novelist [fl. 1882–1912], by T. C. Hughes.
h Turner, the poet painter, by W. Emsley.

3294 Vol. 40.

a William Cobbett, by T. Newbigging.
b Mental and moral pabulum for juveniles, 1820–70, by L. Clay.
c Notes on the development of the English novel, by H. Taylor.
d Some early Christmas numbers [of the *Illustrated London News* in the 19th cent.], by J. H. Swann.
e Charles Reade and his novels, by W. D. Cobley.
f William Ernest Henley, by L. C. Hartley.
g A great journalist [Daniel Defoe], by J. J. Richardson.
h Donegal abbey and the 'Four Masters', by A. W. Fox. [Michael O'Clery and the three other compilers of the *Annals of Ireland*, 1636]

3295 Vol. 41.

a The impress of Victorian literature, by L. Clay.
b Joseph Stanley, a Manchester pioneer of travel [b. 1815], by J. E. Phythian.
c Thomas Love Peacock, by L. C. Hartley.
d Francis Thompson, by L. C. Hartley.
e Elijah Ridings, a Failsworth poet [d. 1872], by S. Scho-field.

3296 Vol. 42.

a Allan Breac Stewart [b. *c.* 1722] and his associates, by T. Pratt.
b Hazlitt's walks with Coleridge, by J. C. Walters.
c The discovery of the longitude: a romance in navigation, by J. H. Hobbins. [On the work of John Harrison]
d Some personal recollections of Samuel Bamford [poet, d. 1872] by B. A. Redfern.

3297 Vol. 43.

a Andrew Marvell, poet, satirist and politician, by D. E. Oliver.
b The case of Admiral Byng, or judgment by court-martial, by E. E. Minton.
c Boswell's record of Johnson's table-talk, by F. W. E. Barker.
d Waller's plot restudied, by A. W. Fox.
e A 17th cent. miracle [the revival of Anne Greene after hanging, 1650], by A. W. Fox.

3298 Vol. 44.

a Philip Gilbert Hamerton, 1834–94, by E. E. Minton.
b Military ideals of the past: the order of St. John of Jerusalem, by E. E. Minton.

3299 Vol. 45.

a The *Beau Monde: or Literary and Fashionable Magazine*, 1806–9, by T. L. Cooper.
b James Joseph Sylvester [mathematician, d. 1897], by C. L. Barnes.
c Welsh folk-songs and other things of bardic interest, by T. M. Phillips.

d A literary eccentric: Walter Savage Landor, by J. C. Walters.

3300 Vol. 46.

a Henry Liverseege: the Ancoats artist [d. 1832], by W. Butterworth.
b 'Amicus redivivus': an account of George Dyer [d. 1841], by F. W. E. Barker.
c The Robin Hood ballads, by P. Haworth.
d Thomas Rowlandson, caricaturist and satirist, by W. Butterworth.
e Macaulay, by R. Peel.
f The sailing of the *Mayflower*, by E. E. Minton.

3301 Vol. 47.

a Dorothy Wordsworth's journals, by F. W. E. Barker.

3302 Vol. 48.

a Ford Madox Brown and Manchester, by W. Butter-worth.
b The life and times of Charles Swain, poet [d. 1874]: some unpublished letters, by J. C. Walters.
c Coleridge, by W. C. Hall.

3303 Vol. 49.

a The dance of death [in drawings, wood-cuts, etc.], by W. Butterworth.
b Keats, by W. C. Hall.
c George Sheffield [artist, d. 1892], by W. Butterworth.
d A rural walk in bygone Manchester [in early 19th cent.], by J. Holden.

3304 Vol. 50.

a William Byrd, by W. Butterworth.

3305 Vol. 51.

a Hartley Coleridge, by W. C. Hall.
b Elizabeth Canning [d. 1773] and the gypsies, by J. C. Walters.
c Maurice, Kingsley and Hughes, by W. H. Brown.
d Samuel Bamford, by T. M. Phillips.

3306 Vol. 52.

a Sir Charles Hallé and after, by G. Behrens.
b William Cowper, by W. C. Hall.
c James Rhoades, 1841–1923 [poet], by C. L. Barnes.
d Ben Brierley [writer, d. 1896], by W. Butterworth.
e John Taylor: water poet [d. 1653], by R. K. Derbyshire.
f Some letters of eminent men of the 18th cent., by E. McConnell.

3307 Vol. 53.

a The Holbein Society, by C. L. Barnes.
b John Roby [author, d. 1850], by A. W. Fox.
c Benjamin Robert Haydon [d. 1846], by W. C. Hall.

3308 Vol. 54.

a The Rev. Henry Newcome, M.A. [d. 1695], by W. H. Brown.
b Thomas Raikes, a forgotten journalist [d. 1848], by L. C. Hartley.
c Discipline aboard the *London* [*c.* 1859], by A. Eva.
d Niel Gow, 1727–1807 ['The Fiddler'], by A. H. M. Gow.
e The poets-laureate, by C. H. Bellamy.

3309 Vol. 55.

a The Rob Roy of the west [John Rattenbury, smuggler, b. 1778], by A. W. Fox.

3310 Vol. 58.

a A Lancaster literary family [the Binns family from 1747], by T. C. Hughes.

3311 Vol. 59.

a A 17th cent. traveller [Thomas Coryat, d. 1617], by O. H. Shephard.

b *My Confidences* [by Frederick Locker-Lampson, d. 1895], by L. C. Hartley.

c Stanley John Weyman [author, d. 1928], by T. C. Hughes.

3312 Index to publications, catalogue of the library, and list of members 1862-1903, comp. C. W. Sutton and W. R. Credland. 1903.

MANCHESTER STATISTICAL SOCIETY

Founded 1833, for the collection of facts illustrative of the condition of society, and the discussion of subjects of social and political economy.

Transactions, 1900-33 (33 vols. 1901-33):

3313 Vol. for 1900-1.

a Historical sketch of masters' associations in the cotton industry, by S. J. Chapman.

b The growth of foreign competition [in trade during the 19th cent.], by F. Merttens.

3314 Vol. for 1901-2.

a On the effective use of charitable loans to the poor without interest, by M. Hesse. [Includes an account of the history of the Jewish community in Manchester and the development of its communal charities, and of the Manchester Jewish board of guardians, 1873-1900]

b Public house licenses [including the history of the English licensing laws], by Sir W. H. Holdsworth.

c The distribution, growth, and decay of English towns in 1801, and since that date, by T. A. Welton.

3315 Vol. for 1903-4.

a History and development of the Manchester School Board, by C. H. Wyatt.

3316 Vol. for 1904-5.

a The organisation of labour as a political force, by A. H. Gill.

3317 Vol. for 1905-6.

a Growth of municipal expenditure [in Manchester, 1884-1904], by F. Brocklehurst.

b Rise and decline of the free trade movement, by F. Platt-Higgins. [Also published separately, 1905. New edition 1907, with a postscript on the 'dear loaf']

c Ten years experience of the Manchester and Salford county courts [1894-1904], by E. A. Parry.

d Trade societies in the middle ages, by A. Poock.

3318 Vol. for 1906-7.

a A decade of Manchester banking, 1896-1905, by D. D. Fraser.

b Manchester municipal public libraries [a study of their history, 1852-1906], by W. Butterworth.

3319 Vol. for 1908-9.

a The progress of tropical medicine, by Sir R. W. Boyce. [Includes an account of the history of the Liverpool School of Tropical Medicine]

3320 Vol. for 1912-13.

a The economic value of the Ship Canal [opened 1894] to Manchester and district, by J. S. McConechy.

b The question of cash reserves in the English banks [with particular reference to the situation during the period 1880-1911], by H. Mellor.

3321 Vol. for 1913-14.

a Industrial recruiting and the displacement of labour [male and female, 1851-1911], by S. J. Chapman and A. N. Shimmin.

3322 Vol. for 1914-15.

a Occupations of the people of England and Wales in 1911, from the point of view of industrial developments, by T. A. Welton.

3323 Vol. for 1915-16.

a The cotton trade during the Revolutionary and Napoleonic wars, by G. W. Daniels.

3324 Vol. for 1917-18.

a The cotton trade at the close of the Napoleonic war [1812-20], by G. W. Daniels.

b British mercantile marine in its relation to the state [1850-1918], by Sir N. Hill.

3325 Vol. for 1919-20.

a English poor law: its history and modern developments, by A. Poock.

3326 Vol. for 1920-1.

a Some aspects of trade fluctuation [in the building industry, *c.* 1860-*c.* 1910], by Sir W. Beveridge.

b Transport, by A. Watson. [The principal transport agencies in Britain and a brief account of their development]

3327 Vol. for 1921-2.

a Women's wages in the cotton trade [1833-1920], by Dorothea M. Barton.

3328 Vol. for 1923-4.

a Indian factories in the 18th cent., by G. Unwin.

3329 Vol. for 1925-6.

a Early history of the Manchester Statistical Society, by T. Gregory.

3330 Vol. for 1926-7.

a The comparative position of the Lancashire cotton industry and trade, by G. W. Daniels and J. Jewkes. [An inquiry into the extent and character of the depression in the Lancashire cotton industry, 1921-5, and the relation of Lancashire's decline to world conditions]

3331 Vol. for 1928-9.

a The course of employment since the war [in the United Kingdom, 1921-8], by H. Clay.

3332 Vol. for 1929-30.

a Cyclical fluctuations in the railway industry [1870-1928, with particular reference to unemployment figures], by C. D. Campbell.

b Fluctuations in savings bank deposits [from 1864], by T. S. Ashton.

3333 Vol. for 1930-1.

a Recent changes in the overseas trade of the United Kingdom [1913-28], by G. W. Daniels.

b Some problems of the Manchester merchant after the Napoleonic wars [1820-60], by A. Redford.

3334 Vol. for 1931-2.

a The national electricity scheme, by W. Walker. [An account of electrical development and the legislation concerning it from 1882, with particular reference to the Act of 1926]

3335 Vol. for 1932–3.

a Ottawa [agreements, 1932] and international trade, by H. G. Hughes.

b The mobility of labour and the localisation of industry [in the United Kingdom, chiefly between 1921 and 1931], by J. Jewkes.

MANORIAL SOCIETY

Founded 1906, for the preservation and study of manorial records, and to carry out the principal recommendations, so far as manorial records are concerned, of the report of the parliamentary Local Records Committee. Merged with the British Record Society in 1929.

Publications (Monographs):

3336 Nos. 1, 2, 4. Lists of manor court rolls in private hands, ed. A. L. Hardy. 3 vols. 1907–10. [Pt. 1, second edn., P. 1913]

3337 No. 3. 'A mannor and court baron' (Harleian ms. 6714), ed. N. J. Hone, with preface by J. S. Green. 1909.

3338 No. 5. The special Land Tenure Bill of 1911: a critical analysis, by H. W. Knocker, together with some account of Gavelkind and Borough English by the registrar of the Society [C. Greenwood]. P. 1911.

3339 No. 6. 'A concordance of all written lawes concerning lords of mannors, theire free tenantes, and copieholders', by William Barlee; addressed by him to the high sheriff of Essex, in 1578 (State Papers, Domestic, Eliz., vol. 123, no. 14), with biographical preface by the deputy registrar of the Society [A. L. Hardy]. 1911.

3340 No. 7. Kentish manorial incidents, by H. W. Knocker. P. 1912.

3341 No. 8. Facsimile reproduction of 'The order of keeping a court leet and court baron, with the charges appertaining to the same' (1650 edn.), with introductory note by the registrar of the Society [C. Greenwood]. 1914.

3342 No. 9. Modus tenendi Cŭr Barŏn cum visu franci plegii. A reprint of the first edn., 1510, together with translations and introductory note by C. Greenwood. 1915.

3343 No. 10. The relation betweene the lord of a mannor and the coppy-holder his tenant [by Sir Charles Calthorpe]. Reprint of the edn. printed 1635. 1917.

3344 Nos. 11, 12. Descriptive catalogue of manorial rolls belonging to Sir H. F. Burke, with notes and extracts illustrating manorial custom, by E. Margaret Thompson. 2 vols. 1922–3.

3345 No. 13. Manors and the new acts. The freehold tenement, by H. W. Knocker. P. 1926.

3346 No. 14. Manors and the new acts. The freehold tenement: extinguishment of incidents, by H. W. Knocker. Reprinted from the *Law Times*. P. 1926.

3347 No. 15. The ancient 'Greenways' of Suffolk, by H. W. Knocker. Reprinted from the *East Anglian Daily Times*. P. [1928].

3348 No. 16. Catalogue of 'manorial documents' preserved in the muniment room of New College, Oxford, comp. T. F. Hobson. 1929.

MANX SOCIETY

Founded 1899, as the Manx Language Society (Yn Cheshaght Ghailckagh), for the preservation of the Manx language and the study of its literature. Title changed to above form in 1913.

Publications:

3349 Mannin. Journal of matters past and present relating to Mann, vol. 1 (1913–[18]).

a The saint's name Marown in Wales, by J. Rhŷs.

b Manx carvals [carols] and their writers, by P. W. Caine.

c Manx coast sketches, by P. G. Ralfe. 1: Between Fleshwick and Dalby. 2: The coast of the southern Lowland. 3: Port St. Mary to Port Erin.

d Manx folk song, by A. P. Graves.

e Ruskin and Egbert Rydings [letters, 1875–86], ed. Sophia Morrison.

f First appearance of a Viking ship on a Manx monument [a cross-slab from Kirk Maughold], by P. M. C. Kermode.

g Expedition to the Isle of Man: a hitherto unpublished diary by George Borrow [1855].

h Sir William le Scrope, K.G., King of Man, 1393–9, by G. F. Clucas.

i Life in Ballaugh in the [eighteen] forties, by Ellie Shimmin.

j Reminiscences of Manx pioneers [in America], by W. S. Kerruish.

k Old Peel, by G.G.

l Old Manx music, by G. W. Wood.

m T. E. Brown—Egbert Rydings [letters, 1893–7].

n John Wesley and Mann, by Jessie D. Kerruish.

o New letters from T. E. Brown [to Charles Roeder, 1895–7], ed. Sophia Morrison.

p Manx falcons at the coronations: puffins, eagles and bucks, by G. W. Wood.

3350 William Cashen's Manx folk-lore [ed. with biographical introd. by Sophia Morrison]. 1912.

3351 Place-names of the Isle of Man, with their origin and history. 6 pts. 1925–9.

MASONIC STUDY SOCIETY

Founded 1921, to study the symbolism of freemasonry in its various degrees and to investigate its origin and meaning on anthropological lines.

Transactions, vols. 1–11[1] (1922?–33?):

3352 Vol. 4.

a Greater lights in the 18th cent., with some sidelights on early workings, by Sir F. Pollock.

b Masonic charges and some facts to be derived from their study, by H. G. Rosedale.

3353 Vol. 6.

a Freemasonry and social life in the 18th cent., by W. J. Carroll.

3354 Vol. 10.

a Is masonry to-day on the right track?, by T. L. Salisbury. [Includes a general account of the movement in England from the 17th cent.]

3355 Index to the Transactions of the Masonic Study Society, vols. 1–7. Pt. 1: Subject-index. Pt. 2: Contributors. Pt. 3: Books reviewed. P. [n.d.].

[1] Vols. 2 and 5 have not been seen.

MEDICO-LEGAL SOCIETY

Founded 1902, to promote the advancement of medico-legal knowledge in all or any of its branches.

Transactions, vols. 1–26 ([1904]–33), contd. as Medico-Legal and Criminological Review, vol. 1 (1933):

3356 Vol. 5.

a Bills of mortality, by W. A. Brend.

3357 Vol. 7.

a A note upon deodands, by W. W. Westcott.

3358 Vol. 8.

a The ancient office of coroner, by F. J. Waldo.

3359 Vol. 9.

a The Sidney Street affair [1911] in its medico-legal aspect, by C. G. Grant.

3360 Vol. 20.

a The case of John Perry, 1660 [in which he was kidnapped and sold to Turks, but was reputed to have been murdered], by Sir J. Collie.

b Titles of papers and names of speakers, vols. 1–20.

c Index, vols. 1–20.

MERSEYSIDE ASSOCIATION FOR MASONIC RESEARCH

[*See p.* 484]

MIDLAND RECORD SOCIETY

Founded 1894, to collect original and copies of ancient documents, records, maps, plans, and mss. having reference to Birmingham and its neighbourhood; to transcribe and calendar such documents; and to print such documents as may from time to time be decided upon.

Transactions, vols. 4–6 (1901?–3?):

3361 Vol. 4.

a Warwickshire wills [1519–84].

b Wills and administrations of Gibbon, Gibbons, Gibbins, etc. in the 16th cent.

c A herald's summons [1683, to the chief constables of the hundred of Hemlingford].

d Surrender of the abbey and convent of Kenilworth to Henry VIII, 1537, translated into English by W. Wilson and W. F. Carter.

3362 Vol. 5

a Inventory of the goods of Sir Charles Hales of Newland, Coventry, 1618.

b Deeds relating to a property called Ladyland, in Rowley Regis [12 Henry VI—1666].

3363 Vol. 6.

a Birmingham wills [1533–99, by J. Hill. Contd. from vols. 1 and 2].

b Index locorum to the subsidy roll of Warwickshire for 1327, showing the hundred and leet or liberty in which each place is situate, comp. W. F. Carter.

c Index nominum to the subsidy roll of Warwickshire for 1327, comp. E. A. Fry.

d Taxacio XXe in comitatu Warrinici domino rege Edwardo tercio a conquestu concesse anno regni sui primo. [Transcript, Latin, for Brinklow in Knightlow hundred]

MILFORD-ON-SEA RECORD SOCIETY

Founded 1909, for the collection of local information of antiquarian and other interest.

Occasional Magazine, vols. 1–5 (1909–51):

3364 Vol. 1.

a Notes on the origin of 'Milford' and the Domesday records, by W. Ravenscroft.

b The church, etc. [Milford], by A. B. Woodd.

c The village [Milford], by A. B. Woodd.

d Beating the bounds of Milford, by H. E. U. Bull.

e The prisoner of Hurst [Father Paul Atkinson, d. 1729], by W. Ravenscroft.

f Endowed charities of the parish of Milford, by V. D. Harris.

g The Needles rocks, lighthouse, etc., Isle of Wight, by E. L. Agar.

h A note on Anthony Batts [d. 1850] and his poems, by V. D. Harris.

i Parish church of All Saints, Milford-on-Sea, by W. Ravenscroft, A. L. Barker, and A. B. Woodd.

j Notes on salterns, by A. B. Woodd.

k Transcript of a summary of acts of parliament relating to beggars [1678], by V. D. Harris.

l Smuggling, by J. C. N. King.

m The mummers at Milford 50 years ago [*c.* 1862], by C. Rivett-Carnac.

n The Milford secession from the Church of England, 1815–16, by W. Ravenscroft. [On the early Baptist community in Milford]

3365 Vol. 2.

a Col. Peter Hawker [d. 1853] and his connection with Keyhaven, by V. D. Harris.

b Notes on Col. Peter Hawker and his family, by F. Creighton.

c Notes from Mr. Birkett's diaries [1680–89 and 1718–*c.* 1738], by W. S. Sykes.

d Notes in regard to the associations of Dame Alice Lisle with Pennington, by A. B. Woodd.

e Notes on the connection of Dame Alice Lisle with the parishes of Milford and Dibden in the New Forest, by C. Rivett-Carnac.

f The threatened invasion by the French in 1794–8, by W. S. Sykes.

g Keyhaven, by A. C. G. Heygate. [Further article in vol. 5]

h A list of the principal inhabitants of Milford, 1680–90, taken from the tithe account of John Birkett, vicar; to which have been added various details of their holdings traced in some cases down to 1800, by W. S. Sykes.

i Henry Doman [d. 1900] and his poems, by W. Ravenscroft.

j Musical gleanings from the churchwardens' books, by C. F. A. Williams.

k The reference to Milford church in Domesday book, by W. S. Sykes.

l Silk production at Milford, by Agatha Harris.

m Milford and the war [1914–17].

n Hurst castle, by A. C. G. Heygate.

o Recollections of Milford, by A. Cole. [Contd. as 'Some further recollections' in vol. 3, and 'Reminiscences of Milford' in vol. 5]

p Place-names of the ancient parish of Milford, by W. S Sykes.

3366 Vol. 3.

a Notes on the old mill of Milford.

b Milford tithe award and map of 1840.

c A local ritual controversy [*c.* 1882], by V. D. Harris.

d Notes on the older houses of Milford and its neighbourhood, by A. C. G. Heygate.

e Burial records, 1594–1691; memorials inside Milford church; Baptist chapel graves.

f Tombs and memorials inside Milford church, 1923, by A. W. W. Brown.

g Poorhouses in England, with special reference to Milford poorhouse and the relief of the poor in the parish, by V. D. Harris.

h The old church, Hordle, Hants, by W. Ravenscroft.

3367 Vol. 4.

a Arnewood tower, by T. A. Wylie.

b The New Forest 'shakers', by T. A. Wylie.

c Efford mill, by A. B. Woodd.

d The coming of S. Joseph of Aramathea to England, and the way by which he came, by W. Ravenscroft.

e Notes relating to the development of Milford, by V. D. Harris.

f Milford since 1900, by A. C. G. Heygate.

g The Dane stream and Avon Water, by A. W. W. Brown.

h Longford castle, and its connection with Hurst, by A. C. G. Heygate.

i A dispute between Mr. Benjamin Pepper of Milford mill and Mrs. Whitby in 1833–5, by A. C. G. Heygate.

j The New Forest district, by G. B. B. Johnson.

3368 Vol. 5.

a Milford church and its connections with Christchurch priory, by A. Woodd.

b Bishop F. T. McDougall, bishop of Labuan and Sarawak, 1855–68, vicar of Milford, 1881–5, by R. J. Hitchcock.

c The hospital [at Milford-on-Sea, 1900–38], by A. E. Sears.

d All Saints' church, Milford [alterations, etc., 1920–38], by C. F. G. Young and C. A. Finzel.

e A brief account of Lymore [Hants], by P. T. B. Beale with the help of A. Cole.

f The spire of Milford church, by R. T. Cole.

g Notes on the early development of Milford-on-Sea, by A. E. Sears.

h Milford and the war, 1939–45, by S. G. Hooper.

i Milford churchwardens' accounts, 1713–1800, by F. W. Sears.

j Milford church: matters relating to church fabric and finance, 1937–49, by S. G. Hooper.

k Milford church stones, by S. G. Hooper.

l The little silver tray and cover in Milford church, by S. G. Hooper.

m The advowsons of Milford and her neighbours, by S. G. Hooper.

MILL HILL HISTORICAL SOCIETY

Founded 1929, to preserve permanently every kind of historical record relating to Mill Hill and the manor of Hendon (which includes the Watling estate).

Publications:

3369 Transactions, no. 1 (1933).

a Hugh de Cressingham [d. 1297], by N. G. Brett-James.

3370 The story of Goldbeaters and Watling, by A. G. Clarke. *P.* 1931.

3371 Hendon antiquities: a catalogue of deeds, surveys, maps, drawings, prints, photographs and miscellanea relating to the manor of Hendon. *P.* 1931.

MODERN HUMANITIES RESEARCH ASSOCIATION

Founded 1918, as the Modern Language Research Association, for the encouragement of advanced study in modern languages and literature. Title changed to the above form in 1919.

Publications, nos. 1–8:

3372 No. 5. Joseph Ritson [d. 1803], by W. P. Ker. *P.* 1922. [Reprinted from *Bulletin*, no. 14]

3373 No. 7. Shaftesbury in Italy, by B. Croce. *P.* 1924. [On Anthony Ashley Cooper, Earl of Shaftesbury, d. 1713. In Italian]

M.H.R.A.: Bulletin [*from no.* 9 *onwards* Annual Bulletin] of the Association, nos. 1–12 (1927–33):

3374 No. 1.

a English friendships of Sainte-Beuve, by Eva M. Phillips.

3375 No. 2.

a The Eustace legend in medieval England, by J. Murray.

3376 No. 7.

a 13th cent. ms. fragment at Peterborough [dealing with medicinal prescriptions], by A. Bell.

3377 No. 9.

a English history and Italian drama, by E. G. Gardner.

Bibliography [*from* 1923 *onwards* Annual Bibliography] of English Language and Literature, vols. 1–13 (1921–33)

3378 [Lists of each year's publications]

Modern Language Review, vols. 17–28[1] (1922–33):

3379 Vol. 17.

a Richardson, Warburton and French fiction, by R. S. Crane.

b Tristram and the house of Anjou, by R. S. Loomis.

c Queen Elizabeth in a game of 'Truth', by C. R. Baskerville.

d The single combat in certain cycles of English and Scandinavian tradition and romance, by M. Ashdown.

e The Middle English prose psalter of Richard Rolle of Hampole [d. 1349], by Dorothy Everett. [Contd. in vol. 18]

f Some new facts about Shirley [d. 1666], by A. C. Baugh.

g Andrew Marvell: some biographical points, by H. M. Margoliouth.

h Geoffrey of Monmouth and Spanish literature, by W. J. Entwistle.

3380 Vol. 18.

a The single combat in the 'Lai d'Haveloc', by A. Bell.

b An Old English translation of a letter from Wynfrith [i.e. Boniface] to Eadburga (716–7) in Cotton ms. Otho C.1, by K. Sisam.

c Italian influence on the English court masque, by Enid Welsford.

d Andrew Marvell: further biographical points, by P. Legouis.

3381 Vol. 19.

a Was Peter Cunningham a forger?, by W. J. Lawrence. [Relates to his edition (1842) of the revels accounts of Elizabeth and James I]

[1] For previous vols. see under Modern Language Association.

b Literature no 'document', by E. E. Stoll. [Historical value of literature as a reflection of the customs etc. of the time]

c Joshua Steele on speech-melody (1779), by Marie L. Barker.

d A proposal for an English academy in 1660, by E. Freeman.

e The literary activities of the Spanish *emigrados* in England, 1814–34, by E. A. Peers.

f Mr. W. J. Lawrence and Peter Cunningham, by Charlotte C. Stopes.

g Thomas Ravenscroft's theatrical associations, by W. J. Lawrence. [T. Ravenscroft, d. 1635]

3382 Vol. 20.

a 'Memoirs of a gentlewoman of the old school' [Mrs. Ann McTaggart, d. *c.* 1830], by Edith Birkhead.

b Italian influence on English scholarship and literature during the 'Romantic revival', by R. W. King. [Contd. in vol. 21]

c S. T. Coleridge and the London Philosophical Society, by Fannie E. Ratchford.

d Elizabeth Elstob [d. 1756], the learned Saxonist, by Margaret Ashdown.

e Dryden and the English academy, by O. F. Emerson.

f William Baldwin [fl. 1547], by Eveline I. Feasey.

3383 Vol. 21.

a A 13th cent. ms. at Maidstone [including a text of the 'Proverbs of Alfred' and some Anglo-Norman verse], by C. Brown.

b Bartholomew Yong [fl. 1577–98], translator, by T. P. Harrison.

c James Melvill [d. 1614]: an obscure man of letters, by Marjorie A. Bald.

d Gaimar and the Edgar-Aelfðryð story, by A. Bell.

e Yorkshire place-names: York, Ure, Jervaulx, by R. E. Zachrisson.

3384 Vol. 22.

a John Marston, dramatist [d. 1634]: some new facts about his life, by R. E. Brettle.

3385 Vol. 23.

a Sir Walter Scott and Maria Edgeworth: some unpublished letters [1811–30], by Harriet J. and H. E. Butler.

b More's *History of Richard III*, by R. W. Chambers.

3386 Vol. 24.

a 'Young Mr. Cartwright' [d. 1686, actor and benefactor of Dulwich College], by Eleanore Boswell.

b The Trojan legend in England: some instances of its application to the politics of the times, by A. E. Parsons.

3387 Vol. 25.

a The rôles of William Kemp [Shakespearean actor, fl. 1600], by H. D. Gray.

b Goodman's Fields theatre [1729–42], by F. T. Wood.

3388 Vol. 26.

a William Kemp not Falstaff, by T. W. Baldwin.

b Footnotes to 17th cent. biographies: Samuel Pepys, Inigo Jones, Sir Charles Sedley, Thomas Shadwell, William Wycherley, by Eleanore Boswell.

c Milton's first marriage [?1642], by B. A. Wright. [Contd. in vol. 27]

d Arthurian tombs and megalithic monuments, by L. H. Loomis.

3389 Vol. 27.

a Sophie von La Roche's visit to England in 1786, by J. G. Robertson.

b A biographical note on John Dryden, by C. E. Ward.

3390 Vol. 28.

a Fulk Greville, 1st Lord Brooke [d. 1628], by G. Bullough.

b The political 'disloyalty' of Thomas Southerne [d. 1746], by C. Leech.

3391 Modern Language Review, vols. 11–20, general index. 1926.

3392 Modern Language Review, vols. 21–30, general index, by Winifred Husbands. 1938.

The Year's Work in Modern Language Studies. vols. 1–3, 1931–3.

3393 [Each contains a short report by G. J. Williams on Welsh studies]

MODERN LANGUAGE ASSOCIATION

Founded 1892, to emphasize the close relation into which the study of modern languages should be brought with other modern studies, such as English, History, Geography, and Economics, in order to form a complete course of Modern Humanities.

Modern Language Quarterly, vols. 4–7 (1901–4):

3394 Vol. 4.

a The Elizabethan age, by H. F. Heath.

b Henry Vaughan [d. 1695], by Geraldine Hodgson.

Modern Language Review, vols. 1–16[1] (1906 [1905]–21):

3395 Vol. 1.

a English translations of Dante in the 18th cent., by P. Toynbee.

b The authorship of the songs in Lyly's plays, by W. W. Greg.

c The pre-Shakespearean ghost, by F. W. Moorman.

d A pamphlet by Bishop Berkeley hitherto undescribed [relating to a national bank], by E. Dowden.

e Knowledge of Shakespeare on the continent at the beginning of the 18th cent., by J. G. Robertson.

3396 Vol. 2.

a Court performances before Queen Elizabeth, by E. K. Chambers.

b An Anglo-Norman calendar [13th cent.], by H. J. Chaytor.

c Milton's heroic line viewed from an historical standpoint, by W. Thomas. [Contd. in vol. 3]

3397 Vol. 3.

a The date of Chapman's *Bussy D'Ambois*, by T. M. Parrott.

b Notes on some English university plays [16th and 17th cent.], by G. C. M. Smith.

c Spenser and Lady Carey, by P. W. Long.

d Shakespeare's plays: an examination [authorship and date], by E. H. C. Oliphant. [Contd. in vol. 4]

3398 Vol. 4.

a Court performances under James I, by E. K. Chambers.

b Marlowe at Cambridge, by G. C. M. Smith.

c The Areopagus [literary society] of Sidney and Spenser, by H. Maynadier.

[1] For subsequent vols. see under Modern Humanities Research Association.

d Notes on the supposed dramatic character of the *ludi* in the great wardrobe accounts of Edward III, by A. Beatty.

e Anthony Munday, pamphleteer and pursuivant [d. 1633], by J. D. Wilson.

3399 Vol. 5.

a Old Scandinavian personal names in England, by H. C. Wyld.

b 15th cent. carols by John Audelay, by E. K. Chambers and F. Sidgwick. [Contd. in vol. 6]

c John Lyly's relations by marriage, by J. D. Wilson. [2nd pt. in 'Discussions' by A. Feuillerat]

3400 Vol. 6.

a Alexander Montgomerie [d. 1610?], by A. F. Westcott.

b Bacon's poem, *The world*: its date and relation to certain other poems, by H. J. C. Grierson.

c An Anglo-French life of St. Osith, by A. T. Baker.

3401 Vol. 7.

a The date and authorship of *Jacke Jugeler*, by W. H. Williams.

b The centenary of the completion of Cary's *Dante* [1812], by P. Toynbee.

c The 'Athenian Virtuosi' and the 'Athenian Society', by H. R. Steeves.

3402 Vol. 8.

a 15th cent. carols and other pieces, by M. R. James and G. C. Macaulay.

b Fielding's *Champion* [periodical] and Capt. Hercules Vinegar, by J. E. Wells.

c Swift's *Tale of a Tub*, by A. C. Guthkelch. [Contd. in vol. 10]

d An Anglo-Norman apocalypse from Shaftesbury abbey, by J. C. Fox.

e A chronological arrangement of Donne's sermons, by Evelyn M. Spearing.

3403 Vol. 9.

a Early uses of *parliamentum*, by A. B. White.

b [Influence of] Lessing in England, by S. H. Kenwood.

3404 Vol. 10.

a The Ruthwell and Bewcastle crosses, by M. D. Forbes and B. Dickins.

b Walpole and the *Mémoires de Grammont*, by Ruth Clark.

c The date of the old English inscription on the Brussels cross, by A. S. Cook.

d The Welsh 'Troilus and Cressida' and its relation to the Elizabethan drama, by J. S. P. Tatlock.

e Ballad collections of the 18th cent., by Grace R. Trenery.

3405 Vol. 11.

a The authorship of the *Ancren Riwle*, by V. McNabb.

b Political prophecies in the reign of Henry VIII, by Madeleine H. Dodds.

3406 Vol. 12.

a Who was Spenser's Bon Font? [?Ulpian Fulwell, b. 1546], by A. B. Gough.

b Marylebone—Tyburn—Holborn, by R. E. Zachrisson.

c The Georgian Englishman in contemporary Italian eyes, by L. Collison-Morley.

3407 Vol. 13.

a Dryden not the author of *Macflecknoe*, by P. L. Babington.

b The date of *Love's Labour's Lost*, by H. B. Charlton.

c Spenser's 'Blatant Beast', by M. Y. Hughes.

d Dryden's *Macflecknoe*: a vindication, by G. Thorn-Drury.

e A 17th cent. play-list, by A. C. Baugh.

3408 Vol. 14.

a Henry Brooke's *Gustavus Vasa*, by H. Wright.

b Charles Fitzgeffrey, poet and divine [d. 1638], by G. C. M. Smith.

c The King's revels players of 1619–23, by W. J. Lawrence.

3409 Vol. 15.

a The 'free list' and theatre tickets in Shakespeare's time and after, by Alwin Thaler.

b Doors and curtains in Restoration theatres, by A. Nicoll. [2nd pt. by W. J. Lawrence in 'Miscellaneous Notes'. Contd. in vol. 16 by M. Summers]

c Vernacular books in England in the 14th and 15th cent., by Margaret Deanesly.

3410 Vol. 16.

a The origin of the English heroic play, by M. L. Poston.

b An Anglo-Norman poem by Edward II, by P. Studer.

c John (Henry) Scogan [14th or 15th cent.], by W. E. Farnham.

d Thomas Edwards [fl. 1595], author of *Cephalus and Procris, Narcissus*, by Charlotte C. Stopes.

e Political plays of the Restoration, by A. Nicoll.

3411 Modern Language Review, vols. 1–10, general index. 1915.

Modern Language Teaching, vols. 1–15 (1905–19):

3412 Vol. 2.

a French influences in English education, by M. E. Sadler.

3413 Vol. 3.

a Drayton [d. 1631], by H. Ellershaw.

b The development of the legend of the quest of the holy grail, by Mary C. Malim.

3414 Vol. 9.

a French and Flemish surnames in England, by E. Weekley.

3415 Vol. 11.

a The spoken English of the early 18th cent., by H. C. Wyld.

b Learning French in 1670, by Ruth Clark.

3416 Vol. 14.

a Welsh poetry, by A. S. D. Smith.

Modern Languages: a review of foreign letters, science, and the arts, vols. 1–15 (1919–34):

3417 Vol. 1.

a Britain as an Italian province [during the Roman occupation], by T. Okey.

3418 Vol. 4.

a Notes on English influence in the vocabulary of written French, by P. Barbier.

3419 Vol. 6.

a France of the 18th cent. as seen through English eyes, by F. C. Green.

3420 Vol. 10.

a The schism of England: Calderón's play and Shakespeare's [*Henry VIII*], by H. Birkhead.

3421 Vol. 13.

a Language and history, by A. Mawer.

MONMOUTHSHIRE AND CAERLEON ANTIQUARIAN ASSOCIATION

Founded 1847, as the Caerleon Antiquarian Association, for the study and preservation of county monuments and the maintenance of a museum at Caerleon. Title changed to above form in 1854.

Publications:

3422 The lordship, castle and town of Chepstow, otherwise Striguil, with an appendix on the lordship of Caerleon, by J. G. Wood. 1910. [Not seen]

3423 Some features of the monastic buildings disclosed by recent excavations within the precincts of Tintern abbey, by J. G. Wood. *P.* 1912.

3424 Proceedings, 1927–8. *P.* [1929?].

  a Field day at Machen. [Description of the church, list of incumbents, and notes on Castell Meredydd]
  b The lordship of Machen, by Sir J. Bradney.
  c A Roman pipe-burial from Caerleon, by R. E. M. Wheeler.
  d Pedigree roll of Sir Roger Williams [drawn by Thomas Jones of Fountain Gate, Cardiganshire, 1596].

MONUMENTAL BRASS SOCIETY

Founded 1887, as the Cambridge University Association of Brass Collectors, to ensure the better preservation of monumental brasses, to promote the study of, and interest in them, and to compile, with a view to publication, a full and accurate list of all extant brasses, English and foreign, and of all lost brasses, whereof notices or illustrations are to be found. Reconstituted in 1894 with the above title. Suspended 1914–34.

Transactions, vols. 4–6 (1900–14):

3425 Vol. 4.

  a A list of palimpsest brasses, comp. M. Stephenson. [Contd. in vols. 5 and 6]
  b Buckinghamshire notes, by H. K. St. J. Sanderson. [Contd. from vol. 2]
  c Some interesting Essex brasses, by M. Christy and W. W. Porteous.
  d The brasses of Cambridgeshire, by C. J. P. Cave, O. J. Charlton, and R. A. S. Macalister. [Contd. from vol. 3]
  e Zoology on brasses, chiefly from Gloucestershire examples, by C. T. Davis.
  f Additional note on brasses in St. Paul's church, Bedford, by H. K. St. J. Sanderson.
  g Notes. [Includes: The brass to Robert Pursglove, sometime bishop of Hull, d. 1579, in Tideswell church, Derbys.]
  h Additions and corrections. [Includes further notes on the Pursglove brass]

3426 Vol. 5.

  a The monumental brasses of Derbyshire, by H. E. Field. [Contd. from vol. 3]
  b Monumental brasses of Hackney, Mdx., by J. F. Williams.
  c List of brasses in Lancaster parish church, by P. Manning.
  d Note on the brass of Robert Honywode, 1522, in St. George's chapel, Windsor, by A. Oliver.
  e Monumental brasses formerly in Great Marlow church, by M. Stephenson.
  f Cirencester, parish church of St. John the Baptist: brass inscriptions subsequent to 1600, by H. Druitt.

  g Notes on an engraved slab and brass figures in Dunston church, Norf., by E. B. Evans.
  h Gloucestershire notes, by H. Druitt.
  i Brasses in the church of St. Mary, Islington, Mdx., by M. Stephenson.
  j Bibliographical notes, by R. Griffin.
  k List of casements remaining at Christchurch, Hants, by H. Druitt.
  l List of illustrations in Druitt's *Costume on Brasses* and Macklin's *Brasses of England*, arranged topographically.
  m List of Hampshire brasses, by C. J. P. Cave. [Contd. in vol. 6]
  n Brasses in Tattershall church, Lincs., by M. Stephenson. [Contd. in vol. 6]
  o The Sidney tombs at Penshurst and Ludlow, by R. Griffin.
  p Notes on the brasses remaining at Harpenden and Kimpton, Herts., 1909, by H. Druitt.

3427 Vol. 6.

  a Note on an enamelled shield bearing the arms of Barton, by M. Stephenson.
  b Brasses in St. Michael's church, Stamford, Lincs., by T. Sandall.
  c Notes on some recent repairs to brasses, by W. E. Gawthorp. [Additional notes occur later in this vol.]
  d The Dormer tombs at Wing, Bucks., by W. J. Hemp.
  e Note on the brass of William Holyngbroke, 1375, in New Romney church, Kent, by R. Griffin.
  f Brasses commemorative of the Fettiplace family, by J. R. Dunlop.
  g Lost brasses.
  h Kentish items, by R. Griffin.
  i Notes on the brasses and effigies at Burghfield, Berks., by J. C. Smith.
  j List of monumental brasses in Surrey, by M. Stephenson.
  k Note on the Curzon brass at Waterperry, Oxon., by J. C. Smith.

Portfolio, vols. 2–4 (1900–14):

3428 Vol. 2. Containing reproductions of the following brasses:

  a Nicholas of Louth, rector and builder of the chancel 1383. Cottingham, Yorks.
  b Sir John Phelip, 1415, Walter Cookesey, esq. (1407), and their wife Matilda. Kidderminster, Worcs.
  c Edmund fforde, esq., 1439. Swainswick, Som.
  d Sir Richard Byngham, justice of the king's bench, 1476, and widow Margaret. Middleton, Warwicks.
  e Louis Corteville, 1504, and wife Dame Colyne van Caestre, 1496. Museum of Practical Geology, London.
  f Edward Leventhorp, esq., 1551, and wife Elizabeth, engraved *c.* 1600. Sawbridgeworth, Herts.
  g William de Fulburne, canon of St. Paul's, London, 1391. Fulbourn, Cambs.
  h Sir John Lysle, 1407, brass engraved *c.* 1425. Thruxton, Hants.
  i Robert Skern, 1437, and wife. Kingston-upon-Thames, Surr.
  j Sir William Yelverton, justice of the king's bench, and wife Agnes, *c.* 1470. Rougham, Norf.
  k Sir John Arundell, 1561, and wives (Mary Bevyll and Julian Eryssy). Stratton, Cornw.
  l Anne, wife of John Savage, 1605. Wormington, Glos.
  m Sir William de Echingham, 1388. Etchingham, Suss.
  n William Langeton, canon of Exeter, 1413. Exeter cathedral.
  o John Fortey, woolman, 1458. Northleach, Glos.
  p John Fastolff, esq., 1445, and wife, Katherine, 1478. Oulton, Suff.

q Joan (Walrond), wife of Robert Strangbon, 1507. Childrey, Berks.

r John Cutte, mayor of Bristol, 1575, and wife, Joan. Burnett, Som.

s Sir Robert de Cumpton, 1308. Hawton, Notts. [Matrix]

t Richard Torryngton, 1356, and wife, Margaret. Berkhampstead, Herts.

u A knight and lady of the Massyngberd family, *c.* 1400, with altered inscription to Sir Thomas Massyngberde, 1552, and wife Joan. Gunby, Lincs.

v Thomas Harlyng, canon of Chichester and rector of Pulborough, 1423. Pulborough, Suss.

w William Dunche, esq., d. 1597, and wife, Marie. Little Wittenham, Berks.

x Mary, wife of William Bussie, *c.* 1600. Norwich, St. Peter Mancroft.

y A priest, *c.* 1360. North Mimms, Herts.

z William de Lodyngton, justice of the king's bench, 1419. Gunby, Lincs.

aa Sir Thomas Stathum, 1470, and wives, Elizabeth and Thomasine. Morley, Derbys.

bb A civilian and wife, *c.* 1500 (probably Robert Gardiner, 1508, and wife). Norwich, St. Andrew.

cc John Gyfforde and wife, Susan, 1560. Northolt, Mdx.

dd Sir Richard de Boselyngthorpe, *c.* 1310. Buslingthorpe, Lincs.

ee Two priests, *c.* 1430–40. Formerly at Great Marlow, Bucks.

ff Richard Pendilton, 1502. Eversley, Hants.

gg [Arms from] the Earl of Strafforde's vault, 1687. York minster.

hh Richard Martyn and wife, 1402. Dartford, Kent.

ii Robert de Frevile, 1393, and wife, Clarice, 1399. Little Shelford, Cambs.

jj Robert Langton, D.C.L., d. 1524. Queen's College, Oxford.

kk Robert Shiers, esq., 1668. Great Bookham, Surr.

ll Casement, 15th cent. Byland abbey, Yorks.

mm Thomas de Frevile, 1405, and widow, Margaret. Little Shelford, Cambs.

nn Robert Morley, rector, 1492. Walton-on-Trent, Derbys.

oo A civilian and a lady, *c.* 1500. Brown Candover, Hants.

pp Elizabeth Eynns, 1585. York minster.

qq Walter Davy, vicar, *c.* 1460. Poling, Suss.

rr A notary, *c.* 1475. Ipswich, St. Mary tower.

ss Henry Sacheverell, 1558, and wife Isabel. Morley, Derbys.

tt James Cotrel, 1595. York minster.

uu Martin de Hampton, rector of Ickham and prebendary of Wingham, 1306. Ickham, Kent. [Matrix of a cross only]

vv Sir Thomas Urswyk, recorder of London, chief baron of the exchequer, 1479, and wife. Dagenham, Essex.

ww The Annunciation from the brass to William Porter, S.T.B., warden of New College, Oxford, and canon of Hereford, 1524. Hereford cathedral.

xx Robert Cotton, 1591, and wife, Grace. Richmond, Surr.

yy Dame Millicent Meryng, 1419. East Markham, Notts.

zz Hera, wife of Sir Walter Pole, 1423. Sawston, Cambs. [Matrix]

aaa John Wantele, 1424. Amberley, Suss.

bbb Nicholas Carrew, and wife, Isabel, 1432. Beddington, Surr.

ccc Robert Askwith, alderman, 1597. York, St. Crux.

3429 Vol. 3. Containing reproductions of the following brasses:

a A civilian and lady, *c.* 1400. Northamptonshire Architectural Society [1906].

b Richard Delamare, esq., 1435, and wife, Isabel, 1421. Hereford cathedral.

c Robert Whyte, esq., 1512. South Warnborough, Hants.

d William Lawnder, priest, *c.* 1530. Northleach, Glos.

e Thomas Atkinson, 1642. York, All Saints, North Street.

f Casement ascribed to Maud de Burgh, widow of Gilbert de Clare, Earl of Gloucester and Hertford, 1315. Tewkesbury abbey.

g Thomas and Richard Gomfrey, 1399. Dronfield, Derbys.

h William Brome, builder of chapel and benefactor to the church, 1461. Holton, Oxon.

i Sir Edmund Tame, 1534, and wives, Agnes (Greville) and Elizabeth (Tyringham). Fairford, Glos.

j [Arms of] Sir John Whyte, d. 1573. Aldershot, Hants.

k Sir Thomas Burton, d. 1381, and wife, Margery. Little Casterton, Rut.

l Robert Fowler and wife, Alice, 1540. Islington, Mdx. [With palimpsest reverses]

m Henry Savill and wife, Margaret, 1546. Islington, Mdx. [With palimpsest reverses]

n Ralph, Baron Cromwell, lord high treasurer of England, founder of the college, d. 1455, and wife, Margaret, d. 1454. Tattershall, Lincs.

o Joan, Lady Cromwell, d. 1479. Tattershall, Lincs.

p Maud, Lady Willoughby, d. 1497. Tattershall, Lincs.

q A priest, *c.* 1510 (probably John Gyger, provost of the college). Tattershall, Lincs.

r William Moor, provost, 1456. Tattershall, Lincs.

s William Symson, chaplain to Edward Hevyn, d. 1519. Tattershall, Lincs.

t Robert, son of Thomas Russell, *c.* 1390. Strensham, Worcs.

u Sir John Russel, 1405. Strensham, Worcs.

v Thomas Mordon, LL.B., treasurer of St. Paul's, rector of Fladbury, 1458. Fladbury, Worcs.

w Christopher Peyton, esq., 1507, and wife Elizabeth. Isleham, Cambs.

x Sir Robert Peyton, 1518, and wife Elizabeth. Isleham, Cambs.

y John Pen, esq., 1641, and wife Sarah. Penn, Bucks.

z A lady, *c.* 1310. Sedgefield, Durham.

aa A man in armour, of the Compton family, *c.* 1350. Freshwater, Isle of Wight.

bb A priest, *c.* 1370. Watton, Herts.

cc Thomas Peyton, esq., 1484, and wives Margaret (Bernard) and Margaret (Francis). Isleham, Cambs.

dd Robert Smythe, gent., d. 1539, and wife Katherine, d. 1549. Thames Ditton, Surr.

ee William Notte, esq., d. 1576, and wife Elizabeth, d. 1587. Thames Ditton, Surr.

ff Henry de Grofhurst, rector, 1311–62. Horsmonden, Kent.

gg John Boville, esq., 1467, and wife Isabel. Stokerston, Leics.

hh John Tyringham, esq., 1484. Tyringham, Bucks.

ii John Rusche, gent., d. 1498. London, All Hallows, Barking.

jj John Hotham, master in theology, rector, 1361. Chinnor, Oxon.

kk Alexander Chelseye, rector, 1388. Chinnor, Oxon.

ll A wool-merchant and wife, *c.* 1400. Northleach, Glos.

mm Anthony Fetyplace, esq., 1510. Swinbrook, Oxon.

nn Dame Margaret Plumbe, 1575. Wyddiall, Herts.

oo Thomas, Lord Berkeley, and wife Margaret, 1392. Wotton-under-Edge, Glos.

pp Herry Notingham and wife, *c.* 1405. Holme-by-the-Sea, Norf.

qq Sir Hugh Halsham, 1441, and wife Joyce. West Grinstead, Suss.

rr William Langley, rector, 1478. Buckland, Herts.

ss Thomas de Topclyff, and wife, Mabel, 1391. Topcliffe, Yorks.

tt Roger Bothe, esq., 1467, and wife Katherine. Sawley, Derbys.

uu Robert Bothe, esq., 1478, and widow Margaret. Sawley, Derbys.

vv Robert Doughty, 1493, and wife Maud. Metton, Norf.

ww Roger Bozard, gent., 1505, and son William. Ditchingham, Norf.

xx William Strode, esq., and wife Joan, 1649. Shepton Mallet, Som.

yy A lady, *c.* 1370. Winterbourne, Glos.

zz John Ruggewyn, esq., 1412. Standon, Herts.

aaa Thomas Rolf, sergeant-at-law, 1440. Gosfield, Essex.

bbb John Moore, M.A., prebendary of Osmonderley and rector of Sibson, 1532. Sibson, Leics.

ccc Arthur, only son of Philip, Lord Wharton, 1642. Wooburn, Bucks.

ddd John Curteys, lord of the manor, rebuilder of the church, mayor of the wool staple of Calais, 1391, and wife Aubrey. Wymington, Beds.

eee Margaret, wife of Sir Thomas Brounflet, 1407. Wymington, Beds.

fff Sir Thomas Brounflet, cup-bearer to Richard II, and treasurer of the household to Henry IV, 1430. Wymington, Beds.

ggg John Huntingdon, first warden and builder of the choir, 1458. Manchester cathedral.

hhh Henry Huchenson, M.A., fellow, 1573. Oxford, St. John's College.

iii John Glover, M.A., fellow, 1578. Oxford, St. John's College.

3430 Vol. 4. Containing reproductions of the following brasses:

a Matthew de Asscheton, rector of Shillington and Walpole, canon of York and Lincoln, 1400. Shillington, Beds.

b Thomas Wideville, esq., 1435, and wives Elizabeth and Alice; subsequently appropriated for Sir John Dyve, 1535, his mother Elizabeth (Wilde) and wife Isabel (Hastings). Bromham, Beds.

c John Spycer, 1437, and wife Alice. Burford, Oxon.

d Margaret, wife of Gerard Hornebolt, 1529. Fulham, Mdx.

e Richard Brooke, d. 1593, and wife Elizabeth, d. 1599. Whitchurch, Hants.

f Dame Joan de Feversham, and her son John, *c.* 1360. Graveney, Kent.

g John de Campeden, canon of Southwell and warden of St. Cross, 1382. Winchester, St. Cross.

h Roger Dynham, esq., 1490. Waddesdon, Bucks.

i A lady, *c.* 1490. Luton, Beds.

j Richard Bulkley, and wife Elizabeth, *c.* 1530. Beaumaris, Anglesey.

k Richard Middleton, 1575, and wife Jane, 1565. Whitchurch, Denbighshire.

l John Bacon, citizen and woolman, 1437, and wife Joan. London, All Hallows, Barking.

m John Cottusmore, chief justice of the common pleas, 1439, and wife Amice. Brightwell Baldwin, Oxon. [2 brasses]

n Nicholas Gaynesford, esq., d. 1498, and wife Margaret, d. 1503. Carshalton, Surr.

o Thomas Goodryke, bishop of Ely and lord high chancellor, 1554. Ely cathedral.

p A civilian and widow, *c.* 1420. Furneux Pelham, Herts.

q A civilian, *c.* 1480. Chinnor, Oxon.

r Casement for a bishop or prior, 15th cent. Winchester cathedral.

s John Sacheverell, esq., slain at Bosworth in 1485, and wife Joan (Stathum). Morley, Derbys.

t Edmund West, esq., 1618, and wife Theodosia (Tyrrell). Marsworth, Bucks.

u Hawise Botiler, 1360. Norbury, Staffs.

v William de Lound, rector, *c.* 1360. Althorpe, Lincs.

w Walter de Annefordhe, rector, 1361. Binfield, Berks.

x Henry Paris, esq., 1427, and wife Margaret. Hildersham, Cambs.

y Sir Thomas Bullen, K.G., Earl of Wiltshire and Ormond, 1538. Hever, Kent.

z Sir Thomas de Audeley, 1385. Audley, Staffs.

aa A lady, *c.* 1420. London, St. Helen, Bishopsgate.

bb Inscription and crest, the remains of the brass to John Iwardeby, and wife, Katherine, 1436. Great Missenden, Bucks.

cc Thomas Clarell, 1471, and wife Agnes. Lillingstone Lovell, Bucks.

dd The Blakeden-Boothe brass, 1580. Thames Ditton, Surr.

MUSEUMS ASSOCIATION

Founded 1889, for the promotion of better and more, systematic working of museums throughout the kingdom.

Museums Journal, vols. 1–33 (1902–34):

3431 Vol. 2.

a History of the Sunderland museum, by J. M. E. Bowley

3432 Vol. 4.

a Norwich castle museum (established 1824): some notes on the history of its foundation and progress, by T. Southwell.

3433 Vol. 5.

a The Nelson centenary exhibition at the Royal United Service museum, Whitehall, by B. E. Sargeaunt.

b 'Hastings museum', Victoria Institute, Worcester: its history, development and arrangement, by W. H. Edwards.

3434 Vol. 6.

a The Bristol museum and art gallery: the development of the institution, 1722–1906, by W. R. Barker.

b Insignia and plate of Bristol, by W. W. Watts.

3435 Vol. 8.

a Notes on an 18th cent. museum at Great Yarmouth. 'Museum Boulterianum', and on the development of the modern museum, by T. Southwell.

b History of Ipswich museum, by F. Woolnough.

3436 Vol. 11.

a The evolution of English pottery [chiefly during the 18th cent.]: suggestions for a type-collection, by H. S. Page.

3437 Vol. 13.

a Treasure trove at Sheffield [gold and silver coins, Henry VIII to James I].

3438 Vol. 15.

a Origin and development of the axe and adze, by B. H. Mullen.

b Some museums of old London, by W. H. Mullens. [1: The Leverian museum, 1774–1806. 2 (in vol. 17): William Bullock's London museum, *c.* 1795–1819]

c The Wellcome Historical Medical museum, London, by C. J. S. Thompson.

3439 Vol. 20.

a The Winchester city and Westgate museums, by R. W. Hooley.

b Aedes Hartwellianae: the last of an early 19th cent. museum [formed by Dr. John Lee at Hartwell House, near Aylesbury, Bucks.], by E. Hollis.

3440 Vol. 21.

a The Manchester museum, by W. M. Tattersall.

3441 Vol. 22.

a History and classification of Derby porcelain, by F. Williamson.

3442 Vol. 26.

a The stone age in Bournemouth, by R. Quick.
b The dating of English furniture, by E. Hawking.

3443 Vol. 27.

a The gods of the Isle of Man [Celtic myths], by G. R. B. Spain.

3444 Vol. 29.

a Cissbury [Suss.], by T. Sheppard.

3445 Vol. 32.

a William Cookworthy [d. 1780], by A. J. Caddie.

NATIONAL EISTEDDFOD ASSOCIATION

Founded 1860, as the Eisteddfod Council, to publish a volume of the Eisteddfod transactions annually, and such prize compositions as may from time to time be selected. Title changed to the above form in 1880, and to National Eisteddfod Council in 1936.

Cofnodion a chyfansoddiadau buddugol (Transactions), 1900–31:

3446 Cyfrol am 1900.

a Y Monwyson, gan T. H. Roberts. [Accounts of Lewis Morys, Richard Morys, William Morys, and Goronwy Owen]

3447 Cyfrol am 1902.

a The Eisteddfod: a historical sketch, by L. D. Jones.
b Huw Morus: ci waith a'i amserau, gan D. D. Williams. [Hugh Morris: his life and times, with extracts from his works]

Other publications:[1]

3448 Llyfryddiaeth Gymreig o 1801 i 1810, gan C. Ashton. 1908. [Chronological account of all books in Welsh or bearing on Wales published 1801–10]

3449 Deuddeg o feirdd y Berwyn. Dau draethawd gwobrwyedig (1) gan D. D. Williams, (2) gan R. Griffith. 1910. [Twelve bards of Berwyn: essays on Iolo Goch, Gutto'r Glyn, Guttun Owain, Gwerfyl ferch Madog, Owain Gwynedd, Huw Morus, Sion Dafydd Penllyn, Rhys Jones o'r Blaenau, Ann Griffiths, Gwallter Mechain, Myllin, Ceiriog, Jonathan Hughes, Hywel ab Einion Llygliw, Robert Jones Derfel, Hugh Jones o Langwm, Sion Dafydd Las, Elis y Cowper, Owain Meirion, Gwilym Aran, Meurig Idris, Idris Vychan]

3450 Traethodau gan D. D. Williams. 1: Dylanwad y Rhufeiniaid, ar iaith gwareiddiad a gwaedoliaeth y Cymry. 2: Hanes mynachdai gogledd Cymru hyd eu diddymiad. 3: Addysg Cymru yn y canol oesau. 1914. [Essays (also published separately, 1912–14), on 1: Influence of the Romans on the language, civilization, and racial characteristics of Wales. 2: History of the monasteries of North Wales to the dissolution. 3: Welsh education in the middle ages]

3451 A history of the Puritan movement in Wales from the institution of the church at Llanfaches [Llanvaches] in 1639 to the expiry of the Propagation Act in 1653, by T. Richards. 1920.

[1] See also *addenda*, p. 484.

3452 Thomas Charles Edwards, gan D. D. Williams. 1921. [T. C. Edwards, first principal of the University College of Wales, Aberystwyth]

NATURAL HISTORY SOCIETY OF NORTHUMBERLAND, DURHAM AND NEWCASTLE-UPON-TYNE

Founded 1829, for the study of collections and lectures in the Hancock museum. Amalgamated with the Tyneside Naturalists' Field Club in 1903.

Natural History Transactions of Northumberland and Durham [vols. 7–15: and Newcastle-upon-Tyne], vol. 12 (1899–1902), vols. 14–15 (1902–13):

3453 Vol. 14.

a Biographical notes on early botanists of Northumberland and Durham, by J. G. Baker.

Transactions, new ser., vols. 1–8 (1904–32; vol. 7 completed in 1945):

3454 Vol. 1.

a Notes of an old iron smelting furnace at Wheel Birks [Northumb.], by D. Richardson.

3455 Vol. 3.

a Appendix: the Hancock museum [Newcastle-upon-Tyne] and its history, by E. L. Gill.

3456 Vol. 4.

a Notes on neolithic chipping-sites in Northumberland and Durham, by C. T. Trechmann.

3457 Vol. 7.

a Abel Chapman, 1851–1929 [naturalist], by T. R. Goddard.

Extra publication:

3458 History of the Natural History Society of Northumberland, Durham and Newcastle-upon-Tyne, 1829–1929, by T. R. Goddard. [1929?].

NATURAL SCIENCE AND ARCHAEOLOGICAL SOCIETY, LITTLEHAMPTON

Founded 1924 as the Nature and Archaeology Circle, Littlehampton, to enable persons interested in natural history and archaeology to meet and interchange communications and specimens; to explore the district; to develop a taste for the study of zoology, botany, geology, etc., and architectural and other archaeological works, etc. Title changed to above form in 1931.

Reports of Proceedings, 1924–5—1931–2 (4 vols. 1926–33):

3459 Vol. for 1926–7.

a Exploration: Nanny's Croft [Arundel park], 1926–7.

3460 Vol. for 1928–30.

a The War Dyke. [Earthworks of unknown origin, in the neighbourhood of Arundel]

3461 Vol. for 1931–2.

a Report of the archaeological section, 1931–2. [Excavations in 'Shepherd's Garden', Celtic and Romano-British site in Arundel park]

3462 No. 1. A description of the high stream of Arundel, the heads and risings thereof; the sundry kinds of fishes therein in their several haunts; the fishermen and their care and service in preserving the fish in roading time; the swans and eyries and other fowl in their several limits; the water bailiff of the aforesaid high stream in Arundel, his fees, dues and duties. . . . Being the titles of a manuscript written by, or for, the water-bailiff of Thomas Howard, 24th Earl of Arundel, about the year 1637, and preserved in the muniment room at Old Norfolk House, St. James's Square, S.W., ed., with introd., notes, map, and index, by J. Fowler. 1929.

3463 No. 2. Reminiscences of Littlehampton, by Eva Robinson and J. S. Heward, with map, 1852, and transcripts of the parish registers, 1611–1753, by W. H. Challen. [1933].

NAVAL SOCIETY

Founded 1912, to encourage thought and discussion on all subjects connected with naval warfare including strategy, tactics, history and education.

Naval Review, vols. 1–21 (1913–33):

3464 Vol. 1.
a The executive command and staff in naval warfare [mainly an historical survey].
b Remarks on the evolution of naval warfare.
c Cruiser work in the great war [i.e. the Napoleonic wars].

3465 Vol. 2.
a Some historical aspects of home defence.
b Historical abstract of ages of entry into the navy, 1676–1914.
c Protection of trade in past wars.
d The source of Nelson's greatness.

3466 Vol. 3.
a Naval work in the Cameroons [1914].
b The attempted [French] invasion [of England] of 1745.
c The influence of oversea trade on British naval strategy in the past and at present.
d Action off the Falkland Islands: the chase of the German squadron, and the *Kent's* action with the *Nürnberg* [Dec. 1914].
e A fighting instruction [1665].
f The action off the Falkland Islands: the *Cornwall's* share.
g Proceedings of H.M.S. *Cumberland* and the operations in the Cameroons [1914]: extracts from the diary of an officer.
h Combined naval and military operations against Sheikh Seyd, Southern Arabia [1914–15].
i The work of the *Glasgow* and the action off Coronel [1914]: extracts from the letters of officers.
j H.M.S. *Indefatigable*: with the squadron of observation off the Dardanelles during the first six months of the war [1914–15].
k Narrative of proceedings of H.M.S. *Chatham* off east coast of Africa in search of German light cruiser *Königsberg* [1914].
l The Persian Gulf: naval operations in the Shatt-al-Arab, up to and including the surrender of Kurna [Dec. 1914].
m A synopsis of the doings of the Cape of Good Hope squadron, Aug. 1914–Jan. 1915.
n The Persian Gulf: naval operations in Mesopotamia [1915. Contd. in vol. 4].

3467 Vol. 4.
a The observation and blockade of the French fleets during the Napoleonic wars, by J. S. Mackenzie-Grieve.
b Methods of blockade and observation employed during the Revolutionary and Napoleonic wars, by G. E. Cooper.
c The work of the *Glasgow* and the action off the Falkland Islands [1914].
d An account of the search for and ultimate destruction of the German cruiser *Dresden* [March, 1915].
e Proceedings of H.M.S. *Amethyst* while at the Dardanelles [1915].
f A narrative of H.M.S. *Agamemnon* in the Mediterranean, Jan. 1915–March 1917.
g Dardanelles notes: H.M.S. *Prince George* [1915].
h An account of operations in the Dardanelles in 1915: notes from H.M.S. *Prince of Wales*.

3468 Vol. 5.
a The system of convoys for merchant shipping in 1917 and 1918, as seen by the Ministry of Shipping.
b Slow convoys [1917–18].
c The destruction of the *Königen Louise* and the sinking of the *Amphion*, Aug. 5th and 6th, 1914.

3469 Vol. 7.
a The control of shipping during the war [1914–18].
b German battle cruisers' attacks on the Hartlepools [co. Durham], Dec. 16th, 1914.
c The study of naval history. [Reprinted from the *United Service Magazine* of March, 1896]

3470 Vol. 8.
a The place of history in naval education.
b 1807–1917: a comparison [of the blockading systems].
c Naval operations leading to Coronel and the Falkland Islands [1914].
d The Royal Navy on the Caspian, 1918–19.
e The Navy Records Society, by Sir J. R. Thursfield.
f The progress of aircraft [from 1913].
g Sir John Duckworth's expedition to Constantinople [1806–7], by J. H. Rose.
h Expeditions in the Rufiji river [East Africa], 1917.

3471 Vol. 9.
a Naval work in north Russia, 1918–19.
b A backwater: Lake Victoria Nyanza during the campaign against German East Africa.
c Operations in the Crimea, 1919.
d Smashing the Mullah [Mohammed bin Abdilla Hassan, in Somaliland, 1920]: the navy's part.
e The Nile campaign, 1798–1801, by G. D. Latham.
f Narrative of H.M.S. *Caradoc*, 1917–20, by E. L. Markham. [Contd. in vol. 10]

3472 Vol. 10.
a A study in friction [operations of Rear-Admiral Man in the Mediterranean, 1796].
b A study of war [including naval operations in the French Revolutionary and Napoleonic wars, the Dutch war, 1672–4, and the civil war, 1649–51], by Sir R. N. Custance. [Contd. in vols. 11 and 12]
c Lord St. Vincent [John Jervis, Earl of St. Vincent, d. 1823], by C. H. Drage.
d Naval operations in the Mediterranean, 1793–1801, by E. H. Longsdon.
e The boatswain's whistle, by H. R. H. Vaughan.
f The Naval Society and Review and an historical abstract of other service periodicals.
g Jervis and the Spanish fleet [at the battle of Cape St. Vincent, 1797].

h Conversations with Napoleon at St. Helena, recounted in diary form by Lieut.-col. Sir Thomas Reade, deputy adjutant-general of the island. [Includes letters from Nelson, Admiral Lord Keith, Captain T. Troubridge and Captain Alexander M. Ball, 1800]
i Naval history: a comparative table [of naval operations and administrative changes].

3473 Vol. 11.
a Conduct of the Channel fleet in 1779 against superior force.
b Punishments inflicted at sea from the earliest times to the end of the 18th cent., by Sir R. Acland.
c H.M.S. *Canopus*, Aug. 1914–March 1916. [Contd. in vol. 12]
d Naval operations in the Napoleonic war after Trafalgar as illustrating the use of maritime power to assist operations on land, by C. H. Drage.
e Summary punishments [at sea] in the 19th cent.
f The composition of the main fleet in the past and present.
g The wreck of the *Raleigh* [1922].
h Hawke, 1705–81, by J. L. F. Hunt. [Edward Hawke, first Baron]
i The Raleigh lecture on history. National policy and naval strength 16th–20th cent., by H. W. Richmond.
j Crime and punishment in the Royal Navy during the last 50 years, by Sir R. Acland.
k The struggle for the Mediterranean in the 18th cent., by J. H. Rose.

3474 Vol. 12.
a Naval terms and customs and their origin.
b Gibraltar and its value to the British navy as illustrated in the wars of the 18th cent. previous to the French revolution, by J. D. Prentice.
c The corporation of Trinity House of Deptford Strond.
d The naval development of the East India Company.
e The navy in the Russian war, 1854–55.
f The transition from oars to sail.
g Naval gunnery in the early 19th cent.
h The naval war staff, 1912–14.
i The admiralty: its constitutional changes, 1546–1924, by W. H. Henderson.
j Internal organisation and administration of our warships from the Norman conquest to the battle of Trafalgar.
k Journal kept by William Davidson (a seaman) on board a Russian privateer, 1788–9.

3475 Vol. 13.
a Some of Lord Nelson's sayings [being an attempt to summarize the opinions of Nelson on various subjects in the form of extracts from his correspondence, etc. Contd. in vol. 14]
b 'A 1 at Lloyd's': the origin and functions of Lloyd's and Lloyd's register of shipping, by C. E. Fayle.
c Anson's voyage round the world, 1740–44; special service squadron world cruise, 1923–4; flying squadron cruise round the world, 1869–70.
d Rodney and de Guichen [in the West Indies], 1780, by J. H. Owen.
e Robert Blake [d. 1657], by T. M. Napier.
f The loss of the *Royal George*, 1782.
g Lloyd's 'Patriotic fund' [founded 1803], by C. E. Fayle.
h British shipping [industry] and the state [14th–20th cent.]. [Contd. in vol. 14]
i Naval operations in the Red sea, 1916–17. [Contd. for 1917–19 in vol. 14]
j Naval construction and schools of naval architecture, by W. H. Henderson.

3476 Vol. 14.
a The navy and the surrender at Yorktown, 1781, by J. H. Owen.
b The dockyards and the master shipwrights [16th–19th cent.], by A. W. Johns.
c Naval operations of the war of 1688–97 [war of the League of Augsburg], by K. H. S. Cohen.
d The battle of Grenada, 6 July 1779 [American war of independence], by J. H. Owen.
e Naval tactics, 1653–1805.
f The development of naval courts martial [since 1571], by Sir R. Acland. [Reprinted from the *Journal of Comparative Legislation*, 3rd ser., vol. 4]
g A history of H.M. Navigation School, 1729–1926: a study of naval education, by R. K. Dickson.

3477 Vol. 15.
a The Imperial Conference of 1926.
b Operations of the Western squadron [i.e. Channel squadron] 1781–2, by J. H. Owen. 1: Kempenfelt and de Guichen, Dec. 1781. 2: Barrington and de Soulange, 1782.
c Old naval benevolences: the Royal Naval Benevolent Society [founded 1739] and the Royal Navy Club of 1765 and 1785, by W. H. Henderson.
d Howe and d'Estaing in North America, 1778.
e Rodney as a strategist and tactician, by J. R. Henderson. [Another article with the same title, by D. O. Doble]
f Hood at Saint Christopher's, 1782.
g The mutiny in the fleet at Spithead, April 1797: extracts from the journals of Admiral Sir Graham Moore, G.C.B., K.C.M.G.

3478 Vol. 16.
a The French landing in Ireland, Aug. 1798, and the subsequent defeat of the Brest squadron by Sir John Warren, Nov. 1798: extracts from the diary of Admiral Sir Graham Moore.
b Rodney and Grasse, 1782, by J. H. Owen.
c Naval operations in the Mediterranean from 1793 to the English evacuation of the Mediterranean [1796], with special reference to their influence on the campaigns on land, by P. N. Churchill.
d [Extracts from] *Trade and Navigation of Great Britain considered*, by Joshua Gee, London, 1731, 3rd edn., comp. W. H. C. S. Thring.
e Development of [naval] tactics, by Sir R. Custance.
f Typical ships [of the Royal Navy] in 1782 and 1805.
g Steering gear in the old navy [to the 18th cent.], by L. G. Carr Laughton.

3479 Vol. 17.
a War trade and trade war, 1701–13, by G. N. Clark. [Reprinted from the *Economic History Review*, i, no. 2]
b Naval mutinies [17th–18th cent.], by C. Radcliffe.
c The causes of the war of 1812 [with the U.S.A.].
d The British government and neutral rights, 1861–5, by J. P. Baxter. [Reprinted from the *American Historical Review*]
e Neutral commerce in the war of the Spanish succession and the Treaty of Utrecht, by G. N. Clark. [Reprinted from the *British Year Book of International Law*, 1928]
f The neutral corn ships in 1709 [an account of the navy's part in trying to prevent corn reaching France], by J. H. Owen.
g Anson and his importance as a naval reformer, by P. W. Brock.

3480 Vol. 18.
a Trade defence in Indian seas. [Includes a memorandum, dated 1801, on the defence of trade in the Indian Ocean,

and a report by Admiral Sir E. Pellew (afterwards Lord Exmouth) of 1809]

b Some British opinions as to neutral rights 1861–5, by J. P. Baxter. [Reprinted from the *American Journal of International Law*, July, 1929]

c The third destroyer flotilla in China, 1926–8.

d Strategy of the Anglo-Dutch wars of the 17th cent., by M. F. B. Ward.

e The lucky admiral. [Contemporary opinions of George B. Rodney, first Baron, d. 1792]

f Report of the committee on naval manœuvres, 1888.

g The place of India in naval strategy, 1744–83.

h The maritime defences of India under the East India Company, 1763–83.

i His Majesty's Customs [including an historical survey of the Customs service], by T. R. Moore.

j The divisional system [in the Royal Navy], in the 18th cent.

k History and administration of the Channel Islands, by J. G. L. Faed.

3481 Vol. 19.

a Notes on the early days of the Royal Naval War College [1905–6].

b Pages and papers from the life of Admiral of the Fleet Sir Frederick Richards [d. 1912], with some private and some official correspondence. [Contd. in vols. 20 and 21]

c The problem of imperial defence in the 18th cent. in its relation to the American revolution, by W. A. Phillips.

d Howe, by P. Bethell.

3482 Vol. 20.

a Howe [and the battle of 1 June 1794], by H. G. D. de Chair.

b Special aspects of British sea power, 1830–1914, by Sir G. Aston.

3483 Vol. 21.

a Selection of officers for command: a study in the light of the Revolutionary war, 1793–1802.

b Samuel Pepys.

c Monk as a naval commander, by J. May. [George Monck or Monk, Duke of Albemarle, d. 1670]

d Monk as a naval commander, by N. A. Copeman.

e The navy and the capture of Cork and Kinsale, 1690.

3484 Subject index to the Naval Review, vols. 1–9, comp. G. P. Orde. [1922].

Other publications:

3485 A short naval bibliography, comp. E. M. Keate and W. C. B. Tunstall. [1926].

NAVY RECORDS SOCIETY

Founded 1893, to print rare or unpublished works of naval interest.

Publications, vols. 19–71:

3486 Vols. 19, 24. Letters and papers of Admiral of the Fleet Sir Thos. Byam Martin, G.C.B., ed. Sir R. V. Hamilton. Vols. i and iii, 1901–3. [Vol. i: to 1807. Vol. ii: 1808–13 (published 1898). Vol iii: 1812–36 and later]

3487 Vol. 20. The naval miscellany, vol. i, ed. J. K. Laughton. 1902.

a Book of war by sea and land, 1543, by Jehan Bytharne.

b Relation of the voyage to Cadiz, 1596, by Sir William Slyngisbie, ed. J. S. Corbett.

c Glorious England: a relation of the battle of Quiberon bay, 20 Nov. 1759, from the Portuguese.

d Journals of Henry Duncan, captain R.N., 1776–82.

e Extracts from the papers of Samuel, first Viscount Hood [1778–98].

f Letters of the Hon. William Cathcart, captain R.N. [1796–1804].

g Extracts from the journals of Thomas Addison, of the East India Company's service, 1801–29.

h Seizure of Helgoland, 1807. [Official correspondence]

i Miscellaneous letters [1741–1805].

3488 Vol. 21. Dispatches and letters relating to the blockade of Brest, 1803–5, ed. J. Leyland. Vol. ii, 1902. [Vol. i was published in 1899]

3489 Vols. 22, 23, 43, 45, 47. The naval tracts of Sir William Monson [d. 1643] in six books, ed., with a commentary, by M. Oppenheim. 5 vols. 1902–14.

3490 Vol. 25. Nelson and the Neapolitan Jacobins: documents relating to the suppression of the revolution at Naples, June 1799, ed. H. C. Gutteridge. 1903.

3491 Vols. 26, 27, 36, 57. Descriptive catalogue of the naval mss. in the Pepysian library at Magdalene College, Cambridge, ed. J. R. Tanner. 4 vols. 1903–23.

3492 Vol. 28. Selections from the correspondence of Admiral John Markham, 1801–4 and 1806–7, ed. Sir C. Markham. 1904.

3493 Vol. 29. Fighting instructions, 1530–1816, ed., with elucidations from contemporary authorities, by J. S. Corbett. 1905. [See also no. 3499 below]

3494 Vols. 30, 37, 41, 66. Letters and papers relating to the first Dutch war, 1652–4. Vol. iii ed. S. R. Gardiner and C. T. Atkinson; vols. iv–vi ed. C. T. Atkinson. 1906–30. [Vols. i–ii were published in 1899–1900. A separate pamphlet of corrigenda to all vols. was published in 1931]

3495 Vol. 31. Recollections of James Anthony Gardner, commander R.N., 1775–1814, ed. Sir R. V. Hamilton and J. K. Laughton. 1906.

3496 Vols. 32, 38, 39. Letters and papers of Charles, Lord Barham, admiral of the red squadron, 1758–1813, ed. Sir J. K. Laughton. 3 vols. 1907–11.

3497 Vol. 33. Naval songs and ballads, selected and ed. C. H. Firth. 1908.

3498 Vol. 34. Views of the third Dutch war. Portfolio containing 10 coloured plates [1908], with a note on the drawings in the possession of the Earl of Dartmouth illustrating the battle of Sole bay, 1672, and the battle of Texel, 1673, by J. S. Corbett. *P.* 1908.

3499 Vol. 35. Signals and instructions, 1776–94, with addenda to vol. 29, ed. J. S. Corbett. 1908.

3500 Vol. 40. The naval miscellany, vol. ii, ed. Sir J. K. Laughton. 1912.

a Voyage of the *Barbara* to Brazil, 1540, ed. R. G. Marsden.

b The sea scene from *The Complaynt of Scotlande* [1549], ed. A. Moore.

c The taking of the *Madre de Dios*, 1592, ed. C. L. Kingsford.

d A narrative of the battle of Santa Cruz [1657], written by Sir Richard Stayner, rear-admiral of the fleet, ed. C. H. Firth.

e Extracts from a [naval] commissioner's note book, 1691–4.

f The journal of M. de Lage de Cueilly, captain in the Spanish navy during the campaign of 1744, translated from the French by T. G. Carter.

g Sale of dead man's effects [on board H.M.S. *Gloucester*, 1750].
h The mutiny at the Nore: letter from James Watson to Admiral Robert Digby [1797].
i From the letter books of Sir Charles Thompson, bt., vice-admiral [*c.* 1797]. Selected and ed. Sir T. S. Jackson.
j Orders by Sir John Jervis [1796-7].
k Some letters of Lord St. Vincent [1800-1].
l Operations on the coast of Egypt, 1801.
m Memoirs of George Pringle, esq., captain R.N., 1795-1809, written by himself.
n Pedigree of the naval Duncans.
o Operations in the Scheldt, 1809. [Letter from Capt. C. W. Boys to his brother]
p Frustration of the plan for the escape of Napoleon Bonaparte from Bordeaux, July 1815.
q Extract from the journal of Admiral Benjamin William Page [d. 1845].
r 'Well done, *Phaeton*!' [1850], by Sir G. Elliot [1897].

3501 Vol. 42. Papers relating to the loss of Minorca in 1756, ed. H. W. Richmond. 1913.

3502 Vol. 44. The old Scots navy, 1689-1710, ed. J. Grant. 1914.

3503 Vols. 46, 48, 58, 59. Private papers of George, 2nd Earl Spencer, first lord of the admiralty, 1794-1801. Vols. i-ii ed. J. S. Corbett; vols. iii-iv ed. H. W. Richmond. 4 vols. 1913-14.

3504 Vols. 49, 50. Documents relating to law and custom of the sea, 1205-1767, ed. R. G. Marsden. 2 vols. 1915-16.

3505 Vol. 51. The autobiography of Phineas Pett [d. 1638], ed. W. G. Perrin. 1918.

3506 Vols. 52, 53. The life of Sir John Leake, rear-admiral of Great Britain [d. 1720], by S. Martin-Leake, ed. G. Callender. 2 vols. 1920.

3507 Vols. 54, 56. The life and works of Sir Henry Mainwaring [d. 1653]. Vol. i ed. G. E. Manwaring; vol. ii ed. G. E. Manwaring and W. G. Perrin. 2 vols. 1920-22.

3508 Vols. 55, 61. Letters of Admiral of the Fleet the Earl of St. Vincent whilst first lord of the admiralty, 1801-4, ed. D. B. Smith. 2 vols. 1922-7.

3509 Vol. 60. Samuel Pepys's naval minutes, ed. J. R. Tanner. 1926.

3510 Vol. 62. The Keith papers, selected from the letters and papers of Admiral Viscount Keith. Vol. i, ed. W. G. Perrin. 1927. [Vol. ii, ed. C. Lloyd, was published in 1950]

3511 Vol. 63. The naval miscellany, vol. iii, ed. W. G. Perrin. 1928.

a Naval operations in the latter part of 1666, ed. R. C. Anderson.
b The land forces of France, June 1738, ed. Sir H. W. Richmond.
c The action between H.M.S. *Lyon* and the *Elisabeth*, July 1745, by H. H. Brindley.
d The Channel fleet in 1779: letters of Benjamin Thompson to Lord George Germain.
e The engagement between H.M.S. *Brunswick* and *Le Vengeur*, 1 June 1794.
f Letters of Lord Nelson, 1804-5.
g The second capture of the Cape of Good Hope, 1806.
h The salute in the narrow seas and the Vienna Conference of 1815.
i Two letters from Blake to Mountagu, 1656-7, ed. G. E. Manwaring.
j Instructions to Captain Cook for his three voyages.

k The bombardment of Copenhagen, 1807: journal of Surgeon Charles Chambers of H.M. Fireship *Prometheus*.

3512 Vol. 64. The journal of Edward Mountagu, first Earl of Sandwich, admiral and general at sea, 1659-65, ed. R. C. Anderson. 1929.

3513 Vol. 65. Boteler's dialogues [treatises on naval law and practice by Nathaniel Butler, 17th cent.], ed. W. G. Perrin. 1929.

3514 Vols. 67, 68, 70. The Byng papers, selected from the letters and papers of Admiral Sir George Byng, first Viscount Torrington, and of his son, Admiral the Hon. John Byng, and ed. B. Tunstall. 3 vols. 1930-32.

3515 Vols. 69, 71. The private papers of John, Earl of Sandwich, first lord of the admiralty, 1771-82, ed. G. R. Barnes and J. H. Owen. Vol. i: Aug. 1770-Mar. 1778; vol. ii: Mar. 1778-May 1779. 1932-3. [Vols. iii-iv were published in 1936-8]

NEATH ANTIQUARIAN SOCIETY

Founded 1923, to collect, in Neath and district particularly, descriptions of anything of archaeological and antiquarian interest, etc. The Transactions, 1st series, appeared weekly in the Mid-Glamorgan Herald.

Transactions, 2nd ser., vols. 1-3 ([1931?]-33):

3516 Vol. 1.

a Summer excursions. [1: Laugharne. 2: Ynysygerwn and the early days of the tinplate trade. 4: Ramble round Neath—St. Giles' church, the river bridge, and the Longford heraldic stones. 5: Llywel church and Llanthony abbey. 7: Excavations at Neath abbey. 8: Marcross church and Llantwit Major]
b Winter lectures. [1: Study of place-names, by H. J. Randall. 3: Sir William Nott, G.C.B., d. 1845, by G. Jenkins. 4: Life and art of Richard Wilson, R.A., d. 1782, by I. Williams. 5: Welsh place names in the district of Neath. 7: Neath post office, by S. W. Belderson. Also: Early days of the tinplate industry, with particular reference to the Neath district, by R. Jenkins]
c 'Mischellanies' (being notes made in the 17th cent. by Morgan Evan, registrar of Neath), by G. B. Hammond.
d Poor law administration in Neath, in 1838.
e Members' discussion nights. [1: Neath borough seals, by G. A. Taylor. 2: Iolo Morganwg, or Evan Williams, poet, d. 1826: an observation. 3: St. Margaret's, by G. A. Taylor]
f Notes on early technical methods in the tin-plate trade, by R. Jenkins.
g St. Margaret's chapel: monastic or parochial?

3517 Vol. 2.

a Summer excursions, 1931. [1: Llancarvan church, Llanveithin old grange, Llantrithyd church. 2: Briton Ferry. 3: Brecon museum and cathedral. 4: Kenfig castle and Maudlam church. 5: St. David's cathedral. 6: Penlle'r-castell and Carn Llechart. 7: St. Margaret's chapel. 8: Margam abbey, by D. H. Jones, and Newton Nottage church, by E. G. Smith]
b 'Curfew' bell at Neath.
c Parish registers [with special reference to Neath].
d Briton Ferry and Neath early in the 19th cent. [Extracts from *Beauties of England and Wales*, 1815]
e A notable daughter of the vale of Neath [Maria Jane Williams, d. 1873, Welsh historian and writer].

f Tretower Court.

g Winter lectures, 1931–32. [1 : Offa's dyke, by C. Fox. 2 : Members' discussion night—Roman Neath, the site of the town and roads. 3 : Neath parish church, by G. A. Taylor. 4 : The Norman keep, by A. J. Richard. 5 : Piracy along the Welsh coast, by G. Roberts. 6 : The Arthurian legends, by Mary Williams. 7 : The rude stone monuments of South Wales, by W. F. Grimes]

h Borough of Neath : report on ancient monuments.

i Orders and laws for the town of Neath, ordained and sealed 33 Henry VIII, 1542.

3518 Vol. 3.

a Summer excursions. [2 : St. Michael's church, Cwmavon. 3 : Churches of Cheriton, Llanmadoc, and Llangenydd. 4 : Carew cross, castle and church, Pembroke castle, and Manorbier castle. 5 : Kidwelly and Ferryside. 6 : The Grange of Sker. 7 : Merthyr Mawr, Candleston, and Ogmore castles]

b A Cadoxton-Aberpergwm dispute of the 16th cent., by G. A. Taylor. [With a transcript of the award of arbitration in 1593 between the parish of Cadoxton-juxta-Neath and the inhabitants of Glyn Neath and Aberpergwm relating to the maintenance of the parish church]

c Neath manorial records. [Reprint of a schedule in the *Cardiff Welsh Bulletin*, vol. 1, no. 2]

d Lists of deeds and documents relating to Neath and district, Cardiff library collections.

e Neath street names, by G. A. Taylor.

f A notable native of Neath : Captain [Rees Howell] Gronow [d. 1865].

g Neath in 1803. [Extract from *Letters written during a Tour through South Wales in the year 1803 by the Rev. J. Evans, B.A., late of Jesus College, Oxford*]

h Neath borough maces, by G. A. Taylor.

i The Williams of Duffryn genealogical tablets in Cadoxton church, taken from Evans' *Tour of South Wales in 1803.*

j Winter lectures, 1932–3. [1 : Welsh porcelain, by I. Williams. 2 : History of St. Mary's church, Swansea, by W. T. Havard. 3 : Members' discussion night—Henllan stone circle, Melincourt. 4 : Preservation of local records of Wales, by W. Ll. Davies. 5 : The Llandaff gospels, by L. J. Hopkin-James. 6 : How I met Livingstone : an account of the early life of H. M. Stanley, by W. D. Medlicott]

k The early Friendly societies of Neath, by G. A. Taylor.

l A Welsh sailor's letters from the French wars [written by William Davies, 1794–5].

m Extracts from the *Parochialia* of Edward Lhwyd, *c.* 1699.

n Some observations on local pre-historic remains : Henllan 'stone-circle', by D. H. Jones.

o 'The white rose of Scotland' [Katherine Gordon, d. 1537] and the Herbert chapel, Swansea, by G. B. Hammond.

p The development of Neath, by G. E. Evans.

q Early Neath banks, by G. A. Taylor.

r Story of a murder at Neath in 1770 [committed by Henry Thomas], by L. D. Thomas.

s Neath street names, by G. A. Taylor.

t Early Neath, by W. Rees.

u An early Neath abbey works. [Lease of land by Elizabeth Hoby in 1694 for iron works]

v The lordship of Glamorgan. [Extract from *The Historie of Cambria, now called Wales, by Humfrey Lloyd, augmented and continued by David Powell, 1584*]

w The abbey of Neath versus the abbey of Margam [being arbitrations in various disputes, 1208–1428].

x Old Gyfylchi chapel, by T. M. Rees.

y Summer excursions, 1933. [1 : Arthur's Stone and Pennard castle. 2 : Cilybebyll church and parish]

NEW PALAEOGRAPHICAL SOCIETY

Founded 1902, for the publication of facsimiles of Western manuscripts and the furtherance of the study of palaeography. Dissolved 1930.

Facsimiles of ancient manuscripts, etc., ed. E. M. Thompson, G. F. Warner, F. G. Kenyon and J. P. Gilson, ser. 1, vols. 1–2 (1903–12):[1]

3519 Vol. 1. Containing extracts from:

a St. Gregory's pastoral care, in Anglo-Saxon, 890–897(?). Bodleian Library.

b Anglo-Saxon poems, *c.* 950. Exeter chapter library.

c Manumissions, early 12th cent. Exeter chapter library.

d Gospels, early 11th cent. [in Latin; written probably at Winchester]. Cambridge, Trinity College.

e Psalter, 1322–5 [in Latin with 2 series of brief chronological notes; possibly from East Anglia]. Douai, Bibliothèque publique.

f Monastic press-marks, 14th and 15th cent. [Contd. in vol. 2]

g Titchfield [abbey] library catalogue, etc., 1400–5. Duke of Portland's library, Welbeck.

h Charters of Westminster abbey, 1121 and 1151. Westminster abbey muniments.

i Mortuary roll, *c.* 1230 [of Lucy, foundress and first prioress of the priory of St. Cross and St. Mary, Hedingham, Essex]. British Museum.

j Gospels, 8th cent. [St. John, St. Luke, and St. Mark, in the Latin vulgate version; written probably in the north of England]. Durham cathedral library.

k Apocalypse, in French, *c.* 1230 [possibly written and illuminated at St. Albans abbey]. Cambridge, Trinity College.

l Register of Archbishop Peckham, 1280. Lambeth Palace.

m Psalter, *c.* 1340. Lulworth Castle.

n Charter of William Rufus, *c.* 1091 [confirming grant by Walter Giffard, Earl of Buckingham, of his manor of Blakenham to the abbey of Bec]. Eton College.

o Charter of William Rufus, *c.* 1095 [granting lands in Lothian to the church of Durham]. Durham cathedral library.

p Charter of Ranulph Flambard, 1106–28 [bishop of Durham, granting lands to church of Durham]. Durham cathedral library.

q Gospels, 8th cent. [in the Latin vulgate version]. Durham cathedral library.

r Register of privileges of see of Canterbury, 1120; episcopal professions, 1120–63. British Museum.

s Psalter, *c.* 1250 [written in England]. Belvoir Castle, Duke of Rutland's library.

t Capgrave [lives of St. Augustine of Hippo and St. Gilbert of Sempringham by John Capgrave, Augustinian friar of Lynn, *c.* 1451]. British Museum.

u Charter of Queen Matilda, 1106–18 [notifying Ranulf, bishop of Durham, that she has granted to the church of Durham the church of Carham, Northumb.]. Durham cathedral library.

v Charter of Queen Matilda, *c.* 1115 [concerning her grant to the church of Durham of lands in Epping and Nazing, Essex]. Durham cathedral library.

w Charter of Henry de Oilli, 1149 (?) [granting church of St. George in the castle of Oxford to Oseney abbey]. British Museum.

x Thorney mortuary roll, 1216 [of Ralph, abbot of Thorney, Cambs.]. British Museum.

[1] In all titles listed the date is that of the document named, not necessarily the date of the original if the document named is a copy.

y Proclamation, 1258 [of Henry III, in English and French, marking his public acceptance of the barons' reforms]. Public Record Office.

z Lives of saints, by Goscelin, 1100–25 [monk of St. Augustine's, Canterbury]. British Museum.

aa Register of Reading abbey, *c.* 1257. British Museum.

bb Year book, 1350–75 [13–21 Edw. III, in law-French]. British Museum.

cc Register of Titchfield abbey, *c.* 1390. Duke of Portland's library, Welbeck.

dd Prymer, early 15th cent. [a book of hours in English, of the Sarum use]. British Museum.

ee Register, etc., of Bury St. Edmunds abbey, *c.* 1426. British Museum.

ff Westminster abbey charters [charter of Henry II to Gervase, abbot of Westminster, 1156; notification by Gilbert Foliot, bishop of London, of his hearing of a cause between Walter, abbot of Westminster, and Ranulf, clerk, of Feering, Essex, 1176–86; and grant of lands by Christopher, abbot of Waverley, to Baldwin de Cuserigge, 1187–96]. Westminster abbey muniments.

gg Charter of Richard I, 1189 [to Alexander de Barentin, butler to Henry II]. Westminster abbey muniments.

hh Sherborne pontifical, *c.* 992–95. Paris, Bibliothèque Nationale.

ii Passion and miracles of St. Edmund, 1125–50. London, library of G. L. Holford.

jj Chartulary of Boarstall manor, etc., 1444. Library of H. Aubrey-Fletcher, Dorton House, Thame.

3520 Vol. 2. Containing extracts from:

a Charter of Roger de Mortimer, *c.* 1200 [granting lands to Abbey Cwmhir]. London, library of S. A. Snow.

b Charter of King John, 1203 [granting lands in his manor of Weedon Bec, Northants., to the abbot and monks of Bec, in Normandy]. Eton College.

c Anglo-Saxon chronicle, 9th–11th cent. Cambridge, Corpus Christi College.

d Aelfric's Latin grammar, 11th cent. Cambridge, University library.

e Higden, Marco Polo, etc., 1320–52. [The *Polychronicon* of Ralph Higden, and other historical and topographical works written in England before 1352]. British Museum.

f Papal bull, 1213 [to the Irish, commanding them to abide in fealty to King John in virtue of his grant of his kingdom to the Roman church]. Public Record Office.

g Charter of Louis of France, 1216 [granting town of Grimsby to William de Huntingfeld]. British Museum.

h Charter of Henry III, 1227 [granting lands in manor of Weedon Bec, Northants., to abbot and monks of Bec in Normandy]. Eton College.

i Charter of Henry III, 1234 [notifying his foresters of Essex that Gilbert Marshal and his supporters had made peace with him]. British Museum.

j Charter of Henry III, 1246 [notifying his choice of Westminster abbey for his place of burial]. Westminster abbey muniments.

k Charter of Richard, King of the Romans, 1257 [to Hugh le Despenser]. British Museum.

l Psalter, late 10th cent. [in Latin, of St. Jerome's Roman version; probably written at Canterbury]. British Museum.

m Register of Bishop Baldock, 1307. Bishop of London's registry.

n Simon de Boraston [life of], *c.* 1389. Bodleian Library.

o Will of Richard FitzRobert, 1267. British Museum.

p Grant to Bitlesden abbey [Bucks.], 1271–2. British Museum.

q Letters patent of Queen Eleanor, 1280 [to William de Vergers to do fealty in her name to Guy, Count of Flanders, for land in Flanders]. British Museum.

r Letters patent of Edward I, 1305 [pardoning Thomas Burnel of Windsor]. Eton College.

s King Alfred's version of Orosius, 10th cent. Library of Lord Tollemache, Helmingham Hall.

t Psalter, late 12th cent. [written and illuminated in England]. Glasgow University, Hunterian Museum.

u Register of Godstow abbey [near Oxford], *c.* 1450–60. Bodleian Library.

v Quitclaim by J. de St. John, 1306. British Museum.

w Acquittance to Westminster abbey, 1311 [by Henry de Bluntesdon, archdeacon of Dorset]. Westminster abbey muniments.

x Mandate to Westminster abbey, 1311 [by William de Testa, papal nuncio in England]. Westminster abbey muniments.

y Writ of Edward III, 1328 [ordering the abbot of Westminster to deliver to the sheriffs of London the stone of Scone so that it might be returned to Scotland]. Westminster abbey muniments.

z Inspeximus of Edward III, 1331 [restoring honours and lands to Richard de Arundel]. British Museum.

aa Grant by Westminster abbey, 1335 [to Simon, bishop of Worcester]. Westminster abbey muniments.

bb Record of pleas at Glastonbury, 1344. British Museum.

cc Grant of arms by Lord Stafford, 1347. Eton College.

dd Covenant by R[oger] de Mortimer, 1349. Westminster abbey muniments.

ee Defeasance by the abbot of Westminster [Simon Langham], 1357. Westminster abbey muniments.

ff Homilies in Anglo-Saxon, 971. Library of the Marquess of Lothian, Blickling Hall, Norf.

gg The Winton Domesday, *c.* 1150. [Two surveys of Winchester, one made by order of Henry I, 1103–15, the other by Bishop Henry de Blois, 1148]. Society of Antiquaries.

hh Roger of Hoveden, Chronica, *c.* 1200. British Museum.

ii Psalter, early 13th cent. [in Latin; written and illuminated in England]. Cambridge, Trinity College.

jj John Lydgate, Troy Book, etc., 1455–62. British Museum.

kk Grant by W[illiam] de Bury, of London, 1363. Westminster abbey muniments.

ll Bond by Westminster abbey, 1377. Westminster abbey muniments.

mm Acquittance by the chapter of Ely cathedral, 1380. Westminster abbey muniments.

nn Grant in London, 1381 [concerning transfer of property between two groups of citizens]. Westminster abbey muniments.

oo Grant of a villein, 1384. British Museum.

pp Quitclaim in London, 1394. Westminster abbey muniments.

qq Lease to Geoffrey Chaucer, 1399. Westminster abbey muniments.

rr Charter [of Richard II] of incorporation of the minor canons of St. Paul's, London, 1394. College of minor canons of St. Paul's cathedral.

ss Gospels, early 9th cent. [in Latin; written probably in Wales. At the end of the gospels there is the record, in Anglo-Saxon, of a shire-moot, 1017–35, and of a purchase of land, 1052–6]. Hereford cathedral library.

tt Lections from the gospels [written probably at Hereford], 1st half of the 11th cent. Cambridge, Pembroke College.

uu Bible of Bishop Pudsey of Durham, 1153–95 [in Latin, vulgate version]. Durham cathedral library.

vv 'Abbreviatio' of Domesday book, 13th cent. [i.e. Exchequer Domesday]. Public Record Office.

ww Pictorial bible-history [executed in England], 14th cent. Library of the Earl of Leicester, Holkham Hall, Norf.

xx Petition to the privy council by W[illiam] Warbelton, 1431. British Museum.

yy Letter of Henry VI and his privy council to Pope Calixtus III, 1455. British Museum.

zz Indenture between Henry IV and Henry, Prince of Wales, for payment of troops, 1407. Westminster abbey muniments.

aaa Nuncupative will of Richard Seyntbarbe, 1420. British Museum.

bbb Covenant for building a steeple to Walberswick church, Suff., 1426. British Museum.

ccc Grant to the hospital near St. Laurence church, Reading, 1435. British Museum.

ddd Confirmation by Henry VI of franchises of Yarmouth, Isle of Wight, 1440. Yarmouth corporation muniments.

3521 Indices to facsimiles of ancient manuscripts, etc., 1st ser., 1903–12. 1914.

Facsimiles of ancient manuscripts, etc., ser. 2 (13 pts. in 9, 1913–30):

3522 Pt. 1. Containing extracts from:

a St. Augustine on the psalms, *c.* 1088. [Written for William de Carilef, bishop of Durham]. Durham cathedral library.

b Ormesby psalter, *c.* 1300–25. Bodleian Library.

c Papal bull, 1509 [confirming foundation of Christ's College, Cambridge]. Public Record Office.

d Rotuli de dominabus, 1185 [returns of inquisitions taken 31 Hen. II as to wardships etc. due to King from widows and orphans of his tenants in chief]. Public Record Office.

e Curia regis roll, 1194. Public Record Office.

f Charter roll, 1199 [enrolments, in Latin, of royal grants of lands, liberties, honours etc.]. Public Record Office.

3523 Pt. 2. Containing extracts from:

a Psalter, early 8th cent. [in Latin; written probably in the north of England]. Berlin, Königliche Bibliothek.

b Moralized bestiary, late 12th cent. [in Latin; written and illuminated in England]. Bodleian Library.

c English romances (Thornton ms.), 1430–50. Lincoln cathedral library.

d Memoranda roll of the exchequer, 1219–20. Public Record Office.

e Receipt roll of the exchequer, 1220. Public Record Office.

f Originalia roll of the exchequer, 1232–3. Public Record Office.

3524 Pt. 3. Containing extracts from:

a Acts of the Apostles, early 8th cent. [in Latin, vulgate version; possibly written at Minster nunnery in Thanet]. Bodleian Library.

b Psalter, 1st half of the 10th cent. [in Latin with Anglo-Saxon gloss; written possibly at Winchester but glossed more probably at Canterbury]. Bodleian Library.

c Regula S. Benedicti, late 10th cent. [written at St. Augustine's abbey, Canterbury]. British Museum.

d Episcopal professions, 1086–1133 [of obedience to the archbishop of Canterbury]. Canterbury cathedral library.

e Beda, vita S. Cuthberti, 2nd half of the 12th cent. Oxford, University College.

f Psalter, 2nd quarter of the 14th cent. [written in the diocese of Coventry and Lichfield]. London, library of the Earl of Ellesmere.

g Astronomical calendar, 1430 [in English]. British Museum.

h Inquisition on Templars' lands, 1185. Public Record Office.

i Little Black Book of the exchequer, *c.* 1206. Public Record Office.

j Pleas in the exchequer of the Jews, 1244. Public Record Office.

3525 Pt. 4. Containing extracts from:

a Gospels of St. Luke and St. John, 1st half of 8th cent. [vulgate version; probably written in Northumbria]. Bodleian Library.

b Rule of St. Benedict, 8th cent. Bodleian Library.

c Florence of Worcester, with continuation, *c.* 1108 and *c.* 1130. Oxford, Corpus Christi College.

d Records of King's Lynn, 1308. King's Lynn corporation muniments.

e Miracle-plays [Ludus Coventriae], 1468. British Museum.

f Bull of Urban IV, 1264 [commanding archbishop of Canterbury to publish and enforce his decree annulling the Provisions of Oxford]. British Museum.

g Compotus-roll, 1248 [of the manor of Wistow, Hunts.]. British Museum.

h Deed of Prince Edward, 1270 [appointing Richard, King of the Romans, guardian of his children during his absence on the Crusade]. Public Record Office.

3526 Pt. 5. Containing extracts from:

a Anglo-Saxon martyrology, fragment, 9th cent. Arundel Castle.

b Friar Alexander on the Apocalypse, mid 13th cent. Cambridge, University library.

c Prick of conscience, 1405 [middle-English didactic poem doubtfully attributed to Richard Rolle of Hampole]. British Museum.

d Notebook of Nicolas Bishop [citizen of Oxford], 1432. Cambridge, University library.

e Wardrobe-book of Queen Eleanor's household, 1290. British Museum.

f Registrum munimentorum, liber A, *c.* 1293. [Inventory in Latin of records in the exchequer]. Public Record Office.

g Stapleton's calendar (Aquitaine), 1321. [Inventory partly in French, partly in Latin, of docs. in the treasury relating to Aquitaine]. Public Record Office.

3527 Pts. 6 & 7. Containing extracts from:

a Psalter, with Anglo-Saxon version, 1st half of the 11th cent. Paris, Bibliothèque Nationale.

b [Collection of chronological, astronomical and medical writings], 1100–35. Durham cathedral library.

c Ralph de Diceto, minor works, *c.* 1195. British Museum.

d Breviary of Archbishop Chichele, 1414–43. Lambeth Palace.

e Letter of Margaret and Agnes Paston, 1448. British Museum.

f Charter of Richard I, 1189 [to Reading abbey; including the entry of the same deed in a Reading chartulary]. British Museum.

g Exchequer receipt rolls, 1311. Public Record Office.

3528 Pts. 8 & 9. Containing extracts from:

a Gospels, late 8th or early 9th cent. [vulgate version, written probably in Ireland, with Anglo-Saxon additions made in 10th cent.]. British Museum.

b Private letter of R. Roche, 1530–5 (?). British Museum.

c Court-roll of [the Countess of Kent's manor of] Alton, [Hants?], 1338. British Museum.

d Register of Glastonbury abbey, 1361. British Museum.

3529 Pts. 10 & 11. Containing extracts from:

a Gospels [vulgate version; written partly or wholly in England, late 10th cent. Used during the 11th cent. for the entry of records in Anglo-Saxon]. York minster library.

b Psalter (Bury St. Edmunds), mid 11th cent. [in Latin, Gallican version; written for the abbey of Bury St. Edmunds and decorated in the Winchester style]. Rome, Vatican library.

c Bible (Bury St. Edmunds), 2nd quarter of the 12th cent. [in Latin, vulgate version; written for Bury St. Edmunds abbey]. Cambridge, Corpus Christi College.

d Chartulary of Walden abbey [Saffron Walden, Essex], 1387. British Museum.

e Chaucer, Canterbury tales, 1477. Glasgow, Hunterian Museum.

f Minutes of the privy council, 1398 and 1404. British Museum.

g Wardrobe accompt, 1445 [for the expenses of Margaret of Anjou, consort of Henry VI, on her journey to England]. British Museum.

3530 Pts. 12 & 13. Containing extracts from:

a St. Jerome on Isaiah, mid 12th cent. [written in England, possibly Exeter]. Bodleian Library.

b Psalter with commentary, end of 12th cent. [in Latin, Gallican version; commentary of Herbert of Bosham; written apparently for Christ Church, Canterbury]. Bodleian Library.

c St. Augustine, various tracts, end 13th cent. [written by William de Wodecherche of the Cistercian abbey of Robertsbridge, Suss.]. Bodleian Library.

d The Lytlington missal, 1383–84 [executed for Nicolas Lytlington, abbot of Westminster]. Westminster abbey library.

e Bedford psalter and hours, 1414–35 [executed in England for John, Duke of Bedford, brother of Henry V]. Lulworth Castle library (till 1929).

f Ordinances for the royal household, 1454 [economies ordered by the council under the protectorship of Richard, Duke of York]. British Museum.

g Instructions to an English envoy, 1477 [from Edward IV to Alexander Legh, ambassador to James III of Scotland].

3531 Indices to facsimiles of ancient manuscripts, etc., 2nd ser., 1913–30. 1932.

NEWBURY DISTRICT FIELD CLUB

Founded 1870, to amass and diffuse practical information respecting the history, archaeology, and natural history of the district.

Transactions, vols. 5–6 (1911–33):

3532 Vol. 5.

a The Fettiplace family, by J. R. Dunlop.

b Midgham and the Poyntz family, by W. Money.

c Heralds' visitations of Berkshire and the pedigrees of Berkshire families. [Synopsis of Harleian Soc. vols. 56 and 57, no. 2025 above]

d Bucklebury [manor, after 1540] and its owners, by W. Money.

e Norman architecture of Berkshire, by C. E. Keyser.

f Proceedings. [Includes abstracts of papers on the battle of Chalgrove and the death of Hampden, by W. Money; Compton Wynyates, by W. Money; Broughton Castle, by Lord Saye and Sele; Stanton Harcourt, by W. Money; Sutton Courtenay, by P. H. Ditchfield; Steventon, by W. Money; Milton; Bradford-on-Avon, the town's history, by P. H. Ditchfield; and Wayland Smith's cave, by W. H. Belcher]

g Archaeological notes [relating to Newbury], by W. Money.

3533 Vol. 6.

a A Romano-British settlement at Thatcham Newtown, Berks., by W. E. Harris.

b Archaeological notes. [Kintbury skeleton no. 1, by A. R. Sansbury; Kintbury skeleton no. 2, by F. G. Parsons; Speenhamland skeleton, by F. G. Parsons]

c The Ridgeway and the Icknield way in Berkshire, by H. Peake.

d A Berkshire manor [Shaw] at the close of the middle ages, by L. Clare Latham. [Based on the manor account rolls, 1405–1530, and court rolls, 1406–1518. Additional notes by H. Chitty]

e Excavation of the Romano-British well at Thatcham Newtown, by W. E. Harris. [With reports on the objects found therein: six pewter vessels, by R. G. Collingwood; metal objects, by C. H. Desch; animal remains, by Dorothea M. A. Bate]

f Roman road from Durocornovium to Spinae.

g Recent discoveries [prehistoric burial remains] on Boxford common.

h Three unrecognised castle mounds at Hamstead Marshall, by J. N. L. Myres.

i Thatcham Newtown explorations, 1930–1, by W. E. Harris and W. K. Hardy.

j Early iron age remains on Boxford common, Berks., by H. Peake, H. H. Coghlan, and C. Hawkes.

k Bartholomew manor house, Newbury, by W. E. Wynter and A. J. C. Cooper. [Appendix: List of leases granted by dean and canons of Windsor, 1747–1866]

l An earthwork at Ashdown, by H. Peake.

m Romano-British remains in Salcombe Road, Newbury, by H. V. Beer.

n Two early sites in Woodcott and Crux Easton, Hants, by W. K. Hardy.

o Pre-Roman Silchester, by J. B. P. Karslake.

p Further excavations on Boxford common, by H. Peake and H. H. Coghlan.

q Blewburton hill [theories concerning its terraces], by H. Peake.

Special publication:

3534 History of Sandleford priory, by Evelyn E. Myers. 1931.

NEWCASTLE-UPON-TYNE RECORDS COMMITTEE

Founded 1920 (by the Society of Antiquaries of Newcastle upon Tyne), for the publication of records relating to Northumberland and Durham.

Publications, vols. 1–10:

3535 Vol. 1. Extracts from the Newcastle upon Tyne council minute book, 1639–56, ed. Madeleine H. Dodds. 1920.

3536 Vol. 2. Northumberland pleas from the curia regis and assize rolls, 1198–1272, ed. A. Hamilton Thompson. 1922.

3537 Vol. 3. Register of freemen of Newcastle upon Tyne, from the corporation guild and admission books, chiefly of the 17th cent., ed. Madeleine H. Dodds. 1923.

3538 Vol. 4. Northumbrian monuments; or the shields of arms, effigies and inscriptions in the churches, castles and halls of Northumberland, ed. C. H. Hunter Blair. 1924.

3539 Vol. 5. Durham monuments; or the shields of arms, effigies and inscriptions in the churches, castles, and halls of the county of Durham, ed. C. H. Hunter Blair. 1925.

3540 Vol. 6. Register of freemen of Newcastle upon Tyne, from the corporation guild and admission books, chiefly of the 18th cent., ed. A. M. Oliver. 1926.

3541 Vol. 7. Northumberland and Durham deeds from the Dodsworth mss. in Bodley's library, Oxford, ed. A. M. Oliver. 1929.

3542 Vol. 8. Index of wills etc., in the probate registry, Durham, and from other sources, 1540–99, ed. H. M. Wood. 1928.

3543 Vol. 9. A volume of miscellanea. 1930.

a List of transcripts of parish registers of Northumberland and Durham in the public library, Newcastle upon Tyne.

b List of J. C. Hodgson's ms. pedigrees of families in Northumberland and Durham.

c Index to pedigrees recorded in local histories, etc.

d Selections from the Delaval papers [16th–18th cent.] in the Newcastle upon Tyne public library, ed. with introd. by B. Anderton.

e Registers of the Ballast Hills [non-conformist] cemetery, Newcastle upon Tyne [1792–1801, with list of earlier burials], transcribed with introd. by C. E. Whiting.

3544 Vol. 10. Feet of fines, Northumberland and Durham, ed. A. M. Oliver and C. Johnson. 1931 [1933].

NEWCOMEN SOCIETY FOR THE STUDY OF THE HISTORY OF ENGINEERING AND TECHNOLOGY

Founded 1920, to encourage and foster the study of the history of engineering and industrial technology.

Transactions, vols. 1–12 (1922–33):

3545 Vol. 1.

a Introduction to the literature of historical engineering to 1640, by E. W. Hulme.

b Rise and fall of the Sussex iron industry, by R. Jenkins.

c The mystery of Trevithick's London locomotives, by L. St. L. Pendred.

d The invention of roller drawing in cotton spinning, by A. Seymour-Jones.

e Presidential address [on the history of engineering], by A. Titley.

3546 Vol. 2.

a Early history of mechanical handling devices, by G. F. Zimmer. [Additions by the same author in vol. 4]

b The Liverpool and Manchester railway, by C. F. D. Marshall.

c Timothy Hackworth [engineer, d. 1850] and the locomotive, by R. Young.

d The centenary of naval engineering: a review of the early history of our steam navy, by E. C. Smith.

e A holograph letter of Newcomen [1725], communicated by C. Matschoss.

f A note on Brunton's steam horse, 1813, by L. St. L. Pendred.

g Notes on Heaton's steam carriage of 1830, by A. Titley.

h Gurney's railway locomotives, 1830, by E. A. Forward.

i An 18th cent. engineer's [William Reynolds's] sketch book, by H. W. Dickinson.

j Analytical bibliography of the history of engineering and applied science, 1900–20. [Contd. to 1932 in vols. 3, 4, and 6–12]

3547 Vol. 3.

a Simon Goodrich [d. 1847] and his work as an engineer, comp. from his journal and memoranda by E. A. Forward.

b Notes on the early history of steel making in England, by R. Jenkins. [Appendix: Sir Henry Sidney's steel works]

c Notes on old windmills, by A. Titley.

d Indian cotton prints and paintings of the 17th and 18th cent., by G. P. Baker.

e Early history of the coal gas process, by D. Brownlie.

f Notes on Sir George Cayley [d. 1857] as a pioneer of aeronautics, by J. E. Hodgson.

g Savery, Newcomen, and the early history of the steam engine, by R. Jenkins. [Contd. in vol. 4]

h A holograph letter of Faraday [1821], communicated by L. Darmstaedter.

3548 Vol. 4.

a A 16th cent. treadwheel for raising water, by H. A. Sandford.

b Evelyn's 'Circle [or catalogue] of mechanical trades', annotated by A. F. Sieveking.

c The Rastricks [John, d. 1826, and John U., d. 1856], civil engineers, by H. W. Dickinson and A. Lee.

d The four locomotives imported into America in 1829 by the Delaware and Hudson company, by L. F. Loree.

e Works organization in the 17th cent.: some account of Ambrose and John Crowley, by W. A. Young.

f A sketch of the industrial history of the Coalbrookdale district, by R. Jenkins.

3549 Vol. 5.

a Notes on Coalbrookdale, and the Darbys [Abraham, d. 1717, and son, iron manufacturers], by J. W. Hall.

b The discoveries of the Darbys of Coalbrookdale, by T. S. Ashton.

c Notes on original models of the Eddystone lighthouses, by T. Rowatt.

d Early history of the cylinder boring machine, by E. A. Forward.

e Some windmills of Cape Cod, by E. P. Hamilton.

f Notes on a neglected worthy, John Patison of Airdrie [d. 1905], by D. Brownlie.

g George Dixon [fl. 1760], discoverer of gas light from coal, by J. Macfarlan.

h Gun-making handicrafts, by C. E. Greener.

i Chiddingfold glass and its makers in the middle ages, by Brenda C. Halahan.

j Letters of Marc Isambard Brunel, annotated by R. Jenkins.

k Subject list of books and pamphlets relating to the history of technology, published during 1920–25.

3550 Vol. 6.

a Joshua Field's diary of a tour in 1821 through the midlands, with introd. and notes by J. W. Hall.

b Iron-making in the Forest of Dean, by R. Jenkins.

c The history of copper ruby glass, by J. A. Knowles.

d The invention of English flint glass, by E. W. Hulme.

e John George Bodmer [d. 1864], his life and work, particularly in relation to the evolution of mechanical stoking, by D. Brownlie.

f Matthew Murray [engineer, d. 1826]: a centenary appreciation, by G. F. Tyas.

g Fathers of machine cotton manufacture, by F. Nasmith.

h Notes on local [East Anglian] technology, by H. O. Clark. [On flints, monumental brasses, engineering]

i The strangers in Norwich: a page in the history of our ancient textile industry, by W. R. Rudd.

3551 Vol. 7.

a Observations on the rise and progress of manufacturing industry in England, by R. Jenkins.

b Trevithick and Rastrick and the single-acting expansive engine, by A. Titley.

c Thomas Newcomen: a note on his handwriting, by R. Jenkins.

d British railways of 1825, as seen by Marc Seguin, by F. Achard and L. Seguin.

e The first British locomotives of the St. Etienne-Lyon railway, by F. Achard.

f Notes on lead mining and smelting in west Yorkshire, by A. Raistrick.

g Marc Seguin and the invention of the tubular boiler, by F. Achard and L. Seguin.

h Notes on copper smelting, 1567–1616, by H. G. Graves.

3552 Vol. 8.

a Development of the organ, by E. W. Anderson.

b Railway brakes, by T. Rowatt.

c Notes on horse-mills, by H. O. Clark.

d The making and rolling of iron, by J. W. Hall.

e Some episodes in early ocean steam navigation, by E. C. Smith.

f James Sadler, of Oxford [d. 1828], aeronaut, chemist, engineer, and inventor, by J. E. Hodgson.

g Early Stourbridge industries [coal, fireclay, glass, wool, nails, iron, etc.], by H. E. Palfrey.

h Early history of coal-mining in the Black Country and especially around Dudley, by W. J. Jenkins.

i Thomas Lewis and Samuel Owen, two [late 18th cent.] British pioneers of mechanical engineering in Sweden, by C. Sahlin.

3553 Vol. 9.

a Development of railway signalling, by W. H. Deakin.

b Statistical history of the iron trade of England and Wales, 1717–50, by E. W. Hulme. [A table entitled 'Output of the furnaces and forges in England and Wales, 1717–50: lists A–C', was issued separately]

c Prehistoric agriculture in Britain, by E. C. Curwen.

d A chapter in the history of the water supply of London: a Thames-side pumping installation and Sir Edward Ford's patent from Cromwell [1655], by R. Jenkins.

e John Wyatt and the weighing of heavy loads, by W. A. Benton.

f The Rainhill locomotive trials, 1829, by C. F. D. Marshall.

g Pedigree of Thomas Newcomen, by Muriel Hine.

3554 Vol. 10.

a Valve gear of Newcomen's engine, by C. O. Becker.

b 'The art of water-drawing', by R. Jenkins. [See also extra publication 2, no. **3560** below]

c Bell founding, by A. A. Hughes.

d Pioneer [steam] ships of the Atlantic ferry, by E. C. Smith.

e Richard Trevithick and the winding engine, by A. Titley.

f German wild-fire trials at Oxford, 1438, by E. W. Hulme.

g Civil engineering in 1595–7: the building and destruction of a pier at Hastings, by R. Jenkins.

h Diary of John George Bodner [while in England], 1816–17, ed. H. W. Dickinson.

i Agricultural sources of mechanical information, by H. Nicol.

3555 Vol. 11.

a Fire-extinguishing engines in England, 1625–1725, by R. Jenkins.

b Cornish mining: notes from the account book of Richard Trevithick senior, by A. Titley.

c The south Staffordshire and north Worcestershire mining district and its relics of mining appliances, by T. E. Lones.

d The 16th cent. chain pump at Hampton Court, by G. F. Zimmer.

e John Nuttall's sketch book with notes on wrought iron details and wheels for early locomotives, by J. G. H. Warren.

f The first installation of house-to-house [electricity] supply in the United Kingdom [1886–7], by R. E. B. Crompton.

g John Curr [d. 1823], originator of iron tram roads, by F. Bland.

h John Calley [d. 1725], partner of Thomas Newcomen, by J. J. Bootsgeyel.

i Jonathan Hornblower [d. 1815] and the compound engine, by R. Jenkins.

j Francis Thompson's visit to the Cardiganshire mines, 1788, by R. Jenkins.

k Memorials to pioneer Leeds engineers [18th–19th cent.], by E. K. Scott.

3556 Vol. 12.

a Jolliffe and Banks, contractors, by H. W. Dickinson.

b The oliver: iron making in the 14th cent., by R. Jenkins.

c Men of straw: an account of surviving straw handicraft, by T. B. Hennell.

d Early cloth fulling and its machinery, by E. K. Scott.

e Roman mining in Britain, by G. C. Whittick.

f Trevithick's first rail locomotive, by W. W. Mason.

g Coke: a note on its production and use, 1587–1650, by R. Jenkins.

3557 General index to Transactions, vols. 1–10, 1920–21 to 1929–30. [1932].

3558 General index to Transactions, vols. 11–20, 1930–31 to 1939–40, and extra publications, nos. 1–4. [n.d.].

Extra publications, nos. 1–3:

3559 No. 1. Martin Triewald's *Short Description of the Atmospheric Engine*, published at Stockholm, 1734. 1928.

3560 No. 2. R. D'acres's *The Art of Water-drawing*, published by Henry Brome, at the Gun in Ivie Lane, London, 1659 and 1660, with introd. and diagram by R. Jenkins. 1930.

3561 No. 3. Aeronautical and miscellaneous note-book, *c.* 1799–1826, of Sir George Cayley, with an appendix comprising a list of the Cayley papers [mechanical and technical]. 1933.

NORFOLK AND NORWICH ARCHAEOLOGICAL SOCIETY

Founded 1846, to encourage the study of history, architecture, and antiquities; to collect and publish information on the arts and monuments of the county of Norfolk, etc.

Norfolk Archaeology: or miscellaneous tracts relating to the antiquities of the county of Norfolk, vols. 14–25 (1898–1935):

3562 Vol. 14.

a Three manorial extents [relating to Bradcar in Shropham, Banham, and Wykes in Bardwell] of the 13th cent., by W. H. Hudson.

b South Lopham church, by C. R. Manning.

c Notes on the palimpsest brass of Robert Rugge, 1558, in the church of St. John Maddermarket, Norwich, by M. Stephenson.

d Yarmouth and the Cinque ports: report by the bailiffs of the Cinque ports after their visit to Gt. Yarmouth during the free fair, 1574, by W. L. Rutton.

e Some ancient stone fragments [with plaited-work ornamentation] found in Cringleford church, by T. S. Cogswell.

f Recent discoveries in the cathedral church of Norwich [made during the cleaning of the nave], by W. H. St. J. Hope and W. T. Bensly.

g A notebook of Sir Miles Branthwayt in 1605, by W. Rye. [Extracts]

h The course of the Icknield way through Norfolk, by J. C. Tingey.

i Inventories [early- and mid-16th cent.] of the parish church of St. Peter Mancroft [Norwich], by W. H. St. J. Hope.

j Female head-dresses exemplified by Norfolk brasses, by J. L. André.

k Norwich militia in the 14th cent., by W. Hudson. [With transcripts of views of arms and rolls of array for the city leets]

l Mannington Hall [with some notes of its occupants], by R. J. W. Purdy.

m The hundred of Clackclose and the civil war, by L. G. Bolingbroke. [Parish rate books for Riston and Bexwell, 1645–9]

n Mantelpiece [from a demolished Elizabethan mansion] at Fakenham, by W. Rye. [With a pedigree of the Gwyn family of Fakenham]

3563 Vol. 15.

a The 'Land Buyers' Society', by W. Rye. [Transcript of a ms., *c.* 1630, relating to the activities of a land-buying combine in Norfolk]

b Duel between Thomas Berney and Thomas Bedingfield [in Norwich] in 1684, by P. B. Ficklin.

c Note on the church of Cley, by J. T. Micklethwaite.

d The manor of Kenninghall, and its connection with the office of chief butler of England, by F. O. Taylor.

e Blakeney church, by J. O. Scott.

f Church plate in the rural deanery of Depwade, Norf., by E. C. Hopper. [Articles on the church plate of other Norfolk deaneries, by E. C. Hopper, B. de Chair, J. H. Walter, and H. S. Radcliffe, occur in vols. 16–24]

g Household accounts of Kenninghall palace in 1525, by R. Howlett.

h Palimpsest brasses in Norfolk, by M. Stephenson.

i Two Elizabethan inventories [of John West, labourer, 1513, and of Sir Roger Wodehouse, of Kimberley, 1588], by L. G. Bolingbroke.

j Pedigree of Sir Thomas Browne [d. 1682], by C. Williams.

k The journals of John Dernell [1417] and John Boys [1428–9], carters at the Lathes [a home farm of St. Giles' hospital] in Norwich, by J. C. Tingey.

l A fabric roll of the Norwich guildhall, 1410–11, by R. Howlett.

m Dilham 'castle', by H. Brittain. [Ruins of a 15th cent. tower and walls]

n Extracts from the two oldest registers of the parish of Syderstone, Norf., by H. J. Dukinfield Astley.

o A silver-gilt ewer and basin given by Archbishop Parker to the city of Norwich, by W. T. Bensly.

p 'Memoirs of the life of Thomas Martin, gent. [d. 1771], F.A.S., of Palgrave in Suffolk; with an account of the disposal and dispersion of his large and valuable collection of manuscripts, printed books, papers, coins and other curiosities; by John Fenn, esq., M.A., F.A.S., 1784.' [Introductory notice by Sir J. Fenn]

q Some account of the manor or castle of Horsford [and its occupants], by T. Barrett-Lennard.

r Recent excavations at the college of St. Mary in the Fields, Norwich, by G. E. Hawes.

s The Whissonsett cross, by W. G. Collingwood. [An interlaced wheel-cross, probably of pre-Norman origin]

t Armorial glass in old and new Buckenham churches, by Prince Frederick Duleep Singh.

u The [stained glass in the] east window of St. Stephen's church, Norwich, by D. Harford.

3564 Vol. 16.

a The king's house at Thetford, with some account of the visits of King James I to that town, by H. F. Killick. [Additional note: A royal grant of the property to Andrew Pitcarne, 1628, with some details of the latter's career]

b Thetford castle hill, by W. G. Clarke.

c Norwich artillery in the 14th cent., by R. Howlett.

d A quaint old lettered panel at North Walsham [14th cent., possibly from Rugge's Hall at Felmingham, now demolished], by J. H. Reeve.

e An old [early 16th cent.] cannon at the great hospital, Norwich, by W. Rye.

f Earthworks at Mousehold heath, by W. Rye.

g A group of Norman fonts in north-west Norfolk, by H. J. Dukinfield Astley. [Appendix A: Some ancient carved stones in Calverton church, Notts. Appendix B: The Burnham Deepdale font]

h The will of Thomas Browne, mercer, Cheapside, London, father of Sir Thomas Browne of Norwich; remarks on the early life of Sir Thomas Browne together with the oration delivered by him at the inauguration of Pembroke College, Oxford, 1624; also the will of Sir Thomas Browne, 1679, by C. Williams.

i Hautbois Magna [manor and its occupants], by R. J. W. Purdy.

j Sepulchral cross slabs in East Winch church, by E. J. Alvis.

k Norwich and Yarmouth in 1332: their comparative prosperity [with reference to their assessment for tenths and fifteenths], by W. Hudson.

l Notes on Ingham old Hall, by L. G. Bolingbroke.

m Ancient stained glass in the church of St. Peter Hungate, Norwich, by G. A. King.

n Roman villa recently discovered at Grimston, Norf., by H. Laver.

o Notes on Diss and Bressingham churches, by C. R. Manning.

p The hitherto unpublished certificates of Norwich gilds, by J. C. Tingey. [Transcripts with English translations]

q Notes on some 15th cent. glass in the church of Wiggenhall, St. Mary Magdalene, by C. E. Keyser.

r The Dutch congregation in Norwich [being rules relating to their trading and general conduct in the city, *c.* 1755], by W. Rye.

3565 Vol. 17.

a Notes on the ninth iter of Antoninus, with special reference to the sites of Sitomagus and Venta Icenorum, re-considered in the light of the Tabula Peutingeriana, by H. J. Dukinfield Astley. [An attempt to identify Sitomagus with Thetford, and Venta Icenorum with Caistor]

b Church of St. Mary Coslany, Norwich, by J. T. Hotblack.

c Norwich castle mound, by E. J. Tench.

d The 'Norwich taxation' of 1254, so far as relates to the diocese of Norwich, collated with the taxation of Pope Nicholas in 1291, with remarks on the origin of the rural deaneries, and the valuation of the parochial benefices, by W. Hudson. [With transcript of the valuation, 1254, from the Liber Albus of Bury St. Edmunds]

e Notes on the roof of the nave of All Saints' church, Necton, by S. Martin-Jones.

f Description of ancient stained glass in the church of St. Peter Mancroft, Norwich, by G. A. King.

g Richard of Caister [d. 1420], and his metrical prayer, by D. Harford.

h The armorial bearings of the city of Norwich, by J. T. Hotblack.

i Churchman House, St. Giles's Street, Norwich, by Sir P. Eade.

j Notes on the sculptured parapet on the tower of St. Mary's church, Burnham Market, by T. F. Faulkner.

k A history of Coxford priory, by H. W. Saunders. [With extracts from and notes on the Coxford cartulary and a calendar of the same]

3566 Vol. 18.

a Proceedings, 1912. [Includes accounts of Gildencroft Quaker meeting house, the Octagon chapel, the old Congregational meeting house, and St. Helen's hospital, all in Norwich; the abbey of St. Benet at Holm; the Ranworth antiphoner; Oxborough Hall; Houghton Hall]

b Proceedings, 1913. [Includes accounts of St. Bartholomew's church, Heigham; Costessey Hall; No. 4, South Quay, Yarmouth; Yarmouth corporation plate and regalia]

c The last of the Norfolk Derehams of West Dereham, by F. Goldie. [Sir Thomas Dereham, bt., d. 1739]

d Notes on the Lovells of East Harling [in the 16th and 17th cent.], by G. L. Harrison.

e A list of the clergy of Norfolk and their status, 35 Elizabeth, by H. W. Saunders.

f The ancient see of Elmham, by R. Howlett.

g Grants of murage to Norwich, Yarmouth and Lynn, by J. C. Tingey.

h The Norwich subscription for the regaining of Newcastle, 1643, by F. R. Beecheno.

i Village gilds of Norfolk in the 15th cent., by Catherine B. Firth.

j Time-dials in the deanery of Depwade, by A. Cross.

k An account of Blo' Norton Hall, otherwise the manor house of Brome Hall in Blo' Norton, by Prince Frederick Duleep Singh. [Appendix contains a selection of wills of some of the owners of the house]

l Pre-Reformation painted glass in St. Andrew's church, Norwich, by G. A. King.

m The old bridge at Attlebridge, by T. D. Atkinson.

3567 Vol. 19.

a Mural paintings in Fritton church, by A. Cross.

b The last of the bondmen in a Norfolk manor, by Christobel M. Hoare. [The manor and soke of Gimingham in the reign of Elizabeth]

c The solution of a problem [a 16th cent. cryptograph] in the North Elmham register, by E. H. Townsend.

d Estate management at Rainham in the years 1661-86 and 1706, by H. W. Saunders. [The work of Charles, 2nd Viscount Townshend, d. 1738]

e The library of the cathedral church of Norwich, by H. C. Beeching; with an appendix of priory manuscripts now in English libraries, by M. R. James.

f Roman and other remains recently discovered at Sedgeford, by H. Ingleby.

g Notes on some ancient stained glass in Sandringham church, by C. E. Keyser.

h The account of Edmund Carvell and Humfrey Bedyngfelde as the executors of the will of Thomas Karvell, of Wiggenhall, esq., 1559-65, by H. L. Bradfer-Lawrence.

i The possible East Anglian descent of the poet Spenser, by W. Rye.

j The Sucklings' house at Norwich, by F. R. Beecheno. [Contd. in vol. 20]

k Lives of St. Walstan [of Bawburgh], by M. R. James. [The Latin life from Capgrave's *Nova legenda Anglie* and the English metrical life]

l The Camera roll of the prior of Norwich in 1258, compiled by Bartholomew de Cotton, by W. Hudson. [Appendix 1: Acknowledgments of the homagers of the priory of Norwich on the creation of Sir Robert de Langele prior of Norwich at his first coming, 1309. Appendix 2: Supply and distribution of bread in Norwich priory. Appendix 3: The departments of the 'magister celarii' and the 'celerarius']

m Notes on the architecture and wood-carving of the church of St. Mary the Virgin, Wiggenhall, by W. R. Bullmore.

n Proceedings, 1915. [Includes accounts of Mannington Hall and Wolterton House]

o Proceedings, 1916. [Includes accounts of Norwich cathedral and King Edward VI school]

3568 Vol. 20.

a Francis Blomefield's queries in preparation for his history of Norfolk, by G. A. Stephen.

b Reasons agst a general sending of corne to ye marketts in ye champion parte of Norfolke. [Transcript, by T. S. Cogswell, of a treatise *c.* 1631]

c Notes on the early lords of manors in the parish of Shelfanger [11th-15th cent.], by W. R. Harrisson.

d Two hundred years of estate management at Horsford during the 17th and 18th cent., by Sir T. Barrett-Lennard, bt.

e A mediaeval inscription in Acle church, by G. G. Coulton.

f The prior of Norwich's manor of Hindolveston: its early organisation and the right of the customary tenants to alienate their strips of land, by W. Hudson.

g St. John Madder Market, Norwich: its streets, lanes, and ancient houses, and their old-time associations, by L. G. Bolingbroke.

h Robert Baron [poet and dramatist, fl. 1645], by F. R. Beecheno.

i The Drayton communion cup, by J. H. F. Walter.

j The Anglo-Danish village of Martham: its pre-Domesday tenants and their conversion into the customary tenants of a feudal manor in 1101, by W. Hudson.

k Periodical literature relating to Norfolk archaeology, by G. A. Stephen.

l Proceedings, 1917. [Includes accounts of St. Julian's church, Norwich, and Carrow priory]

3569 Vol. 21.

a Manorial history of Little Ellingham, by J. C. Tingey.

b Additional note on the Paston brass at Paston [to Erasmus Paston, d. 1538, and his wife Mary], by M. Stephenson.

c Notes on three palimpsest brasses recently discovered [in the church of St. John de Sepulchre, Norwich, Norwich castle museum, and the church of St. Andrew, East Burlingham], by H. O. Clark.

d Tudor ceiling at 22, St. Giles Street, Norwich, by E. H. Buckingham.

e King John's sword (King's Lynn), by H. Ingleby.

f The earliest roll of household accounts [of Roger de Holm, steward of the manor of Hunstanton] in the muniment room at Hunstanton for the 2nd year of Edward III [1328], by G. H. Holley.

g Literature relating to Norfolk archaeology and kindred subjects, 1916-20, by G. A. Stephen. [Contd. for the period 1923-34 in vols. 22-25]

h Account of St. Peter's Hungate parish, Norwich, by F. R. Beecheno.

i Notes on the Domesday assessment of Norfolk, by J. C. Tingey.

j The first seventy years [1652-1722] of Guestwick Independent church, by B. Cozens-Hardy.

k The Premonstratensian abbey of Langley, with a report on some excavations made on the site on behalf of the

British Archaeological Association, by F. C. Elliston-Erwood. (Reprinted from the *Journal of the British Archaeological Association.*)

l The Norfolk and Norwich silk industry, by W. R. Rudd.

m Assessment of the hundred of Forehoe, Norfolk, 1621: a sidelight on the difficulties of national taxation, by W. Hudson.

n 14th cent. ms. poem on hawking, by B. Cozens-Hardy. [Part of a poem *Le Roman des deduiz* or The romance of sport, by Gace de la Bigne]

o Thomas Blundeville, of Newton Flotman [d. 1606], author and poet, by A. Campling.

p A review of the minute books concerning the erection of the Octagon chapel, Norwich [1753–4], by S. J. Wearing.

q Notes and queries. [Includes a note on officials in the manor of Gimingham-Lancaster, 1574, by Christobel M. Hood]

r Proceedings, 1920. [Includes accounts of 'Old' Crome, and of St. Andrew's church, Hingham]

s Proceedings, 1921. [Includes accounts of Elsing Hall, Melton Constable Hall, Aylsham church, Felbrigg Hall, and Blickling Hall]

t Proceedings, 1922. [Includes accounts of Norwich cathedral precincts, Blakeney church, Cley parish church]

3570 Vol. 22.

a The Norwich case. Particulars relating to the sufferings of Quakers in Norwich, 1682–3, by A. J. Eddington.

b Muster roll and clergy list in the hundred of Holt, *c.* 1523, by B. Cozens-Hardy.

c More Norfolk palimpsest brasses [in the churches of St. Mary, Shelton, St. Andrew, Honingham, St. Mary, Holm-next-the-Sea, All Saints' Woodton, Reedham, and Swardeston], by H. O. Clark.

d Coat of arms [of the Clere and Uvedale families] in St. Stephen's Street, Norwich, by E. A. Kent.

e Note on the sepulchral slab at Hickling church, by B. Cozens-Hardy.

f Five compotus rolls of Blackbergh nunnery [dating from 39 Henry VI to 20 Edward IV], by A. H. Cooke.

g Notes on the Blackfriars' hall, or Dutch church, Norwich, by E. A. Kent.

h A Norfolk shipmaster, 1379–80 [Robert Rust, of Blakeney], by W. Rye. [With an extract from Spelman's *History of Sacrilege* concerning an outrage by the followers of Sir John Arundel on a nunnery near Portsmouth]

i An East Anglian contemporary of Pepys: Philip Skippon, of Foulsham, 1641–92, by Christobel M. Hood. [Extracts from his diary, 1667–77]

j Some recent discoveries at Paston, by Monica Bardswell. [Mural paintings, *c.* 1400, in the church]

k Chapel of St. Clement at Brundall, by F. Johnson.

l Excavation of a barrow at Cley-next-the-Sea, by J. F. Williams.

m The Bainard family in Norfolk [11th to 14th cent.], by L. Landon.

n The scheduling of the Norfolk ancient monuments, by B. Cozens-Hardy. [A list of those worthy of being scheduled under the Ancient Monuments Act, 1913]

o Notes and queries. [Subjects include: Blackfriars' hall, Norwich, by E. A. Kent, and the tomb of Robert Jannys, d. *c.* 1530, in the church of St. George Colegate, Norwich, by J. K. Floyer]

p The priory of Horsham St. Faith, by W. R. Rudd.

q Wall painting at Horsham St. Faith, near Norwich, by E. W. Tristram.

r The barony of Valoignes in Norfolk, by J. C. Tingey.

s The Puritan moderate: Dr. Thomas Thorowgood, S.T.B., 1595–1669, rector of Grimston, Little Massingham, and Great Cressingham, by B. Cozens-Hardy.

t Wall paintings recently uncovered at Seething and Caistor by Norwich, by Monica Bardswell.

u Church of Saint James, Great Ellingham, by E. J. Tench.

v Some early East Anglian wills [of the Anglo-Saxon period], by O. K. Schram. [Anglo-Saxon texts with English translations]

w The Sackfriars' and Blackfriars' conventual buildings in the parishes of St. Andrew and St. Peter Hungate, Norwich: excavations in the winter of 1910–11, by P. A. Nash.

x Notes and queries. [Includes an account of Roughton church]

y Proceedings, 1923. [Includes accounts of Framingham Earl church, Langley abbey, Wilby Hall, East Harling church, South Lopham church, Raynham Hall, and Roman villa at Gaytonthorpe]

z Proceedings, 1924. [Includes an account of Carbrooke church]

aa Proceedings, 1925. [Includes accounts of Earsham church and Gawdy Hall]

3571 Vol. 23.

a Stained and painted glass in the Guildhall, Norwich, by E. A. Kent.

b Norfolk deeds in the Jackson collection, public reference library, Sheffield, by G. A. Stephen.

c An early site at Stoke Ferry [and its pre-historic and Roman remains], by J. F. Williams.

d An ecclesiastical dispute at Westwick *c.* 1450, by B. Cozens-Hardy.

e The Saxon cathedral of Elmham, by A. W. Clapham and W. H. Godfrey.

f The priory of Horsham St. Faith, by W. R. Rudd.

g The building of Raynham Hall [by Sir Roger Townshend, d. 1637], by H. L. Bradfer-Lawrence. [Appendix 1: Transcripts from a book of accounts 1618/19–23. Appendix 2: Transcript of a book of remembrance concerning the buildings, 1622. Appendix 3: Note on the will of William Edge, freemason, d. 1643. Appendix 4: Note on the visit of Charles II to Raynham, 1671]

h The sheriffs of Norfolk [*c.* 1040–1163], by L. Landon. [With a pedigree showing the descent of the manors of Carbrook and Saxlingham]

i The Roman villa of Gayton Thorpe, by D. Atkinson.

j Norfolk satire in the 18th cent., by R. W. Ketton-Cremer.

k The Roman fortified town at Caistor-next-Norwich, by E. A. Kent.

l John Kirkpatrick, antiquary, d. 20 Aug. 1728, aged 42 years, by F. Johnson. [Reprinted from the *Eastern Daily Press*]

m Ecclesiastical discipline at South Creake in 1317, by J. F. Williams.

n Stiffkey alias Stewkey, by H. L. Bradfer-Lawrence. [An account of the village of that name and its manors. Appendix 1: Inventory of the goods of Sir Roger Townshend at his house in Stiffkey, taken 1636/7. Appendix 2: A terrier of Stiffkey, *temp.* Edward I]

o The priory of St. Mary and All Saints, Westacre, and excavations upon its site, by F. H. Fairweather, with an introductory historical note by H. L. Bradfer-Lawrence.

p Notes and queries. [Includes notes on an armorial seal of the Ingaldesthorpe family, *c.* 1250, by H. L. Bradfer-Lawrence]

q Proceedings, 1926. [Includes accounts of Methwold church, Middleton tower, and of the Nar valley and its religious houses]

r Proceedings, 1927. [Includes accounts of Salle Moor Hall and Thorpe Hall]

s Proceedings, 1928. [Includes accounts of Buckenham castle, Hindringham Hall, and the Grey Friars, Little Walsingham]

3572 Vol. 24.

a Portraits of John Elison [minister of the Dutch church, Norwich, 1603–39] and of Mary, his wife, by Rembrandt, by J. C. Tingey.

b A bailiff's roll of Thetford, 1403–4, by J. F. Williams.

c Assize week in Norwich, 1688, by R. W. Ketton-Cremer. [Letter from M. Chamberlayne to William Windham, of Felbrigg]

d Notes on [the parish of] Toftrees, by H. L. Bradfer-Lawrence.

e Notes and queries. [Includes some account of Freebridge: its meaning and site of origin in the so-named hundred, by H. L. Bradfer-Lawrence]

f Houses of the Duke of Norfolk in Norwich, by E. A. Kent.

g Camping: a forgotten Norfolk game, by R. W. Ketton-Cremer.

h Caistor excavations, 1929, by D. Atkinson.

i A memoir of Frederic Johnson, archivist, 1864–1930, by R. H. Teasdel.

j Gaywood Dragge, 1486–7, by H. L. Bradfer-Lawrence. [A terrier of the manor]

k Augustinian priory of Weybourne, by F. H. Fairweather.

l A Norfolk dissenter's letter, 1662 [written by John Collinges], by A. G. Matthews.

m A Norfolk vicar's charm against the ague, by W. R. Dawson. [The deciphering of a charm used by Robert Forbes, vicar of Rougham, d. 1709]

n Church of St. Bartholomew, Ber Street, Norwich, by C. J. W. Messent.

o Two certificates of a solemn penance [to be performed by Robert Martyn, 1525 and 1526], by A. Hamilton Thompson.

p Mediaeval painted glass in Norfolk, by C. Woodforde.

q Proceedings, 1929. [Includes accounts of Bedingham church, and Shelton church]

r Proceedings, 1930. [Includes accounts of Gowthorpe manor, and Mettingham castle, Suff.]

s Proceedings, 1931. [Includes accounts of Baconsthorpe castle and church, Barningham Norwood Hall, Wickmere church, and St. Mary's church, Mildenhall]

3573 Vol. 25.

a Proceedings, 1932. [Includes accounts of Norwich civic regalia and the plate of St. Peter Mancroft; Northwold church; Terrington St. Clement's church, and Walpole St. Peter church]

b The waits of the city of Norwich through four centuries to 1790, by G. A. Stephen.

c Eastern chapels in the cathedral church of Norwich, by D. H. S. Cranage.

d The seven sacrament fonts of Norfolk, by H. S. Squirrell.

e A palimpsest brass at Narborough to John Spelman, esq., 1581, by H. O. Clark.

f William Bateman, bishop of Norwich, 1344–55, by A. Hamilton Thompson. [Appendix: The itinerary of Bishop Bateman]

g Mediaeval glass restored to Cawston church, by C. Woodforde.

h Notes and queries. [Includes an account of a Rogation-tide perambulation in the parish of Great Melton, 1726]

i Mural painting of St. George in St. Gregory's church, Norwich, by E. A. Kent.

j A drawing for Blomefield's *Norfolk* [made 1744]: the tomb of Judge Francis Windham, by R. W. Ketton-Cremer.

k Chamberlains and treasurers of the city of Norwich, 1293–1835, by Mary Grace.

l A Roman site at Santon, by R. R. Clarke.

m A record of old weights and measures in Norfolk, by A. Robinson.

n Medieval painted glass in North Tuddenham church, Norfolk, by C. Woodforde.

o The Greyfriars of Walsingham, by A. R. Martin.

p Norfolk crosses, by B. Cozens-Hardy.

q Constitutions of the hospital of St. Paul (Normanspitel) in Norwich, by E. H. Carter.

r Notes on the archaeology of Markshall, by R. R. Clarke.

s Roof bosses in the chancel of Salle church, by C. J. P. Cave.

t A Roman colony near Brancaster, by G. Ward.

u Notes on the Boleyn family, by W. L. E. Parsons.

v An iron age tumulus on Warborough hill, Stiffkey, by R. R. Clarke and H. Apling.

w Proceedings, 1933. [Includes accounts of the district around St. Clement's, Norwich, of St. Michael's Coslany church, Norwich, and of Norwich high school]

x Proceedings, 1934. [Includes accounts of Elsing church and Hall, Swanton Morley church, Mattishall church, Barton Turf church, and of Ingham old Hall]

3574 General index to vols. 11–20 of Norfolk Archaeology, comp. J. Olorenshaw, and a list of the principal places visited, July 1890–Dec. 1927. 1928.

Other publications:

3575 Marriages recorded in the register of the sacrist of the cathedral church of Norwich, 1697–1754, by T. R. Tallack, F. Johnson, and L. G. Bolingbroke. 1902.

3576 A short calendar of deeds relating to Norwich enrolled in the court rolls of that city, 1285–1306, ed. W. Rye. 1903.

3577 Depositions taken before the mayor and aldermen of Norwich, 1549–67; extracts from the court books of the city, 1666–88, ed. W. Rye. 1905.

3578 State papers relating to musters, beacons, shipmoney, etc. in Norfolk, from 1626, chiefly to the beginning of the civil war, ed. W. Rye, with preface by C. H. Firth. 1907.

3579 Sculptured bosses in the roof of the Bauchun chapel of Our Lady of Pity in Norwich cathedral, described by M. R. James, with introd. by W. T. Bensly. Folio, 1908.

3580 Calendar of the freemen of Great Yarmouth, 1429–1800, comp. from the records of the corporation. 1910.

3581 Sculptured bosses in the cloisters of Norwich cathedral, described by M. R. James, with illustrations of the bosses in the northern alley from drawings by C. J. W. Winter, and introd. by F. Johnson. 1911.

3582 Calendar of the freemen of Lynn, 1292–1836, comp. from the records of the corporation. 1913.

3583 Churches of Norfolk: hundred of Shropham, by T. H. Bryant. 1913.

3584 Churches of Norfolk: hundred of Brothercross, by T. H. Bryant. 1914.

3585 Churches of Norfolk: hundred of Diss, by T. H. Bryant. 1915.

3586 Calendar of Norwich deeds enrolled in the court rolls of that city, 1307–1341, ed. W. Rye. 1915.

NORFOLK AND NORWICH ARCHAEOLOGICAL SOCIETY. GREAT YARMOUTH BRANCH

Founded 1888, *to encourage the study of history, architecture, and antiquities, etc.*

Proceedings, 1928–32 (5 vols. [1929–33]):

3587 Vol. for 1928.

a Visit of the Suffolk Institute of Archaeology. [Includes

notes on Gorleston church and Great Yarmouth parish church]
b Excursion to the Waveney valley. [Includes notes on Mettingham castle and Barsham church]
c Excursion in north Norfolk. [Includes notes on Felbrigg Hall and church]
d Antiquity of man in East Anglia, by J. R. Moir.

3588 Vol. for 1929.

a Roman Britain, a Norfolk Pompeii [Caistor St. Edmund], by I. C. Hannah.
b The story of Caister castle: Yarmouth archaeologists' excursion. [Also includes notes on Ormesby St. Margaret's church and the manor of Ormesby St. Margaret and Michael.]
c Archaeologists and Caistor camp excavations.
d West Suffolk's antiquities: visit to Bury St. Edmunds.
e The abbey at Bury: episodes in its history, by R. H. Teasdel.

3589 Vol. for 1930.

a A Suffolk field day: reminiscences of William Dowsing, the iconoclast, by R. H. Teasdel.
b A second excursion in north Norfolk. [Includes notes on Mannington Hall, and Barningham Norwood church and Hall]
c The medieval parish church, by J. F. Williams.

3590 Vol. for 1931.

a Broadland excursion. [Includes notes on Barton Turf church]
b Wensum valley excursion: Houghton and the Walpoles. [Also includes notes on Elsing Hall]
c West Norfolk, Castle Rising and Holkham.

3591 Vol. for 1932.

a Annual meeting. [Includes a paper on Tudor housekeeping by Barbara McClenaghan]
b Visit of the Norfolk and Norwich Archaeological Society: the story of Caister castle.
c In the Bure valley. Half-day excursion, Potter Heigham's antiquity. [Also includes notes on the episcopal chapel at Ludham Hall]
d History and antiquities of Lavenham and Long Melford, by R. H. Teasdel.
e North Norfolk churches. [Includes the churches of Salthouse, Cley, and Blakeney]

NORFOLK AND NORWICH NATURALISTS' SOCIETY

Founded 1869, for the practical study of natural science and the publication of papers on natural history, especially such as relate to Norfolk.

Transactions, vols. 7–13 (1899–1935):

3592 Vol. 7.

a Sir Thomas Browne [d. 1682] as a naturalist, by W. A. Nicholson.
b Wild-fowl driving in the 16th cent., by T. Southwell.
c Woad as a blue dye, with an account of its bibliography, by C. B. Plowright.
d Memoir of Robert Wigham [Norfolk naturalist, d. 1855], by W. D. Bidwell.
e Unpublished letter from Dr. Thomas Browne to Mr. William Dugdale, by T. Southwell.
f Leaves from an old diary, 1800–2 [of the Rev. Dr. Charles Sutton of the parish of Holme-next-the-Sea, Norf.], by T. Southwell.

g East Anglian geology: historical sketch—dawn of the science of geology, by H. Woodward.
h Some early [17th cent.] Dutch and English decoys, by T. Southwell.

3593 Vol. 8.

a Remains of the neolithic age in Thetford district, by W. G. Clarke.
b Letters from Hamon le Strange [d. 1660] and Robert Marsham [d. 1797] preserved at Blickling Hall, by T. Southwell.
c Notes on the Arctic whale-fishery from Yarmouth and Lynn, by T. Southwell.
d Classification of Norfolk flint implements, by W. G. Clarke.
e Notes on Blakeney harbour, past and present, by C. A. Hamond.
f Norwich castle mound, by J. T. Hotblack.
g Some old-time Norfolk botanists [18th and 19th cent.], by T. Southwell.
h Distribution of flint and bronze implements in Norfolk, by W. G. Clarke.
i Norfolk neolithic harpoon-barbs and triangular knives, by W. G. Clarke.
j Breckland characteristics [past and present], by W. G. Clarke.
k The rural economy, sport and natural history of East Ruston common, by M. C. H. Bird.

3594 Vol. 9.

a Notes on a decayed trawl-fishery [Great Yarmouth], by A. H. Patterson.
b The commons of Norfolk, by W. G. Clarke.
c Sir James Edward Smith [d. 1828] and some of his friends, by Alice M. Geldart.

3595 Vol. 10.

a Preface, 1869–1919. [An account of the history of the Society, by S. H. Long]
b The progress of ornithology, by C. B. Ticehurst.
c The production of fire, by E. Bidwell.

3596 Vol. 11.

a Henry Stevenson [d. 1888], author of *The Birds of Norfolk*, his friends and contemporaries, by J. H. Gurney.
b Norfolk topography in *The Botanist's Guide* [1805], by W. G. Clarke.
c Natural history in Norfolk place-names, by W. G. Clarke.
d Norfolk woodlands, from the evidence of contemporary chronicles, by H. R. Beevor.

3597 Vol. 12.

a The swan roll in the Norwich castle museum, by N. F. Ticehurst.
b Cley-next-the-Sea and its marshes, by B. Cozens-Hardy.
c Swan-marks of east Norfolk [and west Norfolk], by N. F. Ticehurst.
d Museum Boulterianum, by C. D. Sherborn. [Notes on a copy of the museum catalogue of Daniel Boulter, d. 1802]

3598 Vol. 13.

a The Hookers in Norfolk and Suffolk, by Alice M. Geldart. [Sir William Jackson Hooker, d. 1865, and Sir Joseph Dalton Hooker, b. 1817]
b Peddars way [Suffolk and Norfolk], by H. C. Davies.

3599 Index, 1869–1908. [Issued with Transactions, vol. 8, 1909]

NORFOLK RECORD SOCIETY

Founded 1930, to publish and make accessible any documents or records relating to Norfolk, and the city and county of Norwich, and to promote the preservation of such documents and records.

Publications, vols. 1–3:

3600 Vol. 1. Calendar of Frere mss., hundred of Holt, by B. Cozens-Hardy. Muster roll, hundred of North Greenhoe, *c.* 1523, transcribed by Marian Dale. Norwich subscriptions to the voluntary gift of 1662, transcribed, with prefatory note, by Phyllis M. Williams. 1931.

3601 Vol. 2. St. Benet of Holme, 1020–1210. The 11th and 12th cent. sections of Cott. ms. Galba E. ii, the register of the abbey of St. Benet of Holme, transcribed by J. R. West. 1932.

602 Vol. 3. St. Benet of Holme, 1020–1210. Introductory essay on the 11th and 12th cent. sections of Cott. ms. Galba E. ii, the register of the abbey of St. Benet of Holme, by J. R. West. 1932.

NORTH OF ENGLAND EXCAVATION COMMITTEE

Founded 1924, for the encouragement of excavation of sites in the North, the recording of facts obtained, and the co-ordination of excavation work in the northern counties.

1st–4th Reports, 1924–32 (4 vols. [1926–33]):

3603 1st Report.

a [Report on excavations at the Roman forts of Rudchester (Vindobala), and Great Chesters (Aesica)]

3604 2nd Report.

a Investigations of Roman wall construction, 1926–8.
b The line of the Roman wall through Newcastle [as investigated], 1928.
c Work on the Roman wall near Newcastle, 1928.

3605 3rd Report.

a [Report on work on the line of the Roman wall through and near Newcastle, 1929–30]

3606 4th Report.

a [Reports on investigations of the Roman wall between Whittle Dene and Cawhill; and excavations at Newcastle, Dunstanburgh castle and Housesteads]

NORTH STAFFORDSHIRE FIELD CLUB

Founded 1865, as the North Staffordshire Naturalists' Field Club, for the study of natural history, archaeology, and history, particularly relating to the county of Stafford. Title changed to North Staffordshire Field Club and Archaeological Society in 1877, and to above form in 1897.

Annual Report and Transactions, vols. 35–49, *contd. as* Transactions and Annual Report, vols. 50–67 (1901–33):

3607 Vol. 35.

a Notes on the folk-lore of north Staffordshire, chiefly collected at Stone, by W. W. Bladen.

3608 Vol. 36.

a The *Limes Britannicus*, by T. Barns.
b Our own county [being notes on the history of Staffs. down to the 17th cent.], by F. J. Wrottesley.
c Journal of proceedings. Excursions. [Includes accounts of Tamworth castle and church]

3609 Vol. 37.

a Staffordshire Domesday book, by A. T. Daniel.
b Holy Cross [church], Ilam, by H. G. Hopkins.
c Tatenhill church, by A. Scrivener.

3610 Vol. 38.

a Journal of proceedings. Excursions. [Includes accounts of St. Mary's, Stafford, Bradley and Penkridge churches]

3611 Vol. 39.

a Origin of the manor, village, and tribal communities, by F. J. Wrottesley.
b Chartley earthworks and castle, by A. Scrivener.
c Weston-upon-Trent church, by A. Scrivener.
d Cartulary of Dieu-la-Cres abbey, by W. Beresford.
e Journal of proceedings. Excursions. [Includes an account of Doveridge church, Derbys.]

3612 Vol. 40.

a Notes on Celtic remains found at the Upper House, Barlaston, by L. Wedgwood.
b Journal of proceedings. Excursions. [Includes accounts of Shrewsbury, Rushton, Marton and Astbury churches, Ches., and Norbury church, Staffs.]

3613 Vol. 41.

a [The history of the Club], by W. D. Spanton.
b Old church towers of Staffordshire, by J. H. Beckett. [Contd. in vols. 42–50, 53, and 55]
c Journal of proceedings. Excursions. [Includes accounts of Buildwas abbey and Wenlock priory; the Isle of Man; Arbor Low stone circle, Derbys.; and St. John's church and the cathedral, Chester]

3614 Vol. 42.

a An ancient churchyard cross at Rolleston, by C. Lynam.
b Some ancient sites in north Staffordshire, by T. Barns.
c Celtic survivals in the place-names of north Staffordshire, by T. Barns. [Further article in vol. 45]
d Journal of proceedings. Excursions. [Includes accounts of Horton and Eccleshall churches]

3615 Vol. 43.

a Suggested site of Mediomanum, by T. Barns.
b Traditional history in Staffordshire, by S. A. H. Burne.
c Journal of proceedings. Excursions. [Includes accounts of Lilleshall church, Salop, and Cleulow cross, Ches.]

3616 Vol. 44.

a Church of St. John Baptist, Mayfield, by C. Lynam.
b Some points on which the history of England touches Staffordshire, by W. Beresford.

3617 Vol. 45.

a The Stone common lands, by W. W. Bladen.
b Sandon, All Saints' church, by A. Scrivener.
c Staffordshire during the civil wars, by F. J. Wrottesley.
d Vanished hunting grounds of north Staffordshire, by S. A. H. Burne.
e Journal of proceedings. Excursions. [Includes accounts of Church Mayfield and the Rolleston family, and of Tamworth parish church]

3618 Vol. 46.

a The making of Mercia, by T. Barns.
b Roman camp at Chesterton, by S. A. H. Burne.
c Mr. Edward Arblaster's note-book, 1719, by T. Barns.
d A Staffordshire story of the 17th cent. [concerning recusants]: fact or fiction?, by J. L. Cherry.
e Prehistoric time measurement in Britain: an astronomical study of some ancient monuments, by A. M. McAldowie.

f Blurton chapel and its endowments, by S. W. Hutchinson.

g Journal of proceedings. Excursions. [Includes accounts of Audley church; a tumulus at Winkhill; the remains of Repton priory; and Oxford]

3619 Vol. 47.

a Site of the 'old' castle [Chesterton or Trentham?], by S. A. H. Burne.

b English mediaeval armour, 1300–1500, by J. H. P. O'Connor.

c Monumental brasses of Staffordshire, by C. Masefield. [Postscript in vol. 49]

d Journal of proceedings. Excursions. [Includes accounts of Tutbury church and castle, Polesworth church, Stowe church, and St. Kenelm's church in Halesowen]

3620 Vol. 48.

a Staffordshire parishes in their geographical aspect, by S. A. H. Burne.

b Architectural story of Lichfield cathedral, by H. E. Savage.

c The castle of Lichfield, by T. Barns.

d The date of Croxden [abbey], by F. A. Hibbert.

e Parish life in mediaeval Cheadle, by C. Masefield.

f Notes on the Bawd stone, near Rockhall, on the Roaches, by A. M. McAldowie.

g Journal of proceedings. Excursions. [Includes accounts of Checkley church, Uriconium, and Wroxeter church]

3621 Vol. 49.

a Longton in 1833, from the journal of Peter Orlando Hutchinson.

b Extracts from a Staffordshire [coal-]mining note book of the 18th cent., by J. T. Stobbs.

c Excavations at Castle hill, Audley, by A. Scrivener.

d The Roman station at Rocester, by T. Barns.

e Notes on Darlaston, by A. Huntbach.

f Souling, clementing, and catterning: three November customs of the western midlands, by Charlotte S. Burne.

g Excavations on the site of Wall (Letocetum), by C. Lynam.

h First list of Roman coins from Wall, by N. C. Dibben. [Contd. in vol. 50]

3622 Vol. 50.

a Annals of an old parsonage [in the Ironmarket of Newcastle], by J. W. Dunne.

b Ronton priory, by F. A. Hibbert.

c Journal of proceedings. Excursions. [Includes an account of Caverswall church]

3623 Vol. 51.

a Kidsgrove tower, by C. Lynam.

b Late Gothic in church design, by J. H. Beckett.

c Scandinavian place-names in north Staffordshire, by H. V. Thompson.

d Neolithic flints from a chipping-floor at Cannock wood, near Rugeley, by T. C. Cantrill and G. M. Cockin.

e Journal of proceedings. Excursions. [Includes an account of Abbey Hulton]

3624 Vol. 52.

a Annual address [On the manor of Tunstall], by A. Huntbach.

b Church of S. Giles, Cheadle, destroyed 1837, by J. H. Beckett.

c Croxden abbey and Musden grange, by F. A. Hibbert.

d The borough seal of Newcastle-under-Lyme, by T. Pape.

e Five Staffordshire parsons [Egerton Harding, Thomas Fernyhough, Robert Fenton, John Fernyhough, Clement

Leigh, all of St. Giles, Newcastle-under-Lyme, 1698–1853], by J. W. Dunne.

f Church dedications of Staffordshire, by F. J. Wrottesley.

3625 Vol. 53.

a The Stafford knot [on the county badge], by T. Pape.

b Shakespeare in Staffordshire, by T. Pape.

3626 Vol. 54.

a Notes on Arbor Low, by W. Hind.

b Early glass-workers at Eccleshall, by A. A. Rollason.

c Dialect of the Staffordshire moorlands, by J. Clark.

d Early Staffordshire maps, by S. A. H. Burne. [Contd. in vol. 60]

e Heraldic glass at Whitmore Hall, by T. Pape.

f John Smith's iron tablet [tombstone, 1614], by T. Pape.

3627 Vol. 55.

a St. Peter's church, Norbury, by R. V. H. Burne.

b Newcastle-under-Lyme pottery, by T. Pape.

c Some notes on Thomas Alleyne [d. 1558], by H. M. Fraser. [Additional notes in vol. 59]

3628 Vol. 56.

a A short history of parish church registers, by P. W. L. Adams.

b The coaching age in Staffordshire, by S. A. H. Burne.

3629 Vol. 57.

a The Cromptons and their monuments at Stone, by T. Pape.

b A footnote to the history of Stone, by H. M. Fraser.

c Armorial glass in north Staffordshire, by S. A. H. Burne.

d Armorial glass in the parish of Leigh, by T. Pape.

e Three old halls [Biddulph, Little Moreton, Pooley], by J. H. Beckett.

3630 Vol. 58.

a Thomas Wolfe, master potter of Stoke-upon-Trent, 1751–1818, by P. W. L. Adams.

b An old plan of Stafford [early 17th cent.], by H. L. E. Garbett.

c Armorial glass of Checkley church, by T. Pape.

d The mystery of the Leek town lands, by W. F. Challinor.

e The 'Forty-five' in Staffordshire [from papers in the possession of W. S. Parker-Jervis].

f Journal of proceedings. Excursions. [Includes accounts of Brocton and the Chetwynd family, Bellaport old hall and the Cotton family, and Leigh church]

3631 Vol. 59.

a Court rolls of the manor of Tunstall. [Contd. in vols. 60–66]

b Primitive sundials in north Staffordshire, by T. Pape.

c The Gerard coat-of-arms, by T. Pape.

3632 Vol. 60.

a The Staffordshire campaign of 1745, by S. A. H. Burne.

b The birth centenary of the author of *John Halifax, gentleman* [Dinah Mulock], by T. Pape. [Supplementary note in vol. 61]

3633 Vol. 61.

a Monumental inscriptions in Madeley church, by B. T. Houghton.

b Armorial glass at Broughton, by T. Pape.

3634 Vol. 62.

a Parochial documents, with special reference to the Whitworth mss., by S. A. H. Burne.

b Wulfhere, King of the Mercians, by H. M. Fraser.

c Armorial glass at Pillaton Hall, by T. Pape.

3635 Vol. 63.

a Notes on the history of Mercia, by H. M. Fraser.
b Roman discoveries at Hales, by T. Pape.

3636 Vol. 64.

a Quaint customs and superstitions in north Staffordshire and elsewhere, by E. Deacon.
b Saxon masonry in Sussex, by J. H. Beckett.
c The ancient corporation of Cheadle, by T. Pape.
d Excavation of a round barrow at Swinscoe, by T. Pape.

3637 Vol. 65.

a The glass industry in the Burnt Woods [Eccleshall], by T. Pape.

3638 Vol. 66.

a George Washington's ancestors and their memorials in England, by T. Pape.
b Motto *Salve magna parens*: Dr. Johnson's Lichfield forebears and Dr. Johnson's academy, by P. Laithwaite.
c Recent investigations of the hill fort and camp at Maer, by B. B. Simms.

3639 Vol. 67.

a The Horton brook [and Horton manor], by E. E. Myott.
b Recent population movements in north Staffs., by W. R. Matheson.
c Place names of the Staffordshire–Cheshire border, by W. Smith.

Other publications:

3640 Jubilee volume, 1865–1915, ed. S. A. H. Burne, J. T. Stobbs, and H. V. Thompson. 1916.

a A record of 50 years, by W. D. Spanton.
b Report on archaeology, by C. Lynam. [The work of the archaeology section, 1866–1916]

NORTHAMPTONSHIRE NATURAL HISTORY SOCIETY AND FIELD CLUB

Founded 1876, to encourage a taste for natural history, and to facilitate its study. An archaeological section was formed in 1897, and an historical and genealogical section in 1919.

Journal, vols. 11–27 (1901–34):

3641 Vol. 11.

a Northamptonshire Exploration Society, 1st annual report. [Includes accounts of the Anglo-Saxon cemetery at Holdenby, a Roman villa at Harpole, and a tumulus at Sywell]
b 'Burghley House by Stamford town', by S. S. Campion.
c Drayton House, by R. G. Scriven.
d Are there any indications of palaeolithic man in the immediate neighbourhood of Northampton?, by T. W. Freckelton.
e The past and future work of the Society, by R. G. Scriven.
f Corby pole fair, by S. S. Campion.
g Discovery of a Romano-British pottery kiln at Corby, by B. Thompson.

3642 Vol. 12.

a Progress of botany and geology during the 19th cent., by G. C. Druce.
b Excursion to Castle Yard and Marston Trussell. [Includes an account of the earthwork at Sibbertoft]
c Excursion to Rushton and Rothwell. [Includes an account of the Triangular Lodge, Rushton]
d Anglo-Saxon cemetery at Kettering, by T. J. George.

e The Hazelrig mansion, Northampton, by A. Adcock.
f Growth of local government in Northampton, by A. Adcock.
g English pottery in Northampton museum, by T. J. George.
h Church of the Holy Sepulchre, Northampton, by C. H. Poynton.
i Iron roads of Northamptonshire, by C. A. Markham. [An account of old railways]
j Duston's ancient cemetery, by T. J. George.
k Gothic architecture in Northamptonshire, by R. P. Brereton.

3643 Vol. 13.

a History of St. John's hospital [Northampton], by C. H. Poynton.
b Some bronze mirrors found in Great Britain, by T. J. George.
c Kingsthorpe church.
d Priory of St. Andrew, Northampton, by R. M. Serjeantson.
e Archaeological excursion to Fawsley, by W. Morgan.
f The date of the second tract by Martin Marprelate, commonly called the *Epitome*, by W. Pierce.
g Capital punishment in Northamptonshire, by A. Adcock.
h Abbey of St. James, Northampton, by R. M. Serjeantson.
i Rockingham Castle and forest, by W. Law.

3644 Vol. 14.

a Battle of Northampton [1460], by R. M. Serjeantson.
b Opening of a round barrow at Rushden, by T. J. George.
c The castle of Northampton, by R. M. Serjeantson.
d The king's park at Northampton, by E. F. Leach.
e Botanologia of Northamptonshire [being an account of the life and work of John Morton, d. 1726, naturalist], by G. C. Druce.

3645 Vol. 15.

a Delapré abbey, by R. M. Serjeantson.
b Anglo-Saxon cemetery at Holdenby, by E. Thurlow Leeds.
c History of the water supply of Northampton, by B. Thompson.
d The Grey friars of Northampton, by R. M. Serjeantson. [Contd. in vol. 16]

3646 Vol. 16.

a The Black friars of Northampton, by R. M. Serjeantson.
b Hospital of St. John, Northampton, by R. M. Serjeantson. [Contd. in vol. 17]

3647 Vol. 17.

a Roads of Northamptonshire, by C. A. Markham.
b The central ornaments of the Northampton market square, by B. Thompson.

3648 Vol. 18.

a Leper hospitals of Northampton, by R. M. Serjeantson.
b Ancient fortifications of Northampton, by R. W. Brown.
c The town walls [of Northampton]: where the stone came from, by B. Thompson.
d Early man in Northamptonshire, with particular reference to the late Celtic period as illustrated by Hunsbury camp, by T. J. George. [Contd. in vol. 19]

3649 Vol. 19.

a An early Northampton natural history society [1860], by B. Thompson.
b Formation of the Society, by G. C. Druce.
c The Roman occupation [chiefly of Northamptonshire], by T. J. George.

d Northamptonshire printing, printers, and booksellers, by R. W. Brown. [Contd. in vol. 20. Reproduced from *Book Auction Records*, xiv, pt. 3]

3650 Vol. 20.

a Invasions of the Saxons and Angles and the part Northamptonshire played in them, by T. J. George.
b Notes on the George Hotel, Northampton, by A. Adcock.
c Ms. sources of history of Northamptonshire, by Joan Wake.
d Compton Wynyates, by H. W. Harrison.

3651 Vol. 21.

a A chronologically-arranged history of the Washingtons, by H. W. Harrison.
b The evolution of British breeds of cattle, by W. A. Stewart.
c The Boroughs, Northampton, by A. Adcock.
d Illustrations of Northamptonshire in the Northampton public library. [Catalogue. Contd. in vols. 22 and 23]
e A forgotten chapter in the history of the boot manufacturing industry [the use of machinery by M. I. Brunel, *c.* 1810], by A. Adcock.

3652 Vol. 22.

a The murder of Becket: Fitzurse, of Bulwick, the chief assassin, by A. Adcock.
b Witchcraft in Northamptonshire, by A. Adcock.
c Northampton's *liber custumarum*, by A. Adcock.

3653 Vol. 23.

a Ancient cemeteries at Pytchley, by H. W. Harrison.
b 'Nun' mills, *alias* 'Quyn Johns', Northampton, by R. W. Brown. [With note by B. Thompson on other local mills]

3654 Vol. 24.

a Curious Northamptonshire characters, by R. W. Brown.
b 'Old mountains' [earthworks in Astwell parish], by H. W. Harrison.
c Arbury hill 'camp' a fallacy, by B. Thompson and H. W. Harrison.

3655 Vol. 25.

a Anglo-Saxon cemetery at Kettering, by C. A. Markham.
b John Clare's library, by R. W. Brown.
c Crowland abbey, by Frances M. Page.
d The land utilization of Northamptonshire, by E. E. Field.
e Crowland abbey, by H. W. Harrison.
f The parish of Abington, by E. E. Field and B. Thompson.
g Abington village, by E. E. Field.
h Old New-Abington, by R. W. Brown.

3656 Vol. 26.

a John Dryden's association with Northamptonshire, by G. E. Glazier.
b Abington church, by R. W. Brown.
c Corn mills: a study in evolution, by B. Thompson.
d Water mills and windmills, by B. Thompson.
e Bench ends of Great Brington church, by H. O. Cavalier.
f Abington manor house, by R. W. Brown.
g A history of Northampton, by H. Lee.
h The Harlestone book of tythe accounts [during the incumbency of John Clendon, 1710–56].
i Thomas Randolph, a neglected poet, 1605–34, by Mrs. R. W. Brown.
j Elizabeth Woodville, Queen of England, a figure of romance and tragedy, 1435–92, by Mrs. R. W. Brown.
k The fee farm of Northampton, by W. J. Hull.

3657 Vol. 27.

a Katherine Parr, 1513–48, the 6th and surviving wife of Henry VIII, by Mrs. R. W. Brown.

b Stained glass windows, by H. W. Harrison.
c Northamptonshire families, by H. I. Longden.
d Plumpton, 'a very insignificant parish', by L. W. Wilsden.
e History of Northampton, by Tobias Coldwell, town clerk of Northampton, 1618–52.
f The hundreds of Northamptonshire, by Helen M. Cam.
g Parish registers of Hardwick [1559–1780], by R. W. Brown.
h The story of the windmill [in Northants.], by F. C. Gill.
i Register of marriages, baptisms, and burials in the parish church of Duston, 1692–1756, by D. Gardam.

NORTHAMPTONSHIRE RECORD SOCIETY

Founded 1920, to preserve historical records relating to Northamptonshire, and to publish transcripts of documents of both local and general interest, with introductions by competent authorities.

Publications, vols. 1–6:

3658 Vol. 1. Quarter sessions records of the county of Northampton: files for 1630, 1657, 1657–8, ed. Joan Wake, introd. by S. A. Peyton. 1924.

3659 Vol. 2. Henry of Pytchley's book of fees, ed. W. T. Mellows. 1927.

3660 Vol. 3. A copy of papers relating to musters, beacons, subsidies, etc. in the county of Northampton, 1586–1623, ed. Joan Wake, introd. by J. E. Morris, genealogical note by H. I. Longden. 1926.

3661 Vol. 4. Facsimiles of early charters from Northamptonshire collections, ed. with introd. and notes by F. M. Stenton. 1930.

3662 Vol. 5. The earliest Northamptonshire assize rolls, 1202 and 1203, ed. with introd. by Doris M. Stenton. 1930.

3663 Vol. 6. Kettering vestry minutes, 1797–1853, ed. with introd. by S. A. Peyton. 1933.

NORWICH SCIENCE GOSSIP CLUB

Founded 1870, as Science Gossip and Literary Club, to promote among members a spirit of enquiry and investigation by means of papers on scientific and literary subjects, and by occasional excursions to places of interest. Title changed to Science Gossip Club in 1874 and to the above form in 1904.

Report of Proceedings, [1900]–1914 (14 vols. [1901–14]):

3664 Vol. for 1901–2.

a Notes on the Society of United Friars; or, Norwich science gossip a century ago, by E. A. Kent.
b Education and the municipality, by D. O. Holme. [Includes the history of the organization of education in England]

3665 Vol. for 1903–4.

a Good King Harry and bad Queen Bess, by W. Rye.
b Norwich cathedral, by W. P. Cooper.
c George Borrow: his life and works, by E. Peake.
d The strangers [Dutch and Walloon] in Norwich, by W. R. Rudd.

3666 Vol. for 1904–5.

a Electrical engineering: early history and recent development, by F. M. Long.

b A dilettante's diary, 1767 [Dr. Silas Neville], by L. G. Bolingbroke.

c Old English silver spoons, by J. H. Walter.

3667 Vol. for 1905–6.

a The life and works of Sir Thomas Browne, by E. Peake.

3668 Vol. for 1906–7.

a Lord Byron, by H. Crosse.

3669 Vol. for 1908–9.

a Schools and scholarship in medieval Norwich, by L. G. Bolingbroke.

b Early man in Norfolk, by H. H. Halls.

c The Norfolk and Suffolk company of comedians and the Fisher family, by J. Carver.

3670 Vol. for 1909–10.

a Norwich the 'Venta Icenorum' of the Romans, by J. T. Hotblack.

3671 Vol. for 1910–11.

a The life history of a stained glass window, by G. A. King.

3672 Vol. for 1911–12.

a Norwich guilds, by J. T. Hotblack.

b Troublous times in Norfolk in the 15th cent., by W. Rye.

c Norwich master weavers of the 18th cent. and their trade, by W. R. Rudd.

3673 Vol. for 1913–14.

a The development of the Norfolk broads, by F. D. Wheeler.

OFFA FIELD CLUB

Founded 1888.

Transactions, 1923–32 (7 vols. 1923–[33?]):

3674 Vol. for 1923.

a Excursion to St. Martin's and neighbourhood.

b Excursion to Selattyn and neighbourhood.

c Excursion to the Breiddens.

d Excursion to Uriconium.

3675 Vol. for 1924.

a 'Old Oswestry' [hill fort].

3676 Vol. for 1925.

a Third excursion: Llangynog and Pennant.

3677 Vol. for 1926.

a Second excursion: Rednal and West Felton.

b Fifth excursion: Chester.

3678 Vol. for 1927–8.

a Fifth field excursion: Watts dyke.

b Sixth field excursion: Erbistock [Denbighshire].

3679 Vol. for 1929–30.

a Third field excursion: Offa's dyke.

b Fifth field excursion: Battlefield and Haughmond.

c Sixth field excursion: the Gaer and Montgomery. [An account of Montgomery castle]

d Seventh field excursion: Much Wenlock.

e Third field excursion: Strata Marcella, Caus castle.

f Sixth field excursion: the Berth and Nesscliff hill. [Chiefly an account of the Berth earthworks]

OLD STAFFORD SOCIETY

Founded 1925, to examine buildings, books, documents, and other papers and objects of historical or general interest connected with the town and surrounding district of Stafford; and to collect, collate and record information and photographs of historical, archaeological, scientific or other interest relating to the town and neighbourhood.

Transactions, 1928–33 (6 vols. reproduced from typewriting, 1928–33):

3680 Vol. for 1928.

a Staffordshire antiquities, by F. J. Cope. [Includes a list of the religious houses of the county, giving details of foundation, founder, order, and dedication]

3681 Vol. for 1929.

a A great mediaeval landlord, by J. B. Frith. [Brief history of the Stafford family, its estates and their administration]

b St. Mary's church, by S. A. Cutlack.

c Seal of the Friars Minor or Grey friars of Stafford, by F. J. Cope.

3682 Vol. for 1930.

a Ancient Stafford: extracts from a ms. written by William Jones [d. 1895], prepared for publication by F. J. Cope.

b The records of the borough of Stafford [described, with extracts], by F. J. Cope. [Contd. in vols. for 1931, 1932, 1933]

3683 Vol. for 1931.

a Joan Eaton's cross, by F. J. Cope. [On the name of the road-fork south-west of Church Eaton]

b The Whitworth mss. in the Salt library. 1: Autobiography of Richard Whitworth [d. 1811]. 2: An account of family affairs. [The autobiography ends *c*. 1768 and contains no mention of his parliamentary career. The 'account' is composed entirely of ornithological observations, 1773–1806]

c List of the burgesses of the borough of Stafford at the election in Mar. 1765 [with notes].

3684 Vol. for 1932.

a The twelfth Baron Stafford. [Notes on his descent]

b Arrest of the Duke of Monmouth at Stafford, 1682.

c The castle of Stafford, by G. G. Irvine.

d Reminiscences of an old Stafford resident.

3685 Vol. for 1933.

a Remarks [heraldic and genealogical] on the monument of the last Earl of Stafford [John Paul Howard, d. 1762, in Westminster abbey], by F. J. Cope.

b Notes on the ancient buildings and streets of Stafford, by P. T. Dale.

OPTICAL SOCIETY

Founded 1899, to promote and advance the theory and practice of optical science. Amalgamated in 1932 with the Physical Society of London.

Transactions, vols. 1–33 ([1901–32]):

3686 Vol. 4.

a Presidential address [on the past, present, and future of optical science and industry], by C. V. Drysdale.

3687 Vol. 6.

a Early literature of optics, by S. P. Thompson.

3688 Vol. 8.

a Evolution of artificial lighting, by C. V. Drysdale.

3689 Vol. 9.

a Development of the science of physiological optics in the 19th cent., by M. H. E. Tscherning.

3690 Vol. 13.

a Evolution of eyeglasses and spectacles, by M. W. Dunscombe.
b Recent advances in optical projection work, by R. S. Wright.

3691 Vol. 15.

a The Thomas Young oration [on the life and work of Thomas Young, d. 1829], by Sir J. Crichton-Browne.

3692 Vol. 16.

a Optical or visual signalling [including an historical account of signalling], by W. Ettles.

3693 Vol. 23.

a The mechanical construction of the microscope from a historical standpoint, with special reference to certain instruments now in the Science Museum, South Kensington, by A. Pollard.

3694 Vol. 24.

a The birth of kinematography and its antecedents, by W. Day.
b Surveying and navigational instruments from the historical standpoint, by L. C. Martin.
c Early telescopes in the Science Museum from an historical standpoint, by D. Blaxandall.

3695 Vol. 25.

a Contributions to the history of the spectacle trade from the earliest times to Thomas Young's appearance [late 18th cent.], by M. von Rohr.
b The circular dividing engine of Edward Troughton, 1793, by D. Blaxandall.

3696 Vol. 26.

a Additions to our knowledge of old spectacles: a summary of papers published 1923–4, by M. von Rohr.
b A peep into Herschel's workshop, by W. H. Steavenson.
c Catalogue of instruments made and (or) used by Sir William Herschel, as preserved at Slough and examined there in 1924, by W. H. Steavenson.

3697 Vol. 28.

a Contributions to the history of English opticians in the first half of the 19th cent. (with special reference to spectacle history), by M. von Rohr.

3698 Vol. 29.

a The stereoscope, by R. S. Clay.

3699 Vol. 30.

a Development of spectacles in London from the end of the 17th cent., by T. H. Court and M. von Rohr.
b History of the development of the telescope from about 1675 to 1830 based on documents in the Court collection, by T. H. Court and M. von Rohr. [See also vol. 32 below]

3700 Vol. 31.

a Contributions to the history of the Worshipful Company of Spectaclemakers, by T. H. Court and M. von Rohr.

3701 Vol. 32.

a New knowledge of old telescopes, by T. H. Court and M. von Rohr. [See also vol. 30 above]
b Young's theory of colour vision, by Sir J. H. Parsons.

3702 Subject index of the Transactions, vols. 1–25, by A. F. C. Pollard. 1926.

3703 Subject index of the Transactions, vols. 26–27, by A. F. C. Pollard. [1926].

OXFORD BIBLIOGRAPHICAL SOCIETY

Founded 1922, for the discussion and elucidation of questions connected with books, printed or manuscript; the promotion and encouragement of studies and researches in book-lore; and the exhibition of rare or remarkable books, bindings, or illustrations.

Proceedings and Papers, vols. 1–3 (1923–33):

3704 Vol. 1.

a Index to Rawlinson's collections (*c.* 1700–50) for a new edition of Wood's *Athenae Oxonienses*, by S. and Margaret A. Gibson.
b Leonard Digges [d. *c.* 1571] and his books, by E. F. Bosanquet.
c Worcester College library, by C. H. Wilkinson.

3705 Vol. 2.

a Proof reading by English authors of the 16th and 17th cent., by P. Simpson.
b Bibliography of the works of Samuel Daniel, 1585–1623, with an appendix of Daniel's letters, by H. Sellers.
c Humphrey Moseley, publisher [d. 1661], by J. C. Reed.
d Magdalen College library, by G. R. Driver.

3706 Vol. 3.

a Philip Bliss, 1787–1857, editor and bibliographer, by S. Gibson and C. J. Hindle.

OXFORD HISTORICAL SOCIETY

Founded 1884, for the publication of literature illustrative of the history of the university and city of Oxford, and of the neighbouring county.

Publications, vols. 41–95:

3707 Vol. 41. Studies in Oxford history, chiefly in the 18th cent.: a series of papers by J. R. Green and G. Roberson, ed. C. L. Stainer. 1901.

3708 Vols. 42, 43, 48, 50, 65, 67, 72. Remarks and collections of Thomas Hearne. Vols. v–xi, 1901–21. [Vol. v: 1714–16, ed. D. W. Rannie. Vols. vi–viii: 1717–25, ed. under the superintendence of the committee. Vols. ix–xi: 1725–35, ed. H. E. Salter. Vols. i–iv: 1705–14, were published in 1884–97]

3709 Vols. 44, 62, 79. The Flemings in Oxford: being documents selected from the Rydal papers in illustration of the lives and ways of Oxford men, 1650–1700, ed. J. R. Magrath. 3 vols. 1904–24. [Vol. i: 1650–80. Vol. ii: 1680–90. Vol. iii: 1691–1700]

3710 Vol. 45. The ancient kalendar of the university of Oxford, from documents of the 14th to the 17th cent., together with *Computus manualis ad usum Oxoniensium*, from C. Kyrfoth's edition, Oxon., 1519/20, ed. C. Wordsworth. 1904.

3711 Vol. 46. Oxford silver pennies, 925–1272, described by C. L. Stainer. 1904.

3712 Vol. 47. Collectanea, 4th series. 1905.

a Description of Oxford, from the hundred rolls of Oxfordshire, 1279, ed. Rose Graham.

b Oxford church notes, 1643–4, by R. Symonds, with additions of 1656–61, ed. Rose Graham.

c Three consecrations of college chapels: Lincoln, 1631, ed. A. Clark; Brasenose, 1666, ed. F. Madan; Queen's, 1717, ed. J. R. Magrath.

d Thomas Baskerville's account of Oxford, written in 1683–6, ed. H. Baskerville.

e Bill of costs of Charles Ellis, London agent to the mayor of Oxford for the coronation of George IV, 1821, ed. F. Williams.

f Coaching in and out of Oxford, 1820–40, by William Bayzand, guard of the *Mazeppa* coach.

3713 Vol. 49, 51. Eynsham [abbey] cartulary, ed. H. E. Salter· 2 vols. 1907–8.

3714 Vols. 52, 53, 54. Brasenose College quatercentenary monographs. 2 vols. in 3. 1909. [Vol. i: Essays on the site, name, arms, and annals of the college, by F. Madan; the architectural history, by E. W. Allfrey; the benefactions, plate, estates, advowsons, and pictures, by A. J. Butler. Vol. ii, pt. 1: The history of the college, to 1803, by I. S. Leadam, R. W. Jeffery, G. H. Wakeling, and R. Lodge. Vol. ii, pt. 2: The history, contd. to 1900, by H. C. Wace, J. Buchan, A. J. Jenkinson, T. H. Ward, and F. Madan]

3715 Vol. 55. Brasenose College register, 1509–1909. 2 vols. 1909. [Generally bound together. Vol. i: List of members. Vol. ii: Additions and corrections, college lists, index]

3716 Vol. 56. The obituary book of Queen's College, Oxford, an ancient Sarum kalendar, with the obits of the founders and benefactors of the college, ed. with introd., notes, and appendixes by J. R. Magrath. Folio. 1910.

3717 Vols. 57, 81, 82. Catalogue of portraits in the possession of the university, colleges, city, and county of Oxford, comp. Mrs. R. L. Poole. 3 vols. 1912–26.

3718 Vols. 58–61.Enactments in parliament specially concerning the universities of Oxford and Cambridge, the colleges and halls therein, and the colleges of Winchester, Eton and Westminster, ed. L. L. Shadwell. 4 vols. 1912. [Vol. i: 37 Edw. III–13 Anne. Vol. ii: 1 Geo. I–11 Geo. IV. Vol. iii: 11 Geo. IV–31 & 32 Vict. Vol. iv: 32 & 33 Vict.–1 & 2 Geo. V]

3719 Vol. 63. A subsidy collected in the diocese of Lincoln in 1526, ed. H. Salter. 1909.

3720 Vol. 64. The Oxford deeds of Balliol College, ed. H. E. Salter. 1913.

3721 Vols. 66, 68, 69. A cartulary of the hospital of St. John the Baptist [Oxford], ed. H. E. Salter. 3 vols. 1914–17.

3722 Vols. 70, 73. Mediaeval archives of the university of Oxford, ed. H. E. Salter. 2 vols. 1920–21.

3723 Vol. 71. Munimenta civitatis Oxonie, ed. H. E. Salter. 1920.

3724 Vol. 74. Chapters of the Augustinian canons, ed. H. E· Salter. 1922.

3725 Vol. 75. Surveys and tokens, ed. H. E. Salter. 1923.

a Survey of Oxford in 1772, with maps and plans, ed. H. Salter. 1912.

b Sport and pastime in Stuart Oxford, by P. Manning.

c Subsidies and taxes [1543–1667, including a hearth tax, 1665, and poll tax, 1667], by H. E. Salter.

d Oxford tradesmen's tokens, by E. Thurlow Leeds.

3726 Vol. 76. Registrum annalium collegii Mertonensis, 1483–1521, ed. H. E. Salter. 1923.

3727 Vols. 77, 78. Early science in Oxford, by R. T. Gunther. 2 vols. 1923. [Vol. i: Chemistry, mathematics, physics and surveying. Vol. ii: Astronomy. Subsequent vols. not issued to the Soc.]

3728 Vol. 80. Snappe's formulary and other records, ed. H. E. Salter. 1924. [John Snappe, doctor of decrees, fl. 1397–1404]

3729 Vol. 83. Oxford city properties, by H. E. Salter. 1926.

3730 Vol. 84. The dean's register of Oriel, 1446–1661, ed. G. C. Richards and H. E. Salter. 1926.

3731 Vol. 85. Oriel College records, by C. L. Shadwell and H. E. Salter. 1926.

3732 Vol. 86. Merton muniments, selected and ed. P. S. Allen and H. W. Garrod. Folio. 1928.

3733 Vol. 87. Oxford council acts, 1583–1626, by H. E. Salter. 1928. [For 1626–65 see **3738** below. Further vols. in progress]

3734 Vol. 88. The Boarstall cartulary [1444, drawn up for Edmund Rede, jun., of Boarstall House], by H. E. Salter, with the assistance of A. H. Cooke. 1930.

3735 Vols. 89–91. Cartulary of Oseney abbey, by H. E. Salter. Vols. i–iii, 1929–31. [Vols. iv–vi were published 1934–6]

3736 Vol. 92. Cartulary of the mediaeval archives of Christ Church, by N. Denholm-Young. 1931.

3737 Vols. 93, 94. Registrum cancellarii Oxoniensis, 1434–67, by H. E. Salter. 2 vols. 1932.

3738 Vol. 95. Oxford council acts, 1626–65, by M. G. Hobson and H. E. Salter. 1933.

Other publications:

3739 Catalogue of a loan collection of portraits of English historical personages who died prior to 1625, exhibited under the auspices of the Oxford Historical Society. 1904.

3740 Illustrated catalogue [of the above]. 1904.

3741 Objects and work of the Oxford Historical Society. *P.* 1911.

OXFORD SOCIETY
OF HISTORICAL THEOLOGY

Founded 1891, as the Society of Historical Theology in succession to the Taylerian Society, of London, for the furtherance of theological study, particularly by the use of the historical method. The word 'Oxford' was added in 1920.

Abstract of Proceedings (27 vols. [1901?–33?]):

3742 Vol. for 1900–1.

a Wycliffe's doctrine of dominion, by H. Rashdall.

3743 Vol. for 1911–12.

a The early Bampton lectures, 1780–1831, by T. C. Snow.

3744 Vol. for 1915–16.

a Archbishop Bancroft and the Elizabethan church, by A. Fawkes.

OXFORD UNIVERSITY ANTIQUARIAN SOCIETY

Founded 1893, as the Oxford University Brass-Rubbing Society, for the study of monumental brasses and kindred subjects. Title changed to above form in 1900.

Publications:

3745 Oxford Journal of Monumental Brasses, vol. 2 (1900–12).

a Monumental brasses, past and present, in Eton College chapel, by T. E. Harwood.
b The value of despoiled slabs, by H. W. Macklin.
c Notes on some early matrices in the eastern counties, by E. M. Beloe.
d Monumental brasses at Corpus Christi College, Oxford, by G. O. Smith.
e Notes. [Including: Brass of Sir John Drayton, Dorchester, Oxon., d. 1417]
f Monumental brasses in St. Michael's church and Exeter College chapel, Oxford, by A. A. Hunt.
g Some military garments other than plate armour, by Viscount Dillon.
h Brasses of ecclesiastics in the 14th cent., by R. A. Raven.
i Brasses at North Moreton, Berks., by J. E. Field.
j Monumental brasses of the chapel of St. George in Windsor Castle, by H. G. de Watteville.
k Palimpsest brasses from Quarrendon, Bucks., and Stanton St. John, Oxon., by P. Manning.
l The Huchenson brass at St. John's College, Oxford, by V. Hope. [Henry Huchenson, fellow of St. John's, d. 1573, and brothers]

3746 Oxford Portfolio of Monumental Brasses, pt. 4 (1901).

a William de Herleston, rector, 1353. Sparsholt, Berks.
b A civilian, *c.* 1400. St. Michael's, St. Albans.
c Lady Philippa Byschoppesdon, 1414. Broughton, Oxon.
d John Bloxham, B.D., 1387, and John Whytton, *c.* 1420. Merton College, Oxford.
e Robert Ingylton, esq., and wives Margaret, Clemens, and Isabella, 1472. Thornton, Bucks.

3747 Oxford Portfolio of Monumental Brasses, pt. 5 (1901).

a Incised slab to John —, priest, *c.* 1330. Westwell, Kent.
b Reginald de Malyns and two wives, *c.* 1380. Chinnor, Oxon.
c Roger Gery, LL.B., rector, 148—, engraved *c.* 1456. Whitchurch, Oxon.
d William Disney, esq., and Margaret Joiner his wife, *c.* 1556, and Richard Disney, and wives Nele and Janne, *c.* 1580, on reverse of Flemish inscription, 1518. Norton Disney, Lincs.
e Mary, wife of Richard Fiennes, esq., 1666.

OXFORD UNIVERSITY JUNIOR SCIENTIFIC CLUB

Founded 1882, for the discussion of scientific subjects.

Transactions, new ser., nos. 10–35 (1902–12):

3748 Nos. 22–24.
a William Harvey, by A. S. MacNalty.

3749 Nos. 31–32.
a Wollaston [W.H., d. 1828], his life and work, by W. H. Barrett.

Transactions, 3rd ser., nos. 1–10 (1919–23):

3750 No. 8.
a The British dye industry, 1914–21, by F. A. Mason.

Transactions, 4th ser., nos. 1–10 (1923–7):

3751 No. 5.
a Cave hunting in the Mendips [with an account of some of the remains discovered], by E. K. Tratman.

3752 No. 7.
a The Tradescants [John, the elder, d. 1638, and John, the younger, d. 1662] and their collection, by R. T. Gunther.

3753 No. 8.
a The blocking of Zeebrugge [1918], by A. F. B. Carpenter.

Robert Boyle lectures:

3754 9th Lecture. The rise of the experimental method in Oxford, by C. Allbutt. 1902.

OXFORDSHIRE ARCHAEOLOGICAL SOCIETY

Founded 1852, as the Archaeological Society of North Oxfordshire, for the study and preservation of the antiquities, ecclesiastical, civil, and military, of Oxfordshire and portions of the adjoining counties. Title changed to Archaeological and Natural History Society of North Oxfordshire in Report for 1856–7, though North Oxfordshire Archaeological Society was frequently used thereafter. The above form was adopted in 1887.

Publications, nos. 41–78 (1901–33):

3755 No. 41. Reports, 1900.
a Annual excursion, 1900. [Includes notes on visits to Beckley, Studley priory, Charlton-on-Otmoor, Islip, and Wood-Eaton]
b 'Rood screen' in the parish church of St. Mary the Virgin, Charlton-on-Otmoor, by C. E. Prior.
c Juxon's rectory at Somerton, by G. E. Barnes. [William Juxon, afterwards archbishop of Canterbury]
d Murderous affray near Stonor in 1535, by M. T. Pearman.

3756 No. 42. Transactions. Notices manorial and ecclesiastical of the parish of Nuffield, by M. T. Pearman. 1901.

3757 No. 43. Transactions. History of the parish of Black Bourton, otherwise Burton Abbots, by Mary G. Lupton. 1903.

3758 No. 44. Reports, 1902.
a Annual excursion, 1901. [Includes notes on visits to Broughton castle, Wroxton abbey, and Shotteswell church]
b Reminiscences of John Dunkin [d. 1846], by E. R. Massey.
c Culham sanctuary, by M. T. Pearman.

3759 No. 45. Reports, 1902.
a Church of S. James, A. and M., Somerton.
b Juxon coat of arms at Somerton rectory, by G. E. Barnes.
c A Watlington court roll of the 15th cent., by M. T. Pearman.
d Juxon's arms (glass), by E. Green and T. Garner.
e An account of the parish registers of Merton and of the recovery of a missing portion, by E. R. Massey.
f Oxfordshire preparations for the Prince of Orange [1688], by A. Ballard.

3760 No. 46. Reports, 1903.
a Fritwell: restoration of the parish church in 1864, by G. E. Barnes.

b Dedications of old churches, with some notes as to village feasts and old customs in the deaneries of Islip and Bicester, by C. E. Prior. [Contd. for the deaneries of Woodstock, Deddington, and Witney in no. 47, 1904; for the deaneries of Chipping Norton, Cuddesdon, and Oxford in no. 49, 1905; and for the deaneries of Aston and Henley in no. 52, 1906]

3761 No. 47. Reports, 1904.
a Annual excursion, 1904. [Includes notes on visits to Minster Lovel, Asthall, Swinbrook, Widford, and Burford, by G. E. Barnes]
b Altar tomb, S. aisle, Minster Lovel, by C. Price.
c Acrostic brass inscription on the floor of St. Kenelm's, Minster Lovel, by C. Price.

3762 No. 48. Transactions. Notes on Swincomb, by M. T. Pearman. 1906.

3763 No. 49. Reports, 1905.
a Notes on the Globe room at the Reindeer inn, Banbury, by W. Potts.

3764 No. 50. Transactions. Seven Somerton court rolls [1482–1573], by A. Ballard. 1906.

3765 No. 51. Transactions. Charlton-on-Otmoor open fields, by C. E. Prior. 1907.

3766 No. 52. Reports, 1906.
a John Milton, and Foresthill, by E. Greaves.
b The assize of bread in Oxfordshire in the 19th cent., by A. Ballard.

3767 No. 53. Reports, 1907.
a Notes on Wigginton church, by A. D. Mozley.
b Notes on South Newington church and frescoes, by C. J. Whitehead.
c The open fields of Fritwell, by A. Ballard.
d The vicar's school at Bicester in the 17th cent., by E. R. Massey.

3768 No. 54. Reports, 1908.
a Annual excursion, 1908. [Includes notes on a visit to the church and Roman villa at Northleigh]
b Watlington town hall, by H. Salter.
c Notes on the open fields of Oxfordshire, by A. Ballard.

3769 No. 55. Reports, 1909.
a A charter of Dorchester abbey [1163], by H. E. Salter.
b The Black Death at Witney, by A. Ballard.
c Descent of the family of Barentyne in Oxfordshire, [1233] to 1485, by W. D. Macray.
d Notes of Oxfordshire wills at Lincoln, communicated to W. D. Macray by J. Mearns.

3770 No. 56. Reports, 1910.
a Notes on an Oxfordshire benefice [Charlton-on-Otmoor], by C. E. Prior.
b Three surveys of Bladon [Domesday, 1279, 1606], by A. Ballard.
c Oxfordshire surveys of 1387, by H. Salter.

3771 No. 57. Reports, 1911.
a Romano-British site at Astrop, King's Sutton, by C. Overy.
b Words and sayings from a mid-Oxon. parish [Charlton-on-Otmoor], by C. E. Prior.
c Tackley in the 16th and 17th cent., by A. Ballard.

3772 No. 58. Reports, 1912.
a Annual excursion, 1912. [Includes an account of the battle of Edgehill, 1642, by W. Potts]

b The clergy of the Woodstock deanery and the settlement of 1559, by S. S. Pearce. [Contd. for the deaneries of Witney and Bicester in no. 60, Chipping Norton and Deddington and peculiars of Banbury and Cropredy in no. 62, Henley and Aston and peculiar of Dorchester in no. 64; Oxford and peculiar of Newington with Britewell in no. 65; Cuddesdon and peculiars of Langford, Thame, and Great Milton in no. 66]
c Old method of annual division of common land at Bloxham, by W. D. Macray.
d Neolithic pottery from Buston farm, Astrop, by E. Thurlow Leeds.

3773 No. 59. Reports, 1913.
a South Newington vicarage.
b The management of open fields, by A. Ballard.
c A certificate of the Oxford clergy, 1593, by S. S. Pearce.

3774 No. 61. Reports, 1915.
a Index to the Transactions and Reports, 1853–1915.

3775 No. 63. Reports, 1917.
a Woodeaton [manor], by Miss Taylor.

3776 No. 67. Reports, 1921–2.
a A popular lecture on the history of Watlington, by H. E. Salter.

3777 No. 68. Reports, 1923.
a Three 16th cent. clerical wills, by S. S. Pearce. [Robert Kinge, bishop of Oxford; Hugh Coren, archbishop of Dublin; Walter Wright, archdeacon of Oxford].

3778 No. 69. Reports, 1924.
a Recusants in Oxfordshire, 1603–33, by H. E. Salter.

3779 No. 70. Reports, 1925.
a Churchwardens' presentments, 1520, by H. E. Salter. [Deaneries of Aston, Bicester, Deddington, Woodstock, Witney, Chipping Norton, and Cuddesdon]

3780 No. 71. Reports, 1926.
a The Rollright stones: some facts and some problems, by T. H. Ravenhill.

3781 No. 72. Reports, 1927.
a Parish church of Woodstock and an episode of the civil war, by S. S. Pearce.

3782 No. 73. Reports, 1928.
a The manor of Headington, by Evangeline Evans.

3783 No. 74. Reports, 1929.
a A Romano-British settlement near Bloxham, by W. F. J. Knight.
b Selections from notes on the heraldry in Oxfordshire churches, by Mrs. Hautenville Cope.

3784 No. 75. Reports, 1930.
a Marston church, by G. N. Clark.
b A visitation of Oxfordshire in 1540, by H. Salter.
c The barony of Coggs, by G. A. Moriarty.
d Coggs priory, by H. Salter.
e The dispossessed religious of Oxfordshire, by G. Baskerville.

3785 No. 76. Reports, 1931.
a Architectural notes on the 1931 excursion. [Includes accounts of Byfield church, Fawsley House and church, and Canons' Ashby church and House, all in Northants., and Deddington church and 'castle'], by F. E. Howard.
b Old ruined church at Bixbrand, by H. T. Morley.
c St. Mary's college in Oxford for Austin canons, by Evangeline Evans.

3786 No. 77. Reports, 1932.

    a Architectural notes on the 1932 excursion. [Includes accounts of Claydon House, Middle Claydon church, and Hillesden church], by F. E. Howard.

3787 No. 78. Transactions. Churchwardens' accounts of St. Michael's church, Oxford, by H. E. Salter. 1933.

OXFORDSHIRE RECORD SOCIETY

Founded 1919, for the publication of documents relating to the history of Oxfordshire.

Oxfordshire Record Series, vols. 1–15:

3788 Vol. 1. Chantry certificates, ed. and transcribed by Rose Graham, and Edwardian inventories of church goods, ed. Rose Graham from transcripts by T. Craib [all relating to Oxfordshire]. 1919.

3789 Vols. 2, 4, 11. Parochial collections made by Anthony à Wood and Richard Rawlinson. Transcribed by F. N. Davis. 1 vol. in 3. 1920–29.

3790 Vol. 3. Newington Longeville charters, transcribed and ed. with introd. by H. E. Salter. 1921.

3791 Vol. 5. Glympton: the history of an Oxfordshire manor, by H. Barnett. 1923.

3792 Vol. 6. Churchwardens' accounts of Marston, Spelsbury, Pyrton, ed. F. W. Weaver and G. N. Clark. 1925. [Supplement: 'Open fields and inclosure at Marston', by G. N. Clark]

3793 Vol. 7. The early history of Mapledurham, by A. H. Cooke. 1925.

3794 Vol. 8. Adderbury 'rectoria'. The manor at Adderbury belonging to New College, Oxford; the building of the chancel, 1408–18; account rolls, deeds and court rolls, transcribed and ed. with introd. by T. F. Hobson. 1926.

3795 Vol. 9. The manors and advowson of Great Rollright, by R. Jeffery. 1927.

3796 Vol. 10. Churchwardens' presentments in the Oxfordshire peculiars of Dorchester, Thame, and Banbury, ed. S. A. Peyton. 1928.

3797 Vol. 12. Feet of fines for Oxfordshire, 1195–1291, transcribed and calendared by H. E. Salter. 1930.

3798 Vols. 13, 14. A collection of charters relating to Goring, Streatley, and the neighbourhood, 1181–1546, in the Bodleian Library, with a supplement, ed. T. R. Gambier-Parry. 1 vol. in 2. 1931–2.

3799 Vol. 15. Saxon Oxfordshire: charters and ancient highways, ed. G. B. Grundy. 1933.

PARISH REGISTER SOCIETY

Founded 1896, to print the parish registers of England and Wales. Dissolved 1934, its assets being transferred to the Society of Genealogists.

Publications, nos. 35–84:

3800 No. 35. Registers of Stapleton, Salop, 1546–1812, transcribed by Miss E. C. Hope-Edwardes, ed. H. Stokes. 1901.

3801 No. 36. Registers of Huggate, Yorks., 1539–1812, transcribed by Edith Hobday. 1901.

3802 No. 37. Registers of Morden, Surr., 1634–1812, transcribed and ed. F. Clayton. 1901.

3803 No. 38. Registers of Clunbury, Salop, 1574–1812, transcribed by W. G. Clark-Maxwell. 1901.

3804 No. 39. Registers of Moreton Corbet, Salop, 1580–1812, transcribed by T. R. Horton, ed. W. G. D. Fletcher. 1901.

3805 No. 40. Registers of Hopton Castle, Salop, 1538–1812, transcribed by E. D. Elton, ed. W. G. D. Fletcher. 1901.

3806 No. 41. Registers of Hughley, Salop, 1576–1812, transcribed by E. Collett, ed. W. G. D. Fletcher. 1901.

3807 No. 42. Registers of Merstham, Surr., 1538–1812, transcribed by R. I. Woodhouse, assisted by A. J. Pearman and T. Fisher. 1902.

3808 No. 43. Registers of Headon, Notts., 1566–1812, transcribed by Edith Hobday. 1902.

3809 No. 44. Registers of Tarrant Hinton, Dors., 1545–1812, transcribed by A. S. Newman. 1902.

3810 No. 45. Registers of Canon Frome, Herefs., 1680–1812, transcribed by M. Hopton. *P.* 1903.

3811 No. 46. Registers of Munsley, Herefs., 1662–1812, transcribed by M. Hopton. 1903.

3812 No. 47. Registers of Moulton, Northants., transcribed and ed. S. J. Madge. Vol. i: baptisms, 1565–1812, with calendar of Moulton parish documents. 1903.

3813 No. 48. Registers of Coleby, Lincs., 1561–1812, transcribed by Mrs. Tempest and W. F. Curtoys. 1903.

3814 No. 49. Registers of Boughton-under-Blean, Kent: baptisms, 1558–1624; marriages, 1558–1626; burials, 1558–1625, transcribed by J. A. Boodle. 1903.

3815 No. 50. An appendix to a list of parish registers: being a continuation of the list issued in 1900 by G. W. Marshall. *P.* 1904. [See also no. 3826 below]

3816 No. 51. Registers of Weddington, Warwicks., 1663–1812, transcribed by E. A. Fry. *P.* 1904.

3817 No. 52. Registers of Glasbury, Brec., 1660–1836, transcribed by T. Wood. 1904.

3818 No. 53. Register of Solihull, Warwicks., vol. i: 1538–1668, transcribed by R. Savage, P. E. Martineau, and E. A. Fry, and ed. E. A. Fry. 1904.

3819 No. 54. Registers of Chester cathedral, 1687–1812, transcribed by T. Hughes, revised by T. C. Hughes. 1904.

3820 No. 55. Registers of Stratford-on-Avon, Warwicks.: burials, 1588—1622–3, transcribed by R. Savage. 1905. [For baptisms and marriages see vols. published 1897–8]

3821 No. 56. Registers of Farnham, Yorks., 1569–1812, transcribed by F. Collins. 1905.

3822 No. 57. Registers of Haslemere, Surr.: baptisms, 1594–1812; marriages and burials, 1573–1812, transcribed and ed. J. W. Penfold. 1906.

3823 No. 58. Register of Selattyn, Salop [1557–1812], transcribed by the Hon. Mrs. Bulkeley-Owen. 1906.

3824 No. 59. Registers of Almer, Dors., 1538–1812, transcribed by E. A. Fry. 1907.

3825 Nos. 60, 68. Registers of Bruton, Som., 1554–1812, ed. D. L. Hayward. 2 vols. [1907]–11.

3826 No. 61. An appendix to a list of parish registers compiled in 1900 by G. W. Marshall, revised to the end of 1907 by R. M. Glencross, and superseding the appendix issued in 1904 [no. 3815 above]. *P.* 1908.

3827 No. 62. Register of Saint Martin's chapel in Fenny Stratford, co. Buckingham, 1730–1812, transcribed and ed. W. Bradbrook. [1908].

3828 No. 63. Register of Hanham and Oldland, Glos., 1584–1681, transcribed by P. Carlyon-Britton, ed. E. A. Fry. [1908].

3829 No. 64. Register of St. Mary, Leicester, 1600–1738, transcribed by H. Hartopp. 1909.

3830 No. 65. Registers of Mickleover, 1607–1812, and of Littleover, 1680–1812, Derbys., transcribed by Ll. Ll. Simpson. 1909.

3831 No. 66. Registers of Halesowen, Worcs., 1559–1643, transcribed by Edith Hobday. 1910.

3832 No. 67. Register of Bruera church, formerly in the parish of St. Oswald, Ches., 1662–1812, ed. W. F. Irvine. 1910.

3833 No. 69. Registers of Swanage, Dors., 1563–1812, transcribed by Ll. Ll. Simpson. 1912.

3834 No. 70. Registers of Blewbury, Berks., 1588–1813, transcribed by J. F. Fry. 1913.

3835 No. 71. Registers of Durston, Som., 1712–1812, ed. R. G. Bartlett. 1914.

3836 No. 72. Registers of St. Michael Church, Som., 1695–1812, ed. R. G. Bartlett. 1914.

3837 No. 73. Registers of Denchworth, Berks., 1540–1812, ed. E. R. Nevill. 1914.

3838 No. 74. Registers of Sutton, Surr., 1636–1837, ed. W. B. Bannerman. [1915?].

3839 No. 75. Registers of Coulsdon, Surr. [1653–1812], ed. W. B. Bannerman. 1916.

3840 No. 76. Registers of Beddington, Surr. [1538–1673], ed. W. B. Bannerman. [1917].

3841 No. 77. Registers of Stoke D'Abernon, Surr. [1619–1812], ed. W. B. Bannerman. [1917].

3842 No. 78. Registers of Lullingstone, Kent [1578–1812], ed. W. B. Bannerman. [1918].

3843 No. 79. Registers of Horton Kirbie, Kent [baptisms, marriages, 1684–1812; burials, 1678–1810], ed. W. B. Bannerman. [1918].

3844 No. 80. Registers of Little Woolstone, Bucks. [baptisms, burials, 1596–1813; marriages, 1596–1810], transcribed by W. Bradbrook, ed. W. B. Bannerman. [1919].

3845 No. 81. Registers of Great Woolstone, Bucks. [baptisms, 1538–1811; marriages, 1538–1750, 1789; burials, 1538–1810], transcribed by W. Bradbrook, ed. W. B. Bannerman. [1919].

3846 No. 82. Registers of Hollesley, Suff. [baptisms and marriages, 1623–1812; burials, 1637–1812], ed. W. B. Bannerman. [1920].

3847 Nos. 83, 84. Registers of Newton Longville, Bucks. [1560–1840], transcribed and arranged by W. Bradbrook, ed. W. B. Bannerman. 2 vols. [1921–2].

PETERBOROUGH NATURAL HISTORY, SCIENTIFIC AND ARCHAEOLOGICAL SOCIETY

Founded 1871, to cultivate a taste for the study of natural history and kindred subjects.

30th–60th Annual Reports, 1901–31[1] (1901–32):

3848 32nd Report.
a The Becket chapel at Peterborough, by W. Fickling.
b Local and district inn signs and their strange origins, by D. Glenn.

3849 33rd Report.
a Thorpe Achurch-cum-Lilford, by C. E. Weston.

3850 34th Report.
a Plan of the barracks at Norman Cross. [Building erected 1796–7 for French prisoners-of-war; demolished 1816. Also published separately]
b Notes on Eye, Northants., by S. Egar.
c 'A steeple hunt': a trip to Peterborough district a hundred years ago, ed. C. Dack. [Includes descriptions of the chapel of Guyhirn, Thorney Heathens, Crowland bridge and church, Peterborough cathedral and Burghley House, 1807]

3851 35th Report.
a 'A steeple hunt' [its authorship], by W. Fickling.
b Sketch of the life of Thomas Worlidge [d. 1766], etcher and painter, with a catalogue of his works, by C. Dack.

3852 36th Report.
a Coins, medals, and local tradesmen's tokens of the 17th, 18th and 19th cent. in the Peterborough museum, [a catalogue comp.] J. A. M. Vipan, [together with] a short history of the issue of tradesmen's tokens, by C. Dack. [Also published separately, 1911]

3853 37th Report.
a Markets, guilds and fairs of Peterborough, by W. T. Mellows. [Also published separately, 1909]

3854 38th Report.
a The notable doings as star chamber victim, lawyer, statesman, lord chief justice, ambassador, and political exile, of Oliver St. John [d. 1673], the builder of Thorpe Hall, by C. H. Poynton. [Also published separately, 1910]

3855 39th Report.
a Thornhaugh, by J. R. H. Duke. [Also published separately, 1911?]
b Weather and folk lore of Peterborough and district, by C. Dack. [Also published separately, 1911]

3856 40th Report.
a Good Friday and Easter local customs, by C. Dack. [Also published separately, 1911]
b Thomas White, D.D., bishop of Peterborough, 1685–90, by C. Dack. [Also published separately, 1911]

3857 41st–43rd Reports.
a History of Roman Chesterton as interpreted by discoveries made on the site, by G. W. Abbott. [Also published separately, 1914?]

3858 45th–47th Reports.
a Shields of arms on Peterborough guildhall, and their history, by W. H. Lord. [Also published separately, 1919?]

[1] Reports for 1901 (30th) and 1902 (31st) have not been seen.

b The story of the crossed keys and the crossed swords [from the Peterborough coat-of-arms], by W. H. Lord.
c The Montagues and Peterborough, by W. H. Lord.
d The Ormes [and Peterborough], by W. H. Lord.

3859 48th Report.
a Heraldic antelope, St. John's church, by W. H. H. Lord.
b An old local Norman knight of the Peterborough district [Gervase de Barnack, 12th cent.], by W. H. H. Lord.

3860 49th Report.
a Further discoveries in Anglo-Saxon cemeteries at Woodston, Hunts., and details of a bronze age burial, by G. W. Abbott.

3861 50th Report.
a Buckden Palace and its owners, by R. H. Edleston.

3862 51st Report.
a Overton Waterville, by W. T. Mellows.
b St. Tibba [fl. 696], by W. O. F. Hughes. [Also published separately, 1924?]

3863 52nd–53rd Reports.
a Monumental brasses, by R. H. Edleston. [Contd. in the 54th, 57th–58th and 59th–60th Reports]
b The granges of the abbey of Peterborough, by W. T. Mellows. [Also published separately, 1925?]

3864 54th Report.
a Silver plate in the monastery of Peterborough, by W. T. Mellows.
b Hinchingbrooke and its owners, by the Earl of Sandwich.
c The knights of Peterborough barony, by W. T. Mellows.
d A description of the escutcheons [of the knights of Peterborough], by W. H. Lord.

3865 55th Report.
a Holywell-cum-Needingworth, by J. A. Ross.
b English history as illustrated by the royal arms, by D. J. Proby.

3866 56th Report.
a The abbots of Peterborough, by W. T. Mellows. [Also published separately, 1929?]

3867 57th–58th Reports.
a Water highways of antiquity: river problems 40,000 years ago [the Ouse and the Nene], by J. R. Garrood.
b Commemoration of Mary, Queen of Scots: engravings and pictures in Peterborough museum.
c 18th cent. Peterborough playbills. [Facsimiles]
d Notes on the manorial history of Chesterton, Cambs.
e Buckden Palace.

3868 59th–60th Reports.
a The university of Stamford, by E. G. de S. Wood.

Extra publication:

3869 Notes on old Peterborough [in the 19th cent.], by A. Percival. *P.* 1905.

PHILOLOGICAL SOCIETY

Founded 1842, to promote the study and knowledge of the structure, the affinities, and the history of languages; and to do anything that may advance these ends.

Transactions, 1899–1932 (8 vols. 1902–33):

3870 Vol. for 1907–10.
a The survival of Anglo-Saxon names as modern surnames, by W. W. Skeat.

b An Old English version of Leofric, Earl of Mercia [d. 1057], by A. S. Napier.
c The evolution of the Canterbury tales, by W. W. Skeat.

3871 Vol. for 1917–20.
a Leicestershire place-names, by A. C. Wood.

3872 Vol. for 1925–30.
a Some ancient building terms, by Beatrice S. Snell. [Reprinted in the *Journal* of the Royal Institute of British Architects, vols. 34 and 36]
b The Severn and other Wye rivers [origin of names], by E. D. P. Evans.
c The meaning of 'minster' in place-names, by E. D. P. Evans.

Publications, including:

3873 No. 1. A grammar of the dialect of Lorton, Cumb., historical and descriptive, with an appendix on the Scandinavian element, dialect specimens and a glossary, by B. Brilioth. [1913].

PIPE ROLL SOCIETY

Founded 1883, to print pipe rolls and other documents, originally prior to 1200, later to the end of John's reign.

Publications, vols. 25–38:

3874 Vols. 25–34, 36–38. The great rolls of the pipe for the 22nd–34th year of the reign of Henry II, 1175–6—1187–8. 13 vols. 1904–25.

3875 Vol. 35. Rotuli de dominabus et pueris et puellis de xii comitatibus (1185). With introd. and notes by J. H. Round. 1913.

Publications, new ser., vols. 1–11 (also numbered 39–49 in continuation of the above):

3876 Vols. 1–3, 5–6, 8–9. The great rolls of the pipe for the 2nd–7th and the 9th–10th year of the reign of Richard I, Michaelmas 1190–5 and 1197–8, ed. Doris M. Stenton. 7 vols. 1925–32.

3877 Vol. 4. The great roll of the pipe for the 14th year of the reign of Henry III, Michaelmas 1230, ed. C. Robinson. 1927.

3878 Vol. 7. The chancellor's roll for the 8th year of the reign of Richard I, Michaelmas 1196, ed. Doris M. Stenton. 1930.

3879 Vol. 10. The great roll of the pipe for the 1st year of the reign of John, Michaelmas 1199, ed. Doris M. Stenton. 1933.

3880 Vol. 11. The memoranda roll of the king's remembrancer for Michaelmas 1230–Trinity 1231, ed. C. Robinson. 1933.

PLAINSONG AND MEDIAEVAL MUSIC SOCIETY

Founded 1888, to publish facsimiles of important mss., translations of foreign works on the subject, adaptations of plainsong to English words, and such other works as may be desirable.

Publications:

3881 St. Gregory and the Gregorian music, by E. G. P. Wyatt. 1904.

3882 Introduction to the Gregorian melodies: a handbook of plainsong, by P. Wagner. 2nd edn., completely revised and enlarged. Pt. 1: Origin and development of the forms of the liturgical chant up to the end of the middle ages, translated by Agnes Orme and E. G. P. Wyatt. [1907?].

3883 Early English harmony from the 10th to the 15th cent., illustrated by facsimiles of mss., with a translation into modern musical notation. Vol. ii: Transcriptions and notes, ed. H. V. Hughes. 1913. [Vol. i: Facsimiles, ed. H. E. Wooldridge, was published in 1897]

3884 Antiphonale Sarisburiense: a facsimile of a ms. of the 13th cent., with a dissertation and analytical index by W. H. Frere. 24 pts. 1901-24. [The dissertation and analytical index were reissued separately, 1927]

3885 Pars antiphonarii: a facsimile of a ms. of the 11th cent. in the chapter library at Durham, ed. W. H. Frere. 1923.[1]

3886 Missa 'O quam suavis' for five voices, by an anonymous English composer, c. 1500 (Cambridge University library ms. Nn vi. 46), transcribed and ed., with introd. and explanatory notes, by H. B. Collins. 1927.

3887 Catalogue of the Society's library. 1928.

3888 Worcester mediaeval harmony of the 13th and 14th cent., transcribed, with introd., facsimiles, and notes, by A. Hughes, with a preface by I. Atkins. 1928.

3889 The use of plainsong [including a short account of its history], by E. T. Cook. 1928.

3890 Bibliotheca musico-liturgica: a descriptive handlist of the musical and Latin-liturgical mss. of the middle ages, preserved in the libraries of Great Britain and Ireland, by W. H. Frere. Vol. i, pt. 2, 1901; vol. ii, 1930-32. [Vol. i, pt. 1 was published in 1894]

3891 The Old Hall manuscript [being works by composers of the reign of Henry VI, 1422-61, for St. George's chapel, Windsor], transcribed and ed. A. Ramsbotham. Vol. i: Introduction, Gloria in Excelsis, Motets. 1933.

PLYMOUTH INSTITUTION AND DEVON AND CORNWALL NATURAL HISTORY SOCIETY

Founded 1812, as the Plymouth Institution. Amalgamated in 1851 with the Devon and Cornwall Natural History Society (which published nothing of historical interest) to promote the cultivation of useful knowledge, to encourage habits of research, and to afford opportunities for persons of various pursuits to communicate with each other, by the reading of essays on literary and scientific subjects, and discussing the same.

Annual Reports and Transactions, vols. 13-17 (1899-1937):

3892 Vol. 13.
 a Presidential address [on the history of the Institution], by W. H. K. Wright.
 b Notes on [the history of] engineers, contractors, and navvies, by W. Hirst.
 c Presidential address [on the history of the Institution], by H. M. Evans.
 d A three towns fighting family [the Elphinstone family], by W. Hirst.
 e Benjamin Robert Haydon [d. 1846], historical painter, native of Plymouth, by W. H. K. Wright.
 f Some Plymouth charities early this century [the 19th], by P. Prance.
 g Presidential address [on the history of the Institution], by C. S. Jago.

[1] Not seen.

h Charles Mathews [comedian, d. 1835] in the west, by W. H. K. Wright.
 i The domestic life of the Edwardian period [14th cent.], as shown by its architecture, manners, and customs, by B. P. Shires.
 j Mediaeval municipalities, by W. B. R. Caley.
 k Norman architecture, by J. T. Fouracre.
 l Costume, past and present, by J. T. Fouracre.
 m The metamorphoses of James Bagg [d. 1638], by H. E. Duke.
 n Some seamen and voyages of the 17th cent. [includes an account of Robert Blake, d. 1657, and William Dampier, d. 1715], by K. B. Ferguson.

3893 Vol. 14.
 a George Borrow and his Cornish associations, by R. A. J. Walling.
 b Hill forts and camps, by R. Burnard.
 c The coinage of Britain, by J. E. Square.
 d Human bones from a cave at Cattedown, Devon, by J. Beddoe.
 e Sir John Hawkins, by R. A. J. Walling.
 f Presidential address [on the story of Dartmoor], by R. H. Worth.
 g Some further peeps at old Plymouth, by W. H. K. Wright.
 h Presidential address [on the history of chemistry], by J. D. Turney.
 i A sea dog of the olden time [Christopher Mings, d. 1665], by W. P. Drury.
 j St. Boniface and his times, by F. H. Colson.
 k The titles of our Devon churches, by M. J. Burns.

3894 Vol. 15.
 a The stannaries [to 1586], by R. H. Worth.
 b Breton invasions of Plymouth [14th-15th cent.], by C. W. Bracken.
 c 'Diamond' Pitt, of Boconnoc [Governor Thomas Pitt, d. 1726], by R. A. J. Walling.
 d George Borrow, by R. A. J. Walling.
 e Presidential address [on the centenary of the Institution], by H. P. Prance.
 f Plymouth one hundred years ago [c. 1800], or some links with the past, by W. H. K. Wright.
 g Oliver Cromwell in the west, by G. P. Dymond.
 h Place-names of the west and their origin, by G. P. Dymond.
 i St. Budeaux: its manors and first church, by H. M. Evans.
 j Mediaeval guilds, by W. H. Burgess.
 k Women writers of the west, by W. H. K. Wright.
 l The making of New England, by W. H. Burgess.
 m The study of history, by C. R. Warren.

3895 Vol. 16.
 a The power of poetry in history, by R. S. Conway.
 b Sir Ferdinando Gorges [d. 1647] and Plymouth fort in Elizabethan times, by W. H. Burgess.
 c John de Trevisa: a Cornish militant cleric, by H. S. Hill.
 d Woman's work, by Emma Scott.
 e Men of the South Hams [district of Devon], by P. G. Bond.
 f Presidential address [on the history of entomology], by C. W. Bracken.
 g St. Budeaux: life history and work of its patron saint, Budoc, by H. M. Evans.
 h Presidential address [on the history of medicine], by G. Jackson.

3896 Vol. 17.
 a Presidential address [on the history of music], by W. P. Weekes.

b The day of the private banker [17th–19th cent.], by A. P. Pearce.
c The [Sir Joshua] Reynolds bicentenary celebrations: some reflections, by W. L. Munday.
d Old Plymouth inns, by C. W. Bracken.
e The moorland Plymm: 36 years after, by R. H. Worth. [On archaeological discoveries since 1889]
f Plymouth street and place names, by C. W. Bracken.
g Place-names in west Devon, by J. J. Alexander.
h Richard Burthogge, the Plymouth philosopher [d. 1694], by P. Ferry.
i The moorstone age, by R. H. Worth. [On the uses of moorland granite in Devon and Cornwall]
j A peep into Plymouth's archives [15th–18th cent.], by H. V. Prigg.
k The treatment of the poor in Holbeton 200 years ago [1730–44], by J. J. Beckerlegge.
l A new first chapter for the history of Plymouth, by R. H. Worth. [On prehistoric Plymouth]
m Notes on social life and customs in Plymouth and Plymouth Dock in the 18th cent., by J. E. Pillar.
n Sir William Snow Harris [d. 1867], by S. G. Monk.
o Four hundred years of municipal finance in Plymouth [1532–1932], by J. J. Beckerlegge.
p Huguenot churches of Plymouth and Stonehouse, by C. W. Bracken.
q Matthias Dunn [d. 1901]: the fisherman naturalist of Mevagissey, by E. Ford.
r Trevithick, the Cornish engineer: a centenary study, by J. J. Beckerlegge.
s St. Budeaux: its documents and its treasures, by T. A. Hancock.
t Romance of some old Plymouth deeds [14th–18th cent.], by C. W. Bracken.
u Captain Hambly's book [an 18th cent. notebook containing information on the history of Plymouth], by J. J. Beckerlegge.
v Dartmoor tracks, by R. H. Worth.
w Church towers of Devon, by G. W. Copeland.
x Address at the opening of the session 1935–6 [on the history of local government], by A. L. Strachan.
y Plympton records [overseers' accounts, 1780–1824; workhouse accounts, 1775–93], by J. J. Beckerlegge.
z Jonathan Nash Hearder [d. 1876], by S. G. Monk.

POWYS-LAND CLUB

Founded 1867, to collect and print the historical, ecclesiastical, genealogical, topographical, and literary remains of Montgomeryshire.

Collections Historical and Archaeological relating to Montgomeryshire and its borders, vols. 32–43 (1902–34):

3897 Vol. 32.
a Montgomeryshire screens and roodlofts, by D. R. Thomas.
b History of the parish of Llandysilio, by T. Pryce. [Previous pt. in vol. 31. Contd. in vol. 33]
c Pryce (Newtown Hall) correspondence, etc. [17th cent. Contd. from vol. 31]
d History of the parish of Guilsfield (Cegidva), by T. S. Jones and R. Owen. [Contd. from vol. 31]
e Mallwyd parochial registers [1582–1610. Contd. from vol. 30]
f Ancient fonts of Powysland, by H. H. C. Summers.
g A parochial account of Newtown, by R. Williams.
h The register of Trefeglwys [1625–1723, transcribed by E. Edwards. Contd. in vol. 33]

i The castles of Caereinion, by D. R. Thomas.
j Llanfyllin old church, 1706, by D. R. Thomas.
k Wanten, Wantyn, or Wanton Dyke, in the parish of Kerry; with some remarks on upper and lower 'short ditches', by J. M. E. Lloyd.
l Discovery of bronze axe-heads near Dinas Mawddwy, by H. H. C. Summers.
m Find of an ancient game stone near Oswestry, by H. H. C. Summers.

3898 Vol. 33.
a Montgomeryshire reredoses, by D. R. Thomas.
b The association for the prosecution of felons, Welshpool [founded 1807], by C. E. Howell.
c History of the parish of Carno, by Mrs. A. Davies.
d Llandrinio in the 15th cent.: two poems by Gutto'r Glyn, c. 1430–70, by D. R. Thomas.
e Llandrinio, 1809–46, by D. R. Thomas.
f The Rowley Morris deeds [being bonds, feoffments, marriage settlements, leases and other documents relating to Montgomeryshire, 1560–1620], by D. R. Thomas.
g A Trefeglwys charter: charter of Gruffuth ap Cynan [d. 1137] to the abbey of Haughmond.
h A Blayney deed: conveyance of land in Bettws parish from David Lloyd ap Thomas to David Lloyd Blayney, 1583, by C. Herbert.
i Welshpool parish book (Pool Middle), 1765–84, by T. S. Jones.
j Richard Roberts, C.E., of Llanymynech [d. 1864].

3899 Vol. 34.
a History of the parish of Llanyblodwel, by I. Watkin.
b [Manors of] Street-Marshal, Tirymynech, and Deytheur enclosure act, 28 Geo. III, 1788.
c Humphreys wills at St. Asaph, 1700–1800.
d The Ordovices and ancient Powys, by D. R. Thomas.
e Llanllugan parochial registers [1603–22, 1628–33, 1670–1702, 1731–90. Contd. in vol. 35]
f Perambulations of the boundaries of Churchstoke parish, by T. M. Owen.
g Terrier of the registers, church plate and documents in the archdeaconry of Montgomery [1906], by D. R. Thomas. [Contd. in vol. 35]
h Welshpool tithe commutations, 1840.

3900 Vol. 35.
a History of the parish of Llanmerewig, by R. Gibbings and B. E. Jones. [Contd. in vol. 37]
b Gwenwynwyn [d. 1218?]—traitor or patriot?, by R. V. Dymock.
c Parish of Llandrinio: additional notes on the Griffithses of Trederwen, by W. A. Griffiths.
d A Llandrinio deed, 1595 [re sale of land].
e History of the parish of Hyssington, by J. B. Willans.
f A notable musician, Richard Carte [d. 1891], by H. Ll. Howell.
g History of the parish of Snead, by J. B. Willans.

3901 Vol. 36.
a Welshpool registers: extracts from the old registers of St. Mary's church [1634–1701, 1708–36], with annotations by Mary N. Owen.
b Borough of Montgomery: the Flos lands, by C. S. Pryce.
c The policy of the princes of Powys after Bleddyn [1087–1200], by R. G. V. Dymock.
d Two 15th cent. alms-dishes, by W. Ll. Elliott.
e William Burton [d. 1657] on Mediolanum, with notes and introd. by B. E. Jones.
f Montgomeryshire wills at Somerset House, 1720–87.
g Old Welsh church customs, by D. R. Thomas.
h Montgomeryshire wills at St. Asaph [1651–1729], by D. C. Ll. Owen.

i Owen Lawgoch, a Powysland hero [?14th cent.]. Welsh cave legends and the story of Owen Lawgoch, by Sir J. Rhys. Owen Lawgoch [as] Yeuain de Galles [d. 1378?]: some facts and suggestions, by E. Owen. [See also vol. 37]

j Walter Griffithes of Llanvillinge [d. 1702], by T. G. Jones.

3902 Vol. 37.

a The Cistercian nunnery of Llanllugan, by E. Owen.

b Decayed and decaying industries of Powysland, by J. M. Pearson.

c Survey of the lordship of Halcetor, co. Montgomery, dated 30 June 1609, ed. E. A. Lewis.

d History of the parish of Mainstone, by E. S. M. Pryce.

e Early Montgomeryshire wills at St. Asaph and Somerset House relating to the parishes of Llandysilio, Llandrinio, and Guilsfield [16th–18th cent.], by W. A. Griffiths.

f Forden Union during the Napoleonic wars, 1795–1816, being extracts from the minute books. [Concerning the poor of 'Montgomery and Pool united district'], by J. G. Morris and Mary N. Owen.

g The rising of 1294: was Madoc [d. 1331?] a Prince of Powys?, by R. G. V. Dymock.

h Llanwnog church: monument to Matthew Pryce [d. 1699] of Park Penprice.

i Ancient monuments of Radnorshire: the Royal Commission's inventory, by B. E. Jones.

j Montgomeryshire folk-lore, by J. M. Pearson.

k Owen Lawgoch-Yeuain de Galles [d. 1378?], by J. H. Davies. [See also vol. 36]

l Lhwyd's Parochialia [being 'A summary of answers to parochial queries in order to a geographical dictionary etc. of Wales', by Edward Lhwyd, keeper of the Ashmolean Museum, in 1697].

3903 Vol. 38.

a History of the parish of Llanfyllin 1861–1915, by J. M. Dugdale.

b Llanerfyl: inscribed stone, shrine and reliquary, by D. R. Thomas.

c The poor, 1685–1734: a transcript of a number of old indentures discovered at the Oswestry house of industry, by H. H. C. Summers.

d Welshpool landmarks: an account of the old houses of Pool town and its suburbs, by R. Owen.

e The Gorther [district east of the Severn], by D. R. Thomas.

f Rev. Littleton Brown [d. 1749], vicar of Kerry, by J. B. Willans.

g Lay subsidy rolls for hundreds of Deythur and Pool, 39 Elizabeth and 3 James I, and extracts from Harleian mss. *re* inquisition *post mortem*, copied W. A. Griffith.

h Caus Castle's historic associations, by W. S. Jones.

3904 Vol. 39.

a The registers of Kerry [1602–1812], by J. B. Willans.

3905 Vol. 40.

a Owen Glyndwr [b. 1359], by A. G. Bradley.

b Hill camps of Montgomeryshire east of the Severn, by I. T. Hughes.

c Tumulus at Garthbeibio, Montgomeryshire, by R. E. M. Wheeler.

d Short account of the family of Griffiths of Llandisilio, Glanhavren, Trederwen, Feibion Gynwas, and Keel, by W. A. Griffiths.

e Boundaries of Montgomery [in 1839], by W. E. Jones.

f Rowland Williams, D.D. [d. 1870], by J. R. Pryce.

g Montgomery church, by W. E. Jones.

h William Bowman [d. 1892], surgeon and scientist, by H. Ll. Howell.

i Excavations of the Powysland Club at the Forden Gaer [earthwork], by F. N. Pryce and T. D. Pryce. [Contd. in vol. 41]

j Churchstoke and its townships, by G. Mountford.

k Former Kerry landowners [18th cent.], by J. B. Willans.

l Essays on the historical geography of the Shropshire-Montgomeryshire borderland, by E. E. Evans.

3906 Vol. 41.

a The bronze age in Montgomeryshire: the Tir y Mynach or 'Guilsfield' hoard, by J. Ward. [Contd. in vol. 43]

b Montgomeryshire bells, by H. B. Walters.

c Coronation of George IV [1821; celebrations in Welshpool], by Mary N. Owen.

d History of the parish of Llansilin, by E. Hughes.

e Roads of old Montgomeryshire, by J. B. Willans.

f Map of the Trehelig common fields [end 18th cent.], by E. G. Bowen.

g The Powys *inquisitiones*, 1293–1311, by T. P. Ellis.

3907 Vol. 42.

a Lymore, Montgomery, by A. B. Waters.

b Lymore and Black Hall, by Mary N. Owen.

c The fort at Caersws and the Roman occupation of Wales, by T. D. Pryce.

d Montgomeryshire manuscripts in the National Library of Wales.

e Sketch of Roman Powysland, by F. N. Pryce.

f The Mostyns of Dolycorsllwyn, Cemmaes, by J. B. Willans.

g The manor of Halcetor, by G. Mountford.

h Cann Office: its history and archaeology, by B. H. St. J. O'Neil.

i Suggestions concerning the purpose of 'hill-top camps', by R. U. Sayce.

j 'The customs of Powys' (B.M. Add. ms. 9867), by T. P. Ellis.

k Excavation of a barrow on Caebetin hill, Kerry, by H. N. Jerman.

3908 Vol. 43.

a From moss to Macadam: a study of the inter-relation of roads and human society in the Kerry region, by H. N. Jerman.

b The river trade of Montgomeryshire and its borders, by A. S. Davies.

c The castle and borough of Llanidloes, by B. H. St. J. O'Neil.

d The Biggs family of Churchstoke, etc., by J. B. Willans.

e Ty-Ucha [old house in Cwm Llech], by M. F. H. Lloyd and R. Richards.

f Breiddin hill camp excavations, 1934, by B. H. St. J. O'Neil.

Other publications:

3909 Montgomeryshire records, from 'Collections historical and archaeological relating to Montgomeryshire and its borders'. 1911.

3910 Welshpool. Powys-land museum catalogue. 1922.

PREHISTORIC SOCIETY OF EAST ANGLIA

Founded 1908, for the investigation of questions relating to pre-history, principally those of the stone age of Britain (not restricted to East Anglia).

Proceedings, vols. 1–7 (1911–35):

3911 Vol. 1.

a The flint implements of sub-crag man, by J. R. Moir [with report by the special committee].

b The chronology of the stone age, by W. A. Sturge.

c Animistic forms in certain flints, showing human work, by W. Underwood.

d Recent discoveries in palethnology and the works of early man, by W. Underwood.

e The patina of flint implements, by W. A. Sturge.

f Implements of sub-crag man in Norfolk, by W. G. Clarke.

g Implements in a sand-stratum at Lyng, by H. W. Cockrill.

h The natural fracture of flint and its bearing upon rudimentary flint implements, by J. R. Moir.

i The chipping of flints by natural agencies, by F. N. Haward.

j The occurrence of a human skeleton in a glacial deposit at Ipswich, by J. R. Moir.

k Description of the Ipswich skeleton, by A. Keith.

l Implements of the later palaeolithic 'cave' periods in East Anglia, by W. A. Sturge.

m The bearing of the Drayson theory on the problems presented by striated neolithic flints, by W. A. Sturge.

n Prehistoric human remains at Little Cornard, Suff., by H. D. Hewitt.

o Some Barnham palaeoliths, by W. G. Clarke.

p Flint implements of man from the middle glacial gravel and the chalky boulder clay of Suffolk, by J. R. Moir.

q Roman interments at Scole, by W. A. Dutt.

r The red crag shell portrait, by Marie C. Stopes [with report by the special committee].

s Pygmy flints from Cornwall, by E. L. Arnold.

t Norfolk implements of palaeolithic 'cave' types, by W. G. Clarke.

u The problem of the eoliths, by F. N. Haward.

v A discovery of pleistocene bones and flint implements in a gravel pit at Dovercourt, Essex, by W. Underwood.

w A defence of the 'humanity' of the pre-river valley implements of the Ipswich district, by J. R. Moir.

x A late palaeolithic site on Wretham heath, near Thetford, by J. E. Marr.

y The fractured flints of the eocene 'bull-head' bed at Coe's pit, Bramford near Ipswich, by J. R. Moir.

z Notes on the implements from the factory sites at Peppard, Oxon., by A. E. Peake.

aa Some implements of 'Cissbury type' found in Norfolk, by J. S. Warburton.

bb An early Norfolk trackway: the 'drove' road, by W. G. Clarke and H. D. Hewitt.

cc Some aspects of striation, by W. G. Clarke.

dd Flint industries in north Cornwall, by H. G. O. Kendall.

ee Some details of flint fracture, by J. R. Moir.

ff The red crag shell portrait: a comment on the report of the committee, by M. Christy.

gg Some suggestions for organised research on flint implements, by A. Schwartz.

hh Implements [flint] from a station at Cranwich, Norf., by H. H. Halls.

ii The clay with flints, by A. W. Jamieson.

jj A workshop site of primitive culture at Two-mile-bottom, Thetford, by F. N. Haward.

kk Surface implements of palaeolithic type, by R. A. Smith.

ll An east to west trackway across Norfolk, by W. Rye.

mm The discovery of a flint 'workshop-floor' in Ivry Street, Ipswich, by J. R. Moir.

3912 Vol. 2.

a Further discoveries of flint implements of man beneath the base of the red crag of Suffolk, by J. R. Moir.

b Middle glacial and pre-crag implements in south Norfolk, by H. G. O. Kendall.

c Spade-work in north-west Suffolk [the excavation of a barrow near Thetford], by Louisa L. F. Caton.

d Two north-west Suffolk floors [or occupation-levels at Eriswell and Barnham common], by W. G. Clarke.

e A workshop floor near Porthcurno, Cornw., by J. G. Marsden.

f A neolithic site near Thetford, by H. D. Hewitt.

g Some experiments on patination, by H. D. Hewitt.

h Peddar's way [an early trackway in Norfolk], by W. G. Clarke.

i The occurrence of palaeoliths in north-east Lancashire, by T. E. Nuttall.

j A cave site at Nettlebed, S. Oxon, by A. E. Peake.

k Implements of Les Eyzies-type and a working-floor in the Cray valley, by R. H. Chandler.

l High-level finds in the upper Thames valley, by R. A. Smith.

m Surface changes since the palaeolithic period in Kent and Surrey, by H. Dewey.

n A series of mineralised bone implements of a primitive type from below the base of the red and coralline crags of Suffolk, by J. R. Moir.

o 'Coast finds' by Major Moore at Felixstowe ferry, by Nina F. Layard.

p Some palaeolithic pits and periods in Hertfordshire, etc., by H. G. O. Kendall.

q A description of the sub-crag detritus-bed, by A. Bell.

r A prehistoric flint-pit at Ringland, by W. G. Clarke.

s An ancient interment at Mannington, by C. S. Tomes.

t Some earthworks and standing stones in East Anglia, in relation to a prehistoric solar cultus, by S. E. Dixon.

u The pliocene deposits of the south-east of England, by W. J. L. Abbott.

v Cone cultures of the Wensum valley. A: Hellesdon, by W. G. Clarke and H. H. Halls. B: Sparham and Lyng, by J. E. Sainty.

w A series of pre-palaeolithic implements from Darmsden, Suff., by J. R. Moir.

x The Norfolk sub-crag implements, by W. G. Clarke.

y The gravel at No Man's Land common, Herts., by A. E. Peake.

z Windmill hill, Avebury, and Grime's Graves, by H. G. O. Kendall.

aa The implements and cores of Crayford, by R. H. Chandler.

bb The pleistocene succession in England, by A. S. Kennard.

cc Recent excavations at Grime's Graves, by A. E. Peake.

dd Are Grime's Graves neolithic?, by W. G. Clarke.

ee Flint and other stone implements found at Mary Tavy, Devon, by G. W. Smallwood.

ff Chipped flints from below the boulder clay at Hertford, by H. G. O. Kendall.

gg Some supposed gun flint sites, by R. H. Chandler.

hh Some 'flat-faced' palaeoliths from Farnham, by H. Bury.

ii A 'Cissbury type' station at Great Melton, by W. G. Clarke and H. H. Halls.

jj The position of prehistoric research in England, by J. R. Moir.

kk Plateau deposits and implements, by R. A. Smith.

ll A prehistoric site at Kimble, S. Bucks., by A. E. Peake.

mm Our neighbours in the neolithic period, by R. A. Smith.

nn The ancestry of the Mousterian palaeolithic flint implements, by J. R. Moir.

oo A flint implement factory near Milverton, Som., by C. F. Moysey.

pp The flaking and flake characteristics of a pre-red crag rostro-carinate flint implement, by J. R. Moir.

qq The Icknield way in East Anglia, by W. G. Clarke.

rr Flint implements from the ploughlands of south-west Leicestershire, by A. J. Pickering.

ss The fracturing of flints by natural agencies in geological deposits, by J. R. Moir.

l An Acheulean palaeolithic workshop site at Whitlingham, near Norwich, by J. E. Sainty, with geological notes on the site, by P. G. H. Boswell. [Reprinted, 1926]

m An association of thin butted celts with leaf-shaped arrowheads at Drow hill, Capstone North, Kent, by J. Turner.

n Further report on the epi-palaeolithic factory site at Lower Halstow, Kent, by J. P. T. Burchell. [See also above and below]

o Observations on the provenance of the Thames valley pick, Swalecliffe, Kent, by F. H. Worsfold.

p Upper palaeolithic man in East Anglia, by J. R. Moir.

q Nova et vetera: a plea for a new method in palaeolithic archaeology, by Dorothy A. E. Garrod.

r Further researches in the forest bed of Cromer, by J. R. Moir.

s The Kelling flaking site, by J. E. Sainty.

t A final account of the investigations carried out at Lower Halstow, by J. P. T. Burchell.

u Note on Le Moustier flints from Acton, West Drayton and Iver, by J. G. Marsden.

v Early palaeolithic workshop site at Stonecross, Luton, Chatham, by J. Turner.

w Note on recent excavations in Kent's Cavern, Torquay, by H. G. Dowie.

3916 Vol. 6.

a Palaeolithic implements from the cannon-shot gravel of Norfolk, by J. R. Moir.

b The flint industries of Bapchild, by H. G. Dines.

c Pin Hole cave excavations, Creswell Crags, Derbys.: discovery of an engraved drawing of a masked human figure, by A. L. Armstrong.

d Neolithic pottery and other remains from Pangbourne, Berks., and Caversham, Oxon., by S. Piggott.

e Discoidal polished flint knives: their typology and distribution, by J. G. D. Clark.

f The problems of the [Norfolk] crag, by J. E. Sainty.

g A double-ended rostro-carinate flint implement, by J. R. Moir.

h The Clactonian industry at Swanscombe, by R. H. Chandler.

i The dimensions of flint implements, by A. S. Barnes.

j St. Acheul implements from high-level gravel at Denham, Bucks., by J. G. Marsden.

k Pigmy burins in Surrey and Sussex, by W. Hooper.

l Palaeolithic Thames deposits, by H. Dewey.

m Palaeolithic implements of Nidderdale, Yorks., by E. R. Collins.

n Palaeolithic implements found near Coventry, by F. W. Shotton.

o Ancient man in the Gipping-Orwell valley, Suff., by J. R. Moir.

p A hand-axe from beneath the Norwich crag, by J. R. Moir.

q Upper and lower palaeolithic man in east Yorkshire, by J. P. T. Burchell.

r Early neanthropic man and his relation to the ice age, by J. P. T. Burchell.

s A remarkable quartzite implement, by B. Brotherton.

t Further discoveries of flint instruments in the brown boulder clay of north-west Norfolk, by J. R. Moir.

u Excavations in the Pin Hole cave, Creswell Crags, Derbys., by A. L. Armstrong.

v A late upper Aurignacian station in north Lincolnshire, by A. L. Armstrong.

w The early bronze flint dagger in England and Wales, by W. F. Grimes.

x Notes on the beaker pottery of the Ipswich museum, by J. G. D. Clark.

y A skeleton of the early bronze age found in the fens [i.e. Southery Fen, Norf., with a note on the early Fenland waterways], by T. C. Lethbridge and G. Fowler.

z Bronze age settlements in Norfolk, by H. Apling.

aa Early iron age settlement on Jack's hill, Great Wymondley, Herts., by C. F. Tebbutt.

3917 Vol. 7.

a The culture of pliocene man, by J. R. Moir.

b Evolution and distribution of the [flint] hand-axe in north-east Ireland, by J. P. T. Burchell and J. R. Moir.

c Modes of prehension of some forms of upper palaeolithic implements, by A. S. Barnes.

d The Percy Sladen trust excavations, Grime's Graves: interim report, 1927–32, by A. L. Armstrong.

e Neolithic pottery from Larne, by S. Piggott and V. G. Childe.

f Curved flint sickle blades of Britain, by G. Clark.

g Prehistoric archaeology in Wales since 1925, by W. F. Grimes.

h A 'handled beaker' from Bodney, Norf., by S. E. Glendenning.

i A Hallstatt settlement at West Harling, Norf., by H. Apling.

j The distribution of man in East Anglia, c. 2300 B.C.–50 A.D.: a contribution to the prehistory of the region, by C. Fox.

k Implements from high-level gravel near Canterbury, by R. A. Smith.

l Norfolk palaeolithic discoveries, by J. E. Sainty.

m Hand-axes from glacial beds at Ipswich, by J. R. Moir.

n Mesolithic sites of the north-east coast of England, by A. Raistrick.

o Early settlement at Runcton Holme, Norf. Pt. 1: The first occupation: neolithic and beaker remains, by J. G. D. Clark. Pt. 2: The second occupation: a peasant settlement of the Iceni, by C. Hawkes.

p Bell-barrows, by L. V. Grinsell.

q Flint implements from the 'stone bed' of the north Norfolk coast, by J. E. Sainty.

r A giant hand-axe from Sheringham, Norf., by J. R. Moir.

s Implements from the higher raised beaches of Sussex, by J. B. Calkin.

t A palaeolithic succession at Farnham, Surr., by A. G. Wade and R. A. Smith.

u Excavations in a dry valley in Beer, S.E. Devon, by Gertrude and R. MacA. Woods.

v The mutual relations of the British neolithic ceramics, by S. Piggott.

w Grime's Graves: report on the excavation of pit 12, by A. L. Armstrong.

x A bronze age spear-head found in Methwold Fen, Norf., by H. and M. E. Godwin, J. G. D. Clark, and M. H. Clifford.

Extra publication:

3918 Report on the excavations at Grime's Graves, Weeting, Norf., Mar.–May, 1914, ed. W. G. Clarke. 1915.

PRESBYTERIAN HISTORICAL SOCIETY OF ENGLAND

Founded 1913, to promote the study of the history of Presbytery in England, and to collect manuscripts, books, portraits, paintings, and objects relating thereto.

Journal, vols. 1–5 (1914–35):

3919 Vol. 1.

a Edward VI granting a charter to the Presbyterians, by W. Carruthers. [With an early 17th cent. painting of the occasion] b Summary of early English Presbyterian contendings [16th cent.], by A. H. Drysdale.

c English Presbyterianism and the Book of Common Prayer, 1662, by E. G. Atkinson.

d English Presbyterian trust-deeds, by J. H. Colligan.

e Edward Irving and Marcus Dods: an additional document [1830], ed. W. Carruthers.

f Pre-ejection foundations. I: Horningsham, the oldest nonconformist meeting house in England, by R. S. Robson.

g The Horningsham tradition, by E. G. Atkinson.

h New light on the story of the old Scots church, London [later Trinity church, Islington], by A. Jeffrey. [Completed by J. K. Craig]

i Two biographies [of J. R. Brown, d. 1860, and J. H. Young, d. 1855] from the fasti of the church which is being prepared by W. B. Shaw.

j Pre-ejection foundations. II: Dagger Lane, Hull, compiled from its communion rolls, records, and registers, reputed the oldest nonconformist ones in England, by R. S. Robson.

k John Noble, of Penruddock [d. 1708], and notes on Penruddock church, by J. H. Colligan.

l A biography [of the Rev. Peter Lorimer, d. 1879] from the fasti of our church, by W. B. Shaw.

m The Solemn League and Covenant: its divisive influence, by R. D. McGlashan.

n Records of the English [Presbyterian] church at the Hague [to 1822], by E. G. Atkinson.

o Presbyterianism in Brighton, by I. Wells.

p Presbyterianism in the Isle of Man, by J. Davidson.

q The Association oath rolls of 1696, by E. G. Atkinson.

r Pre-ejection foundations. III: Theobalds in Cheshunt, Herts., by R. S. Robson.

s Ulster's share in the founding of the American Presbyterian church, by R. D. McGlashan.

3920 Vol. 2.

a Puritanism in 1604, by E. G. Atkinson.

b Veitch [William, d. 1722] and Northumberland, by R. S. Robson.

c Tyldesley chapel [Lancs.], by C. B. Tyldesley.

d St. George's, Croydon. I: Presbyterianism in Croydon, by R. S. Robson. II: A walk round St. George's, by Mrs. W. W. D. Campbell.

e Humphrey Fenn's confession of faith [1631], by E. G. Atkinson.

f 'Oxendon', London, by R. S. Robson. [On the forerunners of the Oxendon Street chapel and their ministers, 1737–1920]

g The Huguenots and English Presbyterianism, by Mrs. W. W. D. Campbell.

h Rev. Timothy Nelson [d. 1830], by J. H. Colligan.

i Richard Baxter's 'via pacis', by F. J. Powicke.

j Early English Presbyterianism and the reformed church of France, by Mrs. W. W. D. Campbell.

k The Founders' Hall [Lothbury] meeting, by P. O. Williams.

l A Presbyterian poet, Mark Akenside [b. 1721], by R. S. Robson.

m The old meeting, Whitehaven, by J. H. Colligan.

n Early Presbyterianism in the Channel Isles, by Mrs. W. W. D. Campbell.

o A tradition of St. Columba, by H. Hunter.

p The minute book of the war committee of the Stewartry of Kirkcudbright [1640–1].

q Sir Walter Scott and Presbyterianism, by J. S. Henderson.

r William Veitch and Birdhopecraig, by J. Nichol.

s 'Islington' [meeting], London, by R. S. Robson.

t Presbyterianism in Bath.

u Early Presbyterianism at Tunbridge Wells, from information supplied by Edith F. Ellen.

3921 Vol. 3.

a John Quick, 1636–1706, by Mrs. W. W. D. Campbell.

b Canonbury pulpit, by P. O. Williams.

c *History of the New Presbyterians* [1660, 2nd edn.], by Mrs. W. W. D. Campbell.

d Hackney pulpit, by P. O. Williams.

e Seven archbishops [John Tillotson, Thomas Secker, Archibald Campbell Tait, Frederick Temple, Randall Thomas Davidson, William Dalrymple Maclagan, Cosmo Gordon Lang], by R. S. Robson.

f The shorter catechism [1648], by Mrs. W. W. D. Campbell.

g The United Presbyterian contribution to the Presbyterian church of England, by J. S. Henderson.

h Ancient and interesting sites [of meeting-houses in Newcastle-upon-Tyne], by C. Smith.

i The Westminster assembly and the Baptists [c. 1644], by W. T. Whitley.

j John Knox's two sons.

k Henry Thomson, M.A., D.D. [fl. 1799–1861].

l Our heritage, by R. S. Robson. I: The Presbyterian church in England. II: The synod of the United Presbyterian church. [Notes on the origin of Presbyterian churches in England]

m Foreign mission origins.

n James I and Pierre du Moulin (père), by Mrs. W. W. D. Campbell.

o The true text of the larger catechism, by S. W. Carruthers.

p Presbyterianism in Sunderland, by R. Hyslop.

q Presbyterianism in Northumberland, by C. Smith.

3922 Vol. 4.

a Presbyterianism and nationality, by J. D. Mackie. [Also issued separately as the fifth annual lecture, *P.* 1927]

b London at worship, 1689–90, by D. Maclean. [Extracts from a ms. by the Rev. Robert Kirk, d. 1692. Also issued separately as the sixth annual lecture, *P.* 1928]

c The early history of Shaw Street congregation, Liverpool, by W. J. Couper.

d Aston Tirrold Presbyterian church: the story of 200 years, by R. D. Whitehorn.

e Earle and Herle and the *Microcosmography*, by J. D. Ogilvie. [On the claims of John Earle and Charles Herle as its author]

f Royalist or republican, the story of the engagement of 1649–50, by J. D. Ogilvie. [On the struggle between the Presbyterians and the army. Also issued separately as the seventh annual lecture, *P.* 1929]

g The story of Presbyterianism on Holy Island, by C. Smith. [Also issued separately (probably as the eighth annual lecture), *P.* 1930?]

h New light on the life and family of the Rev. John Baker, of Hackney and of Salters' Hall [d. 1762], by Lillian W. Kelley.

i Francis Rous, 1579–1659, by T. F. Kinlock.

j Records. Letters from Samuel Clark to Philip Doddridge, 1723–29. Introd. and notes by Lillian W. Kelley.

3923 Vol. 5.

a The Geneva service book 1555, by J. H. Colligan. [With reply by W. D. Maxwell. Also issued separately, without the reply, as the ninth annual lecture, *P.* 1931]

b A forgotten Newcastle divine [James Murray, d. 1782]: strange sermons and satires, by C. Smith.

c Edward Irving preaching in Britannia Fields [London], summer 1832: a portrait by Faithful Christopher Pack, by Lillian W. Kelley.

d An old London register [of baptisms at Wells Street, 1751–1863, described with extracts], by W. B. Shaw.
e The 'old' version of the Scottish psalter, by A. Fulton.
f Rev. Edward Bowles, 1617–1662, by T. Gray.
g The Horsley bi-centenary, 1732–1932, by R. S. Robson.
h The contribution of English Presbyterianism to foreign missions [1844–1933], by S. W. Carruthers.
i 'Fasti' of English Presbyterian theological students, 1845 [Andrew Hamilton, d. 1900; John Sinclair, d. 1903; the Rev. George Lillie, d. 1881; the Rev. Robert Henderson, d. 1910; Norman Macbeth, R.S.A., d. 1888; Adam Steward, d. 1881; John Ogilvy Moore, d. 1879], by W. B. Shaw.
j Edmund Calamy, 1671–1732, and the Camisards [a group of Huguenot refugees settled in London, 1706], by O. M. Griffiths.
k Quatercentenary of Thomas Cartwright, the father of English Presbyterianism, 1535–1603, by C. Smith.

Annual Presbyterian Lectures, nos. 2–9:

3924 No. 2. The Westminster assembly—and after, by J. H. Colligan. *P.* [1924].

3925 No. 3. Two church movements: Anglican and Scottish. A comparison of the Anglo-Catholic revival and the Free church of Scotland, by P. C. Simpson. *P.* [1925].

3926 No. 4. Matthew Henry [Presbyterian, 1662–1714], by P. O. Williams. *P.* [1926].

No. 5. See **3922a** above.

No. 6. See **3922b** above.

No. 7. See **3922f** above.

No. 8. See **3922g** above.

No. 9. See **3923a** above.

PRINT COLLECTORS' CLUB

Founded 1921, to afford to a certain number of those who are interested in etching and engraving an opportunity of connecting themselves with the Royal Society of Painter-Etchers and Engravers, one of whose objects is 'the promotion of engraving in all its forms'.

Publications, nos. 1–12:

3927 No. 1. The British school of etching [17th–20th cent.], by M. Hardie, with foreword by F. Short. [1921].

3928 No. 4. British mezzotints [17th–19th cent.], by F. Short. [1925?].

3929 No. 5. Woodcuts and wood engravings, by N. Rooke. 1926.

3930 No. 6. Bookplates [15th–19th cent.], by J. F. Badeley. 1927.

3931 No. 7. Samuel Palmer [d. 1881], by M. Hardie. 1928.

3932 No. 8. Thomas Rowlandson [d. 1827] and George Morland [d. 1804], by S. Image. 1929.

3933 No. 9. History of the Royal Society of Painter-Etchers and Engravers, 1880–1930, by F. Newbolt. 1930.

3934 No. 11. Thomas Bewick [d. 1828], by S. Image. 1932.

3935 No. 12. The etchings of William Strang [d. 1921] and Sir Charles Holroyd [d. 1917], by C. Dodgson. 1933.

RADNORSHIRE SOCIETY

Founded 1930, for the study of all such subjects as shall be found to interest a sufficient number of members. The Society has an archaeological section.

Transactions, vols. 1–3 (1931–3):

3936 Vol. 1.
a Schedule of Radnorshire place names: parish of Llanyre, by C. L. D. Venables-Llewelyn.
b Llanfaredd [place names], by R. Williams.
c Parish of Aberedw [place names], by R. Williams.
d Llandrindod parish [place names].
e Parish of Knighton [place names], by W. Hatfield.

3937 Vol. 2.
a Wechelen, the hermit of Llowes [12th cent.], by D. S. Davies.
b Old Llandrindod parish church register, 1734–1812, by G. Thomas.
c Domesday book in Radnorshire and the border, by Sir C. Venables-Llewelyn.
d Radnorshire school log books, by J. Mostyn. [Contd. in vol. 3]
e Parish of Disserth and the township of Trecoed [place names], by D. Jones.
f Cefnllys parish [place names], by T. P. Davies.
g Parish of Llanbadarn-Fynydd [place names], by F. W. Sibley.

3938 Vol. 3.
a Radnorshire wills [1383–1656], by D. S. Davies.
b Dr. John Dee [d. 1608], by Sir J. Bradney.
c Nantmel tithe [1719].
d The old Wye bridge at Newbridge-on-Wye, by Sir C. Venables-Llewelyn.
e Parish of Llanbister [place names], by A. J. Moseley.
f Place names in the Llangunllo district, by W. S. Bryans.

RAILWAY CLUB

Founded 1899, for the collection and preservation of books, maps, plans, etc., relative to the history and working of railways.

Railway Club Journal, new ser., vols. 1–10 (1902–11):

3939 Vol. 1.
a Railway medals and tokens, by G. W. J. Potter. [Supplementary to no. **3947**]

3940 Vol. 2.
a The Belvoir Castle edge-railway, by G. W. J. Potter.
b The Haigh foundry [established 1810 at Wigan], by G. W. J. Potter.

3941 Vol. 3.
a History of the South Eastern and Chatham railway and its locomotives, by G. F. Burtt.
b The Whitby and Pickering railway [opened 1835], by G. W. J. Potter.
c Railway travelling in 1844, by G. W. J. Potter.

3942 Vol. 4.
a Notes towards a railway bibliography [covering the history of railways. Contd. in vols. 5 and 6]

3943 Vol. 5.
a Early railway maps, by S. Kirkwood.
b Early railway maps, by G. W. J. Potter.
c The first Railway Club [founded 1855], by E. G. Ryder.

d Railways 40 years ago [1866], by J. T. Lawrence.
e Bradshaw 60 years ago [1846], by S. Kirkwood.

3944 Vol. 7.

a Thomas Edmondson [d. 1851, inventor of the railway ticket system], by G. W. J. Potter.

3945 Vol. 8.

a The locomotives of the Lancashire and Yorkshire railway, by H. L. Hopwood. [Contd. in vol. 9]
b Sixty years ago: the L. & N.W.R. in 1849, by J. B. Chirnside.
c Colour in its relation to railway signalling, by G. W. J. Potter.

3946 Vol. 10.

a Locomotive development in the Edwardian era, by J. F. Gairns.
b Early standard locomotive types, by H. L. Hopwood.
c Railway history in the middle ages (1860–80), by W. J. Scott.

Railway Club Library, vols. 1–3:

3947 Vol. 1. Railway medals and tokens, by G. W. J. Potter. P. 1901. [See also no. 3939a above]

3948 Vol. 2. The North London railway, by A. J. Chisholm. P. 1902.

READING LITERARY AND SCIENTIFIC SOCIETY

Founded 1878, as the Redlands Literary and Scientific Society, for the promotion of literary and scientific culture. Title changed to the above form in 1880. Dissolved 1930.

Reports, 1901–5 (3 vols. 1901–5):

3949 Vol. for 1901.

a Buckle: the philosopher of history, by F. W. Stansfield.
b Addison and his associates, by A. H. Cunningham.

Other publications:

3950 Quarter centenary, 1880–1905. P. [1905].

3951 Annual report, 1913–14, historical retrospect, 1880–1914, and proceedings, 1905–14. 1 vol. [1914].

a Historical retrospect, 1880–1914.
b Ufton Court, by H. H. Jones.
c Parish church of St. Laurence, Reading, by E. O. Farrer.
d Parish church of St. Mary the Virgin, Reading, by W. T. Bilson.

3952 Report and proceedings, 1925–6. 1 vol. [1926].

a Local literary celebrities, by E. O. Farrer.

RECORD SOCIETY FOR THE PUBLICATION OF ORIGINAL DOCUMENTS RELATING TO LANCASHIRE AND CHESHIRE
(Lancashire and Cheshire Record Society)

Founded 1878, to transcribe and publish original documents relating to the counties of Lancaster and Chester

Publications, vols. 41–83:

3953 Vol. 41. Some court rolls of the lordships, wapentakes, and demesne manors of Thomas, Earl of Lancaster, in the county of Lancaster, for the 17th and 18th years of Edward II, 1323–4, ed. W. Farrer. 1901.

3954 Vol. 42. Manchester sessions. Notes of proceedings before Oswald Mosley (1616–30), Nicholas Mosley (1661–1672), and Sir Oswald Mosley (1734–39), and other magistrates, ed. E. Axon. Vol. i: 1616–22/3. 1901. [No more published]

3955 Vol. 43. Miscellanies relating to Lancashire and Cheshire, vol. 4. 1902.

a A list of the freeholders in Cheshire, 1578, ed. W. F. Irvine. 1902.
b The earliest ordination book of the diocese of Chester, 1542–7 and 1555–8, ed. W. F. Irvine. 1895.
c Index to wills, inventories, administration bonds and depositions, etc., in testamentary suits, in the diocesan registry of Chester, 1621–1700, ed. W. H. Price. 1902.

3956 Vol. 44. Index to the wills and inventories now in the probate registry at Chester, 1781–90, with an appendix containing a list of the 'infra' wills (or those in which the personalty was under £40), between the same years, ed. W. F. Irvine. 1902. [Contd. in vols. 45, 62, 63, 78, and 79. An index for the period 1761–80 was published as vols. 37 and 38, 1898–9]

3957 Vol. 45. Index to the wills and inventories—, 1791–1800, ed. W. F. Irvine. 1902. [Continues vol. 44 above]

3958 Vols. 46, 50, 60. Final concords of the county of Lancaster, from the original chirographs, or feet of fines, in the Public Record Office, London, pts. ii–iv, ed. W. Farrer. 1903–10. [Pt. ii: 1307–77. Pt. iii: 1377–1509. Pt. iv: 1510–58. Pt. i: 1191–1307, was published as vol. 39 in 1899. All 'pts.' are separately paginated]

3959 Vols. 47, 49. Calendar of the Lancashire assize rolls in the Public Record Office, London, transcribed and calendared by J. Parker. 1 vol. in 2. 1904–5.

3960 Vols. 48, 54, 70. Lancashire inquests, extents, and feudal aids, ed. W. Farrer. 3 vols. 1903–15. [Pt. i: 1205–1307. Pt. ii: 1310–33. Pt. iii: 1313–55]

3961 Vols. 51, 55. Rolls of the freemen of the city of Chester, transcribed and ed. J. H. E. Bennett. 1 vol. in 2. 1906–8. [Pt. i: 1392–1700. Pt. 2: 1700–1805]

3962 Vol. 52. Miscellanies relating to Lancashire and Cheshire, vol. 5. 1906.

a An index to the wills and inventories now preserved in the probate registry at Chester, commonly called 'infra' wills, being those in which the personalty was under £40, between the years 1590 and 1665, ed. W. F. Irvine. 1906.
b Calendar of wills, inventories, administration bonds, citations, accounts and depositions in testamentary suits, in the diocesan registry of Chester, 1701–1800, ed. W. H. Price. 1905.
c Hearth tax returns for the city of Chester, 1664–5, transcribed and ed. F. C. Beazley. 1906.

3963 Vols. 53, 56, 57, 61, 65, 69, 73, 77. Marriage licences granted within the archdeaconry of Chester in the diocese of Chester, ed. W. F. Irvine. 8 vols. 1907–24. [Vol. i: 1606–16. Vol ii: 1616–24. Vol. iii: 1624–32. Vol. iv: 1639–44. Vol. v: 1661–67. Vol. vi: 1667–80. Vol. vii: 1680–91. Vol. viii: 1691–1700]

Vol. 58. Pedigrees made at the visitation of Cheshire, 1613. [See Harleian Soc., vol. 59, no. 2027 above]

3964 Vol. 59. Accounts of the chamberlains and other officers of the county of Chester, 1301–60, ed., with introd., by R. Stewart-Brown. 1910.

3965 Vols. 62, 63. Index to the wills and administrations (including the 'infra' wills) now in the probate registry, at Chester, for the years 1801–10, both inclusive, ed. R. Stewart-Brown. 2 vols. 1911–12. [Pt. i: A to L. Pt. ii: M to Z. Continues vols. 44 and 45 above]

3966 Vol. 64. *Liber Luciani de laude Cestrie*, written about the year 1195. Extracts from the ms. transcribed and ed. M. V. Taylor. 1912. [Together with 'Some obits of abbots and founders of St. Werburgh's abbey, Chester', extracted from a Bodleian ms. and annotated by M. V. Taylor]

3967 Vol. 66. List of Lancashire wills proved within the archdeaconry of Richmond and now in the probate court at Lancaster from 1793 to 1812; also a list of wills proved in the peculiar of Halton from 1793 to 1812, ed. H. Fishwick. 1913. [A list of wills proved in the archdeaconry of Richmond, 1748–92, and in the peculiar of Halton, 1615–92, was published as vol. 23 in 1891]

3968 Vol. 67. Calendar of that part of the collection of deeds and papers of the Moore family of Bankhall, co. Lanc., now in the Liverpool public library, by J. Brownbill, with an appendix containing a calendar of a further portion of the same collection, now in the University of Liverpool School of Local History and Records, by Kathleen Walker. 1913.

3969 Vol. 68. Ledger-book of Vale Royal abbey, ed. J. Brownbill. 1914.

3970 Vol. 71. Lancashire and Cheshire cases in the court of star chamber, ed. R. Stewart-Brown. Pt. i. 1916. [No more published]

3971 Vol. 72. Royalist composition papers, being the proceedings of the committee for compounding, 1643–60, so far as they relate to the county of Lancaster, extracted from the records in the Public Record Office, London. Vol. v: P–R, ed. J. Brownbill. 1917. [Vols. i–iv, ed. J. H. Stanning, were published as vols. 24, 26, 29, and 36 in 1891–8]

3972 Vols. 74, 75, 80, 81, 83. Marriage bonds for the deaneries of Lonsdale, Kendal, Furness, and Copeland, part of the archdeaconry of Richmond, now at Lancaster. Pts. i–vi. 1920–33. [Pt. i: 1648–1710, ed. J. Brownbill. All subsequent pts. include Amounderness. Pt. ii: 1711–22, ed. R. Stewart-Brown. Pt. iii: 1723–8; pt. iv: 1729–34; pt. v: 1734–8, ed. W. F. Irvine. Pt. vi: 1738–45, of bonds 'now preserved at Preston', ed. R. Dickinson, was published as vol. 100 in 1949. All 'pts.' are separately paginated]

3973 Vol. 76. Calendar of persons commemorated in monumental inscriptions, and of abstracts of wills, administrations, etc., contained in books relating to Lancashire and Cheshire, comp. and ed. F. C. Beazley. 1922.

3974 Vols. 78, 79. Index to the wills and administrations (including the 'infra' wills) now in the probate registry at Chester, for the years 1811–20, both inclusive, ed. W. A. Tonge. 2 vols. 1928. [Pt. i: A–L. Pt. ii: M–Z. Continue vols. 44, 45, 62, and 63 above]

3975 Vol. 82. Marriage bonds of the ancient archdeaconry of Chester, now at Chester. Pt. i: 1700–1706/7, ed. W. A. Tonge. 1933. [Pt. ii: 1707–11, ed. W. F. Irvine, was published as vol. 85 in 1935. Pt. iii: 1711–15, and pt. iv: 1715–19, both ed. P. H. Lawson, were published as vols. 97 and 101 in 1942–49. All 'pts.' are separately paginated]

ROCHDALE LITERARY AND SCIENTIFIC SOCIETY

Founded 1878, for literary and scientific studies bearing more particularly on local matters: archaeology, antiquities, geology, meteorology, local history, dialect and dialect writers, Roman remains, etc.

Transactions, vols. 7–17 (1903–31):

3976 Vol. 7.
a The place-name 'low', by W. H. Sutcliffe.
b Manchester's contribution to the chemistry of the 19th cent., by J. H. Brittain. [Contd. in vol. 9]
c A Lancashire chemist [John Mercer, d. 1866], by W. H. Pennington.
d Notes on the Butterworths of Belfield [1594–1728], by H. Fishwick.
e Notes on the lives of Samuel Crompton, the inventor, and John Bradshaw, the regicide, with reference to Hall-i'-th'-Wood and Bradshaw Hall, near Bolton, by I. Renshaw.
f Rochdale manor inquisition (survey), 1610, by H. Fishwick.

3977 Vol. 8.
a The Whitburn Hot-pot [an ancient marriage custom], by G. H. Ashworth.
b Shakespeare's London, by H. Fishwick.
c John Ruskin, social reformer, by F. P. Wright.

3978 Vol. 9.
a Rochdale newspapers, by W. W. Hadley.
b Two reputed manor houses of Rochdale, by H. Fishwick.
c Note on inscriptions on gravestones in the parish churchyard, Rochdale, by J. R. Ashworth.

3979 Vol. 10.
a Stone celt or axe found at Castle hill, Rochdale, by S. S. Platt.
b The Lancashire possessions of the Knights of St. John of Jerusalem, hundred of Salford, by H. Fishwick.

3980 Vol. 11.
a Prehistoric relics from the hills lying due east of Burnley, by G. B. Leach.
b Querns and other corn-grinding stones [found] in Rochdale and district, by J. L. Maxim. [Contd. in vols. 12, 13, and 15]
c Notes on the index to inscriptions on gravestones in the churchyard of the parish church of St. Chad, Rochdale, by J. R. Ashworth.
d Index to the inscriptions, comp. R. J. Gordon.
e The Piltdown (Sussex) skull; some important discoveries in prehistoric archaeology, by W. A. Parker.

3981 Vol. 12.
a Water corn mills in Rochdale and district [and the early history of corn-grinding], by J. L. Maxim.
b Notes on an old building at 'Hollows', Shawclough, by J. L. Maxim.
c First assessment lists for the townships of Castleton (1759), the Lordship side of Butterworth (1763), and the township of Spotland (1750), by R. J. Gordon.
d A chat about S. Mary's graveyard [and on the inscriptions on the gravestones], by Emma Baldwin.
e The Volunteer movement in Rochdale [16th to 20th cent.], by E. L. Taylor.
f Reminiscences of Whitworth [Lancs.] and its doctor [James Eastwood Taylor] fifty years ago [1860s], by J. E. Phythian.
g The early wool trade of Rochdale [16th to 18th cent.], by E. L. Taylor.

h Notes respecting fragments of stained glass windows formerly in Trinity chapel, Rochdale parish church, and now in the Rochdale museum, by R. Schofield.

3982 Vol. 13.

a The Rochdale grammar school [founded 1564], by E. L. Taylor.

b The highway through Rochdale and its coaches [18th and 19th cent.], by J. R. Ashworth.

c The lawsuit 'Dearden v. Maden', 1830 and 1833, by E. L. Taylor. [Case turned on whether or not some waste land originally formed part of the manorial lands of Rochdale]

d The surname 'Rochdale', by H. Brierley.

e A note on an index to the gravestones and the names in the New Burial Ground, by J. R. Ashworth.

f Rochdale's main roads: the history of turnpikes, by A. P. Wadsworth.

g Notes on some Lancashire crosses, by J. Cleworth.

h Discovery of a bloomery at Birches, Healey, by J. L. Maxim.

i Rochdale and Peterloo [1819], by G. E. Leach.

3983 Vol. 14.

a Old sun-dials in or near the ancient parish of Rochdale, by R. Heape.

b Richard Rome Bealey: a Lancashire poet [b. 1828], by R. Muschamp.

c Notes on Rochdale public houses and their signboards, [17th–19th cent.], by Janet Fishwick.

d Healey Hall: its dated and inscribed stones, by R. Heape.

e Two charms against evil spirits found at Cross Lees, Syke, and Meadow Head, Wolstenholme, by J. L. Maxim.

f Examples of dated buildings within the ancient parish of Rochdale, by R. Heape.

g Enclosures of the commons in Rochdale district in the 16th and 17th cent., by A. P. Wadsworth.

3984 Vol. 15.

a The place names Limers Gate, Clegg and Birches, by T. Clegg.

b The Rochdale Literary and Scientific Society, a retrospect, 1878–1923, by W. H. Pennington.

c The Roman road across Blackstone edge, by I. A. Richmond.

d The Byron centenary [the connection of the Byrons with Rochdale], by J. Cleworth.

e Old Rochdale maps [19th cent.], by H. Yarwood.

f History of the Rochdale woollen trade, by A. P. Wadsworth.

3985 Vol. 16.

a Britons, Angles and Norse in the Roch basin, by I. A. Richmond.

b Pack-horse and other ancient tracks in and around Rochdale, by J. L. Maxim.

c Sidelights on Rochdale history, by A. P. Wadsworth. 1: The manor house—a new site. 2: The growth of Rochdale south of the Roch. 3: The Rochdale woollen industry in the 17th cent. 4: A Rochdale inventor [John Kay d. 1779].

d Two Roman coins found on Blackstone edge, by I. A. Richmond.

e Rochdale long-case clockmakers [18th and 19th cent.], by C. Stott.

f Jubilee lecture. Place-names and history, by A. Mawer.

3986 Vol. 17.

a The great wheel of Shore and an unrecorded dated stone, by J. Priestnall.

b Discoveries on the hills around Rochdale, by J. H. Price.

[Includes account of an ancient road over Blackstone edge]

c Broadfield and the environs thereof eighty years ago [1850], by H. Brierley.

d Note on the life and writings of Sir Henry H. Howorth [d. 1923], by J. H. Brittain.

e Discovery of a shale armlet on Flint hill, near Blackstone Edge, by J. W. Jackson.

f Note on John Roby [d. 1850], by J. Fishwick.

3987 Index to the Transactions, vols. 1–17, comp. C. Stott. 1933. [Published with Transactions, vol. 18, dated 1934]

ROCHESTER AND DISTRICT NATURAL HISTORY SOCIETY

Founded 1878, as the Rochester Naturalists' Club, for the study of the natural sciences. The club lapsed in 1915, and was re-formed in 1920 as the Rochester and District Naturalists' Club. Title changed to the above form in 1925–6.

Rochester Naturalist, vols. 3–6 (1900–32):

3988 Vol. 3.

a A city with a history [Rochester], by W. Mackay.

b The antiquity of man, and its connection with survivals of paganism in the 20th cent., by F. J. Bennett.

c Men and implements of the old stone age, by G. W. Bancks.

d Cobham church and college, by Clara E. Pye.

e Allington castle, by C. H. Fielding.

f The Friars, Aylesford, by C. H. Fielding.

g Some literary associations of Kent, by F. R. Wilson.

h Our roads from prehistoric times to the present day, by F. J. Bennett.

i Some market crosses, by F. W. Clarke.

3989 Vol. 4.

a Sir John Hawkyns' hospital at Chatham, by H. F. Wingent.

b Excursion to Burham. [Includes an account of Burham church]

c The evolution of weapons, by H. Sills.

d A peep into chemical history, by P. Mathews.

e The Arthurian legend, by P. K. Wilson.

f A brief summary of our knowledge in regard to the higher antiquity of prehistoric man, by W. H. Cook.

3990 Vol. 6.

a Ecclesiological notes [relating to West Kent], by F. M. H. Roper.

b Benjamin Harrison of Ightham (1857–1921), archaeologist, by W. H. Cook.

c An ancient boat from Murston, by G. E. Dibley.

d Geological notes on the Murston discovery, by J. H. Evans.

e Archaeological discoveries and researches in the regional survey area [achieved by the South-Eastern Union of Scientific Societies], by J. H. Evans.

f Megalithic monuments of the Medway valley, by J. H. Evans.

g A Romano-British cist at Northumberland Bottom, by R. F. Jessup.

h Archaeological discoveries in the area [Kent], by N. C. Cook.

i List of recent literature of local interest [including history and topography, biography, prehistoric archaeology, and Roman archaeology, published 1926–8], by R. F. Jessup.

j Local Kentish churches [erected prior to the 16th cent., within a 10 mile radius of Rochester], comp. J. H. Bolton.
k An early bead necklace found at Higham, by H. S. Toms.
l Sectional records. Archaeology, by N. C. Cook. [Notes on miscellaneous discoveries in Kent]

ROXBURGHE CLUB

Founded 1812, to hold annual dinners, at the second of which it was resolved that each member 'should reprint some scarce piece of antient lore to be given to the members'. This, and 'bibliomania generally', are the principal objects of the Club, which in 1828 began to print additional books in its corporate capacity.

Publications, including:

3991 No. 139. The game of ombre, by Lord Aldenham. 3rd edn. 1902.

3992 No. 140. The Gowrie conspiracy. Confessions of George Sprot [1608], ed. A. Lang. 1902.

3993 No. 141. The epistle of Othea to Hector, or the boke of knyghthode, translated from the French of Christine de Pisan with a dedication to Sir John Fastolf, K.G. by Stephen Scrope, esquire, ed. G. F. Warner. 1904.

3994 No. 142. The nobility of women, by William Bercher, 1559, ed. with introd. and notes by R. W. Bond. Folio. 1904. Addenda, glossary and index. 1905.

3995 No. 143. The castell of labour, translated from the French of Pierre Gringore by Alexander Barclay, reprinted in facsimile from Wynkyn de Worde's edition of 1506 with the French text of 1501 and an introd. by A. W. Pollard. 1905.

3996 No. 144. The academy of armory, or a storehouse of armory and blazon, second volume, by Randle Holme, 1682, ed. I. H. Jeayes. 1905.

3997 No. 145. The pilgrimage of the life of man, Englished by John Lydgate, 1426, from the French of Guillaume de Deguileville, 1330, 1355, ed. F. J. Furnivall, with introd., notes, glossary and indexes by Katharine B. Locock. 1905.

3998 No. 146. Titus and Vespasian, or the destruction of Jerusalem, in rhymed couplets [mid 14th-cent.], ed. J. A. Herbert. 1905.

3999 No. 147. 'The Club' [founded by Sir Joshua Reynolds], 1764–1905, by Sir M. E. G. Duff. 1905.

4000 No. 148. Letters of Philip Gawdy, of West Harling, Norfolk, and of London, to various members of his family, 1578–1616, ed. with introd. and notes by I. H. Jeayes. 1906.

4001 No. 149. Lord Byron and his detractors, by J. Murray [being a criticism of *Astarte* by Lord Lovelace]. 1906.

4002 No. 150. The pageants of Richard Beauchamp, Earl of Warwick, reproduced in facsimile from the Cottonian ms. Julius E. IV, in the British Museum, with introd. by William, Earl of Carysfort. 1908.

4003 No. 151. The mirrour of the blessed lyf of Jesu Christ: translation of the Latin work entitled *Meditationes vitae Christi*, attributed to Cardinal Bonaventura, made before 1410 by Nicholas Love, prior of the Carthusian monastery of Mount Grace [fl. 1415], ed. L. F. Powell. 1908.

4004 No. 152. Femina [being a treatise on teaching French to English children], now first printed from a unique ms. in the library of Trinity College, Cambridge, by W. A. Wright. 1909.

4005 No. 153. Letters written by Charles Lamb's 'princely woman the thrice noble Margaret Newcastle' to her husband; by his 'fine old Whig' William Plumer to the third Duke of Portland and Lord William Bentinck; also by his 'old Bencher' Samuel Salt, from originals at Welbeck Abbey, together with a reprint of a rare pamphlet entitled *Considérations sur l'état actuel de la France au mois de juin, 1815; par un Anglais* [i.e. F. A. Elia], ed. R. W. Goulding, with an introductory note by the Duke of Portland. 1909.

4006 No. 154. Survey of the lands of William, first Earl of Pembroke, transcribed from vellum rolls in the possession of the Earl of Pembroke and Montgomery, with introd. by the transcriber C. R. Straton, and a preface by the Earl of Pembroke and Montgomery. 1 vol. in 2. 1909.

4007 No. 155. The Trinity College apocalypse. A reproduction in facsimile of ms. R.16.2 in the library of Trinity College, Cambridge, with preface and description by M. R. James. Folio. 1909.

4008 No. 156. The benedictional of St. Æthelwold, bishop of Winchester, 963–84, reproduced in facsimile from the ms. in the library of the Duke of Devonshire at Chatsworth, with text and introd. by G. F. Warner and H. A. Wilson. Folio. 1910.

4009 No. 157. Correspondence of Edmund Burke and William Windham, with other illustrative letters from the Windham papers in the British Museum, ed. J. P. Gilson. 1910.

4010 No. 160. Ballads and broadsides chiefly of the Elizabethan period, and printed in black letter, most of which were formerly in the Heber collection, and are now in the library at Britwell Court, Bucks., ed. with notes and introd. by H. L. Collmann. Folio. 1912.

4011 No. 161. Songs, ballads, and instrumental pieces composed by Henry VIII, collected and arranged by the Lady Mary Trefusis, to which is prefixed a list of the king's instruments. Folio. 1912.

4012 No. 162. The treatise of Walter de Milemete, *De nobilitatibus, sapientiis, et prudentiis regum*, reproduced in facsimile from the unique [14th cent.] ms. preserved at Christ Church, Oxford, together with a selection of pages from the companion [14th cent.] ms. of the treatise *De secretis secretorum Aristotelis*, in the library of the Earl of Leicester, at Holkham Hall, with introd. by M. R. James. Folio. 1913.

4013 No. 163. A transcript of the registers of the Worshipful Company of Stationers 1640–1708, ed. G. E. B. Eyre. 3 vols. 1913–14. [Vol. i: 1640–55. Vol. ii: 1655–75. Vol. iii: 1675–1708]

4014 No. 164. The Edmondes papers: a selection from the correspondence of Sir Thomas Edmondes, envoy from Queen Elizabeth at the French court, ed. G. G. Butler. 1913.

4015 No. 165. The letters of Thomas Burnet to George Duckett, 1712–22, ed. D. N. Smith. 1914.

4016 No. 166. The royal commission on the losses and services of American loyalists, 1783–5, being the notes of Daniel Parker Coke, M.P., one of the commissioners during that period, ed. H. E. Egerton. 1915.

4017 No. 167. Letters to Henry Fox, Lord Holland, with a few addressed to his brother Stephen, Earl of Ilchester, ed. the Earl of Ilchester. 1915.

4018 No. 168. The Melvill book of roundels [1612], ed. with introd. by G. Bantock and H. O. Anderton. 1916.

4019 No. 169. The Chaundler mss. Introduction on the life and writings of Thomas Chaundler, and an appendix containing descriptions of the Trinity College and New College mss., with extracts therefrom, ed. M. R. James. 1916.

4020 No. 170. Lives of Lady Anne Clifford, Countess of Dorset, Pembroke, and Montgomery (1590–1676), and of her parents, summarized by herself, with introd. by J. P. Gilson. 1916.

4021 No. 173. Correspondence of the Scots commissioners in London, 1644–6, ed. H. W. Meikle. 1917.

4022 No. 174. Lord Howard of Effingham and the Spanish Armada, with exact facsimiles of the 'Tables of Augustus Ryther', 1590 [being 11 charts of the successive engagements between the English and Spanish fleets] and the engravings of the hangings of the House of Lords, by John Pine, 1739, with introd. by H. Y. Thompson. Folio. 1919.

4023 No. 175. La estoire de Seint Ædward le rei. The life of St. Edward the Confessor, reproduced in facsimile from the unique [13th cent.] ms., together with some pages of the ms. of the life of St. Alban at Trinity College, Dublin, with introd. by M. R. James. 1920.

4024 No. 176. The Sherborne missal. Reproductions of full pages and details of ornament from the missal executed between 1396 and 1407 for Sherborne abbey church, and now in the library of the Duke of Northumberland at Alnwick Castle, with introd. by J. A. Herbert. Folio. 1920.

4025 No. 177. Illustrations of the book of Genesis, being a complete reproduction in facsimile of the ms., British Museum, Egerton 1894, with introd. by M. R. James. 1921.

4026 No. 178. A Peterborough psalter and bestiary of the 14th cent., described by M. R. James. Folio. 1921.

4027 No. 180. The apocalypse in Latin and French (Bodleian ms. Douce 180), described by M. R. James. 1922.

4028 No. 181. Papers of devotion of James II, being a reproduction of the ms. in the handwriting of James II now in the possession of B. R. Townley Balfour, with introd. by G. Davis. 1925.

4029 No. 182. The herbal of Apuleius Barbarus from the early 12th cent. ms. formerly in the abbey of Bury St. Edmunds, described by R. T. Gunther. 1925.

4030 No. 184. Vulgaria, by William Horman, first printed by Richard Pynson in 1519, with introd. by M. R. James. 1926.

4031 No. 185. Two [14th cent.] East Anglian psalters at the Bodleian Library, Oxford. Folio. 1926.

  a The Ormesby psalter, ms. Douce 366, described by S. C. Cockerell.

  b The Bromholm psalter, ms. Ashmole 1523, described by M. R. James.

4032 No. 187. A selection from the papers of George III, in the royal archives at Windsor Castle, embracing the period from the 1st day of November, 1781, to the 20th day of December 1783, the whole ed. J. Fortescue. 1 vol. in 2. 1927.

4033 No. 188. The Roxburghe Club: its history and its members, 1812–1927, by the Hon. C. Bigham. 1928.

4034 No. 189. The Guthlac roll. Scenes from the life of St. Guthlac of Crowland, by a 12th cent. artist, reproduced from Harley roll Y6 in the British Museum, with introd. by Sir G. Warner. 1928.

4035 No. 190. The bestiary, being a reproduction in full of ms. I i.4.26 in the university library, Cambridge, with supplementary plates from other sources, and a preliminary study of the Latin bestiary as current in England, ed. M. R. James. 1928.

4036 No. 191. Marvels of the east. A full reproduction of the three known [ms.] copies [of the 11th and 12th cent.], with introd. and notes by M. R. James. Folio. 1929.

4037 No. 192. The work of W. de Brailes, an English illuminator of the 13th cent., by S. C. Cockerell. Folio. 1930.

4038 No. 193. The double bottom or twin-hulled ship of Sir William Petty, ed. the Marquess of Lansdowne. 1931.

4039 No. 194. Letters of Edward, Prince of Wales, 1304–5, ed. Hilda Johnstone. 1931.

4040 No. 195. Le chanson de Roland. Reproduction phototypique du manuscrit Digby 23 de la Bodleian Library d'Oxford, éditée avec un avant-propos par le comte Alexandre de Laborde; étude paléographique de Ch. Samaran. 1932.

4041 No. 196. The Dublin apocalypse, ed. M. R. James. 1932.

4042 No. 198. John Locke. Directions concerning education, being the first draft of his *Thoughts concerning Education* now printed from Additional ms. 38771 in the British Museum, with introd. by F. G. Kenyon. 1933.

ROYAL ANTHROPOLOGICAL INSTITUTE OF GREAT BRITAIN AND IRELAND

Founded 1871, as the Anthropological Institute of Great Britain and Ireland, for the promotion of the study of the science of man, by the amalgamation of the Anthropological Society of London and the Ethnological Society of London. Title changed to the above form in 1907.

Journal, vols. 31–63 (1901–33):

4043 Vol. 31.

  a A collection of palaeolithic implements from Savernake, by E. Willet.

4044 Vol. 32.

  a The oldest bronze-age ceramic type in Britain: its close analogies on the Rhine; its probable origin in central Europe, by J. Abercromby.

4045 Vol. 33.

  a A recent discovery of palaeolithic implements in Ipswich, by Nina F. Layard. [Reports on further excavations at Ipswich occur in vols. 34 and 36]

  b Skulls from the Danes' graves, Driffield [Yorks.], by W. Wright.

4046 Vol. 35.

  a The chronology of prehistoric glass beads and associated ceramic types in Britain, by J. Abercromby.

  b The origin of 'eolithic' flints by natural causes, especially by the foundering of drifts, by S. H. Warren.

  c Notes on a recently discovered British camp near Wallington, by N. F. Robarts.

4047 Vol. 36.

  a Copper and its alloys in prehistoric times, by W. Gowland.

4048 Vol. 37.

a A series of skulls, collected by John E. Pritchard, from a Carmelite burying-ground in Bristol, by J. Beddoe.

4049 Vol. 38.

a Anthropology in the 18th cent., by D. J. Cunningham.
b Report on the Hythe crania, by F. G. Parsons.

4050 Vol. 39.

a Deneholes and other chalk excavations: their origin and uses, by J. W. Hayes.
b Patrick Cotter [d. 1806], the Bristol giant, by E. Fawcett.

4051 Vol. 40.

a Some eoliths from Dewlish [Dors.] and the question of origin, by C. J. Grist.
b The arrival of man in Britain in the pleistocene age, by W. B. Dawkins.
c Report on the Rothwell [near Kettering] crania, by F. G. Parsons.

4052 Vol. 41.

a Cup- and ring-markings: their origin and significance, by H. J. Dukinfield Astley.
b Some Saxon bones from Folkestone, by F. G. Parsons.
c Prehistoric and aboriginal pottery manufacture, by J. W. Hayes.
d Classification of the British stone age industries, and some new well-marked horizons and cultures, by W. J. L. Abbott.

4053 Vol. 42.

a Classification of the prehistoric remains of eastern Essex, by S. H. Warren.
b Report on the skeleton found near Walton-on-Naze, by A. Keith.
c Metals in antiquity, by W. Gowland.
d An account of the discovery and characters of a human skeleton found beneath a stratum of chalky boulder clay near Ipswich, by J. R. Moir and A. Keith.

4054 Vol. 43.

a Coldrum [Kent] monument and exploration, 1910, by F. J. Bennett.
b Report on human remains found by F. J. Bennett in a megalithic monument at Coldrum, Kent, by A. Keith.
c Paviland cave: an Aurignacian station in Wales, by W. J. Sollas.
d Some bronze age and Jutish bones from Broadstairs, with type contours of all the bronze age skulls in the Royal College of Surgeons museum, by F. G. Parsons.

4055 Vol. 44.

a Discovery of a human skeleton in a brick-earth deposit at Halling, Kent, by W. H. Cook.
b Report on human and animal remains found at Halling, Kent, by A. Keith.
c The Cheddar man: a skeleton of late palaeolithic date, by C. G. Seligman and F. G. Parsons.
d Flint-finds in connection with sand, by R. A. Smith.
e Some recent work on later quaternary geology and anthropology, with its bearing on the question of 'pre-boulder-clay man', by A. Irving.
f The experimental investigation of flint fracture and its application to problems of human implements, by S. H. Warren.

4056 Vol. 45.

a The bronze age invaders of Britain, by A. Keith.
b Saxon graveyard at East Shefford, Berks., by H. Peake and E. A. Hooton.

4057 Vol. 46.

a Geographical distribution of anthropological types in Wales, by H. J. Fleure and T. C. James.
b Evolution of the earliest palaeoliths from the rostro-carinate implements, by J. R. Moir.

4058 Vol. 47.

a Some human and animal bones, flint implements, etc. discovered in two ancient occupation-levels in a small valley near Ipswich, by J. R. Moir.

4059 Vol. 48.

a Anthropology and our older histories. 1: A review of some archaeological and anthropological evidences, by H. J. Fleure. 2: A sketch of references to early movements of peoples in the older histories, by H. J. Fleure and L. Winstanley.

4060 Vol. 49.

a The occurrence of humanly-fashioned flints, etc., in the 'middle glacial' gravel at Ipswich, by J. R. Moir.
b A stone-axe factory at Graig-Lwyd, Penmaenmawr, by S. H. Warren.

4061 Vol. 50.

a Some early neanthropic types in Europe and their modern representatives, by H. J. Fleure.
b The occurrence of flint implements of man in the glacial chalky boulder clay of Suffolk, by J. R. Moir.

4062 Vol. 51.

a The Long Barrow race and its relationship to the modern inhabitants of London, by F. G. Parsons.
b Excavations at the stone-axe factory of Graig-Lwyd, Penmaenmawr, by S. H. Warren.
c Some early British remains from a Mendip cave, by L. S. Palmer.
d Description of a human cranium dredged from the bed of the river Trent, and a comparison of this with ancient and modern British skulls, by R. J. Gladstone.
e An early Chellean-palaeolithic workshop-site in the pliocene 'forest bed' of Cromer, Norf., by J. R. Moir.

4063 Vol. 52.

a The anthropology of the Chiltern Hills, by W. Bradbrooke and F. G. Parsons.

4064 Vol. 53.

a A sepulchral cave at Tray Cliff, Castleton, Derbys., by A. L. Armstrong, with a report on the skeletal remains by A. Low.
b The pleistocene deposits and their contained palaeolithic flint implements at Foxhall Road, Ipswich, by P. G. H. Boswell and J. R. Moir.
c Exploration of Harborough cave, Brassington, by A. L. Armstrong, with a report on the animal remains by J. W. Jackson.

4065 Vol. 55.

a A flint chipping floor at Aberystwyth, by R. Thomas and E. R. Dudlyke.
b Excavations at Mother Grundy's parlour, Creswell Crags, Derbys., 1924, by A. L. Armstrong, with a report on the animal remains by J. W. Jackson.
c Further discoveries of early Chellean flint implements in the Cromer forest-bed of Norfolk, by J. R. Moir.

4066 Vol. 58.

a Introduction of civilization into Britain, by H. J. E. Peake.

4067 Vol. 60.

a Megaliths and beakers, by H. J. Fleure and H. J. E. Peake. [The origins of megalithic culture]

4068 Vol. 62.

a The nomenclature of copper and its alloys, by T. A. Rickard.

4069 Vol. 63.

a The implementiferous gravels of Warren hill [Suff.], by J. D. Solomon.

Man: a monthly record of anthropological science, vols. 1–33 (1901–33):

4070 Vol. 2.

a Recent excavations at Stonehenge, with inferences as to the origin, construction, and purpose of that monument, by W. Gowland.
b Pigmy flint implements from the sand-beds at Scunthorpe, Lincs., by R. A. Gatty.
c Stonehenge: an enquiry respecting the fall of the trilithons, by A. L. Lewis.

4071 Vol. 3.

a Some ancient subterranean chambers recently discovered at Waddon, near Croydon, Surr., by G. Clinch.
b Note on the palaeolithic gravel of Savernake forest, Wilts., by C. Reid.
c Remarkable wells in the county of Antrim in the year 1683, as described by Richard Dobbs, esq., of Castle Dobbs, communicated by R. Casement.
d Stone circles in Derbyshire, by A. L. Lewis.

4072 Vol. 4.

a On the occurrence of stone implements in the Thames valley between Reading and Maidenhead, by Ll. Treacher.
b [The megalithic monument at] Coldrum, Kent, and its relation to Stonehenge, by G. Clinch.
c Excavations at Caerwent, Mon., by T. Ashby.

4073 Vol. 5.

a An excavation in Kemerton camp, Bredon hill, by B. C. A. Windle.

4074 Vol. 6.

a Investigations at Knowle Farm pit [Savernake], by H. G. O. Kendall. [An account of palaeolithic implements discovered there]
b A correction [relating to the above] and a note on the gloss on flint implements, by H. G. O. Kendall.
c Flint supplies of the ancient Cornish, by H. G. O. Kendall.

4075 Vol. 7.

a Flint supplies of the ancient Cornish, by S. H. Warren.
b Note on some palaeolithic and neolithic implements from east Lincolnshire, by S. H. Warren.

4076 Vol. 8.

a Notes on excavations at Oliver's Camp near Devizes, Wilts., by Maud E. Cunnington.

4077 Vol. 9.

a Notes on a late Celtic rubbish heap near Oare, Wilts., by Maud E. Cunnington.
b A remarkable feature in the entrenchment of Knap hill camp, Wilts., by Maud E. Cunnington.

4078 Vol. 10.

a A mediaeval earthwork in Wiltshire [near Devizes], by Maud E. Cunnington.

b The pit dwellings at Holderness, by W. Greenwell and R. A. Gatty.
c A skeleton found in a gravel pit at Overbury, Worcs., by N. Devereux.
d Report on the exploration of the palaeolithic cave-dwelling known as La Cotte, St. Brelade, Jersey, by E. T. Nicolle and J. Sinel. [Contd. in vol. 12]

4079 Vol. 11.

a Additional notes upon the British camp near Wallington, by N. F. Roberts and H. C. Collyer.
b Report on human crania from peat deposits in England, by W. L. H. Duckworth and L. R. Shore.

4080 Vol. 12.

a Excavation of a cave containing Mousterian implements near La Cotte de St. Brelade, Jersey, by R. R. Marett and G. F. B. De Gruchy.
b The discovery of a skeleton and 'drinking cup' at Avebury, by Maud E. Cunnington.

4081 Vol. 13.

a Excavations on Beacon hill, Hants, in August, 1912, by C. L. Woolley, with a prefatory note by Lord Carnarvon.
b Description of vase found on Nunwell down, Isle of Wight, by O. G. S. Crawford, with a report on the associated cranium and femur, by A. Keith.
c Note on certain obsolete [household] utensils in England, by J. Edge-Partington.
d Pygmy flints in the Dee valley [Scotland], by H. M. L. Paterson.

4082 Vol. 14.

a Flint implements of Moustier type and associated mammalian remains from the Crayford brick-earths, by R. B. Higgins, with a note by R. A. Smith.
b Excavation of a barrow called La Hougue de Vinde, situated at Noirmont, Jersey, by R. R. Marett and G. F. B. De Gruchy.
c Standing stones and stone circles in Yorkshire, by A. L. Lewis.
d The striation of flint surfaces, by J. R. Moir.

4083 Vol. 15.

a John Batman's title deeds [1835, for property on the west side of Port Phillip, now including Melbourne, Australia], by Sir G. Warner and J. Edge-Partington.

4084 Vol. 16.

a A strange stone object from a bronze-age interment in Essex, by M. Christy.
b Discovery of some human bones, etc., of neolithic and later date, in the Ipswich district, by J. R. Moir.

4085 Vol. 17.

a The Piltdown skull, by T. E. Nuttall.
b Finger grips: an interpretation of worked hollows found on many surface flints, by Nina F. Layard.

4086 Vol. 18.

a Bronze and tin in Cornwall, by C. Reid.

4087 Vol. 19.

a A piece of carved chalk [possibly representing a woolly mammoth], by J. R. Moir.
b The latest prehistoric mare's nest, by Sir H. H. Howorth. [A correction of the above article]
c Killicks, by R. M. Nance. [The evolution of the anchor, with particular reference to west Cornwall]
d Posthumous deformation of fossil human skulls, by S. Hansen.
e A piece of carved chalk from Suffolk, by J. R. Moir. [An answer to the article by Sir H. H. Howorth above]

4088 Vol. 20.

a Stone circle, Eyam moor, by J. S. Wilson.
b Note on a stone mould from South Wales, by Maud E. Cunnington.
c An early neolithic 'floor' discovered at Ipswich, by J. R. Moir. [With a report on the non-marine mollusca, by A. S. Kennard and B. B. Woodward, and on the plants, by Eleanor M. Reid]
d An uncharted village in Cornwall [Mulfra hill, near Penzance], by C. E. Vulliamy.
e Notes on the recent discovery of a human figure sculptured on a capstone of the dolmen of Déhus, Guernsey, by T. W. M. De Guérin.

4089 Vol. 21.

a The date of rosette-stamped ware found in Britain, by Maud E. Cunnington.
b A recent discovery of rock sculpture in Derbyshire, by G. A. Garfitt.
c A remarkable flint implement from Piltdown, by Sir R. Lankester.
d A series of rostro-carinate implements not hitherto described, by J. R. Moir.
e A note on some brooches from Wiltshire, by Maud E. Cunnington.

4090 Vol. 22.

a Note on a long barrow in Wales [Llanigon, Brec.], by C. E. Vulliamy.
b An early palaeolithic flint implement from West Runton, Norf., by J. R. Moir.
c The red crag flints of Foxhall, by S. H. Warren.
d The ice age and man in Hampshire, by L. S. Palmer.
e Stonehenge: notes on the midsummer sunrise, by E. H. Stone.
f Remarks on Mr. Stone's paper on the date of Stonehenge, and on the dating of megalithic structures by astronomical means generally, by B. T. Somerville.
g Excavation of a long barrow in Breconshire, by C. E. Vulliamy.
h Stonehenge: notes on the midsummer sunrise: a reply [to B. T. Somerville's article], by E. H. Stone.

4091 Vol. 23.

a Two bone harpoons from Hornsea, E. Yorks., being the report of a committee of the Council of the Royal Anthropological Society.
b The discovery of an undisturbed [neolithic] midden and fire hearth at Chark, near Gosport, by J. H. Cooke.
c Further evidences of Maglemose culture in east Yorkshire, by A. L. Armstrong.

4092 Vol. 24.

a Man and the ice age [with particular reference to the Ipswich area], by J. R. Moir.
b Stonehenge: the Heel stone, by E. H. Stone.

4093 Vol. 25.

a Solutrean flint implements in England, by J. R. Moir.
b The purpose of Stonehenge, by E. H. Stone.

4094 Vol. 26.

a Stonehenge: the supposed blue stone trilithon, by E. H. Stone.
b Man and the ice age [with particular reference to East Anglia], by J. R. Moir.
c Britain during the last forest-phase, by O. G. S. Crawford.
d Stonehenge: concerning the sarsens, by E. H. Stone.
e The origin of the socketed bronze celt, by H. S. Harrison.

4095 Vol. 27.

a Stonehenge: concerning the sarsens, by E. H. Goddard.
b Report on the excavation of a bronze age tumulus at Dunstable, Beds., by C. D. Forde, with a report on the human remains found in no. 5 barrow at Dunstable, by G. E. Smith. [Contd. in vol. 28 by G. C. Dunning]
c New views on the 'Dawn Man' of Piltdown, by F. Frassetto.
d A note on proto-neolithic implements from the Chiltern Hills, by C. E. Vulliamy.

4096 Vol. 28.

a Deneholes or drainage pits and their relation to Grime's Graves, or first antler-pick period, by W. M. Newton.
b Excavation of an early iron age site at Knighton hill, near the White Horse hill, Berks., by S. Piggott.

4097 Vol. 29.

a The problem of the pre-Chellean industries, by C. E. Vulliamy.
b Excavation of an unrecorded long barrow in Wales [near Glasbury, Rad.], by C. E. Vulliamy.
c A remarkable object [possibly a sling-stone] from beneath the red crag [Bramford, near Ipswich], by J. R. Moir.

4098 Vol. 30.

a Note on pottery fragments from Essex and Alderney, by T. D. Kendrick. [Portions of 'bar-lip' bowls and their possible origins]
b Corn-customs in Wales, by I. C. Peate.
c A hand-axe from the upper chalky boulder clay [of East Anglia], by J. R. Moir.

4099 Vol. 31.

a The Helston calvarium, by L. H. D. Buxton.
b Discovery of a Saxon sword in Wales, by C. E. Vulliamy.
c An ornamented spearhead of the late La Tène period from the Thames at London, by T. D. Kendrick.
d Report on human skeleton from a depth of 13 ft. near Grosvenor Road, Westminster, by M. L. Tildesley.
e Further hand-axes from the Cromer forest bed, by J. R. Moir.
f The late bronze age in western Europe, by E. E. Evans.
g Note on the distribution of Romano-British and Saxon elements of population in Britain in the 6th cent., by T. C. Lethbridge.

4100 Vol. 32.

a A primitive transitional hand-axe from beneath the red crag [at Ipswich], by J. R. Moir.
b The Towednack gold hoard, by C. Hawkes.
c Notes on some flint daggers of Scandinavian type from the British Isles, by J. G. D. Clark.
d Celtic art in Britain, by E. Thurlow Leeds.

4101 Vol. 33.

a Mesolithic sites on the Burtle Beds, near Bridgwater, Som., by G. Clark.
b The breast plough [its use in Britain], by G. E. Fussell.

Occasional papers:

4102 No. 4. Description of the test specimen of the rostro-carinate industry found beneath the Norwich crag, by Sir R. Lankester. *P.* 1914.

4103 No. 7. The hill figures of England, by Sir Flinders Petrie. *P.* 1926.

4104 No. 9. Anglo-Saxon skull contours, by F. G. Parsons. [66 plates.] 1928.

ROYAL ARCHAEOLOGICAL INSTITUTE OF GREAT BRITAIN AND IRELAND

Founded 1845, in consequence of a schism in the British Archaeological Association [q.v.], for the encouragement of intelligent research into British antiquities and vigilant care for their preservation. 'Royal' was added in 1866.

Archaeological Journal, vols. 58–89[1] (1901–33):

4105 Vol. 58.

a The Gilbertine priory of Watton, in the East Riding of Yorkshire, by W. H. St. J. Hope.

b Recently discovered mural paintings in English churches, by C. E. Keyser.

c Hardham church, and its early paintings, by P. M. Johnston.

d Current archaeology. [Includes accounts of excavations of Roman remains at Caerwent, Verulamium, and West Wickham, Kent, and also of the remains of Romsey abbey, Hants]

e Parish churches of Northamptonshire: illustrated by wills, *temp.* Henry VIII, by J. C. Cox.

f Documents relating to the parish church of All Saints, Bristol, by E. G. C. F. Atchley.

g Current archaeology. [Includes an account of excavations at Silchester, 1900]

h The armiger, by E. M. Chadwick.

i The cairn and sepulchral cave at Gop, near Prestatyn, by B. Dawkins.

j Notes upon clay tobacco pipes of the 17th cent. found in Bristol, by F. G. H. Price.

k Current archaeology. [Excavations at Hayles abbey]

l Nottingham castle, by E. Green.

m A note on the arms of Colchester and Nottingham, by W. H. St. J. Hope.

n Saxon churches of the St. Pancras [Canterbury] type, by C. R. Peers.

o Wollaton and Hardwick Halls, by J. A. Gotch.

p Proceedings. Annual meeting at Nottingham, 1901. [Includes accounts of St. Mary's church and St. Peter's church, Nottingham, carved stones in Calverton church, the pictures at Wollaton Hall, the church of St. Mary Magdalen, Newark, St. Giles' church, Holme, and Bottesford church]

4106 Vol. 59.

a Mediaeval pottery found in England, by R. L. Hobson.

b Fonts with representations of the seven sacraments, by A. C. Fryer. [Contd. in vols. 70 and 87]

c Horse armour, by Viscount Dillon.

d Notes on some Nottinghamshire bells, by J. J. Raven.

e Current archaeology. [Includes accounts of excavations at Lewes priory, and Caerwent]

f Prehistoric horses of Europe and their supposed domestication in palaeolithic times, by R. Munro.

g Castle guard, by J. H. Round.

h Notes upon the signs of pawnbrokers in London in the 17th and 18th cent., by F. G. H. Price.

i Current archaeology. [Excavations at Silchester]

j Bigbury camp and the Pilgrims' Way, by W. B. Dawkins.

k The early potters' art in Britain [pre-Roman, Roman, and Saxon], by T. M. Hughes.

l Church of the Friars Minor in London, by E. B. S. Shepherd.

m Exchequer annuity tallies, by P. Norman.

n The Benedictine nunnery of Little Marlow, by C. R. Peers.

o An Elizabethan tazza belonging to the church of St. Michael, Southampton, by E. H. Goddard.

[1] Vols. 58–86 are also described as 2nd ser., vols. 8–36.

p The Premonstratensian abbey of St. Mary, Blanchland, Northumb., by W. H. Knowles.

q Two hoards of Roman coins found in Somersetshire in 1666, by F. Haverfield.

r Proceedings. Annual meeting at Southampton, 1902. [Includes accounts of St. Michael's church, Southampton, St. Cross hospital, Winchester, and Winchester castle]

4107 Vol. 60.

a Fonts with representations of baptism and the Holy Eucharist, by A. C. Fryer.

b The New Forest: its afforestation, ancient area, and law in the time of the Conqueror and his successors, by W. J. C. Moens.

c Claverley church [Salop] and its wall-paintings, by P. M. Johnston.

d English fortresses and castles of the 10th and 11th cent., by W. H. St. J. Hope.

e Armour notes, by Viscount Dillon.

f Pile structures in the Walbrook near London Wall, by F. W. Reader.

g Remarks on the primitive site of London, by F. W. Reader.

h A Roman lighthouse [at Garreg, on the Dee], by T. Ely.

i The king's pantler, by J. H. Round.

j Liskeard, Legio, by F. Haverfield. [The origin of the theory of the connection of the town with a Roman legion]

k Note on a wall-painting in Claverley church, Salop, by W. H. St. J. Hope. [An answer to the article by P. M. Johnston]

l Burnham abbey, Bucks., by H. Brakspear.

m Proceedings. Annual meeting at York, 1903. [Includes brief accounts of some of the glass in York minster and of buildings of historical interest in that city]

4108 Vol. 61.

a The Roman villa at Box, Wilts., by H. Brakspear. [With notes on objects found, by E. H. Goddard]

b College caps and doctors' hats, by E. C. Clark.

c Yorkshire plate and goldsmiths, by T. M. Fallow.

d Architectural account of Swalcliffe church, Oxon., by C. E. Keyser.

e Ransom, by Viscount Dillon. [Some notes on its use in the middle ages]

f Notes on some English paxes, including an example recently found in Ipswich, by Nina F. Layard.

g Historical traditions at Wells, 1464, 1470, 1497 [relating to the monument of Joan, Viscountess de Lisle, the visit of Edward IV, and the visit of Henry VII, respectively], by C. M. Church.

h A newly discovered English mediaeval chalice and paten [1527–8], by H. P. Mitchell.

i Notes on the abbey church of Glastonbury, by W. H. St. J. Hope.

j Proceedings. Annual meeting at Bristol, 1904. [Includes brief accounts of buildings of historical interest in Bristol]

k The early working of alabaster in England, by W. H. St. J. Hope.

l The college of Fotheringhay, by J. C. Cox.

m Barriers and foot combats, by Viscount Dillon.

n Pre-Roman roads of northern and eastern Yorkshire, by W. B. Dawkins.

4109 Vol. 62.

a Notes on the origin and uses of low-side windows in ancient churches, by H. B. Pim.

b Prehistoric London: especially concerning the late Celtic settlement, as represented in the Guildhall museum, by G. F. Lawrence.

c The rack [and its use, and other forms of torture, with names of sufferers in the 16th cent.], by Viscount Dillon.

d Armour in wills, by Viscount Dillon.

e The characteristics and classification of the church towers of Somerset, by R. P. Brereton.

f Notes on a sculptured tympanum at Kingswinford church, Staffs., and other early representations in England of St. Michael the archangel, by C. E. Keyser.

g Symbolism in Norman sculpture at Quenington, Glos., by Josephine Knowles.

h Supplementary notes on the Norman tympana at Quenington church, by C. E. Keyser.

i Shorthampton chapel [Oxon.], and its wall-paintings, by P. M. Johnston.

j Sir William Dugdale [1605–85], Garter, by E. Brabrook.

k Proceedings. Annual meeting at Tunbridge Wells, 1905. [Includes a brief account of Bodiam castle]

l The Lippen wood Roman villa, West Meon, Hants: report of preliminary excavations, May–Aug. 1905, by A. M. Williams. [Further articles in vol. 64]

m Notes on fibulae, by F. Haverfield. 1: Further examples of Aucissa. 2: Shield shaped fibulae.

n Notes on the nave of Chepstow parish church, by C. Lynam.

4110 Vol. 63.

a The great ford across the lower Thames: (a) the extensive line of British stakes protecting the ford across the Thames at Brentford, (b) did Caesar cross here?, (c) were the Coway stakes in existence B.C.?, by M. Sharpe.

b Origine anglaise du style flamboyant français, par C. Enlart.

c Notes on fonts, by A. C. Fryer. A: Additional notes on leaden fonts. B: Additional notes on fonts with representations of the seven sacraments.

d The 11th-cent. east-ends of St. Augustine's, Canterbury, and St. Mary's, York, by J. Bilson.

e Excavations [of a Roman settlement] in Hayling island, by T. Ely.

f The Cistercian abbey of Beaulieu, in the county of Southampton, by W. H. St. J. Hope and H. Brakspear.

g Notes on Worcestershire bell-founders, by H. B. Walters.

h Notes on the effigy of John Caperon, rector of Rendlesham [1349–75], by A. C. Fryer.

i The evolution of Worcester, by J. W. Willis Bund.

j The making of Place house at Titchfield, near Southampton, in 1538, by W. H. St. J. Hope.

k Proceedings. Annual meeting at Worcester, 1906.

4111 Vol. 64.

a The besague or moton [the identification of these parts of armour], by Viscount Dillon.

b The feather staff, by Viscount Dillon.

c A French purchase of English alabaster in 1414, by J. Bilson. [Text of two documents relating to a purchase by the abbey of Fécamp]

d Excavations [on the Roman site] at Corbridge-on-Tyne, by C. L. Woolley. [Further articles in vols. 65 and 66]

e A Roman bas-relief from Bremenium [now High Rochester, Northumb.], by R. Cagnat.

f The chronology of Henry II's charters, by J. H. Round.

g A day's excursion among the churches of south-east Norfolk, by C. E. Keyser.

h Illustrated notes on the church of St. Candida and Holy Cross at Whitchurch Canonicorum, Dors., by Edith K. Prideaux.

i Some alabaster sculptures of Nottingham work, by W. H. St. J. Hope.

j Proceedings. Annual meeting at Colchester, 1907. [Includes brief accounts of Colchester and of Hedingham church and castle]

k The town charters and other borough records of Colchester, by W. G. Benham.

l The destruction of Camulodunum by Boadicea, by H. Laver.

m The Essex Sackvilles, by J. H. Round.

n Traces of Saxons and Danes in the earthworks of Essex, by I. C. Gould.

o Church chests of the 12th and 13th cent. in England, by P. M. Johnston.

4112 Vol. 65.

a Consecration crosses and the ritual connected with them, by E. S. Dewick.

b The Stroud Roman villa, Petersfield, Hants: report on first season's excavation, 1907, by A. M. Williams. [Further article in vol. 66]

c Architectural notes on the chapel of the hospital of St. James, Tamworth, by C. Lynam.

d The evolution and distribution of some Anglo-Saxon brooches, by R. A. Smith.

e Holdenby, Northants.; its manors, church and house, by A. Hartshorne.

f Excavations on the site of the Roman fortress at Pevensey, 1907–8, by L. F. Salzmann.

g The Anglo-Saxon Chronicle, its origin and history, by Sir H. H. Howorth. [Contd. in vols. 66 and 69]

h The transition between the palaeolithic and neolithic civilizations in Europe, by R. Munro.

i The gun called Policy, by Viscount Dillon. [The use of dummy guns, with particular reference to the siege of Boulogne, 1548]

j Arms and armour in Shakespeare, by Viscount Dillon.

k The Tudor battle flag of England, by Viscount Dillon.

l Additional notes on leaden fonts: the Haresfield bowl, by A. C. Fryer. [Supplementary article in vol. 78]

m South Wales and the religious orders, by J. W. Willis Bund.

n Proceedings. Annual meeting at Durham, 1908. [Includes brief accounts of the cathedral and castle]

4113 Vol. 66.

a Chantry chapels in England, by P. Biver and F. E. Howard.

b Some account of the library at the Kepier school, Houghton-le-Spring [founded by Bernard Gilpin, 1574], by R. W. Ramsey.

c The gold chains, pendants, paternosters and zones of the middle ages, the Renaissance and later times, by A. Hartshorne.

d An outline of the history of gunpowder and that of the hand-gun, from the epoch of the earliest records to the end of the 15th cent., by R. C. Clephan.

e Notes on Durham, York, and Manchester in prehistoric times, by W. B. Dawkins.

f The architecture of the Cistercians, with special reference to some of their earlier churches in England, by J. Bilson.

g Haughmond abbey, Salop, by W. H. St. J. Hope and H. Brakspear.

h The symbolism of the crocodile in the middle ages, by G. C. Druce.

i The rood-screen of Moulton church, Lincs., by A. Vallance.

j Proceedings. Annual meeting at Lincoln, 1909. [Includes brief accounts of Somerton castle and of the churches of Tattershall, Navenby, Heckington, Sleaford, Long Sutton, Gedney, Holbeach, and Whaplode]

4114 Vol. 67.

a The priory church of St. Mary and St. Oswin, Tyne-mouth, Northumb., by W. H. Knowles.

b Tombs of the school of London at the beginning of the 14th cent., by P. Biver.

c Some examples of English alabaster tables in France, by P. Biver.

d Notes on some early crucifixes, with examples from Raydon, Colchester, Ipswich and Marlborough, by Nina F. Layard.

e Note on a bone crucifix found in London, and some others, by F. W. Reader.

f The military handgun of the 16th cent., by R. C. Cle-phan.

g Screens and roof-lofts in the parish churches of Oxford-shire, by F. E. Howard.

h Church plate of the diocese of Lincoln, by E. M. Sympson.

i The site of the Saxon cathedral church of Wells, by W. H. St. J. Hope.

j Building at Westminster abbey, from the great fire (1298) to the great plague (1348), by R. B. Rackham.

k The amphisbaena [dragon-like mythological animal] and its connexions in ecclesiastical art and architecture, by G. C. Druce.

l Proceedings. Summer meeting at Oxford, 1910. [Includes accounts of Dorchester abbey church, Ewelme hospital and church, the colleges of the university, the origin of mediaeval universities (with special reference to Oxford), Broughton church and castle, Bloxham church, and Burford church and priory]

m Proceedings. Autumn meeting at Westminster, 1910. [An architectural account of the abbey]

4115 Vol. 68.

a Fan-vaults, by F. E. Howard.

b A Roman villa near Henley, by T. Ashby.

c Ordnance of the 14th and 15th cent., by R. C. Clephan.

d Roman inscriptions at Bitterne [Hants] and Minster Acres [Northumb.], by F. J. Haverfield.

e White tawers, by A. Betts. [An attempt to explain the term]

f A sword-blade and a cinquedea [dagger] in the Ashmo-lean Museum, Oxford, by C. Ffoulkes.

g Notes on the Holy Blood of Hayles [given to the abbey by Edmund, Earl of Cornwall, 1295], by W. H. St. J. Hope. [A discussion of documents connected with its disappearance]

h Notes on the history of the heraldic jall or yale, by G. C. Druce and W. H. St. J. Hope.

i Crypts of the churches of St. Peter in the East and of St. George within the Castle, Oxford, by C. Lynam.

j Note on the tessellated pavements found at Medbourne, Leics., and in Broad Street, London, by A. H. Lyell.

k Proceedings at monthly meetings. [Includes papers by J. H. Wilkinson and Sir H. H. Howorth on Oliver Crom-well's head, later published as *The Embalmed Head of Oliver Cromwell in the possession of the Rev. H. R. Wilkinson*, 1911]

l [Norman colonies in] Glamorgan and Pembroke, by J. W. Willis Bund.

m Sanctuaries and sanctuary seekers of Yorkshire, by J. C. Cox.

n Registers of John Gynewell, bishop of Lincoln, for the years 1347-50, by A. Hamilton Thompson. [Appendix 1: Comparative tables of institutions in the various arch-deaconries and deaneries of Lincoln diocese, 23 Sept. 1347-31 Dec. 1350. Appendix 2: List of benefices vacated by death in Lincoln diocese, 25 Mar. 1349-24 Mar. 1350. Appendix 3: Table of all institutions in Lincoln diocese from 25 Mar. 1349 to 24 Mar. 1350]

o The Confessor's shrine in Westminster abbey church, by W. R. Lethaby.

p Proceedings. Summer meeting at Cardiff, 1911. [Includes accounts of Cardiff castle, Llandaff cathedral, the stone cross slabs of Glamorgan, St. Donat's castle, Llantwit Major church, Ewenny priory, Caldey priory, Carew castle, and of the bishop's palace and the cathedral, St. David's]

q Proceedings. Autumn meeting at Westminster, 1911. [An account of the abbey by W. H. St. J. Hope]

4116 Vol. 69.

a The figure-sculpture of the west front of Exeter cathedral church, by Edith K. Prideaux.

b Inlaid tiles of Westminster abbey, by P. B. Clayton.

c Suit of armour [belonging to Henry VIII] in the Tower of London, by Viscount Dillon.

d An outfit for the profession of an Austin canoness at Lacock, Wilts., in 1395, and other memoranda, by W. G. Clark-Maxwell.

e Accounts of the constables of the village of Stathern, Leics. [1630-49], transcribed and ed. E. L. Guilford.

f Extracts from the documentary history of the Tower of London [c. 1087-1532], by H. Sands. [Contd. in vol. 70]

g Notes on the development of the Tower of London, [c. 1087-1532], by C. R. Peers.

h Caerleon, Caerwent, Gellygaer, and Cardiff castle, by J. Ward.

i Sources of error in assigning objects found in sands and gravels to the age of those deposits, with special reference to the so-called eoliths, by T. McK. Hughes.

j Proceedings. Spring meeting at the Tower of London, 1912. [With a brief account of its structure]

k Monumental effigies sculptured by Nicholas Stone [d. 1647], by A. C. Fryer. [With a topographical index. Contd. in vol. 77]

l Accounts of the iron-works at Sheffield and Worth in Sussex, 1546-9, by M. S. Giuseppi. [With extracts from Miscellanea of the Exchequer and Exchequer Accounts Various]

m The caladrius and its legend, sculptured upon the 12th-cent. doorway of Alne church, Yorks., by G. C. Druce. [With an account of the legend concerning the caladrius, a prophetic bird, and various representations of it in mss.]

n The defeat of the ninth legion, A.D. 60 [by Boudicca], by T. D. Pryce.

o The Hunsbury hill [Northants.] finds [with particular reference to the iron currency-bars and the bronze brooches], by R. A. Smith.

p Proceedings. Summer meeting at Northampton, 1912. [Includes accounts of the churches of St. Peter, St. Sepulchre and St. Giles, Northampton; the churches at Geddington, Rushton and Rothwell; Liddington bede-house; Rockingham Castle; the churches at Raunds, Higham Ferrers, Rushden, and Lowick; Drayton House; Northamptonshire earthworks; Fotheringhay church; ancient roads and bridges in Northamptonshire; Brix-worth church and Cogenhoe church]

q Proceedings at monthly meetings. [The Corbridge excava-tions, 1912, by R. H. Foster]

4117 Vol. 70.

a The 15th cent. glass in the church of St. Michael, Ashton-under-Lyne, by P. Nelson.

b Excavation [on the site of a Roman villa] near West Marden, Suss., by T. Ely.

c An account of a flint factory, with some new types of flints, excavated at Peppard Common, Oxon., by A. E. Peake.

d Kensworth church, Herts., by W. G. Smith.

e Excavations [of earthworks] at The Buries, Repton, by F. G. Simpson and G. A. Auden.

f Gauntlets, by Viscount Dillon.

g English brick buildings of the 15th cent., by J. K. Floyer.

h Some examples of Nottingham alabaster-work of the 15th cent., by P. Nelson.

i Fonts sculptured by Nicholas Stone, by A. C. Fryer.

j Is Ruthwell Cross an Anglo-Celtic work?, by W. R. Lethaby.

k Painted glass of Exeter cathedral and other Devon churches, by F. M. Drake.

l Sir William Sharington's work at Lacock, Sudeley and Dudley, by W. G. Clark-Maxwell. [Sir William Sharington, d. 1553. Article also printed in the *Wiltshire Archaeol. and Nat. History Magazine*, vol. 38]

m Degradation and reduction from knighthood, by Viscount Dillon.

n Proceedings. Spring meeting at Windsor Castle, 1913. [With an account of its history and structure]

o The parish churches and religious houses of Northamptonshire: their dedications, altars, images and lights, by R. M. Serjeantson and H. I. Longden. [With an alphabetical list of Northamptonshire parish churches, and extracts from wills relating to them, *c*. 1510–58]

p Church architecture in Devon, by A. Hamilton Thompson.

q Proceedings. Summer meeting at Exeter, 1913. [Includes accounts of Forde abbey, Ottery St. Mary church, Exeter cathedral and guildhall, Devonshire civic regalia, Grimspound (Dartmoor), Crediton church, Holcombe Rogus court, Cullompton church, Bradfield House, St. Saviour's church (Dartmouth), Paignton church, Compton Castle, Torre Abbey, and Dartington Hall]

r Proceedings at monthly meetings. [Evidences of the use of a building unit or symbolical dimension, found at Glastonbury abbey, and in some other medieval churches, by F. B. Bond]

s Proceedings. Autumn meeting at Stonehenge and Old Sarum, 1913. [Includes accounts of Stonehenge and of Old Sarum castle and cathedral site]

4118 Vol. 71.

a Dudley castle, by H. Brakspear.

b The last days of the Roman wall [in the 5th cent. A.D.], by H. H. E. Craster.

c Great crosses of the 7th cent. in northern England, by Sir H. H. Howorth.

d Effigies in English churches attributed to Bernini, by A. C. Fryer.

e Nicholas Stone's school of effigy-makers, by A. C. Fryer. [Henry Stone, d. 1653, Nicholas Stone, the younger, d. 1647, John Stone, d. 1667]

f Pestilences of the 14th cent. in the diocese of York, by A. Hamilton Thompson. [Appendix 1: Institutions in the archdeaconries of York, Cleveland, East Riding, and Nottingham, from the autumn of 1347 to 31 Dec. 1350. Appendix 2: Institutions for the years 1361–2 and 1369. Appendix 3: Benefices vacated by death in the archdeaconries of York, Cleveland, East Riding, and Nottingham. Appendix 4: Institutions in the archdeaconry of Richmond, 1349, 1361, 1362 and 1369. Appendix 5: Institutions in the archdeaconries of York, Cleveland, East Riding, and Nottingham, from 25 Mar. 1349 to 24 Mar. 1349/50]

g The cloister of Southwark priory and other early cloisters, by W. R. Lethaby.

h Some examples of English mediaeval alabaster-work, by P. Nelson. ['Some further examples' in vol. 74]

i Three pre-Reformation fonts in London [St. Dunstan's, Stepney, St. Bartholomew-the-Great, Smithfield, and St. Ethelreda, Ely Place], by A. C. Fryer.

j The author of the Bayeux embroidery, by W. Tavernier.

k Proceedings. Spring meeting in London, 1914. Visit to the churches of St. Bartholomew-the-Great, St. Helen, Bishopsgate, St. Katherine Cree, and to Southwark cathedral.

l Heraldry and sculptures of the vault of the Divinity School at Oxford, by W. H. St. J. Hope. [With a descriptive list of bosses on the vault]

m An illuminated pedigree of the Ferrers family, made in 1612, and presented to the Worshipful Company of Farriers in that year, by R. Garraway Rice.

n The construction of mediaeval roofs, by F. E. Howard.

o An early 17th-cent. silver-mounted wooden bowl; with some notes on an old City company [the company of Merchants of Muscovia, afterwards the Russia company], by H. D. Ellis.

p Proceedings. Summer meeting at Derby, 1914. [Includes accounts of the Romano-British town of Wall or Letocetum, Lichfield cathedral, Tutbury church and castle, Wingfield manor house, the churches at Sawley and Morley, Croxden Abbey, Wootton Lodge, the churches at Norbury and Ashbourne, Repton priory, the churches at Melbourne and Breedon, Arbor Low earthwork, Haddon Hall, Tideswell church, Bolsover Hall and Hardwick Hall]

4119 Vol. 72.

a Carvings of mediaeval musical instruments in Exeter cathedral church, by Edith K. Prideaux.

b Archbishop Roger's cathedral at York and its stained glass, by W. R. Lethaby. [Roger of Pont L'Evêque, archbishop of York, 1154–81]

c The Codex Amiantinus [*c*. 716 A.D.]: its history and importance, by Sir H. Howorth.

d A procession of Queen Elizabeth to Blackfriars [1600, for the marriage of Anne Russell to Lord Herbert], by Viscount Dillon. [An identification of the personages in the painting of the event]

e The Chesterfield armour in the Metropolitan Museum of Art, New York, by Viscount Dillon.

f The Romano-British names of Ravenglass and Borrans (Muncaster and Ambleside), by F. J. Haverfield. [An attempt to define Iter X in the Antonine itinerary]

g Some abnormal and composite human forms in English church architecture, by G. C. Druce.

h The Vallum [and Hadrian's Wall], by R. H. Forster.

i Some Roman roads in the South Downs, by A. H. Allcroft.

j The will of Master William Doune, archdeacon of Leicester [d. 1361], by A. Hamilton Thompson.

k Merton parish church, by P. M. Johnston.

4120 Vol. 73.

a The chronicle of John of Worcester, previously assigned to Florence of Worcester, by Sir H. H. Howorth.

b Was the Anglo-Saxon an artist?, by G. B. Brown.

c Pre-Norman churches and sepulchral monuments of Nottinghamshire, by A. Du B. Hill.

d The Warwick effigy [of Richard Beauchamp, Earl of Warwick, d. 1439], by Viscount Dillon.

e A monumental effigy [in St. Michael's church, Chenies, Bucks.] of Bridget, Countess of Bedford [d. 1600], by A. C. Fryer.

f An ambassador to Russia in the early 17th cent. [Richard Lee, d. 1610], by Viscount Dillon.

4121 Vol. 74.

a The Norman school and the beginnings of Gothic architecture. Two octopartite vaults: Montvilliers [abbey of Benedictine nuns, Normandy] and Canterbury [cathedral], by J. Bilson.

b The first castle of William de Warrenne [first Earl of Surrey, d. 1088, at Lewes], by A. H. Allcroft.

c The evidence of Saxon land charters on the ancient road-system of Britain, by G. B. Grundy.

d A Purbeck marble effigy of an abbot of Ramsey of the 13th cent., by P. Nelson.

e The perjury [of Harold] at Bayeux, by W. R. Lethaby. [An interpretation of the Bayeux tapestry]

f Notes on colleges of secular canons in England, by A. Hamilton Thompson. [Appendix: The statutes of the new collegiate church of St. Mary, Leicester, 1355–6 and 1490–1]

4122 Vol. 75.

a Roman Leicester, by F. J. Haverfield. [Appendix 1: The Roman name of Leicester and the derivation of the name 'Leicester'. Appendix 2: List of Roman pavements and other structures found in Leicester]

b Some painted glass [early 16th cent.] from a house at Leicester, by G. McN. Rushforth.

c The ancient highways and tracks of Wiltshire, Berkshire and Hampshire, and the Saxon battlefields of Wiltshire, by G. B. Grundy.

d Notes on some family relics of the Jacobite rebellion, 1745 [relating to Captain Robert Blake, d. 1802], by V. B. Crowther-Beynon.

e Late mediaeval sculpture from the church of St. Peter, Tiverton: its testimony to the art of the early 16th cent. in England, by Edith K. Prideaux.

f Statutes of the college of St. Mary and All Saints, Fotheringhay, by A. Hamilton Thompson. [Full Latin text]

g English alabasters of the embattled type, by P. Nelson.

4123 Vol. 76.

a The elephant in mediaeval legend and art, by G. C. Druce.

b Inscriptions upon mediaeval bells, by A. H. F. Boughey.

c Earliest type of English alabaster panel carvings, by P. Nelson.

d The Roman circus in Britain: some new identifications, by A. H. Allcroft.

e Some 15th cent. English alabaster panels, by P. Nelson.

f The Virgin triptych [English alabaster-work, *c*. 1430] at Danzig, by P. Nelson.

g Saxon land charters of Wiltshire, by G. B. Grundy. [Contd. in vol. 77]

h Proceedings. Autumn meeting at St. Albans, 1919.

4124 Vol. 77.

a Celtic place-names in England, by O. G. S. Crawford.

b The palace or manor-house of the bishops of Rochester at Bromley, Kent, with some notes on their early residences, by P. Norman.

c English mediaeval alabaster carvings in Iceland and Denmark, by P. Nelson.

d 'Groma': the ancient land-surveying instrument, by F. Tandy, from notes supplied by Dr. M. Della Corte.

e Some unpublished English mediaeval alabaster carvings, by P. Nelson.

f The circle and the cross, by A. H. Allcroft. [An attempt to solve the problem of the derivation of the word 'church'. Contd. in vols. 78–85]

g Proceedings. Summer meeting at Devizes, 1920. [Includes accounts of Stonehenge, Bishops Cannings church, Wansdyke, the circles, church and manor house at Avebury, Silbury hill, and the churches at Edington and Steeple Ashton]

4125 Vol. 78.

a Notes on the incised effigies of Derbyshire and Staffordshire, by A. Oliver. [Appendix 1: Heraldry of the effigies.

Appendix 2: List of the effigies. Appendix 3: Persons represented by the effigies]

b Place-names, by O. G. S. Crawford.

c Saxon land charters of Hampshire with notes on place and field names, by G. B. Grundy. [Contd. in vols. 81, 83, and 84]

d Cocking, Suss., and its church, by P. M. Johnston.

e Ancient burial-places: a suggestion, by T. Cyriax. [The possible motives behind the structure of neolithic tombs]

f The pre-Conquest church at Lydd, Kent, by F. C. Elliston-Erwood.

g An interdict on Dover, 1298–9, by Rose Graham.

h The stall work of Bristol cathedral, by Mary P. Perry.

i Dwellers in Wiltshire in prehistoric times, by Sir W. B. Dawkins.

j Some evidences of the defences of Roman Gloucester [Glevum], by St. C. Baddeley.

k The mediaeval marriage market, by C. Moor.

l Lines of communication and their relation in pre-Roman times to the valleys of tributaries of the Humber, by E. K. Clark.

m Proceedings. Summer meeting at Gloucester, 1921. [Includes accounts of Gloucester cathedral, Deerhurst priory church, Tewkesbury abbey church and domestic architecture, Bredon church, Flaxley abbey, Chedworth Roman villa, Uley Bury tumulus and camp, and Gloucester cathedral glass]

4126 Vol. 79.

a Bardney abbey [Lincs.], by H. Brakspear.

b Roman mausolea of the 'cart-wheel' type [and an example of one excavated on Mersea Island, Essex], by A. W. Clapham.

c Durham cathedral: the chronology of its vaults, by J. Bilson.

d Notes on the mechanism of clocks, by W. E. Miller.

e The periodic plagues of the second half of the 14th cent. and their effects on the art of glass-painting, by J. A. Knowles.

f Proceedings. Summer meeting at Ripon, 1922. [Includes accounts of Ripon minster, Jervaulx abbey, Wensley church, Bedale church, Patrick Brompton church, Fountains abbey, and Tanfield church]

g Proceedings. Autumn meeting at Dartford, 1922.

4127 Vol. 80.

a Alabaster tombs of the Gothic period, by A. Gardner. [With a list of examples of alabaster effigies]

b The Grey friars of Greenwich [established 1482], by A. R. Martin. [Appendix: Extracts from wills referring to the Greenwich friars 1482–1534]

c English brick buildings, Henry VII–VIII, by J. K. Floyer.

d Proceedings. Summer meeting at Norwich, 1923. [Includes brief accounts of Wymondham abbey church, Castleacre earthworks, church, and priory, and of the churches of Attleborough, Ranworth, Sall, Cley, Barton Turf, Tunstead, Worstead, and Trunch]

4128 Vol. 81.

a The relation of the prehistoric to the pleistocene and historic periods, by Sir W. B. Dawkins.

b Pre-Reformation vestments in Catholic churches in Monmouthshire, by R. H. D'Elboux.

c Church screens of Dorset, by E. T. Long.

d Proceedings. Summer meeting at Winchester, 1924. [Includes accounts of Winchester cathedral church and its history, Romsey abbey, Roman Winchester, St. Cross hospital, Winchester College, Portchester, the medieval religious houses of Hampshire, Old Basing church and castle, Sherborne priory, and medieval Winchester]

4129 Vol. 82.

a The cult of Mithra in Britain and the Rhineland in the first century A.D.: evidence from tombstones for its place of origin, and its inter-relations with primitive Christianity, by W. J. Williams.

b Some unpublished English mediaeval alabaster carvings, by P. Nelson.

c The clothing and arming of the Yeomen of the Guard from 1485 to 1685, by C. R. Beard.

d Proceedings. Annual meeting at Newcastle-on-Tyne, 1925. [Includes accounts of the Chesters museum and its Roman relics, the Roman forts of Cilurnum (or Chesters) and Borcovicus (or Housesteads), Durham cathedral, Hexham priory church, Blanchland abbey church and monastic buildings, Alnwick parish church and castle, Iona and its influence on Northumbria, Bamburgh castle and parish church, Dunstanburgh castle, and St. Andrew's church, Newcastle]

e Proceedings. Autumn meeting at Leeds, Kent, 1925.

4130 Vol. 83.

a Pre-Conquest carved stones in Lincolnshire, by D. S. Davies.

b The legend of the Green Tree and the Dry Tree [and its treatment in mediaeval literature], by Miss M. R. Bennett.

c Some undescribed English alabaster carvings, by P. Nelson.

d The priory of Dartford and the manor house of Henry VIII, by A. W. Clapham.

e Two records of plate and vestments removed from Beaulieu abbey in 1399, by Rose Graham.

f The cathedral church of St. David's, by E. W. Lovegrove.

g Proceedings. Summer meeting at Birmingham, 1926. [Includes accounts of churches and other buildings of historical interest in the neighbourhood of Birmingham, Coventry, Warwick, and Kenilworth]

h Proceedings. Visit to Rochester. [Includes an account of the cathedral and castle]

4131 Vol. 84.

a The college of St. Mary Magdalene, Bridgnorth, with some account of its deans and prebendaries, by W. G. Clark-Maxwell and A. Hamilton Thompson. [With a list of deans and canons *c.* 1161–1545, and biographical notes upon the former]

b Architectural remains of the mendicant orders in Wales, by A. W. Clapham.

c Painted windows [early 16th cent. Flemish] in the chapel of the Vyne in Hampshire, by G. McN. Rushforth.

d Some additional specimens of English alabaster carvings, by P. Nelson.

e The choir stalls, Winchester cathedral, by A. W. Goodman and T. D. Atkinson.

f The order of St. Antoine de Viennois and its English commandery, St. Anthony's, Threadneedle Street, by Rose Graham. [Appendix 1: Inventorium bonorum et jocalium Sancti Antonii, 1499, with a brief glossary. Appendix 2: A note on some seals of St. Antoine de Viennois. Appendix 3: A note on documents relating to the buildings of St. Anthony's and the site, and some extracts from the documents]

g Proceedings. Summer meeting at Cambridge, 1927. [Includes an account of Ely cathedral and of numerous colleges and places in and around Cambridge]

h Proceedings. Autumn meeting at Canterbury, 1927.

4132 Vol. 85.

a Documentary evidence relating to the building of the cathedral church of Wells (*c.* 1186–1242), by J. Armitage Robinson.

b Notes on the earlier architectural history of Wells cathedral, by J. Bilson.

c The technique of stained glass, by F. M. Drake.

d Holes in the skulls of prehistoric man and their significance, by T. W. Parry.

e The Stantons of Holborn [monumental sculptors, 17th–18th cent.], by Katharine A. Esdaile. [Thomas, d. 1674; William, d. 1705; Edward, b. *c.* 1680]

f Socketed and looped iron axes from the British Isles, by H. N. Rainbow.

g Winstone church, Glos., by W. H. Knowles.

h Proceedings. Summer meeting at Shrewsbury, 1928. [Includes accounts of the abbey, castle, and churches at Shrewsbury, Wenlock priory, Tong church, Ludlow castle, Wroxeter, and of the 15th cent. chantry foundations of Shropshire]

i Proceedings. Autumn meeting at Westminster abbey, 1928.

4133 Vol. 86.

a The kingdom of Kent, by C. W. C. Oman.

b Rievaulx abbey: the shrine in the chapter house, by C. R. Peers.

c Roman lighthouses at Dover, by R. E. M. Wheeler.

d The Saxon-shore fortress at Dover, by E. G. J. Amos and R. E. M. Wheeler.

e The abbot's parlour, Thame Park, by W. H. Godfrey. [Part of the abbot's lodging of Thame abbey]

f Antiquities from the middle Thames, by G. F. Lawrence.

g Some mediaeval hospitals of east Kent, by W. H. Godfrey.

h Unusual forms of *terra sigillata* [or Samian ware], by J. A. Stanfield.

i The Dominican priory at Canterbury, by A. R. Martin. [Appendix 1: The site after the dissolution. Appendix 2: Valuation of the site in 1539. Appendix 3: Particulars for a grant to John Harrington, 1559. Appendix 4: List of documents relating to the Blackfriars]

j [Louis François] Roubiliac [d. 1762], by Katharine A. Esdaile.

k Gundulf's cathedral and priory church of St. Andrew, Rochester: some critical remarks upon the hitherto accepted plan, by F. H. Fairweather. [Gundulf, d. 1108, bishop of Rochester]

l Minster Court, Thanet, by P. K. Kipps.

m Proceedings. Summer meeting at Canterbury, 1929. [Includes a brief historical account of Canterbury and accounts of the cathedral, castle, St. Augustine's abbey, the Dane John, medieval walls, St. John's hospital, and various churches of the city, Dover castle, Richborough castle, the hospital of St. Nicholas, Harbledown, Roman Ospringe and Faversham, and Hythe church]

4134 Vol. 87.

a Walter Morgan's illustrated chronicle of the war in the Low Countries, 1572–4, by Sir C. W. C. Oman.

b Mattersey priory, Notts., by C. R. Peers.

c A contract to rebuild the chancel of Sandon church, Herts. [1348], by Rose Graham.

d Wansdyke, by Sir C. Oman.

e Wall-paintings of the 16th and early 17th cent. recently discovered in Bosworth House, Wendover, Bucks., by F. W. Reader.

f Mediaeval brass lecterns in England, by C. C. Oman. [Appendix A: Notes on the post-Reformation histories of some of the examples. Appendix B: The present condition of the lecterns. Appendix C: Mediaeval brass lecterns formerly in England and now lost. Additions and corrections in vol. 88] g The Belgae of Gaul and Britain, by C. Hawkes and G. C. Dunning. [Appendix 1: List of pedestal-urns in Britain. Appendix 2: List of bead-rim bowls in Britain]

h The Penyston seal, by W. J. Hemp.

i St. Henry of Finland [fl. 1150]: an Anglo-Scandinavian saint, by T. Borenius.

j Proceedings. Summer meeting at Bath, 1930. [Includes accounts of the history of Bath, the Roman baths, Bath abbey, Lacock Abbey, Corsham Court, Sherborne castle, abbey and hospital of St. John, Sherborne School, Glastonbury abbey, Malmesbury abbey, the bishop's palace and cathedral at Wells, Worlebury camp, the hospital of Chapel Plaister, Hazlebury manor, and Longleat]

4135 Vol. 88.

a The Cistercian order in Ireland, by A. Hamilton Thompson, A. W. Clapham and H. G. Leask.

b Continental affinities of British neolithic pottery, by V. G. Childe.

c Neolithic pottery of the British Isles, by S. Piggott.

d The date of the Lady chapel at Wells, by J. Armitage Robinson.

e The abbey of St. Mary, Malling, Kent, by F. H. Fairweather.

f A barrow at Dunstable, Beds., by G. C. Dunning and R. E. M. Wheeler.

g English brass lecterns of the 17th and 18th cent., by C. C. Oman.

h Miscellaneous notes concerning English alabaster carvings, by W. L. Hildburgh.

i A Romano-British cemetery at Baldock, Herts., by W. P. Westell.

j Proceedings. Summer meeting at Dublin, 1931. [Includes accounts of the history of Dublin and of its civic regalia, charters, and mss., Christ Church cathedral, and St. Patrick's cathedral]

4136 Vol. 89.

a The four Roman camps at Cawthorne, North Riding of Yorks., by I. A. Richmond.

b Notes on St. Anthony the Great [b. c. 250], by P. Flemming. [1: St. Anthony and English medicine. 2: St. Anthony and the pig. 3: St. Anthony in English art]

c Bigberry camp, Harbledown, Kent, by R. F. Jessup.

d Tudor mural paintings in the lesser houses in Bucks., by F. W. Reader.

e The long barrows of Lincolnshire, by C. W. Phillips.

f The Roman signal station at Goldsborough, near Whitby, by W. Hornsby and J. D. Laverick. [Appendix 1: List of coins found at Goldsborough, by H. H. E. Craster. Appendix 2: Human remains, by Sir A. Keith]

g Pottery from the Roman signal-stations on the Yorkshire coast, by M. R. Hull.

h Prehistoric Britain in 1931 and 1932: a review of periodic publications, by C. Hawkes.

i Proceedings. Summer meeting at King's Lynn, 1932. [Includes accounts of the history of King's Lynn, and of St. Margaret's church, King's Lynn; Castle Rising, Thorney abbey, Crowland abbey; the churches of Spalding, Whaplode, Holbeach, Walsoken, Wisbech, Walpole St. Peter, and Long Sutton; Marham abbey; Boston town and church; and Middleton Towers]

ROYAL ARTILLERY INSTITUTION

Founded 1838, to afford instruction and information for the officers of the regiment on all subjects of professional and scientific interest.

Proceedings, vol. 27–vol. 32, no. 3 (1900–5), *contd. as* Journal of the Royal Artillery, vol. 32, no. 4–vol. 60 (1905–34):

4137 Vol. 27.

a The strategic geography of Europe at the accession of Queen Victoria [1837] and in 1899, by T. M. Maguire.

b The last guns fired in anger in England [1745], by R. Saunders.

c Leaves from the diary of Capt. (afterwards Lt.-col.) A. R. Wragge, R.A., during the Crimean war, by Mrs. T. M. Maguire.

d The Arracan expedition, 1825 [in the first Burmese war], from the diary of an artillery officer [Lieut. W. C. J. Lewin], by J. H. Leslie.

e The Boer war, 1899–1900, by L. R. Kenyon. [Contd. in vol. 28]

f The Boer position at Magersfontein covering their investment at Kimberley, by G. F. MacMunn.

g A Heavy battery at the relief of Ladysmith, by C. E. Callwell.

h [History of] the Royal Military Repository [Woolwich, 1778–1900], by H. B. Stanford.

i The battle of Diamond Hill as it appeared from the 82nd battery, R.F.A., June 11th and 12th, 1900, by W. H. Connolly.

j The 2nd Brigade Division, Royal Field Artillery, in the Natal campaign, 1899–1900, up to the relief of Ladysmith, by J. A. Coxhead.

k The strength and cost of Cromwell's army in 1654, ed. C. Dalton.

l No. 4 Mountain battery, Royal Artillery, in the Boer war, 1899–1900, by C. A. Ker.

m Historical retrospect of events leading to the Boer war, 1899–1900, by F. G. Stone.

4138 Vol. 28.

a The Dickson memoirs, series 'A': 1294–1794; being a collection of manuscripts, letters, prints, books, maps, etc., gathered together by Sir Alexander Dickson, collated and annotated by R. H. Murdoch. [Contd. in vol. 29. Also published separately, 1903]

b Some notes on the corps of R.A. drivers, raised 1794, reduced 1821, by J. C. Dalton.

c Returns showing casualties and expenditure of ammunition in the Royal Artillery during the campaign in South Africa, 1899–1901.

d Contrasts in the conditions of warfare at the beginning of the 19th and 20th cent. and some deductions as to possible tactical formations for the future, by J. F. Cadell.

e Col. Sir Robert Barker, F.R.S., commander-in-chief in Bengal, 1700–73, by C. Dalton.

f Early artillery [13th–16th cent.], by T. M. Kough.

4139 Vol. 29.

a Narrative of a Boer taken prisoner at Taungs, on S.W. borders of Transvaal, during the war in South Africa, 1899–1900, by Sir C. Parsons.

b Returns showing casualties and expenditure of horses and ammunition in the Royal Artillery during the campaign in South Africa, 1899–1902.

4140 Vol. 30.

a Nelson and Napoleon: a criticism of sea power, by C. H. Wilson. [Napoleon's expedition to Egypt, 1798]

b Record of work carried out by the artillery branch of the head-quarters staff, South African war, 1899–1902.

4141 Vol. 31.

a Pack artillery in 1819, by G. F. MacMunn.

b An account of a visit to some of the battle fields of Natal, by F. Waldron.

c Two regimental institutions the Royal Artillery Institution and the Department of Artillery Studies], by J. R. J. Jocelyn. [Contd. in vol. 32]

d The campaign of Corunna: a sketch, by C. H. Wilson.

e Royal Artillery Mounted Rifles in South Africa [1901–2], by T. S. Baldock.

f Our earliest cannon, 1314–46, by H. W. L. Hime.

4142 Vol. 32.

a An epitome of the Afghan war, 1878–9 and 1879–80, by J. H. V. Crowe.

b An a count of the Royal Artillery regimental plate in the R.A. mess, Woolwich, by F. B. R. Toms.

c Extract from letter of Capt. John Charlton, R.A. [written 1809 describing the retreat to Corunna], by Sir C. S. B. Parsons.

d The north-west frontier of India [including an historical account], by G. F. MacMunn.

e A description, with illustrations, of the arms, orders, decorations and medals of Maj.-gen. Sir Alexander Dickson, Royal Artillery [d. 1840], by J. H. Leslie.

f The connection of the ordnance department with national and royal fire-works [16th–19th cent.], including some account of Sir Martin Beckman [d. 1702], Col. Henry John Hopkey [fl. 1706–28], and Sir William Congreve [b. 1828], by J. R. J. Jocelyn.

4143 Vol. 33.

a A brief summary of the Chitral campaign, 1895, by E. Nash.

b Retreat from Kabul, 6–13 Jan. 1842, by A. Keene.

c The Royal Artillery in the siege of Gibraltar, 1779–83, by J. A. FitzGibbon. [Contd. in vol. 34]

d The battle of Busaco [1810], by C. W. C. Oman.

4144 Vol. 34.

a Remarks upon the early history and dates of formation of the companies of Royal Artillery, 1705–57, by J. H. Leslie.

b Notes upon the origin, formation, and subsequent development of the Madras Horse Artillery, represented in 1907 by J, M, P, and R batteries, Royal Horse Artillery, comp. J. H. Leslie.

c The British artillery at Waterloo, June 18, 1815, by A. F. Becke.

d Remarks concerning the Royal Artillery at the battle of Talavera, July 27–28, 1809, by J. H. Leslie. [Contd. in vol. 35]

e An historical sketch of the battle of Maida [1806], by C. W. C. Oman.

4145 Vol. 35.

a Wreck of the Union-Castle S.S. *Newark Castle* on a voyage from Durban to Mauritius with troops 12 Mar. 1908, by J. C. Dalton.

b An old time drill-book [1690], by Sir T. P. Larcom.

4146 Vol. 36.

a Albuerra [battle, 1811], by C. W. C. Oman.

b Notes on the history of recruiting during the 18th cent., by A. V. Langton.

c Note upon the artillery units engaged at the battle of Waterloo, 1815, by J. H. Leslie.

d The application of the strategic advanced guard in the Waterloo campaign, 1815, by A. F. Becke.

e Old time gunnery [from a treatise on gunnery written in 1674], by A. A. McHardy.

4147 Vol. 37.

a Emoluments and expenses of the junior officer during the period of the 'long wars' of the second and third Georges, by H. C. C. D. Simpson.

b A short history of Kane's *List of Officers of the Royal Regiment of Artillery* [originally compiled and published by John Kane in 1815], by J. H. Leslie.

c The battle of Barrosa, March 5th, 1811, by C. W. C. Oman.

d Notes on the war in the Peninsula, 1808–10, including the Girón diaries (ed. J. Arzadun), by J. C. Dalton.

e The Crimea revisited, by H. T. Arbuthnot.

4148 Vol. 38.

a The battle of Fuentes de Onoro, May 3rd–5th, 1811, by C. W. C. Oman.

b Our 13th cent. gunpowder, by H. W. L. Hime.

c The tiger's den [being an account of the British capture of Seringapatam, 1799], by A. K. Hay.

d The Gold Coast Artillery Corps, 1851–63, by J. J. Crooks.

4149 Vol. 39.

a The date of the introduction of the tangent scale in the Royal Artillery, by Sir H. W. Barlow.

b Tradition in the Royal Regiment of Artillery and how it can best be preserved, by J. H. Leslie. [Includes short biographical accounts of various 19th cent. officers and accounts of various actions in the 19th cent. in which the Royal Artillery was engaged]

4150 Vol. 40.

a Cromwell as an imperialist, by J. A. Cramb.

b Ancient [18th cent.] anticipations of modern artillery material, by Sir H. W. Barlow.

c Guns and gunners: a brief review up to 1815, by J. H. Mitchell.

d Swedish medals granted to the Rocket brigade, R.H.A., for the battle of Leipzig, Oct. 16–18, 1813, by J. H. Leslie.

4151 Vol. 41.

a The inspection of warlike stores [including a short history of ordnance inspection], by 'Inspector'.

b The diary of the great European war of 1914[–16], by W. M. Ogg. [Contd. by F. C. Morgan in vols. 42 and 43]

c A visit to some of the battlefields of the Sutlej campaign, 1845–6, together with an account of the services of the artillery in the four battles of that campaign, by W. B. R. Sandys.

d The Grand Army and [Napoleon's projected] invasion [of England] in 1805, by C. H. Wilson.

4152 Vol. 42.

a Field Marshal Earl Roberts.

b Centenary of the battle of Waterloo. [A list of officers of the Royal Artillery present at the battle]

c A visit to the battlefields of Chillianwalla and Gujrat, 1849, together with the account of the services of the artillery in those battles, by W. B. R. Sandys.

d Some aspects of great campaigns: Waterloo, by R. G. Cherry.

e Some aspects of great campaigns: the Crimean war, by R. G. Cherry.

f The army and the nation [including accounts of the part played by the army in the civil war, 1642–7, and in the revolution of 1688], by F. G. Stone.

g An examination of 'The travels of master-gunner Edward Webbe' [reputedly] sometime chief master-gunner of the French army in the field [published 1590], by H. W. L. Hime.

4153 Vol. 43.

a An account of the battels, sieges, etc., wherein Lieut.-gen. Albert Borgard [d. 1751] hath served. From a ms.

in the Royal Artillery Institution library, by Sir J. H. Lefroy. [Reprinted from *Proceedings*, vol. 13, 1884]

b Remarks on the services of Lieut.-gen. Albert Borgard, by H. W. L. Hime.

c Jonas Watson, first lieutenant-colonel of the Royal Regiment of Artillery [d. 1741], by H. W. L. Hime.

d The work of the R.E. in the field [1914–16], by C. G. Martin.

e The great North Sea battle and its lessons [Jutland, 1916. Reprinted from the *Journal of the United States Artillery*, July–Aug., 1916].

f An intelligence report on the French frontier, 1775 [by J. C. Pleydell], ed. C. B. Thackeray.

g Personal recollections of Florence Nightingale in reference to her reforms for the soldier, by G. J. H. Evatt.

h The British army in Germany [during the war of Liberation], 1813, by H. W. L. Hime.

4154 Vol. 44.

a The minor campaign in East Africa [1914–17], by G. P. A. Phillips.

b Our artillery [including an account of the history of the regiment], by H. W. L. Hime.

c Two Ordnance Office episodes [17th cent.], by H. W. L. Hime.

4155 Vol. 45.

a The history and traditions of the Royal Artillery, by E. A. P. Hobday.

b Surveys of the English coast, 1779–93, from records of reports made by the Inspector of Royal Artillery on the coast defences of England, by A. E. Macrae.

c Ordnance on the allied front: developments in artillery during the war [1914–18], by J. E. W. Headlam.

d Actions performed by the artillery of the 5th Army [1914–18], by H. C. C. Uniacke.

e The taking of Jerusalem [1917], by a Battery Commander and F. R. Barry.

f The German [economic] invasion of England, 10th–16th cent., by F. G. Stone.

g With the Field Artillery from trench [November, 1917] to open warfare [April, 1918] on the western front, by W. H. F. Weber.

h The battle in Palestine, commencing Aug. 9th, 1918, as seen from the R.G.A. advancing in support of the left flank, by F. P. Hutchinson.

i Some old [19th cent.] gunnery experiments, by T. W. Saidler.

4156 Vol. 46.

a Five-inch howitzers ['F' battery] in Damaraland [S.W. Africa, 1914–15], by A. S. Mehan.

b Siege artillery in the 15th cent., by J. C. Coley-Bramfield.

c The work of the Heavy Artillery 21st Corps in Palestine, Feb. to Sept. 1919, by F. P. Hutchinson.

d A tactical study of the Field Artillery group in retreat [in France, Mar.–April, 1918], by W. H. F. Weber.

e Invention and development of the shrapnel shell, by A. Marshall.

f Artillery at Anzac in the Gallipoli campaign, April–Dec., 1915, by C. Cunliffe Owen. [See also correspondence in vol. 47]

4157 Vol. 47.

a The Cameroons campaigns, 1914–16, by A. H. W. Haywood.

b A history of artillery [including its history before the R.A. was founded and a history of the regiment 1716–83], by R. Flenley.

c Episodes during the battle-fighting on the western front [involving various units of the Royal Artillery], by Sir

H. C. C. Uniacke. [Contd. from *The Gunner* (old issue), Nov. 1919 ?]

d Some aspects of great campaigns: 1914 in the west, by R. G. Cherry.

e Gallipoli strategy, by C. H. Wilson.

4158 Vol. 48.

a Our artillery in Italy [1917–18], by A. G. Rolleston.

b The history of the Supreme War Council from its creation, Nov. 7th, 1917–Nov. 11th, 1918, translated by E. M. Hutchinson [from the *Revue militaire générale*, Feb. 1921].

c Artillery experiences of the campaign in Italy, Oct. 1917–Nov. 1918, by L. F. Garratt.

d Soldiering under John Company: an officer [Robert Bell] in the Madras Artillery 1779–1820, by Miss H. M. Poynter. [Reprinted from *The Pioneer Mail*, July, 1921]

e Military intelligence and incidents connected therewith during the war [1914–18], by Sir G. M. MacDonogh.

f Bombardment of the Hartlepools [co. Durham], 16 Dec. 1914, by L. Robson.

g Sidelights on Waterloo, by C. H. Wilson.

4159 Vol. 49.

a The northern blockade [of Germany, 1914–18], by Sir D. R. S. de Chair.

b Development of artillery tactics, 1914–18, by C. N. F. Broad.

c Reflections on the cavalry campaign in Palestine [1918], by G. A. Weir.

d A Field Artillery group in the general advance [Sept.–Nov. 1918], by W. H. F. Weber.

4160 Vol. 50.

a A Field Artillery group in the surprise [Oct.–Dec. 1917], by W. H. F. Weber.

b British Heavy and Siege batteries in France, Aug.–Nov. 1914, by A. F. Becke.

c The [Royal Artillery] regiment: some remarks upon its origin and early history, by J. H. Leslie. [Contd. in vol. 53]

d The Rock [of Gibraltar]: its connection with the R.A., by J. C. Dalton. [Contd. in vol. 51]

e Reminiscences of 40 years of peace and war [in the Royal Artillery, late 19th cent.], by R. Bannatine-Allason.

f Artillery equipments used in the field during the last 25 years [1899–1924], by Sir S. von Donop.

g The Royal Military Academy [1741–1923], by Sir W. Gillman.

h Coaching notes; with some memories of old days on the Woolwich coach, by G. H. A. White.

i R.A. officers' theatricals at Woolwich, 1822–1900, by J. R. J. Jocelyn.

4161 Vol. 51.

a The tale of a button [being the history of the design of the regimental button, reprinted from the *Royal Army Ordnance Corps Gazette*].

b [History of the] R.A. drag hunt, comp. M. H. Dendy.

c The [army] reforms of Haldane in 1906–7, by M. N. T. Gubbins.

d The north-western frontier of India today [including an historical account], by Sir G. F. MacMunn.

e The services of the Royal Regiment of Artillery in the Peninsular war, 1808–14, by J. H. Leslie. [Chapters 4–5: 1810–14. Contd. in vol. 53. Chapters 1–3 were published separately as pamphlets, 1908–12]

f The evolution of artillery in the Great war, by A. F. Brooke. [Contd. in vols. 52 and 53]

g Medals awarded to officers of the Royal Regiment of Artillery for service in the Peninsular war, 1808–14, by J. H. Leslie.

4162 Vol. 52.

a The battle of Romani [1915], by Sir G. F. MacMunn.
b 41 [Brigade], R.F.A., 11 Nov. 1914, by A. F. Becke.
c Our cannon at the battle of Cressy, 1346, by H. W. L. Hime.
d The stand at Le Cateau, 26 Aug. 1914, by C. De Sausmarez.
e The Bombay Horse Artillery in Persia, and the [Indian] mutiny, 1857–9, by J. C. Dalton.
f The story of the Sikhs and the recent troubles [1920s], by Sir G. F. MacMunn.

4163 Vol. 53.

a The passing of the [rank of] driver [in the Royal Artillery], by G. H. A. White.
b The story of a gallant fiasco, [the attack on] Walcheren, 1809, by J. C. Dalton.

4164 Vol. 54.

a [The British attack on] Buenos Aires and Monte Video, 1806, 1807, by J. C. Dalton.
b British conduct of war in the 18th cent., 1793–1801, by G. M. Orr.
c The 'Ross' collection [including various medals, weapons and other relics of Field-Marshal Sir Hew Dalrymple Ross, G.C.B., d. 1868, and General Sir John Ross, G.C.B., d. 1905], by J. H. Leslie. [Reprinted in vol. 7 of the *Journal* of the Soc. for Army Historical Research]
d 'N' battery, R.H.A., at the battle of Hyderabad, Scinde [Sind], 24 Mar. 1843, by G. M. Spencer-Smith.

4165 Vol. 55.

a N/5 R.A. in the Zulu war of 1879, by J. C. Dalton.
b Growth of artillery training [since 1860], by C. A. L. Brownlow.
c The battle of Cambrai, Nov. 20th–30th, 1917, by H. D. De Pree.
d E/B R.H.A. ['E' battery, 'B' brigade] at Maivand, 27 July 1880 [2nd Afghan war], by H. B. Latham.
e Military administration in the Palestine campaign [1914–1918], by W. G. Lindsell.
f The real British attitude towards Afghanistan [an historical account], by Sir G. MacMunn.
g [British capture of] Louisbourg 1745 and 1758, and historical restrospect, by J. C. Dalton.

4166 Vol. 56.

a 8th August, 1918 [battle of Amiens], by Sir A. Montgomery-Massingberd.
b [British siege of] Belleisle, 1761, by J. C. Dalton.
c The services of the Royal Artillery in the first Boer war, 1880–81, by J. F. de F. Shaw.
d The romance of the first Afghan war [1839–42], by Sir G. MacMunn.
e Lord Horne as an army commander [Henry Sinclair Horne, Baron Horne, d. 1929], by Sir H. Anderson.
f The Rocket Service [R.H.A.] and the award of the Swedish decorations for Leipzig [1813], by H. B. Latham.
g The Master-Gunner of St. James's Park [being the history of a military appointment, 1263–1929], by T. J. Edwards.
h The 'honour' titles of batteries in the Royal Regiment of Artillery, by J. H. Leslie. [Contd. in vol. 57]

4167 Vol. 57.

a The bombardment of the Hartlepools, Dec. 16th, 1914, by F. A. Yorke.
b A subaltern of artillery in the eighties, by Sir G. MacMunn.
c The development of artillery survey, by A. F. V. Jarrett.
d The Board of Ordnance [history of], by O. F. G. Hogg.

e General Sir John Lefroy, Colonel Commandant, Royal Artillery, 1817–90, by C. Ffoulkes.
f The conquest of Sind, by Sir G. MacMunn.
g Royal Regiment of Artillery: succession list of colonels commandant [1722–1930], comp. J. Sandilands.
h Bengal, Madras and Bombay Artillery: succession list of colonels commandant prior to amalgamation with the Royal Artillery, comp. J. Sandilands. [Bengal Artillery, 1824–58; Madras Artillery, 1833–53; Bombay Artillery, 1845–59]

4168 Vol. 58.

a The coming of the creeping barrage, by A. F. Becke.
b Colonel Thomas Lumsden, C.B., Bengal Horse Artillery, 1808–43: Woolwich cadet, soldier, traveller, envoy, by J. C. Dalton.
c The Afridi operations, 1930–31, by G. V. Dreyer.
d Oliver Cromwell, by R. P. Waller.
e The 38th (Welsh) Division in the last five weeks of the Great war, by H. D. De Pree. [Contd. in vol. 59]
f Townshend's campaign [in Mesopotamia, 1915], by C. O. Head.

4169 Vol. 59.

a Gallipoli revisited, by W. R. E. Harrison.
b The dawn of ordnance administration [12th–16th cent.], by O. F. G. Hogg.
c In the ranks of the Bengal Horse Artillery [being an account of the memoirs of Quartermaster-sergeant N. W. Bancroft, fl. 1837–97], by Sir G. MacMunn.

4170 Vol. 60.

a Marlborough's battlefields illustrated: Malplaquet, by A. H. Burne.
b The Waterloo batteries [showing the descents and modern designations of the Royal Horse Artillery Troops and of the Field Brigades, Royal Artillery, that were present at Waterloo], comp. A. F. Becke.
c Education and the army: a brief historical sketch, by A. L. Pemberton.
d Incidents of the past [including the Bombay and Bengal Horse Artillery in the Mahratta war, 1817–19; the Bengal Horse Artillery's march over the Hindu Khush, 1839; and various incidents in the Indian mutiny and the 2nd Afghan war, 1878–80], by A. S. Cotton.
e The Crimean campaign through the light of the Great war, by C. O. Head.
f Sir John Moore [d. 1809], by J. F. C. Fuller.

Other publications:

4171 The Forbes Macbean correspondence, being letters on regimental business to and from Forbes Macbean, R.A., 24 Feb. 1757–14 June 1779, ed. Sir H. L. Geary. [Published as supplement to *Proceedings*, vol. 28, 1901–2]

4172 The Wright letters, being a collection of letters written by Major Jesse Wright, R.A., and others, during the Duke of York's campaigns in the Low Countries, 1793–4, ed. F. A. Whinyates. [Published as supplement to *Proceedings*, vol. 28, 1901–2]

4173 Calendar of inscriptions upon monuments, tombstones, etc., relating to officers of the Royal Artillery. [Published in parts as supplements to vols. 27 and 29 of *Proceedings*, 1900–1 and 1903]

4174 The Dickson manuscripts, being diaries, letters, maps, account books, with various other papers of Maj.-gen. Sir Alexander Dickson, series 'C', 1809–18, ed. J. H. Leslie. 1905–12. [Ends 1813. For earlier material in this collection see no. 4138a]

4175 Catalogue of the Royal Artillery Institution library (military section). 1913.

4176 Accessions to the library (military section) of the R.A. Institution, since the publication of the catalogue in 1913. *P.* [1922?]. [Contains accessions up to 1921]

4177 List of officers of the Royal Regiment of Artillery, vol. ii: 1862–1914. New edn. 1914. [Vol. i of the new edn., apparently intended to supersede the pre-1862 portion of Kane's *List* (revised edn. 1899), was not published]

4178 The story of 'G' troop, Royal Horse Artillery, by H. M. Davson. 1914.

4179 The Royal Regiment of Artillery at Le Cateau, 26 Aug. 1914, by A. F. Becke. 1919.

4180 History of the 20th Divisional Artillery, 1914–19, comp. E. G. Earle. 1919.

4181 Narrative of the 5th Divisional Artillery, 1914–18, by A. H. Hussey. 1919.

4182 [1]A short history of the 27th battery, R.F.A., by C. M. Vallentin. 1919.

4183 History of the 91st (siege) battery, R.G.A., Dec. 1915–11 Nov. 1918, by W. F. Christian. 1920.

4184 A short history of the 72nd brigade, R.F.A., 1914–19, by J. W. Stirling and F. W. Rickey. 1920.

4185 29th Divisional Artillery war record and honours book, 1915–18, by R. M. Johnson. 1921.

4186 Some pages from the history of 'Q' battery, R.H.A., in the Great war, by A.H.B. 1922.

4187 The story of the Royal Regiment of Artillery, by C. A. L. Graham. 1928.

4188 The history of the Royal Artillery from the Indian mutiny to the Great war, vol. i: 1860–99, by Sir C. Callwell and Sir J. Headlam. 1931. [Vol. ii: 1899–1914, by Sir J. Headlam, was published in 1937]

ROYAL ASIATIC SOCIETY OF GREAT BRITAIN AND IRELAND

Founded 1823, as the Asiatic Society of Great Britain and Ireland, for the investigation of subjects connected with, and the encouragement of, science, literature, and the arts, in relation to Asia. 'Royal' was added in the same year. Absorbed the Society of Biblical Archaeology in 1919.

Journal, new ser., 1901–33 (33 vols. 1901–33):

4189 Vol. for 1903.
a Cup-marks as an archaic form of inscription, by J. H. Rivett-Carnac.

4190 Vol. for 1904.
a Index to Journal, 1889–1903.

4191 Vol. for 1910.
a Miscellaneous communications. The tomb [in Agra, India] of John Mildenhall [adventurer, d. 1614], by E. A. H. Blunt.

4192 Vol. for 1918.
a 'Jang Nafuskh' and 'The red thread of honour', by A. C. Yate. [The destruction, in 1840 during the first Afghan war, of a small British force commanded by Lieut. Walpole Clarke, and a Baluchi ballad composed upon the occasion, with an English translation by L. Dames]

[1] Not seen.

4193 Vol. for 1919.
a Graves of Europeans in the Armenian cemetery at Isfahan [Persia, including those of William Bell, d. 1624, English agent at the court of Shāh Abbās, and the Rev. Edward Pagett, d. 1703, fellow of Trinity College, Cambridge], by T. W. Haig.

4194 Vol. for 1922.
a The provision of funds for the East India Company's trade at Canton during the 18th cent., by H. B. Morse.

Other publications:

4195 Centenary volume of the Society, 1823–1923, comp. and ed. F. E. Pargiter. 1923. [Contains a brief history of the Society, 1823–1923, and indexes to *Transactions*, 1827–33, and *Journal*, 1834–1923]

4196 Index of the contents of the Journal, 1920–29. [1934].

4197 Index of the contents of the Journal, 1930–39. [1940?].

ROYAL CENTRAL ASIAN SOCIETY

Founded 1901, as the Central Asian Society, for the encouragement of interest in central Asia. Absorbed the Persia Society in 1928. 'Royal' added 1931.

Journal, vols. 1–20 (1914–33):

4198 Vol. 1.
a Sir Alfred Lyall and the understanding with Russia [the Anglo-Russian convention, 1907], by Sir H. M. Durand.

4199 Vol. 6.
a An old route to India [via Aleppo and Basra, and some early travellers thereon], by F. D. Harford.

4200 Vol. 7.
a The new Levant company [founded 1918, and its predecessor, 1581–1825], by Sir M. de Bunsen.
b Cyprus, by R. Mitchell.

4201 Vol. 8.
a Military mission to north-west Persia, 1918, by L. C. Dunsterville.
b How Sir Richmond Shakespear set free the Russian slaves at Khiva [1840], by J. Shakespear.

4202 Vol. 9.
a The British military mission to Turkistan, 1918–20, by Sir W. Malleson.

4203 Vol. 10.
a The Knights of St. John in Rhodes and Asia Minor, by G. Bagnani.
b Extraterritoriality in China, by H. B. Morse. [Reprinted in vol. 12 and in *Some Problems of the Chinese Republic*, 1927]
c The romance of Aden, by H. Wilberforce-Bell.
d Caspian naval expedition, 1918–19, by D. Norris.

4204 Vol. 12.
a Some early travellers in Persia and the Persian Gulf, by Sir A. T. Wilson.

4205 Vol. 13.
a Extraterritoriality in China, by H. G. W. Woodhead.
b Aden, by H. Wilberforce-Bell.
c Military operations in Transcaspia, 1918–19, by D. E. Knollys.

4206 Vol. 16.

a Some hitherto unpublished despatches of Capt. John Malcolm, His Britannic Majesty's envoy at the court of H.I.M. the Shah of Persia, Dec. 1799–May 1801 [addressed to Henry Dundas, later Lord Melville].

4207 Vol. 17.

a The Melville papers. Letters from Maj. John Morrison relative to Bengal and Persia [1783–5, addressed to William Pitt and Henry Dundas].

4208 Vol. 18.

a British and Russian relations with modern Persia, by Rosita Forbes.

b Weihaiwei, by Sir R. Johnston.

c What the surrender of extraterritoriality [in China] will mean to us, by Sir H. Fox.

d The Iraq treaty, 1930, by S. G. Vesey-FitzGerald.

ROYAL CORNWALL POLYTECHNIC SOCIETY

Founded 1833, as the Cornwall Polytechnic Society, to promote the advancement of science and of the fine and industrial arts and technical and general education. 'Royal' added 1835.

Sixty-ninth–Seventy-fifth Annual Report (1901–7):

4209 70th Report.

a Cornwall, the nursery of the steam engine, by H. Davey.

4210 71st Report.

a Address [on the development of mining, iron, steel and machinery in Britain in the 19th cent.], by Sir J. Alleyne.

4211 72nd Report.

a Ancient mining districts of Cornwall [Lelant, St. Ives and Zennor], by F. J. Stephens.

4212 73rd Report.

a Stone memorials in the west: who built them, when, and why? A new astronomical theory, by S. R. John.

b An early chapter in the history of Cornwall: Cornish and Egyptian monuments, by Sir N. Lockyer.

c Busts, paintings, etc., in possession of the Society.

Seventy-sixth–Hundredth Annual Report, new ser., vols. 1–7 (1909–33):

4213 Vol. 1 (76th–78th Reports).

a Address [on a mining engine set up at Rosewarne in 1763, and on the cavalry, artillery and infantry of Cornwall in 1806], by J. D. Enys.

b William Pennington Cocks [d. 1878, naturalist], by F. H. Davey.

c Cassiterides and Ictus—where were they?, by T. Peter.

d 'The coming of the saints', by E. Howard. [The first arrival of Christianity in Britain, with particular reference to Joseph of Arimathea]

e Index to Annual Reports, 66–75, 1898–1907, comp. F. H. Davey. [Index, 1896–1957, published 1960]

f Nevil Northy Burnard [d. 1878, sculptor], by F. H. Davey.

g History of the Cornish [mining] engine, by H. Davey.

h Boulton and Watt, by H. Fox. [Letters and extracts from letters received by Thomas Wilson of Chacewater, financial agent of Boulton and Watt, concerning the defence of their patents in Cornwall, 1794–1800]

i Cornwall and Brittany, by T. Hodgkin. [The Cornish migration to Brittany]

j Charles William Peach [d. 1886, geologist], by F. H. Davey.

4214 Vol. 2 (79th–81st Reports).

a Perran Round and the Cornish drama, by H. Jenner.

b Christian worship in St. Pirran's oratory in the 6th and 7th cent., by H. Jenner.

c Some historical and other notices of mining in the northern part of the parish of St. Agnes, by J. H. Collins.

d Portrait gallery of the Royal Cornwall Polytechnic Society. 1: Sir Charles Lemon, bt. [d. 1868, M.P.]. 2: Lord de Dunstanville [d. 1836, M.P.]. 3: Davies Gilbert [d. 1839, M.P., F.R.S.].

e History in Cornish place-names, by H. Jenner.

f Portrait gallery of the Royal Cornwall Polytechnic Society. 1: Sir Richard Rawlinson Vyvyan, bt. [d. 1879, M.P., F.R.S.]. 2: John Samuel Enys [né Hunt, d. 1872]. 3: Edward William Wynne Pendarves, M.P. [d. 1853].

g Dingerein and the Geraints, by H. Jenner. [The place, Dingerein, and the three Geraints, princes of Damnonia, in legends and early records]

h Alabaster carvings in the chapel of St. Michael's Mount, by H. Jenner.

i The hut clusters of Chysauster, by H. Jenner.

j Governors of St. Mawes castle, 1557–1847, by F. J. Stephens.

k Admiral Sir Richard Spry, 1746–75 [and the Spry family of Place, St. Anthony in Roseland], by F. J. Stephens.

l Portrait gallery of the Royal Cornwall Polytechnic Society. 1: John St. Aubyn, first Baron St. Levan [d. 1908, M.P.]. 3: Caroline Fox [d. 1871, diarist].

4215 Vol. 3 (82nd–84th Reports).

a Materials for a history of the church and parish of St. Crantock, by W. J. Stephens.

b Portrait gallery of the Royal Cornwall Polytechnic Society. 1: George Croker Fox [d. 1850]. 2: John Taylor [d. 1863, F.R.S., mining engineer]. 3: John Williams [d. 1849, F.R.S.].

c Historical synopsis of the Royal Cornwall Polytechnic Society for 81 years, 1833–1913, by W. Ll. Fox, with index by H. Fox. 1915. [Issued with 82nd Report]

d Tin and tungsten in the west of England [and the mine yields, chiefly in the 19th cent.], by J. H. Collins.

e Portrait gallery of the Royal Cornwall Polytechnic Society. 1: Charles Fox [d. 1878, scientific writer].

f Irish immigration into Cornwall in the late 5th and early 6th cent., by H. Jenner.

4216 Vol. 4 (85th–89th Reports).

a The dedication of churches [with special reference to Cornwall], by H. Jenner.

b Portrait gallery of the Royal Cornwall Polytechnic Society. 1: William Henry Edgcumbe, 4th Earl of Mount Edgcumbe [d. 1917]. 2: The Rev. John Rogers, canon of Exeter [d. 1856]. 3: Richard Taylor [d. 1883, mining engineer].

c The royal house of Damnonia, by H. Jenner.

d Celtic words in Cornish dialect, by R. M. Nance.

e Portrait gallery of the Royal Cornwall Polytechnic Society. 1: The Rev. Saltren Rogers, hon. canon of Truro [d. 1905]. 2: Leonard Henry Courtney, Lord Courtney of Penwith [d. 1918]. 3: The Right Rev. William Boyd Carpenter, lord bishop of Ripon, canon of Westminster [d. 1918].

f The dukes and earls of Cornwall, by H. Jenner.

g Ship-modelling as a craft [with particular reference to church-ships], by R. M. Nance.

h Portrait gallery [of the Royal Cornwall Polytechnic Society]. 1: Lieut.-General Sir Richard Hussey Vivian, bt., 1st Baron Vivian [d. 1842]. 2: Thomas Charles Agar

Robartes, 6th Viscount Clifden, 6th Baron Mendip and 2nd Baron Robartes [d. 1930]. 3: Sir Joseph Whitwell Pease, bt. [d. 1903, M.P.].

i Castle-an-Dinas [hill-fort] and King Arthur, by H. Jenner.

j The manor of Arwenack, by F. J. Bowles.

k Portrait gallery of the Royal Cornwall Polytechnic Society. 1: Sir William Henry Preece [d. 1913, F.R.S., electrical engineer]. 2: Sir John St. Aubyn, 5th baronet [d. 1839, M.P., F.R.S.].

4217 Vol. 5 (90th–93rd Reports).

a A Cornish oration in Spain in 1600 [made by Richard Pentry, member of the English college, Valladolid, on the occasion of Philip II's visit to the city], by H. Jenner.

b Folk-lore recorded in the Cornish language, by R. M. Nance.

c Robert Were Fox [d. 1877, F.R.S., scientific writer].

d The Rev. John Sterling [d. 1844, author].

e The Right Rev. John Gott, bishop of Truro [d. 1906].

f Falmouth and the Great war, by W. Ll. Fox.

g Mine and anti-submarine operations carried out during the [1914] war, off the Cornish coast, by E. J. Moseley.

h Carn Brea [and its prehistoric remains], by E. W. Newton.

i Cornish streams and bridges: a contribution to local topography, by C. G. Henderson.

j William Clift [d. 1849, F.R.S., first Conservator of the Hunterian Museum].

k Henry Charlton Bastian [d. 1915, F.R.S., physician].

l The mining coinage of Cornwall, by E. W. Newton.

m Boulton [d. 1809] and Watt [d. 1819] in Cornwall, by A. K. H. Jenkin.

n Augustus John Smith [d. 1872, M.P., lessee of the Scilly Islands].

o The Right Hon. Sir William Molesworth, bt. [d. 1855, M.P.].

4218 Vol. 6 (94th–97th Reports).

a War prisoners at Falmouth and district [from the 18th cent.], by W. Ll. Fox.

b The china clay industry [with particular reference to Cornwall], by J. M. Coon.

c War prisoners in Cornwall, by W. Ll. Fox.

d Some Cornish medical worthies, by J. H. Rowe.

e General notes on ancient mining in Cornwall, by F. J. Stephens.

f John Couch Adams [d. 1892, F.R.S., astronomer].

g William Philip Dymond [d. 1878, engineer and meteorologist].

h Some miscellaneous scraps of Cornish, by H. Jenner.

i Abandoned Cornish mines, by E. W. Newton.

j Commander James Liddell, R.N. [d. 1889], by W. J. P. Burton.

k Summary of the history of Perran foundry [1750–1850], by W. T. Harper.

l Tributers [in Cornish mining]: their uses and abuses, by A. K. H. Jenkin.

m Cornish inventions, by J. H. Rowe.

n Historical documents in the Duchy of Cornwall office, by R. L. Clowes.

o Jonathan Hornblower [the younger, d. 1815] and the compound engine, by R. Jenkins.

4219 Vol. 7 (98th–100th Reports).

a Cornish fellows of the Royal Society, by J. H. Rowe.

b Abandoned Cornish mines: the mines of St. Just, by W. Thomas.

c Topography of the parish of St. Keverne, by C. Henderson.

d The Robartes family of Lanhydrock, by J. H. Rowe.

e Michael Loam [d. 1871], engineer, by E. Loam.

f Ancient mining districts of Cornwall: notes on the geology, minerals and mines of the Liskeard district within an area of five to six miles, by F. J. Stephens.

g Swanpool mine [Falmouth district], by W. T. Hooper.

h Cornish foundries: what they have achieved [in the 19th cent.], by S. Michel.

Extra publication:

4220 The Royal Cornwall Polytechnic Society: a short summary of its work, during the first 100 years of its existence, by E. W. Newton. 1932.

ROYAL ECONOMIC SOCIETY

Founded 1890, as the British Economic Association, to promote the study of economic science. Title changed to the above form in 1902.

Economic Journal, vols. 11–43 (1901–33):

4221 Vol. 11.

a The Taff Vale Railway case [Taff Vale Railway Co. *v.* Amalgamated Society of Railway Servants, 1900], by M. Barlow.

b The new Companies Act, 1900, by M. Barlow.

c The Factory and Workshops Act Amendment Bill [1900], by Mona Wilson.

d Report of the local taxation commission [1901], by C. P. Sanger.

e Insurance of industrial risks, 1897–1901, by M. Barlow.

f The British salt trade in the 19th cent., by J. M. Fells.

g Economic effects of the Tramways Act of 1870, by V. Knox.

4222 Vol. 12.

a Relief of the poor in Jersey, by Beatrice Lander.

b Local authorities and the housing problem in 1901, by Lettice Fisher.

c A Derbyshire farmer's budget, 1723–4, by A. Hughes.

d Report on the manufacture of matches in Great Britain, 1897–1902, by G. H. Wood.

4223 Vol. 13.

a Early stages of English public house regulation, by C. M. Isles.

b The grainmilling industry: a study in organisation [from the end of the 19th cent.], by H. Macrosty.

c Some neglected British economists [late 18th and early 19th cent.], by E. R. A. Seligman.

4224 Vol. 14.

a The assize of bread, by S. and Beatrice Webb.

b Employment of women in paper mills [in the latter half of the 19th cent.], by B. L. Hutchins.

c Britain's place in foreign markets [1889–1901], by A. W. Flux.

d The latest chapter in the history of trade unionism [1888–1904], by H. B. L. Smith. [With a letter by J. M. Ludlow]

4225 Vol. 15.

a The Unemployed Workmen Bill [1905], by H. B. L. Smith.

b Robert Owen and co-operation, by F. Podmore.

c Report of the royal commission on coal supplies [1905], by J. Macaulay.

d The present position of the land tax [including a brief historical account], by A. Hook.

e Three Birmingham relief funds: 1885, 1886, and 1905, by F. Tillyard.

f Note on the statistics of the woollen industries [1865–1904], by A. L. Bowley.

4226 Vol. 16.

a The study of economic history, by L. L. Price.
b The 'Treasury Order Book' [established 1667], by W. A. Shaw.
c The report of the royal commission on trade disputes, by W. M. Geldart.
d Variations in the editions of J. S. Mill's *Principles of Political Economy*, by Miriam A. Ellis.
e The colonial lands of Natal, by R. Ababrelton.
f The progress of the small holdings movement [1890–1906], by R. Winfrey.
g Industrial organisation in the woollen and worsted industries of Yorkshire, by J. H. Clapham.

4227 Vol. 17.

a Evolution of an industrial town [Coventry], by C. H. d'E. Leppington.
b Correspondence of Ricardo with Maria Edgeworth [1822–3].
c Final report of the miners' eight-hour day committee [1907], by T. I. Jones.
d The present position of political economy [including an historical survey], by W. J. Ashley.

4228 Vol. 18.

a Report from the select committee on home work, House of Commons, 1907, by B. L. Hutchins.
b [On the authorship of] *An Essay on the Causes of the Decline of Foreign Trade ... Begun in the year 1739*, by E. C. K. Gonner.
c Report of the Central Unemployment Body for London [upon its work, 1906–7], by R. H. Tawney.

4229 Vol. 19.

a Trade unions in the tinplate industry, by J. H. Jones.
b The apprenticeship question [*c.* 1901–9], by R. A. Bray.
c The Patents and Designs Act, 1907, by G. Schuster.

4230 Vol. 20.

a Lot-meadow customs at Yarnton, Oxon., by R. H. Gretton. [See also 4232a below]
b The historical basis of English poor-law policy, by Helen Bosanquet.
c The transference of the worsted industry from Norfolk to the West Riding, by J. H. Clapham.
d Report of the departmental committee on the Employment of Children Act, 1903, by N. B. Dearle.

4231 Vol. 21.

a Women and unemployment [*c.* 1910], by Jeannette Tawney.
b The National Insurance Bill [1911], part 2: Unemployment, by W. J. Ashley.
c The government's scheme for insurance against unemployment [1911], by R. Lennard.
d Ricardo and Torrens, by E. R. A. Seligman and J. H. Hollander.
e Unrest among workpeople [and its late 19th and early 20th cent. causes], by J. G. Newlove.
f The Railway Conciliation scheme, 1907, and the report of the royal commission thereon, by W. T. Stephenson.
g The industrial evolution of a manufacturing village [Hebden Bridge, Yorks.], by S. C. Moore.

4232 Vol. 22.

a Historical notes on lot-meadow customs at Yarnton, Oxon., by R. H. Gretton.

b The depreciation of British home investments [late 19th and early 20th cent.], by 'a stockbroker'. [Contd. in vols. 23 and 24]
c Economic changes in the textile and dress industries of the United Kingdom [late 19th and early 20th cent.], by A. G. Doubt.
d The rise and fall of the indigo industry in India, by Asiaticus.
e The minimum wage, past and present, by E. Hubbard.
f A narrative of the coal strike [1912], by D. H. Robertson.
g Co-partnership in industry, by C. R. Fay.
h Some recent [20th cent.] developments of poor relief, by W. A. Bailward.

4233 Vol. 23.

a Towards the solution of the casual labour problem [a consideration of the Labour Exchanges Act], by F. Keeling.
b Comparative economic history and the English landlord, by W. J. Ashley.
c Finance of railway nationalisation in Great Britain, by R. A. Lehfeldt.
d The feeding and medical treatment of school children [a consideration of the Education (provision of meals) Act and the Education (administrative provisions) Act, 1907], by A. M. Carr-Saunders.
e Some factors affecting the incidence of the National Insurance contributions, by J. Cunnison.
f The Trades Board Act [1908] at work, by S. C. Moore.
g English town development in the 19th cent., by F. Tillyard.

4234 Vol. 24.

a The Leeds municipal strike [1913–14], by A. Greenwood [with a note by M. E. Sadler].
b The assessment of wages in the West Riding of Yorkshire in the 17th and 18th cent., by H. Heaton.
c An experiment in decasualisation: the Liverpool Docks Scheme [1912], by L. S. Woolf.
d A 17th cent. labour exchange [Threadneedle St., London], by W. H. Beveridge.
e Fluctuations in the [personnel of the] woollen and worsted industries of the West Riding, by S. Brierley and G. R. Carter.
f Rural factories in Wales [19th and 20th cent.].
g War and the financial system, Aug. 1914, by J. M. Keynes.
h The influence of the war [1914] on employment, by D. Henderson. [Contd. in vol. 25]

4235 Vol. 25.

a The analysis of a rural population [in Warwickshire, 1891–1911], by C. H. d'E. Leppington.
b Clothing the allies' armies [1914–15], by G. R. Carter.
c The law relating to trade with the enemy, by G. E. Toulmin.
d The early records of a great Manchester cotton-spinning firm [McConnel, Kennedy and Sandford, since 1795], by G. W. Daniels.
e Home industries in the Scottish highlands and islands, by G. B. Brown [with a note by W. R. Scott on Scottish rural industries, 1914–15].
f Non-parliamentary industrial legislation [i.e. by provisional and statutory orders, determinations, and bye-laws], by F. Tillyard.
g The coal strike in South Wales [1915], by G. R. Carter [with supplementary article by the same].
h The housing of the Scottish farm servant, by J. D. Smith.
i Some factory statistics of 1815–16, by J. H. Clapham.
j Valuation of Manchester cotton factories in the early years of the 19th cent., by G. W. Daniels.

4236 Vol. 26.

a Monetary difficulties of early colonisation in New Zealand, by H. D. Bedford.
b Women traders in medieval London, by Annie Abram.
c The Spitalfields acts, 1773-1824, by J. H. Clapham.

4237 Vol. 27.

a Industrial Ireland under free trade, by C. H. Oldham.
b Housing conditions in London [1916], by Helen Bosanquet.
c Industrial unrest [1917], by E. Cannan.
d Loans and subsidies in time of war, 1793-1914, by J. H. Clapham.

4238 Vol. 28.

a The wool trade in war time [1914-18], by Dorothy M. Zimmern.
b The bank restriction of 1797, by R. G. Hawtrey.
c Government [economic] control in war and peace, by A. C. Pigou.

4239 Vol. 29.

a The monopoly in alcoholic drink, by J. S. Eagles.
b The reports of the coal industry commission [under Mr. Justice Sankey], by H. D. Henderson.
c Notes on labour unrest [1919], by T. Wilson.
d Archdeacon Cunningham [d. 1919], by H. S. Foxwell [with addition by Lilian Knowles].
e The railway strike [1919], by H. D. Henderson.

4240 Vol. 30.

a Adam Smith on public debts, by J. S. Nicholson.
b British exports and the barometer, by W. H. Beveridge. [On the correspondence of barometric statistics and production and export figures during the 18th, 19th and early 20th cent.]
c The public finances of Ireland [chiefly in 1918-19, with retrospect to the Act of Union], by C. H. Oldham.
d The Guild Socialists, by H. Reynard.
e Early price associations in the British iron industry, by T. S. Ashton.
f Europe after the great wars, 1816 and 1920, by J. H. Clapham.

4241 Vol. 31.

a Corn prices and the corn laws, 1815-46, by C. R. Fay.
b The place of rye in the history of English food, by W. Ashley.
c Weather and harvest cycles, by W. H. Beveridge. [With table of wheat prices in western Europe, 1500-1869]
d The present position of industrial women workers [1921], by B. L. Hutchins.

4242 Vol. 32.

a The alleged exhaustion of the soil in medieval England, by R. Lennard.
b Was rye ever the ordinary food of the English?, by A. G. L. Rogers.
c Some causes of the increase of population in the 18th cent. as illustrated in London, by M. Dorothy George.

4243 Vol. 33.

a Grouping under the Railways Act, 1921, by W. M. Acworth.
b An 18th cent. combination in the copper-mining industry [the Cornish Metal Company, 1785-92], by G. C. Allen.
c Ricardo's ingot plan [of currency reform]: a centenary tribute, by J. Bonar.
d Early Liverpool cotton imports and the organisation of the cotton market in the 18th cent., by S. Dumbell.
e The trading accounts of a London merchant [John Stubs of Newton-le-Willows] in 1794, by G. W. Daniels.

4244 Vol. 34.

a The income of tenants on a Scotch open-field farm in the 18th cent. [at Dunachton], by Isabel F. Grant.
b The sale of corn in the 19th cent., by C. R. Fay.
c The beginnings of the Liverpool cotton trade, by S. Dumbell.
d Alfred Marshall, 1842-1924, by J. M. Keynes [with a bibliographical list of Marshall's writings].
e The war's influence upon village life [after 1918], by C. H. d'E. Leppington.
f A retrospect of free trade doctrine, by W. Ashley.
g Sir Thomas Gresham and the foreign exchanges, by H. Buckley.

4245 Vol. 35.

a Economic theorists among the servants of John Company, 1766-1806, by J. C. Sinha.
b The sale of corn in the 19th cent., by S. Dumbell.
c A contribution to the study of London's retail meat trade [1924], by W. R. Dunlop.

4246 Vol. 36.

a A narrative of the general strike of 1926, by D. H. Robertson.

4247 Vol. 37.

a The crisis in the Lancashire cotton industry [after 1918], by G. W. Daniels and J. Jewkes.

4248 Vol. 39.

a The public regulation of wages in Great Britain [20th cent.], by H. Clay.

4249 Vol. 40.

a Adam Smith and the dynamic state, by C. R. Fay.
b Has foreign investment paid?, by A. M. Samuel.

4250 Vol. 41.

a Labour mobility in the South Wales and Monmouthshire coal-mining industry, 1920-30, by B. Thomas.
b The changed outlook in regard to population, 1831-1931, by E. Cannan.
c Interest and usury in a new light, by H. Somerville.

4251 Vol. 42.

a Savings and usury: a symposium, by E. Cannan, P. Adarkar, B. K. Sandwell and J. M. Keynes. [Contd. under the title 'Usury and the canonists' by L. Dennis and H. Somerville]

Economic History (a supplement to the Economic Journal), vols. 1-2 (1926-33):

4252 Vol. 1.

a The development of Ruskin's views on interest, by Clara E. Collet.
b The Irish staple organisation in the reign of James I, by G. O'Brien.
c The consumption of tobacco since 1600, by A. Rive.
d Economy of a Norfolk parish [Mattishall] in 1783 and at the present time, by J. A. Venn.
e The social effects of the agricultural reforms and enclosure movement in Aberdeenshire, by Isabel F. Grant.
f The Potteries in the industrial revolution, by V. W. Bladen.
g The domestic system in the early Lancashire tool trade, by T. S. Ashton.
h The cotton market in 1799, by S. Dumbell.
i Price control and the corn averages under the corn laws, by C. R. Fay.
j The yield and price of corn in the middle ages, by W. H. Beveridge.
k An early exposition of 'final utility': W. F. Lloyd's lecture

on 'the notion of value' (1833) reprinted. [Ed. R. F. Harrod]

l The general strike during one hundred years, by A. Plummer.

m Family endowment and the birth-rate in the early 19th cent., by J. S. Blackmore and F. C. Mellonie.

n The combination laws reconsidered, by M. Dorothy George.

o The London coal-heavers: attempts to regulate waterside labour in the 18th and 19th cent., by M. Dorothy George.

p The last years of the Irish currency, by G. O'Brien.

q The change in farm labourers' diet during two centuries, by G. E. Fussell.

r Note on the labour exchange idea in the 17th cent., by P. S. Belasco. [See also below]

s Neglected aspects of the enclosure movements, by M. Aurousseau.

t The coal-miners of the 18th cent., by T. S. Ashton.

u A pre-Bank of England English banker, Edward Backwell [d. 1683], by R. D. Richards.

v The Association of the Manufacturers of Earthenware, 1784–6, by V. W. Bladen.

w 'Scotch cattle' [secret societies of employees] and early trade unionism in Wales, by E. J. Jones.

x The London cheesemongers of the 18th cent., by G. E. Fussell.

y A further note on labour exchanges in the 17th cent., by F. A. Norman and L. G. Lee. [See also above]

z Some accounts of individual Highland sporting estates [i.e. grouse moors, after 1918], by Isabel F. Grant.

aa Urban death-rates in the early 19th cent., by Barbara Hammond.

bb The population problem during the industrial revolution: a note on the present state of the controversy, by T. H. Marshall.

cc John Stuart Mill's attitude to neo-Malthusianism [i.e. birth-control], by N. E. Himes.

dd The pioneers of banking in England, by R. D. Richards.

ee Theories of the velocity of circulation of money in earlier economic literature, by W. M. Holtrop.

ff A plea for theory in economic history, by E. F. Heckscher.

gg Methods of industrial organisation in the west midlands, 1860–1927, by G. C. Allen.

hh A short history of tobacco smuggling, by A. Rive.

ii The early history of registry offices [in the 17th and 18th cent.]: the beginnings of advertisement, by M. Dorothy George.

jj A 'turn-out' [or strike] of Bolton machine-makers in 1831, by G. W. Daniels. [Contd. in vol. 2]

kk 'Bidentes Hoylandie': a mediaeval sheep farm [being an analysis of the sheep-farming records of Crowland, 1258–1322], by F. M. Page.

4253 Vol. 2.

a Wheat measures in the Winchester rolls, by W. H. Beveridge.

b The 'stop of the exchequer' [1672], by R. D. Richards.

c Housing of the rural population in the 18th cent., by G. E. Fussell and Constance Goodman.

d The localisation of the cotton industry [in Lancashire, Derbyshire, Cheshire], by J. Jewkes.

e Samuel Crompton's census of the cotton industry in 1811, by G. W. Daniels.

f An early factory community [established by Samuel Greg at Styal, Ches., 1784], by Frances Collier.

g Combination in the west of Scotland coal trade, 1790–1817, by H. Hamilton.

h The exchequer in Cromwellian times, by R. D. Richards.

i The profits of the Guinea trade, by S. Dumbell. [An examination of Gomer Williams' researches into late 18th and early 19th cent. slaving accounts]

j Two towns' enclosures [Sheffield and Lambeth, late 18th and early 19th cent.], by Barbara Hammond.

k The coming of general limited liability [an account of the legal position of joint-stock enterprise until the acts of 1855–7], by H. A. Shannon.

l The genesis of American engineering competition, 1850–70, by D. L. Burn.

m The Public Works Act, 1863, by W. D. Henderson.

n The assize of bread in London during the 16th cent., by Frieda J. Nicholas.

o The Bank of England and the South Sea company, by R. D. Richards.

p History of Covent Garden market [London], by C. E. Wallis.

q The Albion steam flour mill [opened at Blackfriars, London, 1786], by D. A. Westworth.

r The first five thousand limited companies and their duration, by H. A. Shannon.

s The dispute concerning the Plymouth pilchard fishery, 1584–91, by A. L. Rowse.

t Masons' wages in mediaeval England, by D. Knoop and G. P. Jones.

u Mr. Pepys and the goldsmith bankers, by R. D. Richards.

v Farmers' calendars from Tusser to Arthur Young [i.e. 1557–1800], by G. E. Fussell.

w An early Victorian business forecaster in the woollen industry, by H. Heaton. [On the monthly economic surveys in the *Leeds Mercury*, 1835–44, and the reports of Edward Baines, the proprietor]

x The question of the [gold or silver monetary] standard in the eighteen-fifties, by R. S. Sayers.

4254 Index to the Economic Journal, vols. 1–10. 1901.

4255 Index to the Economic Journal, vols. 11–20. 1911.

4256 Index to the Economic Journal, vols. 21–30. 1922.

4257 Index to the Economic Journal, vols. 31–40. 1934.

Other publications:

4258 The state in relation to railways: papers read at the congress of the Society, 1912. 1912.

a Parliament and the railways, by E. Cleveland-Stevens.

4259 First essay on population, 1798, by Thomas Robert Malthus. With notes by J. Bonar. 1926. [A typefacsimile]

4260 Studies in economic history: the collected papers [published and unpublished] of George Unwin, ed., with introductory memoir, by R. H. Tawney. 1927.

a Some economic factors in general history.

b The aims of economic history.

c The teaching of economic history in university tutorial classes.

d The teaching of history in schools.

e The mediaeval city [with special reference to London].

f Mediaeval gilds and education.

g London tradesmen and their creditors.

h The economic policy of Edward III.

i The Merchant Adventurers' company in the reign of Elizabeth.

j Chapters from a history of commerce [relating to intercontinental trade routes centring in the Levant pre-1000 A.D., nomadic and caravan trade, and early medieval gilds and the beginnings of settled trade].

k The history of the cloth industry in Suffolk.

l Commerce and coinage in Shakespeare's England.

m Introduction to *National Power and Prosperity*, by Conrad Gill [1916].

n Introduction to *The Poor Husbandman's Advocate to Rich*

Racking Landlords, by Richard Baxter [ed. F. J. Powicke, 1926].
o Indian factories in the 18th cent.
p Reviews of books.
q Miscellaneous papers.
r List of published works of George Unwin.

ROYAL EMPIRE SOCIETY

Founded 1868, as the Colonial Society, to promote the increase and diffusion of knowledge respecting the colonies, dependencies and possessions of the Crown, and the Indian Empire, and the preservation of a permanent union between the mother country and the various parts of the British Empire. The word 'Royal' was added in 1869. In 1870 the name 'Royal Colonial Institute' was adopted. Title changed to above form in 1928, and to Royal Commonwealth Society in 1958.

Proceedings, vols. 32–40 (1901–9):

4261 Vol. 32.
a Recent observations in Western Australia [1895–1900], by Sir G. Smith.
b Impressions of the British West Indies [with particular reference to the sugar industry, *c.* 1900], by H. de R. Walker.

4262 Vol. 34.
a Australia and naval defence [1889–1903], by Senator Matheson.
b Our colonial kingdoms, by H. G. Parsons. [Historical survey of the British imperial system as a congeries of kingdoms under a common crown]

4263 Vol. 35.
a Ceylon from 1896 to 1903, by J. Ferguson.
b The development of West Africa by railways [1896–1904], by F. Shelford.

4264 Vol. 37.
a The progress and problems of the East Africa protectorate, by Sir C. Eliot.
b Australian immigration, by W. James.

4265 Vol. 38.
a St. Helena, by J. C. Melliss.
b A link of empire: the Royal Colonial Institute, by A. R. Colquhoun.
c Some phases of Canada's development, by W. L. Griffith.
d The trend of Victoria's progress, by T. Bent.

4266 Vol. 39.
a Twelve months of imperial evolution [being some account of subjects discussed at the colonial conference of 1907], by R. Jebb.
b Nyasaland, by Sir A. Sharpe.
c Cotton growing and Nigeria, by C. A. Birtwistle.

United Empire: the Institute journal, new ser., vols. 1–24 (1910–33):

4267 Vol. 1.
a The evolution of the high commissioner, by C. de Thierry.
b The Falkland Islands and its dependencies, by W. L. Allardyce.
c The colonisation of the Caribbean, by F. Cundall.
d The New Hebrides, by E. G. Rason.

e Progress of Rhodesia, by Sir L. Michell. [Statistics for 1908–9]

4268 Vol. 2.
a A notable naval duel, 1812, by G. Stronach. [The *Shannon* and the *Chesapeake*]
b The Imperial Department of Agriculture [founded 1898] in the West Indies, by Sir D. Morris.
c Industrial development of Canada, by E. T. Powell.
d The origins of the New Zealand nation, by G. H. Scholefield.
e Newfoundland and the naval movement in Canada, by P. T. McGrath. [A brief account of the organization of the Newfoundland Naval Reserve]
f The new day in Rhodesia [a survey of its development, 1897–1911], by C. Boyd.
g Sierra Leone and its commercial expansion, by T. J. Aldridge.
h Trade development in Nigeria [1904–11].
i British diplomacy and Canada: the Ashburton treaty [1842], by D. A. Mills.
j Expansion of British influence in the Malay peninsula [1910–11], by T. H. Reid.
k The fight between the *Randolph* [American privateer] and the *Yarmouth* [Royal Navy, 7 Mar. 1778], by N. D. Davis.

4269 Vol. 3.
a Colonials at Westminster [i.e. M.P.s of colonial birth, from the 18th cent.], by C. de Thierry.
b Master-builders of Greater Britain. [2: Sir George Grey, d. 1898, governor of South Australia, New Zealand and South Africa, by Sir E. im Thurn. 3: Lord Durham, d. 1840, governor-general of Canada, by C. P. Lucas. 4: Admiral Arthur Phillip, d. 1814, governor of New South Wales, by J. D. Rogers. 5: Matthew Flinders, d. 1814, explorer, by P. E. Lewin. 6: John Macarthur, d. 1834, founder of the Australian wool trade, by J. D. Rogers. 9: Guy Carleton, Lord Dorchester, d. 1808, governor of Quebec, by H. E. Egerton. 10: Sir Isaac Brock, d. 1812, major-general, by C. P. Lucas. 11: Joseph Howe, d. 1873, Nova Scotian statesman, by J. D. Rogers. 12: John Graves Simcoe, d. 1806, governor of Upper Canada, by C. P. Lucas]
c West Indian progress [in trade, 1910–11], by A. E. Aspinall.
d Products of the Empire. [1: Rubber, by E. Salmon. 2: Wool, by J. C. Reid]
e Distinguished West Indians in England, by C. de Thierry.
f Some old British settlements in South Africa, by A. W. Tilby.

4270 Vol. 4.
a Master-builders of Greater Britain. [13: Edward Gibbon Wakefield, d. 1862, colonial reformer, by H. E. Egerton. 14: Charles Sturt, d. 1869, Australian explorer, by Sir E. im Thurn. 15: Bishop George Augustus Selwyn, d. 1878, by W. O. B. Allen. 16: James Bruce, 8th Earl of Elgin, d. 1863, governor-general of Canada, by W. L. Grant. 17: Sir Stamford Raffles, d. 1826, colonial governor, by Ethel Colquhoun. 19: Cecil John Rhodes, d. 1902, by E. M. Cook. 20: Thomas Douglas, 5th Earl of Selkirk, d. 1820, pioneer of emigration in western Canada, by P. E. Lewin. 21: John MacKenzie, d. 1899, missionary and statesman, by A. W. Tilby. 22: Sir Bartle Frere, d. 1884, by A. B. Tucker. 23: Sir Alexander Mackenzie, d. 1820, Canadian explorer, by P. E. Lewin. 24: Charles Poulett Thomson, Lord Sydenham, d. 1841, governor of Canada, by H. E. Egerton.]
b Products of the Empire. [3: Gold, by S. Merry]

c Some missionary pioneers in South Africa, by A. W. Tilby.

d The Livingstone centenary, by A. W. Tilby. [An account of the career and work of David Livingstone]

e [Edward Gibbon] Wakefield and the colonial reformers, by R. C. Mills.

f British contributions to Argentine progress, by H. A. Cartwright.

g A voyage to Australia and back in [18]52, by S. Cookson.

4271 Vol. 5.

a Master-builders of Greater Britain. [25: William Charles Wentworth, d. 1872, Australian statesman, by J. Munro. 26: Lord Charles Somerset, d. 1831, governor of Cape Colony, by H. T. Pooley. 28: Sir Harry Parkes, d. 1885, diplomatist, by B. Brenan. 29: Sir Frederick Weld, d. 1891, colonial governor, by G. H. Scholefield. 30: Sir Frederick Baker, d. 1893, African explorer, by A. S. White. 31: Sir Harry Smith, d. 1860, soldier and governor of Cape Colony, by E. M. Cook. 32: Sir William Molesworth, d. 1855, politician, by H. E. Egerton]

b British interests in Argentina, by H. Gibson. [Contains a brief account of the River Plate campaigns of 1806 and 1807]

c 'The battle of Muddy Flat', April 4, 1854, by C. J. Dudgeon. [An account of an engagement between Chinese Imperial troops and the Shanghai Volunteer Corps]

d Maori sovereignty: the deputation to London, by G. H. Scholefield. [A brief account of the 'King' Maori movement]

4272 Vol. 6.

a The Nova Scotia baronets, by E. Lewin. [The first British settlement of Nova Scotia, established by Sir William Alexander, 1621, and the order of the Baronets of Nova Scotia, 1624]

b The war in East and West Africa [1914], by H. T. M. Bell.

c Australia and the war [1914–18], by J. M. Myers.

d Great Britain and the Persian Gulf [c. 1900–15], by H. T. M. Bell.

e The work of the navy in the war [1914–15], by H. W. Wilson.

f Kindred societies, past and present. [1: The Imperial Federation League 1884–93, by W. B. Worsfold. 2: The Imperial Federation (Defence) Committee, 1894–1906, by A. H. Loring. 3: The British Empire League, established 1895, by C. F. Murray. 4: The Society of Comparative Legislation, established 1895, by Sir C. P. Ilbert. 5: The Victoria League, established 1901, by E. B. Sargant. 7: The League of the Empire, established 1901, by Sir F. Pollock. 8: The Empire Parliamentary Association, established 1911, by H. d'Egville. 10: The National Service League, established 1902, by R. Mac-Leod]

g The rebellion in South Africa [led by Beyers and De Wet, 1914], by H. T. M. Bell.

h The New Zealanders on service: first days in Gallipoli, by G. H. Scholefield.

i The taking of German South-West Africa [by South African forces], by W. B. Worsfold.

j The campaign in the Cameroons [1914–15]: a letter from an officer on service.

k Empire and money market: the romance of a three hundred years' alliance, by E. T. Powell. [Chiefly an account of the development of British finance]

4273 Vol. 7.

a The King's dominion of the islands: major and minor West Indian [historical] notes, by T. H. McDermot.

b The spirit of Empire, 1798–1916, by Kathleen F. Doughty.

c Russia and Britain [a brief account of relations between the two countries, 1844–1916], by Vedette.

d The integration of the Empire, by Sir H. Wilson.

e 'News of battles' [a brief historical account of war-correspondents], by D. H. M. Reid.

f Britain's work in the Far East, by R. I. Hope. [The establishment of a university at Hongkong, 1907–12]

4274 Vol. 8.

a Joseph Chamberlain as I knew him, by H. F. Wilson.

b The cradle of Empire: Newfoundland, by H. F. Reeve.

c Richard Hakluyt: a pioneer of colonisation, by F. Watson.

d The [Maltese] order of St. Michael and St. George [founded 1818], by E. C. Stembridge.

e The Euphrates valley railway project [1831–85], by D. C. Boulger.

f The jubilee of Canadian confederation [1867], by J. M. Sloan.

g 'The milestones of African civilization', by R. Williams. [Chiefly an account of the discovery of copper deposits at Katanga, Belgian Congo, and the subsequent railway development]

h British East Africa [its progress, 1897–1916], by H. R. Tate.

i The Colonial Nursing Association, 1896–1917: its origin, foundation, work and aim, by Mabel W. Piggott.

j Place names of the Empire, by Sir C. Lucas.

4275 Vol. 9.

a The Pacific and its political settlement, by Sir William Macgregor.

b 'The British Empire' [the first use of the expression], by C. H. Firth.

c Naval operations in central Africa [1915], by G. B. S. Simson.

d The jubilee of the Royal Colonial Institute [founded 1868, as the Royal Colonial Society], by A. W. Tilby.

e Thomas Dundas [d. 1794], empire builder, by C. Bruce.

f The British Empire at war [1914–18], by Sir G. Aston.

g Past and present members of the Royal Colonial Institute [1868–1918].

4276 Vol. 10.

a Three English artists in Australia [John Webber, d. 1793; William Westall, d. 1850; John Glover, d. 1849], by W. Moore.

b West Indian federation: its historical aspect, by A. E. Aspinall.

c General Berrangé's march across the Kalahari [with a South African force, 1915, from Kimberley to Rehoboth, in German South-West Africa], by C. E. S. King.

d Australian interests in the New Hebrides, by F. H. L. Paton.

e Problems of reconstruction in the Pacific [1919, with an historical survey of the development of international interests there], by G. H. Scholefield.

f The Imperial position in 1919, by W. Lang. [The problem of federation]

g Railway development in Australia, by T. R. Johnson.

h An ill-starred imperialist: a footnote to history, by W. Lang. [William Paterson, d. 1719, and the Darien colonisation scheme]

i Our West Indian colonies, by T. H. MacDermot.

j An historic tour: the Prince of Wales in Canada [1919], by J. S. Mills.

4277 Vol. 11.

a Conference or cabinet? Resolutions of the Imperial Conference [with particular reference to the resolutions of the conferences of 1907 and 1917], by R. Jebb.

b The administration of the Empire, by W. B. Worsfold.

[Problems of Imperial collaboration after the 1914–18 war]

c South Africa in 1802–4: a forgotten diary [of Augusta de Mist], by Ethel L. McPherson.

d The government of the British Commonwealth [with particular reference to the constitutional resolution of the Imperial Conference of 1917], by H. D. Hall.

e The artist of the goldfields [of Australia], by W. Moore. [A brief account of the life and work of Samuel Thomas Gill, fl. 1846–53]

f The navy on the Tigris [1914–18], by E. J. H. Boosé.

g The royal tour [by the Prince of Wales, 1920]. 2: Australasia, the Pacific and the West Indies, by J. S. Mills.

h Malta and sea power, by A. Bartolo.

i The Samoan mandate [1920], by Sir J. Allen.

4278 Vol. 12.

a The father of Australian sculpture [Charles Summers, d. 1878], by W. Moore.

b The Indian Marine [founded 1613], by C. de Thierry.

c The romance of Ashanti, by Sir F. Fuller. [An historical account of the confederation and of its relations with Britain]

d Who would not be an Australasian?, by C. Imrie. [An account of an engagement at Orakau, New Zealand, between British forces and Maoris led by Rewa Te Paerata, 1864]

e South African agriculture and its development, by F. B. Smith.

f Common counsels: an appreciation of the Empire Conference [1921], by J. S. Mills.

g Sir Richard Burton [d. 1890, a brief account], by J. G. Baker.

h Arthur Phillip [d. 1814: some facts concerning his early history], by E. M. Green.

i India and some problems, by Viscount Chelmsford. [The working of the administration under the author's viceroyalty]

4279 Vol. 13.

a The National Service League [and its work, 1902–14], by G. F. Shee.

b The birth of the overseas Empire, by Lord Morris. [The settlement of Newfoundland]

c The historian of Jamaica [Edward Long, d. 1813], by T. H. MacDermot.

d Empire trade development [1800–1921], by Sir P. Ll. Greame.

e The Prince [of Wales] in India [1921–2], by J. S. Mills.

f In justice to an empire founder, by Sir J. A. Cockburn. [Sir Francis Bacon, and his downfall]

g The fibre industry in East Africa, by A. Wigglesworth.

h The Washington Conference [1921–2], by Lord Lee of Fareham.

i Economic problem of British tropical Africa [1920–2], by Sir H. Leggett.

j Colonisation in British Guiana [from the early 17th cent.], by C. Clementi.

k British West Indies, by W. Ormsby-Gore. [An account based on the visit of the British government's mission, 1921]

l Cecil Rhodes: a great Englishman, by Sir H. Wilson.

m The political constitution of Jamaica, by T. H. Mac-Dermot.

n Canadian city names, by P. D. Meadows-Wood.

4280 Vol. 14.

a The third assembly of the League of Nations, by Sir J. Cook.

b Canada and the Empire, by Sir C. Stuart. [Chiefly an account of the early history of Canada, 1608–1791]

c The south-east coast of Africa and its development, by A. M. Miller.

d Francis Bacon as an empire builder, by Sir J. Cockburn.

e The North-West company [1779–1821] and the fur trade, by E. Lewin.

f The Dingaan treaties of 1837 and 1838 regarding the cession of Port Natal, South Africa, by I. J. Rousseau.

g Some recent phases of Indian politics, by Sir M. O'Dwyer. [1: Revolutionary movements, 1921. 2: Alkali movement in the Punjab. 3: Protective duties. 4: The Kenya controversy]

4281 Vol. 15.

a Forgotten pages. 1: The crowning of Cetywayo [as king of the Zulus by Theophilus Shepstone, 1873], by Nomad.

b A pioneer empire-builder: Sir Humphrey Gilbert [d. 1583], by Eva M. Tenison.

c Forgotten pages. 2: The Jamaica case, by Nomad. [Edward John Eyre, governor, and the negro rebellion of 1865]

d Forgotten pages. 3: The making of a province [Baluchistan, by Sir Robert Groves Sandeman, d. 1892], by Nomad.

e Bristol: Empire city, by E. W. Lennard.

f Our ambassador to India [Sir Thomas Roe, d. 1644], by R. F. Truscott.

g Forgotten pages. 4: Great Britain, Egypt and the Sudan [1800–99], by Nomad.

h Old Cape Town: 1845 and 1860, seen through women's eyes, by E. L. McPherson. [Extracts from letters by Mrs. Fanny Parkes and Lady Duff Gordon]

i The founding of Natal [1824], by Katherine F. Doughty.

4282 Vol. 16.

a Forgotten pages. 5: The mad Mullah of Somaliland [fl. 1899–1920], by Nomad.

b Hydro-electric development in Ontario, Canada, by W. C. Noxon.

c Tasmania: the development of a new country [from 1803], by R. E. Snowden.

d Forgotten pages. 8: Two South American adventures, by Nomad. [The British attacks on Buenos Aires, 1806, and Monte Video, 1807]

e Forgotten pages. 9: The Panjdeh scare, by Nomad. [Anglo-Russian rivalry in Afghanistan, 1885–7]

f The Prince [of Wales] in two continents [Africa and South America, 1925], by J. S. Mills.

4283 Vol. 17.

a Lord Ashburton and the treaty of 1842 [between the United States and Great Britain]: a vindication, by G. F. Jeanes.

b Scotland's secretary: how a high office was lost, by W. Lang.

c The truth about Captain Cook [the circumstances of his death], by Sir J. Carruthers.

d Forgotten pages. 10: The *Malacca* case, by Nomad. [The seizure of the P. & O. mail steamer *Malacca* by Russia during the Russo-Japanese war]

e The birthplace of Rhodes [Bishop's Stortford], by W. B. Worsfold.

f Sir Stamford Raffles, 1826–1926, by E. Salmon.

g The Imperial Conference [1926], by J. S. Mills.

4284 Vol. 18.

a The Conference [1926] and the future, by E. Salmon.

b The North Devons. Historic regiment in old Sydney, by M. Cox-Taylor.

c Cyprus, our newest colony, by W. Bevan.

d New Zealand's literary associations, by H. Bolitho.

e George Canning and William Blake [their patriotism], by E. Salmon.

f Some impressions of New Zealand in 1868 [based on the author's diary], by J. H. Hubback.

g On the track of a plague, by C. Hose. [An account of research into the causes of beri-beri. Contd. in vol. 19]

4285 Vol. 19.

a The racial problem in South Africa. Territorial segregation, by P. A. Silburn.

b The bombardment of Alexandria [by the British, 1882], as seen by C. F. Moberley Bell, on H.M.S. *Condor*.

c Economics and administration in British East Africa, by Sir H. Leggett.

d Links with the Iron Duke, by J. Paine. [Associations with, and relics of, the Duke of Wellington]

e The battle of St. George's Caye [British Honduras, between British and Spanish naval forces, 1798], by Sir J. Burdon.

f An account of the descent made by the Spaniards on the settlement of Honduras in the year 1798. [A contemporary compilation from various sources]

g The British Empire: then and now, 1868–1928, by H. Gunn.

h British Columbia's early explorers, by Eugenie Perry.

i The search for the Niger in the 1820s: some account of Dixon Denham, soldier, explorer and administrator, 1786–1828, by D. Hollis.

j Captain James Cook, R.N.: the greatest of navigators and ocean explorers, by H. Gunn.

k Bermuda's literary associations, by T. H. MacDermot.

4286 Vol. 20.

a Australia's contribution to the arts, by Beatrice Tildesley.

b The Indian navy, by H. Winckler.

c The Prince's tour: the great cycle completed [in British East Africa], by J. S. Mills.

d The last trek [by Boers from the Transvaal to Portuguese Angola, 1874–7], by G. H. Lepper.

e Iraq, by Sir P. Cox. [The creation and development of the kingdom, 1914–27]

f Lord Milner and the unified command: a chapter in the history of the Great war, by W. B. Worsfold.

g Tristan da Cunha: original documents illustrating its history and that of its 'flag', by E. H. Fairbrother.

h Captain Cook and British Columbia, by Sir J. S. Allen.

i Woodes Rogers [d. 1732, governor of the Bahamas], by B. M. H. Rogers.

4287 Vol. 21.

a Afghanistan and the Pathan border, by Sir H. Grant. [A brief outline of relations between Great Britain and Afghanistan]

b The West Indian sugar crisis [the position in 1930], by Lord Olivier.

c Ceylon's proposed new constitution, by Sir W. Woods.

d The Pungwe route to S. Rhodesia, by Mrs. T. Jollie. [The beginning of the railway from Beira to Southern Rhodesia, 1890]

e Wolfe's admiral [Sir Charles Saunders, d. 1775], by E. Salmon.

f West Indian sugar crises, 1800–1930, by C. W. Guillebaud.

g The Kelsey papers: an unsolved riddle in early Canadian history, by G. F. Jeanes. [Henry Kelsey, d. 1729, Canadian explorer, and governor of Fort York, Hudson's Bay]

4288 Vol. 22.

a With Captain Scott to the Antarctic, by H. G. Ponting [photographer to the expedition].

b Captain George Maclean: a centenary study, by J. Hardy. [Relations between the governors of Cape Coast Castle, Gold Coast, and the Ashanti kingdom, 1821–38]

c The Indian problem: Indian politics since 1919, by J. Coatman.

d The Indian problem: the Indian Civil Service, by Sir P. Fagan.

e Greater Rhodesia, by Mrs. T. Jollie. [A brief outline of the development of Southern and Northern Rhodesia]

f Sir James Russell [d. 1674]: defender of Nevis, by J. W. Damer-Powell.

g Thomas Aldworth [d. 1615]: founder of British India, by J. W. Damer-Powell.

4289 Vol. 23.

a The debt of the British Empire to medical research, by F. E. Fremantle.

b The Milner period in South Africa, by C. Headlam.

c The Imperial crown [and its jewels], by E. F. Twining.

d The race for Manica [Mashonaland, 1890–91, between British and Portuguese for concessions in the goldfield], by Ethel T. Jollie.

e 'For all prisoners and captives', by A. M. Wilson. [The capture of Edward Wilson, d. 1832, seaman, by Algerine pirates]

f Joseph Brant—Thayendanegea [chief of the Iroquois, d. 1807].

g The native question in Nigeria, by A. N. Cook.

h Richard Steel [fl. 1613–27]: a forgotten envoy to Persia, by J. W. Damer-Powell.

i Warren Hastings, by Sir E. Cotton.

j Terrorism in India [its genesis and development, 1897–1930], by Sir C. Tegart.

4290 Vol. 24.

a The Warren Hastings bi-centenary: historic commemoration in Westminster school.

b The Falkland Islands: centenary of the southern Atlantic outpost of Empire, by E. R. Yarham.

c The Ottawa agreements [1932] and their implications, by Sir B. Morgan.

d Britain's work in Iraq, by Sir H. Dobbs.

e What Ottawa achieved, by M. MacDonald.

f The crossing of the Blue Mountains [Australia, by Gregory Blaxland, William Lawson and Charles Wentworth, 1813], by H. Davies.

g John Guy [d. 1628?]: founder of Newfoundland.

h Tasmania's first governor [David Collins, d. 1810]: memories of old Hobart town, by M. Cox-Taylor.

i For the centenary of Adam Lindsay Gordon [d. 1870], by L. Sladen. [Includes a brief account of Gordon's life]

j Sidelights on the life of Captain Cook, by Sir C. Bennett.

k Early records of Tristan da Cunha: the discovery in New London, by D. M. Gane.

l Bushman's River Pass: an incident in South Africa of sixty years ago, by J. W. Lydekker. [An engagement in Natal, between a small force under the command of Major A. W. Durnford and the Ama-Hlubi tribe, 4 Nov. 1873]

m The Mount Everest expedition [1933]. 1: The climb, by H. Ruttledge. 2: The flight, by L. V. S. Blacker.

Monographs, nos. 1–2:

4291 No. 1. Imperial defence and trade, by F. A. Kirkpatrick. 1914. [Not exclusively concerned with the British Empire]

4292 No. 2. Democracy and empire. The applicability of the dictum that 'a democracy cannot manage an empire' to the present conditions and future problems of the British Empire, especially the question of the future of India, by A. E. Duchesne. 1916. [2nd edn. 1917]

Bibliographies, nos. 1–6:

4293 No. 1. Select bibliography of publications on foreign colonisation (German, French, Italian, Dutch, Portuguese, Spanish, and Belgian) contained in the library of the Royal Colonial Institute, comp. Winifred C. Hill, with introd. by the librarian [E. Lewin]. *P.* 1915.

4294 No. 2. Select list of recent publications illustrating the constitutional relations between the various parts of the British Empire, comp. E. Lewin. *P.* 1926.

4295 No. 3. Select bibliography of recent publications illustrating the relations between Europeans and coloured races, comp. E. Lewin. 1926.

4296 No. 4. Select list of publications illustrating the communications of the overseas British Empire, with special reference to Africa generally and the Baghdad railway, comp. E. Lewin. 1927.

4297 No. 5. Hastings bi-centenary. Select list of printed publications relating to Warren Hastings, comp. Vera Ward. *P.* 1932.

4298 No. 6. List of publications on the constitutional relations of the British Empire, 1926–32, comp. E. Lewin. 1933. [Published in conjunction with the Royal Institute of International Affairs]

Imperial Studies monographs, nos. 1–8:

4299 No. 1. Political unrest in Upper Canada, 1815–36, by Aileen Dunham. 1927.

4300 No. 2. British West African settlements, 1750–1821: a study in local administration, by Eveline C. Martin. 1927.

4301 No. 3. British colonial policy and the South African republics, 1848–72, by C. W. de Kiewiet. 1929.

4302 No. 4. British policy and Canada, 1774–91: a study in 18th cent. trade policy, by G. S. Graham. 1930.

4303 No. 5. Colonial admiralty jurisdiction in the 17th cent., by Helen J. Crump. 1931.

4304 No. 6. Education for Empire settlement: a study of juvenile migration, by A. G. Scholes. 1932.

4305 No. 7. The provincial system in New Zealand, 1852–76, by W. P. Morrell. 1932.

4306 No. 8. Railway and customs policies in South Africa, 1885–1910, by J. Van der Poel. 1933.

Other publications:

4307 First supplementary catalogue of the library of the Royal Colonial Institute, comp. J. R. Boose. 1901.

4308 The after-war settlement and employment of ex-service men in the overseas Dominions, by Sir R. Haggard. 1916. [An account of his mission to South Africa, Rhodesia, East Africa, Australia, New Zealand and Canada, 1916]

4309 Land settlement for ex-service men in the overseas Dominions, by C. Turnor, 1920.

4310 The Empire at war [1914–18], ed. Sir C. Lucas. 5 vols. 1921–26. [Vol. i traces the development of colonial self-defence, and of Imperial co-operation during war-time, 1816–1914. Vol. ii: Canada, Newfoundland, the West Indies, Bermuda and the Falkland Islands. Vol. iii: Australia, New Zealand and the Pacific Islands. Vol. iv: West Africa, East Africa, Central Africa, South Africa, African islands, Somaliland and the Sudan. Vol. v: The Mediterranean colonies, Egypt and Palestine, Aden, India, Ceylon, Malaya and China]

4311 Imperial studies in education. Papers read at the Imperial Studies Conference, 1924, ed. Eveline C. Martin. 1924.

4312 Overseas official publications, being a quarterly bulletin of official publications issued in the overseas British Empire or relating thereto. Vols. i–v: Dec. 1926–Nov. 1931. 1927–32.

4313 Diamond jubilee souvenir of the Royal Colonial Institute, now the Royal Empire Society, ed. E. Salmon. [1928].

4314 Subject catalogue of the library of the Royal Empire Society, formerly Royal Colonial Institute, by E. Lewin. 3 vols. 1930–32. [Vol. i: British Empire generally, and Africa. Vol. ii: Commonwealth of Australia, the Dominion of New Zealand, the South Pacific, general voyages and travels, and Arctic and Antarctic regions. Vol. iii: Dominion of Canada and its provinces, the Dominion of Newfoundland, the West Indies and colonial America]

4315 Terrorism in India [1897–1932], by Sir C. Tegart. 1932.

ROYAL GEOGRAPHICAL SOCIETY

Founded 1830, as the Geographical Society of London, for the advancement of geographical science. The word 'Royal' was added to the title in the same year. The words 'of London' were abandoned about 1852, except on the reverse of the medals (designed in 1836) and on devices based thereon.

Geographical Journal, including the Proceedings, vols. 17–82 (1901–33):

4316 Vol. 17.
  a In commemoration of the reign of Queen Victoria, Empress of India. 1: President's address, by Sir C. R. Markham. [Progress of geographical discovery during the reign of Victoria]. 2: Progress of exploration and the spread and consolidation of the Empire in America, Australia and Africa, by Sir G. T. Goldie. 3: Advances in Asia and Imperial consolidation in India, by Sir T. H. Holdich.
  b Can Hawkins' 'Maiden Land' be identified as the Falkland Islands?, by B. M. Chambers. [See also 4358a and 4358d below]

4317 Vol. 18.
  a Geographical conditions affecting British trade, by G. G. Chisholm.

4318 Vol. 21.
  a Commemoration of the reign of Queen Elizabeth. 1: President's address, by Sir C. R. Markham. [Development of scientific geography in the reign of Elizabeth]. 2: Sir Walter Raleigh, by E. Gosse. 3: Francis Drake, by J. Corbett. 4: William Gilbert and terrestrial magnetism, by S. P. Thompson. 5: Exhibition of books, maps, etc.

4319 Vol. 23.
  a The impetus and direction of geography in the 19th cent., by Baron F. von Richthofen.
  b The geographical pivot of history, by H. J. Mackinder. [European civilization and its struggle against Asiatic invasion]

4320 Vol. 24.
  a Description of an astrolabe, by S. A. Ionides.

4321 Vol. 26.

a Moorcroft and Hearsey's visit to Lake Mansarowar [Tibet] in 1812, by H. Pearse. [William Moorcroft, d. 1825, veterinary surgeon and traveller; Hyder Young Hearsey, d. 1840]

4322 Vol. 27.

a The Ordnance Survey maps from the point of view of the antiquities on them, by F. J. Haverfield.
b Wrecks of the Spanish Armada on the coast of Ireland, by W. S. Green.

4323 Vol. 28.

a The economic geography and development of Australia, by J. W. Gregory.
b Twenty-five years' geographical progress [since 1881], by Sir G. T. Goldie.

4324 Vol. 29.

a The inclosure of common fields considered geographically, by G. Slater.

4325 Vol. 31.

a Admiral Sir Leopold M'Clintock, K.C.B. [d. 1907, explorer], by Sir C. R. Markham.
b The story of London maps, by L. Gomme.

4326 Vol. 33.

a Notes on an early American Arctic expedition [1753], by H. E. Bryant.
b Fifty years of Nile exploration [1858–1908], and some of its results, by Sir W. Garstin.

4327 Vol. 34.

a The western Pacific: its history and present condition, by Sir E. F. im Thurn.
b A 16th cent. map of the British Isles.
c Changes on the east coast of England within the historical period. 1: Yorkshire, by T. Sheppard.

4328 Vol. 35.

a Some recent changes in the course of the Trent, by B. Smith.
b Geographical factors that control the development of Australia, by J. W. Gregory.
c Cambridgeshire rivers, by W. Cunningham.

4329 Vol. 37.

a David Thompson, a great geographer [d. 1857], by J. B. Tyrrell.

4330 Vol. 38.

a Foundation and development of British Guiana, by J. A. J. De Villiers.
b A forgotten navigator: Captain (afterwards Sir) John Hayes [d. 1838], and his voyage of 1793, by Ida Lee.

4331 Vol. 39.

a Major Gordon Laing, and the circumstances attending his death [1826, in Timbuktu], from the narrative of M. Bonnel de Mézières.
b Review of the results of twenty years of Antarctic work originated by the Society [1893–1912], by Sir C. R. Markham.

4332 Vol. 40.

a The distribution of early bronze age settlements in Britain, by O. G. S. Crawford.
b New Drake documents discovered by Mrs. Zelia Nuttall.

4333 Vol. 41.

a David Livingstone, centenary of his birth: Livingstone as an explorer, by Sir H. H. Johnston.

4334 Vol. 42.

a Lost geographical documents, by Sir C. R. Markham.
b Statistical study of wheat cultivation and trade, 1881–1910, by J. F. Unstead.
c Voyages of Capt. William Smith and others to the South Shetlands [1819–22], by Ida Lee (Mrs. C. B. Marriott).

4335 Vol. 43.

a The geographer and history, by E. Huntington.
b Nottinghamshire in the 19th cent.: the geographical factors in the growth of population, by B. C. Wallis.

4336 Vol. 44.

a Lost explorers of the Pacific, by B. Thomson.
b A 17th cent. cartographer [Charles Wilde d. 1688], by W. Foster.
c Famous maps in the British Museum, by J. A. J. De Villiers.

4337 Vol. 45.

a European influence in the Pacific, 1513–1914, by Sir E. im Thurn.

4338 Vol. 46.

a History of the gradual development of the groundwork of geographical science, by Sir C. R. Markham.
b Earthquakes in Great Britain, 1889–1914, by C. Davison.

4339 Vol. 47.

a Railway development in Africa, present and future, by Sir C. Metcalfe, bt.
b Sir Allen Young [d. 1915, Arctic explorer], by Sir C. R. Markham.

4340 Vol. 48.

a The mapping of the earth, past, present, and future, by E. A. Reeves.
b Tercentenary of Richard Hakluyt.

4341 Vol. 49.

a Hakluyt and [Richard] Mulcaster, by F. Watson.
b Thirty years' work of the Society [1880–1910], by J. S. Keltie.

4342 Vol. 50.

a The pilgrimage of Symon Semeonis [14th cent. Irish Franciscan]: a contribution to the history of mediaeval travel, by M. Esposito. [Includes a description of London and other English towns. Contd. in vol. 51]

4343 Vol. 51.

a Routes from the Panjab to Turkestan and China recorded by William Finch (1611), discussed by Sir A. Stein.
b Halley's magnetic variation charts, by E. A. Reeves.
c British interests in Spitsbergen. [Correspondence of the Society with the secretary of state for foreign affairs at the time of the treaty of Brest Litovsk, 1917]
d The London Society's map, with its proposals for the improvement of London, by Sir A. Webb.
e Mr. Carmichael: an early traveller in the Syrian desert [1751], by D. Carruthers and F. D. Harford.

4344 Vol. 52.

a Raleigh, died 29 Oct. 1618, by E. A. Benians.
b Notes on the early history of the mariner's compass, by M. Esposito.

4345 Vol. 53.

a The political status of Spitzbergen [from 1596], by Sir M. Conway.
b The physiographic control of Australian exploration, by G. Taylor.

c The earliest maps of the New York region, by E. Heawood.
d War work of the Society [1914–18].
e Population changes in the eastern part of the South Wales coalfield, by A. E. Trueman.

4346 Vol. 54.
a Geographical work with the army in France [1915–18], by H. S. L. Winterbotham.
b Hondius [Dutch cartographer] and his newly-found map of 1608, by E. Heawood.
c Geological work on the western front [1915–18], by W. B. R. King.

4347 Vol. 56.
a Evolution of the Hastings coastline, by E. M. Ward.

4348 Vol. 57.
a Two early monuments to Capt. Cook [erected in Hawaii, 1825 and 1837], by Lord C. N. Hamilton.
b The death of Mungo Park [at Boussa, Nigeria].
c The history of the chronometer, by R. T. Gould.
d Sir Richard Francis Burton, born 1821, by A. H. Sayce.
e The world before and after Magellan's voyage, by E. Heawood.

4349 Vol. 58.
a South Persia and the Great war, by Sir P. Sykes.
b Notes on the technique of boundary delimitation, by A. R. Hinks. [Includes material relating to Uganda–Congo–German East Africa, Alaska, South Australia and Victoria, Canada and the United States]

4350 Vol. 59.
a Jan Mayen island, by J. M. Wordie.
b Archaeology and the Ordnance Survey, by O. G. S. Crawford.
c Capt. Shakespear's last journey [across Arabia, 1914], by D. Carruthers.

4351 Vol. 60.
a Influence of geography on the growth of London, by C. E. N. Bromehead.

4352 Vol. 61.
a A history of steamboat navigation on the upper Tigris, by R. E. Cheeseman.
b The influence of man as an agent in geographical change, by R. L. Sherlock.
c Air survey and archaeology, by O. G. S. Crawford.

4353 Vol. 62.
a Mercator's large map of the British Isles: copy found at Rome.
b King Alfred's system of geographical description in his version of Orosius, by E. D. Laborde.
c A hitherto unknown world map of A.D. 1506, by E. Heawood.

4354 Vol. 63.
a The use of watermarks in dating old maps and documents, by E. Heawood.
b The work of John Cary [fl. 1769–98, cartographer], and his successors, by Sir G. Fordham.

4355 Vol. 64.
a An interesting collection of early maps [in the possession of the Society], by E. Heawood.

4356 Vol. 65.
a The first sighting of the Antarctic continent [in 1820, by Edward Bransfield, d. 1852], by R. T. Gould.

4357 Vol. 66.
a Southesk's journey through the west [of Canada, 1859], by J. N. Wallace.

4358 Vol. 67.
a Did Sir Richard Hawkins visit the Falkland Islands?, by H. Henniker-Heaton.
b Saxton's general map of England and Wales [c. 1580], by Sir H. G. Fordham.
c Geography and prehistoric earthworks in the New Forest district, by H. Sumner.
d Hawkins' Maiden Land and the Falkland Islands: a reply to Mr. Henniker-Heaton, by B. M. Chambers.

4359 Vol. 68.
a Purchas and his *Pilgrimes* [1625], by Sir W. Foster.
b Some early county maps, by E. Heawood.
c The British Isles in the nautical charts of the 14th and 15th cent., by M. C. Andrews.

4360 Vol. 69.
a Ships of early explorers, by G. S. L. Clowes.
b The two-hundredth anniversary of the birth of General Roy [d. 1790, an originator of the Ordnance Survey], by Sir C. Close.
c Note on a map of the British Isles by Pietro Coppo [c. 1525], by R. Almagià.
d Captain Cook's ships. [A list of drawings and engravings]

4361 Vol. 70.
a A note on the 'Quartermaster's map', 1644 [engraved by Hollar], by Sir G. Fordham.

4362 Vol. 71.
a Some surveys and maps of the Elizabethan period remaining in manuscript, by Sir G. Fordham.
b Nathaniel Carpenter [d. 1628], and English geography in the 17th cent., by J. N. L. Baker.

4363 Vol. 72.
a The Gilbert map of c. 1582–3.
b Lessons of the Gilbert map, by R. P. Bishop.
c William Bourne [d. 1583]: a chapter in Tudor geography, by Eva G. R. Taylor.
d The mariner's astrolabe, by R. T. Gunther.
e Bouvet Island [in the Antarctic, 1825–1927].

4364 Vol. 73.
a Captain James Cook and the Sandwich Islands, by Sir H. Newbolt.
b Captain Cook and the founding of British power in the Pacific, by J. H. Rose.
c Cook as a hydrographical surveyor, by H. P. Douglas.
d Captain Cook as an astronomer, by Sir F. Dyson.

4365 Vol. 74.
a Roger Barlow: a new chapter in early Tudor geography, by Eva G. R. Taylor. [Some account of Barlow's *Geography*, 1540–1, and the circumstances in which it was written]
b Agriculture and economic geography in the 18th cent. [in England], by G. E. Fussell. [With a select bibliography]

4366 Vol. 75.
a Hondius's portraits of Drake and Cavendish.
b The missing draft project of Drake's voyage of 1577–80, by Eva G. R. Taylor.
c Major James Rennell, 1742–1830 [explorer and geographer], by R. Rodd.
d Samuel Purchas, by Eva G. R. Taylor.

4367 Vol. 76.

a The old English mile, by Sir C. Close.

b The centenary meeting: addresses on the history of the Society, by Sir C. Close, H. R. Mill, D. Freshfield, Sir F. Younghusband and the Marquess of Zetland.

4368 Vol. 77.

a Further notes on the old English mile, by J. B. P. Karslake.

b Master [Richard] Hore's journey of 1536 [to Newfoundland], by Eva G. R. Taylor.

4369 Vol. 78.

a The Anglo-Italian Somaliland boundary [and its demarcation, 1929–30], by J. H. Stafford.

b The glacial drifts of Essex and Hertfordshire, and their bearing upon the agricultural and historical geography of the region, by S. W. Wooldridge and D. J. Smetham.

c A 16th cent. ms. navigating manual in the Society's library [of Italian origin, with a general account of contemporary rutters or pilot books], by Eva G. R. Taylor.

4370 Vol. 79.

a John Adams and his map of England [*c.* 1680?], by E. Heawood.

b Distribution of urban population in Great Britain, 1931, by C. B. Fawcett.

c Speeches at the unveiling of the Shackleton memorial, by H. R. Mill and the Marquess of Zetland.

4371 Vol. 80.

a The formation of Dungeness foreland, by W. V. Lewis.

b Human geography of the Fenland before the drainage, by H. C. Darby.

c Historical geography of the town and roads of Whitby, by W. G. East.

4372 Vol. 81.

a Early maps of Great Britain. 1: The Matthew Paris maps, by J. B. Mitchell. 2: The [Richard] Gough map [14th cent.], by R. A. Pelham. 3: Aegidius Tschudi's maps, by E. Heawood.

b The urbanization of the Shetland Islands, by A. C. O'Dell.

4373 Vol. 82.

a A Roman bridge in the Fens [Nordelph, Norf.], by E. J. A. Kenny.

b Changes in land utilization in the south-west of the London basin, 1840–1932, by E. C. Willatts.

c The agrarian contribution to surveying in England [in the 16th and 17th cent.], by H. C. Darby.

d Woutneel's map of the British Isles, 1603, by E. Lynam. [Hans Woutneel, Flemish bookseller, fl. 1585–1607]

4374 General index to the first twenty volumes of the Geographical Journal, 1893–1902. 1906.

4375 General index to the second twenty volumes of the Geographical Journal, 1903–12. 1925.

4376 Third general index to the Geographical Journal, vols. 41–60, 1913–22. 1930. [Fourth general index, vols. 61–80, and fifth general index, vols. 81–100, were published 1935–51]

Other publications:

4377 Maps and map-making: three lectures delivered under the auspices of the Society, by E. A. Reeves. 1910.

4378 Review of British geographical work, 1889–1912, by O. J. R. Howarth. *P.* 1913.

4379 Some account of the Raleigh and Geographical Club, by Sir C. R. Markham. Seventh edition. Revised by J. S. Keltie. *P.* 1913.

4380 East Africa: an address to the Society on 28 Jan. 1918, by General Smuts. 1918. [Includes a brief account of the campaign against the Germans, 1916–17]

4381 The record of the Royal Geographical Society, 1830–1930, by H. R. Mill. 1930.

Reproductions of early engraved maps:

4382 The map of the world on Mercator's projection by J. Hondius, Amsterdam, 1608 [25 sheets folio], with a memoir by E. Heawood [*P.* folio]. 2 vols. 1927.

4383 English county maps [16th–17th cent.] in the collection of the Society [21 sheets folio]. Introd. and notes by E. Heawood [*P.* folio]. 2 vols. 1932.

a 1: England and Ireland. Anon.

b 2: Chester, by Saxton.

c 3: Durham, by Saxton.

d 4: Hampshire, by Saxton.

e 5: Hertfordshire, by Saxton.

f 6: Lancashire, by Saxton.

g 7: Surrey, by Norden.

h 8: Sussex, by Norden.

i 9: Hampshire, by Norden.

j 10: Eastern half of Kent, by Symonson.

k 11: Surrey. Anon.

l 12: Hertfordshire. Anon.

m 13: Northamptonshire. Anon.

n 14: Leicestershire and Rutland. Anon.

o 15: Warwickshire. Anon.

p 16: Staffordshire. Anon.

q 17: Essex. Anon.

r 18: Kent and Sussex, by Camden.

s 19: Sussex, by Speed.

t 20: Cheshire, by Speed.

u 21: Part of a set of playing cards with county maps. Anon.

Reproductions of early ms. maps:

4384 The portolan chart of Angellino de Dalorto, 1325 [4 sheets folio], with a note on the surviving charts and atlases of the 14th cent., by A. R. Hinks [*P.* folio]. 2 vols. 1929.

ROYAL HISTORICAL SOCIETY

Founded 1868, as the Historical Society, to promote and foster the study of history by assisting in the publication of rare and valuable documents, and by the publication from time to time of volumes of transactions and publications. Title changed to above form in 1872. Absorbed the Camden Society in 1897.

Transactions, new ser., vols. 15–20 (1901–[6]):

4385 Vol. 15.

a The later history of the Ironsides, by C. H. Firth.

b Correspondence of an English diplomatic agent [William Perwich] in Paris, 1669–77, by M. Beryl Curran.

c The *denarius sancti Petri* in England, by O. Jensen. [Contd. in vol. 19]

4386 Vol. 16.

a Some materials for a new edition of Polydore Vergil's 'History', by F. A. Gasquet.

b The internal organisation of the Merchant Adventurers of England, by W. E. Lingelbach.

c The high court of admiralty in relation to national history, commerce, and the colonisation of America, 1550–1650, by R. G. Marsden.

d State papers of the early Stuarts and the Interregnum, by Mrs. S. C. Lomas.

e An unknown conspiracy against Henry VII [1503], by I. S. Leadam. [See also vol. 18 below]

f Social conditions of England during the wars of the roses, by V. B. Redstone.

4387 Vol. 17.

a The English Premonstratensians, by F. A. Gasquet.

b The intellectual influence of English monasticism between the 10th and the 12th cent., by Rose Graham.

c Royalist and Cromwellian armies in Flanders, 1657–62, by C. H. Firth.

d Development of industry and commerce in Wales during the middle ages, by E. A. Lewis.

e Italian bankers and the English crown, by R. J. Whitwell.

f Bondmen under the Tudors, by A. Savine.

4388 Vol. 18.

a Canning and Spanish America, by E. M. Lloyd.

b The holy maid of Kent [Elizabeth Barton, d. 1534], by A. D. Cheney.

c The finance of Malton priory [Yorks.], 1244–57, by Rose Graham.

d A supposed conspiracy against Henry VII [1503], by J. Gairdner. [See also vol. 16 above]

e The midland revolt and the inquisitions of depopulation of 1607, by E. F. Gay.

f The minority of Henry III, by G. J. Turner. [Contd. in 3rd ser., vol. 1]

4389 Vol. 19.

a The beginnings of the king's council, by J. F. Baldwin.

b The English occupation of Tangier, 1661–83, by Enid Routh.

c Beverley town riots, 1381–2, by C. T. Flower.

d Inclosure of common fields in the 17th cent., by Ellen M. Leonard.

e Polydore Vergil in the English law courts, by I. S. Leadam.

f The case of Dr. Crome [Edward Crome, d. 1562], by R. H. Brodie.

g Bondmen in Surrey under the Tudors, by H. E. Malden.

h English ships in the reign of James I, by R. G. Marsden.

4390 Vol. 20.

a Mr. Canning's rhyming 'despatch' to Sir Charles Bagot [1826], by Sir H. Poland.

b Canning and the secret intelligence from Tilsit, July 6–23, 1807, by J. H. Rose.

c The northern policy of George I to 1718, by J. F. Chance.

d Beginnings of the Anglo-Portuguese alliance, by Violet Shillington.

e The study of 19th cent. history, by P. Ashley.

f The rebellion of the earls, 1569, by Rachel R. Reid.

Transactions, 3rd ser., vols. 1–11 (1907–17):

4391 Vol. 1.

a A contemporary drawing of the burning of Brighton in the time of Henry VIII [1514], by J. Gairdner.

b The northern treaties of 1719–20 [and George I's part in their negotiation], by J. F. Chance.

c Commercial relations of England and Portugal, 1487–1807, by Annie B. W. Chapman.

d The diaries (home and foreign) of Sir Justinian Isham, 1704–36, by H. I. Longden.

e Some Elizabethan penances in the diocese of Ely, ed. H. Hall.

4392 Vol. 2.

a The ballad history of the reigns of Henry VII and Henry VIII, by C. H. Firth.

b The eclipse of the Yorkes [1760–70], by B. Williams.

c Diary of an Elizabethan gentlewoman [Margaret, Lady Hoby, d. 1633], by Evelyn Fox.

d The Bardon papers: a collection of contemporary documents relating to the trial of Mary, Queen of Scots, 1586, by C. Cotton.

e The siege of Madras, 1746, and the action of La Bourdonnais, by G. W. Forest.

4393 Vol. 3.

a An address on the occasion of the commemoration of the bicentenary of William Pitt, Earl of Chatham, by F. Harrison.

b The ballad history of the reigns of the later Tudors, by C. H. Firth.

c Sir Otho de Grandison, 1238?–1328, by C. L. Kingsford.

d Causes of the war of Jenkins' Ear, 1739, by H. W. V. Temperley.

e English traders and the Spanish Canary inquisition in the Canaries during the reign of Queen Elizabeth, by Leonora de Alberti and Annie B. W. Chapman.

f The origin of the *Regium donum* [a pension paid by the crown to Presbyterian ministers in Ireland], by C. E. Pike.

4394 Vol. 4.

a The finance of Lord Treasurer Godolphin [Sidney Godolphin, 1st Earl, d. 1712], by I. S. Leadam.

b Sources for the history of Sir Robert Walpole's financial administration, by H. Hall.

c The two Sir John Fastolfs [Sir John Fastolf of Caister and Sir John Fastolph of Nacton], by L. W. V. Harcourt.

d Concerning the Historical Manuscripts Commission, by R. A. Roberts.

e The Duc de Choiseul and the invasion of England, 1768–70, by Margaret C. Morison.

f The estate book of Henry de Bray of Harlestone, Northants., 1289–1340, by Dorothy Willis.

g The collection of ship money in the reign of Charles I, by Miss M. D. Gordon.

4395 Vol. 5.

a The ballad history of the reign of James I, by C. H. Firth.

b Respublica Christiana, by J. N. Figgis. [The mediaeval conception of the church]

c The intrigue to deprive the Earl of Essex of the lord lieutenancy of Ireland [1676–7], by C. E. Pike.

d Notes on the Agincourt roll, by J. H. Wylie.

e The possession of Cardigan priory by Chertsey abbey: a study in some mediaeval forgeries, by H. E. Malden.

f Relations between England and the northern powers, 1689–97. Pt. 1: Denmark, by M. Lane.

4396 Vol. 6.

a The family as a political unit [with special reference to Scottish history], by W. Cunningham.

b The reign of Charles I, by C. H. Firth.

c Some aspects of Castlereagh's foreign policy, by C. K. Webster.

d Parish clergy of the 13th and 14th cent., by H. G. Richardson.

e The Commonwealth charters, by B. L. K. Henderson.

f The Eastland company in Prussia, 1579–85, by A. Szelagowski and N. S. B. Gras.

g Records of the English African companies, by H. Jenkinson.

4397 Vol. 7.

a The guildry and trade incorporations in Scottish towns, by W. Cunningham.

b The development of the study of 17th cent. history, by C. H. Firth.

c England and the Polish-Saxon problem at the congress of Vienna, by C. K. Webster.

d Castlereagh's instructions for the conferences at Vienna, 1822, by J. E. S. Green.

e The pedigree of Earl Godwin, by A. Anscombe.

f Some mercenaries of Henry of Lancaster, 1327–30, by V. B. Redstone.

g Side-lights upon the assessment and collection of mediaeval subsidies, by J. F. Willard.

h The order of the Holy Cross (Crutched Friars) in England, by E. Beck.

4398 Vol. 8.

a Presidential address [a survey of the study of 17th cent. history], by C. H. Firth.

b The authenticity of the 'Lords' Journals' in the 16th cent., by A. F. Pollard.

c John Wycliffe, the reformer, and Canterbury Hall, Oxford, by H. S. Cronin.

d Mounted infantry in mediaeval warfare, by J. E. Morris.

e Prégent de Bidoux's raid in Sussex in 1514 and the Cotton ms. Augustus 1 (1), 18, by A. Anscombe.

f Secular aid for excommunication, by R. C. Fowler.

g Manuscripts at Oxford relating to the later Tudors, 1547–1603, by F. J. Routledge.

4399 Vol. 9.

a Presidential address [relations between England and the Netherlands], by C. H. Firth.

b The Despenser war in Glamorgan [1321], by J. C. Davies.

c The errors of Lord Macaulay in his estimation of the squires and parsons of the 17th cent., by P. H. Ditchfield.

d A suggestion for the publication of the correspondence of Queen Elizabeth with the Russian Czars, by Inna Lubimenko.

e The historical side of the Old English poem of 'Widsith', by A. Anscombe.

f History of the Canadian archives, by A. G. Doughty.

4400 Vol. 10.

a Presidential address [the study of English foreign policy], by C. H. Firth.

b The influence of the writings of Sir John Fortescue, by Caroline A. J. Skeel.

c Sources available for the study of mediaeval economic history, by E. Lipson.

d An unedited Cely letter of 1482, by H. E. Malden. [George Cely, merchant of the staple at Calais, to Sir John Weston, prior of the Knights of St. John in England, at Naples]

e The burning of Brighton by the French [*temp.* Henry VIII], by L. G. Carr Laughton.

4401 Vol. 11.

a Presidential address [English policy towards Austria], by C. H. Firth.

b The mission of M. Thiers to the neutral powers [Britain, Russia and Austria] in 1870, by J. H. Rose.

c The India Board, 1784–1858, by W. Foster.

d The treason legislation of Henry VIII, 1531–34, by Isobel D. Thornley.

e The Derwentdale plot, 1663, by H. Gee.

f Duelling and militarism, by A. F. Sieveking.

g The historical manuscripts at Lambeth, by C. Jenkins.

Transactions, 4th ser., vols. 1–16 (1918–22):

4402 Vol. 1.

a Presidential address [the development of rumour in times of political or military crisis], by C. W. C. Oman.

b Traces of primitive agricultural organisation as sug-

gested by a survey of the manor of Martham, Norf., 1101–1292, by W. Hudson.

c Wellington, Boislecomte, and the congress of Verona, 1822, by J. E. S. Green.

d Correspondence of the first Stuarts with the first Romanovs, by Inna Lubimenko.

e The Ceylon expedition of 1803, by V. M. Methley.

f The establishment of the great farm of the English customs, by A. P. Newton.

g The place of the council in the 15th cent., by T. F. T. Plucknett.

h The system of British colonial administration of the Crown colonies in the 17th and 18th cent. compared with the system prevailing in the 19th cent., by H. E. Egerton.

i The constitutional development of South Africa, by L. S. Amery.

j The constitutional development of Canada, by E. M. Wrong.

4403 Vol. 2.

a National boundaries and treaties of peace, by C. Oman.

b British and allied archives during the war. [Reports on their condition, 1918. Includes: England, by H. Hall; Scotland, by R. K. Hannay; Ireland, by H. Wood; Wales, by J. Ballinger]

c The metropolitan visitation of the diocese of Worcester by Archbishop Winchelsey in 1301, by Rose Graham.

d The relations of Henry, Cardinal York [d. 1807] with the British government, by W. W. Seton.

e The Whigs and the Peninsular war, 1804–14, by G. Davies.

f The question of the Netherlands in 1829–30, by G. W. T. Omond.

g The trial of Sir Walter Raleigh, by Sir H. L. Stephen.

4404 Vol. 3.

a British and allied archives during the war. Series II. [Includes: The Canadian war records, by H. P. Biggar; Australia's records of the war; The Union of South Africa, by C. G. Botha]

b The English in Russia during the second half of the 16th cent., by Mildred Wretts-Smith.

c Unpublished documents relating to town life in Coventry, by Mary D. Harris. [Royal and other correspondence relating to Coventry, and the diary of Robert Beake, mayor, 1655]

d The Black Death in Wales, by W. Rees.

e The Commons' journals of the Tudor period, by J. E. Neale.

4405 Vol. 4.

a Some mediaeval conceptions of ancient history, by Sir C. W. C. Oman.

b Status of *villani* and other tenants in Danish East Anglia in pre-Conquest times, by W. Hudson.

c The council of the west [or the council in the western parts, established 1539], by Caroline A. J. Skeel.

d Illustrations of the mediaeval municipal history of London from the Guildhall records, by A. H. Thomas.

e Notes from the ecclesiastical court records at Somerset House, by F. W. X. Fincham.

f The extent of the English forest in the 13th cent., by Margaret L. Bazeley.

g Norse settlements in the British islands, by A. Bugge.

4406 Vol. 5.

a The embassy of William Harborne to Constantinople, 1583–8, by H. G. Rawlinson.

b Year books and plea rolls as sources of historical information, by H. G. Richardson.

c The political theory of the Indian mutiny, by F. W. Buckler. [See reply in vol. 7]

d The influence of the industrial revolution (1760–90) on the demand for parliamentary reform, by Gwen Whale.

e Practical notes on historical research, by Sir F. Piggott.

f The origin and growth of the office of deputy-lieutenant, by Gladys S. Thomson.

g English establishments on the Gold Coast in the second half of the 18th cent., by Eveline C. Martin.

4407 Vol. 6.

a The relations of Great Britain with Guiana, by G. C. Edmundson.

b The birth of an American state, Georgia: an effort of philanthropy and Protestant propaganda, by R. A. Roberts.

c The system of account in the wardrobe of Edward I, by C. Johnson.

d The English colony in Rome during the 14th cent., by E. Re.

e Portraits of historians, by Sir C. H. Firth.

f The east midlands and the second civil war, May–July, 1648, by E. W. Hensman.

4408 Vol. 7.

a Edward I and his tenants-in-chief, by Eleanor C. Lodge.

b The struggle of the Dutch with the English for the Russian market in the 17th cent., by Inna Lubimenko.

c Courts and court rolls of St. Albans abbey, by A. E. Levett.

d Some aspects of mediaeval travel, notably transport and accommodation, with special reference to the wardrobe accounts of Henry, Earl of Derby, 1390–93, by Grace Stretton.

e The English province of the order of Cluny in the 15th cent., by Rose Graham.

f A reply to Mr. F. W. Buckler's 'The political theory of the Indian mutiny', by D. Dewar and H. L. Garrett.

4409 Vol. 8.

a William IV of Orange and his English marriage, by P. Geyl.

b Debates in the House of Lords, 1628, by Frances H. Relf.

c Financial administration under Henry I, by G. H. White.

d Coal-mining in the 17th cent., by Asta Moller.

e Devonshire ports in the 14th and 15th cent., by Frances A. Mace.

f The beginning of the dissolution: Christchurch, Aldgate, 1532, by Eliza Jeffries Davis.

g Experiments in exchequer procedure, 1200–32, by Mabel H. Mills.

h The exchequer year, by H. G. Richardson. [See also supplementary note in vol. 9]

4410 Vol. 9.

a Presidential address, by T. F. Tout. [The history of the Society]

b Irish parliaments in the reign of Edward II, by Maude V. Clarke.

c An episode in Anglo-Russian relations during the war of the Austrian succession [with special reference to the activities of Friedrich Lorentz, fl. *c.* 1744, British representative at Berlin], by Sir R. Lodge.

d The authorship of the *Defensor Pacis*, by Marian J. Tooley.

e The making of a Crown colony: British Guiana, 1803–33, by Lillian M. Penson.

f The cattle trade between Wales and England from the 15th to the 19th cent., by Caroline Skeel.

g The foundations of English history, by F. M. Stenton. [Sources for early English history]

4411 Vol. 10.

a The reign of Henry III: some suggestions, by E. F. Jacob.

b Illustrations of English history in the mediaeval registers of the parlement of Paris, by H. G. Richardson.

c The diplomatic service under William III, by M. Lane.

d Reforms at the exchequer, 1232–42, by Mabel H. Mills.

e The duchy of Cornwall: its history and administration, 1640–60, by Mary Coate.

f Some attempts at imperial co-operation during the reign of Queen Anne, by W. T. Morgan. [A British attack on Canada, 1711]

g General and provincial chapters of the English Black monks, 1215–1540, by W. A. Pantin.

4412 Vol. 11.

a The human side of mediaeval records, by T. F. Tout.

b The Public Record Office and the historical student: a retrospect, by A. E. Stamp.

c Anglo-Russian relations during the first English revolution, by Inna Lubimenko.

d The merchant adventurers of Bristol in the 15th cent., by Eleanora M. Carus-Wilson.

e A study in the history of Clare, Suff., with special reference to its development as a borough, by Gladys A. Thornton.

f The will of Polydore Vergil, by E. A. Whitney and P. P. Cam. [Chiefly an account of his life and work]

g The origins of parliament, by H. G. Richardson.

h The transformation of the keepers of the peace into the justices of the peace, 1327–80, by Bertha H. Putnam.

i Administration of the diocese of Ely during the vacancies of the see, 1298–9 and 1302–3, by Rose Graham.

j The system of account in the wardrobe of Edward II, by J. H. Johnson.

k The imprisonment of Lord Danby in the Tower, 1679–1684, by A. M. Evans.

l Relations of William III with the Swiss Protestants, 1689–97, by L. A. Robertson.

m Lord Palmerston's policy for the rejuvenation of Turkey, 1839–41, by F. S. Rodkey.

4413 Vol. 13.

a Public records of Ireland before and after 1922, by H. Wood.

b King Stephen's earldoms, by G. H. White.

c Spanish resistance to the English occupation of Jamaica, 1655–60, by Irene A. Wright.

d The proposed Anglo-Franco-American treaty of 1852 to guarantee Cuba to Spain, by A. A. Ettinger.

e The later history and administration of the customs revenue in England, 1671–1814, by B. R. Leftwich.

f William Huskisson and the controverted elections at Liskeard in 1802 and 1804, by G. S. Veitch.

4414 Vol. 14.

a The mission of Henry Legge to Berlin, 1748, by Sir R. Lodge.

b Forfeitures and treason in 1388, by Maude V. Clarke.

c The borough business of a Suffolk town (Orford), 1559–1660, by R. A. Roberts.

d English architecture in the 17th and 18th cent., by Sir R. Blomfield.

e English neutrality in the war of the Polish succession: a commentary upon *Diplomatic Instructions, vol. 6, France, 1727–44*, by Sir R. Lodge.

f The Elibank plot, 1752–3, by Sir C. Petrie.

g The humanitarian movement of the early 19th cent., to remedy abuses on emigrant vessels to America, by K. A. Walpole.

h Economic aspects of the negotiations at Ryswick [1697], by W. T. Morgan.

4415 Vol. 15.

a Sir Benjamin Keene, K.B. [d. 1757]: a study in Anglo-Spanish relations in the earlier part of the 18th cent., by Sir R. Lodge.

b William of Ely, the king's treasurer, ?1195–1215, by H. G. Richardson.

c Wilkins's *Concilia* and the 15th cent., by E. F. Jacob.

d Edmund Dudley [d. 1510], minister of Henry VII, by D. M. Brodie.

e Queen Elizabeth and the siege of Rouen, 1591, by R. B. Wernham.

f The transference of lands in England, 1640–60, by H. E. Chesney.

g The secret service under Charles II and James II, by J. Walker.

h The Polwarth papers: a commentary upon the Historical Manuscripts Commission's report (1911–31), by Sir R. Lodge.

4416 Vol. 16.

a The treaty of Seville, 1729, by Sir R. Lodge.

b Bede as a classical and a patristic scholar, by M. L. W. Laistner.

c Ranulf Flambard and early Anglo-Norman administration, by R. W. Southern.

d Woburn abbey and the dissolution of the monasteries, by Gladys S. Thomson.

e The office of the English resident ambassador: its evolution as illustrated by the career of Sir Thomas Spinelly, 1509–22, by Betty Behrens.

f The economic and social effect of usury laws in the 18th cent., by Sybil Campbell.

g The English factory at Lisbon: some chapters in its history, by Sir R. Lodge.

Camden new series:

4417 Vol. 62. The Clarke papers: selections from the papers of William Clarke, secretary to the council of the army, 1647–9, and to General Monck and the commanders of the army in Scotland, 1651–60, ed. C. H. Firth. Vol. iv. 1901. [Vols. i–ii were published by the Camden Soc. as new ser., vols. 49 and 54, 1891–4. Vol. iii was published by the Royal Historical Soc. in 1899 as Camden new ser., vol. 61]

Camden 3rd ser., vols. 3–48:

4418 Vol. 3. Despatches and correspondence of John, 2nd Earl of Buckinghamshire, ambassador to the court of Catherine II of Russia, 1762–5, ed. with introd. and notes by Adelaide D'A. Collyer. Vol. ii. 1902. [Vol. i was published in 1900 as 3rd ser., vol. 2]

4419 Vol. 4. Camden miscellany, vol. 10. 1902.

a Journal of Sir Roger Wilbraham, solicitor general in Ireland and master of requests, 1593–1616, together with notes in another hand, 1642–9, ed. H. S. Scott. 1902.

b Travels and life of Sir Thomas Hoby, of Bisham Abbey, written by himself, 1547–64, ed. E. Powell. 1902.

c Prince Rupert at Lisbon [a contemporary narrative and correspondence relating to the reception of the Prince's fleet, 1649], ed. S. R. Gardiner. 1902.

4420 Vol. 5. Despatches of William Perwich, English agent in Paris, 1669–77, ed. M. Beryl Curran. 1903.

4421 Vols. 6, 10, 12. Collectanea Anglo-Premonstratensia: documents drawn from the original register of the order and the transcript of another register, arranged and ed. F. A. Gasquet. 3 vols. 1904–6.

4422 Vol. 7. Select despatches from the Foreign Office archives relating to the formation of the third coalition against France, 1804–5, ed. J. Holland Rose. 1904.

4423 Vol. 8. The Presbyterian movement in the reign of Elizabeth, as illustrated by the minute book of the Dedham classis, 1582–9, ed. R. G. Usher. 1905.

4424 Vol. 9. State trials of the reign of Edward I, 1289–93, ed. T. F. Tout and Hilda Johnstone. 1906.

4425 Vol. 11. Acts and ordinances of the Eastland [Merchants] company, ed. Maud Sellers. 1906.

4426 Vol. 13. Camden miscellany, vol. 11. 1907.

a Some unpublished letters of Gilbert Burnet, the historian [to George Saville, Earl of Halifax, 1680], ed. Helen C. Foxcroft. 1907. [Cancelled title-page gives editor's name as Foxwell]

b Extracts from the papers of Thomas Woodcock (*ob.* 1695), ed. G. C. M. Smith. 1907.

c Memoirs of Sir George Courthop, 1616–85, ed. Sophia C. Lomas. 1907.

d The Commonwealth charter of the city of Salisbury, Sept. 1656, ed. H. Hall. 1907.

4427 Vol. 14. The relation of Sydnam Poyntz, 1624–36 [an autobiography], ed. A. T. S. Goodrick. 1908.

4428 Vol. 15. Diary of the Rev. Ralph Josselin, 1616–83, ed. E. Hockliffe. 1908.

4429 Vols. 16, 19. Despatches from Paris, 1784–90, selected and ed. from the Foreign Office correspondence by O. Browning. 2 vols. 1909–10. [Vol. i: 1784–7. Vol. ii: 1788–90]

4430 Vol. 17. The Bardon papers: documents relating to the imprisonment and trial of Mary, Queen of Scots, ed. C. Read, with prefatory note by C. Cotton. 1909.

4431 Vol. 18. Camden miscellany, vol. 12. 1910.

a Two [16th cent.] London chronicles from the collections of John Stow, ed. C. L. Kingsford. 1910.

b Life of Sir John Digby, 1605–45, ed. G. Bernard. 1910.

c Iter bellicosum. Adam Wheeler his account of 1685 [Monmouth rebellion], ed. H. E. Malden. 1910.

d Common rights at Cottenham and Stretham, Cambs., ed. W. Cunningham. 1910.

4432 Vols. 20, 21. John of Gaunt's register [1371–5], ed. S. Armitage-Smith. 2 vols. 1911.

4433 Vol. 22. The official diary of Lieut.-Gen. Adam Williamson, deputy-lieutenant of the Tower, 1722–47, ed. J. C. Fox. 1912.

4434 Vol. 23. English merchants and the Spanish inquisition in the Canaries [*temp.* Eliz. I], ed. Leonora de Alberti and Annie B. W. Chapman. 1912.

4435 Vol. 24. Selections from the correspondence of Arthur Capel, Earl of Essex, 1675–7, ed. C. E. Pike. 1913. [Continues Camden Soc. new ser., vol. 47, published in 1890]

4436 Vol. 26. The official papers of Sir Nathaniel Bacon of Stiffkey, Norf., as J.P., 1580–1620, ed. H. W. Saunders. 1915. [Additional papers occur in *Camden miscellany*, vol. 16, published in 1936]

4437 Vol. 27. The estate book of Henry de Bray, of Harleston, Northants. *c.* 1289–1340, ed. Dorothy Willis. 1916.

4438 Vol. 28. Autobiography of Thomas Raymond [1610–81], and memoirs of the family of Guise of Elmore, Glos., ed. G. Davies. 1917.

4439 Vols. 29, 30. The Stonor letters and papers, 1290–1483, ed. C. L. Kingsford. 2 vols. 1919. [See also vol. 34 below]

4440 Vol. 31. The Nicholas papers: correspondence of Sir Edward Nicholas, secretary of state, ed. Sir G. F. Warner.

Vol. iv: 1657–60. 1920. [Vols. i–iii, covering the period 1641–56, were published by the Camden Soc. as new ser., vols. 40, 50, 57, in 1886, 1892, and 1897]

4441 Vols. 32, 35, 36, 38, 39, 43. British diplomatic instructions, 1689–1789. Vols. i–vi, 1922–30. [Vols. i and v: Sweden, 1689–1727 and 1727–89, ed. J. F. Chance. Vols. ii, iv, vi: France, 1689–1721, 1721–27, and 1727–44, ed. L. G. Wickham Legg. Vol. iii: Denmark, ed. J. F. Chance. Vol. vii: France, 1745–89, was published in 1934]

4442 Vol. 33. Parliamentary papers of John Robinson, 1774–1784, ed. W. T. Laprade. 1922.

4443 Vol. 34. Camden miscellany, vol. 13. 1924.

  a Gesta Dunelmensia, 1300, ed. R. K. Richardson. 1924.
  b Supplementary Stonor letters and papers, 1314–1482, by C. L. Kingsford. 1923.
  c Devereux papers, with Richard Broughton's memoranda, 1575–1601, ed. H. E. Malden. 1923.
  d Voyage of Captain William Jackson, 1642–5, ed. V. T. Harlow. 1923.
  e The English conquest of Jamaica: an account of what happened in the island of Jamaica, from May 20, 1655, when the English laid siege to it, up to July 3, 1656, by Captain Julian de Castilla, translated and ed. Irene A. Wright. 1923.

4444 Vol. 37. Camden miscellany, vol. 14. 1926.

  a Spanish narratives of the English attack on Santo Domingo, 1655, transcribed, translated, and ed. Irene A. Wright. 1926.
  b Embajada Española: an anonymous contemporary Spanish guide to diplomatic procedure in the last quarter of the 17th cent., translated and ed. H. J. Chaytor.
  c The will of Peter de Aqua Blanca, bishop of Hereford, 1268, ed. C. E. Woodruff. 1926.
  d The ransom of John II, King of France, 1360–70, ed. Dorothy M. Broome. 1926.
  e Historia sive narracio de modo et forma mirabilis parliamenti apud Westmonasterium, 1386, per Thomam Favent [fl. 1394–1400] clericum indictata, ed. May McKisack. 1926.

4445 Vol. 40. The *Vita Wulfstani* of William of Malmesbury, to which are added extant abridgments of this work and the miracles and translation of St. Wulfstan, ed. R. R. Darlington. 1928.

4446 Vol. 41. Camden miscellany, vol. 15. 1929.

  a A transcript of 'The red book', a detailed account of the Hereford bishopric estates in the 13th cent., ed. A. T. Bannister. 1929.
  b Edward II, the lords ordainers, and Piers Gaveston's jewels and horses, 1312–13, ed. R. A. Roberts. 1929. [A report to Pope Clement V by papal nuncios sent to compose differences that had arisen after Gaveston's death]
  c Table of Canterbury archbishopric charters [1330], transcribed and ed. Irene J. Churchill. 1929.
  d An early admiralty case (1361), ed. C. Johnson.
  e Select tracts and table books relating to English weights and measures, 1100–1742, ed. H. Hall and Frieda J. Nicholas. 1929.
  f An English prisoner [? Sir William Codrington] in Paris during the Terror, 1793–4, ed. V. T. Harlow.

4447 Vol. 42. Notes of the debates in the House of Lords officially taken by Robert Bowyer and Henry Elsing, clerks of the parliaments, 1621, 1625, 1628, ed. Frances H. Relf. 1929.

4448 Vol. 44. Private correspondence of Chesterfield and Newcastle, 1744–6, ed., with introd. and notes, by Sir R.

Lodge. Pt. 1: Chesterfield at the Hague. Pt. 2: Chesterfield at Dublin. 1930.

4449 Vols. 45, 47. Documents illustrating the activities of the general and provincial chapters of the English Black monks, 1215–1540, ed. W. A. Pantin. Vols. i–ii, 1931–3. [Vol. iii was published in 1937]

4450 Vol. 46. British diplomatic representatives, 1689–1789, ed. D. B. Horn. 1932. [Continued for the period 1789–1852 in Camden 3rd ser., vol. 50, published 1934]

4451 Vol. 48. The diplomatic correspondence of Richard II, ed. E. Perroy. 1933.

Other publications:

4452 Bibliography of the historical works of Dr. Creighton, late bishop of London, Dr. Stubbs, late bishop of Oxford, Dr. S. R. Gardiner, and Lord Acton. Ed. W. A. Shaw. 1903.

4453 Catalogue of the library of the Royal Historical Soc. 1915.

4454 Magna Carta commemoration essays, ed. H. E. Malden, with a preface by Viscount Bryce. 1917.

  a Preface [on the place of Magna Carta in English law and politics], by Viscount Bryce.
  b Magna Carta, 1215–1915, by W. S. McKechnie.
  c Innocent III and the great charter, by G. B. Adams.
  d 'Barons' and 'knights' in the great charter, by J. H. Round.
  e Magna Carta, c. 39: *Nullus liber homo*, etc., by Sir P. Vinogradoff.
  f *Per iudicium parium vel per legem terrae*, by F. M. Powicke.
  g Magna Carta and common law, by C. H. McIlwain.
  h The influence of Magna Carta on American constitutional development, by H. D. Hazeltine.
  i Magna Carta and Spanish mediaeval jurisprudence, by R. Altamira.
  j Financial records of the reign of John, by H. Jenkinson.

4455 Repertory of British archives. Pt. 1: England, comp. H. Hall. 1920.

4456 List and index of the publications of the Royal Historical Society, 1871–1924, and of the Camden Society, 1840–97, ed. H. Hall. 1925.

4457 Bibliography of British history: Stuart period, 1603–1714, ed. G. Davis. 1928. Issued under the direction of the Royal Historical Soc. and the American Historical Association.

4458 Bibliography of British history: Tudor period, 1485–1603, ed. C. Read. 1933. Issued under the direction of the American Historical Association and the Royal Historical Soc.

ROYAL INSTITUTE OF BRITISH ARCHITECTS

Founded 1834, as the Institute of British Architects, for the general advancement of civil architecture and the promotion of the acquirement of knowledge of the various arts and sciences connected therewith. Absorbed the Architectural Society in 1842, and the Society of Architects in 1925. Title changed to above form in 1866.

Journal, 3rd ser., vols. 8–41 (1901–34):

4459 Vol. 8.

  a Education in building [with particular reference to mediaeval English masons], by W. R. Lethaby.

4460 Vol. 9.

a Architectural discoveries of 1901 at Stonehenge, by D. J. Blow.

4461 Vol. 10.

a Some points of interest in our old churches, by W. Millard.
b A Pugin student's tour in the Cotswolds, by C. W. Smith. [Cotswold architecture]
c The architectural development of London, by O. Fleming.

4462 Vol. 11.

a Lead architecture, by J. S. Gardner.
b Sir John Vanbrugh: architect and dramatist, by R. P. Oglesby.
c Plaster decoration, by J. D. Crace.
d The statues of Wells, with some contemporary foreign examples, by E. S. Prior.
e English architecture of the 15th cent., by W. H. Wood.
f Screens and screen work in the English church, by F. B. Bond. [Contd. in vol. 12]

4463 Vol. 12.

a English church architecture in its relation to English history, by H. C. Windley.
b The evolution of [English] domestic architecture, by R. P. S. Twizell.
c Description of the tower and spire of St. Nicholas' cathedral, Newcastle-on-Tyne, by W. H. Wood.

4464 Vol. 13.

a Furniture [its development in England from the middle ages to the present day], by E. G. Dawber.
b Leadwork [with particular reference to English lead-covered spires], by F. W. Troup and L. Weaver.
c Plaster-work [with particular reference to decorative plaster ceilings], by G. P. Bankart and L. A. Turner.
d George Devey [d. 1886, architect]: a biographical essay, by W. H. Godfrey.

4465 Vol. 14.

a Sundry draughts and plans by Huntingdon Smithson [d. 1648, architect], of Bolsover, by M. B. Adams.
b Devonshire churches, by H. Reed.

4466 Vol. 15.

a The present condition of St. Paul's cathedral [1907, with a brief survey of the conditions under which it was built], by M. Macartney.
b The story of a [17th cent.] wood-carver [Phillip Wood] of St. Paul's, by W. J. Gribble.
c Architecture of the bridges of London, by B. Pite.
d Church of the Holy Trinity, Twynham, commonly called Christchurch priory, Hampshire, by G. J. Coombs.
e Romano-British precedents for some English romanesque details, by C. F. Innocent.

4467 Vol. 16.

a The development of house design in the reigns of Elizabeth and James, as illustrated by contemporary architectural drawings, by J. A. Gotch.
b Heraldry in relation to architecture, by E. B. Kirby.
c Church of St. Nicholas, Stevenage, Herts., by W. Millard.
d Excavations at Corstopitum, Northumb., by W. H. Knowles.

4468 Vol. 17.

a The site of the Globe theatre of Shakespeare on Bankside as shown by maps of the period, by G. Hubbard.
b The Greek revival in England, by L. B. Budden.

c Ashburnham House and the precincts of Westminster abbey, by H. Sirr.
d [John] Carr of York [d. 1807], by S. D. Kitson.
e Ancient painted glass of York minster, by G. Benson.
f House and garden: an essay on the treatment of gardens in connection with buildings, by J. A. O. Allan.

4469 Vol. 18.

a Notes on the architectural history of Lincoln minster from 1192 to 1255, by F. Bond and W. Watkins.
b The monumental work of the Cosmati at Westminster abbey, by C. Formilli.
c St. Katharine's church, Ickleford, Herts., by W. Millard.
d Mr. Thorpe, clerk of Her Majesty's works (1600), by H. Sirr.
e St. Mary's church, Baldock, Herts., by W. Millard.
f The Burlington-Devonshire collection of drawings, with special reference to the relations between Inigo Jones and John Webb, by J. A. Gotch.
g East Anglian cathedrals: a study of romanesque, by J. L. Ball.
h John Thorpe [fl. 1570–1610] and Roland Stickles, and architectural drawings of their times, by H. Sirr.
i Architecture of Cambridge, by W. S. Purchon.
j Contemporary information relating to 17th and 18th cent. architects, by H. Sirr.
k Lincoln cathedral: the new reading, by J. Bilson.
l The interleaved copy of Wren's *Parentalia* [1750] with ms. insertions, by L. Weaver.
m The design and construction of belfry stages and spires in stone and brick, by H. L. Honeyman.
n Life and work of Professor Cockerell [d. 1863], by E. Prestwich.
o Ewan Christian [d. 1895, architect]: a memoir, by J. S. Adkins.

4470 Vol. 19.

a Church of St. Mary, Ashwell, Herts.: its structural development, by W. Millard.
b Collegiate architecture, by E. Warren.
c The Royal Institute library and some of its contents, by C. H. Townsend.
d Architects from George IV to George V, by M. B. Adams.
e Architecture of Oxford, by W. S. Purchon.
f Inigo Jones in history and tradition, by H. Sirr.

4471 Vol. 20.

a Church of St. Ippolyts, Herts., by W. Millard.
b The buildings of St. Mary's guild, Lincoln, locally known as John Gaunt's stables, by W. Watkins.
c Catalogue of drawings attributed to Inigo Jones, preserved at Worcester College, Oxford, and at Chatsworth, by J. A. Gotch.
d The preservation of ancient monuments, by W. J. Davies.

4472 Vol. 21.

a Old painted glass in the parish churches of York, by G. Benson.
b Church of St. Mary, King's Walden, Herts., by W. Millard.
c St. Mary's guild, Lincoln, and mediaeval builders, by W. Watkins.
d Stained glass, by N. Heaton.
e The development of London and the London building acts, by W. R. Davidge.

4473 Vol. 22.

a The rebuilding and the workmen of St. Paul's cathedral from the accounts, by J. M. W. Halley.
b English church monuments, by J. Williams.

c The evolution of the architectural competition, by H. V. Lanchester. [Also printed in *Architectural Association Notes*, vol. 39, no. 123a above]

4474 Vol. 23.

a The study of mediaeval architecture, by C. H. Moore.

4475 Vol. 24.

a The study of Anglo-Saxon art, by B. Pite.
b Two designs for proposed work at Cambridge by Robert Adam between 1784 and 1789, by A. T. Bolton.

4476 Vol. 25.

a The place of St. Paul's in art, by B. Pite.
b George Edmund Street's sketches at home and abroad, by W. Millard. [G. E. Street, d. 1881, architect]
c The rebuilding of London after the great fire of 1666, by W. G. Bell.
d Augustus Welby Pugin: a sketch, by H. Sirr.

4477 Vol. 27.

a London town-planning schemes in 1666, by S. Perks. [With the full text of John Evelyn's '*Londinum Redivivum* or London Restored']
b A war memorial of the last century [the Wellington Needle, near Taunton], by J. W. Simpson.

4478 Vol. 28.

a The library and collections of the Royal Institute of British Architects, by R. Dircks.
b Westminster abbey: an attempt to read the story of the north transept façade from an examination of ancient prints, by S. H. Seager.
c Some newly found drawings and letters of John Webb, by J. A. Gotch.

4479 Vol. 29.

a Ancient monuments and historical buildings in charge of H.M. Office of Works. [List]
b London clubs, by S. C. Ramsey.
c Exhibition of 17th cent. architectural drawings. [Speeches by J. A. Gotch and Sir B. Fletcher]
d The first half-century of the R.I.B.A. [founded 1834], by J. A. Gotch.
e The work of the mediaeval builder, by G. B. Brown.
f Life and work a century ago: an outline of the career of Sir John Soane, by A. T. Bolton.

4480 Vol. 30.

a Westminster hall roof, by W. Harvey.
b Oxford: a school of architecture, by H. C. Corlette. [With reproductions from E. H. New's prints]
c The law of building outside London, by A. N. C. Shelley.
d Some observations on the character and genius of Sir Christopher Wren, by P. Waterhouse.
e The artist and the man [Sir Christopher Wren], by Sir R. Blomfield.
f John Nash, 1752–1835, by W. H. Nash.
g Architectural education a century ago: being an account of the office of Sir John Soane, with special reference to the career of George Basevi [d. 1845] his pupil, by A. T. Bolton.

4481 Vol. 31.

a An Australian architect of last century: Arthur Ebden Johnson [d. 1895], by J. H. Harvey.
b English architecture, by H. C. Corlette.
c Preservation of ancient monuments and historic buildings, by Sir F. Baines.
d Architecture in Canada, by P. E. Nobbs.
e English Gothic architecture of the 19th cent., by H. S. Goodhart-Rendel.

f The scheme for a Thames embankment after the great fire of London, by S. Perks.
g Historical sketch of Oxford, by E. P. Warren.
h A note on architectural training in the past, with special reference to England, by P. Waterhouse.

4482 Vol. 32.

a Planning for good acoustics, by H. Bagenal.
b Shop fronts and their treatment, by A. J. Davis.
c Pre-Norman free standing stone crosses, by J. Hall.
d The architect in history: his training, status and work, by M. S. Briggs.

4483 Vol. 33.

a The sociological basis of architecture, by S. C. Ramsey.
b Inigo Jones as a collector, by W. G. Keith.
c Lincoln cathedral, by Sir C. Nicholson and Sir F. Fox.
d Sir John Vanbrugh, 1664–1726, by A. T. Bolton.
e The works of Sir Thomas Graham Jackson, R.A. [d. 1924, architect], by H. S. Goodhart-Rendel.
f An architectural history of the Bank of England, by H. R. Steele.
g Raynham Hall, Norf., by Sir R. Blomfield.

4484 Vol. 34.

a Artistic craft guilds of the middle ages, by J. A. Knowles.
b History of the palace of Westminster, by T. Wilson.
c Nicholas Hawksmoor, by H. A. Tipping.
d Burlington architectus, by F. Kimball. [Architectural designs by Richard Boyle, d. 1753, 3rd Earl of Burlington and 4th of Cork. Contd. in vol. 35]

4485 Vol. 35.

a Humphrey Repton, 1752–1818 [landscape gardener], by H. C. Hughes.
b Ancient bridges, by G. H. Jack.
c Inigo Jones: a modern view, by J. A. Gotch.
d A walk around Bath, by M. A. Green. [An architectural survey]
e Dorchester House, by C. Hussey.
f The manor house of north Derbyshire, by E. W. Chapman.

4486 Vol. 36.

a Lincoln's Inn old hall, by Sir J. Simpson.
b [Henry] Bell of Lynn: a contemporary of Sir Christopher Wren, by J. F. Howes.
c The work of George Wittet [d. 1926, consulting architect to the Government of Bombay]: an appreciation, by J. Begg.

4487 Vol. 37.

a Winchester Palace: built by Sir Christopher Wren for Charles II, 1683–5, by A. T. Bolton.
b Architects' drawings of 1800–1851, by A. E. Richardson.

4488 Vol. 38.

a The royal barge: notes on the original drawings by William Kent [d. 1748], in the library of the Royal Institute of British Architects, by A. E. Richardson.
b The first 'sprinkler' system at Drury Lane theatre, by A. V. Sutherland-Graeme.
c The work of Sir Robert Lorimer [architect, d. 1929], by F. W. Deas.
d Manor houses of Sussex, by R. F. Tatchell.
e The college of the vicars choral at Hereford, by S. E. D. Bower.

4489 Vol. 39.

a Notes on 'The New Bridge' at Ferrybridge, John Carr of York, architect, 1797, by A. Booth.

b St. George's chapel, Windsor [and works of repair to it], by Sir H. Brakspear.

c William Kent's designs for the Houses of Parliament, 1730-40, by F. Kimball.

4490 Vol. 40.

a The work of William Wilkins, R.A. [architect, d. 1839], by A. B. Pite.

b The tomb of Sir Justinian Isham of Lamport, and the drawings in the Isham collection in the R.I.B.A. library, by Katharine A. Esdaile.

c A Repton portfolio, by J. Summerson. [Drawings done by or associated with Humphrey Repton, d. 1818, John Adey Repton, d. 1860, and George Stanley Repton, d. 1858]

d The architectural antecedents of Sir Christopher Wren, by G. Webb.

e 17th cent. buildings in search of an architect. 1: [Some account of Sir Balthazar Gerbier D'Ouvilly, b. 1591], by A. E. Richardson. 2: [Edward Marshall, b. 1598], by Katharine A. Esdaile.

f Architecture of Cambridge: the 19th cent., by B. Pite.

g Architecture of Cambridge: prior to the 19th cent., by G. Webb.

4491 Vol. 41.

a The architects of Wentworth Castle and Wentworth Woodhouse, together with a brief description of their clients, by A. Booth.

b The planning of London past and present, by W. R. Davidge.

c William Morris, by J. W. Mackail.

d The English public school plan [in its development from 1870] and the new Merchant Taylors' school [Rickmansworth], by W. G. Newton.

e The strip drawings [of Knightsbridge and Piccadilly in 1934 compared with those of Knightsbridge in 1811, by Salway, and Piccadilly in 1820, by Tallis].

f Organs and organ cases, by S. E. Dykes-Bower.

g Painted screens of Norfolk, by Olive M. Briggs.

Other publications:

4492 The designers of our buildings, by L. C. Cornford, with foreword by W. J. Locke. 1921.

4493 The bicentenary of the death of Sir Christopher Wren. Exhibition catalogue. *P.* [1923].

4494 Sir Christopher Wren, 1632-1723. Bicentenary memorial volume, 1923. [Essays by various contributors on aspects of Sir Christopher Wren and his works, with particular reference to his parish churches, St. Paul's cathedral, his plan for London, and his buildings at Oxford and Cambridge]

4495 The Society of Architects, founded 1884, incorporated 1893, amalgamated with the R.I.B.A. 1925, by C. McA. Butler. [1926?].

ROYAL INSTITUTE OF INTERNATIONAL AFFAIRS

Founded 1920, as the British Institute of International Affairs, to advance the science of international politics, economics, and jurisprudence and the study, classification and development of the literature of these subjects; to provide and maintain means of information upon international questions and promote the study and investigation of international questions; and generally to encourage and facilitate the study of international questions. Title changed to the above form in May 1926.

British Year Book of International Law, 1920-33 (14 vols.):

4496 Vol. for 1920-1.

a Professor Oppenheim [d. 1919, Whewell Professor of International Law at Cambridge], by E. A. Whittuck.

b British prize courts and the war, by Sir H. E. Richards.

c The legal position of merchantmen in foreign ports and national waters, by A. H. Charteris.

d Changes in the organization of the Foreign and Diplomatic Service [from 1856].

e The legal administration of Palestine under the British military occupation, by N. Bentwich.

f Submarine warfare [1914-18], by A. P. Higgins.

g The peace treaty [1919-20] in its effects on private property, by E. J. Schuster.

h International labour conventions, by Sir J. Macdonell.

i The late Dr. T. J. Lawrence [d. 1919, lecturer and writer on international law], by A. P. Higgins.

4497 Vol. for 1921-2.

a The jurisdiction of the Permanent Court of International Justice, by Sir H. E. Richards.

b The Permanent Court of International Justice and compulsory jurisdiction, by B. C. J. Loder.

c Submarine cables and international law, by A. P. Higgins.

d Mandated territories: Palestine and Mesopotamia (Iraq), by N. Bentwich.

e Judicial recognition of states and governments, and the immunity of public ships, by A. D. McNair.

f Prize court procedure [in Great Britain], by E. S. Roscoe.

g The [14th cent.] roll *De superioritate maris Angliae*: the foundation of the Stewart claim to the sovereignty of the sea, by T. C. Wade.

h Protectorates and mandates, by T. Baty.

i The work of the League of Nations [1920], by R. Berkeley.

j Notes. [Includes: British American pecuniary claims commission, established in 1910—its antecedents and its work, 1910-14, by Sir C. Hurst]

4498 Vol. for 1922-3.

a The international status of the British self-governing Dominions, by M. M. Lewis.

b The territoriality of bays, by Sir C. Hurst.

c Enemy ships in port at the outbreak of war, by A. P. Higgins.

d Angary [an historical account of the requisitions o shipping], by C. Ll. Bullock.

e Submarines at the Washington conference, by R. F. Roxburgh.

f Immunity of states in maritime law, by W. R. Bisschop.

g Notes. [Includes: The Washington conference, 1921-2, by H. W. Malkin]

4499 Vol. for 1923-4.

a Air bombardment [with particular reference to the war of 1914-18], by J. M. Spaight.

b Whose is the bed of the sea? Sedentary fisheries outside the three-mile limit [and British theories concerning them], by Sir C. J. B. Hurst.

c Prize case notes in the days of [William Scott, Baron] Stowell [d. 1836], by C. J. B. Gaskoin.

d The mandate over Nauru Island [in the Pacific, conferred on 'His Britannic Majesty', 1919], by A. H. Charteris.

4500 Vol. for 1924.

a The *Trent* [case, 1861] and the *China* [case, 1916]: the removal of enemy persons from neutral vessels, by H. W. Malkin.

b Notes. [Includes: The liquor treaty between the British Empire and the United States of America, 1923]

c Decisions, opinions, and awards of international tribunals in 1923–4. [Includes: Anglo-American pecuniary claims arbitration award. The Robert E. Brown claim, undertaken on his behalf by the United States on account of the denial of real property rights acquired by him in 1895 in South Africa]

4501 Vol. for 1925.

a The treaty-making power of the Dominions, by M. M. Lewis.

b The obligatory jurisdiction of the Permanent Court of International Justice, by P. J. Baker.

c Ships of war as prize, by A. P. Higgins.

4502 Vol. for 1927.

a The inner history of the declaration of Paris [1856], by H. W. Malkin.

b The doctrine of continuous voyage, 1756–1815, by O. H. Mootham.

c Retaliation in naval warfare [with particular reference to the war of 1914–18], by A. P. Higgins.

4503 Vol. for 1928.

a The treatment of mails in time of war [with particular reference to the war of 1914–18], by A. P. Higgins.

b Neutral commerce in the war of the Spanish succession and the treaty of Utrecht, by G. N. Clark.

4504 Vol. for 1929.

a Extraterritoriality in China [with particular reference to British jurisdiction], by Sir S. Turner.

b British policy and the regulation of European rivers of international concern, by Ruth Bacon.

c Notes. [Includes: The mandate for Transjordan, and an agreement varying its execution, 1928]

d Index to vols. 1–10 [i.e. 1920–1—1929].

4505 Vol. for 1930.

a The Indian states [and their position], by D. B. Somervell.

b The optional clause [of the statute of the Permanent Court of International Justice; the British signature and reservations], by Sir J. Fischer-Williams.

c The proposed amendments to the covenant of the League of Nations [1929], by C. A. W. Manning.

d Notes. [Includes: The International Copyright conference, 1928]

4506 Vol. for 1931.

a The court of chancery and recognition 1804–31, by P. L. Bushe-Fox.

b Notes. [Includes: British reservations to the General Act of the League of Nations]

4507 Vol. for 1932.

a Unrecognized states: cases in the admiralty and common law courts, 1805–26, by P. L. Bushe-Fox.

b British and American policy and the right of fluvial navigation, by Ruth E. Bacon.

c Notes. [Includes: The Statute of Westminster]

4508 Vol. for 1933.

a The rule of unanimity: the practice of the council and assembly of the League of Nations, by J. Stone.

Journal, vols. 1–9 (1922–30), *contd. as* International Affairs, vols. 10–12 (1931–3):

4509 Vol. 1.

a The Egyptian question, by V. Chirol. [Anglo-Egyptian relations, 1882–1922]

b Nationality in relation to the British Commonwealth of Nations, by J. Fischer-Williams.

c Lord Esher's proposals for the limitation of armaments [1922], by Sir F. B. Maurice.

d The Permanent Court of International Justice, by Lord Phillimore.

e The Genoa conference [1922], by W. Harris.

4510 Vol. 2.

a The balance of power, by A. F. Pollard. [The development of the doctrine in Europe]

4511 Vol. 3.

a Fiscal policy [of the post-war world] and international relations, by A. E. Zimmern.

b The draft treaty of Mutual Assistance [1923], by Viscount Cecil of Chelwood.

c Flag discrimination, by C. Tennyson. [Preferential treatment to ships under the national flag, with particular reference to Great Britain]

d The political situation in Iraq [1918–24], by B. H. Bourdillon.

e The Geneva protocol of 1924 for the pacific settlement of international disputes, by J. Fischer-Williams.

4512 Vol. 4.

a Wahabism and British interests [in Arabia], by D. G. Hogarth.

b The problem of the Rhineland [in relation to the treaty of Versailles, 1919–20], by E. L. Spears.

c The colour problem in Africa, by H. A. Wyndham.

d The practical working of the mandates system, by W. E. Rappard.

e Locarno and British interests, by W. Steed.

4513 Vol. 5.

a Sanctions, by W. Arnold-Forster. [The international sanction of the League covenant]

b Trade treaties and capitulations in Morocco [with particular reference to Britain and France], by M. B. Milne.

c Allied debts, 1702–1914, by J. D. Woodruff. [Appendix: Extracts from minutes of various meetings of the directors of the Bank of England and records of personal interviews between the governor of the Bank and the chancellor of the exchequer, Mr. Pitt]

d The Anglo-Soviet treaties of 1924: recital of events which led to their final conclusion, by A. Ponsonby.

e Nationalism in Canada [1924], by G. M. Wrong.

f Some thoughts on Indian polity [with particular reference to the constitution of 1919 and its working], by S. Reed.

4514 Vol. 6.

a Some aspects of the Imperial conference [1926], by L. S. Amery.

b British memorandum on China. Text of memorandum communicated by H.M. chargé d'affaires at Peking on Dec. 16, 1926, to the representatives of the Washington Treaty Powers; together with the text of a memorandum communicated to the U.S. embassy in London on May 28, 1926.

c The Imperial conference [an historical outline to 1926, with particular reference to Canada], by Sir R. Borden.

d The situation in Egypt [1922–7], by P. G. Elgood.

e Naval disarmament [and the Geneva conference, 1926], by W. C. Bridgeman.

f The Economic conference [1927]: prospects of practical results, by Sir A. Salter.

g The work of the eighth assembly of the League of Nations [1927], by Sir H. Young.

4515 Vol. 7.

a Report on the second conference of the Institute of Pacific Relations, held at Honolulu in July 1927.

b The place of law in international affairs [with particular reference to article 36 of the statute of the Permanent Court of International Justice and the Locarno agreement, 1925], by Sir J. Fischer-Williams.

c The problems of the Indian States [from 1773], by the Maharajah of Patiala.

d Model treaties [commended to the League of Nations, 1928] for the pacific settlement of disputes: mutual assistance and non-aggression, by Sir J. Fischer-Williams.

4516 Vol. 8.

a Sir A. Bailey's gift to the Royal Institute [of International Affairs of an annual income of £5,000 in 1928].

b The freedom of the seas, by Viscount Cecil and W. Arnold-Forster. [The development of the doctrine]

c The industrial aspect of reparations [1924–8], by H. Quigley.

d The reparation problem [1919–29], by R. H. Brand.

e Report of the commission on the closer union of the eastern and central African dependencies, by J. H. Oldham.

f Influence of aviation on international affairs [1926–29], by P. R. C. Groves.

g A problem of Arabian statesmanship, by A. J. Toynbee. [The relations of Ibn Sa'ud with the Wahhābīs and Great Britain, 1921–8]

h Canada and the problem of naval disarmament [1928–9], by W. Chipman.

i Reparation: the Young report [1929], by C. R. S. Harris.

j Anglo-Russian relations, by Sir B. Pares.

k The tenth assembly of the League of Nations, by Viscount Cecil of Chelwood.

l Anglo-American relations, by T. Buesst.

4517 Vol. 9.

a The International Postal Service, by F. H. Williamson.

b The third biennial conference of the Institute of Pacific Relations, Kyoto, Oct. 31 to Nov. 8, 1929, by A. J. Toynbee.

c A comparison of the American and British party systems, by J. K. Pollock.

d The economic relations between Great Britain and the Argentine Republic, by Sir M. Robertson.

e The Hague conference and non-German reparations, by G. Glasgow.

f Europe and the United States: the problem of sanctions, by P. Kerr, Marquess of Lothian.

g The political situation in India [1929–30], by Sir S. Reed.

h The London naval conference, 1930, by J. R. Mac-Donald.

i The international status of India [1930], by L. Sundaram.

j The Permanent Court of International Justice and its place in international relations, by A. Hammarskjöld.

k Economic and social movements underlying antagonisms in the Pacific, by J. B. Condliffe.

l The present position in Malta [1930, with particular reference to the Roman Catholic church], by Sir A. Bartolo.

m The eleventh assembly of the League of Nations, by H. Dalton and Mary Hamilton.

n The problem of the West African liquor traffic, by H. A. Wyndham.

4518 Vol. 10.

a The present situation in Palestine [1930], by A. J. Toynbee.

b The Indian round table conference [1930–1], by W. W. Benn.

c The convention on financial assistance [1930], by Sir H. Strakosch.

d Treaty revision and the future of the League of Nations, by Sir J. Fischer-Williams.

e The Dominions of the British Commonwealth in the League of Nations [1920–30], by Sir W. H. Moore.

f The private manufacture of arms, ammunition and implements of war [with reference to the League of Nations, 1921–31], by D. Carnegie.

g The international wheat situation [1931], by F. L. McDougall.

h The problem of disarmament in the light of history, by H. A. Smith. [The proposals of Alexander I (1816), Napoleon III (1863), the Russian repudiation of the treaty of Paris (1870), and the Hague peace conference (1899)]

i The twelfth assembly of the League of Nations, by the Earl of Lytton.

j Anglo-French relations [1914–31], by S. King-Hall.

4519 Vol. 11.

a Judicial reform and the Egyptian settlement, by H. E. Garle.

b The international aspect of the coal problem, by W. A. Lee.

c India and the franchise problem [with particular reference to the India franchise committee, 1932], by the Marquess of Lothian.

d Monetary reconstruction [and Britain, 1918–32], by G. Cassel.

e The Imperial economic conference [at Ottawa, 1932: the economic situation in the Empire prior to its meeting], by L. S. Amery.

4520 Vol. 12.

a The termination of the Iraq mandate, by Sir N. Davidson.

b War debts, by Sir A. Salter.

c The problem of constitutional reform in India [with particular reference to the opposition to the proposals for a constitution, 1933], by Lord Lloyd of Dolobran.

d Indian public opinion on the White Paper [Proposals for Indian Constitutional Reform, 1933], by Sir Tej Bahadur Sapru and Zafrulla Khan.

e The British Commonwealth Relations conference, 1933: a personal impression, by G. M. Gathorne-Hardy.

Other publications:

4521 History of the peace conference of Paris, ed. H. W. V. Temperley. 6 vols. 1920–24.

4522 Dates of political events and treaties during the year ending June 1, 1922. P. [1922?].

4523 The world after the peace conference, by A. J. Toynbee. 1925.

4524 Survey of International Affairs:

1920–23, and 1924. 2 vols. 1925–6. [By A. J. Toynbee]

1925. 3 vols. 1927–8. [Vol. i, on the Islamic world since the peace settlements, by A. J. Toynbee; vol. ii by C. A. Macartney and others; supplement, being a chronology of international events and treaties, 1920–25, comp. Miss V. M. Boulter]

1926–32. 7 vols. 1928–33. [Vols. for 1926 and 1927 by A. J. Toynbee; subsequent vols. by A. J. Toynbee assisted by Miss V. M. Boulter]

4525 China and foreign powers: an historical view of their relations, by Sir F. Whyte. 1927. [Chatham House monograph no. 1. Revised edn. issued as Monograph no. 2, 1928]

4526 Naval disarmament: a brief record from the Washington conference to date, by H. Latimer. 1930. [Chatham House monograph no. 3]

4527 The conduct of British Empire foreign relations since the peace settlement, by A. J. Toynbee. 1928.

4528 Documents on international affairs, 1928–32, ed. J. W. Wheeler-Bennett assisted, in vols. for 1931 and 1932, by S. A. Heald. 5 vols. 1929–33.

4529 Consolidated index to the Survey of International Affairs, 1920–30, and supplementary volumes [i.e. nos. 4523 and 4527 above, and to Documents on International Affairs, 1928–30], by V. M. Boulter and M. Franklin, 1932.

4530 The international gold problem: collected papers. A record of the discussions of a study group of members of the Royal Institute of International Affairs, 1929–31. 1931.

4531 World agriculture: an international survey. A report by a study group of members of the Royal Institute of International Affairs. 1932.

4532 Monetary policy and the depression. A first report on international monetary problems by a group of the Royal Institute of International Affairs. 1933.

4533 Problems of imperial trusteeship. Native education: Ceylon, Java, Formosa, the Philippines, French Indo-China, and British Malaya, by H. A. Wyndham. 1933.

List of publications on the constitutional relations of the British Empire, 1926–32, comp. E. Lewin. 1933. [Published in conjunction with the Royal Empire Society. See no. 4298 above]

ROYAL INSTITUTION OF CORNWALL

Founded 1818, to encourage literature and to promote knowledge in natural science, archaeology, ethnology, and the fine and industrial arts, especially in relation to Cornwall.

Journal, vols. 14–23 (1900–34):

4534 Vol. 14.

a The Celtic saints [of Cornwall], by S. Baring-Gould.

b Cornubiana, pt. 3, by S. Rundle. [Includes accounts of relics of Cornish saints, the Great Work mine at Godolphin, and various examples of Cornish folk-lore]

c A catalogue of saints connected with Cornwall, with an epitome of their lives, and list of churches and chapels dedicated to them, by S. Baring-Gould. [Contd. from vol. 13. Contd. in vols. 15–17]

d Notes on the church of St. Just-in-Penwith, by T. C. Peter.

e Notes on the parliamentary history of Truro, by P. Jennings. [Contd. from vol. 13. Contd. in vols. 18–20]

f Notes on St. Michael's Mount, by T. C. Peter.

g The Harlyn explorations, by W. Iago.

h The Romans in Cornwall, by R. N. Worth.

i Stone circles of Cornwall and of Scotland: a comparison, by A. L. Lewis.

j Cornish chairs, by S. Rundle.

k Notes on the churches of St. Mylor and Mabe, by T. C. Peter.

l The occurrence of flint flakes, and small stone implements in Cornwall, by F. Brent. [Contd. from vol. 9]

4535 Vol. 15.

a Annual excursion, 1901. [Includes an account of St. Michael Penkivel church]

b Part register of St. Buryan college, *temp.* Dean Robt. Knollys, 1473–85.

c The Harlyn burials in the light of recent archaeological discoveries in Europe, etc., by D. G. Whitley.

d Ancient earth-fenced town and village sites of Cornwall, by O. B. Peter.

e Mural paintings in Cornish churches, by J. D. Enys, T. C. Peter, and H. M. Whitley.

f Report on bones from Harlyn bay, by J. Beddoe.

g Footprints of vanished races in Cornwall [palaeolithic men, pigmies, dolmen builders, and the Ivernians or Iberians], by D. G. Whitley.

h The expansion of Truro [1100–1790], by P. Jennings.

i An inventory of the jewels, ornaments, vestments, etc., belonging to the priory of St. Michael's Mount, Cornwall [comp. early 16th cent.], by H. M. Whitley.

4536 Vol. 16.

a Annual excursion, 1903. [Includes an account of Probus parish church]

b An exploration of Tregaer Rounds [earthwork], by S. Baring-Gould, R. Burnard, J. K. Anderson, and J. D. Enys.

c The builders and the antiquity of our Cornish dolmens, by D. G. Whitley.

d St. Piran's old church [Perranzabuloe], by T. C. Peter.

e Steam in relation to Cornwall [being a history of the use of steam-power in Cornwall, and including *The Miner's Friend; or an Engine to raise Water by Fire*, by Thomas Savery, 1702], by Sir E. Durning-Lawrence.

f The mayoralty of Truro, 1538–[1794], by P. Jennings. [Contd. in vol. 17]

g Notes on the church of St. Ives, by T. C. Peter.

h The stannaries of Cornwall, by H. W. Fisher.

4537 Vol. 17.

a Cornish numismatics, by P. W. P. Carlyon-Britton.

b Old Kea church, by H. M. Whitley.

c St. Michael's Mount and the Domesday survey, by T. Taylor.

d Bevile of Drennick and Woolston [pedigree], by T. Taylor.

e Notes on tin ownership in Cornwall, by G. H. Chilcott.

f Notes on the church, etc., parish and antiquities of S. Constantine, by W. B. Mayne. [Contd. in vol. 20]

g Address of the president [on the early years of the Royal Institution of Cornwall], by R. Pearce.

h The founding, endowing and extinction of the collegiate church of St. Stephen, and the priory of St. Stephen, at Launceston, by O. B. Peter.

i Churchwardens' accounts of the parish of Camborne, by T. Peter.

4538 Vol. 18.

a Defence of the Helford river, 1643–6, by C. Vyvyan.

b Francis Tregian [d. 1608], by T. Taylor.

c Cornish place-names, by H. Jenner.

d The rebellion of Cornwall and Devon in 1549, by W. J. Blake.

e Launceston priory, Cornwall: notes from mss. in the Bodleian Library, translated and abstracted by O. B. Peter.

f Notes on an unrecorded cromlech in north Cornwall [at Davidstow], by H. Dewey.

g Parentage and ancestry of Ralph Allen [d. 1764], the 'man of Bath', by J. H. Rowe.

h St. Pirran's oratory [Perranzabuloe], Perranporth, by M. B. Collins.

i Richard, King of the Romans [Earl of Cornwall, d. 1272]: his descendants, by T. Taylor.

4539 Vol. 19.

a Some antiquities at Lewannick, by F. Nicholls and H. Dewey.

b Some possible Arthurian place-names in west Penwith, by H. Jenner.

c Index to Cornish transcripts [of parish registers, etc.] at Exeter and Bodmin, by J. Nicholls.

d Some prehistoric earthworks of unknown origin near Boscastle, by H. Dewey.

e Flint axe-head from St. Enoder parish, by C. E. Cardew.

f Descriptions of Cornish manuscripts, by H. Jenner. 1: The Borlase manuscript [a collection relating to the Cornish language in the handwriting of Dr. William Borlase, d. 1772].

g Notes on the smelting of tin at Newham, Truro, in 1703–11, by J. S. Henderson.

h The hobby horse, by T. Peter.

i Government of the isles of Scilly [being a report of a case heard before Lord Mansfield, 1756].

j Some notes on old Mevagissey, by J. H. Harris.

k A history of Cornwall, 1529–39, by W. J. Blake.

l St. Allen crosses, by W. J. Stephens.

m Wendron church, by W. A. Mathews.

n Monastery bishoprics of Cornwall, by T. Taylor.

o Provisional lists of ancient Cornish monuments, as adopted by the county committee, 23 July 1913.

p Valuation for a muster, giving the names of all persons in the hundred of Pydar (21 parishes) who advanced to Henry VIII divers sums of money by way of loans, copied by W. J. Stephens.

q Sir N[icholas] Slanning's regiment in [the] great civil war, copied by T. Peter.

4540 Vol. 20.

a Descriptions of Cornish manuscripts, by H. Jenner. 2: The 14th cent. charter endorsement [consisting of 42 lines of verse in Cornish on the back of a land conveyance deed].

b The Cornish rebellion of 1497, by W. J. Blake.

c St. Kew crosses, by W. J. Stephens.

d A tabular statement of the Earls and Dukes of Cornwall, 1068–1914, by O. Peter.

e Cornish folk-lore notes, by T. Peter.

f The Easter book of St. Just-in-Penwith, 1588–96 [being an account of the various offerings made by parishioners to the vicar], by T. Taylor.

g The Easter sepulchre and its uses, with some remarks on the dramatic element in church services, by H. Jenner.

h St. Piran's oratory [Perranzabuloe]: an attempt to trace its history and to show that it was a mediaeval pilgrim shrine, by T. F. G. Dexter.

i Excavation of the old parish church of Perranzabuloe [St. Piran's oratory], by T. F. G. Dexter.

j Notes on flints and other stone implements from south-west Penwith, by J. G. Marsden.

k Summer excursion, 1920. [Includes an account of the hermitage at Roche rocks by H. Jenner.]

l The west-country goldsmiths, by H. H. Mills.

m An incident in Cornwall in 1715 [in connection with the Jacobite rebellion], by H. Jenner.

4541 Vol. 21.

a The Kea chalice and paten, by H. H. Mills.

b Flint implements of Le Moustier type from Camborne, by J. G. Marsden.

c The *Men Scrifa* [or inscribed stone on Busullow downs], by H. Jenner.

d The arms of Cornwall: the two wrestlers, by Sir R. Edgcumbe.

e Summer excursion, 1922. [Includes an account of the church of St. Mary Magdalene, Launceston]

f The Bodmin Gospels [late 9th or early 10th cent.], by H. Jenner.

g Some unrecorded prehistoric sites in west Penwith, by J. G. Marsden.

h Church inventories, 1549 [of the hundred of Kirrier], by T. Taylor.

i The manumissions [of serfs, written on the fly-leaves and margins] in the Bodmin Gospels, by H. Jenner.

j A Roman milestone at Breage, by H. Jenner.

k St. Michael's Mount, by Lord St. Levan.

l A Launceston assize sermon of 1635, by Miss M. F. Wadmore.

m Meane-on-Tol or 'Maen Rock', etc., Constantine, by W. B. Mayne.

4542 Vol. 22.

a The British village at Carwen, near Blisland, by R. D. Greenaway.

b Four Cornish folk-tales, by R. M. Nance.

c Some notes on churchwardens' account-books, by H. R. Jennings.

d The hurling game: a study in the popular survival of magical ritual, by R. D. Greenaway.

e Tintagel castle in history and romance, by H. Jenner.

f The Cassiterides, and the ancient trade in tin, by T. A. Rickard.

g Palaeologus [being the story of Theodore Palaeologus, a Greek who lived in Landulph in the early 17th cent.], by G. F. Tregelles.

h Poor Law administration in the 18th cent., by H. R. Jennings.

i Andrew Boorde on Cornwall, *c.* 1540, by R. M. Nance.

j Records of St. John's hospital near Helston, by C. Henderson.

k Cornish history in mine plans and cost books [chiefly 18th–19th cent.], by A. K. H. Jenkin.

l Tristram, King Rivalen and King Mark, by J. H. Rowe. [Contd. in vol. 23 under the title 'King Arthur's territory (in Cornwall)']

4543 Vol. 23.

a Records of the borough of Truro, before 1300, by C. Henderson.

b A clue to the early history of the parishes of Madon and Paul, by G. H. Doble.

c The history of great Wheal Vor [tin mine], by A. K. H. Jenkin.

d From Watt to Parsons, or the rise of steam power, by Viscount Falmouth.

e Tregagle, in fact and tradition, by Barbara O. Spooner. [John Tregagle, d. 1655]

4544 General index to the Journal and Reports of the Royal Institution of Cornwall, 1818–1906, comp. C. R. Hewitt. 1907.

Other publications:

4545 The St. Columb green book [containing parish records from 1585 to date], by T. Peter. [Published as supplement to vol. 19, pt. 1, of the *Journal*, 1912]

ROYAL INSTITUTION OF GREAT BRITAIN

Founded 1799, to diffuse the knowledge and facilitate the general introduction of useful mechanical inventions and improvements, and to teach the application of science to the common purposes of life.

Notices of the Proceedings, with abstracts of discourses delivered at evening meetings, vols. 16–27 (1900–33):

4546 Vol. 16.

a Epitaphs, by Sir M. E. G. Duff.

b Roman defences of south-east Britain, by V. Horsley.

c George III as a collector, by R. R. Holmes.
d King Alfred, by Sir F. Pollock.
e Runic and Ogam characters and inscriptions in the British Isles, by G. F. Browne.
f Pictorial historic records, by Sir B. Stone.
g Gases at the beginning and end of the century, by J. Dewar.

4547 Vol. 17.

a George Romney and his works, by Sir H. Maxwell.
b Dictionaries, by J. A. H. Murray.
c Westminster abbey in the early part of the 17th cent., by J. Armitage Robinson.

4548 Vol. 18.

a The scientific study of dialects, by J. Wright.
b Walter Pater [d. 1894], by A. C. Benson.
c Fifty years of explosives, by Sir A. Noble.
d The Guildhall library [in the city of London], by C. Welch.

4549 Vol. 19.

a Centenary of Davy's discovery of the metals of the alkalis, by T. E. Thorpe.
b The scientific work of William Thomson, Lord Kelvin, by J. Larmor.
c Ancient and mediaeval projectile weapons other than fire arms, by Sir R. Payne-Gallwey.
d The letters of Queen Victoria, by Viscount Esher.

4550 Vol. 20.

a The road: past, present and future, by Sir J. H. A. Macdonald.
b Electricity supply: past, present and future, by A. A. C. Swinton.
c Sir William Herschel [astronomer, d. 1822], by Sir G. H. Darwin.
d Lord Lister, by Sir W. MacEwen.

4551 Vol. 21.

a The archives of Westminster abbey, by E. H. Pearce.
b A lecture on the plan which it is proposed to adopt for improving the Royal Institution and rendering it permanent, by Humphry Davy [1810]. Reprint.

4552 Vol. 22.

a Authors' dedications in the 17th cent., by H. H. Henson.
b Cellulose and chemical industry, 1866–1916, by C. F. Cross.
c The Brontës: a hundred years after, by J. H. B. Browne.
d Food production and English land [c. 1870–1918], by Sir A. D. Hall.
e Medicine and the war [1914–18], by G. Adami.

4553 Vol. 23.

a Researches of a musical antiquarian, by Sir F. Bridge. [Settings for London cries by Thomas Weelkes, Orlando Gibbons and Richard Dering]
b Chronicles of Cornhill, by L. Huxley. [An outline history of the *Cornhill Magazine*]

4554 Vol. 24.

a The growth of the telescope, by W. J. S. Lockyer.
b Stained glass of York minster, by W. F. Norris.
c Faraday as a chemist, by Sir W. J. Pope.
d Index to vols. 13–24.

4555 Vol. 25.

a Wireless within the Empire, by W. H. Eccles. [The development of wireless communications, 1911–26]
b English illuminated manuscripts, by Sir F. G. Kenyon.
c Old Hampton Court palace revealed, by E. Law. [A survey, c. 1870–1927, of rediscovered portions of the palace]
d Carlyle as a historian, by G. M. Trevelyan.

4556 Vol. 26.

a English civilization from Alfred to Harold, 900–1066, by R. W. Chambers.
b Some scientific instrument makers of the 18th cent. [in England, with particular reference to Benjamin Martin, d. 1782, and George Adams the elder, d. 1773], by R. S. Whipple.
c Joseph Priestley and his place in the history of science, by Sir P. Hartog.

4557 Vol. 27.

a [Michael Faraday] commemorative meeting at the Queen's Hall. [Includes speeches on aspects of Faraday and his work and a commemorative oration by Sir W. Bragg. Also issued separately in 1932 as *Report on the Faraday celebrations, 1931*]
b The work of Sir Charles Parsons [d. 1931, engineer], by Sir A. Ewing.
c Michael Faraday and electro-chemistry, by Sir H. Hartley.
d The Roman [Antonine] wall in Scotland, by Sir G. Macdonald.
e The ancient monuments of England, by Sir C. Peers.

Other publications:

4558 Catalogue of the library [of the Royal Institution]. Additions to the second volume [of the classified catalogue by B. Vincent, 2 vols. 1857–82], 1882–1904 [?1905].

4559 Additions to the library of the Royal Institution, 1905–09 [?1910].

4560 Additions to the library of the Royal Institution, 1910–14. P. [?1915].

4561 Faraday centenary exhibition, 23 Sept. to 3 Oct. 1931. Souvenir catalogue and guide. [1931].

4562 A reproduction of some portions of Faraday's diary [relating to experiments made in the year 1831]. P. [1931].

4563 Faraday's diary, being the various philosophical notes of experimental investigation made by Michael Faraday during the years 1820–62 and bequeathed by him to the Royal Institution of Great Britain, ed. T. Martin, foreword by Sir W. H. Bragg. Vols. i–iv: 1820–47. 1932–3. [Vols. v–vii: 1847–62, and index were published in 1934–6]

ROYAL INSTITUTION OF SOUTH WALES

Founded 1835, as the Swansea Philosophical and Literary Institution, for the cultivation and advancement of the several branches of natural science; the elucidation of the history and antiquities of Wales; the encouragement of literature and the fine arts; and the general diffusion of knowledge. Title changed to above form in 1839. The Institution's Reports for 1901–19 include the reports and transactions of the Swansea Scientific Soc., q.v.

Annual Reports, 1900–33 (31 vols. 1901–[33]):

4564 Vol. for 1907–8.

a The antiquity of the Gorsedd, by N. Lockyer.
b Some measurements in South Wales [chiefly of Arthur's Stone, Gower], by N. Lockyer. [This, together with the article above, was also published separately, 1908]

4565 Vol. for 1920–1.

  a Two holy wells of Gower: Llangavelach and Cefn Bryn, by W. Ll. Morgan.

4566 Vol. for 1921–2.

  a The Gnoll stones [from Neath].

  b Find of Roman coins at Skewen, Glam. Abridged from a paper read before the Royal Numismatic Society by G. A. Taylor.

4567 Vol. for 1922–3.

  a Carn at Penyralltwen [Pontardawe, Glam.], by W. Ll. Morgan.

4568 Vol. for 1923–4.

  a Recent cave explorations in Gower: Worms Head cave, by W. Riches; Culver hole (Llangennydd), by H. E. David.

  b Chapel of St. Margaret [Coed Franck], Cadoxton, by W. H. Jones.

4569 Vol. for 1924–5.

  a Record of our Institution's activities, by W. Ll. Morgan. Knelston [church]. Broken pottery found at Hafod. Local place names.

  b Excavations at Neath abbey, by G. A. Taylor.

4570 Vol. for 1925–6.

  a Chapel of St. Margaret, Coed Franck [Cadoxton]: notes on the excavations, by G. B. Hammond.

  b The town wall of Swansea, by W. H. Jones.

4571 Vol. for 1926–7.

  a Penwyllt cave, near Craig-y-Nos, by P. G. Stevens.

  b Kittle Hill cave, by W. Riches.

Other publications:

4572 Catalogue of coin specimens. 1904.

4573 Catalogue of antiquities. 1913.

ROYAL MEDICAL AND CHIRURGICAL SOCIETY

[see p. 484]

ROYAL NUMISMATIC SOCIETY

Founded 1836 as the Numismatic Society of London, for the study of the history of the coinage of all countries and all ages, and especially that of the United Kingdom and Ireland and of the British Dominions beyond the seas. Title changed to above form in 1904.

Numismatic Chronicle and Journal of the Society, 4th ser., vols. 1–20 (1901–20):

4574 Vol. 1.

  a A numismatic history of the reign of Henry I, 1100–35, by W. J. Andrew. [See also vol. 2]

4575 Vol. 2.

  a Bedwin and Marlborough and the moneyer, Cilda [11th cent.], by P. Carlyon-Britton.

  b A rare sterling of Henry, Earl of Northumberland [d. 1152], by P. Carlyon-Britton.

  c A find of silver coins of Edward IV–Henry VIII, by L. A. Lawrence.

  d Remarks on the last silver coinage of Edward III [1369–1377], by F. A. Walters.

  e The cross and pall on the coins of Alfred the Great, by Sir J. Evans.

  f Coins of William I and II and the sequence of the types, by P. Carlyon-Britton.

  g The silver coinage of the reign of Henry VI, by F. A. Walters.

  h Coins of Edgar [d. 975], and Henry VI, by H. A. Grueber.

  i 'A numismatic history of the reign of Henry I' by W. J. Andrew: [a criticism] by C. G. Crump and C. Johnson. [See vol. 1 above]

  j Some unpublished 17th cent. [tradesmen's] tokens, by W. G. Searle.

4576 Vol. 3.

  a The coinage of William Wood, 1722–33, by P. Nelson.

  b A find of silver coins at Colchester, by H. A. Grueber.

  c The gold coinage of the reign of Henry VI, by F. A. Walters.

  d A find of coins of Alfred the Great, at Stamford, by H. A. Grueber.

4577 Vol. 4.

  a The coinage of William I and William II, by F. Spicer.

  b The coinage of Richard II, by F. A. Walters.

4578 Vol. 5.

  a A recent find of Roman coins in Scotland, by G. Macdonald.

  b Roman coins from Croydon, by G. F. Hill.

  c A hoard of Edward pennies found at Lochmaben, by G. Macdonald.

  d The coinage of Henry IV, by L. A. Lawrence.

  e A find of coins at Oswestry, by R. Ll. Kenyon.

  f Edward the Confessor and his coins, by P. Carlyon-Britton.

  g The coinage of Henry IV, by F. A. Walters.

  h A numismatic question raised by Shakespeare [*Merry Wives of Windsor*, act I, scene 1], by Sir J. Evans.

  i A find of coins of Stephen and Henry II at Awbridge, near Romsey, by H. A. Grueber.

  j Anglo-Gallic coins [1154–1436], by L. M. Hewlett. [Contd. in vols. 6, 8, 12, and 19]

4579 Vol. 6.

  a The silver medal or map of Sir Francis Drake, by Sir J. Evans.

  b The coinage of Henry V, by F. A. Walters.

  c Roman silver coins from Grovely Wood, Wilts., by G. F. Hill. [Reprinted in the *Wiltshire Archaeol. and Nat. History Magazine*, vol. 35]

  d The re-coinage of 1696–97, by T. H. B. Graham.

4580 Vol. 7.

  a Reign and coinage of Carausius [Roman emperor in Britain], 287–93, by P. H. Webb.

  b A silver badge of Thetford, by Maria M. Evans.

  c Anglo-Saxon coins found in Croydon, by T. Bliss.

  d Romney penny of Henry I, by A. S. Yeames.

  e William Hole, or Holle, cuneator of the mint [fl. 1600–1630], by H. A. Grueber.

  f A find of early Roman bronze coins in England [Croydon], by F. A. Walters.

4581 Vol. 8.

  a A large hoard of gold and silver ancient British coins of the Brigantes, found at South Ferriby, Lincs., in 1906, by B. Roth.

  b Cromwell's silver coinage [*c.* 1656–8], by T. H. B. Graham.

  c Memorial medal of Anne Eldred [d. 1678], by Maria M. Evans.

  d Two hoards of Roman coins, by G. F. Hill. 1: Bronze coins of the Tetrarchy, from the Brooklands motor-track,

Weybridge. 2: Silver coins of the late 4th cent. from Icklingham, Suff.

e The coins of Ecgbeorht [King of the West-Saxons, d. 839] and his son, Athelstan, by Sir H. H. Howorth.

f A silver plaque of Charles I as prince [*c.* 1614–15], by Maria M. Evans.

g Note on William Holle [fl. 1600–30], cuneator of the mint, by Helen Farquhar.

h A find of English silver coins [*temp.* Edward I, Edward III, Richard II, Henry IV, Henry V and Henry VI] in Hampshire, by F. A. Walters.

i A find of coins at Bridgnorth [*temp.* Mary, Elizabeth I, James I, and Charles I], by R. Ll. Kenyon.

j Nicholas Hilliard [d. 1619], 'embosser of medals of gold', by Helen Farquhar.

4582 Vol. 9.

a A unique ancient British gold stater of the Brigantes (? a pattern), by B. Roth.

b Simon's dies in the Royal Mint museum [Thomas Simon, d. 1665], with notes on the early history of coinage by machinery, by W. J. Hocking.

c The coinage of the reign of Edward IV, by F. A. Walters. [Contd. in vols. 10 and 14.]

d Memorial medal of Josias Nicolson [*c.* 1680–85], by Maria M. Evans.

e A find of English coins [*temp.* Edward VI, Mary, Elizabeth I, James I, and Charles I] at Constable Burton [Yorks.], by G. C. Brooke.

4583 Vol. 10.

a A find of Roman denarii at Castle Bromwich, by G. C. Brooke.

b The coin-types of Ethelred II, by H. A. Parsons. [See also below]

c Chronology in the short-cross period [reigns of Richard I and John], by G. C. Brooke. [See also vol. 16]

d Mr. Parsons' arrangement of the coin-types of Ethelred II, [a criticism] by G. C. Brooke. [See above]

e Mr. G. C. Brooke on 'The coin-types of Ethelred II', a reply, by H. A. Parsons.

f Charles I: the trials of the pyx, the mint-marks and the mint accounts, by H. Symonds.

g Indexes to vols. 1–10, 1901–10, fourth series.

4584 Vol. 11.

a A hoard of Roman and British coins from Southants, by G. F. Hill.

b Charles II's hammered silver coinage, by T. H. B. Graham.

c The Stamford find and supplementary notes on the coinage of Henry VI, by F. A. Walter.

d Notes on [the coinage of] the reign of William I, by G. C. Brooke.

e A find of nobles of Edward III, at East Raynham, Norf., by G. C. Brooke.

f Bristol mint of Henry VIII and Edward VI, by H. Symonds.

4585 Vol. 12.

a Palmer's Green [London] hoard, by H. A. Grueber. [Pennies of reign of Henry III]

b The Edwinstowe [Notts.] find of Roman coins, by G. C. Brooke.

c The quarter-angel of James I, by H. A. Grueber.

d Hoards of Roman gold coins found in Britain, by H. H. E. Craster. 1: 2nd and 4th cent. hoards found at Corbridge, 1908–11.

4586 Vol. 13.

a The first Corbridge find [Roman gold coins 4th cent.], by H. A. Grueber.

b Two hoards of Edward pennies recently found in Scotland, by G. Macdonald.

c Tables of bullion coined under Edward I, II and III, by A. Hughes, C. G. Crump, and C. Johnson.

d Medallions, true and false, of Mary, Queen of Scots, and Charles I, by Helen Farquhar.

e The Douglas [Isle of Man] find of Anglo-Saxon coins and ornaments, by H. A. Grueber.

f English mint engravers of the Tudor and Stuart periods, 1485–1688, by H. Symonds.

g Epigraphical data for the arrangement of the coin-types of William II, Henry I, and Stephen, by G. C. Brooke.

4587 Vol. 14.

a The Steppingley [Beds.] find of English coins [chiefly *temp.* Henry III], by L. A. Lawrence and G. C. Brooke.

b Edward VI and [the existence of a mint at] Durham House, by H. Symonds.

c Nicholas Briot [d. 1646] and the civil war, by Helen Farquhar.

4588 Vol. 15.

a Some irregular coinages of the reign of Stephen, by G. C. Brooke.

b The Irish coinages of Henry VIII and Edward VI, by H. Symonds.

c Hoard of nine Anglo-Saxon pennies found in Dorsetshire, by R. C. Lockett.

d The pyx trials of the Commonwealth, Charles II and James II, by H. Symonds.

4589 Vol. 16.

a The mint of Queen Elizabeth and those who worked there, by H. Symonds.

b Silver counters of the 17th cent., by Helen Farquhar. [Contd. in 5th ser., vol. 5]

c Some light coins of Charles I, by H. Symonds.

d More chronology of the short-cross period [*c.* 1189–*c.* 1247], by L. A. Lawrence. [See also vol. 10]

4590 Vol. 17.

a The Elizabethan coinages for Ireland [1558–9, 1561, 1600–1], by H. Symonds.

b Pennies of Edward I, II, and III [issued between 1279 and 1350], by J. Shirley-Fox and H. B. E. Fox.

4591 Vol. 18.

a The coinage of Henry VII, by L. A. Lawrence.

4592 Vol. 19.

a The Lark Hill (Worcester) find [chiefly coins of the reign of Henry II], by L. A. Lawrence.

b Two medals of Englishmen [Tanfield Vachell, d. 1705; William Villiers, 2nd Earl of Jersey, d. 1721], by G. F. Hill.

c The martlet and rose half-groats of Henry VII, by G. C. Brooke and L. A. Lawrence.

d Halfpence and farthings of Henry VIII, by L. A. Lawrence.

4593 Vol. 20.

a The coinage of Offa [d. 796], by R. C. Lockett.

b A find of coins of Edgar [959–75], Eadweard II [975–8], and Ethelred II [978–1016] at Chester, by G. F. Hill.

c Indexes to vols. 11–20, 1911–20, fourth series.

Numismatic Chronicle and Journal of the Society, 5th ser., vols. 1–13 (1921–33):

4594 Vol. 1.

a Notes on two place-names on the Anglo-Saxon coins, by L. Woosman.

b A second specimen of the crown of the rose [struck by order of Henry VIII, 1526], by L. A. Lawrence.

c The Irish silver coinages of Edward IV, by H. Symonds.

d A hoard of coins found at Perth [chiefly 15th cent.], by G. Macdonald.

4595 Vol. 2.

a A hoard of coins chiefly of King Stephen, by L. A. Lawrence.

b Charles I: a three-pound piece of Shrewsbury, by L. A. Lawrence.

c Anglo-Saxon acquisitions of the British Museum [1893–1921], by G. C. Brooke. [Contd. in vols. 3–5]

4596 Vol. 3.

a A new type of penny of Edward I, by L. A. Lawrence.

b The English and Irish coinages of 1542–4, by G. C. Brooke.

c John Rutlinger [d. 1609] and the phoenix badge of Queen Elizabeth, by Helen Farquhar.

4597 Vol. 4.

a The company of Moneyers under Queen Elizabeth, by R. A. Coates.

4598 Vol. 5.

a The Linchmere [Suss.] hoard [late 3rd cent. coins mainly of Carausius, Roman emperor in Britain, 287–93], by P. H. Webb.

b Hoard of silver coins found at Welsh Back, Bristol [mainly of Elizabeth, James I, Charles I and Charles II], by L. W. G. Malcom.

c Edward Courtenay [Earl of Devonshire, d. 1556, medal of], by G. F. Hill.

d A mint at Wroxeter? [during the Roman occupation of Britain], by G. F. Hill.

e The two mints at York, by L. A. Lawrence.

4599 Vol. 6.

a Mint accounts and documents of Edward IV, by H. Symonds.

b Forgery of English copper money in the 18th cent., by F. P. Barnard.

c The coinage of Edward III from 1351, by L. A. Lawrence. [Contd. in vols. 9, 12 and 13]

4600 Vol. 7.

a Unpublished 17th cent. [tradesmen's] tokens, by W. Gilbert.

b A find of Roman coins at Clapton-in-Gordano, Som., by F. S. Salisbury.

c Notes on the coinage of Roman Britain under the first Tetrarchy [late 3rd cent.], by L. Laffranchi.

d Leicester hoard of 'Tealby' pennies of Henry II, by L. A. Lawrence.

e The first coinage, or 'Tealby' type, of Henry II, by G. C. Brooke.

f Two finds of ancient British coins, by G. C. Brooke. 1: Westerham, Kent. 2: Chute, Wilts.

4601 Vol. 8.

a The pennies and halfpennies of 1344–51, by J. Shirley-Fox.

b A hoard of English and foreign sterlings found at Derby [mainly coins of Edward I, II and III], by L. A. Lawrence.

c Issuers of 17th cent. London tokens, by K. Rogers.

d A lost coinage in the Channel Islands, by Helen Farquhar.

e The royalist mints of Truro and Exeter, 1642–6, by Mary Coate.

4602 Vol. 9.

a Tables of bullion coined from 1377 to 1550, by Ethel Stokes.

b The law of treasure-trove, past and present, by C. S. Emden.

c Notes on certain Anglo-Saxon coin-types, by Sir C. W. C. Oman.

d A find of nobles at Horsted Keynes, Suss. [*temp.* Edward III and Henry IV, V and VI], by G. C. Brooke.

4603 Vol. 10.

a Privy marks in the reign of Henry V, by G. C. Brooke.

b A find of coins of Carausius and Allectus [Roman emperors in Britain, 287–96] from Colchester, by A. H. F. Baldwin.

c The Forlorn Hope medal of Charles I, by Helen Farquhar.

d Indexes to vols. 1–10, 1921–30, fifth series. [Vol. 20 of this series, published 1940, contains indexes to vols. 11–20, 1931–40]

4604 Vol. 11.

a Late 4th cent. currency in Britain, by F. S. Salisbury.

b The mint of Berwick-on-Tweed under Edward I, II and III, by C. E. Blunt.

c A find of nobles [*temp.* Henry V and VI], at Borth, Card., by G. C. Brooke.

d Two unpublished English medals, by G. C. Brooke. [1:] State of Britain (1714–15) medal. [2:] Restoration (Gigantomachia) medal, 1660.

e The Durham hoard of Edward I–III, by L. A. Lawrence.

4605 Vol. 12.

a An alleged proclamation of Queen Elizabeth, dated March 4, 1562, regarding the coinage, by Sir C. Oman.

b The Shrewsbury mint in the reign of Richard I, and the silver mine at Carreghova, by W. C. Wells.

c Thomas Simon [d. 1665], 'one of our chief gravers', by Helen Farquhar.

4606 Vol. 13.

a A rose-marked pound of Queen Elizabeth, by A. Mallinson.

b The Terling treasure [4th cent. gold and silver coins found at Chelmsford, Essex], by B. H. St. J. O'Neil.

c Notes on the Terling and other silver hoards found in Britain, by J. W. E. Pearce.

ROYAL SOCIETY FOR PROMOTING NATURAL KNOWLEDGE
(The Royal Society)

Founded 1662, to promote, by the authority of experiments, the sciences of natural things and of useful arts, to the glory of God the creator, and the advantage of the human race.

Proceedings, vols. 68–75 (1901–5):

4607 Vol. 69.

a An attempt to ascertain the date of the original construction of Stonehenge from its orientation, by Sir N. Lockyer and F. C. Penrose. [Reprinted in the *Journal of the Royal Institute of British Architects*, 3rd ser., vol. 9]

4608 Vol. 75.

a Obituaries of deceased fellows, chiefly for the period 1898–1904, with a general index to previous obituary notices. [Obituaries to 1931 appeared as separately paginated appendices to the *Proceedings*. For obituaries post-1931 see no. **4625** below]

**Proceedings, ser. A, containing papers of a
mathematical and physical character,
vols. 76–142 (1905–33):**

4609 Vol. 76.

a Observations of stars made in some British stone circles,
by Sir N. Lockyer. [Contd. in vols. 77, 80 and 82]

4610 Vol. 81.

a Note on two recently compiled calendars of papers of the
period 1606–1806 in the archives of the Royal Society, by
A. H. Church.

4611 Vol. 107.

a Life statistics of fellows of the Society, by Sir A.
Schuster.

**Proceedings, ser. B, containing papers of a
biological character, vols. 76–113 (1905–33):**

4612 Vol. 91.

a Some rostro-carinate flint implements and allied forms,
by Sir E. R. Lankester.

4613 Vol. 92.

a A remarkable flint implement from Selsey Bill, by Sir
R. Lankester.

Other publications:

4614 Index to the Proceedings (old series), vol. 1–75, 1800–
1905. 1913.

4615 Index to the Proceedings (1905–30) and to the Philosophical Transactions (1901–30). 1932.

4616 Index to the Proceedings and Philosophical Transactions, 1931–40. [1942].

4617 Catalogue of scientific papers (1800–83), vol. 12, supplement. 1902.

4618 Catalogue of scientific papers (1884–1900), vols. 13–19.
1914–25.

4619 Catalogue of scientific papers (1800–1900), subject
index. 3 vols. 1908–14. [Vol. i: Pure mathematics.
Vol. ii: Mechanics. Vol. iii: Physics, pt. 1: Generalities,
heat, light, sound; pt. 2: Electricity and magnetism]

4620 Catalogue of a collection of early printed books in the
library of the Society. 1910.

4621 Catalogue of the periodical publications in the library of
the Society. 1912.

4622 The signatures in the first journal-book and the charter-
book of the Society, being a facsimile of the signatures
of the founders, patrons and fellows of the Society from
the year 1660 down to the present time. 1912.

4623 Record of the Society [containing an account of its
history, lists of officers and fellows, etc.]. 2nd edn., 1901;
3rd edn., entirely revised and rearranged, 1912.

4624 Obituary notices of fellows of the Society, reprinted from
the year-book of the Society, 1900, 1901, with an index
to the obituaries published in the Proceedings from 1860
to 1899. 1901. [Reprinted with additions in *Proceedings*,
vol. 75]

4625 Obituary notices of fellows of the Society, 1932–5.
2 pts. 1932–5.

4626 The scientific papers of Sir William Herschel, including
early papers hitherto unpublished; with a biographical
introduction compiled mainly from unpublished material,
by J. L. E. Dreyer. 2 vols. 1912.

4627 The celebration of the two hundred and fiftieth anniversary of the Society, July 15–19, 1912. 1913.

4628 The scientific work of Spencer Pickering, F.R.S. [d.
1920], by T. M. Lowry and Sir J. Russell, with a
biographical notice by A. Harden. 1927.

ROYAL SOCIETY FOR THE
ENCOURAGEMENT OF ART,
MANUFACTURES AND COMMERCE
(Royal Society of Arts)

*Founded 1754, as the Society for the Encouragement of
Arts, etc. Title changed to the above form in 1908.*

Journal, vols. 49–82 (1900–34):

4629 Vol. 49.

a Address [on the origin, development and aim of scientific
societies], by Sir J. Evans.
b The siege of Ladysmith, by W. T. Maud.
c Some features of railway travelling past and present, by
F. McDermott.
d Evolution of form in English silver plate.
e The growth and trend of Indian trade—a 40 years' survey, by H. J. Tozer.

4630 Vol. 50.

a Address [on the scientific discoveries of the 19th cent.],
by Sir W. H. Preece.
b History of the rosary in all countries, by H. Thurston.
c Origin and history of carriages, by A. Chancellor.
d The past and present connection of England with the
Persian Gulf, by T. J. Bennett.
e History of personal jewellery from pre-historic times, by
C. Davenport. [Also published separately, 1902]

4631 Vol. 51.

a Artistic fans, by Hannah Falcke.
b Swordsmanship considered historically and as a sport, by
E. Castle.

4632 Vol. 52.

a Early painting in miniature, by R. R. Holmes.
b Pewter and the revival of its use, by A. L. Liberty.

4633 Vol. 53.

a West country screens and rood-lofts, by F. B. Bond.
b Aspects of ancient and modern embroidery, by A. S. Cole.
[Also published separately, 1905]

4634 Vol. 54.

a Address [on the industrial development of England since
the 11th cent.], by Sir O. Roberts.
b The horseless carriage, 1885–1905, by C. Johnson.
c Barry centenary, 1806–1906. [James Barry, painter,
d. 1806]
d English royal heraldry, by C. Davenport.
e Development of water-marking in hand-made and
machine-made papers, by C. Beadle.
f Cut glass, by H. Powell.
g Early history of the London guilds.

4635 Vol. 55.

a Medieval stained glass: its production and decay, by
N. Heaton.
b Exhibitions in Great Britain and Ireland since 1890, by
Sir H. T. Wood.
c Romanesque ornament, by F. H. Jackson.
d History of the development of electric motive power, by
S. Thompson.

4636 Vol. 56.

a Lord Clive and his part in the foundation of the Indian Empire, by Sir S. C. Bayley.

b Developments in the art of jewellery, by Mrs. Hadaway.

c Development of colonial self-government in the 19th cent., by A. B. Keith.

d Banners in pageantry, by G. W. Eve.

4637 Vol. 57.

a Address [on the education of naval architects in the 19th cent.], by Sir W. H. White.

b Hand-made papers of different periods, by C. Beadle and H. P. Stevens.

c English furniture: its design and construction—ancient and modern, by P. A. Wells.

4638 Vol. 58.

a An old English waterway [the Kennet and Avon canal], by T. B. Grierson.

b Birthplace of the Royal Society of Arts [Rawthmell's Coffee-house in Henrietta Street, Covent Garden].

c Miniatures, by C. Davenport.

d The port of Dover, by A. T. Walmisley.

e Industrial England in 1754, by Sir H. T. Wood. [Also published separately, 1910]

f Halley and his comet, by H. H. Turner.

g The restoration and recent discoveries at Guildhall, London, by S. Perks.

h Art and history of British leadwork, by L. Weaver. [Also published separately, 1910]

4639 Vol. 59.

a A new view of Roman London, by R. A. Smith.

b The Royal Society of Arts, by Sir H. T. Wood. [Contd. in vols. 60 and 61. Also published separately, 1913]

4640 Vol. 60.

a The inventions of John Kay, 1704–70, by Sir H. T. Wood.

b The British silk industry: its development since 1903 [i.e. 1903–10], by F. Warner.

c The loom and spindle: past, present and future, by L. Hooper. [Also published separately, 1912]

4641 Vol. 61.

a The art of miniature painting, B.C. 1500 to the present day, by C. Davenport. [Also published separately, 1913]

b List of officers of the Royal Society of Arts [1754–1912].

c Charcoal ironworks, by H. B. Wheatley.

4642 Vol. 62.

a History of colour printing, by R. A. Peddie.

b Shakespeare's life and work, by Sir S. Lee.

c The technique of glass-painting in medieval and Renaissance times, by J. A. Knowles.

d The Channel tunnel and its early history, by J. C. Hawkshaw.

4643 Vol. 63.

a Domestic metal-work of the 18th cent., by W. A. Young.

b History and practice of the art of printing, by R. A. Peddie. [Also published separately, 1915]

c The Indian army, by A. C. Yate.

d House-building, past and present, by M. H. B. Scott. [Also published separately, 1915]

4644 Vol. 64.

a Origin of English measures of length, by Sir C. M. Watson.

b The common lands of London: the story of their preservation, by L. W. Chubb.

c The England of Shakespeare, by P. H. Ditchfield.

d History of the safety-lamp, by F. W. Hardwick and L. T. O'Shea.

e Surveying, past and present, by E. A. Reeves.

4645 Vol. 65.

a Progress in the metallurgy of copper [since the 18th cent.], by H. C. H. Carpenter. [Also published separately, 1918]

b English commerce with India, 1608–58, by W. Foster.

c The freedom of the seas, by G. Fiennes.

4646 Vol. 67.

a The work of the British Army Veterinary Corps at the front, by Sir F. Smith.

b English carpets, by A. F. Kendrick.

c The rubber industry, past and present, by B. D. Porritt.

4647 Vol. 68.

a A stained glass tour [being a survey of medieval stained glass in England and France], by C. H. Sherrill.

b The architecture and decoration of Robert Adam and Sir John Soane, 1758–1837, by A. T. Bolton. [Also published separately, 1920]

4648 Vol. 69.

a Origin and development of the research associations established by the Department for Scientific and Industrial Research, by A. Abbott.

4649 Vol. 70.

a Processes of engraving and etching, by A. M. Hind.

4650 Vol. 71.

a The Strand and the Adelphi: their early history and development, by J. Slater.

b History of children's and invalids' carriages, by S. J. Sewell.

4651 Vol. 72.

a The work of the Royal Botanic Gardens, Kew, by A. W. Hill.

b The archives of the Honourable East India Company, by W. Foster.

4652 Vol. 73.

a The motor-car: its birth, its present, and its future, by R. E. Crompton.

b Miniature of William Shipley [d. 1803], founder of the Society.

c Government botanic gardens, by Sir D. Prain.

d Wallpaper: its history, production and possibilities, by H. G. Dowling.

e William Sturgeon [d. 1850] and the centenary of the electromagnet, by J. A. Fleming.

f Radiological research: a history, by V. E. Pullin. [Also published separately, 1925]

4653 Vol. 74.

a Furniture of Hampton Court and other royal palaces, by I. C. Goodison.

b Ornament in Britain [from prehistoric times], by C. R. Peers. [Also published separately, 1926]

4654 Vol. 75.

a History by excavation [the value of scientific excavation], by R. E. M. Wheeler.

4655 Vol. 76.

a The Royal Society of Arts: its services to trade and training, by Sir P. Magnus.

b Enamels, secular and ecclesiastic, by H. de Koningh.

c Trinity House: its history and work, by Sir A. Clarke.

4656 Vol. 77.

  a Fifty years of British industry [1878–1928], by Sir G. Sutton.

  b History of the Royal Indian Marine, by Sir E. J. Headlam.

4657 Vol. 78.

  a Alfred Stevens [d. 1875]: sculptor, painter, architect, by D. S. MacColl.

  b The portrait in our later monumental sculpture [16th–18th cent.], by Katharine A. Esdaile.

  c Wedgwood's busts in black basalt, by Katharine A. Esdaile. [Josiah Wedgwood, d. 1795]

  d The Radcliffe Observatory [Oxford], by Katharine A. Esdaile.

  e Josiah Wedgwood, F.R.S., 1730–95, potter, inventor, and man of science, by H. Barnard.

  f Temple Bar [London].

  g Aids to navigation, by F. G. Cooper. [Also published separately, 1930]

  h Three master etchers: Rembrandt, Meryan, Whistler. Lecture 3: The etchings and drypoints of James Abbott McNeill Whistler, 1834–1903, by H. J. L. Wright. [The three lectures were also published as a separate pamphlet, 1930]

4658 Vol. 79.

  a The building of the Mansion House [London], by S. Perks.

  b The restoration of St. George's chapel, Windsor, by A. Baillie.

  c The art of the bridge builder, by G. H. Jack.

  d John Zoffany in India, 1783–9, by Sir W. Foster.

4659 Vol. 80.

  a The development of lighthouses [from earliest times], by D. A. Stevenson.

  b William Hogarth, by H. Hubbard.

4660 Vol. 81.

  a The design and construction of buildings in relation to fire risks, by M. E. Webb.

  b The bridges of London—past, present, and future, by J. Benskin.

  c Heraldry [its origin and development], by Sir G. W. Wollaston.

  d Goldsmiths' and silversmiths' work—past and present, by W. A. Steward. [Also published separately, 1933]

4661 Vol. 82.

  a Colour block prints, by H. Hubbard.

  b Costume in history, with special reference to dress design in the 18th and 19th cent., by Mrs. H. Richardson.

  c Developments in type founding since 1720, by H. D. Caslon.

  d Deep diving and under-water rescue, by Sir R. H. Davis.

  e Life and work of William Morris, by P. Bloomfield.

Other publications:

4662 Directory of the Royal Society of Arts, ed. Sir H. T. Wood. 1909. [Contains a short account of the history of the Society, 1754–1909]

ROYAL SOCIETY OF LITERATURE OF THE UNITED KINGDOM

Founded 1823, for the advancement of literature, by the publication of inedited remains of ancient literature, and of such works as may be of great intrinsic value, but not of that popular value which usually claims the attention of publishers.

Transactions, 2nd ser., vols. 22–37 (1900–19):

4663 Vol. 22.

  a The study of familiar letters as an aid to history and biography, by S. Davey.

  b Influence of Chaucer upon the language and literature of England, by J. S. Phené.

  c The poet Cowper and his surroundings, by W. Bolton.

  d John Keats, by O. Browning.

  e The letters of Lady Mary Wortley Montagu [d. 1762], by S. Davey.

4664 Vol. 23.

  a The literary forgeries of the 18th cent., by W. Bolton.

4665 Vol. 24.

  a S. T. Coleridge as a Lake poet, by E. H. Coleridge.

  b The relation of poetry to history, with special reference to Shakespeare's English historical plays, by S. Davey.

4666 Vol. 25.

  a The letters of Charles Lamb, by S. Davey.

  b Some old Shakespearians (from Reed's ms. note-books), by E. Dowden. [Isaac Reed, d. 1807]

  c Edmund Spenser, by P. W. Ames.

  d Lord Byron, by E. H. Coleridge.

  e 16th cent. women students, by Charlotte C. Stopes.

4667 Vol. 26.

  a The letters and autobiographical writings of Oliver Goldsmith, by S. Davey.

  b Some contributors to Tottel's *Miscellany* [1557], by F. St. J. Corbett.

4668 Vol. 27.

  a A 15th cent. devotion: the 'Golden litany of the Holy Magdalen' (Douce ms. 42), by W. E. A. Axon.

  b Books from the library of Ben Jonson, by R. W. Ramsey.

  c Note on Ben Jonson's books, by R. W. Ramsey.

  d Roger Bacon [d. 1294] and Francis Bacon [d. 1626]: a comparison, by H. Candler.

4669 Vol. 28.

  a Anna Jane Vardill Niven [d. 1852], the authoress of 'Christobell', the sequel to Coleridge's 'Christabel', with a bibliography, by W. E. A. Axon, and an additional note on 'Christabel', by E. H. Coleridge.

  b Sir Richard Fanshawe [d. 1666], by J. W. Mackail.

  c The friends in Shakespeare's sonnets, by Charlotte C. Stopes.

4670 Vol. 29.

  a Some Spanish influences in Elizabethan literature, by M. Hume.

  b Literary martyrdoms, by P. H. Ditchfield.

  c John Donne: poet and preacher, by the Hon W. M. Sinclair.

4671 Vol. 30.

  a Lady Betty Molyneux [née Capel] and her husbands [Samuel Molyneux, d. 1728, and Nathaniel St. André, d. 1776], by F. R. Harris.

4672 Vol. 31.

  a English domestic drama, by A. E. Morgan.

  b Nicholas Amhurst, 1697–1743 [journalist], by C. E. Wade.

4673 Vol. 32.

  a The canon of De Quincey's writings, with references to some of his unidentified articles, by W. E. A. Axon.

  b Boy-actors under the Tudors and Stewarts, by J. A. Nairn.

c The Burbages, founders of the modern stage, by Charlotte C. Stopes.

d William Allingham [d. 1889, poet], by A. P. Graves.

e Swift, Stella, and Vanessa, by Margaret L. Woods.

4674 Vol. 33.

a George Crabbe, by F. J. Foakes-Jackson.

4675 Vol. 34.

a Warburton's notes on Neal's *History of the Puritans*, by H. Henson.

b Catharine Trotter [d. 1749], the precursor of the blue stockings, by E. Gosse.

4676 Vol. 35.

a A great mistress of romance: Ann Radcliffe, 1764–1823, by M. Summers.

b Currents of English drama in the 18th cent., by A. E. Morgan.

4677 Vol. 36.

a The Graal legend: some interpretations and a suggestion, by D. F. de l'H. Ranking.

b Gray's notes on [the poems of Charles] Churchill [published in 1764], with introd. by E. Gosse.

Essays by Divers Hands, being the transactions of the Society, new ser., vols. 1–12 (1921–33):

4678 Vol. 2.

a Some memorialists of the period of the Restoration, by Sir H. M. Imbert-Terry. [James Wellwood, d. 1727; Sir Richard Bulstrode, d. 1711; and Ann, Lady Fanshawe, b. 1625]

4679 Vol. 4.

a William Cory [d. 1892], by J. Drinkwater.

b Chivalry and the sea [in English naval history], by J. H. Rose.

c Saints' lives written in Anglo-French: their historical, social and literary importance, by A. T. Baker.

4680 Vol. 6.

a The Royal Society of Literature: an outline, by the Marquess of Crewe.

4681 Vol. 7.

a The reminiscences of a chancellor [William Cowper, d. 1723, first Earl Cowper] and his wife, by Sir H. Imbert-Terry.

b Inigo Jones: a modern view, by J. A. Gotch.

c The miracle play in mediaeval England, by J. M. Manly.

4682 Vol. 8.

a Edward Young, LL.D., poet, 1683–1765, by Marjorie Bowen.

4683 Vol. 9.

a John Bunyan, by W. L. Courtney.

4684 Vol. 10.

a Charlotte Carmichael Stopes [d. 1929, authoress]: some aspects of her life and work, by F. S. Boas. [Appendix: A biographical list of the writings of Charlotte Carmichael Stopes, comp. Gwendoline Murphy]

4685 Vol. 11.

a Lord Elgin and the marbles, by C. Pollock.

b London coffee-houses and the beginnings of Lloyd's [*c.* 1686–7], by W. R. Dawson.

4686 Vol. 12.

a Some English Utopias, by H. Child.

Other publications:

4687 Chronicon Adae de Usk, 1377–1421, ed. with a translation and notes by Sir E. M. Thompson. 2nd edn. 1904.

4688 Queen Elizabeth and the Levant company: a diplomatic and literary episode of the establishment of our trade with Turkey [1595], ed. H. G. Rosedale. 1904.

4689 Milton memorial lectures, 1908, ed. with introd. by P. W. Ames. 1909.

a Portraits of Milton, by G. C. Williamson.

b Milton and the liberty of the press, by W. E. A. Axon.

c Milton: his religion and polemics, ecclesiastical as well as theological, by H. G. Rosedale.

d The Society and the study of Milton [1823–1908], by Sir E. Brabrook.

4690 Venus and Anchises (Brittain's Ida) and other poems by Phineas Fletcher, ed. from a Sion College ms. by Ethel Seaton, with preface by F. S. Boas. 1926.

4691 The eighteen-seventies [and English literature]: essays by fellows of the Royal Society of Literature, ed. H. Granville-Barker. 1929.

ROYAL SOCIETY OF MEDICINE

Founded 1907, by the amalgamation of the Royal Medical and Chirurgical Society (q.v.), the Medical Society, and other principal medical societies of London, for the cultivation of physic and surgery and of the branches of science connected with them.

Proceedings, vols. 1–26 (1907–33):

4692 Vol. 6.

Section of the history of medicine:

a A down survey manuscript of William Petty. Note by Sir W. Osler.

b Notes on early portraits of John Banister [physician and surgeon, d. 1610], of William Harvey, and the Barber Surgeons' visceral lecture in 1581, by D'A. Power.

c Medical allusions in the writings of Francis Bacon, by G. W. Steeves.

d Old English herbals, 1525–1640, by H. M. Barlow.

e The Lady Sedley's receipt book, 1686, and other 17th cent. receipt books, by L. Guthrie.

f The hospital and chapel of St. Mary Roncevall at Charing Cross, by J. Galloway.

g Further notes on Thomas Dover [physician, d. 1742], by J. A. Nixon.

h John Avery [surgeon, d. 1855], by M. Yearsley.

Odontological section:

i James Gordon of Bristol [dentist, d. 1864]: an echo from the past, by G. R. Shiach.

4693 Vol. 7.

Section of the history of medicine:

a Roman medicine and Roman medical inscriptions in Britain, by H. Barnes.

b The medical education and qualifications of Oliver Goldsmith, by Sir E. Clarke.

c Two early 18th cent. treatises on tropical medicine [being a French manual and *The Sea-surgeon or the Guinea Man's vade mecum*, by T. Aubrey, 1729], by A. J. Chalmers and R. G. Archibald.

d A note on Nathaniel Highmore, M.D. [d. 1685], and his memorial tablet in Purse Caundle church, Dors., by W. de C. Prideaux.

e A relic of the king's evil in the Surgeon-general's library, Washington, D.C., by F. H. Garrison.
f Dr. Thomas Spens: the first describer of the Stokes-Adams syndrome, by C. E. Lea.

4694 Vol. 8.

Balneological and climatological section:

a Presidential address: Old London's spas, baths and wells, by S. Sunderland.

Section of the history of medicine:

b Oliver Goldsmith and medicine, by R. Crawfurd.
c A Westmorland medical superstition [relating to tench and tench-men, with particular reference to the diary of Sir Daniel Fleming, of Rydal, d. 1701], by G. C. Peachey.
d The apothecary in England from the 13th to the close of the 16th cent., by C. J. S. Thompson.
e William Withering [d. 1799], M.D., F.R.S., by A. R. Cushny.
f Thomas Baynton [surgeon], 1761-1820, by J. A. Nixon.
g William Bromefield [surgeon], 1713-92, by G. C. Peachey.
h Lionel Lockyer [quack, d. 1672], by H. A. Colwell.

4695 Vol. 9.

Section of epidemiology and state medicine:

a An analysis of Gloucestershire statistics, 1901-10, by J. M. Martin.

Section of the history of medicine:

b Harvey, by N. Moore.
c Note on an autograph letter [from James Douglas, physician, d. 1755], describing inoculation of smallpox in Carlisle in 1755, by H. Barnes.
d Anthony Askew [d. 1774], M.D., F.R.S., and his library, by H. Barnes.
e Some notes on Edmund Harman, king's barber, 1509(?)-1576, by D'A. Power.
f The rate of mortality in the British army 100 years ago, by A. Chaplin.
g Joshua Ward, 1685-1761 [quack], by H. S. Bennett.
h Sir John Finch [physician, d. 1682] and Sir Thomas Baines [physician, d. 1681], by A. Malloch.

4696 Vol. 10.

Section of the history of medicine:

a A revised chapter in the life of Dr. William Harvey, 1636, by D'A. Power.
b The medical history of the exiled Stuarts, by J. Rae.
c A review of the medical literature of the dark ages, with a new text of about 1110, by C. Singer.

4697 Vol. 11.

Section of the history of medicine:

a The letters of Boerhaave to Cox Macro [physician, d. 1767], by D'A. Power.
b John Halle [surgeon, d. 1568] and 16th cent. consultations, by D'A. Power.
c The first printed documents relating to modern surgical anaesthesia, by Sir W. Osler.

4698 Vol. 12.

Section of epidemiology and state medicine:

a Thomas Sydenham [d. 1689] as an epidemiologist, by M. Greenwood.

Section of the history of medicine:

b Evidences of disease in Shakespeare's handwriting, by R. W. Leftwich.
c Survey of medical manuscripts in the British Isles dating from before the 16th cent., by Dorothea W. Singer.

4699 Vol. 13.

Section of the history of medicine:

a History of baths and bathing in Britain before the Norman conquest, by C. F. Sonntag.
b History of medical education in the universities of Oxford and Cambridge, 1500-1850, by A. Chaplin.

4700 Vol. 14.

Section of the history of medicine:

a The prehistoric trephined skulls of Great Britain, together with a detailed description of the operation probably performed in each case, by T. W. Parry.

4701 Vol. 16.

General reports:

a Jenner centenary. Edward Jenner [d. 1823], by Sir W. Hale-White.

Section of the history of medicine:

b The medical services of Henry V's campaign of the Somme in 1415, by G. E. Gask.
c The Black Death in England and Wales as exhibited in manorial documents, by W. Rees.

4702 Vol. 17.

Section of epidemiology and state medicine:

a A survey of the mortality due to child-bearing in London from the 17th cent., by R. Dudfield.
b Note upon the provision for lying-in women in London up to the middle of the 18th cent., by G. C. Peachey.

Section of the history of medicine:

c British medical arrangements during the Waterloo campaign, by H. A. L. Howell.

4703 Vol. 18.

Section of epidemiology and state medicine:

a The health of London in the 18th cent., by J. Brownlee.

4704 Vol. 19.

Section of the history of medicine:

a The medical staff of Edward III, by G. E. Gask.
b [Francis] Glisson [d. 1677] as an orthopaedic surgeon, by E. M. Little.

Section of odontology:

c Origin and growth of the Odontological Society, by J. L. Payne.

4705 Vol. 20.

Section of the history of medicine:

a The London dentist of the 18th cent., by Lilian Lindsay.
b Eighteen letters written by Edward Jenner to Alexander Marcet between the years 1803-14, presented to the library of the Society by Dr. William Pasteur, by W. G. Spencer.
c The place of the Tudor surgeons in English literature, by Sir D'A. Power.
d [James] Wolveridge's *Speculum Matricis* (1671), with notes on two copies in the Society's library, by H. R. Spencer.
e English physicians—'Doctorati'—at the University of Padua in the Collegio Veneto Artista, 1617-1771, by E. Morpurgo.

4706 Vol. 21.

Section of the history of medicine:

a Francis Home, 1719-1813, first professor of *materia medica* in Edinburgh, by W. E. Home.
b The gild of barber surgeons of the city of York, by G. A. Auden.

c A medical adventurer: biographical note on Sir James Wylie, bt., M.D., 1758–1854, by R. Hutchison.

4707 Vol. 22.

Section of the history of medicine:

a Beginnings of the literary renaissance of surgery in England, by Sir D'A. Power.

b The company of barber surgeons and tallow chandlers of Newcastle-on-Tyne, by F. C. Pybus.

c Notes on the early history of the veterinary surgeon in England, by F. Bullock.

d The medical aspect of the mediaeval monastery in England, by P. Flemming.

e The Withering letters in the possession of the Society, by Sir W. Hale-White. [William Withering, physician, d. 1799]

4708 Vol. 23.

Section of anaesthetics:

a Henry Hill Hickman [pioneer of anaesthesia in surgery, d. 1828], by Lord Dawson of Penn.

Section of epidemiology and state medicine:

b The disappearance of malaria from England, by S. P. James.

Section of the history of medicine:

c Armorial bearings of the Worshipful Society of Apothecaries, by T. V. Dickinson.

d English physicians in Russia in the 16th and 17th cent., by W. J. Bishop.

e The medical Boswells, by Sir W. Hale-White.

f Two unpublished autograph letters of Edward Jenner on the subject of vaccination, by H. R. Spencer.

4709 Vol. 24.

War section:

a Some remarks on the evolution of naval hygiene, by A. E. Malone.

Section of the history of medicine:

b Some factors in the reform of the treatment of the insane, by H. J. Norman.

c Thomas Trapham (Cromwell's surgeon) and others, by G. C. Peachey.

4710 Vol. 25.

Section of epidemiology and state medicine:

a The General Register Office [with particular reference to William Farr, statistician, d. 1883], by M. Greenwood.

b William Budd [d. 1880]: a forgotten epidemiologist, by E. W. Goodall.

Section of the history of medicine:

c The work of Richard Lower, 1631–91 [anatomist and physiologist], by K. J. Franklin.

d The morphology of state medicine in Great Britain, by H. Williams.

4711 Vol. 26.

Section of the history of medicine:

a Robert Knox [d. 1862], anatomist, scientist and martyr, by A. S. Currie.

b John Green Crosse [surgeon, d. 1850], of Norwich, by Sir J. Thomson-Walker.

c The autobiography of British medical men, by W. J. Bishop.

United services section:

d Yellow fever, as seen by medical officers of the Royal Navy in the 19th cent., by S. F. Dudley.

e The story of a small campaign: medical arrangements during the Burma campaign, 1931, by J. W. West.

Other publications:

4712 Portraits of Dr. William Harvey. 1913.

4713 Royal Society of Medicine. Record of the events and work which led to the formation of that Society by the amalgamation of the leading medical societies of London with the Royal Medical and Chirurgical Society [being extracts from the *Medico-Chirurgical Transactions*, 1905–7]. 1914.

ROYAL STATISTICAL SOCIETY

Founded 1834, as the Statistical Society of London, to collect, arrange, digest and publish facts illustrating the condition and prospects of society in its material, social and moral relations. Title changed to the above form in 1887.

Journal, vols. 64–96[1] (1901–33):

4714 Vol. 64.

a Statistics of wages in the United Kingdom during the last hundred years, by A. L. Bowley and G. H. Wood. [Contd. from vol. 63. Contd. in vols. 65, 68, 69 and 73]

4715 Vol. 65.

a Tonnage statistics of the decade 1891–1900, by J. Glover.

b A financial retrospect, 1861–1901, by R. Giffen.

c Factory legislation [of the 19th cent.] considered with reference to the wages etc. of the operatives protected thereby, by G. H. Wood.

d Wages in York in 1899, from B. S. Rowntree's investigations, communicated by A. L. Bowley.

e Wool prices in Great Britain, 1883–1901, by R. J. Thompson.

4716 Vol. 66.

a Agricultural wages in England and Wales during the last 50 years, by A. W. Fox.

b The growth and direction of our foreign trade in coal during the last half century, by D. A. Thomas.

c A decade of London pauperism, 1891–1901, by W. Chance.

4717 Vol. 67.

a The accounts of the colleges of Oxford, 1893–1903, with special reference to their agricultural revenues, by L. L. Price.

4718 Vol. 68.

a Estimates of agricultural losses in the United Kingdom during the last 30 years [since 1875], by R. H. L. Palgrave.

b Progress of Friendly societies and other institutions connected with the Friendly Societies Registry Office during 1894–1904, by E. W. Brabrook.

c The introduction of the words 'statistics', 'statistical' into the English language, by G. U. Yule.

4719 Vol. 69.

a Rise and development of local legislation by private bill, by the Earl of Onslow.

b The changes in the marriage- and birth-rates in England and Wales during the past half century; with an inquiry as to their probable causes, by G. U. Yule.

c Statistics of population and pauperism in England and Wales, 1861–1901, by C. S. Loch.

4720 Vol. 70.

a An inquiry into the rent of agricultural land in England and Wales during the 19th cent., by R. J. Thompson.

b The assize of bread at Oxford, 1794–1820, by A. Ballard.

[1] Vols. 73–96 are described as 'new series'.

4721 Vol. 71.

  a Changes in the wages of domestic servants during 50 years, by W. T. Layton.

4722 Vol. 72.

  a Real wages and the standard of comfort since 1850, by G. H. Wood.

  b A statistical note on birth registration in Scotland previous to 1855; suggested by inquiries as to verification of birth for old age pensions, by G. T. Bisset-Smith.

4723 Vol. 73.

  a Occupations in England and Wales, 1881, and 1901.

4724 Vol. 74.

  a The fatality of fractures of the lower extremity and of lobar pneumonia: a study of hospital mortality rates, 1751–1901 [at the London Hospital], by M. Greenwood and R. H. Candy.

4725 Vol. 75.

  a The course of prices at home and abroad, 1890–1910, by R. H. Hooker.

  b An old exchequer tally, by E. Clarke.

  c The rate of interest since 1844, by R. A. Macdonald.

4726 Vol. 76.

  a The population of England in the 18th cent., by E. C. K. Gonner.

4727 Vol. 77.

  a The course of real wages in London, 1900–12, by Frances Wood.

4728 Vol. 78.

  a The progress of the United Kingdom from the war of the French Revolution to 1913, by Lord Welby.

  b Progress of Friendly societies and other provident institutions, 1904–14, by E. Brabrook.

4729 Vol. 82.

  a The paper pound of 1797–1821.

  b The fertility of various social classes in England and Wales from the middle of the 19th cent. to 1911, by T. H. C. Stevenson.

4730 Vol. 85.

  a Progress of British agriculture [1866–1921], by R. H. Rew.

  b Note on *An Account of the Number of People in Scotland in 1755* by Alexander Webster, one of the ministers of Edinburgh.

  c Francis Galton [d. 1911], by R. H. Rew.

4731 Vol. 86.

  a Changes in the birth-rate and in legitimate fertility in London, 1911–21, by T. T. S. de Jastrzebski.

4732 Vol. 89.

  a The growth of mortality due to motor vehicles in England and Wales, 1904–23, by P. G. Edge.

  b The growth of textile businesses in the Oldham district, 1884–1924, by T. S. Ashton.

4733 Vol. 91.

  a [John] Graunt [d. 1674] and [Sir William] Petty [d. 1687], by M. Greenwood. [Contd. in vol. 96]

4734 Vol. 92.

  a Rickman's second series of 18th cent. population figures, by G. T. Griffith. [John Rickman, d. 1840]

4735 Vol. 95.

  a Overseas trade of the United Kingdom, 1924–31, by H. W. Macrosty.

4736 Vol. 96.

  a Production, output per head, prices and costs in the iron and steel industry, 1924–31, by R. W. B. Clarke.

4737 General index to the Journal, vols. 51–71, 1888–1908. 1908.

4738 General index to the Journal, vols. 72–87, 1909–24. 1926.

4739 General index. Journal of the Royal Statistical Society, vols. 88–102, 1925–39. 1941.

Other publications:

4740 Catalogue of the library. 1908.

4741 Catalogue of the library. 1921.

ROYAL UNITED SERVICE INSTITUTION

Founded 1831, as the Naval and Military Library and Museum, for the promotion and advancement of naval and military science and literature. Title changed to United Service Museum in 1824, to United Service Institution in 1839, and to the above form in 1860.

Journal, vols. 45–78 (1901–33):

4742 Vol. 45.

  a The execution of Charles I, by Sir R. F. D. Palgrave.

  b The premier field-marshal of England [Lord George Hamilton, Earl of Orkney, d. 1737], by C. Dalton.

  c Medal presented by Major-general John Small, lieutenant-governor of Guernsey, to John Breton, pilot of H.M.S. *Crescent*, 1794.

  d Nelson relics, by Earl Nelson.

  e Correspondence. [Includes: Wolfe and Townshend and the attack on Quebec]

4743 Vol. 46.

  a Officers' shoulder-belt plates (latter part of the 18th cent.), by S. M. Milne.

  b Anchors: old forms and recent developments, by A. S. Thompson.

  c The Duke of Wellington and the Punjaub campaign. [Wellington's letter to Dalhousie, 22 Jan. 1849]

  d Voyage of the *Charming Nancy*, 1776, by F. A. Whinyates. [A code of rules drawn up by a group of officers in Burgoyne's expeditionary force for their own observance during the voyage to America]

  e The doctrine of continuous voyage: its origin and development from the Seven Years war (1756) to the Boer war, by A. G. Leech.

  f General Wolfe's advice to a newly-joined ensign [Hugh Lord, d. 1829] in 1756, by C. Dalton.

4744 Vol. 47.

  a An Elizabethan army [being a description of a plate in *The Image of Ireland* by John Derry, 1581].

  b The first appearance of Britannia on medals and coins; why adopted, by C. Dalton.

4745 Vol. 49.

  a The Somaliland operations, June 1903–May 1904, by F. C. Owen.

  b To Lhasa with the Tibet expedition, 1903–4, by H. A. Iggulden.

  c Capture at sea: modern conditions and the ancient prize laws, by D. Owen.

4746 Vol. 50.

a Cromwell as a soldier, by P. A. Charrier.

b The Chitral campaign, by H. Rowan-Robinson. [An account of the British expedition against the usurping Mihtar, Amir-ul-Mulk, and his Pathan allies, 1895]

4747 Vol. 51.

a [Letter written by Signal Midshipman John Wells, H.M.S. *Britannia*, 30 Oct. 1805, in facsimile]

b The reconstitution of our Indian army: its composition in the past and in the present, by F. H. Tyrrell.

4748 Vol. 52.

a Whitehall palace and the execution of Charles I, by E. Sheppard.

b Facsimile of a letter from a French naval officer describing the battle of Trafalgar, with a signed plan showing the disposition of the two fleets at noon on the day of the battle.

c Lord Nelson's signal, by B. E. Sargeaunt.

4749 Vol. 53.

a General Sir John Moore, by H. D. Hutchinson.

b A forgotten hero [Stringer Lawrence], by G. J. Harcourt.

c The battle of Preston Pans, by H. W. Pearse.

d The command of the sea: what is it? Four essays, by A. B. N. Churchill, T. L. Shelford, T. Fisher, and R. F. Phillimore.

e The execution and burial of Charles I, by E. Sheppard.

f The war in the Peninsula, 1808–14: valuable notes from recently discovered diaries of the war, now being published in *El Imparcial* of Madrid. Précis by J. C. Dalton.

g The expedition to Sicily, 1718, under Sir George Byng, by H. W. Richmond.

h The French raid on Ireland, 1798, and short sketches of other attempts and landings on the coast of the United Kingdom, by H. W. Pearse.

i The Spanish succession war in Spain with special reference to the British action, by J. H. Anderson.

4750 Vol. 54.

a Waterloo, and the De Lancey memorandum, by C. W. Robinson. [Sir William De Lancey, d. 1815, deputy quarter-master general of the army under Wellington]

b The organisation of Wellington's Peninsular army, 1809–14, by C. W. C. Oman.

c Prince Rupert as a cavalry leader, by Sir G. Arthur. [Also printed in the *Cavalry Journal*, vol. 5]

d A story of a British flag [captured from the 69th at Quatre Bras].

4751 Vol. 55.

a The progress and failure of the expedition from Canada, June–Oct. 1777, by H. Belcher.

b The last of the East Indiamen, by W. B. Whall.

c Samuel Greig [d. 1788] grand admiral in the Imperial Russian navy, by N. Beklemisheff.

d The first Afghan war, 1838–42, by Bruce Hay.

e Colonel Harwood's 'Advice' to Charles I on the defence of the country. [Sir Edward Harwood, d. 1632]

f The strategical aspects of English castles, by W. H. St. J. Hope.

g The organization of the British Board of Admiralty, translated from the *Marine Rundschau* by H. Wylly.

h The Nelson touch at Trafalgar, by G. W. Cobb.

4752 Vol. 56.

a The 'Highland emigrants' and their comrades [regiment raised in N. America, 1775, by authority of General Gage, and an account of the siege of Quebec in 1775–6], by R. E. Key.

b The development of sailing ship tactics compared to that of steam tactics, with a glance into the future, by E. Wilde.

c Peninsular recollections, 1811–12, by Cornet Francis Hall [with a note on Hall by E.G.H. Contd. in vol. 57]

d Letters to George III from Lieut.-general Viscount Townshend, contributed by C. Dalton.

e Sir Isaac Brock [d. 1812], the hero of Upper Canada, by C. W. Robinson.

f Courts martial of the Peninsular war, by C. Oman.

4753 Vol. 57.

a Regimental bands: their history and rôle of usefulness, by J. M. Rogan.

b General Robert Craufurd and his critics, by A. H. Craufurd.

c The *Shannon* and the *Chesapeake*, June 1, 1813, by H. J. G. Garbett.

d Administration of the English and French armies in the Crimea, by R. D. Barbor.

e The revival and training of light infantry in the British army, 1757–1806, by J. F. C. Fuller.

f Some military aspects of the Roman occupation of Caerleon, by Sir A. Mackworth.

g Coast fortresses during the Napoleonic war, 1803–5, by W. R. James.

h The bombardment of Kagoshima by the British fleet, Aug. 1863, by T. Okuda.

i Report of the committee appointed by the Admiralty to examine and consider the evidence relating to the tactics employed by Nelson at the battle of Trafalgar.

j The true account of Saratoga, by A. W. H. Lees.

k British military administration in the 18th cent., by G. C. Merrick.

4754 Vol. 58.

a Baron de Roll [d. 1813, adjutant-general to the Comte d'Artois and colonel of a Swiss regiment in the British service], by M. Johnson.

b The foreign element in the British army, 1793–1815, by C. T. Atkinson.

c Diary of Charles Dudley Madden, lieutenant, 4th Dragoons, Peninsular war, 1809–11.

d Co-operation of the arms at sea during the 17th cent., by Lieut. de vaisseau Castex. [On the use of guns and fire-ships]

e The Irish brigade in the service of France, 1691–1791, by F. H. Skrine.

f An account by an eye-witness of the expedition against St. Malo in May and June, 1758, by J. Porter.

4755 Vol. 59.

a Lord Hood, 1724–1816, by G. E. Cooper.

b Coast fortresses [in N. America and W. Indies] during the American war of independence, by W. R. W. James.

c Journal kept by Lieut. and Adj. Hunt of the 7th (or Queen's Own) Light Dragoons, during the regiment's absence on the [Britanno-Russian] expedition to north Holland, 1799.

d The battle of Cape St. Vincent, from journal and memoranda of Lieut. William Bryan Wyke.

e Journal of the Bhurtpore campaign of 1805, by Cornet George McCall.

f Maj.-general Sir H. R. R. Gillespie, K.C.B. [d. 1814], by W. H. Wilkin.

g Letters by Col. Caillaud and Maj. Carnac written to Col. Eyre Coote, then in Madras, describing the operations in Bengal in 1760 and 1761.

4756 Vol. 60.

a British armies in Flanders, by the Hon. J. Fortescue.

b Sidelights on Waterloo, by F. H. Skrine.

c Research work for regimental histories, by C. R. B. Barrett.

d Notes on the evolution of uniform, 1660–1882, by D. Hastings-Irwin.

e A brace of British pirates [John and Robert Nutt, early 17th cent.], by C. Case-Horton.

f Journal of the siege of Louisburg, by Lieut. W. A. Gordon.

g Standing orders, regulations and instructions by Thomas Graves, esq., captain of His Majesty's ship *Magicienne* in the year 1792.

h Journal of Capt. William Smith of the 11th Light Dragoons during the Peninsular war.

i Extract from the journal of Lt.-col. Sir William Gomm, a quarter-master-general to the army under the Duke of Wellington, June 15th, 1815.

j An account of the action of Dominique and Guadaloupe, 1782.

k Concerning figure-heads, by C. Field.

l The British capture of Genoa, 1814, by C. T. Atkinson.

m Letters concerning the 44th regiment during the retreat from Cabul in the first Afghan war.

n Diary of Lt. C. F. Trower, 33rd Bengal Native Infantry, during the Afghan war of 1842.

4757 Vol. 61.

a Diary of First Lieut. William Swabey, R.A., 28 July–31 Oct., 1807 [expedition against Copenhagen], ed. J. H. Leslie.

b Letters from the Peninsula during 1812–14, ed. the Hon. H. N. Shore.

c Extract from the diary of an English boy at Smyrna 1807 [during the British passage of the Dardanelles].

d Letter from hospital at Minden [1759, giving an account of the battle].

e The march of Craufurd's light brigade to Talavera, July 28–9, 1809: an old legend corrected from the papers of Sir John Bell, by C. Oman.

f Journal of the siege of Gibraltar, 1727.

g Account of the battle of Meanee [1843, during the conquest of Sind], by C. Waddington.

h The second capture of Pondicherry in 1778.

i The capture of Manilla in 1762.

j The expedition to Plattsburg, upon Lake Champlain, Canada, 1814 [with an account from the journal of General Sir Frederick Philipse Robinson], by C. W. Robinson.

k The methods of blockade and observation employed during the Revolutionary and Napoleonic wars, by G. E. Cooper.

l The 53rd regiment in the Nepal war [1814, from the diaries of Capt. Charles Chepmell and Lieut. Henry Sherwood], by C. Chepmell.

m The training of the new army, 1803–5, by J. F. C. Fuller.

n Gibraltar [its capture and defence by British forces, 1704], by C. Field.

o Journal kept by Lieut. Hough, 22 March 1812—13 May 1813 [relating to the Peninsular war], ed. J. H. Leslie.

4758 Vol. 62.

a Pipeclay afloat. Some account of the duties and organization of marine detachments in the 18th cent., by C. Field.

b The missing fifteen years (1625–40) in the life of Robert Blake, admiral and general at sea, by C. R. B. Barrett.

c An authentick narrative of the campaign in Flanders, 1744.

d Some account of the British operations against the Carlists, 1836–7, by C. Field.

e Naval operations in the Mediterranean during the Anglo-Dutch war, 1652–4, by R. C. Anderson.

f The King William III flag [a relic of 1688], by C. R. B. Barrett. [Further discussed in letter by C. Field and answer by C. R. B. Barrett]

g Sea power and the American war of independence, by the Hon. Sir E. Fremantle.

h Irish troops in the service of France, 1691–1791, by C. N. Watts.

i Naval operations in the Mediterranean, 1793–1801, by J. S. Mackenzie-Grieve.

j Extracts from a journal of the campaigns of 1803 and 1804 in India, kept by Cornet George Call, 27th Light Dragoons.

k The marines in the great naval mutinies, 1797–1802, by C. Field.

l A hundred years ago: the Mahratta and Pindari war, by R. G. Burton.

m From the order book of Ferdinand of Brunswick [referring to a British contingent, 1759–62].

4759 Vol. 63.

a Irish troops in the service of Spain, 1709–1818, by C. Oman.

b Some obscure passages in the life of Maj.-gen. Robert Craufurd, by W. Verner.

c Salutes and saluting, naval and military, by C. Field.

d British sea power and international law, by T. M. Maguire.

e The British with Turenne in Alsace, 1674–5, by T. E. Compton.

f The undertaker's charges for conducting the burial of a naval officer in Westminster abbey, Oct. 1811.

g Some British side shows [campaigns in the war of the Spanish succession and the Seven Years war], by W. D. Bird.

h The treaty of Tilsit and India, 1807–43, by A. C. Yate.

i The field marshal [a brief account of the office], by D. H. Irwin.

j The expedition to Portugal, 1589, by C. S. Goldingham.

k Our early regiments of marines [in the 17th cent.], by C. Field.

l Missing battle honours, by C. T. Atkinson.

m The European brigade under Sir Archibald Alison in the Ashanti war, 1873–4, by C. W. Robinson. [Contd. in vol. 64]

n The expedition to Ostend in 1798: blowing up the gates of the Bruges canal, by G. E. Manwaring.

o A regrettable incident [defeat of British troops by Hyder Ali in Madras, 1780], by E. E. Forbes.

p The light infantry company of yore [changes in uniform and equipment, 1783–1858], by A. D. L. Cary.

q Some survivals in military costume, by F. H. Tyrrell.

4760 Vol. 64.

a The rank and office of admiral, by C. Field.

b Naval prize money, by C. S. Goldingham.

c English strategy in the war of the Austrian succession, by H. W. Richmond.

d The Hague: the past [English exiles in], by Captivus.

e Briton and Turk in the Aegean sea, 1807–1914, by Lord Teignmouth.

4761 Vol. 65.

a The Dardanelles, 1807 and 1915: a strategical parallel, by W. D. Bird.

b Development of Malta as a first-class naval base since its inclusion in the British Empire, by G. A. Ballard.

c Lord Collingwood, 1748–1810, by J. L. Bedale.

d Walcheren and Gallipoli: a comparison, by B. M. Ward.

e Who guided the stormers to the lesser breach at Ciudad-Rodrigo?, by Lord Teignmouth.

f A naval centenary [the publication in 1820 of Sir Howard Douglas's *Naval Gunnery*], by F. L. Robertson.

4762 Vol. 66.

a A naval comparison, 1807–1917 [i.e. systems of blockade], by V. H. Danckwerts.
b The Irish rebellions of 1798 and of today: a comparison, by C. N. Watts.
c The British German legion, 1855–6, by A. Egerton.
d Old memorials of British seamen and soldiers in London.
e Naval costume past and present, by R. N. Suter.
f Battle honours of the British army and their anomalies, by R. W. Knollys. [Contd. in vol. 67]
g Napoleon and the British navy, by Lord Teignmouth.
h With the Murmansk expeditionary force [British troops in Russia 1918–19], by W. K. M. Leader.
i French prisoners at Norman Cross [1808].

4763 Vol. 67.

a Captain Cook's chronometer. [Correspondence by R. T. Gould]
b Old naval customs and expressions, by H. H. Smith.

4764 Vol. 68.

a A record of the battles and engagements of the British armies in France and Flanders, 1914–18, by E. A. James.
b The deflection of strategy by commerce in the 18th cent., by C. E. Fayle.
c The right to march under arms in the city of London.
d The battle of Velez Malaga, 1704, by L. G. Carr Laughton.
e Economic pressure in the war of 1739–48, by C. E. Fayle.
f The first battle of the Falklands [a British naval settlement, 1765–70, and its expulsion by the Spaniards], by H. M. S. Turner.

4765 Vol. 69.

a [Capt. James] Douglas of the *Royal Oak*, an episode in the history of the Royal Scots [during the Dutch raid in the Medway, 1667], by L. G. Carr Laughton.
b Memories of the old pipeclay army [i.e. infantry of the line, 1837–c. 1870], by J. G. Downing.
c The past and future of the Royal Indian Marine, by H. L. Mawbey.

4766 Vol. 70.

a Old military customs still extant, by C. T. Tomes.
b Under sail and steam: the Channel squadron in 1872, by L. G. Carr Laughton.
c The taking of Tobago, 1793, by F. G. Cardew.
d The ancestry of Nelson's ships, by R. A. Hopwood.
e The Dillon regiment [1653–1920, being mainly a record of its service under the French government], by L. G. Dillon.

4767 Vol. 71.

a The Corps of Commissionaires [founded 1859 to assist army and navy pensioners], by A. Wilson.
b The loss of the *Revenge* [1591], by W. C. Castle.
c Promotion by merit in the navy: an historical review, by C. N. Robinson.
d Payment of soldiers: its origin and history, by T. J. Edwards.
e Naval reviews: milestones in warship development, by C. N. Robinson.
f Nelson's tutor [Samuel, Lord Hood, d. 1816], by P. C. Standing.

4768 Vol. 72.

a H.R.H. Frederick, Duke of York [d. 1827]: a centenary appreciation, by W. H. Wilkin.
b The birth of the regular army [in the 18th cent.], by D. H. Lennox-Conyngham.
c The origin of the West India regiment, by G. M. Orr.
d Wolfe's early career, by A. C. Whitehorne.

e Trinity House and its relation to the Royal Navy, by A. W. Clarke.

4769 Vol. 73.

a Naval traditions, by Sir R. Phillimore.
b The Cardwell system, by Sir E. A. Altham.
c Captain Nelson and Colonel Moore: a study of leadership in a combined operation [the conquest of Corsica, 1794], by G. A. Martelli.
d Bibliography of British military music, by J. Paine.

4770 Vol. 74.

a Naval bases and sea power, by C. J. C. Little.
b The work of the British navy in the Far East [including accounts of clashes between Chinese revolutionaries and pirates and British naval forces, 1925–7], by L. O. I. MacKinnon.
c Battleship life in the early eighties, by H. H. Paynter.
d The sergeant-major [a brief account of the office], by T. J. Edwards.
e The Board of Trade and the fighting services [from the 18th cent.], by E. J. Foley.
f The provost services from 1809 to the present day, by H. Bullock.
g A pre-war example of 'sanctions' [the blockade of Montenegro and Albania and the occupation of Scutari by international (including British) forces, 1913], by H. P. W. G. Murray.
h Military musical relics, by J. Paine.

4771 Vol. 75.

a A Pioneer battalion in the Great war [1914–18], by Jet.
b A midshipman in the Egyptian war [1882], by H. H. Paynter.
c The navy in the Persian gulf [an historical account beginning with the origin of British interests there], by R. St. P. Parry.
d The capture of Barcelona, 1705, by H. FitzM. Stacke.
e The piracy of S.S. *Haiching* [an incident off the China coast, 1929].
f The centenary of the first naval gunnery school [1830–1930].
g Propaganda in war [with particular reference to Lord Northcliffe and British propaganda in 1918], by H. M. Horne.
h An early example of propaganda: a French account of Trafalgar [originally in *Le Moniteur*, translated in the *Naval Chronicle*, 1805].
i The pipers of the British army, by J. Paine.
j The change in the naval situation [the political and strategical aspect of Britain's position from the end of the 19th cent. to 1930], by Sir R. Webb.
k Salvage operations at Scapa Flow [1924–9].

4772 Vol. 76.

a The north-west frontier of India, by Sir G. MacMunn. [Includes a brief historical account of its defence by British forces]
b Eight years of British control in Iraq [1922–30], by Jundi. [Also reply by Taiyari]
c The work of the Royal Air Force at Aden [including a short account of the protectorate, 1839–1918], by the Hon. R. A. Cochrane.
d The work of our China gunboats, by H. J. Tweedie.
e The Royal United Service Institution, 1831–1931, by E. Altham.
f The banqueting house of Whitehall palace, by E. Fraser.
g A hundred years of the Royal Navy, by W. N. T. Beckett.
h A hundred years of the British army, by H. G. de Watteville.
i A hundred years of service aviation, by H. A. Jones.

j General Sir Howard Douglas, first chairman of the Royal
United Service Institution, by Sir J. S. Douglas, bt.
k The foundations of the Indian army, by E. B. Maunsell.
l The shako, by H. FitzM. Stacke.
m The merchant navy in war [14th-20th cent.], by G.
Norman-Jones.

4773 Vol. 77.

a An Indian navy in the making [a brief historical survey],
by P. A. Mare.
b The making of our modern artillery [1860-99], by H. de
Watteville.
c Robert Blake, general and admiral [d. 1657], by R. H.
Beadon.
d The design of regimental badges and buttons, by H. G.
Parkyn.
e Aircraft attacks on warships: an historical summary
[1914-18], by O. Stewart.
f The British navy in South Africa [1797-1932], by W. L.
Speight.
g General Lord Hill [d. 1842], by R. G. Thurburn.
h The records of the Victoria Cross, by J. Paine.
i The Royal Army Clothing Department [1855-99, with a
brief history of the clothing of the army, 1660-1909], by
H. de Watteville.
j Sail training for the navy [including a short historical
account], by G. C. Steele.
k South Persia during the Great war [British activities,
1916-21], by F. A. Hamilton.

4774 Vol. 78.

a The Auxiliary Patrol in war [1914-18], by H. S. Lecky.
b Recent operations in Kurdistan [by the Royal Air Force,
1930-32], by A. G. R. Garrod.
c Tercentenary of the Royal Scots (the Royal Regiment)
[1633-1933], by Sir E. A. Altham.
d Battle of the Marne, 1914, by Sir J. E. Edmonds.
e An historic reverse in Afghanistan: Maiwund, 1880
[being extracts from the diary of Lt.-col. H. Anderson,
1st Bombay Grenadiers].
f Uniforms of the British army, by H. FitzM. Stacke.

Cavalry Journal, vols. 1-23 (1906-33):

4775 Vol. 1.

a British cavalry, 1853-1903, by Sir E. Wood.
b Cromwell's cavalry, by W. H. Greenly.
c Cavalry in battle, by P. A. Charrier. 1: Marston Moor
[1644].
d The scoutmaster-general, by H. G. Purdon. [A brief
historical account of the office]

4776 Vol. 2.

a Cavalry exploits: General Lake's pursuit of Holkar [after
the defence and relief of Delhi, 1804], by G. F. MacMunn.
b Fathers of the Indian cavalry: James Skinner [d. 1841],
by H. W. Pearse.
c Horse Grenadiers [16th-18th cent.], by R. M. Holden.
d The action of Campo Mayor [Spain, 1811], by R. M.
Holden. [Reproduced from *Royal United Service Institution Journal*, Feb. 1900]
e Balaclava.
f The native cavalry of India, by W. W. Norman. [A brief
history of their organisation, 18th-19th cent.]
g Cavalry swordsmanship in 1854 [in India], by H. J.
Landon.

4777 Vol. 3.

a Fathers of the Indian cavalry: Gardner of Gardner's
Horse, by H. W. Pearse.
b Tactics and training of cavalry, 1640-1760, by H. C.
Malet.

c Famous leaders of cavalry, by H. de B. De Lisle. 2: Oliver
Cromwell.
d History of the bayonet, by B. E. Sargeaunt.

4778 Vol. 4.

a Fathers of the Indian cavalry: Lieut.-general Sir John
Hearsey [d. 1865], by H. W. Pearse.
b The battle of Warburg [1760, and the Marquis of
Granby], by H. Pearse.
c A short history of the Guides cavalry, by J. E. B.
Johnson.
d The cavalry division in the Egyptian campaign of 1882,
by W. H. Birkbeck.
e William Cavendish [d. 1676], Duke of Newcastle, K.G.,
by B. E. Sargeaunt.

4779 Vol. 5.

a General Sir Banastre Tarleton, bt., G.C.B. [d. 1833], by
W. H. Pearse.
b A short account of the work of the Egyptian cavalry
during the Atbara and Omdurman campaigns [from an
officer's unpublished diary].
c Colonel Sir Augustus S. Frazer, K.C.B., F.R.S., Royal
Horse Artillery [d. 1835], by R. H. Mackenzie.
d Charge of the 23rd Light Dragoons at Talavera [1809],
by C. Battine.
e Sir Hope Grant [d. 1875], by H. W. Pearse.
f A brilliant cavalry exploit: an incident in the Seven
Years war, by H. Garbett. [The 15th or King's regiment
of Hussars at Emsdorff, 1760]

4780 Vol. 6.

a The Poona Horse, by R. W. Grimshaw.
b Captain Lewis Edward Nolan (15th Hussars) [d. 1854,
writer on cavalry], by C. R. B. Barrett.
c The London and Westminster Light Horse Volunteers
[1779-1829], by B. E. Sargeaunt.
d *'Regi adsumus coloni'*, by H. Fortescue. [The formation of King Edward's Horse or the King's Oversea
Dominions regiment, 1901]
e Hodson of Hodson's Horse, by R. H. Mackenzie.
f The work of the cavalry at Sobraon, Feb. 10, 1846, by
H. C. Wylly.
g Cavalry sabretaches, by D. H. Irwin.
h General Sir John Floyd, bt., 1748-1818, by Sir H. Floyd.
i The British cavalry at Benavente, 29 Dec. 1808, by P. A.
Charrier.
j Battle of Naseby [1645], by J. Vaughan.
k Major-general Sir Robert Rollo Gillespie, K.C.B. [d.
1814], by H. Pearse.
l The 3rd (King's Own) Light Dragoons at Moodkee and
Ferozeshah [1845], by A. E. H. Ley.
m Lieut.-col. Charles Taylor (20th Light Dragoons) [d.
1808], by C. R. B. Barrett.

4781 Vol. 7.

a Trooper Thomas Brown[d. 1746] of Dettingen fame, by
C. Dalton.
b Brigadier-general John Jacob, C.B. [d. 1858] (the Seidlitz
of the Sind army), by H. Garbett.
c Regimental medals [19th cent.], by D. H. Irwin.
d Early cavalry barracks in Great Britain, by C. R. B.
Barrett.
e Brig.-general C. R. Cureton, C.B., A.D.C. [d. 1848], by
R. H. Mackenzie.
f Stapleton Cotton [d. 1855], Viscount Combermere,
field-marshal, by N. M. Smyth.
g The extinct cavalry regiments of the British army.
[Comp. from an article by A. E. Sewell in *Royal United
Service Institution Journal*, 1887]
h An old cavalry training manual [being *Regulations for the
Cavalry*, 1795].

i Portrait of a captain, 15th Light Dragoons [possibly Gen. Sir David Dundas, d. 1820].
j Notes. [Includes: The Royal Dragoons, their 250th anniversary; The observatory at Waterloo]
k Battle of the Boyne [1690], by P. C. Standing.
l A Dragoon officer's experiences at Salamanca [1812], by C. Dalton. [Transcript of a letter written by Norcliffe Norcliffe, d. 1862]
m The Cape Mounted Rifles, by Q.L.

4782 Vol. 8.

a The 16th Lancers at Aliwal: a comparison, by P. C. Standing.
b The use of mounted infantry in America, 1778–80, by H. Belcher.
c Field-marshal the Marquis of Anglesey, K.G., G.C.B. [d. 1854], by H. C. Wylly.
d Lieut.-general Sir John Elley, K.C.B., K.C.H. [d. 1839], by R. H. Mackenzie.
e Sir Ralph Abercromby, the hero of Alexandria [d. 1801], by N. M. Smyth.
f The Aden troop [formed in 1855], by P. F. Norbury.

4783 Vol. 9.

a The opening of the campaign of 1815, by a cavalry general officer.
b Walter Hamilton, V.C., of the Guides [d. 1879], by R. H. Mackenzie.
c The 18th Hussars at Croix d'Orade [1814].
d Notes. [Includes: The lance cap (i.e. cap worn by lancers), 1816–45]
e [The battle of] El Bodon, Sept. 25, 1811, by W.H.R.
f General Sir Robert Wilson [d. 1849], by C. Battine.
g Notes. [Includes: The evolution of Light Dragoons' head-dresses]

4784 Vol. 10.

a Lieut.-general Richard Hussey, 1st Lord Vivian, G.C.B., G.C.H. [d. 1842], by R. H. Mackenzie.
b The attack on the 1st Cavalry Brigade at Nery, Sept. 1st, 1914, by T. T. Pitman.
c With the 4th Cavalry Division in Palestine, Sept. 1918.
d Saluting in the time of George IV, by H. Payne.
e Moss-troopers.
f The Royal North Devon Hussars [1914–18], by A.C.M.
g The Machine Gun Corps (Cavalry) in France, 1916–18, by T. Preston. [Contd. in vols. 11–13]
h Badges worn by British cavalry regiments, by H. G. Parkyn.
i Major Norman Ramsay [d. 1815], by R. H. Mackenzie.
j Ramadi [an engagement with the Turks during the Mesopotamian campaign, 1917].
k Cavalry in Mesopotamia, in 1918, by Sir H. D. Fanshawe.
l Operations of 1st Cavalry Brigade, Afghanistan, May 7–Aug. 27, 1919, by J. R. V. Sherston.
m Some critics of cavalry and the Palestine campaign, by G. A. Weir.

4785 Vol. 11.

a Operations of the mounted troops of the Egyptian expeditionary force [in the Sinai peninsula, Palestine and Syria, 1916–18], by W. J. Foster. [Contd. in vols. 12 and 13]
b Historical records of British cavalry, by J. Paine.
c General Charles [William Stewart], 3rd Marquess of Londonderry, by R.H.
d The 5th Cavalry Brigade at Cerizy, Aug. 28th, 1914, by R. G. H. Howard-Vyse.
e The cavalry cocked hat, by E. Fraser.

4786 Vol. 12.

a Origin of the Yeomanry, by Sir R. Hardy.

b Changes in the Yeoman Cavalry, by F. H. D. C. Whitmore.
c General outline of cavalry operations on the western front, by T. T. Pitman.
d A letter book of General Sir James Steward Denham during his cavalry service, 1760–1839, by H. G. Parkyn.
e A female Light Dragoon [Sarah Taylor, fl. 1800–14].
f The romance of the drum banner, by E. Fraser.
g Dates of raising the existing regular regiments of the British cavalry.
h Disbanded cavalry regiments, by H. G. Parkyn. [Contd. in vol. 13]
i A cavalry episode in the advance to the Marne [1914], by C. Burnett.
j Notes on the work of the Independent Air Force during the war.

4787 Vol. 13.

a A short history of the Royal Deccan Horse.
b The 9th Hodson's Horse at Cambrai, 1917, by C. H. Rowcroft.
c Cavalry in the '45, by W. Little.
d Standards and guidons, by E. Fraser.
e The advance on Mosul, Oct. 1918, from the squadron commander's point of view, by A. Hammond.
f *Militarie instructions for the cavallrie* [1644]. [Extracts] comp. by F. H. D. C. Whitmore. [Contd. in vol. 14]
g The part played by the British cavalry in the surprise attack on Cambrai, 1917, by T. T. Pitman.
h British cavalry swords, by H. Payne.
i Operations of the 2nd Cavalry Division (with Canadian Cavalry Brigade attached) in the defence of Amiens March 30–April 1, 1918, by T. T. Pitman.
j The Prince of Wales's Own Scinde Horse, by E. B. Maunsell. [Contd. in vol. 14]
k A daylight bombing raid [over Mannheim, 1918], by L. A. Pattinson.
l Oliver Cromwell as a cavalry instructor, by Sir R. Hardy.

4788 Vol. 14.

a The 21st Light Dragoons, 'The Royal Foresters', by W. E. Manners.
b A remarkable mediaeval horse [Morocco, owned by one Banks, a showman, fl. 1588–1637].
c A cavalry charge in the western desert: the Dorset Yeomanry at Agagia [1916].
d Inventions in war [being brief extracts from the *Illustrated London News*, August, 1855, relating to (1) Lubbock's reconnoitring reflector, and (2) Captain Disney's war projectile].
e The Arab rebellion: a disaster [involving the Manchesters] and a cavalry rear-guard action [by the Scinde Horse, 1920], by E. B. Maunsell.
f A cavalry fight near Aleppo, Oct. 26, 1918, by W. J. Lambert.
g Yeomanry badges, by H. G. Parkyn. [Contd. in vol. 15]
h Disbanded cavalry regiments: the 28th to 33rd Light Dragoons, by H. G. Parkyn.
i The capture of the Mont des Cats, Oct. 1914 [by the Second Cavalry Division].
j Maiwand [battle, 1880], by E. B. Maunsell.

4789 Vol. 15.

a Cavalry in the 'Forty-five', by C. H. F. Thompson.
b A sidelight on the Indian mutiny [being a transcript of a letter from a native adjutant of the 3rd Irregular Cavalry, Soobhan Khan, to his commanding officer, 1858].
c Cavalry in bush warfare [East Africa, 1917–18], by W. K. Fraser-Tytler.

4790 Vol. 16.

a The 31st Duke of Connaught's Own Lancers, 1817–1923, by A. Campbell-Ross.

b Waterloo letters from the Royal Scots Greys. [Transcripts from the letter-book of Sir James Stewart Denham, d. 1839]

c The charge [of the 10th Hussars] at El Teb [Sudan], Feb. 29th, 1884.

d Cambrai [1917: the work of the 4th and 5th Cavalry Divisions], by E. B. Maunsell.

e The nine days which saved Natal to Britain, by Sir N. Smyth. [The journey from Durban to Grahamstown, 1842, by Richard King]

f The capture of Togoland [1914], by F. C. Bryant.

g The Bengal Irregular Cavalry.

h Hyder Ally [d. 1782]: the Lion of Mysore, by H. C. Wylly.

i In the footsteps of Wellington [some relics and associations], by J. Paine.

j Morgan Charles Chase [d. 1868, of the 1st Madras Light Cavalry], by R. A. Addington.

k The North Somerset Yeomanry, by W. Shakespeare.

l Nolan and the Light Brigade [at Balaclava, 1854], by F. E. Whitton.

m The Prince Albert Victor's Own Cavalry (Frontier Force), by C. B. D. Strettell.

4791 Vol. 17.

a The charge of the Scots Greys at Waterloo.

b Field-marshal Jean Louis, Earl Ligonier [d. 1770], by H. C. Wylly.

c The mottoes of the cavalry, by E. Fraser.

d Notes on the remounting of the Madras Cavalry [1785–1802] in the days of the company bahadur, by R. A. Addington. [Contd. for 1802–13 in vol. 19]

e The surrender of Kazimain [Baghdad, 1917].

f General Sir John Floyd, bt. [d. 1818], by H. C. Wylly.

g Corunna [1809]: a study in waste, by J. Goddard.

h Horse racing through the ages [in England], by T. R. Badger.

i Old British cavalry shoulder belt plates and buttons, by H. G. Parkyn.

4792 Vol. 18.

a The Yorkshire Hussars, by T. Preston.

b One of Eliott's Light Horse [George Caesar Hopkinson, b. 1738], by H. C. Wylly.

c Operations carried out by the Mhow Cavalry Brigade on Dec. 1st, 1917 [at Cambrai].

d The Royal North-West Mounted Police now the Royal Canadian Mounted Police [1873–].

e A great cavalryman [John Gaspard Le Marchant, d. 1812, major-general], by A. R. Godwin-Austen.

f British women soldiers in war [from the 17th cent.], by E. W. Sheppard.

g The ancestors of the tank, by J. F. C. Fuller. [The evolution of armoured vehicles for use in war]

h A family regiment in the Peninsular war, by T. C. Dalton. [Notes on members of the Dalton, Dalbiac, and Luard family in the Queen's Own Dragoons]

i The Madras Cavalry, by E. J. Shearer.

j A government stud farm [1798–1811] in the days of the company bahadur, by R. A. Addington.

k Jousts, tourneys and tilts, by F. E. Whitton.

l The 14th [Hussars] in fact and fiction [being a bibliography of the regiment], by J. Paine.

m Bihar Light Horse (the oldest volunteer cavalry regiment in India), by H. B. Ellis.

n The soldier's bride, by E.W.S. [A history of married families in the army, 18th and early 19th cent.]

o An incident in the China war of 1860, by H. C. Wylly. [British cavalry in the action at Pa-Li-Chiao]

4793 Vol. 19.

a 'Purchase' and the cavalry arm, by P. C. Standing. [The purchase of commissions and the abolition of the system in 1871]

b Some military fallacies—and facts [relating to James Wolfe and Sir John Moore], by H. C. Wylly.

c Old cavalry stations: Ipswich, by B. G. Baker.

d Bad boys, by A. R. Godwin-Austen. [Cadet disorders at the Royal Military College at Marlow, 1802–12]

e 'Bonnie Dundee', by E. W. Sheppard. [John Grahame, of Claverhouse, d. 1689, Viscount Dundee]

f Mounted forces of the British Empire and mandated territories [1928].

g General Sir William Keir-Grant, K.C.B., G.C.H. [d. 1852], colonel 2nd Royal Dragoons, by H. C. Wylly.

h Corporal Shaw [d. 1815] of the 2nd Life Guards at Waterloo, by E. Fraser.

i Indian cavalry standards, by H. Bullock. [Contd. in vol. 20]

4794 Vol. 20.

a [British cavalry charge at] Almenara, July 27, 1710.

b 'The horseman Peel', by H. Machell. [Anecdotes concerning John Peel, d. 1854, huntsman]

c General Sir Edward Kerrison, bt., K.C.B., G.C.H. [d. 1853], colonel 14th Hussars, by H. C. Wylly.

d An early Indian equitation school [in the Madras Presidency, early 19th cent.], by R. A. Addington.

e An army list of 1799, by J. Aye.

f The romance of military bands, by T. J. Edwards.

g War medals of the British cavalry [1650–1919], by M. L. Ferrar.

h Battle of the Aisne [1914], from a cavalry point of view, by T. T. Pitman.

i The British cavalry of the Honourable East India Company, by H. C. Wylly.

j Cavalry at sea, by G. A. Ballard. [The wreck of the cavalry transport *Neera* in the Red Sea, 1884]

k Old cavalry stations: Canterbury, by B. G. Baker.

l Cavalry and Magna Charta, by P. C. Standing. [The military strategy of the baronial party, 1215]

m Battle-honours of the cavalry, comp. K. R. Wilson.

n Cavalry bands, by J. Paine.

o Life in the cavalry in 1830, by J. Aye.

p The Middlesex Yeomanry.

q Old cavalry stations: Norwich, by B. G. Baker.

r The army reserve of officers in the year 1740, by H. C. Wylly.

s The Oudh campaign of 1859, by Hyderabad.

t Battle-honours of the cavalry militia, and yeomanry, by K. R. Wilson.

4795 Vol. 21.

a 'Lake and victory', by E. B. Maunsell. [Gerard Lake, d. 1808, Viscount Lake of Delhi. Accounts of the battle of Delhi, 1803, the siege of the fort at Agra, and the battle of Laswari, 1803. Further articles on Lake's armies and on the results of Laswari appear in vol. 22]

b Army derivations: how our military vocabulary has been collected all over the world, by J. Aye.

c Cavalry in the trenches [in France, 1915], by T. T. Pitman.

d Old cavalry stations: York, by B. G. Baker.

e Yeomanry regiments, 1931.

f Cavalry at 'Barnet field' [1471], by P. C. Standing.

g Australia's greatest inland explorer [Charles Sturt, d. 1869], by Sir N. M. Smyth.

h Elixem, 1705: a missing cavalry battle-honour, by H. FitzM. Stacke.

i The cavalry at Arras, 1917, by T. Preston.

j Old cavalry stations: Colchester, by B. G. Baker.

k Cavalry battle honours, by T. J. Edwards. 1: The origin of battle honours. [Contd. in vols. 22 and 23]

l A rogues' gallery, by J. Aye. [Some examples of corruption in army administration, 17th and 18th cent.]

m Modes of using the firearm in the cavalry from early time to present date, by H. Payne.

4796 Vol. 22.

a Exploits of the 8th Hussars, by J. Paine. [An account of some histories of the regiment]

b Cavalry in France, March–April, 1918, by T. Preston. [Contd. in vol. 23]

c Fishguard [and the French invasion], 1797, by K. R. Wilson.

d Old cavalry stations: Woolwich, by B. G. Baker.

e Chivalry [as an institution in Europe: a general account], by E. W. Sheppard.

f 'The officer's lady', by E. W. Sheppard. [War experiences of officers' wives in the 19th cent.]

g Something about [Robert Smith] Surtees [d. 1864], by H. Machell.

h Senlac field, by C. F. Marriott.

4797 Vol. 23.

a The Scinde Irregular Horse, by E. B. Maunsell.

b Some little known British commanders of the past, by E. W. Sheppard. 1: Lord Hill, 1772–1842. 2: Marquess of Hastings, 1754–1826.

c Old cavalry stations: Royal Windsor, by B. G. Baker.

d A cock-pit in Flanders, by A. H. Burne. [Accounts of the battles of Landen, 1693, and Elixem, 1705]

e 'Muddling through', by J. Aye. [Army administration in the 18th cent.]

f British cavalry in Kurram [N. India] and Khost [Afghanistan, 1853–97], by B. M. Mahon.

Other publications:

4798 Catalogue of the library of the Royal United Service Institution. Accessions, 1898–1904. 3 vols. 1901–5.

4799 Catalogue of the library (to January 1st, 1908). Pt. 1, 1908; pt. 2 [subject index, n.d.].

4800 Catalogue of the library. Accessions, 1908–16. 8 vols. [1910–17].

4801 The story of Whitehall palace, told by the Viscount Dillon. 3rd edn. *P.* 1905.

4802 Catalogue of the exhibition of Nelson relics, in commemoration of the centenary of the battle of Trafalgar, comp. A. Leetham and B. E. Sargeaunt. *P.* 1905.

4803 Index to subjects and names of authors appearing in the Journal of the Royal United Service Institution, 1887–1906 (vols. 31–50), 1907–16 (vols. 51–61). 2 vols. 1907–19.

4804 An account of Lord Nelson's signal 'England expects that every man will do his duty', by B. E. Sargeaunt. *P.* 1908.

4805 Calendar of military mss. in the Institution, comp. Sir L. Hale. *P.* 1914.

4806 Catalogue of naval mss. in the library of the Institution, comp. H. Garbett. [1914].

4807 Official catalogue of the Royal United Service Museum, comp. Sir A. Leetham. 8th edn., ed. E. L. Hughes. [1932].

4808 The Royal Marine Artillery, 1804–1923, by E. Fraser and L. G. Carr Laughton. 2 vols. 1930. [Vol. i: 1804–59. Vol. ii: 1859–1923]

4809 The Iraq Levies, 1915–32, by J. G. Browne. 1932.

4810 The Loyal North Lancashire regiment, by H. C. Wylly. 2 vols. 1933. [Vol. i: 1741–1914. Vol. ii: 1914–19]

RUTLAND ARCHAEOLOGICAL AND NATURAL HISTORY SOCIETY

Founded 1902, to promote and encourage a taste for archaeology, natural history, and kindred subjects. The first nine Reports issued by the Society contain little of historical interest, accounts of meetings and texts of papers being printed in the privately published Rutland Magazine and County Historical Record, 5 vols. 1903–12. The Tenth–Fifteenth reports are entitled Annual Report and Transactions.

First–Thirtieth Annual Report, 1902–32 (6 vols., 15 pamphs., [1904]–33):

4811 10th Report.

a Village life, from churchwardens' accounts, with special reference to Witham-on-the-Hill church estate book, 1548, by D. S. Davies.

b Pictorial composition and the drawings of George Barret, 1767–1842, by F. S. Robinson.

c All Saints' church, Oakham, by A. Hamilton Thompson.

d Deene church and Kirby Hall [Northants.], by A. Hamilton Thompson.

e Stapleford Park [Leics.], by J. A. Gotch.

f North Luffenham church and North Luffenham Hall, by E. A. Irons.

g Abraham Johnson [d. 1649], of South Luffenham, by E. A. Irons.

4812 11th Report.

a Robert Browne [d. 1633] of Little Casterton, founder of the Brownists, by R. M. Serjeantson.

b A glance at the history of the English coinage, by V. B. Crowther-Beynon.

c Hospital chapel, Oakham [the chapel of the hospital of St. John and St. Anne], by E. A. Irons.

d Architecture of the chapel of St. John and St. Anne [Oakham], by A. Hamilton Thompson.

e Uppingham church, by E. A. Irons and E. M. Moore.

f Apethorpe Hall [Northants.], by J. A. Gotch.

g Whissendine church, by H. F. Traylen.

4813 12th Report.

a Our parish churches, by F. W. Bull.

b Furness abbey [Lancs.], by J. P. W. Lightfoot.

c Hornfield, by E. A. Irons.

d Fotheringhay church [Northants.], by A. Hamilton Thompson.

e Liddington church, by A. Hamilton Thompson.

f Liddington bede house, by A. Hamilton Thompson.

g Gretton church [Northants.], by A. Hamilton Thompson.

h Upton [near Peterborough], by H. F. Traylen.

i Saxon stones and stone crosses in Lincolnshire, by D. S. Davies.

4814 13th Report.

a History of the legend of St. Alban [d. 304?], by W. R. L. Lowe.

b The turf maze at Wing, by E. A. Irons.

c Wing church, Rutland, by A. Hamilton Thompson.

d Tansor [church, Northants.], by A. Hamilton Thompson.

e Warmington [Northants.], by A. Hamilton Thompson.

f Melton Mowbray, by B. H. Smith.

g Seaton church, Rutland, by B. E. Foyster.

h Harringworth [Northants.], by B. E. Foyster.

i Church of St. Martin, Stamford Baron [Northants.], by H. F. Traylen.

j Burghley House, Stamford, by H. F. Traylen.

k The Phillips collection of Stamford books and pamphlets, by T. Sandall.

l An account of some of the charters of the corporation of Stamford, by T. Sandall.

4815 14th Report.

a Rights of sanctuary in medieval days, by R. M. Serjeantson.

b The home of William Shakespeare, by C. J. B. Scriven.

c Sir Robert Cawdrie: rector of South Luffenham, 1571–1587, by E. A. Irons.

d Whitwell church, by E. A. Irons.

e Normanton church, by E. A. Irons.

f Little Casterton, by F. T. Johnson.

g Some Anglo-Saxon personal ornaments, with special reference to Rutland finds, by V. B. Crowther-Beynon.

4816 15th Report.

a Churchyards, by D. S. Davies.

b History of the Stamford grammar school, with some particulars of a quarrel between the mayor of Stamford in 1729 and the then headmaster, by T. Sandall.

c Caldecott church, by A. Hamilton Thompson.

d Pickworth, by E. A. Irons.

e Ketton church, by A. H. Snowden.

f Monumental brasses, with special reference to Leicestershire and Rutland, by A. B. McDonald.

4817 22nd–24th Reports.

a The ancient Saxon family of Wingfield, by T. Sandall·

b Some old accounts of the churchwardens and overseers of St. Mary's parish, Stamford, 1701–1837, by T. Sandall.

4818 25th–26th Reports.

a Symbolism in medieval church architecture, by H.C.B. Foyster.

b Roman roads in Britain, by M. Hutton.

4819 27th–28th Reports.

a St. Peter's church, Tickencote, by W. St. G. Coldwell·

4820 29th–30th Reports.

a Local history and local records, by Joan Wake.

ST. ALBANS AND HERTFORDSHIRE ARCHITECTURAL AND ARCHAEOLOGICAL SOCIETY

Founded 1845, as the St. Albans Architectural Society, to collect and publish information on the history and antiquities of the county. Title changed in the St. Albans Architectural and Archaeological Society in 1850 and to the above form in 1897.

Transactions, 1895–1914, new ser., vols. 1–2 (1898–1915) and vols. for 1924–32, 9 vols. (1924–33):

4821 Vol. 1.

a History of the monastery of St. Mary de Pré [near St. Albans], by W. Page.

b Gateway at the Pemberton almshouses, St. Albans, by S. F. Clarkson.

c Notes and memoranda on some Hertfordshire churches at the beginning of this century, by H. R. W. Hall.

d Notes on the church of St. Mary, Watford, by O. W. Davys.

e Cassiobury, by H. Fowler.

f Notes on Sarratt church, by F. T. Davys.

g The parochial chapel of St. Andrew, formerly attached to St. Alban's abbey, by W. Page.

h Conventual church of S. Mary and S. Helen, Elstow [Beds.], by O. W. Davys.

i The collegiate church of S. Paul, Bedford, by H. Fowler.

j Lady Cathcart [d. 1787] and her husbands, by W. J. Hardy.

k St. Peter's church, St. Albans, by W. C. Morgan.

l Romano-British kiln discovered at Radlett, by W. Page.

m Cups, circles and other marks on Hertfordshire churches, by V. H. W. Wingrave.

n Excavations on the site of Verulam [1898–1900], by W. Page.

o The father of inland navigation [Francis Egerton, 3rd Duke of Bridgewater, d. 1803], by S. F. Clarkson.

p St. Albans as a village community, by A. C. Bickley.

q Old inns of St. Albans, by F. G. Kitton.

r The Black Death and its effects, with special reference to St. Albans, by Mrs. J. T. Knight.

s Note on the inscription in Ashwell church, by C. Johnson.

t Dr. Richard Lee [d. 1684] of Hatfield, and his son, Richard Lee [d. 1725] of Essendon, by H. R. W. Hall.

u Sandridge parish accounts [1686–1780], by H. R. W. Hall.

v The clock tower, St. Albans: its origin and history, by F. G. Kitton.

w Notes on Hatfield, by W. Page.

x The lesser domestic architecture of Hertfordshire, by A. W. Anderson.

y Notes on the mural decoration at the old White Hart inn, St. Albans, by F. G. Kitton.

z Mural paintings at Rothamsted, by V. T. Hodgson.

aa English medieval armour as exemplified by Hertfordshire brasses, etc., by C. H. Ashdown.

bb St. Michael's pulpit [St. Albans], by F. W. K. Tarte.

4822 Vol. 2.

a Ornamental carving in Herts. churches, by A. W. Anderson.

b St. Wulfstan and his connection with St. Alban's abbey, by Mrs. F. B. Henderson.

c Early pigeon-houses (columbaria), by G. Mourat.

d The parish church of St. Leonard's, Sandridge, by J. Griffith.

e Dates in the history of St. Leonard's church, Sandridge, by J. A. Cruikshank.

f Vicars of Sandridge (Sandrugge), Herts., by H. T. Fowler.

g Humphrey, Duke of Gloucester [d. 1447], by Maude C. Knight.

h Salisbury Hall [near London Colney, Herts.], by C. H. Ashdown.

i The great gateway of St. Albans monastery, by C. H. Ashdown.

j ''Tis sixty years since' [being a history of the Society], by H. R. W. Hall.

k Kingsbury castle, by W. Page.

l St. Stephen's church [St. Albans], by A. W. Anderson.

m Roman pavements in Verulam, by C. H. Ashdown.

n Hertfordshire fonts, by H. P. Pollard.

o Records of recent archaeological finds in Herts., by G. E. Bullen. [1: Cistercian ware jug from Kensworth. 2: Early leaden seal matrix of the bailiwick of St. Albans. 3: Armorial pendants from St. Albans. 4: Weapons and other relics from the battles of St. Albans. 5: Anglo-Saxon remains from Kings Walden and Toddington]

p Excavations on the site of Verulam, 1913–14, by C. V. Bicknell.

4823 Vol. for 1924.

a The infirmary of St. Albans abbey, by W. Page.
b The ivory fragment from Orchard House [St. Albans], by Sir E. Wigram.
c The chapter house at St. Albans, by Sir E. Wigram.
d A 15th cent. manuscript in St. Albans abbey, by G. R. Owst.
e Notes on Rickmansworth, by T. Bevan.
f The Bacon monument [in St. Michael's church, St. Albans], by Sir E. Wigram.
g The schoolmaster printer of St. Albans [unidentified printer, fl. 1479–86], by C. H. Ashdown.

4824 Vol. for 1925.

a The completion of St. Albans abbey, by Sir E. Wigram.
b The Franciscans in Hertfordshire, by G. R. Owst.
c Some Notts. and Lincs. Easter sepulchres, by E. Woolley.
d Lilley people in literature, by F. A. Hibbert.
e Hertfordshire parish registers, by C. E. Jones.

4825 Vol. for 1926.

a George Tankerfield [Protestant martyr, burned 1555], by Sir E. T. A. Wigram.
b St. Albans abbey: excavations on the site of the great cloister and adjacent buildings, 1924, by E. Woolley.
c Everyday life in medieval St. Albans: some notes on a 15th cent. register of wills [the Stoneham register], by G. R. Owst.
d Watford parish church: some further research, by Helen Rudd.
e Remarks on Richard of Wallingford [abbot of St. Albans, 1326–35], by H. H. Turner.
f Richard of Wallingford, the abbot, by W. A. Wigram.
g Early clocks and horologes: Richard of Wallingford's clock, by R. P. Howgrave-Graham.
h Wallingford's scientific instruments, by R. T. Gunther.

4826 Vol. for 1927.

a Catalogue of field names occurring on the Hertfordshire estates of the Earl of Verulam, and mentioned in documents preserved at Gorhambury, comp. C. Moor.

4827 Vol. for 1928.

a The Edwardine reformation in a Hertfordshire parish [Baldock], by F. E. Croydon.
b Churchwardens' accounts, with special reference to those of Bushey, by Helen Rudd.
c A study of the character of Abbot Thomas de la Mare [of St. Albans, d. 1396], culled from 'Gesta Abbatum', by E. Woolley.
d The brass of Thomas de la Mare, St. Albans abbey church: description, by E. Woolley.
e Some books and book-owners of 15th cent. St. Albans: a further study of the Stoneham register, by G. R. Owst.
f Hemelhempstead market, 1620–60, by J. Gladstone.

4828 Vol. for 1929.

a A picture in St. Albans cathedral [of the Last Supper], by W. H. Fairbairns.
b St. Albans in the early 19th cent., by E. S. Kent.
c The wooden watching loft in St. Albans abbey church, by E. Woolley.
d Queen Eleanor of Castile [d. 1290, wife of Edward I], by H. M. M. Lane.
e Symbolism of the brass of Thomas de la Mare, by H. O. Cavalier.
f A Hertfordshire trial for witchcraft [of Jane Wenham of Walkern, 1712], by C. E. Jones.

4829 Vol. for 1930.

a The preliminary excavation of Verulamium, 1930, by

Mrs. R. E. M. Wheeler. [Contd. for 1931–2 in the vols. for 1931–2]
b King James I and St. Albans abbey, by H. O. Cavalier.
c The Ramryge chantry in St. Albans abbey church, by E. Woolley.
d Romano-British cemetery at The Grange, Welwyn, by W. P. Westell.
e The great tower of St. Albans abbey church, by J. C. Rogers.
f Neolithic site at Oxhey, near Watford, by N. Davey.

4830 Vol. for 1931.

a The old almshouses of Watford, by Helen Rudd.
b 'The male journey' of St. Albans, Thursday, May 22nd, 1455 [being an account of the battle of St. Albans], by Hilda M. M. Lane.
c St. Albans abbey church: the painted wood vault over the presbytery and the saint's chapel, by J. C. Rogers.
d Excavation of Roman material at Hamper mills, near Watford, by N. Davey.
e Roman and pre-Roman discoveries at Newinn, by W. P. Westell.

4831 Vol. for 1932.

a Gorhambury: 1561–1652, by Hilda M. M. Lane.
b Roman tile and pottery kiln at Black Boy pits, St. Stephen, near St. Albans, by N. Davey.
c The goldsmiths at St. Albans abbey during the 12th and 13th cent., by C. C. Oman.
d Bridge Hall, Sandridge, by H. C. Andrews.
e Excavations at Baldock in 1932, by E. S. Applebaum.
f Eglwys Cymmin [Carm.], and its connection with St. Albans abbey, by C. E. Jones.
g Feet of fines for Harpenden, Henry VIII to James II (1509–1688), by B. P. Scattergood.

Other publications:

4832 Report on the muniments of the Gape family [of St. Albans, 16th–17th cent.], by J. V. Lyle. *P.* 1905.

4833 Records of the old archdeaconry of St. Albans: a calendar of papers, 1575–1637, by H. R. W. Hall. 1908.

ST. PAUL'S ECCLESIOLOGICAL SOCIETY

Founded 1879, for the study of matters relating to church history, art and architecture, liturgiology, church music and other kindred subjects, and to fill the gap left by the dissolution of the Ecclesiological Society (originally the Cambridge Camden Society).

Transactions, vols. 5–10[1] (1900–38):

4834 Vol. 5.

a The *pileus quadratus*: an enquiry into the relation of the priest's square cap to the common academical catercap and to the judicial corner-cap, by N. F. Robinson.
b Notes on harvest thanksgivings and certain other votive offices, by E. G. C. F. Atchley.
c The right of the archbishop of York to crown the queen-consort, by L. G. Wickham Legg.
d John Wesley in London churches, by H. C. Richards.
e St. Olave's, Hart Street, by P. Norman.
f All Hallows, Barking, by P. Norman.
g Mediaeval parish-clerks in Bristol, by E. G. C. F. Atchley.

[1] For index, see the *Transactions* of the revived Ecclesiological Society, new ser., vol. 1, pt. 4 (1945).

h An inventory of church goods belonging to the parish of St. Martin, Ludgate [*c.* 1400], by E. S. Dewick.

i Notes on the monumental brasses of Kent, by M. Stephenson.

j The Reformation and the inns of court, by R. J. Fletcher.

k Jesus mass and anthem [in England in the late 15th and early 16th cent.], by E. G. C. F. Atchley.

l A ms. evangelistarium [written *c.* 1270] which belonged to an English house of the Black friars, by E. S. Dewick.

m Church of St. Andrew Undershaft, by P. Norman.

n Church of St. Katherine Cree [Aldgate], by P. Norman.

o Mediaeval screens and rood-lofts, by F. B. Bond.

p Fragment of Anglo-Saxon benedictional preserved at Exeter cathedral, by S. F. H. Robinson.

q Inventory of the parish church of Bledlow in 1783, by J. Wickham Legg.

r Fragment of a mass-book from Burton Latimer, Northants., by E. S. Dewick.

s Church of St. Lawrence, Jewry, by P. Norman.

t Church of All Hallows, Lombard Street, by P. Norman.

4835 Vol. 6.

a London church services in and about the reign of Queen Anne, with the rules of the religious society of St. Giles', Cripplegate, by J. Wickham Legg.

b Mediaeval parish records of the church of St. Nicholas, Bristol, by E. G. C. F. Atchley.

c Church of St. James, Garlickhithe, by P. Norman.

d Notes on the churches of Hertfordshire, by A. W. Anderson.

e Form of consecration of the church and churchyard of Fulmer [Bucks.], in 1610, as used by William Barlow, bishop of Lincoln, by J. Wickham Legg.

f Church of St. Peter upon Cornhill, by P. Norman.

g London church bells and bell-founders, by H. B. Walters.

h Concerning three eucharistic veils of western use, by N. F. Robinson.

i Some inventories of the parish church of St. Stephen, Bristol [15th and 16th cent.], by E. G. C. F. Atchley.

j The pulpitum and rood-screen in monastic and cathedral churches, by A. Vallance.

k Church of St. Martin, Ludgate, by P. Norman.

l Church of St. Michael, Paternoster Royal, by P. Norman.

m Winchester cathedral: an account of the building and of the repairs now [*c.* 1906–10] in progress, by T. G. Jackson.

4836 Vol. 7.

a History and remains of the Augustinian abbey of Lesnes [Kent], by A. W. Clapham.

b St. Mary Magdalene chapel, Kingston-upon-Thames, by T. Garratt.

c St. Benet, Paul's Wharf, by P. Norman.

d Christ Church, Newgate Street, by P. Norman.

e St. John of Jerusalem, Clerkenwell, by A. W. Clapham.

f Obedientiars' accounts of Glastonbury and other religious houses [*temp.* Henry VII and VIII], by C. T. Flower.

g Church of St. Stephen, Walbrook, by P. Norman.

h Two 16th cent. pontificals formerly used in England, by F. C. Eeles.

i St. Mary-le-Bow, by P. Norman.

j St. Mary Abchurch, by P. Norman.

k A Norman prayer gild, by J. K. Floyer.

l Church of St. Magnus the Martyr, by P. Norman.

m Church of St. Mary-at-Hill, by P. Norman.

n The Pilgrims' Way [Surrey] and the *Pilgrim's Progress*, by H. P. K. Skipton.

o The relation of painted glass to other colour-decoration in English churches, by G. Webb.

p Three mediaeval hospitals of London, by A. W. Clapham.

q Early professions of canonical obedience to the see of Canterbury, by C. E. Woodruff.

r Notes on consecration crosses, by E. S. Dewick.

4837 Vol. 8.

a Church of St. Michael, Cornhill, by P. Norman.

b The nonjurors [1690–1784], by H. P. K. Skipton.

c The colour-rule of Pleshy college [Essex], 1394–5 [on the use of liturgical colours in the Church in England], by W. St. J. Hope.

d A ms. Sarum missal of the 15th cent., probably used in or near Canterbury, now in the library of St. Augustine's College, Canterbury, by F. C. Eeles.

e Church of St. Giles, Cripplegate, on the south side of Fore Street, by P. Norman.

f Parish gilds of the later 14th cent., by H. F. Westlake.

g 'The abbot is dead: long live the abbot!', by E. H. Pearce. [Proceedings at Westminster abbey on the death of the abbot, Thomas de Henle, 1344]

h Church plate received in the jewel house in the Tower of London [*temp.*] Edward VI, by T. Craib.

i Churches of St. Mary Aldermary and St. Mildred, Bread Street, by P. Norman.

j An inventory of Pleshy college [Essex], 1527, by Sir W. St. J. Hope and C. Atchley.

k Ewelme [church, Oxon.], by J. A. Dodd.

l Church graffiti [1350–1550], by R. L. Hine.

m The Marian collects of thanksgiving for reconciliation with Rome [1556], by F. C. Eeles.

4838 Vol. 9.

a Some more Bristol inventories [chiefly of All Saints', Bristol, 1395–96, 1469–70 and 1554], by E. G. C. F. Atchley.

b Ancient and modern methods of engraving brasses, by W. E. Gawthorp.

c Low side windows [in churches]: a new theory [as to their origin], by A. D. Sharp.

d Church of St. Sepulchre without Newgate, by P. Norman and G. J. B. Fox.

4839 Vol. 10.

a An account of the college of minor canons of St. Paul's cathedral, by M. F. Foxell.

b St. Helen's church, Bishopsgate, by A. D. Sharp.

c Early sun dials: Roman and Anglo-Saxon, and mass-clocks, by A. R. Green.

d The charter of the college of minor canons of St. Paul's cathedral in London [1394], by M. F. Foxell.

e Plan of Glastonbury abbey church dedicated to the Blessed Virgin Mary and St. Peter and St. Paul, restored to the year 1539, showing suggested arrangements, by A. E. Henderson.

f The miracles of Archbishop Winchelsey [d. 1313], by C. E. Woodruff.

SAMUEL PEPYS CLUB

Founded 1903. A dining club. Dinners are followed by papers on the diarist, his friends, and his times, together with songs and music of the period.

**Occasional Papers, 1903–14, 1917–23
(2 vols. 1917–25):**

4840 Vol. 1.

a Notes on the portraits of Samuel Pepys, by L. Cust.

b Notes on some distinctive features in Pepys's portraits, by S. P. Cockerell.

c The cataloguing of the Pepysian manuscripts, by J. R. Tanner.

d The Pepys ballads, by F. Sidgwick.

e Who performed lithotomy on Mr. Samuel Pepys?, by D'A. Power.

f Why Samuel Pepys discontinued his diary, by D'A. Power. [An account of Pepys's visual troubles]

g The medical history of Mr. and Mrs. Samuel Pepys, by D'A. Power.

h Gladiatorial stage fights in the time of Pepys, by E. Castle.

i Musical instruments mentioned by Pepys, by Sir F. Bridge.

j Francesco Corbetta [guitar-player, d. *c.* 1700], by Sir F. Bridge.

k Pepys and the city of London, by Sir F. H. Green.

l A musical trio: Captain [Henry] Cooke [d. 1672], Tom Edwards [Pepys's clerk, d. 1681] and Mr. Pepys, by J. C. Bridge.

m Davenant's 'operas' acted during the later years of the Commonwealth [1656-8], by H. B. Wheatley.

n A clerical friend of Pepys [Dr. William Fuller, d. 1675], by Sir E. Clarke.

o Notes on the false messiah, Sabbatai Zevi [d. 1676], by S. P. Cockerell.

p The growth of the fame of Samuel Pepys, by H. B. Wheatley.

4841 Vol. 2.

a Pepys and Shakespeare, by Sir S. Lee.

b Kenrick Edisbury, surveyor of the navy, 1632-8, by J. C. Bridge.

c The birthplace of Pepys, by W. H. Whitear.

d Pepys and [William] Hewer [d. 1715], by P. Norman.

e Pepys and the law, by G. Whale.

f Pepys and the church (with special reference to the church of St. Olave [Hart St., London]), by T. Wellard.

g Notes on Samuel Pepys's 'admiralty journal' [1673-9], by J. R. Tanner.

h Spanish books in the library of Samuel Pepys, by S. Gaselee.

i Documents relating to the prize goods taken from the Dutch in 1665, ed. P. Norman.

j Memoirs of Samuel Pepys, esq., F.R.S. [Sir Walter Scott's review of the first edition of the diary].

k Henry Benjamin Wheatley, D.C.L., F.S.A. [d. 1917].

l Samuel Pepys Cockerell, F.S.A. [d. 1921].

m Sir Frederick Bridge, C.V.O. [d. 1924], master of the Pepys Music Club.

SCARBOROUGH PHILOSOPHICAL AND ARCHAEOLOGICAL SOCIETY

Founded 1827, as the Scarborough Philosophical Society, to promote the study of archaeology, also of literary, scientific and philosophical subjects. Absorbed the Scarborough Archaeological Society in 1853, when the title was changed to the above form.

Reports, 1901-26[1] (17 vols. 1901-26):

4842 Vol. for 1902.

a Prehistoric Britons, by J. A. Hargreaves.

4843 Vol. for 1903.

a Scarborough: 18th and 19th cent. Résumé of lectures by M. T. Whittaker.

[1] No more found.

4844 Vol. for 1905.

a Things local and peculiar. Résumé of J. Irving's lecture touching the Scarborough museum from its inception until now.

4845 Vol. for 1908.

a Prehistoric man in the Scarborough district, by J. Rowntree.

4846 Vol. for 1920-2.

a Bronze age weapons in the Scarborough museum, by T. Sheppard.

SELBORNE SOCIETY

Founded 1888 (?), to bring about an appreciation, on the part of the public, of the value of science to the community and to promote the study of natural history and antiquities.

Nature Notes, vols. 12-29 (1901-25):

4847 Vol. 13.

a A 'White' family Bible [with genealogical entries], by E. A. Martin.

4848 Vol. 15.

a An old appreciation of Gilbert White [in *Blackwood's Magazine*, 1840, with some notes on portraits of the White family], by R. Holt-White.

4849 Vol. 20.

a Alfred Russel Wallace [naturalist, d. 1913].

b A list of bibliographies of the writings of Gilbert White, by H. B. Watt.

4850 Vol. 21.

a Unpublished letter of Gilbert White [to his niece, Mary White, 1780].

b St. Michael's chapel, Torquay, by P. F. Visick.

4851 Vol. 22.

a The story of St. Alban's abbey, by W. P. Westell.

4852 Vol. 23.

a Catalogue of the Gilbert White exhibition [1912].

4853 Vol. 24.

a An Elizabethan theatre-programme [for *England's Joy* at the Swan playhouse, 1602], by W. Martin.

b Selborniana. [Gilbert White's portrait]

c The personal characteristics of Gilbert White, by R. Holt-White.

d Rushlights, by W. M. Webb.

e Light of other days, by W. R. Butterfield. [Brief notes on rush-candles]

4854 Vol. 25.

a The candle tax [1709], by S. C. Spink.

b Sussex draught oxen, by W. R. Butterfield.

c Selborniana. [Portrait of Gilbert White]

d Selborniana. [Gilbert White's fellowship at Oriel College, Oxford]

4855 Vol. 28.

a Some trials of the early banker [being a few incidents relating to the firm of Backhouse and Co. of Darlington, in the early 19th cent.], by M. Phillips.

b Gilbert White and Ringmer, by J. C. Wright.

c Herbs and herbalists, by P. J. Ashton.

d The passing of Cloth Fair [London, being an account of its demolition], by K. C. Thomson.

4856 Vol. 29.

  a Food control in the middle ages [with particular reference to the statute *De cibariis utendis*, 1336], by S. C. Spink.
  b Tunbridge Wells and its story, by P. J. Ashton.
  c Two letters of Gilbert White to Thomas Pennant [d. 1798, naturalist], by W. M. Webb.
  d Gilbert White as a botanist, by D. B. Morris.

Other publications:

4857 A nature calendar, by Gilbert White, ed. with introd. by W. M. Webb. 1911.

SELDEN SOCIETY

Founded 1887, to encourage the study and advance the knowledge of the history of English law.

Publications (excluding Year Books of Edw. II):

4858 Vol. 13. Select pleas of the forest [from the eyre rolls and other mss. in the Public Record Office and British Museum, 1209–1300], ed. G. J. Turner. 1901.

4859 Vol. 14. Beverley town documents [mainly 14th–16th cent.], ed. A. F. Leach. 1900.

4860 Vol. 15. Select pleas, starrs, and other records from the rolls of the exchequer of the Jews, 1220–84, ed. J. M. Rigg. 1902. [Also published by the Jewish Historical Soc. of England]

4861 Vols. 16, 25. Select cases before the king's council in the star chamber, commonly called the court of star chamber, ed. I. S. Leadam. 2 vols. 1903–11. [Vol. i: 1477–1509. Vol. ii: 1509–44]

4862 Vols. 18, 21. Borough customs, ed. Mary Bateson. 2 vols. 1904–6.

4863 Vols. 23, 46, 49. Select cases concerning the law merchant. 3 vols. 1908–32. [Vol. i: Local courts, 1270–1638, ed. C. Gross. Vol. ii: Central courts, 1239–1633, ed. H. Hall. Vol. iii: Supplementary central courts, 1251–1779, ed. H. Hall]

4864 Vol. 28. Select charters of trading companies, 1530–1707 [from the patent rolls in the Public Record Office], ed. C. T. Carr. 1913.

4865 Vol. 30. Select bills in eyre, 1292–1333, ed. W. C. Bolland. 1914.

4866 Vols. 32, 40. Public works in mediaeval law, ed. C. T. Flower. 2 vols. 1915–23. [Entries mainly from coram rege rolls, relative to the maintenance of roads, bridges, sewers, and other local public works]

4867 Vol. 35. Select cases before the king's council, 1243–1482, ed. I. S. Leadam and J. F. Baldwin. 1918.

4868 Vol. 44. The *Liber pauperum* of Vacarius [1149], ed. F. de Zulueta. 1927.

4869 Vol. 47. Year books of Edward IV. 10 Edw. IV and 49 Henry VI, 1470, ed. Nellie Neilson. 1931.

4870 Vol. 48. Select cases in the exchequer of pleas [1236–1304], ed. H. Jenkinson and Beryl E. R. Formoy. 1932.

4871 Vol. 50. Year books of Henry VI. 1 Hen. VI, 1422, ed. C. H. Williams. 1933.

4872 Vol. 51. Select cases in the exchequer chamber before all the justices of England, 1377–1461, ed. M. Hemmant. 1933. [Vol. ii: 1461–1509, was published in 1948]

Year Books series, Year Books of Edward II, vols. 1–9, 11–19 (vol. numbers in the Publications series are shown in square brackets):

4873 Vol. 1. 1 and 2 Edw. II, 1307–9, ed. F. W. Maitland. 1903. [17]

4874 Vol. 2. 2 and 3 Edw. II, 1308–9 and 1309–10, ed. F. W. Maitland. 1904. [19]

4875 Vol. 3. 3 Edw. II, 1309–10, ed. F. W. Maitland. 1905. [20]

4876 Vol. 4. 3 and 4 Edw. II, 1309–11, ed. F. W. Maitland and G. J. Turner. 1907. [22]

4877 Vols. 5, 7, 8. The eyre of Kent, 6 and 7 Edw. II, 1313–14. 3 vols. 1910–13. [24, 27, 29. Vols. i–ii ed. F. W. Maitland, L. W. V. Harcourt, and W. C. Bolland. Vol. iii ed. W. C. Bolland]

4878 Vol. 6. 4 Edw. II, 1310–11, ed. G. J. Turner. 1914. [26]

4879 Vol. 9. 4 Edw. II, 1311, ed. G. J. Turner. 1926. [42. Year Books series, vol. 10, for 5 Edw. II, 1311, Publications vol. 63, was issued in 1947]

4880 Vol. 11. 5 Edw. II, 1311–12, ed. W. C. Bolland. 1915. [31]

4881 Vol. 12. 5 Edw. II, 1312, ed. W. C. Bolland. 1916. [33]

4882 Vol. 13. 6 Edw. II, 1312–13, ed. Sir P. Vinogradoff and L. Ehrlich. 1918. [34]

4883 Vol. 14, pt. 1. 6 Edw. II, 1312–13, ed. Sir P. Vinogradoff and L. Ehrlich. 1921. [38]

4884 Vol. 14, pt. 2. 6 Edw. II, 1313, ed. W. C. Bolland. 1927. [43]

4885 Vol. 15. 6 and 7 Edw. II, 1313, ed. W. C. Bolland. 1918. [36]

4886 Vol. 16. 7 Edw. II, 1313–14, ed. W. C. Bolland. 1922. [39]

4887 Vol. 17. 8 Edw. II, 1314–15 [*recte* 1315], ed. W. C. Bolland. 1925. [41]

4888 Vol. 18. 8 Edw. II, 1315 [*recte* 1314], ed. W. C. Bolland. 1920. [37]

4889 Vol. 19. 9 Edw. II, 1315–16, ed. G. J. Turner and W. C. Bolland. 1929. [45]

Other publications:

4890 Table talk of John Selden, ed. F. Pollock, from a ms. hitherto uncollated, belonging to Lincoln's Inn, together with an account of Selden and his work by E. Fry. 1927.

4891 A bibliography of abridgements, digests, dictionaries, and indexes of English law to the year 1800, by J. D. Cowley. 1932.

SETTE OF ODD VOLUMES

Founded 1878. A dining club.

Opuscula, including:

4892 No. 35. The early history of the Royal Society [1645–84], by H. B. Wheatley. 1905.

4893 No. 39. A bit of 18th cent. romance, being an episode in the life of Lady Mary Fitzgerald, née Hervey [d. 1815], by H. C. Marillier. To which is added an appendix, with notes. 1910.

4894 No. 48. The mirror of the century, by W. F. Lord. 1902. [English novelists of the 19th cent.]

4895 No. 51. Thomas Chaloner, scholemaster [of Shrewsbury school, d. 1664], by P. Addleshaw. 1904.

4896 No. 54. An old city company: a sketch of the history and conditions of the Skinners' company of London, by L. B. Sebastian. 1906.

4897 No. 57. John White, [bishop] of Winchester [d. 1560], by J. B. Wainewright. 1907.

4898 No. 59. The Spanish match in the light of recent works and the consideration of a private ms. relating thereunto [being a discussion on Prince Charles's visit to Spain in 1623 in connection with his proposed marriage to the Infanta], by H. G. Rosedale. 1908.

4899 No. 60. A Salopian worthy [Abraham Causton, fl. 1818]; or, a week in Eldorado, by P. Addleshaw. 1909.

4900 No. 64. Centenary of William Makepeace Thackeray: [a paper] by C. P. Johnson [with a catalogue of exhibits]. 1911.

4901 No. 68. Music in the time of Elizabeth, by F. Keel. 1914.

4902 No. 70. The manor of Pellipar [belonging to the Skinners' company of London, 17th–19th cent.]: an episode in the plantation of Ulster, by L. B. Sebastian. 1919.

4903 No. 71. Lodowick Muggleton [d. 1698], by G. C. Williamson. 1919. [Includes a list of his writings and of those of William Reeve]

4904 No. 75. Jeremiah Horrox [astronomer, born *c.* 1619], by R. T. Gould. 1923.

4905 No. 76. An odd bibliography, being a list of all the publications of Ye Sette of Odd Volumes from 1878 to 1924, comp. R. Straus. 1925.

4906 No. 78. Crime and insanity, by Sir M. Craig. *P.* 1924. [Includes the McNaghten case 'rules']

4907 No. 79. The press-gang, by A. Hildesley. 1925.

4908 No. 81. Frederick, Baron Corvo [b. 1860], by A. J. A. Symons. *P.* 1926.

4909 No. 83. Some other Odd Volumes [being an account of societies founded on the model of the Sette of Odd Volumes at Chelmsford, Nottingham, Boston (U.S.A.), and Hong Kong], by G. C. Williamson. 1927.

4910 No. 86. The Old Bailey, by G. D. Roberts, with a prefatory note by ye Lord Chief Justice of England [Lord Hewart]. 1928.

4911 No. 89. Some criminal curiosities, by R. Oliver. 1930. [Not seen]

4912 No. 90. Medieval pilgrims' badges, by T. Borenius. 1930.

4913 No. 91. The mistery of St. George of the Armourers, comp. S. H. Pitt. 1931. [The origin and growth of the Worshipful Company of Armourers and Brasiers of London]

4914 No. 93. Wine in Shakespeare's days and in Shakespeare's plays, by A. L. Simon. 1931.

4915 No. 94. *The Toast*, an heroic poem [written by Dr. William King, *c.* 1732], by H. Williams. 1932.

SHAKESPEARE ASSOCIATION

Founded 1916, *to promote the study and interpretation of Shakespeare; to advance Shakespearian research, and to help forward investigations in dramatic and other literature, history, bibliography, and the various branches of learning bearing on the poet and his work; to publish papers and monographs on Shakespearian subjects.*

Shakespeare Association facsimiles, nos. 1–7:

4916 No. 1. *A Dialogue concerning Witches and Witchcraftes* (1593), by George Gifford, with introd. by Beatrice White. 1931.

4917 No. 2. Everard Guilpin: *Skialetheia* [*or a shadow of truth, in certaine epigrams and satyres* (1598)]. 1931.

4918 No. 3. *A Health to the Gentlemanly Profession of Serving Men* (1598), by I.M., with introd. by A. V. Judges. 1931.

4919 No. 4. J. Norden: *Vicissitudo Rerum* (1600), with introd. by D. C. Collins. 1931.

4920 No. 5. *A Short Treatise of Hunting* (1591), by Sir Thomas Cockaine, with introd. by W. R. Halliday. 1932.

4921 No. 6. G. Silver: *Paradoxes of Defence* (1599), with introd. by J. D. Wilson. 1933. [Treatise on fencing]

4922 No. 7. *Present Remedies against the Plague*, etc. [1593], with introd. by W. P. Barrett. 1933.

Other publications:

4923 Shakespeare and his Welsh characters, by A. E. Hughes. [Reprinted from the *Transactions of the Hon. Society of Cymmrodorion*, 1917–18.] *P.* [1918?].

4924 Shakespeare's *Tempest* as originally produced at court, by E. Law. *P.* [1921?].

4925 The 17th cent. accounts of the masters of the revels, by Charlotte C. Stopes. *P.* 1922.

4926 The beginning of the English secular and romantic drama, by A. W. Reed. *P.* 1922.

4927 In commemoration of the first folio tercentenary: a resetting of the preliminary matter of the first folio, with a catalogue of Shakespeariana exhibited in the hall of the Worshipful Company of Stationers, illustrative facsimiles, and introd. by Sir I. Gollancz. 1923.

4928 1623–1923: studies in the first folio, written for the Association in celebration of the first folio tercentenary, by M. H. Spielman, J. D. Wilson, Sir S. Lee, R. C. Rhodes, W. W. Greg, A. Nicholl, with introd. by Sir I. Gollancz. 1924.

4929 A series of papers on Shakespeare and the theatre, together with papers on Edward Alleyn and early records illustrating the personal life of Shakespeare, by members of the Association. 1927.

  a Edward Alleyn, by W. W. Greg.
  b The development of Shakespeare's stagecraft, by C. M. Haines.
  c Shakespeare's actors, by G. B. Harrison.
  d Shakespeare as man of the theatre, by J. Isaacs.
  e Shakespeare and the Elizabethan stage, by G. H. Cowling.
  f Shakespeare's audience, by Muriel St. C. Byrne.
  g Early records illustrating the personal life of Shakespeare, by Charlotte C. Stopes.

4930 Lewes Lavater: Of ghostes and spirites walking by nyght (1572), with introd. and appendix by J. D. Wilson and May Yardley. 1929.

4931 The disputed revels accounts reproduced in collotype facsimile, with a paper read before the Shakespeare Association by A. E. Stamp. 1930.

4932 Production and stage management at the Blackfriars theatre, by J. Isaacs. *P.* 1933.

SHAKESPEARE CLUB
(STRATFORD-UPON-AVON)

Founded 1874, to read, study, and discuss the works of the poet and the historical memories of his town and neighbourhood; also to encourage the delivery of original papers relating thereto, and in other ways to do honour to the memory of the poet. The Club is the descendant of the Shakespearean Club, founded in 1824, which became the Royal Shakespearean Club in 1830, and ceased operations in 1866.

Summary of Papers, 1905–25 (19 vols. [1906?–25?]), *contd. as* Annual Report, together with a summary of papers, and the Shakespeare sermon, 1925–33

(8 vols. [1926?–33?]), *all reprinted from the* Stratford-upon-Avon Herald:

4933 Vol. for 1905–6.[1]

　a Shakespeare clubs at Stratford-on-Avon: celebrations in honour of the poet, by G. M. Bird.

4934 Vol. for 1906–7.[1]

　a The date and occasion of *The Tempest*, by H. G. Fiedler.
　b Sports and pastimes of Shakespeare's day, by H. S. Ward.

4935 Vol. for 1907–8.

　a Ecclesiastical dramas of the middle ages, by S. Cooper·
　b The Elizabethan play-house, by W. Poel.

4936 Vol. for 1908–9.

　a Notes on the portraits of Shakespeare, by W. S. Brassington.

4937 Vol. for 1909–10.

　a Shakespeare's dramatic predecessors, by S. Cooper.
　b The evolution of an Elizabethan house, by J. H. Bloom.

4938 Vol. for 1910–11.

　a Shakespearean frauds, by W. Jaggard.
　b Shakespeare the actor, by W. S. Brassington.

4939 Vol. for 1912–13.

　a The masque as an art type, by R. T. R. Milliken.
　b The twin partnership of Beaumont and Fletcher, by S. Cooper.

4940 Vol. for 1913–14.

　a Heraldry in Shakespeare's plays, with a note upon the arms of the town of Stratford-upon-Avon, by W. S. Brassington.

4941 Vol. for 1914–15.

　a Social life in Shakespeare's day, by R. W. Wright-Henderson.
　b Shakespeare and wayfaring life, by F. C. Wellstood.[With notes from the Stratford-upon-Avon chamberlain's accounts relating to players at Stratford in Shakespeare's time]

4942 Vol. for 1915–16.

　a Quartos, folios, and other early editions of Shakespeare, by C. Clark.
　b Shakespeare and Warwickshire, by Mrs. Rose.

4943 Vol. for 1917–18.

　a The Elizabethan playhouse and its descendants, by W. Martin.
　b The *Tempest* as originally produced at court [1611], by E. Law.

¹ Not seen.

4944 Vol. for 1918–19.

　a Dr. John Hall, of Stratford-upon-Avon [b. 1575], by R. W. Leftwich.
　b Elizabethan tavern life, by C. Clark.
　c Henry, 3rd Earl of Southampton, lord of Shakespeare's love, by Charlotte C. Stopes.

4945 Vol. for 1919–20.

　a David Garrick: his modern treatment of Shakespeare, by A. Bond.
　b Notes on Stratford-upon-Avon before Shakespeare's time, by Mrs. E. Scriven.
　c Rambles among the old records of Stratford-upon-Avon [7th–16th cent.], by F. C. Wellstood.
　d The contemporary recognition of Shakespeare's eminence, by Sir S. Lee.

4946 Vol. for 1920–21.

　a John Shakespeare [father of William Shakespeare], by E. I. Fripp.
　b Shakespeare at Hampton Court and at the peace conference of 1604, by E. Law.

4947 Vol. for 1921–3.

　a Shakespeare's enemies, by W. Jaggard.
　b Stratford-upon-Avon when John Ward, M.A., was vicar, 1622–81, by Sir D'A. Power.

4948 Vol. for 1923–4.

　a Richard Quyny [d. 1602] bailiff of Stratford-upon-Avon, and friend of William Shakespeare, by E. I. Fripp.
　b Michael Drayton and some of his friends, by B. Newdigate.

4949 Vol. for 1924–5.

　a Early history of the Shakespeare Club [1768–1845], by F. C. Wellstood.
　b 'The Bear' and 'The Swan' inns [Stratford-upon-Avon] in Shakespeare's time, by E. I. Fripp.

4950 Vol. for 1927–8.

　a Shakespeare and Tudor economic life, by H. G. Smith.
　b Music in Shakespeare's day, by C. M. Edmunds.

4951 Vol. for 1928–9.

　a Elizabeth, the inspiration of her age, by H. G. Smith.

4952 Vol. for 1931–2.

　a The songs in Shakespeare and songs of his time, by F. H. Wood.
　b The influence of the audience on Shakespeare's dramatic art, by R. M. Goodfield.
　c Queen Elizabeth and her court, by H. Baker.

4953 Vol. for 1932–3.

　a Elizabeth and England, by C. May.

SHEFFIELD LITERARY AND PHILOSOPHICAL SOCIETY

Founded 1822, to promote polite literature and science. Dissolved 1932.

78th–109th Annual Report (32 vols. 1901–32):

4954 79th Report.

　a The influence of Sheffield upon the hymnology of the 19th cent., by J. Julian.
　b The presidents of the Society, 1823–50, with glimpses of Sheffield society at the period of its formation, by D. Parkes.

4955 81st Report.

a West Cornwall facts, fancies and fables of 50 years ago [*c.* 1850], by J. Julian.

4956 94th Report.

a Humour in the British parliament during four centuries, by W. J. Morrison.

4957 96th Report.

a The early [i.e. pre-Norman] history of the district as shown by the Christian monuments, by C. F. Innocent.

4958 97th Report.[1]

a Edward Law [d. 1838]: a notable Sheffield sculptor of the past, by B. H. Hoole.

4959 99th Report.[1]

a Old Sheffield, by H. Richardson.

4960 101st Report.

a Early history of old Sheffield plate, by E. Howarth.

Other publications:

4961 Sheffield Literary and Philosophical Society: a centenary retrospect, 1822–1922, by W. S. Porter. 1922.

SHROPSHIRE ARCHAEOLOGICAL AND NATURAL HISTORY SOCIETY
(Shropshire Archaeological Society)

Founded 1877, by the amalgamation of the Shropshire Archaeological Society (founded in the same year) and the Shropshire and North Wales Natural History and Antiquarian Society (founded 1835), for the printing of the historical, ecclesiastical, genealogical, topographical, geological, and literary remains of Shropshire, and other purposes. The Shropshire Parish Register Society [q.v.] was incorporated in 1923.

Transactions, 3rd ser., vols. 1–10, *also styled* **original ser., vols. 24–33 (1901–10):**

4962 Vol. 1.

a Samuel Pepys and his music, by J. C. Bridge.
b The provosts and bailiffs of Shrewsbury, by J. Morris. [Contd. in 3rd ser., vols. 2–6]
c Manor of Ruyton-of-the-eleven-towns, by R. Ll. Kenyon. [See also **4965**i below]
d The rebellion of Robert de Belesme [1102], by T. Auden.
e A 14th cent. roll of names, preserved among the Shrewsbury gild-merchant rolls, ed. C. H. Drinkwater.
f Two Shrewsbury burgess rolls, *temp.* Henry III, ed. C. H. Drinkwater.
g Some petitions to the bailiffs of Shrewsbury [1582–1682], by W. G. D. Fletcher.
h Where was Fethanleag?, by T. Auden.
i Sequestration papers of Sir John Weld, senior [d. 1666], and Sir John Weld, junior [d. 1681], of Willey, ed. W. Phillips.
j Township of New Ruyton, by R. Ll. Kenyon.
k Township of Old Ruyton, by R. Ll. Kenyon.
l Township of Coton, by R. Ll. Kenyon.
m A list of Shropshire wills at Somerset House, London, 1641–60. [Contd. in 3rd ser., vol. 2]
n Institutions of Shropshire incumbents, ed. W. G. D. Fletcher. [Diocese of Lichfield certificates of induction, 1563–1602, and extracts from the *Libri Institutionum,*

[1] For these years the abstracts of papers, usually part of the Report, were printed separately, with their own pagination.

1615–48. Certificates for the diocese of Lichfield, for 1605–34, together with extracts from the *Libri Institutionum* for Hereford and Lichfield dioceses, 1556–1680, are given in 3rd ser., vol. 5. Induction certificates for Hereford diocese, 1589–1634, occur in 3rd. ser., vol. 8, and for 1634–1759 in 4th ser., vol. 2. The Hereford certificates for 1759–1816, together with those for the diocese of Coventry and Lichfield, 1634–1816, occur in 4th ser., vols. 4–7]

o Francis Throgmorton, a prisoner in Shrewsbury, 1597–8, by W. Phillips.
p Sequestration papers of Sir Thomas Edwardes, bt. [d. 1660], ed. E. C. Hope-Edwardes.
q A glossary of some difficult or obsolete words found in the first series, by C. H. Drinkwater. [Contd. in 3rd ser., vol. 2]
r Will of William Fytzherberd, of Tong, 1451, ed. E. Calvert.
s Salop house of correction, and provision for the poor, 1598, ed. W. Phillips. [Relates to the proposed establishment of a house of correction at Shrewsbury]

4963 Vol. 2.

a Sequestration papers of Sir Orlando Bridgeman [d. 1674], ed. E. R. O. Bridgeman and C. G. O. Bridgeman.
b Shrewsbury gild merchant and other rolls of the 14th cent., ed. C. H. Drinkwater. [Contd. in 3rd ser., vol. 3]
c Township of Shelvock, by R. Ll. Kenyon.
d Township of Wikey, by R. Ll. Kenyon.
e Township of Shotatton, by R. Ll. Kenyon.
f Township of Eardiston, by R. Ll. Kenyon.
g The capture of Lord Thomas Grey in Shropshire [1554], by W. Phillips.
h On wearing the bonnet in the royal presence [in the 16th cent.], by W. G. D. Fletcher.
i Church bells of Shropshire, by H. B. Walters. [Contd. in 3rd ser., vols. 4–10, and 4th ser., vol. 1]
j Two royal paramours [Sibil Corbet and Rosamond de Clifford, 12th cent.], by T. Auden.
k The castle of Wem, by the Hon. G. H. F. Vane.
l The members of parliament for Wenlock [1472–1880], by H. T. Weyman.
m Township of Felton, by R. Ll. Kenyon.
n Township of Haughton, by R. Ll. Kenyon.
o Township of Rednal, by R. Ll. Kenyon.
p Township of Sutton, by R. Ll. Kenyon.
q Township of Tedsmere, by R. Ll. Kenyon.
r Will of Henry Bishop, vicar of Moreton Corbet, 1539, ed. W. Phillips.

4964 Vol. 3.

a Battle of Shrewsbury [1403], by J. H. Wylie.
b Sequestration papers of Thomas Smalman of Wilderhope [d. 1693], by W. G. D. Fletcher.
c Giraldus Cambrensis in Shropshire, by T. Auden.
d Churchwardens' accounts of the parish of Worfield [1500–1648], ed. H. B. Walters. [Contd. in 3rd ser., vols. 4, 6, 7, 9 and 10, and 4th ser., vol. 2]
e Five hundred years ago [the battle of Shrewsbury, 1403], by J. H. Wylie.
f Arms and clothing of the forces at the battle of Shrewsbury, by Viscount Dillon.
g Some additional documents relative to the battle of Shrewsbury, by W. G. D. Fletcher.
h Owen Glyndwr and the battle of Shrewsbury, by J. Parry-Jones.
i Battlefield church, by D. H. S. Cranage.
j Battlefield college, by W. G. D. Fletcher.
k Alleged relics from Battlefield, by H. R. H. Southam.
l Carved memorials on the tower of Battlefield church, by W. Phillips.

m A bibliography of Battlefield, by W. G. D. Fletcher.

n Shropshire five hundred years ago [*c.* 1403], by Henrietta M. Auden.

o Two exchequer suits respecting tithes of the rectory of Shifnal, and certain payments for the poor inhabitants, 1585, by W. G. D. Fletcher.

p The lords-lieutenant of Shropshire [1403-1898], by W. Phillips. [Contd. in 3rd ser., vol. 4]

q Authority for Sir Richard Ottley, kt., to search for hidden treasures [1669], by W. Phillips.

r Shropshire justices of the peace, 1590, ed. W. Phillips.

s Living descendants of Hotspur in Shropshire [1903], by W. G. D. Fletcher.

t Our Lady of Pity [Battlefield church], by T. Auden. [Contd. in 3rd ser., vol. 4]

u Stained glass formerly in Battlefield church, by W. G. D. Fletcher.

4965 Vol. 4.

a Parish documents of the county of Salop, by the Hon. G. H. F. Vane.

b Stretton court rolls of 1566-7 (a fragment), ed. C. H. Drinkwater.

c Subsidy roll for the hundreds of Purslow and Clun, 1641, ed. F. C. Norton.

d The founder [David Holbache d. *c.* 1423] and first trustees of Oswestry grammar school, by the Hon. Mrs. Bulkeley-Owen.

e A [Shrewsbury] burgess roll and a gild merchant roll of 1372, ed. C. H. Drinkwater.

f Accounts of the churchwardens of Wem [1683-1737], by the Hon. G. H. F. Vane.

g Manor of Sandford and Woolston, by R. Ll. Kenyon.

h Township of Twyford, by R. Ll. Kenyon.

i Additional notes on the history of the manor of Ruyton-of-the-eleven-towns, by R. Ll. Kenyon.

j Chantry chapels in Ludlow church, by H. T. Weyman.

k Will of John Talbot, 1st Earl of Shrewsbury, 1452, ed. with introd. and notes by the Hon. G. H. F. Vane.

l Palmers' gild of Ludlow: inventories of jewells and stuff in the 16th cent., ed. C. H. Drinkwater.

m Living descendants of Henry VII in Shropshire [1904], by W. G. D. Fletcher.

n Will of Lewys Taylour, pastor of Moreton Corbet, dated 1623, ed. W. Phillips.

o Who was the Lady Alice Stury?, by J. R. Burton.

4966 Vol. 5.

a Shrewsbury gild merchant rolls of the 14th and 15th cent., ed. C. H. Drinkwater.

b The Shropshire lay subsidy of 1327, with introd. by W. G. D. Fletcher. [Contd. from 2nd ser., vol. 11. Contd. in 3rd ser., vols. 6 and 7]

c Two Shrewsbury gild merchant rolls, 1501-10, ed. C. H. Drinkwater.

d Dodmore, by H. T. Weyman.

e Shropshire-men at the French wars of 1346-7, by W. G. D. Fletcher.

f Records of proceedings before the coroners of Salop, 1295-1306: a fragment, ed. C. H. Drinkwater.

g Shrewsbury burgess roll of 1416-17, ed. C. H. Drinkwater.

h Extracts from the note-book of a Shropshire vicar [the Rev. Robert Goodwin, vicar of Cleobury Mortimer], 1656-91, ed. Frances C. Baldwyn-Childe.

i A find of [16th and 17th cent.] coins at Oswestry, by R. Ll. Kenyon.

j Documents relating to estates of papists within the town and liberties of Shrewsbury, 1706-22, ed. W. G. D. Fletcher.

k The topographical history of Shrewsbury, by the Rev. J. Blakeway, ed. W. Phillips. [Contd. in 3rd ser., vols. 6 and 7]

l Salopian book-plates, by F. R. Ellis.

m Sequestration papers of Humphrey Walcot [d. 1650], by J. R. Burton.

n Inventories of religious houses of Shropshire at their dissolution, by W. G. D. Fletcher.

o Will of Thomas Gamel of Shrewsbury, 1355, ed. W. Phillips.

p St. Mary Magdalen's chapel, Shrewsbury, by W. Phillips.

q Notes on Wenlock, by Henrietta M. Auden.

r Certificate of a gild or chantry in St. Alkmund's church, Shrewsbury, 1388/9, ed. W. G. D. Fletcher.

4967 Vol. 6.

a Will of Katherine Bonell, widow of Thomas Lowe of Shrewsbury, 1461, ed. W. G. D. Fletcher.

b Sequestration papers of Thomas Pigott of Chetwynd [d. 1666], ed. W. G. D. Fletcher.

c Notes on the parish of Worthen and Caus castle, by L. J. Lee, ed. W. Phillips.

d Sir Richard de Sandford, of Sandford, 1306-47, by W. G. D. Fletcher.

e Shropshire feet of fines, 1218-48, ed. W. G. D. Fletcher. [Contd. from 2nd ser., vol. 10. Contd. in 3rd ser., vol. 7, and 4th ser., vols. 1, 4, and 6]

f The mayors of Shrewsbury, 1638-89, by J. Morris. [Contd. in 3rd ser., vol. 10, and 4th ser., vols. 2-4, and 9]

g The college of Tong, by J. E. Auden.

h Escapades of Richard Peshall of Chetwynd [fl. 1408-27], by W. G. D. Fletcher.

i History of Chirbury [from notes by W. Phillips], ed. Flora A. MacLeod.

j Bury walls, Hawkstone, by D. R. Thomas.

k Deed relating to Montgomery castle, 1301, ed. C. H. Drinkwater.

l Worthen communion plate, by C. H. Drinkwater.

4968 Vol. 7.

a Owen Glyndwr and Sycharth [Den.], by T. Auden.

b The Herberts of Cherbury, by Florentia C. Herbert.

c Montford bridge: tolls, customs, etc., 1285-1412, by C. H. Drinkwater.

d Wigley, by H. T. Weyman.

e A Bitterley broil in 1718: Booton *v.* Langford, by J. R. Burton.

f The Augustinian friars, Shrewsbury, by C. H. Drinkwater.

g The library of More church, by W. G. Clark-Maxwell.

h Upper Millichope, by E. C. Hope-Edwardes.

i Terrier of the parish of Diddlebury, 1637, ed. Evelyn H. Martin.

j The first bailiffs of Ludlow [13th cent. onwards]: an early chapter in the history of the borough, by H. T. Weyman.

k Early Salopian [tobacco] pipes, by T. H. Thursfield.

l Shropshire earthworks, by E. S. Cobbold.

m Charles II and Tong, by J. E. Auden. [Contd. in 3rd ser., vol. 8]

n Shrewsbury paving and other accounts, 1269-70: a roll preserved among the borough records, ed. C. H. Drinkwater.

o Ecclesiastical history of Shropshire during the civil war, Commonwealth and Restoration, by J. E. Auden. [Contd. in 3rd ser., vols. 8-10]

p Some proceedings at the Shropshire assizes, 1414, ed. W. G. D. Fletcher.

q Deed relating to the reparation of the Clive chapel, 1578, ed. W. G. D. Fletcher.

4969 Vol. 8.

a The last stand of Caractacus, by A. Heber-Percy.
b Poynton chapel, by J. A. Morris.
c Three early Shropshire charters [*c.* 1190–1314], ed. W. G. D. Fletcher.
d Notes on Alberbury, by Henrietta M. Auden.
e Notes on Kinlet, by the Rev. J. B. Blakeway [d. 1826], ed. Frances Baldwyn-Childe.
f Notes on some Shropshire royal descents, by W. G. D. Fletcher.
g Documents relating to Tong college, by J. E. Auden. [Contd. in 3rd ser., vol. 9]
h Muster rolls of the hundreds of Bradford, Munslow, etc. 1532–40, ed. from transcript by J. Beacall by C. H. Drinkwater. [Contd. in 3rd ser., vol. 9]
i Clun and its neighbourhood in the first civil war [1642–6], by A. M. Auden. [Contd. in 3rd ser., vol. 9]
j Sequestration papers of Sir Thomas Eyton [d. 1659], of Eyton-on-the-Wealdmoors, ed. W. G. D. Fletcher.
k Extent of the manor of Cheswardine, and a moiety of the manor of Childs Ercall, 1280, ed. W. G. D. Fletcher.
l Four Shropshire inquisitions *post mortem* [Elizabeth, daughter of John Lestrange, 1383; Sir Thomas de Roos of Hamelak, 1384; John Wareyn of Ightfield, 1413; Sir Roger Trumpyngton of Aldemere, 1416], ed. W. G. D. Fletcher.
m Haughmond abbey, by H. R. H. Southam.
n Order concerning rogues and vagabonds, 1571, ed. C. H. Drinkwater.

4970 Vol. 9.

a Notes on Albrighton near Shifnal, by H. F. J. Vaughan
b Shropshire hermits and anchorites, by Henrietta M. Auden.
c Visitations of Wenlock priory in the 13th cent., by W. G. D. Fletcher.
d History of the manor of Westhope, by Evelyn H. Martin. [Further notes occur in 4th ser., vol. 1]
e The Stone House, near St. Mary's church, Shrewsbury, by J. A. Morris.
f Two elections for Bishop's Castle in the 18th cent. [1741 and 1753], by J. R. Burton.
g Hopton Wafers, by J. Payton.
h Three Mytton letters [*c.* 1644–8], with introd. and notes by J. E. Auden. [Contd. in 3rd ser., vol. 10]
i The rural deanery of Clun in the 17th cent., by W. G. Clark-Maxwell.
j Admiral Sir Francis Geary, 1709–96, by Sir W. N. M. Geary.
k Some notes on a ms. of the Vulgate formerly belonging to Haughmond abbey, ed. C. H. Drinkwater.
l Wigmore castle, by T. Auden.
m Shropshire grants of arms, by W. G. D. Fletcher.
n A find of [16th–17th cent.] coins at Bridgnorth [1908], by R. Ll. Kenyon.
o Shropshire entries in the state papers, ed. W. M. M. Sellwood.

4971 Vol. 10.

a Shropshire and the royalist conspiracies, 1648–60, by J. E. Auden.
b Haughmond abbey, by W. H. St. J. Hope and H. Brakspear.
c History of Wrockwardine, by Florentia C. Herbert. [Contd. in 4th ser., vols. 1, 5, 8, and 9]
d Certificates of the Shropshire chantries under the acts of 37 Hen. VIII [1545] and 1 Edw. VI [1547], ed. with introd. by A. Hamilton Thompson. [Notes and appendices occur in 4th ser., vol. 1]
e Human remains found at Shrewsbury [1910], by T. Auden and J. A. Morris.

f Kinlet churchwardens' accounts, 1713–19, ed. Frances C. Baldwyn-Childe.
g Index of papers published in the 3rd ser. of the Transactions, 1901–10, comp. Flora A. MacLeod.

Transactions, 4th ser., vols. 1–12, *also styled original series*, vols. 34–45 (1911–30):

4972 Vol. 1.

a Anglo-Saxon charters relating to Shropshire, by W. H. Stevenson and W. H. Duignan.
b The family of Astley of Aston in the parish of Wem, by R. C. Purton.
c The Ottley papers, 2nd series: Commonwealth and Restoration, transcribed by W. Phillips and ed. J. E. Auden.
d The advowson of Clun in the 12th and 13th cent., by W. G. Clark-Maxwell.
e Some local church dedications in their bearing on local church history, by W. G. Clark-Maxwell.
f The choir ceiling of Ludlow church, by H. T. Weyman.
g 'The parish book' of St. Chad's, Shrewsbury, 1722–85, by J. A. Morris. [Contd. in vols. 2, 3, and 7]
h Will of Thomas Pendrell [1669], ed. J. E. Auden.

4973 Vol. 2.

a Four letters from Shropshire to Prince Rupert [1644], ed. J. E. Auden.
b Plan of Tong college: notes by N. W. Howard-McLean.
c The Ketlebys of Steple, by R. C. Purton.
d History of several families connected with Diddlebury, by Evelyn H. Martin. 1: The Baldwyns.
e The expulsion of Oxford students in 1768, by W. G. D. Fletcher. [See also below]
f Sequestration papers of Richard Oakeley of Oakeley [d. 1653], ed. W. G. D. Fletcher.
g Shropshire clergy who contributed to the free and voluntary present to his Majesty, 1662, by W. G. D. Fletcher.
h War services of some Shropshire officers in the king's army [1642–8], by J. E. Auden.
i Sir Francis Ottley and the royalist attempt of 1648, ed. J. E. Auden.
j Certificate of ordination by a Shropshire Presbyterian classis [1652], with notes by J. E. Auden.
k Shropshire institutions, 1648–59, annotated by J. E. Auden and W. G. D. Fletcher. [Contd. in 'Miscellanea' section, 4th ser., vol. 4]
l [Excavations at Uriconium (Wroxeter)], by J. P. Bushe-Fox, J. A. Morris and D. Atkinson. [Contd. in 4th ser., vols. 3–5, 9, 10–12, and 46]
m Thomas Jones, the expelled Oxford student, by W. G. D. Fletcher. [See also above]

4974 Vol. 3.

a Oswestry tenures, 17th cent., transcribed with introd. and notes by R. C. Purton.
b Coston [manor], by H. Weyman.
c Early deeds [13th–15th cent.] relating to lands on Claremont, Shrewsbury, ed. W. G. D. Fletcher.
d Devolution of the manor of Edgmond in the 14th and following centuries, by C. G. O. Bridgeman.
e Some account of Sidbury, by R. C. Purton.
f A Shrewsbury divine of the 18th cent. [the Rev. Job Orton, d. 1783], by T. Auden.
g The earliest book of the Drapers' company, Shrewsbury [1461–1608], ed. Irene M. Rope and Lily F. Chitty. [Contd. in 4th ser., vols. 4, 9–11]
h The Walters at Ludlow: an Elizabethan plan [of a part of Bringewood forest leased to Edmund Walter, of Mary Vale, d. 1594], by H. T. Weyman.
i Wattlesborough castle, by S. Leighton.
j History of several families connected with Diddlebury,

by Evelyn H. Martin. 2: The Cornewalls. 3: The Littletons.

k Notes on the inscriptions of the S. Bernard windows in S. Mary's, Shrewsbury, by A. Moriarty. [See also 4th ser., vol. 8]

l The family of Hoggins, of Great Bolas, by W. G. D. Fletcher. [Contd. in 4th ser., vol. 4]

m Notes on the rural deanery of Stottesdon, 1275–1375, by J. Payton.

n Hanwood monumental inscriptions, by Lily F. Chitty.

4975 Vol. 4.

a William Cartwright, nonjuror [d. 1799], and his chronological history of Shrewsbury, ed. W. Phillips.

b John Oakeley's notes on Lydham, ed. with introd. by R. R. James.

c A roll of a forest court of Hogstow forest, 1521, ed. T. E. Pickering.

d Sequestration papers of Sir Thomas Wolryche, kt. and bt., of Dudmaston [d. 1668], ed. W. G. D. Fletcher.

e A 13th cent. Whetmore charter of Hugh de Donvile, ed. R. R. James.

f History of Knockin, by the Rev. J. B. Blakeway [Bodleian Library Blakeway mss., vol. 11], ed. Henrietta M. Auden.

g The Wolley family of Wood Hall, by H. E. Forrest.

h Sequestration papers of Sir Thomas Whitmore, kt. and bt., of Apley [d. 1653], ed. W. G. D. Fletcher.

i The true story of the marriage of 'the Lord of Burleigh' and Sarah Hoggins [1790], by W. G. D. Fletcher.

4976 Vol. 5.

a Members of parliament for Bridgnorth [to 1880], by H. T. Weyman.

b Burwarton [manor of, from Bodleian Library Blakeway mss., vol. 10], with notes and additions by R. C. Purton and R. R. James.

c Two Salopian deeds, ed. R. R. James. 1: A licence for Edward Foxe to alienate lands in Novers, Cainham, Snytton and Bennet's Ende to Richard Churchman [1596]. 2: Fine between George Hayes and Thomas Garlicke, complainants, and James Kettleby, deforciant, concerning lands in Stepple, Neen Savage, Nash and Cleobury Mortimer [6 Geo. II].

d Rev. Francis Leighton, 1747–1813, by Frances C. Baldwyn-Childe.

e Contemporary letter as to the death of Lord Clive [1774], by A. South.

f Ludlow castle in 1631, by Caroline A. J. Skeel.

g Sutton, near Shrewsbury, by J. A. Morris.

h Parish registers of Sutton [1709–1870, with extracts from registers of the bishops of Hereford].

i Old Shropshire houses and their owners: Whitton; Marshe Manor; Braggington; Dinthill; Whitley; Plas-y-court, by H. E. Forrest.

j Sir John Burgh, lord of Mawddwy, 1414–71, by Frances C. Baldwyn-Childe.

k Early Quakerism in Shropshire, by T. Auden.

l List of English words usual in the marches of Wales (17th cent.), by Caroline A. J. Skeel.

m The Goughs of Newton-on-the-Hill, by A. V. Gough.

4977 Vol. 6.

a Register of boys admitted to Shrewsbury school, 1636/7–1664, ed. J. E. Auden.

b Deed of consecration of the school chapel in the Old schools, Shrewsbury, 1617, transcribed by C. H. Drinkwater with introd. by W. G. D. Fletcher.

c The old church of Llanfairwaterdine, with some account of its destruction and an interpretation of the inscription formerly in the rood-screen, by W. G. Clark-Maxwell.

d Two celebrated Salopian surgeons: Sir Caesar Hawkins, bt. [d. 1786], and his brother Pennell Hawkins [d. 1791], with some account of their ancestors and descendants, by R. R. James.

e The borough of Clun, by R. Ll. Clun.

f [On] the register of the council in the marches of Wales, 1569–91, published by the Honourable Society of Cymmrodorion, 1916, by Caroline A. J. Skeel.

g Notes on the history of the Oakeley family, by E. F. Oakeley.

h Grant from William Lyster to his son-in-law Nicholas Waryng and Cristiana his wife, in tail, of all his lands in Frankwell, Shrewsbury, 1494, ed. J. de C. Laffan.

i Some Shropshire incidents in the 15th cent. [including an account of a quarrel between the Plowden and Walcot families], by H. T. Weyman.

j The romance of Shrewsbury school register [being notes on some of the scholars], by A. C. Yate.

k Holgate and the Cressetts, by R. C. Purton.

l Bromcroft in the parish of Diddlebury, and its owners, by Evelyn H. Martin.

m Old Shropshire houses and their owners: The Lynches, Yocklreton; Bentall, near Ford; Ford Hall; Ford House; Mansion House, Ford, by H. E. Forrest.

n Shrewsbury show, by R. Ll. Kenyon.

o Borough-English and the manor of Ford, by Henrietta M. Auden.

4978 Vol. 7.

a The names of boys admitted to Shrewsbury school, 1734–46 [with supplemental names of scholars, 1746–98], ed. J. E. Auden.

b Oswestry borough gaol, by R. Ll. Kenyon.

c The Penderel annuities in 1665, by Henrietta M. Auden.

d Sequestration papers of Sir Thomas Harris, 3rd bt. of Boreatton [d. c. 1661], and of Lady Anne Harris, his stepmother, ed. W. G. D. Fletcher.

e The statue of Edward III, on the tower of the abbey church, Shrewsbury, by H. R. H. Southam.

f Lord Clive [d. 1774] and the Rev. Dr. William Adams of Shrewsbury, by H. R. H. Southam.

g Extracts from a manuscript book in the library at Sweeney Hall [Old Book of Remarkable Occurences of Bailiffs, Mayors and Sheriffs of ye Towne and County of Salop], ed. Rachel Leighton.

h Old Shropshire houses and their owners: Charlton Hill; Eyton on Severn; High Ercall Hall; Old Hall, Wellington; Dothill; Arleston; Hadley manor house; Lee Hall, Ellesmere, by H. E. Forrest.

i The manor of Rorrington, by O. Wakeman.

j Kingsland and Shrewsbury show, by J. Barker.

k Dame Margaret Eyton's will, 1642, by C. S. Betton.

l An order of the council in the marches, 1571, by Caroline A. J. Skeel.

m Medical men in practice in Shropshire, 1779–83, by R. R. James.

n Sequestration papers of John Yonge the elder of Pimley [d. 1655] and of John Yonge his son, ed. W. G. D. Fletcher.

o Bishop's transcripts at Hereford [1600–60], by F. C. Norton.

p A muster roll of Sheriff Hales, 1539, ed. A. T. Michell.

4979 Vol. 8.

a The family of Marston, of Afcote, etc., by Evelyn H. Martin. [Contd. in 4th ser., vols. 9 and 10]

b The mediaeval hospitals of Bridgnorth, by W. G. Clark-Maxwell.

c Deed relating to property belonging to the hospital of St. John the Baptist, Shrewsbury, 1610, ed. C. H. Drinkwater.

d Old Shropshire houses and their owners: Eaton Mascot; Golding; Frodesley Hall; The Lodge, Frodesley; Stanwardine Hall (Baschurch); Berwick, Shrewsbury; Abcott Manor; Lower Woodcote; Upper Woodcote; Oak Farm, Woodcote; Orleton, Wellington, by H. E. Forrest.

e Berwick almshouses: will of Sir Samuel Jones, founder, 1673, ed. R. R. James.

f Wills of the Prynce family [1598–1772], ed. H. E. Forrest.

g Notes on the glass, S. Mary's, Shrewsbury, by A. J. Moriarty. [See also 4th ser., vol. 3]

h Chancery proceedings, 1697–8: William Scarlett and Abigail his wife *v.* Henry Smallman, and John Bayley and Susan his wife, ed. W. G. D. Fletcher.

i Chantries of St. Leonard's church, Bridgnorth, by W. G. Clark-Maxwell.

j Alcaston manor, by J. A. Morris.

k Church of St. Michael within the castle, Shrewsbury, by W. G. D. Fletcher.

l The Thornes family of Thornes Hall, by H. E. Forrest.

m Some Shropshire grants of arms [1562–1881], ed. W. G. D. Fletcher.

n Six 15th cent. roundels in the Shrewsbury museum, by A. Moriarty.

o Deed concerning lands in Alveley parish, 1386, ed. W. G. Clark-Maxwell.

4980 Vol. 9.

a Whitton Court, by H. T. Weyman.

b Richard Baxter [d. 1691] in Bridgnorth, by W. G. Clark-Maxwell.

c Charles I: a three-pound [coin] of Shrewsbury [1642], by L. A. Lawrence.

d Bridgnorth: the bridge and its chapel, by W. G. Clark-Maxwell.

e The life of William Baxter [d. 1723], written by himself for the sake of his children, ed. J. E. Auden. [Contd. in 4th ser., vol. 10]

f The Baxter family of Eaton Constantine, by W. G. D. Fletcher. [Contd. in 4th ser., vol. 10]

g Roland Gosenell, prior of Wenlock, 1521–6, by Rose Graham.

h The monks of Much Wenlock after the suppression [1540], by W. G. Clark-Maxwell.

i Terrier of the vicarage of Wroxeter, 1765, by H. Hobson.

j Old Shropshire houses and their owners: Worthen Hall; Hampton Hall, Worthen; Newnham; Lower Newton; Lea Hall; Langley Hall, Acton Burnell, by H. E. Forrest.

k A grant by Walter de Lacy to Ludlow church [*c.* 1230], by H. T. Weyman.

4981 Vol. 10.

a Shropshire members of parliament [1290–1885], by H. T. Weyman. [Contd. in 4th ser., vols. 11 and 12]

b Welsh shrievalty papers among the Bridgewater mss., by Caroline A. J. Skeel.

c The Lord Calvin [fl. 1644–5], by F. Pember.

d The family of James of Mainstone, by C. S. James.

e Patent of peerage granted to Sir Francis Richard Sandford, K.C.B., 1891.

f Old timber-framed houses: principles of construction, by H. E. Forrest.

g The rural deanery of Ludlow in the 16th cent., by A. J. Knapton.

h Briefs for Shropshire churches, etc. [1661–1748], by H. R. H. Southam.

i The building of the church of Great Bolas, 1726–9, by W. G. D. Fletcher.

j Notes on prehistoric implements, by Lily F. Chitty. [1: Stone and bronze implements from the Clee hills. 2: Perforated stone axe-hammer from the Severn near Montford Bridge. 3: Perforated stone axe-hammer from Aston, near Oswestry]

k The Hoar stone or Marsh Pool circle, by Lily F. Chitty.

l Detton, by R. C. Purton.

m Certificates of residence, *temp.* Charles I: entries relating to the Smallman family, by H. R. H. Southam.

n Shropshire inquisitions *post mortem* [a list, 1216–1649, together with the inquisitions for Thomas Corbet, 1310, and Nicholas Sonford, 1415], by W. G. D. Fletcher.

o Excavations at the White abbey, Alberbury, by Lily F. Chitty.

p Inscriptions in the churchyard [and church], Eaton-under-Haywood, by Lilian H. Hayward.

q A letter of Thomas Cooke, 1655, ed. R. R. James.

r Bronze dirk found near the Whetstones circle, Montgomeryshire–Shropshire border, with notes on the neighbouring antiquities, by Lily F. Chitty.

s The D. G. Goodwin collection of antiquities, by Lily F. Chitty.

t Two cinerary urns of the bronze age from Little Ryton, near Condover, by R. C. C. Clay.

4982 Vol. 11.

a The Grey friars of Bridgnorth, by W. G. Clark-Maxwell.

b The King's Head and town walls in Mardol, Shrewsbury, by J. A. Morris.

c Will of Admiral John Benbow, 1702, ed. W. G. D. Fletcher.

d Report by Sir Frederick Kenyon on a collection of charters, rolls and papers [12th–18th cent.] from Ashridge Park, co. Buckingham, belonging to representatives of the late Lord Brownlow.

e Old Shropshire houses and their owners: Ledwych Court, Bitterley; Park Hall, Bitterley; Lupencote, Bitterley; Crow Leasow, Bitterley; Alkington; Bellaport Old Hall, Market Drayton; Snytton, Bitterley, by H. E. Forrest.

f References to Wales and the marches in the Penshurst Place mss. [16th cent.], by Caroline A. J. Skeel.

g The Dettons of Wheathill, by R. C. Purton.

h Dug-out canoes from Shropshire, by Lily F. Chitty.

i Three sepulchral stones discovered at Wroxeter in 1752: an address by Dr. John Ward, vice-president of the Royal Society in 1755, with introd. by J. A. Morris.

j The rural deanery of Wenlock in the 16th cent., by A. J. Knapton.

k Clergy list of the archdeaconry of Salop in Hereford, 1563, by A. J. Knapton.

l Mediaeval enclosures in Shropshire, by Henrietta M. Auden.

m Rural settlement in Shropshire: a geographical interpretation, by Dorothy Sylvester.

n Alberbury priory, by Rose Graham and A. W. Clapham.

o Roman bridge at Wroxeter, by J. A. Morris.

p Bronze implements found near Castle Bryn Amlwg, Bettws-y-Crwyn, by Lily F. Chitty.

q Local bequests in the will of John Jones of London and Hampton-on-Thames, 1692, ed. B. Garside.

4983 Vol. 12.

a The minister's library in Tong church, by J. E. Auden.

b Notes on recent acquisitions to the prehistoric section, Shrewsbury museum, by Lily F. Chitty.

c The Grey friars of Shrewsbury, by A. J. Moriarty.

d The riddle [of the hill camp] of Abdon Burf, by G. R. H. Webster.

e The rural deaneries of Burford, Stottesdon, Pontesbury and Clun in the 16th cent., by A. J. Knapton.

f Shrewsbury members of parliament [1295–1918], by H. T. Weyman. [Contd. in 4th ser., vol. 47]

g Local peculiar courts of Shropshire, by J. E. Auden. [Contd. in vols. 46 and 47]

h Old Shropshire houses and their owners: Coton Hall; Nordeley Regis Manor; The Hay, Alveley, by H. E. Forrest.

i Small perforated stone adze from High Hatton, Stanton-upon-Hine Heath, by Lily F. Chitty.

j Wilderhope [16th cent. manor house], by J. A. Morris.

k Clive House, College Hill, Shrewsbury, by J. A. Morris.

l Index of papers published in the 4th ser. of the Transactions, 1911–30, comp. R. C. Purton.

m Calendar of Shropshire wills and administrations, deposited in the Shrewsbury district probate registry [17th–19th cent.], extracted by R. C. Purton.

Transactions, vols. 46–47, *continuing the above*, (1931–3):

4984 Vol. 46.

a Bridgnorth castle and Ethelfleda's tower, by W. Watkins-Pitchford.

b Manor of Oldbury, near Bridgnorth, by R. C. Purton.

c Flint flakes from the Shrewsbury and Wellington district, by T. C. Cantrill.

d Another Elizabethan clergy list, by A. J. Knapton. [Refers mainly to the Shropshire portion of the diocese of Hereford]

e Austin friars and the town drainage [Shrewsbury], by J. A. Morris.

f William Burnel [d. 1304], fellow of Merton College, Oxford; provost and dean of Wells, etc., by A. L. Browne.

g Buildwas abbey: the survey of 1536, by W. G. Clark-Maxwell.

h Old Shropshire houses and their owners: Aston Botterell; Bedstone Manor; Chelmarsh and the Mortimers, by H. E. Forrest.

i Bury walls, Hawkstone, by J. A. Morris.

j Robert Burd of Tong [d. *c.* 1680], by J. E. Auden.

k Adderley and its church, by F. A. Hibbert.

l The Shropshire pigs of Roman lead, by G. C. Whittick.

m Mainstone pewholders [*c.* 1562–1728], by C. S. James.

n Standing stones on Stapely hill, by G. Mountford.

o Putlog holes in Bridgnorth castle, by W. Watkins-Pitchford.

p [Calendar of] St. Mary's (Shrewsbury) wills and administrations [17th–19th cent.], ed. W. G. D. Fletcher and T. Plummer.

4985 Vol. 47.

a An inquisition in Salop, 1655, by virtue of a commission from the Protector, ed. H. E. Evans.

b Lieut.-col. William Reinking in Shropshire [*c.* 1644–5], by J. E. Auden.

c Manor of Acton Burnell, by R. C. Purton.

d Deeds relating to an estate behind the walls, Shrewsbury [1272–1614], ed. R. C. Purton.

e Archaeological notes, by Lily F. Chitty. 1: Bronze looped palstave from Whixall Moss, north Shropshire. 2: Stone implement reported from Buildwas. 3: Gold standard weight of James I from Uffington.

f Note on the water supply of Uriconium [Wroxeter], by R. W. Pocock.

g Mytton[s] of Halston, by Evelyn H. Martin, revised and ed. J. E. Auden.

h A 16th cent. Shrewsbury school inventory, by J. B. Oldham.

i Stottesdon, by R. C. Purton.

j Old Shropshire houses and their owners: Walliborne Hall; Gibbons' Mansion, Shrewsbury, by H. E. Forrest.

k Wroxeter excavations, by J. A. Morris.

Other publications:

4986 Shrewsbury burgess roll, abstracted and ed. H. E. Forrest. 1924.

SHROPSHIRE PARISH REGISTER SOCIETY

Founded 1898, to print Shropshire parish registers from their first commencement to 1812. Incorporated with the Shropshire Archaeological and Natural History Society in 1923.

Shropshire parish registers, diocese of Hereford, vols. 1–19 (1900 [1898]–1943):

4987 Vol. 1. [Registers of Shipton, 1538–1812; Ford, 1589–1812; Hughley, 1576–1812; Hanwood, 1559–1763; Wolstaston, 1601–1812; Tasley, 1563–1812; Sidbury, 1560–1812.] 7 pts. separately paginated and indexed. 1900 [1898–1900].

4988 Vol. 2. [Registers of Sibdon Carwood, 1582–1812; Hopton Castle, 1538–1812; More, 1570–1812; Clunbury, 1574–1812.] 4 pts. separately paginated and indexed. 1901 [1898–99].

4989 Vol. 3. [Registers of Lydham, 1596–1812; Edgton, 1722–1812; Monk Hopton, 1698–1812; Chelmarsh, 1557–1812; Neenton, 1558–1812; Billingsley, 1625–1812.] 6 pts. separately paginated and indexed. 1903 [1900–3].

4990 Vol. 4. [Registers of Stanton Lacy, 1561–1812; Bitterley, 1658–1812.] 2 pts. separately paginated and indexed. 1903 [1900–2].

4991 Vol. 5. [Registers of Bromfield, 1559–1812; Greete, 1663–1812; Bedstone, 1719–1812; Middleton Scriven, 1728–1812; Deuxhill and Glazeley, 1718–1812; Habberley, 1598–1812; Cardeston, 1663–1812; Ratlinghope, 1755–1812.] 8 pts. separately paginated and indexed. 1909 [1903–9].

4992 Vols. 6, 7. Alberbury register. 1 vol. in 2. 1902 [1902–7]. [Pt. 1: 1564–1733. Pt. 2: 1733–1812]

4993 Vol. 8. [Registers of Chirbury, 1629–1812; Church Stretton, 1661–1812.] 3 pts. separately paginated and indexed. 1911 [1903–11].

4994 Vol. 9. [Registers of Cleobury Mortimer, 1601–1812; Hopton Wafers, 1660–1812.] 2 pts. separately paginated and indexed. 1909 [1904–9?].

4995 Vol. 10. [Register of Claverley, 1568–1812, marriages to 1837.] 1907 [1905–7].

4996 Vol. 11. [Register of Worthen, 1558–1812.] 1909 [1907–9].

4997 Vol. 12. [Registers of Pontesbury, 1538–1812; Westbury, 1637–1812.] 2 pts. separately paginated and indexed. 1909.

4998 Vols. 13, 14. [Register of Ludlow.] 1 vol. in 2. 1912–15 [1910–15]. [Pt. 1: 1558–1719. Pt. 2: 1719–1812]

4999 Vol. 15. [Registers of Diddlebury, 1583–1812; Munslow, 1538–1812.] 2 pts. separately paginated and indexed. 1912 [1910–12].

5000 Vol. 16. [Registers of Oldbury, 1582–1812; Church Preen, 1680–1812; Badger, 1660–1812; Burford, 1558–1812; Willey, 1644–1812; Neen Sollars, 1678–1812; Milson, 1678–1812.] 7 pts. separately paginated and indexed. 1915 [1912–15].

5001 Vol. 17. [Registers of Neen Savage, 1575–1812; Kinlet, 1657–1840; Stokesay, 1559–1812, marriages to 1837; Wistanstow, 1638, 1661–1812, marriages to 1837.] 4 pts. separately paginated and indexed. 1920 [1916–20].

5002 Vol. 18. [Registers of Hopesay, 1660–1812, marriages to 1837; Onibury, 1577–1812, marriages to 1837; Meole

Brace, 1660–1812, marriages to 1837.] 4 pts. separately paginated and indexed. 1929 [1919–29].

5003 Vol. 19. [Registers of Abdon, 1560–1812, marriages to 1838; Norbury, 1560–1812; Eaton-under-Heywood, 1660–1812, marriages to 1837; Easthope, 1624–1812, marriages to 1837; Stoke St. Milborough, 1654–1812, marriages to 1837.] 5 pts. separately paginated and indexed. 1943 [1932–43].

Shropshire parish registers, diocese of Lichfield, vols. 1–19 (1900 [1898]–1931):

5004 Vol. 1. [Registers of Battlefield, 1663–1812; Pitchford, 1558–1812; Smethcote, 1609–1812; Stapleton, 1546–1812; Moreton Corbet, 1580–1812; Albrighton, near Shrewsbury, 1649–1812; Broughton, 1705–1812.] 7 pts. separately paginated and indexed. 1900 [1898–1900].

5005 Vol. 2. [Registers of Harley, 1590–1812; Sheinton, 1658–1812; Cressage, 1605–1812; Kenley, 1682–1812; Cound, 1562–1812; Longdon-upon-Tern, 1692–1812; Grinshill, 1592–1812.] 7 pts. separately paginated and indexed. 1901 [1898–1901].

5006 Vol. 3. [Registers of Albrighton near Wolverhampton, 1558–1812; Boningale, 1698–1812; Donington, 1556–1812; burial register of White Ladies, 1816–44.] 4 pts. separately paginated and indexed. 1901 [1899–1901].

5007 Vol. 4. [Registers of Fitz, 1559–1812; Frodesley, 1547–1812; Uppington, 1650–1812; Tong, 1629–1812; Adderley, 1692–1812.] 5 pts. separately paginated and indexed. 1903 [1900–3].

5008 Vol. 5. [Registers of Astley, 1692–1812; Withington, 1591–1812; Stirchley, 1658–1812; Uffington, 1578–1812; Ruyton-in-the-eleven-towns, 1719–1812; Leebotwood, 1547–1812; Longnor, 1586–1812.] 7 pts. separately paginated and indexed. 1905 [1903–5].

5009 Vol. 6. [Register of Condover, 1570–1812.] 1906 [1904–6].

5010 Vol. 7. [Registers of Montford, 1662–1812; Clive, 1671–1812; Sheriffhales, 1557–1812; Hordley, 1686–1812.] 4 pts. separately paginated and indexed. 1909 [1906–9].

5011 Vol. 8. [Registers of Wrockwardine, 1591–1812; Moreton Say, 1691–1812.] 2 pts. separately paginated and indexed. 1907 [1906–7].

5012 Vol. 9. [Register of Wem, 1583–1744.] 1908 [1906–7].

5013 Vol. 10. [Registers of Wem, 1745–1812, with index for 1583–1812; Edstaston, 1712–1812; Newtown, 1779–1812.] 3 pts., the first continuing vol. 9, the others separately paginated and indexed. 1908.

5014 Vol. 11. [Registers of Wroxeter, 1613–1812; Hodnet, 1656–1812; Weston under Red Castle in the parish of Hodnet, 1565–1812.] 3 pts. separately paginated and indexed. 1911 [1910–11].

5015 Vol. 12. [Register of St. Mary's Shrewsbury, 1584–1812.] 1911.

5016 Vol. 13. [Registers of Edgmond, 1669–1812; Tibberton, 1719–1812; Waters Upton, 1547–1812; Great Bolas, 1582–1812; Eaton Constantine, 1684–1812.] 5 pts. separately paginated and indexed. 1913 [1912–13].

5017 Vol. 14. [Registers of Leighton, 1661–1812; Atcham, 1619–1812, marriages to 1837; Buildwas, 1665–1812, marriages to 1837; Berrington, 1559–1812, marriages to 1837.] 4 pts. separately paginated and indexed. 1921 [1915–21].

5018 Vols. 15, 16, 17. St. Chad's, Shrewsbury. 3 vols. 1913–18. [Registers. Vol. i: 1616–1717. Vol. ii: 1717–81, marriages

to 1754. Vol. iii: Marriages, 1756–1812; baptisms and burials, 1781–1812]

5019 Vol. 18. [Registers of Dawley Magna, 1666–1812, marriages to 1837; Norton-in-Hales, 1572–1880.] 2 pts. separately paginated and indexed. 1927 [1923–7].

5020 Vol. 19. [Registers of Myddle, 1541–1813, marriages to 1837; Lee Brockhurst, 1566–1838; Acton Burnell, 1568–1812, marriages to 1838.] 3 pts. separately paginated and indexed. 1931 [1925–31].

Shropshire parish registers, diocese of St. Asaph, vols. 1–8 (1906 [1899]–1922):

5021 Vol. 1. [Registers of Melverley, 1723–1812; Selattyn, 1557–1812.] 2 pts. separately paginated and indexed. 1906 [1899–1906].

5022 Vol. 2. [Registers of Whittington, 1591–1812; Halston, 1686–1897.] 2 pts. separately paginated and indexed. 1910 [1899–1910].

5023 Vol. 3. [Registers of Kinnerley, 1677–1812; Knockin, 1661–1812; Llanyblodwel, 1695–1812.] 3 pts. separately paginated and indexed. 1913 [1905–13].

5024 Vols. 4–7. [Registers of Oswestry.] 4 vols. 1909 [1904]–14. [Vol. i: 1558–1669. Vol. ii: 1669–1727, burials to 1750. Vol. iii: Baptisms, 1727–1812; marriages, 1727–54. Vol. iv: Burials, 1750–1812; marriages, 1754–1812]

5025 Vol. 8. [Registers of Llanymynech, 1666–1812; St. Martin's, 1579–1812, marriages to 1837.] 2 pts. separately paginated and indexed. 1922 [1917–22].

Other publications:

5026 Shropshire parish registers. Nonconformist registers, transcribed and ed. G. E. Evans. 1903. Containing registers of the following, each separately paginated:

  a High Street church, Shrewsbury, 1692–1812.
  b Swan Hill chapel, Shrewsbury, 1767–1812.
  c Dodington Presbyterian chapel, Whitchurch, 1708–1812.
  d Wem Presbyterian chapel, 1755–1814.
  e Bridgnorth Stoneway chapel, 1765–1812.
  f Oswestry old chapel, 1780–1812.
  g Old dissenting chapel, Oldbury, 1715–45, 1759–1813.
  h Independent chapel, Ellesmere, 1787–1811.
  i Claremont Baptist meeting-house, Shrewsbury, 1766–1808.
  j Society of Friends, Shrewsbury, 1657–1834.

5027 Shropshire parish registers. Roman Catholic registers, transcribed by W. Kinsella, with introd. by H. F. J. Vaughan, ed. W. G. D. Fletcher. 1913. Containing baptismal registers of the following:

  a St. Mary, Shrewsbury, 1775–1837.
  b SS. Peter and Paul, Newport, 1785–1837.
  c Acton Burnell, 1769–1838.
  d St. Francis, Plowden, 1826–37.
  e St. Mary, Mawley Hall, 1763–1831.

5028 Shropshire parish registers. Nonconformist and Roman Catholic registers. 1922. Containing registers of the following:

  a Bridgnorth Castle Street Baptist chapel, 1779–1836.
  b Broseley, Birch Meadow chapel, Particular Baptist, 1794–1835.
  c Clee Hill (parish of Caynham) Wesleyan chapel, 1796–1829.
  d Hadnall and Clive Independent chapels, 1798–1837.
  e Llanyblodwel, Smyrna Independent chapel, 1825–36.
  f Ludlow Corve Street (and Old Street) Independent chapel, 1802–36.

g Market Drayton Independent chapel, 1776–1836.
h Wem, Chapel Street Independent chapel, 1785–1836.
i Lyth Hill and Dorrington Independent chapel, 1808–1837.
j Ditton Priors Wesleyan chapel, 1801–34.
k Westbury, Minsterley Independent chapel, 1806–37.
l Prees, Whixall Independent chapel, 1805–23.

SOCIÉTÉ DES GENS DE DROIT DE JERSEY

Founded 1899, to promote the study of law and the protection and interests of its members.

Publications:

5029 Les commentaires sur l'ancienne coutume de Normandie par Jean Poingdestre, lieutenant-bailli de Jersey, 1668–76, avec une notice biographique de l'auteur, éd. E. T. Nicolle. 1907.

5030 Les lois et coutume de l'île de Jersey, par Jean Poingdestre, éd. E. T. Nicolle, A. M. Coutanche, C. W. D. Aubin, et C. S. Harrison. 1928.

SOCIÉTÉ GUERNESIAISE

Founded 1882, as the Guernsey Society of Natural Science, for (a) the study and investigation of the archaeology and history, folklore and language, geology and meteorology, and the fauna and flora of the bailiwick of Guernsey, (b) the holding of meetings for the reading and discussion of papers and the exhibition of objects of interest, (c) the publication of Transactions and of such papers and notes on the aforesaid matters as may be deemed worthy of record. The words 'and Local Research' were added to the original title in 1889. Title changed to above form in 1922.

Report and Transactions, vols. 4–11 (1901–33):

5031 Vol. 4.
a An excursion to St. Pierre-du-Bois, by G. T. Derrick.
b Ancient names of the bays, creeks, rocks, etc. on and near the coast of Guernsey and the other islands of the bailiwick, with notes, by R. H. Tourtel.
c Jerbourg and its fortifications: a contribution to Guernsey history, by G. T. Derrick.
d The Vale church and priory, by G. E. Lee.
e The early history and first siege of Castle Cornet, by T. W. M. De Guérin.
f The Castel church, by G. E. Lee.

5032 Vol. 5.
a Alderney archaeology. [Correspondence with the admiralty relating thereto]
b The English garrison of Guernsey from early times, by T. W. M. De Guérin.
c The antiquities of Alderney, by G. T. Derrick.
d The chapel of Saint Apolline, by G. E. Lee.
e St. Peter-Port in bygone times, by C. Cox, revised and ed. G. T. Derrick.
f Le Colombier [and the ruins of a manorial pigeon-house], Torteval, by T. W. M. De Guérin.
g Guernsey crosses, by T. W. M. De Guérin.
h The old Guernsey lamp, or crâsset, by J. S. Hocart.

5033 Vol. 6.
a Feudalism in Guernsey, by T. W. M. De Guérin.
b Some important events in Guernsey history, by T. W. M. De Guérin.

c Our statue-menhirs and those of France and Italy, by T. W. M. De Guérin.
d Our hereditary governors, by T. W. M. De Guérin.
e An eminent Guernseyman: Sir Henry De Vic [d. 1672], by Edith Carey.
f Recent pre-historic researches in Jersey, by E. T. Nicolle.
g Note on a deposit of glacial clay and its contents, by A. Collenette.
h Some historical and architectural notes on the priory at Lihou, by S. C. Curtis.
i An account of the discovery and examination of a cist or dolmen of a type novel to Guernsey, by S. C. Curtis.

5034 Vol. 7.
a Amias Andros [d. 1674] and Sir Edmund, his son [d. 1714], by Edith F. Carey.
b Church plate of the deanery of Guernsey, by S. C. Curtis. [Contd. in vol. 8]
c Notes on some old documents [1338–1478], formerly in the possession of Sir Edgar MacCulloch, by T. W. M. De Guérin.
d The evolution of the town church [St. Peter-Port], by S. C. Curtis.
e The chevauchée de St. Michel [a Guernsey custom and its origins], by Edith F. Carey. [See also Société Jersiaise, *42me Bulletin annuel*, **5056c** below]
f Report on the discovery of two cists on the beach near Rousse tower, by T. W. M. De Guérin.
g The pleistocene period in Guernsey, by A. Collenette.

5035 Vol. 8.
a A forgotten episode [concerning Peter Bailleul in 1688], by Edith Carey.
b Notes on some marks on silver-plate peculiar to the Channel Islands, by S. C. Curtis. [Further notes occur in vol. 10]
c Silver plate for domestic purposes, used in Guernsey before the 18th cent., by Edith F. Carey.
d The beginnings of Quakerism in Guernsey, by Edith Carey.
e Evidence of man in Guernsey during the bronze and early iron age, by T. W. M. De Guérin.
f Notes on the early constitutional history of the Channel Islands, by T. W. M. De Guérin.
g The evolution of the country churches, by S. C. Curtis.
h Notes on the recent discovery of a human figure sculptured on the capstone of the dolmen of Déhus, Guernsey, by T. W. M. De Guérin.
i Social life in Guernsey in the 16th cent., with special reference to the Reformation, by Edith Carey.

5036 Vol. 9.
a List of dolmens, menhirs and sacred rocks, compiled from Guernsey place-names, with legends, etc., by T. W. M. De Guérin.
b The currency of Guernsey in historical times, by S. C. Curtis.
c Les monnaies gauloises des Iles de la Manche, par A. Bourde de la Rogerie.
d The first Lord De Saumarez and his diplomatic work in the Baltic, 1808–13, by J. W. Parkes.
e Sketch of Alderney history, by W. Rolleston.
f The accounts of Thomas Guille, esq., captain and receiver to Richard Neville, Earl of Warwick, 1450–2.
g Les seigneurs de Sausmarez et leurs tenants.
h Increase Mather [d. 1723]: a sidelight on Guernsey in the 17th cent., by B. T. Rowswell and Edith F. Carey.
i Sculptured stone found in a dolmen in Alderney, by T. W. M. De Guérin.
j Château des Marais, by Edith F. Carey.

k The town church [St. Peter-Port], by Edith F. Carey.
l Cornet Street [St. Peter-Port], by Edith F. Carey.
m Les Caretiers [being estates formerly possessed by the family of that name], by Edith F. Carey.
n Royalistes et parlementaires des Iles de la Manche à St. Malo en 1644, by A. Bourde de la Rogerie.
o The tomb of a former governor of the Islands [Philip d'Albini or d'Aubigny, d. 1236] at Jerusalem.
p Succession of Madelaine, Lady de Carteret [1743], by Sir H. De Sausmarez.
q Excavations in Alderney, by R. R. Marett and T. W. M. De Guérin.
r Historical pitfalls for local students, by Edith F. Carey.
s The megalithic culture of Guernsey, by T. W. M. De Guérin.

5037 Vol. 10.

a Considerations on the ecclesiastical position in the Channel Islands, and particularly in Guernsey, by Sir H. De Sausmarez.
b Peter Le Mesurier, governor of Alderney, 1793–1803, by Edith F. Carey.
c Elizabeth College, 1563–1824, by W. Rolleston.
d Elizabeth College, 1826–1926, by Christine Ozanne.
e The economic and historic rôle of the Channel Islands in the Angevin empire of the 13th and 14th cent., by D. T. Williams. [Chiefly a résumé of the article in the *27me Bulletin* of the Société Jersiaise]
f The frescoes at the Castel church and St. Apolline, by S. C. Curtis.
g The village community of Alderney, by Susan Harris. [Reprinted from the *Sociological Review*, Oct. 1926]
h Adventures of a Channel Islander [William Chepmell, of Jersey, d. 1798] in France in the 18th cent., by Christine Ozanne.
i The priory of the Vale, by Edith F. Carey.
j Low-side windows in Guernsey churches, by S. C. Curtis.
k Merchants' marks of the Channel Islands, by N. V. L. Rybot, with notes concerning the owners of the various merchants' marks mentioned, by Edith F. Carey.
l Heraldry in the Channel Islands, by N. V. L. Rybot.
m Heraldry in Guernsey, comp. with the co-operation of E. F. Carey, by N. V. L. Rybot.
n La Plaiderie [or old court house, St. Peter-Port], by Edith F. Carey.
o The Tupper medal [presented to John Tupper of Guernsey, b. 1658, for services at the battle of La Hogue, 1692], by S. C. Curtis.
p Channel Islands' seals of a non-heraldic or sub-heraldic character, 1167 to 1536, by N. V. L. Rybot.
q Extracts from the diary of Elisha Dobrée [b. 1756, of Guernsey], transcribed and arranged by J. P. Warren. [Contd. in vol. 11]

5038 Vol. 11.

a Contemporary accounts of the explosion at Castle Cornet, Dec. 1672, by Christine Ozanne.
b Settlements and field systems in Guernsey, by Susan Harris. [Reprinted from *Studies in Regional Consciousness*]
c Report on excavations in Alderney, May 1929–April 1930.
d Neolithic pottery in Guernsey, by G. H. Plymen, with notes by S. C. Curtis.
e Some primitive sculptures of the Channel Islands, by N. V. L. Rybot.
f The Sausmarez family in the Channel Islands before 1350, by Sir H. W. De Sausmarez.
g Jean de la Marche, 1585–1631. Pt. 1: The diary. Pt. 2: His life, by T. W. M. De Guérin. Pt. 3: The Presbyterian system, by W. Rolleston.

h A trip to Guernsey in 1798 [made by William Taylor Money, d. 1832], by W. T. Money; introd. and notes by Edith F. Carey.
i Naval impress in Guernsey: letters of Lord St. Vincent, by Sir H. W. De Sausmarez.
j La famille Martelle, par A. Bourde de la Rogerie.
k Some letters of Mrs. Richard Sausmarez [d. 1802], with notes by W. Rolleston.
l The *extentes* of 32 Henry III (1248) and of 5 Edward III (1331), by Sir H. W. De Sausmarez.
m Guernsey megaliths: their secrets revealed by night, by Florence Ayscough.

Other publications:

5039 Jubilee of the Société Guernesiaise. General index to the Transactions, 1882–1932, comp. S. C. Curtis. 1934.

SOCIÉTÉ JERSIAISE

Founded 1873, to study the language and antiquities of the island, and to publish historical documents.

26me–47me Bulletin annuel (1901–22), *contd. as* Bulletin annuel, 1923–33 (1923–33):

5040 26me Bulletin.

a Quatrième excursion archéologique. Guernesey. [Includes: Le Château Cornet; L'église de St. Pierre-Port; Le prieuré de Lihou]
b Appendice. Lettre sous sceau, du 4 mars 1485, contenant inspeximus des chartes de Richard II et du chapitre de l'abbaye du Mont St. Michel pour la dotation de la chapelle de Ste. Marie de la Perelle (Ste. Appolline). [Transcript with translations]
c Liste des gouverneurs, lieut.-gouverneurs et députés-gouverneurs de l'île de Jersey, 1461–1749, par J. A. Messervy. [Contd. for 1749–1850 in *27me Bulletin*]
d Notices sur quelques anciennes familles jersiaises: Journeaux.
e Douze contrats des XIVe et XVe siècles [relating chiefly to the St. Martin family who held the fief of Trinity in the 14th and 15th cent.].

5041 27me Bulletin.

a Liste des lieut.-gouverneurs et des députés-gouverneurs de 1850 à 1900, due à l'obligeance de . . . E. T. Nicolle.
b Notices sur quelques anciennes familles jersiaises: Romeril, de la Fontaine, Trinité; Lemprière, de St. Jean; Chevalier, de St. Hélier.
c Essai de bibliographie jersiaise: catalogue d'auteurs qui ont écrit sur Jersey, par E. Duprey.
d Mélanges. Quatre ordres du conseil, du 16e siècle, non enregistrés à Jersey. 4 lettres [1521–30] de Messire Hugh Vaughan, gouverneur. Ancienne généalogie des familles de Barentin, Payn et Lemprière.
e Documents relatifs à un procès au sujet d'armoiries [de Samarès] en 1567.
f Lettre inédite de Messire Philippe de Carteret, bailli de Jersey, 1682–93. [Addressed to Samuel Pepys, 1687]

5042 28me Bulletin.

a Liste des receveurs-généraux de l'île de Jersey [1320–1899], par J. A. Messervy.
b Notices sur quelques anciennes familles jersiaises: Hue.
c Laurens Baudains [d. 1611], et sa famille, par J. A. Messervy.
d Documents relating to the re-establishment of the ancient jurisdiction, 1652–3, by E. T. Nicolle.
e Les émeutes de 1730. [An account, from a ms. of the Rev. Philip Morant, concerning riots over a proposed reduction of money in Jersey]

f Renseignements sur quelques sceaux de gardiens, baillis etc., des Iles Normandes qui se trouvent aux Archives Nationales de France, recueillis par A. Le Coy de la Marche, et dont les empreintes se trouvent au musée de la société.

g La Chapelle de Notre Dame des Pas, by E. T. Nicolle.

h Documents relating to the appointment of a dean of Jersey in 1728-9.

i Documents relatifs aux Iles conservés à la bibliothèque de Caen: archives du Calvados. [Includes: 1: Donation en 1221 à l'abbaye de la Ste. Trinité à Caen par William de Salinelles d'une vavassorie à Jersey. 2: Sentence prononcée en l'année 1270 en faveur de l'abbaye de la Ste. Trinité à Caen. 3: Lettre (de l'an 1270) de Jean d'Essey, évêque de Coutances, ordonnant au doyen de Jersey d'admonester Regnaud de Carteret. 4: Abbaye de la Ste. Trinité, Caen. Jean de Newent, lieutenant d'Otho de Grandison, gouverneur des Iles, rend compte du revenu de l'abbaye dans les Iles, 15 avril 1302]

j Quelques notes sur Mauger de Carteret, 1066-87, par P. J. de Carteret.

5043 29me Bulletin.

a Notices sur quelques anciennes familles jersiaises: Falle, de Maufant; Le Geyt.

b Documents concerning the transfer of the ecclesiastical jurisdiction over the Channel Islands from the see of Coutances to those of Salisbury and Winchester, with comments thereon. [Includes: 1: Bull of Alexander VI transferring the Islands from Coutances to Winchester and cancelling a previous bull which annexed them to Salisbury, 20 Jan. 1499. 2: Bull of Alexander VI transferring the islands of Jersey and Guernsey from Coutances to Salisbury, 28 Oct. 1496. 3: Letter of Henry VII to the bishop of Winchester signifying that Jersey and Guernsey had by papal bull been detached from the see of Coutances and annexed first to Salisbury and then to Winchester, 25 Oct. 1499]

c Note on the portrait of Major Francis Peirson [d. 1802], by E. T. Nicolle.

d Lettres inédites relatives à la bataille de Jersey, 1781. [Letters from Thomas and William-Charles Lemprière to their father Charles Lemprière, seigneur of Rozel and lieutenant-bailli, and from Thomas Pipon, of La Moye, procureur-général, to Charles Lemprière and General Conway, governor of Jersey]

e Etude sur les titres civils et ecclésiastiques à Jersey depuis le quinzième siècle.

f Anciens contrats. [Contracts, 1367-82, relating to the manors of Rozel, Samarès, etc., the parties being members of the Lemprière, Barentin, and Payn families]

g Documents concernant Jean Lemprière, gouverneur de Jersey, 1500 à 1502.

5044 30me Bulletin.

a Liste des connétables de St. Hélier [1524-1904] et de St. Sauveur [1462-1904], par J. A. Messervy.

b Rapport des excursions locales, septembre et octobre, 1904. [Includes accounts of the following manors: Ponterrin, St. Saviour; Diélament; Les Augrès.

c Notices sur quelques anciennes familles jersiaises: Fondan, de St. Pierre; Dumaresq, de Gros-Puits et de Ponterrin, St. Sauveur, de St. Hélier et de St. Pierre.

d Jersey under the Commonwealth, by E. T. Nicolle. [Report from Colonel Martin, member of the Council of State, to Parliament touching certain proposals relating to the government of the island, 1652]

e The report of the royal commissioners [Sir Edward Conway and Sir William Bird] sent to Jersey in 1617, by E. T. Nicolle. [Transcript of a portion of the report]

f Mélanges. [1: Acte de la cour royale en date de 1516 au

sujet de l'essiage dû par les pêcheurs au seigneur du prieuré de St. Clément. 2: Lettre émanant du Comité du Parlement nommant Michael Lemprière bailli de Jersey, 1643. 3: Lettre de Messire William Parkhurst, bailli de Jersey, 1622-4, à son lieut., Hugh Lemprière, seigneur de Diélament, 1623]

5045 31me Bulletin.

a Liste des connétables de St. Clément [1531-1905] et de Grouville [1531-1905], par J. A. Messervy.

b Notices sur quelques anciennes familles jersiaises: Le Breton; D'Auvergne; Falle, de Maufant, St. Sauveur.

c Documents concerning the proceedings of the royal commissioners of 1531, by E. T. Nicolle. [Transcripts]

d Testament de Brelade Alexandre [connétable de St. Brelade. Transcript of will, 1539, with English translation]

e Recettes de M. Samuel De La Place [recteur de Ste. Marie, 1600-c. 1620].

f The church of St. Saviour. [With notes, by A. Curry, on its restoration, 1903-5]

5046 32me Bulletin.

a Liste des connétables de St. Martin [1490-1907] et de la Trinité [1531-1907], par J. A. Messervy.

b Notices sur quelques anciennes familles jersiaises: Robin; Pipon, de St. Pierre et de Noirmont, par J. A. Messervy.

c A genealogical sketch of the family of Philippe de Gorrequer, of St. Brelade's parish. [With a memoir of Colonel Gideon Gorrequer, military secretary to Sir Hudson Lowe at St. Helena, and a letter concerning the death of Napoleon I]

d Report of the commissioners, Robert de Norton and Guillaume de la Rue, dated April 15, 1331, on the condition of Gorey castle and the mills, by P. N. Richardson. [Latin transcript]

e Contrat de 1513 incorporant un jugement de la cour royale au sujet du fief Levesque à Ste. Marie. [Transcript]

f Excursion locale, septembre, 1906. [Includes an account of the manor of Malletière, by E. T. Nicolle]

g Notes sur l'origine de quelques noms de localités et de vingtaines, etc., par J. A. Messervy. [Contd. in 33*me Bulletin*]

h The restoration of St. Brelade's church, 1895-1900, by J. A. Balleine. [Appendix: Notes on the colours of the South-West Regiment of the Jersey Militia]

5047 33me Bulletin.

a Liste des connétables de St. Brelade [1527-1908] et de St. Laurens [1525-1908], par J. A. Messervy.

b Notices sur quelques anciennes familles jersiaises: Jutize, et De Carteret, de Grouville; Hamon, ou Hammond, par J. A. Messervy.

c Comptes de Clement Dumaresq, connétable de la paroisse de St. Clement [1702-5].

d Cartographie jersiaise, par D. A. Mills. [Reproductions, with notes and appendices]

5048 34me Bulletin.

a Liste des connétables de St. Jean [1524-1909] et de Ste. Marie [1505-1909], par J. A. Messervy.

b Le traité de St. Clair-sur-Epte [911] et les Iles Normandes, par E. T. Nicolle.

c Copies de vieux contrats [1367-1550].

d Philip Jean, artist, 1755-1802, by E. T. Nicolle. [With a list of his works exhibited at the Royal Academy]

e Observations of General Dumouriez on the attacks made on Jersey by the French in 1779 and 1781. [Reprinted from *Dumouriez and the defence of England against Napoleon*, by J. Holland Rose and A. M. Broadley]

f Translation of a Public Record Office copy of the letters patent 18 Charles I (19 April 1643) granting to Sir George de Carteret the fiefs and manors of Meleschers, Grainville and Noirmont.

g Patente accordée à Benjamin La Cloche, seigneur de Longueville, au sujet de l'incorporation des fiefs de Longueville et du Buisson, etc. [1617].

h Letters patent, dated 12 Jan. 1649, granting to Elie De La Place the fiefs of Anneville, Everard and Lemprière.

5049 35me Bulletin.

a Liste des connétables de St. Pierre [*c.* 1524–1910] et de St. Ouen [1531–1910], par J. A. Messervy.

b Notice sur la famille Brevint.

c Listes complémentaires de procureurs-généraux [1323–1650], vicomtes [1309–1786], avocats-généraux [1367–1635] et receveurs-généraux [1224–1430], par J. A. Messervy. [With a document concerning the appointment of John Lemprière as receiver of the Duke of Bedford, 'seigneur des îles', 1430]

5050 36me Bulletin.

a Report on the work done at the dolmen of La Pouquelaie Faldouet, St. Martin, July 1910, by E. T. Nicolle and J. Sinel.

b Report of the exploration of the palaeolithic cave-dwelling known as La Cotte, St. Brelade, Jersey, by E. T. Nicolle and J. Sinel. [Further reports on La Cotte appear in *Bulletins* 37, 38, 40, and 42–44]

c Liste des recteurs de l'île de Jersey, par J. A. Messervy. [Contd. in *Bulletins* 37–42. Supplement in *Bulletin* for 1926]

d Supplément à la liste des baillis, lieutenants-baillis et juges-délégués [1258–1831], par J. A. Messervy. [Supplements the list in the 23*me Bulletin*, 1898]

5051 37me Bulletin.

a Reparations for his Māties castles of Mont Orgueil and Elizabeth in the isle of Jersey, beginning from the 10th of Julie Aᵒ. 1634. [Transcript]

b Accounts of John de Roches, keeper of Jersey, for the year 1329; of John de Carteret, receiver, for the year 1349–50; also an inventory of the stores in Mont Orgueil castle in 1337, by E. T. Nicolle. [Transcripts]

c Ordonnance de 1462 pour la garde du château de Mont Orgueil et la police de l'île de Jersey. [Transcript]

d The estate and orders militarye of the castle (Mont Orgueil) and ile of Jarzye taken 1562 and since. [Transcript of a ms. belonging to Sir John Peyton, governor of Jersey, 1603–28]

e Petition, dated June 4th, 1524, from the jurats, dean, rectors, constables and others to Cardinal Wolsey, by E. T. Nicolle. [Transcript]

f Rental de Thomas de St. Martin [*c.* 1515], par E. T. Nicolle. [Transcript]

g The prehistoric cave-dwelling, 'Cotte à la chèvre', St. Ouen, by J. Sinel.

h A description of teeth of palaeolithic man from Jersey, by A. Keith and F. H. S. Knowles.

i Archaeological researches at La Motte, Oct. 1910, by E. T. Nicolle and J. Sinel. [Report for 1912 in 38*me Bulletin*]

j Notice sur le torque d'or trouvé à Jersey et sur les torques hélicoïdaux, par E. T. Nicolle.

5052 38me Bulletin.

a Remarks on the excavations at La Motte, by A. Dunlop.

b Note on the relative ages of the two neolithic horizons of La Motte, by J. Sinel.

c Report on human crania in the museum of the Société Jersiaise, by A. Keith.

d Report on the exploration of the dolmen at Les Monts Grantez, St. Ouen, Sept. 1912, by E. T. Nicolle, R. G. Warton and J. Sinel.

e Evolution of our parish churches: introduction. [The churches of Grouville, St. Clement and St. Peter]

f L'origine du nom Jersey, par C. Oberreiner.

g Notes sur l'origine de quelques noms de localités et de fiefs, etc., par J. A. Messervy.

h The communion service plate of Elizabeth castle.

5053 39me Bulletin.

a Rollo, Duke of Normandy, by E. B. Renouf.

b Account of the stay in Jersey of Russian troops, 1799–1800. [Extracts from the diary of Mary Dumaresq, wife of Lieut.-general John Le Couteur]

c St. Saviour's church, by R. G. Warton.

d St. Ouen's church, by R. G. Warton.

e St. Brelade's church, by R. G. Warton.

5054 40me Bulletin.

a Extraits des anciens rôles de la cour royale. [A case of robbery in 1542, etc.]

b Notes sur quelques contrats du commencement du 17me siècle.

c Exploration of a tumulus at Les Platons, Trinity, March 1914, by H. J. Baal and J. Sinel.

d Exploration of 'La Hougue Mauger', Oct. 1914, by H. J. Baal and J. Sinel.

e St. Martin's church, by R. G. Warton.

5055 41me Bulletin.

a The neolithic horizon of Les Mielles, in St. Ouen's bay, by J. Sinel.

b St. Helier's parish church, by R. G. Warton.

c Notice sur la famille Patriarche.

d Copies de vieux contrats et autres lettres. [Includes contracts between Guillaume Nicholas and Philipot de St. Martin, 1336, and John de Vinchelez and John Le Cornu, priest, 1467; a letter from the court of Jersey to John Le Marchant, 1340; and a letter from the court to Thomas Lemprière, of Diélament, 1573]

5056 42me Bulletin.

a Greffiers de la cour royale de Jersey [1299–1892].

b Rapports des sections. 1916. [Includes: The prehistoric station at 'La tête des Quenvais', by T. W. Attenborough, H. J. Baal and J. Sinel]

c The chevauchée de St. Michel, by Edith F. Carey. [An answer to criticisms of the original article in *Report and Transactions*, vol. 7, of the Société Guernesiaise, no. 5034e above]

d Notice sur les Lemprières, seigneurs de Diélament, par J. A. et Mme. Messervy.

e St. Lawrence's parish church, by R. G. Warton.

f Church plate of the deanery of Jersey, by S. C. Curtis.

5057 43me Bulletin.

a Liste des enregistreurs des contrats, etc. [1602–1901].

b Liste des jurés-justiciers [1801–73]. [Contd. from 24me and 25*me Bulletins*. Concluded in 44*me Bulletin*]

c Notes relatives à quelques fiefs situés à St. Helier, par J. A. et Mme. Messervy. [Contd. in 44*me Bulletin*]

d The first Jersey botanist, Dr. William Sherard [d. 1728], by T. W. Attenborough and S. Guitou. [Chiefly an account of plants identified in Jersey by Sherard but includes a brief biography]

e The bronze age in Jersey, by E. T. Nicolle.

f St. John's parish church, by R. G. Warton.

5058 44me Bulletin.

a Liste des doyens de l'île de Jersey [1180–1906], par J. A. Messervy. [Appendice: Thomas de Soulement, doyen de Jersey, 1534–41, demande aux Etats de respecter ses droits]

b Les premiers habitants de Jersey, par C. Oberreiner.

c The entries relating to Jersey in the great rolls of the exchequer of Normandy of 1180 (Stapleton's transcript of the rolls, vol. 1, pp. 25 and 26), by G. F. B. De Gruchy. [With notes and references appended]

d An account of the families of de St. Martin and De La Cour, seigneurs of Trinity, by T. W. M. De Guérin. [Appendix: Notes and extracts from 15th cent. documents relating to the de St. Martin family and Trinity manor]

e Messire Walter Ralegh, gouverneur de Jersey, 1600–3, par R. R. Lemprière.

f Trinity parish church, by R. G. Warton.

5059 45me Bulletin.

a Avocats de la cour royale. [Liste, 1523–1817. Appendice: Ordinances au sujet des avocats, 1534–1689. Contd. in *46me Bulletin*]

b Rapports des sections. 1919. [Includes: Le Couperon dolmen, Rozel, etc., par H. J. Baal]

c L'occupation de Jersey par les comtes de Maulevrier, 1461–8, par E. T. Nicolle. [Appendices: Selection of official French documents relating to Jersey, 1462–8]

d St. Mary's parish church, by R. G. Warton.

e Texte de la proclamation à Jersey du roi Charles II [1649].

5060 46me Bulletin.

a La carrière d'Edouard de Carteret (1519?–1601), vicomte, avocat-général et procureur-général de Jersey, et bailli de Serk, par R. R. Lemprière. [Appendices include: Star chamber proceedings, Henry VIII, Clement Lemprière and others v. Edward de Carteret]

b Sir John Peyton's Booke of disbursements upon the castells of Jersey [1617–19] (S.P. Dom. Add. James I, vol. 42, no. 7).

c Notes on the early constitutional history of the Channel Islands: the charter of 1179 and the vicomte of Guernsey, by T. W. M. De Guérin.

d Blazon, or written description, of the arms of the lords and keepers of the isles and of the governors of Jersey, by N. V. L. Rybot.

5061 47me Bulletin.

a Notes sur quelques noms de baptême donnés autrefois à Jersey, par Mme. Messervy.

b Liste de dénonciateurs [1525–1914], par Mme. A. Messervy.

c Some account of the Jersey revolution of 1769 and of the political parties in Jersey at the end of the 18th cent., by E. T. Nicolle.

d Trinity manor, by A. Riley.

e Notice sur la famille Du Pré, par Mme. A. Messervy.

5062 Bulletin, 1923.

a Le cinquantenaire de la Société Jersiaise, 1873–1923: aperçu sur son origine, son rôle et ses travaux, par E. T. Nicolle.

b Célébration du cinquantenaire. [Includes: Les sources de la conquête de l'Angleterre]

c 'Le victoriale' and the [Spanish] attack on Jersey in 1406, by E. T. Nicolle. ['Le victoriale', a Spanish chronicle celebrating the exploits of Pero Niño, Count of Buelna, c. 1378–1450, by Gutière Diaz de Gamez]

d Précis historique sur le fief des arbres. Le fief 'qui fut à l'évêque d'Avranches', et la propriété connue sous le nom d'Avranches, par A. Messervy.

5063 Bulletin, 1924.

a Rapports des sections. 1923. [Includes: Discovery of a

bee-hive hut at La Sergenté, St. Brelade, by E. T. Nicolle; Grosnez Hougue, by N. V. L. Rybot]

b Report on the discovery of a neolithic ossuary at St. Brelade, by J. D. Hill. [With a report on the human remains by Sir A. Keith]

c L'occupation de Jersey par le comte de Maulevrier: une enquête faite à Jersey en décembre 1463 par le capitain du château du Mont Orgueil au sujet des menées d'un Anglais nommé Jehan Hareford, par R. R. Lemprière. [Transcript from a ms. in the Musée Condé, Chantilly]

5064 Bulletin, 1925.

a The capture of Sark by the French in 1549 and its recapture in 1553 by a Flemish corsair, by E. T. Nicolle. [Appendices include letters from the Constable de Montmorency to the Duc d'Estampes, 1549, and between the Emperor Charles V and the Imperial ambassadors in England, 1553–4]

b La Hougue Bie: (A) In legend and history, with appendices of historical documents, by E. T. Nicolle. (B) The prehistoric monument. 1: The site and structure of the grave-mound. 2: The discovery of the prehistoric burial chamber. 3: Detailed description of the tomb, with note on the accompanying map. 4: Report on the examination of the floor of the dolmen, with special notes on the pottery and on the desecration of the tomb. 5: Report on the human and animal remains found in the dolmen, by H. W. M. Tims and Sir A. Keith. 6: An appreciation of the pre-historic monument by Z. Le Rouzic, curator of the Miln museum, Carnac. (C) The fabrics of the chapels, by E. T. Nicolle and N. H. Harris.

5065 Bulletin, 1926.

a The court of the fief and seigneurie of Noirmont, by G. F. B. De Gruchy. [Appendix: Specimens from the rolls, c. 1550–c. 1630]

b Les vicissitudes d'un juré-justicier [Guillaume le Breton] au 14e siècle. [Transcripts of documents in Warwick Castle]

c Grosnez castle, by N. V. L. Rybot and E. T. Nicolle.

5066 Bulletin, 1927.

a The family of Walsh or Wallis and the seigneurie de St. Germain, by G. F. B. De Gruchy. [With transcripts of documents relating to the Walsh family in the archives of Warwick Castle]

b Nouvelle extente des commissaires pour les fieux 1645–6. [Transcript]

c Early Protestant refugees in the Channel Islands, by H. M. Godfray.

d La famille Payn, de St. Laurent, par A. Messervy.

e Sketches of 16th cent. history from the 'Chroniques de Jersey', by G. T. Messervy.

5067 Bulletin, 1928.

a The importance of the Channel Islands in British relations with the continent during the 13th and 14th cent.: a study in historical geography, by T. Williams. [With a bibliography]

b Les colombiers de Jersey, par E. T. Nicolle.

c Famille Bisson, de St. Brelade et St. Laurent, par A. Messervy.

d Extracts from protests and sworn declarations made before Peter de Ste. Croix, notary public, Jersey, 1739–44, by A. C. Saunders.

e Heraldry in the Channel Islands, by N. V. L. Rybot. [Contd. in *Bulletin* for 1929]

5068 Bulletin, 1929.

a Charles Robin [fl. 1766–83], pioneer of the Gaspé fisheries, by A. C. Saunders. [Appendix: Remarks on the settlements in Lower Canada since the conquest]

b Letters of Charles II [to the States of Jersey, etc. relating to island affairs, 1645–50], by E. T. Nicolle.

c Archaeological researches at the Minquiers, July, 1928, by A. D. B. Godfray.

d Restes d'un monument mégalithique à la pointe de la Coupe, par C. Burdo.

5069 Bulletin, 1930.

a Report on excavation of the Dolmen des Géonnais at Vinchelez de Bas, by H. J. Baal.

b The corsairs of Jersey, by A. C. Saunders.

c The seigneurs and manor of Longueville, by C. Langton. [Appendix A: The arms of Nichol (Nicholle) at Longueville manor. Appendix B: Journal of the Rev. W. B. Bateman, late 19th cent.]

d Report on the reparations and investigations in Mont Orgueil castle, 1921–9, by N. V. L. Rybot. [Contd. for 1930 in *Bulletin* for 1931, and for 1931–3 in *Bulletin* for 1933]

5070 Bulletin, 1931.

a Rear Admiral Philip de Carteret [d. 1796], by A. C. Saunders.

b Famille de Vinchelez, par Julia M. Marett.

c Elizabeth castle: reparation and restoration of the oratory of Saint Helier, commonly known as 'The hermitage'.

d Seigneurs of Samarès, by C. Langton. [With documents relating to the manor, 11th–19th cent.]

5071 Bulletin, 1932.

a Diary of a visit to Jersey, Sept. 1798 [written by William Taylor Money].

b Le Vesconte family and the Royal Navy, by G. W. Younger.

c Copie de la patente octroyée par Charles II à Laurens Hamptonne, donnée au château Elizabeth le 28 janvier 1649, signée par le roi et portant le grand sceau d'Angleterre.

d Two Celtic glass beads [found at St. Aubin's bay].

e Pinnacle Rock: preliminary report on the excavations, by A. D. B. Godfray and C. Burdo.

f The Dolmen de Faldouet [near Gorey castle], by N. V. L. Rybot. [With a list of objects from the dolmen]

5072 Bulletin, 1933.

a The royal mace of the bailiff of Jersey, by R. Mollet.

b Josué Ahier, 1619–93, rector of St. Lawrence, 1650–51, 1655–93, by P. Ahier.

c Documents from La Hague manor, by G. F. B. De Gruchy.

d Les Ecrehous: a report on the expedition of 1928 to the islet which is called the 'maître île', by N. V. L. Rybot. [Includes an examination of the site occupied by mediaeval religious buildings]

e Bénitiers [arched recesses built into the structure of private dwellings] in Jersey, by G. S. Knocker and G. A. Kelly.

f Dolmen de la Hougue Bie: nature and provenance of material, by A. E. Mourant.

Publications, 16–20:

5073 Nos. 16, 17, 19, 20. Actes des Etats de l'île de Jersey, 1676–1745. 4 vols. 1901–6. [Actes des Etats, 1524–1675, appeared as *Publications* 12–15, 4 vols. 1897–1900. See also no. 5077 below]

5074 No. 18. Rolls of assizes held in the Channel Islands in 2 Edw. II, 1309. 1903.

Other publications:

5075 'Ancient petitions of the chancery and the exchequer' ayant trait aux Iles de la Manche [*c.* 1291–1454], conservées au Public Record Office à Londres. 1902.

5076 Journal de Jean Chevalier [1643–51]. 9 fascicules· [1906?]–1914.

5077 Actes des Etats de l'île de Jersey, 1746–1800. 11 vols. 1907–17.

5078 Cartulaire des Iles Normandes: recueil de documents conservés aux archives du département de la Manche et du Calvados, de la Bibliothèque Nationale, du Bureau des Rôles, du château de Warwick, etc. 6 fascicules. 1918–24.

5079 Catalogue of the museum of the Société Jersiaise, comp. R. G. Warton. [1923].

5080 The town of St. Helier, its rise and development, by E. T. Nicolle, preface by R. R. Marett. [1931].

5081 La Hougue Bie, Jersey. [Abridgement of the report in *Bulletin* for 1925 by E. T. Nicolle.] 1933.

SOCIETY FOR ARMY HISTORICAL RESEARCH

Founded 1921, to encourage research into army antiquities, into matters connected with regimental history, uniforms, dress and equipment of the past, old military customs and traditions, the art of war in bygone days, pictures, prints, medals, relics, and other subjects of similar interest.

Journal, vols. 1–12 (1921–34):

5082 Vol. 1.

a Old printed army lists, by J. H. Leslie. [Contd. in vols. 2 and 3]

b [The attack on] Ticonderoga, 1758, by L. Butler.

c A 'Royal American' [being extracts from the letters of Captain George Bent, d. 1803, relating to the West Indies], by M. Bent.

d The battle of Culloden, 1746, as described in a letter from a soldier of the royal army, by W. H. Anderson.

e Notes on two old jackets of the 8th Light Dragoons and 19th Lancers, by H. G. Parkyn.

f Regimental nicknames, by W. Y. Baldry.

g Feversham's account of the battle of Entzheim, 1674, by C. T. Atkinson.

h A duel of 1807 [between Brevet-major Alexander Campbell and Captain Alexander Boyd], by Sir C. Oman.

i Mediaeval artillery in a former expeditionary force overseas, by R. J. Macdonald. [An account of the ordnance employed by English armies in France, late 14th and early 15th cent.]

j Irish troops at Boulogne in 1544, by Viscount Dillon.

k A contemporary ballad on Culloden, by C. H. Firth.

l Disbanded regiments: the New Brunswick Fencibles, afterwards the 104th Foot, by W. Y. Baldry and A. S. White.

m The evolution of the gorget, by H. Oakes-Jones.

n The Royal Military Academy, Woolwich, in 1809, by V. Hodson.

o A contribution towards a bibliography of proclamations of military interest, 1511–1641, by M. J. D. Cockle.

p The siege and capture of Boulogne, 1544 [B.M. Cotton ms. Calig. E. iv. 57–58], with notes by J. H. Leslie.

q The English soldier of the 16th cent., by Viscount Dillon. [Extracts from reports on England by Venetian ambassadors]

r Disbanded regiments: the 100th Foot, by W. Y. Baldry and A. S. White.

s The arms of the Board of Ordnance, by J. H. Leslie.

t 18th cent. notices of uniform, by P. Sumner.

u Military war-cries, by E. A. P. Hobday.

v Cavalry drum banners, by Sir A. Leetham.

w Regimental colours: the Buffs (East Kent regiment), by J. H. Leslie.

x The expedition against Martinique, 1762 [being a letter by Brigadier Hunt Walsh], with notes by W. Y. Baldry.

y Flogging in the army, by Sir C. H. Firth.

z British war medals which have been awarded to women, by J. H. Leslie.

5083 Vol. 2.

a Historical notes on the ancient and present constitution of the Ordnance, hastily collected on reading Mr. [Edmund] Burke's bill for suppressing that Board [1780, Anon.], with notes by J. H. Leslie.

b Officers of the past. 1: General Sir Ralph Abercromby, K.B. [d. 1801], by H. Parker.

c A barrack library of 1839, by F. J. Hudleston.

d Badges of English county militia regiments, by H. G. Parkyn.

e Military supporters [heraldic], by G. R. Bellew.

f The 18th (or Royal Irish) regiment of Foot in North America, 1767-75, by G. E. Boyle.

g Hessian troops in the American war of independence, by W. Y. Baldry.

h Colonel James Berry's regiment, 1650-60, by Sir C. H. Firth.

i Notes on two cavalry standards of Cromwell's time, by E. Fraser.

j Some regimental medals of the 88th Connaught Rangers, and 94th regiments, by H. F. N. Jourdain.

k Extracts from standing orders in the garrison at Gibraltar, established by General H.R.H. the Duke of Kent, governor, 1803.

l War medals and decorations of Major-general Sir Alexander Dickson, G.C.B. [d. 1840] and General Sir Collingwood Dickson, V.C., G.C.B. [d. 1904], by J. H. Leslie.

m Officers of the past. 2: General Sir James Fergusson, G.C.B. [d. 1865], by R. B. Crosse.

n The order of merit [a regimental award for good conduct]: 5th regiment of Foot, 1767-1856, by A. Brewis.

o The Baraset cadet college [near Calcutta], East India [and disturbances which took place there, 1810], by V. Hodson.

p The colours of the 71st Foot, by R. E. S. Prentice.

q Concerning old prints relating to the British army, by R. V. Steele.

r The 'jingling johnny' [war trophy] of the 88th Connaught Rangers, by H. F. N. Jourdain.

s Disbanded regiments, by W. Y. Baldry. 1: Pearce's Dragoons, 1706-13. 2: The Royal Corsican Rangers, 1803-16. 3: An Irish corps of invalids.

t Short biographies: Major Thomas Henry Shadwell Clerke, K.H., 1790-1849, by A. Brewis; Lt.-general the Hon. Alexander Mackay, 1717-89, by J. H. Leslie.

u [The storming of] Cartagena, 1741, by C. Field.

v The fort of St. Johns on the river Richelieu, Canada, by R. C. Alexander.

5084 Vol. 3.

a Canton memorial [in honour of members of British forces who died there], 1858-61, by N. Shaw.

b Battle of Dettingen, 1743. [Letter by Sam Davies, foot-boy to Major Philip Honywood]

c Officers of the past. General Sir Philip Honywood, K.B. [d. 1752], by H. Parker.

d The arms of Major Thomas Ross, Royal Artillery [d. 1794], by J. H. Leslie.

e The wit and wisdom of General George Monck, first colonel of the Coldstream Guards, subsequently Duke of

Albemarle, by Eva M. Tenison. [Extracts from Monck's *Observations upon Military and Political Affairs*, 1671]

f The term 'point blank', by Lord Cottesloe.

g Short biographies: Colonel Jean Pierre Galiffe, C.B., 60th Rifles, 1767-1847, by L. Butler; Lt.-general Sir John Clavering, K.B., 1722-77, by J. H. Leslie.

h The English red coat, by Viscount Dillon.

i Aden [attacked by Portuguese in] 1512 and [captured by the British in] 1839, by H. Wilberforce-Bell.

j The siege of Gibraltar by the Spaniards, 1727 [from contemporary sources], with introd. and notes by J. H. Leslie.

k Diary of Lieutenant C. Gillmor, R.N.; Portugal, 1810, with introd. and notes by H. N. Edwards.

l A warrant for musters in Suffolk [*c*. 1605], ed. Lord Cottesloe.

m The diary of James Miller, 1745-50 [relating chiefly to the Jacobite rebellion and to operations against the French in the Carnatic], with introd. and notes by J. H. Leslie.

n Army inspection returns, 1753-1804, by P. Sumner. [Contd. in vols. 4-6]

o Transport and the second Mysore war, by H. Dodwell.

5085 Vol. 4.

a Notes on class catalogue, no. 50 (military), in the Department of mss., British Museum, by E. Fyers.

b A survey, or muster, of the armed and trayned companies in London, 1588 and 1599, with notes by J. H. Leslie.

c The king's body-guard of the yeomen of the guard, 1485-1920.

d A new ballad to an old tune, *Tom of Bedlam* [*c*. 1660], with notes by Sir C. Firth.

e Infantry recruiting instructions in England in 1767, by Sir B. Seton.

f Notes on some British officers who served in the Portuguese artillery, 1762-80, by J. T. Botelho.

g The Honorable the Board of Ordnance, 1299-1855, by J. H. Leslie.

h Rules and orders of the Honourable Artillery Company, by G. G. Walker.

i Battle of Falkirk, 17 Jan. 1745/6, by H. N. Edwards.

j Monuments and memorials of soldiers in London city churches, by J. H. Leslie. [Contd. in vol. 6]

k The orderly book of Captain Daniel Hebb's company in the Loveden Volunteers (Lincolnshire), 1803-8, with introd. by W. K. Fane.

l A general court martial in 1708, with notes by J. H. Leslie.

m The siege and capture of Bristol by the royalist forces in 1643, with introd. by Sir C. Firth and notes by J. H. Leslie.

5086 Vol. 5.

a Reminiscences of a Woolwich cadet of 1802, by 2nd Captain Frederick Robertson [d. 1873], with notes by J. H. Leslie.

b A recruiting scheme of 1777 [proposed by Lockhart Gordon], by J. M. Bulloch.

c The order of precedence of regiments, by A. S. White.

d Letters of Captain Philip Browne, 1737-46, with notes by J. H. Leslie.

e Schellenberg and Blenheim, 1704: roll of casualties in General Sir Richard Ingoldsby's regiment of Foot, now the Royal Welsh Fusiliers, contrib. Lord Cottesloe, with notes by J. H. Leslie.

f The *lancespessade* and the history of the 'lance' rank, by J. M. Kendall.

g Articles of war, 1627, with introductory notes by H. Bullock.

h A short memorial of northern actions during the war there, 1642-4, by Sir Thomas Fairfax [d. 1671].

i Army uniforms in a stained glass window in Farndon church, Ches., *temp.* Charles I, by C. Field.
j Diary of Major Thomas Downham, Royal Horse Artillery, in the Peninsula, 1811–12.
k Lodging the colour, by H. Oakes-Jones.
l Standing orders for the army, 1755. [Contd. in vol. 6]

5087 Vol. 6.
a Plan for the defence of the Bermudas, submitted by Lt.-colonel Robert Donkin in 1780, with introd. by J. C. Dalton.
b The old march of the English army, by H. Oakes-Jones.
c An unidentified portrait [of an English officer], by H. Oakes-Jones.
d Cromwell's regiments, by Sir C. H. Firth.
e 'The British Grenadiers', by D. N. Smith. [Reprinted from the *Household Brigade Magazine*]
f Pictures of the death of Major-general James Wolfe, by J. C. Webster. [Reprinted from the *Transactions of the Royal Society of Canada*]
g The taking of Quebec, 1759, by J. H. Leslie.
h A treatise on the art of war, by Thomas Audley [d. 1544], contributed by W. St. P. Bunbury.
i The charter of the company of Gunmakers, London [with description of the proof plate from *A History of Firearms*, by H. B. C. Pollard].
j Battle of Fontenoy, 1745. [Letter by Charles James Hamilton]
k Battle of Warburg [1760]: a ballad, with introductory note by Sir C. H. Firth.
l Old army customs, by A. Wilson.
m The king's marshalmen, by C. L. Gordon. [Reprinted from the *Household Brigade Magazine*]
n Our present knowledge of past British uniform dress, by P. W. Reynolds.
o Will of Captain Robert Keayne [d. 1656], founder of the Military Company of Massachusetts, with notes by J. H. Leslie.
p The 'Cumberland' society, by Sir G. Dalrymple-White.
q The Loyal and Friendly Society of the Blew and Orange, by J. H. Leslie.
r The strategy of Harold Hardrada in the invasion of 1066, by G. A. Auden.
s The mystery of [Thomas] Walker's ear: a story of the 28th regiment of Foot in 1764 [in Canada, with particular reference to the billeting problem], by A. L. Burt. [Reprinted from the *Canadian Historical Review*]

5088 Vol. 7.
a The colours of the British marching regiments of Foot in 1751, by J. H. Leslie. [Contd. in vols. 8–10]
b Adventures of Serjeant Benjamin Miller, during his service in the 4th battalion, Royal Artillery, 1796–1815, with introd. by M. R. Dacombe and Benedicta J. H. Rowe.
c The diary of Lieutenant John Barker, 4th (or the King's Own) regiment of Foot, from Nov. 1774 to May 1776, with a biographical note by J. C. Dalton.
d Captured flags in the Royal Hospital, Chelsea, by F. W. Barry.
e Egypt, 1801: a letter from [George Slater] a serjeant of the 28th Foot, to his mother, at Longroyd-bridge, near Huddersfield.
f Castles. 1: Pontefract, Yorks., by J. H. Leslie.
g Fort Ticonderoga, by S. H. P. Peel.
h Battle of Minden, 1 Aug. 1759. [A contemporary account]
i The death of Major-general Wolfe: letter from Captain Samuel Jan Hollandt [d. 1801], with introd. and notes by A. G. Doughty. [Reprinted from the *Canadian Historical Review*]

j The order of shooting wt the crossbow. A [16th cent.] poem by M. Beele, in sixteen seven-line stanzas, with introd. by Viscount Dillon.
k Graves of British soldiers at Concord, Massachusetts, U.S.A., by A. French.
l How the colours of the 55th Foot were saved at Bergen-op-Zoom, in March, 1814: a letter [by Major George Goodall, 1843] contrib. H. M. McCance.
m Dress in the Indian army in the days of John Company, by Sir G. MacMunn. [Contd. in vol. 8]
n The Frampton Volunteers, 1798 to 1802, by G. B. Michell.
o The printed articles of war of 1544, transcribed from the only known copy, with notes by J. H. Leslie.

5089 Vol. 8.
a Campaigning in 1793: Flanders, by J. H. Leslie. [Chiefly extracts from the diary of Thomas Howard Fenwick, d. 1797]
b Bibliography of the military writings of Sir Charles Firth.
c Artillery services in North America in 1814 and 1815, being extracts from the journal of Colonel Sir Alexander Dickson, K.C.B. [d. 1840], commanding Royal Artillery, with introd. and notes by J. H. Leslie.
d Alexander Forsyth, 1769–1843 [inventor of the percussion system in fire arms], by Lord Cottesloe.
e Soldiering and circuses, by J. M. Bulloch. [The career of Philip Astley, d. 1814]
f General Sir William Howe's operations in Pennsylvania, 1777: the battle of the Brandywine Creek, 11 Sept., and the action at Germantown, 4 Oct., by E. W. H. Fyers. [Contd. in vol. 9]

5090 Vol. 9.
a Diary and letters of Arthur Moffatt Lang, 1st Lieutenant, Bengal Engineers: India, 1857–8, ed. J. H. Leslie and F. C. Molesworth. [Contd. in vols. 10 and 11]
b Canadian sketches in 1805–6 [by Colonel Sempronius Stretton].
c The model room in the Royal Arsenal at Woolwich, by O. F. G. Hogg.
d The points of war [a short musical phrase sounded as a signal], by J. H. Leslie.
e Relative rank in the Royal Navy and the army [a letter from the admiralty, 1747].
f Articles of war, 1642.
g The home-coming of the king's colour of the 2nd battalion 69th (or the South Lincolnshire regiment) of Foot, captured by the French at Quatre Bras, 16 June 1815, by J. H. Leslie.
h Yeomen cavalry, by G. R. Codrington.
i The earliest 'establishment' (1661) of the British standing army, contrib. Lord Cottesloe with introd. and notes by J. H. Leslie.
j Two private letters from Major-general Sir John Moore, K.B., with notes by J. F. C. Fuller.

5091 Vol. 10.
a The march of the siege-train from Ferozepore to Delhi, Aug.–Sept. 1857: the journal of 1st Lieutenant W. J. Gray, Bengal Artillery, with notes by J. H. Leslie.
b A prisoner of war in India, 1782–4, by Lieut.-col. Robert Cameron [d. 1826], with introd. and notes by P. R. Cadell.
c The papers of General the Rt. Hon. Sir George Murray, G.C.B., G.C.H. [d. 1846], by M. R. Dobie.
d Major-general Sir David Ochterlony, bt., G.C.B., 1758–1825, by F. G. Cardew.
e The defences of London in 1643, with introd. and notes by J. H. Leslie.

f Brigadier-general Sir Charles MacCarthy, kt., 1764–1824, by D. D. Daly.

g The epaulet, by F. G. Blakeslee.

h Materials for a history of the Bombay army, by J. H. Leslie.

i The re-organisation of the infantry of the line, 1 July 1881, by M. L. Ferrar.

j The Goodwood troop of Yeomen Artillery [formed in 1817], by J. H. Leslie.

k An early experiment in bayonet fighting [1817], by A. C. T. White.

l Grenadier companies in the British army (with two original letters on the subject [between Carteret and John, Earl of Stair, 1743]).

m Dress of the Madras Light Infantry regiments, by F. H. Tyrrell.

5092 Vol. 11.

a The arms of Robert Timpson, of the city of Exeter, captain in the 22nd regiment of Foot [1767].

b The Tower of London: a military store-house, by C. Ffoulkes.

c The first Sikh war, 1845–6: the battle of Ferozeshah, 21 Dec. 1845; the battle of Sobraon, 10 Feb. 1846; two letters contrib. by the Marquess of Sligo [from Lieut.-col. the Hon. Thomas Ashburnham]; with notes by J. H. Leslie.

d The castle of Inniskilling in 1593–4. [Two letters describing its assault and capture, from *The History of Enniskillen*, by W. C. Trimble]

e The Warwickshire militia in 1759–60.

f Forerunners of the army council, by O. F. G. Hogg.

g Antient military words, by J. H. Leslie. [Extract from *The Theorike and Practicke of Moderne Warres*, by Robert Barret, 1598]

h The revolt in Kashmir, 1846, by R. R. Sethi.

i Note on the battle of Dettingen, 16 June (O.S.) 1743, by J. H. Leslie.

j The loss and recapture of St. John's, Newfoundland, in 1762, by W. H. Fyers.

k Statutes and acts of parliament—army—from 1225 to 1761, with notes by J. H. Leslie. [Extracts from *The Statutes at Large*, 1761. Contd. in vol. 12]

l Before Waterloo, 1815: a fragment from the diary of 1st Lieutenant William Bates Ingilby, Royal Horse Artillery, 24 March to 25 May, 1815.

m The trial of Raja Lal Singh, 1846, by R. R. Sethi.

n Swords of the British army, by C. Ffoulkes and E. C. Hopkinson. [Contd. in vol. 12]

5093 Vol. 12.

a Waterproofing soldiers' great-coats [with particular reference to the process of John Maberly, d. 1845], by J. M. Bulloch.

b Names, numbers, and errors. Tongres and Melle: two stories amended, by C. T. Atkinson. [The identification of regiments taking part in the defence of Tongres, 1703, and in the action at Melle. 1745]

c The treaty of Bhyrowal or second treaty of Lahore, Dec. 1846, by R. R. Sethi.

d Militia regiments of Great Britain: a calendar of their records and histories.

e The royal citadel of Plymouth, by F. W. Pfeil.

f An early war diary, 1415 [by an anonymous priest who was present at Agincourt, being an extract from *A History of the Battle of Agincourt, and of the Expedition of Henry the Fifth into France, in 1415*, by Sir Harry Nicolas, 1832]

g The Bank of England picquet, by W. M. Acres.

h Military battle prints, by C. de W. Crookshank.

i The Peninsular war: letters (1811–13) of Robert Garrett

Ensign 2nd (or the Queen's Royal) regiment, 6 March 1811; Lieutenant, 7th regiment (or Royal Fuzileers), 2 Oct. 1812.

j Bibliography of works by the late Viscount Dillon, comp. J. G. Mann.

k Some extracts from a military work of the 18th cent. [the *Continuation of the History of the late War in Germany between the King of Prussia and the Empress of Germany and her Allies*, by Major-gen. Henry Lloyd, 1781], with a note by B. H. Liddell-Hart.

l Notes on the history of the Royal Small Arms Factory, Enfield Lock, by Lord Cottesloe.

m When promotion was slower still: the commission of enquiry in 1838, by W. Miles.

n The era of army purchase, by H. Biddulph.

o The North Lancashire regiment [in the 18th cent.], by J. M. Bulloch.

p Wellington's staff at Waterloo, by Sir J. E. Edmonds.

5094 General index, vols. 1–12, 1921–33. [n.d.]

Special numbers, 1–3:

5095 No. 1. Tangier, 1680: the diary of Sir James Halkett [major in Dumbarton's regiment, d. 1684], with introd. and notes by H. M. McCance. *P.* 1922.

5096 No. 2. The orderly book of Lord Ogilvy's regiment in the army of Prince Charles Edward Stuart, 10 Oct. 1745 to 21 April 1746, with explanatory notes by Sir B. Seton. 1923.

5097 No. 3. The army list of 1740, reprinted by the Soc. with a complete index of names and of regiments. 1931.

SOCIETY FOR NAUTICAL RESEARCH

Founded 1910, to encourage research into nautical antiquities, into matters relating to sea-faring and ship-building in all ages and among all nations, into the language and customs of the sea, and into other subjects of nautical interest.

Mariner's Mirror, vols. 1–19 (1911–33):

5098 Vol. 1.

a Eminent marine artists, by H. Parker. 1: The two Van de Veldes.

b The last of the East Indiamen [1850–70], by W. B. Whall.

c Decks and their definitions [in the 18th and 19th cent.]., by A. Moore.

d Captain Nathaniel Boteler [fl. 1619–41, author of *Six Dialogues about Sea Service between an High Admiral and a Captain at Sea*], by L. G. Carr Laughton.

e The Union flag, by W. G. Perrin.

f Mediaeval ships in painted glass and on seals, by H. H. Brindley. [Further articles, entitled 'Mediaeval ships', appear in vols. 2–4]

g The victualling instructions of 1697, by J. R. Tanner.

h A 15th cent. trader, by R. M. Nance. [A description of a Flemish drawing]

i An early-Victorian windfall, by W. Senior. [The capture of 'pirates' off the Moluccas by Captain Sir Edward Belcher, of H.M.S. *Samarang*, in 1844, and his petition for reward]

j A bibliography of nautical dictionaries, comp. L. G. Carr Laughton.

k The Union flag, by Sir R. M. Blomfield. [An amplification of the article by W. G. Perrin above]

l Eminent marine artists, by H. Parker. 3: Peter Monamy [d. 1749].

m Round-sterned ships [16th–19th cent.], by A. Moore and R. M. Nance.

5101 Vol. 4.

a The development of the capital ship, by G. Robinson. [Contd. in vols. 6 and 7]

b Accounts and inventories of John Starlyng, clerk of the king's ships to Henry IV, by A. Moore.

c Figure-heads and beak-heads of the ships of Henry VIII, by H. S. Vaughan.

d Two ships on bench-ends in west country churches [Bishop's Lydeard and East Budleigh], by H. H. Brindley.

e The *Great Harry*, by W. B. Whall.

f Naval executive titles: commadore or commodore?, by Sir R. M. Blomfield.

g 'Patience' [14th cent. poem: its nautical allusions], by G. Callender. [Further article by L. G. Carr Laughton]

h The Devonport figure-heads, by D. Owen.

i Neptune as defendant, by W. Senior. [Actions for assault and battery brought as a result of 'Crossing the line' observances, 1801 and 1851]

j The laws of Oleron [being a summary of the version in the mid-14th cent. Oak Book of Southampton], by A. B. Wood.

k The master's whistle, by G. Robinson.

l Eighty-gun three-deckers, by R. C. Anderson.

m The Budleigh bench-end, by G. Callender [being an answer to the article above by H. H. Brindley].

n An artist's notes at the battle of the Nile, by L. Paul. [Notes on some sketch-books owned by William Anderson, marine artist, d. 1837]

5102 Vol. 5.

a British ships through Dutch spectacles [17th cent.], by R. M. Nance.

b Some heresies with regard to decks, by R. C. Anderson.

c Some 15th cent. ship pictures, by A. H. Moore. [Notes on a pilot's guide for the coasts of England and Wales, and its illustrations]

d Documents: The inventory of the *Great Bark*, 1531, contrib. L. G. Carr Laughton.

e Miches, capsquares, and trunnion-bands, by G. Callender.

f Cromsters [16th–17th cent. craft], by R. M. Nance.

g An early naval chest [probably *c.* 1670–80], by L. G. Carr Laughton.

h The whistle as a naval instrument, by G. E. Manwaring.

i Document: Grog [and its connection with Admiral Vernon], contrib. L. G. Carr Laughton.

j The first English yachts, 1660, by C. G. 't Hooft.

k The Hull whaling trade, by T. Sheppard.

l *Jack Junk* [or a cruize on shore; a humorous poem by the author of the *Sailor Boy*, 1813], by O. Hartelie.

5103 Vol. 6.

a Extracts [1699–1700 and 1717] from a slaver's log [belonging to Walter Prideaux, merchant-captain], by F. C. P. Naish.

b The ancient breech-loading gun [being an account of one found at Bridlington, Yorks.], by G. Robinson.

c Extracts from the log of a salt-trader [Walter Prideaux] 1717–18, by F. C. P. Naish.

d Early naval ordnance, by W. G. Perrin.

e Early reefs, by H. H. Brindley.

f The first naval uniform for officers: the story of the blue and white costume of 1748, by G. E. Manwaring.

g Two new sets of sailing and fighting instructions [*c.* 1689 and 1690], by R. C. Anderson.

h Whaling relics [being carved pieces of whalebone and ivory], by T. Sheppard.

i Documents: Regulations about salutes, 1702, contrib. W. G. Perrin.

j Old pilot books and sailing directions, by H. S. Vaughan.

k [Sir Edward] Pellew and the departure of the Bantry expedition, Dec. 1796, by G. E. Cooper.

l British naval flags of command, by Sir R. M. Blomfield.

m [Inventory of] a barge of Edward III, by A. Moore.

n 'The Rutter of the sea' [*c.* 1528, being a translation by Robert Copland, fl. 1508–47, of a French treatise], by W. Senior.

o A new portrait of Anson, by G. Callender.

p By-paths in naval literature [being extracts from a pamphlet *The Life and Adventures of Matthew Bishop, of Deddington, in Oxfordshire, 1701 to 1711*, 1744], by C. N. Robinson.

q Henry VIII's *Great Galley* [1515], by R. C. Anderson.

r An unknown painting of the *Sovereign of the Seas*, by G. E. Manwaring.

s Brigantines, by E. A. Dingley. [The derivation of the name]

t An early Scandinavian model boat and crew [found at Roos Carrs, near Withernsea, Yorks., in 1836], by T. Sheppard.

u Transport of troops by sea [with particular reference to the sinking of the transport *Lord Shelburne*, 1787], by E. Fyers.

v 'A pirate's journal' [written by William Davidson when aboard a Russian pirate ship in the Mediterranean, 1798], by F. K. Ingram.

w The *Prince Royal* of 1610, by R. C. Anderson.

5104 Vol. 7.

a By-paths in naval literature [18th and 19th cent.], by C. N. Robinson.

b A forgotten life of Sir Francis Drake, by G. Robinson. [An attempt to reassess his character and the Doughty affair in the light of *A New, Authentic, and Complete Account of a Voyage round the World, undertaken and performed by Sir Francis Drake, in the 'Pelican'*, 1784]

c The East India Company—and interlopers, by H. S. Vaughan.

d Brigantines, by R. M. Nance.

e Sidelights on the slave trade, by G. E. Cooper. [The cases of Gregson *v.* Gilbert, 1783, and Tatham *v.* Hodgson, 1796]

f Comparative naval architecture, 1670–1720, by R. C. Anderson.

g Gwyn's book of ships, by E. A. Dingley. [An account of a ms. book of ship drawings by Edward Gwyn, coach herald painter, *c.* 1780]

h Drake and his detractors, by G. Callender [being a reply to the article above by G. Robinson].

i Sea power and the winning of British Columbia, by J. H. Rose.

j The preamble to the articles of war, by L. G. Carr Laughton.

k Galleys and runners [*c.* 1707], by Sir J. Corbett.

l English and Dutch privateers under William III, by G. N. Clark.

m Documents: Captain's orders for a ship of the Indian navy, about 1855, contrib. D. C. Roe.

n Square-rigged vessels with two masts, by H. H. Brindley and A. Moore.

o By-paths in naval literature, by C. N. Robinson. [An account of a pamphlet *England's Safety, or a Bridle to the French king*, 1693, by Captain George St. Lo]

p 17th cent. 'profiteering' in the Royal Navy, by Isobel G. Powell.

q The *Victory* after Trafalgar, by F. J. Roskruge.

r The trial and death of Thomas Doughty [1578], by G. Robinson.

s Drake at the suit of John Doughty, by W. Senior.

t Documents: Captain's orders of H.M.S. *Superb*, 1803–4.

u The maritime school at [Ormond House] Chelsea [1779–1830], by H. T. A. Bosanquet.

v Popham's expedition to Ostend in 1798, by G. E. Manwaring.

w H.M. Brigantine *Dispatch*, 1692–1712, by L. G. Carr Laughton.

x More doubts about decks, by R. C. Anderson. [A criticism of the third of G. Robinson's articles on the development of the capital ship]

y Some ships of 1541–2, by R. M. Nance.

z The Whitstable oyster fishery, by Beryl Couper.

aa Document: A privateer commission of 1798, contrib. L. G. Carr Laughton.

5105 Vol. 8.

a The *Mayflower*, by J. W. Horrocks.

b A day in Westminster hall, 1797, by G. E. Cooper. [Three law cases, Keate *v.* Temple, Macdonald *v.* Pasley, and Sparenburgh *v.* Bannatyne, relating to the Royal Navy]

c *The Mariner's Marvellous Magazine* [*or the Wonders of the Ocean*, 1809], by O. Hartelie.

d The state of Nelson's fleet before Trafalgar, by T. H. Rose.

e The boatswain's whistle, by G. E. Manwaring.

f County naval free schools on waste land [being an unrealized project of Jonas Hanway, d. 1786, philanthropist], by T. A. Bosanquet.

g Some additions to the brigantine problem, by R. C. Anderson.

h Some ballads and songs of the sea, by J. Leyland.

i Document: Midshipmen extra and volunteers [being an order from the Board of Admiralty to the Navy Board, 1676], contrib. W. G. Perrin.

j The last Lord Camelford, by G. E. Cooper. [The shooting of Charles Peterson by Lord Camelford at English Harbour, Antigua, 1798]

k Graffiti of mediaeval ships, from the church of St. Margaret's-at-Cliffe, Kent, by A. B. Emden.

l The Chatham Chest under the early Stuarts, by Isobel G. Powell.

m H.M.S. *Victory* [and her predecessors], by E. Fraser.

n Wicker vessels, by R. M. Nance.

o The pre-historic boat from Brigg [Lincs.], by T. Sheppard.

p Documents: A proposal for naval reforms *c.* 1773, contrib. by W. G. Perrin.

q A model of Henry Hudson's *Halve Maen*, by G. C. E. Crone.

r *An Abridgement of all Sea-lawes* [1613, by William Wellwood, d. 1622], by A. R. G. McMillan.

s Document: Carved work of the *Victory*, 1765, contrib. by E. Fraser.

t Naval chaplains in the early Stuart period, by Isobel G. Powell.

u The *Keying*, by H. H. Brindley. [An account of a Chinese junk which arrived in the Thames in 1848]

v The dress of the British seaman; from the earliest times till 1600, by G. E. Manwaring. [Contd. for 1600–1748 in vols. 9 and 10]

w Document: Captain's orders for H.M.S. *St. George*, 1745, contrib. H. R. H. Vaughan.

x Auxiliary oars, by R. C. Anderson.

y A scale model of the *Sovereign of the Seas* of 1637, by H. B. Culver.

5106 Vol. 9.

a Notes on the development of bands in the Royal Navy, by W. G. Perrin.

b Early [17th cent.] ship surgeons, by Isobel G. Powell.

c Fresh light on Drake [from *Elegias de Varones Illustres*

de Indias, by Juan de Castellaños, d. 1607], by G Callender.

d The royalists at sea in 1648, by R. C. Anderson.

e Shantying and shanties, by L. G. Carr Laughton.

f Document: The auditing of navy accounts under Edward IV, contrib. by A. P. Newton.

g The lord admiral's 'whistle of honour', by G. E. Manwaring.

h The great ship of 1419, by L. G. Carr Laughton.

i Notes on the preservation of H.M.S. *Victory* and her restoration to the Trafalgar condition, by Sir P. Watts.

j Notes on Pepys's Admiralty journal of 1674–9, by J. R. Tanner.

k Document: Signalls to be observed for the better keeping company with His Majties ship, the *Bridgwater* [1715], contrib. by R. Sinclair.

l John Rastell's voyage in the year 1517, by A. W. Reed. [With transcripts of his proceedings against John Ravyn in the court of requests arising out of the failure of the project]

m A transformation in armament [*temp.* Henry VIII], by F. L. Robertson.

n Document: Naval medal, 1677, communicated by D. B. Smith.

o Drake's voyage of circumnavigation: some of the original sketches, by Florence E. Dyer.

p The rank of commander, R.N., by L. G. Carr Laughton.

q Document: [A letter from the lords of the admiralty to the secretary of state concerning an incident between a press-gang and the master of a merchant-ship, 1718], contrib. L. G. Carr Laughton.

r With the grand fleet in 1780, by G. Callender. [An account of the command of Admiral Sir Francis Geary]

s The Admiralty building [London], by D. B. Smith.

t John Cunningham's journal [1824–5], by L. G. Carr Laughton. [John Cunningham, naval surgeon, b. 1771]

u The early naval lieutenant, by Isobel G. Powell.

v Document: The safeguard of the sea, 1442 [a transcript of an ordinance made by the Commons], contrib. by G. E. Manwaring.

5107 Vol. 10.

a The writing of naval history, by L. G. Carr Laughton.

b The mace of the admiralty court, by W. Senior.

c Early books on shipbuilding and rigging, by R. C. Anderson.

d Naval satire and caricature, by J. Leyland.

e Notes. [Includes: Nelson at Nicaragua; Views and charts of the coasts of 'New Albion', etc., made during Vancouver's voyage; Sir William Batten, d. 1667; Nelson and George Campbell, admiral, fl. 1781–1803]

f The Elizabethan sailorman, by Florence E. Dyer.

g 'Shipkeepers' and minor officers serving at sea in the early Stuart period, by Isobel G. Powell.

h H.M.S. *Victory*. Report to the *Victory* technical committee of a search among the admiralty records [to ascertain the condition of the ship when in action at Trafalgar], by L. G. Carr Laughton.

i Robert and Ralph Dodd, marine painters, by G. W. Younger. [Robert Dodd, d. 1816?; Ralph Dodd, d. 1822].

j The department of the accountant-general of the navy, by C. M. Bruce.

k Notes. [Includes: H.M.S. *Endeavour* and foreign suspicion; The bugle and the bugler in the Royal Navy]

l John the painter, by W. Senior. [James Aitken, incendiary, d. 1777]

m Dampier's voyage of 1703, by B. M. H. Rogers.

n Documents: Shipbuilding abuses in the 17th cent., contrib. by E. W. H. Fyers.

o Notes. [Includes: H.M.S. *Coventry*, a Spanish privateer captured and taken into the navy, 1658; Courts-martial being extracts, 1710–11, from the *Journal* of Vice-admiral John Baker; Captain Samuel Sturmy, 1633–69; Coronation procession, 1661]

5108 Vol. 11.

a The study of ship models, by L. G. Carr Laughton.
b The story of the machine vessels [i.e. ships employed as explosive missiles], by E. W. H. Fyers.
c Sir Anthony Deane [d. 1721], by A. W. Johns.
d Notes. [Includes: Early yachts in England]
e The shipwrights of the royal dockyards, by N. Macleod.
f The old dockyard at English Harbour, Antigua, by H. R. H. Vaughan.
g An earl's voyages in the late 14th cent., from the evidence of [Henry, Earl of Derby's] household account books, by Grace Stretton.
h Notes. [Includes: References to ships, etc., in early English wills; Dampier's debts]
i Shipwright officers of the royal dockyards, by N. Macleod.
j H.M.S. *Britannia*, 1700, by L. G. Carr Laughton.
k Burghley's notes on the Spanish Armada, by Florence E. Dyer.
l Document: Beds in troopships, contrib. by Miss Fairbrother.
m Notes. [Includes: The first printed list of sea-officers, 1700]

5109 Vol. 12.

a The *Pearl's* brigade in the Indian mutiny, by E. Fraser.
b The arrival of the Dutch and British in the Indian ocean, by G. A. Ballard.
c Notes. [Includes: The *Britannia* model; The fight of the *Mary Rose* with Algerian pirates, 1669]
d The lord high admiral and the Board of Admiralty, by W. G. Perrin.
e The Flanders galleys: some notes on seaborne trade between Venice and England, 1327–1532, by H. G. Rawlinson.
f Saluting the quarterdeck, by L. G. Carr Laughton.
g Document: Instructions for a muster master, 1692.
h Notes. [Includes: Mediaeval rudders; A ship-yard sketch-book by William Anderson, 1757–1837]
i Sailors of the civil war, the Commonwealth and the Protectorate, by Sir C. H. Firth.
j Effect of the Anglo-Dutch wars of the 17th cent. on Indian ocean developments, by G. A. Ballard.
k Sir John Kempthorne [d. 1679] and his sons, by G. A. Kempthorne.
l Captain [John] Tyrrell [d. 1694] and the East India Company, by J. G. Bullocke.
m Van de Velde memorial.
n Notes. [Includes: Nelson's monument on the Portsdown hills]
o History of wood-preserving in shipbuilding, by F. Moll.
p The general situation in the Indian ocean during the early Georgian period, by G. A. Ballard.
q 'Capital ship' [the expression and its use in the 17th cent.], by L. G. Carr Laughton.
r Naval administration of the interregnum, 1641–59, by A. C. Dewar.
s Phineas Pett, by A. W. Johns. [An account of seven 17th cent. members of the Pett family, all bearing the name Phineas]
t Notes. [Includes: The Free Shipwrights of London in the 17th cent. (see also vol. 14, no. 1, Notes); Martin Frobisher and Dr. John Dee; Saluting in the Royal Navy]

5110 Vol. 13.

a The first and second Anglo-French conflicts in the Indian ocean [during the war of the Austrian succession and the Seven Years war], by G. A. Ballard.
b Sir Henry Penrice [d. 1752] and Sir Thomas Salusbury [d. 1773, both judges of the admiralty court], by W. Senior.
c The lord high admiral and the administration of the navy, by E. S. de Beer.
d Captain William Hawkeridge [b. *c.* 1590] and his voyage in search of a north-west passage in 1625, by M. Christy.
e Documents: Instructions for the porter at the Navy Office, 1687; Lieutenants' instructions, 1677; The loss of the *Ville de Paris*, 1782.
f The last battlefleet struggle in the Bay of Bengal [1783], by G. A. Ballard.
g Captain John Strong, privateer and treasure hunter [fl. 1689–91], by Florence E. Dyer.
h Harwich dockyard, by L. H. St. C. Cary.
i Documents contrib. by D. B. Smith. [Includes: Kite balloon ships, being letters to the admiralty from Charles Henry Knowles, concerning his project, 1803]
j Notes. [Includes: Square and round tucks in the 17th cent.; Brig *Garland*, being extracts from its journal, 1833]
k The Suffolk and Norfolk beach yawls, by E. R. Cooper.
l The Hughes-Suffren campaign [being a refutation of the article above by G. A. Ballard], by Sir H. W. Richmond. [Sir Edward Hughes, d. 1794, vice-admiral; Pierre-André de Suffren-Saint Tropez, d. 1788, rear-admiral of the French navy]
m Naval uniform of 1748, by D. B. Smith.
n The journal of Commander Thomas Colby, R.N., 1797–1815, by E. Fraser.
o The judges of the high court of admiralty [biographies, *temp.* Edward IV–1875], by W. Senior.
p Hughes and Suffren, by G. A. Ballard. [Reply to the article by Sir H. W. Richmond. Further discussion appears in vol. 14, no. 1, Notes]
q Castles in the sea, by G. Robinson. [A further article on the development of the capital ship]
r Documents: Returns by Cornelis Johnson, the king's gun-maker, of the supply and repair of ordnance in the navy, 1 Aug. 1512–10 Feb. 1513; Watchmen in the dockyards, 1670.
s Notes. [Includes: Captain Cook, being an account of the disposal of his remains]

5111 Vol. 14.

a European rivalry in the Indian seas, 1600–1700, by C. R. Boxer. [A criticism of the articles in vols. 12 and 13 by G. A. Ballard]
b The vice-admiral and the rear-admiral of the United Kingdom, by W. G. Perrin. [See also Notes in no. 2 of this vol.]
c The principal officers of the navy [16th and 17th cent.], by A. W. Johns.
d Documents: Reports of Pepys's speech in the House of Commons, March 5th, 1668; The lord lieutenant of Ireland and his yacht, 1822–3; The cutting down of the *Sovereign* in 1651.
e Notes. [Includes: Commonwealth 'frigates'; Some reforms in the Victualling Office, 1700 and 1711]
f Naval armament in the 13th cent., by F. W. Brooks.
g The way of a ship, by L. G. Carr Laughton. [Some account of the management of a sailing ship, with explanations of the technical terms]
h Notes. [Includes: The King's Regulations and Admiralty Instructions; An Anglo-Danish incident in 1694, being an encounter in the Downs between Niels Barfod, of the *Gyldenlöve*, and an English division under Sir Cloudesley Shovell (a fuller account appears in Notes in no. 3 of this vol.); 'Wynewes', being an attempt to explain a mediaeval nautical term]

i The journal of Grenvill Collins [1676–8, relating chiefly to actions against Algerian pirates], by Florence E. Dyer.

j English galleys in 1295, by R. C. Anderson. [With transcripts from accounts for building expenditure in Southampton]

k Some unpublished accounts of Cook's death, by R. T. Gould.

l The royalists at sea in 1649, by R. C. Anderson.

m Gunnery, frigates, and the line of battle, by L. G. Carr Laughton.

n Nautical time [its earliest use in English ships], by H. Harries.

o Bligh's notes on Cook's last voyage [in a copy of an account published 1784], by R. T. Gould. [William Bligh, admiral, d. 1817]

5112 Vol. 15.

a The king's ships and galleys, mainly under John and Henry III, by F. W. Brooks.

b Thomas Eldred [fl. 1558–*c.* 1600], merchant, by A. D. Harrison. [See correction in Notes in no. 4 of this vol.]

c Notes. [Includes: Master shipwrights of Chatham dock-yard; Early two-masted ships in England]

d The black battlefleet: some notes on the mid-Victorian transformation in battleship design, by G. A. Ballard.

e Master John Dee, Drake, and the straits of Anian, by E. G. R. Taylor.

f The Cinque Ports [and their origin], by F. W. Brooks. [With transcripts of charters of 1206, and the charter of 1278]

g Captain John Narbrough [d. 1688] and the battle of Solebay, by Florence E. Dyer.

h Midshipman W. G. Anderson [d. *c.* 1803], by D. B. Smith. [Extracts from his letters, 1798–1802]

i The sandbanks of Yarmouth and Lowestoft, by H. M. Evans.

j The 17th cent. frigate, by G. Robinson.

k The unveiling of the Van de Velde memorial. [Ceremony included a brief general address by Sir G. Hope on the two Van de Veldes]

l Naval administration and the raising of fleets under John and Henry III, by F. W. Brooks.

m British battleships of 1870: the *Minotaur* and *Agincourt*, by G. A. Ballard.

n Document: Instructions for captains, 1663.

o Notes. [Includes: Sea fencibles]

5113 Vol. 16.

a The loss of the *Lapwing*, post office packet [in action with the American privateer *Fox*, 1812], by H. H. Brindley. [Transcript of a letter by Henry Senior, d. 1861]

b British battleships of 1870: the *Northumberland* and *Achilles*, by G. A. Ballard.

c Sands, gats and swatchways [channels of water between sandbanks] between Harwich and the Nore, by H. M. Evans. [See also Notes in nos. 3 and 4 of this vol.]

d Document: Commodore Johnstone's improvements, 1779 [relating to the fitments of ships of war], contrib. by D. B. Smith.

e Notes. [Includes: The evacuation of Naples, 1806; Loss of *Megaera*, store ship, on St. Paul's island, 1871]

f More light on Drake [with special reference to the voyage of circumnavigation], by E. G. R. Taylor. [With transcript of John Winter's report, 1579]

g Lord Cochrane's secret plans [for destroying the French fleet, 1812], by P. W. Brock.

h British battleships of 1870: the *Warrior* and *Black Prince*, by G. A. Ballard.

i Document: Medical officers' uniform [1805].

j British battleships of 1870: the *Bellerophon* and *Hercules*, by G. A. Ballard.

k The battle of Damme [between English and French forces], 1213, by F. W. Brooks.

l The navy as penitentiary, by W. Senior. [Naval service as a means of correction for minor criminals in the early 19th cent., and a case of the problem of discharge]

m The Kentish flats and southern channels, by H. M. Evans.

n The third Dutch war in the East, 1672–4, by C. R. Boxer. [With transcripts of English and Dutch accounts of naval actions]

o Annual general meeting of the Society. [Includes a transcript of the will of Robert Blake]

p Document: Fremantle and Trafalgar [being a letter written before action by Thomas Francis Fremantle, then commanding H.M.S. *Neptune*]

q Notes. [Includes: The ship's-council on the expedition of Pet and Jackman on July 27th, 1580, in the Kara sea; Navigation instruction in 1677]

5114 Vol. 17.

a Trincomali, by L. H. S. Cary. [An account of Dutch, French and British interests in Ceylon, with particular reference to Trincomali, 1639–1815]

b British battleships of 1870: the *Lord Clyde* and *Lord Warden*, by G. A. Ballard.

c British battleships of 1870: the *Monarch*, by G. A. Ballard.

d The royalists at sea in 1650, by R. C. Anderson.

e Portrait of the *Sovereign* [*of the Seas*], by G. S. L. Clowes.

f The *Henri Grace à Dieu* [being a report of a lecture by L. G. Carr Laughton].

g Document: The lord high admiral's council [1702–5], contrib. by D. B. Smith.

h Blake's reduction of the Scilly Isles in 1651, by J. R. Powell.

i The shipping gallery in the Liverpool museums, by C. Carter.

j The privateering voyages of the *Tartar* of Bristol [1778–1779], by B. M. H. Rogers.

k British battleships of 1870: the *Captain*, by G. A. Ballard.

l The Hinchingbrooke drawings of the action between the *Lyon* and the *Elisabeth* [a French man of war], 1745, by H. H. Brindley.

m Documents: The rank of master and commander [1746], by D. B. Smith; Bounty ships, 1581–94, by J. W. Damer-Powell.

5115 Vol. 18.

a British battleships of 1870: the *Prince Consort*, *Caledonia* and *Ocean*, by G. A. Ballard.

b Papers relating to the Westminster fish market, 1750–1, by M. Lewis.

c The Long Sand and Southern channels, by H. M. Evans.

d Blake's reduction of Jersey in 1651, by J. R. Powell.

e Notes. [Includes: The *Henry Grace à Dieu*'s mast and sail plan]

f The Bideford polackers [ships], by V. C. Boyle.

g The *Royal Sovereign*, 1685, by L. G. Carr Laughton.

h Captain Christopher Myngs in the West Indies [1656–1663], by Florence E. Dyer.

i The *Constant Warwick* [1645–91], by A. W. Johns.

j British battleships of 1870: the *Royal Oak* and *Royal Alfred*, by G. A. Ballard.

k Notes. [Includes: Lieut. Henry Thomas Dundas Le Vesconte, d. 1845?]

l The Greenwich portrait of Sir Francis Drake, by G. Callender.

m Trawling under sail on the north-east coast, by E. Dade.

n Flag signalling for yachts [in the 19th cent.], by H. P. Mead.

o The London East India company's first expedition [to Bantam, Java, in 1601], by H. B. Butcher.

p The seaman's bookshelf on the eve of the Restoration, by E. G. R. Taylor. [Works on nautical science from a bookseller's catalogue, 1656]

q 'Carpenter' master shipwrights [17th and 18th cent.], by C. Knight.

5116 Vol. 19.

a British battleships of 1870: the *Zealous* and *Repulse*, by G. A. Ballard.

b Sir William Monson consults the stars, by E. G. R. Taylor. [Consultations by Monson and others with Simon Forman, astrologer, d. 1611]

c The Cinque Ports' feud with Yarmouth in the 13th cent., by F. W. Brooks.

d Letters from Sir Samuel Hood, 1780–2, by J. H. Owen.

e Notes on sail in the 19th cent., by R. Grenfell.

f Have the *Mayflower*'s masts been found?, by R. C. Anderson.

g British battleships of 1870: the *Hector* and *Valiant*, by G. A. Ballard.

h The old Yorkshire yawls, by E. Dade.

i Woodes Rogers' privateering voyage of 1708–11, by B. M. H. Rogers.

j Samuel Pepys, by E. Chappell.

k Document: Acre 1840 [being a letter by Lieutenant Lord Frederick Herbert Kerr describing the British bombardment and capture of the town, held by an Egyptian force]

l British battleships of 1870: the *Resistance* and *Defence*, by G. A. Ballard.

m Some letters of Admiral the Hon. Samuel Barrington [1770–79].

n H.M. Bark *Endeavour* [being chiefly correspondence relating to her, 1768], by C. Knight.

o Sources of plans of British fishing boats, by H. I. Chapelle.

p The four-masted ship *Transit* [1800–10], by W. R. Chaplin.

q The story of the semaphore [in the early 19th cent.], by H. P. Mead.

r Notes. [Includes: Early two-masted ships in England]

s Annual general meeting of the Society. [Includes an address by Sir R. Mansell on the work, past and present, of Trinity House]

t Where was Pepys Island?: a problem in historical geography, by B. M. Chambers.

Occasional publications, nos. 1–3:

5117 No. 1. A treatise on rigging written about the year 1625, from a ms. at Petworth House, ed. R. C. Anderson. 1921.

5118 No. 2. The wooden world, by Edward Ward. First published 1707. Reprinted from the edition of 1751 with a foreword by G. Callender. 1929.

5119 No. 3. The lengths of masts and yards, etc. 1640. (Containing also sizes of cables, anchors, standing rigging, boats and sails.) From a ms. formerly at Petworth House and now in the Science Museum, ed. G. S. L. Clowes. 1931.

Other publications:

5120 The Chelengk [Turkish decoration conferred on Nelson]. *P.* [1929].

5121 The portrait of Peter Pett [d. 1670?] and the *Sovereign of the Seas*, by G. Callender. 1930.

SOCIETY FOR THE PROMOTION OF ROMAN STUDIES

Founded 1910, to deal with the archaeology, art, and history of Italy and the Roman Empire down to about the year A.D. 700.

Journal of Roman Studies, vols. 1–23 (1911–33):

5122 Vol. 1.

a Roman London, by F. Haverfield.

5123 Vol. 2.

a The Corbridge gold find of 1911, by G. Macdonald.

b British centurions, by H. Dessau.

c Some representative examples of Romano-British sculpture, by F. Haverfield and H. S. Jones.

d Notes on the Roman coast defences of Britain, especially in Yorkshire, by F. Haverfield.

e The Roman fort at Huntcliff, near Saltburn, by W. Hornsby, R. Stanton and others.

5124 Vol. 3.

a Roman and native remains in Caledonia, by J. Curle.

b A Romano-British house near Bedmore barn, Ham hill, Som., by I. H. Beattie and W. J. Phythian-Adams.

5125 Vol. 4.

a Roman silver in Northumberland, by F. Haverfield.

5126 Vol. 5.

a Roman silver coins found at Corstopitum [near Corbridge-on-Tyne, 1906–12], by H. H. E. Craster.

5127 Vol. 6.

a A bronze bust of a Iulio-Claudian prince (? Caligula) in the museum at Colchester; with a note on the symbolism of the globe in imperial portraiture, by Mrs. S. A. Strong.

5128 Vol. 7.

a Woodeaton [Oxon., a Romano-British site], by M. V. Taylor.

b A Cybele altar in London, by E. M. W. Tillyard.

5129 Vol. 8.

a Professor Haverfield: a bibliography, by G. Macdonald.

5130 Vol. 9.

a The Agricolan occupation of North Britain, by G. Macdonald.

b Roman Colchester, by R. E. M. Wheeler and P. G. Laver.

c The Caractacus stone on Exmoor, by F. A. Bruton.

5131 Vol. 10.

a A Romano-British cemetery at Barnwood, Glos., by St. C. Baddeley.

b The date of Agricola's governorship of Britain, by R. K. McElderry.

c The vaults under Colchester castle: a further note, by R. E. M. Wheeler. [See vol. 9]

d The *Notitia Dignitatum*, by J. B. Bury.

e A decorative bronze Silenus-mask from Ilkley, by A. M. Woodward.

f Romano-British dovecots, by C. D. Chambers.

5132 Vol. 11.

a The building of the Antonine wall: a fresh study of the inscriptions, by G. Macdonald.

b Hadrian's wall: a history of the problem, by R. G. Collingwood.

c A Roman fortified house near Cardiff, by R. E. M. Wheeler.

d Roman Britain in 1921 and 1922, by M. V. Taylor and R. G. Collingwood. [Reports for 1923–32 appear in vols. 12, 14–19, and 21–23]

5133 Vol. 12.

a Tacitus, Agricola, *c.* 24, by J. B. Bury. [The military operations of Agricola as governor of Britain in A.D. 81]

b The governors of Britain from Claudius to Diocletian, by D. Atkinson.

c The Roman evacuation of Britain, by R. G. Collingwood.

5134 Vol. 13.

a The army reforms of Diocletian and Constantine and their modifications up to the time of the *Notitia Dignitatum*, by E. C. Nischer.

b The British frontier in the age of Severus, by R. G. Collingwood.

c Commodus-Hercules [cult] in Britain, by M. Rostovtseff, with an appendix on the evidence of coins, by H. Mattingly.

d The pottery of a Claudian well at Margidunum [Notts.], by F. Oswald.

5135 Vol. 14.

a Niall 'of the Nine Hostages' in connexion with the treasures of Traprain Law and Ballinrees [Coleraine], and the destruction of Wroxeter, Chester, Caerleon and Caerwent, by Sir W. Ridgeway.

b A note on the Peutinger Table and the fifth and ninth iters, by O. G. S. Crawford.

c Britannia on Roman coins of the 2nd cent. A.D., by Jocelyn Toynbee.

d The Fosse [Way], by R. G. Collingwood.

5136 Vol. 15.

a Further notes on Britannia coin-types, by Jocelyn Toynbee.

b Roman York: excavations of 1925, by S. N. Miller. [Report for 1926–7 in vol. 18]

5137 Vol. 16.

a Note on some fragments of imperial statues and of a statuette of Victory [found in Britain], by G. Macdonald.

b The pottery of a 3rd cent. well at Margidunum, by F. Oswald.

5138 Vol. 17.

a The date of the *Notitia Dignitatum*, by F. S. Salisbury.

b Circular bath-buildings in connection with cohort forts, by Mary C. Fair.

5139 Vol. 19.

a Bowls [of terra sigillata] by Acaunissa from Birdoswald, Mainz and Cologne, by F. Oswald.

5140 Vol. 20.

a A new diploma for Roman Britain [issued in A.D. 122, granting citizenship to Gemellus, an auxiliary], by F. N. Pryce.

b The decorated work of the potter Bvtrio, by F. Oswald. [Examples of terra sigillata ware, including some found in Britain]

5141 Vol. 21.

a Hadrian's wall, 1921–30, by R. G. Collingwood.

b Woodeaton coins, by J. G. Milne.

c Bowls of Acaunissa from the north of England, by F. Oswald.

d Notes on some Roman British pigs of lead, by G. C. Whittick.

5142 Vol. 22.

a Bibliography of Sir George Macdonald's published works.

b Three Caistor[-next-Norwich] pottery kilns, by D. Atkinson.

c Roman garrisons in the north of Britain, by E. Birley.

d Some notes on Roman coast defences [in Britain], by J. P. Bushe-Fox.

e Hoards of Roman coins found in Britain and a coin survey of the Roman province, by H. Mattingly.

f Notes on building-construction in Roman Britain, by R. E. M. Wheeler.

g John Horsley [Presbyterian divine and author of *Britannia Romana*, d. 1732], by Sir G. Macdonald.

5143 Vol. 23.

a The Roman evacuation of Britain, by H. S. Schultz.

b The *Notitia Dignitatum* and the western mints, by F. S. Salisbury. [The date of the *Notitia Dignitatum* and of the duration of Roman government in Britain submitted to numismatic evidence]

c A few notes on the currency of Britain, by J. G. Milne.

Other publications:

5144 A classified catalogue of the books, pamphlets and maps in the library of the Societies for the Promotion of Hellenic and Roman studies, by J. Penoyre. 1924.

SOCIETY OF ANTIQUARIES OF LONDON

Founded 1572, for the study of antiquity and the history of former times. Suppressed by James I, but continued to meet until c. 1660. Refounded 1707. Incorporated by royal charter 1751.

Proceedings, 2nd ser., vols. 18–32 ([1901]–20):

5145 Vol. 18.

a [Roman stone coffin found at Braintree, Essex, by G. F. Beaumont]

b [Romano-British remains in the upper Thames valley near Wallingford, Dorchester, Oxford and Eynsham, by F. Haverfield]

c [Documents of the parish of Feckenham, Worcs., by J. W. Willis Bund]

d Romano-British camp and cemetery at Hardham, Suss., by R. Garraway Rice.

e Roman causeway at Strood, Kent, by G. Payne.

f Roman interments discovered at 'The Brook', Chatham, by G. Payne.

g [Excavations at Warter priory, Yorks., by W. H. St. J. Hope]

h [Medieval altar frontal from Baunton, Glos., by W. H. St. J. Hope]

i Celtic interments discovered at Shorne [Kent], by G. Payne.

j [An order for the defence of the coast, 1625, by C. T. Martin]

k An inscribed Roman ingot of Cornish tin, and Roman tin-mining in Cornwall, by F. Haverfield.

l Excavation at Pule hill, near Marsden, on the Huddersfield and Manchester road, by E. Kitson Clark.

m [15th cent. tilting helm, by Viscount Dillon]

n Roman altar and other sculptured stones found at Cirencester, 1899, by W. J. Cripps.

o [A plaster head and bronze medallion of Sir Thomas Lovell, d. 1524, by L. H. Cust]

p [Choir screen in Tattershall church, Lincs., by Mrs. Sympson]

q [Excavations of tumuli at Hunstanton, Norf.], by T. McK. Hughes.

5146 Vol. 19.

a [State swords of the city of Lincoln, by J. G. Williams]
b [Wall-paintings at Rothamstead manor house, Harpenden, Herts., by C. E. Keyser]
c Queen's cross and St. Peter's church, Northampton, by C. A. Markham.
d Norman tympanum in Hawkesworth church, Notts., by J. R. Allen.
e History of the chapel porch of Magdalen College, Oxford, by R. T. Günther.
f [Roman interments at Enfield, Mdx., by R. A. Smith]
g The Cogenhoe family and Cogenhoe church, Northants., by A. Hartshorne.
h [Inscribed stone found at Llystyn Gwyn, Caern., by J. Rhys]

5147 Vol. 20.

a [Anglo-Saxon silver ornaments found at Trewhiddle, Corn., 1774, by R. A. Smith]
b [Letters patent of Edward I, 1303, *re* lands at Covenham, Lincs., by G. W. Kitchin]
c English spinet of the 17th cent. made by Charles Haward, by W. Dale.
d Ancient British iron currency, by R. A. Smith.
e Palaeolithic implements from the river Arun and the western Rother, Suss., by R. Garraway Rice.
f [Samuel Mearne, fl. 1668, and his book-bindings, by C. Davenport]
g [17th cent. rolls of Norfolk swan-marks, by W. Minet]
h A Lambeth salt-cellar of the company of Parish-clerks, by Sir J. Evans.

5148 Vol. 21.

a [Leaden grave crosses discovered near the Grey Friars monastery, Newgate Street, London, by F. G. H. Price]
b [15th–17th cent. death's-head spoons and silver spoons of provincial makes, by H. D. Ellis. Contd. in vol. 23]
c [Saxon bronze casting found at Pershore, Worcs., by C. R. Peers]
d [Antiquities found at Ham hill, Som., by H. St. G. Gray]
e Excavations at Kirklees priory, Yorks., by G. J. Armytage.
f [Prehistoric remains found at Haslemere, Surr., and pottery from late Celtic graves, by J. Hutchinson]
g [Sculptured representation of Hell Cauldron, probably late 12th cent., found at York, by J. Bilson]
h The [Roman] wreck on Pudding-pan Rock, Herne Bay, Kent, by R. A. Smith. [Contd. in vol. 22]
i [A tumulus containing urns of the bronze age, near Sunningdale, Berks., by O. A. Shrubsole]
j A burial place of the bronze age at Sulham, Berks., by O. A. Shrubsole.
k Timekeepers of the ancient Britons, by R. A. Smith.
l [Mottisfont priory, Hants, by C. R. Peers]
m [English medieval embroideries in the British Museum and the Victoria and Albert Museum, by W. R. Lethaby]

5149 Vol. 22.

a [Human remains found in the crypt of Canterbury cathedral supposed to be those of Archbishop Becket, d. 1170, by M. Beazeley]
b [A collection of pilgrims' signs or amulets, by Sir J. Evans]
c [Excavation of Harborough cave, near Brassington, Derbys., by W. S. Fox and R. A. Smith]
d Compton church, Surr., by H. T. Turner.
e Report of the Red Hills [Essex] exploration committee. [Contd. in vol. 23. See also vol. 30]

f A relief representing the crucifixion in the parish church of St. Dunstan, Stepney, by O. M. Dalton.
g [An early medieval latten door knocker from Lindsell, Essex, by M. Christy]
h [Excavations in the cloister of Durham abbey, by W. H. St. J. Hope]
i A penny of St. Aethelberht, King of East Anglia [d. 794], by P. W. P. Carlyon-Britton.

5150 Vol. 23.

a [A manuscript book of the Horners' company of London, 1455–1635, by H. G. Rosedale]
b [Roman villa at Cromhall, Glos., by E. Conder]
c A Roman inscribed tile from Plaxtol, Kent, by F. Haverfield.
d 'The Corbridge pottery shop' and other notes on Samian ware, by F. Haverfield.
e [Medieval pottery from Basing House, Hants, by R. L. Hobson]
f [Bronze age hoard dredged from the Thames off Broadness, by R. A. Smith]
g Report of the committee for excavations at Old Sarum. [Contd. in vols. 24–28]
h Burkat Shudi [d. 1773] and his harpsichords, by W. Dale.
i [A stone coffin and other Roman burials found at Old Ford in east London, by R. A. Smith]
j Easthorpe church, Essex, by H. Laver.
k A prehistoric route in Yorkshire, by E. Kitson Clark.
l Excavations at Corbridge, by F. Haverfield. [Contd. in vols. 24–26]
m Romano-British finds near Kettering, Northants., by F. W. Bull.

5151 Vol. 24.

a Down pits in the Isle of Wight, by P. Stone.
b [Excavation of a tumulus at Eyebury, near Peterborough, by E. Thurlow Leeds. Contd. in vol. 27]
c [Excavation of the Holy Well of St. Constantine, north Cornwall, by P. Williams]
d Some notes on Watling Street and its relation to London, by W. Page.
e [Excavation in 1868 of an Anglo-Saxon cemetery at Uncleby, East Riding of Yorks., by R. A. Smith]

5152 Vol. 25.

a [Exchequer tallies, by H. Jenkinson]
b [16th cent. English altar frontals from Cotehele House, Corn., by W. H. St. J. Hope]
c Porters, Southend, Essex, and its sculptured panels, by H. C. Smith.

5153 Vol. 26.

a An original exchequer account of 1304 with private tallies attached, by H. Jenkinson.
b The wheel of the ten ages of life in Leominster church, by G. McN. Rushforth.
c Flint implements from the surface near Avebury: their classification and dates, by H. G. O. Kendall.
d [The private chapel of the Earl Ferrers at Staunton Harold, Leics., by R. Burrough]
e Romano-British potteries in mid-Somerset, by A. Bulleid.
f Visitations of religious houses by William Alnwick, bishop of Lincoln, 1436–49, by A. Hamilton Thompson.

5154 Vol. 27.

a [An iron currency bar from Salmonsbury camp, Bourton-on-the-Water, Glos., by R. A. Smith]
b [Bronze vessels, including water-clocks, of the early iron age, discovered at Wotton, Surr., 1914, by R. A. Smith. Reprinted in *Surrey Archaeological Collections*, xxix]

c Maiden Bower [camp], Beds., by W. G. Smith.
d [13th cent. stained glass in Lanchester church, co. Durham, by J. T. Fowler]

5155 Vol. 28.

a Excavations on Hackpen hill, Wilts., by H. G. O. Kendall.
b [The shrine of St. Edward at Westminster, by H. F. Westlake]
c [Jacobean roundels, by H. C. Smith]
d [The seals of the abbey of Waltham Holy Cross, Essex, by W. St. J. Hope]
e Maurice Johnson, F.S.A., 1688-1755, and the early meetings of the Society, by L. Weaver.
f [London topography in stained glass, *c.* 1623, in the chapel of Lincoln's Inn, by W. Martin]
g [The tombs of two bishops in Salisbury cathedral, by Sir W. St. J. Hope]
h Bishop Flambard's great wall at Durham, *c.* 1120, by W. T. Jones and J. T. Fowler.

5156 Vol. 29.

a [A box of coin weights made for Henry Somerset, 5th Earl of Worcester, d. 1646, by Sir C. H. Read]
b An Anglo-Saxon cemetery at Wheatley, Oxon., by E. Thurlow Leeds.
c Notes on Southwick priory, Hants, by W. Dale.
d A set of standard troy weights, dated 1588, by L. A. Lawrence.
e [The history of the Society, from the anniversary address by Sir A. J. Evans]
f [Discovery of a pre-Conquest window, with early painting on the internal splays, in Witley church, Surr., with notes on other recent discoveries of early paintings on window-splays, by P. M. Johnston. Reprinted in *Surrey Archaeological Collections*, xxxi]
g [English book of ornamental engravings of 1548, by C. Dodgson]

5157 Vol. 30.

a The fountain at Leez priory [Little Leighs, Essex], by M. E. Hughes-Hughes.
b The Essex Red Hills as salt-works, by R. A. Smith. [See also vol. 22]
c [An enamelled lid at All Souls College, Oxford, of the mid 14th cent., by Joan Evans]
d [Prehistoric and Anglo-Saxon remains from Howletts, near Bridge, Kent, by R. A. Smith]
e [Anglo-Saxon remains from Islip, Northants., by R. A. Smith]
f The plan and arrangement of the first cathedral church of Canterbury, by Sir W. St. J. Hope.
g Notes on the early history, form and functions of Paul's Cross, by W. P. Baildon.

5158 Vol. 31.

a [Flint implements from the palaeolithic floor at Whipsnade, by R. A. Smith]
b Avebury [Wilts.] and Grime's Graves [Norf.], by H. G. O. Kendall.
c [Helmets in Little Chart church, Kent, by V. Farquharson]

5159 Vol. 32.

a The chronology of flint daggers, by R. A. Smith.
b [The ancient manor house of the bishopric of Winchester at Esher, by J. K. Floyer]
c English alabaster tables, by W. L. Hildburgh.
d [Silchester and its relations to the pre-Roman civilization of Gaul, by J. B. P. Karslake]
e Elizabethan madrigals, by E. H. Fellowes.

Antiquaries Journal, *continuing the above,* vols. 1–13 (1921–33):

5160 Vol. 1.

a Stonehenge: report on the exploration, by W. Hawley. [Contd. in vols. 2–6 and 8]
b John Plummer, master of the children [of the Chapel Royal, 1445], by C. Johnson.
c The discovery of engravings upon flint crust at Grime's Graves, Norf., by A. L. Armstrong.
d Excavations at Frilford [Berks.], by L. H. D. Buxton.
e Site of the battle of Ethandun [878], by E. A. Rawlence.
f Wayland's smithy, Berks., by C. R. Peers and R. A. Smith.
g Notes on some English alabaster carvings, by W. L. Hildburgh.
h Two relic-holders from altars in the nave of Rievaulx abbey, Yorks., by C. R. Peers.
i Ancient settlements at Harlyn bay [Corn.], by O. G. S. Crawford.
j Observations on the polygonal type of settlement in Britain, by J. B. P. Karslake.
k A hoard of iron currency-bars found on Worthy down, Winchester, by R. W. Hooley.

5161 Vol. 2.

a A village site of the Hallstatt period in Wiltshire, by Maud E. Cunnington.
b Roman remains at Welwyn [Herts.], by G. M. Kindersley.
c A prehistoric invasion of England [800–700 B.C.], by O. G. S. Crawford.
d Roman spoons from Dorchester [Dors.], by O. M. Dalton.
e A hoard of bronze discovered at Grays Thurrock [Essex], by C. H. Butcher.
f Avebury ditch, by A. D. Passmore.
g Four Suffolk flint implements, by J. R. Moir.
h The seal of Robert Fitz Meldred [fl. 1200], by W. A. Littledale.
i Further discoveries of the neolithic and bronze ages at Peterborough, by E. Thurlow Leeds.
j On Coldharbour [as a place-name], by J. B. P. Karslake.
k Notes on early British pottery, by E. Thurlow Leeds.
l An account relating to Sir John Cobham, 1408, by Sir H. C. Maxwell Lyte.
m The age of Stonehenge, by T. R. Holmes.
n Hallstatt pottery from Eastbourne, by W. Budgen.
o Roman Cardiff: supplementary notes, by R. E. M. Wheeler.
p Roman coffins discovered at Keynsham [Som.], 1922, by H. St. G. Gray.

5162 Vol. 3.

a English medieval alabaster carvings, by W. L. Hildburgh. [Contd. in vols. 4, 8, and 10]
b The siege of Berkhampstead castle in 1216, by J. M. Kendall.
c Early Anglo-Saxon weights, by R. A. Smith.
d The age of Stonehenge deduced from the orientation of its axes, by E. H. Stone.
e Flint celts from Dorset, by H. G. O. Kendall.
f The Parish Clerks' company's plate, by E. A. Ebblewhite.
g Distribution of Roman remains in Cornwall, by R. D. Greenaway.
h The source of the stones of Stonehenge, by H. H. Thomas.
i Discovery of a Roman burial at Radnage, Bucks., by C. O. Skilbeck.
j An indulgence inscription in Clapton church, Glos., by G. McN. Rushforth.

k The Roman road, Rowhook, Suss., to Farley Heath, Surr., by S. E. Winbolt.

5163 Vol. 4.

a Sculptured cornices in churches near Banbury and their connexion with William of Wykeham, by C. E. Keyser.
b The age and origin of the Wansdyke, by A. D. Passmore.
c Pottery finds at Wisley [Surr.], by R. A. Smith.
d Roman milestones in Cornwall, by R. G. Collingwood.
e An Anglo-Saxon cremation-burial of the 7th cent. in Asthall barrow, Oxon., by E. Thurlow Leeds.
f The problem of Wansdyke, by A. F. Major.
g Notes on mural paintings of St. Christopher in English churches, by H. H. Brindley.
h Medieval seal matrices, by C. H. Hunter Blair.
i Seal matrices with screw-out centres, by H. S. Kingsford.
j Discoveries near Cissbury, Suss., by G. R. Wolseley and R. A. Smith.
k Notes on the shrine of St. Swithun formerly in Winchester cathedral, by J. D. Le Couteur and D. H. M. Carter.

5164 Vol. 5.

a The trunnion celt in Britain, by W. J. Hemp.
b Pre-Roman finds at Folkestone, by S. E. Winbolt.
c The Beeston Tor [Staffs.] hoard, by R. A. Smith. [Includes 50 silver Anglo-Saxon coins and two silver brooches]
d Disputes between English and foreign glass-painters in the 16th cent., by J. A. Knowles.
e Flint tools of the iron age, by H. G. O. Kendall.
f English wall-papers of the 16th and 17th cent., by H. Jenkinson.
g Bronze crowns and a bronze head-dress from a Roman site at Cavenham Heath, Suff., by Nina F. Layard.
h Anglo-Saxon finds at Warwick, by P. B. Chatwin.
i Three bronze instruments from the Edgebold brick-yard, Meole Brace, Salop, by Lily F. Chitty.
j A gun-flint factory site in south Wilts., by R. C. C. Clay.

5165 Vol. 6.

a Some additions to the plan of the Benedictine priory church of St. Mary, Blyth, Notts., by F. H. Fairweather.
b Excavations on the Akeman street, near Asthally [Asthall Leigh], Oxon., Feb.–June, 1925, by C. G. Stevens and J. N. L. Myres.
c A 'dug out' canoe from south Wales: with notes on the chronology, typology, and distribution of monoxylous craft in England and Wales, by C. Fox.
d Excavations in Alderney, by R. R. Marett and T. W. M. De Guérin.
e Use of Arabic and Roman numerals in English archives, by H. Jenkinson.
f Two early British bronze bowls, by R. A. Smith.
g Ancient bridges in Herefordshire and their preservation, by G. H. Jack.
h A dated medieval bell from Minchinhampton, Glos. [1515], by H. B. Walters.
i The Saxon cathedral of Elmham [Norf.], by A. W. Clapham and W. H. Godfrey.
j 13th cent. English bells, by H. B. Walters.

5166 Vol. 7.

a An 'encrusted' urn from Wales; with notes on the origin and distribution of the type, by C. Fox.
b The construction and use of wheel dials, by Sir J. R. Findlay.
c An Anglo-Saxon hut on the Car Dyke at Waterbeach, [Cambs.], by T. C. Lethbridge.
d Excavations at Alchester [Wendlebury, Oxon.], by C. Hawkes. [Contd. by J. H. Iliffe in vols. 9 and 12]

e The Richborough coins and the end of the Roman occupation, by F. S. Salisbury.
f The history of the Worshipful Company of Glaziers, by J. A. Knowles.
g Bronze implements from the city of London, by R. E. M. Wheeler.
h Excavations on the site of the priory church and monastery of St. Peter, Eye, Suff., by F. H. Fairweather.
i London shipbuilding, 1295, by C. Johnson.
j A neolithic site at Abingdon, Berks., by E. Thurlow Leeds. [Contd. in vol. 8]
k A late bronze age urn-field at Pokesdown, Hants, by R. C. C. Clay.
l A late palaeolithic settlement in the Colne valley, Essex, by Nina F. Layard.

5167 Vol. 8.

a The Willow Moor bronze hoard, Little Wenlock, Salop, by Lily F. Chitty.
b The Roman kilns of Farnham, Surr., by A. G. Wade.
c Roman temple at Worth, Kent, by W. G. Klein and R. A. Smith.
d A Saxon cemetery at Luton, Beds., by W. Austin, with notes by T. W. Bagshawe and F. G. Parsons.
e Excavations at Wookey Hole and other Mendip caves, by H. E. Balch.
f Cross-head from Berrow church, Som., by W. D. Caröe.
g A 'Romano-Celtic' temple near Harlow, Essex; and a note on the type, by R. E. M. Wheeler.
h A bronze age refuse pit at Swanwick, Hants, by C. F. Fox. [Contd. in vol. 10]
i A Romano-British settlement at Springhead, Kent, by R. F. Jessup.
j An early hall at Chilham castle, Kent, by A. W. Clapham.
k Early iron age site at Findon Park, Findon, Suss., by C. Fox and G. R. Wolseley.
l Anglo-Saxon sun dials, by A. R. Green.

5168 Vol. 9.

a A Roman pipe-burial from Caerleon, Mon., by R. E. M. Wheeler.
b The priory of St. Leonard of Stanley, Glos., by C. Swynnerton.
c Akeman street and the river Cherwell, by B. H. St. J. O'Neil.
d Seven sacraments compositions in English medieval art, by G. McN. Rushforth.
e A Roman villa at Newport, Isle of Wight, by P. G. Stone. [Pt. 2: Pottery, by G. A. Sherwin]
f Report on recent excavations in London. I: The Midland Bank site, Princes Street, E.C., by E. B. Birley.
g Early London fire-appliances, by J. B. P. Karslake.

5169 Vol. 10.

a Report on the excavations at Glastonbury abbey, by C. R. Peers, A. W. Clapham, and E. Horne.
b Stonehenge and the two-date theory, by Mrs. B. H. Cunnington.
c Examples of Claudian terra sigillata from London, by J. A. Stanfield.
d Ship-burial in the Isle of Man, by P. M. C. Kermode.
e A polished hand-axe from West Runton, Norf., by J. R. Moir.
f A 15th cent. sword and a medieval bronze figure from Westminster abbey, by L. E. Tanner.
g Flint implements of upper palaeolithic facies from beneath the uppermost boulder clay of Norfolk and Yorkshire, by J. R. Moir and J. P. T. Burchell.

5170 Vol. 11.

a The Winchester Anglo-Saxon bowl, by W. J. Andrew and R. A. Smith.

b The date of Cissbury camp [Suss.], being a report on excavations undertaken for the Worthing Archaeological Society, by E. C. Curwen and R. P. R. Williamson.

c Roman objects from Stanwix [Cumb.] and Thatcham [Berks.], by R. G. Collingwood.

d Recent discoveries in the minsters of Ripon and York, by C. R. Peers.

e The Sacred Tree motive on a Roman bronze from Essex, by A. B. Tonnochy and C. F. C. Hawkes.

f An illuminated charter of free warren dated 1291, by C. Clay.

g Two 'dug-out' boats from Wales, by W. F. Grimes. [The section on the Llandrindod Wells boat was reprinted in *Radnorshire Society Transactions*, vol. i]

h Notes on the history in the 17th cent., of the portraits of Richard II, by Mrs. R. L. Poole.

i A seal of Edward II for Scottish affairs, by H. Jenkinson.

j Lydney castle, Glos., by D. A. Casey.

k Palaeolithic implements from Kirmington, Lincs., and their relation to the 100-foot raised beach of late pleistocene times, by J. P. T. Burchell.

l Excavations at Colchester, by C. Hawkes.

m Chastleton camp, Oxon., a hill fort of the early iron age, by E. Thurlow Leeds.

n An iron-age site near Radley, Berks., by E. Thurlow Leeds.

o A sword and helm in Westminster abbey, by J. G. Mann.

p A West Alpine and Hallstatt site at Southchurch, Essex, by A. G. Francis.

5171 Vol. 12.

a Excavations at Hollingbury camp, Suss., by E. C. Curwen.

b The age of Stonehenge: a criterion, by G. Engleheart.

c Was there a second Belgic invasion (represented by bead-rim pottery)?, by Mrs. B. H. Cunnington. [See also below]

d Eastern chapels in the cathedral church of Norwich, by D. H. S. Cranage.

e Two helmets in St. Botolph's church, Lullingstone, Kent, by J. G. Mann.

f The Mull hill circle, Isle of Man, and its pottery, by S. Piggott.

g The date of the plano-convex flint knife in England and Wales, by J. G. D. Clark.

h The prehistoric pottery sites of the Lincolnshire coast, by H. H. Swinnerton.

i Roman blast furnace in Lincolnshire, by I. C. Hannah.

j Seven charters of Henry II at Lincoln cathedral, by V. H. Galbraith.

k Bronze age settlements and a Saxon hut near Bourton-on-the-Water, Glos., by G. C. Dunning.

l A destroyed cycle of wall paintings in a church [Winterbourne Dauntsey] in Wilts., by T. Borenius.

m Medieval alabasters from Naworth castle [Cumb.], by E. Maclagan.

n The second Belgic invasion: a reply to Mrs. B. H. Cunnington [see above], by C. Hawkes and G. C. Dunning.

5172 Vol. 13.

a Excavations at Castlelaw, Midlothian, and the small forts of north Britain, by V. G. Childe.

b Notes on the megalithic monuments in the Isles of Scilly, by H. O'N. Hencken.

c An altar to the mothers in Lund church, near Kirkham, Lancs., by J. P. Droop.

d Excavations on Thundersbarrow hill, Suss., by E. C. Curwen.

e Pottery from the Romano-British site on Thundersbarrow hill, by K. P. Oakley.

f Early Saxon penetration of the upper Thames area, by E. Thurlow Leeds.

g An heraldic agreement of 1580, by W. G. Clark-Maxwell.

h Report on an early bronze age site in the south-eastern fens, by J. G. D. Clark.

i Trial-excavations in the so-called 'Danish camp' at Warham, near Wells, Norf., by H. St. G. Gray.

j Three late bronze-age barrows on the Cloven way [Colbury barrow, Landford barrow (in Plaitford), and Plaitford barrow, Hants], by J. P. Preston and C. Hawkes.

k Plough coulters from Silchester, by J. B. P. Karslake.

Archaeologia, vols. 57-83 (1900-33):

5173 Vol. 57.

a An illuminated and emblazoned copy of the statutes from Edward III to Henry VI, illustrating the genealogy of the family of Fitzwilliam of Mablethorpe, Lincs., by A. Higgins.

b An examination of the grave of St. Cuthbert in Durham cathedral church in March, 1899, by J. T. Fowler.

c A ms. collection of ordinances of chivalry of the 15th cent. belonging to Lord Hastings, by Viscount Dillon.

d A defence of the liberties of Chester, 1450, by H. D. Harrod.

e Excavations on the site of the Roman city at Silchester, Hants, in 1899, by W. H. St. J. Hope and G. E. Fox. [Contd. in vols. 58-62]

f Remains of a Roman silver refinery at Silchester, by W. Gowland.

g Lacock abbey, Wilts., by H. Brakspear.

h Notes on the buildings, books and benefactors of the library of the dean and chapter of Wells, by C. M. Church.

i Sir John de Pulteney [d. 1349] and his two residences in London, Cold Harbour and the Manor of the Rose, together with a few remarks on the parish of St. Laurence Poultney, by P. Norman.

j Charters of the manor of Meonstoke [Hants], by T. F. Kirby.

k Excavations at Caerwent, Mon., on the site of the Roman city of Venta Silurum, by A. T. Martin and T. Ashby. [Contd. in vols. 58-62, and 64. Contd. by V. E. Nash-Williams in vol. 80]

l Recent discoveries in Romsey abbey church, by C. R. Peers.

m A portable sundial of gilt brass made for Cardinal Wolsey, by L. Evans.

n Cardiff castle: its Roman origin, by J. Ward.

o Notes on the heraldic glass in Great Malvern priory church, by R. W. Paul.

p The early metallurgy of silver and lead. Pt. 1: Lead, by W. Gowland. [Includes an account of the Roman use of lead in Britain]

5174 Vol. 58.

a Recent excavations at Stonehenge, by W. Gowland, with a note on the nature and origin of the rock fragments found in the excavations, by J. W. Judd.

b Some familiar letters of Charles II and James, Duke of York, addressed to their daughter and niece [Charlotte Fitzroy], Countess of Litchfield [written *c.* 1681-4], by Viscount Dillon.

c The destroyed church of St. Michael, Wood Street, in the city of London, with some notes on the church of St. Michael, Bassishaw, by P. Norman.

d Charters of the manor of Ropley, Hants, by T. F. Kirby.

e The St. Albans school of painting, mural and miniature. Pt. 1: Mural painting, by W. Page.

f The London Charterhouse and its old water supply, by W. H. St. J. Hope.

g The castles of the Conquest, by J. H. Round.

h Charters of Harmondsworth, Isleworth, Heston, Twickenham, and Hampton-on-Thames, by T. F. Kirby.

i Brougham castle, Westmld., by E. Towry Whyte.

j Garnier de Nablous [d. 1192], prior of the Hospital in England, and grand master of the order of St. John of Jerusalem, by J. H. Round.

k A morse ivory tau cross head of English work of the 11th cent., by C. H. Read.

l Recent discoveries in the cloister of Durham abbey, by W. H. St. J. Hope, with introd. by J. T. Fowler.

m Excavations at Arbor Low [stone circle, Derbys.], by H. St. G. Gray.

n The medieval library of the Benedictine priory of St. Mary, in Worcester cathedral church, by J. K. Floyer.

5175 Vol. 59.

a Chancery proceedings of the 15th cent., by C. T. Martin.

b The hauberk of chain mail and its conventional representations, by J. G. Waller.

c Records of the manor of Durrington, Wilts., by T. F. Kirby.

d Roman and later remains found during excavations on the site of Newgate prison, by P. Norman.

e The imagery and sculptures on the west front of Wells cathedral church, by W. H. St. J. Hope, with suggestions as to the identification of some of the images by W. R. Lethaby.

f Notes on some probable traces of Roman fulling in Britain, by G. E. Fox.

g Notes on 14th cent. conveyancing, by T. F. Kirby.

h The island of Ictis [the Isle of Wight, and the ancient trade with Britain for tin], by C. Reid.

i Notes on the Augustinian priory of St. Bartholomew, West Smithfield [London], by E. A. Webb.

5176 Vol. 60.

a The brass of Sir Hugh Hastings [d. 1347] in Elsing church, Norf., by A. Hartshorne, with a note by W. H. St. J. Hope.

b Excavations in an Anglo-Saxon burial ground at Mitcham, Surr., by H. F. Bidder, with notes on crania and bones found there, by W. L. H. Duckworth.

c The loss of King John's baggage train in the Well-stream in October, 1216, by W. H. St. J. Hope.

d The palace of Westminster in the 11th and 12th cent., by W. R. Lethaby.

e Recent discoveries in connexion with Roman London [chiefly of the Roman wall], by P. Norman and F. W. Reader. [Contd. in vol. 63]

f Early iron age burials in Yorkshire, by W. Greenwell.

g An Anglo-Saxon cemetery in Ipswich, by Nina F. Layard.

h Clerical life in the 15th cent. as illustrated by proceedings of the court of chancery, by C. T. Martin.

i Sculptures in Lincoln minster: the judgment porch and the angel choir, by W. R. Lethaby.

j The treasury of God and the birthright of the poor; or facts illustrating the origin of 'parsons' and 'vicars' in England, by O. J. Reichel.

k The great almery for relics in the abbey church of Selby [Yorks.], with notes on some other receptacles for relics, by W. H. St. J. Hope.

l The episcopal ornaments of William of Wykeham and William of Waynflete, sometime bishops of Winchester, and of certain bishops of St. Davids, by W. H. St. J. Hope.

m The Cistercian abbey of Stanley, Wilts., by H. Brakspear.

n Funeral effigies of the kings and queens of England [Edward the Confessor to James I], with special reference

to those in the abbey church of Westminster, by W. H. St. J. Hope, with a note on the Westminster tradition of identification, by J. Armitage Robinson.

5177 Vol. 61.

a Stone circles of east Cornwall, by H. St. G. Gray.

b Inventory of the goods of the collegiate church of the Holy Trinity, Arundel, 1 Oct., 9 Hen. VIII (1517), by W. H. St. J. Hope.

c Chronology of the British bronze age, by O. Montelius.

d Three inventories: the Earl of Huntingdon, 1377; Brother John Randolf, 1419; Sir John de Boys, 1426, by W. P. Baildon.

e The round church of the Knights Templar at Temple Bruer, Lincs., by W. H. St. J. Hope.

f The castle of Ludlow [Salop.], by W. H. St. J. Hope.

g A late-Celtic mirror found at Desborough, Northants., and other mirrors of the period, by R. A. Smith.

h The White conduit, Chapel Street, Bloomsbury, and its connexion with the Grey Friars' water system, by P. Norman and E. A. Mann.

i The ancient topography of the town of Ludlow, Salop, by W. H. St. J. Hope.

j The later history of the Steelyard in London [1598–1865], by P. Norman.

k A late-Celtic village near Dumpton Gap, Broadstairs [Kent], by H. Hurd.

l The origin, evolution and classification of the bronze spear-head in Great Britain and Ireland, by W. Greenwell and W. P. Brewis.

m Wooden monumental effigies in England and Wales, by A. C. Fryer.

n Excavation of the site of Basing House, Hants, by C. R. Peers.

o The music in the painted glass of the windows in the Beauchamp chapel at Warwick, by C. F. Hardy.

5178 Vol. 62.

a The manor of Eia, or Eye next Westminster, by W. L. Rutton.

b Fellows of the Society who have held the office of Director, by Sir E. W. Brabrook.

c Church of Edward the Confessor at Westminster, by J. Armitage Robinson.

d St. Paul's school before Colet [c. 1111–1512], by A. F. Leach.

e The stone bridge at Hampton Court, by C. R. Peers.

f The discovery of prehistoric pits at Peterborough, and the development of neolithic pottery, by G. W. Abbott and R. A. Smith.

g Canterbury cathedral choir during the Commonwealth and after, with special reference to two oil paintings, by W. D. Caröe.

h Exchequer tallies [13th cent.], by H. Jenkinson.

i Pleistocene man in Jersey, by R. R. Marett.

j Notes on an Anglo-Saxon cemetery at Market Overton, Rut., by V. B. Crowther-Beynon, with a supplementary note by E. Thurlow Leeds.

k A wardrobe account of 16–17 Richard II, 1393–4, by W. P. Baildon.

l A palaeolithic industry at Northfleet, Kent, by R. A. Smith.

m The discovery of the remains of Henry VI in St. George's chapel, Windsor Castle, by W. H. St. J. Hope.

n Plan of the first cathedral church of Lincoln, by J. Bilson.

o A late-Celtic and Romano-British cave-dwelling at Wookey Hole, near Wells, Som., by H. E. Balch and R. D. R. Troup. [Contd. in vol. 64]

p Lake-dwellings in Holderness, Yorks., discovered by Thos. Boynton, 1880–1, by R. A. Smith.

5179 Vol. 63.

a Late-Celtic antiquities discovered at Welwyn, Herts., by R. A. Smith.

b Jousting cheques of the 16th cent., by C. Ffoulkes.

c Wall paintings in the infirmary chapel, Canterbury cathedral, by W. D. Caröe.

d Topography of the Dominican [Blackfriars] priory of London, by A. W. Clapham.

e The ancient paintings in the Hastings and Oxenbridge chantry chapels, in St. George's chapel, Windsor Castle, by W. H. St. J. Hope and P. H. Newman.

f The date of Grime's Graves [Norf.] and Cissbury flint mines [Suss.], by R. A. Smith.

g The distribution of the Anglo-Saxon saucer brooch in relation to the battle of Bedford, 571, by E. Thurlow Leeds.

h Further observations on prehistoric man in Jersey, by R. R. Marett.

i Plan of the church and monastery of St. Augustine, Bristol, by R. W. Paul.

5180 Vol. 64.

a Some 14th cent. accounts of iron works at Tudely, Kent, by M. S. Giuseppi.

b The plan of St. Bartholomew's, West Smithfield, and the recent excavations, by E. A. Webb.

c Stratification at Swanscombe [Kent]: report on excavations made on behalf of the British Museum and H.M. Geological Survey, by R. A. Smith and H. Dewey.

d The use of Samian pottery in dating the early Roman occupation of the north of Britain, by J. P. Bushe-Fox.

e Bess of Hardwick's buildings and building accounts [Elizabeth Talbot, Countess of Shrewsbury, d. 1608], by B. Stallybrass.

f Malmesbury abbey [Wilts.], by H. Brakspear.

5181 Vol. 65.

a Effigies of Saxon bishops at Wells, by J. Armitage Robinson.

b The funeral, monument, and chantry chapel of Henry V, by W. H. St. J. Hope.

c Ancient deeds and seals belonging to Lord de l'Isle and Dudley [12th–15th cent.], by C. L. Kingsford.

5182 Vol. 66.

a The complete building accounts of the city churches (parochial) designed by Sir Christopher Wren, by L. Weaver.

b Remarks on the churches of the Domesday survey, by W. Page.

c Researches at Rickmansworth [Herts.]: report on excavations made on behalf of the British Museum, by R. A. Smith.

d Recent Roman discoveries in London, by F. Lambert.

e The last testament and inventory of John de Veer, 13th Earl of Oxford [d. 1513], by Sir W. H. St. J. Hope.

f Topography of the Cistercian abbey of Tower Hill, by A. W. Clapham.

g Contracts for the tomb of the Lady Margaret Beaufort, Countess of Richmond and Derby [d. 1509], mother of Henry VII and foundress of the colleges of Christ and St. John in Cambridge; with some illustrative documents, by R. F. Scott.

h Recent discoveries in the abbey church of St. Austin at Canterbury, by Sir W. St. J. Hope.

i Mary de Sancto Paulo [Mary of St. Pol, Countess of Pembroke, d. 1377], foundress of Pembroke College, Cambridge, by H. Jenkinson.

j Heraldry in the cloisters of the cathedral church of Christ at Canterbury, by R. Griffin.

5183 Vol. 67.

a Recent discoveries of medieval remains in London, by P. Norman.

b Origin of the neolithic celt, by R. A. Smith.

c Notes on the palaeolithic floor near Caddington [Herts. and Beds.], by W. G. Smith.

d The site, fauna, and industry of La Cotte de St. Brelade, Jersey, by R. R. Marett.

e The feast of the five kings [Edward III of England, Peter de Lusignan, King of Cyprus, David of Scotland, John of France and Waldemar IV of Denmark, in London 1363–4], by C. L. Kingsford.

f The trousseaux of Princess Philippa, wife of Eric, King of Denmark, Norway and Sweden [daughter of Henry of Lancaster afterwards Henry IV, d. 1430], by W. P. Baildon.

g The dorter range at Worcester priory, by H. Brakspear.

5184 Vol. 68.

a Our Lady of the Pew: the king's oratory or closet in the palace of Westminster, by C. L. Kingsford.

b Quire screens in English churches, with special reference to the 12th cent. quire screen formerly in the cathedral church of Ely, by Sir W. St. J. Hope.

c The Sarum consuetudinary and its relation to the cathedral church of Old Sarum, by Sir W. St. J. Hope.

d Portions of a 'temporale' of 1350–80, by G. F. Browne.

e Roman roads and the distribution of Saxon churches in London, by R. A. Smith.

5185 Vol. 69.

a Westminster abbey: the old Lady chapel and its relation to the Romanesque and Gothic churches, by H. F. Westlake.

b The origins and forms of Hertfordshire towns and villages, by W. Page.

c Roll of arms belonging to the Society, *temp.* Henry VIII, *c.* 1540, by M. Stephenson and R. Griffin.

d Roll of household accounts of Sir Hamon le Strange of Hunstanton, Norf., 1347–8, by H. le Strange.

e Roman Cirencester, by F. Haverfield.

5186 Vol. 70.

a Wardrobe and household accounts of Bogo de Clare, 1284–6, by M. S. Giuseppi.

b A set of Elizabethan heraldic roundels [c. 1587] in the British Museum, by R. Griffin and M. Stephenson.

c Two forfeitures in the year of Agincourt [relating to the property of Henry le Scrope (executed 1415), and that of Richard Gurmyn (burnt 1415)], by C. L. Kingsford.

d Paris Garden [Southwark] and the bear-baiting, by C. L. Kingsford.

5187 Vol. 71.

a Hardknot castle [Cumb.] and the 10th Antonine itinerary, by R. G. Collingwood.

b London houses of the early Tudor period, by C. L. Kingsford.

c Recent excavations in London, by F. Lambert. [1: King William Street. 2: London Wall. 3: Moorfields]

d Hoards of neolithic celts [from Norfolk and Kent], by R. A. Smith.

e Heraldry in the Chicheley porch of the cathedral church of Christ at Canterbury, by R. Griffin.

f The Llynfawr [Glam.] and other hoards of the bronze age, by O. G. S. Crawford and R. E. M. Wheeler.

g A Romano-British homestead in the Hambledon valley, Bucks., by A. H. Cocks.

h The priory of St. Leonard of Stanley, Glos., in the light of recent discoveries documentary and structural, by C. Swynnerton.

i An archaeological survey of Oxfordshire, by P. Manning and E. Thurlow Leeds.

5188 Vol. 72.

a Medieval seals of the bishops of Durham, by C. H. Hunter Blair.
b Flint implements of special interest, by R. A. Smith.
c The devastation of Bedfordshire and neighbouring counties in 1065 and 1066, by G. H. Fowler.
d Weaverthorpe church [Yorks.] and its builder, by J. Bilson.
e The monastery of St. Milburge at Much Wenlock, Salop, by D. H. S. Cranage.
f Unpublished plans of Dover harbour [1495–1847], by W. Minet.
g Pottery from the waste heap of the Roman potters' kilns discovered at Sandford, near Littlemore, Oxon., in 1879, by T. May.
h Bath Inn or Arundel House [Strand, London], by C. L. Kingsford.

5189 Vol. 73.

a Essex House [Strand, London], formerly Leicester House and Exeter Inn, by C. L. Kingsford.
b Wharram-le-Street church, Yorks., and St. Rule's church, St. Andrews, by J. Bilson.
c An Anglo-Saxon cemetery at Bidford-on-Avon, Warws., by J. Humphreys, J. W. Ryland, E. A. B. Barnard, F. C. Wellstood, and T. G. Barnett. [Contd. in vol. 74]
d The architecture of the Premonstratensians, with special reference to their buildings in England, by A. W. Clapham.
e A Saxon village near Sutton Courtenay, Berks., by E. Thurlow Leeds. [Contd. in vol. 76]
f Instances of orientation in prehistoric monuments in the British Isles, by B. Somerville.
g Excavations at some Wiltshire monasteries [Braden-stoke, Monkton Farley and Kington priories], by H. Brakspear. [Reprinted in the *Wiltshire Archaeol. and Nat. History Magazine*, vol. 43]
h The bronze sword in Great Britain, by W. P. Brewis.

5190 Vol. 74.

a Monumental effigies made by Bristol craftsmen, 1240–1550, by A. C. Fryer.
b Flints from the Sturry gravels, Kent, by H. Dewey and R. A. Smith.
c A London merchant's house and its owners, 1360–1614 [Asselyn's Wharf], by C. L. Kingsford.
d Elizabethan Sheldon tapestries, by J. Humphreys.
e An alabaster table [medieval] of the Annunciation with crucifix: a study in English iconography, by W. L. Hildburgh.
f Examples of Anglian art [*c*. 670–*c*. 867], by R. A. Smith.
g The inscribed and sculptured stones of Lindisfarne, by C. R. Peers.
h Medieval tallies, public [exchequer] and private, by H. Jenkinson.

5191 Vol. 75.

a The Roman baths at Bath; with an account of [recent] excavations, by W. H. Knowles.
b Letters of confraternity [between monasteries etc.], by W. G. Clark-Maxwell. [Contd. in vol. 79]
c The perforated axe-hammers of Britain, by R. A. Smith.
d The Roman house at Keynsham, Som., by A. Bulleid and E. Horne.
e Fromond's chantry at Winchester college, by H. Chitty.
f The order of Grandmont and its houses in England, by Rose Graham and A. W. Clapham.

5192 Vol. 76.

a Prehistoric and Roman settlements on Park Brow [Suss.], by G. R. Wolseley, R. A. Smith and W. Hawley.
b The Armourers' company of London and the Greenwich school of armourers, by C. Ffoulkes.
c Flint arrow-heads in Britain, by R. A. Smith.
d Bosses on the vault of the quire of Winchester cathedral, by C. J. P. Cave.
e Wall-paintings in Croughton church, Northants., by E. W. Tristram and M. R. James.
f Excavations at Chun castle, in Penwith, Cornw., by E. Thurlow Leeds. [Contd. in vol. 81]
g Excavation of a tumulus at Lexden, Colchester, by P. G. Laver.
h Excavations at Merton priory [Surr.], by H. F. Bidder and H. F. Westlake. [Reprinted in *Surrey Archaeological Collections*, xxxviii]
i The great astrolabe and other scientific instruments of Humphrey Cole [fl. 1570–80], by R. T. Gunther.

5193 Vol. 77.

a Early chessmen of whale's bone excavated in Dorset [Witchampton], by O. M. Dalton.
b An account of the expenses of Eleanor, sister of Edward III, on the occasion of her marriage to Reynald, Count of Guelders, by E. W. Safford.
c Deerhurst priory church [Glos.], by W. H. Knowles.
d Post-Reformation ecclesiastical seals of Durham, by C. H. Hunter Blair.
e Pre-Roman remains at Scarborough, by R. A. Smith.
f St. Augustine's abbey church, Canterbury, before the Norman conquest, by C. R. Peers and A. W. Clapham.
g The carved stones at Breedon on the Hill [church], Leics., and their position in the history of English art, by A. W. Clapham.
h Reculver [Kent]: its Saxon church and cross, by C. R. Peers.
i Some clocks and jacks, with notes on the history of horology, by R. P. Howgrave-Graham.
j The decoration of the Beauchamp chapel, Warwick, with special reference to the sculptures, by P. B. Chatwin.

5194 Vol. 78.

a Seals of the religious houses of Yorkshire, by C. Clay.
b Roman London: its initial occupation as evidenced by early types of terra sigillata, by T. D. Pryce and F. Oswald.
c The Roman amphitheatre at Caerleon, Mon., by R. E. M. Wheeler and Tessa V. Wheeler.
d An investigation of two Anglo-Saxon kalendars (missal of Robert of Jumièges and St. Wulfstan's homiliary), by Sir I. Atkins.
e The Sheldon tapestry weavers and their work, by E. A. B. Barnard and A. J. B. Wace.

5195 Vol. 79.

a The iconography of St. Thomas of Canterbury [d. 1170], by T. Borenius. [Contd. in vols. 81 and 83]
b The uranical astrolabe and other inventions of John Blagrave of Reading [d. 1611], by R. T. Gunther.
c Roof bosses in the nave of Tewkesbury abbey, by C. J. P. Cave.
d Corfe castle [Dors.]: its history, construction, and present condition, by S. Toy.
e The epigraphy of medieval English seals, by H. S. Kingsford.

5196 Vol. 80.

a A bronze cauldron from the river Cherwell, Oxon., with notes on cauldrons and other bronze vessels of allied types, by E. Thurlow Leeds.

b Romano-Celtic art in Northumbria, by R. G. Collingwood.

c Excavations at Kingsdown camp, Mells, Som., by H. St. G. Gray.

d The chambered cairn of Bryn Celli Ddu [Anglesey], by W. J. Hemp.

5197 Vol. 81.

a A west country school of masons [of the 12th cent.], by Sir H. Brakspear.

b The Easby [Yorks.] cross, by M. Longhurst.

c 14th cent. glass at Wells [Som.], by J. Armitage Robinson.

5198 Vol. 83.

a An examination of two Anglo-Saxon manuscripts of the Winchester school: the missal of Robert of Jumièges, and the benedictional of St. Aethelwold, by J. B. L. Tolhurst.

b Roof bosses in the transepts of Norwich cathedral church, by C. J. P. Cave.

c Kidwelly castle, Carm.; including a survey of the polychrome pottery found there and elsewhere in Britain, by C. Fox and C. A. R. Radford; with an inventory of the polychrome pottery found in England, by G. C. Dunning.

d The abbot's house at Battle [Suss.], by Sir H. Brakspear.

e The bronze spear-head in Great Britain and Ireland, by E. E. Evans.

f The round castles of Cornwall, by S. Toy.

g Discoveries in the nave of Westminster abbey, by L. E. Tanner and A. W. Clapham.

h An excavation by H.M. Office of Works at Chysauster [Chysoyster], Cornw., by H. O'Neill Hencken.

i London customs houses during the middle ages [14th cent.], by Mabel H. Mills.

Reports of the research committee, nos. 1-10:

5199 Nos. 1, 2, 4. Excavations on the site of the Roman town at Wroxeter, Salop, by J. P. Bushe-Fox. 3 vols. 1913-16.

5200 No. 3. Excavations at Hengistbury Head, Hants, by J. P. Bushe-Fox. 1915.

5201 No. 5. Excavation of the late-Celtic urn-field at Swarling, Kent, by J. P. Bushe-Fox. 1925.

5202 Nos. 6, 7, 10. First, second and third reports on the excavation of the Roman fort at Richborough, Kent, by J. P. Bushe-Fox. 3 vols. 1926-32.

5203 No. 8. Report on the excavation of the Roman cemetery at Ospringe, Kent, by W. Whiting, W. Hawley and T. May. 1931.

5204 No. 9. Report on the excavation of the prehistoric, Roman, and post-Roman site in Lydney Park, Glos., by R. E. M. Wheeler and Tessa V. Wheeler. 1932.

5205 Vetusta monumenta quae ad rerum Britannicarum memoriam conservandam Societas Antiquariorum Londoni sumptu suo edenda curavit, vol. 7. Large folio. [1892?]-1906.

a Pt. 1: The [early 13th cent.] tomb of an archbishop [probably Hubert Walter] recently opened in the cathedral church of Canterbury, by W. H. St. J. Hope. [1892?].

b Pt. 2: The atchievements [*sic*] of Edward, Prince of Wales (the 'Black prince'), in the cathedral church of Canterbury [i.e. relics of the Prince hanging above his tomb], by W. H. St. J. Hope. 1895.

c Pt. 3: The royal gold cup of the kings of France and England, now preserved in the British Museum [14th cent., belonged originally to Charles VI of France and then to Henry VI of England], by C. H. Read. 1904.

d Pt. 4: The obituary roll of John Islip, abbot of Westminster, 1500-32, with notes on other English obituary rolls, by W. H. St. J. Hope. 1906.

Other publications:

5206 An archaeological survey of Northants., by T. J. George. P. 1904.

5207 General index to Proceedings, 2nd ser., vols. 1-20, with a classified list of illustrations. 1908. [Index to vols. 21-32 was published in 1938]

5208 Illustrated catalogue of the exhibition of English medieval alabaster work held in the rooms of the Society, 1910. 1913.

5209 The excavations at Old Sarum. P. [1913].

5210 The excavations at Wroxeter, Shropshire. P. [1913].

5211 The Antiquaries Journal, general index, vols. 1-10. 1934.

SOCIETY OF ANTIQUARIES OF NEWCASTLE-UPON-TYNE

Founded 1813, to inquire into antiquities in general, but especially into those of the North of England, and of the counties of Northumberland, Cumberland, and Durham in particular.

Proceedings, new ser., vols. 9-10 (1899-1902):

5212 Vol. 9.

a Re-opening of St. Cuthbert's tomb [in Durham cathedral], by E. J. Taylor.

b Croft [Yorks., St. Peter's church].

c Hurworth [co. Durham].

d Sockburn [co. Durham].

e Dinsdale church [co. Durham].

f Middleton Low Hall [co. Durham].

g Rothbury church [Northumb.].

h Alnham [Northumb.].

i Whittingham [church, Northumb.].

j Hirst [Northumb.], by W. W. Tomlinson.

k Woodhorn church [Northumb., by W. W. Tomlinson].

l [History of the castle, Newcastle-upon-Tyne, by C. J. Bates]

m Church briefs, by J. Bailey. [Contd. in new ser., vol. 10]

n A list of the proprietors of the New Assembly Rooms, Newcastle [with biographical notes], by J. Robinson.

o A Palmyrene inscription illustrating the epitaph of Regina [a British freed woman] in the South Shields museum, by T. Hodgkin.

p Three old documents [including a grant of land by Robert Anderson, esq., of Newcastle, to Ralph Fowler, merchant, of the same, 1630], by J. Ventress.

q Note on the orderly book of the 2nd battalion of Northumberland Militia, 1798-99, by W. W. Tomlinson.

r Heraldic visit to Seaton Delaval [Northumb.] at the end of the 19th cent., by S. S. Carr.

s Stamfordham [church, Northumb.].

t An early [18th cent.] 'award on umpirage' of Gabriel Reed relating to the 'Petty Knowes' in Redesdale, by T. Stephens.

u The Lacys of Tynemouth, Newcastle and Eden Lacy, by S. S. Carr.

v Harbottle castle [Northumb.], by D. D. Dixon.

w Alwinton church [Northumb.].

x Hepple Wood House [includes an account of Hepple pele].

y Mount Grace priory [Yorks.].

z Whorlton church and castle [Yorks.].

aa Norton church [co. Durham].

bb Billingham church [co. Durham].
cc Greatham hospital [co. Durham].

5213 Vol. 10.

a Newton Cap bridge, near Bishop Auckland, by J. Thompson.
b Pardon [1660] to Robert Ellison.
c Hepple pele [Northumb.], by D. D. Dixon.
d East Shaftoe [Northumb.].
e The clergy of Newcastle and Gateshead in 1774, by C. E. Adamson.
f Bishop Middleham [co. Durham].
g Sedgefield [co. Durham].
h Redmarshall [co. Durham].
i Great Stainton.
j Stannington [Northumb.].
k Will of Thomas Ogle [d. 1648] of Dublin, *alias* of Tritlington.
l A small hoard of [Roman] coins from Carrawburgh.
m The charity schools of the 18th cent., by H. E. Savage.
n Brinkburn priory [Northumb.].
o Morpeth and Bothal [Northumb.].
p Tynemouth [church and castle, Northumb.].
q [Documents relating to the bishopric of Durham, 13th–19th cent.]
r Egliston abbey and Barnard Castle [co. Durham].

Proceedings, 3rd ser., vols. 1–10 (1903–22):

5214 Vol. 1.

a [A number of documents relating to co. Durham, 13th–19th cent.]
b Chipchase castle.
c Wallsend (Segedunum).
d Roman altar to 'Oceanus' and altar base from the Tyne bridge [Newcastle].
e Mitford [Northumb.].
f The ancient British camp known as 'The Castles' near Hamsterley, Durham, by E. Wooler.
g Roman tablet from the Tyne at Newcastle, by R. O. Heslop.
h Ulgham, Widdrington, and Chibburn [Northumb.].
i Bishopwearmouth tythe barn, by J. Robinson.
j A civil war letter [printed, from Rotterdam] of 17 Dec. 1642, relating to Newcastle, by H. A. Adamson.
k Ancient Piercebridge [co. Durham], by E. Wooler.
l Notes from a Delaval 'diary', by H. H. E. Craster. [Ms. in the Rawlinson collection, written by Lady Elizabeth Livingstone, b. 1649, later wife of Robert Delaval]
m Town walls of Newcastle, by R. O. Heslop.
n Old deeds relating to Newcastle [16th–19th cent.].
o Ancroft, Ford, and Etal [Northumb.].
p Askerton castle [Cumb.].
q Bewcastle [Cumb.].
r St. Helen's Auckland [co. Durham].
s A Roman centurial stone from West Denton [Northumb.], by R. O. Heslop.

5215 Vol. 2.

a Seven civil war tracts of local interest, 1642–9. [Notes and abstracts of their contents]
b Index to later Northumbrian inquisitions *post mortem* [15 Hen. VIII—21 Charles I], by Miss M. T. Martin.
c Some Orde deeds [at Ford Castle], by H. E. Craster.
d [Mss. relating to the building of Holy Island fort in 1675–6]
e The Catrail [an ancient earthwork extending from Galashiels in Scotland to Peel Fell, Northumb.], by E. Wooler.
f Jesmond. [Suit in 1404 concerning the presentation to the chapel there]
g Coldingham, Fast castle, etc. [Scotland].

h Pre-historic burials near Bamburgh, by E. A. Filby.
i Darlington market cross [co. Durham], by E. Wooler.
j [Notes on the history of Chester-le-Street, co. Durham]
k Bellingham [Northumb.].
l Brancepeth [castle and church of St. Brandon, co. Durham].
m Ancient remains discovered at Grindon hill, near Sunderland, by J. Robinson.
n Wolsingham church and parish [co. Durham], by E. Wooler.
o Old Park, co. Durham [and its owners], by J. Thompson.
p Dog spits, etc., by M. Phillips.
q [Reprint of a tract relating to the blowing up of two wrecks in Tynemouth harbour, 1673]
r 'Pilgrimage' along the line of the Roman wall [Wallsend to Bowness-on-Solway].
s Ripon.
t The Tyne foreshore [being notes on the Alderley mss. relating to a suit of the corporation of Newcastle against the dean and chapter of Durham, 1668–70].
u Gainford [co. Durham].
v St. Andrew's, Winston [co. Durham].
w Raby castle [co. Durham].
x Lanchester [co. Durham].

5216 Vol. 3.

a Manners and customs in our grandfathers' days [18th and 19th cent.], by M. Phillips.
b Buryness [Byrness, Northumb.] register of baptisms and burials [1797–1812].
c [Extracts relating chiefly to the Hexham riots, 1761, from] a ms. diary of John Dawson of Brunton.
d Epitaphs in Wallsend old churchyard.
e Aycliffe [co. Durham].
f Heighington [co. Durham].
g Three ancient documents relating to Northumberland and one [1380] belonging to Sir Algernon Legard, bt.
h Refoundation charter of Syon abbey [1557].
i Norham [church and castle, Northumb.].
j Discovery of pre-historic burials at Fatfield, co. Durham, by R. H. Jeffreys.
k Northumbrian wills [abstracts] from the city act books, and from the probate registry, at York.
l Antonine wall.
m A Jacobean book of arms [1617], by C. Hunter Blair.
n Ancient local documents. [Includes the will of Eleanor Hornby, 1537, of Newcastle, and selections from Gateshead parish accounts, early 18th cent.]
o Kirkby Stephen. [Includes accounts of Wharton Hall and Pendragon castle, in Mallerstang]
p Bolam and Whalton [Northumb.].
q Holy Island [i.e. Lindisfarne].

5217 Vol. 4.

a [Grant from the crown of chapels and chantry lands in co. Durham, 1586]
b Local muniments. [Includes an 'indenture of Sir John de Cromwell and Sir Robert de Umfraville, Earl of Angus, concerning the custody of the parts of Northumberland', 1319–20]
c Street nomenclature on Oliver's plan of Newcastle in 1830, by R. O. Heslop.
d Miscellanea. [Includes a selection of letters relating to Elswick colliery, 1698–1732]
e Stanwick St. John's church [Yorks.].
f [A petition of Sir Ralph Gray, of Chillingham, 1620, from chancery proceedings]
g The 'praetorium' at Chesters (Cilurnum), by Mrs. T. H. Hodgson.
h The rectorial, or great, tithes of Long Houghton, by J. C. Hodgson.

i Miscellanea. [Will of Richard Wright of Langley, near Durham, 1684]

j The Barras mill, Newcastle, by J. D. Walker. [A grant of the mill and close at Barras bridge, by the mayor and commonalty, 1503]

k Miscellanea. [Includes extracts from the pipe rolls, 1336–38, relating to repairs to the castle of Newcastle]

l Alnwick [Northumb.].

m Lower Teesdale. [Includes accounts of Croft, Hurworth, Sockburn, Dinsdale, Middleton St. George, Egglescliffe, Longnewton, Sadberge, and Haughton-le-Skerne]

n Miscellanea. Seaton Delaval. [A few letters of the Delaval family, chiefly relating to parliamentary elections in 1715]

o Miscellanea. [Deeds and other documents relating to co. Durham, 17th cent.]

5218 Vol. 5.

a The palatinate boroughs of Durham, by E. Wooler.

b The manor of Coniscliffe [co. Durham], by E. Wooler.

c [Notes on the brass matrix of the 14th cent. seal of Ralph, the farrier, etc., of the bishop of Durham, and on horse-shoes in general]

d Houghton-le-Spring [co. Durham].

e Elsdon [Northumb.].

f Notices on the devotion to, and relative popularity of saints in Northumberland, in early times, as indicated by the dedications of the churches, by J. C. Hodgson.

g The market cross of Newcastle, commonly called the White cross, by R. O. Heslop.

h Discoveries *per lineam valli* [Hadrian's Wall, between Birdoswald and Appletree turret], by F. G. Simpson.

i Memorandum on the material available for a history of the Society, by H. H. E. Craster.

j Inventory of books and papers preserved in the diocesan registry, Durham, with notes of similar documents in other depositories, comp. H. H. E. Craster.

k Segedunum [being a note on recent discoveries at Wallsend], by W. S. Corder.

l Deodatus Threlkeld, of Newcastle, watchmaker [d. 1733], by J. C. Hodgson.

5219 Vol. 6.

a Two 18th cent. Newcastle worthies, by J. C. Hodgson. 1: Samuel Hallowell, surgeon [d. 1760]. 2: William Newton, architect [d. 1798].

b Seaham [co. Durham].

c Newminster abbey [near Morpeth].

d Cartington oak coffin, etc. [probably bronze age].

e [Documents of the early 18th cent. relating to the Derwentwater family. Contd. in 3rd ser., vol. 7]

f Mitford, Hartburn, and Wallington [Northumb.].

g Corstopitum.

h Stockton[-on-Tees, co. Durham].

i Bewcastle [Cumb.].

j Finchale priory [co. Durham].

k Frenchman's Row [Heddon, Northumb.]: an episode in the French revolution. [The temporary settlement in Northumberland of French refugee clerics, 1796–1802]

5220 Vol. 7.

a [Proceedings in the sheriff's court, Newcastle, between Henry Maddison and Nicholas Cole, 1601]

b Reports. 1: Pre-Roman remains in Upper Coquetdale, by P. Brewis and D. D. Dixon. 2: Roman monuments, etc. in Northumberland, by F. G. Simpson and P. Newbold.

c Old Hartley colliery [Northumb., 1774–1808], by W. W. Tomlinson.

d Centenary of the safety lamp: local helpers of Sir Humphry Davy, by J. Oxberry.

e St. Nicholas's cathedral church, Newcastle-upon-Tyne.

f Armour notes, with some account of the tournament, by R. Coltman Clephan.

g A prehistoric implement [a polished stone axe], by A. Watts.

h Incumbents of Stannington [Northumb., 1100–1909], comp. J. C. Hodgson.

i Monumental inscriptions in Bath abbey connected with Northumberland and Durham, by J. C. Hodgson.

j Roman fort near Northallerton? [Brief discussion of the evidence]

k The collar of 'esses', by W. H. Cullen. [With a list of collars of SS on monumental effigies in England. Contd. in 4th ser., vols. 8 and 10]

l The Williams family of Newcastle [18th cent. glass manufacturers], by J. C. Hodgson.

m Thomas White, of Woodlands, arboriculturist [d. 1811], by J. C. Hodgson.

n Denis Grenville, dean of Durham, 1684–1703. [A letter, dated 1682]

o The Whites of Woodlands and the Rev. John Hodgson [d. 1845], by J. Oxberry.

5221 Vol. 8.

a Miscellanea. [Deeds of houses in Newcastle]

b Two chapters from the history of Upper Coquetdale, by J. C. Hodgson. 1: Cartington. 2: Harbottle.

c Miscellanea. [Correspondence of John Bell of Gateshead, 1843–57]

d George Marsh the elder [d. 1760] and George Marsh the younger [d. 1795], successively rectors of Ford [Northumb.], by J. C. Hodgson.

e Notes on the chantry chapel and cantarists of Alnwick castle, 1362–1548, by J. W. Fawcett.

f The statute merchant and statute staple seals of Newcastle, York and Westminster, by C. H. Hunter Blair.

g Deeds, etc., relating to Northumberland [17th–18th cent., a list].

h Northumbrian and Novocastrian epitaphs in Westmorland, by J. W. Fawcett.

i Richard Peck, an 18th cent. coal viewer [d. 1746], by J. C. Hodgson.

j Early Northumbrian deeds [12th–16th cent., in the Public Record Office].

k Rev. Robert Patten [d. 1733]: cleric, rebel, historian, by J. W. Fawcett.

l Bishop Neile's subscription book, 1617–28, by W. Brown.

m Notices of the lay rectory of Ovingham [Northumb.], by J. H. Hinde.

n A sixteenth-cent. Newcastle clergy list [chronological, 1501–1600], by J. W. Fawcett.

5222 Vol. 9.

a An interleaved copy of Lilly's *Merlini Anglici Ephemeris*, 1648, containing the diary of Maj. John Sanderson of Hedleyhope, from Jan. to Dec. 1648, written on the interleaves.

b Minor historians and topographical writers of Northumberland [17th–19th cent.], by J. C. Hodgson.

c Miscellanea. [Includes a list of the abbots of Alnwick, 1147–1540]

d The Coleman deeds [being an abstract of a collection of deeds of the 17th–19th cent. relating to co. Durham, Northumberland or Newcastle].

e [Will of Margaret Conyers, of Durham, 1724]

f [Notes on the township of Spittle, Ovingham, by J. C. Hodgson]

g Chantries in Northumberland, by J. W. Fawcett.

h ['Distribution of the Papists' Horses within the county

of Northumberland to the severall Officers of the Militia', *c.* 1688–90]

i Pummer colliery, near Barnsley, Yorks.

j Lord lieutenants of Northumberland. [List, 1552–1918]

k Traces of the celtic pantheon found during the Corbridge excavations, 1906–14, by G. R. B. Spain.

l Thomas Slack, Newcastle printer [fl. 1764], by J. Oxberry.

m Notices of Reynold Gideon Bowyer, sometime archdeacon of Northumberland [d. 1826], by J. C. Hodgson.

n Ancient effigy in St. Nicholas's church, Newcastle, by R. Coltman Clephan.

o Vicars of Ponteland [Northumb., 1297–1895], by H. M. Wood.

p Effigies in St. Mary's church, Stamfordham [Northumb.], by C. Hunter Blair.

q The sculptured reredos, Stamfordham church, by A. Hamilton Thompson.

r Early schools, etc., in Northumberland, by J. W. Fawcett.

5223 Vol. 10.

a John Scafe, a Northumbrian minor poet [d. 1856], by J. C. Hodgson.

b Roman pottery from Chester-le-Street, by G. R. B. Spain.

c Fowberry, Northumb. [abstracts of title, 1587–1816, relating to property there], by J. W. Fawcett.

d An old bell [1610] at Gateshead Fell church [co. Durham], by J. Oxberry.

e John Brough Taylor, F.S.A. [d. 1825], a Sunderland antiquary, by J. C. Hodgson.

f Tynemouth priory.

g Seaton Delaval Hall [and church, Northumb.].

h High Warden hill [and prehistoric camp].

i 'The Castles' [prehistoric] camp, Weardale.

j Newcastle, St. Andrew's church.

k Minor historians and topographers of the county of Durham [17th–19th cent.], by J. W. Fawcett. [Contd. in 4th ser., vol. 2]

l [Abstract of a collection of deeds of 1669–1793 relating to property at Hamsterley in Weardale, by J. W. Fawcett]

m Hunstanworth [co. Durham]: its geography and history, by J. W. Fawcett.

n An excavation at Chesters [Cilurnum] in Oct. 1921.

o [Earthworks near Bolam, Northumb., by T. Ball]

p Bedlington church [Northumb.].

q Butsfield township, by Satley, co. Durham, by J. W. Fawcett.

r Whickham church.

s The Rev. Thomas Hobbes Scott [d. 1860], by J. W. Fawcett.

t The Unthanks of Unthank [Alnham].

u Note on a pillar stoup from Easby abbey, Yorks., by C. H. Hunter Blair.

v Early Tardenois remains at Bamburgh, etc., by F. Buckley.

w Seaham church, by A. Hamilton Thompson.

x Whitburn [church], by A. Hamilton Thompson.

y West Boldon [church], by A. Hamilton Thompson.

z Hilton castle, by A. Hamilton Thompson.

aa The manor of Consett [co. Durham], by J. W. Fawcett.

Proceedings, 4th ser., vols. 1–6 (1923–35):

5224 Vol. 1.

a Hill and plateau forts near Otterburn [Northumb.], by T. Ball.

b Incumbents of St. Hild's, South Shields [1256–1917], by H. T. Giles.

c Sedgefield rectors [1085–1923], by H. T. Giles.

d Old Benwell tower chapel and its graveyard, by J. W. Fawcett.

e Mote hills in south Northumberland, by T. Ball.

f Lanchester collegiate church and its deans [1283–1532], by J. W. Fawcett.

g Early earthworks in Northumberland, by R. C. Hedley.

h The collegiate church of Chester-le-Street, co. Durham, and its deans [1311–1544], by J. W. Fawcett.

i The collegiate church of Darlington, co. Durham, and its vicars and deans [1309–1534], by J. W. Fawcett.

j Abstracts of documents relating to the county of Durham [in the possession of Lady Lawson-Tancred].

k Cells and hermitages in co. Durham, by J. W. Fawcett.

l The office of coroner with reference to those of the county palatine of Durham, and especially of Chester ward, by J. W. Fawcett.

m Lord lieutenants of the county of Durham [1536–1884], by J. W. Fawcett.

n John Stokoe [d. 1852], Napoleon's Northumbrian surgeon, by A. Brewis.

o Sir John Duck [d. 1691], the butcher baronet of Durham, by J. W. Fawcett.

p Some rectilinear earthworks in Northumberland, by T. Ball.

q Miscellanea. [Includes: An award for the division of Cresswell, 1595]

r Three generations of London booksellers [of the Vaillant family, 1686–1802] and their descendant, Paul Vaillant of Hexham [d. 1816], by J. C. Hodgson.

s Warkworth [Northumb.].

t Langley castle.

u Whitley castle [Roman camp, Northumb.].

v On the pedigree of Cotesworth of the Hermitage [West Acomb, Northumb.], by J. C. Hodgson.

w Forgotten or ruined churches or chapels in co. Durham, by J. W. Fawcett.

x Heddon-on-the-Wall church [Northumb.].

y Ovingham church [Northumb.].

z Piercebridge, Stanwick, and Staindrop [co. Durham].

aa The manor of Satley [co. Durham], by J. W. Fawcett.

bb The trenches at Chesters, Oct. 30th, 1924.

5225 Vol. 2.

a [Transcript of notes of the contents of documents in the Durham cathedral treasury, by J. C. Hodgson]

b Blue Crag promontory fort, Colwell, North Tyne, Northumb., by T. Ball.

c The rectors of Redmarshall [co. Durham, 1258–1914], by H. T. Giles.

d Willimoteswyke castle [Northumb.], by J. Gibson.

e A section across Dere street [Roman road], near Swinburn, Northumb., by T. Ball.

f Deeds relating to land in Upperdean Bridge [Newcastle], by A. M. Oliver.

g The manor of Crook Hall, by Leadgate, co. Durham, by J. W. Fawcett.

h The compilation of parish clergy lists, with special reference to the diocese of Durham, by J. W. Fawcett.

i Miscellanea. [Includes exchequer depositions, 1607, on behalf of Joshua Delavall, plaintiff, against Thomas and Mabel Middleton, defendants]

j The manor of Pontop, co. Durham, by J. W. Fawcett.

k Archdeacon Thorpe's visitation of Northumberland, 1792–3, by J. W. Fawcett.

l Naworth castle [Cumb.], by J. Gibson.

m Finchale priory, near Durham.

n Monumental inscriptions of St. Hild's churchyard, South Shields, by H. T. Giles. [Contd. in 4th ser., vols. 3, 4, and 6]

o Ripon minster [Yorks.], by A. Hamilton Thompson.

p Fountains abbey [Yorks.], by A. Hamilton Thompson.

q A Shipley charter [a grant of Ysouda, daughter of Wido the glazier, c. 1219-44, to the convent of St. Mary of Coldstream], by F. W. Dendy.

r Cloisters; with special reference to Newminster, by H. L. Honeyman.

s Miscellanea. [Includes exchequer depositions concerning Kirkwhelpington parsonage, 1583, and the Edward the Sixth grammar school at Morpeth, 1630]

5226 Vol. 3.

a The friction match and what it superseded: a centenary review, by J. Oxberry.

b Norham castle [Northumb.], by C. H. Hunter Blair.

c Ingram church [Northumb.].

d Greaves Ash [near Linhope, a prehistoric site].

e The topography of Bamburgh.

f Bamburgh Friars, Magdalene chapel and leper hospital, by R. G. A. Hutchinson.

g Grave slabs at Newminster, by C. H. Hunter Blair.

h Lanchester: the Roman fort.

i The Causey arch at Tanfield [co. Durham], by H. L. Honeyman.

j Notes and miscellanea. 17th cent. colliers [extracts from the *London Gazette*].

k Head of a [Romano-British] statue from Benwell.

l North country apprentices: a list of Durham and Northumberland men who served their apprenticeships with the Drapers company, London, 1615-50, by H. M. Wood. [Contd. for 1651-75 in 4th ser., vol. 4, and for 1676-1700 in vol. 5]

m Donations to the museum: Roman altar from Hexham.

n Bronze age burial at West Wharmley [Northumb.], by R. C. and W. P. Hedley.

o Hilton castle, co. Durham, by H. L. Honeyman.

p Roman Newcastle: the investigation committee's reports.

5227 Vol. 4.

a Armorial glass in Stannington church [Northumb.], by C. H. Hunter Blair.

b [Notes on ancient trackways in the Rothbury district, Northumb., by E. R. Newbigin]

c Opening of barrows in Swinburne Park [Northumb.], by T. Ball.

d Manside cross and Gunners Box camp [earthwork], by H. L. Honeyman.

e Note upon a shield of arms at Bewcastle, by C. H. Hunter Blair.

f The Society's collection of coins: catalogue of the British section, by J. D. Cowen.

g Frescoes in Escombe church [co. Durham], by T. Ball.

h The 'vallum' crossings [of Hadrian's wall], by H. L. Honeyman.

i The Roman fort at Newbrough [Northumb.], by F. G. Simpson.

j The making of Grey Street [Newcastle], by J. Oxberry.

k Two deeds of Tobias, bishop of Durham [1595-1606].

l Hadrian's wall: a system of numerical references, by R. G. Collingwood.

m Woolworkers and their processions in Gateshead, Newcastle and elsewhere, by F. W. Dendy.

n Armorials in the parish church of St. Mary, Gateshead, by C. H. Hunter Blair.

o Tumuli south of Bamburgh castle [Northumb.], by R. H. Hodgkin.

p Sun-dials at Escombe [church, co. Durham], by T. Ball.

q An Anglo-Saxon 'hanging-bowl' from a burial of the pagan period in Northumberland, by J. D. Cowen.

r The Blackhall deeds [being a calendar of sixteen deeds, 1538-1748, connected with the estate of Blackhall,

Hexhamshire, Northumb.], by H. L. Honeyman and F. W. Dendy.

s Crosses at Escombe church [co. Durham], by T. Ball.

5228 Vol. 5.

a Notes from Greenwich Hospital northern estates reports, 1821-3, by J. Oxberry.

b Newcastle-upon-Tyne oar-mace, by T. Wake.

c Local muniments. Some Northumberland and Durham deeds [17th-18th cent.].

d The Kemble family, by H. Oswald.

e The portraits of James Allan, the Northumbrian piper [d. 1810], by G. Askew.

f A mid 18th-cent. Presbyterian minister's pocket-book [the Rev. Robert Trotter, d. 1807], by J. Oxberry.

g Kirkheaton [manor-house].

h Mount Grace priory [Yorks.], by C. C. Hodges.

i Excavations near the Moot Hall [Newcastle], by J. Charlton.

j The Dixon collection [of prehistoric antiquities, chiefly flints], by J. D. Cowen.

k The 'vallum' crossings: a criticism of the stone transport theory of their purpose, coupled with an alternative explanation, by W. W. Gibson.

l Corbridge manor house [Northumb.], by W. P. Hedley and J. Charlton.

m 1814-17: notes from the diary of a Sunderland youth, by J. Oxberry.

n John Horsley [d. 1732], by J. W. Duff.

5229 Vol. 6.

a Roman stones in the Black Gate [Newcastle], by J. D. Cowen.

b Ludworth tower, by W. H. Knowles.

c The last days of the old Roman wall at Rudchester, by H. L. Honeyman. [Correspondence, 1752, relating to the construction of the military road from Newcastle to Carlisle]

d Effigy in Bishopwearmouth parish church, by C. H. Hunter Blair.

e Prehistoric earthworks on Doddington and Norton moors [Northumb.], by W. P. Hedley.

f List of prioresses of the Benedictine nunnery of S. Bartholomew of Newcastle [1227-1540].

g The incised rocks of Doddington district, by E. R. Newbigin.

h Doddington church, by H. L. Honeyman.

i Microlithic and other industries of the Wear valley, by H. Preston.

j Northern museums. 1: Municipal museum, Gateshead, by W. H. Young.

k The Hon. Lord Algernon Percy's election book, 1774, by T. Wake.

l The Ellsnook tumulus near Rock, by R. C. Bosanquet.

m Northern museums. 2: Alnwick Castle museum [and some of its exhibits], by J. D. Cowen.

n A note on the Benedictine nunnery at Holystone, by K. G. Hall.

o Elizabeth Elstob [d. 1756], Saxon scholar and author, by J. Oxberry.

p Museum notes. [Includes: A rare brooch from Benwell Roman camp]

q Busks as love-tokens, by R. P. R. Lyle and R. C. Bosanquet.

r The Society's 15th cent. fede-ring brooch, by T. Wake.

s Consecration cross at the Saxon church of St. Lawrence, Bradford-on-Avon, Wilts., by W. A. Ingledew.

t The execution of John Hall [Jacobite, 1716], by E. L. Guilford.

u James Allan's organ pipes. [James Allan, d. 1810, Northumbrian piper] v Notes on the Roman bridge and station at Piercebridge, by J. E. Hodgkin.

w Roman camps near High Rochester from the air, by K. St. Joseph.

x The Roman tombs near High Rochester, by R. C. Bosanquet.

y Report on a trial excavation at Old Bewick [earthworks], Sept. 1934, by J. Charlton.

z Notes on a former ownership of the Luttrell psalter, by O. J. Charlton.

aa Habitancum [Roman fort at Risingham], Bremenium [Roman fort at High Rochester], and Corseside.

bb The Hesleyside standard goblet, by O. Charlton and T. Wake. [Goblet of Northumbrian glass, *c.* 1761–78]

cc A note on two cup and ring-marked rocks at Fowberry park, by W. B. Davison.

dd John Bell [d. 1860], an inveterate collector, by J. Oxberry.

ee Buildings of the Carmelites or White friars of Newcastle, by K. G. Hall.

ff Cup marked rocks on Chirnells moor, Rothbury, by Nancy Newbigin.

gg Museum notes. [A Roman glass linen-smoother]

Archaeologia Aeliana: or miscellaneous tracts relating to antiquities, new ser., vols. 23–25 (1902–4):

5230 Vol. 23.

a Excavations at Chesters, by F. Haverfield.

b Tynemouth priory, to the dissolution in 1539, with notes of Tynemouth castle, by H. A. Adamson.

c On 'low side windows', by J. F. Hodgson.

d Researches into the origin of the name 'Ogle', by Sir H. A. Ogle.

e Local muniments [being an abstract of documents relating to the history of Newcastle and other parts of Northumb.], by R. Welford. [Contd. in new ser., vol. 24; 3rd ser., vols. 5, 12, and 13]

f The Boutflowers of Apperley, by D. S. Boutflower.

5231 Vol. 24.

a Excavations on the line of the Roman wall in Northumberland, by T. Hodgkins.

b Recent discoveries in the chapel of Raby castle [co. Durham], by J. P. Pritchett.

c The Brumell collection of charters, etc. [relating chiefly to the estates of the Northumbrian family of Ogle and to Burradon in Tynemouthshire, *c.* 1200–1828], by J. C. Hodgson.

d Abstract of deeds in the muniment room, Kirkleatham Hall [Yorks.], relating to the chantry of the B.V.M. in Chester-le-Street church [co. Durham], by T. M. Fallow.

e Proofs of age of heirs to estates in Northumberland, by J. C. Hodgson. [Contd. from vol. 22. Contd. in 3rd ser., vol. 3]

f Extracts from privy seal dockets relating principally to the north of England, by F. W. Dendy.

g Seaton Sluice [Northumb.], by W. W. Tomlinson.

h The 'Craster tables' [a Northumbrian roll of arms comp. 1631–2], by J. C. Hodgson.

5232 Vol. 25.

a Local muniments [eighteen documents relating to the disposal of lands in Northumb., 1197–1488], by W. Brown.

b Notes on a recent examination of certain structural features of the great tower or keep, of the castle of Newcastle, by R. O. Heslop.

c Ancient deeds relating to Gunnerton [Northumb.], by W. B. Hornby.

d The Villiers family as governors of Tynemouth castle and owners of the lighthouse, by H. A. Adamson.

e Early monumental remains of Tynemouth, by S. S. Carr.

f Discovery of Roman inscriptions, etc., at Newcastle. 1: A Roman altar to 'Oceanus' and altar base from the Tyne bridge, by R. O. Heslop and R. Mowat. 2: An inscribed slab, mentioning the 2nd, 6th, and 20th legions, from the river Tyne, by R. O. Heslop and F. Haverfield. 3: Two stone coffins of the Roman period, in one of them human bones and an urn, by F. W. Rich.

g Sources of Testa de Nevill, by J. C. Hodgson.

h Coupland castle [Northumb.], by M. Culley.

i Excavations on the line of the Roman wall in Northumberland: the Roman camp at Housesteads, by R. C. Bosanquet.

Archaeologia Aeliana, 3rd ser., vols. 1–21 (1904–24):

5233 Vol. 1.

a An account of Jesmond [Northumb.], by F. W. Dendy.

5234 Vol. 2.

a Purchases at Corbridge fair in 1298, by F. W. Dendy.

b The Killingworths of Killingworth [Northumb.], by F. W. Dendy.

c John Lomax, ejected from Wooler, Northumb., in 1662, with some account of his family, by M. Phillips.

d Documents relating to an incident at Newcastle after the battle of Flodden [1513], by R. O. Heslop.

e 17th and 18th cent. owners of Bewick [Northumb.], by J. C. Hodgson.

f Additional notices of the Walk-mill in the parish of Warkworth [Northumb.], by J. C. Hodgson.

g The flail and its varieties, by T. M. Allison.

h Notes on pre-historic burials on Tyneside and the discovery of two cists of the bronze period in Dilston park, by J. P. Gibson.

i The ancestry of Admiral Lord Collingwood [d. 1810], by J. C. Hodgson.

j The Presbyterian church at Morpeth, by W. Woodman.

k The murder of William Delaval in Northumberland in 1618, by H. H. E. Craster.

l A northern roll of arms [*c.* 1580], by H. H. E. Craster.

5235 Vol. 3.

a Early Newcastle typography, 1639–1800, by R. Welford. [Contd. in 3rd ser., vol. 4]

b Art and archaeology: the three Richardsons [Thomas Miles Richardson, d. 1848; Moses Aaron Richardson, d. 1871; George Bouchier Richardson, d. 1877], by R. Welford. [Contd. in 3rd ser., vol. 5]

c The Black Death in the palatinate of Durham, by F. Bradshaw.

d Corstopitum [Corbridge]: report of the excavations, by C. Leonard Woolley. [Contd. in 3rd ser., vol. 4 by R. H. Forster, and in vols. 5–9 and 11–12 by W. H. Knowles and R. H. Forster]

e An unpublished Northumbrian hundred roll [1274], by H. H. E. Craster.

f The capricorn of the 2nd legion, surnamed Augusta, and the goat of the 23rd regiment Royal Welsh Fusiliers, by R. Mowat.

g A book of north country arms of the 16th cent., with introd. and notes by C. Hunter Blair.

h Kepier school, Houghton-le-Spring [co. Durham], and its library, by R. W. Ramsay.

5236 Vol. 4.

a Exchequer commissions and depositions relating to Northumberland, by F. W. Dendy.

b An episode in the history of a Morpeth family [family of Marr, 1725], by J. C. Hodgson.

5247 Vol. 15.

a Early Northumbrian Christianity and the altars to the 'di veteres', by F. Haverfield.

b Thomas Cradock's estate, by D. S. Boutflower. [Thomas Cradock d. 1690]

c Remains of John Horsley, the historian [d. 1732], by J. C. Hodgson.

d Unpublished letters of Richard Dawes [d. 1766], sometime master of the grammar school and of the hospital of the Blessed Virgin Mary in Newcastle-upon-Tyne, by J. C. Hodgson.

e George Tate [d. 1871], the historian of Alnwick, by J. C. Hodgson.

5248 Vol. 16.

a Honorary members of the Society: a list [of those] elected during the first century of its existence [1813–1913]; annotated, with an introd. by J. Oswald.

b St. Elgy's chantry in All Saints' church, Newcastle-upon-Tyne, by A. M. Oliver.

c The manor and township of Ovington [Northumb.], by J. C. Hodgson.

d Notes on some place-names of Northumberland and co. Durham, by A. Mawer.

e Diary of Maj. Sanderson of Hedleyhope, for 1648, by J. Oxberry.

f Four unpublished letters of Dr. Richard Neile [d. 1640], bishop of Durham, by J. C. Hodgson.

5249 Vol. 17.

a Catalogue of inscribed and sculptured stones of the Roman era in possession of the Society (3rd edn.), by R. Blair.

b Thomas Slack of Newcastle, printer, 1723–84, founder of the *Newcastle Chronicle*, by J. Hodgson.

c Uthred of Boldon [c. 1315–96], by R. B. Hepple.

d Ancestry of John Hodgson Hinde [d. 1869], by J. C. Hodgson.

e The Clervaux chartulary, with abstracts of the deeds contained in it which relate to the property of the family of Clervaux in the county palatine of Durham, by A. Hamilton Thompson.

f An account of the family of Dagnia, of Newcastle and Shields, glass-makers, by H. M. Wood.

g A note upon medieval seals with special reference to those in Durham [cathedral] treasury, by C. H. Hunter Blair.

h Monastery of the Black friars, Newcastle-upon-Tyne, by W. H. Knowles.

5250 Vol. 18.

a Early Northumbrian history in the light of its place-names, by A. Mawer.

b Architectural characteristics of the parish churches of Northumberland, by A. Hamilton Thompson.

c Archbishop Savage's visitation of the diocese of Durham, *sede vacante*, 1501, by A. Hamilton Thompson.

d Shawdon [Northumb.] court rolls [1708, 1717 and 1719], by J. C. Hodgson.

e Notes on the Fenwicks of Brenkley [Northumb.], by A. F. Radcliffe.

f John Cunningham, pastoral poet, 1729–73: recollections and some original letters, by J. Hodgson.

g The manor and tower of Bitchfield [Northumb.]. 1: The manor, by J. C. Hodgson. 2: The tower, by J. Oswald and W. P. Brewis.

h Books of the companies of Glovers and Skinners of Newcastle-upon-Tyne, by A. Hamilton Thompson.

5251 Vol. 19.

a The company of Saddlers of Newcastle, by J. C. Hodgson.

b Notes on the old glass in St. John's church, Newcastle, by R. J. S. Bertram, A. Hamilton Thompson, and C. H. Hunter Blair.

c The lordship, manor and township of Beanley [Northumb.], by J. C. Hodgson.

d The hospital of St. Lazarus and the manor of Harehope [Northumb.], by J. C. Hodgson.

e Benwell Tower, Newcastle, by W. H. Knowles.

f Points in the architectural history of the priory church at Tynemouth, by C. C. Hodges.

g The 'Black Dyke' in Northumberland: an account of the earthwork, by G. R. B. Spain.

h Seals of Newcastle-upon-Tyne, by C. H. Hunter Blair.

i Deeds of St. Andrew's church, Newcastle-upon-Tyne, by A. M. Oliver.

j Minute-book and papers formerly belonging to the Mercers' company of the city of Durham, by A. Hamilton Thompson.

5252 Vol. 20.

a The manor and township of Shipley [Northumb.], by J. C. Hodgson.

b The manors of Brandon and Branton [Northumb.], by J. C. Hodgson.

c An altar from South Shields, now at Oxford, by R. G. Collingwood.

d A Roman inscribed slab from Hexham, and the worship of Concordia, by R. G. Collingwood.

e Seals of Northumberland and [co.] Durham, by C. H. Hunter Blair. [Contd. in 3rd ser., vol. 21]

5253 Vol. 21.

a The manor and township of Titlington [Northumb.], by J. C. Hodgson.

b The Merchants' company of Alnwick, by J. C. Hodgson and H. M. Wood.

c Otterburn: the tower, hall and dene, and the lordship, or manor, of Redesdale, by H. Pease.

d The masters of Horsley's school, Newcastle-upon-Tyne, by A. R. Laws.

e The baronies of Bolbec, by A. M. Oliver.

f Monumental inscriptions in Kirknewton church and churchyard [Northumb.], by J. C. Hodgson.

g Conventina's well [on Hadrian's wall], by J. R. Harris.

h British brooches of the Backworth type in the Black Gate museum, Newcastle, by W. P. Brewis.

i Some Bingfield deeds, by H. H. E. Craster.

j The diary of Timothy Whittingham [d. 1682] of Holmside [co. Durham], by J. C. Hodgson.

k Conventual buildings of the priory of Hexham, with a description of a recently discovered twin capital from the cloisters, by C. C. Hodges.

Archaeologia Aeliana, 4th ser., vols. 1–10 (1925–33):

5254 Vol. 1.

a Roman Durham [co.], by J. A. Petch.

b The township of Knitsley, co. Durham: its geography and history, by J. W. Fawcett.

c The microlithic industries of Northumberland, by F. Buckley.

d Notices on the family of Spearman, by J. C. Hodgson.

e Fenwick of Bywell: an episode in the history of that family [late 17th cent.], by J. C. Hodgson.

f Early carved stones at Hexham, by W. G. Collingwood.

g Roman Rudchester: report on excavations, by W. P. Brewis.

h Northern minstrels and folk drama, by Madeleine H. Dodds.

i Young of Etherdacre, by A. F. Radcliffe.

j The ancient cross of Rothbury [Northumb.], by C. C. Hodges.

k The oldest version of the Customs of Newcastle-upon-Tyne, by C. Johnson.

l Simondburn church, Northumb., by C. C. Hodges.

m Some Anglo-Saxon records of the see of Durham, by H. H. E. Craster.

n The pallium of S. Cuthbert, by F. W. Buckler.

o North country clockmakers of the 17th to 19th centuries, by C. L. Reid.

5255 Vol. 2.

a The castle, Newcastle-upon-Tyne, by W. H. Knowles.

b Roman inscriptions and sculptures belonging to the Society, by R. G. Collingwood.

c Featherstone castle, Northumb., by J. Gibson.

d Newspaper advertisements relating to the goldsmiths of Newcastle of the 18th cent., by F. Buckley.

e The 'Newcastle' galley, 1294, by R. J. Whitwell and C. Johnson.

f The excavations at Aesica, by M. R. Hull.

5256 Vol. 3.

a The Greenwell deeds preserved in the public library, Newcastle-upon-Tyne, calendared by J. Walton, with an introd. by A. Hamilton Thompson. [Documents ranging from 1137 to 1823 chiefly concerned with Kelloe, co. Durham, and its neighbourhood. See also vol. 7]

5257 Vol. 4.

a Armorials of the county palatine of Durham, by C. H. Hunter Blair.

b Potteries on the Tyne and other northern potteries during the 18th cent., by F. Buckley.

c The golden pots: notes on a series of socketed stones in Redesdale [Northumb.], by H. L. Honeyman.

d Six silver ring-brooches of the 14th cent. from Northumberland, by W. P. Brewis.

e Notes on the Roman wall at Denton Bank, Great Hill, and Heddon-in-the-Wall, Northumb., by W. P. Brewis.

f Excavations at Benwell (Condercum), by J. A. Petch. [Contd. in 4th ser., vol. 5]

g Finchale priory [co. Durham], by C. R. Peers.

5258 Vol. 5.

a The descent of the manor of Ellington [Northumb.], by G. G. Baker-Cresswell and H. H. E. Craster.

b Notes on pre-historic pottery and a bronze pin from Ross Links, Northumb., by W. P. Brewis and F. Buckley.

c A bronze age burial at Kyloe, Northumb., by W. P. Brewis.

d John Pigg [d. 1688], Newcastle's Puritan town surveyor, by J. Oxberry.

e Church of St. Mary Magdalene, Mitford, Northumb., by C. C. Hodges.

f Church of St. Bartholomew, Whittingham, Northumb., by C. C. Hodges.

g Embleton vicarage [Northumb.], by H. L. Honeyman.

h St. Mary's chapel and the site of St. Mary's well, Jesmond [Northumb.], by W. P. Brewis.

5259 Vol. 6.

a Medieval effigies in co. Durham, by C. H. Hunter Blair.

b The Little Book of the birth of St. Cuthbert, commonly called the Irish life of St. Cuthbert, translated with notes by Madeleine H. Dodds.

c The tile pavements at Newminster abbey, by H. L. Honeyman.

d Thomas Bewick [d. 1828]: a centenary appreciation, by T. Wake.

e Dr. John Lingard's notes on the Roman wall [dated 1800 and 1807], transcribed and annotated by R. C. Bosanquet.

f Notes on Hadrian's first and second boundaries in Britain, by W. P. Brewis.

g The river-names of Northumberland and Durham, by A. Mawer.

5260 Vol. 7.

a Medieval effigies in Northumberland, by C. H. Hunter Blair.

b A contemporary record of the pontificate of Ranulf Flambard, by H. H. E. Craster.

c The watch and clock-makers of Northumberland and Durham of the 17th and 18th centuries recorded in newspapers, directories etc., by F. Buckley.

d Roger Bertram's lands in Brenkley and Benwell [Northumb.], by A. F. Radcliffe.

e A second calendar of Greenwell deeds [including many non-local deeds], by F. W. Dendy, A. M. Oliver and C. H. Hunter Blair.

f Prior Leschman's chantry chapel in Hexham priory church, by C. H. Hunter Blair.

g The treasure vault of the Roman fort at Benwell (Condercum), by G. R. B. Spain.

h The Northumbrian bag-pipes, by G. V. B. Charlton.

i Excavations on Hadrian's wall west of Newcastle-upon-Tyne, by E. B. Birley. [Contd. in 4th ser., vols. 8 and 9 by F. G. Simpson and E. Birley, and in vol. 10 by E. Birley, W. P. Brewis and J. Charlton. The articles in vols. 9 and 10 form the reports for 1931 and 1932 of the North of England Excavation Committee]

5261 Vol. 8.

a Julius Verus and Hadrian's wall, by Sir G. Macdonald.

b The Walbottle (Throckley) hoard of Roman coins, by W. P. Hedley.

c The renaissance heraldry of Northumberland, by C. H. Hunter Blair.

d Trefoil rear-arches, by H. L. Honeyman.

e Bronze age settlement of the north of England, by A. Raistrick.

f Early furniture in the keep and Black Gate, Newcastle-upon-Tyne, by T. Wake.

g Introduction to the excavations of Chesterholm-Vindolanda, by E. Birley. [Contd. in 4th ser., vol. 9]

h The bath-house at the fort of Chesters (Cilurnum), by Sir G. Macdonald.

i The Capheaton bowl [Anglo-Saxon 'hanging bowl'], by J. D. Cowen.

5262 Vol. 9.

a Cavaliers and covenanters: the Crookham affray of 1678, by R. C. Bosanquet.

b Notes on a series of unrecorded incised rocks at Lordenshaws [Northumb.], by E. R. Newbigin.

c Origins of the Northumbrian pipes, by G. Askew.

d The cathedral church of St. Nicholas, Newcastle-upon-Tyne: a chronicle history by H. L. Honeyman, with a note on the furniture and pictures by T. Wake.

e Warkworth castle [Northumb.], by G. Reavell.

f Conjectural construction of turret no. 18a on Hadrian's wall, by W. P. Brewis.

g Excavations at Housesteads, by E. Birley and J. Charlton, with a note on the coins by W. P. Hedley. [Contd. in 4th ser., vol. 10]

5263 Vol. 10.

a John Horsley, scholar and gentleman [d. 1732], by Sir G. Macdonald.

b John Horsley and his times, by R. C. Bosanquet.

c Excavation of a cave at Bishop Middleham, [co.] Durham, by A. Raistrick.

d The castle of Durham in the middle ages, by C. E. Whiting.

e Norman decoration in Durham cathedral, by R. A. Cordingley.

f Members of parliament for Northumberland, Oct. 1258–Jan. 1327.

g John Bell's plan of St. Nicholas church, Newcastle [1831–2], by H. L. Honeyman.

h Two bronze swords from Ewart Park, Wooler, by J. D. Cowen.

i West Lilburn chapel, by H. L. Honeyman.

Other publications:

5264 General index to Archaeologia Aeliana, 2nd ser., vols. 17–25, 3rd ser., vols. 1–21, and to the Proceedings of the Society, 2nd ser., vols. 6–10, 3rd ser., vols. 1–10, being the publications of the Society from 1895–1924. 1925. [Archaeologia Aeliana, 4th ser., vol. 12 (1935) contains author and subject index to vols. 1–12 of the same series]

5265 The register of baptisms, marriages and burials solemnized in the ancient parish church of Elsdon, Northumb., 1672–1812, transcribed T. Stephens. 1903.

5266 Letters of Cadwallader John Bates [d. 1902, on antiquarian and archaeological matters], ed. M. Culley.

5267 The castle of Newcastle-upon-Tyne: a short descriptive guide to the Black Gate museum and Heron pit, by P. Brewis. *P.* 1914. [See note to following vol.]

5268 The cathedral church of St. Nicholas, Newcastle-upon-Tyne, by T. Wake. *P.* 1932. [Other short guides to the cathedral and castle were published by the Soc. but have not been found]

The book of the pilgrimage of Hadrian's wall, July 1st to 4th, 1930, comp. R. G. Collingwood. n.d. [See Cumberland and Westmorland Antiq. and Archaeol. Soc., no. **1231** above]

SOCIETY OF ARCHITECTS

Founded 1884, for the promotion and advancement of architectural art and practice, and its allied arts, sciences and crafts. Amalgamated with the Royal Institute of British Architects in 1925.

Architects' Magazine, vols. 1–7 (1900–7):

5269 Vol. 1.

a English architecture of the 19th cent., by G. A. T. Middleton.

b Some English cathedrals: Wells, Lincoln and Ely, by M. B. Adams.

5270 Vol. 2.

a Notes on Tideswell church, Derbys., by A. J. Thompson.

b Winchester cathedral: recent reparations to the nave roof, by A. R. Galbraith.

c Some ancient Hampshire palaces, by S. W. Kershaw.

5271 Vol. 3.

a The Strand [London], and its history, by A. Oliver.

b A famous city church: St. Giles, Cripplegate [London].

5272 Vol. 4.

a Robert Adam, architect and artist, by P. Fitzgerald.

b An old Cotswold mansion house [at Painswick, Glos.].

c The city of Coventry, by A. J. Brookes.

d Merton Abbey [Surr.]: its Nelson traditions.

e Peterborough cathedral: its architectural glories.

5273 Vol. 5.

a The church of Westminster abbey.

b Some historic buildings in the city of London, by T. R. Croger.

c The use of metalwork in mediaeval and modern lighting appliances, by G. W. Pridmore.

d The Costessey estate: an interesting Norfolk mansion.

5274 Vol. 6.

a The monasteries of the city of London.

b Paul's cross [London].

c Architecture of the Cotswolds in the 16th and 17th cent., by E. Marsland.

d Painted rood screens of East Anglia, by E. F. Strange.

e Shakespeare and old London, by T. R. Croger.

f The Elizabethan stage: old Blackfriars theatre.

g Concerning Waltham abbey [Essex].

h Blackfriars bridge: an old architectural feud.

i Willington church [Beds.].

5275 Vol. 7.

a An idyllic minster of the west country: Wells cathedral.

b Waltham abbey and the Essex cathedral.

c Two Benedictine minsters [Gloucester and Norwich cathedrals], by E. W. H. Piper.

d Recent discoveries at Hexham abbey [Northumb.].

Journal, including Transactions and Architectural Notes, new ser., vols. 1–15 (1907–22):

5276 Vol. 1.

a The passing of Crosby Hall [London].

b Hayles abbey, Glos. [Photographs of 13th and 15th cent. roof bosses]

c Burford [Oxon.], by H. F. Trew.

5277 Vol. 2.

a St. Guthlac's cell: discovery at Croyland abbey [Lincs.].

b After 25 years. [The inception, rise and progress of the Society. Reprinted from the *Building News*]

c Some old doorways, by H. Walker.

d Some wrought-iron inn signs, by G. Trotman.

e The Society's visit to Rochester. [Includes a description of the cathedral]

5278 Vol. 3.

a Some fonts from East Anglia and the midlands, by H. Walker.

b Ancient and modern ecclesiastical wood carving, by H. Walker.

c Ancient homesteads [half-timbered houses].

d Door knockers, by H. Walker.

5279 Vol. 4.

a The evolution of form in silver plate, by P. Macquoid.

b Hawton and its Easter sepulchre, by H. Walker.

c Some notes on English oak.

d Prelate architects of Lambeth Palace, by S. W. Kershaw.

e Barnack church, Northants., by H. Walker.

5280 Vol. 6.

a The Parthenon of England [Salisbury cathedral], by E. W. H. Piper.

b Some notes on Southwell cathedral, by H. Gill.

c Winchester cathedral, by E. W. H. Piper.

d Westminster abbey, by C. W. Ball.

e Some Devon parish churches of the 15th cent., by F. E. Howard.

f St. Alban's abbey, by E. W. H. Piper.

5281 Vol. 7.

a Church plate, by C. A. Markham.

b St. Mary-at-Hill [London], by F. M. Cashmore.

c The Society of Architects, 1884–1913, by C. McA. Butler.

d The rise and development of Norman architecture, by B. Fraser. [Synopsis only]

e Sussex houses of the archbishops, by S. W. Kershaw.

5282 Vol. 8.

a Roman and mediaeval discoveries in London, by F. Izant.

5283 Vol. 9.

a Ye olde grammar school, Bulwell [Notts., founded 1667], by H. Gill.

5284 Vol. 14.

a The city companies [of London] and their halls, by H. W. Wills.

5285 Vol. 15.

a Old Beaupré [Glam.], by F. W. Rees.

b Discoveries at Glastonbury abbey, by B. Bond.

c The study of ancient painted glass, by J. A. Knowles.

Architecture: the journal of the Society, vols. 16 [1]–3[1] (1922–5):

5286 Vol. 16 [1].

a Some portraits of Wren, by Sir L. Weaver.

b Robert and James Adam, by Sir A. Poynter.

5287 Vol. 2.

a Some London high-streets, by V. M. Christy.

b Waterloo bridge, by A. R. Dent.

c Old Regent Street special number, containing among other essays:

d The architecture of Regent Street, by H. J. Birnstingl.

e John Nash, town planner, by P. Abercrombie.

f The Bank of England, by A. R. Dent.

g Manchester, by J. Swarbrick.

h Wapping, by A. R. Dent.

5288 Vol. 3.

a [Sir Charles] Barry and the Greek revival, by A. R. Dent.

b East Meon [Hants] court house, by Gertrude Bone.

SOCIETY OF COMPARATIVE LEGISLATION

Founded 1894, to promote knowledge of the course of legislation in different countries, more particularly in the several parts of H.M. dominions and in the United States.

Journal, new ser., vols. 3–18 (1901–18):

5289 Vol. 3.

a Influence of English law and legislation upon the native laws of India since 1772, by W. H. Rattigan.

b History of the law of nature: a preliminary study, by Sir F. Pollock. [Contd. from vol. 2]

5290 Vol. 4.

a Naval or victualling stores: the right of pre-emption [being an account of the history of the Naval Prize Act], by R. G. Marsden.

5291 Vol. 5.

a History of comparative jurisprudence, by Sir F. Pollock.

5292 Vol. 6.

a Great jurists of the world. 5: Francis Bacon [d. 1626], by J. E. G. de Montmorency.

[1] Continued as an independent publication by the proprietors of *The Builder*.

5293 Vol. 7.

a The fate of the Roman-Dutch law in the British colonies, by R. W. Lee.

5294 Vol. 8.

a Great jurists of the world. 6: Thomas Hobbes [d. 1679], by J. E. G. de Montmorency.

b Censorship of stage plays, by W. F. Craies.

c Influence of national character and historical environment on the development of the common law, by J. Bryce.

5295 Vol. 9.

a Hobbes and Locke: the social contract in English political philosophy, by Sir F. Pollock.

b Great jurists of the world. 10: Richard Zouche [d. 1661], by C. Phillipson.

5296 Vol. 10.

a French law within the British Empire. Historical introduction: the field of its operation, by A. Wood-Renton.

5297 Vol. 11.

a Great jurists of the world. 13: Lord Stowell [William Scott, d. 1836], by N. Bentwich.

b Notes on land taxation in England [in the Roman and Anglo-Saxon periods], by W. P. B. Shepheard. [Contd. in new ser., vol. 12]

5298 Vol. 14.

a Spanish law in the British Empire, by C. E. Reis.

b The meaning of truth in history, by Viscount Haldane of Cloan.

5299 Vol. 15.

a Prize law, by R. G. Marsden.

5300 Vol. 16.

a Sir John Fortescue [d. 1476?], by H. J. Randall.

5301 Vol. 17.

a Sir William Blackstone [d. 1780], by J. E. G. de Montmorency.

b The civic position of women at common law before 1800, by Rose Graham.

5302 Vol. 18.

a Archdeacon Paley [d. 1805] as a jurist, by G. G. Alexander.

Journal, 3rd ser., vols. 1–15 (1919–33):

5303 Vol. 1.

a Origin and growth of income tax [1798–1918], by H. B. Cox.

b The foundation of the Bombay high court [1670–1726], by P. B.-M. Malabari.

5304 Vol. 2.

a The neutrality of the Channel Islands during the 15th, 16th and 17th cent., by E. T. Nicolle.

5305 Vol. 4.

a The development of naval courts martial [since 1571], by Sir R. Acland.

5306 Vol. 7.

a The 17th and 18th cent. privy council in its relations with the colonies, by H. E. Egerton.

5307 Vol. 8.

a The enlightenment of Lord Mansfield [William Murray, 1st Earl of Mansfield, d. 1793], by Lord Shaw of Dunfermline.

5308 Vol. 13.

a Bibliography of the English law of property, with special reference to property legislation from 1922 to 1927.
b Disraeli and the constitution, by W. I. Jennings.
c John Selden [d. 1654] and Jewish law, by I. Herzog.

Other publications:

5309 Journal. Index to vols. 1–15, new series. *P*. 1915. [Issued as Journal, new ser., no. 34, but separately paginated. The index to new ser., vols. 16–18 was published in 1939, and the index to 3rd ser., vols. 1–20 in 1940]

5310 Legislation of the Empire: being a survey of the legislative enactments of the British dominions, 1898–1907, ed. C. E. A. Bedwell, with preface by the Earl of Rosebery, and introd. by Sir J. Macdonell. 4 vols. 1909.

SOCIETY OF DORSET MEN IN LONDON

Founded 1904, for the promotion in London of friendly intercourse and good fellowship among Dorset folk by meetings, the fostering of a fuller knowledge of the history, folk-lore, literature, art, music, natural history, and antiquities of the county.

Year Book 1904–5—1932 (25 vols. [1905–32]):

5311 Vol. for 1913–14.

a A tale of North Poorton, by F. J. Pope. [The attempt by Thomas Paul to defraud the son and grandsons of Roger Symes, husbandman, of their tenement rights, *c*. 1690]

5312 Vol. for 1914–15.

a Three Dorset doctors, by Sir F. Treeves. [Thomas Sydenham, d. 1689; Francis Glisson, d. 1677; Nathaniel Highmore, d. 1685]
b The Dorsetshire regiment, by Sir W. Watts.
c The old cross [1516] at Rampisham, by A. Pope.

5313 Vol. for 1916.

a The Dorset Verdun, by Sir F. Treeves. [The siege of Lyme Regis, 1644]
b Lewis Tregonwell [d. 1832], the Dorset squire who founded a 'pleasure city' [Bournemouth], by C. H. Mate.
c The Dorsets in the Great war, by H. Pouncy. [Contd. in Year Books for 1917–18, 1918–19, 1919–20]

5314 Vol. for 1917–18.

a Dorset seventy years ago [1846, with particular reference to the state of the agricultural labourer], by Sir F. Treeves.
b Dorset's coinage [being tokens, 17th–19th cent.], by H. Symonds.
c An old West Indian burial ground of the Dorset regiment [English Harbour, Antigua], by J. S. Udal.

5315 Vol. for 1919–20.

a Old Dorchester [17th cent.], by Sir F. Treeves.
b The 'good old days' in Dorset, by J. A. J. Housden. [Notes on the county in the 16th cent.]

5316 Vol. for 1921.

a The folk-lore of William Barnes[d. 1886], by J. S. Udal.

5317 Vol. for 1922.

a Wimborne St. Giles, by E. F. Adams. [A brief description of the house]

5318 Vol. for 1923.

a The war poetry of Matthew Prior, by F. E. Hansford.
b Sergeant William Lawrence [d. 1868], a Waterloo veteran, by N. L. N. Acland.
c Memories of Weymouth and Melcombe Regis [in the 19th cent.], by J. R. Tomkins.
d Some records of ye olde Dorset of five and six centuries ago, by H. Clench. [Transcripts of deeds, etc. 1234–1582. Contd. in Year Book for 1927]

5319 Vol. for 1924.

a Winterbourne Came, Dorchester, by T. H. Rogers. [A brief account of the village and church]
b Witchhampton, by Mary S. Homer. [Extracts from an account book, 1749–78, kept by the executor of Martyn Hutchins]

5320 Vol. for 1925.

a The western circuit in the 16th cent., by Sir M. Shearman. [Records of the diet of Thomas Walmysley, justice of the common pleas, in Dorchester, 1596–1600]
b Alfred Stevens, of Blandford [d. 1875]: the perfection of Victorian art, by R. Southern.
c The Wessex Theocritus: William Barnes, Dorset's dialect poet, by W. M. Parker.
d John Baverstock Knight [artist, d. 1859], by F. Knight.
e The proclaiming of Charles II at Sherborne [being an extract from *Mercurius Publicus*, no. 21, 1660].

5321 Vol. for 1927.

a Forgotten byways in Dorset [being the villages of Purse Caundle, Stourton Caundle, Caundle Haddon and Bishop's Caundle], by Alys F. Serrell.
b History of Wollaston House, Dorchester.
c Dorset men in the battle of Sedgmoor, 6 July 1685, by H. Clench. [Chiefly transcripts of letters by Thomas Chafin, of Chettle, to his wife]
d Reginald Pole [d. 1558], dean of Wimborne and cardinal, by S. C. Ryley.

5322 Vol. for 1928.

a Bridport trade tokens, by A. G. Eveleigh.
b Hardys and Keatses: two Dorset families.
c The diary [1784–1840] of a Dorset farmer [Henry Kaines, of Manston], ed. Janet Pinhorn.

5323 Vol. for 1930.

a Judge Jeffreys at Lyme [being the mayor's accounts for his entertainment, Sept. 1685].
b The parliamentary representation of Dorset from the reign of Edward I, by W. Clark.
c Sir James Thornhill [d. 1734], by F. H. Newberry.

5324 Vol. for 1931.

a Hutchins of the Water-guard, Poole, 1798, by H. S. Carter. [Extracts from records kept by Charles Hutchins, revenue officer]
b Elementary education in Dorset 100 years ago, by H. Harding.
c Some literary luminaries of Dorset, by H. F. V. Johnstone.
d The ancient hospital of St. Margaret's, Wimborne Minster, by S. C. Ryley.

5325 Vol. for 1932.

a The Lady Macbeth of Wessex [Ælfthryth, d. 1000, wife of King Edgar], by E. U. Ouless.
b Roads and ports of Dorset, by F. C. Warren.
c Thomas Bastard [d. 1618], a Dorset poet, by D. R. Leggatt.
d Sherborne old castle, by Blanche Carter.

SOCIETY OF GENEALOGISTS

Founded 1911, as the Society of Genealogists of London, to promote and encourage the study of genealogy, heraldry and topography, and, in particular, to collect, index and provide its members and associates with information on these subjects. Title changed to the above form in 1924.

Genealogists' Magazine, vols. 1–6 (1925–34):

5326 Vol. 1.

a An index to six various versions of the so-called roll of Battle abbey, with especial reference to the corroboration of most of their statements to be obtained from Domesday book, Wace's chronicle, and other sources, by W. Rye. [Contd. in vols. 2–5]

b Origins of the Fitzmaurices, Barons of Kerry and Lixnaw, by G. H. Orpen.

c A key pedigree: Nutter of Reedley, Pendle, Lancs., by Lord Farrer.

d Ms. accessions Jan. 1925 [to the library of the Society. Contd. in vols. 2–6. Lists of books and mss. added to the library before 1925 are given in the First–Thirteenth Annual Reports]

e English entries in Irish records, by T. U. Sadleir.

f History of the Washington family, by H. I. Longden. [Contd. in vol. 2]

g The [George] Washington bookplate, by C. H. Crouch.

h The English background of the New England settlements, by G. A. Moriarty.

5327 Vol. 2.

a Discoveries in the diocesan registry, Wells, Som., by R. Holworthy. [Extracts from the diocesan records of the 16th and 17th cent.]

b Smithett pedigree (Smythcot *alias* Chamberleyn, 1396–1573), by J. L. Smithett.

c Genealogical material in the Guildhall [London] records, by A. H. Thomas.

d An addition to the 'Plantagenet roll', by W. T. J. Gun. [The descendants of Penelope Perrott and Sir William Lower, d. 1615]

e Palmer of Little Chelsea [London], by J. Brownbill.

f Points for pedigrees from the pardon rolls [1574], by T. C. Dale.

g Notes on Sir William Huddersfield [lawyer, d. 1499], by W. P. Haskett-Smith.

h The descendants of George Walker, governor of Derry [d. 1690], by T. U. Sadleir.

i The Renvoize (French Huguenot) family, by W. Bradbrooke.

5328 Vol. 3.

a Knights of Edward I, by C. Moor.

b Direct female lines in history [with particular reference to the descent of Queen Victoria], by W. T. J. Gun.

c Oliver Cromwell's Stuart descent, by L. Griffith.

d The register of a private school for boys at St. Peter's Hill, London, 1650, by G. Hart.

e The Boys family in Virginia: early Kentish settlers, by C. Boyce.

f Notes on Sir Christopher Wren and his family, by Maud Roberts-West. [Contd. in vol. 4]

g Ancestry of Thomas Gray the poet, by C. H. Crouch.

5329 Vol. 4.

a The records of New Romney, by R. Holworthy.

b The wife of Walter the sheriff [*temp.* Henry I], by G. A. Moriarty.

c The plate of Magdalen College, Oxford [during the Commonwealth], by T. C. Dale.

d Ightham Mote, Kent [and its builder], by W. P. Haskett-Smith.

e Alexander Pope and the Angel Inn, Andover, by Grace Hart.

f A merchant [Thomas Lee] in Virginia in 1634, by T. C. Dale.

g Manor court ordinances [for Winterton, Lincs., 1625], by H. W. Atkinson.

h Zouch Turton (1759–1814): a short memoir by his grandson, W. H. Turton.

5330 Vol. 5.

a The succession to baronies by writ of summons, by W. T. J. Gun.

b Pedigrees of Coningham and Sterling, by Sir H. L. L. Denny.

c Notes concerning the Washington family: wife of the Rev. Lawrence Washington [Amphillis Twigden, d. 1655?], by H. I. Longden.

d The genealogical value of early English newspapers, by C. D. P. Nicholson.

e Eton records, by R. A. Austen-Leigh.

f *Clavis regni* [the great seal of England], by J. Harvey Bloom.

g Three 17th cent. clerical families [Sparke, Brett and Williamson], by W. Bradbrooke.

h The baronet's badge, by F. W. Pixley.

i Cheam school, by Maud Roberts-West.

j A side-light on customary tenure in the 17th cent., by W. A. C. Sandford-Thompson. [An action in chancery in 1650 between Anne, Countess of Pembroke, and her customary tenants in Westmorland]

k Testamentary papers at Sarum [from the diocesan records], communicated by C. R. Everett.

l Notes on the ancestry of the Rt. Hon. Sir William A. Waterlow [d. 1913], lord mayor of London, by Sir H. L. L. Denny.

m Drapers' company of London, by P. Boyd. [Notes on the records of the company from the point of view of the genealogist]

n Origin of the surname of Horton.

o Scottish merchants at Memel [Prussia, 17th–early 19th cent.], by P. von Gerbhardt.

p Northamptonshire families, by H. I. Longden.

q Stowe and the Grenvilles, by R. Dew.

r British families in Norway, by T. Width.

s A romance of sixteen quarterings, by H. Ewart. [Some episodes relating to the Ewart family in the 18th cent.]

t The succession to the crown, by W. T. J. Gun.

u Records and record searching in Jersey, by C. Langton.

v Grinling Gibbons [d. 1721, and his English origin], by G. Sherwood.

w Somerset testamentary documents hitherto unlisted, by H. R. Phipps.

x Le Vesconte family, of Jersey, and the Royal Navy, by G. W. Younger. [See also Société Jersiaise, *Bulletin Annuel, 1932*]

y Genealogical gleanings from Westminster abbey, by L. F. Tanner.

z St. John of Bletsoe, by J. Brownbill.

aa Inscriptions in the churchyard of St. Margaret's, Westminster. [Contd. in vol. 6]

bb Members of parliament of the 15th cent., by J. C. Wedgwood.

cc A bibliography of monumental inscriptions in the city and county of London. [Contd. in vol. 6]

5331 Vol. 6.

a The English colony in Virginia in 1618, by T. C. Dale.

b 17th cent. nonconformists, by A. G. Matthews.

c The case of Ankarette Twynyho [her conviction for murder at the instance of George, Duke of Clarence, 1477], by A. R. Bayley.

d Some families with a long East Indian connexion, by V. C. P. Hodson.

e Irish genealogy, by W. Clare.

f Companions of the Conqueror at the battle of Hastings.

g Manorial records, by H. W. Knocker.

h The family of Comber, of Wotton, by J. Comber.

i The English ancestry of William Bradford, governor of Plymouth colony, by W. B. Browne.

j Sources of Anglo-Jewish genealogy, by W. S. Samuel.

k The manor of Gobions, Romford, Essex, and its owners, by E. A. Roe.

l Printed visitations and county pedigrees, by E. N. Geijer.

m India Office records, by V. C. P. Hodson.

n The 64 quarterings of Charles II, by C. Evans. [Contd. as 'The ancestry of Charles II']

o Domesday tenants-in-chief, by F. M. Stenton.

p Ex-president Hoover's English descent, by C. G. Bunting.

q South Newington and the Giffards, by G. A. Moriarty.

r The Cotgreave pedigree forgeries, by R. Stewart-Brown.

s Pedigrees of villeins and freemen in the 13th cent., by Helen Cam.

t The alleged descent of the Marshalls from Dermot Mac Murrough, by L. Griffith. [See below]

u Theatrical families, by J. M. Bulloch.

v The alleged descent of the Marshalls from Dermot Mac Murrough, by G. S. Cary. [See above]

w Gypsy blood [and traces of it in English families], by C. P. Hawkes.

x Ulster Office records, by T. U. Sadleir.

y Trinity House petitions [1797-1854], by E. P. Stapleton.

z Inscriptions in St. Katherine-by-the-Tower [London].

aa Sir John Cox Hippisley [d. 1825, and his ancestry], by I. F. Jones.

bb Notes on the church of Fornham St. Martin, Bury St. Edmunds, Suff., by G. W. Younger.

cc The early Lancashire Turtons up to 1400, by W. H. Turton.

dd Errors in a visitation pedigree [of William Heyward, mayor of Norwich, 1664], by A. F. Rowe.

ee Monumental inscriptions in the churchyard of St. Leonard, Shoreditch.

ff The early Maynards of Devon and St. Albans: notes collected by Constance D. Saunders.

5332 Index of persons and places in [*Genealogists' Magazine*] vols. 1 to 4, April 1925 to December 1928. *P.* 1930.

5333 Index of persons and places in [*Genealogists' Magazine*] vol. 5, March 1929 to December, 1931. *P.* 1932.

5334 Index of persons and places in [*Genealogists' Magazine*] vol. 6, March 1932 to December 1934. *P.* 1935.

Other publications:

5335 Calendar of chancery proceedings, Elizabeth, being those suits omitted from the printed calendars published in 1827-30 by the Record Commissioners, comp. R. Holworthy. *P.* 1913.

5336 Catalogue of parish registers in the possession of the Society, 1924. [1924?]

5337 The inhabitants of London in 1638, ed. from ms. 272 in the Lambeth Palace library, by T. C. Dale. 2 vols. 1931.

SOCIETY OF GLASS TECHNOLOGY
[*see p.* 485]

SOCIETY OF SOMERSET FOLK

Founded 1901, *as Somerset Men in London, to foster a fuller knowledge of county art, literature and music, by means of lectures and entertainments. Title changed to Somerset Folk in London in 1921, and to above form in 1923.*

First-Twentieth Annual Report (1901-21):

5338 9th Report.

a Recent discoveries in Wookey Hole cavern, by H. E. Balch.

5339 10th Report.

a Hugh Sexey, of Bruton [d. 1620], by W. A. Knight.

5340 11th Report.

a Stone crosses of Somerset, by A. S. Macmillan.

b Thomas Coryate, the Odcombe leg-stretcher [d. 1617], by H. Scott.

5341 12th Report.

a Sir John Popham, speaker of the House of Commons and lord chief justice [d. 1607], by J. King.

5342 13th Report.

a Somerset and Oxford [the foundation of Wadham College], by J. Read.

b Ilminster and the Spekes, by J. Street.

5343 14th Report.

a Before Trafalgar: the man who made Nelson possible [Admiral Robert Blake, d. 1657], by S. R. Littlewood.

5344 15th Report.

a The Somerset Light Infantry: story of the famous regiment, by R. S. Clarke.

5345 16th Report.

a Phases of the story of the Somerset regiment, by R. S. Clarke.

b Saint Dunstan, by J. Armitage Robinson.

c The woollen industry in Somerset, by Miss D. Biddick.

d Montacute [village], by C. A. Palmer.

5346 17th Report.

a Somerset worthies, no. 3: Roger Bacon [d. 1294], by C. Tite.

b Charles Moore, the Somerset geologist [d. 1881].

c Witchcraft in Somerset [being a transcription of an account of various witch-trials of 1664 composed by the Rev. J. Glanville and published 1681].

5347 18th-19th Reports.

a Somerset and Cambridge [University], by J. Read.

b Notes on Somerset bells [extracted from *Church Bells of England*, by H. B. Walters].

5348 20th Report.

a Old village customs, by Mrs. F. French.

b The hundreds of Somerset, with some glimpses of early village life [chiefly in Anglo-Saxon times], by D. Macmillan.

c Locus Dei [Hinton Charterhouse], by F. S. Gray.

Somerset Year Book, nos. 21-32, continuing the above (1922-33):

5349 No. 21.

a William Kingston, armless fighter, farmer and family man [d. 1831].

b Somerset artists.

c A prison for one [the Round house, Castle Cary].

5350 No. 22.

a A Somerset writer of hymns: Godfrey Thring [d. 1903], by A. T. Thring.
b Somerset epitaphs relating to trades, professions, occupations, etc., collected and classified by A. S. Macmillan.
c Ralph Allen of Prior Park [d. 1764], by W. T. J. Gun.
d A hunted king [Charles II], in Wessex, by 'Warren'.
e Mendip mines of long ago: lead and coals, being extracts from *The Agreeable Historian, or the Complete English Traveller* by Samuel Simpson, gent. from London, printed by R. Walker, in Fleet Lane, 1746, communicated by R. S. Churchill.

5351 No. 23.

a [John Hanning] Speke, the explorer [d. 1864], by W. T. J. Gun.
b Curious Somerset epitaphs, comp. A. S. Macmillan.
c Glastonbury abbey and the early Christian foundation, by F. B. Bond.
d A Somerset parson's diary: the Rev. James Woodforde [d. 1803].
e Somerset church bench-ends, by D. M. Cary.

5352 No. 24.

a Letters from a Somerset sailor, Henry Churchill, 1845–1859, communicated by his nephew.
b Tom Poole of Nether Stowey [d. 1837]: a famous Somerset worthy, by W. G. Harris.
c Chard: byeways of its history; its M.Ps, 1313–28, by W. G. W. Watson.
d Old stones at Bruton [church and bridge], by W. B. Jones.

5353 No. 25.

a Farleigh castle and the Hungerfords, by G. Lansdown.
b Woodspring priory, by W. G. W. Watson.
c Leaves from old Somerset chronicles [Sir Anthony Herbert's *Book of Husbandry*, *c.* 1534; Leland's *Itinerary*; Camden's *Britannia*; the *Diary* of Celia Fiennes, *c.* 1697], by J. Read.

5354 No. 26.

a Monmouth in Somerset [1685], by D.P.

5355 No. 27.

a Lady Huntingdon's circle in Bath [Selina Hastings, Countess of Huntingdon, d. 1791], by A. W. Knight.
b Tramping Tom of Odcombe [Thomas Coryate, d. 1617], by J. S. Bull.

5356 No. 28.

a Charterhouse on Mendip, by M. E. Board.

5357 No. 29.

a Frome and its fringes, by D. M. Cary.
b The Monmouth rebellion [1685], by F. A. J. Harding.

5358 No. 30.

a Bath through the ages, by M. Frazer.
b A Somerset grazier in the 18th cent.: Robert Brown of Hill farm [author of *The Compleat Farmer : or the Whole Art of Husbandry*, 1759], by G. E. Fussell.
c Weston-super-Mare in the 19th cent., by Dorothy H. Rowlands.
d Old fonts of Somerset, by A. V. Gandy.

5359 No. 31.

a John Locke, 1632–1704, by W. T. Jones.
b William Wallwyn, parish warden [of Kilmersdon, early 17th cent.], by W. G. Jolliffe, 3rd Baron Hylton.

5360 No. 32.

a Elizabeth Pepys [d. 1669], by E. Chappell.

b William Dampier, buccaneer and geographer, 1651–1715.
c Walter Bagehot, 1826–77, by W. Vowles.
d Hannah More, 1745–1833, by A. Holland.
e Westonzoyland church, by M. Page.

SOCIOLOGICAL SOCIETY

Founded 1903, to promote study and research in sociology, and for this purpose to co-operate with specialists and workers in all branches of the social sciences. Incorporated with Le Play House to form the Institute of Sociology in 1930.

Sociological Papers, vols. 1–3 (1905–7):

5361 Vol. 1.

a The origin and use of the word sociology, by V. V. Branford.

5362 Vol. 2.

a Some guiding principles in the philosophy of history, by J. H. Bridges.

Sociological Review, vols. 1–25 (1908–33):

5363 Vol. 1.

a The sociological view of history, by H. A. L. Fisher.

5364 Vol. 3.

a The religious order [Benedictine, Franciscan etc.] in the west, by C. D. Burns.
b The beginning of modern socialism, by G. Wallas.
c The doctrine of *laissez faire*, by Grace Kemeys-Tynte.

5365 Vol. 4.

a The highways of England: their growth and relation to civics, by G. Montagu.

5366 Vol. 5.

a Charles Dickens and the social movement, by B. L. Hutchins.
b Society and liberalism in England and Germany [in the 19th cent.], by H. Levy.

5367 Vol. 8.

a Westminster: an interpretative survey [being a history of the city of Westminster].

5368 Vol. 10.

a The drift to revolution. [England from the time of Adam Smith to 1919]

5369 Vol. 14.

a The steel industry of South Yorkshire, by C. H. Desch.

5370 Vol. 16.

a A scheme of British culture periods, and of their relation to European cultural developments, by C. Dawson.

5371 Vol. 18.

a Charles Darwin and the theory of evolution: a sociological study, by G. Spiller.
b The industries of Reading: a study in regional development, by W. F. Morris.
c Influence of foreign nationalities on the life of the people of Merthyr Tydfil, by J. R. Williams.
d The village community of Alderney, by S. Harris.

5372 Vol. 19.

a Progress of education in England, by J. Reeves.

5373 Vol. 21.

a A 14th cent. regional survey [being a poll tax return or 1379 for Craven, Yorks.], by A. Raistrick.

5374 Vol. 22.

  a Sir William Petty's views on London [in 1682], by E. A. J. Johnson.

5375 Vol. 25.

  a Rural settlement in Domesday Shropshire: a geographical interpretation, by Dorothy Sylvester.

SOMERSET RECORD SOCIETY

Founded 1886 (an offshoot of the Somersetshire Archaeological and Natural History Society), to seek out, edit and print such documents as bear upon the history of Somerset and will aid the future historian of the county.

[Publications] vols. 16–47 (1901–33):

5376 Vols. 16, 19, 21. Somerset medieval wills, ed. F. W. Weaver. 3 vols. 1901–5. [Vol. i: 1383–1500. Vol. ii: 1501–30, with some Somerset wills, 1363–1491, at Lambeth. Vol. iii: 1531–58]

5377 Vol. 17. *Pedes finium*, commonly called feet of fines, for Somerset, 1347–99, by E. Green. 1902. [Contd. in vol. 22 below. For earlier fines see vols. 6, 11, and 12, published in 1892–8]

5378 Vol. 18. *Bellum civile*. Hopton's narrative of his campaign in the west, 1642–4, and other papers, ed. C. E. H. Chadwyck-Healey. 1902. [Ralph Hopton, d. 1652]

5379 Vol. 20. Certificate of musters in Somerset, 1569, extracted, with notes, by E. Green. 1904.

5380 Vol. 22. *Pedes finium*, commonly called feet of fines, for Somerset, Henry IV–Henry VI, by E. Green. 1906.

5381 Vols. 23, 24, 28, 34. Quarter sessions records for Somerset. 4 vols. 1907–19. [Vols. i–iii ed. E. H. Bates Harbin, vol. iv ed. M. C. B. Dawes. Vol. i: 1607–25. Vol. ii: 1625–39. Vol. iii: 1646–60. Vol. iv: 1666–77]

5382 Vol. 25. A cartulary of Buckland priory, ed. F. W. Weaver. 1909.

5383 Vol. 26. A feodary of Glastonbury abbey, ed. F. W. Weaver, with introd. by C. H. Mayo. 1910.

5384 Vol. 27. Proceedings in the court of star chamber, Henry VII and Henry VIII, ed. Gladys Bradford. 1911.

5385 Vols. 29, 30. The register of Nicholas Bubwith, bishop of Bath and Wells, 1407–24, ed. T. Scott Holmes. 1 vol. in 2. 1914.

5386 Vols. 31, 32. The register of John Stafford, bishop of Bath and Wells, 1425–43, ed. T. Scott Holmes. 1 vol. in 2. 1915–16.

5387 Vol. 33. Documents and extracts illustrating the history of the honour of Dunster, selected and ed. Sir H. C. Maxwell-Lyte. 1917–18 [1918].

5388 Vol. 35. Two registers formerly belonging to the family of Beauchamp of Hatch, ed. Sir H. C. Maxwell-Lyte. 1920. [Both compiled in 14th cent., containing extents, custumals, etc.]

5389 Vols. 36, 41, 44. Somersetshire pleas from the rolls of the itinerant justices, ed. L. Landon. Vols. ii–iv. 1923–9. [Vol. ii: 41–57 Hen. III. Vol. iii: 1–7 Edw. I. Vol. iv: Civil pleas, 8 Edw. I. Vol. i, to 41 Hen. III, ed. C. E. H. Chadwyck-Healey, was published in 1897]

5390 Vol. 37. Life of Richard Kidder, D.D., bishop of Bath and Wells [d. 1703], written by himself, ed. Amy E. Robinson. 1924.

5391 Vol. 38. The accounts of the chamberlains of the city of Bath, 1568–1602, ed. F. D. Wardle. 1923.

5392 Vol. 39. Collectanea I: a collection of documents from various sources, arranged by T. F. Palmer. 1924.

  a Glastonbury abbey in 1322, ed. Sir H. C. Maxwell-Lyte.

  b Glastonbury abbey and the church of West Pennard, ed. R. Flower.

  c The *Historia minor* and the *Historia major* of Wells, ed. J. Armitage Robinson.

  d Household roll of Bishop Ralph, 1337, ed. J. Armitage Robinson, with appendix by A. Hamilton Thompson.

  e Summons of the Green Wax to the sheriff of Somerset and Dorset, ed. T. Bruce Dilks.

  f Visitation of religious houses and hospitals, 1526, ed. Sir H. Maxwell-Lyte.

5393 Vol. 40. Medieval wills from Wells in the diocesan registry, Wells, 1543–6, 1554–6, ed. Dorothy O. Shilton and R. Holworthy. 1925.

5394 Vol. 42. Muchelney memoranda, ed. from a breviary of the abbey, by B. Schofield, with an essay on Somerset medieval calendars by J. Armitage Robinson. 1927 [1929].

5395 Vol. 43. Collectanea II: a collection of documents from various sources, arranged by T. F. Palmer. 1928 [1929].

  a Act book of the archdeacon of Taunton [1623–4], transcribed and ed. C. Jenkins.

  b Documents of the Laudian period, ed. J. Armitage Robinson. [Proceedings against Beckington churchwardens, 1635, etc.]

  c List of escheators for Somerset and Dorset, comp. Sir H. Maxwell-Lyte.

5396 Vol. 45. Mendip mining laws and forest bounds, by J. W. Gough. 1931.

5397 Vol. 46. Wells city charters, by Dorothy O. Shilton and R. Holworthy. 1932.

5398 Vol. 47. Wulfric of Haselbury, by John, abbot of Ford, [with Dom Jerome Porter's English life of St. Wulfric, 1632], ed. with introd. and notes by M. Bell. 1933.

Other publications:

5399 Historical notes on some Somerset manors formerly connected with the honour of Dunster, by Sir H. C. Maxwell-Lyte. 1931.

SOMERSETSHIRE ARCHAEOLOGICAL AND NATURAL HISTORY SOCIETY

Founded 1849, for the collection and publication of information on archaeology and natural history, particularly in connection with the county of Somerset, and the maintenance of the museum and library at Taunton castle.

Proceedings, vols. 47–78 (1901–33):

5400 Vol. 47.

  a Presidential address, by G. F. Browne. [Includes an account of the Alfred jewel discovered near Athelney, 1693]

  b St. Mary Redcliffe, Bristol, by J. R. Bramble.

  c Hospital of St. John, Bristol, by J. Latimer.

  d St. Peter's hospital, Bristol, by J. J. Simpson.

  e Church of St. John the Baptist, Bristol, by H. C. M. Hirst.

  f Whitchurch, by E. Buckle.

  g Stanton Drew church, by H. T. Perfect.

  h Chew Magna [church], by E. Buckle.

g Crowcombe church, by H. C. Young.
h Crowcombe church house.
i Halsway manor house, by W. H. P. Greswell.
j St. Decuman's church, by C. H. Heale.
k Nettlecombe Court, by F. Hancock.
l Trull church.
m Pitminster church.
n Report on the Wick barrow [Stogursey] excavations, by H. St. G. Gray. [Also published separately, 1909]
o Barlwich priory [Brompton Regis], by F. W. Weaver.
p Glastonbury abbey: report on discoveries made during excavations, by F. B. Bond. [Contd. in vols. 55–62, 65, and 72]
q Excavations at Norton camp, near Taunton, by H. St. G. Gray.

5408 Vol. 55.
a Wookey church, by E. B. Cook.
b [Wells cathedral]
c The bishop's palace [Wells], by T. Scott Holmes.
d Compton Martin church, by J. Cairns.
e Chewton Mendip church.
f St. Cuthbert's church, Wells, by J. Beresford.
g Courts leet and the court leet of the borough of Taunton, by H. B. Sheppard. [Also published separately, 1909]
h The gold torc found at Yeovil, 1909, by H. St. G. Gray. [Also published separately, 1909]
i The first cathedral church of Wells, and the site thereof, by W. H. St. J. Hope.
j The clock and quarter jacks in the cathedral church of Wells, by C. M. Church.
k Excavations at the 'amphitheatre', Charterhouse-on-Mendip, by H. St. G. Gray.
l Historical notes on Priddy and its lead mines, by J. Coleman.
m Excavations at Downend, near Bridgwater, by A. G. Chater and A. F. Major.
n Ancient type of huts at Athelney, by H. Laver.

5409 Vol. 56.
a Church of St. John Baptist, Yeovil, by E. H. Bates Harbin.
b Barwick church.
c Ham hill camp and quarries.
d Chantry House, Stoke-under-Ham.
e Stoke church.
f Tintinhull church.
g Ilchester church, by E. H. Bates Harbin.
h Limington church.
i History of the manor of Newton Surmaville, by E. H. Bates Harbin.
j Structural notes on Taunton castle, by J. H. Spencer. [Also published separately, 1911]
k Notes on archaeological remains found on Ham hill, by H. St. G. Gray.
l The 'Cantoche' [Quantock] of Domesday (1086), by W. H. P. Greswell.
m Court rolls of the manor of Curry Rivel in the years of the Black Death, 1348–9, with a translation of the rolls of the courts for those years, by J. F. Chanter.
n The *Taunton Castle* privateer [built 1790], by H. Symonds.

5410 Vol. 57.
a Frome parish church, by W. E. Daniel.
b Elm church, by F. B. Bond.
c The Murtry hill stones.
d Nunney church, by W. E. Daniel.
e Mells church.
f Kilmersdon and its church.
g Hemington church.

h Beckington church, by F. B. Bond.
i Wellow church, by F. B. Bond.
j Norton St. Philip church, by F. B. Bond.
k Lullington church.
l Monmouth at Philip's Norton [1685], by Helen C. Foxcroft.
m Taunton tokens of the 17th cent., by H. Symonds.
n Roman remains found at Puckington, by H. St. G. Gray.
o Tangier and Gibraltar [districts of Taunton], by J. H. Spencer.
p Report on excavation work at Brinscombe, Weare, by A. F. Major.
q Glaston, Glastonia, Glastonbury [the derivation of the place-name], by W. H. P. Greswell.

5411 Vol. 58.
a Presidential address, by W. B. Dawkins. [On some points in the prehistoric archaeology of Somerset]
b Wellington parish church, by F. B. Bond.
c Burlescombe church, by F. B. Bond.
d Holcombe Court, by E. H. Bates Harbin.
e Kittisford church, by F. B. Bond.
f Nynehead church.
g Bradford-on-Tone church.
h Bishop's Hull church, by R. C. W. Raban.
i Bishop's Hull manor house, by J. H. Spencer.
j Milverton church, by F. B. Bond.
k A third John de Courcy [? 13th cent.], by H. Hall.
l Hamdon or Ham hill: notes on its early occupation—and afterwards, by R. H. Walter.
m Pomparles [bridge], Glastonbury, by J. Morland.
n An early portion of the churchwardens' accounts of All Saints, Nynehead, 1668–84, by W. de C. Prideaux.

5412 Vol. 59.
a Glastonbury abbey ['evidences of a hidden symbolism in the plan'], by F. B. Bond.
b Alford church, by P. H. Milne.
c Queen Camel church, by F. B. Bond.
d West Camel church, by F. B. Bond.
e North Cadbury church.
f Trial-excavations at Cadbury castle [camp], S. Somerset, by H. St. G. Gray.
g Somerset scratch dials, by E. Horne. [Contd. in vols. 62 and 63]
h The prebend of Cudworth cum Cnolla, by G. A. Allan.
i Roman remains found at Barrington, by H. St. G. Gray.
j Coleridge cottage, Clevedon, by Lady Elton.

5413 Vol. 60.
a Bath abbey church.
b South Wraxhall manor house.
c The Roman thermae at Bath, by A. J. Taylor.
d Bath in the 18th cent., by M. A. Green.
e Englishcombe church, by C. W. Shickle.
f The Wansdyke.
g Langridge [parish], by C. W. Shickle.
h Correspondence of Bishop Oliver King [d. 1503] and Sir Reginald Bray [d. 1503], by J. Armitage Robinson.
i Church of St. John the Evangelist, Milborne Port, by C. E. Ponting.
j John of Pitney [14th cent.], by J. Armitage Robinson.
k Church bells of Somerset, their history, use, and founders, by G. de Y. Aldridge.

5414 Vol. 61.
a Thomas Boleyn, precentor of Wells [d. 1472], by J. Armitage Robinson.
b Monumental effigies in Somerset, by A. C. Fryer. [Contd. in vols. 62–72 and 74–76]
c The north chapel of St. Andrew's church, Curry Rivel, by G. W. Saunders; with notes on the heraldry of the

chancel and the will of John de Urtiaco, 1340, by E. H. Bates Harbin.

d Wells wills [1539–41] (Serel collection), by F. W. Weaver.

e Deeds relating to Stavordale priory and the family of Sanzaver [13th cent.], by E. H. Bates Harbin.

f Somerset trade tokens, 17th cent.: new types and varieties and corrections of former lists, by H. St. G. Gray and H. Symonds. [Also published separately, 1915]

g Sir Ralph de Midelney, d. 1363, by D. M. Ross.

h Notes on the heraldry in Chubb's *Maps of Somerset* [1572–1914], by F. Were.

i Roman remains found at West Coker, by H. St. G. Gray.

5415 Vol. 62.

a Memories of St. Dunstan [d. 988] in Somerset, by J. Armitage Robinson.

b The priory of St. Michael on the Steep Holme, by E. H. Bates Harbin.

c Hoard of Roman coins found at Yeovil, 1916, by H. St. G. Gray.

5416 Vol. 63.

a John Botreaux of Trent [d. 1444] and his chantry, by E. H. Bates Harbin.

b The burgesses of Bridgwater in the 13th cent., by T. Bruce Dilks.

c The Black Death in Somersetshire, 1348–9, by E. H. Bates Harbin.

d The Arthur Hull collection, Chard, by H. St. G. Gray. [Includes a description of a virginal by Charles Rewallin, 1675, and accounts of many Roman, British, English and Irish coins of all periods, and of 17th to 19th cent. tradesmen's tokens]

5417 Vol. 64.

a Presidential address, by F. J. Haverfield. [The character of the Roman empire as seen in west Somerset]

b The foundation charter of Witham Charterhouse [*c.* 1181], by J. Armitage Robinson.

c Walter Fichet's grant of lands to Simon Michel, *c.* 1300, by E. H. Bates Harbin.

d Two early English responds discovered at Shepton Mallet church, by F. J. Allen.

e A piscina and part of a reredos at Downside farm, Shepton Mallet, by F. J. Allen.

f The heronries of Somerset, by J. Wiglesworth.

5418 Vol. 65.

a Church of St. Mary, Ottery.

b Burci, Falaise, and Martin, by Sir H. C. Maxwell-Lyte. [Serlo de Burci, fl. 1068; William de Falaise, fl. 1100–7; Martin, husband of Serlo de Burci's daughter. Explains the devolution of Serlo de Burci's property in Somerset]

c A by-path of the civil war, by H. Symonds. [Documents describing a rising around Brent Knoll caused by the outrages of royalist troops, 1645]

d Discovery of Roman remains at 'Stanchester' in the parish of Stoke-sub-Hamdon, by R. H. Walter.

5419 Vol. 66.

a Chedzoy church.

b Westonzoyland church.

c The Mump, Boroughbridge.

d Cannington Court and priory.

e Stogursey church.

f East Quantockshead.

g Gothelney manor, by S. Evans.

h Medieval building: documents and what we learn from them, by A. Hamilton Thompson.

i Ancient Bridgwater and the river Parrett, by W. H. P. Greswell.

j Bridgwater wills, 1310–1497, by T. Bruce Dilks.

k Curci [Norman family of, 11th–13th cent.], by Sir H. C. Maxwell-Lyte.

l Church bells of Somerset, by H. B. Walters.

5420 Vol. 67.

a St. Bartholomew's church, Crewkerne.

b St. George's church, Hinton, by A. Hamilton Thompson.

c Barrington church.

d Barrington Court.

e South Petherton [church of SS. Peter and Paul, and 'King Ina's Palace'].

f Martock church.

g Merriott church.

h Norton-sub-Hamdon church.

i Stoke-under-Ham [fives court and church].

j Montacute [church, priory and house], by A. Hamilton Thompson.

k Excavations at Murtry hill, Orchardleigh Park, by H. St. G. Gray. [Contd. in vol. 75]

l Somerset volunteers of the 18th cent., by H. Symonds.

5421 Vol. 68.

a Weston-in-Gordano church, by F. B. Bond.

b Clevedon Court, by A. Elton.

c Clapton-in-Gordano [church], by F. B. Bond.

d Portbury [church], by F. B. Bond.

e Church of St. Andrew, Backwell, by F. B. Bond.

f Church of St. Bridget, Chelvey, by F. B. Bond.

g Nailsea Court, by C. E. Evans.

h Tickenham church, by F. B. Bond.

i Yatton church, by F. B. Bond.

j Congresbury [vicarage and church], by F. B. Bond.

k Burrington church of the Holy Trinity, by F. B. Bond.

l Wrington All Saints church, by F. B. Bond.

m The ethnology of Somerset, by Sir W. B. Dawkins.

n Trial-excavations at Cadbury camp, Tickenham, by H. St. G. Gray.

o The [river] Brue at Glastonbury: the Roman road, Pons perilis, and Beckery mill—a regional survey, by J. Morland.

p Roman coffins discovered at Keynsham, by H. St. G. Gray.

q Fitzurse [family of], by Sir H. C. Maxwell-Lyte.

r Heraldry on a tomb of the Nortons in Abbotsleigh church, by F. Were.

5422 Vol. 69.

a Tarr steps [ancient bridge across the Barle], by Sir W. B. Dawkins.

b New views respecting Stonehenge, by A. Herbert.

c Anglo-Saxon coins found at Wedmore in 1853, by H. Symonds.

d Descent of the manor of Sandford Orcas, by E. A. Fry and J. W. D. Thorp.

e Archaeological remains, Ham hill, south Somerset, by H. St. G. Gray.

5423 Vol. 70.

a The lord mayor's chapel [Bristol], by Mary P. Perry.

b Church of St. Gregory (now St. Nicholas), Whitchurch, by A. Hamilton Thompson.

c Roman remains, Keynsham.

d Stanton Drew [stone circle], by C. Lloyd Morgan.

e St. Mary Redcliffe church [Bristol], by H. Brakspear.

f Bristol cathedral, by A. Hamilton Thompson.

g The antiquity of man, by W. J. Sollas.

h The course of Wansdyke through Somerset; with an itinerary, by A. F. Major.

i The prebend of Yatton, by J. Armitage Robinson.

j Part of a hoard of Roman coins found on Sandford hill, by H. St. G. Gray.

k Catalogue of documents in the exchequer at Taunton castle, by A. J. Hook. [Also published separately, 1926]
l Excavations at Ham hill, south Somerset, by H. St. G. Gray. [Contd. in vols. 71, 72, and 75]

5424 Vol. 71.

a Church of All Saints, Langport, by D. M. Ross.
b Muchelney abbey, by A. Hamilton Thompson.
c Church of St. Andrew, Aller.
d Church of St. Andrew, High Ham.
e Somerton.
f Lytescary.
g Kingsbury Episcopi, church of St. Martin, by J. E. Forbes.
h Church of St. Catherine, Swell.
i Church of St. Andrew, Curry Rivel.
j Pageantry [history of], by M. F. C. Trevilian.
k Three lords of Aller [12th and 14th cent.], by D. M. Ross.
l Langford manor, Fivehead, by W. A. K. Matteson.
m The effigy of 'John de Middleton' at Wells, by J. Armitage Robinson.
n Barrington Court, by J. E. Forbes.

5425 Vol. 72.

a Church of St. John the Baptist [Glastonbury].
b Church of the Blessed Virgin Mary, Meare, by A. Hamilton Thompson.
c Wedmore church, by A. Hamilton Thompson.
d Church of St. Mark at Mark, by A. Hamilton Thompson.
e West Pennard, church of St. Nicholas.
f Butleigh, church of St. Leonard.
g Somerset drainage, by R. N. Grenville.
h Glastonbury abbey excavations, by T. Fyfe. [Contd. in vol. 73]
i Medieval embroidery in Somerset churches, by E. Horne.
j The mound, Glastonbury: report of the excavation committee, by A. Bulleid and J. Morland.
k Archaeological remains found at Middlezoy, by H. St. G. Gray.
l Excavations at Chelm's Combe, Cheddar: Chelm's Combe shelter, by H. E. Balch; human remains, by N. C. Cooper; the pottery [and bone and flint implements], by R. C. C. Clay.

5426 Vol. 73.

a Whitchurch Canonicorum [Dors.].
b Ford abbey [Devon].
c Combe St. Nicholas.
d Whitelackington, church of St. Mary.
e Old Chard, by J. W. Gifford.
f History of Combe St. Nicholas, by G. de Y. Aldridge.
g Notes on Tatworth [parish], by F. E. W. Langdon.
h Thomas Chard, D.D., last abbot of Ford [d. 1544], by D. J. Pring.
i Whitelackington and the Duke of Monmouth in 1680, comp. H. St. G. Gray.
j The historical evidence as to the Saxon church at Glastonbury, by J. Armitage Robinson.
k Two 17th cent. manor houses [Writhlington manor and Hassage manor house, Wellow], by H. G. H. Jolliffe, Baron Hylton.
l Bridgwater and the insurrection of 1381, by T. Bruce Dilks.
m Doubtful dedications of Somerset churches, by J. Armitage Robinson.
n Michell of Cannington [family of], by G. B. Michell.

5427 Vol. 74.

a Glastonbury abbey excavations, by C. R. Peers, A. W. Clapham, and E. Horne. [Contd. in vols. 75, 77, and 78]
b Thomas Chard, abbot of Ford [d. 1544], by Sir H. C. Maxwell-Lyte.

c Saxon cemetery at Camerton, by E. Horne.
d The Porlock stone circle, Exmoor, by H. St. G. Gray.
e The manor houses of Hardington and Vallis, by H. G. H. Jolliffe, Baron Hylton.
f The Witham Carthusians on Mendip, by J. W. Gough.
g Excavations at the caves, Cheddar, by R. F. Parry. [Contd. in vol. 76]
h The Roman site at Westland, Yeovil, by C. A. R. Radford.

5428 Vol. 75.

a Worlebury camp, by H. St. G. Gray.
b The excavations on the site of the Roman legionary fortress at Caerleon [Mon.], by V. E. Nash-Williams.
c Church of SS. Peter and Paul, Bleadon, by L. T. Powys-David.
d Church of St. James [Winscombe], by F. C. Eeles.
e Weston-super-Mare, by E. A. Baker.
f Notes on the medieval stained glass at Winscombe and East Brent, by F. C. Eeles.
g Kilmersdon manor-house, by H. G. H. Jolliffe, Baron Hylton.
h Armour in Somerset churches, by F. H. Cripps-Day.
i Excavations at Kingsdown camp, Mells, by H. St. G. Gray.

5429 Vol. 76.

a St. John's church, Yeovil, by J. Goodchild.
b Sherborne [abbey, Dors.].
c Church of St. Mary, Bradford Abbas [Dors.], by F. C. Eeles.
d Church of St. Andrew, Yetminster [Dors.], by F. C. Eeles.
e Maiden castle [Dors.], by H. St. G. Gray.
f Church of St. Mary, Limington, by E. Glanfield.
g Manor House, West Coker, by Sir M. Nathan.
h Some village families [from West Coker], by Sir M. Nathan.
i Inscription to Flavius Valerius Severus found at Stoke-under-Ham, 1930, by H. St. G. Gray.
j Consecration crosses on Somerset and Dorset churches, by F. C. Eeles.
k Babington House and High Downside, by H. G. H. Jolliffe, Baron Hylton.
l Excavation of Pool Farm barrow, West Harptree, by E. Horne.

5430 Vol. 77.

a St. George's church, Bicknoller, by F. C. Eeles.
b Sampford Brett church, by F. C. Eeles.
c Carhampton [church], by F. C. Eeles.
d Luccombe church, by F. C. Eeles.
e Nettlecombe church.
f Withycombe church, by F. C. Eeles.
g Old Barrow camp, Exmoor, by H. St. G. Gray.
h Wootton Courtenay church, by F. C. Eeles.
i Battlegore, Williton [earthworks], by H. St. G. Gray.
j Cleeve abbey: recent discoveries, by F. C. Eeles.
k The Nettlecombe font with representations of the seven sacraments, by A. C. Fryer.
l The disused ancient clock in Porlock church: a striking clock without face or hands, by F. J. Allen.
m West country hobby-horses and cognate customs, by H. W. Kille.
n Rude stone monuments of Exmoor (Somerset portion), by H. St. G. Gray. [Contd. in vol. 78]
o Monumental brasses in Somerset, by A. B. Connor. [Contd. in vol. 78]
p Barton Grange [in the parishes of Pitminster and Corfe], by A. W. Vivian-Neal.
q The Lytes of Lytescary, by Sir H. C. Maxwell-Lyte.

5431 Vol. 78.
a Nunney church, by F. C. Eeles.
b Church of St. John Baptist, Frome, by F. C. Eeles.
c Beckington church, by F. C. Eeles.
d Hazelbury manor [Wilts.], by G. Kidston.
e Ancient monuments in Somerset, by Sir C. R. Peers.
f Longleat [manor house], comp. H. St. G. Gray.
g Notes for the history of Frome, by J. O. Lewis.
h Somerset incumbents, 1354–1401, by Sir H. C. Maxwell-Lyte. [Also published separately, 1932]
i Martin Strong, vicar of Yeovil, 1690–1720, by J. Goodchild.

Other publications:

5432 Taunton castle: notes on its construction and history, by D. P. Alford.[1] 1906.

5433 Parish register of Horsington, 1558–1836, ed. W. E. Daniel.[1] 1907.

5434 Guide to the Charbonnier collection of pewter in Taunton castle museum, by T. Charbonnier.[1] 1st edn. 1908; 2nd enlarged edn. 1912.

5435 Descriptive list of the printed maps of Somersetshire, 1575–1914, with biographical notes and illustrations, by T. Chubb. 1914.

5436 The western rebellion [1685], by R. Locke.[1] 1927. [Facsimile reprint of the edn. of 1782].

5437 Saxon charters and field names of Somerset, by G. B. Grundy. Pts. 1–6. 1928–33. [Issued as supplements to the *Proceedings*, vols. 73–78]

5438 Index to papers in the Proceedings of the Society on monumental effigies of Somerset, by A. C. Fryer. 1932.

5439 Members of parliament for the county of Somerset [1258–1832], by Sophia W. Bates Harbin. Pt. 1. 1933. [Issued as a supplement to the *Proceedings*, vol. 78]

5440 A short index, chiefly topographical, to the Proceedings, vols. 1–80, 1849–1934, to which is added a parochial index to the inventory of Somerset church plate published in the Proceedings, 1897–1913. 1937.

SOMERSETSHIRE ARCHAEOLOGICAL AND NATURAL HISTORY SOCIETY, BATH AND DISTRICT BRANCH

Founded 1903.

Proceedings, 1904–33 (6 vols. 1909 [1904]–33):

5441 Vol. for 1904–8.
a Roman baths [at Bath], by H. H. Winwood.
b Wellow [church] and Stoney Littleton [tumuli].
c Bath [abbey], by S. A. Boyd.
d Notes on Englishcombe, by T. S. Bush.
e Exploration of barrows, Hampton down, by G. J. Grey.
f St. Catherine's, Batheaston.
g Shepton Mallet [parish church] and Croscombe [church].
h Bitton [church, Glos.].
i Exploration of tumulus, Hampton down, by G. J. Grey.
j Exploration on Claverton down, by H. H. Winwood.
k Explorations on Lansdown, by T. S. Bush. [Contd. in vol. for 1909–13]
l Roman coins found during the Lansdown explorations, by H. St. G. Gray.
m Beckington.
n Houses in Bath, by M. A. Green.

[1] Not seen.

o Exploration of a bank in Norwood's field, Claverton down, by G. J. Grey.
p Taunton [St. James's church, St. Mary Magdalen church, and the castle].
q An incised stone at Holcombe church, by E. Horne.
r Roman remains in Hot Bath Street [Bath], by A. J. Taylor.
s Glastonbury abbey, by F. B. Bond.

5442 Vol. for 1909–13.
a Lacock [church, Wilts.].
b Gloucester [church of St. Mary de Crypt and the cathedral].
c Roman road, Stratton-on-the-Fosse, by E. Horne.
d Barrows on Charmy down, by T. S. Bush.
e Chelvey Court, by St. D. Kemeys-Tynte.
f Discoveries [chiefly Roman coffins] in Bath and vicinity, 1911, by T. S. Bush.
g Extracts [*re* Lansdown] from the Rev. John Skinner's mss. at the British Museum.
h Great Chalfield [manor house], Broughton Gifford [manor house and church], and Westwood [church, Wilts.].
i Colerne [church], North Wraxall [church], and Castle Combe [church, Wilts.].
j Roman jar found on Hampton down, by H. H. Winwood.
k Roman sculpture recently found at Nettleton Scrub, Castle Combe [Wilts.], by G. J. Grey.
l Discoveries [chiefly Roman coins, pottery, etc.] at the Royal Mineral Water Hospital, Bath, June, 1912, by T. S. Bush.
m Stanton Prior [church], and Priston [church].
n Discoveries near St. Michael's church [Bath], by A. J. Taylor.
o Summary of the Lansdown operations, 1905–12, by T. S. Bush.

5443 Vol. for 1914–18.
a Holcombe [church], by E. Horne.
b Amesbury [abbey church, Wilts.].
c Scratch dials in the Bath district, by E. Horne.
d Gargoyles on Somersetshire and Wiltshire churches, by G. J. Grey.
e Bath abbey: discovery of part of the Norman triforium arcade in the west wall of the former transept (south), now the east wall of the south aisle of the choir, by F. B. Bond.
f Roman sculpture at Nettleton Scrub, near Castle Combe [Wilts.], by F. Haverfield.
g Hodshill, Southstoke: Roman coffin and skeleton, by T. S. Bush.
h Stratton-on-the-Fosse [church].
i [Hinton priory, and Road church]
j Holy wells of Somerset, by E. Horne.
k Turf monuments of England, by M. H. Scott.
l History of Monkton Combe, by D. L. Pitcairn.
m The old glass at Westwood church, Wilts., by E. Horne.
n Early records of the parish of Charlcombe and its people, by T. S. Bush.
o [Bath] abbey, by S. A. Boyd.
p The Roman thermae of Bath, by A. J. Taylor.
q Abbey Church House [Bath], by S. A. Boyd and M. A. Green.
r The Bluecoat school and Masonic hall [Bath].
s Burial mounds of Ireland, by G. Norman.
t Discovery of two stone coffins [one at Priston, the other at Midford], by C. J. Calvert and G. J. Grey.
u St. John's hospital [Bath].
v Southstoke.
w No. 30 Royal Crescent and 7 The Circus [houses in Bath], by M. A. Green.

x Weston [Bath].
y History of Claverton, by D. L. Pitcairn.

5444 Vol. for 1919–23.

a Syston and Pucklechurch [Glos.].
b Celtic crosses, by G. Norman.
c Corsham and Lacock [Wilts.].
d Wells.
e [The discovery of the Loretto chapel, Glastonbury abbey, by F. B. Bond]
f From Norman to Perpendicular [a description of the restoration of Somerset churches in the 15th cent.], by E. Horne.
g Lyncombe, 970, by H. Parry.
h Cirencester [Glos.].
i Henbury and Westbury-on-Trym [Glos.].
j Northumbrian crosses, by G. Norman.
k The craft of the English medieval masons, by J. E. Barton.
l Brasses in churches at Beckington, Cirencester, and St. Mary Redcliffe, Bristol, by H. Parry.
m Sherborne [Dors.].
n [The Roman baths at Bath, by A. J. Taylor]
o Farleigh castle, by G. Lansdown.
p Manorial dovecotes and fishponds, by E. Horne. [Reprinted by the Soc. of Somerset Folk in *Somerset Year Book* no. 22 (1923)]
q Brasses in the church of St. Mary, Fairford, Glos., by H. Parry.
r Roman site at Limpley Stoke [Wilts.], by A. T. Wicks.
s Fortified dwelling houses in England in the middle ages, by C. H. Bothamley.

5445 Vol. for 1924–8.

a Roman Somerset, by E. Horne.
b Recent discoveries in the Mendip caves [prehistoric remains], by J. A. Davies and E. K. Tratman.
c The misericords and stall work in Bristol cathedral, by Mary P. Perry.
d Longleat [house, Wilts.].
e Ilminster and Barrington.
f Shaftesbury [Dors.] and Wardour castle [Wilts.].
g The Roman house at Keynsham, by E. Horne.
h Bowood [house, Wilts.].
i Deerhurst and Tewkesbury [Glos.].
j The antiquities of Bradford-on-Avon [Wilts.], by W. H. M. Clarke.
k Camerton Saxon cemetery, by E. Horne. [Contd. in vol. for 1929–33]
l Ancient and picturesque Claverton, by G. J. Grey.

5446 Vol. for 1929–33.

a Somerset fonts, by Violet Gandy.
b Saxon and Norman Charlcombe, by G. J. Grey.
c Chard and Forde abbey.
d Bradford-on-Avon [Wilts.].
e Burial mounds and stone monuments in Somerset, by Elsie Russ.
f Old Dutch houses at Topsham, Devon, and elsewhere, by G. J. Grey.
g *The Bloody Assize* [pamphlet first published 1689], by E. Horne.
h Thornbury castle [Glos.].
i Tintinhull.
j 18th cent. architecture of Bath, by M. Green.
k Early plans of Bath, by R. W. M. Wright.
l Bath printers of the 18th cent., by Elsie Russ.
m Chedworth Roman villa [Glos.].
n Church of St. Michael the Archangel, Bawdrip.
o The romance of the old turnpike roads, by G. J. Grey.

SOMERSETSHIRE ARCHAEOLOGICAL AND NATURAL HISTORY SOCIETY, NORTHERN BRANCH

Publications:

5447 Collections for a parochial history of Chew Magna, by F. A. Wood. 1903.

SOUTH WALES AND MONMOUTH RECORD SOCIETY

Founded 1929, for the collection, preservation and publication of historical documents and other historical materials and works relating to the counties of Glamorgan, Monmouth, and Brecon.

Publications:

5448 No. 1. The storie of the Lower Borowes of Merthyrmawr, by John Stradling, ed. H. J. Randall and W. Rees. 1932. [An account, written 1598–1601, of various lawsuits concerning title to the Lower Burrows]

SOUTHAMPTON CIVIC SOCIETY

Founded 1924, to stimulate interest in the history, tradition and future development of the town.

Publications:

5449 Southampton: a civic survey, being a report of the civic survey committee of the Society under the chairmanship of E. M. Jack, ed. P. Ford. 1931. [Contains chapters on the history and street- and place-names of Southampton]

SOUTHAMPTON RAMBLING CLUB

Founded 1891, to promote the study of the antiquities and natural history of Hampshire.

Proceedings and other information, 1909–32. (24 vols. 1910–33):

5450 Vol. for 1909.

a Winchester [castle hall].
b Portchester.
c Warnford.
d Whitchurch.
e Paultons.

5451 Vol. for 1910.

a Eldon and Michelmersh.
b Farley Chamberlayne.
c Hound and Hamble.
d Stanbridge Earls.
e Baddesley.
f Boarhunt.

5452 Vol. for 1911.

a Merdon castle.
b Easton and Martyr Worthy.
c Moor Court and Broadlands.
d Old Sarum.
e Southampton.

5453 Vol. for 1912.

a Southwick.
b Alresford and Bishop's Sutton.
c Hursley.
d Christchurch.
e Salisbury.

5454 Vol. for 1913.
   a Winchester [cathedral].
   b Headbourne Worthy.
   c West Tisted.
   d Romsey.
   e Carisbrooke castle.
   f Eling.
   g Southampton [Tudor house].

5455 Vol. for 1914.
   a Romsey.
   b Houghton.
   c Christchurch.
   d Newport.
   e Broughton.
   f Southampton [St. Michael's church].

5456 Vol. for 1915.
   a Bishop's Waltham.
   b Nursling.
   c Dibden.
   d Clausentum.
   e Netley [abbey].

5457 Vol. for 1916.
   a Millbrook.
   b Stoneham.
   c Chilworth.
   d Northwood.
   e Luzborough.

5458 Vol. for 1917.
   a Itchen.
   b Romsey.
   c Botley.
   d Otterbourne.

5459 Vol. for 1918.
   a Romsey.
   b Grove Place.
   c Moor Court and Nursling.
   d Baddesley.

5460 Vol. for 1919.
   a Bursledon.
   b St. Cross.
   c Highwood.
   d Eling.

5461 Vol. for 1920.
   a Southampton [early water supply].
   b Mottisfont.
   c Marwell manor.
   d Highwood.
   e Durley.

5462 Vol. for 1921.
   a Cutthorn and Lordswood.
   b Romsey.
   c Compton.
   d Hamble and Hound.
   e [Early history of Romsey Extra and Hursley, by Mrs. Suckling]
   f Timsbury.
   g Titchfield.

5463 Vol. for 1922.
   a Wonston, Hunton and Stoke Charity.
   b Brockenhurst and Boldre.
   c Michelmersh.
   d Tidbury Ring [earthwork].

5464 Vol. for 1923.
   a Portchester.
   b Eldon.
   c Easton and Martyr Worthy.
   d St. Leonard's and Buckler's Hard.
   e Rowner.

5465 Vol. for 1924.
   a Winchester [castle hall].
   b Barton Stacey and Bullington.
   c Newport.
   d Ampress and Buckland Rings [earthworks].
   e Upham.
   f Wickham.

5466 Vol. for 1925.
   a Winchester [college].
   b Netley [abbey].
   c Boarhunt.
   d Stockbridge.
   e Twyford [Roman villa].
   f Dibden.
   g Brading.
   h Winchester [St. Peter's church] and Chilcomb.

5467 Vol. for 1926.
   a Twyford.
   b Toot hill [earthwork].
   c Newport [Roman villa].
   d Southwick.
   e Droxford.
   f Robert Pollock [d. 1827].

5468 Vol. for 1927.
   a Meonstoke and Corhampton.
   b King's Somborne and Ashley.
   c Gatcombe.
   d Bishop's Waltham.

5469 Vol. for 1928.
   a Winchester [St. John's church].
   b Fawley.
   c Headbourne Worthy and King's Worthy.
   d Portchester.
   e Ellingham and Moyles Court.
   f Alice Lisle and the Duke of Monmouth, by W. J. Andrew.

5470 Vol. for 1929.
   a Lymington.
   b East Wellow.
   c Quarr and Binstead.
   d Wymering.
   e Romsey.
   f Otterbourne.
   g Baddesley.

5471 Vol. for 1930.
   a Romsey.
   b Farley Chamberlayne.
   c Arreton.
   d Beaulieu heath.
   e Minstead.
   f Beaulieu abbey.
   g The Winchester Anglo-Saxon bowl, and Oliver Cromwell's Battery, by W. J. Andrew.

5472 Vol. for 1931.
   a Portsmouth [cathedral].
   b Sloden.
   c Shalfleet and Newtown.

d St. Catherine's hill [earthwork].
e Farley Mount, by W. J. Andrew.
f Northwood.
g Clausentum [Bitterne] and the early history of Southampton, by W. J. Andrew.

5473 Vol. for 1932.
a Winchester [West Gate].
b Merdon and Hursley.
c Godshill.
d Mottisfont.
e Kimbridge manor house.
f Nursling.
g Carisbrooke.
h St. Cross.

SOUTHAMPTON RECORD SOCIETY

Founded 1905, *to print and publish the more interesting and important of the ancient documents of the borough, and to prepare and publish other works, such as books of plans or collections of essays, calculated to elucidate the history of Southampton.*

Publications:

5474 Vols. 1, 2, 4, 6. Court leet records, transcribed and ed. F. J. C. Hearnshaw and D. M. Hearnshaw. 1 vol. in 4. 1905–8. [Pt. 1: 1550–77; pt. 2: 1578–1602; pt. 3: 1603–24; pt. 4: supplement, containing glossary of select terms, notes on syntax and dialect, and indexes]

5475 Vol. 3. Maps and plans of old Southampton, ed. with notes by W. H. Rogers. [1907?].

5476 Vol. 5. Leet jurisdiction in England, especially as illustrated by the records of the court leet of Southampton, by F. J. C. Hearnshaw. 1908.

5477 Vols. 7, 9. Charters of the borough of Southampton, ed., with introd. and notes, by H. W. Gidden. 2 vols. 1909–1910. [Vol. i: 1199–1480. Vol. ii: 1484–1836]

5478 Vol. 8. The history and antiquity of Southampton, with some conjectures concerning the Roman Clausentum, by John Speed, written about 1770; ed., with introd., notes and index, by Elinor R. Aubrey. 1909.

5479 Vols. 10–12. The oak book of Southampton, of *c*. 1300, transcribed and ed., with translation, introd. and notes, etc., by P. Studer. 3 vols. 1910–11. [Vol. i: Anglo-French ordinances of the ancient guild-merchant of Southampton, etc. Vol. ii: 14th cent. version of the rolls of Oleron. Vol. iii: Supplement, containing notes on the Anglo-French dialect of Southampton (early 14th cent.), glossary, and indexes]

5480 Vols. 13, 14, 17. The black book of Southampton, transcribed and ed., with translation, introd., notes, etc., by A. B. Wallis Chapman. 3 vols. 1912–15. [Vol. i: *c*. 1388–1414. Vol. ii: *c*. 1414–1503. Vol. iii: *c*. 1497–1620]

5481 Vol. 15. The port books of Southampton, or (Anglo-French) accounts of Robert Florys, water-bailiff and receiver of petty-customs, 1427–30, transcribed and ed., with notes, introd., glossary, etc., by P. Studer. 1913.

5482 Vol. 16. Books of examinations and depositions, 1570–94, transcribed by Gertrude H. Hamilton; introd. by Elinor R. Aubrey. 1914.

5483 Vol. 18. The sign manuals, and the letters patent of Southampton to 1422, ed., with introd., notes, and index, by H. W. Gidden. Vol. i. 1916. [For vol. ii see no. 5485 below]

5484 Vols. 19, 21, 24, 25. The assembly books of Southampton, ed., with introd., notes, and index, by J. W. Horrocks. 4 vols. [Vol. i: 1602–8. Vol. ii: 1609–10. Vol. iii: 1611–14. Vol. iv: 1615–16]

5485 Vol. 20. The letters patent of Southampton, 1415–1612, ed., with introd., notes, and index, by H. W. Gidden. Vol. ii. 1919. [Continues no. 5483 above]

5486 Vol. 22. Letters of the 15th and 16th cent., from the archives of Southampton, ed. R. C. Anderson. 1921.

5487 Vol. 23. The assize of bread book, 1477–1517, ed. R. C. Anderson. 1923.

5488 Vol. 26. The book of examinations, 1601–2, with a list of ships belonging to Southampton, 1570–1603, ed. R. C. Anderson. 1926.

5489 Vols. 27, 28, 30. The book of remembrance of Southampton, ed., with introd., notes and index, by H. W. Gidden. 3 vols. 1927–30. [Vol. i: 1440–1620. Vol. ii: 1303–1518. Vol. iii: 1483–1563]

5490 Vols. 29, 31, 34, 36. The book of examinations and depositions, 1622–44, ed. R. C. Anderson. 4 vols. 1929–1936. [Vol. i: 1622–7. Vol. ii: 1627–34. Vol. iii: 1634–9. Vol. iv: 1639–44]

5491 Vols. 32, 33. The miscellaneous papers of Capt. Thomas Stockwell, 1590–1611, ed. J. Rutherford. 2 vols. 1932–3. [Relating to municipal affairs and to the Southampton estates of Sir Oliver Lambert]

SOUTH-EASTERN UNION OF SCIENTIFIC SOCIETIES

Founded 1896, *to systematise scientific work among the affiliated societies; to impart greater impetus to scientific research; and, in general, to promote the study and advancement of science by co-operation. The Union has an archaeological section.*

South Eastern Naturalist [from 1928 the South Eastern Naturalist and Antiquary], being the proceedings and transactions of the Union, 1901–33 (28 vols. 1901–33):

5492 Vol. for 1902.
a Leprosy in the middle ages, by J. Hutchinson.
b Eolithic flint implements, by E. R. Harrison.

5493 Vol. for 1903.
a A late Keltic cemetery at Harlyn bay [Corn.], by R. A. Bullen.

5494 Vol. for 1904.
a Allington castle [Kent], by D. C. Falcke.
b The Friars, Aylesford [Kent], by C. H. Fielding.
c The meridional position of megaliths in Kent, compared with those of Wilts., and also with those of earthworks and churches, by F. J. Bennett.
d The abbey and St. Leonard's tower at West Malling [Kent], by G. M. Livett.
e A few notes on the corporation museum, Maidstone, formerly Chillington manor house, by J. H. Allchin.

5495 Vol. for 1905.
a The law of treasure trove as it affects archaeological researches, by W. Martin.

b Antiquities of Reigate [Surr.], by E. Penfold.
c Gatton [Surr.] in the past, by S. W. Kershaw.

5496 Vol. for 1906.

a Sea erosion and coast protection, by E. A. Martin.
b Pevensey [castle, Suss.] and its lords, by E. E. Crake.
c Michelham, a Sussex priory, by E. E. Crake.

5497 Vol. for 1907.

a Side streams in archaeology [events in the history of Woolwich, Plumstead and Eltham], by W. T. Vincent.

5498 Vol. for 1908.

a Gilbert White and Sussex, by W. H. Mullens.
b Mediaeval timber houses of Kent and Sussex, by J. E. Ray.
c Hastings castle, by H. Sands.

5499 Vol. for 1909.

a The records of Southampton, by F. J. C. Hearnshaw.
b Prehistoric memorials of Hampshire, by W. Dale.
c Hospital of St. Cross [Winchester], by N. C. H. Nisbett.
d Wolvesey castle, by N. C. H. Nisbett.

5500 Vol. for 1910.

a The Pilgrims' way between Farnham and Albury [Surr.], by J. G. N. Clift.
b The interpretation of maps of the 16th and 17th cent., by W. Martin.
c Charterhouse [school, Godalming, Surr.], by O. H. Latter.

5501 Vol. for 1911.

a The abbey church of St. Albans, by Mrs. W. Plomer-Young.

5502 Vol. for 1912.

a A review of the development of small arms, by J. E. Price.
b Parish church of Folkestone, by J. B. Walton.

5503 Vol. for 1913.

a The Temple [London], by W. Martin.

5504 Vol. for 1914.

a The alum trade in the 15th and 16th cent., and the beginnings of the alum industry in England, by R. Jenkins.

5505 Vol. for 1915.

a Brighton's lost river, by E. A. Martin.
b The study of place names, with illustrations from the south-east of England, by A. Bonner.
c The connection of Kew with the history of botany, by G. S. Boulger.

5506 Vol. for 1916.

a Prehistoric man, by F. W. Keeble.
b Review of British coinage [from the early Britons to Henry VIII] with special reference to that of the south-eastern district of England, by A. Archibald.

5507 Vol. for 1917.

a Skulls and jaws of ancient man, and his implements, by E. A. Martin.
b London tokens [18th cent.], by W. Dale.
c Notable trees and old gardens of London, by B. D. Jackson.

d The association of the Chelsea physic garden with the history of botany, by G. S. Boulger.

5508 Vol. for 1918.

a Romano-British mints, by P. H. Webb.

5509 Vol. for 1919.

a The public woodlands of London: the story of the work of the city corporation in saving open spaces, by L. W. Chubb.

5510 Vol. for 1922.

a History of lichens in the British Isles, by A. L. Smith.

5511 Vol. for 1923.

a Prehistoric man in Kent, by R. A. Smith.
b The story of some common garden plants, by D. Prain.

5512 Vol. for 1925.

a Barfrestone church [Kent], by A. H. Reade.

5513 Vol. for 1926.

a Essex before the Saxons, by R. A. Smith.
b Dr. Wm. Gilberd [d. 1603], of Colchester, author of *De Magnete*, by C. E. Benham.

5514 Vol. for 1928.

a Some understandings in the study of archaeology, by W. Martin.
b History of the regional survey movement, by C. C. Fagg.
c Archaeology of the Medway valley, by A. E. Hurse.
d Palaeolithic site at Bapchild, near Sittingbourne, by H. G. Dines.

5515 Vol. for 1929.

a The pre-Roman inhabitants of southern England, by Sir A. Keith.
b The pre-history of village churches, by A. H. Allcroft. [Contd. in vol. for 1931]
c The Blackpatch [Suss.] excavations, by J. H. Pull.

5516 Vol. for 1930.

a The Crusades [1096–1272] and pilgrimages, by W. E. St. L. Finny.
b Some correlations between the prehistory of Hampshire and Africa, by L. S. Palmer.

5517 Vol. for 1931.

a Archaeological surveys, by H. J. E. Peake.
b The kings and kingdom of Wessex [519–940], by W. E. St. L. Finny.
c Pre-Roman Winchester, by J. P. Williams-Freeman.

5518 Vol. for 1932.

a British field-archaeology, past and future, by R. E. M. Wheeler.
b Medieval games and gaderyngs at Kingston-upon-Thames, by W. E. St. L. Finny.

5519 Vol. for 1933.

a Viking period antiquities in England, by T. D. Kendrick.

Other publications:

5520 A survey and record of Woolwich and West Kent, containing descriptions and records, brought up-to-date, of the geology, botany, zoology, archaeology and industries of the district, with a brief photographic commentary, in commemoration of the 12th annual congress, 1907, of the Union. General editors: C. H. Grinling, T. A. Ingram, B. C. Polkinghorne. 1909.

SOUTHEND-ON-SEA AND DISTRICT ANTIQUARIAN AND HISTORICAL SOCIETY

(Southend-on-Sea Antiquarian Society)

Founded 1920, to encourage the study of antiquities and to examine and record all evidence of historic and prehistoric remains of antiquarian interest within the hundred of Rochford.

Transactions, vols. 1–2 (1921–34):

5521 Vol. 1.
a 'Porters' [house at Southend], by C. Nicholson.
b Prittlewell priory: its story from the 12th to the 16th cent., by J. W. Burrows.
c Essex windmills, by J. Turner.
d Local government in the 13th cent., with special reference to Rochford hundred, by Helen M. Cam.
e The Roman and Saxon settlements, Southend-on-Sea, by W. Pollitt. [Appendix A: Report on three skulls from ancient cemetery at Southend-on-Sea, by A. Keith. Appendix B: Archaeological evidences (pre-Norman) found in the Rochford hundred]
f The compotus of the manor of Earl's Fee, Prittlewell, 1515, by J. F. Nichols.
g Milton Hall [manor] in 1500, by J. F. Nichols.
h Notes on the history of Southchurch, by J. F. Nichols.
i New lights on the history of Milton hamlet, by J. F. Nichols.
j Eastwood and its church, by W. A. Mepham.
k A shell-mound on a prehistoric creek at Southchurch, Essex, probably belonging to the beaker period of the bronze age, by A. G. Francis.
l Regular canons of the order of St. Augustine, by Rose Graham.
m Milton Hall [manor]: 'extent' of 1309 and an inventory of 1278, by J. F. Nichols.

5522 Vol. 2.
a When the 'old town' was Leigh [i.e. Leigh-on-Sea in the first half of the 19th cent.], by H. N. Bride.
b Farming operations in the 14th cent., by J. F. Nichols.
c Prittlewell camp: report of excavations, by W. A. Mepham.
d A causeway at the prehistoric settlement of Southchurch, Essex, by A. G. Francis.
e The East Saxons of Prittlewell, by W. Pollitt.
f Place-names of Rochford hundred, by P. H. Reaney.
g Milton Hall, the compotus of 1299, by J. F. Nichols.
h Local historical problems, by J. W. Burrows. Was the *Mayflower* a Leigh vessel? Why did the Peasants' revolt [1381] originate in south-east Essex? Where was the battle of Assandune fought [1016]?
i Great Wakering, by W. A. Mepham.
j The Dutch invasion of the Thames, 1667: Edward Gregory's report.
k 15th-cent. house: no. 13 North Street, Prittlewell, by L. Freeborn.
l Prints, paintings, and drawings of Rochford hundred, by R. W. Higgs.
m Sir Stephen Glynne's notes on the churches of Prittlewell and Leigh.

SOUTHPORT LITERARY AND PHILOSOPHICAL SOCIETY

Founded 1881. Dissolved 1914.

Proceedings, 1900–1906 (6 vols. [1901–6]):

5523 Vol. for 1900–1.
a Old halls of Lancashire and Cheshire, by H. Taylor.

5524 Vol. for 1901–2.
a Some contemporaries of Shakespeare, by J. T. Foard.
b Cromwell and the army, by J. Openshaw.

5525 Vol. for 1902–3.
a The mystery of the Casket letters, by G. E. Johnson.
b The contribution of journalism to literature, by F. Riley.

5526 Vol. for 1903–4.
a The literary work of Sir Walter Raleigh, by G. E. Johnson.
b The real life of Shakespeare, by J. T. Foard.
c Life and writings of Capt. John Smith [d. 1631], by E. Ackroyd.
d Margaret Paston: domestic life during the wars of the roses, by W. W. Cannon.
e The novels of Benjamin Disraeli: their literary and political importance, by W. Permewan.
f Some literary reminiscences of Lancashire, by J. Bromley.

5527 Vol. for 1904–5.
a An Old English chronicle [Geoffrey of Monmouth's], and its influence on English literature, by A. Dall.
b The black art, by J. Openshaw.

5528 Vol. for 1905–6.
a Some historical aspects of trades unionism, by A. Dall.
b George Selwyn [d. 1791] and his letters, by H. Farr.
c Historical memoirs, by G. B. Hertz.

SOUTHPORT SOCIETY OF NATURAL SCIENCE

Founded 1890, to encourage and stimulate the study of various branches of natural science in the town and neighbourhood.

Fifth—Twenty-seventh Report (23 vols. 1901–33):

5529 7th Report.
a A neolithic interment, by G. W. Chaster.

5530 8th Report.
a Martin mere, by H. Brodrick.

5531 11th Report.
a A recently discovered skeleton in Scoska cave, Littondale, by J. B. Barnes and H. Brodrick.

5532 12th Report.
a General index to papers in First–Twelfth Reports.

STAFFORDSHIRE PARISH REGISTER SOCIETY

Founded 1900, to preserve the contents of the parochial registers in the county of Stafford by transcribing and printing them.

Publications:

5533 Alstonfield parish register [1538–1812]. 1902–6.

5534 Haughton parish register [1570–1812]. 1902–6.

5535 Barton under Needwood parish register [1571–1812]. 1902–9.

5536 Standon parish register, 1558–1812. 1902–6.

5537 Castle church, Stafford, parish register [1568–1812]. 1903.

5538 Milwich parish register [1573–1711]. 1904.

5539 The registers of Hamstall Ridware [1598–1812]. 1904–6.

5540 Berkswich with Walton parish register, 1601–1812. 1905.

5541 Tatenhill parish register, 1563–1812. 1905.

5542 Barlaston parish register, 1573–1812. 1905.

5543 Pipe Ridware parish register [1561–1812]. 1905. [Index issued separately]

5544 Brewood parish register. Vol. i: 1562–1649. 1906. [No more published, 1967]

5545 Trentham parish register [1558–1812], copied by S. W. Hutchinson. 1 vol. in 2. 1906.

5546 Rocester parish register, 1565–1812. 1 vol. in 2. 1906–9.

5547 Eccleshall parish register [1573–1667]. 1 vol. in 2. 1907–10.

5548 Ellastone parish register, 1538–1812. 1 vol. in 2. 1907–12.

5549 West Bromwich parish register. Vol. i: 1608–58. 1909. [No more published, 1967]

5550 Stowe parish register. Vol. i: 1613–89. 1909. [No more published, 1967]

5551 Hints parish register, 1558–1812. 1910.

5552 Croxden parish register, 1674–1812, also Bradley-in-the-Moors parish register, 1674–1812. 1912.

5553 Rowley Regis parish register, 1539–1812. 1 vol. in 3. 1912–15.

5554 Burslem parish register, 1578–1812. 1 vol. in 3. 1913.

5555 Wolstanton parish register, 1624–1812. 1 vol. in 2. 1914.

5556 Blymhill parish register, 1561–1812. 1914.

5557 Stoke-upon-Trent parish register, 1629–1812. 1 vol. in 4. 1914–27.

5558 Betley parish register, 1538–1812. 1916.

5559 Tamworth parish register. Pt. 1: 1558–1614. 1917. [No more published, 1967]

5560 Leek parish register. Pt. 1: 1634–95. 1919. [No more published, 1967]

5561 Bucknall-cum-Bagnall parish register, 1762–1812. 1920.

5562 Penn parish register, 1570–1754. 1921.

5563 Gnosall parish register [burials and baptisms, 1572–1699; marriages, 1572–1785; payments for lestalls, i.e. burial within the church, 1669–99]. 1922.

5564 Tipton parish register, 1513–1736. 1923.

5565 Norton-in-the-Moors parish register, 1574–1751. 1924. [Contd. as Norton-le-Moors parish register, 1754–1837, published 1943]

5566 Rugeley parish register. Pt. 1: 1569–1722. 1928. [No more published, 1967]

5567 Mucklestone parish register. Pt. 1: 1555–1701. 1929. [No more published, 1967]

5568 Tettenhall parish register. Pt. 1: 1602–1744. 1930. [No more published, 1967]

5569 Newcastle-under-Lyme parish register. Pt. 1: 1563–1705. 1931. [Pt. 2: 1705–70, published 1939]

5570 Wolverhampton parish register. Pt. 1: 1539–1660. 1932. [Index issued separately. A further vol., containing marriages only, 1660–1734, was published in 1952]

5571 Weston-under-Lizard parish register, 1654–1812. 1933.

SUFFOLK INSTITUTE OF ARCHAEOLOGY AND NATURAL HISTORY

Founded 1848, as the Bury and West Suffolk Archaeological Institute, to collect and publish information on the archaeology and natural history of Suffolk, and to oppose and prevent any injuries with which ancient monuments, within the county, may be threatened, and to collect accurate drawings, plans, and descriptions thereof. Title changed to above form in 1853.

Proceedings, vols. 11–21 (1901–33):

5572 Vol. 11.
  a The condition of the archdeaconries of Suffolk and Sudbury in 1603.
  b A Suffolk captain of the time of Queen Elizabeth [Thomas Cheston], by J. H. Josselyn.
  c Flint-work inscription on Blythburgh church, by Sir W. R. Gowers.
  d Annual excursion. [Includes a paper on Ickworth and Little Saxham by S. H. A. Hervey]
  e Excursion to Little Wenham.
  f Conversazione at Ipswich. [Includes a paper on the parentage of Cardinal Wolsey by V. B. Redstone]
  g Gild of S. Peter in Bardwell [being extracts from mss. relating to the gild], comp. F. E. Warren.
  h A pre-Reformation village gild [the gild of S. Peter in Bardwell], by F. E. Warren.
  i Extent of Hadleigh manor, 1305, by Lord J. Hervey.
  j *Nomina villarum*, Suffolk, 1316 [the returns of the names of the lords of townships for the purpose of effecting military levies].
  k Neolithic Suffolk, by E. R. H. Hancox.
  l Hadleigh.
  m Kersey, by W. Fickling.
  n Polstead church.
  o Assington church and the Hall.
  p Ash Bocking, by M. B. Cowell.
  q Tudenham St. Martin, by V. B. Redstone.
  r Records of Sudbury archdeaconry, by V. B. Redstone. [Also published separately, 1902]
  s Notes on Suffolk castles, by V. B. Redstone.
  t Notes on some east Suffolk neoliths, by W. A. Dutt.
  u Lowestoft china factory, by H. C. Casley.

5573 Vol. 12.
  a Chapels, chantries and gilds in Suffolk, by V. B. Redstone.
  b Haughley Park and the Sulyards, by A. Dimock.
  c The Tollemaches of Bentley, by Mrs. C. Roundell.
  d The Tollemaches of Helmingham, by Mrs. C. Roundell.
  e Helmingham Hall at the close of the 19th cent., by Mrs. C. Roundell.
  f Excursions, 1904. [Includes an account of Lydgate castle and manor]
  g Taxation of Ipswich for the Welsh war, 1282, by E. Powell.
  h An Ipswich worker of Elizabethan church plate [Jeffrey Gilbert], by H. C. Casley.
  i The Chaucer-Malyn family, Ipswich, by V. B. Redstone.
  j Aldeburgh, by V. B. Redstone.
  k Debenham: its halls and manors.

l Crabbe as a botanist, by J. Groves. [George Crabbe, d. 1832]

m Summer excursion, 1906. [Includes an account of the Warbanks, earthworks near Cockfield]

n Calendar of pre-Reformation wills, testaments, probates, administrations, registered at the probate office, Bury St. Edmunds, ed. V. B. Redstone. [See also vol. 13 below]

5574 Vol. 13.

a Anglo-Saxon cemetery, Hadleigh Road, Ipswich, by Nina F. Layard.

b Nicholas of Kenton [d. 1468], by F. S. Stevenson.

c Discovery of Roman remains at Aldeburgh, May 1907, by C. Ganz.

d Extracts from the diary of Sir James Thornhill, May 16th, 1711.

e The Booke of Subscriptions (1663–1705) [being a record of oaths taken by members and officers of the corporation of Bury St. Edmunds], by W. Symonds.

f Tabular lists from [V. B.] Redstone's calendar of Bury wills, by C. Partridge. [See also vol. 12 above]

g Suffolk workers of Elizabethan church plate, by H. C. Casley.

h Annual excursion, 1907. [Includes an account of Mettingham castle and church]

i Discovery of prehistoric implements at Danecroft, Stowmarket, by St. J. F. M. Fancourt.

j Presbyterian church government in Suffolk, 1643–7, by V. B. Redstone.

k The Warbanks [earthworks] at Cockfield, 1908, by E. Hill.

l List of rectors [c. 1200–1898] with sundry documents relating to church matters at Barton Mills, by E. Powell.

m St. Edmund's Bury [in medieval times] and town rental for 1295, by V. B. Redstone.

n Middleton: a mural painting [in the church], by C. Ganz.

o The Norfolk helmet [over the tomb of Thomas Howard, 3rd Duke of Norfolk, d. 1554] in Framlingham church, by C. Ganz.

p Drury helmet, Hawstead church [the helmet of Sir William Drury, d. 1557], by C. Ganz.

q Lindsey castle and chapel.

r Architectural details of Lindsey chapel, by H. J. Wright.

s Discovery of Roman remains at Old Newton [near Stowmarket], by C. W. Low.

t Calendar of the muniments of the borough of Sudbury, by Ethel Stokes and Lilian Redstone. [Also published separately, 1909]

u First ministers' account of the possessions of the abbey of St. Edmund [1539–40], by Lilian J. Redstone.

v Annual excursion, 1909. [Includes an account of Freston Tower, by C. R. Durrant]

5575 Vol. 14.

a A few notes on an iron Anglo-Saxon brooch supposed to have been found at Hoxne, by C. W. Low.

b Calendar of exchequer depositions by commission during the reigns of Elizabeth and James I, relating to Suffolk, by R. F. Bullen.

c Earthwork near Butley, by H. St. G. Gray.

d St. Peter's church, Sudbury, by B. Oliver.

e All Saints' church, Sudbury.

f Early Sudbury clothiers, by V. B. Redstone.

g Early Sudbury records, by Ethel Stokes.

h A bailiff's roll of the manor of Lawshall, 1393–4, by H. W. Saunders.

i The Blois mss. [containing pedigrees of Suffolk families, Suffolk church notes, and a Suffolk armoury, all compiled in the 17th cent.], by E. Farrer.

j Brome Hall, by the Hon. A. Rosamund Bateman-Hanbury.

k Ipswich port books, by V. B. Redstone.

l Eye castle, by H. A. Harris.

m Note on the Red Book of Eye, by F. E. Warren.

n Hardwick House, Bury St. Edmunds, by Lilian J. Redstone.

o Cullum letters [16th–18th cent.], by V. B. Redstone.

p The wodewose in East Anglian church decoration, by H. D. Ellis.

q Hintlesham Hall, by J. S. Corder.

r Site of Rumburgh priory, by V. B. Redstone.

s South Elmham deanery, by V. B. Redstone.

t House of the Knights Templars, Dunwich, by V. B. Redstone.

5576 Vol. 15.

a Pre-palaeolithic man, by J. R. Moir.

b Hadleigh deanery and its court.

c Robert Bloomfield, the Suffolk poet [d. 1823].

d Melton old gaol, by V. B. Redstone.

e Edwardstone: its church and priory.

f Whelnetham Magna: suit *re* advowson, 1286, by E. Powell.

g Muster rolls of the [Suffolk] territorials in Tudor times, by E. Powell. [Contd. in vols. 16, 18, and 19]

h Suffolk county records.

i Extracts from the sessions order book, 1639–51.

j Slavery and serfdom in England with special reference to East Anglia, by F. E. Warren.

k The liberty of St. Edmund, by Lilian J. Redstone.

l The ancient chapel of Bures.

m Cratfield church: the font, by A. J. Bedell.

n Suffolk under arms [being the military history of the county], by V. B. Redstone.

o Accounts and diary of Rev. John Rhodes, rector of Barton Mills, 1662–7, by E. Powell.

p Early Suffolk wills [enrolled at Ipswich 1284–1660], by V. B. Redstone.

5577 Vol. 16.

a Yaxley Hall: its owners and occupiers, by E. Farrer.

b The old minster at South Elmham, classified and described by J. T. Micklethwaite.

c Barnardiston vaults in Kedington church, by W. H. B.W.

d Wulcy of Suffolk, by V. B. Redstone.

e Ancient flint implements of Suffolk, by J. R. Moir.

f Notes on Bury corner posts [in houses], by J. S. Carder.

g Extracts from the Chevallier papers, 1728–62, by Frances E. M. Chevallier.

h Mary Beale, by G. Milner-Gibson-Cullum.

i St. Fursey [7th cent.], by F. E. Warren.

5578 Vol. 17.

a Flint tools showing well-defined finger-grips, by Nina F. Layard.

b The font at Monks' Soham, by C. Morley.

c Inventories of the college of Stoke-by-Clare taken in 1534 and 1547–8, transcribed and annotated by Sir W. St. J. Hope.

d Suffolk 'Dane stones', by C. Morley.

e *Nonarum inquisitiones* for Suffolk [a subsidy granted to Edward III, 1341], by W. A. Wickham.

f Notes on St. Mary the Virgin, Coddenham.

g Notes on Needham Market church, by E. T. Lingwood.

h The Venerable Francis Mason [d. 1621], *Vindex ecclesiae Anglicanae*, rector of Sudbourne cum Orford, by H. W. B. Wayman.

i Origin, purposes, and development of parish gilds in England, by H. F. Westlake.

j The Ampton sealed book [being a copy at Ampton of the prayer-books known as 'sealed books' which were corrected by a specially appointed commission, 1661, in accordance with the 'book annexed' to the Act of Uniformity], by W. A. Wickham.

k Freckenham: notes and theories on the village and its unrecorded castle, by C. Morley.
l Excursion to Hadleigh.

5579 Vol. 18.

a Traces of Saxon architecture yet remaining in Suffolk, by C. Morley.
b St. Botolph (Botwulf) and Iken, by F. S. Stevenson.
c Henry Coggeshall of Orford: inventor and mathematician, by H. W. B. Wayman.
d Hepworth and its rectors, by T. T. Methold.
e Subject index of articles, contributions, papers, published in the Proceedings of the Institute, 1898–1921, vols. 10–17 inclusive, comp. R. F. Bullen.
f Clovesho. 1: The councils [of the early English church] and the locality, by C. Morley. 2: Clovesho disclosed [as being at Mildenhall], by H. A. Harris. 3: The witan of Godmundesley [747]: an evidence of locality, by F. S. Stevenson.
g The parsons and patrons of Ampton, by W. A. Wickham.
h Circular towers, by C. Morley.
i The sea port of Frostenden. 1: Its place in history, by C. Morley. 2: The Danish quay discovered, by E. R. Cooper.
j Part of the Peddar way in Suffolk, by H. C. Hill.
k Thorndon before the Conquest, by H. A. Harris.
l The Essex and Suffolk border, by J. H. Round.

5580 Vol. 19.

a The Suffolk shore: Yarmouth to Aldeburgh, by J. A. Steers.
b Sequestrations in Suffolk [of clergy, 1642–60], by F. R. Bullen.
c A chancery case illustrating life in Clare at the end of the 16th cent., by Gladys A. Thornton.
d Excavations on the site of the Augustinian alien priory of Great Bricett, by F. H. Fairweather.
e The present state of the Elmham controversy [on the site of the Anglo-Saxon see of Elmham], by F. S. Stevenson.
f The Suffolk coast: Orford Ness, by J. A. Steers. [Includes an account of the development of the bar at Orford Ness from the 12th cent.]
g A check-list of the sacred buildings of Suffolk to which are added gilds, by C. Morley.
h Suffolk muster roll, 1579: part of hundred of Babbeogh, transcribed by E. C. Powell.
i Combretonium and Brettenham, by H. C. Hill.
j St. Saviour's hospital, Bury St. Edmunds, by E. R. Burdon.
k Medieval mural paintings, by H. A. Harris.
l List of Suffolk churches associated with mural paintings, by H. A. Harris.
m Some pedigrees of Denny, Le Dennys, etc., by H. L. L. Denny.
n The Burgate Hall charters, by E. Farrer.

5581 Vol. 20.

a The island of Lothingland, 1584, by V. B. Redstone.
b Letheringham abbey, by E. Farrer.
c Early archdeacons of Norwich diocese [1070–1214], by L. Landon.
d Suffolk limiters [begging friars], by Lilian J. Redstone. [Also published separately, 1928]
e Notes on some families and brasses at Great Thurlow and Little Bradley, by H. C. Andrews.
f St. Peter's Hall, South Elmham, by E. Farrer.
g List of [Suffolk] deeds recently acquired by the Institute, comp. E. R. Burdon, with introd. by E. Farrer.
h Notes on Suffolk manuscript books [chiefly the manu-

script of the Canterbury Tales, Harl. ms. 7335], by Lilian J. Redstone.
i Excursions. [Includes accounts of Gorleston, and Crows Hall]
j Debenham church, by V. B. Redstone.
k The family of William Sancroft, archbishop of Canterbury, by C. Boyce.
l Windmills, with special reference to those in Suffolk, by A. Woolford.
m The Dunthorne mss. [including material relating to the parishes of Dennington, East Bergholt, Debenham, and Copdock], by E. Farrer.
n Everard, bishop of Norwich, by L. Landon.
o Suffolk courts in English, by Sybil Andrews and Lilian J. Redstone. [Extracts from a 16th cent. English translation of the Latin records of various Suffolk manorcourts held 1399–1480. Also published separately, 1929]
p Screenwork in Suffolk, by W. W. Lillie. [Contd. in vol. 21]
q The lord lieutenancy of Suffolk under the Tudors.
r Third excursion. [Includes an account of St. Martin's church, Nacton, by E. R. Hancox]
s The seal of a prior of Stoke-by-Clare, by E. Farrer.
t Chapel of St. Nicholas, Gipping, by P. J. Turner.
u Great Ashfield cross, by H. C. Hill.
v Kedington cross, by H. C. Hill.

5582 Vol. 21.

a Early Suffolk heraldry, by E. Farrer.
b Restoration and reconstruction of All Saints, Thorndon, by H. A. Harris.
c Two unusual subjects in ancient glass in Long Melford church, by C. Woodforde. [See also below]
d Mediaeval glass in Yaxley church, by C. Woodforde.
e Stained glass in the east window of Yaxley church, by H. A. Harris.
f S. Robert of Bury St. Edmunds, by H. C. Hill.
g Moulton pack-horse bridge, by A. A. Watkins.
h Ancient sun alignments: the meaning of artificial mounds and mark stones, by H. Hudson, with a commentary by F. A. Bennett. [On the early history of astronomy]
i Swan-marks of Suffolk, by N. F. Ticehurst.
j The retable at Thornham Parva, by W. W. Lillie.
k Seals of the priory of Stoke-by-Clare, by E. Farrer.
l Notes by [L. W.] H. Whitehead with reference to paper on glass in Long Melford church. [See above]
m The gaol at Bury St. Edmunds, by Mary D. Lobel.
n Additions to André Réville's account of events at Bury St. Edmunds following on the revolt of 1381 [in his *Le soulèvement des travailleurs d'Angleterre*], by Mary D. Lobel.
o A detailed account of the 1327 rising at Bury St. Edmunds and the subsequent trial, by Mary D. Lobel.
p The 15th cent. [painted] glass in Blythburgh church, by C. Woodforde.
q The Roman villa at Castle Hill, Whitton, Ipswich, by J. R. Moir and G. Maynard.

Other publications:

5583 The ship-money returns for the county of Suffolk, 1639–1640 (Harl. mss. 7540–7542), transcribed and ed. V. B. Redstone. 1904.

5584 Suffolk churchyard inscriptions, copied from the Darby transcription (made about 1825–34), by C. Partridge. Reprinted from [i.e. issued as supplement to] Proceedings, vols. 15, 17, and 18, 1913–23.

5585 The household book of Dame Alice de Bryene, of Acton Hall, Suffolk, Sept. 1412–Sept. 1413, with appendices, translated by Marian K. Dale, ed. V. B. Redstone. 1931.

SUNDERLAND ANTIQUARIAN SOCIETY

Founded 1899, *for inquiry into antiquities in general, more especially to investigate all matters of historical character connected with Sunderland and district.*

Antiquities of Sunderland and its vicinity, vols. 1–18 (1902–31):

5586 Vol. 1.

a Sunderland church and parish, by J. Robinson.
b Sunderland sacramental tokens, by R. Hyslop.
c A peep into an old Monkwearmouth ratebook [1776–84], by J. T. Middlemiss.

5587 Vol. 2.

a The history of the parish boundaries in the borough of Sunderland and the neighbourhood, by T. Randell.
b The natural boundary between Bishopwearmouth and Sunderland parishes, by G. W. Bain.
c Notes on the rectors of Bishopwearmouth, 1200–1900, by H. M. Wood.
d Some Saxon remains at Monkwearmouth church, by J. Patterson.

5588 Vol. 3.

a Sunderland ferry, by J. T. Middlemiss.
b Extracts from Monkwearmouth parish registers [1658–1812], by H. M. Wood.
c Notes on Dalden tower and the village of Dalton-le-Dale, by R. A. Aird.
d Extracts from Whitburn parish registers [1597–1795], by J. Patterson.
e Rectors of Whitburn [1245–1901].
f The family of Goodchild of Pallion Hall: their ancestors, descendants, and relatives, by H. R. Leighton.
g Rowland Wetherald, printer (1727–91), by B. R. Hill.

5589 Vol. 4.

a Post office development in Sunderland, 1830–1903, by G. W. Collinson.
b A Sunderland newspaper about 70 years ago [*The Sunderland Herald and Shields and Stockton Observer*, 1836], by J. T. Middlemiss.
c Some historic houses in Sunderland, by J. Robinson.
d History of the Sunderland moor as recorded in the minute book of the ancient corporation of the borough of Sunderland [1764–1853], by B. Morton.
e Notes on the life and works of John Laurence, rector of Bishop Wearmouth, 1721–32, by G. O. Bellewes. [Contd. in vol. 10]
f The records of two Newbottle families [the Chiltons and the Bates], by H. R. Leighton.
g Assembly Garth and Trafalgar Square [Sunderland], merchant seamen's houses, by B. Morton.

5590 Vol. 5.

a The topography of Southwick, by G. W. Bain.
b Roman road and remains at Bishopwearmouth, by J. Robinson.
c Depositions in a lawsuit against the freemen and stallingers about 1730, by T. Randell.
d The volunteer movement in Sunderland in the time of the Napoleonic wars, by J. Patterson.
e 'The antient chappel in the Corn Market, Sunderland-near-the-sea' [the first Dissenters' place of worship in Sunderland, erected *c*. 1711], by G. W. Bain.
f The Rev. Samuel Turner [d. 1854], sometime minister of the Corn Market chapel, by J. T. Middlemiss.

5591 Vol. 6.

a Silksworth and St. Leonard's chapel, by J. Patterson.
b A visit to Silksworth Hall.

c The Secession meeting house in Spring Garden Lane and some of its ministers, by R. Hyslop.
d A critical enquiry into the origin and status of the freemen and stallingers of Sunderland, by V. Ritson.
e Early days of banking in Sunderland [1768–1857], by G. W. Bain.

5592 Vol. 7.

a Early printing presses of Sunderland [1771–1830], by G. W. Bain.
b The memorial stone, supposed to be that of Tidfirth, the last bishop of Hexham [d. *c*. 821], by C. C. Hodges.
c The priory of Finchale, by J. Patterson.
d Potteries of Sunderland and neighbourhood, by W. R. Ball.
e Some account of St. George's Square [Sunderland], and the people connected therewith, by C. L. Cummings.

5593 Vol. 8.

a Extracts from the registers and overseers' account books of Boldon parish [1583–1848], by J. Patterson.
b Rectors of Boldon [1311–1906], by J. Patterson.
c Some account of Sunderland bridge, by J. T. Middlemiss.
d The topography of Bishopwearmouth, by G. W. Bain. [Contd. in vol. 11]

5594 Vol. 9.

a The Sunderland subscription library, by J. J. Kitts.
b Extracts from the Houghton registers [1563–1812], by H. M. Wood.
c A chapel of ease: the early records of St. John's church, Sunderland [1769–1830], by V. Ritson.
d Local paper mills, by J. P. Cornett.
e The Hutton family (papermakers), by R. M. Richardson.

5595 Vol. 10.

a History of the Sunderland Beef-steak Club, founded 1828, by G. W. Bain.
b The old Presbyterian chapel in Maling's Rigg, by R. Hyslop.
c Notes on the parish of Seaham, by R. A. Aird.
d A sketch of the life of Sir Cuthbert Sharp [d. 1849], with a bibliography of his writings, by B. R. Hill.
e The Poor laws, with special reference to the old Sunderland workhouses, by J. J. Kitts.
f Notes on Bowmaker's mill [1736–1908], by R. Hyslop.

5596 Vol. 11.

a Riding the stang [an ancient punishment], by G. T. Brown.
b Tunstall, by M. Laverick.

5597 Vol. 12.

a Thomas Dixon [d. 1880] and his correspondents, by J. Patterson.
b Early history of the water supplies of Sunderland and South Shields, by G. B. Gibbs.
c Notes on the cross-slab at St. Paul's church, Jarrow, by J. D. Rose.
d The birthplace of the Venerable Bede, by J. Patterson.

5598 Vol. 13.

a Family notices from the *Newcastle Courant*, 1745–1800, relating to Sunderland and district, by E. Dodds and H. M. Wood.

5599 Vol. 14.

a Recent finds of pre-historic remains at Hasting hill, near Offerton, by C. T. Trechmann.
b Notes on, and deductions from bones found at Hasting hill, near Sunderland, by T. C. Squance.
c Remarks on two pre-historic skulls, one found in a cave

at Ryhope and the other dredged from the bed of the river Wear, by T. C. Squance.

d Visit to Dalton-le-Dale and Easington, by R. A. Aird.

e Sherburn hospital, by J. J. Kitts.

5600 Vol. 15.

a Recent discoveries at Seaham church: some extracts from the parish register [1762–1812], by R. A. Aird.

b Some Sunderland poets [1783–1901], by J. T. Middlemiss.

c Prehistoric remains in the county of Durham, by C. T. Trechmann.

d Historical origin of some proverbs and familiar allusions, by G. W. Bain.

5601 Vol. 16.

a Pre-historic anthropology, by T. C. Squance.

b Paul Jones [d. 1792] and his connection with the north-east coast, by G. T. Brown.

c Non-parochial burial places in Sunderland, by J. Rutherford.

d Historical sketch of the Jewish congregation in Sunderland, by S. Daiches.

e Reminiscences of William Thackray of Sunderland, 1844–1915, by J. A. C. Deas.

5602 Vol. 17.

a Types of Saxon churches in the county of Durham, by D. S. Boutflower.

b Historical account of the Londonderry (Seaham and Sunderland) railway, by G. Hardy.

c Wearmouth worthies, by F. C. Macdonald. 1: Links with Archdeacon Paley [d. 1805]. 2: The Rev. Canon Miles, rector of Monkwearmouth church [d. 1891].

d List of books printed in Sunderland from the earliest known [1752] to 1830, by G. W. Bain.

5603 Vol. 18.

a Lumley castle, by R. A. Aird.

b Note on the Dales of Dalton [1502–1725], by T. C. Dale.

c Notes on the owners of Pallion, 1572–1815, by T. C. Dale.

d The place-name of Sunderland, by C. L. Cummings.

e North country hermits and hermitages, by J. J. Wilkinson.

f The dates of the monastic remains at St. Peter's church, Monkwearmouth, by J. Hall.

SURREY ARCHAEOLOGICAL SOCIETY

Founded 1854, to collect and publish information of all kinds on archaeological subjects relating to the county.

Surrey Archaeological Collections, relating to the history and antiquities of the county, vols. 16–41 (1901–33):

5604 Vol. 16.

a Notes on the manor and parish of Woodmansterne, by F. A. H. Lambert.

b The shell keep at Guildford castle, by H. E. Malden.

c Female head-dresses as exemplified by Surrey brasses, by J. L. André.

d Accounts of the overseers of the poor of Paris Garden, Southwark, 17 May 1608 to 30 Sept. 1671, by P. Norman.

e Preparations by the county of Surrey to resist the Spanish Armada, by A. R. Bax, from the original mss. in the Public Record Office.

f Send church and the chapel of Ripley, by P. M. Johnston.

g Church plate of Surrey, by T. S. Cooper. [Contd. from vol. 15. Also published separately with preceding articles in 1902]

h Notes. [Includes: The Presbyterian congregation at Kingston-upon-Thames]

5605 Vol. 17.

a Wotton church, by F. R. Fairbank.

b Rectors of Merstham, by A. J. Pearman.

c The manor of Ewood and the iron-works there in 1575, by M. S. Giuseppi.

d Weybridge parish registers, by Eleanor Lloyd.

e Note on two drawings by John Evelyn of Wotton House in 1640.

f Holmbury hill and the neighbourhood, by H. E. Malden.

g The names of those persons in Surrey who contributed to the loan of King Charles I [1626], communicated by A. R. Bax.

h Parliamentary survey of church lands in Surrey, made between 1649–58, from the original records preserved in the archiepiscopal library at Lambeth, by A. R. Bax.

i Some further notes on the restoration of Warlingham church in 1893–4, by P. M. Johnston.

j Wandsworth churchwardens' accounts, 1558–73, by C. T. Davis. [Contd. for 1574–1630 in vols. 18–20]

k Notes. [Includes: 1: The place-name Guildford. 5: Prehistoric chambers discovered at Waddon, near Croydon]

5606 Vol. 18.

a Thunderfield castle [earthworks], by H. E. Malden.

b Parliamentary survey of Guildford castle in 1650, communicated by A. R. Bax.

c Rake in Witley, with some notices of its former owners and of the ironworks on Witley and Thursley heaths, by M. S. Giuseppi.

d Notes on the architecture of Rake House, by R. Nevill.

e Notes on the history of the manor of Witley, by E. Foster.

f The church of Witley and Thursley chapel-of-ease, by P. M. Johnston.

g The archdeacons of Surrey, comp. H. E. Malden.

h The lay subsidy assessments for Surrey in 1593 or 1594, transcribed by A. R. Bax. [Contd. in vol. 19]

5607 Vol. 19.

a Roman coins from Croydon (Constantius II, Constans, Magnentius, and Gallus), by G. F. Hill.

b Ashted and the de Mara chantry, by H. E. Malden.

c Note on a late Keltic burial ground recently discovered at Haslemere, by E. W. Swanton.

d The corporation in Godalming, by R. Nevill. [With an appendix including the letters patent of inspeximus of charter of Elizabeth I, 25 Jan. 1574/5, by Charles II, 1 Mar. 1665/6, and extracts from the corporation records]

e Notes. [Includes: 1: The old taverns of Surrey. 4: St. Mary's church, Blechingley. 5: The churches of Letherhead, Mickleham, Fetcham, and Ashtead, as they were forty years ago. 7: Rectors of Merstham]

5608 Vol. 20.

a Stoke D'Abernon church, by P. M. Johnston. [With a list of 12th and 13th cent. church chests in England. Supplementary notes on Stoke D'Abernon church occur in vol. 21]

b Rental of the manor of Merstham in the year 1552, communicated by Lord Hylton. [Transcript]

c The earthworks at Lagham, by H. E. Malden.

d Recent and former discoveries [of prehistoric, Romano-British and Anglo-Saxon remains] at Hawkshill, by R. A. Smith.

e Presentations to benefices in Surrey during the Commonwealth, 1651–9, communicated by A. R. Bax.

f Remains of an ancient building at Rotherhith, by P. Norman.

g Villenage in the weald of Surrey, by H. E. Malden.

h The manor house, Byfleet, by Frances T. Mitchell.

i Notes on the architecture of the manor house, Byfleet, by E. P. Warren.

j Notes. [Includes: 1: An anchorite's cell at Letherhead church. 2: Discovery of ancient pottery near Farnham in 1906. 4: Recent discoveries of prehistoric pottery at Wallington]

5609 Vol. 21.

a Excavations in an Anglo-Saxon burial ground at Mitcham, by H. F. Bidder; with notes on crania and bones found there, by W. L. H. Duckworth.

b Remarks on the antiquities discovered in the Mitcham cemetery, by R. A. Smith.

c Further inventories of the goods and ornaments of the churches in Surrey in the reign of King Edward the Sixth, by R. A. Roberts. [Contd. in vols. 22–24. For preceding article see vol. 4]

d West Clandon church, by P. M. Johnston.

e West Horsley Place and the literary associations of West Horsley, by H. E. Malden.

f The symbolism of the goat on the Norman font at Thames Ditton, by G. C. Druce.

g The family of John Perior, charter-warden of Godalming, and the manor of Ashurst in Godalming, by P. Woods.

h Iron gates at Carshalton Park, by G. Clinch.

i Churchwardens' accounts of Weybridge, 1622–1701, by Eleanor Lloyd.

j The Weybridge bucket [of the Hallstatt period], and prehistoric trade with Italy, by R. A. Smith.

k The river Wandle in 1610, by M. S. Giuseppi. [A commission of *ad quod damnum* relating to the project of William Heliar, archdeacon of Barnstaple, to supply London with water from the Wandle]

l Romano-British remains at Cobham, by R. A. Smith. [Contd. in vol. 22]

5610 Vol. 22.

a Some armorial ledgers in the cathedral church of St. Saviour, Southwark, and the persons they commemorate, by A. R. Bax.

b The civil war in Surrey, by H. E. Malden.

c The parsonage or rectory manor of Godalming, and a 14th-cent. custumal thereof, by P. Woods.

d Notes on Temple Elfold, by C. H. Jenkinson.

e Notes on the Lumley monuments at Cheam, by G. Clinch.

f West Horsley church, by P. M. Johnston.

g A hoard of Roman bronze coins of the Tetrarchy, from the Brooklands motor-track, Weybridge, by G. F. Hill.

5611 Vol. 23.

a Some minor features of the Chaldon paintings, by G. C. Druce.

b Burningfold in Dunsfold [manor], by H. E. Malden.

c Notes on the architecture of Burningfold, by P. M. Johnston.

d Inventory of a Surrey farmer [John Potter, of Thorpe], 1637, by G. Clinch.

e Notes on the history and architecture of Farley church, by P. M. Johnston.

f A 14th cent. rental of the principal manor of Godalming; with some remarks on cotholders, by P. Woods.

g Notes on the manor and manor house of Walton-on-the-Hill, by W. P. D. Stebbing.

h Surrey wills in the prerogative court of Canterbury in 1609, by Ethel Stokes.

i The site of the Globe playhouse of Shakespeare, by W. Martin.

j Early wooden tallies relating to Surrey, by C. H. Jenkinson.

5612 Vol. 24.

a The British stronghold of St. George's hill, Weybridge, by E. Gardner.

b Surrey wills proved in the prerogative court of Canterbury in 1610, by Ethel Stokes.

c Remarks upon some carved heads on a doorway in Wotton church (in connection with the great Interdict of 1208, and the form of the papal tiara), by P. M. Johnston.

d The old manor house of Croydon, commonly known as the archbishop's palace, by B. Fletcher and J. M. Hobson.

e Wandsworth churchwardens' accounts, 1631–9, by C. T. Davis.

f Eolithic man in west Surrey, by F. Lasham.

g The tower of St. Mary's church, Bletchingley, by C. R. B. King.

h Notes. [Includes: John Perior, the charter-warden, d. 1599, and the manor of Ashurst in Godalming]

5613 Vol. 25.

a Surrey chantries, by T. Craib.

b A list of monumental brasses in Surrey, comp. M. Stephenson. [Contd. in vols. 26–33. Additions and corrections in vol. 40]

c Henry Needler [d. 1718], a forgotten poet and philosopher of Surrey, by A. R. Bax.

d A modern church record [dating from 1829]; being notes from the register of the rural dean of the south-east district of Stoke, by F. R. Fairbank.

e Some prehistoric and Saxon antiquities found in the neighbourhood of Weybridge, by E. Gardner.

f The battle of Ockley, 852.

5614 Vol. 26.

a Lingfield college, by T. Craib.

b Notes from a Carshalton vestry book [1691–1746], by Hilda Fosberry.

c Stoke D'Abernon church: some recent discoveries [relating to the pre-Conquest structure], by P. M. Johnston.

d Notes. [Includes: 2: A series of finds at Ewell, being coins, chiefly Roman and mediaeval]

5615 Vol. 27.

a A late Surrey chronicler (Surrey and the Revolution, 1688), by H. Jenkinson. [Extracts from a ms. volume by Lawrence Lee, of Godalming, d. 1735]

b Rectors and vicars of Surrey parishes (supplementing and correcting the lists in Manning and Bray), by H. E. Malden.

c Great Bookham church, by P. M. Johnston.

d A palatinate seal of John, Earl of Warenne, Surrey and Stratherne, 1305–47, by Sir W. H. St. J. Hope.

e Billeting in Surrey in the 17th and 18th cent., by D. L. Powell.

f A discovery at Merton priory [of a Norman arch, being part of the original buildings], by P. M. Johnston.

g Notes. [Includes: 4: An ancient Richmond wharf]

5616 Vol. 28.

a Kitlands in Capel, by H. E. Malden. [The descent of the estate]

b Sir Thomas Cawarden [d. 1559], by T. Craib.

c Chertsey abbey after the dissolution, by H. Jenkinson and F. P. White.

d A Roman building found at Compton, by M. Stephenson.

e London south of the Thames, by T. Codrington.

f Notes. [Includes: 1: The Militia Act in Surrey in the 18th cent.]

5617 Vol. 29.

a Blechingley churchwardens' accounts, 1546-52, by T. Craib.

b A 18th cent. journey through Surrey and Sussex [made by Dr. John Burton, d. 1771], by H. E. Malden.

c A hoard of Roman coins found at Normandy, near Ash, by M. Stephenson.

d The Greate House, called Coles, otherwise Coles alias Frenches, formerly in Bridge Street, Godalming, by P. Woods.

e Notes. [Includes: 1: Quartering and movements of soldiers in Surrey, 1781-2. 5: The commission for sewers in Surrey in the reign of Elizabeth. 6: Customs of the manor of Kennington]

5618 Vol. 30.

a Notes on some Surrey pedigrees, by F. Turner.

b Abstract of original returns of the commissioners for musters and the loan in Surrey [1522], by T. Craib.

c 'The waters of Redewynd', by Lucy Wheeler. [The identification of some of the features of the 'plan of Chertsey abbey demesne' in the Chertsey cartulary]

d Inventory of Abbot's hospital, Guildford, 1633, by P. Palmer.

e Hognel money and hogglers, by U. Lambert.

f Notes. [Includes: Abinger registers: churchyard fencing, and lease of ground for a pew]

5619 Vol. 31.

a A Carew household book, by H. Lambert. [Accounts of the household of Sir Francis Carew, of Beddington, d. 1611]

b Mr. Jasper Yardeley [d. 1639], second master of Abbot's hospital, Guildford, by P. Palmer.

c Dunsfold and its rectors, by S. L. Ollard. [Contd. in vol. 32]

d Addington charters of St. Mary Overie, by F. Turner, and a St. Mary Overie charter in Banstead, by H. E. Malden.

e Notes. [Includes: 3: Inquisition upon the state of the embankments and water courses in Bermondsey, 1464. 4: Notes from Wotton parish registers]

5620 Vol. 32.

a Inventories of Abbot's hospital, Guildford, 1709, 1731, 1778, 1792, 1820, 1825, by P. Palmer.

b Two Banstead recoveries (1468 and 1517) and a fine (1573), by Sir H. Lambert.

c The crypt and chapel of Lambeth Palace: notes on their history and architecture, by P. M. Johnston.

d Notes. [Includes: 1: Note on a helmet lately in the Lumley chapel at Cheam. 3: Deeds concerning land in Surrey and Sussex, 1682-1736. 5: A Beddington inventory of furniture, 16th cent.]

5621 Vol. 33.

a Banstead in the middle of the 18th cent., by Sir H. Lambert.

b Notes on some farms in Capel [being Misbrook, Broomells and Broome Hall, and Moorhurst], by H. E. Malden.

c Manuscript maps of Surrey; with a list of known examples in the Public Record Office, by R. L. Atkinson.

d Well House farm, Banstead, by P. M. Johnston.

e Notes. [Includes: 9: Richmond: a discovery at Wardrobe Court. 14: Surrey historical notes, epitaphs, wills, etc. collected by the late A. Ridley Bax, F.S.A.]

5622 Vol. 34.

a Some account of St. Mary's, the parish church of Wimbledon, by Sir T. G. Jackson.

b The foundations of Merton priory, by H. F. Westlake and H. F. Bidder.

c Tyting House, and its priest's oratory, by J. E. C. Piper.

d Banstead maps, by Sir H. Lambert.

e The Frome Copse glass-house, Chiddingfold, discovered Sept. 1921, by Brenda C. Halahan.

f A mediaeval undercroft at Reigate, by G. M. Livett.

g Albury old church, by P. M. Johnston.

h Notes. [Includes: Epsom: an old track near the Wells; An account of church and other goods at Newark priory, 30 Henry VIII; Weybridge and Byfleet: traces of old ironworks]

5623 Vol. 35.

a Bronze age urns of Surrey, by E. Gardner.

b Surrey wills proved in the prerogative court of Canterbury in 1611, by Ethel Stokes.

c The Rowhook–Farley heath branch of Stanley street, by S. E. Winbolt.

d Surrey bill-headings, by Dorothy O. Shilton and R. Holworthy.

e Mediaeval pottery kiln discovered at Cheam, by C. J. Marshall.

f The site of the Saxon church at Kingston, by G. H. Freeman.

g A triple-banked enclosure on Chobham common, by E. Gardner.

5624 Vol. 36.

a Guide to archives and other collections of documents relating to Surrey. General introduction and scheme, by H. Jenkinson. [See also no. 5659a below]

b The annals of Southwark and Merton, by M. Tyson. [A study of two mss. from the priories of Southwark and Merton, with an appendix comparing passages from each]

c Sir Richard Onslow, 1603-64, M.P. and a member of Cromwell's House of Lords, by the Earl of Onslow.

d A Cheam school bill in 1766, by Sir H. C. M. Lambert.

e Surrey place-names, by A. Bonner. [Contd. in vol. 37]

f A Carshalton camp, by Mrs. J. E. Birch.

g The historical geography of the wealden iron industry, by H. E. Malden. [Some corrections to the monograph by M. C. Delany]

h General notes and documents. [Includes: Pre-Conquest churches in Surrey]

5625 Vol. 37.

a Diary of Sir Thomas Dawes, 1644, by V. B. Redstone.

b Thomas, 2nd Earl of Onslow [d. 1827], and Guildford Onslow, M.P. [d. 1882], by the Earl of Onslow.

c A burial of the iron age and a series of early iron age occupation sites at Waddon, Croydon, by P. Row.

d Charlwood church and its wall-paintings, by P. M. Johnston.

e St. Leonard's [chapel], Preston (Banstead), by Sir H. C. M. Lambert.

f The Hart's Horn inn at Ash, by H. R. Huband.

g Mediaeval stone heads in Surrey churches, by L. G. Fry.

h Discoveries of mural paintings [c. 1572-80] at Bramley, by P. M. Johnston.

i Roman and Saxon finds. [Includes an account of Saxon skeletons found at Banstead]

j Mediaeval and general notes. [Includes: Unrecorded incumbents of Pirbright; The riverside parks at Richmond]

k Excavation [of a Roman site] at Ashtead, by A. W. G. Lowther. [Contd. in vol. 38]

l The Banstead court roll in the reigns of Richard II and Henry IV, by H. C. M. Lambert. [Contd. for reigns of Henry V and Henry VI in vol. 38]

m Excavations of a Roman camp at Farley heath, Albury, 1926, by S. E. Winbolt.

n Parliamentary surveys of Surrey, by S. J. Madge.
o The Saxon church at Kingston, by W. E. St. L. Finney.
p A Romano-British burial ground at Wotton, by W. Hooper.
q Vernon House, Farnham, by H. R. Huband.
r Surrey museums, by D. Grenside.

5626 Vol. 38.

a Surrey swan-marks, by N. F. Ticehurst.
b Admiral Sir Richard Onslow, bt., G.C.B. [d. 1817], by the Earl of Onslow.
c A founder's hoard of prehistoric bronze implements discovered in Shunaway plantation, Coulsdon, by P. Row.
d The repair of old Malden church, by T. F. Ford.
e An inundation in Surrey in 1323, by M. Weinbaum.
f Prehistoric, Roman and Norman notes. [Includes: Excavation of Banstead heath earthworks]
g Mediaeval and general notes. [Includes: Cheam Court farm, Cheam; Vicars of Reigate; The will of a Newdigate rector (John Baynyne), 1540]
h Bondmen at Reigate under the Tudors, by W. Hooper.
i Excavations at Holmbury camp, April 1930, by S. E. Winbolt.
j The parish and curates of Capel, by H. E. Malden.
k Mounds in Clapham and Balham, by A. Bonner.
l Farnham and the bishops of Winchester: the charter of 1249 [granted by Bishop William de Ralegh to the townspeople], by E. Robo.
m Romano-British occupation site on the Downs at Ashtead, by A. W. G. Lowther.
n The rectory and advowson of Letherhead church, and the advowson of Ashtead, by H. E. Malden.
o The laye brethrens statutes [of Shene charterhouse, late 15th or early 16th cent.], by C. P. Matthews. [Contd. in vol. 39]

5627 Vol. 39.

a The Saxon cemetery at Guildown, Guildford, by A. W. G. Lowther.
b Notes on parliamentary representation in Surrey, by H. E. Malden.
c Three Surrey speakers [of the House of Commons, being Richard Onslow, d. 1571, Richard Onslow, first Baron Onslow, d. 1717, and Arthur Onslow, d. 1768], by the Earl of Onslow.
d Seals of the Cluniac monastery of Bermondsey, by Rose Graham.
e Answers made to the visitation articles of Dr. Willis, bishop of Winchester, from the parishes in Surrey excluding the peculiars of Canterbury, 1724–5, abridged and annotated, by H. E. Malden.
f Witley and Thursley churches: recent discoveries [of Saxon windows], by P. M. Johnston.
g Notes. [Includes: The armorial window at Cranleigh church]

5628 Vol. 40.

a An account of the buildings of Newark priory with a note on its founder's [Ruald de Calna's] family, by C. M. H. Pearce.
b The lords-lieutenant of Surrey, by the Earl of Onslow.
c Some Surrey bell-barrows, by L. V. Grinsell.
d Roque's map of Surrey [and its date of publication], by W. Hooper.
e Excavations at Hascombe camp, Godalming, June–July 1931, by S. E. Winbolt.
f The Roman road on the Surrey-Kent boundary, by J. Graham.
g Notes. [Includes: Inhumation burials, probably Romano-British, at Eashing; The Domesday mill at Betchworth]

5629 Vol. 41.

a The Pilgrims' way from Shere to Titsey as traced by public records and remains, by E. Hart.
b Some account of the Surrey manors held by Merton College and Corpus Christi College, Oxford, in the 17th cent., by Sir H. Lambert.
c The pigmy flint industries of Surrey, by W. Hooper.
d Dry Hill camp, Lingfield, by S. E. Winbolt and I. D. Margary.
e Bronze-iron age and Roman finds at Ashtead, by A. W. G. Lowther.
f The Surrey roll of the [fifteenth and tenth] tax of 1332, by J. F. Willard.
g Notes. [Includes: The Saxon cemetery at Guildown, Guildford; The family of de la Puilles and the Poyles]

5630 Surrey Archaeological Collections. General index to vols. 1–20. 1914.

5631 Surrey Archaeological Collections. General index to vols. 21–38. 1934.

Other publications:

5632 The church plate of Surrey, by T. S. Cooper. 1902.

5633 Waverley abbey, by H. Brakspear. 1905.

5634 A schedule of antiquities in Surrey, by P. M. Johnston, with the assistance of R. Nevill, H. E. Malden, and others. 1913.

5635 Ancient stained and painted glass in the churches of Surrey, illustrated by A. V. Peatling [and ed. from his notes by F. C. Eeles]. 1930.

SURREY PARISH REGISTER SOCIETY

Founded 1903, *for the publication of the older registers of the parishes in Surrey which have not already been printed. Dissolved* 1932 (?).

Publications, vols. 1–16:

5636 Vols. 1, 3. Registers of Richmond, ed. J. C. C. Smith. 2 vols. 1903–5. [Vol. i: 1583–1720. Vol. ii: 1720–80]

5637 Vol. 2. Registers of Godalming [1582–1688], ed. H. C. Malden. 1904.

5638 Vol. 4. Registers of Farleigh [1679–1812], ed. R. Garraway Rice; Tatsfield [1679–1812], transcribed and ed. W. B. Bannerman; Wanborough [1561–1675], transcribed by P. G. Palmer, and ed. in conjunction with W. B. Bannerman; Woldingham, 1765–1812, transcribed and ed. R. Garraway Rice. 1906.

5639 Vol. 5. Registers of Addington [1559–1812], Chelsham [1669–1812], Warlingham [1653–1812], transcribed and ed. W. B. Bannerman. 1907.

5640 Vol. 6. Registers of Gatton [1599–1812], Sanderstead [1564–1812], transcribed and ed. W. B. Bannerman. 1908.

5641 Vol. 7. Registers of Chipstead [1656–1812], Titsey [1579–1812], transcribed and ed. W. B. Bannerman.

5642 Vol. 8. Registers of Coulsdon [1653–1812], ed. W. B. Bannerman; Haslemere, pt. 1: 1573–1812, transcribed and ed. J. W. Penfold. 1910. [See also vol. 9]

5643 Vol. 9. Registers of Stoke D'Abernon [1619–1812], ed. W. B. Bannerman; Haslemere, pt. 2: 1573–1812, transcribed and ed. J. W. Penfold. 1911. [See vol. 8]

5644 Vol. 10. Registers of Beddington [1538–1673], ed. W. B. Bannerman; Morden, 1634–1812, transcribed and ed. F. Clayton. 1912.

5645 Vols. 11–13. Register of Putney, transcribed by Amy C. Hare, ed. W. B. Bannerman. 1 vol. in 3. 1913–16. [Pt. i: 1620–1734. Pt. ii: 1735–1812. Pt. iii: 1774–1870, and index]

5646 Vols. 14, 15. Registers of Caterham [1543–1812], transcribed by R. R. B. Bannerman, ed. W. B. Bannerman. 1917–18.

Extra volumes, 1–2:

5647 Vol. 1. Registers of Merstham, 1538–1812, transcribed by R. I. Woodhouse, assisted by A. J. Pearman and T. Fisher. 1914.

5648 Vol. 2. Registers of Sutton [1636–1837], ed. W. B. Bannerman. 1915.

SURREY RECORD SOCIETY

Founded 1913, to use the county and county history as a central idea for a series of trustworthy texts drawn from archives.

Publications, vols. 1–12, etc.:

Vols. 1, 6. Registrum Johannis de Pontissara. 1 vol. in 2. 1913–24. [Comprises nos. 1, 4, 6, 9, 12, 14, 16, 19, 20 of the Society's publications. See Canterbury and York Soc., no. 842 above]

5649 Vol. 2. Court rolls of the manor of Carshalton, Edward III–Henry VII. 1916. [No. 8 of the Society's publications]

5650 Vol. 3. Surrey musters [1544–1684]. 1914–19. [Nos. 2, 10, 11, 13 of the Society's publications]

5651 Vol. 4. Surrey wills. Archdeaconry court, Herringman register [1595–1608]. 1915–20. [Nos. 3, 7, 15 of the Society's publications]

5652 Vol. 5. Surrey wills. Archdeaconry court, Spage register [1484–90]. 1921 [1922]. [No. 17 of the Society's publications]

5653 Vol. 7. The pipe roll for 1295, Surrey membrane. 1924. [No. 21 of the Society's publications]

5654 Vol. 8. Parish register of Wimbledon [1538–1812]. 1924. [Issued in conjunction with the John Evelyn Club of Wimbledon. No. 22 of the Society's publications]

5655 Vol. 9. Parish registers of Abinger [1559–1806], Wotton [1596–1812], and Oakwood chapel [1696–1814]. 1927. [No. 25 of the Society's publications]

5656 Vol. 10. Surrey apprenticeships from the registers in the Public Record Office, 1711–31. 1921. [No. 30 of the Society's publications]

5657 Vol. 11. Surrey taxation returns, fifteenths and tenths; being the 1332 assessment and subsequent assessments to 1623. Introd. by J. F. Willard and H. C. Johnson. 1922–32. [Nos. 18, 33 of the Society's publications]

5658 Vol. 12. Chertsey cartularies. Vol. i, being the first portion of the cartulary in the Public Record Office, with notes from that at the British Museum. 1933 [1915–33]. [Nos. 5, 27, 34 of the Society's publications]

5659 Guide to archives and other collections of documents relating to Surrey. *Comprises the following pts., being nos. 23, 24, 26, 28, 29, 31, 32 of the Society's publications:*

a General introduction and scheme, by H. Jenkinson. 1925.
b The Public Record Office, by M. S. Giuseppi. 1926.
c Parish records, civil and ecclesiastical, by Dorothy L. Powell. 1927.
d List of court rolls, with some notes of other manorial records, by Dorothy L. Powell. 1928.
e Borough records, by Dorothy L. Powell. 1929.
f Records of schools and other endowed institutions, by Dorothy L. Powell. 1930.
g Quarter sessions records, with other records of the justices of the peace for Surrey, by Dorothy L. Powell, with introd. by H. Jenkinson. 1931.
[All but the first two were also issued (in smaller size and, in some cases, with slightly different title-pages) by the Surrey County Council]

SURTEES SOCIETY

Founded 1834, for the publication of inedited mss. illustrative of the intellectual, moral, religious, and social condition of those parts of England and Scotland included, on the east, between the Humber and the Forth and, on the west, between the Mersey and the Clyde, a region which constituted the ancient kingdom of Northumbria.

Publications, vols. 103–147:

5660 Vol. 103. Extracts from the account rolls of the abbey of Durham, ed. J. T. Fowler. Vol. iii. 1901. [Vols. i–ii were published in 1898–9]

5661 Vols. 104, 110. Wills and administrations from the Knaresborough court rolls, ed. F. Collins. 2 vols. 1902–5. [Vol. i: 1507–1607. Vol. ii: 1607–68, with index to original wills, etc., at Somerset House]

5662 Vol. 105. Extracts from the records of the company of Hostmen of Newcastle-upon-Tyne [1595–1901], ed. F. W. Dendy. 1901.

5663 Vol. 106. Testamenta Eboracensia. A selection of wills from the registry at York. Vol. vi: 1516–51, ed. J. W. Clay. 1902. [Vols. i–v were published in 1836–84]

5664 Vol. 107. Rites of Durham; being a description or brief declaration of all the ancient monuments, rites, and customs belonging or being within the monastical church of Durham before the suppression, written 1593, ed. J. T. Fowler. 1903.

5665 Vol. 108. Memorials of Beverley minster: the chapter act book of the collegiate church of S. John of Beverley, 1286–1347; with illustrative documents and introduction by A. F. Leach. Vol. ii. 1903. [Vol. i was published in 1898]

5666 Vol. 109. Register of Walter Giffard, archbishop of York, 1266–79, ed. W. Brown. 1904.

5667 Vol. 111. Records of the committees for compounding, etc. with delinquent royalists in Durham and Northumberland, 1643–60, ed. R. Welford. 1905.

5668 Vols. 112, 142. Wills and inventories from the registry at Durham. Pts. iii–iv. 1906–29. [Pt. iii, ed. J. C. Hodgson. Pt. iv, ed. H. M. Wood. Pt. i, entitled 'Wills and inventories illustrative of the history, manners, language, statistics etc. of the northern counties of England from the 11th cent. downwards', and pt. ii were published in 1835–60]

5669 Vol. 113. Records of the northern convocation [1279–1714], ed. G. W. Kitchin. 1907.

5670 Vol. 114. Register of William Wickwane, archbishop of York, 1279–85, ed. W. Brown. 1907.

5671 Vol. 115. Memorials of the church of SS. Peter and Wilfrid, Ripon. Vol. iv, consisting of the Ingilby ms., ed. J. T. Fowler. 1908. [Vols. i–iii were published in 1882–8]

5672 Vols. 116, 121. North country wills; being abstracts of wills relating to the counties of York, Nottingham, Northumberland, Cumberland, and Westmorland at Somerset House and Lambeth Palace, ed. J. W. Clay. 2 vols. 1908–12. [Vol. i: 1383–1558. Vol. ii: 1558–1604]

5673 Vol. 117. The Percy chartulary [containing conveyances of Percy family property], ed. Miss M. T. Martin. 1911.

5674 Vol. 118. Six north country diaries, ed. J. C. Hodgson. 1910.

   a Journal of John Aston (of Aston, Cheshire, d. 1650), 1639.
   b Selections from the diary of Christopher Sanderson, of Barnard Castle (b. 1615), 1640–88.
   c Diary of Jacob Bee of Durham (d. 1711), 1681–1707.
   d Diary of the Rev. John Thomlinson (d. 1761), 1717–22.
   e Diary of Thomas Gyll (of Barton, Yorks., d. 1780), 1748–78.
   f Diary of Nicholas Brown (d. 1797), 1767–96.

5675 Vol. 119. Richard D'Aungerville, of Bury [bishop of Durham, 1333–45]: fragments of his register, and other docs., ed. G. W. Kitchin. 1910.

5676 Vols. 120, 125. York memorandum book, ed. Maud Sellers. 2 vols. 1912–15. [Pt. i: 1376–1419. Pt. ii: 1388–1493]

5677 Vols. 122, 133, 144, 146. Visitations of the north, or some early heraldic visitations of, and collections of pedigrees relating to, the north of England. 4 vols. 1912–22. [Pt. i: 1552–61. Pt. ii: 1563–67. Pt. iii: c. 1480–1550. Pt. iv: Yorkshire and Northumberland, 1575]

5678 Vols. 123, 128. Register of John Le Romeyn, archbishop of York, 1286–96 [Pt. ii: and of Henry of Newark, archbishop of York, 1296–99], ed. W. Brown. 2 vols. 1913–17.

5679 Vol. 124. North country diaries (second series), ed. J. C. Hodgson. 1915.

   a Journal of Sir William Brereton (of Handforth, Ches., d. 1661), 1635.
   b Autobiography (in verse) of Sir John Gibson (of Welburn, Yorks., d. 1665), 1655.
   c Jacob Bee's chronicle of births, marriages and mortality, 1630–1711.
   d Mark Browell's diary, 1688. (Mark Browell, of Newcastle, d. 1729.)
   e The family of Mark Akenside the poet (d. 1770).
   f Two letters of Bishop Warburton (d. 1779), 1755–6.
   g Northern journeys of Bishop Richard Pococke (d. 1765), 1760.
   h Diary of John Dawson of Brunton, 1761.

5680 Vol. 126. Register of the priory of St. Bees, ed. J. Wilson, 1915. [In conjunction with the Cumb. and Westmld. Antiq. and Archaeol. Soc.]

5681 Vol. 127. Miscellanea, Vol. II. 1916.

   a Two 13th cent. assize rolls for co. Durham, ed. K. C. Bayley.
   b North country deeds, ed. W. Brown.
   c Documents relating to diocesan and provincial visitations from the registers of Henry Bowet, 1407–23, and John Kempe, 1425–52, ed. A. Hamilton Thompson.

5682 Vol. 129. The York mercers and merchant adventurers, 1356–1917, ed. Maud Sellers. 1918.

5683 Vol. 130. Memorials of the abbey of St. Mary of Fountains. Vol. iii: Bursars' books, 1456–9, and memorandum book of Thomas Swynton, 1446–58, ed. J. T. Fowler. 1918. [Vols. i–ii were published in 1863–78]

5684 Vol. 131. Northumbrian documents of the 17th and 18th cent., comprising the register of the estates of Roman Catholics in Northumberland and the correspondence of Miles Stapylton [d. 1685, auditor and commissioner of Bishop Cosin, of Durham], ed. J. C. Hodgson. 1918.

5685 Vol. 132. Horae Eboracenses: the prymer or hours of the Blessed Virgin Mary, according to the use of the illustrious church of York, with other devotions as they were used by the lay-folk in the northern province in the 15th and 16th cent., ed. C. Wordsworth. 1920.

5686 Vol. 134. Percy bailiffs' rolls of the 15th cent. [relating to manors of the earls of Northumberland], ed. J. C. Hodgson. 1921.

5687 Vol. 135. Durham protestations, or the returns made to the House of Commons in 1641/2 for the maintenance of the Protestant religion for the county palatine of Durham, for the borough of Berwick-upon-Tweed, and the parish of Morpeth, ed. H. M. Wood. 1922.

5688 Vol. 136. Liber vitae ecclesiae Dunelmensis. A collotype facsimile of the original ms., with introductory essays and notes. Vol. i: Facsimile and general introduction, ed. A. Hamilton Thompson. 1923. [No more published, 1967]

5689 Vol. 137. Early deeds relating to Newcastle-upon-Tyne, ed. A. M. Oliver. 1924.

5690 Vols. 138, 141. Register of Thomas of Corbridge, archbishop of York, 1300–4, ed. W. Brown and A. Hamilton Thompson. 2 vols. 1925–8.

5691 Vol. 139. Fasti Dunelmenses: a record of the beneficed clergy of the diocese of Durham down to the dissolution of the monastic and collegiate churches, ed. D. S. Boutflower. 1926 [1927].

5692 Vol. 140. Rituale ecclesiae Dunelmensis. The Durham collectar. A new and revised edition of the Latin text with the interlinear Anglo-Saxon version, ed. U. Lindelöf, with introd. by A. Hamilton Thompson. 1927.

5693 Vol. 143. The statutes of the cathedral church of Durham, with other documents relating to its foundation and endowment by King Henry the Eighth and Queen Mary, ed. A. Hamilton Thompson from the Latin text prepared by J. M. Falkner. 1929.

5694 Vol. 145. Register of William Greenfield, archbishop of York, 1306–15, ed. W. Brown and A. Hamilton Thompson. Pt. i. 1931. [Concluded in four further vols., called pts. ii–v, published in 1934–40]

5695 Vol. 147. Register of Richard Fox, bishop of Durham, 1494–1501, ed. Marjorie P. Howden. 1932.

SUSSEX ARCHAEOLOGICAL SOCIETY

Founded 1846, to promote the study of archaeology in all its branches, especially within Sussex.

Sussex Archaeological Collections relating to the history and antiquities of the county, vols. 44–74 (1901–33):

5696 Vol. 44.

   a Hoard of Roman coins found near Eastbourne in 1899, by F. Haverfield.

b Pre-Reformation [and Elizabethan] vicars of Cuckfield, by J. H. Cooper. [Contd. from vol. 43. Contd. for the 17th cent. in vols. 45 and 46, for the 18th in vol. 50]

c Fonts in Sussex churches, by J. L. André.

d The services of barons of the Cinque Ports at the coronation of the kings and queens of England, and the precedency of Hastings port, by C. Dawson. [See no. 5731 below]

e Inventories of goods of the smaller monasteries and friaries in Sussex at the time of their dissolution.

f Hardham church, and its early [wall] paintings, by P. M. Johnston.

g Notes on the family of Chaloner of Cuckfield, by F. W. T. Attree.

h Note on the Sussex Domesday, by J. H. Round.

i Terrier for the vicarage of Westdean with Binderton annexed, 1615, by R. Garraway Rice.

j Notes on an early map of Atherington manor [1606], with some remarks upon the ancient chapel attached to Bailie's Court, by P. M. Johnston.

k Extracts from the churchwardens' accounts of St. Peter's the Less, Chichester, by F. H. Arnold.

l The play acted by the 'Tipteers' at West Wittering, Chichester, by J. I. C. Boger.

m Notes on the life of St. Richard of Chichester [d. 1252], by J. H. Cooper.

n Notes and queries. [Includes: 1: Mural paintings in Sussex churches, by P. M. Johnston. 6: Poll for the election of two barons to represent the town and port of Seaford, 25 Mar. 1761, by R. Garraway Rice]

5697 Vol. 45.

a Ancient stones found in Ringmer, by W. H. Legge.

b Churchwardens' accounts of St. Andrew's and St. Michael's, Lewes, 1522–1601, by H. M. Whitley.

c The correspondence of John Collier [d. 1760], five times mayor of Hastings, and his connection with the Pelham family, by W. V. Crake.

d The household goods, etc., of Sir John Gage, of West Firle, Sussex, K.G., 1556, by R. Garraway Rice.

e A forgotten industry: pottery at Ringmer, by W. Martin.

f A religious census of Sussex in 1676, by J. H. Cooper.

g A 16th cent. rate book of the corporation of Pevensey, by W. Hudson.

h Painted glass from a window in the church of St. Thomas-a-Becket, Brightling, by W. C. Alexander.

i Pedigree of Hoo, by H. Hall.

j Ancient cultivations, by R. Blaker.

k Priesthawes [Westham], by H. M. Whitley.

l Notes and queries.[Includes: 1: Sir Thomas Bowyer, bt., 1583–1650, M.P. for Bramber, and his family, by J. Patching]

5698 Vol. 46.

a Sussex iron work and pottery, by C. Dawson.

b Extracts relating to Sussex ordnance from a carrier's account book, 1761, by W. P. Breach.

c Three East Sussex churches: Battle, Icklesham, Peasmarsh, a study of their architectural history, by G. M. Livett. [Contd. in vols. 47 and 48]

d Bodiam castle, by H. Sands.

e Testament and will of Agnes Morley, widow, foundress of the free grammar school at Lewes, 1511–12, by R. Garraway Rice.

f The 'Barton' or 'Manor' farm, Nyetimber, Pagham, by H. L. F. Guermonprez and P. M. Johnston.

g A Roman inscription from Worthing, by F. Haverfield.

h Earl Swegen [d. 1052] and Hacon Dux, by H. Hall.

i The Coverts [family], by J. H. Cooper. [Contd. in vols. 47 and 48]

j Borough of Horsham market deed [1756, and three Horsham wills of 1574, 1593, and 1601], by P. S. Godman.

k The church of Lyminster and the chapel of Warringcamp, with some notice of the dependent manors, by P. M. Johnston.

l Notes and queries. [Includes: 1: Norman carvings at Shermanbury church, by P. M. Johnston]

5699 Vol. 47.

a The priory of Shulbred, by E. L. Calverley.

b The Sussex Colepepers [family], by F. W. T. Attree and J. H. L. Booker. [Contd. in vol. 48]

c Catalogues of portraits at Compton Place and at Buxted Park, by Lord Hawkesbury.

d Earl Roger de Montgomery and the battle of Hastings, by P. M. Johnston.

e The Chichester inquest [of service] of 1212, by J. H. Round.

f A pre-Conquest coffin-slab from Arundel Castle, by P. M. Johnston.

g Notes and queries. [Includes: 4: Thomas Johnson, d. 1744, and the Charlton hunt, by F. H. Arnold]

5700 Vol. 48.

a Extracts from the first book of the parish of Southover [16th–18th cent.], by W. Hudson.

b Papal bullae found in Sussex, by A. P. Boyson.

c Extracts from the household account book of Herstmonceux castle, 1643–9, by T. Barrett-Lennard.

d Ancient coats of arms in Chichester cathedral, by R. H. Codrington.

e Masons' and other incised marks in New Shoreham church, by E. F. Salmon.

f Notes and queries. [Includes: 6: A pre-Conquest graveslab at Bexhill, by P. M. Johnston. 7: Two [New] Shoreham antiquities: the borough seal and a market charter, 1608, by E. F. Salmon]

5701 Vol. 49.

a Documents relating to Pevensey castle, by L. F. Salzmann.

b Shulbrede priory, by A. Ponsonby.

c Notes from the act books of the archdeaconry court of Lewes [1581–1641], by W. C. Renshaw.

d The Cluniac priory of St. Pancras at Lewes, by W. H. St. J. Hope.

e Cuckfield families: the Wardens, by J. H. Cooper.

f Inscriptions in the churchyard and crypt of St. Clement's and in the Croft chapel and burial ground, Hastings, transcribed by A. R. Bax.

g A supposed pre-Conquest font at Waldron, by P. M. Johnston.

h The Combers of Shermanbury, Chichester and Allington, by J. Comber.

i Notes and queries. [Includes: 1: Notes connected with the history of West Blatchington church, by W. C. Renshaw. 2: Derick Carver, executed 1555, by W. C. Renshaw]

5702 Vol. 50.

a A short account of Rye church, by J. Borrowman.

b Notes from the act books of the court for the deanery of South Malling [17th cent.], by W. C. Renshaw.

c St. Martin's church, Chichester, by E. E. Street.

d Notes on the family of Michelborne, by F. W. T. Attree.

e A Pynson indulgence of 1523 [i.e. printed by Richard Pynson], by J. Fraser.

f Wall painting in a house at Rye formerly known as 'The Old Flushing Inn', by P. M. Johnston and H. Sands.

g Index to some wills proved and administrations granted in the peculiar of the deanery of South Malling [1560–

1567], and index to 216 other Sussex wills [16th cent.], by R. Garraway Rice.

h Assessment of the hundreds of Sussex to the King's tax in 1334, showing their local organisation and economic condition, by W. Hudson.

5703 Vol. 51.

a Return of conventicles in Sussex, 1669, and King Charles' licences for nonconformists, 1672, by J. H. Cooper.

b The Chichester Grey Friars' church, now the Guildhall, by W. V. Crake.

c Chartulary of St. Mary's hospital, Chichester, by A. Ballard.

d Extracts from the memoirs of Sir George Courthop, 1616-85, by F. G. Courthope.

e Excavations at Pevensey, 1906-7, by L. F. Salzmann. [Contd. for 1907-8 in vol. 52]

f Two Sussex inventories [of James Stilwell, d. 1677, and Elizabeth Capron, d. 1747], by P. S. Godman.

g Rood-loft piscina in Eastbourne parish church, by W. Budgen.

h A return of the members of parliament for the county and boroughs of Sussex [1761-1801], by A. H. Stenning. [Contd. from vol. 35]

i A commission to arm and array the clergy in 1400, by W. Hudson.

j Extracts from the vestry book of the parish of New Shoreham, 1707-79, by E. F. Salmon.

k Notes and queries. [Includes: 1: Lewes nonconformity in the early 18th cent., by J. E. Ray. 2: Notes on the bells of Withyham church, by W. W. Starmer]

5704 Vol. 52.

a Bishop's palace, Chichester, by I. C. Hannah.

b Cuckfield briefs [1625-38], by J. H. Cooper.

c Bolebroke House, by W. D. Scull.

d Extracts from Mr. John Baker's Horsham diary [1771-7], by W. S. Blunt.

e An allotment of sittings in Sedlescombe church [1632], by P. S. Godman.

f Inquisitions *post mortem* [for Sussex], *temp.* Henry VII, James I and Charles I, by F. W. T. Attree.

g Dixter, Northiam: a 15th cent. timber manor house, by J. E. Ray.

h Inscriptions in New Shoreham church, by E. F. Salmon.

i Tortington church and priory: notes on their history and architecture, by P. M. Johnston.

j Inventories of parochial documents. [St. Peter's, Bexhill, comp. J. E. Ray; East Dean and Friston, comp. A. A. Evans; Jevington, comp. E. E. Crake; Ringmer, comp. W. H. Legge; Waldron, comp. W. J. H. Crofts]

k Notes and queries. [Includes: 2: Skeletons found near Eastbourne, by J. E. Ray]

5705 Vol. 53.

a East Sussex churches in 1586, by W. C. Renshaw.

b The Sussex coast line, by A. Ballard.

c Selsey or Pagham harbour, by J. Cavis-Brown.

d The inning of Pevensey levels, by L. F. Salzmann.

e Church of SS. Peter and Paul, Bexhill, by J. E. Ray.

f Cuckfield families: the Michells, by F. W. T. Attree.

g Excavations at Chanctonbury ring, 1909, by G. S. Mitchell.

h Ancient [wall] paintings at 'Pekes', Chiddingly, by P. M. Johnston.

i A series of rolls of the manor of Wiston, by W. Hudson. [See also vol. 54]

j A Sussex knight's fee [Robert Peverel], by J. H. Round.

k The honour of Petworth, by J. Dawtrey.

l Survey of the Sussex estates of the dean and chapter of Canterbury, 1671, by C. E. Woodruff.

m Sussex church plate, by J. E. Couchman. [Contd. in vols. 54 and 55, and in vol. 56, 'Notes and queries' 2]

n Inventories of parochial documents. [Contd. in vols. 54-56 and 64]

o Notes and queries. [Includes: 9: Samuel Gott, 1613-71, by C. Thomas-Stanford]

5706 Vol. 54.

a The prebendal school at Chichester, by I. C. Hannah.

b The manor of Keymer with some ecclesiastical notes, by W. C. Renshaw.

c 'Bridge' [house], Lynchmere, by P. M. Johnston.

d Leedes [family] of Wappingthorne, by Eleanor Lloyd.

e Extracts from the parish registers of Bosham, by K. H. MacDermott.

f Old Buckhurst [the home of the Sackville family], by W. D. Scull.

g Visitations and inventories of the King's free chapel of Bosham, by H. M. Whitley. [Appendix 1: Extract from the statutes of the synod of Exeter, held under Bishop Quivil, 1287. Appendix 2: Indentura de ornamentis in libera capella regia de Boseham]

h Early churchwardens' accounts, Arlington [1455-79], by L. F. Salzmann.

i The porch at Cowdray, with some account of its builder [Sir William Fitzwilliam, Earl of Southampton, d. 1542], by W. V. Crake.

j A series of rolls of the manor of Wiston. 1: The agriculture of the 14th cent., by P. S. Godman. 2: Miscellaneous notes [the manor under the de Bavent, de Braose and Sherley families; rectors and chaplains of Wiston, etc.], by W. Hudson.

k Notes and queries. [Includes: 1: The dedication of St. Anne's church, Lewes, by F. B. Stevens; 4: Pews in Brighton and East Grinstead churches, by W. C. Renshaw. 5: Licenses for nonconformists in South Malling deanery, 1701-17, by W. C. Renshaw]

5707 Vol. 55.

a Crawley, by I. C. Hannah.

b The Stophams, the Zouches, and the honour of Petworth, by J. H. Round.

c Early municipal charters of the Sussex boroughs, by A. Ballard.

d Excavations at the Beltout valley entrenchments, by H. S. Toms.

e Excavations at Selsea, 1911, by L. F. Salzmann.

f A Roman glass inkpot found at Patcham, by A. F. Griffith.

g Notes on early Sussex Quaker registers, by P. Lucas.

h Chithurst church, by P. M. Johnston.

i The ancient deaneries of the diocese of Chichester and their relation to the rapes of the county of Sussex, by W. Hudson.

j Some clergy of the archdeaconry of Lewes and South Malling deanery [16th-18th cent.], by W. C. Renshaw.

k A notice of Maresfield forge in 1608, by W. V. Crake.

l An inventory of the goods and chattels of William Shelley of Michelgrove, 1585, by H. M. Whitley.

m Notes and queries. [Includes: 1: British coin found at Burpham, by L. P. Johnston. 3: Descent of the manor of Eastbourne, by J. H. Round. 4: Note on a Jefferay family seal, by T. Bourke. 5: Ashdown forest in 1632, by W. D. Scull. 6: Bishop's transcripts for the archdeaconry of Lewes, by W. C. Renshaw. 7: Archaeological discoveries in Selsey in 1912, by E. Heron-Allen. 8: 'Bridge', Lynchmere, by P. M. Johnston]

5708 Vol. 56.

a Witnesses from ecclesiastical deposition books [of the archdeaconry court of Lewes], 1580-1640, by W. C. Renshaw.

b An Anglo-Saxon cemetery at Alfriston, by A. F. Griffith and L. F. Salzman. [Supplementary paper by A. F. Griffith in vol. 57]

c The devolution of the Sussex manors formerly belonging to the earls of Warenne and Surrey, by C. G. O. Bridgeman. [Supplement in vol. 57]

d The vicar's close and adjacent buildings, Chichester, by I. C. Hannah.

e The Barhams of Shoesmiths in Wadhurst, by R. G. Fitzgerald-Uniacke.

f Stories of Loxwood [and its houses], by J. C. Buckwell.

g Notes on an ancient house at Steyning, by W. P. Breach.

h Notes and queries. [Includes: 2: A Roman well at Hassocks, by J. E. Couchman. 3: Plumpton and the Springett family, by E. F. Salmon. 5: Exploration of the 'castle' mound, earthwork, at Hartfield, by L. F. Salzman. 6: Samuel Knight, the younger, bellfounder of Reading, Berks., settles at Arundel in 1712, by R. Garraway Rice]

5709 Vol. 57.

a Sussex church bells, by A. D. Tyssen.

b Hastings castle, 1050–1100, and the chapel of St. Mary, by F. H. Baring.

c On Stane street in its passage over the South Downs, by E. Curwen.

d Steyning church, by P. M. Johnston.

e Some Sussex Domesday tenants, by L. F. Salzman. 1: Alvred Pincerna and his descendants.

f Drungewick manor, Loxwood, by J. C. Buckwell.

g Notes and queries. [Includes: 2: Roman urns found at Firle, by W. E. Nicholson. 3: Saxon cremations near Saddlescombe, by H. S. Toms. 4: Order by the court of Sussex quarter sessions, held Jan. 13 and 14, 1684/5, to the sheriff to apprehend William Penn, of Warminghurst, gent, founder of Pennsylvania, by R. Garraway Rice. 6: Old Sussex iron, by G. F. Chambers]

5710 Vol. 58.

a Discovery of wall paintings at Hardham priory, by P. M. Johnston.

b The hundred of Buttinghill, by W. C. Renshaw. [Records of the sheriff's turns, 1613–21, in translation]

c The parish church of All Saints, Herstmonceux, and the Dacre tomb, by J. E. Ray. [Appendix 1: Description of coats of arms at Herstmonceux castle, copied by James Lambert, jun., 2 Nov. 1776, and preserved in Barbican House library, Lewes. Appendix 2: Description of plate of quarterings engraved for Thomas Barrett Lennard, Baron Dacre, by Joseph Edmondson, Mowbray herald. Appendix 3: Will of John Pencell, parson of Herstmonceux, 1485]

d Some earthworks of West Sussex, by A. H. Allcroft.

e The Verrall family of Lewes, by P. Lucas.

f A note on Stane street on Halnaker hill, by E. Curwen.

g Excete and its parish church, by W. Budgen.

h Some Sussex Domesday tenants, by L. F. Salzman. 2: The family of Dene.

i Notes and queries. [Includes: 1: Recent 'finds' at Eastbourne, (i) Romano-British cinerary urns, by J. E. Ray and W. Budgen, (ii) a hoard of Roman coins, by W. Budgen. 3: Roman remains from Ticehurst, by F. Haverfield. 7: Dacre tomb, Herstmonceux: additional notes, by J. E. Ray]

5711 Vol. 59.

a Early history of North and South Stoke, by J. H. Round.

b Canting arms in Sussex, by L. F. Salzman.

c Covered ways on the Sussex downs, by E. Curwen and E. C. Curwen.

d The Sussex place-names in Domesday book which end in '-itun', by A. Anscombe.

e Farnefold [family] of Steyning, by W. P. Breach.

f Sussex musters of 1618, by C. Thomas-Stanford.

g Notes and queries. [Includes: 1: The hundred of Eastbourne, by J. H. Round. 3: The Lords Dacre and their Hoo quarterings, by J. H. Round]

5712 Vol. 60.

a Sussex church music in the past, by K. H. MacDermott. [With a table of musical instruments formerly used in Sussex churches]

b Family of Gratwicke, of Jarvis, Shermanbury and Tortington, by J. Comber.

c Poling and the Knights Hospitallers, by P. M. Johnston. Pt. 1: The village and church. [Contd. in vol. 62. Pt. 2: The preceptory]

d Names of Sussex hundreds in Domesday book, by A. Anscombe.

e Primitive sundials on west Sussex churches, by H. M. Whitley.

f Notes and queries. [Includes: 1: The shrine and relics of St. Richard of Chichester, and relics at Wisborough Green church, by H. M. Whitley]

5713 Vol. 61.

a Conventual buildings of Boxgrove priory, by W. D. Peckham.

b Earthworks of Rewell hill, near Arundel, by E. C. Curwen and E. Curwen.

c Tentative explorations of Rewell hill, by A. H. Allcroft.

d A perambulation of Cuckfield, 1629, by M. H. Cooper.

e Kingston-Buci church, by F. Grayling.

f A 17th cent. account book [of payments made by Elizabeth, widow of John Cowper, d. 1699], by L. J. Hodson.

g Neolithic spoons and bronze loops [found in Sussex], by J. E. Couchman.

h Sanctuary in Sussex, by H. M. Whitley.

i An Elizabethan return of the state of the diocese of Chichester [1563], by V. J. B. Torr.

j Some notes on the family of Alard, by L. F. Salzman.

5714 Vol. 62.

a The Lords Poynings and St. John, by J. H. Round.

b Architectural history of Amberley castle, by W. D. Peckham.

c The manor of Chollington in Eastbourne, with notes on the families of La Warre, De Fokington and De Diva, by W. Budgen.

d The manors of Cowfold, by P. S. Godman. [Shermanbury, Ewhurst, Beeding, Stretham, High Hurst and Walhurst]

e Notes and queries. [Includes: 2: The acre equivalent of the Domesday hide, by E. Sayers. 4: The family of Alard, by J. H. Round]

5715 Vol. 63.

a Notes on the archaeology of Burpham and the neighbouring downs, by E. Curwen and E. C. Curwen.

b The Sussex war dyke: a pre-Roman thoroughfare, by A. H. Allcroft.

c Southwick, by E. F. Salmon.

d The Bulls of Sussex, comp. by L. F. Salzman from materials supplied by Sir W. Bull.

e Long barrows in Sussex, by H. S. Toms.

f The castle of Lewes, by L. F. Salzman. [Further article in vol. 64]

g Sussex Domesday tenants. 3: William de Cahagnes and the family of Keynes, by L. F. Salzman.

h Houghton Place, by W. D. Peckham.

i Notes and queries. [Includes: 1: Some Roman antiquities—Wiston, Chanctonbury and Cissbury, by E.

Curwen and E. C. Curwen. 2: Romano-British habitation site on Kithurst hill, by E. Wight. 3: The mounts at Lewes and Ringmer, by H. S. Toms. 5: The Knights Hospitallers at Poling, by J. H. Round. 6: Poling and Islesham, by W. D. Peckham. 7: Amberley castle measurements, by C. G. O. Bridgeman. 9: An old Lewes map, 1620, by R. Blaker. 11: Notes on Ifield church monumental inscriptions, by H. R. Mosse. 14: Reports of local secretaries, one of which concerns an Anglo-Saxon cemetery on Ocklynge hill]

5716 Vol. 64.

a Sussex lynchets and their associated field-ways, by E. Curwen and E. C. Curwen.

b Sussex deeds in private hands. [Contd. in vols. 66 and 69]

c Alfoldean Roman station, by S. E. Winbolt. [Contd. in vol. 65]

d Notes concerning the Bowyer family, by P. A. Bowyer.

e The story of the old gunpowder works at Battle, by H. Blackman.

f Kingsham [house], near Chichester, by I. C. Hannah.

g Amberley castle measurements, by W. D. Peckham and C. G. O. Bridgeman.

h 'The Old Palace' at West Tarring, by A. B. Packham.

i A coffin chalice and patten [found at East Dean], by A. A. Evans.

j Notes and queries. [Includes: 2: Note on the examination of a barrow on Glynde hill, by B. Currey, E. Curwen and E. C. Curwen. 3: Notes on inhumation and cremations on the London Road, Brighton, by E. Curwen and E. C. Curwen. 4: Roman burial in Aldingbourne, by E. Curwen and E. C. Curwen. 6: Newhaven harbour and a commission appointed for its repair, 1664]

5717 Vol. 65.

a Anne of Cleves' house, Southover, Lewes, by W. H. Godfrey.

b Sussex Domesday tenants. 4: The family of Chesney or Cheyney, by L. F. Salzman.

c Sutton rectory, by W. D. Peckham.

d Blackpatch flint-mine excavation, 1922: report prepared on behalf of the Worthing Archaeological Society, by C. H. Goodman, Marian Frost, E. Curwen and E. C. Curwen.

e 'The Marlipins', New Shoreham, by A. B. Packham. [The house and its owners]

f Press-marks on the deeds of Lewes priory, by V. H. Galbraith.

g Ancient carving [of the Dolmen goddess] from Piltdown, by J. E. Couchman.

h An Elizabethan builder's contract [for Giles Garton's house at Woollavington, 1586], by W. H. Godfrey.

i Pygmy and other flint implements found at Peacehaven, by J. B. Calkin.

j The 'circus' on Park Brow, Sompting, by H. T. Pullen-Burry.

k Notes and queries. [Includes: 1: The Park Brow platforms, by H. S. Toms. 2: Lurgashall parish clerk's fee, by D. Philipson-Stow. 3: The Michells of Cuckfield, by H. F. S. Ramsden]

5718 Vol. 66.

a Horselunges: the manor house, by W. H. Godfrey.

b The manor of Horselunges, by W. Budgen.

c A Roman cemetery at Hassocks, by J. E. Couchman.

d Some Sussex miracles, by L. F. Salzman.

e Sedgwick castle, by S. E. Winbolt.

f Dobell [family] of Streat, by A. F. Radcliffe.

g The old house at Broad Oak, Brede, by E. Austen.

h Customary acres in south west Sussex, by W. D. Peckham.

i Earthworks and Celtic road, Binderton, by E. Curwen and E. C. Curwen.

j Two unrecorded long barrows [on Stoughton down], by E. Curwen and E. C. Curwen.

k Two wealden promontory forts [Philpots camp, West Hoathly, and Henfield], by E. Curwen and E. C. Curwen.

l Saddlescombe manor, by A. O. Jennings.

m The court hall, Rye, by A. F. de P. Worsfield.

n Some notes on Anglo-Saxon antiquities from High down, near Worthing, by A. F. Griffith.

o Find of celts at Bognor, by H. L. F. Guermonprez.

p Notes and queries. [Includes: 3: The dedication of West Hoathly church, by Mary S. Holgate. 4: Notes on the situation of Horeappeltre common, Heathfield, by D. MacLeod. 6: The Burrell mss., by W. D. Peckham. 7: The family of Chesney, by L. F. Salzman]

5719 Vol. 67.

a Michelham priory, by W. H. Godfrey.

b Gun founding at Heathfield in the 18th cent. [from records of the Fuller family], by H. Blackman.

c The Cissbury earthworks, by H. S. Toms and Christine Toms.

d Two notes on Roman Sussex, by S. E. Winbolt. [1: Bignor bath recovered. 2: Southwick Roman villa site]

e The Linchmere hoard [of Roman and Romano-British coins], by P. W. Webb.

f Harrow hill flint-mine excavation, 1924–5, by E. Curwen and E. C. Curwen.

g The use of scapulae as shovels, by E. C. Curwen.

h Notes on air-photograph of Harrow hill, by O. G. S. Crawford.

i Coats of arms in Sussex churches, by F. Lambarde. [Contd. in vols. 68–74]

j A 13th cent. steelyard weight, by E. Curwen.

k An old Sussex household diary [relating to the establishment of William Frankland of Muntham, 1793–5], by E. W. Cox.

l The family of Marten of Sussex, by A. E. Marten. [Contd. in vol. 68]

m Notes and queries. [Includes: 4: Map of Selsey, 1672, by E. Heron-Allen. 7: The surroundings of Philpots camp, by Mary S. Holgate]

5720 Vol. 68.

a Excavations in the Caburn [earthwork], near Lewes, by E. Curwen and E. C. Curwen.

b Discovery of a Carthaginian coin near the Caburn, by S. Spokes.

c Early history of the honor of Petworth, by L. F. Salzman.

d No. 173, High Street, Lewes, by W. H. Godfrey.

e Notes on the heraldry of Goring and Covert, by F. Lambarde.

f Excavations at Hardham camp, Pulborough, Apr. 1926, by S. E. Winbolt.

g Houses in the close at Chichester, by I. C. Hannah.

h St. Richard de Wych and the vicarage of Brighton, by A. O. Jennings.

i Parish churches of Lewes in the 14th cent., by W. H. Godfrey.

j Miscellaneous earthworks near Brighton: notes and surveys by H. S. Toms.

k Peacock's school, Rye [established 1644], by A. F. de P. Worsfield.

l The Royal Arms (punch house), Chichester, by W. H. Godfrey.

m Some former parishes in Chichester, by W. D. Peckham.

n Manors of the archbishops [of Canterbury] in Sussex, by Mary S. Holgate.

o Notes and queries. [Includes: 2: Some hollow-scrapers from Seaford, by J. G. D. Clark. 7: The divorce of Sir

William Barentyne, 1540, by F. Ward. 9: Battle church plate, by F. Lambarde]

5721 Vol. 69.

a Wilmington priory: an architectural description, by W. H. Godfrey.
b Wilmington priory: historical notes, by W. Budgen.
c Early heraldry of Pelham, by L. F. Salzman.
d Heraldry of Horselunges, by F. Lambarde.
e Notes on some uncommon types of stone implements found in Sussex, by E. Curwen.
f The antiquities of Windover hill [Wilmington], by E. C. Curwen.
g Brambletye [house], by I. C. Hannah and W. D. Peckham.
h A church of St. Anne, Lewes: an anchorite's cell and other discoveries, by W. H. Godfrey.
i Timber exports from the weald during the 14th cent., by R. A. Pelham.
j Roman ironworks near East Grinstead, by E. Straker.
k Notes and queries. [Includes: 2: Two sections through Stane street on Halnaker hill, by S. E. Winbolt. 3: Amberley castle, by W. D. Peckham]

5722 Vol. 70.

a The Lewknor carpet, by F. Lambarde.
b The barbican, Lewes castle, by W. H. Godfrey.
c Origin of the Finches, by J. H. Round.
d Excavations in the Trundle, Goodwood, 1928, by E. C. Curwen.
e The foreign trade of Sussex, 1300–1350, by R. A. Pelham.
f Old Place, Pulborough, by W. D. Peckham. [Contd. in vol. 71]
g An Aynscombe of Mayfield will of 1649, by A. Anscombe. [Thomas Aynscombe, d. 1649]
h The lower and middle palaeolithic periods in Sussex, by L. V. Grinsell.
i The canons' manor of South Malling, by Mary S. Holgate.
j Notes and queries. [Includes: 1: Palaeolith found at West Bognor, by R. A. Smith. 2: Palaeoliths found at Slindon, by J. Fowler. 3: Rubbing stones of flint, by J. G. D. Clark. 4: The micro-burin, or beaked pigmy graver, on Sussex pigmy sites, by W. Hooper. 6: Earthworks on Middle Brow, near Ditchling Beacon, by H. S. Toms. 7: Neolithic camp, Combe hill, Jevington, by E. C. Curwen. 8: Wilmington priory, by W. H. Godfrey. 10: Sussex entries in Surrey registers, by W. H. Challen]

5723 Vol. 71.

a Roof bosses in Chichester cathedral, by C. J. P. Cave.
b The Tompkins diary [1768–1814], ed. G. W. Eustace.
c Excavations in Whitehawk neolithic camp, near Brighton, by R. P. R. Williamson.
d Sussex in the pipe rolls under Henry II, by J. H. Round.
e Mediaeval timber houses at West Hoathly and Forest Row, by I. C. Hannah.
f Some further aspects of Sussex trade during the 14th cent., by R. A. Pelham.
g Badshurst in Lindfield, by Mary S. Holgate. [Charters relating to the locality]
h Excavations at Saxonbury camp, by S. E. Winbolt.
i Wolstonbury [earthworks], by E. C. Curwen.
j West Blatchington church, by I. C. Hannah.
k Notes and queries. [Includes: 2: Lynchet burials near Lewes, by E. Curwen and E. C. Curwen. 3: Thundersbarrow hill earthworks, by E. Curwen and E. C. Curwen. 4: Excavations at Ditchling Beacon, by D. A. Crow]

5724 Vol. 72.

a Brambletye [house], by W. H. Godfrey.
b The rapes of Sussex, by L. F. Salzman.

c Sussex in the bronze age, by L. V. Grinsell.
d The moated homestead, church and castle of Bodiam, by W. D. Simpson.
e Excavations in the Trundle, second season, 1930, by E. C. Curwen.
f The Caburn: its date and a fresh find, by E. C. Curwen.
g Studies in the historical geography of mediaeval Sussex, by R. A. Pelham.
h Prehistoric remains from Kingston Buci, by E. Curwen, with a commentary on the pottery by C. Hawkes.
i Mediaeval houses in Southwater, by I. C. Hannah.
j [Henry] Westall's Book of Panningridge [being accounts for the iron-works in 1546], by E. Straker.
k The manor of Pulborough, by H. Hope-Nicholson.
l A late Celtic settlement on Nore hill, Eartham, by S. E. Winbolt.

5725 Vol. 73.

a Wooden roof bosses in the FitzAlan chapel, Arundel, and in Poling church, by C. J. P. Cave.
b Roman villa at Southwick, by S. E. Winbolt.
c A new Roman road to the coast, by I. D. Margary. 1: The road from Edenbridge to Maresfield through Ashdown forest. [2: The road from Maresfield to Lewes, in vol. 74]
d Floor tiles and kilns near the site of St. Bartholomew's hospital, Rye, by L. A. Vidler.
e A microlithic flaking site at West Heath, W. Harting, by J. G. D. Clark.
f Philpots camp, West Hoathly, by I. C. Hannah.
g Rackham bank and earthwork, by E. Curwen.
h St. Nicholas, Bramber, by E. F. Salmon.
i A bronze steelyard weight, by E. Curwen.
j Notes and queries. [Includes: 1: Some noteworthy flints from Sussex, by E. Curwen]

5726 Vol. 74.

a Pevensey castle, by Sir C. Peers.
b Mediaeval pottery and kilns found at Rye, by L. A. Vidler.
c Parishes of the city of Chichester, by W. D. Peckham.
d Church of St. Mary, Broadwater, by F. Harrison and O. H. Leeney.
e Exportation of wool from Sussex in the late 13th cent., by R. A. Pelham.
f A hoard of Roman coins from a villa-site at Selsey, by E. Heron-Allen.
g [Celtic] agricultural settlement on Charleston Brow, near Firle Beacon, by W. J. Parsons and E. C. Curwen. [With brief descriptions of pottery by C. Hawkes]
h A 15th cent. house at West Tarring, by I. C. Hannah.
i The Saxon hundreds of Sussex, by D. K. Clarke.
j The Thomas-Stanford trust fund. [The article chiefly consists of details concerning the Stanford family of Sussex]
k Notes and queries. [Includes: 2: The boundary between the rapes of Lewes and Bramber, by F. B. Stevens]

Sussex Notes and Queries devoted to the antiquities, documentary records, family history, placenames, folk-lore, customs, etc. of the county, being a quarterly journal, vols. 1–4 (1926–33):

5727 Vol. 1.

a The traditional Roman road, Rowhook–Portslade, by S. E. Winbolt.
b The passage of the Arun at North Stoke, by A. H. Allcroft.
c Old roads from the Sussex coast, by H. E. Malden.
d Sussex and the Ravennate geography, by A. Anscombe.
e Horsham churchwardens' account book: extracts, by R. Garraway Rice. [Contd. in vol. 2]

hh Guns bought for Eastbourne, 1550.

ii Sussex furnaces and forges in 1717.

jj Glyndebourne household memoranda [1672, from the period of John Hay's ownership].

kk A Bodiam charter, 1330.

ll A Sussex stone implement, by E. Curwen.

mm The Roman road from Selsfield to the coast, by F. B. Stevens.

nn The Gage monument, Firle. [Design for the tomb of Sir John Gage and his two wives, *c.* 1595, by Garat Johnson, fl. 1567–91]

oo The family of Kyme in Lewes, by W. H. Godfrey.

pp An Alfriston vicar's sons pressed as soldiers [in 1624, Hugh Walker being vicar].

qq Sussex church plans, 5: St. Mary, Stoughton.

rr The manor of Withdean–Cayliffe. [A rental, *c.* 1600]

ss The Broadhurst gold nobles [a find of coins, *c.* 1351–*c.* 1430, from Broadhurst Manor, Horsted Keynes].

tt Thomas and Brian Twine, by W. H. Godfrey. [Letters of Thomas Twine, d. 1613, physician of Lewes, and Brian Twine, d. 1644, Oxford antiquary and sometime vicar of Rye. Contd. in vol. 3]

uu The first and last heraldic visitations of Sussex [with name index for visitation of 1662–8], by W. D. Peckham.

vv Two probable hundred moot sites, by W. Budgen. [1: Willingdon hundred. 2: Totnore hundred]

ww The Gage brasses at Firle.

xx Three early Cuckfield charters [of the 13th and early 14th cent. found on a court roll of the manor of Tye].

yy Legh Manor, Cuckfield.

zz Sussex church plans, 6: St. James, Friston.

aaa Saxonbury camp, by S. E. Winbolt.

bbb Hove: origin of the name, by E. F. Salmon. [Reply by A. Mawer in vol. 3]

ccc Dr. John Bayly, meteorologist [d. 1815].

ddd A Lewes priory charter [of Ralph, bishop of Chichester, 1091–1125. Latin text]

eee Lewes Old Bank.

fff Sussex church plans, 7: St. Mary the Virgin, Apuldram.

5729 Vol. 3.

a Roman roads in Ashdown, by I. D. Margary.

b Bishop Sherburne and [his attempted suppression of] Shulbrede priory, by W. D. Peckham.

c Sussex church plans, 8: St. Andrew, Alfriston.

d A Brighthelmston 'tarriat' of 1673, by W. C. Wallis. [With transcript]

e Churchwardens' accounts of West Tarring [1514–79], by W. J. Pressey. [Concluded in vol. 4]

f A new Roman site at Wiggonholt, by S. E. Winbolt.

g Sussex ploughs, by F. Harrison.

h Sussex church plans, 9: St. Denys, Rotherfield.

i Coldharbours, by E. G. Godfrey-Faussett. [An attempt to discover the origin of the place-name]

j Long-barrows and bell-barrows in Sussex, by L. V. Grinsell.

k A Celtic enclosure in Ashdown forest, by I. D. Margary.

l King's Standing, Ashdown forest, by I. D. Margary. [An early iron age agricultural settlement]

m Sussex church plans, 10: St. John the Evangelist, Singleton.

n Thomas Smith [d. 1688] and Binderton church.

o Human remains [probably bronze age] recently discovered near the Dyke, by E. C. Curwen.

p Notes on some Sussex place-names, by E. Straker and Mary S. Holgate.

q Western Road, Brighton, by C. S. Clarke.

r The mystery mounds on Camp hill and Stone hill, Ashdown forest, by I. D. Margary.

s Some Sussex examples of English mediaeval art [from the exhibition at the Victoria and Albert Museum, 1930].

t *The Place-names of Sussex.* [Addenda and corrigenda to the 2 vols. published by the English Place-name Soc., 1929–30. Contd. in vol. 4]

u Sussex church plans, 11: St. Mary the Virgin, Ringmer.

v The Black Death in Sussex.

w A 14th cent. hall at Hamsey. [Transcript of the building contract, 1321, in French, with English translation, reprinted from the *Archaeological Journal*, 1867]

x The Sussex manors of Francis Carewe [d. 1607], by Mary S. Holgate. [Transcript of a survey, 1575. Concluded in vol. 4]

y A classification of downland tumuli, by L. V. Grinsell.

z Estcot's farm, East Grinstead, by I. C. Hannah.

aa Documents relating to Uckfield and Framfield. [Including an inventory of the effects of Edward Russell, 1653]

bb Sussex church plans, 12: St. Michael, Newhaven.

cc The borough and mint of Rye in the reign of Stephen, by W. J. Andrew.

dd Salmon's chantry, Arundel, by W. D. Peckham. [Thomas Salmon, usher of the chamber to Henry V, d. 1430]

ee Opal glass. Boric and lead oxides in early glass, by E. Wyndham Hulme.

ff Sussex church plans, 13: St. John the Baptist, Clayton; 14: St. Margaret, Ditchling.

gg St. Bartholomew's [hospital], Winchelsea. [Transcript in English of a letter issued by John, King of Castile and Duke of Lancaster, *c.* 1380–83]

hh Manor of Houndean, by R. Morris.

ii Oldland mill and museum, Keymer, Hassocks, by F. Harrison.

jj How the mill worked, by F. M. Treglown.

kk The Poole memorial in Ditchling church [to Henry Poole, d. 1580], by F. Lambarde.

ll Sussex lands held by English religious houses situated outside the county, by Alice M. Tudor. 1: Land held by Reading abbey in Fernhurst and the neighbourhood. [Contd. in vol. 4]

mm Sussex church plans, 15: St. Botolph (next Bramber).

nn Some bronze age axes, by E. Curwen.

oo 'Katherine', by F. Lambarde. [An attempt to establish the genealogy of Katherine Scales, d. 1505. Further article in vol. 4]

pp A grave-mound cluster on Mill hill, near Rodmell, by L. V. Grinsell.

qq Sussex church plans, 16: St. Michael the Archangel, South Malling.

rr Trayton of Lewes, sketch pedigree [*c.* 1500–1757], by W. H. Godfrey.

ss Collins of New England [the Sussex origins of the family], by R. G. Fitzgerald-Uniacke.

5730 Vol. 4.

a Bronze lion-headed ornament found in Chichester [of probable Romano-British origin], by W. J. Andrew.

b Sussex lands held by English religious houses outside the county. 2: The lands of Godstow abbey in Wiston and Old Shoreham.

c Human remains at the Dyke, by E. Curwen and E. C. Curwen.

d Sussex church plans, 17: Holy Trinity, Cuckfield.

e Charlston manor house, by W. H. Godfrey.

f Suggestions on the lay-out of two Roman roads [Stane street and Shoreham road], by E. G. Godfrey-Faussett.

g Sussex church plans, 18: St. Andrew, Edburton.

h Robert Frye, M.P. for Shoreham, 1385, 1391, 1396/7 and 1399, by G. S. Fry.

i Sussex lands held by English religious houses situated outside the county. 3: The lands of Hyde abbey in Southease, Telscombe and Donnington.

j The distribution of wool merchants in Sussex, *c.* 1330, by R. A. Pelham.

k Three barrows in the parishes of Iford and Rodmell, by E. Curwen.

l Sussex drawings in the Bodleian, by L. F. Salzman.

m Sussex church plans, 19: St. Bartholomew, Rogate.

n Hawis de Poynings [d. 1359], by R. G. Griffiths.

o Roman roads in the Sussex weald, by I. D. Margary.

p Annals of old Rottingdean, by Lucy Baldwin and A. Ridsdale. [Contd. in vol. 5]

q Sussex church plans, 20: Holy Trinity, Poynings; 21: St. Michael and All Angels, Withyham.

r An ancient homestead moat [at Blackham Court, Withyham], by E. Straker.

s Notes on the Sackville monuments in Withyham church, by Katharine Esdaile.

t Further evidence of the methods of transporting produce in mediaeval Sussex, by R. A. Pelham. [The victualling of Pevensey castle, 1326]

u Colin Godman's farm house [in Danehill], by I. C. Hannah.

v Sussex church plans, [22]: St. Mary, Northiam.

w Excavations on the paved road, Henley, by Katherine M. E. Murray.

x Roman and pre-Roman pottery found in Little Horsted, by S. Spokes.

y Yonesmere Pit, by D. MacLeod. [The possible site of the hundred court]

z The distribution of wool merchants in Sussex in 1296, by R. A. Pelham.

aa The Selsey Artillery Volunteers [1798–*c.* 1807], by H. G. Parkyn.

bb Objects found at the Roman ironworks, Ridge hill, East Grinstead, by I. D. Margary.

cc The will of a parish priest [Miles Newbye, of Ardingly] 1545, by J. E. Ray.

dd Sussex church plans, [23]: St. Mary Magdalene, Wartling.

ee A Sussex merchant in London [Gilbert Mayfield, d. *c.* 1397], by L. F. Salzman.

ff A beaker skeleton from Goodwood, by E. Curwen and E. C. Curwen.

gg St. Cuthman: what is known of him?, by E. W. Cox.

hh Sussex church plans, [24]: St. Andrew, Steyning.

ii New Bridge, Wisborough Green, by G. D. Johnston.

jj Horace Walpole in Sussex. [Extracts from *Letters of Horace Walpole*, published by Richard Bently in 1840]

kk Sussex lands held by English religious houses situated outside the county. 4: The advowson of Lancing held by Mottenden, Kent.

ll Sussex church plans, [25]: All Saints, West Dean; [26]: Litlington.

mm Some 11th cent. references to Sussex, by G. Ward.

nn Suspected flint mines on Bow hill, by B. C. Hamilton.

Other publications:

5731 The services of the barons of the Cinque Ports at the coronations of the kings and queens of England, and the precedency of Hastings port, by C. Dawson. [With a note on the titular rank of the barons of the Cinque Ports.] *P.* 1901.

5732 Sussex Archaeological Collections. General index to vols. 26–50, comp. L. F. Salzman. 1914.

5733 Sussex Archaeological Collections and Notes and Queries. General index to vols. 51–75 of the Collections (1908–34) and vols. 1–4 of Notes and Queries (1926–33), comp. E. G. Godfrey-Faussett. 1936. [The 'Bibliographical Index to archaeological matter relating to Sussex, appearing elsewhere than in the publications of the Sussex Archaeological Society', comp. E. Curwen,

which is appended to this vol., continues the lists in vols. 15–18 and 32–33 of the *Collections*; it is contd. to 1940 in *Collections*, vol. 82, published in 1941]

5734 Lewes castle, by W. H. Godfrey. *P.* [1933].

5735 Sussex churches, ed. W. H. Godfrey:

a No. 1. Guide to the church of Holy Trinity, Cuckfield. *P.* 1933.

b No. 2. Guide to the church of St. Mary Magdalene, Wartling. *P.* 1933.

c No. 3. Guide to the church of St. Mary, Eastbourne. *P.* 1933.

SUSSEX RECORD SOCIETY

Founded 1901, to transcribe and publish documents relating to Sussex.

Publications, vols. 1–40:

5736 Vol. 1. Calendar of Sussex marriage licences recorded in the consistory court of the bishop of Chichester for the archdeaconry of Lewes, Aug. 1586–Mar. 1642/3, by E. H. W. Dunkin. 1902.

5737 Vol. 2. An abstract of feet of fines relating to Sussex, 2 Rich. I–33 Hen. III, comp. L. F. Salzmann. 1903.

5738 Vol. 3. A calendar of *post mortem* inquisitions relating to Sussex, 1–25 Eliz., abstracted and translated L. F. Salzmann. 1904.

5739 Vol. 4. Miscellaneous records. 1905.

a Ecclesiastical returns for 81 parishes in East Sussex, 1603, ed. W. C. Renshaw.

b A poll for the election of members of parliament for the county of Sussex, 1705.

c A calendar of entries relating to Sussex in the Harleian mss., comp. L. F. Salzmann.

d Extracts from the episcopal register of Richard Praty, bishop of Chichester, 1438–45, ed. C. Deedes.

5740 Vol. 5. West Sussex protestation returns, 1641–2, transcribed, ed., and indexed by R. Garraway Rice. 1906.

5741 Vol. 6. Calendar of Sussex marriage licences recorded in the consistory court of the bishop of Chichester for the archdeaconry of Lewes, Aug. 1670–Mar. 1728/9, and in the peculiar court of the archbishop of Canterbury for the deanery of South Malling, May 1620–Dec. 1732, by E. H. W. Dunkin. 1907.

5742 Vol. 7. An abstract of feet of fines relating to Sussex, 34 Hen. III–35 Edw. I, comp. L. F. Salzmann. 1908.

5743 Vols. 8, 11. The episcopal register of Robert Rede, *ordinis predicatorum*, bishop of Chichester, 1397–1415, summarized and ed. C. Deedes. 1 vol. in 2. 1908–10.

5744 Vols. 9, 32, 35. Calendar of Sussex marriage licences recorded in the consistory court of the bishop of Chichester for the archdeaconry of Chichester, by E. H. W. Dunkin. 2 vols. in 3. 1909–29. [Vol. i: 1575–1730. Vol. ii, ed. D. MacLeod, pt. 1: 1731–77; pt. 2: 1775–1800]

5745 Vol. 10. The three earliest subsidies for Sussex in 1296, 1327, 1332; with some remarks on the origin of local administration in the county through 'borowes' or tithings, transcribed and ed. W. Hudson. 1910.

5746 Vol. 12. Calendar of Sussex marriage licences recorded in the peculiar courts of the dean of Chichester and of the archbishop of Canterbury: deanery of Chichester, Jan. 1582/3–Dec. 1730; deaneries of Pagham and Tarring Jan. 1579/80–Nov. 1730, by E. H. W. Dunkin. 1911.

5747 Vol. 13. Parish registers of Cuckfield, 1598–1699, ed. W. C. Renshaw. 1911.

5748 Vol. 14. Notes of *post mortem* inquisitions taken in Sussex, 1 Hen. VII to 1649 and after, abstracted and translated by F. W. T. Attree. 1912.

5749 Vol. 15. Parish registers of Bolney, 1541–1812, ed. E. Huth. 1912.

5750 Vol. 16. Abstracts of star chamber proceedings relating to Sussex, Hen. VII to Philip and Mary, transcribed and ed. P. D. Mundy. 1913.

5751 Vol. 17. Parish registers of Ardingly, 1558–1812, ed. G. W. E. Loder. 1913.

5752 Vol. 18. The first book of the parish registers of Angmering, 1562–1687, ed. E. W. D. Penfold. 1913.

5753 Vols. 19, 20. Sussex manors, advowsons, etc., recorded in the feet of fines, 1509–1833, arranged and ed. E. H. W. Dunkin. 1 vol. in 2. 1914–15. [Vol. i: A–L. Vol. ii: M–Z]

5754 Vol. 21. Parish register of Horsham, 1541–1635, transcribed, ed. and indexed by R. Garraway Rice. 1915.

5755 Vol. 22. Parish register of Cowfold, 1558–1812, ed. P. S. Godman. 1916.

5756 Vol. 23. An abstract of feet of fines relating to Sussex, 1 Edw. II–24 Hen. VII, comp. L. F. Salzman. 1916.

5757 Vol. 24. Parish register of East Grinstead, 1558–1661, ed. R. P. Crawfurd. 1917.

5758 Vols. 25, 26. Calendar of Sussex marriage licences recorded in the consistory court of the bishop of Chichester for the archdeaconry of Lewes, and in the peculiar court of the archbishop of Canterbury for the deanery of South Malling, 1772–1837, comp. E. H. W. Dunkin, ed. E. W. D. Penfold. 1 vol. in 2. 1917–19.

5759 Vol. 27. An abstract of the court rolls [1562–1702] of the manor of Preston (Preston Episcopi), by C. Thomas-Stanford. 1921.

5760 Vol. 28. Sussex apprentices and masters, 1710–52, extracted from the apprenticeship books, and ed. and indexed by R. Garraway Rice. 1924.

5761 Vol. 29. Abstracts of Sussex deeds and documents from the muniments of the late H. C. Lane, of Middleton Manor, Westmeston, prepared and ed. W. Budgen. 1924.

5762 Vol. 30. Parish register of Glynde, 1558–1812, ed. L. F. Salzman. 1924.

5763 Vol. 31. Thirteen custumals of the Sussex manors of the bishop of Chichester, and other documents from Libri P and C of the episcopal mss., translated and ed. W. D. Peckham. 1925.

5764 Vol. 33. Sussex inquisitions. Extracts from Rawlinson ms. B. 433 in the Bodleian Library, Oxford, described as *inquisitiones post mortem* relating to Sussex, ed. Mary S. Holgate. 1927.

5765 Vol. 34. The book of John Rowe, steward of the manors of Lord Bergavenny, 1597–1622, comprising rentals of twenty-seven manors in Sussex, etc., ed. W. H. Godfrey. 1928.

5766 Vol. 36. Sussex chantry records, extracted from documents in the Public Record Office relating to the dissolution of the chantries, colleges, free chapels, fraternities, brotherhoods, guilds and other institutions, ed. J. E. Ray. 1931.

5767 Vol. 37. Lathe court rolls and views of frankpledge in the rape of Hastings, 1387–1474, ed. Elinor J. Courthope and Beryl E. R. Formoy. 1931 [1934].

5768 Vols. 38, 40. The chartulary of the priory of St. Pancras of Lewes, ed. L. F. Salzman. 2 vols. 1932–4 [1933–5]. [A supplementary vol. was issued in 1938]

5769 Vol. 39. The Buckhurst terrier [or survey of Lord Buckhurst's manors, etc.], 1597–8, epitomized by E. Straker. 1933 [1934].

SWANSEA SCIENTIFIC SOCIETY

Founded 1877, as the Swansea Geological Society, for the elucidation of the geology, natural history, and antiquities of South Wales. Title changed to above form in 1879. The Society's reports, listed below, are also to be found in the Annual Reports of the Royal Institution of South Wales. In 1920 the Society amalgamated with the Swansea Scientific and Field Naturalists' Society. The publications of the amalgamated Society to 1933 contain little of historical character.

Annual Reports and Transactions, 1899–1919:

5770 Vol. for 1900–1.
a Danes in South Wales, by A. G. Moffat.

5771 Vol. for 1901–2.
a New light on Gower history, by W. Ll. Morgan.
b Old maps [16th–18th cent.] with special reference to South Wales, by C. H. Glascodine.

5772 Vol. for 1904–5.
a The *Via Julia Maritima* in Margam parish, by T. Gray.
b Margam abbey, by T. Gray.
c Prehistoric men of Swansea bay, by Prof. Hepburn and W. Riley.

5773 Vol. for 1905–6.
a The Welshery of Gower: where does it begin?, where is the boundary line?, by W. Ll. Morgan.
b The origin of the place name 'Swansea', by A. G. Moffat.
c Swansea and Nantgarw china, by H. Eccles.

5774 Vol. for 1907–8.
a Three days with the Society, by W. Ll. Morgan. [On stone circles, namely the Trecastle mountain group, the Van group, Careg Ddu group, and the Saeth Maen on the Cribarth. Contd. in vol. for 1908–9]

5775 Vol. for 1909–10.
a Burry Holmes [an island off the west coast of Glamorganshire with the remains of a camp and monastic buildings], by W. Ll. Morgan.

5776 Vol. for 1910–11.
a Castle Ditches [a camp at Col Hugh bay, Llantwit], by W. Ll. Morgan.
b Culver Hole [once a castle and then a pigeon house, at Porteynon, Glam.] and the Salt house [16th cent. mansion], by W. Ll. Morgan.

5777 Vol. for 1911–12.
a Inaugural address [including a description of the ruins of Culver Hole castle, and an account of the excavations at Cil Ivor camp], by W. Ll. Morgan.

5778 Vol. for 1912–13.
a Sir Robert Mansel of Margam and Penrice [d. 1656], by A. G. Moffat.

TEIGN NATURALISTS' FIELD CLUB

Founded 1858, to investigate the natural history (and archaeology) of the valley of the Teign and adjoining districts.

Forty-third—Sixtieth Annual Meeting (3 vols. and 9 pts., 1901–[18]), contd. as Proceedings, 1918–28 (1938) and 1929–31 (1932):

5779 45th Meeting.
a Some stray notes on the terms of the capitulation of Salcombe castle in 1646, and other incidents connected with the Fortescue family, by E. A. S. Elliot.
b [Abstract of an address on prehistoric remains and burials at Harlyn bay, by R. Burnard]

5780 47th Meeting.
a [Brief notes on Throwleigh church and manor], by J. Brooking-Rowe.

5781 48th Meeting.
a A brief note on the ancient tenements of the forest of Dartmoor, by R. Burnard.

5782 49th Meeting.
a A Dartmouth worthy: Thomas Newcomin [d. 1729], by M. Adams.
b [Topsham and its objects of interest, by H. Reed]

5783 51st Meeting.
a Sharpham and its owners, by O. D. Parker.

5784 53rd–54th Meetings.
a Mamhead [its early history and its owners], by S. Grose.

THORESBY SOCIETY

Founded 1889, for the collection and preservation of books, pamphlets, manuscripts and other objects relating to the town and neighbourhood of Leeds, or bearing upon the past or present history of the inhabitants; the transcription, reproduction, and publication of public records and other documents relating to Leeds; the preparation of plans and views of buildings and other objects of interest in the town and the neighbourhood; the preparation and publication of papers on subjects of historical or antiquarian interest, and of biographical and genealogical notices of local worthies; the collection of materials which may be useful in preparing, and also the preparation of, a history of Leeds.

Publications, vols. 6, 8, 10–33 (1901–[33]):

5785 Vol. 6. The Calverley charters, presented to the British Museum by Sir Walter Calverley Trevelyan. Vol. i, transcribed by S. Margerison, ed. W. P. Baildon and S. Margerison. 1904. [No more published]

5786 Vol. 8. The coucher book of the Cistercian abbey of Kirkstall, in the West Riding of the county of York, ed. W. T. Lancaster and W. P. Baildon. 1904.

5787 Vols. 10, 13, 20, 25. Registers of the parish church of Leeds. 1901–23. [Vol. 10: 1667–95, ed. G. D. Lumb. Vol. 13: 1695–1722, with Armley chapel, 1665–1711, and Hunslet chapel, 1686–1724, ed. G. D. Lumb. Vol. 20: 1722–57, ed. G. D. Lumb. Vol. 25: baptisms and burials, 1757–76, marriages, 1754–69, ed. J. Singleton and Emily Hargrave. 3 vols. covering the years 1571–88 and 1612–67 were published in 1889–97]

5788 Vol. 11. Miscellanea. 1904 [1900–4].
a The family of Leathley or Lelay, by W. P. Baildon.
b *Testamenta Leodiensia*, extracted from the probate registry at York, ed. G. D. Lumb. [1531–7. Contd. to 1539 in vol. 15. See also vols. 19 and 27]
c Justice's note-book of Capt. John Pickering, 1656–60, ed. G. D. Lumb. [Contd. in vol. 15]
d Lay subsidies, co. York, West Riding, wapentakes of Aggbrigg and Morley, 1545. [Contd. from vol. 9, published in 1899]
e Plan of Leeds, 1806, by J. R. Ford.
f Some civil war accounts, 1647–50, ed. Ethel Kitson and E. Kitson Clark.
g Churchwardens' accounts, Methley, by E. Kitson Clark.
h A 'Waterloo' map of Leeds, by E. Wilson.
i The life and funeral sermon of the Rev. Richard Stretton, M.A. [d. 1712], first minister of Mill Hill chapel, Leeds, 1672–7, ed. G. D. Lumb.
j Survey of the manor of Leeds [1612], ed. H. T. Kelsey. [Cf. vol. 24]

5789 Vol. 12. Registers of the parish church of Methley, 1560–1812, transcribed and ed. G. D. Lumb. 1903.

5790 Vol. 14. Leeds grammar school admission books, 1820–1900, ed. and annotated by E. Wilson. 1906.

5791 Vol. 15. Miscellanea. 1909 [1905–9].
a The dukedom of Leeds, by G. D. Lumb.
b Hooton Pagnell and its market cross, by E. C. Clark.
c Dr. Timothy Bright [d. 1615]: some troubles of an Elizabethan rector, by H. A. Hall.
d Lay subsidy, wapentake of Skyrack, 1588, ed. W. Brigg.
e Map of Leeds, 1781, by F. Gott.
f The family of John Harrison [d. 1656], the Leeds benefactor, by G. D. Lumb.
g Burials at St. Paul's church, Leeds [1796–1865], ed. G. D. Lumb.
h Some notes on the personal and family history of Robert Waterton, of Methley and Waterton [fl. 1399–1425], by H. A. Hall.
i A local find of over 7,000 Roman coins, by Aquila Dodgson.
j Musters in Claro wapentake, 1535, by W. P. Baildon.
k The Farnley Wood plot [1663], by S. J. Chadwick.
l Notes on cressets, by J. H. Whitham.
m Lay subsidy, wapentake of Agbrigg and Morley, 1588, by W. Brigg.
n Thorp's map of Leeds and district, 1819–21.
o 14th cent. court rolls of the manor of Thorner, by W. T. Lancaster.
p Discovery of ancient foundations and human remains at Temple Newsam, by W. Braithwaite.
q The arms of Leeds, by G. D. Lumb.
r The Swillingtons of Swillington, by A. Beanlands.
s Leeds in prehistoric times, by E. Kitson Clark.
t The early history of Horsforth, by W. T. Lancaster.
u The family of Denison of Great Woodhouse, and their residences in Leeds, by G. D. Lumb.

5792 Vol. 16. Architectural description of Kirkstall abbey, by W. H. St. J. Hope and J. Bilson. 1907.

5793 Vol. 17. History of the parish of Barwick-in-Elmet, by F. S. Colman. 1908.

5794 Vol. 18. Place-names of the West Riding of Yorkshire, by F. W. Moorman. 1910.

5795 Vols. 19, 27. *Testamenta Leodiensia*. Wills of Leeds, Pontefract, Wakefield, Otley, and district, extracted and ed. G. D. Lumb. 2 vols. 1913–30. [Vol. i: 1539–53. Vol. ii: 1553–61]

5796 Vol. 21. Letters addressed to Ralph Thoresby, F.R.S., printed from the originals in the possession of the Yorkshire Archaeological Society, ed. W. T. Lancaster. 1912.

5797 Vol. 22. Miscellanea. 1915 [1912–15].

a Northumbria after the departure of the Roman forces, by H. E. Savage.

b Find of Roman coins in Leeds, by T. Pickersgill and Aquila Dodgson.

c John Thoresby [d. 1679], by G. D. Lumb.

d Poems of 'Pendavid Bitterzwigg' (a satire on Leeds of the 18th cent.), ed. G. D. Lumb.

e Wills of Leeds and district, transcribed R. B. Cook. [Contd. in vols. 24, 26, and 33]

f Whitkirk register [1600–1]: transcripts at York.

g Adel register [1600]: transcripts at York.

h Subsidy roll of the wapentake of Skyrack, 1610 (and 1629).

i Four early charters of Arthington nunnery, by W. T. Lancaster.

j The Leeds white cloth hall, by H. Heaton.

k Some old deeds relating to Barwick-in-Elmet, by R. B. Cook.

l Extracts from the *Leeds Mercury*, 1721–9, ed. G. D. Lumb. [Contd. for 1729–51 in vols. 24, 26, and 28]

m The early crosses of Leeds, by W. G. Collingwood.

n Yorkshire *c.* 120, according to Ptolemy's geography, by A. S. Ellis.

o 'The tricks of the trade.' Facts and fiction concerning the Yorkshire textile industry, by H. Heaton.

p The committee of charitable uses, Leeds: extracts from the minute-book, commencing 1664.

q General index to the first six volumes of the Miscellanea.

5798 Vols. 23, 29. Registers of the chapels of the parish church of Leeds, transcribed and ed. G. D. Lumb. 2 vols. 1916–28. [Vol. i: St. John's, Holy Trinity, Armley, Beeston, Bramley, Chapel-Allerton, Farnley, Headingley, Holbeck, and Hunslet, 1724–63, and in some cases earlier years. Vol. ii: St. John's, Holy Trinity, Headingley, Bramley, Beeston, Chapel-Allerton and Farnley, 1763–1812, and in some cases later years. Cf. vol. 10 etc. above. Registers for Holbeck, Armley and Hunslet are contd. for 1764–1812 in vol. 31, 1934]

5799 Vol. 24. Miscellanea. 1919 [1915–18].

a Picture of Pontefract castle at Hampton Court palace, by A. S. Ellis.

b A 15th cent. rental of Leeds, by W. T. Lancaster.

c Colonel Edmund Wilson [founder of the Society, d. 1914], by J. Singleton.

d Extracts from an old Leeds merchant's memorandum book, 1770–86, and copies of certain loose papers therein, by J. Singleton.

e Some correspondence of the Maudes of Hollinghall, 1594–9, by W. P. Baildon.

f St. Helen's chapel, Holbeck, by W. T. Lancaster.

g The Maudes of Ilkley, Hollinghall, Brandon, Helthwaite Hill, etc., by W. P. Baildon.

h Church of St. John the Evangelist, New Briggate, Leeds, chiefly concerning the woodwork and carving, by J. E. Stocks.

i The claim of John de Eston [d. 1301, to the Skipton estates of Aveline de Forz], by A. Beanlands.

j The family of Beeston, by W. T. Lancaster.

k Leeds parish church: inscriptions on the tombstones in the churchyard, transcribed about 1890 at the expense of John Stansfeld. [Contd. in vol. 26]

l Leeds and district potteries, by G. D. Lumb.

m A 15th cent. rental of Rothwell, by W. T. Lancaster.

n Survey of the manor of Leeds in 1612: some additions and corrections, by J. Singleton, with notes by W. P. Baildon. [Cf. vol. 11]

o John Miers, the profilist [d. 1821], by G. D. Lumb. [Additional note in vol. 33]

p The tax on bachelors and widowers imposed in 1695, by H. W. Thompson.

q The Nalson family of Altofts and Methley, by G. D. Lumb.

r St. John's church, Leeds: the trustees' (feoffees') account book, 1660–1766, ed. G. D. Lumb.

s Leeds manor house and park, by G. D. Lumb.

t Lease, 1687, of the tithe of hay in Leeds by the Earl of Burlington to Thomas Dixon, ed. G. D. Lumb.

u The consecration service of St. John's church, Leeds, by J. E. Stocks.

v The formation of the Leeds Yeomanry (1817), by Emily Hargrave.

w The Leeds Volunteers (1820), by Emily Hargrave.

x The family of Green of Horsforth, by W. T. Lancaster.

5800 Vol. 26. Miscellanea. 1924 [1919–22].

a The Old Hall, Wade Lane, Leeds, and the Jackson family, by G. D. Lumb.

b Birstall, Gomersal, and Heckmondwike: a genealogical paper, by W. T. Lancaster.

c Ellis of Kiddal, by G. D. Lumb.

d The Denison family, by G. D. Lumb.

e The Old Hall, Burmantofts, by G. D. Lumb.

f Lotherton chapel, by G. E. Kirk.

g The manor court of Leeds Kirkgate-cum-Holbeck, by W. T. Lancaster.

h A Leeds malefactor of 1752, by Emily Hargrave. [An account of a robbery committed in the house of William Fearn, of Leeds, clothworker]

i Notes on the importation of English wool into Ireland as affected by the Union, by C. T. Clay.

j The return made by the Leeds commissioners to the archbishop of York in respect of the poor benefices in Leeds and the bounty of Queen Anne [1716], copied by R. J. Wood.

k Anderton rents, 1708; notes on Leeds chapel; the vicarage of Leeds [1697]; copy of a letter written by Rev. Geo. Plaxton [1716, rector of Barwick]. (Copied from a ms. formerly belonging to W. Cookson.)

l York or East Bar, Leeds, by G. D. Lumb.

m Turner in Yorkshire: his wanderings and sketches, by H. E. Wroot.

n The family of Wridlesford or Woodlesford, by C. T. Clay.

o A 15th cent. rental of Pontefract, ed. G. D. Lumb.

p The arms of Leeds, by W. B. B. Turner.

q The Shilletos of the West Riding of Yorkshire, by R. J. Shilleto.

r Notes on the early pedigree of the Copley family, by W. P. Baildon. [Contd. in vol. 28]

s Some hitherto unpublished letters of Ralph Thoresby, transcribed and annotated by Emily Hargrave.

t The last shop with bow windows in Briggate, Leeds, by G. D. Lumb.

5801 Vol. 28. Miscellanea. 1928 [1923–7].

a A dialect in architecture: some buildings of the 17th cent. in the parish of Halifax, by T. F. Ford.

b Extracts from the *Leeds Mercury*, 1742–60 [1742–51; *Leeds Intelligencer*, 1755–63], ed. G. D. Lumb. [Contd. in vol. 33]

c The Washington shield at Selby abbey, by W. B. B. Turner.

d Anthony Hunton, M.D. [d. *c.* 1624], an Elizabethan physician, and his connexion with Harrogate, by W. J. Kaye.

e A change-ringing controversy [at Wakefield, 1779], by Emily Hargrave.

f Note on clerical strikes, by A. Hamilton Thompson.

g 15th cent. rentals of Barwick and Scholes (from the Parlington ms. entitled 'Coppie of the coucher', translated by W. T. Lancaster).

h The early Leeds Volunteers [1757–1814], by Emily Hargrave.

i Musical Leeds in the 18th cent., by Emily Hargrave.

j Christopher Saxton, of Dunningley [b. *c.* 1542–4]: his life and work, by Sir G. Fordham.

k The genesis of Warburton's 'Map of Yorkshire', 1720, by W. B. Crump.

l An old case for the opinion of counsel relating to the property of the Thoresby and Briggs families [1686], by G. G. Alexander.

m The custom of the province of York: a chapter in the history of wills and intestacies, by G. G. Alexander.

n Mss. written or possessed by Ralph Thoresby, F.R.S., ed. G. D. Lumb.

o Notes on an armorial window at Adel church, by W. B. B. Turner.

p The family of Lacy of Cromwellbottom and Leventhorpe, by C. T. Clay.

5802 Vol. 30. History and architectural description of the priory of St. Mary, Bolton-in-Wharfedale, with some account of the canons regular of the order of St. Augustine and their houses in Yorkshire, by A. Hamilton Thompson. 1928.

5803 Vol. 32. The Leeds woollen industry, 1780–1820, by W. B. Crump. 1931.

5804 Vol. 33. Miscellanea. [1930–32. Title-page and index added 1935]

a Yorkshire abbeys and the wool trade, by H. E. Wroot.

b A 16th cent. rental [1507] of the manor of Temple Newsam and its appurtenances, ed. G. E. Kirk.

c A rental of the bailiwick of Whitkirk [of the Knights of St. John of Jerusalem, 1523], ed. G. E. Kirk.

d Chapter House records. [Translations by J. Lister of extents of Leeds, Rothwell, Allerton, Kippax, and Ledston, 1341, from originals in the P.R.O.]

e John Harrison [d. 1656], the Leeds benefactor, and his times, by Margaret A. Hornsey.

f Charles Donald Hardcastle [d. 1903, of Leeds, and a paper by him, 'Leeds in my grandfather's days', which appeared in the *Leeds Mercury Supplement*, *c.* 1890].

g William Boyne, F.S.A., numismatist of Leeds and Florence [d. 1893], by G. D. Lumb.

h Wills, inventories and bonds of the manor courts of Temple Newsam, 1612–1701, ed. G. E. Kirk.

i The manorial system and copyhold tenure [with particular reference to the manor of Sherburn, near Leeds, in the 18th cent.], by G. G. Alexander.

j Monuments in St. John's church, Leeds, by G. D. Lumb.

k Monumental inscriptions in the churchyard of St. John the Evangelist, Leeds, copied by G. D. Lumb.

l The tithes of Farnley: an 18th cent. dispute, by W. E. Preston.

m Paganini in Leeds, Jan. 1832, by F. Dawson.

5805 Jubilee index to the publications of the Thoresby Society, 1889–1939, by G. E. Kirk. 1941.

THOROTON SOCIETY

Founded 1897, to promote, generally, the study of the history and antiquities of Nottinghamshire, and to print ancient records relative to the county and an annual illustrated volume of Transactions.

Transactions, vols. 4–36 (1901–33):

5806 Vol. 4.

a Syerston church, by A. W. Bailey.

b Staunton and the Staunton family, by G. W. Staunton.

c [Hawton church]

d [Newark parish church, by C. Brown]

5807 Vol. 5.

a The Retford excursion. [Includes descriptions of Worksop priory church, Blyth priory church, East Retford plate and regalia, and East Retford church]

b Was Mary, Queen of Scots, ever at Hardwick Hall [Derbys.]?, by F. Brodhurst.

c Notes on Osberton, Scofton, Rayton, Bilby, Hodsock, Fleecethorp, etc., by Lord Hawkesbury.

d Priory and church of St. Peter's, Thurgarton, by J. Standish.

e Blyth, by W. Stevenson.

f Car Colston: Dr. Thoroton's headstone, by T. M. Blagg.

g Southwell: pavement, probably pre-Norman, by A. M. Y. Baylay.

5808 Vol. 6.

a Spring excursion. [Includes descriptions of Bunny school and church, East Leake church of St. Mary the Virgin, Costock church, Wysall church, and Willoughby-on-the-Wolds church]

b Autumn excursion. [Includes descriptions of North Muskham church of St. Wilfrid, the manor of Ossington, Laxton church, and Sutton-on-Trent church]

c A Vale of Belvoir family [the Goldings, of Colston Bassett], by W. Stevenson.

d Monuments in Laxton church, by W. Stevenson.

e A find of old bibles at Beeston, by G. Fellows.

f Wollaton Hall, church, and the family of Willoughby, by G. Fellows.

5809 Vol. 7.

a Excursion, 1903. [Includes notes on Gedling church, by R. Whitbread; Gonalston church, by A. M. Y. Baylay; Hoveringham church, by A. M. Y. Baylay; Shelford church, by J. Standish; and Holme Pierrepont church, by H. Gill]

b Sturton-le-Steeple, by Lord Hawkesbury.

c St. Peter's church, East Bridgford, by A. Du Boulay Hill.

d Account of the family called in Latin Cadurcis, in French Chaources, in English Chaworth, by L. Chaworth Musters. [Contd. in vol. 8]

5810 Vol. 8.

a Excursion, 1904. [Includes notes on Skegby church, by G. G. Bonser; Skegby inquisitions, by T. M. Blagg; and Teversal church, by J. Standish]

b The precincts of Nottingham castle, by W. Stevenson.

c Ancient Nottingham pottery, by R. A. Wilde.

d Commissions of escheat, by F. A. Wadsworth.

e Discovery of a Saxon grave-cover, by W. H. Mason.

f Chantries at Edwinstowe, by A. M. Y. Baylay.

5811 Vol. 9.

a Excursion, 1905. [Includes notes on Scrooby, by R. Mellors; Tickhill, Yorks., by W. Stevenson; Tickhill church, by J. Standish; and Roche abbey, Yorks., by G. Fellows]

b Second excursion, 1905. [Includes notes on Holme church, and South Collingham church, by T. M. Blagg]

c Sir Nesbit Willoughby, admiral of the Blue [d. 1848], by Eliza M. Middleton.

d Plumtree church, by A. Du Boulay Hill.

e The endowment of Worksop priory, by C. Brown.

f The arms, crest, and motto of the city of Nottingham and county of the same city, by G. Fellows.

5812 Vol. 10.

a Nuthall church, by H. Gill.
b Strelley church, by A. Du Boulay Hill.
c Monuments in Strelley church, by T. L. K. Edge.
d Stapleford cross, by A. Du Boulay Hill.
e Stapleford church, by G. Fellows.
f Attenborough church, by J. Standish.
g The old streets of Nottingham, by J. Granger. [Contd. in vols. 11–14]
h The Luddites, by J. Russell.
i Crocolana [a Roman station], the Nottinghamshire Brough, by T. C. S. Woolley.
j The palace, Southwell, by H. Gill.
k Muster roll for Newark wapentake, 1595, by T. M. Blagg.
l Henry Kirke White [d. 1806], by J. C. Warren.

5813 Vol. 11.

a Fledborough church, by A. Du Boulay Hill.
b East Markham church, by A. E. Briggs.
c Tuxford church, by J. Standish.
d Beauvale [priory], by C. Brown.
e Hucknall Torkard parish church, by J. H. Beardsmore.
f Account of the family of White of Tuxford and Walling-wells, by Miss M. H. Towry White.
g Notes on the domestic architecture of old Nottingham, by H. Gill.
h A description of Nottinghamshire in the 17th cent., by W. H. Stevenson.
i Kirkby-in-Ashfield, by G. G. Bonser.
j An ancient village site: Whimpton, by T. D. Pryce and F. W. Dobson.

5814 Vol. 12.

a Lowdham church, by A. M. Y. Baylay.
b Woodborough church, by H. Gill.
c Epperstone church and manors, by T. W. Huskinson.
d Oxton and its church, by W. Laycock.
e Calverton church, by A. Du Boulay Hill.
f Margidunum [Roman station], by J. Standish.
g Dr. Robert Thoroton, by T. M. Blagg.
h Screveton church, by J. Standish.
i Beauvale charterhouse, by A. Du Boulay Hill and H. Gill.
j The descendants of Dr. Robert Thoroton, by W. Stevenson.

5815 Vol. 13.

a Mattersey priory, by C. E. Scott-Moncrieff.
b Everton church, by H. Gill.
c Clayworth, by A. W. B. Marshall.
d Church of St. Peter and St. Paul, Sturton-le-Steeple, by G. F. Twycross.
e Littleborough, by T. C. S. Woolley.
f Richard Parkes Bonington [d. 1828], by R. Mellors.
g The old inns of Brewhouse Yard [Nottingham], by H. Gill.
h The manors of Cotgrave, especially the manor-court of St. John of Hierusalem, commonly called 'Shelford St. John's', a little known Notts. 'peculiar', by T. M. Blagg.
i Some Cartwright records [16th–18th cent.], by Mrs. G. Cartwright.
j Nottingham castle: recent explorations and some historical notes, by F. W. Dobson.

5816 Vol. 14.

a St. John Baptist, Stanford-on-Soar, by C. L. V. Baker.
b The church at Normanton-on-Soar, by A. M. Y. Baylay.
c Ratcliffe-on-Soar church, by G. Fellows.
d Tattershall castle and church [Lincs.], by M. Sympson.

e Notes on the topography of north-east Notts., by B. Smith.
f The low side windows of Notts., by H. Gill.

5817 Vol. 15.

a Coddington church, by A. M. Y. Baylay.
b Balderton church, by A. M. Y. Baylay.
c Claypole church, by A. F. Sutton.
d The cathedral church of the Blessed Virgin Mary, Southwell, by A. Hamilton Thompson.
e Certificates of the chantry commissioners for the college of Southwell in 1546 and 1548, with introd. and notes by A. Hamilton Thompson.
f Ancient [17th cent.] documents and letters at Clifton Hall, by Lady Bruce.

5818 Vol. 16.

a Annesley old church, by A. M. Y. Baylay.
b Felley priory, by A. M. Y. Baylay.
c Selston church, by A. S. Buxton.
d St. Mary Magdalene, Sutton-in-Ashfield, by G. G. Bonser.
e Wollaton [Hall] portraits and pictures, by G. Fellows.
f Nottingham in the 18th cent., especially with reference to domestic architecture, by H. Gill.
g Chantry certificate rolls for the county of Nottingham, ed. with introd. and notes by A. Hamilton Thompson. [Contd. in vols. 17 and 18]
h Nottingham town hall, by A. Stapleton.
i The great ditch, St. Mary's hill, Nottingham, by W. Stevenson.
j A guard-room of the town wall of Nottingham, by F. W. Dobson.

5819 Vol. 17.

a Burghley House [nr. Stamford, Lincs.], by A. Hamilton Thompson.
b St. Martin's church [Stamford, Lincs.], by A. Hamilton Thompson.
c St. Mary's church [Stamford], by A. Hamilton Thompson.
d All Saints' church [Stamford], by A. Hamilton Thompson.
e Kelham [church], by A. M. Y. Baylay.
f Averham [church], by A. M. Y. Baylay.
g Upton [church], by H. Gill.
h Rolleston [church], by A. M. Y. Baylay.
i Notts. monumental brasses, by J. Bramley.
j The fight at Willoughby field, 5 July 1648, by G. Fellows.

5820 Vol. 18.

a Sookholm church, by A. S. Buxton.
b Warsop church, by A. Du Boulay Hill.
c Norton Cuckney church, by J. W. Smith.
d Carburton church, by H. Gill.
e Edwinstowe church, by H. Gill.
f The British Museum ms. of the life of Col. [John] Hutchinson [d. 1664], and its relation to the published memoirs, by S. Race.
g Education in the middle ages, by S. Corner.

5821 Vol. 19.

a West Bridgford church, by H. Gill.
b St. Peter's church, Nottingham, by R. Evans.
c Colwick church and monuments, by G. Fellows.
d Colwick Hall and church, by H. Gill.
e East Bridgford church, by A. Du Boulay Hill.
f Nottingham Presbyterian records, by J. C. Warren.
g The shire hall, Nottingham, in the 17th and 18th cent., by H. H. Copnall.
h Nottingham church bells, by J. Bramley.
i A local patron of architecture in the reign of Henry VI

[Radulphus Cromwell, d. 1456, builder of Tattershall castle and church, Lincs., and Wingfield manor-house, Derbys.], by H. Gill.

5822 Vol. 20.

a Notes on the Leen and the buildings on its banks, including the churches of Lenton, Radford, Old Basford, and Bulwell, by H. Gill.
b Church of St. Mary the Virgin, Nottingham, by A. Du Boulay Hill.
c Architectural notes on the church of St. Mary the Virgin, Nottingham, by H. Gill.
d Church windows of Nottinghamshire, by H. Gill.

5823 Vol. 21.

a Church porches and doorways of Nottinghamshire, by H. Gill.
b Notes on the tombs, chapels, images, and lights, in the church of St. Mary the Virgin, Nottingham, by F. A. Wadsworth.
c Abstracts of wills [relating to St. Mary's, Nottingham, 15th cent.].
d Extracts from archdeaconry records [relating to St. Mary's, Nottingham, 16th-17th cent.].
e The family of Hanley, or Handley, of Bramcote, by G. Fellows.
f The Weekday cross at Nottingham, and its associations, by J. P. Briscoe.

5824 Vol. 22.

a Edwalton church, by H. Gill.
b Church of St. George, Barton-in-Fabis: a study in mediaeval mason-craft, by H. Gill.
c Topographical and other early notes about Nottingham, by W. Stevenson.
d The parish churches and houses of friars of Nottingham, their chapels, gilds, images, and lights [extracts from wills prior to 1558 relating thereto], by F. A. Wadsworth.
e Note on an old painting of Southwell minster and Archbishop Booth's chapel, by S. Race.

5825 Vol. 23.

a Linby church, by W. Stevenson.
b The Castle Inn, High Pavement, Nottingham, by H. H. Copnall.
c The Beaumond-cross, Newark, and its date, by W. Stevenson.
d Church of St. Mary, Clifton: a study in mediaeval mason-craft, by H. Gill.
e The priory of St. Mary of Newstead in Sherwood forest, with some notes on houses of regular canons, by A. Hamilton Thompson.

5826 Vol. 24.

a History of the manor of Rampton, by H. Chadwick.
b Church of St. Mary, Orston, by H. Gill.
c St. Leonard's hospital, Newark, by R. F. B. Hodgkinson.
d The development of castle building in England, by J. H. Walker.
e Church of St. Leonard, Wollaton: a study in mediaeval mason-craft, by H. Gill.

5827 Vol. 25.

a Manuscripts of the collegiate church of the Blessed Mary the Virgin of Southwell, transcribed by W. A. James.
b St. Wilfrid's church, Wilford: a study in mediaeval mason-craft, by H. Gill.
c George Green, mathematician, 1793-1841, by Edith M. Becket.
d Booth's chapel, Southwell, by S. Race.
e The manor of Dunham-on-Trent, by H. Chadwick.

5828 Vol. 26.

a Hardwick Hall [Derbys.], by H. Gill.
b Extracts from the records of the borough of Nottingham, by E. L. Guilford. [Contd. in vols. 27-31]
c Gervase Holles [d. 1675], 'a great lover of antiquities', by R. W. Goulding.
d Selston Old Hall, by W. Stevenson.
e The surrender of King Charles I to the Scots [1646], by E. L. Guilford.
f The medallic history of Lord Byron, by F. E. Burton.
g Kingshaugh, by H. Chadwick.

5829 Vol. 27.

a Henrietta, Countess of Oxford [d. 1755], by R. W. Goulding.
b Staunton-in-the-Vale, by H. Gill.
c The rectors of East Bridgford [1255-1898], by A. Du Boulay Hill.
d The rood screen in Balderton church, by A. Du Boulay Hill.

5830 Vol. 28.

a Thrumpton Hall, by H. Gill.
b Radcliffe-on-Soar, Holy Trinity church, by H. Gill.
c Gotham church, St. Lawrence, by H. Gill.
d Oakham castle [Rut.], by J. H. Walker.
e Oakham church [Rut.], by J. H. Walker.
f A Nottingham riot in 1678, by R. J. Burton.
g Some Nottinghamshire and Lincolnshire Easter sepulchres, by E. Woolley.
h St. Michael's, Laxton, by H. Gill.
i Nottinghamshire in 1676: a transcript from the Tanner mss. in the Bodleian Library, by E. L. Guilford.
j Military effigies in Notts. before the Black Death, by H. Lawrance and T. E. Routh.

5831 Vol. 29.

a Churches of Chaddesden and Morley [Derbys.], by E. L. Guilford.
b Extracts from the act books of the archdeacons of Nottingham [1565-1642], extracted and collated by R. F. B. Hodgkinson. [Contd. in vols. 30 and 31]
c The royalist badges of Charles I, by F. E. Burton.
d An itinerary of Nottingham, being information as to the history of the streets, buildings etc., of the city collected from many sources, by J. H. Walker. [Contd. in vols. 30-36]
e The account book [1644-5] of John Hooper, steward to John Holles, 2nd Earl of Clare, transcribed and ed. S. J. Kirk.
f Notes about Sutton Bonington, by W. E. Buckland.
g Account of the Rev. Charles Allen, rector of St. Anne, Sutton Bonington, 1755-95, by W. E. Buckland.
h Hawton church, by F. H. Burnside.

5832 Vol. 30.

a Windmills, by R. Neville.
b St. Mary's church, Bottesford, by F. Walford.
c The life of John Blackner [d. 1816], by J. C. Warren.

5833 Vol. 31.

a Margidunum [Roman camp], by F. Oswald.
b The coins of King Athelstan [d. 940] of the Nottingham mint, by F. E. Burton.

5834 Vol. 32.

a Church of Breedon-on-the-Hill [Leics.], by T. E. Routh.
b Thomas Berdmore [d. 1785], by Lilian Lindsay.
c The open fields of Laxton, by J. D. Chambers.
d Sutton [family] of Sutton-in-Ashfield, by G. G. Bonser.

5835 Vol. 33.

a East Chilwell and Keighton: notes on early settlements, with an attempt to locate a lost village, by A. Cossons.
b All Saints' church, Gedling, by C. M. O. Scott.
c An assessment for St. Mary's church, Nottingham [1637], transcribed by F. A. Wadsworth.
d Church bells of Nottinghamshire, by R. F. Wilkinson. [Contd. in vol. 35]

5836 Vol. 34.

a Nottinghamshire Volunteer medals of the Napoleonic period, by F. E. Burton.
b Nottinghamshire maps of the 16th–18th cent.: their makers and engravers, by F. A. Wadsworth.
c The 18th cent. enclosures of the townships of (Sutton) Bonington St. Michael's, and Sutton St. Anne's, by W. E. Tate.

5837 Vol. 35.

a Haughton Hall, by T. M. Blagg.
b Haughton chapel, by T. M. Blagg.
c Norwell, by T. M. Blagg.
d Owthorpe church, by J. E. H. Wood.
e Sir Cornelius Vermuyden [d. *c.* 1683], by J. Bramley.
f The Leah Gossip diary and letters [1772, 1823 and 1830], with introd. by A. B. Reid. [Contd. in vol. 36]
g Sir Charles Morrison, knight [d. 1599], by C. L. Stevenson.

5838 Vol. 36.

a The Wollaton antiphonale, by A. Du Boulay Hill.
b Nottingham pottery, by A. Parker.
c A young Nottinghamshire soldier of the civil war [William Holles], by A. C. Wood.

Record series, vols. 1–3:

5839 Vol. 1. Seventeenth century parish register transcripts belonging to the peculiar of Southwell, ed. T. M. Blagg. 1903.

5840 Vol. 2. The domesday of inclosures for Nottinghamshire, from the returns to the inclosure commissioners of 1517 in the Public Record Office, ed. with introd., translation and summaries by I. S. Leadam. 1904.

5841 Vols. 3, 4. Abstracts of *inquisitiones post mortem* relating to Nottinghamshire. Vols. i–ii, 1905–14. [Vol. i: 1485–1546, ed. W. P. W. Phillimore. Vol. ii: 1279–1321, ed. J. Standish. Vol. iii: 1321–50, was published in 1939; vol. iv: 1350–1436, was completed in 1952]

TORQUAY NATURAL HISTORY SOCIETY

Founded 1844, for the study of natural science. The Society instituted an archaeological section in 1924.

Journal, vols. 1–3, *contd. as* **Journal of Transactions and Proceedings, vols. 4–6 (1909–34):**

5842 Vol. 1.

a The Torquay Natural History Society: historical notes, by H. J. Lowe.
b Notes on a collection of worked flints from the neighbourhood of North Bovey, recently acquired by the Society, by A. Somervail.
c Tokens, with special reference to those in the museum of the Society, by S. Grose.
d Notes on some points connected with the excavation of Kent's cavern, Torquay, by W. L. H. Duckworth.
e A sketch of the life of William Pengelly [geologist, d. 1894], by Hester F. Julian. [Contd. in vol. 2]

f Historical and national plants, by G. Lee.
g Kent's cavern: some doubts and difficulties, by A. R. Hunt.
h Charters of Totnes priory, by H. R. Watkin.

5843 Vol. 2.

a Plan of Kent's cavern, by H. J. Lowe.
b A 13th cent. deed formerly belonging to Torre abbey, by H. R. Watkin.
c Stone implements from the breccia of Kent's cavern, by H. J. Lowe.
d Dartmoor antiquities and their builders, by H. J. Lowe.
e The caves of Tor Bryan, their excavator [James Lyon Widger, d. 1892], excavation, products and significance, by H. J. Lowe.
f The astronomical clue to the age of the stone implements in Kent's cavern, by R. A. Marriott.
g Norse standards of measurement found locally in architecture of the 11th and 12th cent., by H. R. Watkin.
h The needles of Kent's cavern, with reference to needle origin, by H. J. Lowe.
i The scientific correspondence of Charles Kingsley and William Pengelly, by Hester F. Julian.

5844 Vol. 3.

a Rev. John MacEnery [d. 1841] and Kent's cavern, by H. J. Lowe.
b The *Mayflower* tercentenary and recollections of New England, by Hester F. Julian.
c Kent's cavern anthropology and the ice ages, by H. J. Lowe.
d Blag, Blache, Black and Blake in place-names, by H. R. Watkin.
e Life and labours of Lord Lister [surgeon, d. 1912], by Hester F. Julian.
f The Kingsteignton idol, by H. G. Dowie.

5845 Vol. 4.

a The excavation products of Kent's cavern and their distribution, by H. J. Lowe.
b A note on the [cinerary] urn discovered near Marldon, by H. G. Dowie.
c The origin of the British race, by H. G. Dowie.
d Tormohun and other place-names, by H. R. Watkin.
e Historical sketch [of the Torquay Natural History Society], by H. L. Earl.
f William Pengelly and Kent's hole, by Sir W. B. Dawkins.
g The manor of Tormohun, by H. R. Watkin.
h Cockington and local place-names, by H. R. Watkin.
i Excavation of a cave at Torbryan, by H. G. Dowie.
j Report on a human skull found near the entrance to Kent's cavern, by Sir A. Keith.
k Sources of English history, by F. S. Edmonds.
l Samuel Johnson, by H. L. Earl.

5846 Vol. 5.

a Report on a fragment of a human jaw found in Kent's cavern, by Sir A. Keith.
b A prehistoric burial site at Slapton, by H. G. Dowie.
c Horace Walpole, by H. L. Earl.
d Notes on some Kent's cavern specimens, by Hester F. Julian.
e The story of Cockington: lords of the manor, by H. R. Watkin.
f John Davis, Arctic explorer, by G. Bryce.
g Neolithic flint implements from west Somerset, by C. F. Moysey.
h Robert Louis Stevenson: the man and his work, by T. J. Hardy.
i The 'Blag' culte and the 'virbegna': the possessions of Torre abbey in Woodbury, by H. R. Watkin.
j Ancient man, by J. F. Nall.

k Sir Walter Scott, by T. J. Hardy.

l Origin of the title and office of mayor, by H. R. Watkin.

m Report on excavations in Kent's cavern, 1926–9, by F. Beynon, H. G. Dowie and A. H. Ogilvie.

n Dartmouth: the origin and meaning of the place-name, by H. R. Watkin.

5847 Vol. 6.

a The Pied Piper of Hamlyn and the coming of the Black Death, by E. H. Hankin.

b Sir John Bowring, philologist, politician, and poet [d. 1872], by Hester F. Julian.

c Teignbridge: a chapter in the early history of Newton Abbot, by H. R. Watkin.

d The romance of a great librarian [Sir Anthony Panizzi], by T. J. Hardy.

e Charles Lamb and his circle, by Mrs. V. M. Nosworthy.

f Teign, Teign Bruer, Teign le Gras, Teign Graas, Teign Grace, by H. R. Watkin.

g 'Those Victorians', by T. J. Hardy.

h Some Kent's cavern questions, by A. H. Ogilvie.

i Seven hundred years ago: 1232, the sixth crusade and the south-west of England, by H. R. Watkin.

j Notes on 17th cent. life in a Devonshire village [from parish records], by P. M. B. Lake.

Other publications:

5848 Historical pictorial souvenir of Torquay, by H. R. Watkin. *P.* 1920.

TYNESIDE GEOGRAPHICAL SOCIETY

Founded 1887, to promote the science of geography, with special reference to commerce, emigration, and education, and to the interests of the district.

Journal, vol. 4–vol. 6, no. 3 (1897–1913):

5849 Vol. 4.

a Tenth anniversary of the Society.

b The Soudan in 1885 and 1898, by W. Verner.

c The Royal Niger Company [and Sir George Taubman Goldie. A brief history, from *The Times*].

5850 Vol. 5.

a The development of Rhodesia and its railway system in relation to oceanic highways, by J. T. P. Heatley.

b Persian aspirations [and British and Russian interests, 1890–1907], by E. G. Browne.

5851 Vol. 6.

a A British state in the making: how the plan of empire is filled in, by Sir N. J. Moore. [The development of Western Australia]

UNITARIAN HISTORICAL SOCIETY

Founded 1915, for the study of the history of Unitarian and kindred movements in the United Kingdom and elsewhere; the preservation of registers, manuscripts, plate, pictures, architectural and other records, and antiquities relating to the congregations connected therewith; and for the publication of historical documents and the Transactions of the Society.

Transactions, vols. 1–5 (1917–34):

5852 Vol. 1.

a The deeds of the Free Christian church, Horsham, by R. M. Montgomery.

b An open trust: note on the Ditchling trust deed [for the Free Christian church, 1740].

c The old nonconformity at Norton, Derbys., by C. J. Street.

d Early records of a Presbyterian congregation: the High Pavement, Nottingham, by J. C. Warren.

e The old meeting, Framlingham, by A. Amey.

f An apology for the nonconformist Arians of the 18th cent., by F. J. Powicke.

g The origin and history of the old meeting house, Aberdare, by R. J. Jones.

h The deeds of Westgate chapel, Lewes, by R. M. Montgomery.

i The church book of the General Baptist church of Turners Hill and Horley [Surr.], by W. H. Burgess.

j An historical legal decision [in Bowman *v.* Secular Society, Ltd., 1917].

k The deeds of Essex chapel [Essex Street, Strand, London].

l The old meeting house, Banbury, and its successor the Unitarian church, by A. D. Tyssen.

m The open-trust myth, by W. Whitaker.

n John Pounds [d. 1839, shoemaker and philanthropist], by W. H. Burgess.

5853 Vol. 2.

a From Puritanism to Unitarianism at Lincoln, by J. C. Warren.

b Roger Baldwin [d. 1695, nonconformist minister], by F. Nicholson and E. Axon.

c Some Protestant dissenting congregations ministered to by the Rev. John Baxter Pike, in the years 1780–1810, by C. E. Pike.

d The open trust, by R. M. Montgomery.

e Our Welsh hymn book, by R. J. Jones.

f The Manchester Socinian controversy [and subsequent events, 1825], by H. McLachlan.

g The Presbyterians of Bloxham and Milton, near Banbury, Oxon., by A. D. Tyssen.

h An old pamphlet [*A narrative of the late Proceedings of some Justices and others, Pretending to put in execution the late Act against Conventicles,—in and about the Town of Lewes in Sussex,—etc. Printed in the year 1670*], by R. M. Montgomery.

i Record section. [Includes: A list of ministers residing in and about London in the summer of 1689; A document by a member of the Pilgrim Fathers' church, being a statement of his case written from prison by Thomas Brewer, 1626]

j Nonconformist schools under persecution, 1662–1714, by S. G. Lee.

k The Christian Brethren movement [and its founder Joseph Barker, d. 1875], by H. McLachlan.

l The Hollis family and Harvard College [in the 17th cent.], by C. J. Street.

m Record section. [Includes: A list of west country divines, 1690–1740]

n The manuscripts of William Shepherd [d. 1847, nonconformist minister] at Manchester College, Oxford, by F. Nicholson and E. Axon.

o Pews and benches, by C. E. Pike. [A record of pew-making in a meeting-house dating from 1688]

p 17th cent. Unitarian tracts, by H. McLachlan.

5854 Vol. 3.

a Strata in the formation of Unitarian church tradition, by R. V. Holt.

b The evolution of church government in an English Presbyterian congregation, by C. E. Pike.

c Record section. [Includes: Excommunication among the older Welsh independents; Trust deed of St. Thomas Street chapel, Portsmouth]

d English Unitarian hymn writers, by D. Wright.

e The Mort family in connexion with Lancashire nonconformity, by E. Axon.

f Historical notes on the Stockport Unitarian church, by H. E. Perry.

g Record section. [Includes: A sermon register, 1833–54, kept by Silvanus Gibbs, of sermons delivered in the Unitarian chapel, Devonport]

h The old Hackney [Unitarian] College, 1786–96, by H. McLachlan.

i Unitarian liturgies, by C. E. Pike.

j British and Foreign Unitarian Association centenary exhibition. [An account of some of the exhibits]

k Record section. [Includes: The Kenrick letters, 1773–8, between Samuel Kenrick and his brother John]

l Buxton chapel, by E. Axon.

m More letters of Theophilus Lindsey [d. 1803], by H. McLachlan.

n Record series. [Includes further Kenrick letters. Contd. in vols. 4 and 5]

5855 Vol. 4.

a University Hall, London [subsequently the home of Dr. Williams's library], by W. G. Tarrant and J. Worthington.

b Nonconformity at Coseley [Staffs.], by A. Gordon.

c The Taylors and Scotts of the *Manchester Guardian*, by H. McLachlan.

d Some chapters in the story of *The Inquirer* [a Unitarian newspaper first published in 1842], by W. G. Tarrant.

e Notes on the history of the Eastern Union of Unitarian and other Free Christian churches, by G. R. Jones.

f Our communion plate and other treasures, by G. E. Evans. [Contd. in vol. 5]

g Short sketch of the origin and progress of nonconformity in Walsall, by H. Warnock.

h Notes on 17th cent. Lancashire ministers named Lawton and Walker, by E. Axon.

i The Unitarian church at Sydney, by W. H. Burgess.

j Record section. [Includes: The will of John Cooper, d. 1665, the Cheltenham Unitarian; Two certificates relating to John Crompton, minister, 1659/60, and Samuel Crompton, minister, 1686/7]

k Chapel and service, by R. P. Jones. [The form of worship in Anglican churches before the Oxford movement]

l Hackney College and William Hazlitt, by H. W. Stephenson.

m Diary of a Leeds layman [Joseph Ryder], 1733–68, by H. McLachlan.

n Unitarian ministers of Walsall and their predecessors, by H. Warnock.

o Record section. [Includes: Early Scottish Unitarians, being correspondence between James Purves, d. 1795, and Thomas Fyshe Palmer, d. 1802]

p The history of the Presbyterian academy, Brynllywarch-Carmarthen, 1662–82, by H. P. Roberts. [Contd. in vol. 5]

q James Martineau and Sunday School work, by W. H. Burgess.

r Recollections of Dr. Priestley, by John Ryland, written down by his daughter, Miss Susan Ryland, at her father's dictation, 25 Feb. 1844, with introductory remarks and appended notes by R. A. M. Dixon.

5856 Vol. 5.

a John Knowles [fl. 1646–68] and Henry Hedworth [d. 1705], Unitarian pioneers, by W. H. Burgess.

b The ministers' monthly meeting in the Manchester district [from 1861], by H. E. Perry.

c Priestley's daughter [Sarah Finch, d. 1803?] and her descendants, by R. A. M. Dixon.

d Priestley and the Birmingham riots [1791], by B. M. Allen.

e The claim of Batley grammar school to be the alma-mater of the Rev. Dr. Joseph Priestley, F.R.S., by N. L. Frazer.

f Dr. Joseph Priestley, F.R.S., and the offer to him of French citizenship and membership of the National Assembly of France, by R. A. M. Dixon.

g 'Taking the census', a play written for his grandchildren by the Rev. Joseph Priestley, F.R.S. (previously unpublished), communicated with introductory remarks by R. A. M. Dixon.

h Early Unitarian schoolmasters and schools in Wales, by H. P. Roberts.

i Samuel Taylor Coleridge and Unitarianism, by H. W. Stephenson.

j Our indebtedness to Priestley, by H. J. Rossington.

k Yorkshire nonconformity in 1743, by E. Axon.

l Memorials of an ancient Presbyterian meeting house at Cirencester, by C. H. Clennell.

m Was Dr. Priestley responsible for the dinner which started the 1791 riots?, by R. A. M. Dixon.

n Reply by B. Allen [to the above] and rejoinder by R. A. M. Dixon.

o Record section. [Includes: Letter from Thomas Belsham relating to the Dissenters' Bill, 1779]

p Toxteth Park chapel [Liverpool] in the 17th cent., by L. Hall.

q George's meeting house, Exeter [17th–18th cent.], by A. Hickmott.

r The meeting house at Newcastle-under-Lyme [17th–20th cent.], based on notes collected by G. Pegler.

s Record section. [A petition of Rev. John Knowles, 1665; Letter from Philip Doddridge, 1738; Rev. Thomas Belsham to his sister, 1777; Kenrick letters, 1800–77]

UNIVERSITY OF BRISTOL SPELAEOLOGICAL SOCIETY

Founded 1919, for the discovery and exploration of caves and the investigation of their contents, and the study of prehistoric archaeology.

Proceedings, vols. 1–4 (1919–35):

5857 Vol. 1.

a Report on material found at 'The Cave', Burrington [Som.], by E. Fawcett.

b The Keltic cavern [near Mendip Lodge hill, Som.], by L. S. Palmer. [Further reports in this vol. and in vols. 2 and 4 under the title 'Read's cavern']

c Classification of stone implements, by R. Smith.

d Civilisation of the stone age, by M. C. Burkitt.

e Cave hunting in Somerset, by Sir W. B. Dawkins.

f Kent's cavern [Torquay, Devon], by R. H. Coysh.

g Some prehistoric finds from the Mendips, by H. E. Balch.

h Aveline's hole, Burrington Coombe: an upper palaeolithic station, by J. A. Davies. [Further reports in this vol. and in vol. 2]

i Rowberrow cavern [Som.], by H. Taylor. [Further reports in this vol. and in vol. 2]

j Preliminary report of some recent discoveries at Brean down [Som.], by N. C. Cooper.

k The stratigraphical position of the transitional culture in the south and south-west of England, by L. S. Palmer.

5858 Vol. 2.

a Report on the excavation of Mendip barrows during 1923, by R. F. Read. [Further reports in this vol.]

b First report on Kings Weston hill, Bristol [being an account of the tumuli and prehistoric remains], by E. K. Tratman. [Further reports in this vol.]

c First report on excavations in the Wye valley, by T. F. Hewer. [Further reports in this vol. and vol. 4, with particular reference to Merlin's cave]

d Notes on the Maglemose culture, by M. C. Burkitt.

e Notes on some chisel-like implements from Mendip, by J. A. Davies.

f The Tickenham rock shelter, by J. H. Savory.

g Guy's Rift, Slaughterford, Wilts.: an early iron age habitation, by T. F. Hewer.

h Report on calvarium from Guy's Rift, Slaughterford, Wilts., by L. H. D. Buxton.

i Frank i' th' Rocks cave [Hartington, Derbys.] and other northern caves in relation to the ice ages, by L. S. Palmer and L. S. Lee.

j Notes on some upper palaeolithic implements from some Mendip caves, by J. A. Davies.

k Field work [being a survey of prehistoric features in Somerset and Gloucestershire]. General introduction by E. K. Tratman. [Contd. in vol. 3]

l The upper palaeolithic age in Britain, by Dorothy A. E. Garrod.

m The study of flint flaking, by S. H. Warren.

5859 Vol. 3.

a The Percy Sladen memorial fund excavations at Bury Hill camp, Winterbourne down, Glos., 1926, by J. A. Davies and C. W. Phillips.

b King Arthur's cave, near Whitchurch, Ross-on-Wye, by H. Taylor.

c First report on the excavations at Sun hole, Cheddar. Levels above the pleistocene, by E. K. Tratman and G. T. D. Henderson.

5860 Vol. 4.

a Earthworks on Walton Common down, near Clevedon, by C. W. Phillips.

b Note on an anvil and a palstave found at Flax Bourton, Som., by S. J. Jones.

c The Tynings barrow group [near Blackdown, Som.]: second report [being a continuation of Field work, vol. 3], by H. Taylor.

d A cyst of the beaker period at Corston, near Bath, by H. Taylor.

e Field work, by C. W. Phillips. [A Romano-British site at Wraxall, and Celtic and Anglo-Saxon field systems in Ashton park]

f Note on excavations [of a beaker age site] at Gorsey Bigbury, Charterhouse-on-Mendip, Som., 1931-5, by S. J. Jones.

g Report on excavations at Worship's farm, Redhill, Wrington, Aug. 1933, by E. K. Tratman.

h Recent finds at Solisbury hill camp, near Bath: a Hallstatt-early La Tène site, by J. P. E. Falconer and S. B. Adams.

i Field work, 1933, by E. K. Tratman. [Excavations of prehistoric and Roman structures in Somerset]

j An upper arm bone of a slinger [found in a Roman coffin in Dyrham park], by E. Fawcett.

k Index of vols. 1-4.

UNIVERSITY OF DURHAM PHILOSOPHICAL SOCIETY

Founded 1896, for the promotion of research and the communication and discussion of facts and ideas bearing upon scientific and philosophic questions.

Proceedings, vols. 2-9 (1901-38):

5861 Vol. 2.

a Notes on Durham College, founded by Oliver Cromwell, by G. W. Kitchin.

b The development of mathematics in the 19th cent., by J. T. Merz.

c The Black Death in the palatinate of Durham, by F. Bradshaw.

5862 Vol. 3.

a The strategical importance of the Roman forts Habitancum and Bremenium, by G. R. B. Spain.

b Note on a flint implement found near Newcastle, by J. A. Smythe.

c The Roman city of Corstopitum, by W. H. Knowles.

d Sun and star observations at the stone circles of Keswick and Long Meg [Cumb.], by J. Morrow.

e The metrical life of St. Cuthbert, by J. T. Fowler.

f The Romano-British city of Corstopitum: excavations in 1908, by W. H. Knowles.

g A border pele [Shield Hall, near Hexham, Northumb.]: extract from paper on 'The development of the dwelling in the border counties', by R. J. S. Bertram.

5863 Vol. 4.

a St. Oswin and Tynemouth priory, by H. H. E. Craster.

b The mutual developments of metallurgy and engineering, by H. Louis.

5864 Vol. 5.

a Evolution of the bronze spear and sword in Britain, by P. Brewis.

5865 Vol. 6.

a Some aspects of mining laws under the Roman empire, by H. Louis. [Includes observations on tin-mining in Cornwall]

5866 Vol. 8.

a The application of physics to agriculture from the 16th cent. to the present day, by B. A. Keen.

5867 Vol. 9.

a A flanged bronze celt from Birtley, co. Durham, by A. Raistrick and J. A. Smythe.

b An examination of Roman copper from Wigtownshire and North Wales, by G. C. Whittick and J. A. Smythe.

c Examination [by chemical analysis] of a Roman chisel from Chesterholm, by C. E. Pearson and J. A. Smythe.

d Lead smelting in the north Pennines during the 17th and 18th cent., by A. Raistrick.

e 'Rara avis in terris': the laws and customs of lead mines in west Yorkshire, by A. Raistrick.

f Excavations at Sewell's cave, Settle, Yorks., by A. Raistrick. [With an account of prehistoric and Romano-British finds]

g Roman objects of copper and iron from the north of England, by J. A. Smythe. [A metallurgical study]

VALE OF DERWENT NATURALISTS' FIELD CLUB

Founded 1887, for the practical study of natural history in all its branches.

Notes on the History, Ornithology, Entomology. and Botany of the Vale of Derwent, vols. 4-5 (1903-5):

5868 Vol. 4.

a Derwent vale [Northumberland and Durham], by W. Featherstonehaugh. [Brief historical notes]

b Tanfield parish in the 18th cent., by H. F. Bulman.

c Old rating methods in Whickham parish, by H. F. Bulman.

5869 Vol. 5.

a Shotley Bridge, by F. W. Nicholson.
b An eminent Durham naturalist, Thomas John Bold [d. 1874], by J. W. Fawcett.

Other publications:

5870 Transactions, new ser., vol. 1 (1908–13).

a A brief history of the township of Chopwell, by J. W. Fawcett.
b Sir Ambrose Crowley [fl. 1690–1713, iron-master]: a brief history of Winlaton, by C.L.B.

VASARI SOCIETY

Founded 1905, for the reproduction of drawings by old masters.

[Reproductions], 1905–15 (10 pts. [1905–15]):

5871 Pt. 2.

a (31) Sir Peter Lely: Portrait of [John Maitland,] Duke of Lauderdale [d. 1682].

5872 Pt. 3.

a (20) Lucas Vorsterman: Portrait of Anne Dacres Countess of Arundel and Surrey, 1557–1630.
b (32) Nicholas Hilliard: Design for the Irish seal of Queen Elizabeth.

5873 Pt. 4.

a (35) David Loggan: Portrait of John Wilmot, Earl of Rochester [d. 1680].

5874 Pt. 5.

a (28) Hans Holbein, the younger: Portrait of George Nevill [d. 1535], 3rd Lord Abergavenny.
b (39) Peter Oliver: Portrait of Sir Francis Crane [d. 1636, last lay chancellor of the order of the Garter].

5875 Pt. 6.

a (34) Samuel Cooper: Portrait of Thomas Alcock.

5876 Pt. 10.

a (10) Antonio Canale (Canaletto): View of old London bridge.

[Reproductions], 2nd ser. (14 pts. 1920–33):

5877 Pt. 1.

a (21, 22) George Frederic Watts: Two small figure studies [Mrs. Thoby Prinsep, d. 1887, and Lady Dalrymple].
b (—) Dante Gabriel Rossetti: Elizabeth Siddal [d. 1862].

5878 Pt. 3.

a (10) Rembrandt: View of St. Albans.
b (11) Rembrandt: View of Windsor.
c (19) Thomas Rowlandson: Soirée at the Royal Academy.
d (20) John Hoppner: Portrait of Mrs. Forster.

5879 Pt. 4.

a (19) Sir Joshua Reynolds: Study for the portrait of Jane, Duchess of Gordon [d. 1812].

5880 Pt. 5.

a (15) Wenceslaus Hollar: Westminster and the abbey from the river.

5881 Pt. 9.

a (10) Sir Anthony Van Dyck: Portrait of the artist's wife, Mary Ruthven.

b (14) Hans Holbein the younger: Sir Charles Wingfield.
c (—) Isaac Oliver: Henry Frederick, Prince of Wales [d. 1612].

5882 Pt. 11.

a Index to 2nd series, pts. 1–10.

5883 Pt. 13.

a (12) Jean Auguste Dominique Ingres: The Montagu sisters [Harriet Mary, d. 1867, and Catherine Caroline, d. 1834].

5884 Pt. 14.

a (7) Thomas Girtin: The Savoy ruins.
b (12) Dante Gabriel Rossetti: Portrait of Miss Siddal.

Other publications:

5885 Index to the 1st series, pts. 1–10 (1905–15). *P.* 1920.

5886 Index to the 2nd series, pt. 1 (1920). *P.* 1920.

5887 Index to the 2nd series, pts. 2–3 (1921–2). *P.* [1922?].

VICTORIA INSTITUTE
(or Philosophical Society of Great Britain)

Founded 1865, to investigate important questions of philosophy and science, especially those bearing upon Holy Scripture, and to combat unbelief by directing attention to the evidences of the Divine care for man that are supplied by science, history, and religion.

Journal of Transactions, vols. 33–65 (1901–33):

5888 Vol. 33.

a Eolithic implements, by R. A. Bullen.

5889 Vol. 38.

a The early Celtic churches of Britain and Ireland, by Eleanor H. Hull.

5890 Vol. 43.

a The last century's witness to the bible, by J. Sharp.
b Contents of Journal of Transactions, 1st ser., vols. 1–5, new ser., vols. 6–42. [General index to vols. 1–43 was issued with vol. 44. Vol. 70 contains a list of contents of vols. 44–70]

5891 Vol. 49.

a Some of the relations between science and religion as affected by the work of the last fifty years, by H. Wace.

5892 Vol. 50.

a Prehistoric man: his antiquity and characteristics, by W. Dale.

5893 Vol. 51.

a The philosophy of Bishop Butler [d. 1752], by H. J. R. Marston.

5894 Vol. 52.

a Monumental art in early England, Caledonia and Ireland, by G. F. Browne.

5895 Vol. 53.

a The Roman wall in north Britain, by H. E. Fox.

5896 Vol. 54.

a Christianity in Roman Britain, by W. Dale.

VIKING SOCIETY FOR NORTHERN RESEARCH

Founded 1892, as the Viking Club, being the social and literary branch of the Orkney and Shetland Society of London. Connection with the latter society ended shortly afterwards and the title Viking Club, or, Orkney, Shetland, and Northern Society, was adopted, the objects of the Society including the discussion of papers on northern history, literature, music, art, archaeology, language, folklore, and anthropology, and also the transcription and publication of original documents relating to northern history, etc., and the translation of sagas and other works on northern subjects. Title changed to above form in 1912.

Saga-Book, vols. 2–10 (1898–1929):

5897 Vol. 2.

a Norse place-names in Gower, Glam., by A. G. Moffat.

b Ethandune, 878: King Alfred's campaign from Athelney, by C. W. Whistler.

c Great Clifton cross-shaft, by W. G. Collingwood.

d The Norse lay of Wayland ('Vǫlundarkviða') and its relation to English tradition, by S. Bugge.

e King Eirik of York, by W. G. Collingwood.

5898 Vol. 3.

a Runic tympanum at Pennington, Furness, by W. G. Collingwood.

b Palnatoki [Danish chief, fl. 930–90] in Wales, by A. G. Moffat.

c Gospatrick's Cumberland charter. Viking age cross at Iona, by W. G. Collingwood.

d The Danish camp on the Ouse, near Bedford, by A. R. Goddard.

e Stone circles and other rude stone monuments of Great Britain, by A. L. Lewis.

5899 Vol. 4.

a Traces of Danish conquest and settlement in Cambridgeshire, by E. Hailstone.

b The Danes in Cambridgeshire, by J. W. E. Conybeare.

c Scandinavian *motifs* in Anglo-Saxon and Norman ornamentation, by H. J. Dukinfield Astley.

d The oldest known list of Scandinavian names [being a Northumbrian bidding prayer, early 11th cent.], by J. Stefánsson.

5900 Vol. 5.

a Some illustrations of the archaeology of the Viking age in England, by W. G. Collingwood.

b The [Danish] battle burials at Cannington park [Som.], by C. W. Whistler.

c A Viking ship [represented in ironwork] on a church door [at Stillingfleet, Yorks.], by G. A. Auden.

5901 Vol. 6.

a The sites of three Danish camps and an Anglian burying ground in East Anglia, by B. Lowerison.

b Brunaburh and Vinheith in Ingulf's chronicle and Egil's saga, by C. W. Whistler.

c Rangar Lothbrok and his sons [with particular reference to the 9th cent. Viking raids on England], by A. Mawer.

d Abstract of a paper on antiquities dating from the Danish occupation of York, by G. A. Auden.

e Siward Digri of Northumberland: a Viking-saga of the Danes in England, by A. Olrik.

5902 Vol. 7.

a Norse elements in English dialects: a survey of the study, by G. T. Flom.

b The Scandinavian kingdom of Northumbria, by A. Mawer.

c William Herbert [d. 1847, dean of Manchester] and his Scandinavian poetry, by W. F. Kirby.

d Early English influence on the Danish church, by A. V. Storm.

e Anglo-Saxon silver coins from the 11th cent. in a silver-hoard from Ryfylke, Norway, by A. W. Brøgger.

5903 Vol. 8.

a The cultus of Norwegian saints in England and Scotland, by E. Bull.

b Scandinavian influence in the place-names of Northumberland and Durham, by A. Mawer.

c Thyra, the wife of Gorm the old, who was she, English [and daughter of Ethelred I] or Danish?, by E. Rason.

5904 Vol. 9.

a Manx crosses relating to Great Britain and Norway, by H. Shetelig.

b The English parish before the Norman conquest, by Constance B. Stoney.

5905 Vol. 10.

a The attitude of the Anglo-Saxons to their Scandinavian invaders, by Margaret Ashdown.

b Arthur and Athelstan, by W. G. Collingwood.

c Danes and Norwegians in Yorkshire, by A. H. Smith.

d A Norse camp at Brandon, Suff., by C. Morley.

Year Book, vols. 1–24 (1909–32):

5906 Vol. 1.

a Notes on the Rampside [Lancs.] sword, by H. Gaythorpe.

Other publications:

5907 List of books belonging to the Club, comp. J. Stefánsson. P. [1907].

5908 Essays on questions connected with the old English poem of Beowulf, by K. Stjerna. 1912.

WALPOLE SOCIETY

Founded 1911, to promote the study of the history of British art.

First–Twenty-first Annual Volume[1] (1912–33):

5909 Vol. 1.

a Nicholas Hilliard's treatise concerning 'The arte of limning', with introd. and notes by P. Norman.

b A sketch of English mediaeval figure-sculpture, by E. S. Prior.

c London and Westminster painters in the middle ages, by W. R. Lethaby, with notes on the plates by E. W. Tristram.

d Reynolds' first portrait of Keppel, by (1) Leonard O'Malley, (2) C. H. Collins Baker.

e Turner's 'Isle of Wight' sketch-book, by A. J. Finberg.

5910 Vol. 2.

a The painter HE ('Hans Eworth'), by L. Cust.

b An outline of the history of the De Critz family of painters [1568–1728], by Rachel Poole.

c The romance tiles of Chertsey abbey, by W. R. Lethaby.

d Rood screen of Cawston church, by E. F. Strange.

e The Hatfield tapestries of the seasons, by A. F. Kendrick.

f Hugh Douglas Hamilton [portrait painter, d. 1808], by W. G. Strickland.

g Some of the doubtful drawings in the Turner bequest at the National Gallery, by A. J. Finberg.

[1] After vol. 4 the word 'Annual' is omitted.

5911 Vol. 3.

a Marcus Gheeraerts, father [b. *c.* 1525] and son [*c.* 1561–1635/6], by Rachel Poole.

b Marcus Gheeraerts [the younger], by L. Cust.

c A psalter in the British Museum (Royal ms. 1. D. X), illuminated in England early in the 13th cent., by J. A. Herbert.

d Animals in English wood carvings, by G. C. Druce.

e A painted room of the 17th cent. [in Botolph Lane, Eastcheap, London], by E. W. Tristram.

f Notes on Edmund Ashfield [pastellist, fl. 1674], by C. H. Collins Baker.

g Some leaves from Turner's 'South Wales' sketch book, by A. J. Finberg.

h Notes on [Richard Parkes] Bonington's parents, by C. E. Hughes.

i A further note on Haunce Eworth, by L. Cust.

j Two portraits by Haunce Eworth, by Mary F. S. Hervey.

k Notes on additional HE portraits, by R. W. Goulding.

l George Vertue's note-books and manuscripts relating to the history of art in England: introd. and proposals of a scheme for their publication, by L. Cust, with additional notes and a list of the manuscripts in the British Museum, by A. M. Hind.

5912 Vol. 4. The Welbeck Abbey miniatures, belonging to the Duke of Portland: a catalogue raisonné by R. W. Goulding. 1916.

5913 Vol. 5.

a English 17th cent. portrait drawings in Oxford collections, by C. F. Bell. [Contd. by C. F. Bell and Rachel Poole in vol. 14]

b The etchings of Andrew Geddes [d. 1844], by C. Dodgson.

c Fresh light on some water-colour painters of the old British school, derived from the collection and papers of James Moore, F.S.A. [d. 1799], by C. F. Bell.

d Kilpeck church, by L. Cust.

e A note on Thomas Gainsborough and Gainsborough Dupont comprising a complete list of the works by both artists, by M. H. Spielman.

5914 Vol. 6.

a Two anonymous portraits by Cornelius Johnson [d. *c.* 1664], by A. J. Finberg.

b The Lumley inventories, by L. Cust. [An inventory of the pictures and sculptures belonging to John, Lord Lumley, at Lumley Castle, 1590]

c A Lumley inventory of 1609, by Mary F. S. Hervey.

d Gawen Hamilton [d. 1737] an unknown Scottish portrait painter, by Hilda F. Finberg.

e Liverpool art and artists in the 18th cent., by E. R. Dibdin.

f Further leaves from Turner's 'South Wales' sketch-book, by A. J. Finberg.

g Two early works of Sir Joshua Reynolds [being the portraits of Captain Roberts, R.N., 1747, and Thomas and Maria Neate with their tutor, 1748].

h The papers of the Society of Artists of Great Britain [1759–61].

5915 Vol. 7. The note-book and account book of Nicholas Stone, master mason to James I and Charles I, transcribed and annotated with introd. by W. L. Spiers; together with an appendix containing a transcript of the diary of Nicholas Stone, junr., recording the visit of himself and his brother Henry to France and Italy, in 1638–42. 1919.

5916 Vol. 8.

a Portraits of Sir Walter Raleigh, by L. Cust.

b Wriothesley portraits, authentic and reputed, by R. W. Goulding.

c Francis Towne [d. 1816], landscape painter, by A. P. Oppé.

d A lost monument by Nicholas Stone [to Lady Anne Cutt, d. 1631, at Swavesey church, Cambs.], by H. C. Andrews.

5917 Vol. 9.

a Queen Elizabeth's visit to Blackfriars, June 16, 1600 [with particular reference to the painting by Marcus Gheeraerts], by the Earl of Ilchester, with introd. by L. Cust.

b Canaletto in England [1746–55?], by Hilda F. Finberg. [Additional notes in vol. 10]

c Documents relating to an action brought against Joseph Goupy [artist, fl. 1711–66] in 1738, by C. R. Grundy.

d An authentic portrait [of Charles I as Duke of York] by Robert Peake [fl. 1598–1613], by A. J. Finberg.

5918 Vol. 10.

a Chronological list of portraits by Cornelius Johnson or Jonson, by A. J. Finberg.

b Some contemporary records relating to Francis Place [d. 1728], engraver and draughtsman, with a catalogue of his engraved work, by H. M. Hake.

c Farleigh castle, by R. W. M. Wright.

5919 Vol. 11.

a An English bible-picture book of the 14th cent. (Holkham ms. 666), by M. R. James.

b Two Netherlandish artists in England: Steven van Herwijck [d. 1565–7?] and Steven van der Meulen [fl. 1543–62], by G. F. Hill.

c Edward Pierce [d. 1698], the sculptor, by Rachel Poole.

d Henry Gyles [d. 1709], glass-painter of York, by J. A. Knowles.

e The etchings of Sir David Wilkie [d. 1841], by C. Dodgson.

5920 Vol. 12. Designs by Inigo Jones for masques and plays at court: a descriptive catalogue of drawings for scenery and costumes mainly in the collection of the Duke of Devonshire, with introd. and notes by P. Simpson and C. F. Bell. 1924. [Also published by the Malone Society]

5921 Vol. 13.

a An English mediaeval sketch-book, no. 1916 in the Pepysian library, Magdalene College, Cambridge, by M. R. James.

b The drawings of John White [fl. 1585–93], governor of Raleigh's Virginia colony, by L. Binyon.

c An 18th cent. art chronicler: Sir Henry Bate Dudley, bt. [d. 1824], by W. T. Whitley.

d John White Abbott, of Exeter, 1763–1851, by A. P. Oppé.

5922 Vol. 14.

a The drawings of Matthew Paris [d. 1259], by M. R. James.

b Some Barcheston tapestries [from the factory founded by William Sheldon], by A. F. Kendrick.

c John Sell Cotman's letters from Normandy, 1817–20, ed. H. Isherwood Kay. [Contd. in vol. 15]

5923 Vol. 15.

a The painted windows in the chapel of The Vyne, Hampshire, by G. McN. Rushforth.

b John Bushnell [d. 1701], sculptor, by Katharine A. Esdaile. [Additional notes in vol. 21]

c Tilly Kettle, 1735–86 [portrait-painter], by J. D. Milner.

5924 Vol. 16.

a Mediaeval wall-paintings at Christ Church, Oxford, by M. R. James and E. W. Tristram.

b Horace Walpole's journals of visits to country seats, etc., ed. P. Toynbee.

c A Roman sketch-book by Alexander Cozens [d. 1786], by A. P. Oppé.

5925 Vol. 17.

a Wall-paintings in Eton College chapel and in the Lady chapel of Winchester cathedral, by M. R. James and E. W. Tristram.

b William Peckitt, glass-painter [d. 1795], by J. A. Knowles.

c Richard Crosse, miniaturist and portrait-painter [d. 1810], by B. S. Long.

d English devotional woodcuts of the late 15th cent., with special reference to those in the Bodleian Library, by C. Dodgson.

5926 Vols. 18, 20. Vertue note books, vols. i–ii. 1930–32. [The note-books of George Vertue, d. 1756, relating to artists and collections in England, ed. by a committee appointed by the Society. Vols. iii–x and separate index were published as vols. 22, 24, 26, 29, in 1934–47]

5927 Vol. 19.

a British artists in India, 1760–1820, by Sir W. Foster.

b The glass-paintings of Coventry and its neighbourhood, by B. Rackham.

c Letters and drawings of Nicholas Hawksmoor relating to the building of the mausoleum at Castle Howard, 1726–1742, by G. Webb.

5928 Vol. 21.

a English church monuments, 1536–1625, by J. G. Mann.

b Notes on the life of John Wootton [d. 1764] with a list of engravings after his pictures, by G. E. Kendall.

c English embroideries belonging to Sir John Carew Pole, bt., by A. J. B. Wace.

d Notes on a collection of portrait drawings formed by Dawson Turner [Yarmouth banker, d. 1858?], by S. D. Kitson.

WALSALL HISTORICAL ASSOCIATION

Founded 1922, for the advancement of the study and teaching of history.

Publications:

5929 The history of Rushall Hall, near Walsall, by W. H. Duignan. *P.* 1924.

5930 Social aspects of the Protestant revolution, by W. Cross. *P.* 1924.

5931 Latocetum (Wall), by W. F. Blay. *P.* 1925.

5932 The charter of the corporation of Walsall, with an account of the estates thereto belonging, 1925. [Facsimile reproduction of a book printed in 1774, from the only known copy. Includes several mid-17th cent. surveys]

5933 Glimpses of Walsall history: some 17th cent. documents, by J. Turner. *P.* 1927.

5934 The effigy of Sir Roger Hillary [d. 1400], St. Matthew's church, Walsall, by J. Turner. *P.* 1930.

WALTHAMSTOW ANTIQUARIAN SOCIETY

Founded 1915, for the investigation of local history and antiquities, and the wider dissemination of information on these matters amongst local residents.

Monographs, nos. 1–29:

5935 No. 1. Some account of Forbes' map of High Hall manor, Walthamstow, 1699, by G. E. Roebuck. *P.* folio, 1915.

5936 No. 2. A history of St. Mary's church, Walthamstow, by G. F. Bosworth. *P.* folio, 1916.

5937 No. 3. George Monoux: the story of a Walthamstow worthy, his foundations and benefactions, by G. F. Bosworth. *P.* 1916.

5938 No. 4. The rectory manor of Walthamstow, by G. F. Bosworth. *P.* folio, 1917.

5939 No. 5. Essex Hall, Walthamstow, and the Cogan associations, by G. F. Bosworth. *P.* folio, 1918.

5940 No. 6. The manor of Higham Bensted, Walthamstow, by G. F. Bosworth. *P.* folio, 1919.

5941 No. 7. The manors of Low Hall and Salisbury Hall, Walthamstow, by G. F. Bosworth. *P.* folio, 1920.

5942 No. 8. A history of Walthamstow charities, 1487–1920, by G. F. Bosworth. Folio, 1920.

5943 No. 9. Abstracts of wills relating to Walthamstow, 1335–1559, by G. S. Fry. *P.* folio, 1921.

5944 No. 10. The manor of Walthamstow Toni or High Hall, by G. Bosworth. *P.* folio, 1922.

5945 No. 11. Calendar of deeds relating to Walthamstow, 1595–1890, by S. J. Barns. *P.* folio, 1923.

5946 No. 12. Some Walthamstow houses and their interesting associations, by G. F. Bosworth. *P.* folio, 1924.

5947 Nos. 13, 14, 16. Walthamstow in the 18th cent., being extracts from the vestry minutes, churchwardens' and overseers' accounts, 1710–94, by S. J. Barns. Folio, 1925–7. [Issued in 3 pts., no. 13: 1710–40; no. 14: 1741–71; no. 16: 1772–94]

5948 No. 15. A series of illuminated panels designed by Louisa Puller to illustrate a story book of the manors of Walthamstow and Higham, described by Constance D. Saunders. *P.* folio, 1926.

5949 No. 17. George Monoux: the man and his work, by G. F. Bosworth. *P.* folio, 1927.

5950 No. 18. The Walthamstow tokens, by J. Coxall. *P.* folio, 1927. [18a: Supplement to monograph 18, by J. Coxall. *P.* folio, 1929]

5951 No. 19. Original documents relating to the Monoux family, collected and arranged by G. F. Bosworth and Constance D. Saunders. Folio, 1928.

5952 No. 20. More Walthamstow houses and their interesting associations, by G. F. Bosworth. *P.* folio, 1928.

5953 No. 21. Calendar of deeds relating to Walthamstow, 1541–1862, by S. J. Barns. *P.* folio, 1929.

5954 No. 22. Some chapters in the history of Walthamstow, by G. F. Bosworth. *P.* folio, 1929.

5955 Nos. 23, 27. St. Mary the Virgin, Walthamstow: inscriptions in the church and churchyard. *Ps.* folio, 1930–32. [Pt. i: Churchyard inscriptions, by C. H. Crouch. Pt. ii: Memorials in the church, by S. J. Barns]

5956 No. 24. The place-names of Walthamstow, by P. H. Reaney. Folio, 1930.

5957 No. 25. Walthamstow marriages, 24 Feb. 1650–1 Jul. 1837, abstracted from the parish registers, by G. E. Roebuck. *P.* folio, 1931.

5958 No. 26. The Walthamstow armorial, described by G. E. Roebuck. *P.* folio, 1932.

5959 No. 28. Early days in the Walthamstow district [pre-Norman archaeology], by A. R. Hatley. *P.* folio, 1933.

5960 No. 29. Some more Walthamstow houses and their interesting associations, by G. F. Bosworth. *P.* folio, 1933.

WARHAM GUILD

Founded 1913, for the making of all ornaments of the church and of the ministers thereof according to the use of the Church of England.

Occasional Leaflets:

5961 No. 11. The altar, by F. C. Eeles. *P.* 1916. [A brief historical account. Reprinted 1922]

5962 No. 15. The chancel screen, by F. E. Howard. *P.* 1919.

5963 No. 16. The chalice and paten, by P. Dearmer. *P.* 1920.

5964 No. 17. Some notes on vestments, by E. H. Day. *P.* 1921.

5965 No. 20. Heraldry as an element in church decoration, by E. E. Dorling. *P.* 1925.

5966 No. 21. The aumbry and hanging pyx, by A. S. Duncan-Jones and D. C. Dunlop. *P.* 1925.

5967 No. 22. The episcopal ornaments: an outline, by F. C. Eeles. *P.* 1925.

5968 No. 27. The burse and the corporals, by P. Dearmer.[1]

5969 No. 28. The Warham Guild handbook. Historical and descriptive notes on 'Ornaments of the church and the ministers thereof'. 1932.

WARRINGTON LITERARY AND PHILOSOPHICAL SOCIETY

Founded 1870, for the advancement of literature and science.

Proceedings, 1900–33 (19 vols. 1901–33):

5970 Vol. for 1902–3.
  a Historical sketch of the old parish church, Warrington, by F. W. Willis.
  b The development of the English glee, by L. J. T. Darwall.
  c The life and work of Joseph Priestley, by C. B. R. Kent.

5971 Vol. for 1904–6.
  a A glance at some old Warrington societies, by A. Bennett.
  b The story of English pottery, by H. S. Page.

5972 Vol. for 1907–8.
  a A Warrington poetess: Mrs. Barbauld [Anna Laetitia Aikin, d. 1825], by H. S. Page.

5973 Vol. for 1908–10.
  a Some Devonshire church screens, by H. Congreve.
  b The development of modern banking in England, by J. C. Macdonald.

5974 Vol. for 1910–11.
  a The evolution of our village churches, by H. Congreve.

5975 Vol. for 1912–14.
  a Grappenhall parish church, by H. V. Pigot.
  b Philip Bourke Marston [d. 1887] and his poems, by Emily Ridgway.

5976 Vol. for 1914–16.
  a Stones of Waterloo: a centenary review of the 1815 campaign, by H. H. Taylor.

[1] Not seen.

5977 Vol. for 1918–20.
  a A Lancashire parish [Winwick] in life and history, by M. L. Smith.
  b Papers and addresses given to the Literary and Philosophical Society, 1870–1920.

5978 Vol. for 1920–2.
  a Warrington bridge, by C. H. Madeley.

5979 Vol. for 1922–4.
  a The British dyestuffs industry, by A. T. de Mouilpied.

5980 Vol. for 1927–9.
  a Early Warrington fisheries: an historical sketch, by G. A. Dunlop.
  b Warrington academy [1757–86], by J. Hawthorn.

5981 Vol. for 1931–3.
  a Diary of a Warrington mayor [William Beaumont, d. 1889], by J. Hawthorn.
  b Some Warrington poems [and poets], by S. Jeffery.

WARWICKSHIRE NATURALISTS' AND ARCHAEOLOGISTS' FIELD CLUB

Founded 1854, for the practical study of natural history, geology, and archaeology.

Proceedings, 1900–10 (9 vols. [1901]–11):

5982 Vol. for 1900.
  a St. Mary's hall [Coventry]: recent excavations, by W. Andrews.
  b Recorders of Warwick, by T. Kemp.

5983 Vol. for 1901.
  a Ancient British place-names of Warwickshire, by W. Andrews. [Contd. in vol. for 1903]
  b The Church of England and the progress of art, by A. J. Brookes. [An account of the history of the Church of England and of church architecture]

5984 Vol. for 1902.
  a Extracts from the registers of Tanworth church [1558–1755], by T. Kemp.
  b Guy's cave at Guy's Cliffe his burial place [i.e. the burial place of Guy of Warwick, legendary Anglo-Saxon figure], by S. S. Stanley.

5985 Vol. for 1903.
  a The ancient British language in Warwickshire, by W. Andrews.
  b An account of the market hall, Warwick, with a notice of the ancient booth hall, and the old fairs and markets, by T. Kemp.

5986 Vol. for 1904.
  a Recent progress in geological and archaeological investigations in Warwickshire and neighbourhood, by W. Andrews.

5987 Vol. for 1907.
  a A few facts about Roman roads, particularly in their relation to Warwickshire, by J. I. Bates.

5988 Vol. for 1908.
  a The identification of the Roman roads, by J. I. Bates.
  b A brief history of early geological work in Warwickshire, by F. T. Maidwell. [Contd. in vol. for 1909]

5989 Vol. for 1909.
  a Roman remains in east Warwickshire, by W. Andrews.
  b A Warwick market scene during the Commonwealth, by T. Kemp.

WEARDALE NATURALISTS' FIELD CLUB

Founded 1896, for the practical study of all branches of natural history and the cultivation of a fuller knowledge of the local antiquities.

Publications:

5990 Transactions, vol. 1, pts. 1–2 (1900–4).

a The Romans in Weardale, by W. M. Egglestone.
b Westgate castle in Weardale, by W. M. Egglestone.
c Bradley Hall, Wolsingham, by W. M. Egglestone.
d Gold coins of Edw. III, by H. W. Thorburn.
e The folk-lore of ferns, W. M. Egglestone.

WELLS NATURAL HISTORY AND ARCHAEOLOGICAL SOCIETY

Founded 1888, for the practical study of natural history, archaeology, and kindred subjects.

Annual Reports, 1900–32 (32 vols. [1901?–33?]):

5991 Vol. for 1900.

a Evening meeting. [The old palace of Whitehall, by G. M. Livett]

5992 Vol. for 1901.

a The Wells Blue Schools [founded 1656], by A. T. Powell.
b Books, buildings, benefactors of the library of the dean and chapter [of Wells], by C. M. Church.

5993 Vol. for 1902.

a The place of the bishop of Bath and Wells at the coronation, by C. M. Church.

5994 Vol. for 1904.

a The Carthusian order, and its remains in Somerset, by E. B. Cook.
b Visit of Henry VII to the deanery, Wells, Sept. 30th, 1497, by C. M. Church.

5995 Vol. for 1905.

a Evening meeting. [Excavations of Roman remains at Caerwent]

5996 Vol. for 1906.

a Bells and bell-founding, by F. Sheldon.
b Annual excursion. [High Ham church, Langport, and Muchelney abbey]

5997 Vol. for 1908.

a Evening meeting. Glastonbury lake village, by H. St. G. Gray.
b Mendip nature research committee. Report on cave research [Wookey Hole and its remains], by H. E. Balch and R. D. R. Troup. [Annual accounts of research in caves and elsewhere in the Mendip area appear in subsequent vols.]

5998 Vol. for 1909.

a [Glastonbury abbey, by F. B. Bond]

5999 Vol. for 1910.

a [Old clock and quarter jacks of Wells cathedral church, by C. M. Church]
b Excursion, 1910. [The lake village at Meare]
c Annual excursion. [Includes an account of Bradford-on-Avon Saxon church.]
d Mendip nature research committee. Report on finds of flint implements.

6000 Vol. for 1911.

a Half-day excursion. [Glastonbury abbey]
b Excursion. [Wookey Hole]
c Afternoon meeting. [Wells deanery]
d Mendip nature research committee. Barrows of the neighbourhood. [Contd. in vol. for 1924]

6001 Vol. for 1912.

a Evening meeting. [Somerset: historic and prehistoric, by H. E. Balch]
b Afternoon meeting. [College of vicars choral, Wells, by W. E. Hodgson]
c Half-day excursion. [Meare lake village]
d Annual excursion. [Bristol: Temple church, St. Peter's hospital, and St. Mary Redcliffe]
e An ancient map of Mendip [probably Elizabethan].

6002 Vol. for 1913.

a [Address on three old documents, including a parliamentary survey, of the manor of Wells, Wellesley and Dulcote, 1649, by W. E. Hodgson]
b Afternoon meeting. [Brief historical note on Wells cathedral, by J. Armitage Robinson]

6003 Vol. for 1914.

a [Somerset scratch dials, by E. Horne]
b Half-day excursion. [Worlebury camp and Woodspring priory]
c Annual excursion. [Old Cleeve church and abbey ruins]
d Mendip nature research committee. Neolithic and bronze age flints: recent finds, by H. E. Balch. Barrows on Mendip, by A. T. Wicks.

6004 Vol. for 1915.

a Church towers of Somerset, by F. J. Allen.

6005 Vol. for 1916.

a Holy wells of Somerset, by E. Horne.

6006 Vol. for 1918.

a Early man, by T. W. Morton.

6007 Vol. for 1919.

a Annual excursion. [Churches of Stoke-under-Ham and Martock]
b Mendip nature research committee. Neolithic and bronze age finds from the surface of Mendip, during 1919, by H. E. Balch.

6008 Vol. for 1920.

a Monumental brasses of the 15th cent. in Somerset, by G. H. Mitchell.
b Mendip nature research committee. Two prehistoric Mendip sites, by A. T. Wicks.

6009 Vol. for 1921.

a Half-day excursion to Sherborne.

6010 Vol. for 1922.

a Excursion to Croscombe church.
b Mendip nature research committee. Sir Arthur Keith's report on human and other remains from Ebber.

6011 Vol. for 1923.

a Mendip nature research committee. Roman remains near Wells, by A. T. Wicks.

6012 Vol. for 1924.

a Mendip nature research committee. Report for 1924 [on a prehistoric site at Draycott]. The Tickenham rock shelter.

6013 Vol. for 1925.

a The old watercourse of Wells, by H. E. Balch.

6014 Vol. for 1926.

a Stonehenge traditions, by A. H. Allcroft.

6015 Vol. for 1928.

a Fenny castle [or Castle Hill, near Wells], by A. T. Wicks.

6016 Vol. for 1932.

a Opening of the new museum [with a brief account of its foundation and development, by H. E. Balch].

b The first museum at Wells and some barrow-digging, by A. T. Wicks.

WELSH BIBLIOGRAPHICAL SOCIETY

Founded 1906, to promote and encourage original research in the bibliographical history of Wales, and to publish or support the publication of the results.

Journal, vols. 1–4 (1910–36):

6017 Vol. 1.

a The Trevecka mss. and library, by M. H. Jones.

b A bibliographical note on some of the printed and ms. sources of the medieval history of the Welsh boroughs, by E. A. Lewis.

c The Hengwrt library of printed books.

d John Walters [d. 1797] and the first printing press in Glamorganshire, by 'Cadrawd'.

e The earliest printers of Haverford, 1780–1840, by T. L. James.

f Isaac Carter [fl. *c.* 1718], the pioneer of Welsh printing, by D. R. Phillips.

g The 'circular letters' of the Baptist associations of Wales, 1760–1912, by E. K. Jones.

h Notes on Charles Heath of Monmouth: author, printer, and publisher, *c.* 1788–1831, by W. Haines.

i Rare and early-printed books relating to Monmouthshire, by J. A. Bradney.

j Bibliography of Quaker literature in the English language relating to Wales.

k Thomas Jones the almanacer [d. 1713. Contd. in vol. 2].

l John Jones, Bampton lecturer [d. 1834], by A. O. Evans.

6018 Vol. 2.

a A forgotten Welsh historian (William Davies, 1756–1823), or the fringe of a Glamorgan ms., by D. R. Phillips.

b Parish mss. of Llangyfelach, by W. R. Watkin.

c John Evans and the Welsh bible of 1769, by D. Salmon.

d John Thomas: a forgotten antiquary [d. 1769], by J. E. Lloyd.

e Humphrey Parry of Hackney [d. 1809], by A. O. Evans.

f A howler [concerning the authorship of *The Clergyman's Companion*, 1708], by A. O. Evans.

g Welsh books entered in the Stationers' registers, 1554–1708, by W. Ll. Davies.

h Short-title list of Welsh books, 1546–1700. [Supplement in vol. 4]

i The old-time Welsh school-boy's books, by J. Fisher.

j The first Welsh prayer book, by J. Ballinger.

k Welsh book collectors: the Rev. William Roberts, Nefydd [d. 1872], by E. I. Williams.

l Dr. Michael Roberts [d. 1679]: the corrector for the press of the Welsh bible of 1630, by M. F. Hall.

6019 Vol. 3.

a An address [on some local pamphlets of the 17th cent.], by A. Addams-Williams.

b George Parry [born *c.* 1612], by Sir J. Bradney.

c On Welsh bibles no longer used in churches, by Sir J. Bradney.

d Sir John Henry Scourfield [d. 1876] and his writings, by H. M. Vaughan.

e Mrs. Anne Penry [fl. 1761–80], by H. Lloyd.

f Bygone publishers and printers [from Wales, 1543–1798], by A. Williams.

g An anonymous ms. [of 17th cent. sermons, in the University College library at Bangor], by A. Gordon.

h Dafydd Jones, Treffynon, gan H. Lewis. [David Jones, hymnologist]

i Llyfryddiaeth norwyr Cymru, gan B. Owen. [Bibliography of Welsh seamen]

j Studies in Welsh book-land, by T. Ll. Jones. 1: Old [John] Price [d. 1887]. 2: Hugh Owen, Gwenynog, Mon. [d. 1642].

k Bye-paths in Anglesey bibliography, by T. Ll. Jones.

l Cylchgrawn y Gymdeithas er Taenu Gwybodaeth Fuddiol [Society for the Diffusion of Useful Knowledge, founded 1827], by F. A. Cavenagh. [In English]

m Brython tremadog, gan O. G. Williams. [Bibliographical account of the Welsh newspaper *Y Brython*, 1858–64]

n Enynyddiaeth gynnar y ddeunawfed ganrif, gan M. H. Jones. [Early hymnology of the 18th cent.]

o Dau hen lyfr, gan H. Lewis. [Two old books: (1) *Principles of the Christian Religion*, (2) *Spiritual Hymns*, being additions and corrections to the *Llyfryddiaeth y Cymru*]

p The Association of Welsh Clergy in the West Riding of the county of York, 1822–56, by Sir J. Bradney.

q Joseph Harris, an assay master of the mint [d. 1764], by M. H. Jones.

r Bach ac od, gan O. Ll. Owain. [On a number of small collections of hymns and catechisms for children, temperance societies, etc.]

s Sion Rhydderch yr almanaciwr, 1673–1735, gan B. Owen. [Sion Rhydderch, publisher of almanacs. Additional note on pp. 347–9]

t Nodiadau Uyhryddol gwaith Thomas Wynne y crynwr, gan J. H. Morgan. [Bibliographical notes on the works of Thomas Wynne, Quaker]

u Cyfieithydd 'Hanes pleidiau y byd Crist' nogol' (1808). [On John Evans, author of the *Brief Sketch of the Several Denominations of the Christian World*, with bibliographical details of his work]

6020 Vol. 4.

a Thomas à Kempis and Wales, by A. O. Evans. [Welsh versions of *De imitatione Christi*]

b Blwyddyn cyhocddi *Yn y Lhyvyr Hwnn*, gan I. Williams. [The publication date of *Yn y Lhyvyr Hwnn* identified as 1547]

c Notes on the literary associations of the Aberafan district, by L. Davies.

d Colofn Barddoniaeth y newyddiaduron, 1814–70, gan B. Davies. [The bardic column in Welsh newspapers, 1814–70]

e 'Tomos Glyn Cothi' [Thomas Evans, a Unitarian minister, d. 1833], by Irene George.

f Short-title list of 18th cent. Welsh books. Pt. 1: 1701–10.

g John Peter (Ioan Pedr), 1833–77, by R. T. Jenkins.

h Rhai o lawysgrifau Ellis Wynne a William Wynn, gan Irene George. [Some letters and expenses accounts (in English) of Ellis Wynne, d. 1734, clergyman and author, and William Wynn, d. 1761, poet]

i *Gweledigaetheu y bardd cwsc* [or *The Dreams of the Sleeping Bard*, by Ellis Wynne]: a bibliography, by W. Williams.

j Ellis Wynne's contribution to the literature of the church, by A. O. Evans.

k Gwlad Ellis Wynne, gan B. Owen. [The Ellis Wynne country: Merionethshire]

l Studies in Welsh book-land, by T. Ll. Jones. 3: *Y credadyn bucheddol* [1763, by Risiart ap Robert or Richard Roberts, being a translation of *The Practical Believer*, by John Kettlewell, d. 1695].

m Y gwir er gwaethed yw ... 1684: a Welsh story of the Popish plot [by Thomas Jones 'yr Almanaciwr', d. 1713, bookseller and printer in Shrewsbury].

n Three fragments, by W. Williams. [1: Setting, with additional material, of part of William Middleton's *Rhann o psalmae Davyd*, *c.* 1595–1603. 2: Part of the first edition of *Cerdd lyfr*, by Ffoulke Owens of Nantglyn, 1686. 3: Possibly a fragment of *A Welch Catechisme called the Principles of the Oracles of God, etc.*, by Oliver Thomas and Evan Roberts, 1640]

o A bibliography of translations into Welsh from foreign languages (other than English), up to 1928, by J. J. Jones.

p Caernarvon borough records, by G. Roberts.

q Thomas Jones [bookseller, d. 1713], by Ll. C. Lloyd.

r *Yr Eurgrawn Cymraeg* [periodical]: a correction of its date [of publication, being 1770], by T. Ll. Jones.

s 'Tegid' a Syr S. R. Meyrick, gan D. R. Hughes. [Transcript of a letter, 1837, from John Jones, d. 1852, editor of the works of Lewis Glyn Cothi, to Sir Samuel R. Meyrick]

Other publications:

Bibliography of Welsh ballads printed in the 18th century. 1911. [See Hon. Society of Cymmrodorion, no. **2329** above]

6021 Bibliography of Robert Owen, the socialist, 1771–1858. *P.* 1914.

6022 Select bibliography of Owen Glyndwr, by D. R. Phillips. *P.* 1915.

6023 Rhestr o lyfrau argraffedig yng Nghaerfyrddin gan John Ross rhwng y blynyddoedd 1763 a 1807, gan J. Davies. 1916. [List of books printed in Carmarthen by John Ross, 1763–1807]

6024 Rhestr o lyfrau gan y parch. William Williams, Pantycelyn, a argraffwyd rhwng 1744 a 1800, gan J. H. Davies. 1918. [List of books by the Rev. William Williams, Pantycelyn, printed 1744–1800]

WELSHPOOL FIELD CLUB

Rambles and excursions:

6025 1908.

a Interesting ramble on the Long Mountain.

b Mathrafal and Meifod: historic associations.

c A visit to Powis Castle.

d The Breidden hills: their historical and geological interest.

e Middletown hill and Old Parr's cottage.

Researches and itineraries, 1909–14[1] (6 vols. n.d.):

6026 Vol. for 1909.

a Round about Montgomery [being notes on Montgomery castle and church, and Lymore].

b The Romans at Caersws.

c Guilsfield history: old British camps.

d The Breidden and its archaeology.

6027 Vol. for 1910.

a Round about Montgomery [being notes on Hen Domen, mediaeval? mound and the Gaer, Roman camp].

b A monastic resort [Monksfield].

[1] Vol. for 1913 has not been seen.

c Roman camp or natural mound? Antiquarian's controversy near Llanymynech [Salop.].

d Llanfair's link with the past [being notes on the neighbourhood of Llanfair].

e History of Castle Caereinion.

6028 Vol. for 1911.

a A Welsh hero's reputed birthplace. [Owen de Galles, and Plas-yn-Dinas]

b Historic remains and relics at Forden and Chirbury [Salop.].

c A feudal fortress [Dolforwyn castle] and a familiar legend [of Sabrina].

d A Salopian Roman city [Uriconium] and historic castle [Acton Burnell].

e Lord Cobham [Sir John Oldcastle] and the Lollards.

6029 Vol. for 1912.

a Llandrinio and Alberbury's [Salop.] historic associations.

b Ecclesiastical recollections of Powysland. [Some account of St. Tysilio]

c Meifod re-visited. [Brief notes]

d Is Mathyrafal a lost Roman camp?

e [Prehistoric Britain, by B. Dawkins]

6030 Vol. for 1914.

a The historical associations of Buttington.

b Ludlow's history: a visit to the famous church and castle.

c Roman remains near Llanfair. [Roman camp of Bryn Penarth]

d Whittington castle and Halston [Salop.].

e Pre-historic remains on the Kerry hills [Mont.].

f The origin of druidical circles and round barrows.

WESLEY HISTORICAL SOCIETY

Founded 1893, to promote the study of the history and literature of Methodism and to provide a medium of intercourse for workers in this field.

Proceedings, vols. 3–19 (1902–34):

6031 Vol. 3.

a Sidelights on Methodism and national life: Methodism and Jacobinism at the dawn of the 19th cent., by T. E. Brigden.

b The origin of the name Methodist, by F. C. Wright.

c Bristol Methodist notes, by H. J. Foster. [Contd. from vol. 2. Contd. in vol. 4]

d A portion of Wesley's journal, hitherto unpublished in this form, by R. Green.

e The Oxford Methodists: William [d. 1732] and Richard [d. 1785] Morgan, by C. H. Crookshank.

f Notes from the oldest register of the Great Yarmouth circuit [1785], by J. C. Nattrass.

g Wesley's journal. Notes on the journals of Wesley's visits to Cardiff and the neighbourhood, by R. Butterworth.

h Osmotherley Methodist society's book, commencing 1750, by R. Green.

i The first preaching houses in Birmingham, by R. Green.

j Extracts from the steward's book of the old Octagon chapel, Bradford, by C. A. Federer.

k Notes on Wesley's journal, by C. H. Crookshank. [Contd. in vol. 8]

l Passages in the history of Methodism in Bedford and Devizes, by H. J. Foster.

m The first Methodist society: the date and place of its origin, by T. McCullagh.

n Notes on some portraits of John Wesley, by J. G. Wright. [Contd. in vol. 4]

o [Rev. John] Clayton and Wesley, by R. Green.

p A list (chiefly) of published biographies and biographical notices of John Wesley.

6032 Vol. 4.

a Newspaper notices of early Methodism and Methodists, by W. C. Sheldon.
b A bibliographical catalogue of books mentioned in John Wesley's journals, by F. M. Jackson.
c Notes elucidatory of Wesley's journals, by C. A. Federer.
d An eccentric Bedford evangelist [Timothy R. Matthews, d. 1845], by J. A. Sharp.
e Pit Place, Epsom, by J. Telford.
f Early editions of the Wesleyan hymn-book, by C. D. Hardcastle.
g On travel with Wesley, the preacher: an extract from the journal of William Ripley [fl. 1784], by R. T. Gaskin.
h Wednesbury and West Bromwich as Wesley knew them, by S. Lees.
i Joseph Rule, the White Quaker [d. 1770], by N. Penney.
j William Kingston, of Ditcheat [d. 1831].
k Cornwall in Wesley's journal, by P. Jennings.
l Mrs. [Bridget] Glynne [d. 1799] and John Appleton [fl. 1761] of Shrewsbury.
m Wesley and the North Shields chapel case, by C. A. Federer.
n Minutes of conference for 1749, 1755, 1758, reprinted from John Wesley's ms. copy.

6033 Vol. 5.

a From the archives of Fetter Lane: unpublished letters of John Wesley, by H. J. Foster.
b In and around Castle Cary [Som., being extracts from the *Castle Cary Visitor* illustrating passages of Wesley's journal], by J. E. Winter.
c Deed of settlement, executed by Bartholomew Wesley, 1659.
d [Methodist] class and band tickets, by J. G. Wright.
e Wesley's visits to the Isle of Man.
f The Bowens of Llwyngwayr [Pemb.], by R. Butterworth.
g [Methodist] tune books of the 18th cent., by J. T. Lightwood.
h John Wesley and the Madans.
i Westley Hall [d. 1776], by H. J. Foster.
j Nottingham Methodist notes. 1: John Wesley and the Nottingham general hospital. 2: Early preaching places. 3: Letter written at Nottingham [by John Wesley].
k Bradford Methodist topography.
l In the Isle of Axholme [Lincs.], by H. J. Foster.
m Was Charles Wesley ever curate of Islington?, by E. Crawshaw.
n Parkgate, near Guiseley, Yorks., by C. A. Federer.

6034 Vol. 6.

a The Dorset Wesleys: a pilgrimage to the home of John Wesley, the elder, at Winterbourne Whitchurch, by A. M. Broadley.
b Three letters of William Thompson, first president after the death of Wesley.
c Enoch Wood's busts of Wesley, by R. Green.
d William Ripley, of Whitby [d. 1786], by R. T. Gaskin.
e Six unpublished letters of John Wesley.
f A Methodist preacher's diary for 1799, by H. G. Godwin.
g North Wales in John Wesley's journal, by D. B. Bradshaw.
h Early preaching places in Gainsborough.
i An account of the most remarkable occurrences in the awakenings at Bristol and Kingswood till the brethren's labours began there in 1746, written by John Cennick in April 1750.
j Rev. Jenkin Morgan [fl. 1750] of Rhosymeirch, by R. Butterworth.

6035 Vol. 7.

a Travelling in Wesley's time: some roads, routes and distances, by W. C. Sheldon.
b Wesley's ordinations at Bristol, Sept. 1784, by T. E. Brigden.
c Adams, the Osmotherley priest, by J. C. Nattrass.
d The Rev. John Fletcher, vicar of Madeley: his induction at Hereford [1760], by W. Parlby.
e Methodism in Alnwick [Northumb.], by J. H. Broadbent.
f Wesley as the agent of the S.P.G., by R. Butterworth.
g John Wesley and Margate, by F. F. Bretherton.
h Religious societies in Southwark in the letters of Thomas Day [late 18th cent.], by H. J. Foster.
i William Pritchard [d. 1773] of Bodlewfawr [Anglesey], by R. Butterworth.
j A king's bench case in 1766 on the registration of a Methodist meeting-house under the Toleration Act, by T. Bennett.
k Smith House, Lightcliffe, first headquarters of the Moravians in Yorkshire, and home of Mrs. Elizabeth Holmes of Wesley's journal, by T. E. Brigden.

6036 Vol. 8.

a John Wesley's conversion, by J. A. Beet.
b Excerpts from John Valton's ms. journal [1780–90].
c John Wesley's visits to Warrington, by A. Mounfield. [Contd. in vol. 9]
d John Wesley's visit to Ockbrook [Derbys.], in June, 1741, by A. W. Harrison.
e Methodist beginnings in Barton-on-Humber circuit, by B. A. H. Barley.
f Development of Methodist organization as indicated in the *Lives of the Early Methodist Preachers*, by A. W. Harrison.

6037 Vol. 9.

a The Rev. James Rouquet [d. 1776], by R. Butterworth.
b Correspondence of the Rev. Brian Bury Collins, M.A. (from Jan. 1800, the Rev. Brian Bury) with John, Charles and Sarah Wesley, the Rev. Dr. Witherspoon, the Revs. Rowland Hill, John Newton, Walter Shirley, H. Venn and others, Dr. Beilby Porteus, bishop of Chester, the Countess of Huntingdon and Ladies Darcy Maxwell and A. A. Erskine, 1773–97, ed. and annotated A. M. Broadley.
c The first four volumes of Wesley's sermons, by J. S. Simon.
d Wesley's journeys in mid-Wales, by D. Young.
e The original settlement of the Wesleys.
f John Wesley's visits to Coventry.
g A Methodist sermon register of the 18th cent.
h Wesley's ordinations, by J. S. Simon. [Contd. in vol. 10]
i The Rev. John Pawson, 1737–1806: president of the conference 1793 and 1801, by G. Stampe. [Contd. in vols. 10 and 11]

6038 Vol. 10.

a Whitefield and Bristol, by J. S. Simon.
b George Whitefield and Gloucester, by J. W. Crake.
c Letters of George Whitefield from the collection of George Stampe.
d The ministry of George Whitefield, by the Rev. Dr. Watkinson.
e Some early estimates of Whitefield, by T. E. Brigden.
f John Wesley at Carmarthen, by M. H. Jones.
g Letters from Samuel Bradburn [d. 1816] to John Pritchard.
h John White, 'the patriarch of Dorchester' [d. 1648], by J. S. Simon.
i Notes on early Methodism in Haworth [Yorks.], by J. C. Nattrass.

j Bibliography of the works of George Whitefield, by R. Austin.

k John Wesley's visits to Tunbridge Wells, by F. F. Bretherton.

l Correspondence between William Grimshaw [d. 1763] and the Quakers of Stanbury, near Haworth.

6039 Vol. 11.

a The Rev. Samuel Wesley, M.A. [d. 1735], rector of Epworth, by G. Stampe.

b Samuel Wesley, junior (schoolmaster, high churchman, minor poet), and his circle, 1691–1739, by T. E. Brigden.

c Wesley and Anne Dutton [d. 1765], by A. Wallington.

d John Wesley and field preaching, by J. S. Simon.

e The Conventicle Act [1664–1670] and its relation to the early Methodists, by J. S. Simon.

f The repeal of the Conventicle Act [1812], by J. S. Simon.

g Wesleyan Methodist registers in Somerset House.

h The Rev. John Berridge [d. 1793] and his hymn-book, 1760 and 1785.

6040 Vol. 12.

a The Trevecka letters, 1733–73, by M. H. Jones. [Contd. in vols. 13–15]

b Wesley's letter to Lady Huntingdon on the union of the evangelical clergy, 20 April 1764, by T. E. Brigden.

c Dummer [Hants] and the Oxford Methodists, by R. Butterworth.

d John Wesley's 'Deed of declaration', by J. S. Simon.

e The landmarks of Bishop Asbury's childhood and youth, by W. C. Sheldon. [Francis Asbury, d. 1816]

f John Wesley's first visit to Gateshead, by H. F. Fallaw.

g George Yard chapel, Hull, by T. E. Brigden.

h The evangelicals of Hull [Joseph Milner, d. 1797, and William Wilberforce, d. 1833].

i Books, tracts, pamphlets, etc. [18th cent.] on Methodism in the Bodleian Library, Oxford, by J. T. Lightwood.

j *The Arminian Magazine*, by A. W. Harrison.

k Early history of Methodism in Cheltenham, 1739–1812, by G. H. B. Judge.

6041 Vol. 13.

a Wesley Cottage, Swanage, by T. E. Brigden.

b Soame Jenyns, M.P., 1704–87, by R. Butterworth.

c John Wesley's visits to Stanley and Winchcombe (near Cheltenham), with notes on early Methodism in the neighbourhood, by G. H. B. Judge.

d Richard Viney's memoranda [and diary for] 1744, by M. Riggall. [Contd. in vols. 14 and 15]

e John Wesley's visits to Banbury, by H. G. Godwin.

f John Wesley's visits to Stanley, by G. H. B. Judge.

g Wesley and Winchelsea, by A. N. Walton.

h The death of John Wesley, by J. S. Simon.

i The early societies for the reformation of manners, by J. S. Simon.

6042 Vol. 14.

a The story of Plessey Methodism, by J. C. Nattrass.

b Oliver Goldsmith and Methodism, by T. E. Brigden.

c John Wesley's visit to Mr. Hampson's church, Sunderland, by F. F. Bretherton.

d An early woman preacher: Sarah Crosby [d. 1804], by A. W. Harrison.

e John Wesley's health, by R. Butterworth.

f Quaint records of Liverpool Methodism, 1765–91, by A. G. Bate.

g The press in Newcastle-upon-Tyne in the 18th cent.

6043 Vol. 15.

a John Wesley, and early Methodism in east Sussex, by E. Austen.

b Wesley's visits to Monkwearmouth, by F. F. Bretherton.

c Methodism in Haverfordwest and neighbourhood, by F. F. Bretherton.

d The alleged illiteracy of the early Methodist preachers, by H. Bett.

e Early trust deeds, by J. C. Nattrass. 1: Allendale. 2: Newbegin. 3: Alston.

f William Hunter, early Methodist preacher [d. 1797], by J. C. Nattrass.

g Derby: the old chapel in St. Michael's Lane, by G. A. Fletcher.

h Wesley and politics, by T. E. Brigden.

i John Wesley, Dr. Stonestreet, and early Methodism in Northiam, east Sussex, by E. Austen.

j Early records of John Wesley's own circuit stewards in the first London society, by A. H. Lowe.

6044 Vol. 16.

a Samuel Sebastian Wesley, Mus. Doc., 1810–76.

b The Perronets of Shoreham, Kent, by A. W. Harrison.

c John Wesley, early Methodism in Rye, and Wesley's last open-air service at Winchelsea, by E. Austen.

d West Street chapel, St. Giles, Seven Dials [London], by Florence A. Reeve.

e Compressed notes on Wesley and ordination, by T. E. Brigden.

6045 Vol. 17.

a The Moravian society: Fetter Lane, London, by W. M. Trousdale.

b An unrecorded visit of Wesley to Margate, by F. F. Bretherton.

c Early visits of the founders of Methodism to Herefordshire, 1743–50, by W. Parlby.

d Early meeting places of the Wesleyan Methodists in Hereford, 1770–1840, by W. Parlby.

e Portland chapel, Bristol, by H. J. Foster.

f Old accounts of Leeds circuit [1778 and 1781], by A. W. Harrison.

g Wesley's letters to Rev. Samuel Furley (or Furly) [1754–64].

h The first Methodist martyr: William Seward (1702–40), his grave at Cusop [Herefs.], by W. Parlby.

6046 Vol. 18.

a Early Methodists in Maldon, Essex, by B. R. K. Paintin.

b The Middleham circuit, 1796, by F. F. Bretherton.

c Why the 18th cent. dreaded Methodist enthusiasm, by A. W. Harrison.

d Extracts from the journal of Thomas Edman [d. 1819], by H. G. Godwin.

e Thomas Coke and the origins of Welsh Wesleyan Methodism, by A. H. Williams.

f James Lackington [d. 1815], and Methodism in Budleigh Salterton, by A. N. Walton.

g John Wesley and the magistrate at Rolvenden, Kent, by E. Austen.

h Charles Wesley's house in Bristol, by F. Platt.

i Romance of Hogarth's church: an interesting chapter of Whitehaven Methodist history, by G. H. B. Judge.

j Methodism in Whitehaven, by G. H. B. Judge. [Contd. in vol. 19]

6047 Vol. 19.

a Early Methodism in Bristol, with special reference to John Wesley's visits to the city, 1739–90, and their impression on the people, by W. A. Goss.

b 'A society in Aldersgate Street [London]' (John Wesley's journal, May 24, 1738), by H. W. Mansfield.

c Wesley's visits to Holland [1738, 1783, 1786], by F. F. Bretherton.

d John Wesley's special visit to Ewhurst, east Sussex [1779], by E. Austen.

e Notes on Wesley's journal by Samuel Bradburn [d. 1816, Methodist preacher].

f George Whitefield. Letter from a clergyman [1739], by E. D. Bebb.

g Dr. Thomas Coke [d. 1814] and Wesleyan Methodism in North Wales. [Transcript of a letter, 1806, from Coke to his sister]

h A script portrait of [John] Wesley [by Glück Rosenthal, 1850], by Anna Onstott.

i Inscriptions from Wesley's 'New Room' at Bristol, by C. H. Laws.

j Letters by John and Charles Wesley [1735–74].

k The beginnings of Methodism in the Penrith district, by G. H. B. Judge.

l The first 'Apology' for Methodism [being a pamphlet printed 1733], by F. F. Bretherton.

m Letters [1774–90] from John Wesley to Ann Tindall [d. 1806, of Scarborough].

n New light on Methodism in the Isle of Man [in the late 18th and early 19th cent.], by A. W. Harrison.

6048 Skeleton index to the Publications, 1–4, and Proceedings, vols. 1–16 [including a separate list of John Wesley's letters published in the Proceedings, vols. 1–16], comp. L. T. Daw. [1929–30].

Other publications:

6049 An itinerary in which are traced the Rev. John Wesley's journeys from Oct. 14, 1735 to Oct. 24, 1790, by R. Green. [1907–8].

WHITBY LITERARY AND PHILOSOPHICAL SOCIETY

Founded 1823, to support a museum and to promote the interests of science.

Seventy-eighth—One hundred and fourth Report (26 vols. [1901]–33):

6050 82nd Report.

a Census of coins, etc., in the Whitby museum.

6051 83rd Report.

a List [of prints] and maps, etc., in the Whitby museum.

6052 86th Report.

a List of books, pamphlets, etc., added to the Society's library between August, 1899, and February, 1909.

6053 87th Report.

a Rough guide to the records (mainly local), stored at the Whitby museum.

6054 95th Report.

a Implements of the bronze age in the Whitby museum, by T. Sheppard.

6055 96th Report.

a The flood of August 1917, and other local floods, by J. W. Barry.[1]

6056 97th Report.

a Some abbey problems and discoveries, by J. W. Barry.[1]

6057 98th Report.

a Notes on Whitby's water supplies, by T. H. Woodwark.[1]

b A ford at Whitby, by J. T. Sewell.[1]

6058 99th Report.

a Whitby churchyard, by G. Austen.

b The rise and fall of the jet trade, by T. H. Woodwark.

6059 100th Report.

a Parish church of St. Mary, Whitby, by T. H. Woodwark.[1]

b An account of some mediaeval roads crossing the moors, south and south west of Whitby, by J. T. Sewell.[1]

6060 101st Report.

a The crosses of the North York moors, by T. H. Woodwark.[1] [Also published separately, *P.* 1924]

b Ptolemy's Yorkshire coast in Roman times, by T. English.[1] [Also published separately, *P.*[2]]

6061 102nd and 103rd Reports.

a The Quakers of Whitby, by T. H. Woodwark.[1] [Also published separately, *P.* 1926]

6062 104th Report.

a Some notes on the flood of 1930, by T. H. English, H. P. Kendall, A. S. Frank and D. Peary.

WHITEHAVEN SCIENTIFIC ASSOCIATION

Founded 1866. Affiliated to the Cumberland (and Westmorland) Association 1876–85. Dissolved.

Annual Journal, nos. 3–15 (1901–[1914?]):

6063 No. 4.

a Some aspects of the iron and steel trades of west Cumberland, by G. W. Wilkinson.

6064 No. 5.

a The fire-place, or the evolution of the hearth, by J. F. Curwen.

b Flax: its growth, preparation, manufacture, and uses, by T. G. Mathews.

6065 No. 6.

a Early masters of the British school of painting, by H. J. Dobson.

6066 No. 7.

a St. Bees priory church—past, present, and future, by R. H. Snape.

b Whitehaven harbour works during the last century, by G. Huddleston.

6067 No. 9.

a Cuaran's daughter: a saga of the Norsemen in Cumberland in the 10th cent., by C. A. Parker. [Olaf Sitricson or Cuaran, d. 981, King of Dublin and Deira]

b Fortified dwellings of Cumberland and Westmorland, by J. F. Curwen.

6068 No. 15.

a William Howgill [d. 1824]; or music in Whitehaven 100 years ago, by G. Tootell.

WILLIAM SALT ARCHAEOLOGICAL SOCIETY

Founded 1879, for the editing and printing of original documents relating to the county of Stafford (and of other material relating to the same). Title changed to Staffordshire Record Society in 1936.

Collections for a History of Staffordshire, new ser., vols. 4–12 (11 vols., 1901–9):

6069 Vol. 4.

a Final concords, divers counties, to which Staffordshire

---

[1] These articles, though forming part of the report in each case, have separate pagination, and occasionally separate title-pages. That in the 96th *Report* has title 'Whitby Museum Publications, no. 1'.

[2] Not seen.

tenants are parties, *temp.* James I, abstracted by W. Boyd and revised by the Hon. G. Wrottesley.

b Final concords, Staffordshire [10–13 James I], abstracted by W. Boyd and revised by the Hon. G. Wrottesley. [For final concords 1–9 James I, see old ser., vol. 18, and new ser., vol. 3. Contd. in new ser., vol. 6 (pt. 1), vol. 7, and vol. 10 (pt. 1)]

c Extracts from the plea rolls [*de banco* and *coram rege*, relating to Staffordshire tenants], 34 Hen. VI–14 Edw. IV, translated by the Hon. G. Wrottesley. [For earlier extracts see old ser., vols. 3, 4, 6 (pt. 1), 7, 9–17, and new ser., vol. 3. Concluded, for Hen. VI, Edw. IV, and Rich. II, in new ser., vol. 6 (pt. 1)]

d Muster roll, Staffordshire, 1539, Offlow hundred. [Transcript, by W. Boyd. Contd. for Cuttlestone and Pyrehill hundreds in new ser., vol. 5; for Seisdon and Totmonslow hundreds in new ser., vol. 6 (pt. 1)]

6070 Vol. 5.

a The Giffards, from the Conquest to the present time, by the Hon. G. Wrottesley.

6071 Vol. 6 (pt. 1).

a Inventory of church goods and ornaments taken in Staffordshire in 6 Edw. VI, 1552, archdeaconry of Stafford, by F. J. Wrottesley.

6072 Vol. 6 (pt. 2). History of the family of Wrottesley of Wrottesley, co. Stafford, by the Hon. G. Wrottesley. 1903. Reprinted from *The Genealogist*, new ser., vols. 15–19.

6073 Vol. 7.

a An account of the family of Okeover of Okeover, co. Stafford, by the Hon. G. Wrottesley.

b Early chancery proceedings, Rich. II–Hen. VII, by the Hon. G. Wrottesley. [Contd. for the reign of Elizabeth, by W. K. Boyd, in new ser., vol. 9, and in vols. for 1926 and 1931, and also in vol. for 1938]

6074 Vol. 8. The registers or act books of the bishops of Coventry and Lichfield, book 5, being the second register of Bishop Robert de Stretton, 1360–85; an abstract of the contents by R. A. Wilson. 1905. [See also new ser., vol. 10 (pt. 2)]

6075 Vol. 9.

a The parentage of Sir James de Audley, K.G. [d. 1369], by J. Wedgwood.

b The Burton abbey surveys, by J. H. Round. [An enquiry into their dates, reprinted from *The English Historical Review*, April 1905]

c Chartulary of Dieulacres abbey, with introd. and notes by the Hon. G. Wrottesley.

6076 Vol. 10 (pt. 1).

a The tenure of Draycote-under-Needwood, by J. H. Round.

b Staffordshire suits in the court of star chamber, *temp.* Henry VII and Henry VIII, abstracted by W. Boyd. [Contd. for Hen. VIII and Edw. VI in vols. for 1910 and 1912]

c The forest tenures of Staffordshire, by the Hon. G. Wrottesley.

d Alrewas court rolls, 1259–61, transcribed and ed. W. N. Landor. [Contd. for 1268–9 and 1272–3 in vol. for 1910]

6077 Vol. 10 (pt. 2). The registers or act books of the bishops of Coventry and Lichfield, book 4, being the register of the guardians of the spiritualities during the vacancy of the see, and the first register of Bishop Robert de Stretton, 1358–85; an abstract of the contents by R. A. Wilson. 1907.

6078 Vol. 11.

a History of the Bagot family, by the Hon. G. Wrottesley.

b The identification of the place named Monetville in the Domesday survey of Staffordshire, by W. F. Carter.

c Inquests on the Staffordshire estates of the Audleys, 1273–1308, with introd. and notes by J. Wedgwood. [Inquisitions *post mortem*]

d A review of recent publications of the Deputy Record Keeper, by J. Wedgwood. [Reviews of other calendars, etc. of state papers occur in the following vols.]

6079 Vol. 12. Collections for a history of Pirehill hundred, by Walter Chetwynd of Ingestre, esq., 1679, with notes by F. Parker. 1909. [Contd. in vol. for 1914]

Collections for a History of Staffordshire, 1910–32 (21 vols. in 20, 1910–33):

6080 Vol. for 1910.

a Lane of King's Bromley, formerly of Bentley and the Hyde, by the Hon. G. Wrottesley.

b Notes on Staffordshire families [Abell, Abnett, Adams, Adderley, Addes, Agard, and Aldriche], by W. F. Carter. [Contd. for Arblaster, Heveningham, and Draycote, in vol. for 1925]

6081 Vol. for 1911.

a Liberate rolls, Henry III, relating to Staffordshire, from the transcripts in the Wm. Salt library.

b Calendar of final concords or *pedes finium*, Staffordshire, Ed. I and Ed. II, 1272–1327, transcribed from the Wm. Salt library ms., to which are added the fines of mixed counties which include Staffordshire or in which Staffordshire tenants are interested, 1272–1327.

c Inquisitions *post mortem, ad quod damnum*, etc., Staffordshire, Hen. III, Edw. I and Edw. II, 1223–1327, transcribed from the mss. in the Wm. Salt library and checked by the printed calendars where available. [Contd. for Edw. III in vol. for 1913]

d Testa de Nevill and later feudatories: Staffordshire, 1212–1316, by J. C. Wedgwood.

e Staffordshire cartulary, 1200–1327, by J. C. Wedgwood. [Abstracts of deeds]

6082 Vol. for 1912.

a The *Lists and Indexes* of records at the Public Record Office, by J. C. Wedgwood. [Indicating the value of the first 34 vols. to the local historian, particularly in their relation to Staffordshire]

b The first two generations of the Swynnertons of co. Stafford, 1086–1122.

c The Staffordshire sheriffs, 1086–1912, escheators, 1247–1619, and keepers or justices of the peace, 1263–1702, by J. C. Wedgwood. [A correction by J. H. Round occurs in vol. for 1913 and an addition by G. P. Mander in that for 1919]

6083 Vol. for 1913.

a Notes on the manors of Aston and Walton, near Stone, in the 13th and 14th cent., by G. O. Bridgeman.

b A domestic cartulary of the early 14th cent., by C. Swynnerton. [Mainly concerning the Bromleys of Bromley in Whitmore, Newcastle-under-Lyme]

c Staffordshire coats of arms, 1272–1327, from the rolls of arms in ms. in the British Museum, by J. C. Wedgwood.

6084 Vol. for 1914.

a Harcourt of Ellenhall, by J. C. Wedgwood.

6085 Vol. for 1915. Staffordshire incumbents and parochial records, 1530–1680, by W. N. Landor. 1916.

6086 Vol. for 1916.

 a Wulfric Spot's will, by C. G. O. Bridgeman. [Anglo-Saxon, with translation, and notes on the bequests. Additional notes occur in vol. for 1919]

 b Staffordshire pre-Conquest charters, by C. G. O. Bridgeman.

 c Early Staffordshire history from the map and from Domesday, by J. C. Wedgwood. [Notes by C. G. O. Bridgeman and G. P. Mander occur in vol. for 1919]

 d The Burton abbey 12th cent. surveys, by C. G. O. Bridgeman.

 e The Watling street in Staffordshire, by C. G. O. Bridgeman.

6087 Vols. for 1917, 1920, 1922. Staffordshire parliamentary history from the earliest times to the present day, by J. C. Wedgwood. [Vol. i: 1213–1603. Vol. ii, pt. 1: 1603–1715; pt. 2: 1715–80. The pts. issued as vols. for 1920 and 1922 generally occur bound together. Contd. to 1841 in vol. for 1933, issued 1934]

6088 Vol. for 1919.

 a Notes on the early history of the parish of Blithfield, by D. S. Murray.

 b The Staffordshire hidation, by C. G. O. Bridgeman and G. P. Mander.

 c Notes on Seisdon hundred, etc., arising out of the volume for 1916, by G. P. Mander.

 d P.R.O. *Lists and Indexes*, 13, star chamber proceedings Philip and Mary. Stafford only.

 e Gregory King's Staffordshire note book; being church and parochial notes from the hundreds of Pirehill and Cuttlestone, with some diary matter, chiefly of the years 1679–80, annotated and arranged by G. P. Mander.

6089 Vol. for 1921.

 a Calendar of the manuscripts in the William Salt library, Stafford, by M. E. Cornford and E. B. Miller. [Deeds prior to 1500]

 b Lay subsidy 256/31, hearth tax, Pyrehill hundred, co. Stafford. [The 1666 assessment. Contd. for Seisdon and Offlow hundreds in vol. for 1923; for Totmonslow hundred in vol. for 1925; and for Cuttlestone hundred in vol. for 1927]

6090 Vol. for 1923.

 a Note on the Betley morris dance window, by C. G. O. Bridgeman.

 b Some unidentified Domesday vills, by C. G. O. Bridgeman.

 c Shenstone charters, by H. E. Savage. [Mainly from the Oseney cartulary]

 d Some Ridware armorial glass, by G. P. Mander and T. Pape.

 e Forest pleas in the Staffordshire pipe roll of 13 Hen. II, 1166–7, by C. G. O. Bridgeman.

6091 Vol. for 1924. The great register of Lichfield cathedral known as *Magnum registrum album*, ed. H. E. Savage. 1926.

 Vol. for 1925. [See nos. 6080b and 6089b above]

6092 Vol. for 1926.

 a A register of Stafford and other local wills [1537–58, 1575–83].

 b Ancient earthwork at Huntley Hall near Cheadle, with notes on the descent of the manor of Cheadle, by C. G. O. Bridgeman.

 c Two early Staffordshire charters, with notes by C. Swynnerton. [Relating to Swynnerton church, *c.* 1154–1159, and land in Eccleshall, 1292]

6093 Vol. for 1927.

 a A Gnosall lawsuit of 1395. [Relating to the collegiate church, with a note on its constitution by A. Hamilton Thompson, and a list of prebendaries]

 b The Staffordshire quarter sessions rolls. [With extracts for 1586, and lists of recusants, 1588]

 c Report on excavations at the Roman camp on Ashwood heath, by G. P. Mander.

 d The Stafford coinage of Henry II, 1158–9.

6094 Vol. for 1928.

 a Ancient deeds preserved at the Wodehouse, Wombourne, ed. G. P. Mander. [Calendar, late 12th cent.–1665, with abstracts, 1561–1637, from the lost parish register of Bushbury]

 b Calendar of early charters etc., in the possession of Lord Hatherton, by Henrietta L. E. Garbett. [Contd. in vol. for 1931]

 c Church-wardens' accounts, All Saints' church, Walsall, 1462–1531, transcribed and ed. by G. P. Mander.

6095 Vols. for 1929, 1930, 1932. Staffordshire quarter sessions rolls, ed. S. A. H. Burne. [Calendar. Vol. i: 1581–89. Vol. ii: 1590–93. Vol. iii: 1594–97. Contd. in vols. for 1935, 1940, and 1948–49. All vols. issued in conjunction with the Staffordshire County Council]

6096 Vol. for 1931.

 a An index to the marriage bonds of the peculiar and exempt jurisdictions of (i) Wolverhampton, prior to 1846, (ii) Tettenhall, prior to 1858, now in the diocesan registry, Lichfield, with introd. and notes by G. P. Mander.

 b The enclosure of open fields and commons in Staffordshire, by H. R. Thomas.

 c The Walsall ship money papers [1635–37], with introd. by G. P. Mander.

 d Three letters of Thomas Draxe [vicar of Colwich] concerning the recusants at Colwich [1613].

 e A note on discoveries in the close, Lichfield, in 1932, by J. J. G. Stockley.

 f A list of Staffordshire deputy lieutenants appointed 19 May 1689, by G. P. Mander.

WILTS RECORD SOCIETY

Founded c. 1895.

Publications:

6097 The canonization of St. Osmund [d. 1099, bishop of Salisbury], from the manuscript records in the muniment room of Salisbury cathedral. Ed. with introd., notes and appendices by A. R. Malden. 1901.

6098 The 15th cent. cartulary of St. Nicholas' hospital, Salisbury, with other records, ed. C. Wordsworth. 1902.

WILTSHIRE ARCHAEOLOGICAL AND NATURAL HISTORY SOCIETY

Founded 1853, to collect and publish information on the antiquities of Wiltshire and on the natural history of the county.

Wiltshire Archaeological and Natural History Magazine, vols. 31–46 (1900–34):

6099 Vol. 31.

 a Notes on common lands in and around Durrington, by C. S. Ruddle.

 b Amesbury church: reasons for thinking that it was not the church of the priory, by C. H. Talbot.

c Notes on Amesbury church, by C. S. Ruddle.
d Four letters written by the Rev. George Millard [d. 1740, rector of Calston and of Haselbury, and vicar of Box], 1712–18. [With a report on Box charity, 1834, and the wills of Dame Rachel Speke, 1711, and the Rev. George Miller (Millard), 1740]
e The Society's mss.: Chiseldon.
f The churches of Bulford, Enford, and Fittleton, by C. E. Ponting.
g Wilts. obituary: Lt.-gen. Augustus Henry Lane-Fox-Pitt-Rivers. [Includes a bibliographical list of his books, pamphlets and articles]
h Lacock abbey, by H. Brakspear.
i Ellandune identified [as Wroughton], by T. S. Maskelyne.
j Inaugural address of the Right Rev. the Lord Bishop of Bristol [G. F. Browne] as president of the Society. [Malmesbury and district and its Anglo-Saxon associations]
k Notes on the history of Great Somerford, by F. H. Manley.
l Churches of Sherston, Corston, and Netheravon, by C. E. Ponting.

6100 Vol. 32.

a Bibliography of the great stone monuments of Wiltshire, Stonehenge and Avebury, with other references, by W. J. Harrison.
b The rise and fall of Steeple Ashton as a market town, by E. P. Knubley.
c An episode of the Great Rebellion [being a brief account of the troubles of a royalist clergyman, Thomas Hickman, of Upton Lovell], by J. Harding.
d The old parsonage at Sherston Magna, by W. Symonds.
e The Tropenell cartulary [1464–88], by J. S. Davies.
f Steeple Ashton, Semington, and Whaddon churches, by C. E. Ponting.
g Thomas Stevens [d. 1619, Jesuit missionary], *primus in Indis*, by H. Chitty.
h 'Rowless thing', 'Rowlese tenement', 'Rowley', by T. G. J. Heathcote. [The etymology of a holding in Melksham]
i An English manor [Wilton] in the time of Elizabeth, by C. R. Straton.
j The customs of four manors of the abbey of Lacock [*temp*. Edw. I], by W. G. Clark-Maxwell. [Transcript, with abridged translation and notes]
k General index, vols. 25–32.

6101 Vol. 33.

a Recent excavations at Stonehenge, by W. Gowland, with a note on the nature and origin of the rock-fragments found in the excavations, by J. W. Judd.
b Note on a seal of Ludgershall, by C. Wordsworth.
c Early history of the upper Wylye valley, by J. U. Powell.
d Palaeolithic implements and gravels of Knowle, by W. Cunnington and W. A. Cunnington.
e Palaeolithic flint implements from Knowle, Savernake forest, by S. B. Dixon.
f Purton: a case in the star chamber [1548].
g The Roman villa at Box, by H. Brakspear.
h Notes on Durrington [manor and church], by C. S. Ruddle.
i Durrington and Durnford churches, by C. E. Ponting.
j Letters concerning the boundaries of Cranborne Chace [18th cent.], communicated by Mary Eyre Matcham.
k Erlestoke and its manor lords, by J. Watson-Taylor [Contd. in vol. 34]
l The appropriation of the rectory of Lacock [by Lacock abbey, 1312], by W. G. Clark-Maxwell.
m A letter [written by Dr. William Petre] to Cromwell concerning the surrender of Lacock abbey [1539], by W. G. Clark-Maxwell.

n Offenders against the Statute of Labourers in Wiltshire, 1349, translated [from the assize roll, 26 Edw. III] and communicated by Ethel M. Thompson.
o Pre-historic interments near Porton, by E. A. Rawlence.

6102 Vol. 34.

a Supposed influences of the Eastern church on English ecclesiastical architecture, with special reference to the solid screen in Stockton church, by R. G. Penny.
b Alton Barnes church: a Jacobean tablet of the Decalogue, etc., by C. Wordsworth, with architectural note by C. E. Ponting.
c A contribution to the anthropology of Wiltshire, by J. Beddoe.
d The Westbury acorn cup, by E. H. Goddard.
e Note on a carved figure [or 'Shelah-na-gig'] on the wall of Oaksey church, by E. H. Goddard.
f Wilts. ministers, 1643–62, by C. Wordsworth. 1: List of clergy in Wiltshire, outed, sequestered, or silenced, 1643–60. 2: Supplemental list of intruded ministers, some of whom were ejected in 1660–62. 3: List of Wiltshire clergy whose sons were entered at Oxford colleges, *c*. 1615–47. 4: The Wiltshire voluntary association of Puritan ministers, 1643–62.
g The churches of Marlborough, by C. Wordsworth and C. E. Ponting.
h A relic of pagan Marlborough [a Roman sculptured panel representing Fortuna], by C. Wordsworth.
i Customs of the manor of Winterbourne Stoke, 1574, copied by C. V. Goddard.
j Manor of Alderston and lands in Whiteparish, etc. Seinct Barbe *v*. Knight and others (chancery decree, 1545), communicated by W. F. Lawrence.
k Early gravestones [possibly Norman] found at Trowbridge, by E. H. Goddard.
l The death of the 1st Earl of Salisbury at Marlborough, 24 May 1612: the Gilbertines of S. Margaret's, by C. Wordsworth.
m South Wilts. in Romano-British times, with an appendix on W. H. Stevenson's view [on the location] of Egbert's stone, by J. U. Powell.
n Four terriers of North Wraxall rectory, extracted from the registers of the bishop of Salisbury, by F. Harrison.
o Investigations [of implements from gravel] at Knowle Farm pit, by H. G. O. Kendall.
p Notes on recent discoveries [being chiefly bronze and flint implements and weapons], by A. D. Passmore.
q A letter from Stephen Duck, the thresher-poet, in 1747, by C. Wordsworth, with a bibliographical list of the works of Stephen Duck.
r The 'Journal of a Wiltshire Curate' (1766), and 'Leaves from the Journal of the Poor Wiltshire Vicar of Cricklade' in 1764–5 [composed by J. Heinrich Daniel Zschokke, d. 1848, of Magdeburg], by C. Wordsworth.
s The Saxon church at Bradford-on-Avon, by H. J. Dukinfield Astley.
t Cadnam [and Studley, being an account of how these manors passed from the possession of the Cricklade family into that of the Hungerford family, in the 15th cent.].
u Discoveries [Romano-British and mediaeval] near Fonthill, by B. Stallybrass.
v Tan Hill fair [near Devizes], by Theresa M. Story Maskelyne.

6103 Vol. 35.

a Notes on the opening of a bronze age barrow at Manton, near Marlborough, by Maud E. Cunnington.
b Tithe barn, Place Farm, Tisbury, by E. Towry Whyte.
c Churchwardens' accounts of Mere [1556–1616], transcribed by T. H. Baker.

g A list of prehistoric, Roman and pagan Saxon antiquities in Wilts. arranged under parishes, by E. H. Goddard.

h List of the long barrows of Wiltshire, by Maud E. Cunnington.

i Church of S. John the Baptist and S. Helen, Wroughton, by C. E. Ponting.

j Malmesbury abbey, by H. Brakspear.

k List of altars in Salisbury cathedral, and names of kings of whom there were representations there about the year 1398, by C. Wordsworth.

l List of Wiltshire men extracted from the minute books of the company of Weavers of London, 1653–74, by F. R. Y. Radcliffe.

m Liddington castle (camp), by A. D. Passmore.

n Some bronze age pottery of 'food vessel' type, by A. D. Passmore.

o Copy of a ms. in the possession of Sir Walter Grove, bt. [being a list, *c.* 1642–3, of the inhabitants of certain hundreds in Wiltshire, with sums of money appended to each name] to which is pre-fixed a copy of a lay subsidy [1641] preserved in the Public Record Office.

6107 Vol. 39.

a Old Sarum and Sorbiodunum, by F. Haverfield. [Reprinted, with a few additions, from the *English Historical Review*, vol. 30, no. 117, Jan. 1915]

b Notes on Salisbury cathedral, by C. Wordsworth.

c Huish [manor] and the Doynells.

d Notes. [Includes: The provision of warlike furniture amongst the clergie of the dioces of Sarum besides the Bisshop his owne (14 August 1588); A remarkable house at Chippenham, and the successive houses at Bowden Park]

e The relations of the bishops and citizens of Salisbury (New Sarum) between 1225 and 1612, by Fanny Street.

f The original bederoll of the Salisbury tailors' gild [*c.* 1444], by C. Haskins.

g A forgotten hospital at [Great] Bedwyn [being a transcript of a grant in frank almoin by Walter le Bret of Croftone, to the house of St. John the Baptist of Bedewynde].

h 'Two surveys of the manour of Broad Hinton, 1708/9 and 1751', communicated by Theresa M. Story Maskelyne.

i Elias de Derham's Leadenhall in Salisbury close, 1226–1915, by C. Wordsworth.

j Return for the hundred of Westbury, 1643 [being a transcript of the assessment].

k Notes. [Includes: Portrait of William Windover (merchant and draper of London, d. 1632) discovered at Salisbury]

6108 Vol. 40.

a Early bronze age interment at the Central Flying School, Upavon, by E. H. Goddard.

b Notes on the skeleton found in an early bronze-age burial at Upavon, 1915, by A. Keith.

c Lidbury camp, by Maud E. Cunnington, being an account of excavations carried out by Mr. and Mrs. B. H. Cunnington in 1914.

d Wiltshire newspapers, past and present. [Pts. 1 and 2 by J. J. Slade; pt. 3 by Mrs. H. Richardson. Contd. in vols. 41 and 43 by Mrs. H. Richardson, and in vol. 42 by J. J. Slade]

e Durrington walls, or Long walls [earthworks], by P. Farer.

f Church of St. Michael, Brinkworth, by C. E. Ponting.

g The customs of the manor of Purton (*c.* 1597), transcribed by F. H. Manley.

h Perambulation of Purton, 1733, transcribed by Mrs. T. Story Maskelyne.

i The Lavington manual (*Manuale ad usum Sarum*), by E. F. Bosanquet.

j The [John] Buckler collection of Wiltshire drawings [executed for Sir Richard Colt Hoare].

k Existing materials for Wiltshire bibliography, by E. H. Goddard.

l The church survey in Wilts., 1649–50 [Parliamentary surveys (Lambeth), vol. 14, etc.], communicated by E. J. Bodington. [Concluded in vol. 41]

m The early Norman castle at Devizes, by E. H. Stone.

6109 Vol. 41.

a Notes on the rural deaneries of Marlborough and Cricklade, 1812, by G. F. Tanner.

b Excavation of a late-Roman well at Cunetio (Mildenhall), by J. W. Brooke.

c Notes on pottery from a well on the site of Cunetio [Mildenhall], near Marlborough, by Maud E. Cunnington.

d Notes. [Includes: Certain customs belonging to the manor of Christian Malford, 1614; Customs of the rectory manor of Christian Malford, 1744; Salisbury cathedral, the tombs of 'Bishop Robert Bingham' and 'Bishop William of York'; An index to Hospitallers' properties in Great Britain; A Coppie of a booke of the survey of the Devizes old parke and every man's name in particular taken Aprill the 8th, in the yeare of Our Lord 1654]

e The Society's mss.: abstracts of copies of court rolls and other documents relating to the manors of Bradford and Westwood, by A. W. Stote.

f Roman Wanborough, by A. D. Passmore.

g The Anglo-Saxon bounds of Bedwyn and Burbage, by O. G. S. Crawford.

h Place-names of Wiltshire, by G. B. Grundy. [Suggested emendations of and additions to *The Place-names of Wiltshire, their Origin and History*, by Einar Ekblom, 1917]

i Stone implements of uncommon type found in Wiltshire, by E. H. Goddard.

j Notes on Roman finds in north Wilts., by A. D. Passmore.

k Wansdyke, its course through E. and S.E. Wiltshire, by A. F. Major.

l King's Bowood park, by the Earl of Kerry. [Contd. in vol. 42]

m Notes on the ecclesiastical history of Wroughton, its rectors and vicars, comp. by Theresa M. Story Maskelyne and F. H. Manley.

n The Devil's Den dolmen, Clatford Bottom: an account of the monument and of work undertaken in 1921 to strengthen the north-east upright, by A. D. Passmore.

6110 Vol. 42.

a Widhill chapel and manor, by J. Sadler.

b Notes on field-work in N. Wilts., 1921–2, by A. D. Passmore.

c Notes on field-work round Avebury, Dec. 1921, by O. G. S. Crawford.

d The destruction of the ancient screen at Hullavington [church, 1917], by F. H. Manley.

e Notes. [Includes: Brooches from Cold Kitchen hill, Brixton Deverell; Late bronze age gold bracelet from Clench Common, near Marlborough; The eastward end of Wansdyke]

f Notes on Wiltshire churches, by Sir S. Glynne [*c.* 1850].

g Report of diggings in Silbury hill, Aug. 1922, by W. M. Flinders Petrie.

h Some notes on Trowbridge parish church registers, by A. W. Stote.

i Romano-British villages on Upavon and Rushall downs, excavated by Lt.-col. Hawley, F.S.A. [Abstract of a paper printed in the *Wiltshire Gazette*, 17 July 1899] j The Society's mss.: inventory of the goods of Sir Charles Raleigh, of Downton, 1698.

k The source of the foreign stones of Stonehenge, by H. H. Thomas.

l Notes. [Includes: Survey of the lands of Ferdinand Hughes, of Bromham, 1652; Roman pavement near Avebury; Pits in Battlesbury camp]

m The 'Blue stone' from Boles barrow [Heytesbury], by B. H. Cunnington. [With a transcript of a letter, 1801, by William Cunnington, F.S.A., of Heytesbury, d. 1810]

n Notes on a palimpsest brass from Steeple Ashton church, by E. P. Knubley.

o The method of arranging the stones of Stonehenge, by E. H. Stone.

p An early iron age site on Fifield Bavant down, by R. C. C. Clay. [With reports on the animal remains by J. W. Jackson, on the cereals by R. H. Biffen, and on a skull by Sir A. Keith]

q Wansdyke: report of excavations on its line by new buildings, near Marlborough, by A. F. Major.

r The west of England cloth industry: a 17th cent. experiment in state control, by Kate E. Barford.

s A lost [17th cent.] fragment of Hullavington register restored, by E. H. Goddard.

t The churches of Aldbourne, Baydon, Collingbourne Ducis, and Collingbourne Kingston, by C. E. Ponting.

u Aldbourne manor, chase, and warren, by J. Sadler.

v The village feast or revel, by Theresa M. Story Maskelyne.

6111 Vol. 43.

a Figsbury Rings: an account of excavations in 1924, by Maud E. Cunnington.

b An inhabited site of La Tène I date, on Swallowcliffe down, by R. C. C. Clay.

c A pagan Saxon cemetery at Broadchalke, by R. C. C. Clay. [With a report on the bones by Sir A. Keith]

d Flint implements from the Nadder valley, south Wilts., by R. C. C. Clay.

e Church of St. John the Baptist, Inglesham, by C. E. Ponting.

f The Evans family of north Wilts., by F. H. Manley.

g A complete list of the ancient monuments in Wiltshire scheduled under the Ancient Monuments Act, 1913 (up to March 1925).

h Objects found during excavations on the Romano-British site at Cold Kitchen hill, Brixton Deverill, 1924, by R. de C. Nan Kivell. [Further reports in vol. 44]

i The customs of the manors of Calstone and Bremhill, by the Earl of Kerry.

j The so-called 'Kenward stone' at Chute causeway, by H. St. G. Gray, with an appendix by H. H. Thomas.

k List of bronze age drinking cups found in Wiltshire, by Maud E. Cunnington.

l The Society's mss.: deeds of Seagry House, by F. H. Manley.

m The Woodminton group of barrows, Bowerchalke, by R. C. C. Clay.

n Notes. [Includes: Box, Haselbury, and Ditcheridge rate and valuation, 1628; Early iron age antiquities from N. Wilts.; The Devizes skippet]

o Objects found during excavations on the Romano-British site at Stockton earthworks, 1923, by R. de C. Nan Kivell.

p Notes on recent prehistoric finds, by Maud E. Cunnington.

q The Society's mss.: abstracts of deeds relating to the family of Methuen at Bradford, Corsham, Melksham, Chitterne, and Beckington, by E. P. Knubley.

r The barrows on Middle down, Alvediston, by R. C. C.

Clay. [With a report on a Saxon skull from a barrow, by Sir A. Keith]

s Sheep-farming in Wiltshire, with a short history of the Hampshire Down breed, by G. B. Hony.

t Notes on Purton tithe books [1726, 1788], by S. W. Shaw.

u Guy's Rift, Slaughterford, Wilts.: an early iron age habitation, by T. F. Hewer. [Reprinted from *Proceedings of the Spelaeological Society* (of Bristol) *for 1925*]

v Two bronze age beaker burials at Netheravon, by Maud E. Cunnington.

w Corsham, by H. Brakspear.

x Supplementary report on the early iron age village on Swallowcliffe down, by R. C. C. Clay.

y The barrows on Marleycombe hill, Bowerchalke (1926), by R. C. C. Clay.

6112 Vol. 44.

a Some 18th and 19th cent. Wiltshire tokens, and a Stonehenge medal [1796] in the Society's museum at Devizes, by B. H. Cunnington.

b The collection of ms. copies of monumental inscriptions in the churches and churchyards of Wiltshire, in the Society's library, by E. H. Goddard.

c A Malmesbury abbey manuscript [which includes an abridgement of William of Malmesbury's *Gesta Pontificum*], by Sir R. H. Luce.

d The Society's mss.: abstracts of deeds, etc., of Little Park, Wootton Bassett, by W. Gough.

e A Roman villa at Nuthills, near Bowood, by the Marquess of Lansdowne.

f Polished flint knives, with particular reference to one recently found at Durrington, by R. C. C. Clay.

g Pre-Roman coffin burials, with particular reference to one from a barrow at Fovant, by R. C. C. Clay.

h Thomas Duckett [d. 1766], and Daniel Bull, members for Calne, by L. B. Namier.

i Two shale cups of the early bronze age and other similar cups, by R. S. Newall.

j Beaker and food vessel from barrow no. 25, Figheldean, by R. S. Newall.

k Notes on Clyffe Pypard and Broad Town, by F. Goddard.

l The Society's mss.: Grittleton manor deeds, by F. H. Manley.

m Hoard of British coins found at Chute, by B. H. Cunnington.

n Field work in N. Wilts., 1926–8, by A. D. Passmore.

o Notes on stone implements of material foreign to Wiltshire in the collection of A. D. Passmore, by H. H. Thomas and A. D. Passmore.

p Heytesbury almshouse accounts, 1592, by J. J. Hammond.

q Notes. [Includes: Traces of the Roman road in Conolt Park; Sir John Falstaff and Steeple Langford]

r Sir William Petty [d. 1687], by the Marquess of Lansdowne.

s List of goods destroyed by fire at Marlborough, 1679, transcribed by B. H. Cunnington from the corporation records.

t Trouble with the bakers of Marlborough in 1634, transcribed from the municipal records by B. H. Cunnington.

u Tisbury in the Anglo-Saxon charters, by W. Goodchild.

v Recent excavations at Stonehenge, by B. H. Cunnington.

w Stonehenge: the recent excavations, by R. S. Newall. [Reprinted from *Antiquity*, vol. 3, March 1929]

x Heraldry of the churches of Wiltshire, by R. St. J. B. Battersby. [Contd. in vol. 45]

y Three inventories of plate and furniture belonging to Salisbury cathedral transcribed by J. J. Hammond.

z Lawsuit concerning property of Robert May, of Broughton Gifford, 1598, by G. Kidston.

aa The Society's mss.: Grittleton manor rolls, 1613-25, 1627-47, translated by C. W. Shickle and annotated by F. H. Manley.

6113 Vol. 45.

a The origin and history of the Wiltshire Archaeological and Natural History Society, by B. H. Cunnington.

b Magna Carta in Salisbury cathedral library, by C. Wordsworth.

c Wiltshire wills, etc., still preserved in the diocesan registry, Salisbury, by C. R. Everett.

d The sacraments window in Crudwell church, by G. McN. Rushforth.

e A probable source of the material of some Wiltshire prehistoric axe-hammers, by G. H. Engleheart.

f Church of Shaw-in-Alton, by H. C. Brentnall.

g Romano-British Wiltshire, being a list of sites occupied during the Roman period with the addition of some preRoman villages, by Maud E. Cunnington.

h Glazed flints, by W. J. Arkell.

i The stained glass in Salisbury cathedral, by J. M. J. Fletcher.

j The [Richard] Kemm drawings of Wiltshire churches [1860-68].

k Scratch dials on Wiltshire churches, by R. G. V. Dymock.

l The 'Sanctuary' on Overton hill, near Avebury, by Maud E. Cunnington, being an account of excavations carried out by Mr. and Mrs. B. H. Cunnington in 1930.

m Notes on farming families of the 19th cent. in Wiltshire, by E. Coward.

n Extracts from the accounts of the overseers of the parish of Box, from November 26th, 1727, to April 17th, 1748, extracted by A. S. Mellor.

o Easton down, Winterslow, flint mine excavation, 1930, by J. F. S. Stone.

p A settlement site of the beaker period on Easton down, Winterslow, by J. F. S. Stone.

q Hoard of bronze implements from Donhead St. Mary, and a stone mould from Bulford, in Farnham museum, Dors., by A. D. Passmore.

r Barrow 85 Amesbury [Goddard's list], lat. 51° 9′ 32′7″, long. 1° 44′ 44·8″, by R. S. Newall. [Appendix A: List of ogival daggers with grooves and midrib or thickened at centre other than from hoards. Appendix B: List of grooved whetstones]

s The Society's mss.: various documents presented by the British Record Society, 1930, catalogued by G. Kidston.

t The Act of Uniformity, 1662: declaration by ministers (of Salisbury diocese), transcribed by C. R. Everett.

u Notes. [Includes: 'The Sanctuary' on Overton hill, was it roofed?; Three iron axes found at Downton; The Malmesbury ciborium and cover; Giles Fettiplace, knight, died 11 Mar. 1641, chancery inquisition *post mortem*]

v The *antiqua monumenta* of Bedwyn [being a reference to the Little Bedwyn landbook of A.D. 778], by G. M. Young.

w Tombstone of the Countess Ela, foundress of Lacock abbey, by W. G. Clark-Maxwell.

x Scratch dials on Wiltshire churches, by R. G. V. Dymock: addenda.

y Influence of geology on the past and present of Wiltshire, by E. H. Goddard.

z The disafforesting of Braden, by F. H. Manley.

aa Saxon interments on Roche Court down, Winterslow, by J. F. S. Stone, and a report on the human remains, by M. L. Tildesley.

6114 Vol. 46.

a The demolition of Chisenbury Trendle [earthwork], by Maud E. Cunnington.

b Chisbury camp, by Maud E. Cunnington.

c Notes on the Larmer, Wermere, Ashmore and Tollard Royal ponds, by H. S. Toms.

d The Gorges monument in Salisbury cathedral, by J. M. J. Fletcher. [Sir Thomas Gorges, of Longford Castle, d. 1610]

e Notes on Erchfont manor house, by H. R. Pollock.

f William Gaby [of Netherstreet, merchant], his booke, 1656, 1: The wool trade. [Extracts and notes by E. Coward]

g Wiltshire politicians (*c.* 1700), by the Marquess of Lansdowne.

h Notes. [Includes: Basalt weapon-head from Rotherley down, Rushmore]

i Wiltshire in pagan Saxon times, by Maud E. Cunnington.

j Parliamentary surveys of the crown land in Braden forest, 1651, transcribed by F. H. Manley.

k Some domestic and other bills of the Wyndham family (Salisbury), by C. W. Pugh.

l Excavations in Yarnbury Castle camp, 1932, by Maud E. Cunnington.

m Report on three skeletons from Yarnbury camp, by M. L. Tildesley.

n A middle bronze age urnfield on Easton down, Winterslow, by J. F. S. Stone.

o Excavations at Easton down, Winterslow, 1931-2, by J. F. S. Stone.

p Old Sarum pottery, by F. Stevens.

q Roman remains from Easton Grey, by A. D. Passmore.

r The Wiltshire hundreds, by H. B. Walters.

s Notes on the records and accounts of the overseers of the poor of Chippenham, 1691-1805, by F. H. Hinton.

t Evidence of climate derived from snail shells and its bearing on the date of Stonehenge, by Maud E. Cunnington.

u A subscription book of the deans of Sarum, 1662-1706, by F. H. Manley.

v A terrier of the common fields belonging to Broad Town and Thornhill, 1725, transcribed by E. H. Goddard.

w The Giants' Caves, long barrow, Luckington, by A. D. Passmore.

x Notes. [Includes: Chitterne All Saints churchwardens' accounts, extracts from 1732 onwards; A second Stonehenge 'altar' stone]

y The monasteries of Wiltshire, by Sir H. Brakspear.

z Ivychurch priory, by Sir H. Brakspear.

aa The Wilton hanging bowl [and the origin of hangingbowls in general], by F. Stevens.

bb Three 'Peterborough' dwelling pits and a doublystockaded early iron age ditch at Winterbourne Dauntsey, by J. F. S. Stone.

cc A case of bronze age cephalotaphy on Easton down, Winterslow, by J. F. S. Stone. [Reprinted from *Man*, 1934, nos. 51 and 52]

dd Notes on the early history of Box, by G. Kidston.

ee 'The Highfield pit dwellings', Fisherton, Salisbury, excavated May, 1866, to September, 1869, by F. Stevens.

ff Bishop Giles of Bridport, 1257-62 [bishop of Salisbury], by J. M. J. Fletcher.

gg De Vaux college, Salisbury, founded by Bishop Giles of Bridport, by J. M. J. Fletcher.

Other publications:

Abstracts of Wiltshire *inquisitiones post mortem*. [See British Record Soc., no. 622 above]

6115 The Tropenell cartulary: being the contents of an old Wiltshire muniment chest, ed. J. S. Davies. 2 vols. 1908.

6116 Catalogue of the antiquities in the museum of the Wiltshire Archaeological and Natural History Society at Devizes. Pt. 2, comp. Maud E. Cunnington and E. H. Goddard. 1911. [Pt. 1, comprising the Stourhead collection, was published in 1896]

6117 Church bells of Wiltshire: their inscriptions and history arranged alphabetically by parishes, with a general account of Wiltshire bells and bell-founders, by H. B. Walters. 3 pts. 1927–9.

6118 A calendar of the feet of fines relating to Wiltshire, remaining in the Public Record Office, London, from their commencement in the reign of Richard I (1195) to the end of Henry III (1272), comp. E. A. Fry. 1930.

WINCANTON FIELD CLUB

Founded 1889, for the investigation of art, archaeology, natural history, and geology, with especial reference to Wincanton and neighbourhood. Dissolved c. 1912.

Tenth–Eleventh Annual Report ([1901 ?–2 ?]):

6119 10th Report.
  a The parish church, Sturminster Newton, by J. C. M. Mansel-Pleydell.
  b Catash [hundred], by W. E. Daniel.
  c 'The Dogs' and its owners: with particular reference to the Churchey family in Wincanton, by G. Sweetman.
  d Index to reports [nos. 1–10] of Wincanton Field Club.

6120 11th Report.
  a Résumé of the history of the Club, by G. Sweetman.
  b Notes on Suddon Grange, Wincanton, by G. Sweetman.
  c Notes on the history of [the village of] Abbas and Temple Combe, by J. C. Fox.

WOOLHOPE NATURALISTS' FIELD CLUB

Founded 1851, for the study of the natural history and archaeology of Herefordshire and the districts immediately adjacent.

Transactions, 1900–32 (11 vols. 1903–33):

6121 Vol. for 1900–2.
  a Manorial customs in co. Hereford, by H. C. Beddoe.
  b The Kemble family, by the Hon. J. W. Leigh.
  c Welsh Newton church, by R. Clarke.
  d Pembridge castle, by the Hon. J. W. Leigh.
  e Notes on the suppressed college of Jesuits at Combe, in the parish of Llanrothal, Herefs., by W. Pilley.
  f Hereford city insignia and plate, by J. Carless.
  g Some incidents in Hereford life two hundred years ago [being extracts from the corporation minute book 1693–1701], by J. Carless.
  h Hereford—the civic offices of escheator and customer, by J. Carless.
  i Sir Peter de la Mare [fl. 1370]: a little recorded Herefordshire worthy, speaker of the House of Commons, by J. Carless.
  j The preceptory of Dinmore, by H. F. St. John.
  k Prince Edward's escape from Hereford [1265], by H. Croft.
  l Some archives and seals of Hereford cathedral, by the Hon. J. W. Leigh.
  m Notes on Moor Court, Nunsland, Luntley Court, and Grimsditch, by J. Barker.
  n Pembridge church and belfry, by F. Whitehead.
  o Pembridge church, by J. R. Hewitt.
  p Offa's dyke and Rowe ditch, by H. C. Moore.

  q Notes on the portions of Offa's dyke called the Stone row and Rowe ditch, by J. G. Wood.
  r Old Herefordshire rectories and tithes, by J. Lloyd.
  s Richards castle, by R. Clarke.
  t The 17th cent. restoration of Dore abbey church, by T. Blashill.
  u Arthur's stone, Dorstone, by H. C. Moore.
  v Notes on the Chace and Penyard park in relation to Dean forest, by J. G. Wood.
  w History of Goodrich, by D. Seaton.
  x Herefordshire [survey and history of], by J. Davies.

6122 Vol. for 1902–4.
  a Weather in Herefordshire during the 19th cent., by H. Southall.
  b Westhide, by W. H. Lambert.
  c Yarkhill, by A. G. Jones.
  d Inscribed stones [at Tretower], by H. C. Moore.
  e Tretower castle, by J. O. Evans.
  f Tretower Court, by J. O. Evans.
  g Roman roads and the so-called Julian road in the neighbourhood, by H. C. Moore.
  h The Turpilian stone [in Glanusk park], by H. C. Moore.
  i Watling street in Herefordshire, by H. C. Moore.
  j Primary Roman roads into Herefordshire and Monmouthshire and the crossings of Severn, by J. G. Wood.
  k The ancient harbours of Gwent Iscoed or South Monmouthshire, and the Roman passage thence, by J. G. Wood.
  l The place name of Caerwent, by J. G. Wood.
  m Almeley castle and church, by R. H. Warner.
  n Offa's dyke: the gap in the Weobley district, by A. Watkins.
  o Eardisley and its castle, by R. H. Warner.
  p Craswall priory [and manor], by C. J. Lilwall.
  q Place names of the neighbourhood of Hay, by W. E. T. Morgan.
  r Tintern abbey, by P. Baylis.
  s Short history of Tintern abbey and the lordship of Striguil, by J. G. Wood.
  t Cleobury Mortimer church, by R. Clarke.
  u The Herefordshire Domesday, by A. T. Bannister.
  v The Hereford miracles [being an account of miracles at the tomb of St. Thomas Cantilupe, 1286–1307], by A. T. Bannister.

6123 Vol. for 1905–7.
  a Bredwardine and the 'Wardines' of Herefordshire, by J. G. Wood.
  b The navigation of the Wye, by H. C. Moore.
  c Some Domesday place-names in the neighbourhood of Dean forest, by J. G. Wood.
  d Forms and forming of mote castles in Herefordshire, by E. A. Downham.
  e Rowlestone church, by M. G. Watkins.
  f The Keltic lanes of south Herefordshire, by M. G. Watkins.
  g Birtsmorton Court [Worcs.], by R. H. Warner.
  h Wigmore castle, by J. Davies.
  i The Garden cliff of Westbury-on-Severn, by J. G. Wood.
  j Duxmere [in the parish of Ross], by J. G. Wood.
  k Radnor as a place-name, by J. G. Wood.
  l Short notes on the history of Hampton Court, by R. H. George.
  m A survey of the river Wye from the city of Hereford to Bixwear, by Isaac Taylor, 1763. [Reprint]

6124 Vol. for 1908–11.
  a Wigmore and the west border, by R. H. George.
  b A note on an obscure episode in the history of St. Guthlac's priory, Hereford, by A. T. Bannister.

c Further notes on Craswall priory, by C. J. Lilwall.
d Observations at Craswall priory, by Sir H. H. Howorth.
e Notes on Roman Herefordshire, by G. H. Jack.
f The itinerary of Giraldus Cambrensis, by W. E. T. Morgan.
g Roman road between Monmouth and Gloucester, with a note on the Roman masonry at Donnington, by G. H. Jack.
h Notes on Tretyre church and parish, by W. D. Barber.
i St. Weonard's church, by A. Ley.
j Brunlyas tower, by H. E. Jones.
k [Credenhill church]
l [Brinsop church and court, by C. H. Stoker]
m [Weobley, by Mrs. F. H. Leather]
n Charles I in Breconshire and Radnorshire, by J. Hutchinson.
o Notes on Kimbolton, Stockton, and Berrington, by R. H. George.

6125 Vol. for 1912–13.

a Historic screen [in Partrishow church], by H. Reade.
b Raglan castle [Mon.], by Sir J. A. Bradney.
c Roman towns: Wroxeter or Uriconium, by F. S. Stooke-Vaughan.
d Historic Bishopstone: notes on the rectory, church and village, by R. H. Wilmot.
e Notes on the Herbert tombs [in St. Mary's church, Abergavenny], by H. Reade.
f The mayors of Grosmont [Mon.], by R. H. Evans.
g The origin of Kilpeck, by E. R. Firmstone.
h Kilpeck church: its Norman origin, by J. G. Wood. Additional notes by E. R. Firmstone.

6126 Vol. for 1914–17.

a Gladestry church and parish [Rad.], by A. Bickerton-Evans.
b The strange story of Wisteston chapel, by A. Watkins.
c Notes on the manor and castle of Huntington, by S. C. Watkins.
d Wapley camp, the upper Lugg valley, and Kingsland, by R. H. George.
e Some account of the churches of Vowchurch, Turnastone, St. Margaret's, Urishay, and Peterchurch, by G. Marshall.
f Madley church, by W. E. H. Clarke.
g Herefordshire churchyard crosses, by A. Watkins.
h Rudhall, by H. E. Forrest.
i Ludlow castle and church, by H. T. Weyman.
j The book of Llandaff [comp. *c.* 1133] and Herefordshire place names, by W. D. Barber.
k The Wye free fishery case, by F. R. James.
l Presidential address [on ancient roads and bridges, with special reference to Herefordshire], by G. H. Jack.
m Some notes on Marden church, co. Hereford, by G. Marshall.
n A short account of Freen's Court and its former owners, by G. Marshall.
o Sutton Walls [an ancient camp], and the legend of St. Ethelbert, by A. T. Bannister.
p Notes on the churches of Sutton St. Michael and Sutton St. Nicholas, by R. H. Craft.
q Pembridge and Wapley camp, by R. H. George.
r Herefordshire wayside and town crosses, by A. Watkins.
s Notes on the early history of Goodrich castle, by J. G. Wood.
t A lost cartulary of Hereford cathedral, by A. T. Bannister.

6127 Vol. for 1918–20.

a Early local bee-keeping, by A. Watkins.
b The possessions of St. Guthlac's priory, Hereford, by A. T. Bannister.

c The Crosse, Leominster, by T. Neild.
d Remarks on a Norman tympanum at Fownhope, and others in Herefordshire, by G. Marshall.
e The hospital of St. Katherine at Ledbury, by A. T. Bannister.
f The roof of the vicar's cloister at Hereford, by G. Marshall.
g Points of interest in the vicinity of the site of the ancient castle of Hereford, by A. H. Lamont.
h Llanigon [Brec.] place names, by W. E. T. Morgan.
i Park Hall, Bitterley [Salop], by J. R. Burton.
j 'Titterstone' and 'The Clees' [as place-names], by J. G. Wood.
k Court rolls of Burton, in the parish of Eardisland, co. Hereford, by A. T. Bannister.
l Hereford city walls, by A. Watkins.
m Three early timber halls in the city of Hereford, by A. Watkins.
n Wooden monumental effigies in Herefordshire, by G. Marshall.
o 'Scotland' and the 'Arthur stone' at Dorstone, by J. G. Wood.
p Garway church, by A. Watkins.
q Ross parish church, by R. T. A. Money-Kyrle.
r Brampton Bryan castle, by R. H. George.
s Church of Leintwardine, by G. Marshall.
t All Saints' church, Hereford, by W. E. H. Clarke.
u The Blackfriars monastery and the Coningsby hospital, Hereford, by G. Marshall.
v The king's ditch of the city of Hereford, by A. Watkins.

6128 Vol. for 1921–3.

a Diary [1638–47] of Joyce Jefferies, a resident in Hereford during the civil war, by F. R. James.
b Castles and camps of south Herefordshire, by H. Reade.
c Further notes on the parish of Llanigon, co. Brecon, by W. E. T. Morgan.
d Welsh and English place-names in south Herefordshire, by H. Reade.
e Report on the excavation of a long barrow at Llanigon, co. Brecon, by W. E. T. Morgan and G. Marshall.
f Hereford cathedral organ, by W. E. H. Clarke.
g Deerhurst church and the battle of Tewkesbury [1471], by E. S. Hartland.
h Blackwardine, by G. H. Jack.
i A Huguenot glass works near St. Weonards, Herefs., by B. P. Marmont.
j Fords and ferries of the Wye, by A. H. Lamont.
k Church of Eaton Bishop, co. Hereford, by G. Marshall.
l Some remarks on the ancient stained glass in Eaton Bishop church, co. Hereford, by G. Marshall.
m Notes on the manor of Sugwas, co. Hereford, by G. Marshall.
n A Brobury rent roll of 1716, by H. F. B. Compston.
o The manor of Courtfield, by Sir J. A. Bradney.
p Hall Court [Much Marcle], and Sir John Coke, knt. [d. 1644], by H. Reade.
q Architectural account of Hereford cathedral, by W. E. H. Clarke.
r Colwall and the neighbourhood, by A. H. Bright.
s Pilleth, Nant-y-Groes, and Monaughty [Rad.], by Sir J. A. Bradney.
t Forests and woodland areas of Herefordshire, by S. Robinson.
u Llanvillo (Llanfilo) church [Brec.], by G. I. R. Jones.
v Descriptive catalogue of mss. dealing with St. Katherine's, Ledbury, by A. T. Bannister.
w The manor of Kingsland, by H. Easton.
x Excavations on the site of Ariconium, a Romano-British smelting town in the parish of Weston-under-Penyard, south Herefs., by G. H. Jack [and others].

6129 Vol. for 1924–6.

a Ergyng (Archenfield), by Sir J. A. Bradney.
b Ancient bridges in Herefordshire and their preservation, by G. H. Jack.
c William Langland's birthplace, by A. T. Bannister.
d Observations on earth works, with reference to the Welsh border, by I. T. Hughes.
e Report on the excavations conducted on Midsummer hill camp, by I. T. Hughes.
f Tours and tourists in 17th cent. Herefordshire, by H. Reade.
g Church of Edvin Ralph and some notes on pardon monuments, by G. Marshall.
h Ancient glass in Madley church, co. Hereford, by G. Marshall.
i Excavations on the site of Caplar camp, in the parish of Brockhampton, Herefs., by G. H. Jack and A. G. K. Hayter.
j Bishop Peter de Aquablanca: his last will, his death and burial [1268], by A. T. Bannister.
k Castle Morton, co. Worcester, by C. V. Kennerley.
l Elizabeth Barrett [d. 1861] and Hope End, by A. Watkins.
m Richard's Castle and the Normans in Herefordshire, by A. T. Bannister.
n Church of Richard's Castle, co. Hereford, by G. Marshall.
o Some account books of the first Lord Scudamore [d. 1671] and of the Hereford craft guilds, by H. Reade.
p Field and place names of Coddington, a local study, by W. G. Hamilton.
q The priory of Austin canons at Wormesley, by A. T. Bannister.
r Wormesley church, Herefs., by G. Marshall.
s Ancient chapels in the Palace grounds, Hereford, by J. H. Hoyle.
t Field names in the parish of Brinsop, Herefs., by C. H. Stoker.
u Timber houses of Weobley, by Mrs. F. H. Leather.
v Solers Hope church, Herefs., by G. Marshall.
w The Whittingtons and Solers Hope, by A. T. Bannister.
x Excavations at the Queen stone, by A. Watkins.

6130 Vol. for 1927–9.

a Nicholas Hereford [d. 1417], by M. L. Smith.
b Churches of Brilley and Michaelchurch-on-Arrow and their baldachinos, by G. Marshall.
c Painscastle [Rad.], by W. E. T. Morgan.
d Much Wenlock priory and Buildwas abbey, by E. H. Day.
e The preceptory of the Knights Hospitallers at Dinmore, co. Hereford, by E. H. Day.
f Burghope, Herefs., by G. Marshall.
g Church of the Knights Templars at Garway, Herefs., by G. Marshall.
h St. Giles' chapel, Hereford, by A. Watkins and A. T. Bannister.
i The Fedw stone circle, in the parish of Glascwm, Rad., by G. Marshall.
j Notes on Weston-under-Penyard, by E. R. Holland.
k Penyard castle, in the parish of Weston-under-Penyard, Herefs., by G. Marshall.
l The stone age at Linton, by S. C. Neal.
m Arthur's stone, by A. Watkins.
n Bredwardine church, Herefs., by G. Marshall.
o Ghosts of Much Dewchurch, by H. Reade.
p Sir Walter Pye's monument in St. David's church, Much Dewchurch, by H. Reade. [Sir W. Pye, d. 1635]
q Notes on the derivation of 'Bettws' and 'Yspytty' and the origin of parishes, by W. E. T. Morgan. [2 pts. 2nd pt. by H. Reade]
r Farlow, an ancient Herefordshire parish, by R. Lee-Roberts.

s 10th cent. crucifixion and emblem stones at Llanveyno, by A. Watkins.
t An ancient cottage pottery in Upton Bishop parish, by S. C. Neal.
u 15th cent. effigy of an unknown lady at Ledbury, co. Hereford, by St. C. Baddeley.
v Dog doors in churches and dog tongs, by W. E. T. Morgan.

6131 Vol. for 1930–2.

a Lollardism in the diocese of Hereford from the 14th to the 16th cent., by M. L. Smith.
b Church of St. David at Kilpeck, by W. E. H. Clarke.
c Stretford church, co. Hereford, by G. Marshall.
d Notes on Kingsland church, Herefs., by G. Marshall.
e A medieval tomb at Little Malvern, by W. J. C. Berrington.
f Shrine of St. Thomas de Cantilupe in Hereford cathedral, by G. Marshall.
g Field names of Burghill parish, by O. R. Swayne.
h A pottery site at Pembridge, by G. Marshall.
i Croft church, Herefs., by G. Marshall.
j John Gethin, bridge builder, of Kingsland, Herefs., 1757–1831, by G. H. Jack.
k Hereford place-names and sites, by A. Watkins.
l The early succession of the see of Hereford [deduced from the *Textus Roffensis*], by M. L. Smith.
m Report on the discovery of bronze age cists in the Olchon valley, Herefs., by G. Marshall. [With a report on the human remains by Sir A. Keith]
n The college of Christ of Brecknock [established on the lands and in the buildings of the Dominican friary of St. Nicholas, 1541], by A. E. Donaldson.
o St. David's, and Swansea and Brecon dioceses, by W. E. T. Morgan.
p Tretower Castle and Court, Brec., by G. Marshall.
q An underground mediaeval chamber in Eign Street, Hereford, by E. J. Bettington.

6132 Index to the Transactions, 1852–1911, comp. J. C. Fowler.[1] 1915. [Index, 1912–35, and index of illustrations, 1852–1935, comp. F. Boddington, was published in 1939]

Other publications:

6133 Report of the research committee of the Club: excavations on the site of the Romano-British town of Magna, Kenchester, Herefs., 1912–13 [and 1924–5], by G. H. Jack and A. G. K. Hayter. 2 vols. [1916–26. Also issued with the *Transactions* for 1912–13 and 1924–6]

6134 The old standing crosses of Herefordshire, by A. Watkins. 1930.

WOOLWICH AND DISTRICT ANTIQUARIAN SOCIETY

Founded 1895, as the Woolwich District Antiquarian Society, to encourage the study of antiquities and to examine and record all matters of historic and prehistoric interest; to help to preserve all buildings and landmarks of historical and antiquarian interest, and the amenities and natural beauties of the district. Title appeared in the above form in 1926.

Annual Report, list of officers and members, abstract of proceedings, papers, etc., vols. [6]–24[2] (1901–31):

[1] Not seen.
[2] Vol. 22 was issued as *Occasional Papers, 1920*; vols. 23 and 24 are entitled *Annual Report and Transactions*.

d Matters of local interest in the Lesnes missal, by W. H. Mandy.

e Pleas of the crown for the hundred of Lesnes, by W. H. Mandy.

6151 Vol. 23.

a Collections for the early history of Bexley and Dartford, by W. H. Mandy.

b Flint implements from Shooters Hill, by A. H. A. Hogg.

6152 Vol. 24.

a The identification of Noviomagus with the earthworks at Charlton (with a schedule of Roman remains found in the district), by F. C. Elliston-Erwood.

b The river walls and the ancient commission of sewers, by R. W. Jackson.

Other publications:

6153 Lesnes abbey in the parish of Erith, Kent, by A. W. Clapham; being the complete report of the investigations, architectural and historical, carried out by the Works Committee of the Society during the years 1909–1913. 1915.

6154 The canon from the Lesnes abbey missal, *c.* 1200, with rubrics of much interest. Report of the Society. Supplement to vol. 23. 1925.

WORCESTERSHIRE ARCHAEOLOGICAL SOCIETY

Founded 1854, as Worcester Diocesan Architectural Society, to promote the study and preservation of ecclesiastical and other architectural antiquities, and to form a collection of books, photographs, etc., concerning matters of antiquarian interest. Title changed to Worcester Diocesan Architectural and Archaeological Society in 1875, and to above form in 1911.

Transactions, new ser., vols. 1–9 (1924–33):

6155 Vol. 1.

a Catalogue of papers in the Harvington church chest, by J. Davenport.

b Some notes from cathedral records as to Barnabas Oley [d. 1686, royalist divine], and the restoration of Worcester cathedral, 1660–66, by J. M. Wilson.

c *John Inglesant*, its author [Joseph Henry Shorthouse, d. 1903], and Little Malvern, by H. H. M. Bartleet.

d William Lloyd [d. 1717], bishop of Worcester, by J. W. Willis Bund.

e The earliest register of the parish of Bromsgrove, by E. A. B. Barnard.

f The Harewell triptych [1588] in Besford church, by J. Willis.

6156 Vol. 2.

a Church bells of Worcestershire, by H. B. Walters. [Contd. in vols. 3–8, with an index in vol. 8. These articles are fuller than the pamphlet by the same author on this subject issued by the Society in ? 1901]

b The tenure of Hartlebury [by the bishops of Worcester], by E. H. Pearce.

c The Worcester antiphonar and the cathedral services of the 13th cent., by J. M. Wilson.

d Some old Worcestershire inns, by Mildred Berkeley.

e Parish and church of Kingsnorton; being some record of recent documentary researches, by H. M. Grant and E. A. B. Barnard.

f The parish of Eckington: its church and records, by A. W. Fletcher.

g A glimpse of Worcester cathedral in the reign of Queen Mary: a petition from the dean and chapter to Cardinal Pole, by J. M. Wilson.

h Notes. [Includes: A Worcestershire historical glass commemorating the election of George Durant as M.P. for Evesham, 1768 or 1774; A supposed Roman pottery at Sandlin Farm, Leigh Sinton]

6157 Vol. 3.

a Churchwardens' accounts of the parish of South Littleton, 1548–71, with appendix, 1582–1693, transcribed and annotated by E. A. B. Barnard.

b Monumental brasses of Worcestershire, by F. J. Thacker. [Contd. in vol. 4]

c Saxon finds [from burial-sites] at Blockley, by E. A. B. Barnard.

d A [16th cent.] painted panel and the Harewell triptych in Besford church.

6158 Vol. 4.

a The Dingleys of Charlton, by E. A. B. Barnard.

b The painted glass of Birtsmorton church, by G. McN. Rushforth.

c The Elizabethan settlement at Worcester, 1559–62, by J. Davenport.

d Bibliography of the late J. W. Willis Bund [d. 1928], by E. A. B. Barnard.

e Flint arrow-head from Stone, Kidderminster, by T. C. Cantrill.

6159 Vol. 5.

a The life of Sir John de Wysham [d. 1332], of Clifton-on-Teme, steward of the King's household and justice of North Wales, by R. G. Griffiths. [Appendix 1a: The effigy in Clifton-on-Teme church. Appendix 2a: Sir Michael de Poynings, 'the uncle'. Appendix 3a: Pedigree of Sir John de Wysham]

b The old rural Worcestershire postmen, by Mildred Berkeley.

c Clement Lichfield, last abbot of Evesham, 1514–39, by E. A. B. Barnard.

d Philip Hawford, pseudo-abbot of Evesham (1539), and dean of Worcester (1553–57): his will and inventory, by E. A. B. Barnard.

e Some original documents concerning Worcestershire and the great rebellion, by E. A. B. Barnard.

f The font in Elmley Castle church, by G. McN. Rushforth.

g William Hutton, the Birmingham historian, 1723–1815, by J. Sumner.

6160 Vol. 6.

a The early history of Clifton-on-Teme, by R. G. Griffiths. [Contd. in vols. 7–9]

b Yarranton's works at Astley, by T. C. Cantrill and Marjory Wright. [Andrew Yarranton, d. 1684?, engineer and agriculturist]

c Notes on the Worcester diocese, 1660–62, by J. Davenport.

d Some old Worcestershire stocks, by Mildred Berkeley.

e Survey of Malvern Chase, 1628, transcribed by E. A. B. Barnard.

6161 Vol. 7.

a A mediaeval tomb at Little Malvern, by W. J. C. Berington.

b Excavations on Oliver's Mount, Shrawley Wood, in 1928–30, by S. W. Masterman.

c Some old Worcestershire churches and parochial chapels as noted and illustrated in the Prattinton collections, comp. E. A. B. Barnard. [Contd. in vol. 9]

6162 Vol. 8.

a Some additional notes concerning the Prattinton collections of Worcestershire history, by E. A. B. Barnard.

b The ferries of Worcestershire, by Mildred Berkeley.

c The Worcestershire drawings of E. F. and T. F. Burney.

6163 Vol. 9.

a Old Bewdley and its industries, by Mrs. J. F. Parker.

b Worcestershire scratch dials, by Sir J. Sumner and T. W. Cole.

c The Anglo-Saxon sundial at Pirton, by A. R. Green.

d The sanctus bell at Fladbury, by H. B. Walters.

e The Rouses of Rous Lench, by E. A. B. Barnard.

WORCESTERSHIRE HISTORICAL SOCIETY

Founded 1893, for the collection and publication of materials for compiling a history of the county.

Publications:

6164 *Inquisitiones post mortem* for the county of Worcester, ed. J. W. Willis Bund. 1894–1909. [Pt. 1: 1242–99. Pt. 2: 1300–26]

6165 Bibliography of Worcestershire. Pt. 1: Acts of parliament relating to the county, ed. J. R. Burton and F. S. Pearson. Pt. 2: Classified catalogue of books and other printed matter, with notes, by J. R. Burton. Pt. 3: Works relating to the botany of Worcestershire, comp. J. Humphreys. 1898–1907.

6166 Lay subsidy roll, 1603, for the county of Worcester, ed. J. Amphlett. 1901.

6167 Lay subsidy rolls, 6 and 7 Henry VI, 1427–9, for the county of Worcester, ed. J. Amphlett. 1902.

6168 Episcopal registers, diocese of Worcester. Register of Bishop Godfrey Giffard, Sept. 23, 1268, to Aug. 15, 1301, ed. J. W. Willis Bund. 2 vols. 1902 [1898–1902].

6169 Diary of Francis Evans, secretary to Bishop Lloyd, 1699–1706, ed. D. Robertson. 1903.

6170 The old order book of Hartlebury grammar school, 1556–1752, ed. D. Robertson. 1904.

A calendar of wills and administrations preserved in the consistory court of the bishop of Worcester. 2 vols. 1904 [1899] –1911. [See British Record Soc., Index library, no. 630 above]

6171 The Kyre Park charters [*c.* 1312–*c.* 1734], ed. J. Amphlett. 1905.

6172 Catalogue of manuscripts in the chapter library of Worcester cathedral, comp. J. K. Floyer, ed. and revised by S. G. Hamilton. 1906.

6173 Accounts of the priory of Worcester, 13–14 Hen. VIII, 1521–2, ed. J. M. Wilson, and a catalogue of the rolls of the obedientiaries, prepared by J. H. Bloom and revised and ed. S. G. Hamilton. 1907.

6174 Early compotus rolls [1278–1352] of the priory of Worcester, transcribed and ed. J. M. Wilson and C. Gordon. 1908.

6175 Original charters [8th–17th cent.] relating to the city of Worcester in possession of the dean and chapter, ed. J. H. Bloom. 1909.

6176 Compotus rolls of the priory of Worcester of the 14th and 15th cent., transcribed and ed. S. G. Hamilton. 1910.

6177 *Liber elemosinarii*: the almoner's book of the priory of Worcester [13th–16th cent.], ed. J. H. Bloom. 1911.

6178 *Liber ecclesiae Wigorniensis*: a letter book of the priors of Worcester [14th cent.], ed. J. H. Bloom, collated with the original ms. by Ethel Stokes. 1912.

6179 Court rolls of the manor of Hales, 1270–1307, ed. J. Amphlett, assisted by S. G. Hamilton. 1912 [1910–12].

6180 Court rolls of the manor of Hales, pt. 2 [continuing the above], containing additional courts, 1276–1301, and Romsley courts, 1280–1303, ed. R. A. Wilson. 1933.

6181 Collectanea. 1912.

a Charters from St. Swithun's, Worcester, ed. J. H. Bloom.

b Records of a ruridecanal court of 1300, ed. F. S. Pearson.

c An ancient [13th cent.] rental of Worcester priory, ed. C. Gordon.

d Catalogue of certain rolls in the archives of the dean and chapter of Worcester, ed. J. H. Bloom.

6182 Documents illustrating early education in Worcester, 685 to 1700, ed. A. F. Leach. 1913.

6183 Journal of Prior William More [prior of Worcester, 1518–36], ed. Ethel S. Fegan. 1914 [1913–14].

6184 Corrodies at Worcester in the 14th cent.: some correspondence between the crown and the priory of Worcester in the reign of Edward II concerning the corrody of Alicia Conan, with a summary of the correspondence, ed. J. M. Wilson and Ethel C. Jones. *P.* 1917.

6185 The early occupants of the office of organist and master of the choristers of the cathedral church of Christ and the Blessed Virgin Mary, Worcester, by I. Atkins. 1918.

6186 The *Liber albus* of the priory of Worcester, pts. 1 and 2, priors John de Wyke, 1301–17, and Wulstan de Bransford, 1317–39: a short abstract of all the documents, with indices to the original, and introd., by J. M. Wilson. 1919.

6187 Diary of Henry Townshend of Elmley Lovett, 1640–63, ed. J. W. Willis Bund. 2 vols. 1920 [1915–20].

6188 The parliamentary survey of the lands and possessions of the dean and chapter of Worcester made in or about 1649 in pursuance of an ordinance of parliament for the abolishing of deans and chapters, ed. T. Cave and R. A. Wilson. 1924.

6189 *Liber pensionum prioratus Wigorn.*; being a collection of documents relating to pensions from appropriated churches and other payments receivable by the prior and convent of Worcester and to the privileges of the monastery, ed. C. Price. 1925.

Register of Walter Reynolds, bishop of Worcester, 1308–1313. 1927. [See Dugdale Soc., no. 1408 above]

6190 Register of William de Geynesburgh, bishop of Worcester, 1302–7, ed. J. W. Willis Bund, with an introduction added by R. A. Wilson. 1929 [1907–29].

6191 Register of Thomas de Cobham, bishop of Worcester, 1317–27, ed. E. H. Pearce. 1930.

WORCESTERSHIRE NATURALISTS' CLUB

Founded 1847, for the study and investigation of the natural history, geology, and archaeology of the county of Worcester and adjacent counties.

Transactions, vols. 3–8 (1903–32):

6192 Vol. 3.

a Pre-historic man in Worcestershire (as known by his implements and weapons), by W. H. Edwards.

b Chaddesley Corbett and the Roman Catholic persecution in Worcestershire in connection with the Titus Oates plot, by J. Humphreys.

6193 Vol. 4.

a Some ancient flint implements recently obtained from the county, by F. T. Spackman. [See also no. **6194c** below]
b Bibliography of natural history with special reference to works of local interest, by T. Duckworth.
c Birtsmorton Court and manor and its possessors, by E. R. Dowdeswell.
d The ancient castle of Worcester, by J. W. Willis Bund.
e The work and art of neolithic man, by J. Humphreys.
f Hartlebury Castle and the bishops of Worcester, by H. Yeatman-Biggs.
g Man's earliest implements: eoliths or dawn stones, by W. H. Edwards.
h The Wyntours of Huddington and the Gunpowder plot, by J. Humphreys.
i Clifton-on-Teme and its church, by R. Griffiths.
j Payne's Place, by E. R. Dowdeswell.
k Eastington Hall, by E. R. Dowdeswell.
l Notes on old Worcester to the end of the 13th cent., by J. W. Willis Bund.
m Some stone implements from north Worcestershire, by T. C. Cantrill.

6194 Vol. 5.

a The bishops of Worcester whose pictures exist at Hartlebury Castle, by H. Yeatman-Biggs.
b Manorial and other ancient courts of Worcestershire, by W. W. A. Tree.
c Some additional flint implements from the county, by W. H. Edwards. [See also no. **6193a** above]
d Memorandum of the Berkeleys, Spetchley, Worcs., by P. Ward.
e The rise of the abbey and town of Evesham, by F. T. Spackman.
f The maintenance of Charles II in the city of Worcester in 1651, and the flight of the king after the battle, by F. T. Spackman.
g Some old Worcestershire customs, by W. W. A. Tree.
h The battle of Worcester, by J. W. Willis Bund.
i Some notes on the history of Pull and Bushley, by E. R. Dowdeswell.
j Some notes on the parish of Hanley Castle, by E. R. Dowdeswell.
k Stourton castle, by J. A. Lycett.
l Kinver and its ancient forest, by J. A. Lycett.
m Droitwich, by P. J. Pond.
n Some notes on the folklore of Worcestershire, by E. C. Corbett.
o Some early Worcestershire camps, by J. A. Lycett.
p Elmley Castle, by F. R. Jeffery.
q Some recent discoveries of the remains of prehistoric man, by F. T. Spackman.

6195 Vol. 6.

a Notes on some of the portraits [chiefly of members of the Dowdeswell family] at Pull Court, by E. R. Dowdeswell.
b Some remains of the bronze age at Mathon, by J. E. H. Blake.
c The Chipping Campden area and its industries past and present, by L. Richardson.
d The Sheldon tapestry maps of Worcestershire, 1588, by J. Humphreys.
e British rainfall, with special reference to Worcestershire [and with an account of some 18th and 19th cent. floods], by B. Brotherton.
f The Severn: as it was, as it is, and as it should be, by E. J. Bradley.

g The Commandery [of St. Wulstan], Worcester: notes on a deed of lease, dated 33 Henry VIII, by F. T. Spackman.
h The siege of Worcester, 20 May to 23 July, 1646, by J. W. Willis Bund.
i Worcestershire history in Elizabeth's reign, from the privy council records, by J. Humphreys.
j The cultivation of medicinal herbs: recent development of the industry in Britain, by R. C. Gaut.

6196 Vol. 7.

a Evolution of the parish church in Worcestershire, by J. Humphreys.
b Papers and deeds belonging to the parish of Stone, by H. Howard.
c Iron in antiquity, with special reference to local currency bars and their relation to early British water clocks, by J. N. Friend.
d 'Early man on the hills', by P. H. L'Estrange.
e Roman coins in the Worcester museum, by F. S. Salisbury.
f The Tewkesbury area and its industries, past and present, by L. Richardson.
g Bretforton, by J. E. H. Blake.
h Roman pottery in the Worcester museum, by F. S. Salisbury.
i Gleanings from the diaries of a Bewdley naturalist [George Jordan, d. 1871], by F. R. Jeffery.
j Misericords of Malvern, Ripple and Stratford-on-Avon, by F. C. Morgan.

6197 Vol. 8.

a Notes on the history of the Wyre forest, by E. E. Lea.
b Midsummer hill [earthworks, with a report on the excavations, by I. T. Hughes].
c Some notable Worcestershire wells, by L. Richardson.
d Early history of the water supply of Worcester, by B. Brotherton.
e History of the Worcester waterworks, by T. Caink.

WORCESTERSHIRE PARISH REGISTER SOCIETY

Founded, c. 1913, to publish county parish registers up to the year 1812. Dissolved c. 1916.

Publications:

6198 Register of Worcester cathedral, 1693–1811, transcribed by E. Ophelia Browne, introd. by J. W. Willis Bund, and biographical notes by F. S. Colman. 1913.

6199 Registers of Bushley, in the deanery of Upton, 1538–1812, transcribed by J. Rusling. 1913.

6200 Registers of Churchill in Oswaldslow, in the deanery of Worcester East [1564–1794; marriages to 1839]. 1914.

6201 Registers of Eastham (with Hanley Child and Orleton) with Hanley William, in the deanery of Burford, 1572–1812, transcribed, with introd., by E. E. Lea. 1915.

6202 Registers of Over Areley, 1564–1812, transcribed by H. R. Mayo. 1916.

WORTHING ARCHAEOLOGICAL SOCIETY

Founded 1922, to promote the study of archaeology in all its branches, and especially the proper recording and preservation of local antiquities.

First–Eleventh Annual Report (1923–33):

6203 3rd Report.

a Report of discoveries [of pottery] made at the flint pit

of the corporation, in Waterworks Lane, Broadwater, by C. H. Goodman.

6204 5th Report.

   a Highdown [camp], by C. H. Goodman.

6205 6th Report.

   a Hoard of bronze-age axes found at Worthing, 1928, by Marian Frost.

6206 8th Report.

   a Tarring inclosure award [1811], by C. H. Goodman.

WREN SOCIETY

Founded 1923, to elucidate the career and achievements of the great architect by the searching out and publication of original drawings, documents and facts of proved authenticity relating to his life and works.

Publications, vols. 1–10:[1]

6207 Vol. 1. St. Paul's cathedral: original Wren drawings from the collection at All Souls College, Oxford. 1924.

6208 Vols. 2, 3. St. Paul's cathedral: original Wren drawings from the collection in the library of St. Paul's cathedral. 2 vols. 1925–6.

6209 Vol. 4. Hampton Court palace, 1689–1702. Original Wren drawings from Sir John Soane's museum and All Souls collections. 1927.

6210 Vol. 5. Designs of Sir Chr. Wren for Oxford, Cambridge, London, Windsor, etc.: original Wren drawings from All Souls, Hans Sloane and Sir John Soane collections. 1928.

6211 Vol. 6. The Royal Hospital for Seamen at Greenwich, 1697–1728: original drawings by Sir Christopher Wren, Sir John Vanbrugh, Nicholas Hawksmoor, John James. 1929.

6212 Vol. 7. The royal palaces of Winchester, Whitehall, Kensington, and St. James's, Sir Christopher Wren, architect, 1660–1715; to which are added some additional designs for Hampton Court palace supplementary to vol. 4, with an account of Marlborough House, St. James's park, and two plans of Buckingham House: original drawings by Sir Christopher Wren and Sir John Vanbrugh. 1930.

6213 Vol. 8. Thirty-two large drawings for Whitehall, Windsor, and Greenwich, 1694–8: original Wren drawings purchased by Dr. Stack, F.R.S., in 1749, in the collection at All Souls. 1931.

6214 Vols. 9, 10. The parochial churches of Sir Christopher Wren, 1666–1718. Pt. 1: Reprint of John Clayton's 'Churches of Sir Christopher Wren, 1848', and original Wren drawings, with contemporary engravings collected by Samuel Pepys, now in the Pepysian library at Cambridge. Pt. 2: The description of the churches, 1666–1718, and accounts, with tables of the tradesmen employed; photographic record of the churches as existing, and original Wren drawings supplementary to vol. 9, together with six plates of designs for St. Mary's, Warwick, now at All Souls. 2 vols. 1932–3.

[1] For index to vols. 1–19 see vol. 20, 1943 [1944].

WYCLIF SOCIETY

Founded 1882, to remove from England the disgrace of having left buried in mss. the most important works of John Wyclif. Dissolved 1925.

Publications:

6215 Johannis Wyclif miscellanea philosophica. Vol. i: De actibus anime, Replicacio de universalibus, De materia et forma, with an essay on Wyclif's philosophical system. Vol. ii: De universalibus, Fragmenta, Notae et quaestiones variae, De materia. Now first ed. M. H. Dziewicki. 2 vols. 1902–5.

6216 Johannis Wyclif de civili dominio, liber tertius, with critical and historical notes by J. Loserth; English side-notes by F. D. Matthew. Vols. iii–iv. 1903–4. [Vol. i ed. R. L. Poole, vol. ii ed. J. Loserth, were published in 1885–1900]

6217 John Wyclif's De veritate sacrae scripturae. Now first ed. from the mss. with critical and historical notes by R. Buddensieg. 3 vols. 1905–7.

6218 Johannis Wyclif tractatus de potestate pape. Now first ed. from the mss. with critical and historical notes by J. Loserth; English side-notes by F. D. Matthew. 1907.

6219 Johannis Wyclif de ente librorum duorum excerpta. Libri 1: Tractatus tertius et quartus; libri 11: Tractatus primus et tertius; et fragmentum de annihilatione. Now first ed. M. H. Dziewicki. 1909.

6220 Johannis Wyclif opera minora. Now first ed. from the mss. with critical and historical notes by J. Loserth; English side-notes by F. D. Matthew. 1913.

6221 Johannis Wyclif tractatus de mandatis divinis, accedit tractatus de statu innocencie. Now first ed. from the mss. with critical and historical notes and with an appendix De differentia inter peccatum mortale et veniale, by J. Loserth and F. D. Matthew. 1922.

6222 Rogeri Dymmok liber contra XII errores et hereses Lollardorum, ed. H. S. Cronin. [1922?].

6223 Shirley's catalogue of the extant Latin works of John Wyclif, revised by J. Loserth. P. [1924].

YORKSHIRE ARCHAEOLOGICAL SOCIETY

Founded 1863, as the Huddersfield Archaeological and Topographical Association, to further the collection and preservation of materials for the history and topography of the county of York. Title changed to Yorkshire Archaeological and Topographical Association in 1867, and to the above form in 1893.

Yorkshire Archaeological Journal, vols. 16–31 (1900–34):

6224 Vol. 16.

   a Paver's marriage licences, with notes by J. W. Clay. [Extracts from marriage licences, 1567–1630, formerly preserved in the registry of York, taken from the mss. of W. Paver. Contd. from vol. 14. Contd. in vols. 17 and 20. For 1630–1714 see Record series, vols. 40, 43 and 46, no. 6248 below]

   b Excavation at Pule hill, near Marsden, on the Huddersfield and Manchester road, by E. K. Clark.

   c Notes on the bells of the ancient churches of the West Riding of Yorkshire, by J. E. Poppleton. [Contd. in vols. 17 and 18]

   d Yorkshire deeds. [13th–16th cent. Contd. in vol. 17]

   e 17th cent. builders' contracts, by J. Lister and W. Brown.

   f Yorkshire briefs. [18th–19th cent. Contd. in vols. 17 and 30]

   g Ingleby Arncliffe.

h The Huddersfield Archaeological and Topographical Association founded in 1864, by Sir T. Brooke.
i Palimpsest brass at Winestead, E. Yorks., by M. Stephenson.
j Castle hill, Almondbury: historical notes by Sir T. Brooke.
k Certificates of alleged cures of lunacy by John Smith, of Wakefield, 1615, by M. H. Peacock.
l Five East Riding churches, by A. D. Leadman. [Burnby, Nunburnholme, Kilnwick Percy, Millington, and Givendale Magna]
m Gundrada de Warenne [d. 1085]: a legend, by H. Hall.
n Kirklees priory, by S. J. Chadwick.
o Some pardons or indulgences preserved in Yorkshire, 1412–1527, ed. C. Wordsworth.
p Visitations in the diocese of York, holden by Archbishop Edward Lee, 1534–5.
q The early history of Crayke, by J. T. Fowler.
r Kirklees [priory] charters.

6225 Vol. 17.

a St. Hilda [d. 680], by A. D. H. Leadman.
b Will of Timothy Bright, M.D., rector of Methley and Barwick-in-Elmet, 1615.
c Danby v. Sydenham: a Restoration chancery suit [1660s].
d Humberston's survey [being a survey made in 1570 of the estates of the attainted leaders of the Rising in the North, 1569].
e Early inscription [11th or 12th cent.] in Bilsdale church.
f Notes on Yorkshire churches [written 1856–74], by Sir S. Glynne. [Contd. from vol. 14. Contd. in vols. 18, 20, 23, 24, and 26]
g The feast days of St. Hilda, by G. Buchannan.
h Some legends of St. Nicholas, with special reference to the seal of Pocklington grammar school, by J. T. Fowler.
i Monumental brasses in the North Riding, by M. Stephenson.
j Vescy [family] of Brampton-en-le-Morthen in the parish of Treeton, and their descendants, by C. E. B. Bowles.
k Grave-slab of Abbot Barwick in Selby abbey church, 1526.
l Two Yorkshire charms or amulets: exorcisms and adjurations, by C. Wordsworth.
m The rectory of Fishlake, by F. R. Fairbank.
n Kirklees priory, by S. J. Chadwick.

6226 Vol. 18.

a Monumental brasses in the city of York, by M. Stephenson.
b Ecclesiastical Middlesbrough in medieval times.
c The Rising in the North [1569]: a new light upon one aspect of it.
d Confirmation of a grant of land at Huggate to Watton priory [1235].
e Grants of arms [to various Yorkshiremen, 1469–1658].
f Eggleston abbey, by J. F. Hodgson.
g Nathaniel Reading [d. 1713] and the commissioners of sewers for the level of Hatfield Chace.
h Some Elizabethan visitations of the churches belonging to the peculiar of the dean of York, by T. M. Fallow.
i Mount Grace priory: the founding of the Carthusian order, by H. V. Le Bas; history of the priory, by W. Brown; architectural history, by W. H. St. John.
j The Clifford family, by J. W. Clay.
k An English document of about 1080: privileges of Archbishop Thomas I of York (1070–1100) in the city of York.

6227 Vol. 19.

a Acaster Malbis [manor], and the Fairfax family, by W. P. Baildon.

b Two more Yorkshire pardons [indulgences], or Knaresborough letters of fraternity [1449–1512], by C. Wordsworth.
c The Catterick brass [of Elizabeth, widow of Anthony Catterick, of Stanwick, 1591], by W. Brown.
d Burneston hospital and free school, by H. B. McCall.
e Names of Yorkshire ex-religious, 1573: their pensions and subsidies to the queen thereon, by T. M. Fallow.
f Gilling castle, by J. Bilson.
g The last Earl of Warenne and Surrey, and the distribution of his possessions, by F. R. Fairbank. [John de Warenne, d. 1347]
h Anglian and Anglo-Danish sculpture in the North Riding of Yorkshire, by W. G. Collingwood.
i The Hornes of Mexborough, by J. F. Horne.
j A sculptured representation of hell cauldron found at York, by J. Bilson.
k Evidence of the religious beliefs of the ancient Britons, by J. R. Mortimer.
l Churchwardens' accounts and other documents relating to Howden, by G. E. Weddall.
m Note on a British chariot-burial at Hunmanby, East Yorks., by T. Sheppard.

6228 Vol. 20.

a Documents relating to Handsworth Woodhouse [1339–1683], by S. O. Addy.
b Two early sculptured stones in Birstall church, by G. A. Auden.
c Kirklees priory, by Sir G. Armytage.
d The service of horngarth [a feudal service performed at Whitby], by R. B. Turton.
e The Marmion tomb at Tanfield, by H. B. McCall.
f Excavation of the Roman forts at Castleshaw, West Riding, by F. A. Bruton.
g St. Peter's church, Sheffield.
h St. Nicholas' church, Bradfield.
i The Bailey hill [earthwork], Bradfield, by S. O. Addy.
j St. Mary's church, Ecclesfield.
k Ecclesfield priory.
l St. Mary's church, Welwick, by J. Bilson.
m St. Patrick's church, Patrington, by J. Bilson.
n Anglian and Anglo-Danish sculpture at York, by W. G. Collingwood.
o A selection of documents [13th–15th cent.] belonging to Sir John Lawson, Brough Hall, Yorks.
p Some medieval grave-covers of exceptional or unusual character, in the county of York, by C. C. Hodges.
q Snaith marriage licences [being extracts from the act books of the peculiar court of Snaith, 1596–1628 and 1715–54], by W. Brigg.
r The peculiar of Masham cum Kirkby Malzeard, by H. B. McCall.
s The Tickhill [Yorks.] and Battle [Sussex] monuments, by P. Biver.
t Concerning the surname and arms of the family of St. Paul, by J. F. Horne.
u Monumental brasses in Yorkshire: additions and corrections, by M. Stephenson.
v Poll tax returns for the East Riding, 4 Ric. II [1381], by Eleanor Lloyd.
w Grants of chantry and monastic lands [in Yorkshire], in 1586, by W. Brown.
x Articles on monumental brasses in Yorkshire [published in the *Journal*].
y Notes on Dewsbury church and some of its rectors and vicars, by S. J. Chadwick.
z Blyth priory [Notts.], by J. Bilson.
aa Salley abbey, by S. D. Kitson.
bb Bashall [Hall], by J. W. R. Parker.
cc Browsholme Hall, by J. W. R. Parker.

dd Wensley church, by H. B. McCall.
ee Middleham castle, by W. H. Brierley.
ff Coverham abbey, by H. B. McCall.
gg 12th cent. font at Everingham, by J. T. Fowler.

6229 Vol. 21.

a Newbald church, by J. Bilson.
b Edward Kirkby, abbot of Rievaulx, 1531-3.
c The Redmans of Yorkshire, by J. W. R. Parker.
d The Sterne family, by J. W. Clay.
e Woodcarving in English churches, by F. B. Bond. 1: Misericords. 2: Stalls.
f The Roman forts at Elslack, by T. May.
g Bridlington priory, by E. W. Crossley.
h St. Oswald's church, Flamborough, by E. W. Crossley.
i St. John the Baptist's church, Carnaby, by E. W. Crossley.
j St. Martin's church, Burton Agnes: heraldry, by C. V. Collier.
k All Saints' church, Sherburn-in-Elmet, by S. D. Kitson.
l Steeton Hall: heraldry, by E. W. Crossley.
m Ledston Hall, by S. D. Kitson.
n Opening of two barrows in the East Riding [near Sledmere], by J. R. Mortimer.
o The Fallow papers [of T. M. Fallow, including: Middleham collegiate church, founded 1478; the churches of Marske and Thornaby; sundry wills of vicars of Marske, *temp.* Henry VII and VIII; visitations of Nun Appleton convent in 14th cent.; lists of clergy of Yorkshire taxed in 1526-7].
p Anglian and Anglo-Danish sculpture in the East Riding, with addenda to the North Riding, by W. G. Collingwood.
q Jervaulx abbey [its history and an account of the ruins], by W. H. St. J. Hope and H. Brakspear.
r Dewsbury moot hall, by S. J. Chadwick.
s Account rolls of Dewsbury rectory, 1348-56, and abstract of the earliest remaining court roll of the rectory manor of Dewsbury [1574], by S. J. Chadwick.
t A palimpsest brass relating to Yorkshire [in Cowley church, Mdx., of Walter Pope, d. 1502, and Robert Symson, master of the hospital of St. James, Northallerton, d. 1497], by M. Stephenson.

6230 Vol. 22.

a The church in Ripon [from *c.* 660], by J. T. Fowler.
b The battle of Brunaburh [937], by S. Baring-Gould. [Contd. in vol. 23 by J. J. Brigg]
c Some old West Riding milestones [18th cent.], by R. B. Turton.
d Roseberry Topping [the place-name and its derivation], by R. B. Turton.
e A figure of St. Margaret, supposed to have come from Marton priory, by J. T. Fowler.
f Kilton castle [the foundation of the fief of Kylton, the custodians of the castle, its destruction, and an account of the structure], by W. M. I'Anson.
g An Anglian cemetery at Hobb hill, near Saltburn, by W. Hornsby.
h Heraldic glass from Ingleby Arncliffe and Kirby Sigston churches, by W. Brown.
i A supposed Roman 'camp' near Harrogate, by F. Villy.
j Some notes on the lords of Harewood castle, by J. Parker.
k Howden church: some notes on its architectural history, by J. Bilson.
l The institution of the prebendal church at Howden [in 13th cent.], by W. Brown.
m Proceedings, 1912. [Includes: Harewood castle and church, by S. D. Kitson; Wressle castle, by J. Bilson, E. W. Crossley and C. V. Collier; and articles by A. Hamilton Thompson and W. Brown on the churches of

St. Felix, Felixkirk, St. Mary, Thirsk, St. Wilfrid, South Kilvington, their structure and heraldry and wills relating to them, and on the structure and heraldry of St. Mary's church, Leake]
n Eric Bloodaxe in York [d. *c.* 950], by S. Baring Gould.
o Fangfoss church, by W. D. Wood-Rees.
p The manor-house of the bishops of Durham at Howden, by J. Bilson.
q Medieval highways, streets, open ditches, and sanitary conditions of the city of York, by T. P. Cooper.
r An excavation at Adel [camp of unknown origin], by D. Atkinson.
s Notes. [Includes: Notes of Yorkshire clerics, from the de banco roll, no. 700, 1436, by J. Parker]
t The castles of the North Riding, by W. M. I'Anson.
u The Roman station of Lavatrae (Bowes), by E. Wooler.

6231 Vol. 23.

a The Yorkshire Archaeological Society: an account of its origin in 1863 and of its progress to 1913, by S. J. Chadwick.
b Proceedings, 1913. [Includes: Wighill church, and Bolton Percy church, by J. Bilson]
c Anglian and Anglo-Danish sculpture in the West Riding with addenda to the North and East Ridings and York, and a general review of the early Christian monuments of Yorkshire, by W. G. Collingwood.
d Trial by combat, by W. Brown.
e Notes. [Includes: An intrenchment near Ingleton, of possible medieval origin, by F. Villy]
f The fifteen last days of the world in medieval art and literature, by J. T. Fowler. [With particular reference to a window in All Saints' church, North Street, York]
g Some curious Cymro-Celtic place-names, by W. K. Smith.
h The gentry of Yorkshire at the time of the civil war, by J. W. Clay. [With addenda: Events in Yorkshire during the civil war]
i Notes. [Includes: Slack, Greetland, Cambodunum, being an account of excavations on a Roman camp site at Slack, and at Greetland and the possible identification of the former with Cambodunum, by F. Haverfield]
j Roman Piercebridge [and the Brigantes], by E. Wooler.
k A hoard of Roman coins from Halifax, by A. M. Woodward.
l Catalogue of mss. in the library of the Yorkshire Archaeological Society, 1912, comp. W. T. Lancaster.
m Excavations on the Roman site at Slack, near Huddersfield, in 1913: report by J. Parker, L. Tolson and P. W. Dodd.

6232 Vol. 24.

a St. Helen's church, Sandal Magna [with list of vicars 1154-1909], by J. W. Walker.
b The Mawdes of Riddlesden and Ilkley [16th and 17th cent.], by J. Comber.
c The East Riding clergy in 1525-6 [transcripts from State Papers 17 Hen. VIII], by T. M. Fallow.
d Robert Faucon, rector of Bainton [d. 1661], by W. Brown.
e Mortgage of the manor of Foxton. [Transcript of indenture made between Sir Thomas Lainton, of Sexay, and Edward Wooller, of Staynesby, 1634]
f Notes. [Includes: Slack, Greetland, Cambodunum, being the identification of the site of a Roman discovery at Greetland, 1597, by E. W. Crossley; Wills deposited at Lambeth, and relating to Yorkshire, 1385-1589, by J. Challenor Smith; Notes on an ancient bronze spear-head found at Northallerton, by E. Wooler]
g History of roods, screens, and lofts in the East Riding, by A. Vallance.

h Notes. [Includes: Fragment of early grave-monument at Kirkheaton, *c*. 950–1000, by W. G. Collingwood; The Westow cresset stone, by R. H. Barker]

i Beverley minster: some stray notes, by J. Bilson.

j William Hogeson, 'episcopus Dariensis', 1520–1546, with notes on some errors regarding him, by A. Hamilton Thompson.

k Skipsea castle [the custodians and the structure], by W. M. I'Anson.

l British barrows near Brotton, by W. Hornsby and R. Stanton.

m Some additional brasses in the East Riding, by M. Stephenson.

n Some notes on St. Mary's church, Hull, by J. Bilson.

o A regrouping of the Domesday carucates in the Langbargh wapentake, N.R. Yorks., by W. Hornsby.

p Helmsley castle [history and structure], by W. M. I'Anson.

q Jottings from old Yorkshire [18th cent.], by J. Hutton.

r Ancient heraldry in the deanery of Buckrose, by C. V. Collier and II. Lawrance.

6233 Vol. 25.

a The Saville family [from 1225], by J. W. Clay.

b British barrows round Boulby, by W. Hornsby and J. D. Laverick.

c Pocklington school admission register, 1626–1717, by H. Lawrance.

d Ancient heraldry in the deanery of Dickering, by C. V. Collier and H. Lawrance.

e A Templenewsam inventory, 1565 [of the goods of Matthew Stuart, 4th Earl of Lennox], by E. W. Crossley.

f The lass of Richmond Hill [the genealogy of Frances I'Anson, b. 1766], by W. M. I'Anson.

g Notes on the history of Bainton [church of St. Andrew] and its rectors, by S. L. Ollard.

h The registers of the archdeaconry of Richmond, 1361–1442, ed., with introd. and notes, from the abstract made by Matthew Hutton (B.M., Harl. ms. 6978), by A. Hamilton Thompson. [Contd. for 1442–65 in vol. 30, from ms. Latin 333 in the John Rylands library]

i Coverham abbey [history and structure], by W. M. I'Anson.

j Crambe church, by G. E. Kirk. [With list of vicars]

k Memoirs of Sir Marmaduke Rawden, kt., 1582–1642, by H. F. Killick.

l 'Anima' in Elizabethan English [an explanation of the word], by C. J. Battersby.

m The Domesday valets of the Langbargh wapentake, by W. Hornsby.

n Notes. [Includes: Discovery of a Roman tower in York, by G. Benson; Note on an entrenchment of medieval date between Gargrave and Skipton, by F. Villy]

o St. Mary's church, Beverley, by J. Bilson.

p Register of York castle [concerning prisoners], 1730–43.

q Notes. [Includes: A note on Elland church, by E. W. Crossley]

6234 Vol. 26.

a Excavations at Slack [Roman station], 1913–15, by P. W. Dodd and A. M. Woodward.

b Ancient heraldry in the deanery of Harthill, by C. V. Collier and H. Lawrance.

c 17th cent. plasterwork in the parish of Halifax, by H. P. Kendall.

d The advowson of Lockington and some 18th cent. chancery suits, by P. C. Walker.

e Ancient heraldry in the deanery of Holderness, by H. Lawrance and C. V. Collier.

f Goldsborough Hall, by S. D. Kitson.

g A recently discovered parish register [17th cent., of Huggate church, with notes on the rectors], by S. L. Ollard.

h A transcript of an old Malton document, by C. V. Collier. [Privileges and customs of the burgesses of Malton, 1596]

i Notes on the early generations of the family of Horbury [Saxe of Horbury and his descendants, *c*. 1100–1220], by C. T. Clay.

j The origin of the name of Fountains abbey, by A. Butler.

k The west choir clerestory windows in York minster, by F. Harrison.

l Henry Jenkins of Ellerton-on-Swale [reputed to be aged 157, in 1667], by R. B. Turton.

m Notes. [Includes: The building-inscription from Greta bridge, with a note on the Roman governor L. Alfenus Senecio, 3rd cent. A.D., by A. M. Woodward]

6235 Vol. 27.

a The Keighley family [of Keighley and Inskip, and of Newhall near Otley], by W. P. Baildon.

b Some Yorkshire effigies [chiefly 14th cent.], by W. M. I'Anson.

c Ancient heraldry in the deanery of Bulmer, by H. Lawrance and C. V. Collier.

d The Addy family of Darton and elsewhere in the West Riding, by S. O. Addy.

e The Bedern chapel, York [being the chapel of the college of the sub-chanter and vicars-choral], by F. Harrison.

f A 4th cent. disturbance in the Pennines, by I. A. Richmond. [Evidence of a rising in the Ilkley-Elslack district]

g The Yorkshire Archaeological Society's minster window fund [including Note on the Scrope window, by J. A. Knowles].

h The family of Eland, by C. T. Clay.

i The manor and church of Woolley, by J. W. Walker.

j Parliamentary history of Aldborough and Boroughbridge, by Sir T. Lawson-Tancred, bt.

k Twelve medieval ghost stories [with notes by M. R. James and A. Hamilton Thompson].

l Monumental brasses in the East Riding of Yorkshire, by H. Lawrance.

m The monastic settlement at Hackness and its relation to the abbey of Whitby, by A. Hamilton Thompson.

n Hackness church: note on the earlier building, by J. Bilson.

o Notes. [Includes: A note on the Roman fortifications at Long Preston, by F. Villy]

6236 Vol. 28.

a The east window of Holy Trinity church, Goodramgate, York, by J. A. Knowles.

b The Roman camps at Cawthorn, near Pickering, by F. G. Simpson. [Contd. in vol. 29]

c Ancient heraldry in Yorkshire [deaneries of Ryedale, Cleveland, and Richmond], by H. Lawrance and C. V. Collier.

d Knaresborough cave-chapels [St. Robert's cave and the chapel of Our Lady of the Crag], by J. I. Cummins.

e Corker: an old Northumbrian family, by T. M. Corker.

f Roman lead-mining in Weardale: discovery of bronze lead-pouring ladle, by E. Wooler.

g The parentage of William de Percy [11th cent.], by S. P. H. Statham.

h The Roman fort at Ilkley, by A. M. Woodward.

i The dispersion of the wheel-cross [in Britain, 9th and 10th cent.], by W. G. Collingwood.

j Notes. [Includes: The tower of Silkstone church, its repairing and rebuilding, 14th and 15th cent., by A. Hamilton Thompson]

k The medieval military effigies of Yorkshire, by W. M. I'Anson. [Contd. in vol. 29. Also published separately, 1928]

l Notes on the early Saville pedigree and the Butlers of Skelbrook and Kirk Sandal, by W. P. Baildon. [Contd. in vol. 29]

m The Wakefield mysteries [and the performance of miracle plays generally], by M. H. Peacock.

6237 Vol. 29.

a Bradley, a grange of Fountains [with notes on the Pilkington family, 15th and 16th cent.], by C. T. Clay.

b The chantry chapels of Wakefield, by J. W. Walker.

c The Ripon carvers and the lost choir-stalls of Bridlington priory, by J. S. Purvis.

d Ancient heraldry in the deanery of Catterick, by C. V. Collier and H. Lawrance.

e Notes. [Includes: A cross-fragment at Sutton-on-Derwent, late 10th cent., by W. G. Collingwood]

f Yorkshire and the revolution of 1688 [with particular reference to Thomas Osborne, 1st Earl of Danby], by Miss A. M. Evans.

g The family of Thornhill [being the descendants of Essulf, 12th cent.], by C. T. Clay.

h Architectural history of the church of St. Michael and All Angels, Sutton-on-Derwent, by J. W. Walker.

i The bronze age in West Yorkshire, by A. Raistrick.

j The Templars in Yorkshire, by E. J. Martin. [Contd. in vol. 30]

k Two 15th cent. lists of Yorkshire religious, by J. S. Purvis.

l 17th cent. copies of early Yorkshire charters, by J. S. Purvis.

6238 Vol. 30.

a Iron age sites in the vale of Pickering. [1: Account of the excavation, by Mary K. Clark. 2: Note on deposits exposed at Costa Beck, by Professor Gilligan. 3: The pottery, by M. R. Hull. 4: Mammalian and avian remains from Costa lake dwellings, and from a lake dwelling, Thornton-le-dale, by Dorothea A. Bate]

b 'Customary' milestones, by J. J. Brigg.

c Samian ware from Ilkley, now in the Craven museum, Skipton, by A. Raistrick.

d Finds at Whitkirk church [inscribed grave covers], by G. E. Kirk.

e Roman Yorkshire, by J. P. Droop and M. K. Clark. [Accounts of miscellaneous discoveries in various localities. Contd. in vol. 31]

f Excavations at Knaresborough castle, 1925–8, by S. C. Barber.

g Some Yorkshire field names, by T. S. Gowland.

h William of Rymyngton, prior of Salley abbey, chancellor of Oxford, 1372–3, by J. McNulty.

i Prehistoric burials at Waddington and at Bradley, West Yorks., by A. Raistrick.

j The manor of Wetherby, and lands within the manor, by A. Brett.

k 'The ston bridg over Wharf' at Wetherby, by A. Brett.

l The earthworks [possibly Saxon] at Lofthouse, near Wakefield, by J. W. Walker.

m Notes on the origin of the Fitzalans of Bedale, by C. T. Clay.

n The Burghs of Cambridgeshire and Yorkshire and the Watertons of Lincolnshire and Yorkshire, by J. W. Walker.

6239 Vol. 31.

a A liturgical calendar from Guisborough priory, with some obits, by F. Wormald.

b Bronze age burial, Inglebank gravel pit, Boston Spa, by

Mary K. Clark. [With a report on the human remains, by A. J. E. Cave]

c Preliminary excavation of an earthwork at Easington, West Yorks., by A. Raistrick.

d Stephen of Eston, abbot of Salley, Newminster, and Fountains [d. 1252], by J. McNulty.

e Old parish surnames at Aldborough, by Sir T. Lawson-Tancred, bt.

f Recent discoveries at Ripon cathedral, by W. T. Jones.

g Yorkshire notes, by W. J. Kaye. [A Yorkshire marriage bond of 1522; A stray Barnsley note in an Essex ms., 1590; An ecclesiastical summary of the province and diocese of York in 1603]

h Editorial notes. [Includes: A bronze palstave from Arncliffe in Litton Dale]

i Origin of the family of Warenne, by L. C. Loyd.

j Some remarks on Knaresborough castle, by W. A. Atkinson.

k Iron age relics from East Yorkshire, by T. Sheppard.

l Early bronze measures [1670] from Selby, by T. Sheppard.

m The distribution of mesolithic sites in the north of England, by A. Raistrick.

n Clerical subsidies in the province of York, 1632, 1633 and 1634, by W. J. Kaye. [Transcripts]

o A Roman settlement at Wetherby, by B. J. W. Kent and Mary Kitson Clark.

p The foundation of Warter priory [12th cent.], by N. Denholm-Young.

q Roman remains and roads in West Yorkshire, by A. Raistrick.

r The parliamentary surveys for the North Riding of Yorkshire [subsequent to 'An Act for sale of the Honors, Manors, lands heretofore belonging to the late King, Queen and Prince', 1649], by T. S. Willan.

s The Yorkshire portion of the Lewes chartulary, by C. T. Clay. [Transcript]

t Some invasions of Yorkshire [by the Parisii, the Romans, and the English], by Mary Kitson Clark.

u The Anlaby chartulary [belonging to the Anlaby family, of Neswick Hall, Bainton, and its descendants], by M. R. James.

v The Yorkshire [republican] plot, 1663, by J. Walker.

w Yorkshire men who declined to take up their knighthood, 1 Ric. II (1377) and 16 and 19 Hen. VII (1500 and 1503), by W. J. Kaye.

x The Roman villa at Rudston, E. Yorks., interim excavation: report, by A. M. Woodward.

y The Yorkshire estates of Isabella de Fortibus [d. 1293], by N. Denholm-Young.

Record series, vols. 29–87:[1]

6240 Vols. 29, 36, 57, 78. Court rolls of the manor of Wakefield, vols. i–iv. 1901–30. [Vol. i: 1274–97. Vol. ii: 1297–1309. Vol. iii: 1313–16 and 1286. Vol. iv: 1315–17. Vols. i–ii ed. W. Paley Baildon, vols. iii–iv ed. J. Lister. Contd. for 1322–31 in vol. 109, published in 1945. There is a separate subject index to vol. iv, comp. A. T. Longbotham]

6241 Vol. 30. The chartulary of [the priory of] St. John of Pontefract, ed. R. Holmes. Vol. ii. 1902. [Vol. i was published in 1899]

6242 Vols. 31, 37. Yorkshire inquisitions, ed. W. Brown. Vols. iii–iv. 1902–6. [Vol. iii: 1245, 1282, 1294–1303. Vol. iv: 1300–7. Vols. i–ii, beginning 1241, were published in 1892–8]

[1] Vol. 113, published in 1948, is a catalogue of the record series, 1885–1946, with an introductory chapter on its history, comp. C. T. Clay.

6243 Vols. 32, 35. Index of wills in the York registry. 1902–5. [Vol. 32: Wills, 1620–27. Vol. 35: Wills, 1627–36; administrations, 1627–52. Other vols. covering the period from 1389 were published in 1888–1900. For later wills see no. 6254 below]

6244 Vol. 33. Early Yorkshire schools, by A. F. Leach. Vol. ii: Pontefract, Howden, Northallerton, Acaster, Rotherham, Giggleswick, Sedbergh. 1903. [Vol. i: York, Beverley, Ripon, was published in 1899]

6245 Vol. 34. Yorkshire church notes, 1619–1631, by Roger Dodsworth, ed. J. W. Clay. 1904.

6246 Vol. 38. Index of wills, etc., from the dean and chapter's court at York, 1321–1636; with appendix of original wills, 1524–1724. 1907.

6247 Vols. 39, 50, 63, 65, 69, 76, 83. Yorkshire deeds, vols. i–vii. 1909–32. [12th–17th cent. Vols. i–iii ed. W. Brown. Vols. iv–vii ed. C. T. Clay. Vols. viii–x were published in 1940–55]

6248 Vols. 40, 43, 46. Paver's marriage licences, ed. J. W. Clay. 3 vols. 1909–12. [Extracts from William Paver's transcripts of licences formerly in the registry at York. Vol. i: 1630–44. Vol. ii: 1660–74. Vol. iii: 1674–1714. For earlier licences see *Journal*, vol. 16, no. 6224 above]

6249 Vols. 41, 45, 51, 70. Yorkshire star chamber proceedings. 4 vols. 1909–27. [Vol. i: 1485–1549, ed. W. Brown. Vol. ii: Henry VIII, ed. H. B. McCall. Vol. iii: Mainly Henry VIII, with earlier and later cases, ed. W. Brown. Vol. iv: Henry VIII, ed. J. Lister]

6250 Vols. 42, 52, 62, 67, 82. Feet of fines for the county of York. 1910–32. [Vol. 42: 1327–47, and vol. 52: 1347–77, ed. W. P. Baildon. Vol. 62: 1218–31, vol. 67: 1232–46, vol. 82: 1246–72, ed. J. Parker. Vols. covering the Tudor period were published in 1887–90]

6251 Vol. 44. Three Yorkshire assize rolls for the reigns of King John and King Henry III, ed. C. T. Clay. 1911.

6252 Vol. 47. Selby wills, ed. F. Collins. 1912. [1634–1710, with marriage bonds and licences, 1664–1726]

6253 Vol. 48. Yorkshire monasteries. Suppression papers, ed. J. W. Clay. 1912.

6254 Vols. 49, 60, 68. Index of wills, administrations, and probate acts, in the York registry. 1913–26. [Ed. E. W. Crossley. Vol. 49: 1660–65, with unregistered wills and probate acts, 1633–4, 're infecta' wills, and the wills in bundles A and B. Vol. 60: 1666–72, with wills, etc., in certain peculiars. Vol. 68: 1673–80, with wills etc., in the peculiar of Beeford, 1586–1768. Contd. in vol. 89, published 1934]

6255 Vols. 53, 58. Yorkshire fines for the Stuart period, ed. W. Brigg. 2 vols. 1915–17. [Vol. i: 1603–14. Vol. ii: 1614–25]

6256 Vol. 54. West Riding sessions records, ed. J. Lister. Vol. ii: Orders, 1611–42; indictments, 1637–42. 1915. [Vol. i: sessions rolls, 1597/8–1602, etc., was published in 1888]

6257 Vol. 55. Genealogical history of the family of the late Bishop William Stubbs compiled by himself, ed. F. Collins. 1915.

6258 Vol. 56. The Pudsay deeds: the Pudsays of Bolton and Barforth and their predecessors in those manors, ed. R. P. Littledale. 1916.

6259 Vol. 59. Inquisitions post mortem relating to Yorkshire, of the reigns of Henry IV and Henry V, ed. W. P. Baildon and J. W. Clay. 1918.

6260 Vol. 61. Miscellanea, vol. i. 1920.
　a The preceptory of Newland, ed. E. W. Crossley. [Ministers' accounts, 1539–40; charters; inventories of evidences relating to lands given to the Hospitallers; rentals, and other docs.]
　b Compositions [in Yorkshire] for not taking knighthood at the coronation of Charles I, by W. P. Baildon.
　c A 15th cent. rental of Nostell priory, by W. T. Lancaster.
　d A list of benefices in the diocese of York vacant between 1316 and 1319, by W. Brown.
　e Subscriptions by recusants, 1632–39, by W. Brown.
　f Royalist clergy in Yorkshire, 1642–5, by W. Brown.
　g Presentations to livings in Yorkshire during the Commonwealth, by W. Brown.
　h Extracts from a Yorkshire assize roll, 3 Hen. III, 1219, by W. T. Lancaster.

6261 Vol. 64. The early Yorkshire woollen trade. Extracts from the Hull customs' rolls [1304–1471], transcripts of the ulnagers' rolls [1378–1478], ed. J. Lister. 1924.

6262 Vol. 66. Abstracts of the chartularies of the priory of Monkbretton, ed. J. W. Walker. 1924.

6263 Vols. 71, 72, 75, 77, 79. Archbishop Herring's visitation returns, 1743, ed. S. L. Ollard and P. C. Walker. 5 vols. 1928–31.

6264 Vol. 73. Index of the original documents of the consistory court of York, 1427–1658, and also of the probate and administration acts in the court of the dean of York, 1604–1722, ed. E. W. Crossley. 1928.

6265 Vol. 74. Miscellanea, vol. ii. 1929.
　a Index to the parish register transcripts preserved in the diocesan registry, York, by A. V. Hudson and J. W. Walker.
　b The burges court, Wakefield, 1533, 1554, 1556 and 1579 [transcripts of court rolls], by J. W. Walker.
　c Aldburgh with Boroughbridge. Liberty and soc of Aldburgh near Boroughbridge, 6 Eliz. 1563 [records of the sheriff's turn], by Sir T. Lawson-Tancred, bt., and J. W. Walker.
　d Extracts from the court rolls of the manor of Aldborough, 12–13 Edw. III, 1338–9, by Sir T. Lawson-Tancred, bt., and J. W. Walker.
　e Mills of Boroughbridge [the account of Richard Kildale, supervisor of the mills, *temp.* Hen. VI], by Sir T. Lawson-Tancred, bt., and J. W. Walker.
　f The testamentary documents of Yorkshire peculiars [i.e. the manorial peculiars of Westerdale, 1550–75, and Batley, 1651–94, with list of other known wills and grants in each], by E. W. Crossley.
　g Burton Agnes [book of penalties agreed upon by the jury of the court of Burton Agnes, 1632, transcribed] by C. V. Collier.
　h Reighton manor [book of penalties agreed upon by the jury at the court baron of Reighton manor, 1726, transcribed] by C. V. Collier.
　i Lay subsidy rolls 1 Edw. III [including transcripts for the North Riding and city of York], by J. W. R. Parker.

6266 Vol. 80. Miscellanea, vol. iii. 1931.
　a A selection of monastic rentals and dissolution papers [relating mainly to Bridlington priory and town, and a collection of suppression papers relating to other houses], ed. J. S. Purvis.
　b The chartulary of Tockwith *alias* Scokirk, a cell to the priory of Nostell, ed. Gwenllian C. Ransome.

6267 Vol. 81. Notes on the religious and secular houses of Yorkshire, extracted from the public records by W. P. Baildon. Vol. ii. 1931. [Vol. i was published in 1895]

6268 Vol. 84. Beverley borough records, 1575–1821, ed. J. Dennett. 1933.

6269 Vol. 85. Fasti parochiales, ed. A. Hamilton Thompson and C. T. Clay. Vol. i, being notes on the advowsons and pre-Reformation incumbents of the parishes in the deanery of Doncaster, pt. i. 1933. [Concluded in vol. 107, published 1943]

6270 Vol. 86. A descriptive list of the printed maps of Yorkshire and its ridings, 1577–1900, ed. H. Whitaker. 1933.

6271 Vol. 87. The chartulary of the Cistercian abbey of St. Mary of Sallay in Craven, transcribed and ed. J. McNulty. Vol. i. 1933. [Concluded in vol. 90, published in 1934]

Extra series, vols. 2–5:

6272 Vol. 2. A consolidated index to Paver's marriage licences, 1567–1630, printed in the *Yorkshire Archaeological Journal*. 1912.

6273 Vols. 3, 4. Yorkshire church plate. Begun by T. M. Fallow, completed and ed. H. B. McCall. 2 vols. 1912–15. [Vol. i: City of York and North and East Ridings. Vol. ii: West Riding]

6274 Vol. 5. Historical and architectural description of the priory of St. Mary Magdalene of Monk Bretton, by J. W. Walker. 1926.

Earthworks committee:

6275 Schedule of ancient defensive earthworks in the county of York, as marked on the ordnance survey (excluding Wold dykes or entrenchments) arranged numerically. *P.* folio, 1908.

Roman Antiquities committee, Roman Malton and district, Reports 1–4 and 6:

6276 No. 1. The Roman pottery at Crambeck, Castle Howard, by P. Corder. *P.* 1928.

6277 No. 2. The defences of the Roman fort at Malton, by P. Corder, with contributions by H. Mattingly and M. R. Hull. [n.d.]

6278 No. 3. The Roman pottery at Throlam, Holme-on-Spalding Moor, by P. Corder, with introd. by T. Sheppard. *P.* 1930.

6279 No. 4. A Roman villa at Langton, near Malton, by P. Corder and J. L. Kirk, with contributions by K. B. Blackburn, J. A. Dell, Elisabeth Kitson and H. Mattingly. 1932.

6280 No. 6. The Roman pavements at Rudston, East Riding: a brief description, by I. A. Richmond. *P.* 1933.

Other publications:

6281 Index of the papers contained in vols. 1–17 of the Journal and of the Excursions, 1867–1903, comp. W. F. Lawton. [1904. The Society also published an 'Analytical index of the contents of the first thirty volumes of the Society's Journal', by H. Lawrance, *P.* 1939]

6282 Catalogue of manuscripts in the library of the Yorkshire Archaeological Society, 1912, comp. W. T. Lancaster. 1912.

6283 Churchyard inscriptions [in Yorkshire. A revised list showing when and by whom transcripts were made]. *P.* 1913.

YORKSHIRE ARCHITECTURAL AND YORK ARCHAEOLOGICAL SOCIETY

Founded 1842, as the Yorkshire Architectural Society, to promote the study of ecclesiastical architecture and of antiquities generally; to do all in its power to preserve for posterity the remains of ancient York; and to prevent the disfigurement of the city. Title changed to the above form in 1901.

Proceedings:

6284 Vol. 1 (1933–5).

a The Roman bath discovered in 1930–1 during the reconstruction of the Mail Coach Inn, St. Sampson's Square, York, by P. Corder.

b Notes on some Ainsty churches, by W. H. Dixon. [Bilton, Acaster Malbys, Askham Bryan, Askham Richard, Marston, Acomb, Acaster Selby and Healaugh]

c The birth-place of Guy Fawkes, by A. Raine. [Transcript of an indenture, 1579, between the dean and chapter of York and Edith Fawkes, widow, relating to the lease of a tenement in Stonegate, York]

d Additional notes on the St. William window in York minster, by J. A. Knowles. Pt. I. [Some corrections to the article by J. Fowler in the *Yorkshire Archaeological Journal*, vol. 3, 1875]

e The story of the King's Manor, York, by R. J. A. Bunnett.

f Some notes on the royal monument [possibly of Prince Edward, d. 1484, son of Richard III] in the north chapel of Sheriff Hutton church, by T. B. L. Churchill.

g [Extracts] from an old York chronicle [1578–1709], ed. A. Raine.

YORKSHIRE DIALECT SOCIETY

Founded 1897, to encourage the production of Yorkshire dialect literature; to unite those interested in dialect study, and to assert the value of dialect speech; to investigate the phonology, grammar, vocabulary, and idioms of the Yorkshire dialects; to make records, by means of the phonograph or otherwise, of Yorkshire dialect speech.

Transactions, vols. 1–5 (1898–1936):

6285 Vol. 1.

a The Danish element in the northern folk speech, by C. A. Federer.

b On the word 'Osmond' [meaning iron of high quality], by E. Peacock.

c Anglo-Saxon as an aid to the study of dialects, by T. Clarke.

d Yorkshire dialect as spoken in the West Riding during the 15th and 19th cent., illustrated from the Towneley mysteries and modern dialect literature, by J. H. Green.

e Some place names in the parish of Halifax considered in relation to surrounding natural features, by C. Crossland.

f The Yorkshire dialect and its place in English literature, by J. H. Green.

g Dialect notes from northernmost England [i.e. Northumberland], by R. O. Heslop.

h The Wakefield miracle plays, by F. W. Moorman.

i Ancient Danish 'Mensnames' in Yorkshire, by E. M. Cole.

j Some considerations relating to the study of Old English poetry, by T. G. Foster.

6286 Vol. 2.

a Some features of interest in the phonology of the north, midland and west-northern dialects, by T. O. Hirst.

b The treasures of dialect, with illustrations from the folk-speech of the woldsman, by M. C. F. Morris.

c Some considerations relating to the study of Old English poetry, by T. G. Foster.

d Place names and dialect study, by H. Alexander.

e Appendix to report [being extracts from a work on Yorkshire dialect, *The Praise of Yorkshire Ale*, etc. by George Meriton, 1685], by F. W. Moorman.

f Historical notes on the Sheffield dialect, by J. D. Jones.

6287 Vol. 3.

a Richard Rolle [d. 1349], the Yorkshire mystic, by F. W. Moorman.

b The Scandinavian element in Yorkshire place-names, by A. Goodall.

c William Barnes [d. 1886], the Dorset poet, by A. C. Coffin. [Appendix: The published works of William Barnes]

d The bibliography of Yorkshire dialect literature, by F. J. Taylor.

6288 Vol. 4.

a Two essays on the dialect of Upper Calderdale, by F. H. Marsden. [1: The folk-lore of Calderdale. 2: Notes on the grammar and phonology of the dialect]

b The dialect of North Somerset, by F. C. Perry.

c 'The felon sewe of Rokeby' [a Yorkshire ballad], by G. H. Cowling.

d The rhyming charter of Beverley [c. 1330–31], generally called 'Carta regis Adelstani ecclesiae sancti Johannis Beverlaci', by J. R. Witty.

e The Beverley plays, by J. R. Witty.

f Scandinavian influence in Yorkshire dialects, by E. V. Gordon.

g The Holderness dialect in 1392, by J. R. Witty.

h River names of Yorkshire, by E. V. Gordon and A. H. Smith.

i Bairnsla's best, wi' a bit abaght t'others, by E. G. Bayford. [An account of some Barnsley dialect writers]

j A glimpse of the West Riding dialect of Shakespeare's day, by W. J. Halliday.

k Place-names of North Yorkshire, by A. H. Smith.

l A new glossary of the dialect of Huddersfield district, by W. E. Haigh.

m Notes on the Goathland folk play, by F. W. Dowson.

n A chat about Holderness and the East Riding, by T. C. Jackson.

o Some dialect poets of Cumberland, by F. Warriner.

p Sheep and sheep-scoring, by J. R. Witty.

6289 Vol. 5.

a The dialects of Northumberland, by H. Orton.

b Celtic survivals in the Haworth district, by H. I. Judson.

c Dialect almanacks and dialect writers [of Yorkshire]: a report of two lectures by B. Turner and W. Hampson.

d The Sheffield cutler and his dialect, by B. R. Dyson.

e Two mining account books from Farnley colliery, 1690–1720, by R. Offor.

f A Yorkshire chronicler (William of Newburgh), by B. Dickins.

g Folk-lore of the Plough Stots [teams of mummers and sword dancers], by F. W. Dowson.

Other publications:

6290 Yorkshire dialect poems (1673–1915) and traditional poems, comp. with an historical introd. by F. W. Moorman. 1916.

YORKSHIRE GEOLOGICAL SOCIETY

Founded 1837, as the Geological Society of the West Riding of Yorkshire, to promote and record the results of research in geology and its allied sciences, more especially in Yorkshire. The name was changed to the Geological and Polytechnic Society of the West Riding of Yorkshire in 1838. The above title was adopted in 1905.

Proceedings, vols. 14–22 ([1901]–34):

6291 Vol. 14.

a Notes on the history of the Driffield museum of antiquities and geological specimens, by J. R. Mortimer.

6292 Vol. 15.

a Classified index of the *Proceedings*, vols. 1–14 (1839–1902), by W. L. Carter. [Vol. 26, issued in 1948, is an index to vols. 1–26 (1837–1946), comp. W. Anderson]

6293 Vol. 16.

a Roman remains at Filey, by E. M. Cole.

6294 Vol. 19.

a William Smith [d. 1839]: his maps and memoirs, by T. Sheppard.

b Martin Simpson [d. 1892] and his geological memoirs, by T. Sheppard.

6295 Vol. 22.

a John Phillips [d. 1874, geologist], by T. Sheppard.

YORKSHIRE NATURALISTS' UNION

Founded 1861, as the West Riding Consolidated Naturalists' Society, for the effectual advancement of local natural science. Title changed to the above form in 1877.

The Naturalist, 1901–33 (33 vols.):

6296 Vol. for 1903.

a Notes on some pre-historic jet ornaments from East Yorkshire, by J. R. Mortimer.

b Hull's contribution to science, by T. Sheppard.

6297 Vol. for 1904.

a Neolithic remains in south Durham, by C. T. Trechmann.

6298 Vol. for 1905.

a Pre-historic remains in East Yorkshire.

b Notes on British remains found near the Cawthorne camps, Yorks., by J. R. Mortimer.

c Neolithic remains on the Durham coast, by C. T. Trechmann.

6299 Vol. for 1906.

a Notes on Yorkshire botany in 1727, by H. E. Wroot.

6300 Vol. for 1908.

a Prehistoric remains from Lincolnshire, by T. Sheppard.

b Note on a British burial at Middleton-on-the-Wolds, by J. R. Mortimer.

6301 Vol. for 1909.

a Two ancient burial cairns on Brimham moor, Yorks., by A. L. Armstrong.

6302 Vol. for 1910.

a Neolithic workshops near Bridlington, by T. Sheppard.

6303 Vol. for 1911.

a The evolution of the millstone, by J. R. Mortimer.

b A century's changes in the Sheffield district flora, by C. F. Innocent.

c Notes on the stature, etc., of our ancestors in East Yorkshire, by J. R. Mortimer.

6304 Vol. for 1912.

a Early microscopes [18th cent.], by T. Sheppard.

6305 Vol. for 1914.

a Early history of Filey, by T. Sheppard.
b Yorkshire natural history 200 years ago, by T. Sheppard.

6306 Vol. for 1915.

a Yorkshire's contribution to science, by T. Sheppard.
b A Yorkshire dene hole [near Cottingham, E. Yorks.], by T. Sheppard.

6307 Vol. for 1917.

a Hoard of axes, etc., of the bronze age, from Scarborough, by T. Sheppard.
b Some weapons of the bronze age, recently found in East Yorkshire, by T. Sheppard.
c Old natural history magazines, etc., by T. Sheppard.

6308 Vol. for 1918.

a A Yorkshire rector of the 18th century [John Michell, d. 1793], by Sir A. Geikie.
b Implements of the bronze age in the Whitby museum, by T. Sheppard.
c Neolithic settlement near Scunthorpe, Lincs., by H. E. Dudley.
d Bronze-age weapons in the Doncaster museum, by T. Sheppard.

6309 Vol. for 1919.

a Old scientific magazines, by T. Sheppard.
b The witchery of Gilbert White, by E. A. Woodruffe-Peacock.

6310 Vol. for 1920.

a Neolithic flint implement from Doncaster, by H. H. Corbett.
b Prehistoric implements of bone and flint from Bradfield, S. Yorks., by A. L. Armstrong.

6311 Vol. for 1921.

a Two East Yorkshire bronze axes, by T. Sheppard.
b Bronze age weapons in the Scarborough museum, by T. Sheppard.

6312 Vol. for 1922.

a The Fothergill family as ornithologists [William, d. 1837, Charles, d. 1841, and John, d. 1858], by H. S. Gladstone.
b Hoard of bronze axes from Windsor, by T. Sheppard.

6313 Vol. for 1923.

a Sheep and early man in Britain, by H. E. Forrest.
b Bronze-age mould for casting palstaves, by T. Sheppard.
c Bronze-age weapons [in Hull museum], by T. Sheppard.
d The Maglemose harpoons, by T. Sheppard.
e Prehistoric Bridlington, by T. Sheppard.

6314 Vol. for 1924.

a Remains of early man, by T. Sheppard.

6315 Vol. for 1925.

a A bronze-age earthenware vessel, by T. Sheppard.

6316 Vol. for 1926.

a The water vole in relation to prehistoric man, by F. J. Stubbs.
b Hoard of neolithic axes in East Yorks., by T. Sheppard.

6317 Vol. for 1927.

a Sixty-five years of Yorkshire geology, by E. Hawkesworth.

b Pre-historic gold ornaments found at Cottingham, E. Yorks., by T. Sheppard.
c Lead-mining and smelting in W. Yorks., by A. Raistrick.

6318 Vol. for 1928.

a Coal and iron working in the millstone grit and Yoredale rocks of W. Yorks., by A. Raistrick.
b Bronze age and other pottery from Lincolnshire, etc., by T. Sheppard.

6319 Vol. for 1929.

a British domestic sheep, by H. B. Booth.
b The mining industry in the Huddersfield district, by D. A. Wray.
c Bronze-age beaker from Brough, E. Yorks., by T. Sheppard.

6320 Vol. for 1930.

a The Pennines in history, by H. E. Wroot.
b Palaeolithic man in Yorkshire, by T. Sheppard.
c Clay moulds for bronze age implements, by T. Sheppard.
d Jet ornaments of the bronze age, by T. Sheppard.

6321 Vol. for 1931.

a Shale armlet found near Blackstone Edge, by J. W. Jackson.

6322 Vol. for 1932.

a A cave on Giggleswick Scars, near Settle [containing Romano-British remains], by J. W. Jackson and W. K. Mattinson.
b Relics of the bronze age, by T. Sheppard.

6323 Vol. for 1933.

a Tardenoisian sites on Oxenhope moor, by T. Deans.

YORKSHIRE NUMISMATIC SOCIETY

Founded 1909, as the Yorkshire Numismatic Fellowship, for the study of numismatics, and particularly coins, tokens, medals, etc., relating to Yorkshire. Title changed to the above form in 1913.

Transactions, vols. 1–3, pt. 2 (1910–29):

6324 Vol. 1.

a 19th cent. Hull tokens, by W. Sykes.
b Regal coins struck at York, by T. Pickersgill.
c Yorkshire 17th cent. tokens not in Williamson's 'Boyne', by T. Sheppard.
d Yorkshire tradesmen's tokens of the 17th cent., by T. Sheppard.
e Find of Roman coins in and near Leeds.
f Treasure trove found in Sheffield [chiefly coins of the reigns of Hen. VIII, Edw. VI, Eliz. I, and James I], by E. Howarth.
g Coins in the York museum, by G. Benson.
h Five unpublished 17th cent. tokens of Yorkshire, by T. Sheppard.

6325 Vol. 1. Supplements[1]:

a Hull and East Yorkshire tradesmen's tokens, by W. Sykes.
b List of the 17th cent. tokens of Lincolnshire in the Hull museum, with descriptions of hitherto unpublished tokens and varieties, by T. Sheppard.
c Roman bronze coins found at South Ferriby, Lincs., by T. Pickersgill.

6326 Vol. 2.

a Medals, tokens, etc. issued in connection with William Wilberforce and the abolition of slavery, by T. Sheppard.

[1] Not seen.

b The circulated copper and bronze pence of Queen Victoria, 1837–1901, by J. F. Musham.
c Discovery of a small hoard of Lincolnshire 17th cent. tokens, with an addition to the list, by T. Sheppard.
d Evolution of shipping as illustrated on coins and tokens, by T. Sheppard.
e Yorkshire and Lincolnshire 17th cent. tokens, by T. Sheppard.
f List of Yorkshire medals in the municipal museum at Hull, by T. Sheppard.
g Coins as media for workmen's marks, by J. F. Musham.
h Money scales and weights, by T. Sheppard.
i Catalogue of love tokens and other engraved pieces in the Hull museum, by T. Sheppard.
j Agriculture and its effect on the distribution of recent coins by J. F. Musham.
k Hop growers' tokens, by J. D. Firth.
l Yorkshire tramway tokens and counters, by T. Sheppard.
m Yorkshire 17th cent. tokens: additions to collection, by T. Sheppard.
n Supplemental check-list of the imperial copper and bronze pence of Queen Victoria, by J. F. Musham.
o English regal coins struck at York, by T. Pickersgill.
p Money scales and weights, by J. F. Musham.
q Hoard of silver coins found at Scotton [chiefly *temp.* Edward I and II], by T. Sheppard.
r Commerce and transport numismatics, by T. Sheppard.
s York pennies of Henry III, by T. Sheppard.

6327 Vol. 3, pts. 1–2.
a Yorkshire silver tokens, by T. Sheppard.
b The fauna illustrated on Roman coins, by F. Heeley.
c Archery medals and memoranda.

YORKSHIRE PARISH REGISTER SOCIETY

Founded 1899, to transcribe and print the parish registers in the county of York, and such bishops' transcripts as may be accessible.

Publications, vols. 1–95:

6328 Vols. 1, 11. Registers of St. Michael le Belfrey, York, transcribed and ed. F. Collins. 2 vols. 1899–1901. [Pt. i: 1565–1653. Pt. ii: marriages, 1653–1772; baptisms and burials, 1653–1778]

6329 Vol. 2. Registers of Burton Fleming, otherwise North Burton, 1538–1812, ed. G. E. Park and G. D. Lumb. 1899.

6330 Vol. 3. Registers of the chapel of Horbury in the parish of Wakefield, 1598–1812, ed. J. Charlesworth. 1900.

6331 Vol. 4. Registers of Winestead, in Holderness, 1578–1812, transcribed and ed. N. J. Miller. 1900.

6332 Vols. 5, 18. Registers of Linton-in-Craven, ed. F. A. C. Share. 1 vol. in 2. 1900–3. [Vol. i: 1562–1779. Vol. ii: 1779–1812]

6333 Vol. 6. Registers of Patrington, 1570–1731, ed. H. E. Maddock. 1900.

6334 Vol. 7. Registers of Stokesley, 1571–1750, transcribed and ed. J. Hawell. 1901.

6335 Vol. 8. Registers of Blacktoft, East Yorks., 1700–1812, transcribed and ed. G. E. Weddall; registers of Scorborough [1653–1800], transcribed and ed. A. T. Winn. 1901.

6336 Vol. 9. Parish register of Bingley, 1577–1686, ed. W. J. Stavert. 1901.

6337 Vol. 10. Registers of Kippax, 1539–1812, ed. G. D. Lumb. 1901.

6338 Vol. 12. Registers of Brantingham, East Yorks., 1653–1812, transcribed and ed. G. E. Weddall. 1902.

6339 Vol. 13. Registers of Hampsthwaite: marriages, 1603–1807; baptisms, burials, 1603–1794, transcribed and ed. F. Collins. 1902.

6340 Vol. 14. Registers of Wath-upon-Dearne: baptisms and burials, 1598–1778; marriages, 1598–1779, transcribed and ed. J. W. Clay. 1902.

6341 Vol. 15. Registers of Cherry Burton, 1561–1740, transcribed and ed. A. T. Winn. 1903.

6342 Vol. 16. Registers of Marske in Cleveland: baptisms, marriages, 1570–1812; burials, 1569–1812, transcribed, indexed, and ed. H. M. Wood. 1903.

6343 Vol. 17. Register of Hartshead, 1612–1812, transcribed and ed. Edith B. Armytage. 1903.

6344 Vols. 19, 22. Register of Bolton-by-Bolland, ed. W. J. Stavert. 1 vol. in 2. 1904–5. [Vol. i: 1558–1724. Vol. ii: 1725–1812]

6345 Vol. 20. Registers of Pickhill-cum-Roxby: marriages, 1567–1812; baptisms, 1571–1812; burials, 1576–1812, transcribed, indexed and ed. A. W. Howard; revised by F. Collins. 1904.

6346 Vols. 21, 24, 32, 48. Registers of Howden, transcribed and ed. G. E. Weddall. 3 vols. in 4. 1904–13. [Vol. i: 1543–1659. Vol. ii, pts. 1 and 2: 1543–1725. Vol. iii: 1725–70]

6347 Vol. 23. Registers of Grinton in Swaledale, transcribed by F. W. Slingsby. 1905. [Baptisms and burials, 1640–1807; marriages, 1640–1802]

6348 Vol. 25. Register of Hackness, 1557–1783, transcribed by C. Johnstone and Emily J. Hart. 1906.

6349 Vol. 26. Registers of Ledsham, 1539–1812, ed. J. W. Clay. 1906.

6350 Vols. 27, 34, 51. Registers of Rothwell, ed. G. D. Lumb. 1 vol. in 3. 1906–14. [Pt. 1: 1538–1689; pt. 2: baptisms and burials, 1690–1763, marriages, 1690–1812; pt. 3: 1763–1812, index]

6351 Vol. 28. Register of Gargrave, 1558–1812, ed. W. J. Stavert. 1907.

6352 Vol. 29. Registers of Terrington: christenings, 1600–1812; marriages and burials, 1599–1812, transcribed and indexed by W. Brigg. 1907.

6353 Vols. 30, 40, 53. Register of Thornhill, ed. J. Charlesworth. 1 vol. in 3. 1907–15. [Pt. 1: baptisms, 1580–1742, marriages, 1580–1745, burials, 1580–1678; pt. 2: baptisms, 1743–1812, marriages, 1746–53, burials, 1678–1812, Flockton baptisms, marriages and burials, 1713–1812; pt. 3: marriages, 1754–1812, banns, 1788–1812, Flockton baptisms and burials, 1717–1812]

6354 Vol. 31. Registers of Allerton Mauleverer [marriages, 1557–1812; baptisms, 1562–1812; burials, 1564–1812]; registers of Askham Richard in the Ainsty of York, 1579–1812, transcribed and ed. F. W. Slingsby. 1908.

6355 Vols. 33, 44. Registers of Otley, transcribed and indexed by W. Brigg. 2 vols. 1909–12. [Pt. i: 1562–1672; pt. ii: baptisms, 1672–1753, marriages, 1672–1750, burials, 1672–1751/2]

6356 Vol. 35. Registers of Kirklington, 1568–1812, transcribed by H. B. McCall. 1909.

6357 Vol. 36. Registers of St. Martin, Coney Street, York, 1557–1812, transcribed and ed. R. B. Cook. 1909.

6358 Vols. 37, 45. Registers of Halifax, 1538–93, transcribed and indexed E. W. Crossley. 2 vols. 1910–14. [Vol. i: baptisms. Vol. ii: marriages and burials]

6359 Vol. 38. Register of Settrington, 1559–1812, transcribed and ed. F. Collins. 1910.

6360 Vol. 39. Registers of the chapel of Austerfield, in the parish of Blyth, 1559–1812, transcribed and ed. G. D. Lumb; registers of Cowthorpe [marriages, 1568–1812; christenings and burials, 1568–1797], transcribed F. W. Slingsby. 1910.

6361 Vol. 41. Registers of Holy Trinity church, Goodramgate, York, 1573–1812, transcribed and ed. R. B. Cook. 1911.

6362 Vol. 42. Register of Thirsk in the North Riding, 1556–1721, transcribed and ed. J. Parker. 1911.

6363 Vol. 43. Registers of Danby-in-Cleveland, 1585–1812, ed. and indexed by F. Collins, transcribed by J. B. Walker and F. Collins. 1912.

6364 Vol. 46. Register of Garforth, 1631–1812, transcribed by G. D. Lumb. 1913.

6365 Vols. 47, 55, 69, 92. Registers of St. Andrew's, Kildwick-in-Craven. 4 vols. 1913–32. [Vol. i: 1575–1622, and vol. ii: 1623–78, ed. W. A. Brigg. Vol. iii: 1678–1743, and vol. iv: baptisms, 1744–89; marriages, 1744–54; burials, 1744–71, ed. R. G. C. Livett]

6366 Vol. 49. Register of Darrington, 1567–1812, transcribed and ed. G. D. Lumb. 1913.

6367 Vol. 50. Registers of Harewood, pt. i: baptisms, 1614–1812, marriages, 1621–1812, transcribed and ed. W. Brigg. 1914.

6368 Vol. 52. Register of St. Mary, Bishophill Junior, York, 1602–1812, transcribed B. W. Wood, ed. F. Collins. 1915.

6369 Vol. 54. Register of the chapelry of East Rounton in the parish of Rudby-in-Cleveland, 1595–1837, transcribed and ed. W. T. Robson; register of All Saints, Weston, near Otley, 1639–1812, transcribed, ed. and indexed by J. Singleton. 1916.

6370 Vol. 56. Register of All Saints, Easingwold, 1599–1812, transcribed and ed. G. D. Lumb. 1916.

6371 Vols. 57, 63. Registers of Snaith, transcribed and indexed W. Brigg. 2 vols. 1917–19. [Pt. i: baptisms, 1558–1657, marriages, 1537–1657. Pt. ii: burials, 1537–1656]

6372 Vols. 58, 60, 68, 74. Register of Sheffield, transcribed and ed. C. Drury and T. W. Hall; pt. ii indexed by T. W. Hall, pt. iv by S. E. Cochrane. 4 vols. 1917–24. [Pt. i: baptisms and marriages, 1560–1634/5. Pt. ii: burials, 1560–1634, baptisms, marriages, 1635–53. Pt. iii: burials, 1635–53, baptisms, marriages, 1653–86. Pt. iv: burials, 1653–86; baptisms, marriages, 1687–1703]

6373 Vol. 59. Register of Kirkleatham, 1559–1812, transcribed and indexed J. Charlesworth. 1917.

6374 Vol. 61. Registers of Kilburn, 1600–1812, transcribed and ed. G. D. Lumb. 1918.

6375 Vol. 62. Registers of Crofton, 1615–1812, transcribed and ed. W. Townend. 1918.

6376 Vols. 64, 72. Register of Mirfield. 2 vols. 1919–23. [Pt. i: 1559–1700, transcribed and indexed by W. Brigg. Pt. ii: baptisms and burials, 1700–76, marriages to 1754, transcribed by W. Brigg, ed. G. D. Lumb]

6377 Vol. 65. Register of Emley, 1600–1812, transcribed and ed. J. Charlesworth. 1920. [Vol. ii: 1813–36 issued privately, 1921]

6378 Vol. 66. Register of Addingham, 1612–1812, transcribed and ed. G. D. Lumb. 1920.

6379 Vol. 67. Register of Clapham, pt. i: 1595–1683, transcribed and indexed by J. Charlesworth. 1921.

6380 Vol. 70. Register of St. Crux, York, pt. i: 1539–1716, transcribed and ed. R. B. Cook and Mrs. F. Harrison. 1922.

6381 Vol. 71. Register of Wintringham, 1558–1812, transcribed and ed. A. J. Cholmley. 1922.

6382 Vol. 73. Register of St. Olave, York, pt. i: 1538–1644, transcribed and ed. Mrs. F. Harrison and W. J. Kaye. 1923.

6383 Vol. 75. Register of Kirby Hill, 1576–1812, transcribed and ed. A. B. Browne and J. Charlesworth. 1924.

6384 Vol. 76. Register of Eston, 1590–1812, transcribed, ed. and indexed by W. J. Kaye. 1924.

6385 Vols. 77, 82. Registers of St. Andrew's, Keighley, ed. W. A. Brigg. Vols. i–ii. 1925–7. [Vol. i: Apr. 1562–Sept. 1649. Vol. ii: Oct. 1649–Mar. 1688. Vol. iii issued as vol. 98 (1935): 1687–1736]

6386 Vol. 78. Registers of Heptonstall, vol. i: 1593–1660, ed. and indexed by Edith Horsfall. 1925.

6387 Vol. 79. Register of Hemsworth, 1654–1812, ed. J. Charlesworth. 1926.

6388 Vol. 80. Register of Ripon, pt. i: 1574–1628, transcribed and ed. W. J. Kaye. 1926.

6389 Vol. 81. Register of Maltby, 1597–1812, ed. C. E. Hughes. 1926.

6390 Vol. 83. Register of Ilkley, 1597–1812, transcribed and ed. W. Cooper. 1927.

6391 Vol. 84. Register of Whitby, pt. i: 1600–76, transcribed and ed. J. Charlesworth. 1928.

6392 Vol. 85. Register of Holy Trinity, King's Court (otherwise Christ Church), York [1631–1812], transcribed and ed. W. J. Kaye. 1928.

6393 Vol. 86. Register of Aughton, 1610–1812, transcribed and ed. J. Charlesworth. 1929.

6394 Vol. 87. Registers of Hooton Pagnell, 1538–1812, transcribed C. E. Whiting. 1929.

6395 Vol. 88. Registers of Waddington, 1599–1812, transcribed and ed. J. Parker. 1930.

6396 Vol. 89. Register of Thornton-in-Lonsdale, 1576–1812, transcribed and ed. W. H. Chippindall. 1931.

6397 Vol. 90. Register of Great Ayton, 1600–1812, transcribed, ed. and indexed by W. J. Kaye. 1931.

6398 Vol. 91. Register of Bentham, 1666–1812, transcribed and ed. W. H. Chippindall. 1932.

6399 Vol. 93. Register of Saxton-in-Elmet, 1538–1812, transcribed and ed. G. D. Lumb. 1932.

6400 Vol. 94. Registers of the churches of Ingleton and Chapel-le-Dale, 1607–1812, transcribed W. H. Chippindall. 1933.

6401 Vol. 95. Register of Frickley with Clayton, 1577–1812, transcribed C. E. Whiting. 1933.

YORKSHIRE PHILOSOPHICAL SOCIETY

Founded 1822, for the promotion of natural science and the study of archaeology and antiquities in the county of York and elsewhere.

Annual Report of the Council, 1900–32[1]
(33 vols. 1901–33):

6402 Vol. for 1900.

 a The Treasurer's house, York, by F. Green.
 b Report on excavations in the chancel of St. Mary's abbey church, by W. H. Brierley. [Contd. in Reports for 1901 and 1902]

6403 Vol. for 1901.

 a William Etty [d. 1849, painter], by Miss Moore.
 b Hospital of St. Peter, York, by G. Benson.

6404 Vol. for 1902.

 a Notes on excavations at 25, 26 and 27, High Ousegate, York, by G. Benson.
 b Notes on Clifford's tower, by G. Benson and H. M. Platnauer.

6405 Vol. for 1903.

 a The monks of Marmoutier [at York], by J. Solloway.

6406 Vol. for 1904.

 a The church and parish of St. Martin-cum-Gregory, by G. Benson.
 b Notes on an intrenchment on Holgate hill, York, by G. Benson.

6407 Vol. for 1906.

 a Historical account of the herbarium of the Yorkshire Philosophical Society and the contributors thereto, by H. J. Wilkinson.
 b Notes on an excavation at the corner of Castlegate and Coppergate, by G. Benson.

6408 Vol. for 1907.

 a Selby abbey and its builders, by E. R. Tate.
 b The King's Manor, York, by A. B. Norwood.

6409 Vol. for 1908.

 a Roman pottery in York museum, by T. May. [Contd. in Reports for 1909, 1910 and 1911]
 b A vanishing Yorkshire village [Kilnsea, E. Riding], by J. Backhouse.

6410 Vol. for 1909.

 a Excavations on the site of the N.W. gateway of Eboracum, by G. Benson.

6411 Vol. for 1910.

 a Description of the coins of Edward the Confessor in the collection of the Yorkshire Philosophical Society, by C. Wakefield.

6412 Vol. for 1911.

 a Notes on fire insurance marks, by C. K. Hitchcock.
 b The opening of a tumulus near Pickering, by J. L. Kirk.
 c Note on an inscribed Roman slab [to Lucius Baebius Crescens of Augusta Vindelicum, soldier of the 6th legion], by H. M. Platnauer.

6413 Vol. for 1912.

 a The charm of St. Mary's abbey and the architectural museum, York, by E. R. Tate.

[1] In the Report for 1925 and subsequent years, the papers form a separately paginated section entitled 'Proceedings'.

6414 Vol. for 1913.

 a Coins: especially those relating to York, by G. Benson.
 b Ancient painted glass windows in the minster and churches of the city of York, by G. Benson.

6415 Vol. for 1915.

 a Notes on a cobble-road uncovered under the vaulted archway of St. Leonard's hospital, York, by G. Benson.
 b Yorkshire potteries, pots and potters, by O. Grabham.

6416 Vol. for 1916.

 a Description of the coins of Aethelraed II and Cnut, in the collection of the Yorkshire Philosophical Society, by C. Wakefield.

6417 Vol. for 1917.

 a John Browne, 1793–1877, artist and the historian of York minster, by G. Benson.

6418 Vol. for 1918.

 a Later mediaeval York: the city and county of the city of York from 1100 to 1603, by G. Benson.

6419 Vol. for 1922.

 a Two new Roman memorial stones [discovered in York], by A. Raine.

6420 Vol. for 1923.

 a Yorkshire history in the light of its place-names, by A. Mawer.

6421 Vol. for 1924.

 a John Phillips [d. 1874], the first keeper of the Yorkshire museum, York, by W. E. Collinge.

6422 Vol. for 1925.

 a Some 17th and 18th cent. designs for stained glass windows recently presented to the Yorkshire museum, by J. A. Knowles.
 b Some York notes from the Dodsworth mss. in the Bodleian Library, Oxford, by A. Raine.
 c The York Roman excavations, 1925, by A. Raine.

6423 Vol. for 1926.

 a Two notes on the history of the drama in York in the reigns of Elizabeth and James I, by A. Raine.
 b The earliest extant treaty with an English kingdom [a treaty between Offa of Mercia and Charlemagne, 796], by J. S. Gayner.
 c Technical notes on the St. William window in York minster, by J. A. Knowles.
 d Excavations near the multangular tower, 1926, by A. Raine.

6424 Vol. for 1927.

 a Thomas Magnus [d. 1550], archdeacon of Thest Rydyng, by J. S. Gayner.
 b An Anglian glass vessel in the Yorkshire museum, by C. E. N. Bromehead.

6425 Vol. for 1928.

 a Yorkshire's contribution to the 'Ornithology' of 1678 [by Francis Willughby and John Ray], by J. S. Gayner.
 b The new Roman memorial stone: the sleeping soldier, by A. Raine.

6426 Vol. for 1929.

 a Thomas Allis, osteologist, 1788–1875, by S. Melmore.

Other publications:

6427 Catalogue of the Boynton collection of Yorkshire pottery, by A. Hurst[1]. 1922.

[1] Not seen.

ADDENDA

MERSEYSIDE ASSOCIATION FOR MASONIC RESEARCH

Founded 1922 to explore the history and antiquities of freemasonry and its symbolism.

Transactions, vols. 1–8 (1923–32):

6428 Vol. 1.
  a Origins of gilds and freemasonry [including freemasonry in England], by H. G. Rosedale.
  b The growth of modern ritual [from the 16th cent. onwards], by J. W. Hobbs.
  c 'Masonic old charges', by R. H. Baxter. [Includes appendices listing and classifying old charges]

6429 Vol. 2.
  a Our mediaeval brethren, by J. W. Hobbs. [A similar article by the same occurs in *Trans.* vol. 3 (1923–6) of Somerset Masters' Lodge]
  b The story of the craft [in England], by L. Vibert.

6430 Vol. 3.
  a The origin and meaning of the letter 'G' in freemasonry, by J. T. Thorp.
  b Introduction to the Macnab ms. [an 18th cent. masonic charge], by H. Poole.
  c The 'Macnab ms.', 1722, transcribed by W. Watson.
  d Westminster abbey and its craftsmen, by J. W. Hobbs.
  e Visiting in lodges during the 18th cent., by G. W. Daynes. [A similar article by the same occurs in *Trans.* vol. 3 (1925–7) of Norfolk Installed Masters' Lodge]
  f The development of Gothic architecture in England, by T. T. Rees.

6431 Vol. 4.
  a Catterick [Yorks.] church contract, 1412 [a contract for the building of the church], by H. Poole.
  b The evolution of the second degree, by L. Vibert. [A similar article by the same occurs in *Trans.* vol. 3 (1925–1927) of Norfolk Installed Masters' Lodge]
  c The masonic poem of *c.* 1390: a modernised transcript and some notes, by R. H. Baxter. [Also occurs as **2900b** above]

6432 Vol. 5.
  a The craft in the 18th cent., by A. Heiron.
  b The growth of speculative or symbolical masonry [until 1717], by G. W. Daynes.
  c The old charges, with facsimile of the Dring-Gale ms. [18th cent.], by H. Poole.

6433 Vol. 6.
  a Some aspects of Bro. Wm. Preston's masonic activities, by G. P. G. Hills.
  b Rituals and literature: a general survey [since the 17th cent.], by C. P. Sayles.

6434 Vol. 7.
  a Origins of freemasonry, by T. Keeley. [Includes the origin in England]

6435 Vol. 8.
  a Masonry among prisoners-of-war [including English prisoners in France and French prisoners in England during the Napoleonic wars], by L. Vibert. [A similar article by the same occurs in *Trans.* vol. 4 (1927–30) of Somerset Masters' Lodge]
  b The origin of freemasonry in Britain, by K. E. Keith.
  c What they wore of yore [18th–19th cent. masonic costume], by W. L. Boyden.

ROYAL MEDICAL AND CHIRURGICAL SOCIETY

Founded 1805, for the purpose of conversation on professional subjects, for the reception of communications, and for the formation of a library. Amalgamated in 1907 with the Medical Society and other principal medical societies in London to form the Royal Society of Medicine (q.v.).

Medico-chirurgical Transactions, vols. 84–90 (1901–7):

6436 Vol. 90.
  a Dr. Walter Bayley and his works, 1529–92, by D'A. Power. [Includes a transcript of Bayley's will]

NATIONAL EISTEDDFOD ASSOCIATION

Other publications (*contd. from p. 258 above*):

6437 Hanes llenyddiaeth Gymreig, o 1651 hyd 1850, gan C. Ashton. [n.d. History of Welsh literature, 1651–1850]

6438 Religious developments in Wales, 1654–62, by T. Richards. 1923.

6439 Wales under the penal code, 1662–87, by T. Richards. 1925.

6440 Iolo Morganwg a chywddau'r yychwanegiad, gan G. J. Williams. 1926. [Iolo Morganwg and the additional odes. Preface by Sir J. Morris-Jones]

6441 Wales under the Indulgence, 1672–5, by T. Richards. 1928.

ASSOCIATED ARCHITECTURAL SOCIETIES

Reports and Papers:

6442 Vol. 31. (*See also no.* **153** *above*)
  a Description of the churches visited from Grantham, July, 1911. [Welby, St. Bartholomew; Haydor, St. Michael; Threekingham, St. Peter; Ropsley, St. Peter; Great Ponton, Holy Cross; Colsterworth, St. John Baptist; Burton Coggles, St. Thomas of Canterbury; Irnham, St. Andrew, with notes on Irnham manor; Ingoldsby, St. Bartholomew; and others]

6443 Vol. 32. (*See also no.* 154 *above*)

a Description of churches, etc., visited from Woodhall Spa, June, 1913. [Kirkstead chapel; Tattershall church; Coningsby, St. Michael; Scrivelsby Court; Haltham, St. Benedict; Bucknall, St. Margaret; Tupholme abbey; and others]

SOCIETY OF GLASS TECHNOLOGY

Founded 1916, *for the general advancement of the various branches of glass technology; the reading and discussion of papers; the publication of scientific information; the formation of a library and museum.*

Journal, vols. 1–17 (1917–33):

6444 Vol. 6.

a The British glass industry: its development and outlook, by W. E. S. Turner.

b The medieval glass of York minster, by W. Foxley-Norris.

c The development of coloured glass in England, by H. J. Powell.

d Processes and methods of medieval glass painting, by J. A. Knowles.

6445 Vol. 7

a The [H.M.] Ashley bottle [making] machine: a historical note, by S. English.

6446 Vol. 9.

a The early glasshouses of Bristol, by F. Buckley.

b Glasshouses on the Wear in the 18th cent., by F. Buckley.

c Notes on some old Yorkshire glasshouses, by W. R. Barker.

6447 Vol. 10.

a Glasshouses on the Tyne in the 18th cent., by F. Buckley.

b Old Nottingham glasshouses, by F. Buckley.

c Cumberland glasshouses, by F. Buckley.

6448 Vol. 11.

a Notes on the glasshouses of Stourbridge, 1700–1830, by F. Buckley.

b The glasshouses of Dudley and Worcester, by F. Buckley.

c The Birmingham glass trade, 1740–1833, by F. Buckley.

d Stourbridge fireclays, and the manufacture of glasshouse pots, by M. H. Edwards.

6449 Vol. 13.

a West country glasshouses, by F. Buckley.

b Old Lancashire glasshouses, by F. Buckley.

6450 Vol. 14.

a Notes on various old glasshouses, by F. Buckley. [King's Lynn, Great Yarmouth, Malton, Woolwich, Chester, Hertfordshire, Wales, Sheffield area, and Scotland]

b Old London glasshouses. i: Southwark, by F. Buckley.

6451 Vol. 15.

a Faraday's research on optical glass, by A. Marshall.

b Chapters in the history of the midland glass industry. i: The early history of glass-making in the Stourbridge district, by D. N. Sandilands.

c The birth of Birmingham's glass industry, by D. N. Sandilands.

d The last fifty years of the excise duty on glass [abolished in 1845], by D. N. Sandilands.

e The Spon Lane works [Messrs. Chance Brothers, glass manufacturers, Smethwick], by D. N. Sandilands.

6452 Vol. 16.

a Wealden glass: the old Surrey-Sussex industry, by S. E. Winbolt.

BRITISH NUMISMATIC SOCIETY

British Numismatic Journal and Proceedings:

6453 Vol. 1. (*See also no.* 601 *above*)

a A remarkable groat of Henry VII, by B. Roth.

b Countermarked Spanish dollar for old Canada, 1765, by J. B. Caldecott.

c Illustrations of the coinage. I: Ancient British.

d Two ancient dies [described].

6454 Vol. 2. (*See also no.* 602 *above*)

a Forgery in relation to numismatics, by L. A. Lawrence. [With illustrations of spurious Anglo-Saxon coins. Contd. in vol. 3 with illustrations from later periods, and in vol. 4]

6455 Vol. 3. (*See also no.* 603 *above*)

a Note on 'St. Patrick's pence' [copper halfpence and farthings, 17th cent. Irish], by W. S. Ogden.

b Leather currency, by W. Charlton.

6456 Vol. 4. (*See also no.* 604 *above*)

a An Elizabethan coiner [Sir John Brockett, at Duncannon, nr. Waterford, Ireland], by J. C. Cox.

6457 Vol. 5. (*See also no.* 605 *above*)

a A coin of Offa found in a Viking-age burial at Voss, Norway, by H. Schetelig.

6458 Vol. 8. (*See also no.* 608 *above*)

a Notes on some discoveries of coins in Ireland, by J. B. S. MacIlwaine.

6459 Vol. 9. (*See also no.* 609 *above*)

a Ancient Gaulish coins, including those of the Channel Islands, by B. Roth.

6460 Vol. 10. (*See also no.* 610 *above*)

a An interesting group of decorations of the Peninsular war, by C. Winter. [Medals awarded to Lt.-col. Russell Manners]

b Notes on some Irish coins found at Trim [co. Meath], by J. B. S. MacIlwaine.

6461 Vol. 11. (*See also no.* 611 *above*)

a Note on the 'Blacksmith's' or Kilkenny halfcrowns of Charles I, by J. B. S. MacIlwaine.

6462 Vol. 12. (*See also no.* 612 *above*)

a A coin of Prince Henry of Scotland as Earl of Carlisle in the reign of Stephen, by F. A. Walters.

6463 Vol. 14. (*See also no.* 614 *above*)

a The Ribe hoard [of short-cross coins], by L. A. Lawrence. [Appendix to no. 611d]

6464 Vol. 17. (*See also no.* 617 *above*)

a An emergency coinage in Ireland [*c.* 1642], by Helen Farquhar.

b Some entries of numismatic interest in the master's accounts of the merchant tailors' gild, Dublin, 1553–61, by H. W. Morrieson.

ALDERSHOT ARMY AND NAVY LODGE, No. 1971

Journal, nos. 1–24 (24 *P.* 1908–13):

6465 No. 1.

a The antiquity of Grand Lodge of England, by R. J. Blackham. [Contd. in subsequent numbers]

6466 No. 6.

a The antiquity of the system of degrees in freemasonry, by R. J. Blackham.

6467 No. 13.

   a The origin of the grade of master in freemasonry, by Count Goblet D'Alviella. [Contd. in subsequent numbers]

   b Oracles of the craft. 1: Henry Sadler [b. 1840], of Quatuor Coronati lodge, no. 2076, by R. F. Gould. [2: William Officer, 1826–1906, is in No. 14]

6468 No. 16.

   a The Gather, II, by R. F. Gould. [A list of masonic periodical publications. Contd. in subsequent numbers]

6469 No. 21.

   a Scholars of the craft: Dr. Chetwode Crawley. [Similarly, on Sidney Turner Klein, in No. 24]

6470 No. 22.

   a What is the debt speculative freemasonry owes to the operative society?, by S. S. Stitt.

AUTHORS' LODGE, No. 3456

Founded 1910.

Transactions, vols. 1–5 (1915–30):

6471 Vol. 1.

   a Anthony Sayer, first Grand Master, 1717, by A. F. Calvert.

   b The Worshipful Company of Masons and its connection with freemasonry, by P. H. Ditchfield.

   c The Lodge of Emulation, by E. Poole.

   d Freemasons' lodges among French prisoners of war, by J. T. Thorp.

   e Masonic lodges of Greater Britain [Canada, Australia, New Zealand, S. Africa, India, West Indies], by F. Armitage.

   f Red Apron or Stewards' lodges, by A. F. Calvert.

   g Lodge nights in olden days [from the minutes of Grand Lodge and the Old King's Arms lodge no. 28], by A. F. Calvert. [Another paper on this subject, by the same, occurs in vol. 4. *See also* no. 6483a]

   h Elias Ashmole, 1617–92, by C. Lambert.

   i Two old masonic figures [of wood, on a house at Wooburn Green, Bucks.], by S. Bradgate.

6472 Vol. 2.

   a Peter Gilkes, 1765–1833, by A. F. Calvert.

   b The 'Entered Apprentice's Song', by J. T. Thorp.

   c Some notes on the Royal Arch, by J. S. Green.

   d Freemasonry as depicted in the *Gentleman's Magazine*, by F. Armitage.

   e John Wilkes, 1727–97, by A. F. Calvert.

   f The Worshipful Company of Masons, by E. Conder.

   g The Loge Anglaise, no. 204, of Bordeaux, by E. Heisch.

   h The Emulation and Stability lodges of instruction, by A. F. Calvert.

   i Some masonic maxims of Peter Gilkes, by A. F. Calvert.

   j Was Sir Christopher Wren a mason?, by F. de P. Castells.

   k Masonry in Berkshire, by P. H. Ditchfield.

   l Thomas Dunckerley, 1724–95, by A. F. Calvert.

   m Dunckerley and the Royal Arch in the west, by J. A. Sherren. [A similar article by the same occurs in *Trans.* vol. 8, of Dorset Masters' Lodge]

   n A history of the Grand Stewards, by E. Poole.

   o Old masonic china and glass, by A. F. Calvert.

   p Old masonic medals, by A. F. Calvert.

   q The Levander-York ms.: a newly discovered version of the old charges, by A. F. Calvert. [F. W. Levander's ms. from York]

6473 Vol. 3.

   a Grand Lodge secretaries, by A. F. Calvert.

   b The free, and accepted, masons of the 17th cent., by E. Conder.

   c The first lodge under the English constitution [Antiquity] by A. F. Calvert.

   d Freemasonry in the *Annual Register*, by F. Armitage.

   e Notes from the minute books of two old Dover lodges.

   f The first and last Duke of Wharton: Philip – 'Our sad, glad, mad, bad Brother's name', by A. F. Calvert. [A similar article by the same occurs in *The Masonic Secretaries' Jnl.*, no. 7, of Fratres Calami Lodge]

   g A province of hearts [i.e. lodges in Herts.], by E. Balding.

   h The Mark degree, by T. P. Dorman.

   i The Gregorians [an 18th cent. society claiming affinity to freemasonry], by A. F. Calvert.

   j A great Scots freemason: George Drummond [d. 1766], by A. F. Calvert.

   k Random notes from masonic records [of London and provincial lodges], by A. F. Calvert.

   l Thomas Dunckerley [and lodges on board ships of war], by A. F. Calvert.

6474 Vol. 4.

   a The United Grand Lodge of England: a retrospect, 1717–1813, by G. W. Daynes.

   b The masonic career of Robert Burns, by D. Wright.

   c The Grand Stewards' lodge, by A. F. Calvert.

   d An Indian pioneer of masonry: Edmund Pascal, Madras, 1746–75, by C. H. Malden.

   e George Payne, second Grand Master, 1718 and 1720, by A. F. Calvert.

   f Dr. William Stukeley, F.R.S., by A. F. Calvert.

   g Masonic ritual and rituals, by W. S. Hildesley.

   h The first noble Grand Master [John, Duke of Montagu, d. 1749], by A. F. Calvert. [A similar article by the same occurs in *The Masonic Secretaries' Jnl.*, no. 7, of Fratres Calami Lodge]

   i Early freemasonry in Oxford, by D. Wright.

   j George Parker's *Dissertation on Masonry*, by A. F. Hudson.

   k The story of Great Queen Street, by A. F. Calvert.

   l Freemasonry in Monmouthshire, by F. H. James.

   m Orator John Henley: was he Grand Chaplain?, by A. F. Calvert.

   n The early days of Grand Lodge, by A. F. Calvert.

6475 Vol. 5. History of the lodge, in celebration of its coming-of-age, by A. Rose, 1930.

DORSET MASTERS' LODGE, No. 3366

Founded 1909, *for the association of installed masters who are members of lodges in the province of Dorset and of the London Dorset Lodge, no. 3221.*

Transactions, 1909–33 (21 vols.):

6476 Vol. 1 (1909–10).

   a Is reform of Grand Lodge practicable or desirable?, by S. R. Baskett. [A criticism of Grand Lodge as historically a London creation, and of London's influence in the craft]

6477 Vol. 2 (1910–11).

   a Freemasonry in Madras, by H. Bradley.

   b Two rare and interesting West Country masonic medals, by A. M. Broadley. [The Ralph Allen, Bath, medal, and the medal of the Royal Clarence lodge, Frome. Also occurs in *Trans.* vol. 4 (1907–8) of Leeds Installed Masters' Assn.]

6478 Vol. 3 (1911–12).

    a Origin and history of the Royal Arch degree, by Sir W. Watts.

    b Sir Christopher Wren and Portland, by J. A. Sherren. [With an appendix of docs. relating to the supply of stone from Portland for St. Paul's]

    c Some old certificates [reproduced and described].

6479 Vol. 4 (1912–13).

    a The Noble Order of Bucks [an 18th cent. convivial and political society].

    b The Durnovarian lodge [Dorchester, 1774–1830], by J. A. Sherren.

    c Freemasonry in its relation to the serious pictorial art of the 18th cent., by A. M. Broadley. [Printing and engraving by masons for masonic and other occasions and purposes]

    d Triangular lodge, Rushton, by J. A. Sherren.

    e Masonic clothing and regalia, by F. J. W. Crowe.

    f Rev. W. Mortimer Heath [fl. 1863–1912].

    g Masons' marks, by J. A. Sherren.

6480 Vol. 5 (1913–14).

    a Visit of Bro. W. Stukeley to Dorset in 1723, and the Dorchester amphitheatre, by A. M. Broadley.

    b Bro. Edmund Kean at Dorchester, 1813, by A. M. Broadley.

    c Bro. James Andrews [d. 1913].

    d Freemasonry in Dorset, by J. A. Sherren. [Contd. in subsequent vols. A series of extracts from the minutes of numerous lodges]

    e The two Grand Lodges and their union, by F. Armitage.

    f The Prince of Wales lodge, by Sir W. Watts.

    g William Williams and the Union, 1813, by J. A. Sherren.

6481 Vol. 6 (1914–15).

    a Bro. John Wilkes, M.P., by A. M. Broadley.

    b The Provincial Grand Lodge of Dorset, by J. A. Sherren. [Contd. in vol. 7 for 1915–16]

6482 Vol. 8 (1916–17).

    a Thomas Dunckerley, 1724–95, by A. F. Calvert.

    b The British army: its association with freemasonry past and present, by Sir W. Watts.

6484 Vol. 10 (1918–19).

    a The lady freemason, by Sir W. Watts. [Elizabeth St. Leger (d. 1775), daughter of Lord Doneraile and wife of Richard Aldworth]

    b Masonic china and glass, by J. G. Wallis.

    c Engraved lists of lodges, and etched quarterly communications, by J. A. Sherren.

6485 Vol. 11 (1919–20).

    a Masonic certificates, by J. A. Sherren.

6486 Vol. 14 (1923–4).

    a The three great masonic institutions: Royal Masonic Institution for Girls; Royal Masonic Institution for Boys; Royal Masonic Benevolent Institution, by M. Beachcroft.

    b Freemasonry in the Eastern Archipelago [Malay peninsula], by F. M. Elliott.

6487 Vol. 15 (1924–5).

    a All Souls lodge, no. 170 [Weymouth, formerly Tiverton]: notes on an old minute book, 1770–98, by G. P. Symes.

    b Evolution of the second and third degree, by E. R. Whitfield.

6488 Vol. 16 (1925–6).

    a Byegone customs of the craft [in Ireland], by J. H. Lepper.

6489 Vol. 17 (1926–7).

    a The degrees of pure and ancient masonry, as defined in the articles of Union by J. E. Shum Tuckett.

    b Freemasonry, a speculative science: its origin and purpose, by F. W. Billson.

6490 Vol. 18 (1927–8).

    a Forde abbey.

    b Lodge by-laws in 1814, from the records of the lodge of Amity, Poole.

    c The masonic peace memorial [Freemasons' Hall and Grand Temple], by A. F. Calvert.

6491 Vol. 19 (1928–9).

    a Dunckerley's provincial warrants [i.e. documents issued by a provincial grand master], and some others, by T. M. Carter.

6492 Vol. 21 (1930–1).

    a Freemasonry and the Gothic builders, by F. W. Billson.

6493 Vol. 22 (1931–2).

    a Masonic temples in Dorset, by W. W. R. Hussey.

6494 Vol. 21 (1932–3).

    a Masonry in the Malay peninsula and archipelago, by H. Banner.

    b All Souls chapter, no. 170, Weymouth, by F. W. Burt.

ESSEX MASTERS' LODGE, No. 3256
Transactions, 1 vol. (1925–35):

6495 Vol. 1 (1925–35).

    a Early meetings of the Provincial Grand Lodge of Essex, by F. E. Crate. [2 pts.]

    b Some account of the Provincial Grand Masters of Essex, by R. R. de R. a Ababrelton.

    c Prittlewell priory and its associations, by J. W. Burrows.

    d The lost lodges of Braintree.

    e St. Osyth's priory [and its later owners], by Sir R. Colvin.

FRATRES CALAMI LODGE, No. 3791
The Masonic Secretaries' Journal, nos. 1–7
(1917–19):[1]

6496 No. 1.

    a Sir Edward Letchworth, the doyen of masonic 'brothers of the pen'. [Grand Secretary, 1892–1917)

    b Bi-centenary of Grand Lodge, by A. F. Calvert. [A similar article by the same occurs in *Trans.* vol. 2 of Authors' Lodge]

    c The original of the Grand Stewardship, by A. F. Calvert.

    d The engraved lists of lodges, by A. F. Calvert.

    e United Grand Lodge: a note upon the schism, the separation, and the reunion, by A. F. Calvert.

    f Christopher Cuppage [d. 1804], by A. F. Calvert.

    g The Royal Masonic Benevolent Institution, Royal Masonic Institution for Girls, Royal Masonic Institution for Boys, by A. F. Calvert.

6497 No. 3.

    a The Grand Secretaryship, 1717–1917, by A. F. Calvert.

6498 No. 4.

    a Grand Wardens as operative masons, by E. A. Ebblewhite. [Mason's work at Blenheim by Edward Strong sen., d. 1724, and Edward Strong jun.]

    b Technical training scheme for British interned prisoners [of war] in Switzerland, by H. Billinghurst.

    [1] No more found.

6499 No. 5.

a The city of York [its masonic traditions], by W. R. Makins.

6500 No. 6

a Laurence Dermott and the 'Antients', by M. Rosenbaum. [Against the idea of 'schism' between the 'Antients' and the 'Moderns', and on the work of L. Dermott, Grand Secretary of the 'Antients'; with A. F. Calvert's reply]

b A noted London lodge, no. 28: The Old King's Arms lodge under George III, by A. F. Calvert.

6501 No. 7.

a Ancient usages, by H. J. Oldfield. [Notes from minute books of Hull lodges]

HUMBER INSTALLED MASTERS' LODGE
No. 2494

Founded 1894 (absorbing the Humber Installed Masters' Lodge of Instruction), for the study of freemasonry.

Transactions, pts. 1–8 and vol. 9 (1895–1933):

6502 Pt. 4.

a The four Grand Lodges of the 18th cent., by W. N. Cheesman. [Also occurs in *Trans.* vol. 6 (1909–10) of Leeds Installed Masters' Assn.]

b Old masonic china and glass, by H. Wallis.

6503 Pt. 5.

a Some account of freemasonry in York, by W. R. Makins.

6504 Pt. 6.

a The old charges and the ritual, by R. H. Baxter.

b York lodge, no. 236, its objects of masonic interest, by W. R. Makins.

6505 Pt. 7.

a Bridlington priory, by Canon [J.] Topham.

b Westminster abbey and its craftsmen, by J. W. Hobbs.

c Selby abbey church.

d Cawood castle and church.

6506 Vol. 9.

a History of the masonic charities, by E. C. L. Livesey.

b A glance at the records of two extinct Hull lodges [Rodney, no. 436, and Phoenix, no. 368], by G. L. Shackles.

LEEDS INSTALLED MASTERS' ASSOCIATION

Founded 1904, to encourage masonic research.

Transactions, vols. 1–23[1] (1905–33):

6507 Vol. 1 (1904–5).

a Masonic clothing, by F. J. W. Crowe.

b Freemasonry from 1600 to the Grand Lodge era, by W. J. Hughan. [Reprinted from Lodge of Research, Leicester, *Trans.* no. 2889b above]

c Notes about West Yorkshire lodges. I: Lodge of Fidelity, no. 289, Leeds. [Extracts from minute books occur in vol. 3 (1906–7), rules and bye-laws in vol. 4 (1907–8). Notes on the following Leeds lodges occur in the vols. shown: Philanthropic, no. 304, in vol. 2; Alfred, no 306, in vol. 3; Excelsior, no. 1042, in vol. 4; Goderich, no. 1211, in vol. 5; Defence, no. 1221, in vol. 6]

6508 Vol. 2 (1905–6).

a Masonic musicians and music, by W. H. Griffiths.

[1]Vol. 15 not published.

6509 Vol. 4 (1907–8).

a Lodge of the Nine Muses, no. 235, and its jewels, by E. L. Hawkins.

b An old engraved list of lodges, by A. Gardiner.

c A patriotic West Yorkshire mason [Richard Linnecar, Lodge of Unanimity, no. 202, Wakefield] during the Great Terror (1796–1805), by A. M. Broadley. [An appeal for masonic donations to the Mansion House Fund, 1798]

d Short sketches of three prominent 18th cent. masons, by E. L. Hawkins. [John Theophilus Desaguliers (d. 1744), Thomas Dunckerley (d. 1795), and William Preston (d. 1818)]

6510 Vol. 5 (1908–9).

a Cole's 'Constitutions'. [The 'old charges' engraved by Benjamin Cole, London, first edn. 1728]

b By-laws of the old Talbot lodge, Leeds.

6511 Vol. 6 (1909–10).

a King Edward VII as a mason.

b William Preston [d. 1818].

c The Royal medal of the Lodge of Antiquity.

d Women freemasons.

e The first *Book of Constitutions*. [The historical portion of James Anderson's book, 1723]

6512 Vol. 7 (1910–11).

a The Leeds civic mace, its maker [Arthur Maingee or Mangey, executed for counterfeiting, 1696] and serjeants, by C. H. Wilson.

b Dr. Anderson of the *Constitutions*, by A. F. Robbins. [A reprint of no. 2946a above]

c The Templars and Temple Newsam and Fidelity preceptory, Leeds, by J. W. Stead.

d Index to vols. 1–6.

6513 Vol. 8 (1911–12).

a Masonic certificates: their origin and varieties, by F. J. W. Crowe.

6514 Vol. 9 (1912–13).

a The craft before the establishment of the first Grand Lodge of 1717, by M. Rosenbaum.

b Centenary of the union of the two Grand Lodges on 27 Dec. 1813, by J. E. Cawthorn.

c English printed masonic literature up to 1750, by E. H. Dring. [A reprint of no. 2948e above]

6515 Vol. 10 (1913–14).

a Index, vols. 7–10.

6516 Vol. 11 (1914–15).

a Some account of the Grand Lodge of all England held in York, by W. R. Makins.

b Sir Thomas Gascoigne, bt. [d. 1810], Grand Master of all England, by J. W. Dobson.

6517 Vol. 12 (1915–16).

a *An Account of the Proceedings at the Festival of the Society of Freemasons, 27 Jan. 1813, given to the Earl of Moira previous to his Departure as Governor General of India*, London, 1813. [Reprinted]

b *Bye-laws of the Lodge of Antiquity*, London, 1793. [Reprinted]

c History of the Chapter of Unity, no. 72, and the Alfred chapter, no. 306. [Based on a paper by C. Letch Mason delivered on 9 Nov. 1888]

6518 Vols. 13–14 (1916–17–18).

a Provincial Grand Lodge of West Yorkshire: historical notes. [Includes list of Provincial Grand Masters, deputies, and secretaries, and lists of lodges]

b The work of the Leeds Educational and Benevolent Institution, by C. H. Wilson.

c Golden Lion or Talbot Lodge: notes and minutes.

d Historical sketch of Royal Arch masonry and the celebration of the jubilee of the Philanthropic chapter, no. 304, by W. Watson.

e The Mark degree, by F. G. Harmer. [With special reference to Mark masonry and some of the older Mark lodges in West Yorkshire. Extensive appendix on masons' marks]

6519 Vol. 17 (1920–1).

a The Provincial Grand Lodge library.

6520 Vol. 18 (1921–2).

a Ancient York masonry – a plea for further research, by A. E. Waite.

6521 Vol. 19 (1922–3–4).

a Freemasonry in Lancashire prior to 1825, by E. B. Beesley.

6522 Vol. 20 (1925–6).

a An exact reproduction of the William Watson ms. of 1687, with introd. by W. J. Hughan. [One of the 'old charges', from the edn. of 1891]

b An exact reproduction of the Thomas W. Tew ms., with introd. by W. J. Hughan. [One of the 'old charges', from the edn. of 1892]

c William Horton, first Provincial Grand Master of West Yorkshire, d. 1740.

6523 Vol. 21 (1927–8).

a Masonic verse and music of the 18th cent., by H. Poole.

b Prestonian lecture. Contemporaries of William Preston: masonic teachers of the 18th cent., by J. Stokes. [Wellins Calcott; William Hutchinson; George Smith; J. Ladd; W. Meeson]

6524 Vol. 22 (1929–30).

a The Hughan ms. (an 'old charge'), by H. Poole.

b Summer outing. A sketch of the history of masonry in Leeds in the 18th cent., by H. Poole.

c Summer outing. Notes on Leeds and the places to be visited, by E. Hawkesworth.

d Index, vols. 11–21.

6525 Vol. 23 (1931–2).

a Lodge no. 258 held at the Talbot. Extracts from the minutes. [With lists of members, officers, visitors]

b Some notes on the Talbot inn, by A. Mattison.

NORFOLK INSTALLED MASTERS' LODGE,
No. 3905
Transactions, vols. 1–8 (1920–33):

6526 Vol. 1 (1919–20).

a Past Provincial Grand Masters of Norfolk, by G. W. G. Barnard.

b The *Book of Constitution* [Anderson] in the 18th cent., by E. G. Rose.

c Masonic jewels, by G. W. G. Barnard.

6527 Vol. 2 (1922–4).

a Wymondham church, by J. B. Pomeroy.

b Norfolk freemasonry, 1753–1813, by E. Nash.

6528 Vol. 3 (1925–7).

a The development of the tri-gradal system, by L. Vibert.

b Unanimity lodge, no. 102 [Norwich], 1758–1814, by J. E. A. Sorrell.

c Some masons' marks [on Canterbury cathedral], by R. F. Boileau.

d Ancient Thetford, by C. A. Everitt.

6529 Vol. 4 (1928).

a The stones of Yarmouth, by R. H. Teasdel.

b Masonic benevolence, 1717–1813, by M. Beachcroft.

c Records of the lodge constituted at the Maid's Head, Norwich, 1724, by G. W. Daynes. [Contd. in vol. 6. A reprint of no. 2961c above]

6530 Vol. 5 (1929).

a Medical masons, by D. Rice.

b Notes on the history and antiquities of North Walsham, by J. Shepheard.

c Provincial warrants [relating to the formation of new lodges], by T. M. Carter.

d Notes on the Provincial Grand Lodge building scheme [St. Giles Street, Norwich], by G. W. Daynes.

6531 Vol. 6 (1930).

a Notes on the church of St. Nicholas, East Dereham, by R. H. Teasdel.

b The Royal Masonic Institution for Girls, by M. Beachcroft.

6532 Vol. 7 (1931).

a The Suffolk adventure of a Norfolk lodge [Unanimity, no. 102], 1814–27, by J. E. A. Sorrell.

NOTTS. INSTALLED MASTERS' LODGE,
No. 3593
Transactions, vols. 1–19 (1912–33):

6533 Vol. 2.

a Notes on old Notts. lodges, by J. P. Briscoe. [Early freemasonry in Nottingham; Warren and Newstead lodges. Contd. in vol. 3, Royal Sussex lodge, no. 402, and Union lodge]

b Notts. freemasonry, 1785–1827, by J. O. Manton.

6534 Vol. 3.

a Aprons and other treasures of Grand Lodge, by W. Hammond.

b A great masonic writer [Rev. Dr. George Oliver, d. 1867], by J. P. Briscoe.

6535 Vol. 4.

a 'Speculative, the outcome of operative freemasonry', by J. A. Sherren.

b Emulation lodge of improvement [founded 1823], by G. J. V. Rankin.

6536 Vol. 7.

a Freemasonry in Notts., by Sir Arthur E. Blake.

b Masonic glass and china, by W. J. Wallis.

6537 Vol. 11.

a History of the gilds and freemasonry, by H. G. Rosedale. [Concluded in vol. 12]

6538 Vol. 15.

a Masonry, operative and speculative, by W. S. Hildesley.

b Masonic ritual and rituals, by W. S. Hildesley.

6539 Vol. 16.

a Early masonry in Notts., by H. C. Sheldon.

6540 Vol. 17.

   a Freemasonry in Mansfield and district, by J. H. White.
   b Royal Arch chapter 'No. 68, Justice, Nottingham', 1790–1815, by J. O. Manton.

6541 Vol. 18.

   ɛ Concise history of freemasonry, by F. W. Golby.
   b Notes on freemasonry in India [and Canada], by the Hon. G. V. Monckton-Arundell, Viscount Galway.

SOMERSET MASTERS' LODGE, No. 3746
Founded 1915
Transactions, vols. 1–5 (1915–34):

6542 Vol. 1 (1915–18).

   a Freemasonry a century ago, by F. W. Golby.
   b Evolution of masonic clothing, by G. P. G. Hills.
   c Masonic memoirs [i.e. masonry in Somerset, and especially of John Burnett, b. *c.* 1830, and Henry Brydges, d. 1875].
   d Masonic halls of Bath, by G. Norman and E. Lewis.
   e Masonic lodges of Bath, by G. Norman. [With extracts from minute books. Contd. in later vols.]
   f Perpetual Friendship lodge, no. 135, Bridgwater, by T. Kelway.

6543 Vol. 2 (1919–20).

   a Operative masonry, by Major Gorham.
   b Ancient charges and regulations, by L. Vibert.
   c Bye-laws of the lodge meeting at the Bear inn, Bath [1746–69].
   d The Kennet and Avon canal and its marks, by Major Gorham.
   e Short history of old Taunton lodges, by H. H. Hallett.
   f The Provincial Grand Mark lodge of Somerset, by G. Norman.
   g Notes on the house of Augustinian canons at Bruton and other religious houses in the neighbourhood, by R. T. A. Hughes.

6544 Vol. 3 (1923–6).

   a Notes on craft masonry in Bath and the Masonic Hall, Old Orchard St., by E. Lewis.
   b Burnham church and its altar-piece, by G. L. Porcher.
   c Old ms. rituals belonging to the Sincerity chapter, no. 261, Taunton, by H. H. Hallett.

6545 Vol. 4 (1927–30).

   a William Stukeley [d. 1765], physician, scientist, archaeologist, clerk in holy orders, freemason, by G. Norman.
   b Rev. George Oliver, D.D., and his lecture on masonic rituals [1863], by R. H. Baxter.
   c Freemasonry in Bristol, by R. V. Awdry.
   d Rise of freemasonry in Bristol, and its organisation in the 18th cent., by I. V. Hall.
   e Note on Wells cathedral, by G. Norman.
   f Short account of the lodges of Promulgation, Reconciliation, Stability, and Emulation, by H. H. Hallett.

6546 Vol. 5 (1931–4).

   a Notes on freemasonry in Somerset, by C. R. Bishop.
   b Cleeve abbey, Washford, Som., by C. T. F. Gibbs.
   c Freemasonry in Taunton, 18th cent., by H. H. Hallett.
   d Thomas Dunckerley [d. 1795], by E. Lewis.
   e Craft guilds and merchants' guilds, London, by S. F. Goodall.
   f Woodspring priory, Kewstoke, by H. H. Doorbar.
   g Kewstoke village and church.
   h A span of two centuries, by P. B. Rigg. [On freemasonry in England and Scotland]

SUFFOLK INSTALLED MASTERS' LODGE, No. 3913
Transactions, 11 vols. (1919–36):

6547 Vol. for 1919.

   a Lodge of Unity, no. 71 [Norwich], by G. S. Knocker.

6548 Vol. for 1925.

   a The rise of speculative freemasonry, by G. S. Knocker.
   b Freemasonry in the Channel Islands, 1753–1813, by C. H. Wilson.

6549 Vol. for 1926–8.

   a Freemasonry in Woodbridge, by R. Bentham.
   b Freemasonry in Suffolk, by J. H. Parker.

6550 Vol. for 1929–30.

   a Notes on Apollo lodge, no. 305, Beccles, 1794–1844, by A. W. Youngman.
   b Freemasonry in the two kingdoms before Grand Lodges, by L. Vibert. [See also no. 3230c above]

6551 Vol. for 1931–2.

   a Phoenix lodge, no. 516, Stowmarket, by J. M. Prentice.

6552 Vol. for 1933–6.

   a Freemasonry in Bury St. Edmunds, by J. R. Burdon.
   b Ipswich lodges, and their homes, by J. E. Pierce.

ROYAL ARTILLERY INSTITUTION
Other publications (*contd. from p. 312*)

6553 The history of the Royal Regiment of Artillery, 1815–53, by H. W. L. Hime. 1908.

6554 The history of the Royal Artillery (Crimean period), by Julian R. J. Jocelyn. 1911.

6555 The history of the Royal Artillery and Indian Artillery in the Mutiny of 1857, by J. R. J. Jocelyn. 1915.

BAPTIST HISTORICAL SOCIETY
Extra publications (*contd. from p. 19*)

6556 Minutes of the General Assembly of General Baptist churches of England, with kindred records, ed. with introd. and notes by W. T. Whitley. 2 vols. 1909–10. [Vol. i: 1654–1728. Vol. ii: 1731–1811]

LIBRARY ASSOCIATION
Other publications (*contd. from p. 223*)

6557 History of the public library movement in Great Britain and Ireland, by J. Minto. 1932. [Library Manuals IV]

ROYAL UNITED SERVICE INSTITUTION
Other publications (*contd. from p. 355*)

6558 The 1st King George's Own Light Gurkha Rifles: the Malaun regiment, 1815–1921, by F. L. Petre. 1925.

6559 Historical record of the 14th (King's) Hussars, vol. ii: 1900–22, by J. G. Browne and E. J. Bridges, ed. J. A. T. Miller. 1932. [Vol. i: 1715–1900, by H. B. Blackburne. 1901]

6560 The Poona Horse (17th Queen Victoria's Own Cavalry), vol. i: 1817–1913, by M. H. Anderson, E. S. J. Anderson, and G. M. Molloy; vol. ii: 1914–31, by H. C. Wylly. 2 vols. 1933.

General Index

(The form of the index is explained and abbreviations are listed on p. viii)

Andreas (Kirk Andreas), I.o.M., 2549(d); Knock y Doonee, 2549(m), 2551(v)

Andrew, William Jonathan (d. 1934), 4575(i). *See also* Index of Authors

Andrews, Elizabeth, Quaker (d. 1718), 1832(a)

Andrews, James (d. 1913), 6480(c)

Andros, Amias (d. 1674), 5034(a)

Aneurin (Aneirin), Welsh poet (fl. 603), 2283(a), 2305(c)

Angary, 4498(d)

Angels (coins), as healing-pieces, 612(c). *See also* Quarter-angels

Angevin Empire, and the Channel Islands, 5037(e)

Angles: conquest of Britain by, 995(f); in Devonshire, 1336(o); in Furness and Cartmel, 1187(y); in Roch basin, 3985(a); in Yorkshire, 2375(a)

Anglesey: 17th cent., 60(b); artisan and small farmer in, 69(d); bibliography, 6019(k); Bodlewfawr farm, 6035(i); bronze age, 59(a); Caer Leb, 750(m); churches, 746(g), 750(d); clan-founders, 59(c); clergy, 66(f); court rolls, 66(c); Danes in, 68(b); decorative art, early Christian, 739(q); documents, 64(c), 65(b); ecclesiology, 2291(b); enclosures, 61(a); folk-lore, 56(b); forts, 59(b); megaliths, 2306(a); Methodism, 714(e), 717(s); monasticism, 56(b), 57(b); monumental effigies, 63(c); and national eisteddfod, 59(h); neolithic age, 62(a); non-parochial registers, 59(e); parliamentary representation, 66(d); plea rolls, 72; prehistory, 54(d), 55(a), 63(a), 733(i); Rhuddgaer, lead coffin at, 746(o); Roman remains, 65(a), 2849(b); sessions records, 61(d); settlers, 728(a); shipbuilding, 68(e); Rich. Thomas, preacher, 715(g); tour, 728(o); Twrcelyn commote, 57(a); wills, 64(f). *See also* Anglesey Antiq. Soc. & Fd Club

Anglesey, Marquess of, *see* Paget, Sir Henry William

Anglesey abbey, *see* Bottisham, Cambs.

Anglesey Antiq. Soc. & Fd Club: *Trans.*, 54–69; *Supplements*, 70–72; index, 64(g)

Anglian art, 5190(f)

Anglian burials, burial-grounds, 160(j), 5901(a), 6230(g)

Anglian crosses, 1179(o), 2550(d); fragment, 1167(w); heads, 1196(q), 2120 (e); shafts, 1174(w), 1175(q). *See also* Crosses

Anglian glass vessel, 6424(b)

Anglian sculpture, 1168(p), 6227(h), 6228(n), 6229(p), 6231(c)

Anglian trough, 1168(p)

Anglia Wallia, 731(m)

Anglica Historia (Polydore Vergil), 4386(a)

Anglican orders, 1060–1

Anglo-Belgian treaty, 73(a)

Anglo-Belgian Union, *Anglo-Belgian Notes* contd as *Ann. Rpts*, 73–75

Anglo-Catholic revival, and Free Church of Scotland, 3925

Anglo-Danish sculpture, 6227(h), 6228(n), 6229(p)

Anglo-Danish Soc., *Anglo-Danish Jnl*, 76–77

Anglo-Dutch wars, *see* Dutch wars

Anglo-Egyptian question (1927–30), 2408(a)

Anglo-Egyptian treaty, negotiations, 2406(d)

Anglo-Franco-American treaty, proposed, 4413(d)

Anglo-French commercial treaties, 1631(k), 1632(j)

Anglo-French naval compromise, 2407(a)

Anglo-Hellenic League, *Pamphlets*, etc., 78–81

Anglo-Norman administration, 4416(c)

Anglo-Norman calendar, 3396(b)

Anglo-Norman coinage, 602(d). *See also* Coinage

Anglo-Norman Lit. Circle, *Anglo-Norman Rev.*, 82–84

Anglo-Norman verse, 3383(a), 3410(b)

Anglo-Persian Oil Company, 2411(c)

Anglo-Portuguese alliance, 4390(d)

Anglo-Russian convention, 4198(a)

Anglo-Russian Lit. Soc., *Procs*, 85–90

Anglo-Saxon, *see following entries and* Saxon

Anglo-Saxon architecture, 2062(a), 3007(a); ecclesiastical, 1369(b); Northamptonshire, 149(o); Suffolk, 5579(a)

Anglo-Saxon art, 4120(b); study of, 4475(a)

Anglo-Saxon barrows, 1897(k). *See also* Barrows and tumuli

Anglo-Saxon battlefields, 4122(c)

Anglo-Saxon benedictional, 4834(p)

Anglo-Saxon bones, 4052(b)

Anglo-Saxon bowl, found at Winchester, 2014(b), 5170(a), 5471(g). *See also* Anglo-Saxon hanging bowls

Anglo-Saxon bronze casting, 5148(c)

Anglo-Saxon brooches: from Beeston Tor, 5164(c); evolution and distribution, 4112(d); from Hoxne, 5575(a); saucer type, distribution, 5179(g)

Anglo-Saxon burghs (burhs), 267(c), 1694(g)

Anglo-Saxon burials, burial-grounds: Alfriston, 5708(b); Bidford-on-Avon, 379(b), 5189(c); Blockley, 6157(c); Broadchalke, 6111(c); Burwell, 775(c); Cambridgeshire, 803; Camerton, 5427(c), 5445(k); Droxford, 2007(l); East Shefford, 4056(b); Ellesborough, 99(x); Guildown, Guildford, 5627(a), 5629(g); Holdenby, 3641(a), 3645(b); Hornsea, 2375(a); Ipswich, 5176(g), 5574(a); Kettering, 3642(d), 3655(a); Little Wilbraham, 777(f); Luton, 5167(d); Market Overton, 5178(j); Mitcham, 5176(b), 5609(a,b); Morecombelake, 1399(i); Ocklynge hill, 5715(i); Purley, 1163(f,g); Purton, 6105(o); Soham, 781(h); Suffolk, 803; Uncleby, 5151(e); Wheatley, 5156(b); Winterslow, Roche Court down, 6113(aa); Woodston, 3860(a)

Anglo-Saxon charters: Bedfordshire, 228(b); Brightwell, 247(i); Burmarsh, 2607(k); and Earmundeslea, Berks., 249(b); Hampshire, 2016(a), 4125(c); Mackney, 247(i); meaning of terms, 1644(a); Oxfordshire, 3799; and road-system, 4121(c); Sandtun in, 2605(c); Shropshire, 4972(a); Somerset, 5437; Sotwell, 247(i); Tisbury in, 6112(u); Wiltshire, 4123(g); Worcestershire, 382(a)

Anglo-Saxon chronicle: at Corpus Christi Coll., Camb., 3520(c); and Devon history, 2980(d); origin and history, 4112(g)

Anglo-Saxon churches: co. Durham, 5602(a); Hampshire, 2016(i); Isle of Wight, 2016(i); Kent, 2607(f); St Pancras type, 4105(n); in *Textus Roffensis*, 2606(d). *See also under names of places*

Anglo-Saxon cinerary urn, 1623(j)

Anglo-Saxon civilization, 4556(a)

Anglo-Saxon coins, 1292(b), 4602(c); and battle of Brunanburgh, 620(a); assays and imitations, 617(c); British Museum acquisitions, 4595(c); Cilda, 11th cent. moneyer, 4575(a); Cuthbert pennies, 608(c); double names on, 613(a); of Durham bpric, 97(e); 'Fastolfi moneta', 'Fastolfes mot', on, 620(d); found at, in, *see below*; late, 613(a), 616(c); minted at, in, *see below*; mints, 'uncertain', 606(b); mint-towns, 608(b); Northumbrian regal, 601(c); Odilo, moneyer, of Northumbria, 614(a); of particular rulers, *see below*; place-names on, 4594(a); spurious, 6454(a); symbols on, 613(a); by Torhtulf, 602(j); of Wales, 602(c),

Armathwaite, Cumb., 1175(a), 1180(a)

Armiger (person entitled to bear arms), 4105(h)

Armilla, gold, 760(a)

Arminian Magazine, 6040(j)

Armlets: bronze, 1167(b); shale, 3986(e), 6321(a)

Armley, Leeds, W.R.Yorks., 5787, 5798

Armorial bearings, *see* Arms, heraldic

Armorial glass, stained and painted, 6090(d); Adel church, 5801(o); agreement relating to, 5172(g); Ashton church, 1726(p); Bicknacre priory, 1703(e); Broughton, 3633(b); Buckenham, 3563(t); Checkley church, 3630(c); Colchester museum, 1695(c); Cranleigh church, 5627(g); Ecclesfield church, 2376(r); Great Malvern priory church, 5173(o); Greenwich, Trinity Hosp. chapel, 1897(o); Harlow church, 1695(cc); Hassop Hall, Derbys., 1279(m); Horselunges manor, 5721(d); Ingleby Arncliffe church, 6230(h); Abp Juxon's arms, 3759(d); Kirby Sigston church, 6230(h); Leigh, Staffs., 3629(d); London, Law Society's hall, 663(h); Norwich, 665(h); Pillaton Hall, Staffs., 3634(c); Ridware, 6090(d); Staffordshire, 3629(c); Stamford Baron, 159(n); Stannington church, 5227(a); Whitmore Hall, Staffs., 3626(e)

Armour, *see* Arms and armour; Horse armour

Armoured vehicles, 4792(g)

Armourers, Greenwich school, 5192(b)

Armourers' and Brasiers' company, 2970(q,r), 3060(a), 4913, 5192(b)

Armoury, at Greenwich, 1897(j)

Arms, heraldic, 100(q); antelope in, 3859(a); books of, 1605(e), 3996, 5216(m), 5235(g); borne by, *see below*; canting, 5711(b); carved and sculptured, 518(c), 1164(o), 1168(e), 2122(f), 3516(a); crossed keys and swords in, 3858(b); displayed at, in, on, *see below*; engraved for Lord Dacre, 5710(c); grants, etc., of, *see below*; lawsuit concerning, in Jersey, 5041(e); on books, 2768(a), rolls of, 5185(c), 5234(l); royal, *see* Royal arms; tiger and mirror in, 2590(q)

borne by: Aberafan, 1(e); Apothecaries, 4708(c); Lord Audley of Walden, 776(e); Balliol Coll., Oxf., 3714; Barton family, 3427(a); Board of Ordnance, 5082(s); Booth family, 2112(g); Bristol citizens, 436(m); Bristol city, 430(e), 1097(t); Bristol dean & chapter, 460(i); Bristol, St Augustine's abbey, 460(f); Bristol, St Mark's hosp., 460(g); Bristol, Queen Elizabeth's hosp., 457(f); 3rd D. of Buckingham, 460(h); Channel Islands, lords and keepers of, 5060(d); Clayton family, 2129(b); Clere family, 3570(d); Colchester, 4105(m); Cornwall, 4541(d); Covert family, 5720(e); Cumberland families, 1169(m); Dacre family, 5710(c); Darell family, 2598(f); Derbyshire families, 1283(h), 1288(d), 1290(b); Drapers' company, 2601(j); Durham families, 5257(a); Ewart family, 5330(s); Farley, lords of, 2009(l); Ferrers family, 1294(c); Fitzwilliam family, 5173(a); Flintshire, 1775(e); Gerard family, 3631(b); Wm Gilbert, 1693(h); Gloucester dioc., 446(d); Goring family, 5720(e); Great Torrington, 1345(c); Halifax families, 1966(b), 1992(b); Hanover, 5727(nn); Hull, 1616(a); Hulton family, 2122(e); Jersey, governors of, 5060(d); Abp Juxon, 3759(b,d); Leeds, 5791(q), 5800(p); London city, 516(f); Lyons family, 1097(w); Nichol family, Jersey, 5069(c); north-country families, 5235(g); Northumbrian families, 5231(h), 5234(l), 5238(g); Norwich, 3565(h); Nottingham, 4105(m), 5811(f); Nottinghamshire, 5811(f); Pelham family, 5721(c); Peterborough, 3858(b); Peterborough knights,

Arms, heraldic (*cont.*)

3864(d); Pickering family, 1171(h); Bp Nic. Robinson, 2291(g); Maj. Thos Ross, 5084(d); St Paul family, 6228(t); Scottish families, 2768(a); Shakespeare, 1734(d); Staffordshire families, 6083(c); Stratford-upon-Avon, 4940(a); Suffolk families, 5575(i); Sybill family, 2590(q); Rob. Timpson, 5092(a); Uvedale family, 3570(d); Walrond family, 1337(f); Washington family, 257(b); 5801(c); John Westby, 2122(l); Westmorland families, 1169(m); Whitby, 1617(e); John Whitson, 1096(y); Sir John Whyte, 3429(j); Willoughby family, 1295(c); Yorkshire E.R. families, 1605(e), 1606(b); Sir John and Dame Young, 441(d)

displayed at, in, on: Aughton church, 2120(d); Barton church, Westmld, 1168(e); Berkeley castle, 434(f); Berkshire churches, 271(c); Bewcastle, Cumb., 5227(e); Bristol cath., 431(e); Bristol, Red Lodge, 430(l); Burton Agnes church, 6229(j); Cambridge, 769(d); Cambridgeshire, 811; Canterbury cath., 5182(j), 5187(e); Canterbury, Christ Church gateway, 1851(a); Carmarthen, St Peter's, 2259(d); Channel Islands, 5037(l), 5067(e); Cheshire, 2118(e); Chester, St Bridget's, 1002(b); Chichester cath., 5700(d); Courtenay tomb, Colyton, 1343(c); Curry Rivel church, 5414(c); Derbyshire, 1279(d), 4125(a); Dorset houses, 1391(f); co. Durham, 3539; Ecclesfield church, 2376(r); Felixkirk church, 6230(m); Fenny Stratford, 98(s); Gateshead, St Mary's, 5227(n); Gloucestershire churches, 431(h), 433(j), 434(g), 437(j); Gloucestershire maps, 445(d); Guernsey, 5037(m); Halifax parish church, 1994(b); Hardwick Hall, 1273(d); Hawarden church, 2119(d); Herstmonceux castle, 5710(c); Holt church, 2114(d); Holywell church, 742(n); Huyton church, 2134(e); Leake, 6230(m); London, 518(c); Longford, 3516(a); Northumberland, 3538, 5261(c); Norton tomb, Abbotsleigh, 5421(r); Ormskirk church, 2112(d); Oxford, Divinity School, 4118(l); Oxfordshire churches, 3783(b); Peterborough, 3859(a); Peterborough guildhall, 3858(a); Raby Cote, Cumb., 1164(o); Rochester cath., 2601(g); Romsey town hall, 2015(c); Southampton, Bargate, 2006(f); South Kilvington, 6230(m); Stafford monument, Westminster abbey, 3685(a); Staffordshire, 4125(a); Steeton Hall, 6229(l); E. of Strafford's vault, 3428(gg); Suffolk, 5582(a); Sussex, 5711(b); Sussex churches, 5719(i); Tewkesbury abbey, 432(f); Thirsk, 6230(m); Walthamstow, 5958; Westminster abbey, 2974(d); Wilton church, 6103(o); Wiltshire churches, 6112(x); Winchester cath., 2007(m); Worcestershire churches, 431(h), 433(j); Yanwath, Westmld, 1168(e); Yorkshire, 6232(r), 6233(d), 6234(b,e), 6235(c), 6236(c), 6237(d)

grants, etc., of, 2034, 2035, 2114(g); from British Museum mss, etc., 2039; calendar of printed, 2107(k); to Butler family, of Bewsey and Kirkland, 2121(k); to Rob. Knight of Bromley, 2595(e); in Shropshire, 4970(m), 4979(m); by Lord Strafford (1347), 3520(cc); to Weldisshe of Lynton, 2595(e); in Yorkshire, 6226(e)

See also Armiger; Armorial glass; Badges; Crest; Funeral achievement; Hatchments; Heraldry; Heralds' visitations; Royal arms; Supporters. *For other uses of armorial bearings and heraldry see* Ceilings; Fire-backs; Horse-trappings; House tablets; Ledger-stones; Lewknor carpet; Pendants; Roundels; Seals; Tiles

Arms and ammunition, private manufacture of, 4518(f). *See also* Armaments; Firearms; Small arms

Aumbries, *see* Ambries

Aurignacian stations, floors, 2531(a), 3916(v), 4054

Aust, Glos., 430(h,m), 1096(d)

Austen, Jane, novelist (d. 1817), 1750(b)

Austerfield, W.R.Yorks., 405(c), 6360

Austhwaite, *see* Dalegarth, Cumb.

Austin, *see* Augustinian

Australasia, Prince of Wales's tour, 4277(g)

Australia: and the arts, 4276(a), 4277(e), 4286(a); coinage, 604(g); Congregationalism, 1112(g); development, 2518, 4316(a), 4323(a), 4328(b); discovery, 1957; economic geography, 4323(a); exploration, 1868(a), 4316(a), 4345(b); federal constitution, 2859(a,c); freemasonry, 6471(e); immigration, 4264(b); naval defence, 4262(a); railways, 4276(g); in Royal Empire Soc. subject catalogue, 4314; settlement of ex-service men, 4308; voyage to (1852), 4270(g); and World War I, 4272(c), 4310, 4404(a)

Austria, 4401(a,b)

Austrian Succession, war of: action between H.M.S. *Lyon* and *Elisabeth*, 3511(c), 5114(l); Anglo-French conflicts in Indian Ocean, 5110(a); Anglo-Russian relations, 4410(c); Cartagena stormed, 5083(u); Dettingen, 4781(a), 5084(b), 5092(i); economic pressure, 4764(e); English naval strategy, 4760(c); Flanders campaign, 4758(c); Fontenoy, 5087(j); Holland and England, 2233(b); naval campaign, 3500(f)

Authors' dedications, 17th cent., 4552(a)

Authors' Lodge, No. 3456: history, 6475; *Trans.*, 6471–5

Autobiographies: John Boydell (d. 1804), 1775(h); John Britton (1771–1857), 2952(c); Sir John Gibson (1655), 5679(b); of Halifax, 18th cent., 1995(b); Jos. Metford (1776–1863), 1831(d); Phineas Pett (d. 1638), 3505; Sydnam Poyntz (1624–36), 4427; Thos Raymond (1610–81), 4438; Rev. Rich. Warner (1763–1857), 2952(c); Rich. Whitworth (d. 1811), 3683(b). *See also* Diaries and journals; Memoirs

Autographs, and their validity, 2231(b)

Auvergne, *see* D'Auvergne

Auxiliary Patrol, Royal Navy, 4774(a)

Avebury, Wilts., 216(k), 362(a), 734(d), 1380(a), 5158(b); bibliography, 6100(a); church, 4124(g); ditch, 5161(f); excavation, 546(a), 549(b), 6110(c); flint implements, 5153(c); interment, 6106(a); Kennet avenue, 6106(b); manor-house, 4124(g); Roman pavement, 6110(l); skeleton and drinking-cup, 4080(b); stone circle, 450(b), 4124(g); stones, fallen, 6106(a); Windmill hill, 3912(z), 3913(g)

Aveley, Essex, 1696(o)

Aveline de Forz (d. 1273), 5799(i)

Aveline's Hole, Burrington Combe, *see* Burrington, Som.

Avening, Glos., 443(a), 449(f)

Averham, Notts., 5819(f)

Avery, John, surgeon (d. 1855), 4692(h)

Aviation: in armed services (1831–1931), 4472(i); commercial, 2452(b), 2462(a); effect of, on international affairs, 4516(f). *See also* Aircraft

Aviation mission, to Japan, 2559(a)

Avignon, France, 781(d)

Avignon papacy, 743(b)

Avington, Berks., 252(a)

Avon, river (Upper Avon, flowing to Tewkesbury), 366(c), 371(e). *See also* Kennet & Avon canal

Avon valley, Devon, 1355(e)

Avon Water, *see* Hampshire

Avranches, France, 5062(d)

Awbridge, Hants., 4578(i)

Axbridge, Som., 5404(d)

Axe-hammers: perforated stone, 723(l), 4981(j), 5191(c); prehistoric, of Wiltshire, 6113(e)

Axes, axe-heads: bronze, 2373(d), 3897(l), 6311(a); bronze age, 5729(nn), 6205(a), 6307(a), 6312(b); flint, 3916(p), 3917(b), 4539(e); neolithic, 742(b), 2880(a), 6316(b); Penmaenmawr factory, 747(f), 4060(b), 4062(b); stone, 2110(m), 2552(g), 3979(a). *See also* Hand-axes

Axholme, Isle of, Lincs., 6033(l)

Axminster, Devon, 1105(k), 1355(m); hundred, 1359

Axmouth hundred, Devon, 1359

Axton, Flints., 1775(b)

Aycliffe, co. Dur., 97(a), 5216(e)

Aydon Castle, Northumb., 5236(e)

Aylesbury, Bucks.: charter, 101(i); county hall, 102(e); extent, 101(v); gaol, 102(e); gypsies, 1923(b); Hartwell House museum, 3439(b); hut, semi-underground, 99(p)

Aylesford, Kent, 3988(f), 5494(h)

Ayleston, Leics., 160(f), 2748(c,d), 2753(f), 2756(g)

Aylett, Robert, religious poet (d. 1655?), 1694(c)

Aylsham, Norf., 3569(s)

Aymer (Ethelmar) de Valence, bp (d. 1260), 2009(h)

Aynscombe, Thomas, of Mayfield (d. 1649), 5722(g)

Ayot St Lawrence, Herts., 1592(m,o)

Ayot St Peter, Herts., 1592(r)

Ayton, Great, N.R.Yorks., 6397

B–, R–, author of *Apius and Virginia*, 3163

B–, S–, English Anabaptist (fl. 1575), 196(f)

Babbeogh hundred, Suff., 5580(h)

Babington, Som., 5429(k)

Babraham, Cambs., 760(h)

Bache, The, *see* Warley, W.R.Yorks.

Bachelors, tax on, 5799(p)

Backford, Ches., 2111(f)

Backhall, *see* Southowram, W.R.Yorks.

Backhouse, James, Quaker (d. 1798), 1821(b), 1832(d)

Backhouse & Co., of Darlington, bankers, 4855(a)

Backwell, Som., 5421(e)

Backwell, Edward, banker (d. 1683), 4252(u)

Backworth type brooches, 5253(h)

Bacon, family, 179(c), 184(c)

Bacon, Anthony, diplomatist (d. 1601), 181(c)

Bacon, Francis, 1st Baron Verulam and Vct St Albans (d. 1626), 818(b); and Edw. Alleyn, 182(a); and *Argenis*, 172(d); and Roger Bacon, 4668(d); biographers, 181(b); birth and parentage, 165(a,b), 176(a); and Burghley, 173(a); charges against, 168(b); and Cheltenham rectory, 174(a); death, 174(c), 175(a), 177(b), 178(b), 179(b), 180(a); downfall, 4279(f); and E. of Essex, 166(c); East Anglian M.P., 171(a); empire builder, 4280(d); examination, 183(c); expenses, 176(f,g); and field-sports, 166(a); in France, 172(b); and Gray's Inn, 173(c), 181(d); in Italy, 172(e); as jurist, 5292(a); as K.C., 172(c); letters to, 170(a,c); medical allusions, 4692(c); and money-lenders, 184(d); monument, 4823(f); mystery, 172(a); *New Atlantis*, 2892(c); and Portugal, 175(b); as statesman, 166(b); Dugald Stewart's opinion of, 184(b); Warwickshire relations, 173(b); *The World*, 3400(b). *See also* Bacon Soc.

Baptists (*cont.*)

191(l); diary of lay preacher, 200(w); discipline book, 198(g); disputations, 17th cent., 195(m); doctrines, Welsh, 190(a); and evangelism, 208; and feet-washing, 190(m); under Geo. I, 191(f); graves, in Milford, 3366(e); history, books on, 197(f); and infant baptism, 190(x); letters (1742–1831), 202(b); library, in Barbican, 195(f); licences (1672), 190(q); literature, 190(l); meetings, in city of London, 194(g); militant (1660–72), 190(p); ministers, in England (*c*. 1750), 195(h); ministers, in London (1696), 195(j); minute-book (1719–1806), 201(g); minutes of the General Assembly (1654–1811), 6553; missionary instructions, 190(f); missionary-licence, 193(l); monthly conferences, Leicestershire, 194(d); notable, index to, 196(i); notable, in the Midlands, 199(p); and original sin, 190(m); and parish churches (1641–62), 192(n); periodicals, 194(q); and Pinners' Hall, 197(c); plan for the ministry, 192(b); principles, early, 204(a); prisoners in Devon and Cornwall (1672), 201(b); reasons for dissent, 195(k); and St. Bartholomew's day, 190(c); and Salter's Hall meeting, 194(o); in state papers, 17th cent., 194(l); Ben. Stinton's friends, 190(t); student's programme (1744), 198(k); trust deeds, 201(h); verse writers, 192(k); and Wallis house, Kettering, 197(k); and Westminster assembly, 3921(i); Whitefield's influence on, 201(e). *See also entries above beginning* Baptist *and* Campbellite Baptists; General Baptists; Johnsonian Baptists; McLeanist (Scotch) Baptists; Particular Baptists; Pedobaptists; Welsh Baptists

Baptists of London (Whitley), 200(k)

Baptist Union, 198(i), 200(e)

Baradoun, Henry (15th cent.?), 1472

Baraset, nr Calcutta, cadet college, 5083(o)

Barbados, West Indies, 1107(ee), 1807(h)

Barbara, voyage of, to Brazil, 3500(a)

Barbauld, Mrs, *see* Aikin, Anna Laetitia

Barbellion, W–N–P–, *pseud.*, *see* Cummings, Bruce Frederick

Barber surgeons: Bristol, 450(f); Chester, 997(e); London, 518(b), 3021(a), 3040(a), 4692(b); Newcastle-on-Tyne, 4707(b); York, 4706(b)

Barbican, London, library and baptistery, 195(f)

Barbon, Dr Nicholas (d. 1698), 2974(c)

Barbor, John, brasier, of Salisbury (d. 1404), and wife Alice, 6103(j)

Barcelona, Spain, 814(n), 4771(d)

Barcheston, Warws., 5922(b)

Barclay, Abram Rawlinson (19th cent.), 1833(b)

Barclay, Alexander, poet & divine (d. 1552), 1520, 3995

Barclay, John, writer (d. 1621), 172(d), 183(b), 1074(b)

Barclay, Robert, Quaker apologist (d. 1690), 1824(b)

Barclay mss, 1833(b)

Bardesey, family, *see* de Bardesey

Bardney, Lincs., 154(a,b,m), 524(a), 4126(a)

Bardon papers, 4392(d), 4430

Bards: essays on, 3449; itinerant, 2309(b); legal and social status, 2309(c); Welsh, 2308(c), 3449

Bardsea, Lancs., 1169(j), 1175(t), 1183(l)

Bardsey, island, Caern., 746(l)

Bardsey-cum-Rigton, W.R.Yorks., 2393(d)

Bardwell, Suff., 666(f), 5572(g,h); Wykes, 3562(a)

Barebone, Praise-God (d. 1679), 1105(h)

Barentin, family, 5041(d), 5043(f)

Barentin, Alexander de, butler to Hen. II, 3519(gg)

Barentyne, family, 3769(c)

Barentyne, Sir William (fl. 1540), 5720(o)

Barford, Niels Lauritsen, Danish adm. (fl. 1690–1714), 5111(h)

Barford St Martin, Wilts., 6103(h)

Barforth, N.R.Yorks., 6258

Barfreston, Kent, 517(e), 2607(a), 5512(a)

Barges: inventory, *temp*. Edw. III, 5103(m); royal, 4488(a); Thames type, 5099(x)

Barham, Kent, 2602(a)

Barham, Baron, *see* Middleton, Charles

Barham, family, 5708(e)

Barholme, Lincs., 154(l)

Baring, Alexander, 1st Baron Ashburton, financier & statesman (d. 1848), 4283(a)

Baring, Evelyn, 1st E. of Cromer (d. 1917), 24(b,c), 477(d)

Barkby, Leics.: Hamilton, 157(i)

Barker, John, Presbyterian divine (d. 1762), 3922(h)

Barker, John (d. 1804), 5088(c)

Barker, Joseph, preacher & controversialist (d. 1875), 5853(k)

Barker, Col. Sir Robert, F.R.S. (d. 1789), 4138(e)

Barkham, Berks., 261(d)

Barking, Essex: abbey, 1696(d), 2094; church, 1693(cc), 3006(a); Congregational church, 1108(f); Court House, 1696(s), 1700(j); Eastbury House, 1693(cc), 3085; Uphall camp, 1693(z)

Barkisland, W.R.Yorks., 1966(e), 1985(d), 1995(f)

Barkway, Herts., 1589(x), 1592(s)

Barlaston, Staffs., 3612(a), 5542

Barlborough, Derbys., 507(d)

Barle, river, Som., 5422(a)

Barlee, William (d. 1610), 3339

Barley, Herts., 1594(a)

Barling, Essex, 1694(x)

Bar-lip bowls, 4098(a)

Barlow, family, 2250(c)

Barlow, Edward, *known as* Ambrose, Benedictine (d. 1641), 1024(b), 2641(c)

Barlow, Roger (d. 1554), 1961, 4365(a)

Barlow, William, bp (d. 1613), 4835(e)

Barlwick priory, *see* Brompton Regis, Som.

Barmouth, Mer., 752(b)

Barnack, Northants, 5279(e)

Barnack, Gervase de, of Peterborough (12th cent.), 3859(b)

Barnard, Mrs Ella Pierrepont, 614(f)

Barnard Castle, co. Dur., 5213(r), 5243(a), 5245(b), 5674(b)

Barnard's Inn, London, 3074(a)

Barnes, I.o.W., 2553(d)

Barnes, family, 1818(m)

Barnes, Ambrose, Newcastle Puritan (d. 1710), 1111(k)

Barnes, Richard, bp (d. 1587), 947(b)

Barnes, William, Dorset poet (d. 1886), 5316(a), 5320(c), 6287(c)

Barnes, William, rector of Came (d. 1886), 1383(e), 1392(g)

Barnestone manor-house, *see* Purbeck, Dors.

Barnet, Herts., battle, 4795(f)

Barnham, Suff., 3911(o), 3912(d)

Barnham, Benedict, merchant (d. 1598), 170(b)

Barningham Norwood (Barningham, North), Norf., 3572(s), 3589(b)

Barns, 1354(i), 1368(f), 1372(a). *See also* Tithe barns

Barnscar, Cumb., 1194(h)

Barnsley, W.R.Yorks., 3222(c), 5222(i), 6239(g), 6288(i)

Barnstaple, Devon, 1339(a); archdeaconry, 1727(m); and Armada, 2999(c); and Athelstan, 1352(g); castle, 1350(c); and Charles, Prince of Wales (1645), 1339(g); and Civil war, 1349(g); drama, 1339(h); goldsmiths' guild, 1339(a); music, 1339(e); parish clerks, 1326(o); plaster ceilings, 1339(b); sub-manors, 1339(f)

Barnstaple West, Mass., 1108(o)

Barnston manor-house, *see* Church Knowle, Dors.

Barnwell, Northants, 153(t)

Barnwell Gate, *see* Cambridge

Barnwell priory, *see* Cambridge

Barnwood, Glos., 458(h), 1136(c), 5131(a)

Barometric statistics, and production and export figures, 4240(b)

Baron, Robert, poet & dramatist (fl. 1645), 3568(h)

Baronet's badge, 5330(h)

Baronets of Nova Scotia, 4272(a)

Baronies, succession to, 5330(a)

Barons, and reform (1258), 2239(c)

Barons, in Magna Carta, 4454(d)

Baroose, *see* Lonan, I.o.M.

Barr, Staffs., *see* Staffordshire, Barr beacon

Barracks, 3850(a), 4781(d)

Barret, George, landscape-painter (d. 1842), 4811(b)

Barret, John, nonconformist divine (d. 1713), 1107(l)

Barret, Robert, military writer (fl. 1600), 5092(g)

Barrett (Barrett Lennard), Dacre, of Belhus, Essex (d. 1724), 1714(c)

Barrett-Lennard, Thomas, 16th Baron Dacre (d. 1786), 5710(c)

Barriers, and foot combats, 4108(m)

Barrington, Cambs., 758(cc), 768(d)

Barrington, Som., 1398(c), 5412(i), 5420(c), 5424(n), 5445(e)

Barrington, Samuel, adm. (d. 1800), 3477(b), 5116(m)

Barrington, Sir Thomas (17th cent.), 1696(n)

Barritt, Thomas, saddler-antiquary (d. 1820), 2638(b)

Barrock fell, *see* Hesket, Low, Cumb.

Barrosa, battle, 4147(c)

Barrow camp, *see* Exmoor

Barrow-digging, 6016(b)

Barrowe, Henry, church reformer (d. 1593), 1103(r,v), 1115

Barrowe, Thomas, royal cook (d.1509), 2136(d)

Barrow-in-Furness, Lancs., 211(i,j)

Barrow[-in-Furness] Naturalists' Fd Club & Lit. & Sci. Assn, *Ann. Rpts*, etc., 209–14

Barrow-on-Soar, Leics., 2754(f)

Barrows and tumuli: at, on, near, *see below*; bell-barrows, 3917(b), 5628(c), 5729(j); chambered, 735(i); disc-barrows, 1190(e), 1396(h); long barrows, *see below*; names of, 1278(d); pottery found in, 1375(f); prehistoric, 5246(d); ritual of, 1375(g); Roman, 1696(k); round barrows, *see below*

at, on, near: Abbey Wood, 6147(e); Alvediston, Middle down, 6111(r); Amesbury, 6113(r); Arbor Low, 1281(c); Ashdown Forest, 5729(r); Asthall, 5163(e); Bamburgh castle, 5227(o); Bartlow, 516(l); Barton Mills, 774(a); Bath, Charmy down, 5442(d); Birkrigg, Ulverston, 1177(t); Bourne, Cambs., 763(i); Bowerchalke, 6111(m,y); Brent Pelham, 1590(k); Brightwell heath, Suff., 2532(a); Bristol, Kings Weston hill, 5858(b); Broxbournebury, 1589(b); Bryngwyn, 728(l); Bures, 1693(b); Cambridge, Lord's Bridge, 760(k); Castle Lloyd, Bigning mountain, 907(b); Chadwell St Mary, 1697(p); Chippenham, Lan-

Barrows and tumuli (*cont.*)

hill, 6104(k); Christchurch, 2011(q); Clapham and Balham, 5626(k); Cley-next-the-sea, 3570(l); Colchester, Lexden park, 528(p), 5192(g); Creech, 1368(c); Dane's Graves, Yorks., 1614(d); Derbyshire, 1278(d), 1572(b); Devonshire, 1323(b); Dorset, 1383(b); Dunstable, 4095(b), 4135(f); Easneye, 1588(m); Eglwys Bach, 733(n); Ellsnook, nr Rock, Northumb., 5229(l); Eyam moor, Derbys., 1573(a); Eyebury, 5151(b); Figheldean, 6112(j); Fovant, 6112(g); Garthbeibio, 743(k), 3905(c); Glynde hill, Suss., 5716(j); Gop, 722(j), 2875(e), 4105(i); Graysonlands, Glassonby, 1164(v); Greenwich, 1897(k); Grosnez Hougue, Jersey, 5063(a); Hampshire, 2006(b), 2016(p); Hampton down, Som., 5441(e,i); Heddington, King's Play down, 6104(l); Heytesbury, Boles barrow, 6110(m); Hove, 416(a); Hunstanton, 5145(q); Ibsley common, 398(a); Iford, 5730(k); Kerry, Mont., 3907(k); Knock, Mont., 3907(k); Knocky Doonee, I.o.M., 2551(v); La Hougue de Vinde, Jersey, 4082(b); La Hougue Mauger, Jersey, 5054(d); Lake House, Wilts., 6103(r); Latton, 1692(q); Les Platons, Trinity, Jersey, 5054(c); Lewes, 5715(i); Martinstown, Dorchester, 1372(b); Mendips, 5858(a), 6003(d); Merddyn Gwyn, Pentraeth, Anglesey, 728(g); Netley hill, Bursledon, 2014(h); Newmarket heath, 760(n); Pickering, 6412(b); Plas Heaton, 2887(i); Rickling, 1693(w); Ringmer, 5715(i); Rodmell, 5730(k); Rushden, 3644(b); St Catherine's hill, I.o.W., 2012(a); St Nicholas, Glam., 735(i); Shopland, 1705(n); the Six Hills, Stevenage, 1590(bb); Sizergh fell, 1167(a,k); Sledmere, 6229(n); Somerset, 6000(d); South Charlton, 5246(d); Sponds hill, Ches., 2635(l); Staffordshire, 1278(d); Stanton moor, 1297(a); Stone, Bucks., 99(o); Stoney Littleton, 5441(b); Sunningdale, 5148(i); Sussex downland, 5729(y); Swinburne park, Northumb., 5227(c); Swinscoe, 3636(d); Sywell, 3641(a); Thetford, 3911(c); Tynings, nr Blackdown, Som., 5860(c); Ty'n-y-Pwll, Llanddyfnan, Anglesey, 729(m); Uley Bury, 4125(m); Upavon, 6105(n); West Harptree, Pool farm, 5429(l); Wick, Som., 5407(n); Widford, 1589(t); Wiltshire, 6104(cc); Winkhill, 3618(g); Winterbourne Stoke, 734(d); Woodbury common, 1322(p); Ysceifiog, 746(c)

long barrows: Belas Knap, 457(m,n); Bisley, Glos., 1133(a); nr Glasbury, 4097(b); Lincolnshire, 4136(e); Llanigon, 4090(a), 6128(e); Luckington, Giant's caves, 6114(w); Notgrove, 1134(a); Stoughton down, 5718(j); Sussex, 5715(e), 5729(j); Wiltshire, 6106(h)

round barrows: origin, 6030(f); Ballaterson Cronk, Maughold, I.o.M., 2549(r); Melcombe Bingham, 1384(g); New Forest, 2011(d); Niton, I.o.W., 2553(m)

See also Anglo-Saxon barrows; Bronze age barrows; Iron age tumulus; Romano-British barrows; *and under* Britain, ancient

Barrow-upon-Trent, Derbys., 1274(e)

Barry, Sir Charles, architect (d. 1860), 106(c), 5288(a)

Barry, James, painter (d. 1806), 4634(c)

Barry, Richard, 7th E. of Barrymore, eccentric (d. 1793), 265(d)

Barrymore, Earl of, *see* Barry, Richard

Barsham, Suff., 3587(b)

Barth, Henry, explorer (d. 1865), 18(b)

Barthelmy, –, French refugee (fl. 1852), 265(h)

Bartholomew, bp (d. 1184), 1327(d)

Bell, Sir John, gen. (d. 1876), 4757(e)

Bell, John Browne, publisher (d. 1855), 1764

Bell, Mercy, *see* Ransom, Mary

Bell, Robert, Quaker recording clerk (d. 1776), 1834(b)

Bell, Robert, officer in Madras (fl. 1779–1820), 4158(d)

Bell, William, English agent at the court of Shāh Abās (d. 1624), 4193(a)

Bellamy, family, 2971(f)

Bellamy, John, Puritan publisher (d. 1654), 1109(j)

Bellaport Hall, Salop, 3631(f), 4982(e)

Bell-barrows, *see* Barrows and tumuli

Bellbridge Old House, *see* Sebergham, Cumb.

Bell Brothers' blast-furnaces, 2536(b)

Belleau, Lincs., 152(s)

Belleisle, siege of, 4166(b)

Bellême, Robert of, E. of Shrewsbury (fl. 1073–1112), 4962(d)

Bellerophon, H.M.S., 5113(j)

Bellers, John, Quaker (d. 1725), 1818(j,k), 1823(d)

Bell-founders and bell-founding, 3554(c), 5996(a); Cambridge, 776(d); Gloucestershire, 440(d); London, 4835(g); Whitechapel, 2973(r); Whitford, Flints., 747(i); Wiltshire, 6117; Worcestershire, 4110(g); York, 149(v)

Bell-hangers, English gypsies as, 1936(d)

Bellingham, Lewisham, 2759(a)

Bellingham, Northumb., 929(h), 5215(k)

Bellmen, of Cambridge, 768(b)

Bell metal mortars, 780(d)

Bell-ringing: change-ringing, 2825(cc); change-ringing controversy, 5801(e); orders for, 2132(f)

Bells, 5996(a); 13th cent., 5165(j); Bedfordshire (*c.* 1710), 235(d); curfew bell, Neath, 3517(b); Devon, medieval, 1345(a); Laugharne, cast locally, 919(f); Minchinhampton (1515), 5165(h); Old Weston, Hunts., 825(m); sacring, Essex, 1705(j); sanctus, Fladbury, 6163(d); Welsh Celtic, 746(j); Winchester, 2011(b); Worcestershire, medieval, 147(s), 4110(g). *See also* Church bells; *and* Bell-founders, *etc.*, *above*

Bell's New Weekly Messenger, 1764

Bell's Weekly Messenger, 1764

Belsay, Northumb., 96(l)

Belsham, Thomas, Unitarian minister (d. 1829), 5856(o,s)

Belstead, Suff., 1677(e)

Beltout valley, *see* Eastdean, Suss.

Belts, *see* Zones

Beltz, Samuel, dep. assistant commissary gen. to the forces (d. 1862), 2938(b)

Belvedere, or the garden of the Muses (Badenham), 3209(n),

Belverge, family, 235(a)

Belvoir, Leics., 504(o), 535(d), 536(a), 3940(a)

Belvoir Castle edge-railway, 3940(a)

Benavente, Portugal, battle, 4780(i)

Benbow, John, v.-adm. (d. 1702), 1179(m), 4982(c)

Bench-ends, at or in: Badlesmere, 2605(k); Bishop's Lydeard, 5100(v), 5101(d); Devon, 1727(l); East Budleigh, 5101(d,m); Eynesbury, 822(f); Great Brington, 3656(e); Hawarden, 2119(d); Somerset, 5351(e); Wendens Ambo, 1699(q)

Benedict, Saint (d. 821), 1476, 1496, 3524(c), 3525(b)

Benedictine (Black) monks, 958, 4411(g), 4449

Benedictine nuns, English: Brussels, 940(c); Cambrai, 939(a); Flanders, 933(a); Ghent, 944(a); obituaries, 936(k); Paris, 936(k); Pontoise, 942(b); Preston, 944(a); Winchester, 940(c)

Benedictine rule, 1476, 3524(c), 3525(b)

Benedictionals, *see* Liturgies, Latin rite

Benefices: held by cardinals, in Lincoln, 151(l); Leicestershire, *temp.* Jas I, 151(h); parochial, medieval valuation of, 3565(d); poor, in Leeds, 5800(j); right of presentation, 813(e), 5215(f); sale of presentations, 2377(f); vacant by death, 4115(n), 4118(f)

presentations, admissions, collations, institutions, inductions: Bedfordshire, 231(e); Carmarthenshire, 918(c); Essex (Commonwealth), 1702(h), 1704(o); Leicestershire, 159(f); Lincoln dioc., 147(q), 152(d), 161(f), 162(b), 4115(n); *sede vacante* by chapter of Canterbury, 2616; Shropshire, 4962(n), 4973(k); Surrey (Commonwealth), 5608(e); York dioc., 4118(f); Yorkshire (Commonwealth), 6260(g)

See also Advowsons

Benefit societies, *see* Friendly societies

Benet, Saint, *see* Benedict

Benet, family, 6103(p)

Benet, Sir John (fl. 1676), 1277(e)

Benet, Thomas, *alias* Duggate, Exeter martyr (d. 1531), 1353(n)

Benetheton, Roger, chaplain of Colmworth (d. *c.* 1439), 227(a)

Benfleet, South, Essex, 1692(p)

Benfold, *see* Gosforth, Cumb.

Benfras, Madoc, poet (fl. 1340), 2272(e)

Bengal, 1963, 2226(a), 4138(e), 4207(a), 4755(f)

Bengal, Bay of, 1943, 5110(f)

Bengal Artillery, 4167(h), 5091(a)

Bengal Engineers, 5090(a)

Bengal Horse Artillery, 4169(c), 4170(d)

Bengal Irregular Cavalry, 4789(b), 4790(g)

Bengal Native Infantry, 4756(n)

Bengal Sappers and Miners, 2484(a)

Bengeo, Herts., 1588(i)

Bengeworth, Worcs., 158(f)

Bénitiers (arched recesses in private dwellings), 5072(e)

Bennet, Sir John, of Dawley (b. 1618), 435(k)

Bennet, Thomas, Quaker schoolmaster (d. 1764), 1816(r)

Bennet's Ende, *see* Knowbury, Salop

Bennett, Charles, of Manchester (fl. *c.* 1679), 1017(c)

Bennett, E. Arnold, novelist (d. 1931), 1757

Bennington, Herts., 1588(cc)

Benson, Oxon., 1113(r)

Benson, Rev. George, of Abingdon (d. 1762), 1112(m)

Benson, Martin, bp (d. 1752), 99(d)

Bensted, Sir Edward (fl. 1504–17), 1589(cc)

Bent, Capt. George (d. 1803), 5082(c)

Bentall, Salop, *see* Alberbury with Cardeston

Bentham, W.R.Yorks., *formerly* Lancs., 1196(q), 2706, 6398

Bentham, Jeremy, writer on jurisprudence (d. 1832), 1915

Bentinck, William, 1st E. of Portland (d. 1709), 2867(b)

Bentinck, Lord William Cavendish, gov.-gen. of India (d. 1839), 4005

Bentinck, William Henry Cavendish, 3rd D. of Portland (d. 1809), 4005

Bentley, Staffs., 6080(a)

Bentley, Suff., 5573(c)

Bentley, W.R.Yorks., 1968(k)

Bentley, Jeremy, M.P. for Halifax (fl. 1654), 1992(i)

Bentley, John, Halifax builder (d. 1615), 1991(e)

Bentley, John Francis, architect (d. 1901), 107(a)

Bentley Royd, *see* Sowerby, W.R.Yorks.

Black monks, *see* Benedictine (Black) monks
Blackmoor Vale, Som. and Dors., 1382(c)
Black-more, *see* Cornwall
Blackmore, Richard Doddridge, novelist (d. 1900), 1325(e)
Blackner, John, historian of Nottingham (d. 1816), 5832(c)
Blackpatch, *see* Patching, Suss.
Blackpool, Lancs., 2109(a)
Black Prince, H.M.S., 5113(h)
Blackrod, Lancs., 2678
Blackshaw Clough, *see* Soyland, W.R.Yorks.
Blacksmiths, legends of, 2010(a)
Blackstone, Sir William, legal writer (d. 1780), 819(b,c), 5301(a)
Blackstone Edge, Lancs.: Flint hill, 3986(e), 6321(a); roads, 409(bb), 1972(e), 3984(c), 3986(b); Roman remains, 3984(c), 3985(d)
Blacktoft, E.R.Yorks., 6335
Black Torrington hundred, Devon, 1359
Blackwardine, *see* Stoke Prior, Herefs.
Blackwater, river, 1701(e)
Blackwell, nr Alfreton, Derbys., 1287(d)
Blackwell & Dist. Sci. & Lit. Soc., *Derbyshire Naturalists' Quarterly*, 387–8
Blackwood, Mon., 706(e,f)
Blackwood's Magazine (1818), letter in, 1753
Bladon, Oxon., 3770(b)
Blag, in place-names, 5844(d)
'Blag' culte, 5846(i)
Blagrave, Anthony, of Bulmershe Court, Berks. (d. 1653), 271(b)
Blagrave, John, mathematician (d. 1611), 5195(b)
Blake, Robert, adm. (d. 1657), 3475(e), 3892(n), 4773(c), 5343(a); letters, 3511(i); life (1625–40), 4758(b); reduction of Jersey, 5115(d); reduction of Scilly Isles, 5114(h); will, 5113(o)
Blake, Robert, capt. (d. 1802), 4122(d)
Blake, William, poet & painter (d. 1827), 2846(a), 3118(c), 4284(e)
Blake, in place-names, 5844(d)
Blakeden, Cuthbert (d. 1540), 3430(dd)
Blakeley, Lancs., *see* Blackley
Blakeney, Norf., 3563(e), 3569(t), 3591(e), 3593(e)
Blakenham, Suff., 3519(n)
Blakeway, Rev. John Brickdale, topographer (d. 1826), 4966(k), 4969(e), 4975(f), 4976(b)
Blakhale manor, *see* Carlisle
Blanchland, Northumb., 4106(p), 4129(d)
Bland, Humphrey, military writer (d. 1763), 2465(a)
Blandford, Dors., 1395(b), 5320(b)
Blandford St Mary, Dors., 1377(d)
Blasphemy, law of, 816(b)
Blast-furnaces, 2536(b); Roman, 5171(i)
'Blatant Beast', Spenser's, 3407(c)
Blatchington, West, Suss., 5701(i), 5723(j)
Blaunchflur, *see: Floris and Blaunchflur*
Blaxland, Gregory, explorer (d. 1852), 4290(f)
Blayney, David Lloyd (fl. 1583), 3898(h)
Bleaching and bleachworks, 2652(k)
Bleadon, Som., 5404(c), 5428(c)
Bleak down, *see* Godshill, I.o.W.
Bleasdale, Lancs., 2623(e), 2634(b)
Blechingley, *see* Bletchingley
Bledlow, Bucks., 102(m), 4834(q)

Blencowe Hall, *see* Greystoke, Cumb.
Blenden Hall, merchant-ship, 5098(w)
Blenheim, battle, 5086(e)
Blenheim Palace, Oxon., 216(g), 6498(a)
Blennerhasset, family, 1195(f)
Bletchingley (Blechingley), Surr., 5607(e), 5612(g), 5617(a)
Bletchley, Bucks., 98(k), 99(k), 102(g,t); Etone, 101(r)
Blethin, William, bp (d. 1590), 2282(i)
Bletsoe, Beds., 5330(z)
Blew and Orange, Loyal & Friendly Soc. of the, 5087(q)
Blewburton hill, *see* Blewbury, Berks.
Blewbury, Berks., 254(f), 3834; Blewburton hill, 3533(q)
Blickling, Norf., 3569(s)
Bligh, William, adm. (d. 1817), 5111(o)
Blight, family, 201(p)
Blind Beggar of Alexandria (Chapman), 3198
Blisland, Cornw.: Carwen, 4542(a)
Bliss, Philip, editor & bibliographer (d. 1857), 3706(a)
Blithfield, Staffs., 6088(a)
Blockade, naval: of Brest (1803–5), 3488; comparisons (1807 & 1917), 3470(b), 4762(a); in French Revolutionary and Napoleonic wars, 3467(a,b), 4757(k); of Germany (1914–18), 4159(a); of Montenegro and Albania (1913), 4770(g)
Blockhouse system, Boer war, 2509(b)
Blockley, Worcs., 6157(c)
Blois, *see: Partonope of Blois*
Blois, Henry of, *see* Henry of Blois
Blois, Peter of, *see* Peter of Blois
Blois mss, 5575(i)
Blome, Anne, of Castle Piggin, Abergwili (late 18th cent.), 920(k)
Blomefield, Francis, topographer of Norfolk (d. 1752), 3568(a), 3573(j)
Blomfield, Sir Arthur William, architect (d. 1899), 105(e)
Blomfield, Charles James, bp (d. 1857), 1111(i)
Blo' Norton, Norf., 3566(k)
Blood, Col. Thomas, adventurer (d. 1680), 200(d)
Blood, circulation of, 986(a). *See also* Holy Blood
Bloodaxe, Eric (d. *c*. 950), 6230(n)
Bloody Assize (pamphlet, 1689), 5446(g)
Bloody assizes (1685), 201(c)
Bloomeries, *see* Ironworks
Bloomfield, Robert, Suffolk poet (d. 1823), 5576(c)
Blore with Swinscoe, Staffs., 3636(d)
Blount, family, 702(b)
Blounts manor, Herts., *see* Lowthes
Blowick, Lancs., 2129(c)
Blowing-houses: Glazebrook valley, 1354(f); Meavy, Erme and Avon valleys, 1355(e); Sheepstor Brook, 1354(f), 1355(e); Walkham valley, 1353(m)
Bloxham, Oxon., 458(b), 3772(c), 3783(a), 4114(l), 5853(g)
Bloxham, John, warden of Merton Coll., Oxf. (d. 1387), 3746(d)
Blue Mountains, Australia, 4290(f)
Blue Nile, *see* Nile, Blue
Blue Nuns, *see* Immaculate Conception of Our Lady, order of
Blundell, Nicholas (d. 1736), 2120(k); his diary, 2774(a), *omitted from text*
Blunden, family, 865(k)
Blunden Hall, *see* Bishop's Castle, Salop
Blundeville, Thomas, author & poet (d. 1606), 3569(o)
Bluntesdon, Henry de, archd. of Dorset (fl. 1311), 3520(w)
Bluntisham, Hunts., 200(q)

Blurton, Staffs., 3618(f)

Blutte, family, 2351(i)

Blyborough, Lincs., 147(d)

Blymhill, Staffs., 5556

Blyth, Northumb., 507(d)

Blyth, Notts., 5807(e); priory church, 96(b), 536(a), 5165(a), 5807(a), 6228(z)

Blythburgh, Suff., 531(i), 5572(c), 5582(p)

Blyton, Lincs., 147(d)

Boadicea, *see* Boudicca

Board of Admiralty, *see* Admiralty

Board of Trade, and the fighting services, 4770(e)

Boarhunt, Hants, 2016(bb), 5451(f), 5466(c)

Boars, skulls of, 2102(c)

Boarstall, Bucks., 3519(jj), 3734

Boats: on or belonging to warships, 5098(z); size of (1640), 5119

Boats, ancient, in or from: Baddiley mere, 997(f); Brigg, 1613(c), 5105(o); Murston, 3990(c,d); Warboys fen, 823(g). *See also* Dug-out boats

Boatswain's whistle, 3472(e), 5105(e)

Bobbing, Kent, 2591(h)

Bobbingworth, Essex, 1695(r)

Bocking, Essex, 1632(i), 1697(e), 1701(q), 1703(e)

Bodanan manor, *see* St Teath, Cornw.

Bodelwyddan, Flints., 2878(b)

Bodenham, John (fl. 1600), 3209(n)

Bodiam, Suss., 4109(k), 5698(d), 5724(d), 5728(kk)

Bodlewfawr, *see* Anglesey

Bodley, John, father of the following (d. 1591), 1325(c)

Bodley, Sir Thomas (d. 1613), 170(a,c), 1325(r)

Bodmer, John George, Swiss engineer (d. 1864), 3550(e), 3554(h)

Bodmin, Cornw., 4539(c)

Bodmin Gospels, 4541(f,i)

Bodmin moors, Cornw., stone circles, 544(a), 545(a,d)

Bodney, Norf., 3917(h)

Boerhaave, Herman, scientist (d. 1738), 4697(a)

Boers, trek of, Transvaal to Angola, 4286(d)

Boer war (1899–1902): battlefields in Natal, 4141(b); block-house system, 2509(b); Christiana, defence of, 2464(b); Diamond Hill, 4137(i); events leading to, 4137(m); events (1899–1900), 4137(e); Ladysmith, 4629(b); Magersfon-tein, Boer position at, 4137(f); narrative of Boer prisoner, 4139(a); Natal campaign, 2507(a), 4137(j); Pieter's Hill, 2509(a); railways in, 2511; a retrospect, 2464(a); Royal Engineers in, 2465(d), 2507(a); work of artillery branch of H.Q. staff, 4140(b). *See also* Royal Artillery

Boethius, Ancius Manlius Severinus (d. 524), 1515

Bognor, Suss., 5718(o), 5722(j)

Bogo de Clare, *see* Clare, Bogo de

Bois-le-Comte, Charles Joseph Edmond, comte de, French diplomat (d. 1863), 4402(c)

Boislin, sieur de, *see* Béranger, Isaac de

Boislin trust (1708), 2348(g)

Bokerly dyke, *see* Cranborne Chase

Bolam, Northumb., 5216(p), 5223(o), 5236(e)

Bolas, Great, Salop, 4974(l), 4981(i), 5016

Bolbec, baronies, 5253(e)

Bold, Thomas John, naturalist (d. 1874), 5869(b)

Boldon, co. Dur., 5223(y), 5593(a,b)

Boldre, Hants, 2009(v), 5463(b)

Bolebroke House, *see* Hartfield, Suss.

Boles barrow, *see* Heytesbury, Wilts.

Boley hill, *see* Rochester, Kent

Boleyn, family, 3572(u)

Boleyn, Thomas, prec. of Wells (d. 1472), 5414(a)

Bolingbrooke, Old, Lincs., 2825(c)

Bolingbrooke House, Battersea, 2970(aa)

Bolle, family, 152(q)

Bolling, family, 407(o), 409(ee)

Bolling Hall, *see* Bradford, W.R.Yorks.

Bolney, Suss., 5749

Bolsover, Derbys., 536(a), 1286(a), 1570(d), 4118(p)

Bolton, Lancs.: freemasonry, 3212(b); Hall-i'-th'-Wood, 2110(a), 2117(d), 3976(e); machine-makers' strike, 4252(jj); parish registers, 2692; Quakers, 2650(c)

Bolton, Westmld, 1190(m)

Bolton Abbey, W.R.Yorks., 414(b), 2636(m), 5802

Bolton-by-Bolland, W.R.Yorks., 6258, 6344

Bolton Gate, Cumb., 1177(c)

Bolton in Bowland, *see* Bolton-by-Bolland

Bolton-le-Sands, Lancs., 2684

Bolton, Percy, W.R.Yorks., 6231(b)

Bombay, India, 620(m), 1963, 2501(d), 5303(b)

Bombay army, 5091(h). *See also* Indian army

Bombay Artillery, colonels commandant, 4167(h)

Bombay Horse Artillery, 4162(e), 4170(d)

Bonaventura, Saint (d. 1274), 4003

Bonchurch, I.o.W., 2007(e), 2553(v)

Bondmen: of Gimingham manor, 3567(b); inquisition *re, temp.* Eliz. I, 232(f); at Reigate, 5626(h); of Surrey, 4389(g); Tudor, 4387(f)

Bond of association, *temp.* Eliz. I, 1334(f)

Bonds: *re* Montgomeryshire, 3898(f); Temple Newsam, 5804(h)

Bone-bed (bone-deposit), at Stoke, Ipswich, 3913(r)

Bonedd y Saint, 751(d)

Bone implements, from: Bradfield, Yorks., 6310(b); Chelm's Combe, Cheddar, 5425(l): Suffolk, 3912(n)

Bonell, Katherine, of Shrewsbury (d. 1461), 4967(a)

Bone objects, 1713(d)

Boner, *see* Bonner

Bones, from: Broadchalke Saxon cemetery, 6111(c); Coygan bone cave, 914(k); Grayson-lands tumulus, 1164(w); Harlyn Bay, 4535(f); Rothwell, 76(a). *See also* Anglo-Saxon bones; Human remains; Jutish bones; Pleistocene bones

Bonfire Scar cave, *see* Scales in Furness, Lancs.

Boniface, Saint (d. 755), 3380(b), 3893(j)

Boningale, Salop, 5006

Bonington, Richard Parkes, painter (d. 1828), 5815(f), 5911(h)

Bonner (Boner), Edmund, bp (d. 1569), 850

Bonnet, wearing of, in royal presence, 4963(h)

Bonville, William, 1st Lord B. (d. 1461), 1334(e)

Bonwicke, Ambrose, the younger, non-juror (d. 1714), 810

Book-binders, 2767(a); (1457–1557), 322; the Bowtells, 759(q); Cambridge, 311, 333; Edwards family of Halifax, 1975(g); Oxford, 308, 325; ticket used by, 297(m); York, 274(b)

Book-bindings: Bagford's notes on, 276(c); chained, in St Benedict's church, Camb., 760(f); cloth, 1745(a,b); heraldic, 2768(c); by Sam. Mearne, 5147(f)

Book-case, evolution of, 435(f)

Book clubs, 1113(k), 1761

Book-collecting and book collections, 2778(a), 2789(b)

Book Collector's Quarterly, *see* First Edition Club

Bridge chapels: Bath, 508(e); Bridgnorth, 4980(d); Derby, 1298(b); St Ives, Hunts., 821(e)

Bridge Hall, *see* Sandridge, Herts.

Bridgeman, Sir Orlando, lord keeper (d. 1674), 4963(a)

Bridgeman and Brock, reports of cases by, 2973(ll)

Bridge records, Montford, Salop, 4968(c)

Bridges, 2067(a), 2592(a), 4485(b); building of, 4658(c); iron, 3112(n); maintenance, medieval, 4866; packhorse, 1191(i), 1282(a), 5582(g)

at, in, or over: Aire and Calder (*temp*. Eliz. I & Jas I), 407(i); Aldreth causeway, 821(a); Attlebridge, 3566(m); Barras, nr Newcastle-upon-Tyne, 5217(k); Bath, 508(e); Bideford, 1324(d), 3002(b); Bourn, Cambs., 824(e); Bradford, Yorks., 407(u); Bridgnorth, 4980(d); Bruton, 5352(d); Burton-on-Trent, 700(a,c); Cambridge, 760(k), 762(f); Carmarthen, 918(i); Chester, 1009(c); Colchester, 1700(b); Cornwall, 4217(i); Crowland, 3850(c); Cuckmere river, 1629(d); Culham, 2938(a); Derby, 1298(b); Derbyshire, 1585(b); Dorset, 1375(h); Ferrybridge, 4489(a); Fingringhoe, 1704(r); Furness abbey, 1189(h); Glastonbury, Pomparles, 5411(m); Gloucester, 457(i); Great Salkeld, Eden bridge, 1176(m); Hampton Court, 5178(e); Hanwell, Brynt bridge, 2973(kk); Hereford, 747(q); Herefordshire, 5165(g), 6126(l), 6129(b); Lanercost, 1193(j); London, *see* London, city & environs; Lyme Regis, 1389(h); Maidenhead, 249(c); Monk's bridge, Hadrian's wall, 702(c); Neath, 3516(a); Newbridge-on-Wye, 3938(d); Newcastle-upon-Tyne, 2948(d); Newton Cap, nr Bishop Auckland, 5213(a); Northamptonshire, 4116(p); Rochester, 2597(e,f); St Ives, Hunts., 821(e); Sheffield, Ewden bridge, 2378(w); Sheffield, Ladys bridge, 2376(d); Southwark, 3112(n), 3118(a); Sowerby, 1978(b); Stirk, 1978(b); Sunderland, 5593(c); Swarkestone, Derbys., 1279(e); Tarr steps, Som., 5422(a); Warrington, 5978(a); Warwickshire, 372(a); Wetherby, 6238(k); Windybottom bridge, 2628(d); Worcestershire, 153(i); Worcestershire Avon, 366(c)

See also Bridging: Roman bridges

Bridge Trafford, Ches., 1001(b)

Bridgewater, Duke of, *see* Egerton, Francis

Bridgewater, Earl of, *see* Egerton, John

Bridgewater mss, *see* Egerton, John, 1st Earl of B.

Bridgford, East, Notts.: church, 5809(c), 5821(e); Margidunum, 515(f), 5134(d), 5137(b), 5814(f), 5833(a); rectors, 5829(c)

Bridgford, West, Notts., 5821(a)

Bridging, in World War I, 2514

Bridgnorth, Salop, 866(s); and Rich. Baxter, 4980(b); bridge and chapel, 4980(d); castle, 4984(a,o); Castle Street Baptist chapel, 5028(a); church, 4979(i); coins, 4581(i), 4970(n); Ethelfledd's tower, 4984(a); Grey friars, 4982(a); hospitals, medieval, 4979(b); members of parliament, 4976(a); St Mary Magdalene Coll., 4131(a); Stoneway chapel, 5026(e)

Bridgwater, Som., 217(t); burgesses, 5416(b); Downend, 5408(m); freemasonry, 6542(f); nonconformist academy, 1106(b); Parrett river, 5419(i); and Peasants' revolt, 5426(l); wills, 5419(j)

Bridgwater, H.M.S., 5106(k)

Bridlington, E.R.Yorks.: 17th cent., 1605(d); Austin canons, 155(e); breech-loading gun, 5103(b); neolithic workshops, 6302(a); prehistory, 6313(e); priory, 6229(g), 6237(c), 6266(a), 6505(a); rentals and surveys, 6266(a)

Bridport, Dors., 1374(g), 1379(d), 1389(g), 1391(b), 5322(a)

Bridport, Giles of, bp (d. 1262), 6114(ff,gg)

Brief historical Relation of State Affairs (Luttrell), 3119(b)

Briefs, collections on, 5212(m); (1682–1731), 920(i); Abbot's Ripton, 824(j); Cheshire, 2138(e); Cuckfield, 5704(b); Farcet, 823(k); for Huguenots, 2347(b); Keynsham, 216(h); Lancashire, 2138(e); Langley Burrell, 6104(v); Little Wittenham, 254(d); Pembrokeshire, 2251(a); for Piedmontese (1655), 1112(v); Ruscomb, 255(b); Shropshire, 4981(h); Tollesbury, 1697(m); Woolwich, 6142(c); Yorkshire, 6224(f)

Brief Sketch of the Several Denominations of the Christian world (Evans), 6019(u)

Brief Summe of Geographie (Barlow), 1961, 4365(a)

Briercliffe, Lancs., 2640(c)

Briercliffe, family, 2640(c)

Brierley, Ben, writer (d. 1896), 3306(d)

Brierley, Thomas (b. 1785), 3219(b)

Brigantes, 6231(j); coins of, 2637(b), 4581(a), 4582(a)

Brigantines, 5104(d), 5105(g); derivation of name, 5103(s)

Brigg, Lincs., 1613(c), 2825(u), 5105(o)

Brigg, family, 1976(g)

Brigg mill, *see* Sowerby, W.R.Yorks.

Briggs, family, 5801(l)

Briggs, John, parish clerk of Hurley (d. 1814), 260(b)

Brighouse, W.R.Yorks., 1812(d); Slead Hall, 1996(g). *See also* Hipperholme

Brighouse, family, 1971(e)

Brighstone, I.o.W., 2553(c)

Bright, family, 2377(o)

Bright, Richard, physician (d. 1858), 1926(b)

Bright, Timothy, inventor of shorthand (d. 1615), 5791(c), 6225(b)

Brighthelmston, *see* Brighton, Suss.

Brightling, Suss., 5697(h)

Brightlingsea, family, 1701(e)

Brighton, Suss., 520(g); art galleries, 2768(c); burning, 4391(a), 4400(e); churches, 417(f), 520(g), 5706(k); churches, Presbyterian, 3919(o); coins, 415(g); court roll, 415(g); drove road, 5728(l); earthworks, 5720(j); inhumation, 5716(j); museums, 2768(c); pigmy flint implements, 422(a); prehistory, 419(a); public libraries, 2768(c); lost river, 5505(a); St Bartholomew's chapel, 417(e,f); Steine, 416(e); terrier, 5729(d); vicarage, 5720(h); Western Road, 5729(q); Whitehawk neolithic camp, 5723(c). *See also entries beginning* Brighton & Hove

Brighton, New, *see* New Brighton, Ches.

Brighton & Hove Archaeol. Club, *Brighton & Hove Archaeologist*, 415–17

Brighton & Hove Nat. History & Philosoph. Soc.: *Abstracts of Papers*, 418–29; history, 423(a)

Brighton & Sussex Nat. History Soc., *afterwards* Brighton & Hove Nat. History & Philosoph. Soc., *q.v.*

Brightwalton, Berks., 246(f), 272(g)

Brightwell, Berks., 247(i), 251(a), 261(d)

Brightwell, Suff., 2532(a)

Brightwell Baldwin, Oxon., 3430(m)

Brigstock, Northants, 523(a), 2749(d)

Brigstocke, Thomas, portrait-painter (d. 1881), 905(p)

Brill, Bucks., 101(v)

Brilley, Herefs., 6130(b)

Brimham, W.R.Yorks., 6301(a)

Brimington, Derbys., 1586(a)

Burnett, John (b. *c.* 1830), 6542(c)
Burney, Edward Francis (d. 1848), 6162(c)
Burney, Frances, Mme D'Arblay (d. 1840), 1349(d), 1655
Burney, Thomas Frederick (d. 1785), 6162(c)
Burnham, Bucks., 98(o,z), 4107(l)
Burnham, Som., 6544(b)
Burnham, Richard, Baptist minister (d. 1810), 199(s)
Burnham Deepdale, Norf., 3564(g)
Burnham Market, Norf., 3565(j)
Burningfold manor, *see* Dunsfold, Surr.
Burnley, Lancs., 690(e), 693(a), 694(b), 698(a), 3980(a)
Burnley Lit. & Sci. Club: a retrospect, 694(a); *Trans.*, 681–99
Burns, Robert, poet (d. 1796), 6474(b)
Burnt Woods, *see* Eccleshall, Staffs.
Burpham, Suss., 5707(m), 5715(a)
Burradon, nr Newcastle-upon-Tyne, Northumb., 5231(c)
Burrell mss, 5718(p)
Burrington, Som., 5421(k), 5857(a); Burrington Combe, Aveline's Hole, 5857(h)
Burrough, Leics., 2749(e)
Burrough Island, *see* Devonshire
Burrow, James, of Crosthwaite, Westmld (17th–18th cent.), 1183(m)
Burrow Hall, Lancs., 1196(g); Overborough camp, 2636(f)
Burry Holmes, islet, Glam., 5775(a)
Bursars' books, *see* Accounts
Burscough, Lancs., 2631(j); Martin Hall, 2121(i), 2634(d)
Burse (vestment), 5968
Bursledon, Hants, 5460(a); Netley hill, 2014(h)
Burslem, Staffs., 3623(e), 5554
Burthogge, Richard, Plymouth philosopher (d. 1694?), 3896(h)
Burtle, Som., 4101(a)
Burton, Ches., 994(f), 2113(a)
Burton, Suss., 947(j)
Burton, John, antiquary & physician (d. 1771), 5617(b)
Burton, Sir Richard Francis, writer & explorer (d. 1890), 4278(g), 4348(d)
Burton, Robert, author (d. 1640), 289(f), 1741(a)
Burton, Sir Thomas (d. 1381), and wife Margery (d. *c.* 1410), 3429(k)
Burton, William, antiquary (d. 1657), 3901(e)
Burton Agnes, E.R.Yorks., 1614(e), 5239(b), 6229(j), 6265(g)
Burton Coggles, Lincs., 6442(a)
Burton Fleming, E.R.Yorks., 6329
Burton-in-Lonsdale, W.R.Yorks.: Lowfields, 1196(g)
Burton Latimer, Northants, 4834(r)
Burton Lazars, Leics., hospital of St Lazarus, 5251(d)
Burton manor, *see* Eardisland, Herefs.
Burton-on-Trent, Staffs., 700(a,e), 702(b), 1104(h); Nether Hall, 702(b)
  abbey, 700(b); abbots, 701(c); annals, 701(a); cartulary, 1277(b); Sinai park, 701(b); surveys, 6075(b), 6086(d)
Burton-on-Trent Nat. History & Archaeol. Soc., *Trans.*, 700–2
Burton-upon-Stather, Lincs., 2825(b)
Burwalls camp, Som., *see* Ashton, Long
Burwarton, Salop, 4976(b)
Burwell, Cambs., 775(c), 823(m)
Bury, Hunts., 821(s)
Bury, Lancs., 265, 2633(g), 3216(b)
Bury, John Bagnell, historian (d. 1927), 482(c), 813(g). *See also* Index of Authors
Bury, Richard of, bp (d. 1345), 5675
Bury, William de, of London (fl. 1363), 3520(k)

Bury and W. Suffolk Archaeol. Inst., *afterwards* Suffolk Inst. of Archaeology & Nat. History, *q.v.*
Bury hill, Glos., *see* Winterbourne Down
Bury St Edmunds, Suff., 3588(d); abbey, *see below*; *Booke of subscriptions*, 5574(e); corner posts, 5577(f); freemasonry, 6552(a); gaol, 5582(m); Hardwick House, 5575(n); liberty, 5576(k); medieval, 5574(m); nonconformists, 1103(x); rental, 5574(m); revolt (1381), 5582(n); rising (1327), 5582(o); St James's church, 531(e); St Mary's church, 531(d); St Robert, 5582(f); St Saviour's hosp., 5580(j); wills, 5573(n), 5574(f)
  abbey, 3588(e); abbots, 2971(d); bible, 3529(c); documents, 500; herbal, 4029; *Liber Albus*, 3565(d); possessions, 5574(u); psalter, 3529(b); register, 3519(ee)
Bury Street chapel, London, 1102(b,i), 1104(m), 1105(i), 1107(aa)
Bury walls, Salop, *see* Hawkstone
Busaco, battle, 4143(d)
Buscot, Berks., 262(a)
Bushbury, Staffs., 6094(a)
Bushby, George, Roman Catholic priest (fl. 1681), 1278(i)
Bushel, measure, Elizabethan, 759(f)
Bushell, family, 1107(ee)
Bushell, Thomas, speculator & farmer of the royal mines (d. 1674), 620(k)
Busher, Leonard, pioneer of religious toleration (fl. 1611), 190(i)
Bushey, Herts., 4827(b)
Bushey Park, Mdx, 566(a)
Bushley, Worcs., 6193(j), 6194(i), 6199
Bushman's River Pass, *see* Natal, S. Africa
Bushnell, John, sculptor (d. 1701), 5923(b)
Bushwood, Warws., 363(j)
Busks, as love-tokens, 5229(q)
Buslingthorpe, Lincs., 3428(dd)
Bussey, Lambert de (fl. *c.* 1216), 1194(e)
Bussie, Mary (d. *c.* 1600), 3428(x)
Bussy d'Ambois (Chapman), 3397(a)
Buston, High, Northumb., 5241(e)
Busullow downs, Cornw., 4541(c)
Butchers' companies: London, 3138(b); Newcastle-upon-Tyne, 5246(a)
Butleigh, Som., 5401(i), 5425(f)
Butler, family, 2121(k), 6236(l)
Butler, John Lewis (fl. 1829–42), 709(j)
Butler, Joseph, bp (d. 1752), 1046(h), 5893(a)
Butler (Boteler), Nathaniel, capt. R.N. (fl. 1626), 3513, 5098(d)
Butler, *see* Chief butler of England
Butley, Suff., 5575(c)
Butrio, potter, 5140(b)
Butsfield, *see* Sately, co. Dur.
Butt, John, of Carmarthen, M.P. (d. 1452), 916(f)
Butterfield, William, architect (d. 1900), 113(b)
Buttern hill, *see* Dartmoor, Devon
Butterwick, Westmld, 1185(s)
Butterworth, Lancs., 3981(c)
Butterworth, family, 3976(d)
Butterworth, Edwin, Lancashire topographer (d. 1848), 2627(c)
Butterworth, James, Manchester topographer (d. 1837), 2631(i)
Butterworth End, *see* Norland, W.R.Yorks.
Buttinghill hundred, Suss., 5710(b)

Canada (*cont.*)

disarmament, 4516(h); navy, 4268(e); political unrest (1815–36), 4299; and Prince of Wales, 4276(j); in Royal Empire Soc. subject catalogue, 4314; settlement of ex-service men, 4308; shells manufactured, 2540(a); South-esk's journey, 4357(a); Stretton's sketches, 5090(b); United States boundary, 4349(b); World War I, 4310, 4404(a)

Canale, Giovanni Antonio, *called* Canaletto, painter (d. 1768), 5876(a), 5917(b)

Canaletto, *see* Canale

Canals, 2451(d,e), 2456(a), 2461(a); Gloucester & Berkeley, 1134(b); Kennet & Avon, 1823(b), 4638(a), 6543(d); Lancaster, 1180(c); Manchester Ship, 2451(a), 2454(a), 3320(a); Thames & Severn, 1140(d); W.R.Yorkshire, 1985(g). *See also* Water-ways

Canary Islands, 2569(e), 2584, 4393(e), 4434

Candle-mass, 1(a)

Candleston castle, *see* Merthyr Mawr, Glam.

Candle tax, 4854(a)

Canewdon, Essex, 1693(p)

Cann, Dors., 1384(f)

Canne, John, separatist (fl. 1640), 192(r)

Cannibalism, in ancient Britain, 94(a)

Canning, Elizabeth (d. 1773), 3305(b)

Canning, George, statesman (d. 1827): duel with Castlereagh, 814(g); and intelligence from Tilsit, 4390(b); patriotism, 4284(e); and publication of diplomatic docs., 812(j); rhyming 'despatch', 4390(a); and Spanish America, 4387(f)

Cannington, Som., 5419(d), 5426(n), 5900(b)

Cannock Chase, Staffs., 700(d)

Cannock wood, Staffs., *see* Rugeley

Cannon, 3564(e), 4141(f), 4162(c). *See also* Artillery

Canoes, *see* Dug-out boats and canoes

Canonbury, dist. of Islington, *see* London, metropolitan boroughs: Islington

Canon Frome, Herefs., 3810

Canonization: 12th cent., 657; Bp John de Dalderby, 155(h); Bp Grosseteste, 155(a); St Osmund, 6097

Canon law, 176(b), 2835

Canons, *see* Augustinian canons; Secular canons

Canons' Ashby, Northants, 3785(a)

Canons residentiary, 1338(f)

Canopus, H.M.S., 3473(c)

Canterbury, Kent, 1067(a), 4131(h); archdeaconry, 2587(f), 2603(g); Blackfriars, 4133(i); British Archaeol. Assn congress, 535(g); castle, 4133(m); cathedral, *see below*; cavalry station, 4794(k); Christ Church monastery, *see below*; churches, 4133(m); Congregational church, 1108(p); coinage, 505(h); Dane John, 4133(m); dean & chapter, *see below*; and Dickens, 1600(b); flint implements, 3917(k); Greyfriars, 660, 2596(c); Jews, 2569(b); maps and plans, 1555, 2587(q); monastic houses, 2605(o); pilgrims, 1599(b), 1860(a); psalters, 3520(l), 3524(b); Queningate (Durovernum), 2607(g); road, 1555; St Andrew's church, 2594(c); St Augustine's abbey, *see below*; St Augustine's Coll., 4837(d); St Dunstan's church, Roman cemetery, 2601(d); St John's hosp., 4133(m); St Martin's church, 517(e); St Martin's hill, Roman cemetery, 2602(g); St Pancras church, 2587(o), 4105(n)

cathedral, 4133(m), 5157(f); All Saints' chapel, 1849(a);

Canterbury, Kent (*cont.*)

Black Prince relics, 5205(b); burning and repair, 1867; Chicheley porch, 5187(e); choir, 5178(g); crypt chapel of Our Lady, 2600(j); dean & chapter, *see below*; heraldic badges, 1848(a), 5182(j), 5187(e); human remains, 5149(a); infirmary chapel, 5179(c); library, 277(c), 654(d); masons' marks, 6528(c); pavement, 2604(j); psalter, 1852(c); Queen Ediva's portrait, 2598(a); Reculver columns, 1863(b); St Thomas's shrine, 95; tapestries, 1852(d), 2606(f); tombs, 1862(a), 2589(n), 5205(a); towers, 1847(a), 1848(b), 2607(c); undercroft, capitals, 2607(r); vaults, 4121(a); Warriors' chapel, 1866; windows, 786, 1852(a), 2591(o), 2599(f). *See also* Friends of Canterbury Cath.

Christ Church monastery, 1599(a); chronicles, 782, 2591(e); churches, 2606(h); cult of Becket, 2606(b); deans, priors and monks, 782; Domesday Monachorum, 2607(e); gateway, 1851(a); Wm Glastynbury's chronicle, 2599(f); Hen. of Eastry, prior, 2601(a); manors, 2606(h); monks and their books, 1851(b); petition, 1632(i); psalter, 3530(b); Wm Selling, prior, 2778(a); Rich. Stone, 782, 2605(g); White Book of St Augustine, 2607(e)

dean & chapter: estates, 2600(c), 5705(l); letters, 2604(d); *sede vacante* institutions, 2616; *sede vacante* visitations, 2594(b); *sede vacante* wills, 1705(m), 2612

St Augustine's abbey, 517(e), 4133(m); church, 5182(h), 5193(f); customary, 2078; discoveries and excavations, 2593(t), 2597(d); east end, 4110(d); John Foche, abbot, 2598(d); Thos Ikham, benefactions of, 2599(g); inquisition, 496; plan, 2602(f); register, 495; *Regula S. Benedicti*, 3524(d); Roger II, abbot, 2596(f); St Pancras chapel, 2587(o); St Pancras church, 4105(n); SS. Peter and Paul church, 2587(o), 2588(a); Saxon cross, 2599(l); tombs, 2600(h); walling, 2593(s)

Canterbury, diocese, province, see: act books, 642; administration, 1062; abp's houses in Sussex, 5281(e); abp's manors in Sussex, 517(d), 5720(n); canonical professions of obedience, 2599(c), 4836(q); charters, 4446(c); consistory court records, 2602(c), 2603(g); episcopal professions of obedience, 3519(r), 3524(d); Otford manor-house, 2593(b); peculiar court, marriage licences, 5741, 5746, 5748; prerogative court, wills, 624, 1677(p), 5611(h), 5612(b), 5623(b); and primacy, 152(dd); privileges, 3519(r); probate registry, wills, 639; and Provisions of Oxford, 3525(f); registers, 855, 1109(aa), 3519(l)

Canterbury & York Soc., publs, 827–56. *See also* Cantilupe Soc.

Canterbury Cathedral Chronicle, *see* Friends of Canterbury Cath.

Canterbury Papers, *see* Friends of Canterbury Cath.

Canterbury Tales: Brathwait's comments, 967; Cambridge ms., 963; clerk's tale, 964; eight-text edition, 977; evolution, 972, 3870(c); franklin's tale, 982; Harl. ms., 7334, 975; Harl. ms., 7335, 5581(h); mss of, 964, 980, 3529(e); pardoner's tale, 969, 1555; ploughman's tale, 968; prioress's tale, 978

Cantilupe, Thomas de, Saint, bp (d. 1282), 828, 6122(v), 6131(f)

Cantilupe Soc., publs, 857–9. *See also* Canterbury & York Soc.

Canting arms, 2118(e), 5711(b)

Cantoche, in Domesday, 5409(l)

Canton, China, 4194(a), 5084(a)

Carpets: English, 4646(b); Lewknor, 5722(a)

Carr, family, 2378(y)

Carr, John, architect (d. 1807), 4468(d), 4489(a)

Carrawburgh, Northumb., 5213(l)

Carreg Cennen, Carm., 1(m), 902(a)

Carreghofa, Mont., 864(a), 4605(b)

Carrew, Nicholas (d. 1432), and wife Isabel, 3428(bbb)

Carriages: children's and invalids', 4650(b); history, 4630(c); horseless, *see* Motorcars

Carriers, carters: accounts, 5698(b); journals, 3563(k); token issued by, 610(j)

Carrington House, Westminster, 3112(j)

Carrow, Norf., 528(d), 3568(l)

Carshalton, Surr.: baptisms, Catholic, 950(h); brass, 3430(n); camp, 5624(f); Carshalton Park, 5609(h); manor, court rolls, 5649; vestry book, 5614(b)

Carsington, Roger de, *see* Roger de Carsington

Cartagena, S. America, battle, 5083(u)

Carte, Richard, musician (d. 1891), 3900(f)

Carter, Isaac, pioneer of Welsh printing (fl. *c.* 1718), 6017(f)

Carteret, John, 1st E. Granville (d. 1763), 5091(l)

Carteret, Mauger de, *see* Mauger de Carteret

Carteret, Regnaud de, *see* Regnaud de Carteret

Carteret, *see also* De Carteret

Carters, *see* Carriers

Carthagena, *see* Cartagena

Carthaginian coin, 5720(b)

Carthusian order: in England, 92(g), 1053; founding, 6226(i); remains, in Somerset, 5994(a)

Cartington, Northumb., 5219(d), 5221(b)

Cartmel Fell, Lancs.: Angles in, 1187(y); Beggar's Breeches fields, 1183(b); parish registers, 2670; priory, 1045(d), 1192(z); priory church, 1183(h), 2106(g); St Anthony's chapel, 1175(w,x), 2634(c)

Cartography, 3255(a), 4340(a), 4377; and Marlowe's plays, 1646(a). *See also* Maps and plans

Carts, use of in 14th cent., 2240(b)

Cartularies:
   domestic: Anlaby family, 6239(u); Boarstall manor, 3519(jj), 3734; Bromley family, 6083(b); Clervaux family, 5249(e); Percy family, 5673; Tropenell family, 6100(e)
   of religious houses, etc.: Abingdon, 260(d); Bilsington, 499; Buckland, 5382; Burton, 1277(b); Cerne, 1374(f); Chertsey, 5618(c), 5658; Chester, St Werburgh's, 1035; Chichester, St Mary's hosp., 5703(c); Cockersand, 1020; Coxford, 3565(k); Dale, 1272(k); Darley, 1274(d); Dieulacres, 3611(d), 6075(c); Dunstable, 233; Eynsham, 3713; Fountains, 407(s); Furness, 1032; Hereford cath., 6126(t); Holme Cultram, 1212; Kentish, of order of St John, 2619; Lewes, 5768, 6239(s); Lincoln cath., 2810; Missenden, 225(d); Monkbretton, 6262; Old Wardon, 236; Oseney, 246(e), 3735, 6090(c); Oxford, hospital of St John the Baptist, 3721; Pontefract, 6241; Reading, 3527(f); St Bees, 1165(s), 1166(d); Salisbury, St Nicholas' hosp., 6098; Sallay, 6271; Tockwith, 6266(b); Walden, 3529(d); Warwick, St Mary's, 443(d)

Cartwright, family, 5815(i)

Cartwright, Thomas, Puritan (d. 1603), 3923(k)

Cartwright, William, actor & benefactor of Dulwich Coll. (d. 1686), 3386(a)

Cartwright, William, non-juror (d. 1799), 4975(a)

Carvajal, Maria Fernandez de (fl. 1660), 2582(e)

Carvals (Manx carols), 3349(b)

Carved and sculptured stones, early, in or at: Alderney, 5036(i); Birstall church, 6228(b); Breedon-on-the-Hill, 2754(h), 5193(g); Calverton church, 3564(g), 4105(p); Cardiganshire, 897(a); Cumberland, 1165(f); Hexham, 5254(f); Lincolnshire, 4130(a); Lindisfarne, 5190(g); Manchester cath., 2628(j); Millom, Cumb., 1194(m); Ramsey, I.o.M., 2548(b); Suffolk, 'Dane stones', 5578(d)

Carved wooden spoons, 721(h)

Carvell, Edmund (fl. 1559), 3567(h)

Carver, Derick, Protestant martyr (d. 1555), 5701(i)

Carvings: Cardiganshire churches, 893(n); Exeter cath., 4119(a); Leeds, St John's, 5799(h); Manchester cath., 2127(d). *See also* Alabaster carvings; Carved and sculptured stones; Roof bosses; Sculpture; Wood-carvings

Carvoran, *see* Greenhead, Northumb.

Carwen, *see* Blisland, Cornw.

Cary, Elizabeth, Vctss Falkland (d. 1639), 3179

Cary, Henry Francis, translator of Dante (d. 1844), 3401(b)

Cary, John, cartographer (fl. 1769–98), 4354(b)

Cashen, William (d. 1912), 3350

Cash reserves, in banks (1880–1911), 3320(b)

Casket letters, 2192, 5525(a)

Caspian Sea, 3470(d), 4203(d)

Cass, Aaron (18th cent.), 1111(i)

Cass, Sir John (d. 1718), 2970(m)

Cassiobury Park, Herts., 4821(e)

Cassiterides (tin islands), 509(j), 4213(c), 4542(f)

Castel, Guernsey, 5031(f), 5037(f)

Castell Aber Lleinawg, *see* Penmon, Anglesey

Castellaños, Juan de, Spanish poet (d. 1607), 5106(c)

Castell Coch, Glam., 881(a)

Castell Collen, *see* Llanfihangel Helygen, Rad.

Castell Meredydd, *see* Machen, Mon.

Castell Morgraig, *see* Glamorganshire

Castell of Labour (Gringore), 3995

Castell of Pleasure (Nevill), 1524

Castell Taliorum, *see* Llanhilleth, Mon.

Casterley camp, Wilts., 6106(f)

Casterton, Little, Rut., 3429(k), 4812(a), 4815(f)

Castiglione, Countess (19th cent.), 142(f)

Castile, King of, *see* John of Gaunt; Philip

Castilla, Julian de (17th cent.), 4443(e)

Castle Acre, Norf., 528(n), 4127(d)

Castle-an-Dinas, *see* St Columb, Cornw.

Castle Ashby, Northants, 155(j)

Castle Bromwich, Warws., 4583(a)

Castle Bryn Amlwg, *see* Bettws-y-Crwyn, Salop

Castle Caereinion, *see* Llanfair Caereinion, Mont.

Castle Camps, Cambs., 823(a)

Castle Carlton, *see* Carlton Castle, Lincs.

Castle Carr, *see* Midgley, W.R.Yorks.

Castle Carrock, Cumb., 1182(e); Hallsteads, 1171(q)

Castle Cary, Som., 5349(c), 6033(b)

Castle Combe, Wilts., 5442(i); Nettleton Scrub, 5442(k), 5443(f)

Castle Cornet, Guernsey, 5031(e), 5038(a), 5040(a)

Castle Dobbs, co. Antrim, 4071(c)

Castle Donnington, Leics., 1285(a), 2753(b)

Castle Eden, co. Dur., 1436

Castle Hedingham, Essex, 522(e), 3519(i), 4111(j)

Castle Hewin, Cumb., 1172(m)

Castle How earthwork, Cumb., *see* Bassenthwaite lake

Castle Howard, N.R.Yorks, 1607(b), 5927(c); Crambeck, 6276

Climping, Suss.: Islesham, 5715(i)

Clippers, Liverpool, 2130(b). *See also under* Ships

Clitheroe, Lancs.: in 17th cent., 2646(c); castle, 1992(e); charter, 2651(c); folk-lore, 2639(a); witchcraft, 2632(g)

Clitterhouse manor, *see* Cricklewood, Mdx

Clive, Salop, 4968(q), 5010, 5028(d)

Clive, Robert, Baron C. (d. 1774), 4636(a), 4976(e), 4978(f)

Clock- and watch-makers, 1987(b), 1988(e); Berkshire, 266(h); Bristol, 457(o); Dorset, 1394(i); co. Durham, 5260(c); Gloucestershire, 457(o); Halifax, 1984(g); north country, 5254(o); Northumberland, 5260(c); Prescot, Lancs., 2131(d); Reading and dist. 260(h); Rochdale, 3985(e); York, 152(n)

Clock-jacks, 5193(i), 5408(j), 5999(a)

Clocks, 1988(e), 5193(i); made in Dorset, 1394(i); early, 4825(g); Halifax parish church, 1984(h); long case, 1984(g), 1987(b), 3985(e); mechanism of, 4126(d); Porlock church, 5430(l); Wells cath., 5408(j), 5999(a). *See also* Scratch-dials; Water-clocks

Clock tower, St Albans, 4821(v)

Cloisters, 4118(g), 5225(r); Exeter cath., 1728(j); Great Yarmouth, 528(j); London, St Bartholomew the Great, 2970(k); Newminster, 5225(r); Southwark priory, 4118(g)

Clopton, Cambs., *see* Clapton

Close, William (d. 1813), 211(h)

Close rolls: Edw. I–III, 2109(c); extracts (1238–1339), 267(b); extracts *re* Jews, 2566(h), 2582(d)

Closer union, Eastern and Central Africa: debate on, 20(b); report of committee, 22(c), 2410(b), 4516(e)

Clothall, Herts., 1591(i); Cumberland manor, 1591(n); Quickswood, 1591(j)

Clothes, expenditure on, 1275(a)

Cloth fulling, 3556(d); Roman, 5175(f)

Cloth halls: Halifax, 1968(i), 1984(f); Headcorn, 2593(i)

Clothiers: 17th cent. probate inventories, 408(l); of Sudbury, 5575(f)

Cloth industry, trade: Colchester bays, etc., 1692(o), 1694(e); Suffolk, 93(a), 4260(k); west of England, 6110(r). *See also* Aulnage accounts; Aulnager; *and entries beginning* Wool, Woollen, *etc.*

Clothing, army: (1660–1909), 4773(i); (1914–15), 4325(b); forces at Shrewsbury (1403), 4964(f); Yeomen of the Guard (1485–1685), 4129(c). *See also* Uniform, army

Clough, Arthur Hugh, poet (d. 1861), 2137(c), 2843(b)

Clovelly, Devon: Clovelly Dykes, 2996(c)

Cloven way, *see* Hampshire

Clovesho, councils of, 5579(f)

'Club, The', founded by Sir J. Reynolds and Dr Johnson, 3999

Club-houses, in London, 109(c)

Clubs, *see* Societies and clubs

Clun, Salop, 866(f), 4969(i), 4972(d), 4977(e); deanery, 4970(i), 4983(e); hundred, 4965(c)

Clunbury, Salop, 3803, 4988; Coston manor, 4974(b)

Clungunford, Salop; Abcott manor, 4979(d)

Cluniac order, English province, 525(e), 4408(e)

Clun valley, Salop, 866(q,w)

Cluny abbey, France, 262(d)

Clwyd, vale of, N.Wales, 726(i), 1456(b)

Clyffe Pypard (Cliffe Pypard), Wilts., 6105(j), 6112(k); Bupton, 6103(p)

Clynnog, Caern., 734(h); church, 746(q), 1458(a), 2271(d), 2293(b), 2393(b), 2881(d); monastery, 719(p)

Clyomon and Clamydes, 3174

Clyst, Devon, battle, 1334(e)

Clysters, treatises of, 1488

Cnut, *see* Canute

Coaching and coaches: Jewish calendars, 2567(h); Liverpool, 2127(a); London to Yorkshire, 1986(d); Oxford, 3712(f); Rochdale, 3982(b); Staffordshire, 3628(b); Woolwich, 4160(h)

Coaching inns, 119(a)

Coachmen, in Cambridgeshire probate records, 764(f)

Coal: carbonization experiments, 3278(a); foreign trade in, 4716(b); international problem, 4519(b); royal commission on supplies, 4225(c); utilization, 560(a)

Coalbrookdale, Salop, 3548(f), 3549(a)

Coal-fields, *see* Coal industry

Coal-gas: early history, 3547(e); lighting from, 2649(e), 3549(g)

Coal-heavers, of London, 18th–19th cent., 4252(o)

Coal industry, coal-mines, coal-mining, etc., 2796(a); in 17th cent., 1279(n), 4409(d); colliery records, 1632(e); commission, 4239(b); controls, in Scotland, 4253(g); and eight-hour day, 4227(c); labour in, 4250(a); miners, 18th cent., 4252(t); note-book, 18th cent., 3621(b); population changes in, 4345(e); strikes, disputes, 4232(f), 4235(g)

  at, in: Black Country, 3552(h); Cardiff, 2546; Dudley, Worcs., 3552(h); Elswick (1698–1732), 5217(d); Farnley (1690–1720), 6289(e); Halifax, 1993(f); Hartley, Northumb. (1774–1808), 5220(c); Mendips, 18th cent., 5350(e); Monmouthshire, 4250(a); Pummer, nr Barnsley, 5222(i); Staffordshire, 18th cent., 3621(b); Stourbridge, 3552(g); Wales, 749(c), 2546, 4250(a), 4345(e); Warwickshire, 1882(c); Yorkshire, 6318(a)

  See also Mines, miners, and mining

Coastal changes: Kent, 1604(a); Sussex, 1604(a); Yorkshire, 4327(c)

Coastal formation, Dungeness foreland, 4371(a)

Coastal shipping, Dewisland, 2255(h)

Coast defences: influence of foreign policy, 2468(a); order concerning (1625), 5145(j); Roman, 5123(d), 5142(d); surveys of (1779–93), 4155(b)

Coast erosion, 212(a), 1094(c), 3251(b), 5496(a)

Coasting trade, 2463(a)

Coast-line: Cinque ports, 1874(d); Hampshire, 2014(l); Hastings, 4347(a); Suffolk, 5580(a,f); Sussex, 5705(b)

Coates, Glos., nr Cirencester, 454(m), 456(g)

Coates, Great, Lincs., 151(c)

Coatham, N.R.Yorks., 1094(a)

Coat of arms, the term, 2837(b)

Coats of arms, *see* Arms, heraldic

Cobbett, William, essayist, etc. (d. 1835), 3294(a)

Cobble-road, in York, 6415(a)

Cobham, Kent: church, 506(c), 2069(a), 2665(j), 3988(d); Cobham Park, British oppidum, 2468(d); college, 2589(g), 3988(d); manors, 2589(h)

Cobham, Surr., 5609(l)

Cobham, family, 2591(g)

Cobham, Lord, *see* Oldcastle, Sir John

Cobham, Sir John (d. 1408), 5161(l)

Cobham, Thomas, bp (d. 1327), 148(f), 6191

Cobler's Prophecy (Wilson), 3180

Cochrane, Thomas, 10th E. of Dundonald, adm. (d. 1860), 5113(g)

Cochwillan, *see* Llanllechid, Caern.

Collations to benefices, *see under* Benefices

Collectanea (Lysons), 2951(a)

Collectars, *see* Liturgies, Latin rite: antiphonales

Collections for a History of Staffs., *see* William Salt Archaeol. Soc.

Collects, Marian, 4837(m)

College histories, 514(c)

Colleton, John, Roman Catholic priest (d. 1635), 928(e)

Collier, John, mayor of Hastings (d. 1760), 5697(c)

Collier, John, author & artist (d. 1786), 2773(a)

Collieries, *see* Coal industry

Colliers (coal ships), 5226(j)

Collingbourne Ducis, Wilts., 6110(t)

Collingbourne Kingston, Wilts., 6110(t)

Collinges, John, Norfolk dissenter (d. 1691), 3572(l)

Collingham, South, Notts., 5811(b)

Collingwood, Cuthbert, 1st Baron C., v.-adm. (d. 1810), 4761(c), 5234(i)

Collins, family, 5729(ss)

Collins, Rev. Brian Bury (b. 1752), 6037(b)

Collins, David, first gov. of Tasmania (d. 1810), 4290(h)

Collins, Grenvill, naval capt. & hydrographer (d. 1694), 5111(i)

Collins, William Wilkie, novelist (d. 1889), 1746(a)

Collinson castle, *see* Cumberland

Colly Weston, Northants, 150(s)

Colman, Jeremiah James (d. 1898), 1111(i)

Colmworth, Beds., 227(a)

Colne, Hunts., 824(o)

Colne, Lancs., 202(j), 2662, 2957(b), 3216(a)

Colne Engaine, Essex, 1692(n), 1696(c)

Colne mss of masonic charges, 2957(b)

Colne priory, *see* Earls Colne, Essex

Colne Valley, Essex, 5166(l)

Cologne, Germany, 5139(a)

Cologne merchants, and 1468 crisis, 1633(e)

Colonial administration: by the Admiralty, 4303; in crown colonies, 4402(h)

Colonial Dames, *see* National Soc. of Colonial Dames of America

Colonial history, 2146

Colonial Nursing Assn, 4274(i)

Colonial policy, British: and money supply, 17th–18th cent., 1633(h); and S. African republics, 4301

Colonial records, at Cambridge, 812(h)

Colonial reformers, and Edw. Gibbon Wakefield, 4270(f)

Colonial regiments: Cape Mounted Rifles, 4781(m); King Edward's Horse (the King's Oversea Dominions Regt.), 4780(d); West India, 4768(c)

Colonial self-government, 4636(c)

Colonial Soc., *afterwards* Royal Colonial Soc., *afterwards* Royal Colonial Inst., *afterwards* Royal Empire Soc., *q.v.*

Colonies, British, 2726; crown offices in, 813(j); government of, 2502(a); money supply, 1633(h); and privy council, 5306(a)

Colonization: beginnings, 687(b); British, 2727; of the Caribbean, 4267(c); foreign, publications on, 4293; of New Zealand, 4236(a); of Ulster, 2224(a)

Colour decoration, in English churches, 4836(o)

Colour printing, 4642(a), 4661(a)

Colour problem, 4295, 4512(c)

Colours, liturgical, 4837(c)

Colours, regimental: captured by the French (1816), 5090(g); of 55th Ft (1814), 5088(l); lodging of, 5086(k)

Colours, Roman, 1096(x)

Colour vision, Young's theory, 3701(b)

Colridge (Cadelintona) hundred, Devon, 1333(f)

Colsterworth, Lincs., 6442(a)

Colston Bassett, Notts., 5808(c)

Colt, family, 1698(o)

Colton, Lancs., 1165(r)

Columba, Saint (d. 597), 3920(o)

Columbaria, *see* Pigeon-houses

Columbus, Christopher, Genoese discoverer, (d. 1506), 1958

Colville, James, Lord C. of Culross (d. 1654), 4981(c)

Colwall, Herefs., 6128(r)

Colwell, Northumb., 5225(b)

Colwell, Thomas, printer (16th cent.), 3209(j,p)

Colwich, Staffs., 936(k), 6096(d)

Colwick, Notts., 5821(c,d)

Colwyn Bay, Denb.: Bryn Euryn, 2872(b). *See also* Llandudno, Colwyn Bay & Dist. Fd Club

Colyton, Devon: church, 530(k), 1323(y), 1329(b), 1343(c); nonconformist academy, 1106(b); parish registers, 1315

Combe down, Som., 218(g)

Combe hill, *see* Jevington, Suss.

Combe Martin, Devon, 620(j)

Comber, family, 5331(h), 5701(h)

Comberbach, Ches., 2649(f)

Combermere, Viscount, *see* Cotton, Stapleton

Combe St Nicholas, Som., 5426(c,f)

Combination laws, 4252(n)

Combinations, *see* Trade unionism

Comb Moss, *see* Derbyshire

Combretonium, and Brettenham, Suff., 5580(i)

Combs ditch, *see* Cranborne Chase

Comet, *see* Halley's comet

Comfort, standard of, 4722(a)

Coming of age, proof of, 1286(l)

Commadore (commodore), rank of, 5101(f)

Commander, R.N., rank of, 5106(p), 5114(m)

Commemoracio lamentacionis Beate Marie, 343

Commentaries on the Laws of England (Blackstone), 819(b,c)

Commerce, *see* Trade

Commercial geography, 2416(a)

Commercial history, 2416(a)

Commercial morality, medieval, 2229(g)

Commissioners for public preachers, 1704(o)

Commission of sewers, *see* Sewers

Commissions in army, purchase of, 4793(a), 5093(n)

Committee for compounding, *see* Composition papers

Committee for the Survey of the Memorials of Greater London, *afterwards* London Survey Cttee, *q.v.*

Committee of charitable uses, Leeds, 5797(p)

Commodore, *see* Commadore

Commodus, Roman emperor (d. 192): Commodus-Hercules cult, 5134(c)

Common fields, common lands: balks in, 821(m); enclosure of, *see* Enclosures

at, in, of: Bloxham, 3772(c); Broad Town and Thornhill, 6114(v); Cardiganshire, 894(b); Clifton, Yorks., 1988(c); Durrington, 6099(a); Earley, 267(h); Hayton, 1171(t); London, 4644(b); Stone, 3617(a); Trehelig, 3906(f)

Common law: cases concerning unrecognized states, 4507(a); and civic position of women, 5301(b); development of,

Covenham, Lincs., 5147(b)
Covent Garden, London, 2353(b), 4253(p)
Coventry, Warws., 383(b), 443(b), 5272(c); Baptists, 199(i); Rob. Beake, 4404(c); cathedral, 522(b); churches, 443(e), 4130(g); glass-paintings, 5927(b); hospitals, 368(a); industries, 4227(a); leet book, 513(d), 1485; misericords, 382(e); nonconformist academy, 1105(f); palaeolithic implements, 3916(n); plays, 1540, 1567, 3525(e); priory, 522(b); records, 443(g), 1410; St Mary's hall, 5982(a); town life, 4404(c); and John Wesley, 6037(f)
Coventry, H.M.S., 5107(o)
Coventry and Lichfield, diocese, 3524(f), 4962(n); registers, 6074, 6077
Covered ways, on Sussex downs, 5711(c). *See also* Earthworks
Coverham abbey, *see* Agglethorpe with Coverham, N.R.Yorks.
Covert, family, 5698(i), 5720(e)
Coway stakes, river Thames, 4110(a)
Cowbridge, Glam., 1(h), 707(d)
Cowden, Kent, 2204
Cowdray House (Park), Suss., 928(m), 5706(i)
Cowes, I.o.W., 2010(b)
Cowfold, Suss., 5714(d), 5755; Beeding manor, 5714(d); Ewhurst manor, 5714(d); High Hurst manor, 5714(d); Jarvis, 5712(b); Shermanbury manor, 5714(d); Stretham manor, 5714(d); Walhurst manor, 5714(d)
Cowley, Mdx, 6229(t)
Cowper, family, 1184(e)
Cowper, Elizabeth (17th cent.), 5713(f)
Cowper, William, 1st Earl C. (d. 1723), 4681(a)
Cowper, William, poet (d. 1800), 1821(d), 3306(b), 4663(c)
Cowslade, family, 273(d)
Cowthorpe, W.R.Yorks., 6360
Cox, Benjamin, Baptist (fl. 1595–1646), 195(d)
Coxbench, Derbys., 1282(a)
Coxford, Norf., 3565(k)
Coxwell, Great, Berks., 262(a)
Coxwell, Little, Berks., 262(a)
Coygan, Carm., 914(k)
Coyte, George, London silversmith (fl. 1771–77), 1736(a)
Cozens, Alexander, landscape-painter (d. 1786), 5924(c)
Crabbe, George, poet (d. 1832), 4674(a), 5573(l)
Crabtree, William (17th cent.), 2628(c)
Crackenthorp, family, 1196(f)
Crackenthorpe, Westmld, 1196(h)
Cradock, Sir Matthew (d. 1513), 739(p)
Cradock, Matthew, gov. of Massachusetts (d. 1641), 1106(o)
Cradock, Samuel, cleric & pietist (d. 1706), 1106(o)
Cradock, Thomas (d. 1690), 5247(b)
Craft guilds, 2227(a), 4484(a); Hereford, 6129(o); Lichfield, 1562; London, *see* London, city & environs: companies; Lynn, 1562; Newcastle, 5239(d); Norwich, 2938(e). *See also* Guilds
Craft 'mysteries', 281(c)
Craftsmen, medieval, 1602(a)
Craftsmen's marks, medieval, 2908(a)
Cragg Vale, W.R.Yorks., 1972(d)
Craig Gurtheyrn, *see* Llanfihangel ar Arth, Carm.
Craigie, Pearl, novelist (d. 1906), 3293(e)
Craig Llwyn, *see* Lisvane, Glam.
Craig-y-Nos, Brecon, 744(c)
Craik, Mrs, *see* Mulock, Dinah Maria
Crambe, N.R.Yorks., 6233(j)
Crambeck, *see* Castle Howard, N.R.Yorks.

Cranborne, Dors., 1378(f), 1391(a), 1394(g)
Cranborne Chase, Wilts. and Dors., 1380(e), 1391(a), 1399(g), 6101(j); Bokerly dyke, 402(a), 1391(a), 1398(h); Combs ditch, 402(a), 1398(h)
Cranbrook, Kent, 2598(e), 2599(b), 2603(e), 2605(m)
Crane, Mistress, and Marprelate tracts, 297(i)
Crane, Sir Francis (d. 1636), 5874(b)
Crane, Ralph, scrivener to the King's players (fl. 1625), 292(g)
Crane, Stephen, novelist (d. 1900), 1757
Cranfield, Thomas, pioneer of charity schools (d. 1837), 1111(g)
Cranford, Edward (d. 1431), 511(m)
Cranford series, of illustrated books, 1750(c)
Crania, *see* Skulls
Cranke, James (d. 1780), and James (d. 1826), portrait-painters, 1169(c)
Cranleigh, Surr., 5627(g)
Cranmer, Thomas, abp (d. 1556), 158(m), 2089
Cranmore, West, Som., 5406(b)
Crannogs (artificial islands), 2129(d)
Crantock Rural, Cornw., 4215(a)
Cranwich, Norf., 3911(hh)
Crasset, *see* Cressets
Craster tables (Northumbrian roll of arms), 5231(h)
Craswall, Herefs., 6122(p), 6124(c,d)
Cratfield, Suff., 5576(m)
Craufurd, Robert, gen. (d. 1812), 4753(b), 4759(b)
Craven, W.R.Yorks., 406(y), 5373(a)
Craven, Robert, of Lincoln (fl. 1656), 1830(d)
Craven, William, Earl of C. (d. 1697), 1731(i)
Craven way, Roman road, 409(s)
Crawfurd, John, of St Hill, East Grinstead (d. 1762), 5727(rr)
Crawley, Suss., 2527(a), 5707(a)
Crawley, North, Bucks., 102(r)
Crawley, William John Chetwode, freemason (d. 1916), 6469(a)
Crayford, Kent, 2588(c), 3912(aa), 4082(a), 6135(a)
Crayke, N.R.Yorks., 6224(q)
Crayle, family, 160(a)
Cray valley, Kent, 3912(k)
Creake, South, Norf., 3571(m)
Crebar, Elizabeth, poetess, 1255(b)
Crécy, France, battle, 4162(c)
Credadyn bucheddol (Roberts), 6020(l)
Credenhill, Herefs., 6124(k)
Credit: effects of World War I on, 554(c), 559(a), 586; in medieval trade, 1631(i)
Crediton, Devon: church, 1324(n), 4117(q); Hugh Deane, clerk to governors of corporation 1344(f); hundred, 1344(d); manor, 1344(d); origins, 1344(c); vicars, 1344(e)
Creech, Dors., 1368(c)
Creeping barrage (gun-fire), 4168(a)
Cregneish, I.o.M.: Mull hill circle, 1195(s), 5171(f)
Creighton, Mandell, bp & historian (d. 1901), 4452
Cremations, on London Road, Brighton, 5716(j). *See also* Anglo-Saxon cremations
Crescens, Lucius Baebius, of the VIth legion, 6412(c)
Crescent, H.M.S., 4742(c)
Crespigny, *see* De Crespigny
Cressage, Salop, 5005
Cressets (lamps), 5791(l); Guernsey crasset, 5032(h)
Cresset stones, 1097(q), 1098(j), 6232(h)
Cressett, family, 4977(k)

Cross Canonby, Cumb., 1167(r), 1168(i), 1176(t,u)

Crosse, family, 2127(g)

Crosse, John Green, surgeon (d. 1850), 4711(b)

Crosse, Richard, miniaturist & portrait-painter (d. 1810), 5925(c)

Crosses: 7th cent., 4118(c); to Aldhelm's memory, 1097(l); Anglian, 1179(o); Anglo-Saxon, 1275(j), 2599(l), 4813(i), 5193(h); at, in, near, *see below*; bases, *see below*; Celtic, 5444(b); chrism, 1177(k); churchyard, 1337(a), 3614(a), 6126(g); fragments, *see below*; gable, at Keddington, 161(h); granite, 1323(t); heads, *see below*; leaden, with styca impression, 604(j); names of, 1172(c); portable, bronze or latten foot of, 100(e); pre-Norman, 745(f), 1275(j), 2642(d), 4482(c); relating to Gt Britain and Ireland, in I.o.M., 5904(a); sculptured, 1287(d), 2884(c); shafts, *see below*; sites of, 1172(c); standing, 4482(c), 6134; stone, 217(i), 406(aa), 407(g), 4482(c), 4813(i), 5340(a); Tau-cross capitals, 2607(r); village, 1184(m), 1286(g); wayside, 768(a), 1337(a), 1740(i), 6126(r); wheel, 3563(s)

at, in, near: Abel, Yorks., 1990(d); 'Abbot's way', Dartmoor, 1323(t); Anthorn, Cumb., 1192(m); Beckermet, 1178(g); Bewcastle, 1168(u), 1173(u), 1176(y), 1178(g), 1185(u), 3404(a); Blackwell, nr Alfreton, 1287(d); Brailsford, 1293(a); formerly in Brecon, 723(k); Brussels, 3404(c); Cambridge, 768(a); Carew, Pemb., 3518(a); Carlisle, 1178(g), 1179(o); Cheadle, 2642(d); Cleulow, 3615(c); Cornwall, 1740(i); Cornwall, missing, 1739(pp); Crosthwaite, 1177(k); Cumberland, 1172(c); Dyserth church, 745(f); Easby, Yorks., 5197(b); Escombe church, 5227(s); Exeter, 1337(a); Fernilee Hall, Shall-cross, 1275(j); Gloucester high cross, 430(p); Gosforth, 1180(i); Great Ashfield, 5581(u); Guernsey, 5032(g); Hartside, 1193(l); Herefordshire, 6126(g,r), 6134; Holmsfield, 2377(k); Hyde's cross, Manchester, 2631(h); Isle of Man, 5904(a); Kedington, 5581(v); Keighley, 407(g); King's Newton, 1286(g); Lancashire, 2623(a), 2624(f), 2625(h), 2626(a), 2627(d), 3982(g); Leeds, 5797(m); Lincolnshire, 4813(i); Llandough, 724(m), 753(k); Llantwit Major, 723(e); Long Causeway, 1974(h); Mab's Cross, 2630(f); Maen Achwyfan, 529(d,e), 746(b); Manside, 5227(d); Maughold, 2550(i,j,k); Newark, Beaumond cross, 5825(c); Norfolk, 3573(p); northern England, 4118(c); Northumbria, 5444(j); Nottingham, Weekday cross, 5823(f); Parlooe, 1739(qq); Penrith, Giant's Thumb, 1183(f); Rampisham, 5312(c); Ravenglass, 1184(m); Reculver, 5193(h); Redruth dist., 1739(l); Riva hill, Baildon moor, 406(aa); Rockcliff, Cumb., 1189(r); Rolleston, 3614(a); Rothbury, 5254(j); Ruthwell, 3404(a), 4117(j); St Allen, Cornw., 4539(l); St Kew, Cornw., 4540(c); Sandbach, 529(f), 730(e), 2634(e); Somerset, 217(i), 1097(l), 5340(a); Stapleford, 5812(d); Waberthwaite, 1188(c); Wales, 2884(g); Whibbersley, 2377(k); Whissonnett, 3563(s); Wiltshire, 1097(l); Yorkshire moors, 6060(a)

bases: Dyserth church, pre-Norman, 745(f); Llangefelach, pre-Norman, 723(h); Millom church, 1181(c); Winchester, 2011(j)

fragments: Anglian, at Kendal, 1167(w); Arlecdon, Cumb., 1168(t); from Carlisle abbey, 1164(u); pre-Norman, from Glassonby, 1164(t); Sutton-on-Derwent, 10th cent., 6237(e)

heads: Anglian, 1196(q), 2120(e); Aughton, 2120(e); Bentham, 1196(q); Berrow, 5167(f); morse ivory, 11th cent., 5174(k)

Crosses (*cont.*)

shafts: Anglian, 1174(w), 1175(q); Dacre, 1175(q); Great Clifton, Cumb., 1164(h), 5897(c); Kirkby Stephen, 1175(b,q); Norbury, 1273(c); pre-Norman, 1165(h), 1173(n), 1273(c), 5897(c); rune-inscribed, 1174(w); Saffron Walden, 12th cent., 1705(q); Urswick church, 1173(n); Viking, 1175(b,q)

See also Calvary crosses; Consecration crosses; Eleanor crosses; Market crosses

Cross-fragments, *see* Crosses

Cross-heads, *see* Crosses

Crossing the line, equator ceremony, 5101(i)

Cross Lees, Syke, *see* Rochdale, Lancs.

Crossley, family, 1970(j,k)

Crossley, John, freemason (d. 1830), 3231(c)

Cross-shafts, *see* Crosses

Cross-slabs (slabs incised with a cross): Ballavarkish, I.o.M., 2549(w); East Winch, 3564(j); Glamorganshire, 4115(p); Jarrow, 5597(c); Kirk Maughold, 3349(f); Monmouthshire and S.Wales, 877(a); Ystafell-Fach, 723(o)

Cross Stone, W.R.Yorks., 1991(d)

Crosthwaite, Cumb., 1227; Bristowe hill, 1167(s)

Croston, Lancs., 2114(a), 2654

Crouch, river, Essex, 1713(h)

Crouch End, Mdx, 2975(m)

Croughton, Northants, 524(f), 2394(a), 5192(e)

Crowcombe, Som., 5407(g,h)

Crow Holt wood, *see* Bramhall, Ches.

Crowland (Croyland), Lincs.: abbey, 160(g), 162(j), 3655(c,e), 4136(i), 4252(kk), 5277(a); bridge, 3850(c); church, 3850(c)

Crowle, Worcs., 369(a)

Crow Leasow, *see* Bitterley, Salop

Crowley, Sir Ambrose, ironmaster (d. 1713), 3548(e), 5870(b)

Crowley, John, ironmaster (d. 1728), 3548(e)

Crown: English, and alien merchants, 14th cent., 1632(g); English, and Italian bankers, 4387(e); succession to, in Gt Britain, 5330(t)

Crown, imperial, its jewels, 4289(c)

Crown buildings, in care of Office of Works, 53(b)

Crown colonies, administration of, 4402(h)

Crowndale, Devon, 1336(h)

Crown lands, in Braden forest, 6114(j)

Crown offices, in British colonies, 813(j)

Crown of the rose, *see* Crowns (coins)

Crowns (coins), English: (1551–1901), 6135(b); crown of the rose, 4594(b); Hen. VIII pattern, silver, 601(g); Jas I, 616(h)

Crowns, Roman bronze, 5164(g)

Crows Hall, Suff., 5581(i)

Crowstone Hall, *see* Elland with Greetland, W.R.Yorks.

Croxden, Staffs.: 3620(d), 3624(c), 4118(p), 5552

Croxton, Cambs., 824(m)

Croxton play of the Sacrament, 1554

Croyde, Devon, 1330(g)

Croydon, Surr., 1159(e); to 11th cent., 1163(h); ancient monuments, 1161(c); Bourne flows, 1159(b), 1161(e); coins, 4578(b), 4580(c,f), 5607(a); Grange Wood museum, 528(m); manor-house, 5612(d); mortality rates, 1159(e); Presbyterian church, 3920(d); Roman road, 1162(a); rural handicrafts, 1161(b); stone and bronze celts, 1158(a); tokens, 1161(a); transport, 1162(d)

Croydon Microscop. Club, *afterwards* Croydon Nat. History & Sci. Soc., *q.v.*

Decoys, Dutch and English, 17th cent., 3592(h)

De Crespigny, Daumont (fl. 1673), 2354(h)

De Critz, family, 5910(b)

De Culwen, family, *see* Curwen

De Cundal, family, 1185(s)

de Daillon, Benjamin, Huguenot (d. 1709), 2354(o)

Deddington, Oxon., 3785(a); deanery, 3760(b), 3772(b), 3779(a)

Dedham, Essex, 522(e), 1702(n), 4423

Dedications, *see* Authors' dedications; Church dedications

De differentia inter peccatum mortale et veniale (Wyclif), 6221

De Diva, family, 5714(c)

de Dunstanville, Baron, *see* Basset, Francis

Dee, Dr John, mathematician (d. 1608), 301, 3938(b), 5109(t), 5112(e)

Dee, river, 993(d), 1009(c)

Deeds, 1282(g), 6033(c)

    belonging to: Bath corporation, 219; Lord de l'Isle and Dudley, 5181(c); Markland family, 2652(c); Moore family, 3968; Norris family, 2126(f); Orde family, 5215(c); Oxford, Balliol Coll., 3720; Pudsay family, 6258; Sanderson family, 1169(o); William Salt library, 6089(a); Womborne, the Wodehouse, 6094(a)

    collected by Wm Greenwell, 5256(a), 5260(e)

    relating to: Adderbury, 3794; Alveley, 4979(o); Barwick-in-Elmet, 5797(k); Bedfordshire, 225(c); Bettws, 3898(h); Bingfield, 5253(i); Blackhall estate, Northumb., 5227(r); Brading, I.o.W., 2553(z); Bristol, 448(f), 1096(u), 1098(f); Broomfield church, 1701(j); Buckland Filleigh, 1331(e); Bupton, 6103(p); Cardiganshire, 739(n); Chalford and Colcombe, 457(j); Chelmorton, 1295(b); Chester, 989(f), 1001(f); Chester-le-Street chantry, 5231(d); Claremont, Shrewsbury, 4974(c); Cumberland, 1177(b), 1193(g); Derbyshire, 1272(h); Dorset, 1378(i), 1393(f), 1395(d), 5318(d); Dunkenhalgh, 1036(a); co. Durham, 3541, 5217(o), 5222(d), 5228(c), 5239(b); Durham bpric, 5227(k); Englefield, 270(b); Essex, 1704(i); Ewood estate, 1045(b); Flintshire, 1776; Furness, 1193(g); Gloucester, 447(a); Gloucester, St Peter's abbey, 443(i); Grittleton manor, 6112(l); Gunnerton, Northumb., 5232(c); Hamsterley, 5223(l); Hawarden, 1771(c); Hawksyard, 2377(u); Hazlerigg, 2756(b); Hendon manor, 3371; Hertfordshire, 1592(l); Horsham Free Christian church, 5852(a,b); Hull, 1620(f); Hurley priory, 254(c); Jersey, 5043(f), 5048(c), 5054(b), 5055(d); Kelloe, co. Dur., 5256(a); Kent, 2589(j), 2615; Ladyland, Rowley Regis, 3362(b); Lewes, Westgate chapel, 5852(h); Lewes priory, 5717(f); Liverpool, 2126(f); Llanfihangel Geneu'r Glyn, 737(i); Llandrinio, 3900(d); Llangynfelin, 737(i); London, Essex chapel, 5852(k); Methuen family, 6111(q); Montgomery castle, 4967(k); Montgomeryshire, 3898(f); Neath and dist., 3518(d); Newcastle-upon-Tyne, 5214(n), 5221(a), 5222(d), 5225(f), 5689; Newcastle, St Andrew's church, 5251(i); Norfolk, 3571(b); north country, 5681(b); Northumberland, 3541, 5221(g,j), 5222(d), 5228(c), 5239(b); Norwich, 3576, 3586; Plymouth, 3896(t); Portsmouth, St Thomas Street chapel, 5854(c); Quarr abbey, 2006(l); Quidhampton, 6104(f); Rayne manor, 1693(m); Repton, 1284(f); Repton school, 1280(d); St Martin family, of Trinité, Jersey, 5040(e); Seagry House, 6111(l); Shrewsbury, 4985(d); Shrewsbury, St John's hosp., 4979(c); Shropshire, 4976(c); Southam, Glos., 434(d), 456(h); Staffordshire, 6081(e); Stavordale priory

Deeds (*cont.*)

    and Sanzaver family, 5414(e); Suffolk, 5581(g); Surrey, 5620(c); Sussex, 5620(c), 5716(b), 5761; Titchfield abbey, 2006(l); Torre abbey, 5843(b); Tropenell family, 6105(l); Wales, 919(d); Walthamstow, 5945, 5953; Walton Cardiff, nr Tewkesbury, 438(g); Westmorland, 1177(b), 1193(g); Whitecliff, Brixton Deverell, 6104(u); Wootton Bassett, Little Park, 6112(d); Writtle, 1703(d); Yorkshire, 411, 1620(f), 6224(d), 6247

Deene, Northants, 4811(d)

De ente (Wyclif), 6219

Deerhurst, Glos., 5445(i); church, 431(b,j,k), 455(f), 516(d), 4125(m), 5143(c), 6128(g); priory, 366(d)

Deer parks, 2624(a), 2625(a)

de Essex, family, 260(f). *See also* Essex, family

de Estur, family, 2008(l)

Dee valley, Scotland, 4081(d)

De excidio Britanniae (Gildas), 2335

Defence, H.M.S., 5116(l)

Defence, of British Empire, 2517. *See also* Home Defence; Imperial defence; Naval defence

Defence of Masonry (Clare), 2921, 2951(b)

Defences, *see* Coast defences; Roman defences

Defence work, engineer, in World War I, 2514

Defensio curatorum (Fitz-Ralph), 1512

Defensor pacis, authorship of, 4410(d)

Defoe, Daniel (d. 1731), 1640(b), 2233(a), 2593(e), 3294(g)

De Fokington, family, 5714(c)

de Fynes, family, 2590(f)

Deganwy, Denb., 2872(e), 2875(f)

Degrees, masonic, *see under* Freemasonry

Deguileville, Guillaume de, *see* Guillaume de Deguileville

de Hastings, family, 1174(r). *See also* Hastings, family

Déhus, Guernsey, *see* Paradis

De imitatione Christi, Welsh versions, 6020(a)

Deincourt, family, 1288(h)

De Insula, family, 2008(e)

De invectionibus (Giraldus Cambrensis), 2281

Deira, king of, *see* Olaf Sitricson

Dekker, Thomas, dramatist (d. 1641?), 293(b), 295(a)

de Laci, family, 435(g). *See also* Lacy

De la Cour, family, 5058(d)

Delafield, Thomas, curate of Fingest (18th cent.), 98(x)

de Lage de Cueilly, capt. in Spanish navy (fl. 1744), 3500(f)

De la Mare, Sir Peter, speaker of the House of Commons (fl. 1370), 6121(i)

Delamare, Richard (d. 1435), and wife Isabel, 3429(b)

De la Mare, Thomas, abbot of St Albans (d. 1396), 4827(c,d), 4828(e)

Delamere, Baron, *see* Booth, Sir George

De Lancaster, family, 1173(t)

De Lancey, Sir William (d. 1815), 4750(a)

Delany, Mary Cecilia, 5624(g)

Delapré abbey, Northants, 3645(a)

De la Puilles, family, 5629(g)

De la Roche, family, 734(m)

De laude Cestrie (Lucian), 3966

Delaval, family, 5217(n)

Delaval, Lady Elizabeth, *née* Livingstone (b. 1649), 5214(l)

Delaval, William (d. 1618), 5234(k)

Delavall, Joshua (fl. 1607), 5225(i)

Delaval mss, 3543(d)

Delaware & Hudson railway, 3548(d)

Diplomatic documents, records: at Cambridge, 812(h); publication policy, 812(j)

Diplomatic envoys: British (1689–1852), 4450; in 16th cent., 2236(c)

Diplomatic instructions: (1477), 3530(g); (1689–1789), 4441

Diplomatic procedure, Spanish guide to, 4444(b)

Diplomatic service: organizational changes, 4496(d); under Wm III, 4411(c)

Dippeforda (Stanborough) hundred, Devon, 1335(c)

Diptychs, ivory, 1191(w)

Directions concerning Education (Locke), 4042

Directories: Halifax, 1977(j); Liverpool, 2112(h), 2132(h), 2137(c)

Directories (customaries, ordinaries), *see* Liturgies, Latin rite

Dirk, *see* Daggers

Disafforestation: Braden, 6113(z); Wirral (1376), 2113(f)

Disappointment, The (Southerne), 298(q)

Disarmament: 19th cent., 4518(h); (1917–26), 2400; (1925–31), 2404; draft convention (1930), 2409(d); Lord Esher's proposals, 4509(c); world conference (1932), 2404, 2410(e). *See also* Naval disarmament

Disc barrows, *see* Barrows and tumuli

Discipline, *see* Church discipline; Naval discipline

Discovery, ship, 2322(b)

Diserth, *see* Dyserth

Disney, –, capt. (fl. 1855), 4788(d)

Disney, Richard (16th cent.), 3747(d)

Disney, William (16th cent.), 3747(d)

Dispatch, H.M. brigantine, 5104(w)

Displaying of supposed Witchcraft (Webster), 2644(e)

Dispossessed religious: Derbyshire, 1276(b); Gloucestershire, 455(b), 458(k); Much Wenlock, 4980(h); Oxfordshire, 3784(e); Yorkshire, 6227(e). *See also* Religious houses, suppression of

Disraeli, family, 2567(g)

Disraeli, Benjamin, 1st E. of Beaconsfield (d. 1881), 1146(e), 2582(f), 5308(b), 5526(e)

Diss, Norf., 3564(o); hundred, 3585

Disseisins, 232(e)

Dissenters, *see* Nonconformists

Dissenters Bill (1779), 5856(o)

Dissertation on Masonry (Parker), 6474(j)

Disserth, Rad., 3937(e); Trecoed, 3937(e)

Dissolution of the monasteries, *see* Dispossessed religious; Religious houses, suppression of

Distressed Sion relieved (Keach), 201(n)

Ditcheat, Som., 6032(j)

Ditcheridge, *see* Ditteridge

Ditches: Bran Ditch, 779(c), 780(g); Cambridge, 759(g), 767(a); in and nr Cherry Hinton, 758(n), 760(j); Colchester town ditch, 1697(i); Danes' ditches, 100(a); Danesfield, 100(a); Devil's ditch, 823(l); Hereford, King's ditch, 6127(v); Heronbridge, Roman ditch, 1009(f); in Kerry parish, Mont., 3897(k); Nottingham, St Mary's hill, 5818(i); Saffron Walden, 1693(k); upper and lower 'short ditches', 3897(k); Winterbourne Dauntsey iron age ditch, 6114(bb). *See also* Dykes; Earthworks; Entrenchments

Ditchingham, Norf., 3429(ww)

Ditchley, Oxon., 248(e)

Ditchling, Suss.: church, 5729(ff, kk); church, Free Christian, 5852(b); Ditchling Beacon excavations, 5723(k); earthworks, 5722(j); General Baptists, 200(f); manor and

Ditchling, Suss (*cont.*)
Rivers farm, 5727(f); valley entrenchments, 416(e), 417(c)

Ditteridge (Ditcheridge), Wilts., 6111(n)

Dittisham, Devon, 1340(a)

Ditton Priors, Salop, 5028(j)

Diu Lligwy, Romano-British village, Anglesey, 2874(f)

Diva, *see* De Diva

Dives et Pauper (c. 1405), 299(l)

Dividing engine, *see* Circular dividing engine

Divine Paternoster, 1106(d)

Diving, deep sea, 4661(d)

Divorce: of Sir Wm Barentyne, 5720(o); English gypsy rites, 1806(a); preliminary proceedings, 1272(f)

Dixon, George (fl.1760), 3549(g)

Dixon, Thomas (fl. 1687), 5799(t)

Dixon, Thomas, of Sunderland (d. 1880), 5597(a)

Dixon collection of antiquities, 5228(j)

Dixter manor-house, *see* Northiam, Suss.

Dobbs, Richard, of Castle Dobbs, co. Antrim (fl. 1683), 4071(c)

Dobel, Daniel (fl. 1711), 190(m)

Dobell, family, 5718(f)

Dobrée, Elisha, of Guernsey (b. 1756), 5037(q)

Dobson, Austin (d. 1921), 1755

Dobson cave, *see* Scales, in Furness, Lancs.

Docker, family, 1181(g)

Docks and dockyards, 3476(b); labour in, 2850(a), 4234(c); rating of, 2454(c); royal, 5108(e,i), 5110(r)

at: Abbey Wood (supposed), 6146(c); Chatham, 5112(c); English Harbour, Antigua, 5108(f); Harwich, 5110(h); Liverpool, 2136(g), 2850(a), 2853(a); London, 1873(b), 5099(d)

Doctor and Student (St Germain), 295(l)

Doctor gate (Doctorgate), Roman road, Derbys., 1281(g)

Doctors, *see* Physicians

Doctors' Commons, 3136(b,c,d)

Doctrines of grace, tracts on, 712(b)

Documents on International Affairs, *see* Royal Institute of International Affairs

Dodd, Ralph (d. 1822) and Robert (d. 1816?), marine-painters, 5107(i)

Dodd, William, divine & forger (d. 1777), 2586(a)

Dodding Green, *see* Skelsmergh, Westmld

Doddinghurst, Essex, 1694(o)

Doddington, Northumb. 5229(e,g,h)

Doddridge, Philip, nonconformist divine (d. 1751), 1104(o,hh), 1109(cc), 3922(j), 5856(s)

Dodington, *see* Whitchurch, Salop

Dodington, Christopher (fl. 1657), 2975(u)

Dodington, William (d. 1600), 2975(c)

Dodmore, *see* Ludlow, Salop

Dods, Marcus, Presbyterian divine (d. 1838), 3919(e)

Dodsworth, Roger, antiquary (d. 1654), 6245

Dodsworth mss, 3541

Dog doors, in churches, 6130(v)

Dog Holes caves, *see* Warton with Lindeth, Lancs.

Dog spits, 5215(p)

Dog tongs, 6130(v)

Dolaucothi, Carm., 905(a); Ogofau gold mine, 906(b)

Dolbenmaen, Caern.: Llystyn Gwyn, 727(c), 5146(h)

Dole-gate, at Denny abbey, 777(d)

Doles, Hants, 2012(i)

Estaing, Charles-Hector, comte d'Estaing, French adm. (d. 1794), 3477(d)

Estampes, duc d', *see* Brosse, Jean de

Estate accounts: 14th cent., 102(p); Bannercross, 2377(o); Esholt priory, 407(c); Godinton, 498; Hendon, 2974(z); Hillesden, Bucks., 101(j); by John Hooper, steward to E. of Clare, 5831(e); Oxford colleges, 4717(a); Thornborough, 1633(n); Warwickshire, 1404

Estate books: Hen. de Bray, 4394(f), 4437; Grafton, nr Bromsgrove, 374(a); Hereford bpric, 4446(a)

Estate history, 149(k)

Estate management: Horsford, 3568(d); Rainham, 3567(d); Stafford family, 3681(a)

Estoire de Seint Aedward le Rei, 766(b)

Eston, N.R.Yorks., 6384; Eston Nab, 1095(a)

Eston, John de (d. 1301), 5799(i)

Eston, Stephen of, abbot (d. 1252), 6239(d)

Eston Nab, *see* Eston, N.R.Yorks.

Estur, *see* de Estur

Eswelle, Sanson de, *see* Sanson de Eswelle

Etal, Northumb., 5214(o)

Etchells, Ches., 2632(i)

Etching: British school, 3927; history, 4649(a). *See also* Print Collectors' Club

Etchingham, Suss., 3428(m)

Ethandune, battle, *see* Aethandune

Ethelbert, Saint, king of the East Angles (d. 794), 605(c), 5149(i), 6126(o)

Etheldreda, Saint, queen of Northumbria (d. 679), 136(a)

Ethelmar, *see* Aymer (Ethelmar) de Valence

Ethelred I, king of Northumbria (d. 796), 610(a)

Ethelred II, king of England (d. 1016), 1386(b). *See also under* Anglo-Saxon coins

Ethelred, sub-regulus of Mercia (d. 912), 608(d)

Ethelwold, Saint, bp (d. 984), 4008, 5198(a)

Etherdacre, *see* Easington, co. Dur.

Ethnological Soc. of London, *amalgamated with* Anthropological Soc. of London *to form* Anthropological (*afterwards* Royal Anthropological) Inst. of Gt Britain & Ireland, *q.v.*

Ethnology: and archaeology, 898(a); and linguistic evidence, 481(e); of Somerset, 5421(m)

Etienne de Besançon, Dominican (d. 1294), 1480

Eton College, Bucks., 99(n); bill, 17th cent., 100(y); chapel, 3745(a); letters, 18th cent., 102(q); parliamentary enactments concerning, 3718; property, 2974(l); records, 5330(e); wall-painting, 5925(a)

Etone, *see* Bletchley, Bucks.

Ettrick, family, 1737(a)

Etty, William, painter (d. 1849), 6403(a)

Euangel Nicodemus, 2315(b)

Eucharist, bread of the, 49

Eucharistic veils, Western use, 4835(h)

Euclid, Greek mathematician (3rd cent. B.C.), 316

Euphrates valley, 4274(e)

Eupolemia (Robinson), 296(e)

Eurgrawn Cymraeg, 6020(r)

Europe: 19th–20th cent., 2229(b), 4240(f); bibliographies, 2144, 2165, 2193; bronze age, 4099(f); civilization, and Asiatic invasions, 4319(b); and Peter Munday, 1945; neanthropic types, 4061(a); palaeolithic and neolithic, 4112(h); prehistory, 1873(d), 2241(b); rivers, international, 4504(b); sanctions, 4517(f); strategic geography, 19th cent., 4137(a); wheat prices, 4241(c)

Eustace, Saint (d. c. 118), 3375(a)

Euxton, Lancs., 2131(f), 2132(b)

Eva, wife of Anwel, 63(c)

Evan, Lewis, Welsh preacher (18th cent.), 708(f)

Evangelical Union, Jas. Morison, founder, 1109(w)

Evangelism, in England, 208

Evangelistarium, *see* Liturgies, Latin rite

Evans, family, 6111(f)

Evans, Evan, Welsh poet & antiquary (d. 1789), 918(m)

Evans, Rev. Evan, Welsh Baptist (d. 1827), 1250(a)

Evans, Francis (fl. 1700), sec. to Bp Lloyd of Worcester, 6169

Evans, J– (fl. 1860), 715(b)

Evans, John, curate of Portsmouth (d. 1779), 6018(c)

Evans, John, author (fl. 1812), 3518(g,i)

Evans, John, Baptist minister (d. 1827), 6019(u)

Evans, Morgan, registrar of Neath (fl. 1657–79), 3516(c)

Evans, Thomas (Tomos Glyn Cothi), Unitarian minister (d. 1833), 6020(e)

Evans, Rev. Titus, of Carmarthen (d. 1864), 923(c)

Eveling of Ravenglass, 1187(u)

Evelyn, John, virtuoso (d. 1706): as bibliophile, 297(e); bicentenary, 6141(b); *Circle of mechanical trades*, 3548(b); drawing of Wotton House, 5605(e); *Londinum Redivivum*, 4477(a); and Gabriel Naude, 297(p)

Everard, *see* St Martin, Jersey

Everard of Montgomery, bp (d. 1150), 5581(n)

Evercreech, Som., 5406(f); Small Down camp, 5402(l), 5403(f)

Everest, Mount, 4290(m)

Everill Shaw, *see* Heptonstall, W.R.Yorks.

Everingham, E.R.Yorks., 1618(a), 6228(gg); Everingham Park, Roman Catholic records, 931(d), 934(d,e), 952(e)

Eversholt, Beds., 240

Eversley, Hants, 3428(ff)

Everton, Notts., 5815(b)

Every Man out of his Humour (Jonson), 286(e), 3186

Evesham, Worcs., 216(k), 438(b), 6194(e); abbey, 365(c), 6194(e); battle (1265), 376(a), 438(c); churches, 430(b), 431(h); election, 18th cent., 6156(h); Philip Hawford, pseudo-abbot, 6159(d); incorporation, 367(a); Clem. Lichfield, abbot, 6159(c)

Evesham, Epiphanius, mason (16th cent.), 2607(t)

Evington, Leics., peculiar, 626

Evolution, 349; theory of, and Darwin, 5371(a)

Ewanrigg, Cumb., 1167(o)

Ewart, Northumb., 5263(h)

Ewart, family, 5330(s)

Ewden, W.R.Yorks., 2378(w)

Ewell, Kent, *see* Temple Ewell

Ewell, Surr., 1105(c), 5614(d)

Ewelme, Oxon., 439(b), 4114(l), 4837(k)

Ewenny, Glam., 1(p), 3(g), 437(b), 733(a), 4115(p)

Ewenny, river, Glam., 2(g)

Ewer and basin, given by Abp Parker, 3563(o)

Ewerby, Lincs., 149(a)

Ewhurst, Suss., 6047(d)

Ewhurst manor, *see* Cowfold, Suss.

Ewias Harold, Herefs., 433(b)

Ewloe, Flints., 1773(d), 2290(a,b), 2884(d)

Ewood Bridge, Lancs., 1045(b)

Ewood manor, *see* Newdigate, Surr.

Eworth, Hans, portrait-painter (fl. 1550–75), 5910(a), 5911(i,j,k)

Examinations in history, 2141

Glass, stained and painted (*cont.*)
4979(g); Somerset, 665(a); Stanford-on-Avon, 664(h); Stoke Charity, 2010(q); Stowting, 2607(b); Suffolk, 666(b); Surrey, 5635; Tattershall, 2825(bbb); Temple Ewell, 2606(q); Tewkesbury abbey, 452(k); Thaxted, 763(a); Warwick, Beauchamp chapel, 383(e), 5177(o); Wells cath., 665(d,e), 5197(c); Westlington House, 98(c); Westminster abbey, 5100(f); Westminster, St Stephen's chapel, 662(h); Westwood, 5443(m); Wiggenhall, 3564(q); Winchester cath., 2010(h); Winscombe, 5428(f); Wixford, 385(e); Woolwich, 6140(b); Wrangle, 2825(dd); Yaxley, 5582(d,e); York churches, 4472(a), 6231(f), 6236(a), 6414(b); York minster, 526(e), 666(i), 4107(m), 4119(b), 4468(e), 4554(b), 6234(k), 6235(g), 6284(d), 6414(b), 6423(c), 6444(b); Yorkshire, 664(e), 665(c). *See also* Armorial glass; Glass-painters

Glass beads: Celtic, 5071(d); prehistoric, 4046(a)

Glass bottles, machine for making, 6445(a)

Glasse, Rev. George Henry, classical scholar & divine (d. 1809), 5727(t)

Glasse, Rev. Samuel, theologian (d. 1812), 5727(t)

Glass-houses, *see* Glass industry

Glass industry, glass-workers, glass-works: Chance Brothers, 6451(e); Dagnia family, Newcastle, 5249(f); development, 6444(a); fireclays and pots, 6448(d); flint chippings, 662(b); Williams family, Newcastle, 5220(l)

at, in, etc.: Birmingham, 6448(c), 6451(c); Bristol, 453(j), 1661(a), 6446(a); Chester, 6450(a); Chiddingfold, 662(b), 3549(i), 5622(e); Cumberland, 6447(c); Dudley, 6448(b); Eccleshall, 3626(b), 3637(a); Great Yarmouth, 6450(a); Hertfordshire, 6450(a); King's Lynn, 6450(a); Lancashire, 6449(b); Malton, 6450(a); Nailsworth, 448(a); Nottingham, 6447(b); nr St Weonards, 6128(i); Scotland, 6450(a); Sheffield area, 6450(a); Smethwick, 6451(e); Southwark, 6450(b); Staffordshire, 664(i); Stourbridge and dist., 3552(g), 6448(a), 6451(b); Surrey-Sussex weald, 6452(a); Sussex, 2354(c); on river Tyne, 6447(a); Wales, 6450(a); on river Wear, 6446(b); west country, 6449(a); Woolwich, 6450(a); Worcester, 6448(b); Yorkshire, 6446(c)

See also Society of Glass Technology

Glassonby, Cumb., 1164(t), 1165(x); Grayson-lands, 1164(v,w)

Glass-painters, glass-painting: advertisements, 663(a); Birmingham, 663(b); copyist, 662(f); English and foreign, 16th cent., 5164(d); Essex, 666(c); King's Lynn, 666(a); materials, 662(c); Norwich, 666(a); plague, effects of, 4126(e); technique, 4642(c); York school, 526(f), 662(j). *See also* British Soc. of Master Glass-painters; Glass, stained and painted

Glaston, place-name, 5410(q)

Glastonbury, Som., 1393(a), 1893(d); abbey, *see below*; Beckery mill, 5421(o); borough bicentenary, 1893(e); Brue, river, 5421(o); churches, 1893(h), 5401(a,c,k), 5425(a); and St David, 745(n); French-Walloon church, 2353(m); Grail legend, 1791(c); lake-village, 388(a), 541(a), 1470(a), 1894, 3269(e), 5401(m), 5403(h), 5997(a); Mound, 5425(j); place-name, 5410(q); pleas, 3520(bb); Pomparles, 5411(m), 5421(o); recorders, 1893(f,g); Roman road, 5421(o); Saxon church, 5426(j); streets, 1893(b); and Wm of Malmesbury, 503(a)

abbey, 442(a), 2947(c), 4134(j), 5351(c), 5441(s), 5998(a), 6000(a); 14th cent., 5392(a); building unit, 4117(r); church, 4108(i), 4839(e); consecration crosses, 763(f);

Glastonbury, Som. (*cont.*)
discoveries, 5285(b); excavations, 5169(a), 5407(p), 5425(h), 5427(a); feodary, 5383; Loretto chapel, 5444(e); obedientiar's accounts, 4836(f); register, 3528(d); ruins, 5401(b); Saxon abbots, 503(b); symbolic plan, 5412(a); and West Pennard church, 5392(b)

Glastonbury Antiq. Soc., publs., 1893–4

Glastonia, place-name, 5410(q)

Glastynbury, William, of Christ Church, Canterbury (d. 1448), 2599(f)

Glaze-brook, *see* Devonshire

Glazed pebbles, from Llanbedr, 728(j)

Glazeley, Salop, 4991

Glaziers, companies, etc., of: Chester, 999(d); Exeter, 2964(e); London, 5166(f); Sheffield, 2379(t)

Glazing accounts, 662(h), 663(e)

Gleaston, Lancs., 211(c), 1169(k), 1187(aa)

Gledhill, family, 1985(d)

Glee, development of the, 5970(b)

Glendower (Glyndwr), Owen, Welsh leader (d. 1416?), 905(m), 2208, 3905(a); and battle of Shrewsbury, 4964(h); bibliography, 6022; and Coity castle, 1(f); family, 2314(c); and Sycherth, Denb., 4968(a); and Welsh church, 2278(f)

Glevum, *see* Gloucester: Roman remains

Glisson, Francis, physician (d. 1677), 4704(b), 5312(a)

Globe, symbolism of, in Roman portraiture, 5127(a)

Globe theatre, Southwark, *see* Theatres and playhouses

Gloddaeth, Caern., 2872(b), 2882(l)

Glorious Revolution, *see* Revolution (1688)

Glossop, Derbys., 1286(k), 1287(e)

Gloucester, 432(b,c), 515(d), 1878(c); abbey, St Peter's, 443(i), 452(h), 1895(g), *and see* cathedral *below*; alchemist's laboratory, 1137(c); artists, 446(e); Black Friars, 460(k); bridges, 457(i); cathedral, *see below*; charters, 2748(f); churches, 432(i), 515(e), 1895(e,d), 5442(b); citizens, medieval, 447(b); deeds, 447(a); diocese, *see below*; and Durham, 1137(d); Grey Friars, 460(e); High Cross, 430(p); hospital, St Bartholomew's, 457(i); King's Board, *see* Tibberton, Glos.; King's school, 1895(i); Lanthony priory, 431(i); maces, 430(q); and Monmouth, road between, 6124(g); museum, 436(h); nonconformist academy, 1106(b); plate and insignia, 436(e); priory, St Oswald's, 449(e); Roman remains (Glevum), 436(j), 459(k,l), 1131(a), 4125(j); Southgate chapel, Forbes library, 1111(j); swords, 430(q); vale of, 1096(k); visitations, heraldic, 434(i); water supply, 1133(b); west wall, 459(k); and Geo. Whitefield, 6038(b)

cathedral, 442(b), 515(d), 1895(a), 4125(m), 5275(c), 5442(b); chapter house tombs, 1895(h); glass, stained, 440(c), 444(a), 449(g), 450(j), 1895(a), 4125(m); and Hereford cath., 433(e); Lady chapel, 1895(b); misericords, 434(e); organ, 1895(f); roof bosses, 459(d); tower, 440(e). *See also* Gloucester Cathedral Soc.

Gloucester, diocese: arms, 446(d); consistory court, 452(j); consistory court wills, 632; portraits of bps, 441(f)

Gloucester, Dukes of, *see* Humphry; William Frederick

Gloucester, H.M.S., 3500(g)

Gloucester & Berkeley canal, 1134(b)

Gloucester Cathedral Soc., *Records of Gloucester Cath.*, 1895

Gloucestershire: architecture, 456(c); bell-founders, 440(d); Bisley hundred, archaeology, 457(l); brasses, 504(h), 3425(e), 3426(h); brickmaking, 983(e); cartulary, 455(i);

Holland, William, Moravian (fl. 1746), 718(q)
Holland House, Kensington, 520(c)
Hollandt, Samuel Jan, capt. (d. 1801), 5088(i)
Hollar, Wenceslaus, engraver (d. 1677): Greenwich, view of, 3139; London, engraving of, 3105; London, maps of, 3098, 3099(h); London, unpublished drawings, 3127; as marine artist, 5098(x); 'Quartermaster's map', 4361(a); Westminster and the abbey, 5880(a)
Holles, family, 162(f)
Holles, Gervase, antiquary (d. 1675), 153(m), 162(f), 2799, 5828(c)
Holles, James, vicar of Hurley, Berks. (d. 1552), 260(g)
Holles, John, 2nd E. of Clare (d. 1666), 5831(e)
Holles, Sir Thomas Pelham-, D. of Newcastle, *see* Pelham-Holles
Holles, William (d. 1644), 5838(c)
Hollesley, Suff., 3846
Hollingbury camp, Suss., 415(a), 420(a), 5171(a)
Hollinghall, *see* Ilkley, W.R.Yorks.
Hollinghey, *see* Sowerby, W.R.Yorks.
Hollinghill, Northumb.: Lordenshaws, 5262(b)
Hollins, and Lower Hollins, *see* Warley, W.R.Yorks.
Hollis, family, 197(c), 5853(l)
Holloway, Sir Charles, maj.-gen. (d. 1827), 2464(d)
Hollowell, Samuel, surgeon, of Newcastle-upon-Tyne (d. 1760), 5219(a)
Hollow-scrapers, 5720(o)
Hollyband, Claudius (fl. 1568–97), 282(d)
Holm, Roger de (14th cent.), 3569(f)
Holmbury hill, Surr., 5605(f), 5626(i)
Holme, Norf., nr Norwich, 3566(a), 3601-2
Holme, Notts., 4105(p), 5811(b)
Holme, family, 995(c), 1165(l)
Holme, George (b. *c.* 1671), 995(c)
Holme, Henry (fl. 1745), 1164(j)
Holme, Johanne (d. *c.* 1506), 1275(e)
Holme, John (b. *c.* 1684), 995(c)
Holme, Randle III, genealogist (d. 1700), 995(c), 1001(a), 3996
Holme, Randle IV, genealogist (d. 1707), 995(c), 1001(a)
Holme, Thomas, surveyor-gen. to Wm Penn (d. 1695), 1186(j)
Holme (Howlme), William (d. 1520), 1275(e)
Holme-by-the-Sea, *see* Holme-next-the-Sea
Holme Cultram, Cumb., 1212; abbey, 1176(r), 1212; chapels, 1165(v); churchyard, 1170(t); granges, 1177(h); Raby Cote, 1164(o); Sixteen Men, 1166(j)
Holme-next-the-Sea, Norf., 3429(pp), 3570(c), 3592(f)
Holme-on-Spalding moor, E. R. Yorks., 931(e), 1623(a); Throlam, 1623(b), 6278
Holme Pierrepont, Notts., 5809(a)
Holmes, Mrs Elizabeth, Methodist (d. 1781), 6035(k)
Holmes, Obadiah, Baptist (d. 1682), 194(n)
Holmesdale valley, Kent and Surrey, 2593(k)
Holmesfield, Derbys., 1278(g), 2377(k); Fanshawe Gate, 1584(d), 2379(v)
Holmside, co. Dur., 5253(j)
Holne Chase camp, *see* Devonshire
Holroyd, Sir Charles (d. 1917), 3935
Holroyde, family, 1995(d)
Holt, Denb., 726(m), 736(i), 2114(d); Castle Lyons, 2292
Holt (Nevill Holt), Leics., 2752(g)
Holt, Norf., hundred, 3570(b), 3600
Holt, David, Quaker (d. 1846), 1827(d)
Holton, Oxon., 3429(h)

Holwell (Holewale), Dors., 1392(c)
Holwell, Herts., 1593(k)
Holy Blood of Hayles, 4115(g)
Holy communion, *see* Communion; Holy sacrament; Liturgies, Church of England
Holy Cross, order of, 4397(h)
Holy Cross, Welsh relic of, 2294(a)
Holy days and sabbaths, 198(p)
Holy Grail, *see* Grail legend
Holyhead, Anglesey, 750(i); Caer-y-Twr, 2882(a); Ty Mawr, 2882(a)
Holy Island, *see* Lindisfarne
Holyngbroke, William (14th cent.), 3427(e)
Holy sacrament: bread, 49; represented on fonts, 4107(a); reservation, 38; veils, 4835(h). *See also entries beginning* Communion *and under* Miracle (morality, mystery) plays
Holy Sepulchre, canonesses of, 942(a)
Holy springs, Wormley, Herts., 1595(i)
Holystone, Northumb., 5229(n), 5236(d)
Holy week services, 44
Holywell, Flints., 741(m), 742(n), 930(i), 1773(e)
Holywell, Oxford, 928(i)
Holywell-cum-Needingworth, Hunts., 3865(a)
Holy wells: Bradford dist., 408(m); Cefn Bryn, Gower, 4565(a); Cornwall, 509(g); Gosforth, Holy Well, 1165(e); Llangavelach, Gower, 4565(a); St Constantine, 5151(c); Somerset, 5443(j), 6005(a); Wales, 1450(a), 2875(h). *See also* Wells
Home, Francis, first professor of materia medica in Edinburgh (d. 1813), 4706(a)
Home defence, 3465
Home industries, Scottish highlands and islands, 4235(e)
Home work, report of select committee, 4228(a)
Homilies: Anglo-Saxon, 3520(ff); early English, 1498; English, 12th cent., 1487; Mirk's collection, 1547; St Wulfstan's homiliary, 5194(d)
'Homo planus', and leprosy in Wales, 740(i)
Hondius, Jodocus (d. 1611), 4346(b), 4366(a), 4382
Honest Whore (Dekker), 295(a)
Honeychurch, Devon, 1727(h)
Hongkong, 2496(c), 4273(f), 4909
Honingham, Norf., 3570(c)
Honiton, Devon, 193(i), 1322(h)
Honourable Artillery Company, 5085(h)
Honourable Soc. of Cymmrodorion: *Y Cymmrodor*, 2266–94; *Cymmrodorion Record ser.*, 2334–43; founders, 2306(d); history, 2324(c); index to publs, 2330; *Trans.*, 2295–328; other publs, 2329–33, 2344–5
Honywode, Robert (16th cent.), 3426(d)
Honywood, John (fl. 1745), 1164(j)
Honywood, Sir Philip, gen. (d. 1752), 5084(c)
Honywood, Philip, gen. (d. 1785), 1164(i)
Hoo, family, 5697(i), 5711(q)
Hoo St Werburgh, Kent, 2593(r)
Hood, Robin, legendary outlaw, 406(d), 3209(g), 3300(c)
Hood, Samuel, 1st Vct H., adm. (d. 1816), 3477(f), 3487(e), 4755(a), 4767(f), 5116(d)
Hood game, 1797(e)
Hook, Theodore, author (d. 1841), 3282(e)
Hooke, Richard, vicar of Halifax (d. *c.* 1688), 1968(f)
Hooke, William, Puritan divine (d. 1677), 1110(p)
Hooker, John, *see* Vowell, *alias* Hooker

Hooker, Sir Joseph Dalton, naturalist (d. 1911), 2855(a), 3598(a)

Hooker, Richard, theologian (d. 1600), 1046(b)

Hooker, Sir William Jackson, naturalist (d. 1865), 2855(a), 3598(a)

Hookers (ships), 5099(f)

Hookes, Ellis, Quaker recording clerk (b. 1630), 1807(b)

Hook Norton, Oxon., 522(a)

Hoole, family, 2378(s)

Hooper, John, steward to 2nd E. of Clare (fl. 1644), 5831(e)

Hooton, Elizabeth, Quaker (d. 1672), 1818(g), 1841

Hooton Pagnell, W.R.Yorks., 5791(b), 6394

Hoover, Herbert, president of the U.S.A. (d. 1964), 5331(p)

Hopcar, *see* Leigh, Lancs.

Hope, Derbys.: Brough, 1274(h), 1277(d), 1571(b), 2626(g)

Hope End, Herefs., 6129(l)

Hope Hall, *see* Halifax, W.R.Yorks.

Hope of Health (More), 299(h)

Hopesay, Salop, 5002

Hop-growers' tokens, 6326(k)

Hopkey, Henry John, col. (fl. 1706–28), 4142(f)

Hopkinson, George Caesar, of Eliott's Lt Horse (b. 1738), 4792(b)

Hopkinson, Richard (d. 1505), 1971(b)

Hoppner, John, portrait-painter (d. 1810), 5878(d)

Hopton, family, 1732(a)

Hopton, Ralph, Lord H. (d. 1652), 5378

Hopton and Griffe Grange, Derbys., 1282(k)

Hopton Castle, Salop, 3805, 4988

Hopton Wafers, Salop, 4970(g), 4994

Horbling, Lincs., 149(a)

Horbury, Wakefield, W.R.Yorks., 6330

Horbury, family, 6234(i)

Hordle, Hants, 3366(h)

Hordley, Salop, 5010

Hore, Richard, of London (fl. 1536), 4368(b)

Horham Hall, Essex, 516(i), 1721(g)

Horkesley, Great, Essex, 1703(ff)

Horkesley, Little, Essex, 1705(o)

Horkesley, family, 1705(o)

Horkstow, Lincs., 150(c)

Horley, Oxon., 524(f)

Horley, Surr., 5852(i)

Horley Green, *see* Northowram, W.R.Yorks.

Horman, William, vice-provost of Eton (d. 1535), 4030

Hormead, Little, Herts., 1595(s)

Hornbeamgate manor, Herts., *see* Lowthes

Hornblower, Jonathan Carter, engineer (d. 1815), 3555(i), 4218(o)

Hornblower, Joseph, glass-painter (fl. 1770), 663(b)

Horn-books, 1278(l), 2625(d)

Hornby, Lancs., 931(f), 957(d), 1175(bb), 2697

Hornby, Eleanor (d. *c.* 1537), 5216(n)

Hornchurch, Essex, 1700(m); Dury Fall, 1704(t)

Horndon, West, Essex, 1696(v)

Horne, Surr.: Thunderfield castle, 5606(a)

Horne, family, 6227(i)

Horne, Alexander, gov. of Isle of Man (fl. 1715), 2550(p)

Horne, Henry Sinclair, Baron H. (d. 1929), 4166(e)

Hornebolt, Margaret (d. 1529), 3430(d)

Horners' company, 5150(a)

Hornfield, *see* Exton, Rut.

Horngarth, feudal service, 6228(d)

Horningsea, Cambs., 758(i), 765(a)

Horningsham, Wilts., 3919(f,g)

Horns, 990(d)

Hornsea, E.R.Yorks., 2375(e), 4091(a)

Hornsey, Mdx, 2974(m)

Hornton, Oxon, 524(f)

Horologes, 4825(g)

Horology, 5193(i)

Horrox, Jeremiah, astronomer (d. 1641), 4904

Horse armour, 4106(c)

Horse Grenadiers, 4776(c)

Horseheath, Cambs., 770(c), 779(g)

Horselunges manor, *see* Hellingly, Suss.

Horse-mills, 3552(c)

Horse-racing, 2635(f), 4791(h)

Horses: of Piers Gaveston, 4446(b); palaeolithic European, domestication of, 4106(f); prehistoric, remains of, 2101(a); of Roman Catholics (distributed 1688–90), 5222(h); of Royal Artillery, killed in Boer war, 4139(b); owned by showman, 4788(b)

Horse-shoes, 758(p), 1139(b,d), 5218(c)

Horse-trappings, armorial, 1378(l)

Horsfall, family, 1981(c)

Horsford, Norf., 3563(q), 3568(q)

Horsforth, W.R.Yorks., 5791(t), 5799(x)

Horsham, Suss.: John Baker, 5704(d); chwdns' account book, 5727(e); Free Christian church, 5852(a); market deed, 5698(j); parish registers, 5754; Sedgewick castle, 5718(e); wills, 5698(j)

Horsham St Faith, Norf., 3570(p,q), 3571(f)

Horsington, Som., 5433

Horsley, West, Surr., 3006(a), 5609(e), 5610(f)

Horsley, John, Presbyterian, archaeologist (d. 1732), 5228(n), 5247(c), 5263(a,b); bi-centenary, 3923(g); *Britannia Romana*, 5142(g)

Horsleydown, Bermondsey, Baptist meeting-house, 201(d)

Horsmonden, Kent, 2590(c), 3429(ff)

Horsted, Little, Suss., 5730(x)

Horsted Keynes, Suss., 4602(d)

Horton, Dors., 1397(f)

Horton, Glos., 217(l), 460(a)

Horton, Staffs., 3614(d), 3639(a)

Horton, Yorks., lordship, 408(j)

Horton, family name, 5330(n)

Horton, William (d. 1740), 6522(c)

Horton Baptist Academy, *see* Bradford, W.R.Yorks.

Horton Kirby (Kirbie, Kirkby), Kent, 1269(a), 3843

Horton moor, Northumb., 5229(e)

Horwood, Great, Bucks., 101(e)

Horwood, Little, Bucks., 102(c)

Hospitallers, *see* Knights Hospitallers

Hospitals, medieval: Augustinian leper, 5251(d); Baldock, 1591(i); Bamburgh leper, 5226(f); Bath, 5443(u); Bridgnorth, 4979(b); Bristol, *see under* Bristol; Burneston, 6227(d); Bury St Edmunds, 5580(j); Canterbury, 4133(m); Chapel Plaister, 4134(j); Chatham, 3989(a); Chester, 2132(d); Chichester, 5703(c); Clothall, 1591(i); Coventry, 368(a); Deptford, 3051(b); Durham, 1165(y), 5599(e); Duxford, 758(x); Ely, 822(s); Ewelme, 4114(l); Exeter, 1334(o); Farley, 228(f); Great Bedwyn, 6107(g); Greatham, 5212(cc); Greenwich, 1897(o,q); Guildford, 5618(d), 5619(b), 5620(a); Harbledown, 4133(m); Helston, 4542(j); Hereford, 6127(u); Hertford, 1590(uu);

Inscriptions (*cont.*)

at, in, on: Acle church, 3568(e); Ashwell church, 4821(s); Bardney abbey, 154(m); Bedfordshire, 225(h); Bilsdale church, 6225(e); Colchester castle, 1700(d); Durlston House, Colchester, 1702(g); Eliseg pillar, 729(c); Great Marlow, 98(h); Salisbury cath. buttress, 6103(i); Shrewsbury church windows, 4974(k); south of England, 749(b); Wales, 748(h)

Inscriptions, monumental: indexes to names on, 1326(r), 3973; listed by Yorkshire Archaeol. Soc., 1677(l); recording of, 1125; to R.A. officers, 4173; of Roman Catholics, 938(c)

at, in: Bath abbey, 5220(i); Cambridgeshire, 811; Cheshire, 2111(f), 3973; Devon, 1326(r); co. Durham, 3539; Eaton-under-Haywood, 4981(p); Hanwood, 4974(n); Hastings, 5701(f); Hawarden, 2121(l); Hertfordshire, 1592(q); Ifield, 5715(i); Kirknewton, 5253(f); Lancashire, 3973; Leeds, 5799(k), 5804(k); London, bibliography of, 5330(cc); London, St Katherine by the Tower, 5331(z); Lydd, 2622; Madeley, 3633(a); Melling, Liverpool, 2121(j); Milford, 3366(e); New Shoreham, 5704(h); Northumberland, 3538; Rochdale, 3978(c), 3980(c,d), 3981(d), 3982(e); Rudbaxton, 2257(a); Satley, 1447; Shoreditch, St Leonard's, 5331(ee); South Shields, St Hild's, 5225(n); Suffolk, 5584; Tenterden, 2621; Walthamstow, 5955; Westminster, St Margaret's, 5330(aa); Wiltshire churches and churchyards, 6112(b); Yorkshire, 6283

See also English Monumental Inscriptions Soc.; Epitaphs; Grave-covers; Grave-slabs

Insignia, civic: Bristol, 3434(b); Chester, 996(f); Chesterfield, 1291(f); Gloucester, 436(e); Hereford, 6121(f); Hertford, 1588(dd); Lincoln, 524(h), 2825(z); Macclesfield, 2627(e); Warwick, 513(e)

Insignia, masonic, *see under* Freemasonry

Insignia, of Cambridge Univ. proctor, 759(u)

Inskip, Lancs., 6235(a)

Institute of Actuaries, 2972(h)

Institute of Bankers: *Jnl*, 2414–31, index, 2432; other publ., 2433

Institute of British Architects, *afterwards* Royal Institute of British Architects, *q.v.*

Institute of Christian Religion, 1113(n)

Institute of Marine Engineers: *Ann. Rpts (Trans.)*, 2434–48, index, 2449; foundation, etc., 2441(a)

Institute of Mary, nuns at York, 931(g,i)

Institute of Pacific Relations, conferences, 4515(a), 4517(b)

Institute of Sociology, *see* Sociological Soc.

Institute of Transport, *Jnl*, 2450–63

Institution of Royal Engineers: history, 2498(a); *Professional papers*, 2507–10; *Royal Engineers Jnl*, 2464–506; other publs, 2511–16

Institutions, of chantry priests, 222

Institutions to benefices, *see under* Benefices

Instrument-makers: nautical, 5098(ii); scientific, 594, 4556(b)

Instruments, scientific: by Humph. Cole, 5192(i); of Sir Wm Herschel, 3696(c); of Rich. of Wallingford, 4825(h)

Insula, *see* De Insula

Insurance: fire, 2132(a), 6412(a); industrial risks, 4221(e); marine, 1633(m), 2437(a); mutual insurance societies, 1809(c); National Insurance Bill (1911), 4231(b,c); National Insurance contributions, 4233(e)

Intelligence, engineer, in World War I, 2514

Interdict (1208), 503(f), 5612(c)

Interdict, on Dover, 4125(g)

Interest: rate since 1844, 4725(c); Ruskin's views on, 4252(a); and usury, 4250(c)

Interludes (18th cent. plays), as historical sources, 718(g)

Interludes (Edwards), 2299(b)

Intermediate and Technical (Wales) Act, 2328(a)

Interments, *see* Burials

Internal combustion engine, 2442(c)

Internal combustion machinery, 2444(a)

International Affairs, see Royal Institute of International Affairs

International affairs, relations: (1918–25), 2190; dates of events (1921–2), 4522; documents on (1928–32), 4528–9; effect of aviation on, 4516(f); and fiscal policy (after 1919), 4511(a); in the Pacific, 4517(k); and Permanent Court of International Justice, 4517(j); place of law in, 4515(b); prior to World War I, 1148; study of, 1155; survey of (1920–32), 4524, 4529. *See also* Council for the Study of International Relations; Grotius Soc.; Information Service on International Affairs; Royal Institute of International Affairs

International arbitration, Hen. Richard and, 1113(u)

International Copyright Conference, 4505(d)

International government, in Europe, 2185(b,d)

International Information Cttee, *International Information ser.*, 2517–20

International law: and British sea power, 4759(d); divergent views on, 1902(c); and English common law, 813(m); and submarine cables, 4497(c)

International obligations, British, 2408(m)

International Postal Service, 4517(a)

International relations, *see* International affairs

International Soc. of Philology, Science & Arts, *The Philomath*, 2521–9

Interpretations (*c.* 1561), 48

Intervention, war of, in Russia (1918–19); Crimea, 3471(c): Murmansk expedition, 3471(a), 4762(h); Royal Navy in the Caspian, 3470(d), 4203(d); Transcaspian operations, 4205(c)

Intestacies, and the custom of York province, 5801(m)

Invalids' carriages, 4650(b)

Invasions, of the British Isles, 2466(a). *See also entries beginning* Anglo-Saxon; Belgic; Danes; Irish; Norman; Prehistoric; Roman; *etc.*

Inventions: Cornish, 4218(m); of John Kay, 4640(a); mechanical, 3260(b); scientific, of John Blagrave, 5195(b); war, 4788(d)

Inventories (churches, chapels, religious houses, etc.): (1549–52), 910(m); Arundel, Holy Trinity (1517), 5177(b); Bedfordshire, 27; Bledlow (1783), 4834(q); Bosham, King's free chapel, 5706(g); Bristol, 14th–16th cent. 4838(a); Bristol, St Stephen's, 15th–16th cent., 4835(i); Buckinghamshire, 29; Cornwall, Kirrier hundred, 4541(h); Cranbrook (1509), 2603(e); Crediton, 1324(n); Devon, 37, 1333(g); Dorset (1552), 1371(f); Essex, 1693(o), 1694(r), 1695(l), 1697(l); Exeter, 37; Exeter, St Kieran's (1417), 1333(j); Gloucestershire, 465; Hampshire, 2009(x), 2010(u); High Wycombe, 98(e); Huntingdonshire, 28; Lancashire (1552), 1017(a); Leicestershire, 153(o); Lincolnshire, 156(a); London, St Anthony's, Threadneedle Street (1499), 4131(f); London, St Martin, Ludgate (*c.* 1400), 4834(h); Ludlow, palmers'

League of Nations (*cont.*)
on Financial Assistance (1930), 4518(c); covenant, 2408(f,l), 2413, 4505(c), 4513(a); and dominions of British Commonwealth, 4518(e); Economic Conference (1927), 4514(f); freedom of the seas and, 2238(a); General Act, British reservations, 4506(b); Geneva protocol (1924), 4511(e); model treaties commended to (1928), 4515(d); Mutual Assistance Treaty, draft of (1923), 4511(b); pact of, 2408(l); and private manufacture of arms (1921–31), 4518(f); rule of unanimity, 4508(a); sanctions, 4517(f); and treaty revision, 4518(d); work of (1920), 4497(i). *See also* Permanent Court of International Justice

League of Nations Union, 20(c)

League of the Empire: *Federal Magazine* (incorporating the *Official Rpt of the Federal Conference on Education* and *The All-Red Mail*), 2711–21; *Monthly Record*, 2709–10; *Review and Federal Magazine*, 2722–5; short account of, 4272(f); other publs, 2726–8

Lea Hall, *see* Preston Gobalds, Salop

Leake, Lincs., 2392(d)

Leake, N.R.Yorks., 2386(b), 6230(m)

Leake, East, Notts., 5808(a)

Leake, John (fl. 1667), 3108

Leake, Sir John, r.-adm. (d. 1720), 3506

Leake, Stephen Martin-, *see* Martin-Leake

Lear (Leir), *see*: *History of King Leir*

Learings, *see* Heptonstall, W.R.Yorks.

Learned societies, in London, 594

Leases: to Geoffrey Chaucer (1399), 3520(qq); early (1299), 224(d); of Leicester castle (1686, 1705), 2749(f); in lieu of a will, 1272(e); of Liverpool, fee-farm, 2111(a); of Marlborough, 6106(d); relating to Montgomeryshire (1560–1620), 3898(f); of rectorial profits, 2320(a); of tithe of hay, 5799(t); by dean and canons of Windsor, 3533(k). *See also* Pipe-leases

Leasowe, Ches., 2108(e), 2127(e)

Leather currency, 6455(c); penny, Manx, 2635(e)

Leatherhead (Letherhead), Surr., 5607(e), 5608(j), 5626(n)

Leathersellers' company, 2973(c)

Leathley (Lelay), family, 5788(a)

Leaves from the Journal of the Poor Wiltshire Vicar (Zschokke), 6102(r)

Le Bret, Walter, of Croftone (13th cent.), 6107(g)

Le Breton, family, 5045(b)

Le Breton, Guillaume, juré-justicier of Jersey (14th cent.), 5065(b)

Le Cateau, France, 4162(d), 4179

Lechlade, Glos., 447(f), 450(b)

Lechmere, Sir Nicholas, judge (d. 1701), 147(h)

Leckhampton, Glos., 453(c,d), 1138(a)

Lecky, John, Quaker, of Cork (d. 1839), 1821(a)

Lecky, William Edward Hartpole, historian (d. 1903), 470(e)

L'Ecluse, Jean de (fl. 1612), 1107(v)

Le Cornu, John, priest (fl. 1467), 5055(d)

Le Couperon dolmen, *see* Rozel, Jersey

Le Couteur, Mary, *née* Dumaresq (fl. 1800), 5053(b)

Lecterns: brass, 4134(f), 4135(g); stone, 369(a)

Lectures, nonconformist, in Yorkshire, 1109(p)

Ledbury, Herefs.: church, 448(a,c,d); effigy, 6130(u); hospital, 6127(e), 6128(v)

Le Dennys, family, 5580(m)

Le Despenser, Baron, *see* Dashwood, Francis

Ledger book, Vale Royal abbey, 3969

Ledger stones, armorial, 2603(o), 5610(a). *See also* Grave-slabs

Ledsham, W.R.Yorks., 6349

Ledstone (Ledston), W.R.Yorks., 5804(d), 6229(m)

Ledwych Court, *see* Bitterley, Salop

Lee, family, 865(a)

Lee, Edward, abp (d. 1544), 6224(p)

Lee, Sir Henry, of Ditchley (d. 1611), 248(e)

Lee, Dr John (d. 1866), 3439(b)

Lee, Lawrence, of Godalming (d. 1735), 1108(g), 5615(a)

Lee, Sir Richard, military engineer (d. 1575), 2465(i)

Lee, Richard, ambassador to Russia (d. 1610), 4120(f)

Lee, Dr Richard, of Hatfield (d. 1684), 4821(t)

Lee, Richard, of Essendon (d. 1725), 4821(t)

Lee, Sir Sidney, scholar (d. 1926), 484(b). *See also* Index of Authors

Lee, Thomas, merchant (fl. 1634), 5329(f)

Leebotwood, Salop, 865(j), 5008

Lee Brockhurst, Salop, 5020

Leedes, family, 5706(d)

Lee-Dillon, Harold Arthur, 17th Vct Dillon (d. 1932), 487(d), 5093(j). *See also* Index of Authors

Leeds, W.R.Yorks.: 18th cent., 5804(i); arms, 5791(q), 5800(p); Wm Boyne, 5804(g); Briggate, shop in, 5800(t); British Assn handbook, 583–4; Brotherton library, 1741(c); chapels, 5788(i), 5800(k); charters, 2729(e); church, Baptist, 202(c); churches, 5791(g), 5799(h,r,u), 5804(j); committee of charitable uses, 5797(p); Congregationalism, 1103(p); crosses, 5797(m); Denison family, 5791(u); engineers, 3555(k); extent, 5804(d); Wm Fearn, 5800(h); freemasonry, 2965(c), 6507(c), 6509(a), 6510(a), 6517(c), 6518(c,d), 6524(b), 6525(a); grammar school, 5790; Great Wodehouse, 5791(u); John Harrison, 5804(e); Kirkgate-cum-Holbeck manor, 5800(g); Knight Templary, 6512(c); lease of hay tithe, 5799(t); libraries, 2764(a); mace, its maker and serjeants, 6512(a); manor, 5788(j), 5799(n,s); maps and plans, 5788(h), 5791(e,n), 5799(l); merchant's memorandum book, 5799(d); Methodists, 6045(f); municipal strike, 4234(a); music, 5801(i); old hall, Wade Lane, 5800(a); and Paganini, 5804(m); parish registers, 5787, 5798; places of interest, 6524(c); potteries, 5799(l); prehistory, 5791(s); public institutions, 2763(b); Queen Anne's Bounty, 5800(j); rental, 5799(b); Roman coins, 5797(b), 6324(e); satirical poems, 5797(d); Sherburn manor, 5804(i); Talbot inn, 6525(b); tombstone inscriptions, 5799(k), 5804(k); University library, 1741(c), 2729(f); vicarage, 5800(k); Volunteers, 5799(w), 5801(h); white cloth hall, 5797(j); wills, 5788(b), 5795, 5797(e); woollen industry, 5803; Yeomanry, 5799(v); York or East Bar, 5800(l). *See also following entries and* Thoresby Soc.

Leeds, dukedom, 5791(a)

Leeds, Duke of, *see* Osborne, George William Frederick

Leeds, Edward Rookes, of Royds Hall (d. 1785), 409(dd)

Leeds Educational and Benevolent Institution, 6518(b)

Leeds Installed Masters' Assn, *Trans.*, 6507–25, indexes, 6512(d), 6515(a), 6524(d)

Leeds Intelligencer, 5801(b)

Leeds Mercury: extracts, 5797(l), 5801(b); monthly economic surveys (1835–44), 4253(w)

Leeds Philosoph. & Lit. Soc.: history, 2732; *Procs*, 2729–31

Lee Hall, *see* Ellesmere, Salop

Leek, Staffs., 1104(a), 2624(g), 3630(d), 5560

Leek, national emblem of Wales, 883(a), 2277(d)

Llantwit Major, Glam. (*cont.*)
    725(k), 3516(a), 4115(p); Col Hugh Bay castle ditches, 5776(a); cross of Illtyd, 723(e); ecclesiastical buildings, 872(a); excavations, 735(a), 880(a); Roman villa, 3516(a)

Llantysilio, Anglesey, 68(f)

Llanuwchllyn, Mer., 739(r)

Llanvaches, Mon., 3451

Llanvair Waterdine, Salop, 2277(b), 4977(c)

Llanveithan, *see* Llancarfan, Glam.

Llanveynoe, Herefs., 6130(s)

Llanvihangel, *see* Llanfihangel Abercowin

Llanvillo, *see* Llanfilo

Llanwenog, Card., 730(h), 893(j,k)

Llanwnog, Mont., 752(r), 3902(h)

Llanwrtyd, Brec.: Ystafell-Fach, 723(o)

Llanyblodwel, Salop, 3899(a), 5023, 5028(e)

Llanybyther, Carm., 913(c)

Llanymynech, Salop, 864(a), 3898(j), 5025, 6027(c)

Llanyre, Rad., 3936(a)

Llanystumdwy, Caern., 736(c)

Llaryhchwyn, Caern., 747(d), 2872(i), 2885(a), 2886(a)

Lledrod, Card., 714(l)

Llewelyn, Thomas, Baptist minister (d. 1793), 1240(a)

Lleyn, Caern., 723(n), 743(l)

Lleyn, William, Welsh poet (d. 1587), 2272(e)

Llowes, Rad., 3937(a)

Lloyd, family, 908(k), 2255(k)

Lloyd, Baron, of Dolobran, *see* Lloyd, Sir George Ambrose

Lloyd, David, Quaker (d. 1731), 1809(b)

Lloyd, Rev. Evan, poet (d. 1776), 2280(e)

Lloyd, George, bp (d. 1615), 989(e)

Lloyd, Sir George Ambrose, 1st Baron L. of Dolobran (d. 1941), 24(c)

Lloyd, Henry, maj.-gen. (d. 1783), 5093(k)

Lloyd, Humfrey (d. 1568), 3518(v)

Lloyd, Simon, of Bala (d. 1764), 712(d)

Lloyd, Thomas, lt.-col. (d. 1813), 612(j)

Lloyd, William, bp (d. 1717), 6155(d), 6169

Lloyd's: history, 2438(b); origin and functions, 3475(b); 'Patriotic fund' (1803), 3475(g)

Lloyd's, coffee-house, 4685(b)

Lloyd's register of shipping, 3475(b)

Llwyd, Humfrey, *see* Lloyd

Llwyd, Morgan, of Gwynedd (d. 1659), 1234(a), 2313(b)

Llwyngwayr, Pemb., 6033(f)

Llwynllwyd, *see* Llanigon, Brec.

Llyfryddiaeth y Cymru, 6019(o)

Llyfr y Tri Aderyn (Llwyd), 1234(a)

Llynfawr, *see* Rhigos, Glam.

Llysfaen, *see* Llandrillo-yn-Rhos, Denb.

Llystyn Gwyn, *see* Dolbenmaen, Caern.

Llywarch Hen, Welsh poet (9th cent. ?), 487(b), 2308(c)

Llywel, Brec., 737(a), 3516(a)

Llywelyn (d. 1099), son of Cadwgan, 608(e)

Llywelyn ab Gruffydd, prince of Wales (d. 1282), 731(b), 733(b), 2865(b)

Llywelyn ab Iorwerth (d. 1240), 2865(b)

Loam, Michael, engineer (d. 1871), 4219(e)

Loans: charitable, 3314(a); to the Crown, *temp.* Hen. VIII, 4539(p); in times of war (1793–1914), 4237(d)

Lobley, James, Bradford artist (d. 1888), 406(p)

Local administration, in British West Africa, 4300

Local authorities, and housing problem, 4222(b)

Local government: Essex, Rochfort hundred, 13th cent., 5521(d); Denton, 153(b); Halifax, 1992(c); history, 3642(f); Sussex, through tithings or 'borowes', 5745

Local history: an address, 454(c); bibliography, 2196; and libraries, 2785(a); and local records, 4820(a); ms. sources, 2780(a); teaching of, 2149

Local legislation by private bill, 4719(a)

Local records: local history and, 4820(a); use of, 2310(b); Welsh, 2310(c), 3518(j)

Local Taxation commission, 4221(d)

Local War Records committee (1920–21), 2229(k)

Locarno treaties, 1907(a), 2404, 4512(e), 4515(b)

Lochmaben, Scotland, 4578(c)

Lochmeiler, *see* Camrose, Pemb.

Locke, John, philosopher (d. 1704), 5359(a); *Directions concerning Education*, 4042; library, 1751(a); and Lowndes, 815(e); and modern thought, 470(a); social contract theory, 5295(a); theory of the state, 470(b); and toleration, 202(l)

Locke, Richard, of Burnham, Som. (18th cent.), 5436

Lockerby, William, sandalwood-trader (fl. 1808), 1949

Locker-Lampson, Frederick (d. 1895), 3311(b)

Lockinge, East, Berks., 260(e)

Lockington, Leics., 1285(a)

Lockington, E.R.Yorks., 6234(d)

Lockleys, Herts., 1594(d)

Lockyer, Lionel, quack (d. 1672), 4694(h)

Lockyer, Nicholas, nonconformist divine (d. 1685), 1105(j), 1110(e)

Locomotives: 19th cent., 2507(b); Brunton's, 3546(f); development, 3946(a); early standard types, 3946(b); Gurney's, 3546(h); Tim. Hackworth and, 3546(c); imported into America (1829), 3548(d); of Lancashire & Yorkshire railway, 3944(a); safety valves in, 2447(c); and St Etienne-Lyon railway, 3551(e); of South Eastern & Chatham railway, 3941(a); Trevithick's, 3545(c), 3556(f); trials at Rainhill (1829), 3553(f); wrought iron details and wheels, 3555(e)

Locrine, *see: Tragedy of Locrine*

Loders, Dors., 1399(d)

Lodge, Thomas, author (d. 1625), 178(a), 3160, 3206

Lodge of Research, No. 2429, Leicester: history, etc., 2903(b); *Masonic Papers*, 2916–20; *Masonic Reprints*, 2921–31; *Trans.*, 2888–915, review of *Trans.*, 2889(d); other publs, 2932–6

Lodge Quatuor Coronati, No. 2076, London, 3219(d), 3235, 6467(b); *Ars Quatuor Coronatorum* (*Trans.*), 2937–67, index, 2954(d); other publs, 2968

Lodge rooms, *see under* Freemasonry

Lodges, masonic, *see under* Freemasonry

Lodging the colour, 5086(k)

Lodyngton, William de, justice of the king's bench (d. 1419), 3428(z)

Lofthouse, nr Wakefield, W.R.Yorks., 6238(l)

Lofts, *see* Church lofts; Rood lofts

Loftus, Lord Augustus (d. 1904), 815(k)

Lofty Bishop, lazy Brownist and loyal Author, 1109(z)

Log-books, of: Wm Adams, 2557(a); *Garland*, 5110(j); Abel Hicks, 2255(h); salt-trader, 5103(c); slaver, 5103(a). *See also* School log-books

Loggan, David, artist & engraver (d. 1700?), 759(k), 5873(a)

Lollards, Lollardism: after 1384, 1113(s); in Hereford dioc.,

Long barrow men: of Cotswolds, 984(d); beyond Cotswolds, 985(a); and modern Londoners, 4062(a)
Long barrows, *see* Barrows and tumuli
Longborough, Glos., 451(a)
Longbottom, *see* Yorkshire, West Riding
Longbridge Deverill, Wilts., 1778(a)
Long Causeway, Lancs. and Yorks., 1974(h)
Longchamp, William, bp (d. 1197), 2598(b)
Longcot, Berks., 252(a)
Longdon, Staffs., 1104(d)
Longdon-upon-Tem, Salop, 5005
Longfield, Kent, 104(j)
Longford, *see* Neath, Glam.
Longford Castle, Wilts., 151(n), 1368(d), 3367(h)
Longitude, discovery of, 3296(c)
Longleat, Wilts., 151(n), 218(h), 4134(j), 5431(f), 5445(d)
Longlonde, John, bp (d. 1547), 2093
Long Meg, Cumb., 5862(d)
Longmoor, Hants., 2490(a)
Long Mountain, Mont., 6025(a)
Longnewton, co. Dur., 5217(m)
Longnor, Salop, 865(j), 2892(b), 5008
Long Parliament, 2225(e), 2231(d)
Long Sand channel, 5115(c)
Longshaw earthworks, *see* Hathersage, Derbys.
Longton, Staffs., 3621(a)
Longtown, Cumb., 1829(c)
Longtree hundred, *see* Gloucestershire
Longueville, Jersey, 5048(g), 5069(c)
Longworth, Berks., 248(g)
Lonsdale, Lancs. and Westmld, 1171(l), 1175(s), 1179(i); deanery, 3972; Thirnby manor, 2127(i)
Lonsdale hundred, Lancs., 1017(a), 2626(a)
Looe, Cornw., 1739(ee,ll,oo,qq), 1740(g)
Look about you (1600), 3175
Looking-glass for London and England (1594), 3206
Loom, in bronze age Britain, 1695(u)
Loom weight, from Melandra castle, 2628(d)
Lopez, Ruy (Roderigo), physician (d. 1594), 2568(c)
Lopham, South, Norf., 528(g), 3562(b), 3570(y)
Lord, Hugh (d. 1829), 4743(f)
Lord, Sampson, priest, of Sheffield (d. *c.* 1537), 2377(v)
Lord admiral, lord high admiral: and administration, 5110(c); and Board of Admiralty, 5109(d); council, 5114(g); rank, 5099(i); whistle, 5100(t); 'whistle of honour', 5106(g)
Lord chamberlain, records of, 3209(d), 3210(i)
Lord chancellor, office of, and Jews, 2570(c)
Lord Clyde, H.M.S., 5114(b)
Lordenshaws, *see* Hollinghill, Northumb.
Lord high admiral, *see* Lord admiral
Lord lieutenant, *see* Lieutenancy papers
Lords, House of, *see under* Parliament
Lord's bridge, nr Cambridge, 760(k)
Lord Shelburne, transport, 5103(u)
Lord's Island, Cumb., *see* Derwentwater
Lords journals, *see* Parliament: House of Lords
Lords Ordainers, 4446(b)
Lordswood (Lords Wood), *see* Upton, Hants
Lord Warden, H.M.S., 5114(b)
Lorentz, Friedrich, diplomat (fl. 1744), 4410(c)
Lorica (Gildas), 2335
Lorimer, Peter, Presbyterian divine (d. 1879), 3919(l)
Lorimer, Sir Robert, architect (d. 1929), 4488(c)

Lorna Doone (Blackmore), 1325(e)
Lorton, Cumb., 3873
Lothersdale, W.R.Yorks., 406(n)
Lotherton, W.R.Yorks., 5800(f)
Lothian, Scotland, 3519(o)
Lothingland, Suff., 5581(a)
Lothropp, John, *see* Lathrop
Lot-meadow customs, Yarnton, 4230(a), 4232(a)
Loughborough, Leics., 2904(a)
Loughton, Essex, 1692(k), 1698(w), 1713(e), 1718(b), 1719(a)
Loughton camp, *see* Epping forest
Loughwood, *see* Dalwood, Dors.
Louis of Toulouse, Saint (d. 1297), 657
Louis VIII, king of France (d. 1226), 3520(g)
Louis, Sir Thomas, Bt, r.-adm. (d. 1807), 1354(d)
Louisbourg, Canada, 4165(g), 4756(f)
Louis-Philippe, king of France (d. 1850), 903(c), 2241
Lound, William de (d. *c.* 1360), 3430(v)
Loutfut, Adam (15th cent.), 1513
Louth, Nicholas of (14th cent.), 3428(a)
Louthre, Sir Hugh de (b. *c.* 1287), 1165(m). *See also* Lowther (de Louther)
Love, Nicholas, prior of Mount Grace (fl. 1415), 4003
Loveden hill, *see* Hough on the Hill, Lincs.
Love Feigned and Unfeigned, 3209(b)
Lovelace, Earl of, *see* Milbanke, Ralph Gordon Noel
Lovelich, Henry (fl. 1450), 1544, 1546
Lovell, family, 3566(d)
Lovell, John Hill, Quaker (d. 1855), 1816(k)
Lovell, Sir Thomas, speaker of the House of Commons (d. 1524), 5145(o)
Loventium, *see* Llanio, Card.
Love of King David and fair Bethsabe (Peele), 3168
Love poems, English medieval, 1472
Love's Labour's Lost (Shakespeare), 3407(b)
Love tokens, 614(f), 5229(q), 6326(i)
Low. *For place-names prefixed by* Low *and not found below see under principal name*
Low Countries, *see* Netherlands
Lowdham, Notts., 5814(a)
Lowdin's glass-house, Bristol, 1661(a)
Lowe, Thomas, of Shrewsbury (15th cent.), 4967(a)
Lower. *For place-names prefixed by* Lower *and not found below see under principal name*
Lower, Richard, anatomist & physiologist (d. 1691), 4710(c)
Lower, Sir William, of Treventy (d. 1615), 905(i), 5327(d)
Lower Deerplay, *see* Sowerby, W.R.Yorks.
Lower Willow Hall, *see* Skircoat, W.R.Yorks.
Lowestoft, Suff., 1662(a), 5112(i), 5572(u)
Lowfields, *see* Burton-in-Lonsdale, W.R.Yorks.
Low Hall manor, *see* Walthamstow, Essex
Lowick, Northants, 147(k), 2749(d), 4116(p)
Lowndes, William (d. 1709), 102(m)
Lowndes, William, sec. to the Treasury (d. 1724), 815(e)
Low side windows, *see* Church windows
Lowther, Westmld, 1170(n), 1179(g), 1229
Lowther (de Louther), family, 1179(g). *See also* Louthre, Sir Hugh de
Lowther, Gerard (d. 1597), 1164(c)
Lowther, Sir Gerard (d. 1624), and Sir Gerard (d. 1660), 1165(a)
Lowther, Sir Lancelot (d. 1637), 1165(a)

Maps (*cont.*)
population, distribution maps, 748(d); railway, early, 3943(a,b); in possession of Royal Geograph. Soc., 4355(a); of Wm Smith (d. 1839), 6294(a); watermarks used in dating, 4354(a); in Whitby museum, 6051(a)
of Gt Britain: John Adams's, of England (*c.* 1680), 4370(a); British Isles, 16th cent., 4327; Pietro Coppo's (*c.* 1525), 4360(c); Gough, 14th cent.?, 4372(a); Mercator's, 4353(a); Matthew Paris's, 4372(a); 'Quartermaster's' (1644), 4361(a); Saxton's, of England and Wales (*c.* 1580), 1703(f), 4358(b); Aegidius Tschudi's, 16th cent., 4372(a); Woutneel's (1603), 4373(d)
See also following entry and Field maps; Ordnance Survey; Survey of India; Tapestries; Tithe maps
Maps and plans: Atherington manor (1606), 5696(j); Banstead, 5622(d); Bath, 5446(k); Bedfordshire manors, 240; Birmingham, 385(g); Booth Hall estate, Blakeley, 2628(c); Bradford, 405(l), 406(k); Bristol, 435(c), 450(g), 454(n), 1096(h); Cambridgeshire, 759(d,o); Canterbury, 1555, 2587(q); Carmarthenshire (1730–40), 909(c); Chertsey abbey demense, 5618(c); Cheshire, 2631(a), 4383(b,t); Coventry, 1540; Cornwall, 1739(k); Cumberland, 1181(a); Durham, 4383(c); Dorset, 395(a); Dover harbour (1495–1847), 5188(f); Essex, 4383(q); Exeter, 1354(m); Gloucestershire, 445(d), 457(d), 466; Greenwich, 1898(d), 3139; Hampshire, 395(a), 2012(m), 2014(m), 4383(d,i); Hayton manor, 1170(c); Hendon, 2974(z), 3371; Hertford, Townshend estate, 1591(r); Hertfordshire, 2097(a), 4383(e,l); Horton lordship, 408(j); Isle of Man, 2551 (n,kk); Jersey, 5047(d); Kent, 2592(e), 2600(g), 2605(e), 2607(d), 4383(j,r); Lancashire, 931(a), 2630(a), 4383(f); Leeds, 5788(e,h), 5791(e); Leeds and dist., 5791(h); Leicestershire, 4383(n); Lewes, 5715(i); Littlehampton, 3463; Liverpool, 2113(g), 2116(e); Liverpool, St Nicholas's church, 2125(d); London, *see* London, city & environs; Manchester, 2626(e); Mendip, 6001(e); Milford, 3366(b); Newcastle-upon-Tyne, 5217(c); New York region, 4345(c); Northamptonshire, 4383(m); Nottinghamshire, 5836(b); Oxford, 3725(a); Rochdale, 3984(e); Romney marsh, 2592(l); Rutland, 4383(n); Salford, 2630(j); Selsey, 5719(m); Shipley, 406(l); Somerset, 5435; Southampton, 5475; Stafford, 3630(b); Staffordshire, 1880(c), 3626(d), 4383(p); Surrey, 4383(g,k), 5621(c), 5628(d); Sussex, 4383(h,r,s); Titchfield, 2007(p); Trehelig common fields, 3906(f); Walcot, Som., 216(l); Wales, South, 5771(b); Walthamstow, High Hall manor, 5935; Walworth manor and Newington, Surr., 3141; Warwickshire, 4383(o); Westmorland, 1181(a); Wiltshire, 395(a), 6105(e); world, 4346(b), 4353(c), 4382; Yorkshire, 1615(a), 5801(k), 6270
Maquelone, see: Peare of Provence
Mara, *see* de Mara
Marcet, Alexander John Gaspard, physician (d. 1822), 4705(b)
March, Earl of, *see* Mortimer, Roger de
Marches, *see* Wales, marches of
Marching, in British army, 5087(b)
Marching under arms, in city of London, 4764(c)
Marchwiel, Denb., 1001(c), 2266(b)
Marcigny, Saône-et-Loire, France, 6103(d)
Marcle, Much, Herefs., 6128(p)
Marcross, Glam., 3516(a)
Marcy, family, 1699(j)
Mardale, Westmld, 1165(l), 1192(v)

Marden, Herefs., 6126(m); Freen's Court, 6126(n)
Marden, West, Suss., 4117(b)
Mardol, Shrewsbury, 4982(b)
Mare liberum, principles of, 1903(a)
Maresfield, Suss., 5707(k)
Margam, Glam.: 18th–19th cent., 2(c); abbey, 506(h), 748(l), 749(f), 3517(a), 3518(w), 5772(b); in Carlisle's *Topograph. Dict.*, 5(a); elementary education, 4(h); Mansel family, 904(j); Sir Rob. Mansel, 5778(a); mills, 5(e); mountain, antiquities of, 1(o); Via Julia Maritima, 5772(a). *See also* Aberafan & Margam Dist. Hist. Soc.
Margaret, Saint, of Antioch (4th cent.), 6230(e)
Margaret of Anjou (d. 1482), wife of Hen. VII, 3529(g)
Margaretting, Essex, 662(e), 1698(m,x)
Margate, Kent, 1820(h), 2587(g,h), 6035(g), 6045(b)
Margidunum, *see* Bridgford, East, Notts.
Marham, Norf., 4136(i)
Mariam, *see: Tragedy of Mariam*
Marine artists, 5098(a,l,n,v,x,kk), 5099(g,m) 5100(c) 5101(n)
Marine engineering, 563(a), 2447(c). *See also* Institute of Marine Engineers
Marine engines: cargo-boat, 2434(a); lubrication, 2439(a); some curiosities, 2443(a); torpedo-boat, 2442(a)
Marine insurance, 1633(m), 2437(a). *See also* Lloyd's
Marine refrigeration, 2447(b)
Mariner's Marvellous Magazine, 5105(c)
Mariner's Mirror, see Soc. for Nautical Research
Mariner's Mirrour (Waghenaer, trans. Ashley), 5100(e)
Marines: duties and organization, 18th cent., 4758(c); early regiments, 17th cent., 4759(k); in naval mutinies (1797–1802), 4758(k)
Maritime enterprise, early English, 2236(b)
Maritime law, and immunity of states, 4498(f)
Maritime powers, in 18th cent., 2238(d)
Maritime trade, 2434(b); Essex (1565–77), 1701(l); Exeter, 1334(q), 1878(f); Southampton, 17th cent., 2007(j). *See also* Trade
Mark, Som., 5401(f), 5425(d)
Mark, King, in Cornwall, 4542(l)
Markeaton, Derbys., 1297(c)
Market Bosworth, Leics., 2754(d)
Market crosses, 3004(b), 3988(i); Ambleside, 1192(r); Darlington, 5215(i); Hooton Pagnell, 5791(b); Newcastle-upon-Tyne, 5218(g)
Market Drayton, Salop, 5028(g)
Market hall, Warwick, 5985(b)
Market house, Winster, 1276(f)
Market Lavington, Wilts., 6103(n)
Market Overton, Rut., 5178(g)
Market Rasen, Lincs., 947(g,k)
Markets and fairs: hand (glove) as sign, 999(b); legal status of, 813(h); medieval, England and Wales, 2276(b)
at, in: Adwalton, 408(c); Birmingham, 368(b); Buntingford, 1589(a); Cardiganshire, 898(h); Corbridge, 5234(a); Corby, pole fair, 3641(f); Euxton, 2131(f); Fingringhoe, 1705(i); Hemelhempstead, 4827(f); Horsham, 5698(j); Isle of Man, 2551(e); London, Covent Garden, 4253(p); King's Teignton, 1330(a); Luton, 225(f); Maidenhead, 249(c); Manchester, Acres fair, 2628(h); Norfolk, 3568(b); Okehampton, 1347(b); Peterborough, 3853(a); Ravenglass, 1184(m); Sevenoaks, 2600(d); Shoreham, 5700(f); Stourbridge, 516(f); Tan hill, nr Devizes, 6102(v); Tavistock, goose fair, 2995(c); Warwick,

Micro-burin, beaked pigmy graver, 5722(j)
Microcosmography, authorship of, 3922(e)
Microlithic industry: Durham, 3915(b); Northumberland, 5254(c); Wear valley, Durham, 5229(i)
Microscopes, 3693(a), 6304(a)
Middelburg, Holland, 2569(d)
Middens: Chark, Hants., neolithic, 4091(b); Giltar Point, nr Tenby, 752(n); Isle of Wight, 12th cent., 2553(ii)
Middle. *For place-names prefixed by* Middle *and not found below see under principal name*
Middle, Salop, *see* Myddle
Middle English texts, *see* Early English Text Soc.
Middle English verse and prose, Wheatly ms., 1500
Middleham, N.R.Yorks., 6046(b), 6228(ee), 6229(o)
Middlesbrough, N.R.Yorks., 1092(b), 1095(b), 6226(b)
Middlesex, 2973(t); 19th cent., 2975(e); Commonwealth surveys, 2972(r); Domesday, 1469(a), 2975(e,s); earthworks, 2975(l); Gore hundred, 2975(g); knights of the shire, 2974(o); mummers' plays, 1795(a); parishes, 2975(a); pedigrees, 2033; poll-tax, 2972(s); prehistory, 2975(e); Roman, 1467(a), 2975(e); Saxon, 2969(t). *See also* London & Middlesex Archaeol. Soc.
Middlesex Regiment, 2nd bn Duke of Cambridge's Own, 77th Ft, 613(e)
Middlesex Yeomanry, 4794(p)
Middle Temple, London, 2973(u), 2974(b,q), 5503(a)
Middleton, Essex, 1692(a)
Middleton, Lancs., 2637(g), 2657, 2691
Middleton, Norf., 3571(q), 4136(i); Blackbergh nunnery, 3570(f)
Middleton, Suff., 5574(n)
Middleton, Warws., 357(b), 3428(d)
Middleton, Westmld, 1175(i), 1223; Hawkin, 1187(m)
Middleton, North, Ilderton, Northumb., 5239(f)
Middleton, South, Ilderton, Northumb., 5239(f)
Middleton, Charles, 1st Baron Barham, adm. (d. 1813), 3496
Middleton, Christopher, translator & poet (d. 1628), 1510
Middleton, Jane (d. 1565), 3430(k)
Middleton, John (d. 1623), 2522(a)
Middleton, John de, rector of Wrything (d. *c.* 1350), 5424(m)
Middleton, Mabel (fl. 1607), 5225(i)
Middleton, Richard (d. 1575), and wife Jane (d. 1565), 3430(k)
Middleton, Thomas (fl. 1607), 5225(i)
Middleton, William, Welsh poet (d. 1621), 6020(n)
Middleton Hall, Ilderton, Northumb., 5239(f)
Middleton-in-Lonsdale, *see* Middleton, Westmld
Middleton Low Hall, *see* Middleton St George, co. Dur.
Middleton-on-the-Wolds, E.R.Yorks., 1620(i), 6300(b)
Middleton St George, co. Dur., 1420, 5217(m); Middleton Low Hall, 5212(f)
Middleton Scriven, Salop, 4991
Middletown, Mont., 6025(e)
Middlezoy, Som., 5425(k)
Midelney, Sir Ralph de, soldier (d. 1363), 5414(g)
Midford, Som., 5443(t)
Midgham, Berks., 3532(b)
Midgley, W.R.Yorks.: Brearley Hall, 1966(c); Castle Carr, 1984(d); houses and families, 1991(c); Kershaw House, 1966(c); Lower Brearley Hall, 1985(e); Oats Royd, 1983(d); Upper Brearley Hall, 1985(e)
Midgley, family, 409(k), 1985(e)
Midhurst, Suss., 928(m)
Midland Baptist Coll., 197(l)

Midland circuit, 1286(b)
Midland Record Soc., *Trans.*, 3361–3
Midland revolt (1607), 4388(e)
Midshipmen, Admiralty order concerning, 5105(i)
Midsummer hill, *see* Malvern Hills, Worcs.
Midsummer sunrise, and Stonehenge, 4090(e,h)
Midwifery: bp's licence for, 1166(a); provision for, in London, 4702(b)
Miers, John, profilist (d. 1821), 5799(o)
Mifflin, Warner, Quaker, of Virginia (d. 1798), 1824(h)
Migration, Cornish, to Brittany, 4213(i)
Milan, *see*: *Duke of Milan*
Milbanke, Ralph Gordon Noel, 2nd E. of Lovelace (d. 1906), 4001
Milborne Port, Som., 5413(i)
Milborne St Andrew, Dors., 1398(e)
Milbourne, family, 1692(d)
Milburn, Westmld, 1172(l), 1185(u), 1195(o), 1215
Mildenhall, Suff.: church, 3572(s); councils of Clovesho, 5579(f); Cunetio, 6109(b,c); High Lodge, 3913(cc); Saxon huts, 781(g); Warren hill, 4069(a)
Mildenhall, John, adventurer (d. 1614), 4191(a)
Mildmay, family, 1699(a)
Mile, old English, 4367(a), 4368(a)
Milemete, Walter de, king's clerk (fl. *c.* 1327), 4012
Miles, Charles Popham, canon (d. 1891), 5602(c)
Miles, John, *see* Myles
Milestones: 'customary', 6238(b); in Yorkshire W.R., 6230(c). *See also* Roman milestones
Milford, Hants, 3364(c), 3365(o); 20th cent., 3367(f); advowsons, 3368(m); Baptists, 3364(n), 3366(e); beating the bounds, 3364(d); John Birkett, vicar, 3365(h); burial records, 3366(e); charities, 3364(f); church, *see below*; chwdns' books, 3365(j), 3368(i); development, 3367(e), 3368(g); dispute, 3367(i); Domesday, 3364(a); Efford mill, 3367(c); hospital, 3368(c); houses, 3366(d); inhabitants, 17th cent., 3365(h); and Alice Lisle, 3365(e); Lymore, 3368(e); Bp McDougall, vicar, 3368(b); mill, 3366(a); mummers, 3364(m); place-names, 3365(p); poor-relief, 3366(g); ritual controversy, 3366(c); silk production, 3365(l); tithe award, 3366(b); World War I, 3365(m); World War II, 3368(h)
   church, 3364(b,i), 3368(j); alterations, 3368(d); and Christchurch priory, 3368(a); Domesday, 3365(k); memorials, 3366(e); silver tray, 3368(l); spire, 3368(f); stones, 3368(k); tombs, 3366(f)
Milford-on-Sea Record Soc., *Occasional Magazine*, 3364–8
Miliana of Steyning, *see* Steyning, Miliana of
Militarie Instructions for the Cavallrie, 4787(f)
Militarism, and duelling, 4401(f)
Military administration, British, 4753(k)
Military architecture, Thames defences, 2485(a)
Military bands, 4794(f)
Military Company of Massachusetts, 5087(o)
Military costume, *see* Uniform, military
Military customs, old, 4766(a)
Military discipline, treatise on, 2465(a)
Military effigies, *see* Effigies
Military engineering, *see* School of Military Engineering
Military history, scientific study of, 2467(b)
Military intelligence, World War I, 4158(e)
Military levies: *temp.* Edw. I–II, 1166(q); for Scotch wars, 1615(c)

Place-names (*cont.*)
864(g); west of England, 3894(h); West Penwith, 4539(b). *See also* Guernsey; Isle of Man; Jersey; *and under names of counties and places*

Plague: in Britain, 19th cent., 1687(a); at Carmarthen, 907(e); effects on glass-painting, 14th cent., 4126(e); in Halifax, 1994(a); in London, 1816(a), 3038(a); in Manchester, 1031(a); treatise on (1593), 4922; in York dioc., 4118(f). *See also* Black Death

Plainsong and Mediaeval Music Soc.: library catalogue, 3887; publs, 3881–91

Plaisted, Bartholomew (d. 1767), 1956

Plaitford, Hants: Landford barrow, 5172(j)

Planché, André *or* Andrew (d. *c.* 1804), 1661(d)

Plan for a Universal and Perpetual Peace (Bentham), 1915

Plano Carpini, John de, friar (d. 1252), 1964

Plans, *see* Maps and plans

Plantae Woodfordienses (Warner), 1716(b,d), 1717(f)

Plantagenet, George, Duke of Clarence, *see* George, Duke of Clarence

Plantagenet coinage, of Wales, 602(c)

Plantagenet roll, an addition, 5327(d)

Plants: on Chelsea porcelain, 1663(c); collecting of, 2854(a); common garden, 5511(b); historical and national, 5842(f); of Woodford, 1716(b,d), 1717(f)

Plas Heaton, Denb., 2887(i)

Plas Iolyn, *see* Pentrevoelas, Denb.

Plas Mawr, *see* Conway, Caern.

Plas Penrhyn, *see* Dwyran, Anglesey

Plasterwork, plaster decoration, 2005(a), 4462(c), 4464(c); Binroyd, Norland, 1976(j); Cumberland, 1193(n); Devon, 1331(f); Halifax, 6234(c); Stodmarsh, 2593(d); Westmorland, 1193(n). *See also* Pargetting

Plasterwork ceilings, 1331(f), 1339(b), 4464(c)

Plas-y-Court, *see* Alberbury with Cardeston, Salop

Plas-yn-Dinas, Mont., 6028(a)

Plate, river, campaigns, 52, 4164(a), 4271(b), 4282(d)

Plate, *see* Silver plate

Plateau deposits, 3912(kk)

Platinum, earliest industrial use of, 3265(b)

Platonic tradition, in religious thought, 2845(c)

Platter, Thomas (d. 1582), 3289(a)

Plattsburg, Canada, expedition to, 4757(j)

Plaxtol, Kent, 5150(c)

Plaxton, George, rector of Barwick (fl. 1703), 5800(k)

Play-acting, *see* Drama

Playbills, 296(p), 3867(c)

Player-lists, early, 3209(s)

Players, *see* Actors; Drama companies

Play-houses, *see* Theatres

Playing-cards, 759(v), 4383(u)

Play-list, 17th cent., 3407(e)

Plays, *see* Drama

Playwrights: pre-Shakespeare, 4937(a); Shakespeare's contemporaries, 295(h)

Pleading, rules of, 816(d)

Plea rolls: Anglesey, 72; of medieval county courts, 812(f); of palatinate of Lancaster, 1042; as sources, 4406(b). *See also* Coram rege rolls; De banco rolls; Pleas; Pleas of the crown

Pleas: Flint, 1772; at Glastonbury, 3520(bb). *See also* Plea rolls

Pleasley, Derbys., 1289(e)

Pleas of the crown, Kent, 519(k), 1898(h), 6150(e)

Pleasure gardens: Bath, 218(e); Southwark, Paris garden, 5186(d), 5604(d)

Plegmund, Saint (d. 914), 995(e)

Pleistocene bones, Dovercourt, 3911(v)

Pleistocene deposits: English, and continental chronology, 3913(aa); Ipswich, 4064(b)

Pleistocene man: in Britain, 4051(b); in Jersey, 5178(i)

Pleistocene period: in Guernsey, 5034(g); relation of prehistoric period to, 4128(a)

Pleistocene succession, in England, 3912(bb)

Plenary indulgence, *see* Indulgences

Pleshey, Essex: castle-keep, 1700(p); college, 4837(c,j); earthworks, 1700(t); manor, 1692(u); Plesheybury, Roman finds at, 1698(s)

Plesheybury, Essex, *see* Pleshey

Plesingho, place-name in Essex, 1692(u)

Plessey, Northumb., 6042(a)

Pleydell, John Cleve (b. *c.* 1750), 4153(f)

Pliocene culture, 3917(a)

Pliocene deposits, S.E.England, 3912(u)

Plots, *see* Conspiracies and plots; Gunpowder plot; Popish plot

Plough coulters, from Silchester, 5172(k)

Ploughs, Sussex, 5729(g). *See also* Breast ploughs

Plough Stots (mummers and sword-dancers), 6289(g)

Plowden, Salop, 5027(d)

Plowden, family, 4977(i)

Plumbe, Dame Margaret (d. 1575), 1594(j), 3429(nn)

Plumberow Mount, *see* Hockley, Essex

Plumbers: Chester, 999(a); Sheffield, 2379(t)

Plumer, William (d. 1822), 4005

Plummer, Charles (d. 1927), 484(c)

Plummer, John, master of the Children of the Chapel Royal (fl. 1445), 5160(b)

Plumpton, Northants, 3657(d)

Plumpton, Suss., 5708(h)

Plumpton Hay, Inglewood forest, Cumb., 1168(a)

Plumpton Wall, Cumb.: Voreda, Roman fort, 1176(n)

Plumstead, dist. in Woolwich, *see* London, metropolitan boroughs: Woolwich

Plumtree, Notts., 5811(d)

Plunkett, Francis, Benedictine (17th cent.), 957(a)

Pluralism, in medieval Church, 155(b)

Pluralists, Lincoln dioc., 155(b)

Plym, river, Devon, 3896(e)

Plymouth, Devon, 1727(c), 3893(g), 3896(u); (1800), 3894(f); archives, 3896(j); Breton invasions, 3894(b); Cattedown, 3893(d); charities, 3892(f); china, 1334(j); deeds, 3896(t); Elphinstone family, 3892(d); fort, 3895(b); freemasonry, 2901(a); Huguenot churches, 2360, 3896(p); inns, 3896(d); literary associations, 2761(d); municipal finance, 3896(o); pilchard fishery, 4253(s); place-names, 3896(f); prehistory, 3896(l); royal citadel, 5093(e); social life, 18th cent., 3896(m); street-names, 3896(f)

Plymouth Institution & Devon & Cornwall Nat. History Soc., *Ann. Rpts & Trans.*, 3892–6; centenary, 3894(e); history, 3892(a,c,g)

Plympton, Devon, 3896(y); hundred, 1359

Pneumonia, fatalities from, 4724(a)

Poaching, 253(d), 823(a)

Pocklington, E.R.Yorks., 6225(h), 6233(c)

Pococke, Richard, bp (d. 1765), 5679(g)

Portsmouth, Hants: cathedral, 5472(a); handbook, 574; Jewish congregation, 2568(e); nunnery nr, 3570(h); St Thomas Street chapel, 5854(c)

Port Talbot, Glam., 3(b), 4(b), 5(c)

Portugal: Aden attacked by, 5084(i); and Francis Bacon, 175(b); Wm Braund's trade with, 1633(m); British officers in service of, 5085(f); English commercial relations with, 4391(c); English expedition to (1589), 4759(j); medals granted to British officers by, 612(h,i)

Portuguese books, early translations of, 292(a)

Portway, ancient road, 266(b)

Post, Jacob, Quaker recording clerk (d. 1757), 1834(b)

Postal service: at Bradford, Yorks., 409(o); British, motor transport in, 2459(a); international, 4517(a); in wartime, 4503(a)

Posting, *see* Travelling post; Post-towns

Postling, Kent, 2592(h,i)

Postmasters, of Manchester, 2634(k)

Postmen, rural, of Worcestershire, 6159(b)

Post Office: espionage in, 2971(o); Manchester, 2627(a); Neath, 3516(b); Sunderland, 5589(a)

Post-towns, England and Wales, 918(f)

Potkyn, Constance, of Chalke, Kent (d. 1473), 2604(b)

Potter, John, of Thorpe, Surr. (17th cent.), 5611(d)

Potter Hanworth, Lincs., 148(k)

Potter Heigham, Norf., 3591(c)

Potteries (dist.), during industrial revolution, 4252(f)

Potter-Meols collection, 993(a)

'Potters' (gypsies), of Natland, Kendal, 1919(e)

Potters' art, pre-Roman, 884(a)

Potters Bar, Mdx: Wyllyott's manor, 2973(y)

Potter's field: at Horningsea, 758(i); Roman, near Jesus Coll., Camb., 758(j)

Potters' marks, stamps: on red-glazed Roman ware, 987(f); Roman, found in Chester, 1005(a); on Samian ware, 2629(d)

Potters Marston, Leics., 2751(c)

Potters' tools, of slate, 3913(j)

Pottery: Arretine, in Cambridgeshire, 768(d); bead-rim, 5171(c); beaker, 745(a), 3916(x); Boynton collection, 6427; development of, 694(c); in Dorset county museum, 1375(l); English, 3436(a), 5971(b); Hallstatt, 2012(g), 5161(n); Jutish, in Kent, 2601(b); from late-Celtic graves, 5148(f); manufacture of, 4252(v); masonic, 3215(c), 3224(a); medieval, 4106(a), 5150(e); in Northampton museum, 3642(g); oldest bronze age ceramic type, 4044(a); platinum used in manufacture of, 3265(b); polychrome, 5198(c); prehistoric, 418(a), 4046(a), 4052(c); pre-Roman, 5730(x); rosette-stamped, 4089(a); sepulchral, 1375(f); Wedgwood, 4657(c)

found at, in: Basing House, Hants, 5150(e); Braintree Roman site, 1693(g): Broadwater, 6203(a); Chelm's Combe, Cheddar, 5425(l); Dartford heath, 6145(a); Hafod, 4569(a); Kingston Buci, 5724(h); Lincolnshire, 6318(b); Little Henny, 1704(d); Little Horsted, 5730(x); Lligwy burial chamber, 753(c); London, Nicholas Lane, 2973(q); Mull hill circle, I.o.M., 5171(f); Newtimber hill, Suss., 415(d); Nobottle, Northants, 162(i); Old Sarum, 6114(p); Roos Links, Northumb., 5258(b); Wallington, Surr., 5608(j); Wisley, 5163(c); Yorkshire wolds, 1623(i)

made at, in: Derby, 1297(b); Devon, 1328(c); Gloucestershire, 983(e); Isle of Man, 772(c); Newcastle-under-

Pottery (*cont.*)

Lyme, 3627(b); Nottingham, 5810(c), 5838(b); Rye, 5726(b); Sussex, 5698(a); Yorkshire, 6415(b), 6427

making of (kilns, potteries, sites), at, in: Cheam, 5623(e); nr Horningsea, 758(i); Leeds and dist., 5799(l); Lincolnshire coast, 5171(h); Mill Green, Ingatestone, 1698(b); north of England, 5257(b); Pembridge, 6131(h); Ringmer, 5697(e); Rye, 5725(d), 5726(b); Sunderland and dist., 5592(d); on the Tyne, 5257(b); Upton Bishop, 6130(t); Yorkshire, 6415(b)

See also Bronze age pottery; Celtic pottery; Iron age pottery; Neolithic pottery; Porcelain; Roman pottery; Terra sigillata (Samian ware); *and under* Britain, ancient

Poughill, Cornw., 1726(e)

Poughley, Berks., 249(f)

Poulner, Hants, 1813(c)

Poulton-le-Fylde, Lancs., 2663

Pound (coin), Elizabethan rose-marked, 4606(a)

Pounde, Thomas, Jesuit (d. 1615), 1590(e)

Pound-note (paper pound), 4729(a)

Pounds, John, shoemaker & philanthropist (d. 1839), 5852(n)

Poundstock, Cornw.: Woolston, 4537(d)

Poverty, Abp Peckham's tracts on, 649. *See also* Pauperism; Poor-relief

Poverty figures, criticism of, 548(b)

Powdering, of hair and wigs, 762(a)

Powell, Rice, Parliamentarian, *later* Royalist (fl. 1650), 2326(a)

Powell, Sir Thomas, of Broadway, Carm. (d. 1720), 918(d), 963(f)

Powell, Vavasor, nonconformist (d. 1670), 190(a), 1260(c)

Power, Henry, physician (d. 1668), 1980(a)

Powis Castle, Mont., 743(o), 6025(c)

Powle, Sir Henry, master of the rolls and speaker (d. 1692), 536(h)

Pownall, Thomas, colonial gov. (d. 1805), 2825(ff)

Powtrell, family, 1291(d)

Powys, Powysland: customs of (B.M. Add. ms. 9867), 3907(j); ecclesiastical recollections, 6029(b); inquisitions, 3906(g); and the Ordovices, 726(a), 3899(d); political history, early, 750(b); princes of, their policy, 3901(c). *See also* Montgomeryshire

Powys-land Club: *Collections Hist. & Archaeol.*, 3897–908; excavations by, 747(l); other publs, 3909–10

Poyer, John, Parliamentarian, *later* Royalist (d. 1649), 2326(a)

Poyle, family, 5629(g)

Poynet (Ponet), John, bp (d. 1556), 856

Poynings, Suss., 5730(q)

Poynings, family, 5714(a)

Poynings, Hawis de (d. 1359), 5730(n)

Poynings, Sir Michael de (d. 1359), 6159(a)

Poynton, Salop, 4969(b)

Poyntz, Sydenham, soldier (fl. 1624–50), 4427

Poyston, Pemb., 2257(b)

Prach, Hilary, Quaker (fl. 1676), 1822(a)

Practical Believer (Kettlewell), 6020(l)

Prado y Tovar, Diego de, Spanish navigator (fl. 1605), 1957

Praemunire, statute of, its predecessors, 2231(a)

Praise of Yorkshire Ale (Meriton), 6286(e)

Prasutagus, king of the Iceni (d. *c.* 60), 606(a)

Prattinton collection, Worcestershire drawings, 6161(c), 6162(a)

Praty, Richard, bp (d. 1445), 5739(d)

Prayer guild, Norman, 4836(k)

Sandon, Staffs., 3617(b)
Sandown, I.o.W., 2012(b)
Sandown manor, *see* Sandwich, Kent
Sandridge, Herts.: Bridge Hall, 4831(d); church, 1595(s), 4822(d,e); parish accounts, 4821(u); vicars, 4822(f)
Sandringham, Norf., 3567(g)
Sandsfoot castle, Dors., 1381(e), 1385(c), 1387(d)
Sandtoft, Lincs., 2353(i)
Sandtun, in Saxon charters, 2605(c)
Sandwich, Kent, 517(j), 2607(v); Sandown manor, 2615
Sandwich, Earls of, *see* Montagu, Edward; Montagu, John
Sandwich Islands, 4364(a)
Sandwith, family, 1168(c)
Sandys, family, 98(bb), 1702(l)
Sandys, John (fl. 1704), 1739(r)
Sankey, Great, Lancs., 2138(f)
Sankey, Col. Sir Jerome, M.P. (fl. 1655), 200(p)
Sanson de Eswelle, prior of Hurley (fl. 1238), 254(g)
Sant, John, abbot of Abingdon (fl. 1476), 294(d)
Santa Cruz, Teneriffe, naval battle, 3500(d)
Santo Domingo, English attacks on, 4444(a)
Santon (Kirk Santon), I.o.M., 2551(a)
Santon, Norf., 3573(l), 3913(q)
Santon Downham, Suff., 761(d)
Santwat, I.o.M., battle, 2551(s)
Sanzaver, family, 5414(e)
Sapling, ship's periodical, 2121(c)
Saratoga campaign, 4753(j)
Sark, Channel Islands, 5064(a)
Sarn Helen, Roman road, N.Wales, 2876(a)
Sarratt, Herts., 4821(f)
Sarsens, 243(c), 1710(e)
Sarum, Old, Wilts., 216(g), 734(d), 1397(a), 5452(d); castle, 4117(s); cathedral, 4117(s), 5184(c); excavations, 5150(g), 5209; pottery, 6114(p); Roman road, 435(i); site, 6104(o); and Sorbiodunum, 6107(a)
Satire: naval, 5107(d); in Norfolk, 3571(j)
Satley, co. Dur., 1447, 5224(aa); Butsfield, 5223(q)
Saucer brooch, Anglo-Saxon, 5179(g)
Saumaise, Claude de, professor at Leyden (d. 1653), 289(h)
Saumarez, James, Baron de Saumarez (d. 1836), 5036(d)
Saundby, Notts., 147(d)
Saunders, family, 2249(c)
Saunders, Sir Charles, adm. (d. 1775), 4287(e)
Sausmarez, fief, *see* Guernsey
Sausmarez, family, 5038(f)
Sausmarez, Mrs Richard (d. 1802), 5038(k)
Savage, family, 2591(h)
Savage, Anne (d. *c.* 1605), wife of John Savage, 3428(l)
Savage, Thomas, abp (d. 1507), 5250(c)
Savage, Thomas, Quaker (fl. 1745), 1825(h)
Savernake forest, Wilts., 4043(a), 4071(b); Knowle Farm pit, 4074(a,b)
Savery, Thomas, engineer (d. 1715), 1335(h), 2984(b), 3547(g), 4536(e)
Savery, William, Quaker (fl. 1797), 1830(e)
Savignian order: and Basingwerk abbey, 1459(a); and Furness abbey, 1171(a); and Rushen abbey, 2551(w)
Savile, family, 154(j), 1982(a)
Savile, Sir George, Mq. of Halifax (d. 1695), 4426(a)
Savile, Henry (d. 1617), 278(c)
Savile Green, *see* Halifax, W.R.Yorks.
Savill, Henry (16th cent.), and wife Margaret, 3429(m)

Saville, family, 6233(a), 6236(l)
Savings, and usury, 4251(a)
Savings banks, deposits in, 3332(b)
Savoy, House of, and English court, 477(c)
Savoy, The, Westminster, 1112(m), 2353(b), 3127(b), 5884(a)
Savoy Confession, of English Congregationalists, 1112(m)
Sawbridgeworth, Herts., 1588(h), 3428(f)
Sawley, Derbys., 3429(tt,uu), 4118(p)
Sawley, W.R.Yorks., nr Clitheroe: Salley abbey, 2636(m), 6228(aa), 6238(h), 6239(d), 6271
Sawston, Cambs., 3428(zz)
Sawtry, Hunts., 823(n)
Sawtry St Judith, Hunts., 825(b)
Sawyer, family, 150(h)
Saxe of Horbury (12th cent.), 6234(i)
Saxham, Little, Suff., 5572(d)
Saxlingham, Norf., 3571(h)
Saxlingham Nethergate, Norf., 666(g)
Saxon, *see following entries and* Anglo-Saxon
Saxon abbots, of Glastonbury, 503(b)
Saxon bishops, of Wells, 491, 5181(a)
Saxonbury camp, *see* Frant, Suss.
Saxon coinage, of Wales, 602(c), 2301(a)
Saxones, in the *Excidium Britanniae*, 731(h)
Saxons: in Devon, 1341(b); distribution of, 6th cent., 4099(g); and Essex earthworks, 4111(n); reception of, in Britain, 2278(b); in upper Thames area, 5172(f). *See also* Anglo-Saxons
Saxon shore, 4113(d)
Saxony, 4397(c)
Saxton, Christopher, cartographer (fl. 1570–96), 1703(f), 1708(f), 4358(b), 4383(b,c,d,e,f), 5801(j)
Saxton, Robert (fl. 1613), 409(j)
Saxton-in-Elmet (Saxton with Scarthingwell), W.R.Yorks., 1179(l), 6399
Sayer, Anthony, first grand master of masons (d. 1741), 2937(c), 2960(c), 6471(a)
Sayes Court, Deptford, 6140(c)
Sayle, Charles Edward, of Cambridge Univ. Lib. (d. 1924), 291(d). *See also* Index of Authors
Says (fabrics), from Colchester, 1692(o)
Scafe, John, Northumbrian poet (d. 1856), 5223(a)
Scaife, family, 1195(f)
Scaitcliffe, Lancs., 1970(j,k)
Scaleby, Cumb., 1171(v), 1174(a), 1184(h), 1189(t), 1191(j)
Scalehouse, *see* Skipton, W.R.Yorks.
Scales, Cumb., nr Castle Sowerby, 1195(l)
Scales, Lancs., in Furness: Bonfire Scar cave, 1190(f); Dobson cave, 1190(f)
Scales, Katherine (d. 1505), 5729(oo)
Scamp, Joshua, gypsy (d. 1801), 1930(d)
Scampton, E.R.Yorks., 1617(c,d)
Scandinavian invaders, Anglo-Saxon attitude to, 5905(a)
Scandinavian kingdom of Northumbria, 5902(b)
Scandinavian language, its influence on: Lorton dialect, Cumb., 3873; Northumberland and Durham place-names, 5903(b); Yorkshire dialects, 6288(f); Yorkshire place-names, 6287(b)
Scandinavian model boat, 5103(t)
Scandinavian *motifs*, in Anglo-Saxon and Norman ornamentation, 5899(c)
Scandinavian names, in 11th cent. Northumbria, 5899(d)
Scandinavian personal names, in England, 3399(a)

Tracks and trackways (*cont.*)
  Dartmoor, 3896(v); Devon, 1333(h); Epsom, 5622(h); from Exeter, 1334(u), 1349(c), 1351(h); Great Haldon to Staverton, 1353(h); Hampshire, 2010(e), 4122(c); Norfolk, 3911(bb,ll); Rochdale dist., 3985(b); nr Rothbury, Northumb., 5227(b); nr Saddlescombe, 415(d); Sheffield bridle-road, 2376(e); Suffolk, 92(j); Sussex war dyke, 5715(b); Wiltshire, 4122(c). *See also* Peddar's way; Ridgeway
Trade: Anglo-French, *temp.* Chas II, 2230(a); with Argentina, 4517(d); British overseas, 1637, 3333(a), 4224(c), 4228(b), 4240(b), 4735(a); of British Empire, post-1800, 4279(d); of Chester, medieval, 1005(b); and coinage, 16th–17th cent., 4260(l); colonial, 2582(g); and credit, medieval, 1631(i); crisis in, 15th cent., 1633(e); defence of (1801, 1809), 3480(a); of East India Co. in Canton, 4194(a); between Exeter and Newfoundland, 1354(n); foreign competition, 19th cent., 3313(b); geographical conditions affecting, 4317(a); and High Court of Admiralty, 4386(c); history, 4260(j); and imperial defence, 4291; with India, 17th cent., 4645(b); Indian, 19th cent., 4629(e); international, and Ottawa agreements, 3335(a); and Lancashire cotton industry, 3330(a); laws affecting, 157(d); of Manchester, 19th cent., 3333(b); of Montgomeryshire, 3908(b); Thos Mun's tract on, 1637; and Napoleonic war, 814(d); and naval strategy, 3466(c), 4764(b); neutral, 3479(a), 4503(b); in Nigeria, 4268(b); between Old and New World, 1871(a); of Port of London, 2459(b); with Portugal (to 1807), 4391(c); protection of in war, 3465(c); river-borne, 3908(b); and Royal Soc. of Arts, 4655(a); with Russia, 90(a), 4408(b); settled, beginnings of, 4260(j); and settlement in Africa, 18(a); of Sierra Leone, 4268(g); in South Africa, 8(a); with Spain, 815(l); of Sussex, 13th–14th cent., 5721(i), 5722(e), 5723(f), 5726(e); traffic and carriage, 2434(b); treatise on, 3478(d); with Turkey, *temp.* Eliz. I, 4688; with Venice, 2016(s), 5109(e); voyage proposed to America, 2135(c); in Wales, medieval, 2275(c), 4387(d); and war of 1739–48, 4764(e); and war of Spanish Succession, 1631(j), 3479(a); war-time, 1901(b); in West Indies, 4269(c). *See also following entries and* Markets; Markets and fairs; Overseas markets; *and under names of particular commodities*
Trade and Navigation of Gt Britain considered (Gee), 3478(d)
Trade cards, of instrument-makers, 5098(ii)
Trade companies, guilds, 3317(d); Beverley, 1615(d); charters of (1530–1707), 4864; Chester, 997(e), 999(a,d), 1000(f), 1001(d); Exeter, 1334(l,n); Gateshead, 2938(c); Kendal, 2959(a); Ludlow, 2955(b); Newcastle, 5239(d); Scotland, 4397(a). *See also under names of particular trades*
Trade cycles, 2241(a)
Trade disputes, royal commission on, 4226(c)
Trade fluctuation, in building industry (1860–1910), 3326(a)
Trade numismatics, 6326(r)
Trade routes, intercontinental, pre-1000 A.D., 4260(j)
Traders, English: at Aleppo (1658–1756), 1633(i); in the Canaries, *temp.* Eliz. I, 4393(e). *See also* Merchants
Trades Board Act, 4233(f)
Tradescant, John, naturalist (d. 1638), and son John, traveller & gardener (d. 1662), 3752(a)
Trade signs, 2415(b), 3138(c), 4106(h); of booksellers, 161(c), 278(b)
Trade tokens, *see* Tokens, tradesmen's
Trade Tokens (Boyne, ed. Williamson), 1375(d), 6324(c)

Trade unionism: (1888–1904), 4224(d); historical aspects, 5228(a); in tinplate industry, 546(b), 4229(a); in Wales, early, 4252(w); in West Scotland coal trade (1790–1817), 4253(g)
Trading accounts, *see* Merchants' accounts
Trading with the Enemy Act, 1901(b), 4235(c)
Tradition, Lord Raglan on, 569(a). *See also* Customs (popular) and traditions
Trafalgar, naval battle, 5113(p); French letter describing, 4748(b); French propaganda, 4771(h); Nelson, 4751(h); Nelson's fleet, 4766(d), 5105(d); Nelson's tactics, 4753(i)
Traffic, *see* Institute of Transport
Traffic problem, of London, 2455(a)
Trafford, Thomas, of Bridge Trafford (fl. 1588), 1001(b)
Tragedy of Locrine (1595), 3149
Tragedy of Mariam (1613), 3179
Tragedy of Tancred and Gismund (1591–2), 3183
Tragedy of Tiberius (1607), 3184
Tragical Reign of Selimus (1594), 3151
Train-bands, trained companies, 217(n), 5085(b)
Trallong, Brec., 2272(a)
Tram roads, iron, 3555(g)
Tramways Act, 4221(g)
Tramway tokens, 6326(l)
Traney Clinton, Traney Marsh, Traney Morgan, *see* St Clears, Carm.
Transcaspia, 4205(c)
Transit, four-master, 5116(p)
Transitional culture, 5857(k)
Transjordan, 4504(c)
Transport: air, 2460(b); in Britain, 3326(b); developments (1929–32), 2460(a); early, in E.Riding, 1622(a); history of, 2457(b); medieval, in Cheshire, 1006(c); in Midlands, 2458(b); military, in second Mysore war, 5084(v); military, mechanical, 2499(b); of produce, in medieval Sussex, 5730(t); and science, 561(b); of troops, by sea, 5103(u). *See also* Canals; Railways; Roads; Road transport; Water-borne transport, *etc., and* Institute of Transport
Transvaal, 21(a), 4286(d)
Trapham, Thomas, surgeon (d. *c.* 1683), 4709(c)
Trapraine Law, Haddingtonshire, 5135(a)
Trask, John, divine (fl. 1619), 194(b)
Travel: books on, in catalogue of Royal Empire Soc., 4314; early, in Persia and Persian Gulf, 4204(a); by rail, 1836(b); before railways, 2102(a); Welsh books on, 2866(a); *temp.* John Wesley, 6035(a). *See also following entries and* Pilgrims and pilgrimages
Travel diaries, journals, etc.:
  medieval, 4408(d); northern England and elsewhere, 1184(b); by 13th cent. friars, 1964; to Rome, 1071(a), 1879(a)
  16th cent.: Sir Thos Hoby, 4419(b); Rob. Pedley, in Sussex, 5728(b); John Sanderson, in the Levant, 1960; Sir Edw. Unton, 646(a); Edw. Webbe, 4152(g)
  17th cent.: Aaron Atkinson, in America, 1820(c); Andrew Battell, in Angola, 1941; Thos Bowrey, in bay of Bengal, 1943; Thos Bowrey, in Holland and Flanders, 1953; in England, 298(n); Wm Finch, 4343(a); Geo. Fox, in America, 1815(a); John Fryer, in India and Persia, 1946; to Golconda, 1959; Edw. Haistwell, 1825(f); to Herefordshire, 6129(f); John Jourdain, in Asia, 1944;

Victualling: of Pevensey castle, 5730(t); in Royal Navy, 5098(g)

Victualling Office, reforms, 5111(e)

Vidler, William, Baptist & universalist (d. 1816), 190(d)

Vienna, conferences at (1822), 4397(d)

Vienna, congress of (1814–15), 2185(b), 3511(h), 4397(c)

Views, *see* Drawings; Prints. *For views of London see* London, city & environs: maps, plans, views

Views of old Halls and Castles of Lancashire and Cheshire (Philips), 2639(d)

Viking age: archaeology, in England, 5900(a); burials, 2887(h), 6457(a); camp, 1703(y); cross, 5898(c); cross-shaft, 1175(b); hoard, 1168(v); remains, 5519(a); saga, 5901(e); ships, representations of, 2550(c), 3349(f), 5900(c); site, 750(e); sword, 1173(m), 5906(a)

Viking Club (Orkney, Shetland, and Northern Soc.), *afterwards* Viking Soc. for Northern Research, *q.v.*

Vikings, 2232(b); raids on England, 5901(c)

Viking Soc. for Northern Research: library, 5907; *Saga-Bk*, 5897–905; *Yr. Bk*, 5906; other publs, 5907–8

Villa Faustini, location of, 509(c)

Village feasts, revels, 3760(b), 6110(v)

Village guilds, *see* Religious guilds

Village life: after 1918, 4244(e); Alvingham, 19th cent., 2825(xx); Barrow and Twyford, 1274(e); Blackmoor Vale, 19th cent., 1382(c); Devon, 17th cent., 5847(j); Somerset, Anglo-Saxon, 5348(b)

Villages and village sites: ancient, nr Threlkeld, 1165(c); Berkshire, 259(d); British, 1164(m), 4542(a); Cheshire, 3255(b); Cornwall, ancient, 4535(d); extinct, East Chilwell dist., 5835(a); extinct, Lincolnshire, 2806; Hertfordshire, origins and forms of, 5185(b); origin of, 3611(a); Whimpton, ancient, 5813(j); Wirral, 2131(e). *See also* Hut circle village; Lake-dwellings; *and among* remains, settlements, sites *in entries beginning* Anglo-Saxon, Bronze age, Iron age, Prehistoric, *etc.*

'Villani', in Danish East Anglia, 4405(b)

Villans, *see* Villeins and villeinage

Ville de Paris, H.M.S., 5110(e)

Villeins and villeinage: commutation of services, 225(j); grant of a villein, 3520(oo); pedigrees, 5331(s); in Surrey weald, 5608(g)

Villemarqué, Count (19th cent.), 903(c)

Villiers, family, 5232(d)

Villiers, George, 1st D. of Buckingham (d. 1628), 139(f)

Villiers, William, 2nd E. of Jersey (d. 1721), 4592(b)

Vinchelez, *see* de Vinchelez

Vinchelez de Bas, Jersey: Dolmen des Géonnais, 5069(a)

Vindolanda, *see* Chesterholm, Northumb.

Vinegar, Hercules, prize-fighter (fl. 1739), 3402(b)

Viney, Richard (fl. 1744), 6041(d)

Vineyards, in Wales, 888(b). *See also* Wine, wine trade

Vinheith, *see* Brunanburgh

Viniard of Devotion, 299(h)

Vinogradoff, Sir Paul, historian (d. 1925), 480(f). *See also* Index of Authors

Vintners' company, 3030(a)

Violin makers, Pamphilon family, 1701(g)

'Virbegna', 5846(i)

Virgil (Publius Vergilius Maro, d. 19 B.C.), 1084(a)

Virginal, musical instrument, 5416(d)

Virginia, English colony, 5331(a); Baptist missionaries, 193(d); Boys family, 5328(e); Bristol Quakers, 1817(b); college of

Virginia, English colony (*cont.*)
    William and Mary, 2294(b); Cumberland colonist, 1174(c); Kentish settlers, 193(d), 5328(e); Thos Lee, merchant, 5329(f); Quakers, 1816(c); John White's drawings, 5921(b)

Virginia, *see*: *Apius and Virginia*

Virginia Company, and Shakespeare, 478(b)

Viroconium, derivation of name, 2272(a)

Virtuous Octavia (1598), 3155, 3209(n)

Visions: seen by Quakers, 1814(f), 1817(h); seen by Joseph Fry, 1823(e)

Visitation (Wiggenton), 1104(c)

Visitations, ecclesiastical:
    articles, injunctions, etc., 33, 42; Berkshire archdeaconry, 261(d); Bosham, 5706(g); Cambridgeshire, 824(p); Canterbury archdeaconry, 2587(f); Canterbury prov., by Abp Laud, 151(o); Canterbury prov., *sede vacante*, 2594(b); Carmarthenshire, by Archd. Tenison, 905(h); Chester dioc., 992(a), 1031(c), 1808(g); Colchester rural deanery, 1695(f); Derbyshire, 1280(b); Devonshire, 1332(i); Durham dioc., 5250(c); Ely dioc., religious houses, 778(c); Essex archdeaconry, 1699(b), 1703(z); Furness, 1170(u); Huntingdon archdeaconry, by Card. Pole, 824(h); Kent, 2591(m); Leicestershire, by Abp Laud, 151(o); Lincoln dioc., religious houses, 840, 5153(f); Newcastle and Gateshead, 5213(e); Northumberland, by Archd. Thorpe, 5225(k); Nun Appleton convent, 6229(o); Oxfordshire, 3784(b); St David's, 923(b); Somerset, religious houses and hospitals, 5392(f); Surrey, 5627(e); Wenlock priory, 4970(c); Worcester dioc., 4403(c); Worcester priory, 158(m); York, peculiar of dean of, 6226(h); York dioc., 957(e), 6224(o), 6263; York prov., 5681(c)
    Quakers presented at, 1810(d)
    See also Churchwardens' presentments

Visitations, heraldic, *see* Heralds' visitations

Visscher, Nicholas John (b. *c.* 1580), 3111(c)

Vita S. Cuthberti (Bede), 3524(e)

Vita Wulfstani (William of Malmesbury), 4445

Vivian, Sir Richard Hussey, Bt, 1st Baron V. (d. 1842), 4216(h)

Voclas, Denb., 738(g)

Vølundarkviða, *see* Wayland, Norse lay of

Volunteers, Admiralty order concerning, 5105(i)

Volunteers, Volunteer movement: 18th cent., 2472(c); Bradford, 407(v); Cambridge, 759(l); Dorset, 1378(h), 1387(c); Frampton, 5088(n); Halifax, 1983(f); Isle of Man, Northern Manx and Southern Manx, 2548(c); Leeds, 5799(w), 5801(h); London & Westminster Lt Horse, 4780(c); Loveden, 5085(k); Loyal Masonic, 3216(c); Nottinghamshire, medals, 5836(a); Rochdale, 3981(e); Selsey Artillery, 5730(aa); Somerset, 5420(l); Sunderland, 5590(d). *See also* Militia; Territorial regiments; Yeomanry

Voreda, *see* Plumpton Wall, Cumb.

Vorsterman, Lucas, painter (fl. 1578–1656), 5872(a)

Voss, Norway, 6457(a)

Vowchurch, Herefs., 6126(c)

Vowell, *alias* Hooker, John, antiquary (d. 1601), 1312, 1337(i)

Voyages: 17th cent., 3892(n); books on, in catalogue of Royal Empire Soc., 4314; round the world, 3475(c); Tudor, 2842(a)

Voyages (*cont.*)

of: Anson, 3475(c); Columbus, 1958; Cook, 3511(j),
5111(o); Dampier (1703), 5107(m); Henry, E. of Derby,
14th cent., 5108(g); Drake, his circumnavigation, 1948,
4366(b), 5104(b), 5106(o), 5113(f); Drake, his last,
5099(j); Rob. Harcourt, to Guiana, 1954; Wm Hawkeridge
(1625), 5110(d); John Hayes (1793), 4330(b); Wm Jackson
(1642–5), 4443(d); Magellan, 4348(e); Pet and Jackman,
to Kara Sea (1580), 5113(q); Diego de Prado y Tovar,
towards Australia, 1957; John Rastell (projected, 1517),
5106(l); Vancouver, to 'New Albion', 5107(e)

to: America (1776), 4743(d); Australia and back (1852),
4270(g); Brazil (1540), 3500(a); Cadiz (1596), 3487(b);
the Caribbean (1527–68), 1955; Newfoundland (1536),
4368(b); South Shetlands (1819–22), 4334(c); Spanish
Main (1569–80), 1962; Spitzbergen, 17th cent., 1942

See also Hakluyt Soc. publs

Voyez, John, modeller (fl. 1765–73), 758(a)
Vroom, Henry Cornelius, painter (d. 1640), 5098(n)
Vulgaria (Horman), 4030
Vulgaria (Stanbridge), 1530
Vulgaria (Whittinton), 1530
Vychan, Ithel, of Halkyn (fl. 1301–23), 742(f)
Vyne, The, Hants, 4131(c)
Vyvyan, Sir Richard Rawlinson, Bt (d. 1879), 4214(f)

Waberthwaite, Cumb., 1164(g), 1186(n), 1188(c)
Wace, chronicler (fl. 1170), 5326(a)
Waddesdon, Bucks., 100(h), 3430(h)
Waddington, W.R.Yorks., 1992(e), 6238(i), 6395
Waddon, Dors., 1398(d)
Waddon, Surr., nr Croydon: Celtic burial, 3915(f); chambered
tombs, 1158(c), 4071(a), 5605(k); flints, 1159(a); iron age
sites, 3915(f), 5625(c)
Wade, family, 1986(b)
Wade, Dr Charles (d. 1884), 1589(ee)
Wadeson, Anthony, playwright (fl. 1600), 3175
Wadhurst, Suss.: Shoesmiths, 5708(e)
Wadington, William of (13th cent.), 1475
Wadsworth, W.R.Yorks., 1968(b); Akroyd, 1974(i); Birchen-
lee Carr, 1994(d); Burlees, 1968(d); Ibbotroyd, 1974(i);
Mayroyd, 1967(f); Old Town, 1968(d); Redacre, 1993(c);
Wadsworth Royd, 1996(b)
Wage assessments, 1631(f), 4234(b)
Wages: agricultural, 4716(a); domestic servants, 4721(a); fac-
tory operatives, 4715(c); medieval masons, 2967(d),
4253(t); minimum, 4232(e); real, 4722(a), 4727(a); regu-
lation of, 565(b), 4248(a); in Sheffield, 548(c); statistics,
U.K., 4714(a); women's, in cotton trade, 3327(a); in
York, 4715(d). *See also* Income; Pay; Poor-relief; Poverty
figures
Waghenaer, Lucas Janz, Dutch cartographer (16th cent.),
5100(e)
Wagstaffe, Thomas, Quaker (d. 1802), 1815(d)
Wahābism, Wahhābīs, 4512(a), 4516(g)
Wait, Rev. Patrick (d. 1664), 5239(a)
Waits, in Norwich, 3573(b)
Wake, Margaret, Ctss of Kent (d. 1349), 3528(c)
Wake, William, abp (d. 1737), 2800
Wakefield, W.R.Yorks.: burges courts, 6265(b); change-
ringing, 5801(e); chantry chapels, 6237(b); freemasonry,
6509(c); lunacy cures, 6224(k); manor, 6240; miracle or
mystery plays, 6236(m), 6285(h); wills, 5795

Wakefield, Edward Gibbon, colonial reformer (d. 1862),
4270(a,e)
Wakeley, Herts., 1595(e)
Wakering, Great, Essex, 1694(x), 5522(i)
Wakering, Little, Essex, 1694(x)
Wakerley, Northants, 520(a)
Wakes Colne, Essex, 1696(c)
Walberswick, Suff., 3520(bbb)
Walbottle hoard, 5261(b)
Walbury camp, Hants, 2010(e)
Walcheren, Holland, 4163(b), 4761(d)
Walcot, Lincs.: Catley priory, 2805
Walcot, Som., *see* Bath
Walcot, family, 4977(i)
Walcot, Humphrey, Royalist (d. 1650), 4966(m)
Waldemar IV, king of Denmark (d. 1375), 5183(e)
Walden abbey, *see* Saffron Walden, Essex
Walderslade, *see* Chatham, Kent
Waldron, Suss., 5701(g), 5704(j), 5728(g)
Wales: in middle ages, 1461(a), 2310(e), 2321(b); in 16th cent.,
3(c), 735(h), 2282(f), 4982(f); in 17th cent., 2312(c);
adventurers to the West Indies, 2277(f); ancient monu-
ments, 53(c); Ancient Monuments cttees, 53(e); archaeol.
socs, 53(f); archaeology and various finds, 484(a), 721(c,h),
732(j), 743(i), 745(h), 3917(g), 4099(b), 5166(a); and
Avignon papacy, 743(b); ballads, 1000(e), 2277(f,g), 2329;
Baptists, *see* main *entry and* Welsh Baptists; bardic
columns, in newspapers, 6020(d); bards and bardism,
2308(c), 2309(c), 3449; bibles, 718(a), 1244(a), 2315(b),
6018(c,l), 6019(c); bibliography, 2302(d), 3448, *and see*
Welsh Bibliograph. Soc.; Black Death, 4404(d), 4701(c);
books, 6017(c), 6018(g,h); books, foreign in Welsh,
6020(o); books, school-boy's, 6018(i); books bearing on,
1632(k), 2178, 3448; boroughs, 6017(b); British and
Foreign School Soc., 2327(b); buccaneers, 2277(g);
Calvinistic Methodism, *see* main entry; *Cambrian and
General Advertiser*, 921(h); castles, 755, 2160; catechisms,
6019(r); cathedral cities, 1875(a); cathedral schools,
2280(d); cattle trade, 4410(f); celts, 744(i); charity
schools, 708(d), 2300(d); chronicles, 483(d); church
architecture, 2312(b); church customs, 3901(g); church
dedications, 2302(c); churches, 721(g); churches, founding of, 2273(b); Church of, 2278(f); church organization,
2277(e); and Civil war, 2326(a); clergy, assn of in
W.R.Yorks., 6019(p); clergy, ejected, 1107(p); coinage,
early, 602(c), 608(e), 2301(a); commerce, medieval,
2275(c), 4387(b); corn-customs, 4098(b); council in,
2340, 4977(f,l); court of great sessions, 2277(a); customs
revenue, 2343; *De mirabilibus*, 735(l); *De presenti statu*,
735(h); doctrine of the Trinity and person of Christ,
1248(a); 'dug-out' boats, 5170(g); earthworks, 753(j),
2886(a), 2887(m), 6129(d); economic history, bibliography
of, 1632(k); education, medieval, 3450; education,
secondary, 2328(a); education, voluntary, 2327(b);
education, and Rev. J. Williams of Rhos, 1257(a);
education commission (1846–7), 2275(d); Edw. I in,
2866(b); Edw. I's commission of enquiry, 2276(a);
elegies, 2865(b); English law in, 2266(a); English words
in, 4976(l); evangelization, 1102(aa); felony in, 2312(d);
flint daggers, 3916(w); folk-belief, 1806(b); folk-lore,
2272(d); folk-songs, 2303(a), 3299(c); folk-tales, 1789(a);
forts, 753(j), 2885(l,m), 2886(h); French linguistic
influence, 2314(d); Friends, Religious Soc. of, *see* main

Index of Authors